Writers' & Artists' Yearbook 1998

Ninety-first Year of Issue

A directory for writers, artists, playwrights, writers for film, radio and television, designers, illustrators and photographers

A & C Black · London

© 1998 A & C Black (Publishers) Limited
35 Bedford Row, London WC1R 4JH

The publishers make no representation, express
or implied, with regard to the accuracy of the
information contained in this book and cannot
accept any legal responsibility for any errors or
omissions that may take place.

A CIP catalogue record for this book is available
from the British Library.

ISBN 0-7136-4721-3

Printed and bound in Great Britain by
William Clowes Limited, Beccles and London

Foreword

__Michael Ridpath's__ hugely successful first novel, Free to Trade, was published in 1995 by Heinemann. His second novel, Trading Reality, was published in hardback in 1996 and in paperback in 1997. He is now working on his third novel.

I write this preface as a successful user of *Writers' & Artists' Yearbook*. To explain how, let me tell you a story.

In the summer of 1990 I was working as a bond trader in the City, buying and selling, gossiping on the phone, and writing nothing more than my initials on the bottom of a dealing ticket. I felt a need for something slower, more contemplative, and more creative to do in my spare time. So I began to write a book, just to see whether I liked it.

I did like it. In fact I became obsessed with it. It was a thriller about a bond trader in the City. After a bad day at work where everything had gone wrong, I was able to come home, make a million, nail the bad guys, and get the girl. It was hard work, but fun.

After a year I had finished *Free to Trade*, or so I thought, and I gave it to some well-read friends. They liked the story, but they could see a few small problems: the style, the characterisation and the plot. Oh, and the ending wasn't much good either. In a fury both with them and with myself, I stuffed the draft in a bottom drawer, and went back to watching TV. But I missed my book. Rereading it, I could see they were right. So I started revising.

Two years later, and *Free to Trade* was finished for absolutely the last time. It now didn't just have potential but looked like something I could imagine buying in a bookshop. But how to get it published? I decided to try to secure myself an agent. So I bought the 1993 edition of the *Writers' & Artists' Yearbook* and studied it.

There were dozens of literary agents, but I knew there were many more manuscripts. I decided to be quite methodical about my approach. I drew up a list of 40 agents in order, alternating well-established successful agencies with newer outfits. I read each entry in the *Yearbook* closely, following instructions about sample chapters and synopses carefully. I spent days turning my synopsis into a selling document, and trying to write a pithy, attention-grabbing covering letter. I am convinced this was time well spent, and that it pushed my offering towards the top of the heap of unsolicited manuscripts known as the 'slush pile'.

Fortunately for me, and unfortunately for her, Carole Blake of Blake Friedmann had broken her leg, and so spent more time curled up in bed with her slush pile than she would perhaps have liked. She read my first two chapters and invited me in to the agency for a cup of tea. When she asked me whether she could act for me, I gave the matter five seconds serious consideration, and said 'yes'.

Carole is an excellent agent. She whipped the publishing trade into a frenzy of excitement over my manuscript and secured a near-record advance for me. She also proved skilled in geography, finding publishers in 33 languages (including Latvian and Estonian, but excluding Lithuanian).

So how did I do it? I think it was important that I spent two years revising my first book rather than writing mediocre new ones. Also I was lucky. I know of no foolproof way of getting a first novel published. But there are ways of shortening the odds, and careful use of the *Writers' & Artists' Yearbook* is one of them.

February 1997

Contents

Classified index to listings for quick reference

Literary agents

Art and illustration

Photography and picture research

Societies, prizes and festivals

Preparing for publication

Resources for writers

Publishing practice

Copyright and libel

Finance for writers and artists

Newspapers and magazines

Submitting material

Over a thousand titles are included in the newspapers and magazines section of the Yearbook, almost all of them offering opportunities to the writer. Many publications do not appear in our lists because the market they offer for the freelance writer is either too small or too specialised, or both. We give here some guidelines to bear in mind when submitting material to a newspaper or magazine.

Before submitting a manuscript to any newspaper or magazine it is advisable to first contact the relevant editor. The listings on page 3 give the names of editors for each section of the national newspapers and a quick telephone call to a magazine will establish the name of the relevant commissioning editor.

Magazine editors frequently complain to us about the unsuitability of many manuscripts submitted to them, as well as the omission of return postage. In their own interests, writers and others are advised to enclose postage for the return of unsuitable material.

Study the market

Before submitting manuscripts, always study carefully the editorial requirements of a magazine, not only for the subjects dealt with but for the approach, treatment, style and length. These comments will be obvious to the practised writer but the beginner can be spared much disappointment by buying copies of magazines and studying the market in depth.

The importance of studying the market cannot be overemphasised. It is an editor's job to know what readers want, and to see that they get it. Thus, freelance contributions must be tailored to fit a specific market; subject, theme, treatment, length, etc, must meet the editor's requirements. This is looked at further in *Writing for newspapers* on page 133 and *Writing magazine articles* on page 137.

Editors expect material to be well presented: neatly typed, double-spaced, with good margins, on A4 paper is the standard to aim at. An increasing number of editors are asking writers to submit their articles on disk. Always verify with the editor that your system and theirs are compatible before submission. Most editors also require a hard copy (printout) in addition to the disk. See *Preparing and submitting a manuscript* on page 527 and *Word processing* on page 531.

Illustrations

It is not advisable to send illustrations 'on spec'; check with the editor first. See page 140 for further information; listings of *Picture agencies and libraries* start on page 394.

For a list of magazines and newspapers willing to pay for cartoons, see *Newspapers and magazines which accept cartoons* on page 389, and *A serious look at marketing cartoons* (page 386) offers guidance for success.

Payment

It has always been our aim to obtain and publish the rates of payment offered for contributions by newspapers and magazines. Many publications, however, are reluctant to state a standard rate, since the value of a contribution may be dependent

not upon length but upon the standing of the writer or of the information given. Many other periodicals, in spite of efforts to extract more precise information from them, prefer to state 'by negotiation' or 'by arrangement'.

A number of magazines will accept and pay for letters to the editor, brief fillers and gossip paragraphs, as well as puzzles and quizzes. *Magazines by subject area* on page 121 provides a rough guide to these markets.

Overseas contributions

The lists of overseas newspapers and magazines in the *Yearbook* contain only a selection of those journals which offer a market for the freelance writer. For fuller listings, refer to *Willings Press Guide Volume 2 Overseas*. The overseas market for stories and articles is small and editors often prefer their fiction to have a local setting.

Some overseas magazine titles have little space for freelance contributions but many of them will consider outstanding work. Potential contributors sending material overseas should always enclose return postage in the form of International Reply Coupons (IRCs) when submitting queries or manuscripts. IRCs can be exchanged in any foreign country for stamps representing the minimum postage payable on a letter sent from one country to another.

Using an agent to syndicate material written from overseas is worth considering. Most agents operate on an international basis and are more aware of current market requirements. Again, return postage should always be included.

Newspapers and syndicates

The larger newspapers and magazines buy many of their stories, and the smaller papers buy general articles, through one or other of the well-known syndicates. Another avenue for writers is to send printed copies of stories he or she has had published at home to an agent for syndication overseas. Listings for *Syndicates, news and press agencies* start on page 144. Listings of *National newspapers UK and Ireland* start on page 3, and the names of editors are included in each.

Most of the larger UK and overseas newspapers depend for news on their own staffs and press agencies. The most important overseas newspapers have permanent representatives in Britain who keep them supplied, not only with news of especial interest to the country concerned, but also with regular summaries of British news and with articles on events of particular importance. While many overseas newspapers and magazines have a London office, it is usual for manuscripts from freelance contributors to be submitted to the headquarters' editorial office overseas.

See also ...

• *Regional newspapers UK and Ireland*, page 12
• Newspapers are listed together with magazines for *Australia* (page 107), *Canada* (page 113), *New Zealand* (page 116) and *South Africa* (page 118)
• *USA*, page 120
• *Newspapers and magazines on the Internet*, page 132
• *Recent changes to newspapers and magazines*, page 132
• *Tape-recording interviews*, page 142

National newspapers UK and Ireland

Daily Mail
Northcliffe House, 2 Derry Street, London W8 5TT
tel 0171-938 6000 *fax* 0171-937 3251
Editor Paul Dacre
Daily Mon-Fri 35p Sat 45p
Supplements **Business Day**, **Weekend**

Highest payment for good, exclusive news. Ideas welcomed for leader page articles (500-800 words). Exclusive news photos always wanted. Founded 1896.

City Editor Andrew Alexander
Diary Editor Nigel Dempster
Education Editor Tony Halpin
Features Editor Veronica Wadley
Foreign Editor Tim Jotischky
Health Editor Rory Clements
Industrial Editor David Norris
Literary Editor Jane Mays
Media Editor Sean Poulter
Money Editor Margaret Stone
News Editor Ian MacGregor
Picture Editor Geoff Webster
Political Editor David Hughes
Showbiz Editor Rebecca Hardy
Sports Editor Cameron Kelleher
Travel Editor Cathy Wood
Weekend Editor Aileen Doherty
Women's Editor Diane Hutchinson

Daily Record
Anderston Quay, Glasgow G3 8DA
tel 0141-248 7000 *fax* 0141-204 0770
web site http://www.record-mail.co.uk/rm
London office 1 Canada Square, Canary Wharf, London E14 5AP
tel 0171-293 3000
Editor Terry Quinn
Daily 28p

Topical articles, from 300-700 words; exclusive stories of Scottish interest and exclusive colour photos.

Business Editor Colin Calder
Features Editor Allan Rennie
Financial Editor Colin Calder
Health Editor Tom Little
News Editor Murray Morse
Picture Editor Stuart Nicol
Political Editor Kenny Farquharson
Sports Editor Andy Swinburne
Women's Page Editor Lorna Frame

Daily Sport
19 Great Ancoats Street, Manchester M60 4BT
tel 0161-236 4466 *fax* 0161-236 4535
Editor-in-chief Tony Livesey
Editor Jeff McGowan
Daily Mon-Fri 32p

Factual stories and series. Length: up to 1000 words. Illustrations: b&w and colour photos, cartoons. Payment: £30-£5000. Founded 1988.

Features and News Editor Tony Hore
Letters Editor Belinda Charlton
Sports Editor Mark Smith

Daily Star
Ludgate House, 245 Blackfriars Road, London SE1 9UX
tel 0171-928 8000 *fax* 0171-922 7960
Editor Phil Walker
Daily 28p

Hard news exclusives, commanding substantial payment. Major interviews with big-star personalities; short features; series based on people rather than things; picture features. Payment: short features £75-£100; full page £250-£300; double page £400-£600, otherwise by negotiation. Illustrations: line, half-tone. Founded 1978.

Diary Editor Brian Dunlea
Entertainment Editor Pat Codd
Features Editor Brian Dunlea
Media Editor Linda Duff
News Editor Hugh Whittow
Political Editor Henry Macrory
Sports Editor Phil Rostron
Women's Editor Karen Livermore

The Daily Telegraph
1 Canada Square, Canary Wharf, London E14 5DT
tel 0171-538 5000 *fax* 0171-538 6242
Editor Charles Moore
Daily 40p Sat 75p
Supplements **Appointments**, **Arts & Books**, **Business News**, **Connected**, **Motoring**, **Telegraph Magazine**, **Television & Radio**, **Young Telegraph**, **Weekend**

Articles on a wide range of subjects of topical interest considered. Preliminary

letter and synopsis required. Length: 700-1000 words. Payment: by arrangement. Founded 1855.

Arts Editor Sarah Crompton
City Editor Neil Collins
Education Editor John Clare
Environment Editor Charles Clover
Fashion Editor Hilary Alexandra
Features Editor Corrina Honan
Foreign Editor Patrick Bishop
Health Editor Christine Doyle
Literary Editor John Coldstream
Media Editor Alison Boshoff
News Editor Martin Newland
Picture Editor Bob Bodman
Political Editor George Jones
Sports Editor David Welch

Telegraph Magazine
Editor Emma Soames
Free with Sat paper

Short profiles (about 1600 words); articles of topical interest. Preliminary study of the magazine essential. Illustrations: all types. Payment: by arrangement. Founded 1964.

Electronic Telegraph
web site http://www.telegraph.co.uk/
Editor Ben Rooney
Daily Free to Internet subscribers

Based on *The Daily Telegraph*, contains news, sport, City, features, Internet News, Hyperlinks to Archive. Founded 1994.

The European
200 Gray's Inn Road, London WC1X 8NE
tel 0171-418 7777 *fax* 0171-418 7707
web site http://www.the-european.com
Editor-in-Chief Andrew Neil
Thu 75p

News reports, analytical articles and features on subjects of interest and importance to Europe as a whole, including business affairs, sport, arts, literature, lifestyle, fashion. Illustrations: line, half-tone, colour transparencies, cartoons. Payment: by arrangement.

Arts Editor Chris Holmes
Business Editor Tim Castle
Diplomatic Editor Ian Mather
Economics Editor Thierry Naudin
Features Editor Julian Coman
Letters Editor Roger Evans
News Editor David Meilton
Picture Editor Jeannette Downing
Political Editor Victor Smart
Sports Editor Andrew Warshaw
Technology Editor David Short

The Express
Ludgate House, 245 Blackfriars Road, London SE1 9UX
tel 0171-928 8000 *fax* 0171-260 1654
Great Ancoats Street, Manchester M60 4HB
tel 0161-236 2112
Editor Richard Addis
Daily Mon-Fri 35p Sat 40p
Supplements **Saturday, The Sport, Weekend**

Exclusive news; striking photos. Leader page articles (600 words); facts preferred to opinions. Payment: according to value.

Arts Editor Mal Peachey
Business Editor John Murray
Diary Editor John McEntee
Environment Editor John Ingham
Features Editor Jack Wright
Foreign Editor Mike Graham
Health Editor Liz Wilson
Literary Editor Maggie Pringle
Media Editor David Wigg
News Editor Ian Walker
Political Editor Nicholas Wood
Sports Editor Alex Butler
Women's Editor Rachel Simone

Express on Sunday
Ludgate House, 245 Blackfriars Road, London SE1 9UX
tel 0171-928 8000 *fax* 0171-620 1656
Editor Richard Addis
Weekly 70p

Exclusive news stories, photos, personality profiles and features of controversial or lively interest. Length: 800-1000 words. Payment: top rates. Founded 1918.

City Editor Kirsty Hamilton
Features Editor Jack Wright
Finance Editor John Murray
Literary Editor Maggie Pringle
News Editor Shan Lancaster
Political Editor Peter Obourne
Sports Editor Alex Butler

Express on Sunday Magazine
fax 0171-928 7262
Editor Tessa Hilton
Free with paper

Homes, gardens, cookery, general interest features. Length: 1000 words. Payment: from £250 per 1000 words. Illustrations: colour, half-tone, artwork.

Financial Times
Southwark Bridge, London SE1 9HL
tel 0171-873 3000 *fax* 0171-873 3076
web site http://www.ft.com
Editor Richard Lambert
Daily 75p

Supplements **Companies & Markets, Global Business Outlook, Information Technology, Weekend FT**

Articles of financial, commercial, industrial and economic interest. Length: 800-1000 words. Payment: by arrangement. Founded 1888.

> *Arts Editor* Annalena McAfee
> *Diary Editor* Michael Cassell
> *Features Editor* John Parker
> *Financial Editor* Martin Dickson
> *Foreign Editor* Quentin Peel
> *International Editor* Peter Martin
> *Marketing Editor* John Willman
> *Markets Editor* Philip Coggan
> *News Editor* Julia Cuthbertson
> *Political Editor* Robert Peston
> *Small Businesses Editor* Kathrine Campbell
> *Travel Editor* Robert Thompson
> *Women's Editor* Lucia Van der Post

The Guardian

119 Farringdon Road, London EC1R 3ER
tel 0171-278 2332 *fax* 0171-837 2114
164 Deansgate, Manchester M60 2RR
tel 0161-832 7200 *fax* 0161-832 5351
Editor Alan Rusbridger
Daily Mon-Fri 45p Sat 60p
Supplements **Education, Friday Review, The Guardian 2, Online, Society, The Week, Weekend**

Few articles are taken from outside contributors except on its specialist pages. Length: not exceeding 1200 words. Illustrations: news and features photos. Payment: from £170.83 per 1000 words; from £50.94 for illustrations. Founded 1821.

> *Arts Editor* Claire Armitstead
> *Business Editor* Patrick Donovan
> *Community Affairs Editor* James Meikie
> *Economics Editor* Larry Elliot
> *Education Editor* John Carvel
> *Fashion Editor* Susannah Frankel
> *Features Editor* Roger Alton
> *Foreign Editor* Rosemary Collins
> *Health Editor* Dr Luisa Dillner
> *Literary Editor* Stephen Moss
> *Media Editor* John Mulholland
> *News Editor* Harriet Sherwood
> *Political Editor* Michael White
> *Religious Editor* Madeleine Bunting
> *Science Editor* Tim Radford
> *Sports Editor* Mike Averis
> *Technology Editor* Nicholas Bannister
> *Women's Editor* Sally Weale

Weekend

Editor Deborah Orr
Free with Sat paper

Features on world affairs, major profiles, food and drink, home life, the arts, travel, leisure, etc. Also good reportage on social and political subjects. Illustrations: b&w photos and line, cartoons. Payment: apply for rates.

Guardian Online

web site http://www.guardian.co.uk

The Herald

Caledonian Newspapers Ltd, 195 Albion Street, Glasgow G1 1QP
tel 0141-552 6255 *fax* 0141-552 2288
web site http://www.cims.co.uk/herald
London office Gray's Inn House,
127 Clerkenwell Road, London EC1R 5DB
tel 0171-405 2121
Editor Harry Reid
Daily 48p

Articles up to 1000 words. Founded 1783.

> *Arts Editor* Keith Bruce
> *Associate Editor* John Ryan
> *Business Editor* Bob Sutter
> *Chief Financial Editor* Ronnie Dundas
> *Diary Editor* Tom Shields
> *Economics Editor* Alf Young
> *European Editor* Murray Ritchie
> *Executive Editor* Ron Anderson
> *Features Editor* Jackie McGlone
> *Managing Editor* Bob Jeffrey
> *News Editor* Colin McDiarmid
> *Sports Editor* Iain Scott

The Independent

1 Canada Square, Canary Wharf, London E14 5AP
tel 0171-293 2000 *fax* 0171-293 2435
Editor Andrew Marr
Daily Mon-Fri 40p Sat 50p
Supplements **City+, The Eye, The Independent Magazine, The Independent Tabloid, The Long Weekend, Weekend**

Occasional freelance contributions; preliminary letter advisable. Payment: by arrangement. Founded 1986.

> *Arts Editor* Mark Pappenheim
> *Business Editor* Jeremy Warner
> *City Editor* Tom Stevenson
> *Education Editor* Judith Judd
> *Environment Editor* Nicholas Schoon
> *Features Editor* David Robson
> *Foreign Editor* Andrew Marshall
> *Health Editor* Jeremy Laurancet
> *Labour Editor* Barrie Clement
> *Literary Editor* Boyd Tonkin
> *Media Editor* Rob Brown
> *News Editor* David Felton
> *Picture Editor* David Swanborough
> *Political Editor* Tony Bevins
> *Sports Editor* Paul Newman

The Independent Magazine

Editor Michael Watts
Free with Sat paper

Profiles and illustrated articles of topical interest; all material commissioned. Preliminary study of the magazine essential. Length: 500-3000 words. Illustrations: cartoons; commissioned colour and b&w photos. Payment: by arrangement. Founded 1988.

Independent on Sunday

1 Canada Square, Canary Wharf, London E14 5DL
tel 0171-293 2000 *fax* 0171-293 2043
Editor Rosie Boycott, *Deputy Editor* Stephen Fay
Weekly £1.00
Supplements **Business**, **Real Life**, **The Sunday Review**, **Travel & Money**

News, features and articles. Illustrated, including cartoons. Payment: by negotiation. Founded 1990.

Arts Editor Simon O'Hagan
Environment Editor Geoffrey Lean
Features Editor Sue Matthias
Foreign Editor Ray Whitaker
News Editor Mike McCarthy
Picture Editor David Sandison
Political Editor Stephen Castle
Sports Editor Neil Morton

The Sunday Review

tel 0171-293 2000 *fax* 0171-293 2027
Editor Laurence Earle
Free with paper

Original features of general interest with potential for photographic illustration. Material mostly commissioned. Length: 1000-5000 words. Illustrations: colour transparencies. Payment: £150 per 1000 words.

Irish Independent

Independent House, 90 Middle Abbey Street, Dublin 1, Republic of Ireland
tel (01) 7055333 *fax* (01) 8720304/8731787
Editor Vincent Doyle
Daily 85p

Special articles on topical or general subjects. Length: 700-1000 words. Payment: editor's estimate of value.

Arts Editor Bruce Arnold
Business Editor Frank Mulrennan
Diary Editor Angela Phelan
Features Editor John Spain
News Editor Philip Molloy
Picture Editor Tom Brady
Political Editor Chris Glennon
Sports Editor Karl McGinty

Irish Times

11-15 D'Olier Street, Dublin 2, Republic of Ireland
tel (01) 6792022 *fax* (01) 6719407
Editor Conor Brady
Daily 75p

Mainly staff-written. Specialist contributions (800-2000 words) by commission on basis of ideas submitted. Payment: at editor's valuation. Illustrations: photos and line drawings.

Arts Editor Victoria White
Business Editor Bill Murdoch
Features Editor Caroline Walsh
Finance Editor Cliff Taylor
Foreign Editor Paul Gillespie
Literary Editor John Banville
News Editor Niall Kiely
Picture Editor Dermot O'Shea
Political Editor Dick Walsh
Special Reports Editor Ray Comiskey
Sports Editor Malachy Logan
Supplements Editor Karl Jones

The Irish Times on the Web

web site http://www.irish-times.co.

Mail on Sunday

Northcliffe House, 2 Derry Street, London W8 5TS
tel 0171-938 6000 *fax* 0171-937 3829
Editor Jonathan Holborow
Weekly 85p
Supplements **femail**, **Financial Mail**, **Night & Day**, **Programme**, **You**

Articles. Payment: by arrangement. Illustrations: line, half-tone; cartoons. Founded 1982.

Assistant Editor (Features) Andy Bull
City Editor William Kay
Diary Editor Nigel Dempster
Literary Editor Paula Johnson
News Editor Tom Hendry
Picture Editor Andy Kyle
Political Editor Joe Murphy
Sports Editor Roger Kelly

Night & Day

tel 0171-938 7051 *fax* 0171-937 7488
Editor Simon Kelner
Free with paper

Investigative journalism, profiles, personal columns and book reviews – mostly commissioned. Length: 3000 words for main feature; 1000 words for personal column. Illustrations: colour photos. Founded 1993.

You

Editor Dee Nolan
Features Editor Jane Phillimore
Free with paper

Women's interest features. Length: 500-2500 words. Payment: by arrangement. Illustrations: full colour and b&w drawings commissioned; also colour photography.

The Mirror

1 Canada Square, Canary Wharf, London E14 5AP
tel 0171-293 3000 *fax* 0171-293 3409
Editor Piers Morgan
Daily 28p
Supplements **Mirror Football Mania**, **Mirror TVplus**

Top payment for exclusive news and news pictures. Freelance articles used, and ideas bought: send synopsis only. 'Unusual' pictures and those giving a new angle on the news are welcomed; also cartoons. Founded 1903.

   Business Editor Clinton Manning
   Environment Editor Jeremy Armstrong
   Features Editor Tina Weaver
   Health Editor Jill Palmer
   Letters Editor Jo Dipple
   News Editor Eugene Duffy
   Picture Editor Ron Morgans
   Political Editor Kevin Maguire
   Sports Editor David Balmforth

Morning Star

(formerly Daily Worker)
The Morning Star Co-operative Society Ltd,
1-3 Ardleigh Road, London N1 4HS
tel 0171-254 0033 *fax* 0171-254 5950
e-mail morsta@geo2.poptel.org.uk
Editor John Haylett
Daily 50p

Newspaper for the labour movement. Articles of general interest. Illustrations: photos, cartoons and drawings. Founded 1930.

   Arts & Media Editor Jeff Sawtell
   Diary Editor Mike Ambrose
   Features Editor Paul Corry
   Financial Editor Ian Morrison
   Foreign Editor Paul Donovan
   Health Editor Brian Denny
   Industrial Editor Chris Kasrils
   News Editor Paul Corry
   Political Editor Mike Ambrose
   Sports Editor Amanda Kendal

News of the World

1 Virginia Street, London E1 9XR
tel 0171-782 1000 *fax* 0171-583 9504
Editor Phil Hall
Deputy Editor Rebekah Wade
Sun 55p

Uses freelance material. Payment: by negotiation. Founded 1843.

   Features Editor Ray Levine
   Money Editor Peter Prendergast
   News Editor Greg Miskiw
   Political Editor Eben Black
   Royal Editor Clive Goodman
   Sports Editor Mike Dunn
   Travel Editor David Gordois

Sunday Magazine

Phase 2, 5th Floor, 1 Virginia Street,
London E1 9BD
tel 0171-782 7900 *fax* 0171-782 7474
Editor Judy McGuire
Free with paper

Ideas and material from freelance writers welcomed. Payment: by arrangement. Founded 1981.

The Observer

119 Farringdon Road, London EC1R 3ER
tel 0171-278 2332 *fax* 0171-713 4250
Editor Will Hutton
Sun £1.00
Supplements **Business**, **Life**, **The Observer Review**, **Sport**

Some articles and illustrations commissioned. Payment: by arrangement. Founded 1791.

   Arts Editor Jane Ferguson
   Business Editor Ben Laurance
   City Editor Heather Connon
   Economics Editor William Keegan
   Education Editor Martin Bright
   Fashion Editor Jo Adams
   Features Editor Lisa O'Kelly
   Foreign Editor Leonard Doyle
   Literary Editor Robert McCrum
   Media Editor Richard Brooks
   News Editor Paul Dunn
   Political Editor Patrick Wintour
   Sports Editor Alan Hubbard
   Travel Editor Desmond Balmer

Life

tel 0171-713 4175 *fax* 0171-713 4217
Editor Justine Picardy
Free with paper

Commissioned features. Length: 2000-3000 words. Illustrations: first-class colour and b&w photos. Payment: NUJ rates; £150 per illustration.

The Observer Online

web site http://www.observer.co.uk

The People

1 Canada Square, Canary Wharf, London E14 5AP
tel 0171-293 3000 *fax* 0171-293 3810
Editor Len Gould
Sun 55p
Supplements **TV First!**, **Yes!**

Investigative features, single articles and series considered; pictures should be supplied with contributions if possible. Features should be of deep human interest, whether the subject is serious or light-hearted. Very strong sports following. Exclusive news and news-feature stories also considered. Payment: rates

high, even for tips that lead to published news stories.

Features Editor Tom Petrie
Finance Editor Cathy Gunn
News Editor Danny Buckland
Picture Editor Martin Spaven
Political Editor Nigel Nelson
Sports Editor Ed Barry

Yes!

Editor Tom Petrie
Free with paper

Feature articles. Illustrations: colour. Payment: by arrangement.

Scotland on Sunday

20 North Bridge, Edinburgh EH1 1YT
tel 0131-225 2468 *fax* 0131-220 2443
Glasgow office
tel 0141-332 6163
Editor Brian Groom
Weekly 65p

Features on all subjects, not necessarily Scottish. Payment: £88 per 1000 words. Founded 1988.

Features Editor Stewart Hennessey
News Editor William Paul
Political Editor Kenneth Farquharson

Scotland on Sunday Magazine

Editor Fiona Macleod
Free with paper

The Scotsman

20 North Bridge, Edinburgh EH1 1YT
tel 0131-225 2468 *fax* 0131-226 7420
Editor Martin Clarke
Daily Mon-Fri 42p Sat 50p
Supplements **Business Daily, Property Weekly, Recruitment, The Scotsman Weekend, Sports Weekly**

Considers articles on political, economic and general themes which add substantially to current information. Prepared to commission topical and controversial series from proved authorities. Length: 800-1000 words. Illustrations: outstanding news pictures, cartoons. Payment: by arrangement. Founded 1817.

Arts Editor Douglas Fraser
Business Editor Martin Flanagan
Education Editor Matt Wells
Environment Editor Christopher Cairns
Features Editor Douglas Fraser
Foreign Editor Andrew McCloud
Internet Editor Bob Campbell
Literary Editor Catherine Lockerbie
News Editor Ian Stewart
Political Editor John Penman
Sports Editor Keith Anderson
Women's Editor Gillian Glover

The Scotsman Weekend

Editor Alastair Mcghee
Free with Sat paper
Features, reviews. Illustrated.

The Star

Independent Star Ltd, Star House, 62A Terenure Road North, Dublin 6w, Republic of Ireland
tel (01) 4901228 *fax* (01) 4902193/4902188
Editor Gerard O'Regan
Daily Mon-Sat 60p

General articles relating to news and sport, and features. Length: 1000 words. Illustrations: colour photos. Payment: by negotiation. Founded 1989.

Deputy Editor Danny Smyth
News Editors Dave O'Connell, Bernard Phelan
Picture Editor James Dunne
Political Editor John Donlon
Sports Editor Connie Clinton

The Sun

News Group Newspapers Ltd, Virginia Street, London E1 9XP
tel 0171-782 4000 *fax* 0171-488 3253
Editor Stuart Higgins
Daily 25p
Supplement **Super Goals**

Takes freelance material, including cartoons. Payment: by negotiation. Founded 1969.

Business Editor Isabelle Murray
Education Editor David Wooding
Features Editor Sue Carroll
Foreign Editor Neil Burgess
Health Editor Dr Rosemary Leonard
Letters Editor Sue Cook
News Editor Neil Wallis
Picture Editor Ken Lennox
Political Editor Trevor Kavanagh
Showbiz Editor Andy Coulson
Sports Editor Paul Ridley
Television Editor Peter Willis
Travel Editor Katie Woods
Women's Editor Jane Moore

Sunday Business

3 Cavendish Square, London W1M 0BB
tel 0171-468 6000 *fax* 0171-436 3797
Editor David Rydell
Weekly 85p
Supplements **News Review, Trading Week**

Standalone Sunday newspaper for the business and financial community. Covers all aspects of business news with in-depth features ranging from captains of industry to the entrepreneurial and small business sector. Wide economic coverage, IT news, and personal finance

features. Length: from 200-word news stories to 2500-word features. Payment: by arrangement.

Business Editor George McDonald
Diary Editor James Hipwell
Financial and News Editor Mark Court
Personal Finance Editor Diana Clement
Picture Editor Flora Bathurst
Political Editor Adam Sherwin

The Sunday Business Post

Merchants House, 27-30 Merchants Quay, Dublin 8, Republic of Ireland
tel (01) 6799777 *fax* (01) 6796496/6796498
Editor Damien Kiberd
Weekly £1.00

Features on financial, economic and political topics; also lifestyle, media and science articles. Illustrations: colour and b&w photos, graphics, cartoons. Payment: by negotiation. Founded 1989.

Arts Editor Mariom McKeon
Business Editor Ted Harding
Features Editor Aileen O'Toole
Financial Editor Gail Seekamp
IT Editor Carissa Casey
Media Editor Siobhan O'Connell
News Editor Nick Mulcahy
Political Editor Emily O'Reilly
Sports Editor Brian Carey

Sunday Independent

Independent House, 90 Middle Abbey Street, Dublin 1, Republic of Ireland
tel (01) 8731333 *fax* (01) 8721914
Editor Aengus Fanning
Weekly £1.00

Special articles. Length: according to subject. Illustrations: topical or general interest, cartoons. Payment: at editor's valuation.

Arts Editor Ronan Farren
Business Editor Shane Ross
Diary Editor Tracy Keane
Features Editor Anne Harris
News Editor Willie Kealy
Political Editor Joe O'Malley
Sports Editor Adhamhnan O'Sullivan

Sunday Life

124 Royal Avenue, Belfast BT1 1EB
tel (01232) 264300 *fax* (01232) 554507
Editor Martin Lindsay
Weekly 60p

Items of interest to Northern Ireland Sunday tabloid readers. Payment: by arrangement. Illustrations: colour and b&w pictures and graphics. Founded 1988.

Features Editor Sue Corbett
Photographic Editor Fred Hoare
Sports Editor Jim Gracey
Women's Page Editor Sue Corbett

Sunday Mail

Anderston Quay, Glasgow G3 8DA
tel 0141-248 7000 *fax* 0141-242 3587
web site http://www.record-mail.co.uk/rm
London office 1 Canada Square, Canary Wharf, London E14 5AP
Editor Jim Cassidy
Weekly 55p
Supplements **XS**

Exclusive stories and pictures (in colour if possible) of national and Scottish interest; also cartoons. Payment: above average.

Assistant Editor Andrew Sannholm
Features Editor Rob Bruce
Financial Editor Jim Fyfe
Health Editor Dr Tom Smith
News Editor Brian Steel
Picture Editor David NcNeil
Political Editor Angus Macleod
Showbiz Editor Scott Robinson
Sports Editor George Cheyne
Women's Page Editor Melanie Reid
XS Editor Janette Harkess

Sunday Mirror

1 Canada Square, Canary Wharf, London E14 5AP
tel 0171-293 3000 *fax* 0171-293 3939
Editor Bridget Rowe
Weekly 55p
Supplements **Personal**, **TV Week**

Concentrates on human interest news features, social documentaries, dramatic news and feature photos. Ideas, as well as articles, bought. Payment: high, especially for exclusives. Founded 1963.

City Editor Diane Boliver
Assistant Editor (Features) Shan Lancaster
Assistant Editor (News) Andy Byrne
Executive Editor (Pictures) Paul Bennett
Assistant Editor (Sport) William Bradshaw

Personal

tel 0171-293 3826 *fax* 0171-293 3835
Contact Shan Lancaster, Paul Bennett
Free with paper

Human interest, celebrity articles, and original amusing ideas. Length: 1000 words. Illustrations: colour photos. Payment: articles and photographs high, especially for exclusives. Founded 1988.

Sunday Post

D.C. Thomson & Co. Ltd, 144 Port Dundas Road, Glasgow G4 0HZ
tel 0141-332 9933 *fax* 0141-331 1595
Albert Square, Dundee DD1 9QJ
tel (01382) 223131 *fax* (01382) 201064
185 Fleet Street, London EC4A 2HS
tel 0171-404 0199 *fax* 0171-404 5694
Editor Russell Reid
Weekly 55p

Human interest, topical, domestic and humorous articles, and exclusive news. Payment: on acceptance.

The Sunday Post Magazine

tel (01382) 223131 *ext* 4147 *fax* (01382) 201064
Editor Maggie Dun
Monthly Free with paper

General interest articles. Length: 1000-2000 words. Illustrations: colour transparencies. Payment: varies. Founded 1988.

Sunday Sport

19 Great Ancoats Street, Manchester M60 4BT
tel 0161-236 4466 *fax* 0161-236 4535
Executive Editor Tony Livesey
Editor Jon Wise
Deputy Editor Mark Harris
Weekly 55p

Founded 1986.
   Features Editor Phil Johnson
   News Editor Paul Carter
   Picture Editor Paul Currie
   Sports Editor Marc Smith

Sunday Telegraph

1 Canada Square, Canary Wharf, London E14 5DT
tel 0171-538 5000 *fax* 0171-513 2504
Editor Dominic Lawson
Weekly 70p
Supplements **Appointments, Review, Sunday Telegraph Magazine, RX Magazine**

Occasional freelance material accepted.
   Arts Editor John Preston
   City Editor Neil Bennett
   Diary Editor Mark Inglefield
   Features Editor Rebecca Nicolson
   Literary Editor Miriam Gross
   News Editor Chris Anderson
   Picture Editor Nigel Skelsey
   Sports Editor Colin Gibson
   Women's Editor Kim Fletcher

RX Magazine

tel 0171-538 6208
Editor Mark Edmonds

Sunday Telegraph Magazine

tel 0171-538 7590 *fax* 0171-538 7074
e-mail sunmag@telegraph.co.uk
Editor Rebecca Tyrrel
Free with paper

All material is commissioned. Founded 1995.

The Sunday Times

1 Pennington Street, London E1 9XW
tel 0171-782 5000 *fax* 0171-782 5658
web site http://www.sunday-times.co.uk
Editor John Witherow
Weekly £1.00
Supplements **Appointments, Books, Business, Culture, Money, Sport, Style, The Sunday Times Magazine**

Special articles by authoritative writers on politics, literature, art, drama, music, finance and science, and topical matters. Payment: top rate for exclusive features. Illustrations: first class photos of topical interest and pictorial merit welcome; also topical drawings and cartoons. Founded 1822.
   Arts Editor Helen Hawkins
   Economics Editor David Smith
   Education Editor Judith O'Reilly
   Literary Editor Geordie Greig
   News Editor Mark Skipworth
   News Reviews Sarah Baxter
   Political Editor Michael Jones
   Sports Editor Jeff Randell
   Travel Editor Christine Walker

Culture

Articles and reviews of current performing arts.

Style

Lifestyle articles.

The Sunday Times Magazine

tel 0171-782 7000
Editor Robin Morgan
Free with paper

Articles and pictures. Illustrations: colour and b&w photos. Payment: by negotiation.

The Sunday Times Scotland

Times Newspapers Ltd, 124 Portman Street, Kinning Park, Glasgow G41 1EJ
tel (0141) 420 5100 *fax* (0141) 420 5262
Editor Will Peakin
Free with *The Sunday Times*

News, features and sport. Illustrations: colour photos, cartoons and graphics. Payment: £100 per feature; £50 for illustrations. Founded 1988.

The Sunday Tribune

Tribune Publications plc, 15 Lower Baggot Street, Dublin 2, Republic of Ireland
tel (01) 661 5555 *fax* (01) 661 5302
e-mail stribune@indigo.ie
Editor Matt Cooper

Weekly £1.00
Supplement **Sunday Tribune Magazine**
Newspaper containing news (inc. foreign), articles, features and photo features. Length: 600-2800 words. Illustrations: colour and b&w photos and cartoons. Payment: £100 per 1000 words; £100 for illustrations. Founded 1980.

> *Arts Editor* Ciaran Carty
> *Business Editor* Richard Curran
> *Features Editor* Ros Dee
> *News Editor* Helen Callanan
> *Photo Desk* Sarah Gillespie
> *Sports Editor* Eoghan Corry
> *Sunday Tribune Magazine Editor* Ros Dee

The Times

1 Pennington Street, London E1 9XN
tel 0171-782 5000 *fax* 0171-488 3242
web site http://www.the-times.co.uk
Editor Peter Stothard
Daily Mon-Fri 35p Sat 45p
Supplements **The Directory, Interface, The Times 2, The Times 3, The Times Magazine, Times Sport, Weekend**
Outside contributions considered from: experts in subjects of current interest and writers who can make first-hand experience or reflection come readably alive. Phone appropriate section editor. Length: up to 1200 words. Founded 1785.

> *Arts Editor* Richard Morrison
> *Business Editor* Linsay Cook
> *Economics Editor* Janet Bush
> *Education Editor* John O'Leary
> *Environment Editor* Nick Nuttall
> *Features Editor* Sandra Parsons
> *Foreign Editor* Graham Patterson
> *Health Editor* Jeremy Laurance
> *Industrial Editor* Philip Bassett
> *Literary Editor* Erica Wagner
> *Media Editor* Alexandra Frean
> *News Editor* Graham Duffil
> *Political Editor* Philip Webster
> *Science Editor* Nigel Hawkes
> *Sports Editor* David Chappell
> *Weekend Times Editors* Tim Rice, Gill Morgan

The Times Magazine
Editor Nicholas Wapshott
Free with Sat paper
Features. Illustrated.

Wales on Sunday

Thomson House, Havelock Street, Cardiff CF1 1XR
tel (01222) 583583 *fax* (01222) 583725
Editor Alan Edmunds
Weekly 55p
National Sunday newspaper of Wales offering comprehensive news, features and entertainments coverage at the weekend, with a particular focus on events in Wales. Accepts general interest articles, preferably with a Welsh connection. Founded 1989.

> *Features Editor* Mike Smith
> *News Editor* Mark Hindle
> *Sports Editor* Mark Dawson

Regional newspapers UK and Ireland

Regional newspapers are listed in alphabetical order under region. Some newspapers will accept and pay for letters to the editor, brief fillers, and gossip paragraphs, as well as puzzles and quizzes. National newspaper listings start on page 3. See also Writing for newspapers on page 133.

Belfast

Belfast Telegraph
124-144 Royal Avenue, Belfast BT1 1EB
tel (01232) 321242 *fax* (01232) 554506/554540 (editorial only)
Editor Edmund Curran
Daily 26p
Any material relating to Northern Ireland. Payment: by negotiation. Founded 1870.

Irish News
113-117 Donegall Street, Belfast BT1 2GE
tel (01232) 322226 *fax* (01232) 337505
Editor Tom Collins
Daily 32p
Articles of historical and topical interest. Payment: by arrangement. Founded 1855.

News Letter
46-56 Boucher Crescent, Boucher Road, Belfast BT12 6QY
tel (01232) 680000 *fax* (01232) 664412
Editor Geoff Martin
Daily 32p
Pro-Union. Founded 1737.

Channel Islands

Guernsey Evening Press and Star
Braye Road, Vale, Guernsey,
Channel Islands GY1 3BW
tel (01481) 45866 *fax* (01481) 48972
Editor Graham Ingrouille
Mon-Sat 32p
News and feature articles. Length: 500-700 words. Illustrations: colour and b&w photos. Payment: by negotiation. Founded 1897.

Jersey Evening Post
PO Box 582, Five Oaks, St Saviour, Jersey JE4 8XQ
tel (01534) 611611 *fax* (01534) 611622
Editor Chris Bright
Daily 35p
News and features with a Channel Islands angle. Length: 1000 words (articles/features), 300 words (news). Illustrations: colour and b&w. Payment: £80 (articles/features), £25 (news); £30. Founded 1890.

Cork

Evening Echo (Cork)
Cork Examiner Publications Ltd,
1-6 Academy Street, Cork, Republic of Ireland
tel (021) 272722 *fax* (021) 275477
Editor Brian Feeney
Daily 50p
Articles, features and news for the area. Illustrations: colour prints.

The Examiner
1-6 Academy Street, Cork, Republic of Ireland
tel (021) 272722 *fax* (021) 275477
Editor Brian Looney
Daily 85p
Features. Material mostly commissioned. Length: 1000 words. Payment: by arrangement. Founded 1841.

Dublin

Evening Herald
90 Middle Abbey Street, Dublin 1,
Republic of Ireland
tel (01) 8731333
Editor Paul Drury
Daily 65p

Articles. Payment: by arrangement. Illustrations: line, half-tone, cartoons.

East Anglia

Cambridge Evening News
Winship Road, Milton, Cambs. CB4 6PP
tel (01223) 434438 *fax* (01223) 434415
Editor Robert Satchwell
Mon-Sat 30p

The voice of Mid-Anglia – news, views and sport. Illustrations: colour prints, b&w and colour graphics. Payment: by negotiation. Founded 1888.

East Anglian Daily Times
30 Lower Brook Street, Ipswich, Suffolk IP4 1AN
tel (01473) 230023 *fax* (01473) 211391
Editor Terry Hunt
Daily 37p

Features of East Anglian interest, preferably with pictures. Length: 500 words. Illustrations: colour, b&w. Payment: £50 per feature; illustrations NUJ rates. Founded 1874.

Eastern Daily Press
Prospect House, Rouen Road, Norwich NR1 1RE
tel (01603) 628311 *fax* (01603) 612930
Editor Peter Franzen
London office House of Commons Press Gallery, House of Commons, London SW1A 0AA
tel 0171-219 3384 *fax* 0171-222 3830
Daily 38p

Limited market for articles of East Anglian interest not exceeding 900 words. Founded 1870.

Evening News
Prospect House, Rouen Road, Norwich NR1 1RE
tel (01603) 628311 *fax* (01603) 612930
Editor Bob Crawley
Daily 28p

Interested in local news-based features. Length: up to 500 words. Payment: NUJ or agreed rates. Founded 1882.

East Midlands

Burton Mail
Burton Daily Mail Ltd, 65-68 High Street, Burton on Trent DE14 1LE
tel (01283) 512345 *fax* (01283) 515351
Editor Brian J. Vertigen
Daily 28p

Features, news and articles of interest to Burton and south Derbyshire readers.

Length: 400-500 words. Illustrations: colour and b&w. Payment: by negotiation. Founded 1898.

Chronicle & Echo, Northampton
Northamptonshire Newspapers Ltd, Upper Mounts, Northampton NN1 3HR
tel (01604) 231122 *fax* (01604) 233000
Editor Mark Edwards
Daily 28p

Articles, features and news – mostly commissioned – of interest to the Northampton area. Length/illustrations: varies. Payment: by negotiation. Founded 1931.

Derby Evening Telegraph
Northcliffe House, Meadow Road, Derby DE1 2DW
tel (01332) 291111 *fax* (01322) 253027
Editor Keith Perch
Mon-Sat 29p

Articles and news of local interest. Payment: by negotiation.

The Leicester Mercury
St George Street, Leicester LE1 9FQ
tel (0116) 251 2512 *fax* (0116) 253 0645
Editor Nick Carter
Mon-Sat 27p

Occasional articles, features and news; submit ideas to editor first. Length/payment: by negotiation. Founded 1874.

Nottingham Evening Post
Forman Street, Nottingham NG1 4AB
tel (0115) 948 2000 *fax* (0115) 964 4027
Daily 27p

Material on local issues considered. Founded 1878.

North

Evening Chronicle
Newcastle Chronicle and Journal Ltd, Thomson House, Groat Market, Newcastle upon Tyne NE1 1ED
tel 0191-232 7500 *fax* 0191-232 2256
Editor Alison Hastings
Daily 25p

News, photos and features covering almost every subject of interest to readers in Tyne and Wear, Northumberland and Durham. Payment: according to value.

Evening Gazette
North Eastern Evening Gazette Ltd, Borough Road, Middlesbrough TS1 3AZ

tel (01642) 245401 *fax* (01642) 232014
Editor Ranald Allan
Mon-Sat 24p

News, and topical and lifestyle features. Length: 600-800 words. Illustrations: line, half-tone, colour, graphics, cartoons. Payment: £50 per 1000 words; scale rate or by agreement for illustrations. Founded 1869.

Hartlepool Mail

Northeast Press Ltd, Clarence Road, Hartlepool, Cleveland TS24 8BU
tel (01429) 274441 *fax* (01429) 869024
Editor Christopher Cox
27p Daily

Features of local interest. Length: 500 words. Illustrations: colour, b&w photos, line, cartoons. Payment: by negotiation. Founded 1877.

The Journal

Thomson House, Groat Market, Newcastle upon Tyne NE1 1ED
tel 0191-232 7500 *fax* 0191-261 8869
e-mail journal@ncjlih.demon.co.uk
Editor Mark Dickinson
Daily 32p

News, sport items and features of topical interest considered. Payment: by arrangement.

The Northern Echo

Priestgate, Darlington,
Co. Durham DL1 1NF
tel (01325) 381313 *fax* (01325) 380539
Editor Andrew Smith
Daily 30p

Articles of interest to North-East and North Yorkshire; all material commissioned. Preliminary study of newspaper advisable. Length: 800-1000 words. Illustrations: line, half-tone, colour – mostly commissioned. Payment: by negotiation. Founded 1870.

North-West Evening Mail

Newspaper House, Abbey Road,
Barrow-in-Furness, Cumbria LA14 5QS
tel (01229) 821835 *fax* (01229) 840164/832141
Editor Donald Martin
Mon-Sat 28p

'The Voice of Furness and West Cumbria.' Articles, features and news. Length: 500 words. Illustrations: b&w photos and occasional artwork. Payment: £30 (minimum); £10 for illustrations. Founded 1898.

The Sunday Sun

Thomson House, Groat Market, Newcastle upon Tyne NE1 1ED
tel 0191-201 6330 *fax* 0191-230 0238
Editor Chris Rushton
Weekly 55p

Key requirements: immediate topicality and human sidelights on current problems. Particularly welcomed are special features of family appeal and news stories of special interest to the North-East of England. Length: 200-800 words. Payment: normal lineage rates, or by arrangement. Illustrations: photos and line, cartoons. Founded 1919.

Sunderland Echo

Echo House, Pennywell, Sunderland,
Tyne & Wear SR4 9ER
tel 0191-534 3011 *fax* 0191-534 5975
ad-doc DX60743
web site http://www.sunderland.com/echo
Editor A.G. Hughes
Mon-Sat 28p

Local news, features and articles. Length: 500 words. Illustrations: colour and b&w photos, line, cartoons. Payment: negotiable. Founded 1875.

North West

Bolton Evening News

Newspaper House, Churchgate, Bolton,
Lancs. BL1 1DE
tel (01204) 522345 *fax* (01204) 365068
Daily 28p

Articles, particularly those with South Lancashire appeal. Length: up to 500 words. Illustrations: photos; considered at usual rates. Payment: by arrangement. Founded 1867.

Daily Post

PO Box 48, Old Hall Street, Liverpool L69 3EB
tel 0151-227 2000 *fax* 0151-236 4682
Editor Alastair Machray
Daily 30p

Articles of general interest and topical features of special interest to North West England and North Wales. No verse or fiction. Payment: according to value. News and feature illustrations. Founded 1855.

The Gazette
Blackpool Gazette & Herald Ltd, PO Box 20,
Preston New Road, Blackpool FY4 4AU
tel (01253) 839999 *fax* (01253) 694152
e-mail lindsey_allen@ypn.co.uk
web site http://www.blackpool.com
Director and General Manager Philip Welsh
Daily Mon-Sat 27p

Local news and articles of general interest, with photos if appropriate. Length: varies. Payment: on merit. Founded 1929.

Lancashire Evening Post
Oliver's Place, Fulwood, Preston PR2 9ZA
tel (01772) 254841 *fax* (01772) 880173
Editor Neil Hodgkinson
Daily 27p

Topical articles on all subjects. Area of interest Wigan to Lake District, Lancs, and coast. Length: 600-900 words. Illustrations: colour and b&w photos, cartoons. Payment: by arrangement.

Lancashire Evening Telegraph
Newspaper House, High Street, Blackburn,
Lancs. BB1 1HT
tel (01254) 678678
web site http://www.newsquest.co.uk
Editor Peter Butterfield
Daily 26p

Will consider general interest articles, such as holidays, property, motoring, finance, etc. Payment: by arrangement. Founded 1886.

Liverpool Echo
PO Box 48, Old Hall Street, Liverpool L69 3EB
tel 0151-227 2000 *fax* 0151-236 4682
Editor John Griffith
Daily 28p

Articles of up to 600-800 words of local or topical interest; also cartoons. Payment: according to merit; special rates for exceptional material. This newspaper is connected with, but independent of, the *Liverpool Daily Post*. Articles not interchangeable.

Manchester Evening News
164 Deansgate, Manchester M60 2RD
tel 0161-832 7200 editorial *fax* 0161-834 3814
features fax 0161-839 0968
Editor Michael Unger
Daily 30p

Feature articles of up to 1000 words, topical or general interest and illustrated where appropriate, should be addressed to the Features Editor. Payment: on acceptance.

Oldham Evening Chronicle
PO Box 47, Union Street, Oldham,
Lancs. OL1 1EQ
tel 0161-633 2121 *fax* 0161-627 0905
Editor Philip Hirst
Daily Mon-Fri 30p

News and features on current topics and local history. Length: 1000 words. Illustrations: colour and b&w photos and line. Payment: £20-£25 per 1000 words; £16.32-£21.90 for illustrations. Founded 1854.

Northern Ireland – see Belfast

Scotland

Aberdeen Evening Express
Aberdeen Journals Ltd, PO Box 43, Lang Stracht,
Mastrick, Aberdeen AB15 6DF
tel (01224) 690222 *fax* (01224) 699575
Editor Geoff Teather
Daily 26p

Lively evening paper reading. Illustrations: colour and b&w, cartoons. Payment: by arrangement.

The Courier and Advertiser
D.C. Thomson & Co. Ltd, 80 Kingsway East,
Dundee DD4 8SL
tel (01382) 223131 *fax* (01382) 454590
185 Fleet Street, London EC4A 2HS
tel 0171-242 5086
Daily 30p

Founded 1816 and 1801.

Dundee Evening Telegraph and Post
D.C. Thomson & Co. Ltd, 80 Kingsway East,
Dundee DD4 8SL
tel (01382) 223131 *fax* (01382) 454590
London office 185 Fleet Street, London EC4A 2HS
tel 0171-242 5086 *fax* 0171-404 5694
25p Daily

Edinburgh Evening News
20 North Bridge, Edinburgh EH1 1YT
tel 0131-225 2468 *fax* 0131-225 7302
Editor John McGurk
Daily 25p

Features on current affairs, preferably in relation to our circulation area. Women's talking points, local historical articles; subjects of general interest.

Glasgow Evening Times

195 Albion Street, Glasgow G1 1QP
tel 0141-552 6255 fax 0141-553 1355
web site http://www.cims.co.uk/eveningtimes
London office 127 Clerkenwell Road,
London EC1R 5DB
tel 0171-405 2121 fax 0171-405 1888
Editor John Scott
Daily 30p
Founded 1876.

Inverness Courier

PO Box 13, 9-11 Bank Lane, Inverness IV1 1QW
tel (01463) 233059 fax (01463) 243439
e-mail courier@zetnet.co.uk
Editor John Macdonald
2 p.w. Tue 37p Fri 40p

Articles of Highland interest only.
Unsolicited material accepted.
Illustrations: colour and b&w photos.
Payment: by arrangement. Founded
1817.

The Press and Journal

Lang Stracht, Aberdeen AB9 8AF
tel (01224) 690222
e-mail editor@pj.ajl.co.uk
web site http://www.pressandjournal.co.uk
Editor Derek Tucker
Daily 35p

Contributions of Scottish interest.
Payment: by arrangement. Illustrations:
half-tone. Founded 1748.

The Sun

News International Newspapers, Scotland,
124 Portman Street, Kinning Park,
Glasgow G41 1EJ
tel (0141) 420 5200 fax (0141) 420 5248
Editor Bob Bird
Daily 25p

Scottish edition of The Sun. Illustrations:
transparencies, colour and b&w prints,
colour cartoons. Payment: by arrangement. Founded 1985.

South East

Evening Echo

Newspaper House, Chester Hall Lane, Basildon,
Essex SS9 1RE
tel (01268) 522792 fax (01268) 282884
Editor Martin McNeill
Daily Mon-Fri 30p

Mostly staff-written. Only interested in
local material. Payment: by arrangement.
Founded 1969.

Evening Standard

Northcliffe House, 2 Derry Street, London W8 5EE
tel 0171-938 6000
Editor Max Hastings
Daily 30p

Articles of general interest considered,
1500 words or shorter; also news, pictures and ideas. Founded 1827.

ES Magazine

Editor Adam Edwards
Weekly Free with paper

Feature ideas, exclusively about London.
Payment: by negotiation. Illustrations: all
types.

Kent Messenger

6 and 7 Middle Row, Maidstone,
Kent ME14 1TG
tel (01622) 695666 fax (01622) 757227
Fri 40p

Articles of special interest to Kent, par-
ticularly Maidstone, the Weald and Mid-
Kent areas. Payment: state price.
Illustrations: any format.

Kent Today

395 High Street, Chatham, Kent ME4 4PQ
tel (01634) 830999 fax (01634) 829484
Daily Mon-Fri 25p

Paper with emphasis on news and sport,
plus regular feature pages. National
news; with editions covering the
Medway Towns, Gravesend and Dartford,
Swale, Maidstone. Illustrations: line,
half-tone.

Reading Evening Post

8 Tessa Road, Reading, Berks. RG1 8NS
tel (01734) 575833 fax (01734) 599363
Editor Kim Chapman
Daily 25p

Topical articles based on current local
news. Length: 800-1200 words. Payment:
based on lineage rates. Illustrations: half-
tone. Founded 1965.

The Southern Daily Echo
Newspaper House, Test Lane, Redbridge, Southampton SO16 9JX
tel (01703) 424777 *fax* (01703) 424770
Editor Mike Woods
Daily 30p
News, articles, features, sport. Length: varies. Illustrations: line, half-tone, colour. Payment: NUJ rates. Founded 1888.

The News, Portsmouth
The News Centre, Hilsea, Portsmouth PO2 9SX
tel (01705) 664488 *fax* (01705) 673363
Editor Geoffrey Elliott
Daily 28p
Articles of relevance to southeast Hampshire and West Sussex. Length: 600 words. Illustrations: photos, preferably in colour, cartoons. Payment: £50. Founded 1877.

South West

The Bath Chronicle
Newsquest (Wessex) Ltd, 33-34 Westgate Street, Bath BA1 1EW
tel (01225) 444044 *fax* (01225) 445969
Editor David Gledhill
Mon-Sat 30p
Welcomes local news and features. Length: 200-500 words. Illustrations: colour photos. Payment: 8p-15.7p per printed line; £5 per photo where commissioned. Founded 1760.

Bristol Evening Post
Temple Way, Bristol BS99 7HD
tel (0117) 934 3000
Editor Mike Lowe
Daily 27p
Takes freelance news and articles. Payment: by arrangement. Founded 1932.

The Citizen
Gloucestershire Newspapers Ltd, St John's Lane, Gloucester GL1 2AY
tel (01452) 424442 *fax* (01452) 420664
Editor Spencer Feeney
Daily 30p
Local news and features for Gloucester and its districts. Length: 1000 words (articles/features), 300 words (news). Illustrations: colour. Payment: negotiable.

Dorset Evening Echo
Southern Newspapers plc, 57 St Thomas Street, Weymouth, Dorset DT4 8EU
tel (01305) 784804 *fax* (01305) 760387
e-mail echo@wdi.co.uk
Editor David Lee
Daily 28p

News and occasional features (1000-2000 words). Illustrations: b&w photos. Payment: by negotiation. Founded 1921.

Evening Echo
Richmond Hill, Bournemouth, Dorset BH2 6HH
tel (01202) 554601 *fax* (01202) 292115
Editor Mike Woods
Mon-Sat 28p
Local news and features. Length: up to 500 words. Illustrations: line, half-tone, colour, cartoons. Payment: by arrangement. Founded 1900.

Express & Echo
Express & Echo Publications Ltd, Heron Road, Sowton, Exeter, Devon EX2 7NF
tel (01392) 442211 *fax* (01392) 442294/442287
Editor John Meehan
Mon-Sat 27p
Features and news of local interest. Length: features 500-800 words, news up to 400 words. Illustrations: colour. Payment: lineage rates; illustrations negotiable. Founded 1904.

Gloucestershire Echo
Cheltenham Newspaper Co. Ltd, 1 Clarence Parade, Cheltenham, Glos. GL50 3NZ
tel (01242) 271900 *fax* (01242) 217803
Editor Anita Syvret
Daily 30p
Specialist articles with Gloucestershire connections; no fiction. Material mostly commissioned. Length: 350 words. Payment: £30 per article, negotiable. Founded 1873.

Sunday Independent (West of England)
Southern Newspapers plc, Burrington Way, Plymouth PL5 3LN
tel (01752) 206600 *fax* (01752) 206164
Editor Anna Jenkins
Weekly 55p
News features on West Country topics; features/articles with a nostalgic theme; short quirky news briefs (must be original). Length: 600 words (articles/features), 300 words (news). Illustrations: colour and b&w. Payment: by arrangement. Founded 1808.

Western Daily Press
Bristol Evening Post and Press Ltd, Temple Way, Bristol BS99 7HD
tel (0117) 934 3000 *fax* (0117) 934 3574
Editor Ian Beales
Daily 32p

National, international or West Country topics for features or news items, from established journalists, with or without illustrations. Payment: by negotiation. Founded 1858.

The Western Morning News

Brest Road, Derriford, Plymouth PL6 5AA
tel (01752) 765500 *fax* (01752) 765535
Editor Barrie Williams
Daily 32p

Articles of 600-800 words, plus illustrations, considered on West Country subjects. Founded 1860.

Wales

South Wales Echo

Thomson House, Havelock Street, Cardiff CF1 1XR
tel (01222) 583583/223333 *fax* (01222) 583624
Editor Robin Fletcher
Daily 26p

Evening paper: features, showbiz, news features, personality interviews. Length: up to 700 words. Illustrations: photos, cartoons. Payment: by negotiation. Founded 1884.

The Western Mail

Thomson House, Cardiff CF1 1XR
tel (01222) 223333 *fax* (01222) 583652
Editor Neil Fowler
Daily 35p

Articles of political, industrial, literary or general and Welsh interest are considered. Illustrations: topical general news and feature pictures, cartoons. Payment: according to value; special fees for exclusive news. Founded 1869.

West Midlands

Birmingham Evening Mail

28 Colmore Circus, Queensway,
Birmingham B4 6AX
tel 0121-236 3366 *fax* 0121-625 1105
London office 11 Buckingham Street,
London WC2N 6DF
tel 0171-409 7409 *fax* 0171-495 2742
Editor I. Dowell
Daily 28p

Features of topical Midland interest considered. Length: 400-800 words. Payment: by arrangement. Founded 1870.

The Birmingham Post

PO Box 18, 28 Colmore Circus,
Birmingham B4 6AX
tel 0121-236 3366 *fax* 0121-625 1105
London office 11 Buckingham Street,
London WC2N 6DF
tel 0171-409 7409 *fax* 0171-495 2742
Editor N. Hastilow
Daily 37p

Authoritative and well-written articles of industrial, political or general interest are considered, especially if they have relevance to the Midlands. Length: up to 1000 words. Payment: by arrangement.

Coventry Evening Telegraph

Corporation Street, Coventry CV1 1FP
tel (01203) 633633 *fax* (01203) 550869
Editor Dan Mason
Daily 30p

Topical, illustrated articles, those with a Warwickshire interest particularly acceptable. Length: up to 600 words. Payment: by arrangement.

Express and Star

Queen Street, Wolverhampton WV1 1ES
tel (01902) 313131 *fax* (01902) 319721
Editor Warren Wilson
London office Room 110, Temple Chambers,
Temple Avenue, London EC4Y 0DT
Daily 30p

Founded 1874.

Shropshire Star

Ketley, Telford TF1 4HU
tel (01952) 242424 *fax* (01952) 254605
Editor Andy Wright
Daily 28p

Evening paper: news and features. No unsolicited material; write to features editor with outline of ideas. Payment: by arrangement. Founded 1964.

Sunday Mercury

Colmore Circus, Birmingham B4 6AZ
tel 0121-236 3366 *fax* 0121-233 0271
Editor Peter Whitehouse
Weekly 55p

News specials or features of Midland interest. Illustrations: colour, b&w, cartoons. Special rates for special matter.

Yorkshire/Humberside

Evening Courier
PO Box 19, King Cross Street, Halifax HX1 2SF
tel (01422) 365711 *fax* (01422) 330021
Editor Edward Riley
2 per day Mon-Sat 30p
Articles of local interest and background to news events. Length: up to 500 words. Illustrations: b&w photos. Payment: £25-£40 per article; photos per quality/size used. Founded 1892.

The Evening Press
York and County Press, PO Box 29, 76-86 Walmgate, York YO1 1YN
tel (01904) 653051 *fax* (01904) 612853
Editor Elizabeth Page
Daily 30p
Articles of North and East Yorkshire interest, humour, personal experience of current affairs. Length: 500-1000 words. Payment: by arrangement. Illustrations: line, half-tone, cartoons. Founded 1882.

Grimsby Evening Telegraph
80 Cleethorpe Road, Grimsby, North East Lincolnshire DN31 3EH
tel (01472) 360360 *fax* (01472) 372257
e-mail grimsbytelegraph@dial.pipex.com
web site http://www.grimsbytelegraph.co.uk
Editor Peter Moore
Daily 27p
Considers general interest articles. Illustrations: line, half-tone, colour, cartoons. Payment: by arrangement. Founded 1897.

The Star
York Street, Sheffield S1 1PU
tel (0114) 276 7676 *fax* (0114) 272 5978
Editor Peter Charlton
Daily 27p
Well-written articles of local character. Length: about 500 words. Payment: by negotiation. Illustrations: topical photos, line drawings, graphics, cartoons. Founded 1887.

Telegraph & Argus
Hall Ings, Bradford, West Yorkshire BD1 1JR
tel (01274) 729511 *fax* (01274) 723634
Editor Perry Austin-Clarke
Daily 28p
Evening paper: news, articles and features relevant to or about the people of West Yorkshire. Length: up to 1000 words. Illustrations: line, half-tone, colour. Payment: features from £15; line from £5, b&w photos from £14.40, colour photos from £19.50. Founded 1868.

Yorkshire Evening Post
PO Box 168, Wellington Street, Leeds LS1 1RF
tel (0113) 2432701 *fax* (0113) 2388535
Editor C.H. Bye
Daily Mon-Sat 28p
News stories and feature articles. Illustrations: colour and b&w, cartoons. Payment: by negotiation. Founded 1890.

Yorkshire Gazette & Herald Series
PO Box 29, 76-86 Walmgate, York YO1 1YN
tel (01904) 653051 *fax* (01904) 611488
Editor Bob McMillan
Weekly 40p
Stories, features and pictures of local interest. Payment: varies. Illustrations: line, half-tone, colour.

Yorkshire Post
Wellington Street, Leeds LS1 1RF
tel (0113) 243 2701 *fax* (0113) 238 8537
Editor Tony Watson
London office Ludgate House, 245 Blackfriars Road, London SE1 9UY
tel 0171-921 5000
Daily 38p
Authoritative and well-written articles on new topics or on topical subjects of general, literary or industrial interests. Length: 1200-1500 words. Illustrations: photos and frequent pocket cartoons (single column width), topical wherever possible. Payment: by arrangement. Founded 1754.

Magazines UK and Ireland

Listings for regional newspapers start on page 12 and listings for national newspapers start on page 3. For quick reference, magazines are listed by subject area on page 121. See page 132 for recent changes to newspapers and magazines and for newspapers and magazines on the Internet.

AA Magazine
Redwood Publishing Ltd, 12-26 Lexington Street, London W1R 4HQ
tel 0171-312 2600 *fax* 0171-312 2679
Editor Patrick Devereux
Quarterly Free to members

Articles on motoring, travel and lifestyle. Length: 500-1500 words. Illustrations: colour. Payment: negotiable. Founded 1992.

Accountancy
40 Bernard Street, London WC1N 1LD
tel 0171-833 3291 *fax* 0171-833 2085
e-mail postmaster@theabg@.demon.co.uk
web site http://www.accountancymag.co.uk
Editor Brian Singleton-Green
Monthly £3.75

Articles on accounting, taxation, financial, legal and other subjects likely to be of professional interest to accountants in practice or industry, and to top management generally; cartoons. Payment: £110 per page. Founded 1889.

Accountancy Age
VNU Business Publications, VNU House, 32-34 Broadwick Street, London W1A 2HG
tel 0171-316 9000 *fax* 0171-316 9008
Editor Andrew Pring
Weekly £2.00 (£100 p.a.)

Articles of accounting, financial and business interest. Illustrations: colour photos; freelance assignments commissioned. Payment: by arrangement. Founded 1969.

Achievement
Response Publishing Group plc, 41-45 Goswell Road, London EC1V 7EH
tel 0171-490 0550 *fax* 0171-490 0375
e-mail response@compulink.co.uk
Quarterly £15.00 p.a.

In-depth articles, news and updates on major international projects. Illustrations: first-class photos. Payment: by arrangement.

Active Life
Aspen Specialist Media, Christ Church, Cosway Street, London NW1 5NJ
tel 0171-262 2622
Editor Helene Hodge
Bi-monthly £2.30

Lifestyle advice for the over 50s, including holidays and health, fashion and food, finance and fiction, hobbies and home, personality profiles. Submit ideas in writing. Length: 600-1200 words. Illustrations: colour. Payment: £100 per 1000 words; photos by negotiation. Founded 1989.

Acumen
6 The Mount, Higher Furzeham, Brixham, South Devon TQ5 8QY
tel (01803) 851098
Editor Patricia Oxley
Tri-annual (Jan/May/Sept) £10.00 p.a.

Poetry, literary and critical articles, reviews, literary memoirs, etc, 100pp or more. Send sae with submissions. Payment: by negotiation. Founded 1985.

Aeromodeller
Nexus Special Interests, Nexus House, Boundary Way, Hemel Hempstead, Herts. HP2 7ST
tel (01442) 66551 *fax* (01442) 66998
Editor Alec Gee
13 p.a. £2.35

Articles and news concerning model aircraft. Suitable articles and first-class photos by outside contributors are always considered. Length: 750-2000 words, or by arrangement. Illustrations: photos and line drawings to scale. Payment: by negotiation. Founded 1935.

Aeroplane Monthly

IPC Magazines Ltd, King's Reach Tower, Stamford Street, London SE1 9LS
tel 0171-261 5551 *fax* 0171-261 5269
Editor Richard T. Riding
Monthly £2.70

Articles and photos relating to historical aviation. Length: up to 3000 words. Illustrations: line, half-tone, colour, cartoons. Payment: £50 per 1000 words, payable on publication; photos £10; colour £80 per page. Founded 1973.

Africa Confidential

Blackwell Publishing Ltd, 73 Farringdon Road, London EC1M 3JB
tel 0171-831 3511 *fax* 0171-831 6778
web site africa-confidential.com.uk
Editor Patrick Smith
Fortnightly £202.00 p.a.

News and analysis of political and economic developments in Africa. Unsolicited contributions welcomed, but must be exclusive and not published elsewhere. Length: 1200-word features, 200-word pointers. Payment: £200 per 1000 words. No illustrations. Founded 1960.

Africa: St Patrick's Missions

St Patrick's, Kiltegan, Co. Wicklow, Republic of Ireland
tel (0508) 73233 *fax* (0508) 73281
Editor Rev. Gary Howley
9 p.a. £5.00 p.a.

Articles of missionary and topical religious interest. Length: up to 1000 words. Illustrations: line, half-tone, colour.

African Business

IC Publications Ltd, 7 Coldbath Square, London EC1R 4LQ
tel 0171-713 7711 *fax* 0171-713 7970
Editor Anver Versi
Monthly £2.00

Articles on business, economic and financial topics of interest to businessmen, ministers, officials concerned with African affairs. Length: 400-750 words; shorter coverage 100-400 words. Illustrations: line, half-tone. Payment: £70 per 1000 words; £1 per column cm for illustrations. Founded 1978.

Agenda

5 Cranbourne Court, Albert Bridge Road, London SW11 4PE
tel/fax 0171-228 0700
Editor William Cookson, *Assistant Editor* Anita Money

Quarterly £20.00 p.a. (libraries, institutions and overseas: rates on application)

Poetry and criticism. Contributors should study the journal before submitting MSS with an sae. Illustrations: half-tone. Payment: variable – depends on finances.

Air International

Key Publishing Ltd, PO Box 100, Stamford, Lincs. PE9 1XQ
tel (01780) 55131 *fax* (01780) 57261
Editor Malcolm English
Monthly £2.55

Technical articles on aircraft; features on topical aviation subjects – civil and military; historical aviation subjects. Length: up to 5000 words. Illustrations: colour transparencies/prints, b&w prints/line drawings, cartoons. Payment: £50 per 1000 words or by negotiation; £25 colour, £10 b&w. Founded 1971.

Air Pictorial International

HPC Publishing, Drury Lane, St Leonards-on-Sea, East Sussex TN38 9BJ
tel (01424) 720477 *fax* (01424) 443693/434086
Editor Barry C. Wheeler
Monthly £2.35

Covers all aspects of aviation. Many articles commissioned, and the editor is glad to consider competent articles exploring fresh ground or presenting an individual point of view on technical matters. All articles are illustrated, mainly with photos. Payment: by arrangement.

Amateur Gardening

IPC Magazines Ltd, Westover House, West Quay Road, Poole, Dorset BH15 1JG
tel (01202) 680586 *fax* (01202) 674335
e-mail amateurgardening@ipc.co.uk
Editor G. Clarke
Weekly 90p

Articles up to 700 words about any aspect of gardening. Payment: by arrangement. Illustrations: colour. Founded 1884.

Amateur Photographer

IPC Magazines Ltd, King's Reach Tower, Stamford Street, London SE1 9LS
tel 0171-261 5100 *fax* 0171-261 5404
e-mail amateurphotographer@ipc.co.uk
Editor Keith Wilson
Weekly £1.60

Original articles of pictorial or technical interest, preferably illustrated with either photos or diagrams. Good instruc-

tional features especially sought. Length preferred: (unillustrated) 400-800 words; articles up to 1500 words; (illustrated) 2 to 4 pages. Payment: weekly, at rates according to usage. Illustrations unaccompanied by text considered for covers or feature illustrations – please indicate if we can hold on file. Founded 1884.

Amateur Stage

Platform Publications Ltd, 83 George Street, London W1H 5PL
tel 0171-486 1732 *fax* 0171-224 2215
e-mail cvtheatre@aol.com
Editor Charles Vance
Monthly £2.00

Articles on all aspects of the amateur theatre, preferably practical and factual. Length: 600-2000 words. Illustrations: photos and line drawings. Payment: none. Founded 1946.

Ambit

17 Priory Gardens, London N6 5QY
tel 0181-340 3566
Editor Dr Martin Bax
Quarterly £6.00 inc. p&p (£22.00 p.a. UK; £24/$48 p.a. overseas)

Poems, short stories, criticism. Payment: by arrangement. Illustrations: line, half-tone, colour. Founded 1959.

American Markets Newsletter

175 Westland Drive, Glasgow G14 9JQ
e-mail foconnor@iee.org
Editor Sheila O'Connor
10 p.a. £29.00 p.a. (£53 for 2 years)

Editorial guidelines for US, Canadian and other overseas markets, plus information on press trips, non-fiction/fiction markets and writers' tips. Sample issue £2.95 (payable to S. O'Connor).

AN

(formerly Artists Newsletter)
AN Publications, PO Box 23, Sunderland SR4 6DG
tel (0191) 567 3589 *fax* (0191) 564 1600
e-mail an@anpubs.demon.co.uk
Editor Angela Kingston
Monthly £2.75 (£23.50 p.a.)

Articles, news and features for practising artists and makers. Illustrations: transparencies, colour and b&w photos. Payment: £100 per 1000 words. Founded 1983.

Angler's Mail

IPC Magazines Ltd, King's Reach Tower, Stamford Street, London SE1 9LS
tel 0171-261 5778 *fax* 0171-261 6016
Editor Roy Westwood
Weekly 90p

News items about coarse and sea fishing. Payment: by agreement.

Angling Times

EMAP Pursuit Publishing Ltd, PO Box 231, Bretton Court, Bretton, Peterborough PE3 8EN
tel (01733) 266222/264666 *fax* (01733) 465257
Editor John Kelly
Weekly 83p

Articles, pictures, news stories, on all forms of angling. Illustrations: line, half-tone, colour. Payment: by arrangement. Founded 1953.

The Antique Dealer & Collectors Guide

PO Box 805, London SE10 8TD
tel 0181-691 4820
Editor Philip Bartlam
Monthly £2.75

Articles on antique collecting and art. Length: 1500-2000 words. Payment: £76 per 1000 words. Illustrations: half-tone, colour.

Apollo

1-2 Castle Lane, London SW1E 6DR
tel 0171-233 6640 *fax* 0171-630 7791
Editor Robin Simon
Monthly £7.80

Knowledgeable articles of about 2500 words on art, architecture, ceramics, furniture, armour, glass, sculpture, and any subject connected with art and collecting. Payment: by arrangement. Illustrations: half-tone, colour. Founded 1925.

The Aquarist and Pondkeeper

M&J Publications Ltd, Caxton House, Wellesley Road, Ashford, Kent TN24 8ET
tel (01233) 636349 *fax* (01233) 631239
Editor Dick Mills
Monthly £2.25

Illustrated authoritative articles by professional and amateur biologists, naturalists and aquarium hobbyists on all matters concerning life in and near water, conservation and herpetology. Length: about 1500 words. Illustrations: line, half-tone, colour, cartoons. Payment: by arrangement. Founded 1924.

The Architects' Journal
EMAP Construct, 151 Rosebery Avenue,
London EC1R 4QX
tel 0171-505 6700 *fax* 0171-505 6701
Editor Paul Finch
Weekly £1.80 (£75 p.a.)

Articles (mainly technical) on architecture, planning and building accepted only with prior agreement of synopsis. Illustrations: photos and drawings. Payment: by arrangement. Founded 1895.

Architectural Design
Academy Group Ltd, 42 Leinster Gardens,
London W2 3AN
tel 0171-402 2141 *fax* 0171-723 9540
Editor Maggie Toy
6 double issues p.a. £74.00 p.a. (£53.00 p.a. students)

International magazine comprising an extensively illustrated thematic profile presenting architecture and critical interpretations of architectural history, theory and practice. Uncommissioned articles not accepted. Illustrations: drawings and photos, colour, half-tone, line (colour preferred). Payment: by arrangement. Founded 1930.

Architectural Review
EMAP Construct, 151 Rosebery Avenue,
London EC1R 4QX
tel 0171-505 6725 *fax* 0171-505 6701
e-mail peterd@construct.emap.co.uk
web site www.emap.com/construct/arhome.htm
Editor Peter Davey
Monthly £5.95

Articles on architecture and the allied arts. Writers must be thoroughly qualified. Length: up to 3000 words. Payment: by arrangement. Illustrations: photos, drawings, etc. Founded 1896.

Architecture Today
161 Rosebery Avenue, London EC1R 4QX
tel 0171-837 0143 *fax* 0171-837 0155
Editors Ian Latham and Mark Swenarton
10 p.a. £3.00 Free to architects

Mostly commissioned articles and features on today's European architecture. Length: 200-800 words. Illustrations: colour. Payment: by negotiation. Founded 1989.

Arena
3rd Floor Block A, Exmouth House, Pine Street,
London EC1R 0JL
tel 0171-837 7270 *fax* 0171-837 3906
Editor Ekow Eshun
Monthly £2.70

Profiles, articles on a wide range of subjects intelligently treated; art, architecture, politics, sport, business, music, film, design, media, fashion. Length: up to 3000 words. Illustrations: b&w and colour photos. Payment: £200 per 1000 words; varies for illustrations. Founded 1986.

Army Quarterly & Defence Journal
1 West Street, Tavistock, Devon PL19 8DS
tel (01822) 613577/612785 *fax* (01822) 612785
Editor T.D. Bridge
Quarterly £52.00 p.a. (£138.00 3-yr saver contract)

Articles on a wide range of British, UN, Commonwealth and worldwide defence issues, historical and current; also Quarterly Diary, Defence Contracts, International Defence Reports, book and video reviews. Preliminary letter with synopsis preferred. Length: 1000-4800 words. Illustrations: b&w photos, line drawings, maps. Payment: by arrangement. Founded 1829.

Art & Craft
Scholastic Ltd, Villiers House, Clarendon Avenue, Leamington Spa, Warks. CV32 5PR
tel (01926) 887799 *fax* (01926) 883331
Editor Siân Morgan
Monthly £2.10

Articles offering fresh, creative ideas of a practical nature, based on teaching art, design and technology in the National Curriculum, for the infant/junior school teacher. Articles by teachers for teachers. Illustrations: colour and b&w line drawings. Payment: by arrangement. Founded 1936.

Art & Design
Academy Group Ltd, 42 Leinster Gardens,
London W2 3AN
tel 0171-402 2141 *fax* 0171-723 9540
Editor Nicola Kearton
6 double issues p.a. £68.00 p.a. (£53.00 p.a. students)

International magazine covering the whole spectrum of the arts, with particular emphasis on Contemporary Art. Each issue comprises extensively illustrated thematic features together with critical articles from well-known writers. Feature articles, exhibition reviews and previews, book reviews. Uncommissioned articles not accepted. Illustrations: line, half-tone, colour (colour preferred). Payment: by arrangement. Founded 1985.

Art Business Today

The Fine Art Trade Guild, 16-18 Empress Place,
London SW6 1TT
tel 0171-381 6616 *fax* 0171-381 2596
Editor Anne Beaton
Quarterly £15.00 p.a.

Distributed to the fine art and framing industry. Covers essential information on new products and technology, market trends and business analysis. Length: 800-1600 words. Illustrations: colour photos, cartoons. Payment: by arrangement. Founded 1991.

Art Monthly

Britannia Art Publications Ltd, Suite 17,
26 Charing Cross Road, London WC2H 0DG
tel 0171-240 0389 *fax* 0171-497 0726
Editor Patricia Bickers
10 p.a. £2.85

Features on modern and contemporary visual artists and art history, art theory and art-related issues; exhibition and book reviews. All material commissioned. Length: 1000-2000 words. Illustrations: b&w photos. Payment: features £100-£150; none for photos. Founded 1976.

The Art Newspaper

27-29 Vauxhall Grove, London SW8 1SY
tel 0171-735 3331 *fax* 0171-735 3332
Editor Anna Somers Cocks
11 p.a. £4.50 (£45.00 p.a.)

International coverage of the art market, news, commentary. Length: 200-1000 words. Illustrations: b&w photos. Payment: £120 per 1000 words. Founded 1990.

Art Review

Art Review Ltd, Hereford House,
23-24 Smithfield Street, London EC1A 9LB
tel 0171-236 4880 *fax* 0171-236 4881
Editor David Lee
Monthly £3.50

Art news and features. Commissioned work only. Payment: from £200 per 1000 words. Illustrations: line, half-tone, colour. Founded 1949.

The Artist

The Artists' Publishing Co. Ltd, Caxton House,
63-65 High Street, Tenterden, Kent TN30 6BD
tel (01580) 763673
Editor Sally Bulgin
Monthly £2.10

Practical, instructional articles on painting for all amateur and professional artists. Payment: by arrangement. Illustrations: line, half-tone, colour. Founded 1931.

Artists and Illustrators

The Fitzpatrick Building, 188-194 York Way,
London N7 9QR
tel 0171-700 8500 *fax* 0171-700 4985
Editor Laura Gascoigne
Monthly £2.40

Practical and business articles for amateur and professional artists. Length: 1000-1500 words. Illustrations: colour transparencies. Payment: variable. Founded 1986.

The Asda Magazine

River Publishing, 55 Greek Street,
London W1H 5LR
tel 0171-306 0304 *fax* 0171-306 0314
Editor Linda McKay
Monthly Free

General features on food, health and nutrition; consumer stories. Length: 200-1500 words Payment: £100-£500. Founded 1986.

The Asian Age

Media Asia Europe Ltd, Dolphin Media House,
Spring Villa Park, Spring Villa Road, Edgware,
Middlesex HA8 7EB
tel 0181-951 4401 *fax* 0181-951 4839
Editor M.J. Akbar
Daily 50p

Articles and features of interest to the Asian community; material mostly commissioned. Length: 200-1500 words. Illustrations: b&w photos. Payment: £50 per 1000 words; £40 per photo. Founded 1994.

Asian Times

Ethnic Media Group, 1st Floor, 148 Cambridge
Heath Road, London E1 5QJ
tel 0171-702 8012 *fax* 0171-702 7937
Editor Arif Ali
Weekly 50p

News stories, articles and features of interest to Britain's Asian community. Founded 1983.

Astronomy Now

Pole Star Publications, PO Box 175, Tonbridge,
Kent TN10 4ZY
tel (01732) 367542 *fax* (01732) 356230
Editor Pam Spence
Monthly £2.25

Aimed at amateur and professional astronomers. Interested in news items and longer features on astronomy and some space-related activities. Writers' guidelines available (send sae). Length: 1500-3000 words. Illustrations: line, half-tone, colour. Payment: 5p per word; from £10 per photo. Founded 1987.

Athletics Weekly

EMAP Pursuit Publishing Ltd, Bretton Court, Bretton, Peterborough PE3 8DZ
tel (01733) 261144 *fax* (01733) 465206
Editor Nigel Walsh
Weekly £1.40

News and features on track and field athletics, road running, cross country, fell and race walking. Material mostly commissioned. Length: 1000-3000 words. Illustrations: colour and b&w action and head/shoulder photos, line, cartoons. Payment: varies. Founded 1946.

Attitude

Northern & Shell plc, Northern & Shell Tower, City Harbour, London E14 9GL
tel 0171-308 5090 *fax* 0171-308 5075
Editor James Collard
Monthly £2.20

Men's style magazine aimed primarily but not exclusively at gay men. Covers style/fashion, interviews, reviews. Illustrations: colour transparencies and b&w prints. Payment: £150 per 1000 words; £100 per full page illustration. Founded 1994.

The Author

84 Drayton Gardens, London SW10 9SB
tel 0171-373 6642
Editor Derek Parker
Quarterly £7.00

Organ of The Society of Authors. Commissioned articles from 1000-2000 words on any subject connected with the legal, commercial or technical side of authorship. Little scope for the freelance writer: preliminary letter advisable. Illustrations: line, occasional cartoons. Payment: by arrangement. Founded 1890.

Auto Express

Dennis Publishing Ltd, 19 Bolsover Street, London W1P 7HJ
tel 0171-631 1433 *fax* 0171-917 5556
Editor David Johns
Weekly £1.20

News stories, and general interest features about drivers as well as cars. Illustrations: colour photos. Payment: features £250 per 1000 words; photos, varies. Founded 1988.

Autocar

Haymarket Publishing Ltd, 38-42 Hampton Road, Teddington, Middlesex TW11 0JE
tel 0181-943 5851 *fax* 0181-943 5853
e-mail compuserve 100020.2017
Editor Patrick Fuller
Weekly £1.80

Articles on all aspects of cars, motoring and the motor industry: general, practical, competition and technical. Illustrations: line (litho), colour and electronic (Illustrator). Press day news: Thursday. Payment: varies; mid-month following publication. Founded 1895.

Babycare and Your Pregnancy

(formerly First Steps)
D.C. Thomson & Co. Ltd, 80 Kingsway East, Dundee DD4 8SL
tel (01382) 223131 *fax* (01382) 452491
Editor Irene K. Duncan
Monthly £1.55

Cares about the mother and her needs as well as the baby. Interested in articles on pregnancy, birth and childcare, and fillers. Illustrations: colour transparencies and colour artwork. Length/payment: negotiable. Founded 1994.

Back Street Heroes

PO Box 28, Altrincham, Cheshire WA14 2FG
tel 0161-928 3480 *fax* 0161-941 6897
Editor Karen Tait
Monthly £2.40

Custom motorcycle features plus informed lifestyle pieces. Illustrations: colour, cartoons. Payment: by arrangement. Founded 1983.

Balance

British Diabetic Association, 10 Queen Anne Street, London W1M 0BD
tel 0171-323 1531 *fax* 0171-637 3644
web site http://www.balance.net
Editor Maggie Gibbons
Bi-monthly £1.85

Articles on diabetes or related topics. Length: 1000-2000 words. Payment: by arrangement. Illustrations: colour. Founded 1935.

Ballroom Dancing Times

The Dancing Times Ltd, Clerkenwell House, 45-47 Clerkenwell Green, London EC1R 0EB
tel 0171-250 3006 *fax* 0171-253 6679
Editor Mary Clarke, *Executive Editor* Bronya Siefert
Monthly £1.00

Ballroom and social dancing from every aspect, but chiefly from the serious competitive, teaching and medal test angles. Well-informed freelance articles are occasionally used, but only after preliminary arrangements. Payment: by arrangement.

Illustrations: action photos preferred, b&w or colour. Founded 1956.

The Bank of Scotland Magazine

Brass Tacks Publishing Co. Ltd, 20 York Place, Edinburgh EH1 3EP
tel 0131-558 1542 *fax* 0131-558 1464
e-mail 106025.2652@compuserve.com
Editor Fraser Allen
2 p.a. Free to customers

Lifestyle features with a Scottish flavour, interviews with Scottish celebrities and financial features of Bank products and services. Illustrations: colour transparencies. Payment: varies.

The Banker

Maple House, Tottenham Court Road, London W1P 9LL
tel 0171-896 2525 *fax* 0171-896 2586
e-mail 100617,1135.compuserve.com
Editor Stephen Timewell
Monthly £4.95

Articles on capital markets, trade finance, bank analysis and top 1000 listings. Illustrations: half-tones and full colour of people, charts, tables, maps etc. Payment: by negotiation. Founded 1926.

Baptist Times

PO Box 54, 129 Broadway, Didcot, Oxon OX11 8XB
tel (01235) 512012 *fax* (01235) 512013
Editor John Capon
Weekly 45p

Religious or social affairs material, up to 1000 words. Payment: by arrangement. Illustrations: half-tone, cartoons. Founded 1855.

BBC English

PO Box 76, Bush House, Strand, London WC2B 4PH
tel 0171-257 8110 *fax* 0171-257 8316
e-mail bbcenglish.magazine@bbc.co.uk
Editor Jonas Hughes
Monthly £3.50

BBC World Service magazine for learning English. News, English language features, teaching features and book reviews. Length: 700-1000 words. Illustrations: colour artwork and cartoons. Payment: £60-100; £80. Founded 1963.

BBC Gardeners' World Magazine

BBC Worldwide Publishing, Woodlands, 80 Wood Lane, London W12 0TT
tel 0181-576 3959 *fax* 0181-576 3986
Editor Adam Pasco
Monthly £2.10

Features and ideas on plants, garden design and garden visits. All material commissioned. Study of magazine essential before submitting ideas. Length: varies, mainly 800-1000 words. Illustrations: colour transparencies; all artwork commissioned. Payment: by negotiation. Founded 1991.

BBC GoodFood

BBC Worldwide Publishing, Woodlands, 80 Wood Lane, London W12 0TT
tel 0181-576 2000 *fax* 0181-576 3825
Editor Mitzie Wilson
Monthly £1.55

Recipes from TV and radio, cookery features, food and wine news. No unsolicited material. Length: 700-1400 words. Illustrations: colour photos and line. Payment: by arrangement. Founded 1989.

BBC Homes & Antiques

BBC Worldwide Publishing, Woodlands, 80 Wood Lane, London W12 0TT
tel 0181-576 3490 *fax* 0181-576 3867
Editor Judith Hall
Monthly £2.00

Features on homes and antiques-related subjects. Length: 850-1500 words. Illustrations: colour. Payment: by arrangement. Founded 1993.

BBC Music Magazine

BBC Worldwide Publishing, Room A1004, Woodlands, 80 Wood Lane, London W12 0TT
tel 0181-576 3283 *fax* 0181-576 3292
Editor Fiona Maddocks
Monthly £3.75

Articles, features, news and reviews on classical music. All material commissioned. Length: up to 2000 words. Illustrations: line, half-tone, colour. Payment: £150 per 1000 words; varies for illustrations. Founded 1992.

BBC Top Gear Magazine

BBC Worldwide Publishing, Woodlands, 80 Wood Lane, London W12 0TT
tel 0181-576 2000 *fax* 0181-576 3754
web site http://www.topgear.com
Editor Kevin Blick
Monthly £2.95

Features on any aspect of cars and motoring; car tests. Material mostly commissioned. Length: 1500-3000 words. Illustrations: colour photos and line drawings. Payment: £200 per 1000 words; by agreement for illustrations. Founded 1993.

BBC Vegetarian GoodFood
BBC Worldwide Publishing, Woodlands,
80 Wood Lane, London W12 0TT
tel 0181-576 2000 *fax* 0181-576 3825
Editor Gilly Cubitt
Monthly £1.75

Cooking, nutrition, environmental issues.
Accepts feature ideas; no unsolicited
material. Illustrated, including cartoons.
Payment: by arrangement. Founded
1992.

BBC Wildlife Magazine
Broadcasting House, Whiteladies Road,
Bristol BS8 2LR
tel (0117) 973 8402 *fax* (0117) 946 7075
e-mail wildlifemag@gn.apc.org
Editor Rosamund Kidman Cox
Monthly £2.50

Popular but scientifically accurate articles about wildlife and conservation
(national and international), some linked
by subject to TV and radio programmes.
Two news sections for short, topical biological and environmental stories. Length
of articles: 3000 words. Illustrations: top-
quality colour photos. Payment: £200-
£350 per article; photos according to
reproduction size, £45-£150.

The Beano
D.C. Thomson & Co. Ltd, Albert Square,
Dundee DD1 9QJ
tel (01382) 223131 *fax* (01382) 322214
185 Fleet Street, London EC4A 2HS
tel 0171-242 5086 *fax* 0171-404 5694
Weekly 42p

Comic strips for children. Series, 11-22
pictures. Payment: on acceptance.

Beano Comic Library
D.C. Thomson & Co. Ltd, Albert Square,
Dundee DD1 9QJ
tel (01382) 223131 *fax* (01382) 322214
185 Fleet Street, London EC4A 2HS
tel 0171-242 5086 *fax* 0171-404 5694
2 p.m. 55p

Extra-long comic adventure stories featuring well-known characters from the
weekly *Beano* publication.

Bella
Shirley House, 25-27 Camden Road,
London NW1 9LL
tel 0171-284 0909 *fax* 0171-485 3774
Editor Jackie Highe
Weekly 57p

General interest magazine for women:
practical articles on fashion and beauty,
health, cooking, home, travel; real life
stories, plus fiction up to 2000 words.
Payment: by arrangement. Illustrations:
line including cartoons, half-tone, colour.
Founded 1987.

Best
10th Floor, Portland House, Stag Place,
London SW1E 5AU
tel 0171-245 8700 *fax* 0171-245 8825
Editor Julie Akhurst
Weekly 57p

Short stories. No other uncommissioned
work accepted, but always willing to look
at ideas/outlines. Length: 1300 words for
short stories, variable for other work. Illustrations: line, half-tone, colour, cartoons.
Payment: by agreement. Founded 1987.

Best of British
200 Eastgate, Deeping St James,
Peterborough PE6 8RD
tel/fax (01778) 347003
Editor Ian Beacham
Bi-monthly £2.40

Nostalgic features about life in the 1930s,
1940s and 1950s and personal memories.
Length: 1000 words. Illustrations: colour
and b&w. Payment: £40 (words); £20
(pictures). Founded 1994.

Big!
EMAP Metro, Mappin House, 4 Winsley Street,
London W1N 7AR
tel 0171-436 1515 *fax* 0171-631 0781
Editor Dominic Smith
Fortnightly 95p

Teenage entertainment, aimed at 11-17-
year-olds, covering pop, video, and film
and soap stars. Approach features editor
(Richard Galpin) by phone with ideas for
celebrity interviews, and gossip. All material commissioned. Length: features, 800
words. Illustrations: colour and b&w photos, cartoons. Payment: features £80-£250,
illustrations £80-£250. Founded 1989.

The Big Issue
57-61 Clerkenwell Road, London EC1M 5NP
tel 0171-418 0427
Editor Becky Gardiner
Weekly 80p

Features, news, reviews, interviews – of
general interest and on social issues.
Length: features 500-2000 words. Illustrations: colour and b&w photos and
line. Payment: £150 per 1000 words.
Founded 1991.

The Big Issues

Niall Skelly, 110 Amien Street, Dublin 3,
Republic of Ireland
tel (01) 8553969
Fortnightly £1.00

Articles, features and news on the homeless, unemployed and social issues, plus general articles and celebrity interviews. Length: 800-3000 words. Payment: negotiable. Founded 1994.

Bike

EMAP Nationals, Bushfield House, Orton Centre, Peterborough PE2 5UW
tel (01733) 237111 *fax* (01733) 370283
e-mail richard.fincher@ecm.emap.com
Editor Richard Fincher
Monthly £2.80

'Britain's biggest motorcycle magazine.' Interested in articles, features, news, short stories. Length: articles/features 1000-3000 words. Illustrations: colour and b&w photos, line, cartoons. Payment: £120 per 1000 words; illustrations per size/position. Founded 1971.

Bird Keeper

IPC Magazines Ltd, King's Reach Tower, Stamford Street, London SE1 9LS
tel 0171-261 6201 *fax* 0171-261 6095
Editor Peter Moss
Monthly £2.30

Articles on the care, health and breeding of birds, beginner bird keepers and how-to. Send synopsis of ideas. Length: up to 1200 words. Illustrations: colour photos and transparencies of birds in collections, or how-to. Payment: £65-£85 per 1000 words; £20-£45 per illustration. Founded 1988.

Bird Watching

EMAP Pursuit Publishing Ltd, Bretton Court, Bretton, Peterborough PE3 8DZ
tel (01733) 264666 *fax* (01773) 465939
Editor David Cromack
Monthly £2.35

Broad range of bird-related features. Emphasis on providing accurate information in entertaining ways. Send synopsis first. Length: 1200 words. Illustrations: colour photos, cartoons. Payment: by negotiation. Founded 1986.

Birdwatch

Solo Publishing Ltd, 310 Bow House, 153-159 Bow Road, London E3 2SE
tel 0181-983 1855 *fax* 0181-983 0246
Editor Dominic Mitchell
Monthly £2.35

Topical articles on all aspects of birds and birding, including conservation, identification, sites and habitats, equipment, overseas expeditions. Length: 700-1500 words. Illustrations: colour slides, b&w photos, colour and b&w line. Payment: from £40 per 1000 words; colour: photos £15-£40, cover £70, line by negotiation; b&w: photos £10, line £10-£40. Founded 1991.

Black Beauty & Hair

Hawker Publications, 13 Park House, 140 Battersea Park Road, London SW11 4NB
tel 0171-720 2108 *fax* 0171-498 3023
Editor Irene Shelley
Quarterly £2.00

Beauty and style articles relating specifically to the black woman; celebrity features. No short stories. Length: approx. 1000 words. Illustrations: colour and b&w photos. Payment: £85 per 1000 words; photos £50-£100. Founded 1982.

Bliss

Emap Elan Ltd, Endeavour House, 189 Shaftesbury Avenue, London WC2H 8JG
tel 0171-437 9011 *fax* 0171-208 3591
Editor Ally Oliver
Monthly £1.60

Glamorous young women's glossy magazine. Bright intimate American-style format, with readers' true-life stories (length 1000 words, payment from £50); beauty, fashion, gossip, advice, quizzes (payment by arrangement). Founded 1995.

Blueprint

Christ Church, 35 Cosway Street, London NW1 5NJ
tel 0171-262 2622 *fax* 0171-706 4811
Editor Marcus Field
11 p.a. £3.50

The magazine of modern architecture and design. Interested in articles, features and reviews. Length: up to 2500 words. Illustrations: colour and b&w photos and line. Payment: negotiable. Founded 1983.

BMA News Review

British Medical Association, BMA House, Tavistock Square, London WC1H 9JP
tel 0171-383 6122 *fax* 0171-383 6566
Editor Mark Jessop
GP edition
20 p.a. £52 p.a.
News and features 'for busy GPs'.
Hospital doctors edition
12 p.a. £52 p.a.

News and features 'for busy doctors'. Length: 700-1200 words (features), 100-400 words (news). Illustrations: colour transparencies, colour and b&w artwork and cartoons. Payment: by negotiation. Founded 1966.

Boards
Yachting Press Ltd, 196 Eastern Esplanade, Southend-on-Sea, Essex SS1 3AB
tel (01702) 582245 *fax* (01702) 588434
e-mail 106003.3405@compuserve.com
web site http://www.boards.co.uk
Editor Bill Dawes
Monthly during summer, Bi-monthly during winter £2.50 (10 p.a.)

Articles, photos and reports on all aspects of windsurfing and boardsailing. Payment: by arrangement. Illustrations: line, half-tone, colour, cartoons. Founded 1982.

The Book Collector
(incorporating Bibliographical Notes and Queries)
The Collector Ltd, PO Box 12426, London W11 3GW
tel/fax 0171-792 3492
Editorial Board Nicolas Barker (Editor), A. Bell, J. Fergusson, T. Hofmann, D. McKitterick, Joan Winterkorn
Quarterly £34.00 p.a. ($60.00)

Articles, biographical and bibliographical, on the collection and study of printed books and MSS. Payment: for reviews only. Founded 1952.

Book and Magazine Collector
Diamond Publishing Group Ltd, 43-45 St Mary's Road, London W5 5RQ
tel 0181-579 1082 *fax* 0181-566 2024
Editor Crispin Jackson
Monthly £2.50

Articles about collectable authors/publications/subjects. Articles must be bibliographical and include a full bibliography and price guide (no purely biographical features). Approach in writing with ideas. Length: 2000-4000 words. Illustrations: colour and b&w artwork. Payment: £30 per 1000 words. Founded 1984.

Books in Wales – see Llais Llyfrau

Books Ireland
11 Newgrove Avenue, Dublin 4, Republic of Ireland
tel (01) 2692185 *fax* (01) 260 4927
Editor Jeremy Addis, *Features Editor* Shirley Kelly
Monthly (exc. Jan, Jul, Aug) £2.00 (£20.00 p.a.)

Reviews of Irish-interest and Irish-author books, articles of interest to librarians, booksellers and readers. Length: 800-1400 words. Payment: £35 per 1000 words. Founded 1976.

Books Magazine
43 Museum Street, London WC1A 1LY
tel 0171-404 0304 *fax* 0171-242 0762
Editor Liz Thomson
Bi-monthly £1.50

Reviews, features, interviews with authors. No unsolicited MSS. Payment: negotiable but little bought in. Founded 1987.

The Bookseller
J. Whitaker and Sons Ltd, 12 Dyott Street, London WC1A 1DF
tel 0171-420 6000 *fax* 0171-420 6103
Editor Louis Baum
Weekly £120.00 p.a.

Journal of the publishing and bookselling trades. While outside contributions are welcomed, most of the journal's contents are commissioned. Length: about 1000-1500 words. Payment: by arrangement. Founded 1858.

Bowls International
Key Publishing Ltd, PO Box 100, Stamford, Lincs. PE9 1XQ
tel (01780) 755131 *fax* (01780) 757261
Editor Melvyn Beck
Monthly £2.10

Sport and news items and features; occasional, bowls-oriented short stories. Illustrations: colour transparencies, b&w photos, occasional line, cartoons. Payment: sport/news approx. 25p per line, features approx. £50 per page; colour £25, b&w £10. Founded 1981.

Brewing & Distilling International
52 Glenhouse Road, London SE9 1JQ
tel 0181-859 4300 *fax* 0181-859 5813
Editor Bruce Stevens
Monthly £48.00 p.a. (£80.00/$115.00 p.a. airmail)

Journal for brewers, maltsters, hop merchants, distillers, soft drinks manufacturers, bottlers and allied traders, circulating in over 80 countries. Technical and marketing articles (average 1000 words) accepted, by prior arrangement, from authors with specialist knowledge. Illustrations: line drawings, photos. Payment: by prior agreement with editor. Founded 1865.

Bridge Magazine

Chess & Bridge Ltd, 369 Euston Road,
London NW1 3AR
tel 0171-388 2404 *fax* 0171-388 2407
e-mail chesscentre@easynet.co.uk
web site http://www.bridgemagazine.co.uk
Editor Mark Horton
Monthly £2.95

Articles on bidding and play; instruction,
competitions, tournament reports and
humour. Payment: by arrangement.
Illustrations: line, half-tone. Founded
1926.

British Birds

Fountains, Park Lane, Blunham,
Bedford MK44 3NJ
tel/fax (01767) 640025
Dr J.T.R. Sharrock
Monthly £57.00 p.a.

Original observations relating to birds of
Britain, Europe and North Africa.
Illustrations: line, half-tone, colour.
Payment: none for articles, nominal for
illustrations. Founded 1907.

British Chess Magazine

BCM Chess Shop, 69 Masbro Road,
London W14 0LS
Editor M. Chandler
Monthly £2.50 (£26.00 p.a.)

Commisioned articles, 800-2500 words,
on historical and cultural aspects of
chess. Illustrations: colour, b&w, line,
cartoons. Payment: by arrangement.
Founded 1881.

The British Deaf News

PO Box 12, Carlisle CA1 1HU
tel (01228) 599994 (voice and text)
fax (01228) 41420
Editor Irene Hall
Monthly 85p (£12.00 p.a., members £10.00 p.a.)

Official journal of the British Deaf
Association. Articles, news items, letters
dealing with deafness. Payment: by
arrangement. Illustrations: line, half-tone.
Founded 1955.

British Journal of General Practice

(formerly Journal of the Royal College of General
Practitioners)
14 Princes Gate, Hyde Park, London SW7 1PU
tel 0171-581 3232 *fax* 0171-584 6716
e-mail info@rcgp.org.uk
web site http://www.rcgp.org.uk
Editor Dr A.F. Wright MBE, MD, FRCGP
Monthly £124.00 p.a. (£140 overseas, £158.55 by
airmail)

Articles relevant to general medical practice. Illustrations: half-tone, colour.
Payment: none.

The British Journal of Photography

Timothy Benn Publishing, 39 Earlham Street,
London WC2H 9LD
tel 0171-306 7000 *fax* 0171-306 7017
Editor Reuel Golden
Weekly £1.50

Articles on professional, commercial and
press photography, and on the more
advanced aspects of amateur, technical,
industrial, medical, scientific and colour
photography. Illustrations: line, half-
tone, colour. Payment: by arrangement.
Founded 1854.

British Journal of Special Education

The University of Birmingham, School of
Education, Edgbaston, Birmingham B15 2TT
tel 0121-414 4805 *fax* 0121-414 4865
Editor Christina Tilstone
Quarterly (non-member institutions/individuals
Europe £52.50 p.a., rest of the world £74.00 p.a.)

Official Journal of the National Association
for Special Educational Needs. Articles
by specialists on the education of children and young people with a range of
special educational needs; plus research
findings, and examples of good practice
in education and associated areas: medical, psychological, therapeutic and sociological. Length: about 3000 words. Payment: none. Illustrations: line, half-tone.

British Journalism Review

BJR Publishing Ltd, c/o John Libbey Media,
Faculty of Humanities, University of Luton,
75 Castle Street, Luton, Beds. LU1 3AJ
tel (01582) 743297 *fax* (01582) 743298
Editor Geoffrey Goodman
Quarterly £25.00 p.a. (overseas rates on
application)

Comment/criticism/review of matters
published by, or of interest to, the media.
Length: 1000-3000 words. Illustrations:
b&w photos. Payment: by arrangement.
Founded 1989.

British Medical Journal

BMA House, Tavistock Square,
London WC1H 9JR
tel 0171-387 4499 *fax* 0171-383 6418
e-mail 100730.1250@compuserve.com
web site www.bmj.com
Editor Richard Smith BSc, MB, ChBEd, MFPHM, FRCPE
Weekly £6.70

Medical and related articles. Payment: by arrangement. Founded 1840.

British Printer
Miller Freeman Plc, Sovereign Way, Tonbridge, Kent TN9 1RW
tel (01732) 364422 *fax* (01732) 377362
Editor Jane Ellis
Monthly £70.00 p.a.

Articles on technical and aesthetic aspects of printing processes and graphic reproduction. Payment: by arrangement. Illustrations: offset litho from photos, line drawings and diagrams, cartoons. Founded 1888.

Broadcast
EMAP Media, 33-39 Bowling Green Lane, London EC1R 0DA
tel 0171-505 8014 *fax* 0171-505 8050
Editor Matt Baker
Weekly £2.00

News and authoritative articles designed for all concerned with the UK and international television and radio industry, and with programmes and advertising on television, radio, video, cable, satellite, business. Illustrations: colour, b&w, line, cartoons. Payment: by arrangement.

Brownie
The Guide Association, 17-19 Buckingham Palace Road, London SW1W 0PT
tel 0171-834 6242
Editor Marion Thompson
Monthly £1.15

Official Magazine of The Guide Association. Short articles for Brownies (girls 7-10 years); fiction with Brownie background (500-800 words); puzzles; 'things to make', etc. Illustrations: colour. Payment: £50 per 1000 words; varies for illustrations.

Budgerigar World
The County Press, Bala, Gwynedd LL23 7PG
tel (01678) 520262 *fax* (01678) 521262
Editor Terry A. Tuxford, 145 Western Way, Basingstoke, Hants RG22 6EX
tel (01256) 328898
Monthly £30.00 p.a.

Articles about exhibition budgerigars. Payment: by arrangement. Illustrations: half-tone, colour. Founded 1982.

Building
The Builder Group, Exchange Tower,
2 Harbour Exchange Square, London E14 9GE
tel 0171-560 4141 *fax* 0171-560 4004

e-mail 106173.632@compuserve.com
Editor Adrian Barrick
Weekly £2.20

Covers the entire professional, industrial and manufacturing aspects of the building industry. Articles on architecture and techniques at home and abroad considered, also news and photos. Payment: by arrangement. Founded 1842.

Building Design
30 Calderwood Street, London SE18 6QH
tel 0181-855 7777 *fax* 0181-854 8058
Editor Lee Mallett
Weekly Controlled circulation (£65.00 p.a.)

News and features on all aspects of building design. All material commissioned. Length: up to 1500 words. Illustrations: colour and b&w photos, line, cartoons. Payment: £120 per 1000 words; illustrations by negotiation. Founded 1970.

Built Environment
Alexandrine Press, PO Box 15, 51 Cornmarket Street, Oxford OX1 3EB
tel (01865) 724627 *fax* (01865) 792309
Editors Prof Peter Hall and Prof David Banister
Quarterly £70.00 p.a.

Articles about architecture, planning and the environment. Preliminary letter advisable. Length: 1000-5000 words. Payment: by arrangement. Illustrations: photos and line.

Bunty
D.C. Thomson & Co. Ltd, Albert Square, Dundee DD1 9QJ
tel (01382) 223131 *fax* (01382) 322214
185 Fleet Street, London EC4A 2HS
tel 0171-242 5086 *fax* 0171-404 5694
Weekly 60p

Vividly told picture-story serials for young girls of school age: 16-18 frames in each 2-page instalment; 23-24 frames in each 3-page instalment. Comic strips and features. Payment: on acceptance.

Bunty Library
D.C. Thomson & Co. Ltd, Albert Square, Dundee DD1 9QJ
tel (01382) 223131 *fax* (01382) 322214
185 Fleet Street, London EC4A 2HS
tel 0171-242 5086 *fax* 0171-404 5694
Fortnightly 55p

Picture-stories for schoolgirls, 64 pages (about 140 line drawings): ballet, school, adventure, theatre, sport. Scripts considered; promising artists and scriptwriters encouraged. Payment: on acceptance.

Burlington Magazine
14-16 Duke's Road, London WC1H 9AD
tel 0171-388 1228 *fax* 0171-388 1230
e-mail burlington@compuserve.com
Editor Caroline Elam
Monthly £10.70
Deals with the history and criticism of art; book and exhibition reviews; illustrated monthly Calendar section. Potential contributors must have special knowledge of the subjects treated; MSS compiled from works of reference are unacceptable. Length: 500-3000 words. Payment: up to £100. Illustrations: b&w and colour photos. Founded 1903.

Buses
Coombelands House, Coombelands Lane, Addlestone, Surrey KT15 1HY
tel (01932) 855909 *fax* (01932) 854750
Editor Stephen Morris
Monthly £2.50
Articles of interest to both road passenger transport operators and bus enthusiasts. Preliminary enquiry essential. Illustrations: colour transparencies, half-tone, line maps. Payment: on application. Founded 1949.

Business Life
Premier Magazines, Haymarket House, 1 Oxenden Street, London SW1Y 4EE
tel 0171-925 2544 *fax* 0171-839 4508
Editor Sandra Harris
Monthly Free
Inflight magazine for British Airways. Articles and features of interest to the European business traveller. All material commissioned; approach in writing with ideas. Length: 850-1500 words. Illustrations: colour photos and line. Payment: £300 per 1000 words; £100-£400 for illustrations. Founded 1985.

Business Scotland
Peebles Publishing Group, Bergius House, Clifton Street, Glasgow G3 7LA
tel 0141-331 1022 *fax* 0141-331 1395
Editor Graham Lironi
Monthly Controlled circulation
Features, profiles and news items of interest to business and finance in Scotland. Payment: by arrangement. Founded 1947.

BusinessMatters
GMC Publications, Castle Place, 166 High Street, Lewes, East Sussex BN7 1XU
tel (01273) 477374 *fax* (01273) 486300
Editor Elly Donovan
Bi-monthly £2.50

How to run and market small- to medium-sized businesses. Articles based on case studies; relevant news. Length: 400-2400 words. Illustrations: colour and b&w photos, cartoons. Payment: £50 per 500 words; £50 per illustration. Founded 1992.

Buster
Egmont Fleetway Ltd, Egmont House, 25-31 Tavistock Place, London WC1H 9SU
tel 0171-344 6400 *fax* 0171-388 4020
Fortnightly £1.00
Juvenile comic. Comedy characters in picture strips, for children aged 6 to 12. Full colour. Payment: by arrangement. Founded 1960.

Cage and Aviary Birds
IPC Magazines Ltd, King's Reach Tower, Stamford Street, London SE1 9LS
tel 0171-261 6116 *fax* 0171-261 6095
Editor-in-Chief Peter Moss
Weekly 95p
Practical articles on bird-keeping. First-hand knowledge only. Illustrations: line, half-tone, colour, cartoons. Payment: by arrangement. Founded 1902.

Camcorder User
(incorporating Video Editing and Desktop Video) WV Publications, 57-59 Rochester Place, London NW1 9JU
tel 0171-485 0011 *fax* 0171-482 6269/284 2145
Editor Christine Morgan
Monthly £2.50
Features on film/video-making techniques, specifically tailored to the amateur enthusiast. Material mostly commissioned. Length: 1000-2500 words. Illustrations: colour and b&w; contact editor for details. Payment: by arrangement. Founded 1988.

Campaign
Haymarket Business Publications Ltd, 174 Hammersmith Road, London W6 7JP
tel 0171-413 4036 *fax* 0171-413 4507
e-mail 100560.1626@compuserve.com
Editor Stefano Hatfield
Weekly £2.00
News and articles covering the whole of the mass communications field, particularly advertising in all its forms, marketing and the media. Features should not exceed 2000 words. News items also welcome. Press day, Wednesday. Payment: by arrangement.

Camping Magazine

Garnett Dickinson Publishing, Fitzwilliam Road,
Rotherham S65 1JU
tel/fax (editorial) (01273) 477421
Editor John Lloyd
Monthly £2.20

Covers the spectrum of camping and related activities in all shapes and forms – camping is more than a tent on a site! Lively, anecdotal articles and photos are welcome, but call to discuss your ideas with the editor first. Length: 500-1500 words on average. Illustrations: half-tone, colour. Payment: by arrangement. Founded 1961.

Car

EMAP National Publications Ltd, Abbots Court, 34 Farringdon Lane, London EC1R 3AV
tel 0171-216 6200 *fax* 0171-216 6259
e-mail 101740.3504@compuserve.com
web site http://www.erack.com/car
Editor Rob Munro-Hall
Monthly £3.00

Top-grade journalistic features on car driving, car people and cars. Length: 1000-2500 words. Payment: minimum £260 per 1000 words. Illustrations: b&w and colour photos to professional standards. Founded 1962.

Car Mechanics

Kelsey House, 77 High Street, Beckenham, Kent BR3 1AN
tel 0181-658 3531 or (01733) 203749
fax 0181-650 8035
Editor Peter Simpson
Monthly £2.30

Practical articles on maintaining, repairing and uprating modern cars for DIY plus the motor trade. Preliminary letter outlining feature necessary. Payment: by arrangement. Illustrations: line drawings, colour prints or transparencies. Rarely use words only; please supply text and pictures.

Caravan Magazine

Link House, Dingwall Avenue, Croydon CR9 2TA
tel 0181-686 2599 *fax* 0181-781 6044/760 0973
Editor Barry Williams
Monthly £2.30

Lively articles based on real experience of touring caravanning, especially if well illustrated by photos. General countryside or motoring material not wanted. Payment: by arrangement. Founded 1933.

Carers World

4 Larch Way, Haywards Heath,
West Sussex RH16 3TY
tel/fax (01444) 416866
Editor Jennie Davidson
Bi-monthly £1.50

Factual and informative articles aimed at carers, the disabled and the elderly. Length: up to 800 words. Illustrations: line, half-tone. Payment: by arrangement. Founded 1993.

Caribbean Times

(incorporating African Times)
Ethnic Media Group, 1st Floor,
148 Cambridge Heath Road,
London E1 5QJ
tel 0171-702 8012 *fax* 0171-702 7937
Editor Arif Ali
Weekly 50p

News stories, articles and features of interest to Britain's African-Caribbean community. Founded 1981.

Cat World

Ashdown Publishing, Avalon Court, Star Road, Partridge Green, West Sussex RH13 8RY
tel (01403) 711511 *fax* (01403) 711521
Editor Joan Moore
Monthly £1.95

Bright, lively articles on any aspect of cat ownership. Articles on breeds of cats and veterinary articles by acknowledged experts only. No unsolicited fiction. Illustrations: colour photos, cartoons. Payment: by arrangement; £7.50 per illustration. Founded 1981.

Caterer & Hotelkeeper

Reed Business Information Ltd, Quadrant House, The Quadrant, Sutton, Surrey SM2 5AS
tel 0181-652 8680 *fax* 0181-652 8973/8947
Editor Gary Crossley
Weekly £1.50

Articles on all aspects of the hotel and catering industries. Length: up to 1500 words. Illustrations: line, half-tone, colour. Payment: by arrangement. Founded 1893.

Catholic Gazette

The Chase Centre, 114 West Heath Road,
London NW3 7TX
tel 0181-458 3316 *fax* 0181-905 5780
Editor Fr. Paul Daly
Monthly £1.20

Articles on evangelisation and the Christian life. Length: up to 2000 words. Illustrations: b&w photos, line, cartoons. Payment: by arrangement. Founded 1910.

The Catholic Herald

Herald House, Lambs Passage, Bunhill Row,
London EC1Y 8TQ
tel 0171-588 3101 *fax* 0171-256 9728
Editor Deborah Jones
Weekly 45p

Independent newspaper covering national and international affairs from a Catholic/Christian viewpoint as well as church news. Length: articles 600-1100 words. Illustrations: photos of Catholic and Christian interest, cartoons. Payment: by arrangement.

Catholic Pictorial

Media House, Mann Island, Pier Head,
Liverpool L3 1DQ
tel 0151-236 2191 *fax* 0151-236 2216
Editor David Mahon
Weekly 50p

News and photo features (maximum 800 words plus illustration) of Merseyside, regional and national Catholic interest only; also cartoons. Has a strongly social editorial and is a trenchant tabloid. Payment: by arrangement. Founded 1961.

Catholic Times

1st Floor, St James's Buildings, Oxford Street,
Manchester M1 6FP
tel 0161-236 8856 *fax* 0161-237 5590
Editor Gregory Murphy
Weekly 40p

News (400 words) and news features (800 words) of Catholic interest. Illustrations: colour and b&w photos. Payment: £30-£80; photos £50. Relaunched 1993.

Cencrastus: Scottish & International Literature, Arts and Affairs

Unit One, Abbeymount Techbase, 2 Easter Road,
Edinburgh EH8 8EJ
tel 0131-661 5687
e-mail 106536.755@compuserve.com
Editor Raymond Ross, *Managing Editor* Richard Moore
Quarterly £2.25 (back copies £2.50)

Articles, short stories, poetry, reviews. Payment: by arrangement. Illustrations: line, half-tone. Founded 1979.

Certified Accountant

Cork Publishing Ltd, 19 Rutland Street, Cork,
Republic of Ireland
tel (21) 313855 *fax* (21) 313496
Editor Brian O'Kane
Monthly £2.50

Journal of the Association of Chartered Certified Accountants. Articles of accounting, financial, business, technology and international interest. Illustrations: colour, cartoons. Payment: from £125 per 1000 words; by arrangement for illustrations.

Chapman

4 Broughton Place, Edinburgh EH1 3RX
tel 0131-557 2207 *fax* 0131-556 9565
Editor Joy Hendry
Quarterly £3.70 (£15.00 p.a.)

'Scotland's Quality Literary Magazine.' Poetry, short stories, reviews, criticism, articles on Scottish culture. Illustrations: line, half-tone, cartoons. Payment: £8.00 per page; illustrations by negotiation. Founded 1969.

Chartered Secretary

(formerly Administrator)
16 Park Crescent, London W1N 4AH
tel 0171-580 4741 *fax* 0171-323 1132
e-mail chartsec@dial.pipex.com
web site http://www.icsa.org.uk/icsa/
Monthly £4.00 (£37.00 p.a. post free UK)

Official Journal of The Institute of Chartered Secretaries and Administrators. Practical and topical articles (750-1600 words) on law, finance and management affecting company secretaries and other senior administrators in business, nationalised industries, local and central government and other institutions in Britain and overseas. Payment: by arrangement.

Chat

IPC Magazines Ltd, King's Reach Tower,
Stamford Street, London SE1 9LS
tel 0171-261 6565 *fax* 0171-261 6534
Editor-in-Chief Iris Burton
Weekly 57p

Tabloid weekly for women; fiction. Length: up to 1000 words. Illustrations: half-tone, colour. Payment: by arrangement. Founded 1986.

Chemist & Druggist

Miller Freeman, Miller Freeman House,
Sovereign Way, Tonbridge, Kent TN9 1RW
tel (01732) 364422 *fax* (01732) 361534
e-mail chemdrug@dotpharmacy.com
web site http://www.@dotpharmacy.com
Editor Patrick Grice
Weekly £121 p.a.

'The newsweekly for pharmacy.' News stories and feature items relating to any aspect of community pharmacy or small independent retailing. Length: 1000 or 1500 words (features), up to 300 words

(news). Illustrations: colour. Payment: £110 per 1000 words. Founded 1859.

Chess Monthly
Chess & Bridge Ltd, 369 Euston Road, London NW1 3AR
tel 0171-388 2404 *fax* 0171-388 2407
e-mail chesscentre@easynet.co.uk
web site http://www.chesscenter.com
Executive Editor Malcolm Pein
Technical Editor Jimmy Adams
Monthly £2.95

Tournament reports, news and technical articles. Length: 1-4 pages. Illustrations: colour and b&w. Payment: £15.20. Founded 1935.

Chic
Northern & Shell plc, Northern & Shell Tower, City Harbour, London E14 9GL
tel 0171-987 5090 *fax* 0171-712 0069
Editor Ruth Corbett
Bi-monthly £2.25

In depth human interest articles aimed at women aged over 35. Show business interviews, 'at home' with personalities and stories about ordinary women. Submit written synopsis. Length: 2000-3000 words. Illustrations: all commissioned. Payment: by arrangement. Founded 1995.

Child Education
Scholastic Publications Ltd, Villiers House, Clarendon Avenue, Leamington Spa, Warks. CV32 5PR
tel (01926) 887799 *fax* (01926) 883331
Editor Gill Moore
Monthly £2.50

For teachers, pre-school staff, nursery nurses and parents concerned with children aged 3-8. Articles by specialists on practical teaching ideas and methods, child development, education news. Length: 800-1600 words. Payment: by arrangement. Profusely illustrated with photos, line drawings and cartoons; also large full colour pictures. Founded 1924.

The China Quarterly
School of Oriental and African Studies, Thornhaugh Street, Russell Square, London WC1H 0XG
tel 0171-323 6129 *fax* 0171-580 6836
e-mail chinaq@soas.ac.uk
Editor Dr Richard Louis Edmonds
Quarterly £29/$56 p.a. (£36/$70 institutions, £15/$28 students)

Articles on contemporary China. Length: 8000 words approx.

Choice
Apex House, Oundle Road, Peterborough PE2 9NP
tel (01733) 555123 *fax* (01733) 898487
Editor-in-Chief Sue Dobson
Monthly £2.00

Pre- and retirement magazine for 50+ readership. Positive attitude to life – experiences, hobbies, holidays, finance, relationships. About half the magazine commissioned. Unsolicited material accompanied by an sae will be read. If suggesting feature material, include selection of cuttings of previously published work. Payment: by agreement, on publication. Founded 1974.

Church of England Newspaper
10 Little College Street, London SW1P 3SH
tel 0171-976 7760 *fax* 0171-976 0783
Weekly 45p

Anglican news and articles relating the Christian faith to everyday life. Evangelical basis; almost exclusively commissioned articles. Study of paper desirable. Length: up to 1000 words. Illustrations: photos, line drawings, cartoons. Payment: c. £40 per 1000 words; photos £22, line by arrangement. Founded 1828.

Church of Ireland Gazette
36 Bachelor's Walk, Lisburn, Co. Antrim BT28 1XN
tel (01846) 675743 *fax* (01846) 675743
Editor Rev. Canon C.W.M. Cooper
Weekly 30p

Church news, articles of religious and general interest. Length: 600-1000 words. Payment: according to length and interest. New Series 1963. Founded 1885.

Church Times
33 Upper Street, London N1 0PN
tel 0171-359 4570 *fax* 0171-226 3073
Editor Paul Handley
Weekly 45p

Articles on religious topics are considered. No verse or fiction. Length: up to 1000 words. Illustrations: news photos, sent promptly. Payment: £100 per 1000 words; Periodical Publishers' Association negotiated rates for illustrations. Founded 1863.

Classic & Sportscar
Haymarket Magazines Ltd, 38-42 Hampton Road, Teddington, Middlesex TW11 0JE
tel 0181-943 5000 *fax* 0181-943 5844
Editor Ian Bond
Monthly £2.95

Features on classic cars and sportscars; shows, news and reviews, features and stories. Length: varies. Illustrations: half-tone, colour. Payment: £150 per 1000 words; varies for illustrations. Founded 1982.

Classic Boat

Boating Publications Ltd, Link House, Dingwall Avenue, Croydon CR9 2TA
tel 0181-686 2599 *fax* 0181-781 6535
e-mail 101574.216@compuserve.com
Editor Nic Compton
Monthly £3.10

Cruising and technical features, restorations, events, new boat reviews, practical, maritime history; news. Study of magazine essential: read 3-4 back issues and send for contributors' guidelines. Length: 500-2000 words. Illustrations: colour and b&w photos; line drawings of hulls. Payment: £75-£100 per published page. Founded 1987.

Classic Cars

EMAP National Publications Ltd, Abbots Court, 34 Farringdon Lane, London EC1R 3AU
tel 0171-216 6200 *fax* 0171-216 6227
Editor Robert Coucher
Monthly £2.95

Specialist articles on older cars. Length: from 500-4000 words (subject to prior contract). Illustrations: half-tone, colour, cartoons. Payment: by negotiation.

Classic CD

Future Publishing, 30 Monmouth Street, Beauford Court, Bath BA1 2BW
tel (01225) 442244 *fax* (01225) 462986
e-mail nevans@futurenet.co.uk
Editor Neil Evans
Monthly £3.95

Covers classical music on CD. Aims to inform, educate and entertain, with features on composers and performers, reviews and news. Commissioned material only. Length: up to 2000 words. Illustrations: colour and b&w photos, b&w line, including collage and cartoons. Payment: £125 per 1000 words; colour up to £300, b&w £35 1/8 page. Founded 1990.

Classic Stitches

D.C. Thomson & Co. Ltd, 80 Kingsway East, Dundee DD4 8SL
tel (01382) 462276 *fax* (01382) 452491
Editor Mrs Bea Neilson
Bi-monthly £2.90

Creative needlework ideas and projects; needlework-based features on designers, collections, work-in-progress and exhibitions. Length: 1000-2000 words. Illustrations: colour photos, preferably not 35 mm. Payment: negotiable. Founded 1994.

Classical Music

Rhinegold Publishing Ltd, 241 Shaftesbury Avenue, London WC2H 8EH
tel 0171 333 1742 *fax* 0171 333 1769
e-mail 100546.1127@compuserve.com
Editor Keith Clarke
Fortnightly £2.95

News, opinion, features on the classical music business. All material commissioned. Illustrations: b&w photos and line; colour covers. Payment: minimum £85 per 1000 words; from £40 for illustrations. Founded 1976.

Climber

7th Floor, The Plaza Tower, The Plaza, East Kilbride, Glasgow G74 1LW
tel (01355) 246444 *fax* (01355) 263013
Editor Tom Prentice
Monthly £2.10

Articles on all aspects of mountaineering and hill walking in Great Britain and abroad, and on related subjects. Study of magazine essential. Length: 1500-2000 words, illustrated. Illustrations: colour transparencies/prints. Payment: according to merit. Founded 1962.

Clocks

Nexus Special Interests Ltd.
Editorial address 28 Gillespie Crescent, Edinburgh EH10 4HU
tel/fax 0131-229 5550
Editor John Hunter
Monthly £2.85

Well-researched articles on antique clocks and their makers, clock repair and restoration, and in general anything of interest to knowledgeable horologists. Watches, sundials, barometers and associated scientific instruments are minority interests of readers. Length: 1000-3000 words. Preferred format for copy MS-DOS formatted floppy disk. Illustrations: line, half-tone, colour; no cartoons. Payment: approx. £30 per 1000 words, £5 per b&w photo, £8 per colour print/transparency. Founded 1978.

Clothes Show Magazine

BBC Worldwide Publishing, Woodlands, 80 Wood Lane, London W12 0TT
tel 0181-576 2436 *fax* 0181-576 3379
Editor Jaynie Senior
Monthly £1.70

Articles relating to fashion and beauty in a practical, accessible way. Submit ideas first, in writing, to the editor. Length: 1500-word, 4-page main feature; 400-word, 1-page. Illustrations: commissioned as necessary. Payment: up to £500 for main feature, £150 for 1-page; illustrations £150. Founded 1989.

Coin News

Token Publishing Ltd, PO Box 14, Honiton, Devon EX14 9YP
tel (01404) 831 878 *fax* (01404) 831 895
Editor John W. Mussell
Monthly £2.00

Articles of high standard on coins, tokens, paper money. Length: up to 2000 words. Payment: by arrangement. Founded 1964.

Commando

D.C. Thomson & Co. Ltd, Albert Square, Dundee DD1 9QJ
tel (01382) 223131 *fax* (01382) 322214
185 Fleet Street, London EC4A 2HS
tel 0171-242 5086 *fax* 0171-404 5694
8 p.m. 55p

Fictional war stories told in pictures. Scripts should be of about 135 pictures. Synopsis required as an opener. New writers encouraged; send for details. Payment: on acceptance.

Commercial Motor

Reed Business Publishing, Quadrant House, The Quadrant, Sutton, Surrey SM2 5AS
tel 0181-652 3302/3303 *fax* 0181-652 8969
Editor Brian Weatherley
Weekly £1.30

Technical and road transport articles only. Length: up to 1500 words. Payment: varies. Illustrations: drawings and photos. Founded 1905.

Communicate

Argus Business Media Ltd, Queensway House, Redhill, Surrey RH1 1QS
tel (01737) 768611 *fax* (01737) 760564
Editor Peter Buhlmann
Monthly Controlled circulation

Covers all aspects of telecommunications management: analysis pieces (200-700 words), features (800-1800 words), case studies (1800 words). All material commissioned. Illustrations: colour and b&w photos, line, diagrams. Payment: £180 per 1000 words; illustrations by negotiation. Founded 1980.

Community Care

Reed Business Publishing, Quadrant House, The Quadrant, Sutton, Surrey SM2 5AS
tel 0181-652 4861 *fax* 0181-652 4739
Editor Terry Philpot
Weekly £1.40

Articles of professional interest to local authority and voluntary body social workers, managers, teachers and students. Preliminary letter advisable. Length: 800-1500 words. Payment: at current rates. Illustrations: line, halftone. Founded 1974.

Company

National Magazine House, 72 Broadwick Street, London W1V 2BP
tel 0171-439 5000
Editor Fiona McIntosh
Monthly £2.00

Articles on a wide variety of subjects, relevant to young, independent women. Most articles are commissioned. Payment: usual magazine rate. Illustrated. Founded 1978.

Computer Weekly

Reed Business Information Ltd, Quadrant House, The Quadrant, Sutton, Surrey SM2 5AS
tel 0181-652 3122 *fax* 0181-652 3038
Editor Helena Sturridge, *News Editor* Karl Schneider, Features *Editor* David Evans
Weekly £1.70

Feature articles on computer-related topics for business/industry users. Length: 1200 words. Illustrations: b&w photos, line, cartoons. Payment: £150 per feature; negotiable for illustrations. Founded 1966.

Computing

VNU Business Publications, VNU House, 32-34 Broadwick Street, London W1A 2HG
tel 0171-316 9601 *fax* 0171-316 9160
Editor Peter Kirwan
Weekly £100.00 p.a.

Features and news items on corporate procurement and deployment of IT infrastructure, and on applications and implications of computers and telecommunications. Particular sections address the IT professional career development, and the desktop computing environment. Length: 1600-2200 words. Payment: by negotiation. Illustrations: colour photos, line drawings, cartoons. Founded 1973.

Construction Europe

Southfields, Southview Road, Wadhurst,
East Sussex TN5 6TP
tel (01892) 784088 *fax* (01892) 784086
Editor Paul Marsden
Monthly Controlled circulation

Aimed at contractors, consultants and government/international authorities. Payment: by negotiation.

Contemporary Review

(incorporating the Fortnightly)
Contemporary Review Co. Ltd, Cheam Business Centre, 14 Upper Mulgrave Road, Cheam, Surrey SM2 7AZ
tel 0181-643 4846 *fax* 0181-241 7507
Editor Dr Richard Mullen
Monthly £2.95

Independent review dealing with questions of the day, chiefly politics, international affairs, theology, literature, the arts. Mostly commissioned, but with limited scope for freelance authors with authoritative knowledge. TS returned only if sae enclosed. Intending contributors should study journal first. Length: 2000-3000 words. No illustrations. Payment: £5 per page (500 words), 2 complimentary copies. Founded 1866.

contemporary visual arts

(formerly Contemporary Art)
197 Knightsbridge, 8th Floor North,
London SW7 1RB
tel 0171-823 8373 *fax* 0171-823 7969
Editor Keith Patrick
Quarterly £4.95

Articles and reviews on all aspects of contemporary art; book reviews. Length: articles 1000-2000 words, reviews 1000 words. Illustrations: colour photos. Payment: £100 per 1000 words; none for photos. Founded 1992.

Control & Instrumentation

30 Calderwood Street, London SE18 6QH
tel 0181-855 7777 *fax* 0181-316 3422
Editor Brian J. Tinham BSc, CEng, MInstMC
Monthly £60.00 p.a.

Authoritative main feature articles on measurement, automation, control systems, instrumentation and data processing; also export, business and engineering news. Regular supplement entitled *Sys.Build* details all aspects of system building and system integration – news, projects, feedback, comment and features. Length of articles: 750 words for highly technical pieces, 1000-2500 words main features. Payment: according to value. Illustrations: photos and drawings of equipment using automatic techniques, control engineering personalities, cartoons. Founded 1958.

Cosmetic World News

130 Wigmore Street, London W1H 0AT
tel 0171-486 6757/8 *fax* 0171-487 5436
Editors M.A. Murray-Pearce, Caroline Marcuse, Norman Clare
Bi-monthly £96.00 p.a.

International news magazine of perfumery, cosmetics and toiletries industry. Worldwide reports, photo-news stories, articles (500-1000 words) on essential oils and new cosmetic raw materials, and exclusive information on industry's companies and personalities welcomed. Payment: by arrangement, minimum 10p per word. Illustrations: b&w and colour photos or colour separations. Founded 1949.

Cosmopolitan

National Magazine House, 72 Broadwick Street, London W1V 2BP
tel 0171-439 5000 *fax* 0171-439 5016
Editor Mandi Norwood
Monthly £2.10

Short stories, articles. Commissioned material only. Payment: by arrangement. Illustrated. Founded 1972.

Country

The Country Gentlemen's Association,
Hill Crest Mews, London Road, Baldock,
Herts. SG7 6ND
tel (01462) 490206
Editor Barry Turner
Monthly £2.50

The Magazine of the Country Gentlemen's Association. News and features covering rural events, countryside, leisure, heritage, homes and gardens. Some outside contributors used; approach in writing in the first instance. Payment: by arrangement. Founded 1893.

Country Garden & Smallholding

Broad Leys Publishing Company, Buriton House, Station Road, Newport, Saffron Walden, Essex CB11 3PL
tel (01799) 540922 *fax* (01799) 541367
Editor Helen Sears
Monthly £2.10

The magazine for smallholders. Practical, how-to articles, and seasonal features, on organic gardening, small-scale poultry and livestock keeping, country crafts, cookery and smallholdings. Approach editor in writing with ideas. Length: up to 2000 words. Illustrations: colour and b&w photos, line for instructive articles. Payment: £30 per 1000 words; photos £10, £35 cover. Founded 1975 as *Home Farm*.

Country Homes and Interiors

IPC Magazines Ltd, King's Reach Tower, Stamford Street, London SE1 9LS
tel 0171-261 6451 *fax* 0171-261 6895
Editor Katherine Hadley
Monthly £2.30

Articles on property, country homes, interior designs. Illustrations: colour. Payment: from £250 per 1000 words. Founded 1986.

Country Life

IPC Magazines Ltd, King's Reach Tower, Stamford Street, London SE1 9LS
tel 0171-261 7058 *fax* 0171-261 5139
Editor Clive Aslet
Weekly £2.10 (Special Numbers £2.25)

Illustrated journal chiefly concerned with British country life, social history, architecture and the fine arts, natural history, agriculture, gardening and sport. Length of articles: about 700, 1000 or 1300 words. Illustrations: mainly colour photos, cartoons. Payment: according to merit. Founded 1897.

Country Living

National Magazine House, 72 Broadwick Street, London W1V 2BP
tel 0171-439 5000 *fax* 0171-439 5093
Editor Susy Smith
Monthly £2.50

Up-market magazine for country dwellers and townies who have the country at heart. No unsolicited material and do not send valuable transparencies; magazine cannot accept responsibility for loss of unsolicited material. Illustrations: line, half-tone, colour. Payment: by arrangement. Founded 1985.

Country Quest

7 Aberystwyth Science Park, Aberystwyth, Dyfed SY23 3TN
tel (01970) 611611 *fax* (01970) 624699
Editor Beverly Davies
Monthly £1.50

Illustrated articles on matters relating to countryside, history and personalities of Wales and border counties. No fiction. Illustrated work preferred. Length: 700-1500 words. Payment: by arrangement.

Country Walking

EMAP Pursuit Publishing, Bretton Court, Bretton, Peterborough PE3 8DZ
tel (01733) 264666 *fax* (01733) 465939
Editor Lynne Maxwell
Monthly £2.40

Features and readers' stories. Length: 1000 words on average (features), 800 words (stories), more if commissioned. Illustrations: colour transparencies. Payment: £60 per 1000 words, £35 fee for readers' stories; £15 (1/4 page), £50 (full page). Founded 1987.

The Countryman

Sheep Street, Burford, Oxon OX18 4LH
tel (01993) 822258
Editor Tom Quinn
Bi-monthly £2.30

Every department of rural life except field sports. Copy must be trustworthy, well-written, brisk, cogent and light in hand. Articles up to 1200 words. First-class poetry and skilful sketches of life and character from personal knowledge and experience. Dependable natural history based on writer's own observation. Really good matter from old unpublished letters and MSS. Illustrations: b&w and colour photos and drawings, but all must be exclusive and out of the ordinary. Payment: £60 per 1000 words minimum, usually in excess of this figure, according to merit. Founded 1927.

Country-Side

PO Box 87, Cambridge CB1 3UP
tel/fax (01933) 314672
Editor Dr David Applin
Bi-monthly £12.00 p.a.

Official journal of the British Naturalists' Association (BNA), the national body for naturalists. Original observations on wildlife and its protection, and on natural history generally, but not on killing for sport. Preliminary letter or study of magazine advisable. Payment: 1200 words plus pictures £50, shorter articles pro-rata. Illustrations: photos, drawings, cartoons. Founded 1905.

County

County Magazine Publishers Ltd, PO Box 2486,
Sonning, Reading, Berks. RG4 6YA
tel 0118-969 8884 *fax* 0118-969 8885
Editor Ashlyn Watts
Monthly £1.00

Articles of topical relevance or historical
interest relating to Heart of England
region of Birmingham and Warwickshire
only. Prefer illustrated material. Length:
1200 words. Illustrations: line, half-tone,
colour. Payment: £50 per 1200 words;
according to quality for illustrations.
Founded 1992.

Creative Camera

CC Publishing, 5 Hoxton Square, London N1 6NU
tel 0171-729 6993
Editor David Brittain
Bi-monthly £3.95

Illustrated articles and pictures dealing
with serious photography, sociology of,
history of and criticism of photos; book
and exhibition reviews. Arts Council
supported. Payment: by arrangement.
Illustrations: b&w, colour. Founded 1968.

The Cricketer International

Third Street, Langton Green, Tunbridge Wells,
Kent TN3 0EN
tel (01892) 862551 *fax* (01892) 863755
Editor Peter Perchard
Monthly £2.45

Articles on cricket at any level.
Illustrations: line, half-tone, colour, cartoons. Payment: £50 per 1000 words;
illustrations minimum £17.50. Founded
1921.

The Criminologist

East Row, Little London, Chichester,
West Sussex PO19 1PG
tel (01243) 775552 *fax* (01243) 779278
e-mail jp@barry-rose-law.co.uk
Editor R.W. Stone
Quarterly £36.75 p.a. plus p&p

Specialised material designed for an
expert and professional readership on
national and international criminology,
the police, forensic science, the law,
penology, sociology and law enforcement. Articles welcomed, up to 4000
words, from those familiar with the journal's style and requirements. A preliminary letter with a brief résumé is requested. Payment: according to merit.
Founded 1966.

Critical Quarterly

Address for contributions Kate Mellor,
The London Consortium, PO Box 13843,
London EC1V 0LB
Editor Colin MacCabe
Quarterly £31.00 p.a. (£62.00 p.a. institutions)

Fiction, poems, literary criticism. Length:
2000-5000 words. Interested contributors
should study magazine before submitting
MSS. Payment: by arrangement. Founded
1959.

CTN (Confectioner, Tobacconist, Newsagent)

Maclaren House, 19 Scarbrook Road,
Croydon CR9 1QH
tel 0181-277 5202 *fax* 0181-277 5216
Editor Anne Bingham
Weekly 95p. (£48.00 p.a.)

Trade news and brief articles illustrated
when possible with photos or line drawings; also cartoons. Must be of current
interest to retail confectioner-tobac-
conists and newsagents. Length: articles
600-800 words. Payment: by negotiation.

Cumbria and Lake District Magazine

(formerly Cumbria)
Dalesman Publishing Company Ltd,
Stable Courtyard, Broughton Hall, Skipton,
North Yorkshire BD23 3AE
tel (01756) 701381 *fax* (01756) 701326
e-mail www.yorkshirenet.co.uk/dalesman
Editor Terry Fletcher
Monthly £1.00

Articles of genuine rural interest concerning Lakeland and Cumbria. Short
length preferred. Illustrations: line drawings and first-class photos. Payment:
according to merit. Founded 1951.

Custom Car

Kelsey Publishing Ltd, Kelsey House,
77 High Street, Beckenham, Kent BR3 1AN
tel 0181-658 3531 *fax* 0181-650 8035
Editor Tim Baggaley
Monthly £2.60

Customising, drag racing and hot rods.
Length: by arrangement. Payment: by
arrangement. Founded 1970.

CWU Voice

CWU House, Crescent Lane, London SW4 9RN
tel 0171-622 9977 *fax* 0171-720 2184
web site http://www.101354.1117@compuserve.com
Editors Linda Quinn
Monthly Free to members

Main journal of CWU members. Articles on postal and telecommunications workers in the UK and abroad and on other questions of interest to a trade union readership. Payment: NUJ rates. Illustrations: line and colour. Founded 1920.

Cycling Today

Stonehart Leisure Magazines Ltd,
67 Goswell Road, London EC1V 7EN
tel 0171-410 9410 *fax* 0171-410 9411
Editor Roger St Pierre
Monthly £2.60

Material mostly commissioned. Accepts unsolicited travel/expedition features (UK and abroad), written to style (emphasis on anecdotes and on characters met, rather than bland travelogue) with professional-quality colour transparencies, including cycle action shots; and general cycling news. Interested to hear from health and fitness writers with some knowledge of cycling. Length: features 1500-2000 words, news 150-200 words. Payment: £150 per feature inc. pix; news £20 per item. Founded 1993 as *New Cyclist*.

Cycling Weekly

IPC Magazines Ltd, King's Reach Tower, Stamford Street, London SE1 9LS
tel 0171-261 5588 *fax* 0171-261 5758
Editor Andrew Sutcliffe
Weekly £1.30

Racing and technical articles; topical photos with a cycling interest also considered; cartoons. Length: not exceeding 1500 words. Payment: by arrangement. Founded 1891.

Cyphers

3 Selskar Terrace, Dublin 6, Republic of Ireland
fax (01) 4978866
£6.00 for 3 issues
Editors Leland Bardwell, Pearse Hutchinson, Eiléan Ní Chuilleanáin, Macdara Woods

Poems, fiction, articles on literary subjects, translations. Payment: £10 per page. Founded 1975.

Dairy Farmer and Dairy Beef Producer

Wharfedale Road, Ipswich IP1 4LG
tel (01473) 241122 *fax* (01473) 240501
e-mail dairy-farmer@dotfarming.com
Editor Graeme Kirk
Monthly Controlled circulation

Authoritative articles dealing in practical, lively style with dairy farming. Topical controversial articles invited. Well-written, illustrated accounts of new ideas being tried on dairy farms are especially wanted. Length: normally 800-1400 words with colour photos. Payment: by arrangement.

Dairy Industries International

Wilmington House, Church Hill, Wilmington, Dartford, Kent DA2 7EF
tel (01322) 277788 *fax* (01322) 276474
Editor Rebecca Wright
Monthly £54.00 post free (UK)

Covers the entire field of milk processing, the manufacture of products from liquid milk, and ice cream. Articles relating to dairy plant, butter and cheese making, ice cream making, new product developments and marketing, etc. Payment: by arrangement. Illustrations: colour transparencies/prints and Indian ink diagrams. Founded 1936.

Dalesman

Dalesman Publishing Company Ltd,
Stable Courtyard, Broughton Hall, Skipton, North Yorkshire BD23 3AE
tel (01756) 701381 *fax* (01756) 701326
e-mail www.yorkshirenet.co.uk/dalesman
Editor Terry Fletcher
Monthly £1.25

Articles and stories of genuine rural interest concerning Yorkshire. Short length preferred. Payment: according to merit. Illustrations: line drawings and first-class photos preferably featuring people. Founded 1939.

Dance & Dancers

214 Panther House, 38 Mount Pleasant, London WC1X 0AP
tel/fax 0171-837 2711
Editor John Percival
Monthly £1.75

Specialist features, reviews on modern/classical dance, dancers. Length: by prior arrangement. Payment: by arrangement. Illustrations: line, half-tone; colour covers. Founded 1950.

Dancing Times

The Dancing Times Ltd, Clerkenwell House, 45-47 Clerkenwell Green, London EC1R 0EB
tel 0171-250 3006 *fax* 0171-253 6679
Editor Mary Clarke
Editorial Adviser Ivor Guest
Executive Editor Sue Merrett
Monthly £1.70

Ballet, contemporary dance and all forms of stage dancing, both from general, historical, critical and technical angles. Well-informed freelance articles are occasionally used, but only after preliminary arrangements. Payment: by arrangement. Illustrations: occasional line, action photos always preferred; colour invited. Founded 1910.

The Dandy

D.C. Thomson & Co. Ltd, Albert Square, Dundee DD1 9QJ
tel (01382) 223131 *fax* (01382) 322214
185 Fleet Street, London EC4A 2HS
tel 0171-242 5086 *fax* 0171-404 5694
Weekly 42p

Comic strips for children. 10-12 pictures per single page story, 18-20 pictures per 2-page story. Promising artists are encouraged. Payment: on acceptance.

Dandy Comic Library

D.C. Thomson & Co. Ltd, Albert Square, Dundee DD1 9QJ
tel (01382) 223131 *fax* (01382) 322214
185 Fleet Street, London EC4A 2HS
tel 0171-242 5086 *fax* 0171-404 5694
2 p.m. 55p

Extra-long comic adventure stories featuring the well-known characters from the weekly Dandy publication.

Darts World

World Magazines Limited, 9 Kelsey Park Road, Beckenham, Kent BR3 6LH
tel 0181-650 6580 *fax* 0181-650 2534
Editor Tony Wood
Monthly £1.80

Articles and stories with darts theme. Illustrations: half-tone, cartoons. Payment: £40-£50 per 1000 words; illustrations by arrangement. Founded 1972.

Day by Day

Woolacombe House, 141 Woolacombe Road, London SE3 8QP
tel 0181-856 6249
Editor Patrick Richards
Monthly 80p

Articles and news on non-violence and social justice. Reviews of art, books, films, plays, musicals and opera. Cricket reports. Short poems and very occasional short stories in keeping with editorial viewpoint. Payment: £2 per 1000 words. No illustrations required. Founded 1963.

Dental Update

George Warman Publications (UK) Ltd, Unit 2, Riverview Business Park, Walnut Tree Close, Guildford, Surrey GU1 4UX
tel (01483) 304944 *fax* (01483) 303191
Editor Susan Joyce
10 p.a. £45.00 p.a. (£20.00 p.a. students; £33.00 p.a. vocational trainees)

Clinical articles, clinical quizzes. Illustrations: line, colour. Payment: £50-£100 per 1000 words; £50 cover photos only. Founded 1973.

Derbyshire Life and Countryside

Heritage House, Lodge Lane, Derby DE1 3HE
tel (01332) 347087/8/9 *fax* (01332) 290688
Monthly £1.20

Articles, preferably illustrated, about Derbyshire life, people and history. Length: up to 800 words. Some short stories set in Derbyshire accepted; no verse. Payment: according to nature and quality of contribution. Illustrations: photos of Derbyshire subjects. Founded 1931.

The Dickensian

Dickens House, 48 Doughty Street, London WC1N 2LF
Editor Dr Malcolm Andrews, School of English, Rutherford College, University of Kent, Canterbury, Kent CT2 7NX
fax (01227) 827001
Published by The Dickens Fellowship
3 p.a. £9.50 p.a. (£12.00 p.a. institutions; overseas rates on application)

Welcomes articles on all aspects of Dickens' life, works and character. Payment: none. Send contributions (enclose sae if return required) and editorial correspondence to the editor.

Director

Mountbarrow House, 12-20 Elizabeth Street, London SW1W 9RB
tel 0171-730 8320 *fax* 0171-235 5627
Editor Tim Hindle
Monthly £3.00

Authoritative business-related articles. Send synopsis of proposed article and examples of printed work. Length: 500-3000 words. Payment: by arrangement. Illustrated mainly in colour. Founded 1947.

Dirt Bike Rider

Key Publishing Ltd, PO Box 100, Stamford, Lincs. PE9 1XQ
tel (01780) 755131 *fax* (01780) 757261
Editor Roddy Brooks
Monthly £2.25

Features, track tests, coverage on all aspects of off-road motor-cycling. Length: up to 1000 words. Payment: £80 per 1000 words. Illustrations: half-tone, colour, cartoons. Founded 1981.

Disability Now
Scope, 12 Park Crescent, London W1N 4EQ
tel 0171-636 5020 *fax* 0171-436 4582
Editor Mary Wilkinson
Monthly £16.00 p.a. (£25.00 organisations, £30.00 overseas)

Topical, authoritative articles of interest to people with a wide range of disabilities, carers and professionals; also arts and book reviews. Contributions from people with disabilities particularly welcome. Preliminary letter desirable. Length: up to 1000 words. Illustrations: colour and b&w news photos, cartoons. Payment: from £85 per 1000 words; by arrangement for illustrations. Founded 1957.

Diver
55 High Street, Teddington, Middlesex TW11 8HA
tel 0181-943 4288 *fax* 0181-943 4312
e-mail 100737.2226@compuserve.com
Editor Bernard Eaton
Monthly £2.50

Articles on sub aqua diving and under-water developments. Length: 1500-4000 words. Illustrations: line, half-tone and colour. Payment: by arrangement. Founded 1953.

Doctor
Reed Healthcare, Quadrant House, The Quadrant, Sutton, Surrey SM2 5AS
tel 0181-652 8740 *fax* 0181-652 8701
Editor Jane King
Weekly £2.00

Commissioned articles and features of interest to GPs. Length: various. Illustrations: colour photos – news, features, clinical; some line. Payment: NUJ rates. Founded 1971.

Dogs Today
Pet Subjects Ltd, Pankhurst Farm, Bagshot Road, West End, Nr Woking, Surrey GU24 9QR
tel (01276) 858880 *fax* (01276) 858860
Editor Beverley Cuddy
Monthly £2.80

Study of magazine essential before submitting ideas. Interested in human interest dog stories, celebrity interviews, holiday features and anything unusual – all must be entertaining and informative and

accompanied by illustrations. Length: 800-1200 words. Illustrations: colour, preferably transparencies, colour cartoons. Payment: negotiable. Founded 1990.

Dorset Life – The Dorset Magazine
95 North Street, Wareham,
Dorset BH20 4AE
tel (01929) 551264
Editor John Newth
Monthly £1.50

Articles (500-1200 words), photos (colour or b&w) and line drawings with a specifically Dorset theme. Payment: by arrangement. Founded 1967.

The Downside Review
Downside Abbey, Stratton-on-the-Fosse, Nr Bath, Somerset BA3 4RH
tel (01761) 232 295
Editor Dom Daniel Rees
Quarterly £6.00 (£22.00 p.a.)

Articles and book reviews on theology, metaphysics, mysticism and modernism, and monastic and church history. Payment: not usual.

Drapers Record
EMAP Fashion, 67 Clerkenwell Road, London EC1R 5BH
tel 0171-417 2830 *fax* 0171-417 2832
Editor Sophie Hewitt-Jones
Weekly £1.90

Editorial aimed at fashion retailers, large and small. No unsolicited material. Payment: by negotiation. Illustrations: colour and b&w: photos, drawings and cartoons. Founded 1887.

Early Music
Oxford University Press, 70 Baker Street, London W1M 1DJ
tel 0171-616 5902 *fax* 0171-616 5901
e-mail jnl.early-music@oup.co.uk
web site http://www.oup.co.uk/earlyj
Editor Tess Knighton
Quarterly £9.95 (£40.00 p.a., institutions £58.00 p.a.)

Lively, informative and scholarly articles on aspects of medieval, renaissance, baroque and classical music. Payment: £20 per 1000 words. Illustrations: line, half-tone, colour. Founded 1973.

East Lothian Life
2 Beveridge Row, Belhaven, Dunbar, East Lothian EH42 1TP
tel/fax (01368) 863593
Editor Pauline Jaffray
Quarterly £2.00

Articles and features with an East Lothian slant. Length: up to 1000 words. Illustrations: b&w photos, line, cartoons. Payment: negotiable. Founded 1989.

Eastern Art Report

Eastern Art Publishing Group, 27 Wallorton Gardens, London SW14 8DX
tel 0181-392 1122 fax 0181-392 1422
e-mail easternart@compuserve.com
Managing Editor Sajid Rizvi, Executive Editor Shirley Rizvi
Bi-monthly £10.95 (individual £25.00 p.a., institutions £40.00 p.a.)

Original, well-researched articles on all aspects of the visual arts – Islamic, Indian, Chinese and Japanese; reviews. Length of articles: min. 1500 words. Illustrations: colour transparencies, b&w photos; no responsibility accepted for unsolicited material. Payment: by arrangement. Founded 1989.

Eastern Eye

Ethnic Media Group, 1st Floor, 148 Cambridge Heath Road, London E1 5QJ
tel 0171-702 8012 fax 0171-702 7937
Editor Sarwar Ahmed
Weekly 49p

Articles, features and news of interest to Asians aged 16-36. Length: features, 1800 words. Illustrations: colour and b&w photos. Payment: £80 per 1000 words; photos £10. Founded 1989.

The Ecologist

Agriculture House, Bath Road, Sturminster Newton, Dorset DT10 1DU
tel (01258) 473476 fax (01258) 473748
Editors Nicholas Hildyard and Sarah Sexton
6 p.a. £4.00

Fully-referenced articles on economic, social and environmental affairs from an ecological standpoint. Study magazine first for level and approach. Length: 1000-5000 words. Illustrations: line, half-tone. Payment: by arrangement.

Economica

STICERD, London School of Economics, Houghton Street, London WC2A 2AE
tel 0171-955 7855 fax 0171-242 2357
Editors Prof F.A. Cowell and Dr Alan Manning
Quarterly £21.00 (apply for subscription rates)

Learned journal covering the fields of economics, economic history and statistics. Payment: none. Founded 1921; New Series 1934.

The Economist

25 St James's Street, London SW1A 1HG
tel 0171-830 7000
Editor Bill Emmott
Weekly £2.20

Articles staff-written. Founded 1843.

Edinburgh Review

22 George Square, Edinburgh EH8 9LF
tel 0131-650 4689 fax 0131-662 0053
Editors Gavin Wallace and Robert Alan Jamieson
Bi-Annual £16.00 (£31.50 p.a.)

Fiction, poetry, clearly written articles on Scottish and international cultural and philosophical ideas. Payment: by arrangement. Founded 1969.

Education

17 Park Road, Hampton Hill, Middlesex TW12 1HE
tel/fax 0181-979 9473
Editor George Low
Monthly £32.00 p.a.

Specialist articles on educational administration, all branches of education; technical education; universities; school building; playing fields; environmental studies; physical education; school equipment; school meals and health; teaching aids. Length: 1000 words. Illustrations: photos, cartoons. Payment: by arrangement. Founded 1903; relaunched 1996.

Electrical Review

Reed Business Information Ltd, Quadrant House, The Quadrant, Sutton, Surrey SM2 5AS
tel 0181-652 3113 fax 0181-652 8951
Editor T. Tunbridge
Fortnightly £2.50

Technical and business articles on electrical and control engineering; outside contributions considered. Electrical news welcomed. Illustrations: photos and drawings, cartoons. Payment: according to merit. Founded 1872.

Electrical Times

Reed Business Publishing, Quadrant House, The Quadrant, Sutton, Surrey SM2 5AS
tel 0181-652 3115 fax 0181-652 8972
Editor Steve Hobson
Monthly £2.75

Business and technical articles of interest to contractors and installers in the electrical industries, with illustrations as necessary. Length: 750-1000 words. Payment: £150 per article. Illustrations: line, half-tone, colour, cartoons. Founded 1891.

Electronics Times

Miller Freeman plc, Miller Freeman House,
30 Calderwood Street, London SE18 6QH
tel 0181-855 777 *fax* 0181-855 1793
e-mail 6020@cityscape.co.uk
Editor John Walko
Weekly £3.25 (£85 p.a.)

News, reviews and features on the electronics industry. Length: 2000 words (features), 200 words (news). Illustrations: colour transparencies, colour and b&w artwork and cartoons. Payment: variable. Founded 1978.

Elle (UK)

EMAP Women's Group, 20 Orange Street,
London WC2H 7ED
tel 0171-957 8383
Editor Marie O'Riordan
Monthly £2.30

Commissioned material only. Payment: by arrangement. Illustrations: colour. Founded 1985.

Empire

Mappin House, 4 Winsley Street,
London W1N 7AR
tel 0171-436 1515/1601 *fax* 0171-312 8249
Editor Ian Nathan, *Assistant Editor* Christopher Hemblade
Monthly £2.60

Guide to film and video: articles, features, news. Length: various. Illustrations: colour and b&w photos. Payment: approx. £125 per 1000 words; varies for illustrations. Founded 1989.

The Engineer

30 Calderwood Street, London SE18 6QH
tel 0181-855 7777 *fax* 0181-316 3040
Editor Adèle Kimber
34 p.a. Controlled circulation (£90.00 p.a.)

Articles, features and news on the business and technology of the engineering industry, including profiles, analysis and new products. Length: news up to 200 words, features average 1000 words. Illustrations: colour transparencies or prints, line diagrams, graphs. Payment: £150 per page; £50 per illustration. Founded 1856.

Engineering

Gillard Welch Ltd, Chester Court, High Street,
Knowle, Solihull, West Midlands B93 0LL
tel (01564) 771772 *fax* (01564) 774776
Editor Mike Farish
11 p.a. £5.50

'For innovators in technology, manufacturing and management': features and news. Contributions considered on all aspects of engineering, particularly design. Illustrations: colour. Founded 1866.

English Historical Review

Addison Wesley Longman Higher Education,
Edinburgh Gate, Harlow, Essex CM20 2JE
tel (01279) 623623
Editors Dr J.R. Maddicott and Dr J. Stevenson
5 p.a. £83.00 p.a.

High-class scholarly articles, documents, and reviews or short notices of books. Contributions are not accepted unless they supply original information and should be sent direct to Dr J.R. Maddicott, Editor, EHR, Exeter College, Oxford OX1 3DP. Books for review should be sent to Dr J. Stevenson, Editor, EHR, Worcester College, Oxford OX1 2HB. Payment: none. Founded 1886.

Enterprise

Martin Leach Enterprises Ltd, Selous House,
5-12 Mandela Street, London NW1 0DU
tel 0171-916 1880 *fax* 0171-916 1881
e-mail 100417.3242@compuserve.com
Editor Liz Jones
Bi-monthly £2.25

'The magazine for today's growing businesses': news, features and profiles of companies and people. Length: 1500 words (features). Illustrations: colour transparencies and artwork. Payment: £225 per 1000 words; £300 per illustration. Founded 1991.

Envoi

44 Rudyard Road, Biddulph Moor,
Stoke-on-Trent, Staffs. ST8 7JN
tel (01782) 517892
Editor Roger Elkin
3 p.a. £12.00 p.a.

New poetry, including sequences, collaborative works and translations, reviews, articles on modern poets and poetic style; poetry competitions; editorial criticism of subscribers' poems (with sae) at no charge. Sample copy: £3.00. Payment: 2 complimentary copies. Founded 1957.

ES Magazine – see Evening Standard
in Regional newspapers UK and Ireland,
page 12

Esquire

National Magazine House, 33 Broadwick Street,
London W1V 1FR
tel 0171-439 5000 *fax* 0171-439 5067
Editor Peter Howarth
Monthly £2.70

Quality men's general interest magazine –
articles, features. No unsolicited material
or short stories. Length: various. Illustrations: colour and b&w photos, line.
Payment: by arrangement. Founded 1991.

Essentials

IPC Magazines Ltd, King's Reach Tower,
Stamford Street, London SE1 9LS
tel 0171-261 6970
Editor Karen Livermore
Monthly £1.70

Features, plus fashion, health and beauty, cookery. Illustrations: colour.
Payment: by negotiation. Founded 1988.

Essex Countryside

Market Link Publishing Ltd, Griggs Farm,
West Street, Coggeshall, Essex CO6 1NT
tel (01376) 562578 *fax* (01376) 562581
Editor Andy Tilbrook
Monthly £1.50

Features, profiles and occasional short
stories, all with Essex emphasis. Length:
up to 1200 words. Illustrations: colour
and b&w photos. Payment: negotiable.
Founded 1953.

Estates Gazette

151 Wardour Street, London W1V 4BN
tel 0171 437 0141 *fax* 0171 437 0201
Editor Helen Pearce
Weekly £1.85

Property, legislation, planning, architecture – articles, features and business
news. Length: 1500 words. Illustrations:
colour, line, cartoons. Payment: none.
Founded 1858.

European Bookseller

15 Micawber Street, London N1 7TB
tel 0171 336 6650 *fax* 0171-336 6640
e-mail beishon@ibm.net
web site http://www.axford.com/beishon/eurobook/
Editor Marc Beishon
Bi-monthly £69.00 p.a.

Articles, features, news, statistics for the
European book trade. Publisher profiles,
translation and rights news, book fairs,
electronic publishing, key figure interviews, country focuses, book and CD-
Rom reviews. Length: 200-2000 words.
Illustrations: b&w photos. Payment: £100

per 1000 words; photos by agreement.
Founded 1990.

European Chemical News

Reed Business Information, Quadrant House,
The Quadrant, Sutton, Surrey SM2 5AS
tel 0181-652 3187 *fax* 0181-652 3375
e-mail ecne@rbi.co.uk
Editor John Baker
Weekly £257 p.a. Europe (£295 p.a. overseas)

Articles and features concerning business, markets and investments in the
chemical industry. Length: 1000-2000
words; news items up to 400 words.
Payment: £120-£150 per 1000 words.

European Drinks Buyer

Crier Publications, Arctic House, Rye Lane,
Dunton Green, Sevenoaks, Kent TN14 5HB
tel (01732) 451515 *fax* (01732) 451383
web site http://www.crier.co.uk/crier/general@
crier.demon.co.uk
Editor Edward Hart
Bi-monthly Controlled free circulation

Articles of European interest on business,
marketing, branding, catering, retail, duty
free, EU legislation, packaging, labelling,
product surveys, consumption trends. No
unsolicited material but enquiries for editorial guidelines welcome (enclose
sae/samples of published work). Overseas
correspondents wanted. Length: features,
profiles, interviews, opinion pieces 1000-
2000 words, news 150-500 words. Illustrations: half-tone, colour. Payment: from
£80 per 1000 words; none for illustrations. Founded 1991.

European Frozen Food Buyer

Crier Publications, Arctic House, Rye Lane,
Dunton Green, Sevenoaks, Kent TN14 5HB
tel (01732) 451515 *fax* (01732) 451383
Editor Alwyn Brice
Bi-monthly Controlled free circulation

Articles of European interest on business, marketing, branding, catering,
retail, EU legislation, packaging,
labelling, product surveys, food
hygiene, consumption trends. No unsolicited material but enquiries for editorial guidelines welcome (enclose sae/sam-
ples of published work). Overseas correspondents wanted. Length: features,
profiles, interviews 1000-2000 words,
news 150-500 words. Illustrations: half-
tone, colour. Payment: £100 per 1000
words; none for illustrations. Founded
1989.

European Plastics News

RAPRA Technology Ltd, Shawbury, Shrewsbury, Shropshire SY4 4NR
tel (01939) 250383 *fax* (01939) 251118
Editor Pat Thomas
Monthly £13.00 (£120.00 p.a.)

Technical articles dealing with plastics and allied subjects. Length: depending on subject. Illustrations: b&w or colour photos/diagrams. Payment: by arrangement; none for illustrations. Founded 1929.

Eva

IPC Magazines, King's Reach Tower, Stamford Street, London SE1 9LS
tel 0171-261 5857 *fax* 0171-261 6442
web site http//www.ipc.co.uk
Editor Eve Finlay Dawson
Weekly 45p

For women in the 18-45 age group. Readers' real-life stories. Length: from 400 words. Payment: from £150. Human interest features and celebrity gossip. Payment: by arrangement. Founded 1994.

Eventing

IPC Magazines Ltd, Room 2105, King's Reach Tower, Stamford Street, London SE1 9LS
tel 0171-261 5388 *fax* 0171-261 5429
Editor Kate Green
Monthly £2.60

News, articles, features, event reports and opinion pieces – all with bias towards the sport of horse trials. Mostly commissioned, but all ideas welcome. Length: up to 1500 words. Illustrations: colour and b&w, mostly commissioned. Payment: by arrangement; illustrations £30-£45. Founded 1984.

Everyday Practical Electronics

Wimborne Publishing Ltd, Allen House, East Borough, Wimborne, Dorset BH21 1PF
tel (01202) 881749 *fax* (01202) 841692
e-mail editorial@epemag.wimborne.co.uk
web site www.epemag.wimborne.co.uk
Editor Mike Kenward
Monthly £2.65

Constructional and theoretical articles aimed at the student and hobbyist. Length: 1000-5500 words. Payment: £55-£90 per 1000 words. Illustrations: line, half-tone, cartoons. Founded 1971.

Executive PA

Hobsons Publishing plc, Bateman Street, Cambridge CB2 1LZ
tel (01223) 354551 *fax* (01223) 322850
e-mail executive.pa@hobsons.co.uk
Editor Katrina Hendley
Quarterly Complimentary

Business to business for working senior secretaries. Length: 700-1400 words. Illustrations: colour. Payment: £120 per 1000 words. Founded 1991.

Executive Woman

Saleworld Ltd, 2 Chantry Place, Harrow, Middlesex HA3 6NY
tel 0181-420 1210 *fax* 0181-420 1691/3
Editor Angela Giveon
Bi-monthly £2.25

News and features with a holistic approach to the world of successful working women. Strong business features; articles on management, personnel, networking and mentoring. Length: 500-1000 words. Illustrations: colour and b&w, line drawings. Payment: £150 per 1000 words; £50-£100. Founded 1987.

Express on Sunday Magazine – see Express on Sunday in National newspapers UK and Ireland, page 3

The Face

Exmouth House, Pine Street, London EC1R 0JL
tel 0171-837 7270 *fax* 0171-837 3906
Editor Richard Benson
Monthly £2.00

Articles on music, fashion, films, popular youth culture. Contributors must be familiar with the magazine, its audience and culture. Illustrations: half-tone, colour. Payment: £150 per 1000 words; illustrations approx. £120 per page. Founded 1980.

Family Circle

IPC Magazines Ltd, King's Reach Tower, Stamford Street, London SE1 9LS
tel 0171-261 5000 *fax* 0171-261 5929
Editor Sue James
13 p.a. £1.20

Practical, medical human interest material – mostly commissioned. Payment: NUJ rates.

Family Law

21 St Thomas Street, Bristol BS1 6JS
tel (0117) 923 0600 *fax* (0117) 925 0486
e-mail familylaw@jordans.co.uk
web site http://www.familylaw.co.uk
Editors Elizabeth Walsh and Miles McColl
Monthly £90.00 p.a.

Articles dealing with all aspects of the law as it affects the family, written from a legal or socio-legal point of view. Length: from 1000 words. Payment: by arrangement. No illustrations. Founded 1971.

Family Tree Magazine
61 Great Whyte, Ramsey, Huntingdon,
Cambs. PE17 1HL
tel (01487) 814050
Editor Wendy Smith
Monthly £1.90 (£21.50 p.a.)

Articles on any genealogically related topics. Illustrations: half-tone, line, cartoons. Payment: £25 per 1000 words; by arrangement for illustrations. Founded 1984.

Farmers Weekly
(incorporating Power Farming)
Reed Business Information, Quadrant House,
The Quadrant, Sutton, Surrey SM2 5AS
tel 0181-652 4911 *fax* 0181-652 4005
Editor Stephen Howe
Weekly £1.30

Articles on agriculture from freelance contributors will be accepted subject to negotiation. Founded 1934.

Farming News
30 Calderwood Street, London SE18 6QH
tel 0181-855 7777 *fax* 0181-854 6795
e-mail farmingnews@dotfarming.co.uk
web site http://www.dotfarming.com
Editor Donald Taylor
Weekly £1.40 (£66.00 p.a.)

News, business, technical features and articles. Payment: by arrangement. Founded 1983.

Fashion Forecast International
23 Bloomsbury Square, London WC1A 2PJ
tel 0171-637 2211 *fax* 0171-637 2248
Managing Editor Stephen Higginson
2 p.a. (Feb, Aug) £30.00 p.a. UK/Europe, £40.00 p.a. outside Europe

Hosiery Forecast and Lingerie Forecast are included in each issue. Factual articles on fashions and accessories with forecast trends. Length: 800-1000 words. Illustrations: line, half-tone. Payment: by arrangement. Founded 1946.

FHM (For Him Magazine)
EMAP Metro, Mappin House, 4 Winsley Street,
London W1N 7AR
tel 0171-436 1515 *fax* 0171-312 8191
Editor Mike Soutar
Monthly £2.60

Features, fashion, grooming, travel (adventure) and men's interests. Length: 2000-3000 words. Illustrations: colour and b&w photos, line and colour artwork. Payment: by negotiation. Founded 1987.

The Field
IPC Magazines Ltd, King's Reach Tower,
Stamford Street, London SE1 9LS
tel 0171-261 5198 *fax* 0171-261 5358
Monthly £2.80

Specific, topical and informed features on the British countryside and country pursuits, including natural history, field sports, gardening and farming. Overseas subjects considered but opportunities for such articles are limited. No fiction or children's material. Articles, length 800-2000 words, by outside contributors considered; also topical 'shorts' of 200-300 words on all countryside matters. Illustrations: colour photos of a high standard. Payment: on merit. Founded 1853.

Film Review
Visual Imagination Ltd, 9 Blades Court,
Deodar Road, London SW15 2NU
tel 0181-875 1520 *fax* 0181-875 1588
e-mail star@cix.compulink.co.uk
Editor David Richardson
Monthly £2.40

Interviews, news, and features on new film releases. Reviews of films and videos. Length: 1000-3000 words (features), 4000 words (news). Illustrations: colour and b&w photos. Payment: £80 per 1000 words. Founded 1951.

Financial Accountant
PO Box 752, Dartford, Kent DA2 7UD
tel (01322) 664096 *fax* (01322) 614941
Editor Leon Hopkins
Bi-monthly £12.00 p.a.

Journal of The Institute of Financial Accountants. Articles on accounting, management, company law, data processing, information technology, pensions, factoring, investment, insurance, fraud prevention and general business administration. Length: 1000-2000 words. Illustrations: offset litho (mono or colour). Payment: by arrangement. Founded 1920.

Financial Adviser
FT Magazines Ltd, Maple House,
149 Tottenham Court Road, London W1P 9LL
tel 0171-896 2525 *fax* 0171-896 2591
Editor Kevin O'Donnell
Weekly (£50.00 p.a.) Free to financial intermediaries working in financial services

Topical personal finance news and features. Length: variable. Payment: by arrangement. Founded 1987.

Financial Director

VNU Business Publications, VNU House,
32-34 Broadwick Street, London W1A 2HG
tel 0171-316 9000 *fax* 0171-316 9250
web site http://www.financial-director.vnu.co.uk
Monthly £2.50 (£35.00 p.a.) Free to finance directors

Features on financial and strategic management issues. Length: 1500-2000 words. Illustrations: colour and b&w photos, line drawings. Payment: £150 per 1000 words; photos, variable; line, £250-£300. Founded 1984.

Fire

Queensway House, 2 Queensway, Redhill,
Surrey RH1 1QS
tel (01737) 768611 *fax* (01737) 761685
Editor Simon Hoffman
Monthly £5.25 (£52.90 p.a.)

Articles on firefighting and fire prevention from acknowledged experts only. Length: 850 words. Illustrations: dramatic firefighting or fire brigade rescue colour photos sometimes bought. Also *Fire Europe* (quarterly). Payment: by arrangement. Founded 1908.

Fishing News

Emap Business International, Meed House,
21 John Street, London WC1N 2BP
tel 0171-470 6209 *fax* 0171-831 9362
e-mail timo@meed.emap.co.uk
Editor Tim Oliver
Weekly 80p

News and features on all aspects of the commercial fishing industry. Length: up to 1000 words (features), up to 500 words (news). Illustrations: colour and b&w photos. Payment: £100 per 1000 words; £25 per photo. Founded 1913

Flicks

Flicks Publications Ltd, First floor,
25 The Coda Centre, 189 Munster Road,
London SW6 6AW
tel 0171-381 8811 *fax* 0171-381 1811
e-mail flicks@flicks.co.uk
Editor Nick Thomas
Monthly Free in cinemas (£25.00 p.a.)

Articles, features and reviews on new mainstream film releases; reviews of videos and film tie-ins. Length: 100-1200 words. Illustrations: colour. Payment: by negotiation. Founded 1985.

Flight International

Reed Business Publishing, Quadrant House,
The Quadrant, Sutton, Surrey SM2 5AS
tel 0181-652 3882 *fax* 0181-652 3840
e-mail flight.international@rbi.co.uk
Editor A. Winn
Weekly £2.00

Deals with all branches of aerospace: operational and technical articles, illustrated by photos, engineering cutaway drawings; also news, paragraphs, reports of lectures, etc. News press days: Thu, Fri. Illustrations: tone, line, colour. Payment: by agreement. Founded 1909.

Fly-Fishing & Fly-Tying

Rolling River Publications, Aberfeldy Road,
Kenmore, Perthshire PH15 2HF
tel/fax (01887) 830526
Editor Mark Bowler
8 p.a. £2.00

Fly-fishing and fly-tying articles, fishery features, limited short stories, some fishing travel. Length: 800-1500 words. Illustrations: colour photos. Payment: by arrangement. Founded 1990.

FlyPast

Key Publishing Ltd, PO Box 100, Stamford,
Lincs. PE9 1XQ
tel (01780) 55131 *fax* (01780) 57261
Editor Ken Delve
Monthly £2.80

Articles and features on historic aviation. Particularly interested in personal recollections of flying or visits to interesting aeroplane collections anywhere in the world. Length: up to 3000 words. Illustrations: colour and b&w photos. Payment: £50 per 1000 words; £25 colour; £10 b&w. Founded 1981.

Football Picture Story Library

D.C. Thomson & Co. Ltd, Albert Square,
Dundee DD1 9QJ
tel (01382) 223131 *fax* (01382) 322214
185 Fleet Street, London EC4A 2HS
tel 0171-242 5086 *fax* 0171-404 5694
2 p.m. 55p

Football stories for boys told in pictures.

For Women

Portland Publishing Ltd, 4 Selsdon Way,
London E14 9GL
tel 0171-538 8969 *fax* 0171-538 3690
Editor Ruth Corbett
Monthly £2.95

Women's general interest magazine with erotic emphasis. Features on sex, health and beauty; celebrity interviews; erotic fiction and photos. Submit written synopsis for features; erotic fiction welcomed on spec. Length: 1500-2000

words. Illustrations: colour and b&w photos. Payment: £150 per 1000 words; £150 per illustration. Founded 1991.

Fore!

EMAP Pursuit Publishing Ltd, Bretton Court, Bretton, Peterborough PE3 8DZ
tel (01733) 264666 *fax* (01733) 465221
Editor Paul Hamblin
Monthly £2.25

Interested in off-beat features on golf – thought provoking, fun and occasionally irreverent. Length: up to 1000 words. Illustrations: colour, line, cartoons. Payment: £100 per 1000 words; illustrations per quality/size used. Founded 1993.

Fortean Times

Box 2409, London NW5 4NP
tel/fax 0171-485 5002
web site http://www.forteantimes.com/
Editors Bob Rickard and Paul Sieveking
Monthly £2.50

The journal of strange phenomena, experiences, related subjects and philosophies. Articles, features, news, reviews. Length: 500-3000 words; longer by arrangement. Illustrations: colour photos, line and tone art, cartoons. Payment: by negotiation. Founded 1973.

Fortnight – An Independent Review of Politics and the Arts

7 Lower Crescent, Belfast BT7 1NR
tel (01232) 232353/311337/324141
fax (01232) 232650
e-mail mairtin@fortnite.dnet.co.uk
Editors John O'Farrell and Martin Crawford
Monthly £1.80

Current affairs analysis, reportage, opinion pieces, cultural criticism, book reviews, poems. Illustrations: line, half-tone, cartoons. Payment: by arrangement. Founded 1970.

FourFourTwo

Haymarket Trade and Leisure Publications Ltd, 60 Waldegrave Road, Teddington, Middlesex TW11 8LG
tel 0181-943 5603 *fax* 0181-943 5668
Editor Karen Buchanan
Monthly £2.40

Football magazine with an 'adult' approach: interviews, in-depth features, issues pieces, odd and witty material. Length: 2000-3000 (features), 100-500 words (news/latest score). Illustrations:

colour transparencies and artwork, b&w prints. Payment: £150 per 1000 words. Founded 1994.

FRANCE Magazine

The Square, Stow-on-the-Wold, Glos. GL54 1BN
tel (01451) 831398 *fax* (01451) 830869
e-mail francemag@btinernet.com
Editor Philip Faiers
Quarterly £4.25

An armchair journey to the real France – features and articles ranging from cuisine to customs to architecture to exploring the hidden France. Informed speculative submissions welcome. Length: 800-2500 words. Illustrations: colour transparencies (mounted and captioned). Payment: £100 per 1000 words; £50 per page/pro rata for illustrations. Founded 1989.

Freelance Market News

Sevendale House, 7 Dale Street, Manchester M1 1JB
tel 0161-237 1827 *fax* 0161-228 3533
Editor Angela Cox
11 p.a. £25.00 p.a.

News items on editorial requirements of interest to writers, plus short articles on 'where to sell'. Length: articles up to 700 words. Payment: from £35 per 1000 words. Founded 1963.

Fresh Produce Journal

Lockwood Press Ltd, 430-438 Market Towers, 1 Nine Elms Lane, London SW8 5NN
tel 0171-622 6677 *fax* 0171-720 2047
e-mail fpj.edit@fpj.fruitnet.com
Editor Kathy Miller
Weekly £1.60

Articles dealing with fruit, vegetable and flower trades on the marketing aspects of production but particularly importing, distribution and post-harvest handling; articles should average 500-700 words. Payment: by arrangement. Illustrations: half-tone. Founded 1895.

The Friend

Drayton House, 30 Gordon Street, London WC1H 0BQ
tel 0171-387 7549
Editor Deborah Padfield
Weekly 75p

Material of interest to the Religious Society of Friends and like-minded people; political, social, economic or devotional, considered from outside contrib-

utors. Length: up to 1000 words. Illustrations: b&w or colour prints, b&w line drawings. Payment: none. Founded 1843.

The Furrow

St Patrick's College, Maynooth, Co. Kildare, Republic of Ireland
tel (01) 6286215 *fax* (01) 7083908
Editor Rev. Ronan Drury
Monthly £1.50

Religious, pastoral, theological, social articles. Length: 3000 words. Payment: average £15 per page (450 words). Illustrations: line, half-tone. Founded 1950.

FW

(formerly Fashion Weekly)
EMAP Fashion, 67 Clerkenwell Road, London EC1R 5BH
tel 0171-417 2810 *fax* 0171-417 2812
Editor William Drew
8 p.a. £64.00 p.a.

Fashion business magazine primarily for retailers. Payment: by arrangement. Illustrations: line, half-tone, colour. Founded 1959.

The Garden

Apex House, Oundle Road, Peterborough PE2 9NP
tel (01733) 898100 *fax* (01733) 890657
Editor Ian Hodgson
Monthly £2.75

Journal of The Royal Horticultural Society. Features of horticultural or botanical interest on a wide range of subjects. Commissioned material only. Length: 1200-2500 words. Illustrations: 35mm or medium format colour transparencies, occasional b&w prints, botanical line drawings. Payment: £150 per 1000 words; varies for illustrations. Founded 1866.

Garden Answers

(incorporating Practical Gardening)
EMAP Apex Publications Ltd, Apex House, Oundle Road, Peterborough PE2 9NP
tel (01733) 898100 *fax* (01733) 898433
Editor Adrienne Wild
Monthly £2.00

Commissioned features and articles on all aspects of gardening. Study of magazine essential. Approach by letter with examples of published work. Length: 750 words. Illustrations: colour transparencies and artwork. Payment: by negotiation. Founded 1982.

Garden News

EMAP Apex Publications Ltd, Apex House, Oundle Road, Peterborough PE2 9NP
tel (01733) 898100 *fax* (01733) 898433
Editor Jim Ward
Weekly 75p

Up-to-date information on everything to do with plants, growing and gardening. Illustrations: line, colour, cartoons. Payment: by negotiation. Founded 1958.

Gardens Illustrated

John Brown Publishing, 136-142 Bramley Road, London W10 6SR
tel 0171-470 2400 *fax* 0171-381 3930
Editor Rosie Atkins
Bi-monthly £3.50

Upmarket, inspirational glossy for those interested in garden history, plants and gardening merchandise. Material mostly commissioned; send synopsis, samples of past work and sae to the editor. Length: 1000 words. Illustrations: colour – usually commissioned. Payment: by negotiation. Founded 1993.

Gay Times

Ground Floor, Worldwide House, 116-134 Bayham Street, London NW1 0BA
tel 0171-482 2576 *fax* 0171-284 0329
Editor David Smith
Monthly £2.50

Feature articles, full news and review coverage of all aspects of gay and lesbian life. Length: up to 2000 words. Illustrations: colour, line and half-tone, cartoons. Payment: by arrangement. Founded 1982.

Geographical Journal

Royal Geographical Society (with the Institute of British Geographers), Kensington Gore, London SW7 2AR
tel 0171-591 3025 *fax* 0171-591 3021
Editor Prof V. Gardiner
3 p.a. £25.00 (post free), (£60.00 p.a.)

Papers on all aspects of geography, including some read before the Royal Geographical Society. Length: up to 4500 words. Payment: for reviews. Illustrations: photos, maps and diagrams. Founded 1893.

Geographical Magazine

(under licence from the Royal Geographical Society)
Campion Interactive Publishing Ltd, Unit 2, Utopia Village, 7 Chalcot Road, London NW1 8LX
tel 0171-586 7005 *fax* 0171-483 1774

e-mail geogmag@gn.apc.org
Acting Editor Fiona McWilliam
Monthly £2.45

Topical geography in a broad sense and travel . Illustrations: colour slides, b&w prints or vintage material; maps and graphs always needed; cartoons. Payment: by negotiation. Founded 1935.

Geological Magazine

Cambridge University Press, The Edinburgh Building, Shaftesbury Road, Cambridge CB2 2RU
tel (01223) 312393
Editors Dr C.P. Hughes, Prof I.N. McCave, Dr N.H. Woodcock, Dr M.J. Bickle
Bi-monthly (£176.00 p.a. institutions, £39.00 p.a. students, US$312 USA/Canada/Mexico)

Original articles on all earth science topics containing the results of independent research by experts. Also reviews and notices of current geological literature, correspondence on geological subjects – illustrated. Length: variable. Payment: none. Founded 1864.

Gibbons Stamp Monthly

Stanley Gibbons Ltd, 5 Parkside, Ringwood, Hants BH24 3SH
tel (01425) 472363 *fax* (01425) 470247
Editor Hugh Jefferies
Monthly £1.95 (£23.40 p.a.)

Articles on philatelic topics. Previous reference to the editor advisable. Length: 500-2500 words. Payment: by arrangement, £25 or more per 1000 words. Illustrations: photos, line, stamps or covers.

Gifts International

Nexus Media, Nexus House, Swanley, Kent BR8 8HY
tel (01322) 660070 *fax* (01322) 614904
Editor Kate Gould
Monthly £39.00 p.a. (£46-52 p.a. overseas)

News of gift industry – products, trends, shops; articles on retailing, exporting, importing, manufacturing, crafts (UK and abroad). Illustrations: products, news, personal photos.

Girl About Town Magazine

7-9 Rathbone Street, London W1P 1AF
tel 0171-636 6651 *fax* 0171-255 2352
Editor Bill Williamson
Weekly Free

Articles of general interest to women. Length: about 1100-1500 words. Payment: negotiable. Founded 1973.

Girl Talk

BBC Worldwide Ltd, Room A1130, Woodlands, 80 Wood Lane, London W12 0TT
tel 0181-576 3543 *fax* 0181-576 3267
e-mail gill.smith@bbc.co.uk
Editor Gill Smith
Fortnightly 85p

Highly illustrated magazine for 6-12 year-old girls. No unsolicited articles or features; stories only considered (500 words). Illustrations: colour artwork. Payment: on application. Founded 1995.

Glaucus

Glaucus House, 14 Corbyn Crescent, Shoreham-by-Sea, West Sussex BN43 6PQ
tel (01273) 465433 *fax* (01273) 465433
e-mail 106127.206@compuserve.com
web sites http://ourworld.compuserve.com/homepages/bmlss/index.htm (England)
http://www.ed.ac.uk/~evah01/bmlss.htm (Scotland)
Editor Andy Horton
Quarterly £20.00 p.a.

Official journal of the British Marine Life Study Society, aimed at the popular market. Observations and scientific research on the natural history, and related subjects, of the marine environment surrounding the British Isles. Send sae for Guide to Submissions. Length: up to 2500 words. Illustrations: b&w line, occasional b&w photos. Payment: expenses only. Founded 1990.

Goldlife for 50-Forward

1st Floor, 5 Charterhouse Buildings, Goswell Road, London EC1M 7AN
tel 0171-251 5489 *fax* 0171-251 5490
Editor Miss N. Parmer
Bi-monthly £14.95 p.a.

Celebrity profiles and articles, health, travel and gardening features and news of interest to the over 50s age group. Length: approx. 700 words. Illustrated. Payment: £150 per 1000 words; £20 per illustration. Founded 1989.

Golf Monthly

IPC Magazines Ltd, King's Reach Tower, Stamford Street, London SE1 9LS
tel 0171-261 7237 *fax* 0171-261 7240
Editor Colin Callander
Monthly £2.80

Original articles on golf considered (not reports), golf clinics, handy hints. Illustrations: half-tone, colour, cartoons. Payment: by arrangement. Founded 1911.

Golf Weekly

EMAP Pursuit Publishing Ltd, Bretton Court, Bretton, Peterborough PE3 8DZ
tel (01733) 465223 *fax* (01733) 465221
Editor Bob Warters
Weekly £1.70

News, tournament reports and articles on golf of interest to golfers. Payment: 15p per word published. Illustrations: photos of golf news and new courses.

Golf World

Emap Pursuit Publishing Ltd, Mappin House, 4 Winsley Street, London W1N 7AR
tel (01733) 264666 *fax* 0171-817 9630
Editor David Clarke
Monthly £2.70

Expert golf instructional articles, 500-3000 words; general interest articles, personality features 500-3000 words. Little fiction. Payment: by negotiation. Illustrations: line, half-tone, colour, cartoons. Founded 1962.

Good Housekeeping

National Magazine House, 72 Broadwick Street, London W1V 2BP
tel 0171-439 5000 *fax* 0171-439 5591
Editor Pat Roberts Cairns
Monthly £2.00

Articles of 1000-2500 words on topics of interest to intelligent women. No unsolicited features or stories accepted; approach by letter only. Domestic subjects covered by staff writers. Personal experiences and humorous articles occasionally used. Payment: magazine standards. Illustrations: mainly commissioned. Founded 1922.

GQ

Vogue House, Hanover Square, London W1R 0AD
tel 0171-499 9080 *fax* 0171-495 1679
Editor Angus MacKinnon
Monthly £2.70

Style, fashion and general interest magazine for men. Illustrations: b&w and colour photos, line drawings, cartoons. Payment: by arrangement. Founded 1988.

Gramophone

135 Greenford Road, Harrow, Middlesex HA1 3YD
tel 0181-422 4562 *fax* 0181-869 8403
Editor James Jolly
Monthly £3.95

Features on classical recording artists and hi-fi, with main focus on record reviews. Outside contributions are rarely used.

Granta

2-3 Hanover Yard, Noel Road, London N1 8BE
tel 0171-704 9776 *fax* 0171-704 0474
Editor Ian Jack
Quarterly £7.99 (£24.95 p.a.)

Original fiction, non-fiction and journalism. Length: determined by content. Illustrations: photos. Payment: by arrangement. Founded 1889; new series 1979.

Greetings Magazine

Lema Publishing, Unit No. 1, Queen Mary's Avenue, Watford, Herts. WD1 7JR
tel (01923) 250909 *fax* (01923) 250995
Publisher Malcolm Naish, *Editor* Nicholas Eyriey
10 p.a. £30.00 p.a. (other rates on application)

Official journal of the Greeting Card Association. Articles, features and news related to the greetings card and giftwrap industry. Mainly written in-house; some material taken from outside. Length: varies. Illustrations: line, colour and b&w photos. Payment: by arrangement. Founded 1992.

The Grocer

William Reed Publishing Ltd, Broadfield Park, Crawley, West Sussex RH11 9RT
tel (01293) 613400 *fax* (01293) 610333
e-mail editorial@the-grocer.co.uk
Editor C. Beddall
Weekly 60p

Trade journal: articles or news or illustrations of general interest to the grocery and provision trades. Payment: by arrangement. Founded 1861.

The Grower

Nexus Media Ltd, Nexus House, Azalea Drive, Swanley, Kent BR8 8HY
tel (01322) 660070 *fax* (01322) 667633
Editor Peter Rogers
Weekly £1.30

News and practical articles on commercial horticulture, covering all sectors including fruit, vegetable, salad crop and ornamentals. Founded 1923.

Guiding

17-19 Buckingham Palace Road, London SW1W 0PT
tel 0171-834 6242 *fax* 0171-828 8317
Editor Nora Warner
Monthly £1.25

Official magazine of The Guide Association. Articles of interest to women of all ages, with special emphasis on youth work and the Guide Movement. Articles on simple crafts, games and the

outdoors also welcome. Length: 500-1200 words. Illustrations: line, half-tone, colour, cartoons. Payment: £70 per 1000 words; £100 full colour page, £60 b&w (negotiable).

Hairflair
Hair and Beauty Ltd, 2 Coral Row, Plantation Wharf, London SW11 3UF
tel 0171-738 9911 *fax* 0171-738 9922
Editor Rebecca Barnes
Monthly £1.95

Hair, beauty, fashion – and related features – for the 16-35 age group. Preliminary letter essential. Length: 800-1000 words. Illustrations: colour and b&w photos, occasional line drawings. Payment: £100-£120 per 1000 words. Founded 1985.

Hampshire – The County Magazine
74 Bedford Place, Southampton SO15 2DF
tel (01703) 223591/333457
Monthly £1.60

Factual articles concerning all aspects of Hampshire and Hampshire life, past and present. Length: 400-1000 words. Payment: by arrangement. Illustrations: photos and line drawings.

Harpers & Queen
National Magazine House, 72 Broadwick Street, London W1V 2BP
tel 0171-439 5000 *fax* 0171-439 5506
Editor Fiona Macpherson
Monthly £2.70

Features, fashion, beauty, art, theatre, films, travel, interior decoration – all commissioned. Illustrations: line, wash, full colour and 2- and 3-colour, and photos. Founded 1929.

Health Club Management
Leisure Media Company Ltd, Portmill House, Portmill Lane, Hitchin, Herts. SG5 1DJ
tel (01462) 431385 *fax* (01462) 433909
e-mail catherine@leisuremedia.com
web site www.leisuremedia.co.uk
Editor Catherine Larner
Monthly £48 p.a. with *Leisure Management* magazine

Official publication of the Fitness Industry Association. Articles on the operation of health clubs and sports centres, items on consumer issues and lifestyle trends as they affect club management are all welcomed. Length: up to 1500 words. Illustrations: colour and b&w photos. Payment: by arrangement. Founded 1995.

Health & Efficiency International
Bow House Business Centre, 153-159 Bow Road, London E3 2ST
Editor Helen Ludbrook
Monthly £2.25

Monthly: articles on naturist travel, clubs and beaches. Also well-researched articles on health, piercing and tattooing. Quarterly: articles on the above plus humour and naked lifestyle and relationships. Length: 750-1500 words. Illustrations: line, half-tone, colour transparencies, colour prints, cartoons. Payment: by negotiation. Founded 1900.

Health & Fitness
Nexus Media, Nexus House, Azalea Drive, Swanley, Kent BR8 8HY
tel (01322) 660070 *fax* (01322) 615636
Editor Sharon Walker
Monthly £2.20

Articles on all aspects of health and fitness. Illustrations: line, half-tone, colour. Payment: by arrangement. Founded 1984.

Healthy Eating
Spendlove Centre, Charlbury, Oxfordshire OX7 3PQ
tel (01608) 811266 *fax* (01608) 811380
Editor Jane Last
Bi-monthly £2.50

Articles on health and nutrition, how food affects the body, celebrity food and health stories. Length: 1000-1200 words. Illustrations: colour food photography and illustrations. Payment: £150-£250 per article; £30-£50 for illustrations; £25-£80 for transparencies. Founded 1990.

Helicon Poetry Magazine
Cherrybite Publications, Linden Cottage, 45 Burton Road, Little Neston, South Wirral L64 4AE
tel 0151-353 0967
Editor Shelagh Nugent
Quarterly £2.50 (£9.00 p.a.)

Poems in any style or length. Illustrations: b&w to illustrate poems. Payment: £2 per poem plus free copy. Founded 1995.

Hello!
Wellington House, 69-71 Upper Ground, London SE1 9PQ
tel 0171-667 8721 *fax* 0171 667 8716
Editor Maggie Koumi
Weekly £1.35

News-based features – showbusiness, celebrity, royalty; exclusive interviews. Payment: by arrangement. Illustrated. Founded 1988.

Here's Health

EMAP Élan, 20 Orange Street, London WC2H 7ED
tel 0171-957 8383 *fax* 0171-957 8857
Editor Sheena Miller
Monthly £2.20

Articles on nutrition, alternative medicine, environment and health, natural treatment success stories. Preliminary letter and clippings essential. Length: 750-1800 words. Payment: on publication. Illustrated, including cartoons.

Heritage

Bulldog Magazines Ltd, 4 The Courtyard, Denmark Street, Wokingham, Berks. RG40 2AZ
tel (01189) 771677 *fax* (01189) 772903
Editor Siân Ellis
Bi-monthly £2.95

Features on British topics only: towns and villages to visit, tours/off the beaten track, customs, craftsmen, people, all historic/heritage subjects. Length: 1200 words. Illustrations: colour transparencies. Payment: £100 per 1000 words; illustrations by negotiation. Founded 1984.

Hertfordshire Countryside

Beaumonde Publications Ltd, 4 Mill Bridge, Hertford, Herts. SG14 1PY
tel (01992) 553571 *fax* (01992) 587713
Editor Sandra Small
Monthly £1.25

Articles of county interest. Length: 1000 words. Payment: £25 per 1000 words. Illustrations: line, half-tone, cartoons. Founded 1946.

Hi-Fi News & Record Review

Link House, Dingwall Avenue, Croydon CR9 2TA
tel 0181-686 2599 *fax* 0181-781 6046
e-mail 101574.223@compuserve.com
Editor Steve Harris
Monthly £2.75

Articles on all aspects of high quality sound recording and reproduction; also extensive record review section and supporting musical feature articles. Audio matter is essentially technical, but should be presented in a manner suitable for music lovers interested in the nature of sound. Length: 2000-3000 words. Illustrations: line, half-tone. Payment: by arrangement. Founded 1956.

History

Editorial office History Department, University of Edinburgh, Edinburgh EH8 9JY
tel 0131-650 3785
Published by Blackwell (Oxford) for the Historical Association, 59a Kennington Park Road, London SE11 4JH
tel 0171-735 3901
Editor H.T. Dickinson BA, DipEd, MA, PhD, DLitt
Quarterly (£16.00 p.a. members; £38.00 p.a. non-members)

Historical articles and reviews by experts. Length: usually up to 8000 words. Illustrations: only exceptionally. Payment: none. Founded 1916.

History Today

20 Old Compton Street, London W1V 5PE
tel 0171-439 8315
Editor Gordon Marsden
Monthly £3.15

History in the widest sense – political, economic, social, biography, relating past to present; world history as well as British. Length: articles 3500 words; shorter news/views pieces 600-1200 words. Illustrations: from prints and original photos. Please do not send original material until publication is agreed. Payment: by arrangement. Founded 1951.

Home and Country

104 New King's Road, London SW6 4LY
tel 0171-731 5777 *fax* 0171-736 4061
Editor Amber Tokeley
Monthly £1.40

Official Journal of the National Federation of Women's Institutes for England and Wales. Publishes material related to the Federation's and members' activities; also considers articles of general interest to women, particularly country women, e.g. craft, environment, humour, health, rural life stories, of 800-1200 words. Illustrations: colour and b&w photos and drawings, cartoons. Payment: by arrangement. Founded 1919.

Home and Family

The Mothers' Union, The Mary Sumner House, 24 Tufton Street, London SW1P 3RB
tel 0171-222 5533 *fax* 0171-222 1591
Editor Margaret Duggan
Quarterly £1.10

Short articles related to Christian family life. Payment: approx. £60 per 1000 words. Illustrations: colour photos. Founded 1954.

Home Words

Chansitor Publications Ltd, St Mary's Works,
St Mary's Plain, Norwich, Norfolk NR3 3BH
tel (01603) 615995 *fax* (01603) 624483
Publisher G.A. Knights
Monthly

Illustrated C of E magazine insert.
Articles of popular Christian interest
with an Anglican slant (400-800 words)
with relevant photos; also cartoons.
Payment: by arrangement. Founded
1870.

HomeFlair Magazine

Hamerville Magazines Ltd, Regal House,
Regal Way, Watford, Herts. WD2 4YJ
tel (01923) 237799 *fax* (01923) 246901
Editor Nicola Shannon
Monthly £1.70

Homes' conversions, inspirational looks,
what's new in products and design.
Approach in writing, with samples of
previously published work. Length: up to
1500 words. Payment: £120 per 1000
words. Illustrated. Founded 1990.

Homes and Gardens

IPC Magazines Ltd, King's Reach Tower,
Stamford Street, London SE1 9LS
tel 0171-261 5000 *fax* 0171-261 6247
Editor Julia Watson
Monthly £2.30

Articles on home interest or design.
Length: articles, 900-1000 words.
Illustrations: all types. Payment: generous, but exceptional work required;
varies. Founded 1919.

Homes & Ideas

IPC Magazines Ltd, King's Reach Tower,
Stamford Street, London SE1 9LS
tel 0171-261 7325 *fax* 0171-261 7495
Editor Debbie Djordjevic´
Monthly £1.60

Features on any aspect of style for the
home. Send cuttings to the editor.
Length: by arrangement. Illustrations:
colour photos and drawings. Payment:
NUJ rates plus; illustrations by arrangement. Founded 1993.

Homestyle

RAP Publishing, Vigilant House,
120 Wilton Road, London SW1V 1JZ
tel 0171-233 9989 *fax* 0171-873 8557
Editor Barbara Raine-Allen
Monthly £1.40

Ideas and practical features on home and
garden improvements. Merchandise
reviews. Length: 2 or 4-page spreads.
Illustrations: colour transparencies.
Payment: by negotiation. Founded 1992.

Horse and Hound

IPC Magazines Ltd, King's Reach Tower,
Stamford Street, London SE1 9LS
tel 0171-261 5306 *fax* 0171-261 5429
Editor Arnold Garvey
Weekly £1.45

Special articles, news items, photos, on
all matters appertaining to horses, hunting; cartoons. Payment: by negotiation.

Horse & Pony

EMAP Pursuit Publishing Ltd, Bretton Court,
Bretton, Peterborough PE3 8DZ
tel (01733) 264666 *fax* (01733) 465939
Editor Andrea Oakes
Fortnightly £1.20

All material relevant to young people
with equestrian interests. Payment: on
value to publication rather than length.
Illustrations: colour, with a strong story
line, cartoons. Founded 1970.

Horse and Rider

Haslemere House, Lower Street, Haslemere,
Surrey GU27 2PE
tel (01428) 651551 *fax* (01428) 653888
e-mail h-and-r@remus.com
web site www.equestrian.co.uk
Managing Editor Kate Austin, *Editor* Alison
Bridge
Monthly £2.25

Sophisticated magazine covering all
forms of equestrian activity at home and
abroad. Good writing and technical accuracy essential. Length: 1500-2000 words.
Illustrations: photos and drawings, the
latter usually commissioned. Payment:
by arrangement. Founded 1959.

Horticulture Week

Haymarket Magazines Ltd, 174 Hammersmith
Road, London W6 7JP
tel 0171-413 4595
Editor Vicky Browning
Weekly £1.50 (£63.50 p.a.)

News, technical and business journal for
the nursery and garden centre trade,
landscape industry and public parks and
sports ground staff. Outside contributions considered and, if accepted, paid
for. No fiction. Length: 500-1500 words.
Illustrations: line, half-tone, colour.
Payment: by arrangement.

Hortus

Bryan's Ground, Stapleton, Nr Presteigne,
Herefordshire LD8 2LP
tel (01544) 260001 *fax* (01544) 260015
e-mail hortus@bg.kczltd.co.uk
web site http://www.kcz.co.uk/business/hortus
Editor David Wheeler
Quarterly £30.00 p.a. (UK)

Articles on decorative horticulture: plants,
gardens, history, design, literature, people;
book reviews. Length: 1500-5000 words,
longer by arrangement. Illustrations: line,
half-tone and wood-engravings. Payment:
by arrangement. Founded 1987.

Hospital Doctor

Reed Healthcare Publishing, Quadrant House,
The Quadrant, Sutton, Surrey SM2 5AS
tel 0181-652 8745 *fax* 0181-652 8701
Editor Phil Johnson
Weekly Free to 45,000 doctors. (£70.00 p.a.)

Commissioned features of interest to all
grades and specialities of hospital doctors; demand for news tip-offs. Length:
features 800-1000 words. Illustrations:
colour photos, transparencies, cartoons
and commissioned artwork. Payment:
£120 per 1000 words features, £10 per
100 words news. Founded c.1980.

Hospitality

Pavillon (Publishing) Ltd, Rose Cottage,
Lidwells Lane, Goudhurst, Cranbrook,
Kent TN17 1EJ
tel (01580) 211580 *fax* (01580) 211118
Editor Janet Simpson
10 p.a. £2.60 (£26.00 p.a. UK, £41.00 overseas)

Official magazine of the Hotel Catering &
Institutional Management Association.
Articles for a management readership on
food, accommodation services and related topics in hotels, restaurants, tourism,
educational establishments, the health
service, industrial situations, educational
and other institutions. Illustrations: photos, line, cartoons. Payment: by arrangement. Founded 1980.

Hot Air

The Boathouse, Crabtree Lane, London SW6 6LU
tel 0171-470 2400 *fax* 0171-385 7591
Editor Alex Finer
Quarterly Free

Inflight magazine for Virgin Atlantic
Airways. Sport, trends/lifestyle, celebrities. Length: 1500-3000 words. Illustrations: high quality colour transparencies.
Payment: by negotiation. Founded 1984.

Hot Press

Niall Stokes, 13 Trinity Street, Dublin 2,
Republic of Ireland
tel (01) 6795077/67955091 *fax* (01) 6795097
Fortnightly £1.25

High-quality, investigative stories, or
punchily written offbeat pieces, of interest to 16-39-year-olds, including politics,
music, sport, sex, religion – whatever's
happening on the street. Length: varies.
Illustrations: b&w photos, colour sometimes used. Payment: by negotiation.
Founded 1977.

Hotel and Catering Review

Jemma Publications Ltd, Marino House,
52 Glasthule Road, Sandycove, Co. Dublin,
Republic of Ireland
tel (01) 2800000 *fax* (01) 2801818
e-mail fcorr@homenet.ie
Editor Frank Corr
Monthly £22.00 p.a.

Short news and trade news pieces.
Length: approx. 200 words. Features.
Payment: £80 per 1000 words.
Illustrations: half-tone, cartoons.

House & Garden

Vogue House, Hanover Square, London W1R 0AD
tel 0171-499 9080 *fax* 0171-629 2907
Editor Susan Crewe
Monthly £2.60

Articles (always commissioned), on subjects relating to domestic architecture,
interior decorating, furnishing, gardening,
household equipment, food and wine.

House Beautiful

National Magazine House, 72 Broadwick Street,
London W1V 2BP
tel 0171-439 5500 *fax* 0171-439 5595
Editor Caroline Atkins
Monthly £1.70

Specialist 'home' features for the homes
of today. Preliminary study of magazine
advisable. Payment: according to merit.
Illustrated. Founded 1989.

HouseBuilder

82 New Cavendish Street, London W1M 8AD
tel 0171-580 5588 *fax* 0171-323 0890
Editor Ben Roskrow
11 p.a. £6.00

Official Journal of the House-Builders
Federation and National House-Building
Council. Technical articles on design,
construction and equipment of dwellings,
estate planning and development, and

technical aspects of house-building, aimed at those engaged in house and flat construction and the development of housing estates. Preliminary letter advisable. Length: articles from 500 words, preferably with illustrations. Payment: by arrangement. Illustrations: photos, plans, construction details, cartoons.

HQ: The Haiku Quarterly Poetry Magazine

39 Exmouth Street, Kingshill, Swindon, Wilts. SN1 3PU
tel (01793) 523927
Editor Kevin Bailey
Quarterly £2.60 (£9.00 p.a. UK, £12.00 p.a. non-UK)

A range of experimental and traditional poetry from all over the world. About one third is devoted to haiku, haikuesque, and imagistic poetry. Review section and articles. Payment: small. Commissioned illustrations. Founded 1990.

HU (The Honest Ulsterman)

49 Main Street, Greyabbey, Co. Down BT22 2NF
Editor Tom Clyde
3 p.a. £2.50

Poetry, short stories, reviews, critical articles, poetry pamphlets. Payment: by arrangement. Founded 1968.

i-D Magazine

Universal House, 251-255 Tottenham Court Road, London W1P 0AB
tel 0171-813 6170 *fax* 0171-813 6179£2.20
Editor Avril Mair
Monthly

Youth and general interest magazine: i-Deas, fashion, clubs, music, people. Will consider unsolicited material. Illustrations: colour and b&w photos. Payment: £100 per 1000 words; photos £50 per page. Founded 1980.

Ideal Home

IPC Magazines Ltd, King's Reach Tower, Stamford Street, London SE1 9LS
tel 0171-261 5000
Editor Sally O'Sullivan
Monthly £1.80

Lifestyle magazine, articles usually commissioned. Contributors advised to study editorial content before submitting material. Payment: according to material. Illustrations: usually commissioned. Founded 1920.

The Illustrated London News

20 Upper Ground, London SE1 9PF
tel 0171-805 5555 *fax* 0171-805 5911
Editor Alison Booth
2-3 p.a. £2.50

Two special issues published annually: Summer and Christmas, plus occasional additional issues to tie in with major events. Focuses on London and the UK: culture, the arts, people, dining, fashion, entertainment. All material commissioned but ideas welcome. Founded 1842.

IMAGE

22 Crofton Road, Dún Laoghaire, Co. Dublin, Republic of Ireland
tel (01) 2808415 *fax* (01) 2808300
Editor Jane McDonnell
Monthly £2.20

Short stories of a high literary standard and of interest to women. Length: up to 3000 words. Interviews with actors, writers, etc; human interest stories. Payment: by arrangement. Founded 1974.

In Britain

Premier Magazines, Haymarket House, 1 Oxendon Street, London SW1Y 4EE
tel 0171-925 2544 *fax* 0171-976 1088
Editor Andrea Spain
Monthly £2.75 (£23.95 p.a. UK/Europe; $39.95 p.a. US)

Upmarket features magazine about places and people in Britain. Limited freelance material is accepted. Illustrated. Payment: by arrangement. Founded 1930.

In Dublin

6-7 Camden Place, Dublin 2, Republic of Ireland
tel (01) 4784322 *fax* (01) 4781055
Editor Declan Buche
Fortnightly £1.50

Dublin-related news features, oddball items, humour and interviews. Length: 500-1000 words. Payment: £80 per 1000 words. Illustrated. Founded 1976.

The Independent Magazine – see The Independent in National newspapers UK and Ireland, page 3

Index on Censorship

Lancaster House, 33 Islington High Street, London N1 9LH
tel 0171-278 2313 *fax* 0171-278 1878
e-mail indexoncenso@gn.apc.org
Editor Ursula Owen
Bi-monthly £7.99 (£36.00 p.a.)

Articles up to 3000 words dealing with all aspects of free speech and political censorship. Illustrations: b&w, cartoons. Payment: £60 per 1000 words. Founded 1972.

The Indexer
Society of Indexers, Mermaid House,
1 Mermaid Court, London SE1 1HR
tel 0171-403 4947
e-mail shuter@cix.compulink.co.uk
Editor Janet Shuter
2 p.a. (£40.00 p.a.) Free to members

Journal of the Society of Indexers, American Society of Indexers, Australian Society of Indexers, and Indexing & Abstracting Society of Canada. Articles of interest to professional indexers and providers and users of information in any form. Payment: none. Founded 1958.

Infant Projects
Scholastic Publications Ltd, Villiers House, Clarendon Avenue, Leamington Spa, Warwickshire CV32 5PR
tel (01926) 887799 *fax* (01926) 337322
Editor Jane Morgan
Bi-monthly £2.50

Practical articles suggesting project activities for teachers of children aged 4-8; material mostly commissioned. Length: 500-1000 words. Illustrations: b&w photos and line illustrations, colour posters. Payment: by arrangement. Founded 1978.

Information and Software Technology
UK contact Prof Martin Shepperd, Dept of Applied Computing & Electronics, Bournemouth University, Poole House, Talbot Campus, Fern Barrow, Poole, Dorset BH12 5BB
tel (01202) 595078 *fax* (01202) 595314
Monthly US$657 p.a.

Papers on software design and development and the application of information processing in large organisations, especially multinationals. Length: approx. 5000 words, or by negotiation. Illustrations: line, half-tone. Founded 1959.

The Inquirer
1-6 Essex Street, London WC2R 2HY
tel 0171-240 2384
Editor Keith Gilley
Fortnightly 40p

Journal of news and comment for Unitarians and religious liberals. Articles, liberal and progressive in tone, of general religious, social, cultural and international interest. Length: up to 750 words. Payment: none. Founded 1842.

Inside Edge
9 Whitehall Park, London N19 3TS
tel 0171-561 1606 *fax* 0171-501 1607
Editor Jim Melly
Monthly £2.20

Cricket gossip and unusual stories; satirical humour and serious issues. Read the magazine for style. Length: (features) 1000 words. Illustrations: Unusual cricket photos. Payment: NUJ rates. Founded 1990.

Inspirations
GE Publishing Ltd, 133 Long Acre, London WC2E 9AD
tel 0171-836 0519 *fax* 0171-836 0280
Editor Deborah Barker
Monthly £2.20

Practical features on all aspects of home interest – home design, cookery, crafts, gadgets. Length: 800-2000 words. Payment: by arrangement. Illustrated. Founded 1993.

Insurance Age
EMAP Business Communications,
33-39 Bowling Green Lane, London EC1R 0DA
tel 0171-505 8181 *fax* 0171-505 8187
e-mail johnj@finance.emap.co.uk
web site http://www.emap.com/insurance-age
Publisher and Editor John Jackson
Monthly

News and features on general insurance, personal, commercial, private medical, health and Lloyd's of London. Length: 650 words. Illustrations: transparencies, colour and b&w photos. Payment: by negotiation. Founded 1979.

Insurance Brokers' Monthly
7 Stourbridge Road, Lye, Stourbridge, West Midlands DY9 7DG
tel (01384) 895228 *fax* (01384) 893666
e-mail sadler@dircon.co.uk
web site www.sadler.co.uk/brokers-monthly
Editor Brian Susman
Monthly £3.00

Articles of technical and non-technical interest to insurance brokers and others engaged in the insurance industry. Occasional articles of general interest to the City, on finance, etc. Length: 1000-1500 words. Payment: from £30 per 1000 words on last day of month following publication. Authoritative material written under true name and qualification receives highest payment. Illustrations: line and half-tone, 100-120 screen. Founded 1950.

InterMedia

International Institute of Communications,
Tavistock House South, Tavistock Square,
London WC1H 9LF
tel 0171-388 0671 *fax* 0171-380 0623
Editor Annelise Berendt
Bi-monthly £70.00 p.a.

International journal concerned with
policies, events, trends and research in
the field of communications, broadcasting, telecommunications and associated
issues, particularly cultural and social.
Preliminary letter essential. Illustrations:
b&w line. Payment: by arrangement.
Founded 1970.

International Affairs

Royal Institute of International Affairs, Chatham
House, 10 St James's Square, London SW1Y 4LE
tel 0171-957 5700 *fax* 0171-957 5710
web site http://www.riia.org
Quarterly £16.00 (£40.00 p.a., institutions £59.00
p.a.)

Serious long-term articles on international affairs; more than 100 books reviewed
each quarter. Preliminary letter advisable. Article length: average 7000 words.
Illustrations: none. Payment: by arrangement. Founded 1922.

International Construction

Ground Floor, Montrose House,
412-6 Eastern Avenue, Gants Hill, Ilford,
Essex IG2 6NQ
tel 0181-518 2525 *fax* 0181-518 1020
Editor A.J. Peterson
Monthly Controlled circulation

Articles dealing with new techniques of
construction, applications of construction equipment and use of construction
materials in any part of the world.
Length: maximum 1500 words plus illustrations. Illustrations: line, half-tone,
colour; some 2-colour line illustrations
used, cartoons. Payment: from £150 per
1000 words, plus illustrations.

Internet

EMAP Business Communication, Greater London
House, Hampstead Road, London NW1 7QZ
tel 0171-388 2430 *fax* 0171-383 5578
web site http://www.emap.com/internet
Editor Gail Robinson
Monthly £2.99

Magazine for consumer users, people
who use the net at work and business
users. Articles, news and features and
guide to web sites on the Internet.

Length: 800-1000 words. Illustrations:
colour photos, cartoons. Payment: £150
per 1000 words. Founded 1994.

Interzone

217 Preston Drove, Brighton, East Sussex BN1 6FL
tel (01273) 504710
Editor David Pringle
Monthly £3.00 (£32.00 p.a.)

Science fiction and fantasy short stories,
articles, interviews and reviews. Please
read magazine before submitting. Length:
2000-6000 words. Illustrations: line, half-
tone, colour. Payment: by arrangement.
Founded 1982.

Investors Chronicle

Greystoke Place, Fetter Lane, London EC4A 1ND
tel 0171-405 6969 *fax* 0171-405 5276
Editor Ceri Jones
Weekly £2.20

Journal covering investment and personal finance. Occasional outside contributions for surveys are accepted. Payment:
by negotiation.

IPA Magazine

(formerly Involvement)
42 Colebrooke Row, London N1 8AF
tel 0171-354 8040
Editor Jonathan Hewett
Quarterly £35.00 p.a. (£50.00 p.a. overseas)

Journal of the Involvement & Participation
Association. Articles, mostly commissioned, on participation and involvement
in industry, employee shareholding, joint
consultation, the sharing of information,
labour-management relations, workers
participation, and kindred industrial subjects from the operational angle, with
emphasis on the practice of particular
enterprises, usually written by a member
of the team involved, whether manager or
workers, and with a strong factual background. Length: up to 2500 words.
Payment: by negotiation. Founded 1884.

Ireland of the Welcomes

Irish Tourist Board, Baggot Street Bridge,
Dublin 2, Republic of Ireland
tel (01) 6024000 *fax* (01) 6024335
e-mail iow@failte.travel.ie
Editor Letitia Pollard
Bi-monthly £2.00

Irish items with cultural, sporting or
topographical background designed to
arouse interest in Irish holidays. Mostly
commissioned – preliminary letter pre-

ferred. Length: 1200-1800 words. Payment: by arrangement. Illustrations: scenic and topical, cartoons.

Ireland's Eye

Dominick Street, Mullingar, Co. Westmeath, Republic of Ireland
tel (044) 48868
Monthly 80p

Articles, features, short stories with an Irish flavour; cartoons. Length: max. 1200 words. Payment: £10-£15. Founded 1979.

Ireland's Own

North Main Street, Wexford
tel (053) 22155 *fax* (053) 23801
Editors Gerry Breen and Margaret Galvin
Weekly 50p

Short stories: non-experimental, traditional with an Irish orientation (2000-2500 words); articles of interest to Irish readers at home and abroad (750-1000 words); general and literary articles (750-1000 words). Monthly special bumper editions, each devoted to a particular seasonal topic. Jokes and funny stories always welcome; suggestions for new features considered. Payment: varies according to quality and length. Illustrations: photos, cartoons. Founded 1902.

Irish Farmers Journal

Irish Farm Centre, Bluebell, Dublin 12, Republic of Ireland
tel (01) 4501166 *fax* (01) 4520876
Editor Matthew Dempsey
Weekly £1.00

Readable, technical articles on any aspect of farming. Length: 700-1000 words. Payment: £100-£150 per article. Illustrated. Founded 1948.

Irish Journal of Medical Science

Royal Academy of Medicine, 6 Kildare Street, Dublin 2, Republic of Ireland
tel (01) 6767650 *fax* (01) 6611684
e-mail secretary@rami.iol.ie
web site http://www.iol.ie/~rami/
Monthly £15.00 (EU £70.00 post free; other rates on application)

Official Organ of the Royal Academy of Medicine in Ireland. Original contributions in medicine, surgery, midwifery, public health, etc; reviews of professional books, reports of medical societies, etc. Illustrations: line, half-tone, colour.1st series 1832, 6th series January 1926, Volume 165, 1997.

Irish Medical Times

15 Harcourt Street, Dublin 2, Republic of Ireland
tel (01) 4757461 *fax* (01) 4757468
Editor Dr John O'Connell
Weekly £2.50 (£104.00 p.a.)

Medical articles, also humorous articles with medical slant. Length: 850-1000 words. Payment: £60 per 1000 words. Illustrations: line, half-tone, colour, cartoons.

Irish Printer

Jemma Publications Ltd, 52 Glasthule Road, Sandycove, Co. Dublin, Republic of Ireland
tel (01) 2800000 *fax* (01) 2801818
e-mail fcorr@homenet.ie
Editor Frank Corr
Monthly £22.00 p.a.

Technical articles and news of interest to the printing industry. Length: 800-1000 words. Illustrations: colour and b&w photos. Payment: £80 per 1000 words; photos £30. Founded 1974.

IT (Irish Tatler)

126 Lower Baggot Street, Dublin 2, Republic of Ireland
tel (01) 6623158 *fax* (01) 6619757
Editor Morag Prunty
Monthly £1.95

General interest women's magazine: beauty, interiors, fashion, cookery, current affairs, fiction, reportage and celebrity interviews. Length: 2000-4000 words. Payment: by arrangement.

Jane's Defence Weekly

Sentinel House, 163 Brighton Road, Coulsdon, Surrey CR5 2NH
tel 0181-700 3700 *fax* 0181-763 1007
Editor Carol Reed
Weekly £140.00 p.a.

International defence news; military equipment; budget analysis, industry, military technology, business, political, defence market intelligence. Payment: minimum £150 per 1000 words used. Illustrations: line, half-tone, colour. Founded 1984.

Jazz Journal International

Jazz Journal Ltd, 1-5 Clerkenwell Road, London EC1M 5PA
tel 0171-608 1348/1362 *fax* 0171-608 1292
Publisher and Editor-in-Chief Eddie Cook
Monthly £3.00

Articles on jazz, record reviews. Prospective contributors should tele-

phone or write before submitting material. Payment: by arrangement.
Illustrations: photos. Founded 1948.

Jewish Chronicle

25 Furnival Street, London EC4A 1JT
tel 0171-405 9252
Editor Edward J. Temko
Weekly 50p

Authentic and exclusive news stories
and articles of Jewish interest from 500-
1500 words are considered. There is a
lively arts and leisure section, as well as
regular travel pages. Payment: by
arrangement. Illustrations: of Jewish
interest, either topical or feature.
Founded 1841.

The Jewish Quarterly

PO Box 2078, London W1A 1JR
tel/fax 0181-361 6372 (editorial)
Editor Elena Lappin
Quarterly £3.95 (£15.00 p.a., £17.50 p.a. Europe,
£25.00 p.a. overseas)

Articles of Jewish interest, literature, history, music, politics, poetry, book
reviews, fiction. Illustrations: half-tone.
Founded 1953.

Jewish Telegraph

Telegraph House, 11 Park Hill, Bury Old Road,
Prestwich, Manchester M25 0HH
tel 0161-740 9321 *fax* 0161-740 9325
1 Shaftesbury Avenue, Leeds LS8 1DR
tel (0113) 295 6000 *fax* (0113) 295 6006
Harold House, Dunbabin Road,
Liverpool L15 6XL
tel 0151-475 6666/2222 *fax* 0151-475 2222
43 Queen Square, Glasgow G41 2BD
tel 0141-423 9200/1/2 *fax* 0141-423 9200
Editor Paul Harris
Weekly Man. 30p, Leeds 20p, Liverpool 25p,
Glasgow 40p

Non-fiction articles of Jewish interest,
especially humour. Exclusive Jewish
news stories and pictures, international,
national and local. Length: 1000-1500
words. Payment: by arrangement.
Illustrations: line, half-tone, cartoons.
Founded 1950.

The Journal

CII Journal, 20 Aldermanbury, London EC2V 7HY
tel 0171-417 4435 *fax* 0171-726 0131
Features Editor Liz Loxton
6 p.a. £3.00 Free to members

Journal of the Chartered Insurance
Institute. Technical articles on all aspects
of insurance. Material mostly commis-

sioned. Length: 800-2400 words. Payment:
£140 per 1000 words. Founded 1912.

Journal of Alternative and Complementary Medicine

9 Rickett Street, London SW6 1RU
tel 0171-385 0012 *fax* 0171-385 4566
Editor Graeme Miller
Monthly £2.95 (£33.50 p.a.)

Feature articles (length: up to 2000
words) and news stories (length: up to
250 words). Unsolicited material welcome but not eligible for payment unless
commissioned. Illustrations: line, half-
tone, colour. Payment: by negotiation.
Founded 1983.

Journalist

NUJ, Acorn House, 314 Gray's Inn Road,
London WC1X 8DP
tel 0171-278 7916 *fax* 0171-837 8143
e-mail the.journalist @mcr1.poptel.org.uk
Editor Tim Gopsill
Bi-monthly £2.50 (£12.00 p.a., £20.00 p.a.
overseas)

Magazine of the National Union of
Journalists (mailed to all members).
Accepts material relating to journalism,
trade unionism and general conditions in
the media – newspapers, magazines,
books, broadcasting and electronic.
Mainly contributed by members, and
outside written contributions not paid.

Junior Education

Scholastic Publications Ltd, Villiers House,
Clarendon Avenue, Leamington Spa,
Warks. CV32 5PR
tel (01926) 887799 *fax* (01926) 883331
Editor Mrs Terry Saunders
Monthly £2.50

For teachers, educationalists and students concerned with children aged 7-12.
Articles by specialists on practical teaching ideas and methods, plus in-depth
coverage and debate on news issues in
education. Length: 800-1200 words.
Payment: by arrangement. Illustrated
with b&w photos and line drawings;
includes colour poster. Founded 1977.

Junior Focus

Scholastic Publications Ltd, Villiers House,
Clarendon Avenue, Leamington Spa,
Warks. CV32 5PR
tel (01926) 887799 *fax* (01926) 883331
Editor Kate Element
Monthly £2.50

Aimed at teachers of 7-12 year olds, each issue is based on a theme, closely linked with the National Curriculum. Includes A1 and A3 full-colour posters, 16 pages of photocopiable material and 12 pages of project notes. All material commissioned. Length: 1-4 pages. Illustrations: commissioned b&w line; welcomes samples of work from new illustrators. Payment: £100 per double-page spread; varies for illustrations. Founded 1982.

Just Seventeen
EMAP Élan, 20 Orange Street, London WC2H 7ED
tel 0171-957 8383 *fax* 0171-930 5728
Editor Sam Baker
Monthly £1.50

Articles of interest to girls aged between 12 and 18: fashion, beauty, pop, and various features; real life stories up to 1500 words; quizzes. Payment: £150 per 1000 words. Illustrations: line, half-tone, colour, cartoons. Founded 1983.

Justice of the Peace and Local Government Law
Little London, Chichester, West Sussex PO19 1PG
tel (01243) 775552 *fax* (01243) 779174
Editors F.W. Davies and Mark Watson-Gandy
Weekly £130.60 p.a.

Professional journal. Articles on magisterial and local government law and associated subjects including family law, criminology, medico-legal matters, penology, police, probation (length preferred, under 1400 words). Preliminary letter welcomed although not essential. Payment: articles minimum £12.50 per column except when otherwise commissioned. Founded 1837.

Kerrang!
EMAP Metro Ltd, Mappin House,
4 Winsley Street, London W1N 7AR
tel 0171-436 1515 *fax* 0171-312 8910
Editor Phil Alexander
Weekly £1.50

News, views and reviews; the noise of the new generation. All material commissioned. Illustrations: colour. Payment: by arrangement. Founded 1981.

Keyboard Review
Future Publishing Ltd, Beauford Court,
Monmouth Street, Bath BA1 2BW
tel (01225) 442244
e-mail kr@musicians-net.co.uk
Editor Cliff Douse
Monthly £2.20

Interviews with keyboard/piano players; reviews of new keyboard-related equipment. Length: 900-2500 words. Illustrations: colour transparencies and photos. Payment: £70 per 1000 words. Founded 1985.

Kids Alive! (The Young Soldier)
101 Queen Victoria Street, London EC4P 4EP
tel 0171-236 5222 ext 2345 *fax* 0171-236 3491
e-mail wcry@globalnet.co.uk
Editor Ken Nesbitt
Weekly 20p (£26.00 p.a.)

The Salvation Army's children's weekly. Stories, pictures, cartoon strips, puzzles etc, Christian-based with emphasis on education re addictive substances. Payment: by arrangement. Illustrations: half-tone, line and 3-colour line, cartoons. Founded 1881.

Krino
PO Box 65, Dún Laoghaire, Co. Dublin,
Republic of Ireland
Editor Gerald Dawe, *Associate Editors* Aodan MacPoilin, Eve Patten, Jonathan Williams
2 p.a. £5.00

Poetry; fiction; work-in-progress; critical prose mostly on commissioned basis. Illustrations: line, half-tone. Payment: none, but complimentary copies of the magazine. Founded 1986.

The Lady
39-40 Bedford Street, Strand, London WC2E 9ER
tel 0171-379 4717 *fax* 0171-497 2137
Editor Arline Usden
Weekly 65p

British and foreign travel, countryside, human-interest, celebrity interviews, animals, cookery, art and antiques, historic-interest and commemorative articles (preliminary letter advisable for articles dealing with anniversaries). Length: 900-1200 words; Viewpoint: 600 words. Annual Short Story Competition with prize of £1000 plus. Winning entries printed in magazine. Illustrations: colour transparencies, b&w photos and drawings. Payment: by arrangement. Founded 1885.

Lancashire Magazine
33 Beverley Road, Driffield, Yorkshire YO25 7SD
tel/fax (01377) 253232
Editor Winston Halstead
Bi-monthly £1.20

Articles about people, life and character of all parts of Lancashire. Length: 1500

words. Payment: £30-£35 approx. per published page. Illustrations: line, half-tone, colour. Founded 1977.

Lancet
42 Bedford Square, London WC1B 3SL
tel 0171-436 4981 *fax* 0171-323 6441
Editor Dr Richard Horton
Weekly £3.25

Research papers, review articles, editorials, correspondence and commentaries on the international medicosocial scene. Regular contributors are paid by arrangement; others should consult the editor before submitting. Founded 1823.

Land & Liberty
177 Vauxhall Bridge Road, London SW1V 1EU
tel 0171-834 4266 *fax* 0171-834 4979
Editor Fred Harrison
Quarterly £3.00 (£12.00 p.a.)

Articles on land economics, land taxation, land prices, land speculation as they relate to housing, the economy, production, politics. Study of journal essential. Length: up to 3000 words. Payment: by arrangement. Illustrations: half-tone. Founded 1894.

The Lawyer
Centaur Communications Group,
50 Poland Street, London W1V 4AX
tel 0171-439 4222 *fax* 0171-734 0534
Editor Mary Heaney
Weekly £1.75 (£60.00 p.a.)

News, articles, features and views relevant to the legal profession. Length: 600-900 words. Illustrations: as agreed. Payment: £125-£150 per 1000 words. Founded 1987.

Learned Publishing
17 Orchard Close, Shillingford, Oxon OX10 7HQ
tel/fax (01865) 858799
e-mail alpsp@storrie.demon.co.uk
Editor Eileen Storrie
Quarterly £90.00 p.a. Free to members

Journal of the Association of the Learned and Professional Society Publishers. Articles, reviews and reports on topics and events of interest to academic, medical, scientific and learned society publishers. Editorial, production, copyright, electronic publishing, distribution and marketing issues are all addressed. Length: 1000-5000 words. Illustrations: half-tone, line. Payment: none. Founded 1988; successor to *ALPSP Bulletin*.

The Leisure Manager
The Institute of Leisure and Amenity Management, ILAM House, Lower Basildon, Reading, Berks. RG8 9NE
tel (01491) 874222 *fax* (01491) 874059
Editor Jonathan Ives
Bi-monthly £40.00 p.a. (£50.00 p.a. overseas)

Official Journal of The Institute of Leisure and Amenity Management. Articles on amenity, children's play, tourism, leisure, parks, entertainment, recreation and sports management. Payment: by arrangement. Illustrations: line, half-tone. Founded 1985.

Leisure Painter
63-65 High Street, Tenterden, Kent TN30 6BD
tel (01580) 763315 *fax* (01580) 765411
Editor Irene Briers
Monthly £2.10

Instructional articles on painting and fine arts. Payment: £65 per 1000 words. Illustrations: line, half-tone, colour, original artwork. Founded 1966.

Leisureweek
Centaur Publishing Ltd, St Giles House,
50 Poland Street, London W1V 4AX
tel 0171-494 0300 *fax* 0171-734 2741
e-mail leisure-week@centaur.co.uk
Editor Michael Nutley
Weekly £1.00

News and features relating to the leisure industry. All material commissioned. Length: features from 800 words, news from 200 words. Illustrations: line, half-tone. Payment: by agreement. Founded 1989.

The Library
Incunabula, Humanities & Social Sciences, The British Library, Great Russell Street, London WC1B 3DG
tel 0171-412 7579 *fax* 0171-412 7577
Editor M.C. Davies
Published by Oxford University Press for the Bibliographical Society
Quarterly £65.00 p.a. (£32.00 p.a. to members)

Articles up to 15,000 words as well as shorter Notes, embodying original research on subjects connected with bibliography; reviews. Illustrations: line, half-tone. Payment: none. Founded 1889.

Life – see The Observer in National newspapers UK and Ireland, page 3

Life & Work: Record of the Church of Scotland

121 George Street, Edinburgh EH2 4YN
tel 0131-225 5722 *fax* 0131-220 3113
e-mail lifework@dial.pipex.com
Editor Dr Robin Hill
Monthly 70p

Articles not exceeding 1000 words and news; poems and occasional stories. Study the magazine first. Payment: up to £45 per 1000 words, or by arrangement. Illustrations: photos and line, cartoons.

Lincolnshire Life

PO Box 81, Lincoln LN1 1HD
tel (01522) 527127 *fax* (01522) 560035
Editor Jez Ashberry
Monthly £1.45

Articles and news of county interest. Length: up to 1200 words. Illustrations: b&w and colour photos and line drawings. Payment: varies. Founded 1961.

The Linguist

The Institute of Linguists, Saxon House, 48 Southwark Street, London SE1 1UN
tel 0171-690 9665 *fax* 0171-607 6824
e-mail 100442.2203@compuserve.com
Editor Pat Treasure
Bi-monthly £5.00 (£25.00 p.a.)

Articles of interest to professional linguists in translating, interpreting and teaching fields. Articles usually contributed, but payment by arrangement. All contributors have special knowledge of the subjects with which they deal. Length: 1500-2000 words. Illustrations: line, half-tone.

The Literary Review

44 Lexington Street, London W1R 3LH
tel 0171-437 9392 *fax* 0171-734 1844
Editor Auberon Waugh
Monthly £2.40 (£26.00 p.a.)

Reviews, articles of cultural interest, interviews, profiles, monthly poetry competitions. Material mostly commissioned. Length: articles and reviews 800-1500 words. Illustrations: line and b&w photos. Payment: £25 per article; none for illustrations. Founded 1979.

Live & Kicking Magazine

BBC Worldwide Publishing, Woodlands, Wood Lane, London W12 0TT
tel 0181-576 3254 *fax* 0181-576 3267
Editor Jeremy Mark
Monthly £1.40

Features and news stories on current pop, TV, film and sports stars with teenage appeal. Length: features 1000-1500 words. Illustrations: occasionally commission cartoons and caricatures. Payment: varies. Founded 1993.

Llais Llyfrau/Books in Wales

Welsh Books Council, Castell Brychan, Aberystwyth, Ceredigion SY23 2JB
tel (01970) 624151 *fax* (01970) 625385
Editors R. Gerallt Jones, Katie Gramich, Lorna Herbert Egan
Quarterly £6.00 p.a.

Articles in Welsh and English on authors and their books, Welsh publishing; reviews and book lists. Mainly commissioned. Payment: by arrangement. Founded 1964.

Loaded

IPC Magazines, King's Reach Tower, Stamford Street, London SE1 9LS
tel 0171-261 5000 *fax* 0171-261 5640
e-mail (features) david-bennun@ipc.co.uk
(handbook) danny-plunkett@ipc.co.uk
Editor-in-Chief Alan Lewis
Monthly £2.60

Magazine for men in their twenties. Music, sport, sex, humour, travel, fashion, hard news and popular culture. Address longer features (2000 words) to Features Editor, and shorter items to Handbook Editor. Payment: by arrangement. Founded 1994.

Local Government Chronicle

EMAP Business Publishing, 33-39 Bowling Green Lane, London EC1R 0DA
tel 0171-833 7311 *fax* 0171-837 2725
Editor David Pead
Weekly £2.70

Articles relating to financial, political, legal and administrative work of the local government manager. Payment: by arrangement. Illustrations: half-tone, cartoons. Founded 1855.

The Local Historian

(formerly The Amateur Historian)
7 Carisbrooke Park, Knighton, Leicester LE2 3PQ
tel (0116) 270 5028
British Association for Local History, 25 Lower Street, Harnham, Salisbury, Wilts. SP2 8EY
tel (01722) 332158 *fax* (01722) 413242
web site http://indigo.stile.le.ac.uk/~bon/local_hist/frontpage.html
Editor Dr Margaret Bonney
Quarterly £6.00

Articles, popular in style but based on original historical research, covering methods of research, sources and background material helpful to regional, local and family historians – histories of particular places, people or incidents not wanted. Length: maximum 7000 words. Illustrations: line and photos. Payment: none. Founded 1952.

LOGOS

5 Beechwood Drive, Marlow, Bucks. SL7 2DH
tel/fax (01628) 477577
Editor Gordon Graham
Quarterly £45.00 p.a. (£70.00 p.a. institutions)

In-depth articles on publishing, librarianship and bookselling with international or interdisciplinary appeal. Length: 3500-7000 words. Payment: 25 offprints/copy of issue. Founded 1990.

London Magazine: A Review of the Arts

30 Thurloe Place, London SW7 2HQ
tel 0171-589 0618
Editor Alan Ross, Deputy *Editor* Jane Rye
Bi-monthly £5.99 (£28.50 p.a.)

Poems, stories (2000-5000 words), literary memoirs, critical articles, features on art, photography, sport, theatre, cinema, music, architecture, events, reports from abroad, drawings. Sae necessary. Payment: by arrangement. Founded 1954.

London Review of Books

28-30 Little Russell Street, London WC1A 2HN
tel 0171-209 1101 *fax* 0171-209 1102
e-mail editorial@lrb.co.uk
Editor Mary-Kay Wilmers
Bi-monthly £2.25

Features, essays, poems. Payment: by arrangement. Founded 1979.

Looks Magazine

EMAP Élan, Endeavour House, 189 Shaftesbury Avenue, London WC2H 8JG
tel 0171-957 8383 *fax* 0171-930 4191
Editor Wendy Rigg
Monthly £1.60

Fashion, beauty and hair for 15-24 age range; features, especially with a celebrity bias. No unsolicited material, but ideas welcome. Length: up to 2000 words. Illustrations: colour, b&w. Payment: by arrangement.

M&J

(formerly Mandy/Judy)
D.C. Thomson & Co. Ltd, Albert Square, Dundee DD1 9QJ
tel (01382) 223131 *fax* (01382) 322214
185 Fleet Street, London EC4A 2HS
tel 0171-242 5086 *fax* 0171-404 5694
Weekly 60p

Picture-story paper for schoolgirls. Serials and series in line drawings: 2 and 3 page instalments, 8-9 frames per page. Editorial co-operation offered to promising scriptwriters. Payment: on acceptance.

Make: the magazine of women's art

(formerly Women's Art Magazine)
Women's Art Library, Fulham Palace, Bishops Avenue, London SW6 6EA
tel 0171-731 7618 *fax* 0171-384 1110
e-mail womansart.lib@ukonline.co.uk
Editor Heidi Reitmaier
Bi-monthly £3.00

Interviews, book reviews and exhibition reviews on the work of contemporary and historical women artists. Material mostly commissioned. Length: up to 3000 words. Illustrations: b&w photos, line drawings. Payment: £30 per 1000 words; none for illustrations.

Making Music

Nexus Media Ltd, Nexus House, Swanley, Kent BR8 8HY
tel (01322) 660070 *fax* (01322) 615636
e-mail makingmusic@cerbernet.co.uk
web site http://cerbernet.co.uk/makingmusic/
Editor Paul Quinn
Monthly £18.00 p.a.

Technical, musicianly and instrumental features on rock, pop, blues, dance, world, jazz, soul; little classical. Length: 500-2500 words. Payment: £90 per 1000 words. Illustrations: colour, including cartoons and photos. Founded 1986.

Management Today

174 Hammersmith Road, London W6 7JP
tel 0171-413 4566 *fax* 0171-413 4138
Editor Charles Skinner
Monthly £40.00 p.a.

Company profiles and analysis – columns from 1000 words, features up to 3000 words. Payment: £250 per 1000 words. Illustrations: colour transparencies, usually commissioned. Founded 1966.

Mandy Library

D.C. Thomson & Co. Ltd, Albert Square, Dundee DD1 9QJ
tel (01382) 223131 *fax* (01382) 322214

185 Fleet Street, London EC4A 2HS
tel 0171-242 5086 *fax* 0171-404 5694
Fortnightly 55p

Picture-stories for schoolgirls (about 140 line drawings): adventure, animal, mystery, school, sport. Scripts considered; promising scriptwriters and artists encouraged. Payment: on acceptance.

Marie Claire

European Magazines Ltd, 2 Hatfields,
London SE1 9PG
tel 0171-261 5240 *fax* 0171-261 5277
Editor Juliet Warkentin
Monthly £2.30

Feature articles of interest to today's woman; plus fashion, beauty, health, food, drink and travel. Commissioned material only. Payment: by negotiation. Illustrated in colour. Founded 1988.

Market Newsletter

Focus House, 497 Green Lanes, London N13 4BP
tel 0181-882 3315/6 *fax* 0181-886 5174
Editor John Tracy
Published by Bureau of Freelance Photographers
Monthly Private circulation

Current information on markets and editorial requirements of interest to writers and photographers. Founded 1965.

Marketing Week

St Giles House, 50 Poland Street, London W1V 4AX
tel 0171-439 4222 *fax* 0171-439 9669
web site http://www.marketing-week.co.uk/mw001
Editor Stuart Smith
Weekly £2.10

Aimed at marketing management. Accepts occasional features and analysis. Length: 1000-2000 words. Payment: £150 per 1000 words. Founded 1978.

Mayfair

2 Archer Street, London W1V 8JJ
tel 0171-734 5030 *fax* 0171-734 5030
Editor Steve Shields
Monthly £2.50

Short humorous articles, sport, music, motoring. Payment: by arrangement. Illustrations: colour transparencies to illustrate highly visual feature ideas. Founded 1966.

Medal News

Token Publishing Ltd, PO Box 14, Honiton, Devon EX14 9YP
tel (01404) 831878 *fax* (01404) 831895
Editor Diana Birch
10 p.a. £2.50

Well-researched articles on military history with a bias towards medals. Length: up to 2000 words. Illustrations: b&w preferred. Payment: £20 per 1000 words; none for illustrations. Founded 1989.

Media Week

EMAP Media, 33-39 Bowling Green Lane, London EC1R 0DA
tel 0171-505 8341 *fax* 0171-505 8363
e-mail mweeked@media.emap.co.uk
Editor Susannah Richmond
Weekly £1.85

News and analysis of UK advertising media industry. Illustrations: full colour and b&w. Founded 1985.

Melody Maker

IPC Magazines Ltd, King's Reach Tower, Stamford Street, London SE1 9LS
tel 0171-261 6229 *fax* 0171-261 6706
Editor Allan Jones
Weekly 75p

Technical, entertaining and informative articles on rock and pop music. Payment: by arrangement. Illustrations: line, halftone, colour.

Men Only

2 Archer Street, London W1V 8JJ
tel 0171-292 8000 *fax* 0171-734 5030
Publisher Paul Raymond, *Editor* Mike Collier
Monthly £2.50

High quality glamour photography; explicit sex stories (no erotic fiction); male interest features – sport, humour, entertainment, hedonism! Proposals welcome. Payment: by arrangement. Founded 1971.

Men's Health

Rodale Press Ltd, 7-10 Chandos Street, London W1M 0AD
tel 0171-291 6000 *fax* 0171-291 6060
Editor Phil Hilton
10 p.a. £2.70

Active pursuits, grooming, fitness, fashion, sex, career and general men's interest issues. Length 1000-4000 words. Ideas on any subject welcome. No unsolicited MSS. Payment: by arrangement. Founded 1994.

Methodist Recorder

122 Golden Lane, London EC1Y 0TL
tel 0171-251 8414
Editor Moira Sleight
Weekly 45p

Methodist and Free Church newspaper; ecumenically involved. Limited opportunities for freelance contributors. Preliminary letter advised. Founded 1861.

Middle East International
21 Collingham Road, London SW5 0NU
tel 0171-373 5228 *fax* 0171-370 5956
Editor Steve Sherman
Fortnightly £60.00 p.a. (other rates on application)

Articles (1200-1600 words) and news stories on Middle East and Arab world-related topics. Payment: £80 per 1000 words. Founded 1971.

Military Modelling
Nexus Special Interests, Nexus House, Boundary Way, Hemel Hempstead, Herts. HP2 7ST
tel (01442) 66551 *fax* (01442) 66998
Editor Ken Jones
Monthly £2.30

Articles on military modelling. Length: up to 2000 words. Payment: by arrangement. Illustrations: line, half-tone, colour.

Mind
Oxford University Press, Walton Street, Oxford OX2 6DP
tel (01865) 56767 *fax* (01865) 267773
Editor Prof Mark Sainsbury
Quarterly £7.50 (£25.00 p.a. UK/Europe, $46.00 p.a. rest of world; institution/student rates on application)

Review of philosophy intended for those who have studied and thought on this subject. Articles from about 5000 words; shorter discussion notes; critical notices and reviews. Payment: none. Founded 1876.

Mizz
IPC Magazines Ltd, King's Reach Tower, Stamford Street, London SE1 9LS
tel 0171-261 6319 *fax* 0171-261 6032
Editor Lesley Johnston
Fortnightly 80p

Articles on any subject of interest to teenage girls. Approach in writing. Payment: by arrangement. Illustrated. Founded 1985.

Mobile and Cellular Magazine
Nexus Media, Nexus House, Azalea Drive, Swanley, Kent BR8 8HY
tel (01322) 660070 *fax* (01322) 661257
Editor Peter Sayer
Monthly £38.00 p.a.

Aimed at radio communications professionals – technical features, company profiles and news analysis; cartoons. Length: features up to 1500 words, analysis up to 800 words. Payment: £150 per 1000 words. Founded 1989.

Model Boats
Nexus Special Interests, Nexus House, Boundary Way, Hemel Hempstead, Herts. HP2 7ST
tel (01442) 66551 *fax* (01442) 66998
Editor John L. Cundell
13 p.a. £2.30

Articles, drawings, plans, sketches of model boats. Payment: £25 per page; plans £100. Illustrations: line, half-tone. Founded 1964.

Model Engineer
Nexus Special Interests, Nexus House, Boundary Way, Hemel Hempstead, Herts. HP2 7ST
tel (01442) 66551 *fax* (01442) 66998
Editor Ted Jolliffe
2 p.m. £1.85

Detailed description of the construction of models, small workshop equipment, machine tools and small electrical and mechanical devices; articles on small power engineering, mechanics, electricity, workshop methods, clocks and experiments. Payment: up to £35 per page. Illustrations: line, half-tone, colour. Founded 1898.

Modern Believing
(formerly Modern Churchman)
The Modern Churchpeople's Union, King's College, Cambridge CB2 1ST
tel (01223) 331100
Editor Dr George Pattison
Quarterly £4.00

Covers 'liberal theology in the contemporary world'. Length: up to 3500 words. Intending contributors advised to write to the editor for a copy of instructions to authors. Founded 1911.

Modern Language Review
Modern Humanities Research Association, King's College, Strand, London WC2R 2LS
Quarterly £75.00 p.a. (£90.00 overseas, $180.00 USA)

Articles and reviews of a scholarly or specialist character on English, Romance, Germanic and Slavonic languages and literatures. Payment: none, but offprints are given. Founded 1905.

Modern Painters

Fine Art Journals Ltd, Universal House,
251-255 Tottenham Court Road,
London W1P 9AD
tel 0171-636 6305 *fax* 0171-580 5615
Editor Karen Wright
Quarterly £4.95

Journal of modern fine arts and architecture – commissioned articles and features; also interviews. Length: 1000-2500 words. Payment: £120 per 1000 words. Illustrated. Founded 1986.

Modern Woman

Meath Chronicle Ltd, Market Square, Navan,
Co. Meath, Republic of Ireland
tel (046) 21442 *fax* (046) 23565
Editor Margot Davis
Monthly 50p

Articles and features on a wide range of subjects of interest to women over the age of 18 (e.g. politics, religion, health and sex). Length: 200-1000 words. Illustrations: colour and b&w photos, line drawings and cartoons. Payment: NUJ rates. Founded 1984.

Modus

Hamilton House, Mabledon Place,
London WC1H 9BJ
tel 0171-387 1441 *fax* 0171-383 7230
Editor Geoffrey Thompson
8 p.a. £3.80 (£27.00 p.a.)

Official Journal of the National Association of Teachers of Home Economics and Technology: aimed at teachers and educationists. Articles on the teaching of home economics and technology, including textiles, nutrition, and social and technical background information for teachers. Length: up to 1500 words. Payment: by arrangement. Illustrations: line, half-tone, cartoons.

Mojo

EMAP Metro, Mappin House, 4 Winsley Street,
London W1N 7AR
tel 0171-436 1515 *fax* 0171-637 4925
e-mail mojo@dial.pipex.com
Editor Mat Snow
Monthly £2.95

Serious rock music magazine: interviews, news and reviews of books, live shows and albums. Length: up to 10,000 words. Illustrations: colour and b&w photos, colour caricatures. Payment: £180 per 1000 words; £150-£350 illustrations. Founded 1993.

MoneyMarketing

Centaur Communications Ltd, St Giles House,
50 Poland Street, London W1V 4AX
tel 0171-439 4222 *fax* 0171-734 9379
Editor Grant Ringshaw
Weekly £1.50

News, features, surveys and viewpoints; cartoons. Length: features from 900 words. Illustrations: b&w photos, colour and b&w line. Payment: £150 per 1000 words; colour line £200, b&w line £150. Founded 1985.

Moneywise

Berkeley Magazines Ltd, 10 Old Bailey,
London EC4M 7NB
tel 0171-409 5273 *fax* 0171-409 5261
web site http://www.moneywise.co.uk
Editor Matthew Vincent
Monthly £2.70

Financial and consumer interest features, articles and news stories. Length: 1500-2000 words. Illustrations: willing to see designers, illustrators and photographers for fresh new ideas. Payment: by arrangement. Founded 1990.

The Month

114 Mount Street, London W1Y 6AH
tel 0171-491 7596 *fax* 0171-629 6936
e-mail tim.noble@dial.pipex.com
Editor Tim Noble SJ
Monthly £1.50

Review of Christian thought, and world affairs, with arts and literary sections, edited by the Jesuit Fathers. Preliminary letter desirable. Length: up to 2500 words. Payment: by arrangement. Illustrations: b&w photos. Founded 1864.

More!

EMAP Élan, 20 Orange Street, London WC2H 7ED
tel 0171-957 8383 *fax* 0171-930 4637
Editor Tony Cross
Fortnightly £1.25

Celebrities, fun and sexy features, 'how to' articles aimed at young women. Short erotic fiction. Study of magazine essential. Length: 1800 words. Payment: £150 per 1000 words. Illustrated. Founded 1988.

Mortgage Finance Gazette

Franey & Co. Ltd, 100 Avenue Road,
London NW3 3PG
tel 0171-393 7400 *fax* 0171-393 7466
Editor Liz Salecka
Monthly £45.50 p.a.

Articles on all aspects of bank and building society management, mortgage lending,

retail financial services. Length: up to 2000 words. Payment: by arrangement. Illustrations: line, half-tone. Founded 1869.

Mother & Baby

EMAP Élan, Victory House, Leicester Place, Leicester Square, London WC2H 7BP
tel 0171-437 9011 *fax* 0171-434 0656
Editor Sharon Parsons
Monthly £1.60

Features and practical articles. Length: 1200-2400 words. Payment: by negotiation. Illustrated. Founded 1956.

Motor Boat and Yachting

IPC Magazines Ltd, King's Reach Tower, Stamford Street, London SE1 9LS
tel 0171-261 5333
Editor Alan Harper
Monthly £2.65

General interest as well as specialist motor boating material welcomed. Features up to 2000 words considered on all aspects, sea-going and on inland waterways. Payment: varies. Illustrations: photos (mostly colour and transparencies preferred) and line, cartoons. Founded 1904.

Motor Boats Monthly

Boating Publications Ltd, Link House, Dingwall Avenue, Croydon CR9 2TA
tel 0181-686 2599 *fax* 0181-781 6065
Editor Kim Hollamby
Monthly £2.60

News on motorboating in the UK and Europe, cruising features and anecdotal stories. Mostly commissioned – send synopsis to editor. Length: news up to 200 words, features up to 4000 words. Illustrations: colour transparencies. Payment: by arrangement. Founded 1987.

Motor Caravan Magazine

Link House Magazines Ltd, Link House, Dingwall Avenue, Croydon CR9 2TA
tel 0181-686 2599 *fax* 0181-781 6044
Editor Paul Carter
Monthly £2.20

Practical features, touring features (home and abroad). Length: up to 1500 words. Payment: £35-£40 per page. Illustrations: line, half-tone, colour, cartoons. Founded 1985.

Motor Cycle News

EMAP National Publications Ltd, 20-22 Station Road, Kettering NN15 7HH
tel (01536) 411111 *fax* (01536) 411750
e-mail mcn@mcnl.demon.co.uk

web site http://www.erack.com/mcw
Editor Adam Duckworth
Weekly £1.10

Features (up to 1000 words), photos and news stories of interest to motorcyclists. Founded 1955.

Motorcaravan and Motorhome Monthly (MMM)

14 Eastfield Close, Andover, Hants SP10 2QP
fax (01264) 324794
Editor Mike Jago
Monthly £2.50

Articles including motorcaravan travel, owner reports and DIY. Length: up to 2500 words. Payment: by arrangement. Illustrations: line, half-tone, colour prints and transparencies. Founded 1966 as Motor Caravan and Camping.

Motorcycle International

Myatt McFarlane plc, PO Box 69, Altrincham, Cheshire WA14 2BF
tel 0161-928 3480 *fax* 0161-941 6897
Editor Roger Willis
Monthly £2.50

Motorcycle-related features, news and travel articles. Length: from 1000 words. Illustrations: colour transparencies. Payment: £100 per 1000 words or by negotiation; by negotiation for illustrations. Founded 1985.

Ms London

The Commuter Publishing Partnership, 7-9 Rathbone Street, London W1P 1AF
tel 0171-636 6651
Editor Bill Williamson
Weekly Free

Features and lifestyle pieces of interest to young professional working women. All material commissioned; contributors must live in the capital. Length: 1000-2000 words. Illustrations: no unsolicited illustrations; enquire first. Payment: by negotiation. Founded 1968.

Museums Journal

The Museums Association, 42 Clerkenwell Close, London EC1R 0PA
tel 0171-250 1834 *fax* 0171-250 1929
Monthly £5.00 Free to members (£48.00 p.a. individuals; £72.00 p.a. institutions)

Articles and news items on museum and art gallery policy, administration, architecture and display, notes on technical developments, book reviews. Length: 100-2500 words. Illustrations: line, half-

tone, colour, cartoons. Payment: by agreement. Founded 1901.

Music and Letters
Editorial Dr Nigel Fortune, Prof Tim Carter, Dr Katharine Ellis, Music Department, Royal Holloway, University of London, Egham, Surrey TW20 0EX
tel (01784) 443532
Other matters Oxford University Press (Journals Production), 60 Walton Street, Oxford OX2 6DP
Quarterly£15.00

Scholarly articles, up to 10,000 words, on musical subjects, neither merely topical nor purely descriptive. Technical, historical and research matter preferred. Illustrations: music quotations and plates. Payment: none. Founded 1920.

The Music Review
Editorial Glyneithin, Burry Port, Carmarthenshire SA16 0TA
Other matters Black Bear Press, King's Hedges Road, Cambridge CB4 2PQ
Editor A.F. Leighton Thomas
Quarterly £15.25 (£52.50 p.a.)

Articles from 1500-8000 words dealing with any aspect of standard or classical music (no jazz). Payment: small, by arrangement. Founded 1940.

Music Teacher
Rhinegold Publishing Ltd, 241 Shaftesbury Avenue, London WC2H 8EH
tel 0171-333 1747 *fax* 0171-333 1769
Monthly £2.95

Provides information and articles for both school and private music teachers. Articles and illustrations must both have a teacher, as well as a musical, interest. Length: articles 1000-3000 words. Payment: by arrangement. Founded 1908.

Music Week
Miller Freeman Entertainment Ltd, 8 Montague Close, London SE1 9UR
tel 0171-620 3636 *fax* 0171-401 8035
Editor Selina Webb
Weekly £3.25 (£103.00 p.a.)

News and features on all aspects of producing, manufacturing, marketing and retailing music. Payment: by negotiation. Founded 1959.

Musical Opinion
2 Princes Road, St Leonards-on-Sea, East Sussex TN37 6EL
tel (01424) 715167 *fax* (01424) 712214
Editor Denby Richards
Quarterly (plus 8 supplements) £3.50 (£24 p.a.)

Suggestions for contributions of musical interest, scholastic, educational, anniversaries, ethnic, and also relating to the organ world. Record, video, CD-Rom, opera, festival, book, music reviews. All editorial matter must be commissioned. Payment: on publication. Illustrations: b&w photos, cartoons. Founded 1877.

Musical Times
63B Jamestown Road, London NW1 7DB
tel/fax 0171-482 5697
Editor Antony Bye
Monthly £2.50

Musical articles, reviews, 200-4000 words. All material commissioned. Illustrations: music. Founded 1844.

My Weekly
D.C. Thomson & Co. Ltd, 80 Kingsway East, Dundee DD4 8SL
tel (01382) 223131 *fax* (01382) 452491
185 Fleet Street, London EC4A 2HS
tel 0171-242 5086 *fax* 0171-404 5694
Weekly 48p

Serials, from 30,000-80,000 words, suitable for family reading. Short complete stories of 1000-3500 words with humorous, romantic or strong emotional themes. Articles on television stars and on all subjects of women's interest. Contributions should appeal to women everywhere. Payment: on acceptance. Illustrations: colour and b&w. Founded 1910.

My Weekly Puzzle Time
D.C. Thomson & Co. Ltd, Albert Square, Dundee DD1 9QJ
tel (01382) 223131 *fax* (01382) 322214
Monthly £1.40

Broad range of puzzles appealing mainly to women. Entertainment value more important than intellectual. Payment: by arrangement. No illustrations. Founded 1993.

My Weekly Story Library
D.C. Thomson & Co. Ltd, Albert Square, Dundee DD1 9QJ
tel (01382) 223131 *fax* (01382) 322214
185 Fleet Street, London EC4A 2HS
tel 0171-242 5086 *fax* 0171-404 5694
4 p.m. 55p

35,000-37,500-word romantic stories aimed at the post-teenage market. Payment: by arrangement; competitive for the market. No illustrations.

The National Trust Magazine

The National Trust, 36 Queen Anne's Gate,
London SW1H 9AS
tel 0171-222 9251 *fax* 0171-222 5097
web site http://www.ukindex.co.uk/nationaltrust
Editor Gina Guarnieri
3 p.a. Free to members

News and features on the conservation of historic houses, coasts and countryside in the UK. Length: 1000 words (features), 200 words (news). Illustrations: colour transparencies and artwork. Payment: by arrangement; picture library rates. Founded 1969.

Nationwide Magazine

BLA Group Ltd, 5-8 Hardwick Street,
London EC1R 4RB
tel 0171-278 7603 *fax* 0171-278 6246
Editor Jeanne Griffiths
2 p.a. Free to customers

Home interest and financial articles for Nationwide customers. Founded 1994.

Natural World

20 Upper Ground, London SE1 9PF
tel 0171-805 5555 *fax* 0171-805 5911
Editor Linda Bennett
3 p.a. Free to members

National magazine of The Wildlife Trusts. Short articles on UK nature conservation, particularly the work of The Wildlife Trusts; contributors normally have special knowledge of subjects on which they write. Length: up to 1200 words. Payment: by arrangement. Illustrations: line, colour. Founded 1981.

Naturalist

The University, Bradford BD7 1DP
tel (01274) 384212 *fax* (01274) 384231
e-mail m.r.d.seaward@bradford.ac.uk
Editor Prof M.R.D. Seaward MSc, PhD, DSc
Quarterly £20.00 p.a.

Original papers on all kinds of British natural history subjects, including various aspects of geology, archaeology and environmental science. Length: immaterial. Illustrations: photos and line drawings. Payment: none. Founded 1875.

Nature

Macmillan Magazines Ltd, Porters South,
4-6 Crinan Street, London N1 9XW
tel 0171-833 4000 *fax* 0171-843 4596
web site http://www.nature.com
Editor Philip Campbell
Weekly £4.50

Devoted to scientific matters and to their bearing upon public affairs. All contributors of articles have specialised knowledge of the subjects with which they deal. Illustrations: line, half-tone. Founded 1869.

Nautical Magazine

Brown, Son & Ferguson Ltd,
4-10 Darnley Street,
Glasgow G41 2SD
tel 0141-429 1234 *fax* 0141-420 1694
Editor L. Ingram-Brown MIMgt, MBIM, MRIN
Monthly £27.60 p.a. (£31.80 p.a. overseas)

Articles relating to nautical and shipping profession, from 1500-2000 words; also translations. Payment: by arrangement. No illustrations. Founded 1832.

Needlecraft

Future Publishing Ltd, 30 Monmouth Street,
Bath BA1 2BW
tel (01225) 442244 *fax* (01225) 732398
e-mail needlecraft@futurenet.co.uk
Editor Rebecca Bradshaw
4-weekly £2.99

Mainly project-based stitching designs with step-by-step instructions. Features with tight stitching focus (e.g. technique, personality). Length: 1000 words. Illustrated. Payment: £150-£200. Founded 1991.

.net The Internet Magazine

Future Publishing Ltd, 30 Monmouth Street,
Bath BA1 2BW
tel (01225) 442244 *fax* (01225) 423212
e-mail netmag@futurenet.co.uk
Editor Richard Longhurst
Monthly £3.00

Articles, features and news on the Internet. Length: 1000-3000 words. Payment: £110 per 1000 words. Illustrations: colour. Founded 1994.

New Beacon

RNIB, 224 Great Portland Street,
London W1N 6AA
tel 0171-388 1266
Editor Ann Lee
Monthly £1.60

Articles on all aspects of living with a visual impairment (blindness or partial sight). Published in clear print, braille, disk and tape editions. Length: from 500 words. Payment: by arrangement. Illustrations: half-tone. Founded 1930; as *Beacon* 1917.

New Blackfriars
(incorporating Life of the Spirit)
Blackfriars, 25 George Square, Edinburgh EH8 9LD
tel 0131-668 1776 *fax* 0131-662 0462
Editor Rev. Fergus Kerr OP
Monthly £1.80 (£16.00 p.a.)

Critical review, surveying the field of theology, philosophy, sociology and the arts, from the standpoint of Christian principles and their application to the problems of the modern world. Length: 2500-6000 words. Payment: none. Founded 1920.

New Buckinghamshire Countryside
4 Mill Bridge, Hertford SG14 1PY
tel (01992) 553571 *fax* (01992) 587713
Editor Sandra Small
Bi-monthly £1.25

Articles relating to Buckinghamshire. No poetry. Length: 1000 words. Illustrations: colour transparencies and b&w prints, artwork. Payment: £25 (articles); £20. Founded 1995.

New Christian Herald
Herald House Ltd, 96 Dominion Road, Worthing, West Sussex BN14 8JP
tel (01903) 821082 *fax* (01903) 821081
e-mail media@heraldhouse.co.uk
Weekly 50p

Evangelical Christian paper with strong emphasis on news and current affairs. Features up to 700 words – profiles, the changing church, Christians, and contemporary culture (e.g. media, TV, music); cartoons. No short stories. Payment: £20-£50, depending on length/pictures used.

New Electronics
Findlay Publications Ltd, Franks Hall, Franks Lane, Horton Kirby, Dartford, Kent DA4 9LL
tel (01322) 222222 *fax* (01322) 289577
e-mail editorial@new-elec.demon.co.uk
Editor Louise Joselyn
Fortnightly (£88 p.a. UK, £165 p.a. airmail)

Technical/technology news articles, case studies, and career and skills development articles. Length: 1500 words (features), 800 words (news). Illustrations: colour photos, artwork and cartoons. Payment: £120 per 1000 words. Founded 1968.

New Humanist
Rationalist Press Association, Bradlaugh House, 47 Theobald's Road, London WC1X 8SP
tel 0171-430 1371 *fax* 0171-430 1271
e-mail jim.rpa@humanism.org.uk
Editor Jim Herrick
Quarterly £2.50

Articles on current affairs, philosophy, science, literature and humanism. Length: 1000-3000 words. Illustrations: b&w photos. Payment: nominal; none for photos. Founded 1885.

New Impact
Anser House, Courtyard Offices, 3 High Street, Marlow, Bucks. SL7 1AX
tel (01628) 481581 *fax* (01628) 475570
Managing Editor Elaine Sihera
Bi-monthly £26.00 p.a. (business), £20.00 p.a. (individual)

'Promoting enterprise, training and diversity.' Articles, features and news on any aspect of training, business and women's issues to suit a multicultural audience; also profiles of personalities, short stories. Length: 900-1000 words. Illustrations: b&w photos if related to profiles. Payment: £40 (depending on merit); none for photos. Founded 1993.

New Internationalist
55 Rectory Road, Oxford OX4 1BW
tel (01865) 728181 *fax* (01865) 793152
e-mail newint@gn.apc.org
Editors Vanessa Baird, Chris Brazier, David Ransom, Nikki van der Gaag
Monthly £2.50 (£24.85 p.a.)

World issues, ranging from food to feminism to peace – examines one subject each month. Length: up to 2000 words. Illustrations: line, half-tone, colour, cartoons. Payment: £125 per 1000 words. Founded 1973.

New Law Journal
Butterworth & Co. (Publishers) Ltd, Halsbury House, 35 Chancery Lane, London WC2A 1EL
tel 0171-400 2500 *fax* 0171-400 2583
Editor James Morton
48 p.a. £4.00

Articles and news on all aspects of the legal profession. Length: up to 1800 words. Payment: by arrangement. Founded 1975.

New Library World
MCB University Press, 60-62 Toller Lane, Bradford, West Yorkshire BD8 9BY
tel (01274) 777700 *fax* (01274) 785200
7 p.a. £1249.00 p.a.

Professional and bibliographical articles. Includes Librarians' World (6 p.a.), 16pp newsletter 'for librarians by librarians'. Payment: none. Founded 1898.

New Media Age
Centaur Newsletters, St Giles House,
50 Poland Street, London W1V 4AX
tel 0171-287 9800 *fax* 0171-439 1480
e-mail phil@dwyer.demon.co.uk
Editor Phil Dwyer
Weekly £136 p.a.

News and articles on all areas of the
communications revolution for multimedia companies. Phone first with ideas; no
uncommissioned material. Length: 1200-
3000 (articles), 250-500 words (news).
Illustrations: none. Payment: £150-£170
per 1000 words. Founded 1995.

New Musical Express
IPC Magazines Ltd, 25th Floor, King's Reach
Tower, Stamford Street, London SE1 9LS
tel 0171-261 5000 *fax* 0171-261 5185
Editor Steve Sutherland
Weekly 90p

Authoritative articles and news stories
on the world's rock and movie personalities. Length: by arrangement. Preliminary
letter or phone call desirable. Payment:
by arrangement. Illustrations: action photos with strong news angle of recording
personalities, cartoons.

New Scientist
IPC Magazines Ltd, King's Reach Tower,
Stamford Street, London SE1 9LS
tel 0171-261 7301 *fax* 0171-261 6464
e-mail edit@mail.newsci.ipc.co.uk
web site http://www.newscientist.com
Editor Alun Anderson
Weekly £1.80

Authoritative articles of topical importance on all aspects of science and technology (length: 1000-3000 words); preliminary letter or telephone call desirable. Short items from specialists also
considered for Science, This Week,
Forum and Technology. Intending contributors should study recent copies of
the magazine. Payment: varies but average £300 per 1000 words. Illustrations:
line, half-tone, colour, cartoons.

New Statesman
(formerly New Statesman & Society)
Victoria Station House, 191 Victoria Street,
London SW1E 5NE
tel 0171-828 1232 *fax* 0171-828 1881
Editor Ian Hargreaves
Weekly £1.90

Interested in news, reportage and analysis of current political and social issues

at home and overseas, plus book reviews,
poetry, general articles and coverage of
the arts, environment and science seen
from the perspective of the British Left
but written in a stylish, witty and unpredictable way. Length: strictly according
to the value of the piece. Illustrations:
commissioned for specific articles,
though artists' samples considered for
future reference; occasional cartoons.
Payment: by agreement. Founded 1913.

New Theatre Quarterly
Great Robhurst, Woodchurch, Ashford,
Kent TN26 3TB
Editors Clive Barker and Simon Trussler
Quarterly £13.00 (£27.00 p.a.)

Articles, interviews, documentation, reference material covering all aspects of
live theatre. An informed, factual and
serious approach essential. Preliminary
discussion and synopsis desirable.
Payment: by arrangement. Illustrations:
line, half-tone. Founded 1985; as *Theatre
Quarterly* 1971.

The New Welsh Review
Chapter Arts Centre, Market Road,
Cardiff CF5 1QE
tel/fax (01222) 665529/515014
Editor Robin Reeves
Quarterly £3.60 (£15.00 p.a., £28.00 2 yrs)

Articles, short stories, poems, book
reviews, interviews and profiles.
Especially, but not exclusively, concerned with Welsh writing in English.
Theatre in Wales section. Length: (articles) up to 4000 words. Illustrations:
line, half-tone, cartoons; colour cover.
Payment: £7-£15 per page prose; £8-£20
per poem; £10-£20 per review; £10-£20
per illustration. Founded 1988.

New Woman
EMAP Élan, 20 Orange Street, London WC2H 7ED
tel 0171-957 8383 *fax* 0171-930 7246
Editor Dawn Bebe
Monthly £2.00

Features up to 2000 words. Occasionally
accepts unsolicited articles; enclose sae for
return. No fiction. Payment: at or above
NUJ rates. Illustrated. Founded 1988.

New World
United Nations Association, 3 Whitehall Court,
London SW1A 2EL
tel 0171-930 2931 *fax* 0171-930 5893
4 p.a. £1.00

Review of UN activities, of UNA campaigns and of different viewpoints on major international issues confronting the United Nations. Occasionally takes cartoons. No payment.

Night & Day – see Mail on Sunday in National newspapers UK and Ireland, page 3

19
IPC Magazines Ltd, King's Reach Tower, Stamford Street, London SE1 9LS
tel 0171-261 6410
Editor Lee Kynaston
Monthly £1.70

Glossy fashion and general interest magazine for young women aged 17-22, including beauty, music and social features of strong contemporary interest. All illustrations commissioned. Payment: by arrangement. Founded 1968.

Numismatic Chronicle
Department of Coins and Medals, Fitzwilliam Museum, Cambridge CB2 1RB
tel (01223) 332917 *fax* (01223) 332923
Editor Dr Mark Blackburn
£24.00 per annual volume

Journal of the Royal Numismatic Society. Articles on coins and medals. Articles relating to coins and medals are unpaid, and contributions should reach a high academic standard. Founded 1839.

Nursery World
Lector Court, 151-153 Farringdon Road, London EC1R 3AD
tel 0171-278 7441 *fax* 0171-278 3896
Editor Ruth Beattie
Weekly £1.10

For all grades of primary school, nursery and child care staff, nannies, foster parents and all concerned with the care of expectant mothers, babies and young children. Authoritative and informative articles, 800 or 1600 words, and photos, on all aspects of child welfare and early education, from 0-8 years, in the UK. Practical ideas and leisure crafts. No short stories. Payment: by arrangement. Illustrations: line, half-tone, colour.

Nursing Times and Nursing Mirror
Macmillan Magazines Ltd, Porters South, 4-6 Crinan Street, London N1 9XW
tel 0171-833 4600 *fax* 0171-843 4633
Editor Jane Salvage
Weekly £1.00

Articles of clinical interest, nursing education and nursing policy. Illustrated articles not longer than 2000 words. Contributions from other than health professionals sometimes accepted. Press day, Monday. Illustrations: photos, line, cartoons. Payment: NUJ rates; by arrangement for illustrations. Founded 1905.

The Observer Life Magazine – see Observer in National newspapers UK and Ireland, page 3

Off Licence News
William Reed Publishing Ltd, Broadfield Park, Crawley, West Sussex RH11 9RT
tel (01293) 613400 *fax* (01293) 610320
Weekly £55 p.a.

News and features for the off licence trade. Length: 1000-2000 words (features); news: flexible. Payment: £130 per 1000 words (features). Founded 1970.

Office Secretary
Trade Media Ltd, Brookmead House, Thorney Leys Business Park, Witney, Oxon OX8 7GE
tel (01993) 775545 *fax* (01993) 778884
Editor Danusia Hutson
Quarterly £9.50 p.a.

Serious features on anything of interest to senior secretaries/working women. No unsolicited MSS; ideas only. Illustrations: colour transparencies, cartoons. Payment: by negotiation. Founded 1986.

Occupational Health
Reed Business Information, Quadrant House, The Quadrant, Sutton, Surrey SM2 5AS
tel 0181-652 4669 *fax* 0181-652 8805
e-mail rimsie.mcconiga@rbi.co.uk
Editor Rimsie McConiga
12 p.a. Subscription rates on application

News and features on occupational health-related subjects for the OH profession. Length: 1500-2400 words. Illustrations: colour transparencies. Payment: by arrangement; none. Founded 1947.

OK! Magazine
Northern & Shell plc, Northern & Shell Tower, City Harbour, London E14 9GL
tel 0171-308 5091 *fax* 0171-308 5082
Editor Sharon Ring
Weekly £1.20

Exclusive celebrity interviews and photographs. Submit ideas in writing. Length: 1000 words. Illustrations: colour. Payment: £150-£250,000 per feature. Founded 1993.

The Oldie

45-46 Poland Street, London W1V 4AU
tel 0171-734 2225 *fax* 0171-734 2226
Editor Richard Ingrams
Fortnightly £1.80

General interest magazine reflecting attitudes of older people but aimed at a wider audience. Welcomes features (500-700 words) and ideas on all subjects. No interviews but profiles (900 words) for Still With Us section. Will return MSS if sae enclosed. Illustrations: welcomes b&w and colour cartoons. Payment: approx. £80-£100 per 1000 words; minimum £30 for cartoons. Founded 1992.

Opera

1A Mountgrove Road, London N5 2LU
tel 0171-359 1037 *fax* 0171-354 2700
Editor Rodney Milnes
13 p.a. £2.60

Articles on general subjects appertaining to opera; reviews; criticisms. Length: up to 2000 words. Payment: by arrangement. Illustrations: photos.

Opera Now

241 Shaftesbury Avenue, London WC2H 8EH
tel 0171-333 1740 *fax* 0171-333 1769
Editor Graeme Kay
Bi-monthly £4.95

Articles, news, reviews on opera. All material commissioned only. Length: 150-1500 words. Illustrations: colour and b&w photos, line, cartoons. Payment: £120 per 1000 words. Founded 1989.

Options

IPC Magazines Ltd, King's Reach Tower, Stamford Street, London SE1 9LS
tel 0171-261 5000 *fax* 0171-261 7344
Editor Maureen Rice
Monthly £2.00

Aimed at women aged 25-35. Careers, emotional and sexual matters, health and well-being, women's issues, first-class celebrity interviews and profiles. Mostly commissioned. Length: 1000-3000 words. Payment: by arrangement. Founded 1982.

Orbis

199 The Long Shoot, Nuneaton, Warks. CV11 6JQ
tel/fax/modem (01203) 327440
Editor Mike Shields
Quarterly £15.00 p.a.

Poetry, prose pieces (up to 1000 words), reviews, letters. Annual competition for rhymed poetry. Payment: by arrangement. Illustrations: line. Founded 1968.

The Organ

5 Aldborough Road, St Leonards-on-Sea, East Sussex TN37 6SE
tel (01424) 422225 *fax* (01424) 712214
Editor Dr Brian Hick
Quarterly £17.00 p.a. (£23.00 p.a. overseas)

Articles, 1000-5000 words, relating to any type of organ: historical, technical and artistic; reviews of music, records. Payment: nominal. Illustrations: line, half-tone, colour. Founded 1921.

Organic Gardening

Wardnest Ltd, PO Box 4, Wiveliscombe, Taunton, Somerset TA4 2QY
tel (01984) 623998 *fax* (01984) 623998
Editor Basil Caplan
Monthly £2.15

Articles and features on all aspects of organic gardening. All material commissioned. Length: 600-2000 words. Illustrations: colour and b&w photos, line drawings, cartoons. Payment: by arrangement. Founded 1988.

Our Baby

IPC Magazines Ltd, King's Reach Tower, Stamford Street, London SE1 9LS
tel 0171-261 7986 *fax* 0171-261 6542
web site http://www.ipc.co.uk
Editor-in-Chief Jayne Marsden
Monthly £1.60

Aimed at first-time mums and dads, including product information as well as health news and features on pregnancy and baby care; also readers' birth stories (£25 for 500 words). Material mostly commissioned. Length: varies. Illustrations: brilliant, colour photos of mums- and dads-to-be and newborn babies. Payment: negotiable. Founded 1994.

Our Dogs

Oxford Road Station Approach, Manchester M60 1SX
tel 0161-236 2660 *fax* 0161-236 5534/0892
Editor William Moores
Weekly £1.35

Articles and news on the breeding and showing of pedigree dogs. Illustrations: b&w photos. Payment: NUJ rates; £7.50 per photo. Founded 1895.

Outposts Poetry Quarterly

22 Whitewell Road, Frome, Somerset BA11 4EL
tel/fax (01373) 466653

Editor Roland John
Founder Howard Sergeant MBE
Quarterly £4.00 (£12.00 p.a.)

Poems, essays and critical articles on poets and their work; poetry competitions. Payment: by arrangement. Founded 1943.

Oxford Poetry

Magdalen College, Oxford OX1 4AU
Editors Sinéad Garrigan and Sam Leith
3 p.a. £2.40 (£7.50 p.a.)

Previously unpublished poems, both unsolicited and commissioned. Payment: none. Founded 1983.

Parents

EMAP Élan, Victory House, Leicester Place, London WC2H 7BP
tel 0171-437 9011 *fax* 0171-434 0656
Associate Editor Ruth Beattie
Monthly £1.75

The magazine with smart solutions for today's mums. Articles on pregnancy, childbirth, general family health, food, fashion, child upbringing, development and early education up to age 4, and marital relations. No unsolicited MSS. Illustrations: b&w or colour. Payment: in accordance with national magazine standards; by arrangement for illustrations. Founded 1976.

Parents & Computers

IDG Media, Media House, Adlington Park, Macclesfield SK10 4NP
tel (01625) 878888 *fax* (01625) 850652
e-mail ptc@idg.co.uk
Editor Pam Turnbull
Quarterly £2.25

Articles and features on education and educational computing for parents with children aged 3-11. Length: 1200-2000 words. Illustrations: colour. Payment £100 per page (words); £60. Founded 1995.

Park Home & Holiday Caravan

(formerly Mobile & Holiday Homes)
Link House, Dingwall Avenue, Croydon CR9 2TA
tel 0181-686 2599 *fax* 0181-781 6044
Editor Anne Webb
Monthly £2.00

Informative articles on residential mobile homes (park homes) and holiday static caravans – personal experience articles, site features, news items. No preliminary letter. Payment: by arrangement. Illustrations: line, half-tone, colour transparencies, cartoons. Founded 1960.

PC Direct

Ziff-Davis UK Ltd, Cottons Centre, Hay's Lane, London SE1 2QT
tel 0171-378 6800 *fax* 0171-378 1192
web site http://www.pcdirect.co.uk
Editor Karen Packham
Monthly £1.99

News, features, reviews and technical information for the direct computer buyer. All material commissioned. Length: 500-6000 words. Illustrations: colour photos and illustrations, including computer generated. Payment: £200 per 1000 words; varies for illustrations according to subject/media. Founded 1991.

PC Review

Future Publishing, 30 Monmouth Street, Bath BA1 2BW
tel (01225) 442244 *fax* (01225) 732275
e-mail pcreview@futurenet.co.uk
web site http://www.futurenet.co.uk
Editor Garrick Webster
Monthly £4.99

Features, previews, reviews of PC entertainment – commissioned only, by arrangement with the editor. Illustrations: colour transparencies; ideas for line art, diagrams, charts, etc. Payment: by negotiation.

Peace News

5 Caledonian Road, London N1 9DX
tel 0171-278 3344 *fax* 0171-278 0444
Monthly £1.00

Political articles based on nonviolence in every aspect of human life. Illustrations: line, half-tone. No payment. Founded 1936.

Peninsular Magazine

Cherrybite Publications, Linden Cottage, 45 Burton Road, Little Neston, South Wirral L64 4AE
tel 0151-353 0967
Editor Shelagh Nugent
Quarterly £3.00 (£10.50 p.a.)

Literary magazine. Entertaining and unusual stories and interesting, amusing or informative articles. Length: 1000-3000 words. Payment: £5 per 1000 words plus free copy. Founded 1996.

Pensions World

Tolley Publishing Co. Ltd, Tolley House, 2 Addiscombe Road, Croydon, Surrey CR9 5AF
tel 0181-686 9141 *fax* 0181-760 0588
e-mail stephanie_hawthorne@tolley.co.uk
web site http://www.pensionsworld.co.uk
Editor Stephanie Hawthorne
Monthly £60.00 p.a.

Specialist articles on pensions, investment and law. No unsolicited articles; all material is commissioned. Length: 1500 words. Payment: by negotiation. Founded 1972.

People Management

Personnel Publications Ltd, 17 Britton Street, London EC1M 5NQ
tel 0171-880 6200 *fax* 0171-336 7635
Editor Rob MacLachlan
Monthly £5.00 (£72.00 p.a.)

Journal of the Institute of Personnel and Development. Features and news items on recruitment and selection, training and development; wage and salary administration; industrial psychology; employee relations; labour law; welfare schemes, working practices and new practical ideas in personnel management in industry and commerce. Length: up to 2500 words. Payment: by arrangement. Illustrations: photographers and illustrators should contact art editor.

People's Friend

D.C. Thomson & Co. Ltd, 80 Kingsway East, Dundee DD4 8SL
tel (01382) 223131 *fax* (01382) 452491
185 Fleet Street, London EC4A 2HS
tel 0171-242 5086 *fax* 0171-404 5694
Weekly 48p

Illustrated weekly appealing to women of all ages and devoted to their personal and home interests, especially knitting, fashion and cookery. Serials (60,000-70,000 words) and complete stories (1500-3000 words) of strong romantic and emotional appeal. Stories for children are considered. No preliminary letter required. Illustrations: colour and b&w. Payment: on acceptance. Founded 1869.

People's Friend Library

D.C. Thomson & Co. Ltd, 2 Albert Square, Dundee DD1 9QJ
tel (01382) 223131*fax* (01382) 322214
185 Fleet Street, London EC4A 2HS
tel 0171-242 5086 *fax* 0171-404 5694
2 p.m. 85p

50,000-55,000-word family and romantic stories aimed at 30+ age group. Payment: by arrangement. No illustrations.

Perfect Home

DMG Home Interest Magazines Ltd, Times House, Station Approach, Ruislip, Middlesex HA4 8NB
tel (01895) 677677 *fax* (01895) 676027
Editor Julia Smith
Monthly £1.60

Home-related features: readers' homes, craft, finance, DIY, show houses, product testing/reviews, gardening. Length: 800-1000 words. Payment: by merit. Illustrated. Founded 1992.

Performance Car

EMAP National Publications Ltd, Bushfield House, Orton Centre, Peterborough PE2 5UW
tel (01733) 237111 *fax* (01733) 231137
Editor Brett Fraser
Monthly £2.75

Articles, 2000-3000 words, on all aspects of cars. Payment: by arrangement. Illustrations: half-tone, colour, cartoons. Founded 1983.

Period Living & Traditional Homes

EMAP Élan, Endeavour House,
189 Shaftesbury Avenue, London WC2H 8JG
tel 0171-437 9011 *fax* 0171-434 0656
Editor Clare Weatherall
Monthly £2.60

Articles and features on decoration, furnishings, renovation of period homes; traditional cookery; gardens, crafts, decorating in a period style. Illustrated. Payment: varies, according to work required. Founded 1990.

Personal – see Sunday Mirror in National newspapers UK and Ireland, page 3

Personal Computer World

VNU House, 32-34 Broadwick Street, London W1A 2HG
tel 0171-316 9000 *fax* 0171-316 9313
e-mail pcw@vnu.co.uk
web site www.pcw.co.uk
Editor Ben Tisdall
Monthly £2.95

Articles about computers; reviews. Length: 800-5000 words. Payment: from £130 per 1000 words. Illustrations: line, half-tone, colour. Founded 1978.

Personal Finance

Charterhouse Communications Group plc,
4 Tabernacle Street, London EC2A 4LU
tel 0171-638 1916 *fax* 0171-638 3128
e-mail chartcom@dircon.co.uk
Editor Juliet Oxborrow
Monthly £2.25

Articles and features on savings and investment, general family finance, of interest both to new investors and financially aware readers. All material commissioned: submit ideas in writing to the

editor. Length: 1500-3000 words. Illustrations: colour and b&w photos, colour line drawings. Payment: £150-£200 per 1000 words; £50-£150 for illustrations. Founded 1994.

Perspectives on Architecture

2 Hinde Street, London W1M 5RH
tel 0171-224 1766 *fax* 0171-224 1768
web site http://www.salvo.co.uk/mags/
perspectives.htm
Editor Dr Giles Worsley
Bi-monthly £3.50

Articles on architecture, design, conservation, urban and landscape issues for a general readership. Length: 800-1600 words (articles), 100-250 words (news). Illustrations: colour and b&w photos and colour artwork. Payment: £120 per 800 words; £30-£100 (photos), £150-£300 (artwork). Published in association with The Prince of Wales's Institute of Architecture. Founded 1994.

Petroleum Economist

(incorporating Gas World International)
Petroleum Economist Ltd, Baird House, 15-17 St Cross Street, London EC1N 8VN
tel 0171-831 5588 *fax* 0171-831 4567
Editor Chris Skrebowski
Monthly £12.00 (£95.00 p.a., £120/$195 p.a. USA/Europe)

Full news coverage and technical articles on all aspects of engineering and management in the gas industry. Length: up to 2500 words. Pictures and news items of topical interest accepted. Payment: by arrangement. Founded 1884.

The Pharmaceutical Journal

1 Lambeth High Street, London SE1 7JN
tel 0171-735 9141 *fax* 0171-582 7327
e-mail editor@pharmj.org.uk
Editor D. Simpson FRPharmS
Weekly £3.00

Official Journal of the Royal Pharmaceutical Society of Great Britain. Articles on any aspect of pharmacy may be submitted. Payment: by arrangement. Illustrations: half-tone, colour. Founded 1841.

Photo Answers

EMAP Apex Publications, Apex House, Oundle Road, Peterborough PE2 9NP
tel (01733) 898100 *fax* (01733) 894472
Editor Roger Payne
Monthly £2.20

Aimed at photographic beginners. Little opportunity for freelance writers, but plenty of scope for quality photos. Payment: £25 upwards, depending on size used; colour or mono.

Photo Technique

IPC Magazines, Kings Reach Tower, Stamford Street, London SE1 9LS
tel 0171-261 5100 *fax* 0171-261 5404
Editor Liz Walker
Monthly £2.50

For all photographers seeking to improve their camera, studio and darkroom skills. Aims to inspire the reader with great photography and an editorial tone which doesn't baffle or patronise. Please read magazine before submitting illustrated ideas for step-by-step features and general photo features. Some scope for field testing new equipment. Illustrations: max. 20 prints or transparencies; no prints over 10 x 8in. Payment: £100 per 1000 words; £90 per full page. Founded 1993.

Photon

(formerly photo pro)
Icon Publications Ltd, Maxwell Place, Maxwell Lane, Kelso, Roxburghshire TD5 7BB
tel (01573) 226032 *fax* (01573) 226000
Editor David Kilpatrick
Monthly £2.95

Illustrated features on professional and craft photography. All material commissioned. Length: 750-2500 words. Illustrations: b&w and colour photos. Payment: £50-£300 per feature, including photos. Rights to include one month's recompilation in Icon's World Wide Web Internet photo magazine. Founded 1989.

Picture Postcard Monthly

15 Debdale Lane, Keyworth, Nottingham NG12 5HT
tel 0115-937 4079 *fax* 0115-937 6197
Editor Brian Lund
Monthly £1.95 (£22.00 p.a.)

Articles, news and features for collectors of old or modern picture postcards. Length: 500-2000 words. Illustrations: colour and b&w. Payment: £52 per page; 50p per print. Founded 1978.

Pig Farming

Wharfedale Road, Ipswich IP1 4LG
tel (01473) 241122 *fax* (01473) 240501
Editor Bryan Kelly
Monthly £25.00 p.a.

Practical, well-illustrated articles on all aspects of pigmeat production required,

particularly those dealing with new ideas in pig management, feeding, housing, health and hygiene, product innovation and marketing. Length: 800-1200 words. Payment: by arrangement. Illustrations: line, half-tone, colour, cartoons.

Pilot

The Clock House, 28 Old Town, London SW4 0LB
tel 0171-498 2506 *fax* 0171-498 6920
e-mail compuserve @100126,563
Editor James Gilbert
Monthly £2.60

Feature articles on general aviation, private and business flying. Illustrations: line, half-tone, colour, cartoons. Payment: £100-£800 per article on acceptance; £25 for each photo used. Founded 1968.

The Pink Paper

72 Holloway Road, London N7 8NZ
tel 0171-296 6000 *fax* 0171-957 0046
e-mail editorial @pinkpaper.co.uk
Editor Paul Clements
Weekly Free

National newspaper for lesbians and gay men. Features (500-1500 words) and news (100-500 words) plus lifestyle section (features 700 words) on any gay-related subject. Illustrations: b&w photos and line plus colour 'scene' photos. Payment: £40-£100 for words; £30-£50 for illustrations. Founded 1988.

Planet

PO Box 44, Aberystwyth, Ceredigion SY23 5BS
tel (01970) 611255 *fax* (01970) 611197
Editor John Barnie
6 p.a. £2.50 (£12.00 p.a.)

Short stories, poems, topical articles on Welsh current affairs, politics, the environment and society. New literature in English. Length of articles: 1000-3500 words. Payment: £40 per 1000 words for prose; £25 minimum per poem. Illustrations: line, half-tone, cartoons. Founded 1970-9; relaunched 1985.

Playdays

BBC Worldwide Ltd, Room A1130, Woodlands, 80 Wood Lane, London W12 0TT
tel 0181-576 2693 *fax* 0181-576 2941
Editor Ruth Paley
Fortnightly 95p

Highly illustrated magazine of short stories, poems and activities for children aged 2-6 years old. No written material considered. Illustrations: colour and b&w

artwork. Payment: £100 per page. Founded 1994.

Plays & Players

Northway House, 1379 High Road, London N20 9LP
tel 0181-343 8515 *fax* 0181-446 1410
Editor Sandra Rennie
Monthly £2.50

Articles, reviews and photos on world theatre. Payment: by arrangement. Illustrations: line, photos.

PN Review

(formerly Poetry Nation)
Carcanet Press Ltd, 4th Floor, Conavon Court, 12 Blackfriars Street, Manchester M3 5BQ
tel 0161-834 8730 *fax* 0161-832 0084
e-mail pnr@carcanet.u-net.com
Editor Michael Schmidt
6 p.a. £4.50 (£24.50 p.a.)

Poems, essays, reviews, translations. Payment: by arrangement. Founded 1973.

Poetry Ireland Review/Éigse Éireann

Bermingham Tower, Upper Yard, Dublin Castle, Dublin 2, Republic of Ireland
tel (01) 671 4632 *fax* (01) 671 4634
e-mail poetry@iol.ie
Editor Frank Ormsby
Quarterly £5.00

Poetry. Features and articles by arrangement. Payment: £10 per contribution. Founded 1981.

Poetry London Newsletter

26 Clacton Road, London E17 8AR
tel 0181-520 6693 *fax* 0171-404 3598
e-mail pdaniels@easynet.co.uk
Editors Tamar Yoseloff, Pascale Petit, Katherine Gallagher, Peter Daniels
3 p.a. £9.00 p.a.

Poems of the highest standard, articles/ reviews on any aspect of modern poetry. Contributors must be knowledgeable about contemporary poetry. Payment: £20 or 4 copies of magazine. Founded 1988.

Poetry Nottingham International

13 Bradmore Rise, Sherwood, Nottingham NG5 3BJ
Editor Cathy Grindrod
Quarterly £2.25 (£9.00 p.a. UK, 15.00 p.a. overseas)

Poems; letters; articles up to 500 words on current issues in the poetry world. Payment: complimentary copy. Founded 1946.

Poetry Review
22 Betterton Street, London WC2H 9BU
tel 0171-240 4810 *fax* 0171-240 4818
e-mail poetrysoc@dial.pipex.com
web site http://www.poetrysoc.com/
Editor Peter Forbes
Quarterly £23.00 p.a. (£30.00 p.a. institutions, schools and libraries)

Poems, features and reviews; also cartoons. Send no more than 6 poems with sae. Preliminary study of magazine essential. Payment: £40 per poem.

Poetry Wales
First Floor, 2 Wyndham Street, Bridgend CF31 1EF
Books for review Amy Wack, 20 Denton Road, Canton, Cardiff CF5 1PE
Quarterly £3.00 (£12.00 p.a. inc. postage)

Poems mainly in English and mainly by Welsh people or resident: other contributors (and Welsh language poetry) also published. Articles on Welsh literature in English and in Welsh, as well as on poetry from other countries. Special features; reviews on poetry and wider matters. Payment: by arrangement. Founded 1965.

Police Journal
Little London, Chichester, West Sussex PO19 1PG
tel (01243) 787841 *fax* (01243) 779278
Editor R.W. Stone QPM
Quarterly £51.00 p.a.

Articles of technical or professional interest to the Police Service throughout the world. Payment: by negotiation. Illustrations: half-tone. Founded 1928.

Police Review
Celcon House, 5th Floor, 289-293 High Holborn, London WC1V 7HU
tel 0171-440 4700 *fax* 0171-405 7163
Editor Gary Mason
Weekly £1.25

News and features of interest to the police and legal professions. Length: 200-2000 words. Illustrations: colour and b&w photos, line, cartoons. Payment: NUJ rates. Founded 1893.

The Political Quarterly
Basil Blackwell Ltd, 108 Cowley Road, Oxford OX4 1JF
tel (01865) 791100
Editors Tony Wright MP, House of Commons, Westminster, London SW1A 1AA; and Andrew Gamble, Professor of Politics, University of Sheffield S10 2TU
Literary Editor Bernard Crick, 8A Bellevue Terrace, Edinburgh EH7 4DT
Assistant Editor Gilliam Bromley, PO Box 26, Wheatley, Oxon OX33 1FR
5 p.a. £53.50 p.a.

Journal devoted to topical aspects of national and international politics and public administration; takes a progressive, but not a party, point of view. Send articles to Assitant Editor; send books for review to the Literary Editor. Length: average 5000 words. Payment: c. £60 per article. Founded 1930.

Pony
Haslemere House, Lower Street, Haslemere, Surrey GU27 2PE
tel (01428) 651551 *fax* (01428) 653888
Editor Janet Rising
Monthly £1.20

Lively articles and short stories with a horsy theme aimed at young readers, 8 to 14 years old. Technical accuracy and young, fresh writing essential. Length: up to 800 words. Payment: by arrangement. Illustrations: drawings (commissioned) and interesting photos, cartoons. Founded 1949.

Popular Crafts
Nexus Special Interests, Nexus House, Boundary Way, Hemel Hempstead, Herts. HP2 7ST
tel (01442) 66551
Editor Carolyn Schulz
Monthly £2.25

Covers all kinds of crafts. Projects with full instructions, profiles and successes of craftspeople, news on craft group activities, readers' homes, celebrity interviews, general craft-related articles. Welcomes written outlines of ideas. Payment: by arrangement. Illustrated.

Post Magazine
Timothy Benn Publishing Ltd, 58 Fleet Street, London EC4Y 1JU
tel 0171-353 1107 *fax* 0171-583 6069
Editor Stephen Womack
Weekly £2.00 (£99.00 p.a.)

Commissioned specialist articles on topics of interest to insurance professionals; news, especially from overseas stringers. Length: 1700-2000 words. Illustrations: colour photos, colour and b&w cartoons and line drawings. Payment: £150-£200 per 1000 words; photos £30-£60, cartoons/line by negotiation. Founded 1840.

Poultry World

Quadrant House, The Quadrant, Sutton,
Surrey SM2 5AS
tel 0181-652 4021 *fax* 0181-652 4748
e-mail poultry.world@rbi.co.uk
Editor John Farrant
Monthly £1.90

Articles on poultry breeding, production,
marketing and packaging. News of international poultry interest. Payment: by
arrangement. Illustrations: photos, line.

PR Week

Haymarket Marketing Publications,
174 Hammersmith Road, London W6 7JP
tel 0171-413 4520 *fax* 0171-413 4509
Editor Stephen Farish
Weekly Controlled circulation (£60.00 p.a.)

News and features on public relations.
Length: approx. 800-3000 words.
Payment: £185 per 1000 words. Illustra-
tions: colour and b&w. Founded 1984.

Practical Boat Owner

Westover House, West Quay Road, Poole,
Dorset BH15 1JG
tel (01202) 680593
Editor Rodger Witt
Monthly £2.60

Hints, tips and practical articles for
cruising skippers – power and sail. Send
synopsis first. Payment: by negotiation.
Illustrations: photos or drawings.
Founded 1967.

Practical Caravan

Haymarket Magazines Ltd, 60 Waldegrave Road,
Teddington, Middlesex TW11 8LG
tel 0181-943 5629 *fax* 0181-943 5798
e-mail practicalcaravan@ukbusiness.com
Editor Rob McCabe
Monthly £2.40

Caravan-related travelogues, human
interest features, technical and DIY matters. Length: 1500-2500. Illustrations:
Colour. Payment: £120 per 1000 words;
negotiable. Founded 1967.

Practical Fishkeeping

(incorporating Fishkeeping Answers)
EMAP Apex, Apex House, Oundle Road,
Peterborough PE2 9NP
tel (01733) 898100
Editor Steve Windsor
Monthly £2.10

Hints, tips and practical articles for
cruising skippers – power and sail. Send
synopsis first. Payment: by arrangement.
Illustrations: line, half-tone, high quality

colour transparencies of tropical fish,
cartoons. Founded 1966.

Practical Householder

Nexus Media Ltd, Nexus House, Azalea Drive,
Swanley, Kent BR8 8HY
tel (01322) 660070 *fax* (01322) 667633
Editor John McGowan
Monthly £2.00

Articles about 1500 words in length,
about practical matters concerning home
improvement. Payment: according to
subject. Illustrations: line, half-tone, cartoons. Founded 1955.

Practical Motorist

Crownwheel Publishing Co. Ltd, Frogham,
Fordingbridge, Hants SP6 2HW
tel (01425) 654255 *fax* (01425) 653458
Editor Ewan Scott
£2.25 Monthly

Practical articles on maintaining the
modern car: servicing, repair and tuning
for all makes of cars; also practical hints
and tips. Unsolicited articles welcome
but phone first. Payment: by arrangement. Illustrations: b&w, colour prints or
transparencies, line drawings, artwork.
Founded 1934.

Practical Parenting

IPC Magazines Ltd, King's Reach Tower,
Stamford Street, London SE1 9LS
tel 0171-261 5058 *fax* 0171-261 5366
Editor-in-Chief Jayne Marsden
Monthly £1.60

Articles on parenting, baby and childcare, health, psychology, education, children's activities, personal birth/parenting
experiences. Send synopsis, with sae.
Illustrations: commissioned only; colour:
photos, line, cartoons. Payment: £100-
£150 per 1000 words; illustrations by
agreement. Founded 1987.

Practical Photography

Apex House, Oundle Road, Peterborough PE2 9NP
tel (01733) 898100 *fax* (01733) 894472
Editor Martyn Moore
Monthly £2.60

Features on any aspect of photography
with practical bias. Mostly written by
staff journalists, but freelance ideas welcome. Send brief synopsis only in first
instance. Illustrations: line, half-tone,
colour, cartoons. Payment: from £50 per
1000 words; from £10 b&w or colour.
Founded 1959.

Practical Wireless

PW Publishing Ltd, Arrowsmith Court, Station Approach, Broadstone, Dorset BH18 8PW
tel (01202) 659910 *fax* (01202) 659950
Editor Rob Mannion G3XFD
Monthly 72p

Articles on the practical and theoretical aspects of amateur radio and communications. Constructional projects. Illustrations: in b&w and colour; photos, line drawings and wash half-tone for offset litho. Payment: by arrangement. Founded 1932.

Practical Woodworking

Nexus Special Interests Ltd, Nexus House, Boundary Way, Hemel Hempstead, Herts. HP2 7ST
tel (01442) 66551 *fax* (01442) 66998
Editor Peter Roper
Monthly £2.35

Articles of a practical nature covering any aspect of woodworking, including woodworking projects, tools, joints or timber technology. Payment: £65 per published page. Illustrated.

The Practitioner

30 Calderwood Street, London SE18 6QH
tel 0181-855 7777 *fax* 0181-855 2406
Editor Harvey Jones
Monthly £10.00 (£66.00 p.a. UK, $155.00 p.a. overseas)

Articles of interest to GPs and vocational trainees, and others in the medical profession. Payment: approx. £150 per 1000 words. Founded 1868.

Prediction

Link House, Dingwall Avenue, Croydon CR9 2TA
tel 0181-686 2599 *fax* 0181-781 1159
Editor Jo Logan
Monthly £1.95

Articles on astrology and all occult subjects. Length: up to 2000 words. Payment: by arrangement. Illustrations: for cover use only: large colour transparencies (i.e. not 35mm). Founded 1936.

Prep School

Stone Delf, Mottingham Lane, London SE9 4RW
tel 0181-851 2706 *fax* 0181-851 4914
Editor David Tytler
3 p.a. £9.00 p.a.

Journal of the Preparatory School world: the magazine of IAPS and SATIPS. Articles of educational interest covering ages 4-13. Length: about 1000 words. Illustrations: line, half-tone. Payment: by arrangement.

Pride

Hamilton House, 55 Battersea Bridge Road, London SW11 3AX
tel 0171-228 3110 *fax* 0171-228 3130
Editor Marcia Degia
Monthly £2.20

Celebrity interviews and lifestyle features of interest to young black women; also food, health and fitness, fashion and beauty. Length: 1000-3000 words. Illustrations: colour photos and drawings. Payment: £100 per 1000 words. Founded 1993; relaunched 1994, 1996.

Priests & People

Blackfriars, Buckingham Road, Cambridge CB3 0DD
tel (01223) 359376
Editor Rev. D.C. Sanders OP
Monthly £2.00

Journal of pastoral theology especially for parish ministry and for Christians of English-speaking countries. Illustrations: occasional b&w photos, cartoons. Length and payment by arrangement.

Prima

Portland House, Stag Place, London SW1E 5AU
tel 0171-245 8700
Editor Lindsay Nicholson
Monthly £1.60

Articles on fashion, crafts, health and beauty, cookery; features. Illustrations: half-tone, colour. Founded 1986.

Printing World

Miller Freeman Publishers Ltd, Miller Freeman House, Sovereign Way, Tonbridge, Kent TN9 1RW
tel (01732) 364422 *fax* (01732) 377552
Editor Gareth Ward
Weekly £2.70 (£78.00 p.a., overseas £112.00 p.a.)

Commercial, technical, financial and labour news covering all aspects of the printing industry in the UK and abroad. Outside contributions. Payment: by arrangement. Illustrations: line, half-tone, colour, cartoons. Founded 1878.

Private Eye

6 Carlisle Street, London W1V 5RG
tel 0171-437 4017 *fax* 0171-437 0705
e-mail strobes @cix.compulink.co.uk
web http://www.compulink.co.uk/~private-eye/
Editor Ian Hislop
Fortnightly £1.00

Satire. Payment: by arrangement. Illustrations: b&w, line, cartoons. Founded 1962.

Professional Nurse

Macmillan Magazines Ltd, Porters South,
4-6 Crinan Street, London N1 9SQ
tel 0171-833 4000 *fax* 0171-843 4699
e-mail pn@macmillan.com
Editor Rosemary Rogers
Monthly £35.00 p.a.

Articles of interest to the professional
nurse. Length: articles: 2000-3000 words;
letters: 250-500 words. Payment: by
arrangement. Illustrations: line, half-tone,
colour. Founded 1985.

Professional Photographer

Market Link Publishing Ltd, The Mill,
Bearwalden Business Park, Royston Road,
Wendens Ambo, Saffron Walden, Essex CB11 4JX
tel (01799) 544200 *fax* (01799) 544201
Editor Steve Hynes
Monthly £2.50

Articles on professional photography,
including technical articles, photographer profiles and coverage of issues affecting the industry. Length: 1000-2000
words. Illustrations: colour and b&w
prints and transparencies, diagrams if
appropriate. Payment: from £90 per page
for articles and pro rata for illustrations.
Founded 1961.

Property Week

The Builder Group, Exchange Tower, 2 Harbour
Exchange Square, London E14 9GE
tel 0171-560 4000 *fax* 0171-560-4012
Editor Penny Guest
Weekly £55.00 p.a.

News and features on commercial property, occupational management and
financial issues. Length: by negotiation.
Illustrations: contact art director, Peter
Smith. Payment: £170 per 1000 words;
up to £150-£200. Founded 1982.

Prospect

Prospect Publishing Ltd, 4 Bedford Square,
London WC1B 3RA
tel 0171-255 1281 *fax* 0171-255 1279
e-mail 100643.455@compuserve.com
Editor David Goodhart
Monthly £2.95

Politics and current affairs. Essays, features, special reports, reviews, short stories, opinions/analysis. Length: 3000-
6000 words (essays, special reports,
short stories), 1000 words (opinions).
Illustrations: colour and b&w. Payment:
£150 per 1000 words; £75. Founded
1995.

Publishing News

43 Museum Street, London WC1A 1LY
tel 0171-404 0304
Editor Fred Newman
Weekly £1.80

Articles and news items on books and
publishers. Payment: £80-£100 per 1000
words. Illustrations: half-tone, cartoons.
Founded 1979.

Pulse

Miller Freeman Professional Ltd,
30 Calderwood Street, London SE18 6QH
tel 0181-855 7777 *fax* 0181-855 2406
Editor Howard Griffiths
Weekly £150.00 p.a.

Articles and photos of direct interest to
GPs. Purely clinical material can only be
accepted from medically qualified
authors. Length: up to 750 words.
Payment: £150 average. Illustrations:
b&w and colour photos.

Punch

Liberty Publishing, 100 Brompton Road,
London SW3 1ER
tel 0171-225 6716 *fax* 0171-225 6766
e-mail edit@punch.co.uk
Editor Paul Spike
Weekly £1.00

A satirical and investigative magazine
with cartoons. Illustrations: colour and
b&w. Payment: by arrangement. Founded
1841; relaunched 1996.

Q Magazine

EMAP Metro, Mappin House, 4 Winsley Street,
London W1N 7AR
tel 0171-436 1515 *fax* 0171-312 8247
e-mail q_magazine@dial.pipex.com
web site http://www.erack.com/qweb
Editor David Davies
Monthly £2.60

Glossy modern guide to more than just
rock music. All material commissioned.
Length: 1200-2500 words. Illustrations:
colour and b&w photos. Payment: £180
per 1000 words; illustrations by arrangement. Founded 1986.

Quaker Monthly

Quaker Home Service, Friends House,
Euston Road, London NW1 2BJ
tel 0171-387 3601 *fax* 0171-388 1977
Editor Elizabeth Cave
Monthly 75p (£11.70 p.a.)

Articles, poems, reviews, expanding the
Quaker approach to the spiritual life.
Writers should be members or attenders

of a Quaker meeting. Illustrations: line, half-tone. Payment: none. Founded 1921.

QWF
80 Main Street, Linton, Nr Swadlincote, Derbyshire DE12 6QA
tel (01283) 761042
Editor Jo Good
Bi-monthly £3.75 (£20.00 p.a.)

'Extending the boundaries of women's fiction.' Short stories to appeal to a pre-dominantly female readership and occa-sional articles on writing. Length: up to 3000 words. Illustrations: b&w cover design only. Payment: £5 (articles/fea-tures), £10 or free subscription (short sto-ries); £10 (cover). Founded 1994.

RA Magazine
Royal Academy of Arts, Burlington House, Piccadilly, London W1V 0DS
tel 0171-494 5657 *fax* 0171-287 9023
Editor Nick Tite
Quarterly £4.00

Topical articles relating to the Royal Academy, its history and its exhibitions. Length: 500-1500 words. Illustrations: consult editor. Payment: £100 per 1000 words; illustrations by negotiation. Founded 1983.

Radio Control Models and Electronics
Nexus Special Interests, Nexus House, Boundary Way, Hemel Hempstead, Herts. HP2 7ST
tel (01442) 66551 *fax* (01442) 66998
Editor Kevin Crozier
Monthly £2.25

Well-illustrated articles on topics related to radio control. Payment: £35 per pub-lished page. Illustrations: line, half-tone. Founded 1960.

Radio Times
BBC Worldwide Ltd, Woodlands, 80 Wood Lane, London W12 0TT
tel 0181-576 3999 *fax* 0181-576 3160
web site http://www.radiotimes.beeb.com
Editor Sue Robinson
Weekly 75p

Articles that preview the week's pro-grammes on British television and radio. All articles are specially commissioned – ideas and synopses are welcomed but not unsolicited MSS. Length: 600-2500 words. Payment: by arrangement. Illustrations: in colour and b&w; photos, graphic designs or drawings.

Rail
Emap Apex Publications, Apex House, Oundle Road, Peterborough PE2 9NP
tel (01733) 898100 *fax* (01733) 894472
e-mail rail@ecm.emap.com
Managing Editor Nigel Harris
Fortnightly £1.95

News and in-depth features on current UK railway operations. Length: 2000-3000 words (features), 250-400 words (news). Illustrations: colour and b&w photos and artwork. Payment: £75 per 1000 words; £17 per photo except cover (£70) and Comment (£50). Founded 1981.

Railway Gazette International
Reed Business Information, Quadrant House, The Quadrant, Sutton, Surrey SM2 5AS
tel 0181-652 3739 *fax* 0181-652 3738
Editor Murray Hughes
Monthly £47.00 p.a.

Deals with management, engineering, operation and finance of railways world-wide. Articles of practical interest on these subjects are considered and paid for if accepted. Illustrated articles, of 1000-3000 words, are preferred. A pre-liminary letter is required.

Railway Magazine
IPC Magazines Ltd, King's Reach Tower, Stamford Street, London SE1 9LS
tel 0171-261 5821 *fax* 0171-261 5269
Editor Nick Pigott
Monthly £2.40

Illustrated magazine dealing with all rail-way subjects; no fiction or verse. Articles from 1500-2000 words accompanied by photos. Preliminary letter desirable. Payment: by arrangement. Illustrations: colour transparencies, half-tone and line. Founded 1897.

Rambling Today
1-5 Wandsworth Road, London SW8 2XX
tel 0171-582 6878 *fax* 0171-587 3799
Editor Annabelle Birchall
Quarterly Free to members

Official magazine of The Ramblers' Association. Articles on walking, access to countryside and related issues. Material mostly commissioned. Length: about 1000 words. Illustrations: colour slides. Payment: by agreement. Founded 1935.

Reader's Digest

The Reader's Digest Association Ltd,
Berkeley Square House, Berkeley Square,
London W1X 6AB
tel 0171-629 8144
e-mail excerpts@readersdigest.co.uk
web site http://readersdigest.co.uk
Editor Russell Twisk
Monthly £1.90

Original anecdotes – £200 for up to 150 words – are required for humorous features. Booklet 'Writing for Reader's Digest' available £2.50 post free.

Reality

Redemptorist Publications,
Orwell Road, Rathgar, Dublin 6,
Republic of Ireland
tel (01) 4922488 *fax* (01) 4922654
Editor Rev. Gerry Moloney CSSR
Monthly 80p

Illustrated magazine for Christian living. Articles on all aspects of modern life, including family, youth, religion, leisure. Illustrated articles, b&w photos only. Short stories. Length: 1000-1500 words. Payment: by arrangement; average £25 per 1000 words. Founded 1936.

Red Pepper

Socialist Newspaper (Publications) Ltd,
1A Waterlow Road, London N19 5NJ
e-mail redpepper@online.rednet.co.uk
Editor Hilary Wainwright
Monthly £1.95

Independent radical magazine: news and features on politics, culture and everyday life of interest to the left and greens. Material mostly commissioned. Length: news/news features 200-800 words, other features 800-2000 words. Illustrations: b&w photos, cartoons, graphics. Payment: by arrangement. Founded 1994.

Red Tape

Civil and Public Services Association,
160 Falcon Road, London SW11 2LN
tel 0171-924 2727 *fax* 0171-924 1847
Editor Val Stansfield
10 p.a. 80p Free to members

Well-written articles on Civil Service, trade union and general subjects considered. Length: 750-1400 words. Also photos and humorous drawings of interest to Civil Servants. Illustrations: line, half-tone. Payment: NUJ rates. Founded 1911.

Reform

86 Tavistock Place, London WC1H 9RT
tel 0171-916 2020 *fax* 0171-916 2021 (mark: for 'Reform')
e-mail reform@urc.compulink.co.uk
Editor David Lawrence
Monthly £1.15 (£9.50 p.a.)

Published by United Reformed Church. Articles of religious or social comment. Length: 600-1000 words. Illustrations: line, half-tone, colour, cartoons. Payment: by arrangement. Founded 1972.

Report

ATL, 7 Northumberland Street,
London WC2N 5DA
tel 0171-930 6441 *fax* 0171-925 0529
e-mail newsdesk@atl.org.uk
web site http://www.atl.org.uk
Editor Richard Margrave
8 p.a. £2.50 (£10.00 p.a. UK; £12.00 p.a. overseas)

The magazine from the Association of Teachers and Lecturers (ATL). Features, articles, comment, news about nursery, primary, secondary and further education. Payment: minimum £60 per 1000 words.

Retail Week

EMAP Business Communications, Maclaren House, 19 Scarbrook Road, Croydon, Surrey CR9 1QH
tel 0181-277 5331 *fax* 0181-277 5344
Editor Ian McGarrigle
Weekly Controlled circulation (£80.00 p.a.)

Features and news stories on all aspects of retail management. Length: up to 1000 words. Illustrations: colour and b&w photos. Payment: £120 per 1000 words; photos at market rates. Founded 1988.

The Rialto

PO Box 309, Aylsham, Norwich NR11 6LN
Editor Michael Mackmin
3 p.a. £3.90 (£10.00 p.a., £8.00 p.a. low income)

Poetry and criticism. Sae essential. Payment: by arrangement. Founded 1984.

Ride

Emap National Publications Ltd, Bushfield House, Orton Centre, Peterborough PE2 5UW
tel (01733) 237111 *fax* (01733) 465804
Editor Tim Thompson
Monthly £2.40

Review features on tests of used motorbikes, services and related products. Length: 2000 words (features), 200 words

(news). Illustrations: colour. Payment: £120 per 1000 words (features), £200 per 1000 words (news); £220 per day (photos). Founded 1995.

Right Start
Needmarsh Publishing Ltd, 71 Newcomen Street, London SE1 1YT
tel 0171-403 0840 *fax* 0171-378 6883
Editor Anita Bevan
Bi-monthly £1.50

Features on all aspects of pre-school and infant education, child health and behaviour. No unsolicited MSS. Length: 1200-1500 words. Illustrations: colour photos, line. Payment: varies. Founded 1989.

Rugby World
IPC Magazines Ltd, Kings Reach Tower, Stamford Street, London SE1 9LS
tel 0171-261 6830 *fax* 0171-261 5419
Editor Alison Kervin
Monthly £2.40

Features and exclusive news stories on rugby. Length: approx. 1200 words. Illustrations: colour photos, cartoons. Payment: £120. Founded 1960.

Runner's World
Rodale Press Ltd, 7-10 Chandos Street, London W1M 0AD
tel 0171-291 6000 *fax* 0171-291 6080
Editor Steven Seaton
Monthly £2.40

Articles on jogging, running and fitness. Payment: by arrangement. Illustrations: line, half-tone, colour, cartoons. Founded 1979.

RUSI Journal
Whitehall, London SW1A 2ET
tel 0171-930 5854 *fax* 0171-321 0943
e-mail editorial@rusids.demon.co.uk
web site http://www.almac.co.uk/nmt/rusi-defence
Editorial Manager Alexandra Citron
Bi-monthly £6.00

Journal of the Royal United Services Institute for Defence Studies. Articles on international security, the military sciences, defence technology and procurement, and military history; also book reviews and correspondence. Length: 3000-4000 words. Illustrations: b&w photos, maps and diagrams. Payment: £12.50 per printed page upon publication.

RX Magazine – see Sunday Telegraph in National newspapers UK and Ireland, page 3

Safety Education
Royal Society for the Prevention of Accidents, Edgbaston Park, 353 Bristol Road, Birmingham B5 7ST
tel 0121-248 2000 *fax* 0121-248 2001
Editor Carole Wale
3 p.a. £7.50 p.a. for members of Safety Education Department (£10.50 p.a. non-members)

Articles on every aspect of good practice in safety education including safety of teachers and pupils in school, and the teaching of road, home, water, leisure and personal safety by means of established subjects on the school curriculum. All ages. Commissioned material only. Illustrations: line, half-tone, colour. Payment: by negotiation. Founded as *Child Safety* 1937; became *Safety Training* 1940; 1966.

Saga Magazine
The Saga Building, Middelburg Square, Folkestone, Kent CT20 1AZ
tel (01303) 711523 *fax* (01303) 712699
Editor Paul Bach
Monthly £12.95 p.a.

Articles relevant to interests of 50+ age group, and profiles of celebrities in same age group. Mostly commissioned or written in-house, but genuine exclusives always welcome. Length: 1200-1800 words. Illustrations: colour transparencies, commissioned colour artwork. Payment: competitive rate. Founded 1984.

Sainsbury's: The Magazine
New Crane Publishing, 20 Upper Ground, London SE1 9PD
tel 0171-633 0266 *fax* 0171-401 9423
Editor Michael Wynn Jones
Monthly £1.00

Features: general, food and drink, health and humour; all material commissioned. Length: from 1500 words. Illustrations: colour and b&w photos and line illustrations. Payment: varies; £300 per full page for illustrations. Founded 1993.

Satellite Times
The Stables, West Hill Grange, North Road, Horsforth, Leeds LS18 5HG
tel 0113-258 5008 *fax* 0113-258 9745
Editor Eric Woods
Monthly £2.00

Television and film personality articles and interviews, sports articles, music, competitions. Payment: by negotiation. Founded 1988.

Scale Models International

Nexus Special Interests, Nexus House,
Boundary Way, Hemel Hempstead,
Herts. HP2 7ST
tel (01442) 66551 *fax* (01442) 66998
Editor Kelvin Barber
Monthly £2.10

Articles on scale models. Length: up to
2500 words. Payment: £25-£30 per page.
Illustrations: line, half-tone, colour.

School Librarian

The School Library Association,
Liden Library, Barrington Close, Liden,
Swindon, Wilts. SN3 6HF
tel (01793) 617838
Editor Raymond Astbury, *Review Editor* Keith
Barker, *SL2001 Editor* Mary Mabey
Quarterly Free to members (£45.00 p.a.)

The official journal of the School Library
Association. Reviews of books, CD-Roms
and other library resources from pre-
school to young adult. Articles on school
library organisation, use and skills, and
on authors and illustrators. Length: 1800-
3000 words. Payment: by arrangement.
Founded 1937.

Science Progress

Science Reviews, 41-43 Green Lane, Northwood,
Middlesex HA6 3AE
tel (01923) 823586 *fax* (01923) 825066
e-mail scitech@clac3.ch.kcl.ac.uk
Editor Prof David Phillips and Prof Robin
Rowbury
Quarterly £95.15 p.a. (£105.00 p.a. overseas)

Articles of 6000 words on new scientific
developments, written so as to be intelli-
gible to workers in other disciplines.
Imperative to submit synopsis before
full-length article. Payment: by arrangement. Illustrations: line, half-tone.

Scientific Computing World

IOP Publishing Ltd, Dirac House, Temple Back,
Bristol BS1 6BE
tel 0117-929 7481 *fax* 0117-925 1942
e-mail scicomp@ioppublishing.co.uk
web site http://www.iop.org
Editor Vanessa Spedding
10 p.a. Free to qualifying subscribers

Features on hardware and software
developments for the scientific community, plus news articles and reviews.
Length: 800-2000 words. Illustrations:
colour transparencies, photos, electronic
graphics. Payment: by negotiation.
Founded 1994.

Scootering

PO Box 46, Weston-super-Mare,
Somerset BS23 1AF
tel (01934) 414785
Editor Stuart Lanning
Monthly £2.60

Custom, racing and vintage scooter features, plus technical information. Music
features and related lifestyle pieces.
Payment: by arrangement. Illustrations:
half-tone, colour, cartoons. Founded 1985.

Scotland on Sunday Magazine – see Scotland on Sunday in National newspapers UK and Ireland, page 3

The Scots Magazine

D.C. Thomson & Co. Ltd, 2 Albert Square,
Dundee DD1 9QJ
tel (01382) 223131 *fax* (01382) 322214
Monthly £1.15

Articles on all subjects of Scottish interest. Short stories, poetry, but must be
Scottish. Illustrations: colour and b&w
photos, drawings, cartoons. Payment:
£22 per 1000 words; from £12. Founded
1739.

The Scotsman Weekend – see The Scotsman in National newspapers UK and Ireland, page 3

Scottish Book Collector

c/o 36 Lauriston Place, Edinburgh EH3 9EZ
tel 0131-228 4837 *fax* 0131-228 3904
Editor Jennie Renton
Quarterly £2.50

Articles on collecting Scottish books; lit-
erary/bibliographical articles on books
published in Scotland or by Scottish
writers. Length: 1500-2500 words.
Payment: £25 per article. Founded 1987.

Scottish Educational Journal

Educational Institute of Scotland,
46 Moray Place, Edinburgh EH3 6BH
tel 0131-225 6244 *fax* 0131-220 3151
Editor Simon Macaulay
5 p.a. plus Specials £9.00 p.a.

The Scottish Farmer

The Plaza Tower, East Kilbride, Glasgow G74 1LW
tel (013552) 46444 *fax* (013552) 63013
Editor Alasdair Fletcher
Weekly £1.30

Articles on agricultural subjects. Length:
1000-1500 words. Payment: £80 per 1000
words. Illustrations: line, half-tone,
colour. Founded 1893.

Scottish Field

Special Publications, Royston House,
Caroline Park, Edinburgh EH5 1QJ
tel 0131-551 2942 *fax* 0131-551 2938
Editor Archie Mackenzie
Monthly £2.35

Will consider all material with a Scottish
link and good photos. Payment: by negotiation. Founded 1903.

Scottish Home and Country

42A Heriot Row, Edinburgh EH3 6ES
tel 0131-225 1934 *fax* 0131-225 8129
Editor Stella Roberts
Monthly 75p

Articles on crafts, cookery, travel, personal experience, village histories, country customs, DIY, antiques, farming;
humorous rural stories; fashion, health,
books. Length: up to 1000 words, preferably illustrated. Illustrations: colour
prints/transparencies, b&w, cartoons.
Payment: by arrangement. Founded
1924.

Scouting

The Scout Association, Baden-Powell House,
Queens Gate, London SW7 5JS
tel 0171-584 7030 *fax* 0171-590 5124
Editor David Easton
Monthly £1.25

National magazine of the Scout
Association. Ideas, news, views, features and programme resources for
Leaders and Supporters. Training material, accounts of Scouting events and
articles of general interest with Scouting
connections. Illustrations: photos —
action shots preferred rather than static
posed shots for use with articles or as
fillers or cover potential, cartoons.
Payment: on publication by arrangement.

Screen International

EMAP Business Publishing,
33-39 Bowling Green Lane,
London EC1R 0DA
tel 0171-505 8080 *fax* 0171-505 8117
e-mail boydf@media.emap.co.uk,
100064.2744@compuserve.com
Editor Boyd Farrow
Weekly £1.90

International news and features on every
aspect of films, television and associated
media. Length: variable. Payment: by
arrangement.

Sea Angler

EMAP Pursuit Publishing Ltd, Bretton Court,
Bretton, Peterborough PE3 8DZ
tel (01733) 465307 *fax* (01733) 465436
Editor Mel Russ
Monthly £2.20

Topical articles on all aspects of sea-fish-
ing around the British Isles. Payment: by
arrangement. Illustrations: colour.
Founded 1973.

Sea Breezes

Units 28-30, Spring Valley Industrial Estate,
Braddan, Isle of Man IM2 2QS
tel (01624) 626018 *fax* (01624) 661655
Editor A.C. Douglas
Monthly £1.95

Factual articles on ships and the sea past
and present, preferably illustrated.
Length: up to 4000 words. Illustrations:
line, half-tone, colour. Payment: by
arrangement. Founded 1919.

Select Magazine

EMAP Metro, Mappin House, 4 Winsley Street,
London W1N 5AR
tel 0171-436 1515 *fax* 0171-637 0456
Editor Andrew Harrison
Monthly £2.20

Off-the-wall youth/music feature ideas
for hip 18-25-year-olds. Length: decided
on commissioning. Illustrations: colour
and b&w rock/pop photography with an
arty/provocative bent. Payment: £120 per
1000 words; illustrations £110 per page.
Founded 1990.

She

National Magazine House, 72 Broadwick Street,
London W1V 2BP
tel 0171-439 5000 *fax* 0171-439 5350
Editor Alison Pylkkanen
Monthly £2.00

No unsolicited manuscripts. Ideas with
synopses welcome on subjects ranging
from health and relationships to child
care and careers. Payment: NUJ freelance
rates. Illustrations: photos, cartoons.
Founded 1955.

Ship & Boat International

Royal Institution of Naval Architects,
10 Upper Belgrave Street, London SW1X 8BQ
tel 0171-235 4622 *fax* 0171-245 6959
Editor Richard White
Monthly £50.00 p.a.

Technical articles on the design, construction and operation of all types of
specialised small ships and workboats.

Length: 500-1500 words. Payment: by arrangement. Illustrations: line and half-tone, photos and diagrams.

Ships Monthly
Ships Monthly Ltd, 222 Branston Road, Burton-on-Trent DE14 3BT
tel (01283) 542721 *fax* (01283) 546436
Editor Robert Shopland
Monthly £1.95

Illustrated articles of shipping interest – both mercantile and naval, preferably of 20th century ships. Well-researched, factual material only. No short stories or poetry. 'Notes for Contributors' available. Mainly commissioned material; preliminary letter essential, with sae. Payment: by arrangement. Illustrations: half-tone and line, colour transparencies and prints. Founded 1966.

Shoot
(incorporating 90 Minutes)
IPC Magazines Ltd, King's Reach Tower, Stamford Street, London SE1 9LS
tel 0171-261 6287 *fax* 0171-261 6019
Editor David C. Smith
Weekly 80p

Football magazine for young males. News, features, profiles of big names in football, posters. Length: 300-400 words (features), 100 words (news). Illustrations: colour transparencies, artwork and cartoons. Payment: negotiable. Founded 1969.

Shooting Times and Country Magazine
IPC Magazines Ltd, King's Reach Tower, Stamford Street, London SE1 9LS
tel 0171-261 6180 *fax* 0171-261 7179
Editor John Gregson
Weekly £1.45

Articles on fieldsports, especially shooting, and on related natural history and countryside topics. Length: up to 2000 words. Payment: by arrangement. Illustrations: photos, drawings, colour transparencies. Founded 1882.

The Short Wave Magazine
G8VFH, Arrowsmith Court, Station Approach, Broadstone, Dorset BH18 8PW
tel (01202) 659910 *fax* (01202) 659950
Editor Dick Ganderton
Monthly £2.50 (£25.00 p.a.)

Technical and semi-technical articles, 500-5000 words, dealing with design, construction and operation of radio receiving equipment. Radio-related photo

features welcome. Payment: £55 per page. Illustrations: line, half-tone, cartoons. Founded 1937.

Shout
D.C. Thomson & Co. Ltd, Albert Square, Dundee DD1 9QJ
tel (01382) 223131 *fax* (01382) 200880
185 Fleet Street, London EC4A 2HS
tel 0171-242 5086 *fax* 0171-404 5694
Fortnightly 95p

Colour gravure magazine for 12-16-year-old girls. Pop, film and 'soap' features and pin-ups; general features of teen interest; emotional features, fashion and beauty advice. Illustrations: colour transparencies. Payment: on acceptance. Founded 1993.

The Shropshire Magazine
The Leopard Press Ltd, 77 Wyle Cop, Shrewsbury, Shropshire SY1 1UT
tel (01743) 362175
Editor Pam Green
Monthly £1.00

Articles on topics related to Shropshire, including countryside, history, characters, legends, education, food; also home and garden features. Length: up to 1500 words. Illustrations: b&w photos, line drawings. Payment: £15-£20; illustrations by arrangement. Founded 1950.

Sight and Sound
21 Stephen Street, London W1P 1PL
tel 0171-255 1444 *fax* 0171-436 2327
Editor Nick James
Published by British Film Institute
Monthly £2.70

Topical and critical articles on the cinema of any country; book reviews; reviews of every film theatrically released in London; reviews of every video released; regular columns from the USA and Europe. Length: 1000-5000 words. Payment: by arrangement. Illustrations: relevant photos, cartoons. Founded 1932.

The Sign
Chansitor Publications Ltd, St Mary's Works, St Mary's Plain, Norwich, Norfolk NR3 3BH
tel (01603) 615995 *fax* (01603) 624483
Publisher G.A. Knights
Monthly 5p

Leading national insert for C of E parish magazines. Articles of interest to parishes. Items should bear the author's name and address; return postage essential. Length: up to 400 words. Illustrations: unusual

b&w photos, drawings considered.
Payment: by arrangement. Founded 1905.

Signal, Approaches to Children's Books

Lockwood, Station Road, South Woodchester, Stroud, Glos. GL5 5EQ
tel (01453 87) 3716/2208 *fax* (01453 87) 8599
Editor Nancy Chambers
3 p.a. £4.25 (£12.75 p.a.)

Articles on any aspect of children's books or the children's book world. Length: no limit but average 2500-3000 words. Payment: £3 per printed page. Illustrations: line occasionally. Founded 1970.

The Skier and The Snowboarder Magazine

48 London Road, Sevenoaks, Kent TN13 1AS
tel (01732) 743644 *fax* (01732) 743647
Editor Frank Baldwin
5 p.a. (Sept-May) £2.50

Ski features, based around a good story. Length: 800-1000 words. Illustrations: colour action ski photos. Payment: by negotiation. Founded 1984.

Sky Magazine

Hachette Emap, Mappin House, 4 Winsley Street, London W1N 7AR
tel 0171-436 1515 *fax* 0171-312 8248
Editor Mark Frith
Monthly £2.20

People, movies, music and style. Length: varies. Illustrations: colour and b&w photos. Payment: by arrangement.

Slimmer Magazine

Turret Rai plc, Armstrong House, 38 Market Square, Uxbridge, Middlesex UB8 1TG
tel (01895) 454545 *fax* (01895) 454647
Editor Sarah Stowe
Bi-monthly £1.75

Features on health, nutrition, slimming. Personal weight loss stories. Sae essential. Length: 500 or 1500 words. Payment: £10 per 100 words. Founded 1972.

Slimming Magazine

Victory House, 14 Leicester Place, London WC2H 7BP
tel 0171-437 9011 *fax* 0171-434 0656
Editor Christine Michael
10 p.a. £1.75

Articles on psychology, lifestyle and health related to diet and nutrition. Approach editor in writing with ideas. Length: 1000-1500 words. Payment: by negotiation. Founded 1969.

Smallholder

Hook House, Hook Road, Wimblington, March, Cambs. PE15 0QL
tel/fax (01354) 741182
Editor Liz Wright
Monthly £1.90

Articles of relevance to small farmers about livestock and crops; items relating to the countryside considered. Send for copy. Payment: £20 per 1000 words or by arrangement. Illustrations: line, half-tone, cartoons. Founded 1985.

Smash Hits

Mappin House, 4 Winsley Street, London W1N 7AR
tel 0171-436 1515 *fax* 0171-636 5792
Editor Gavin Reeve
Fortnightly 90p

News interviews and posters of pop, TV and film stars. Illustrations: colour photos. Payment: £100 per page and per photo.

Snooker Scene

Cavalier House, 202 Hagley Road, Edgbaston, Birmingham B16 9PQ
tel 0121-454 2931 *fax* 0121-452 1822
Editor Clive Everton
Monthly £1.50

News and articles about snooker. Payment: by arrangement. Illustrations: photos. Founded 1971.

Solicitors Journal

FT Law & Tax, 21-27 Lamb's Conduit Street, London WC1N 3NJ
tel 0171-420 7500 *fax* 0171-420 7595
Weekly £2.40

Articles, by practising lawyers or specialist journalists, on subjects of practical interest to solicitors. Articles sent on spec should be on computer disk. Length: up to 1800 words. Payment: by negotiation. Founded 1856.

Somerset Magazine

Smart Print Publications Ltd, 23 Market Street, Crewkerne, Somerset TA18 7JU
tel (01460) 78000 *fax* (01460) 76718
Editor Roy Smart
Monthly £1.85

Articles, features with particular reference to county locations, facilities and other interests. Length: 1000-1500 words. Illustrations: line, half-tone, colour (transparencies or prints). Payment: by arrangement. Founded 1977 as Somerset & West.

The Songwriter

International Songwriters Association,
PO Box 46, Limerick City, Republic of Ireland
tel (061) 228837
Editor James D. Liddane
Monthly Available to members only as part of
membership fee

Articles on songwriting and interviews with music publishers and recording company executives. Length: 400-5000 words. Payment: from £75 per page and by arrangement. Illustrations: photos. Founded 1967.

Songwriting and Composing

Sovereign House, 12 Trewartha Road, Praa Sands,
Penzance, Cornwall TR20 9ST
tel (01736) 762826 *fax* (01736) 763328
e-mail songmag@aol.com
web site http://www.icn.co.uk/gisc.html
General Secretary Carole Jones
Quarterly Free to members

Magazine of the Guild of International Songwriters and Composers. Short stories, articles, letters relating to songwriting, publishing, recording and the music industry. Payment: negotiable upon content £25-£60. Illustrations: line, halftone. Founded 1986.

The Spectator

56 Doughty Street, London WC1N 2LL
tel 0171-405 1706 *fax* 0171-242-0603
Editor Frank Johnson
Weekly £2.20

Articles on current affairs, politics and the arts; book reviews. Illustrations: b&w, cartoons. Payment: on merit. Founded 1828.

Speech and Drama

4 Fane Road, Old Marston, Oxford OX3 0SA
tel (01865) 728304
Editor Dr Paul Ranger
2 p.a. £6.50 p.a.

Published by the Society of Teachers of Speech and Drama, the journal covers theatre, drama and all levels of education relating to speech and drama; specialist articles only; preliminary abstract of 300 words; photos welcome. Length: 1500-2000 words. Payment: none, complimentary copy. Founded 1951.

Spoken English

English Speaking Board (International),
26A Princes Street, Southport, Merseyside PR8 1EQ
tel (01704) 501730 *fax* (01704) 539637
Editor Malcolm Dale
£20.00 p.a. (ESB membership inc. 2 issues)

Serious articles (1000-plus words) on spoken English, communication ventures and training, poetry, drama, and English-teaching from primary to university levels, in Britain and overseas. Payment: by arrangement. Founded 1968.

The Sporting Life

Mirror Group Newspapers Ltd, 1 Canada Square,
Canary Wharf, London E14 5AP
tel 0171-293 3000 *fax* 0171-293 3758
web site http://sporting-life.com
Editor Tom Clarke
Daily 85p

National racing daily, with wide news and feature coverage, including bloodstock and betting; plus daily Sports Betting feature on general sports and betting. Also Greyhound Life, a daily pull-out, covering every angle of greyhound racing and betting. Interested in relevant news stories; features, photos and graphics are commissioned. Payment: by negotiation.

Springboard

30 Orange Hill Road, Prestwich,
Manchester M25 1LS
tel 0161-7735911
e-mail leobrooks@compuserve.com
Editor Leo Brooks
Quarterly £8.00 p.a.

Articles on writing, competition news, markets. Winning articles, stories and poems from internal competitions – £45 prize money each quarter. Includes copy of *The Curate's Egg*, poetry submissions for which contributors receive free copy. Founded 1990.

The Squash Player

460 Bath Road, Longford, Middlesex UB7 0EB
tel (01753) 775511 *fax* (01753) 775512
Editor Ian McKenzie
12 p.a. £39.95 p.a.

Covers all aspects of playing squash. All features are commissioned – discuss ideas with editor. Length: 1000-1500 words. Illustrations: unusual photos (e.g. celebrities), cartoons. Payment: £75 per 1000 words; £25-£40 for illustrations. Founded 1971.

The Stage

(incorporating Television Today)
Stage House, 47 Bermondsey Street,
London SE1 3XT
tel 0171-403 1818 *fax* 0171-357 9287
Editor Brian Attwood
Weekly 80p

Original and interesting articles on professional stage and broadcasting topics may be sent for the editor's consideration. Length: 500-800 words. Payment: £100 per 1000 words. Founded 1880.

Stamp Lover
National Philatelic Society,
British Philatelic Centre, 107 Charterhouse Street, London EC1M 6PT
tel 0171-336 0882
Editor Michael Furnell
6 p.a. £1.50

Original articles on stamps and postal history. Illustrations: line, half-tone. Payment: by arrangement. Founded 1908.

Stamp Magazine
Link House Magazines Ltd, Link House, Dingwall Avenue, Croydon CR9 2TA
tel 0181-686 2599 *fax* 0181-781 6044
Editor Richard West
Monthly £2.10

Informative articles and exclusive news items on stamp collecting and postal history. No preliminary letter. Payment: by arrangement. Illustrations: line, half-tone, colour. Founded 1934.

Stand Magazine
179 Wingrove Road, Newcastle upon Tyne NE4 9DA
tel/fax 0191-273 3280
Editors Jon Silkin, Lorna Tracy, Rodney Pybus, Peter Bennet
Quarterly £3.95 inc. p&p (£11.95 p.a.)

Poetry, short stories, translations, literary criticism. Send sae for return. Biennial Short Story Competition for unpublished original short story in English (see page 667) and alternates with biennial Poetry Competition. Payment: £25 per 1000 words of prose; £25 per poem. Founded 1952.

Staple New Writing
Gilderoy East, Upperwood Road, Matlock Bath, Derbyshire DE4 3PD
tel (01629) 583867/582764
Editors Bob Windsor and Donald Measham
4 p.a. £12.00 p.a. (£14.00 Europe and overseas surface mail/£17.50 air overseas)

Mainstream poems and short stories. Payment: £5-£10. Founded 1982.

Steam Classic
Ebony, Trevithick House, Moorswater, Liskeard, Cornwall PL14 4LH
tel (01579) 340100 *fax* (01579) 340200
Editor John Huxley
Bi-monthly £2.10

Features on the history, design and performance of British-built and overseas steam locomotives; news stories and features on present-day steam locomotive preservation. Length: 2000-3000 words. Illustrations: archive and contemporary colour transparencies and b&w photos; apply for list of specific required material (topical material always welcome). Payment: approx. £50 per 1000 words; £20 colour, £10 b&w. Founded 1990.

Studies, An Irish quarterly review
35 Lower Leeson Street, Dublin 2, Republic of Ireland
tel (01) 6766785 *fax* (01) 6762984
Editor Rev. Noel Barber SJ
Quarterly £4.00

General review of social comment, literature, history, the arts. Articles written by specialists for the general reader. Critical book reviews. Preliminary letter. Length: 3500 words. Founded 1912.

Studio Sound
Miller Freeman Entertainment Ltd,
8 Montague Place, London SE1 9UR
tel 0171-620 3636 *fax* 0171-401 8036
Editor Tim Goodyer
Monthly £3.00

Articles on all aspects of professional sound recording. Technical and operational features on the functional aspects of studio equipment; general features on studio affairs. Length: widely variable. Payment: by arrangement. Illustrations: line, half-tone, colour. Founded 1959.

Success Now
(formerly Personal Success)
Sphinx Inc. Ltd, Hope House, 34A Market Square, Bromley, Kent BR1 1NF
tel 0181-402 5252 *fax* 0181-402 4070
Editor Brendan Martin
Quarterly £3.50

Positive and inspirational articles on business and human development; features on success stories of entrepreneurs, famous names and the average person. Length: 1300 words/2 pages to 2100 words/3 pages (features), 200-500 words (news), 600-800 words (short stories). Illustrations: colour photos, artwork and cartoons. Payment: £50-£175 per article. Founded 1993.

94   Newspapers and magazines

Sugar
Attic Futura (UK) Ltd, 17-18 Berners Street,
London W1P 3DD
tel 0171-664 6400 *fax* 0171-636 5055
Editor Marina Gask
Monthly £1.60

Magazine for young women aged 13-17.
Fashion, beauty, entertainment, features.
Interested in real-life stories (1200
words), quizzes. Payment: by arrangement. Opportunities for freelance writers,
illustrators and designers. Founded 1994.

Sunday Magazine – see News of the World in National newspapers UK and Ireland, page 3

The Sunday Post Magazine – see Sunday Post in National newspapers UK and Ireland, page 3

The Sunday Review – see Independent on Sunday in National newspapers UK and Ireland, page 3

Sunday Telegraph Magazine – see Sunday Telegraph in National newspapers UK and Ireland, page 3

The Sunday Times Magazine – see Sunday Times in National newspapers UK and Ireland, page 3

The Sunday Times Scotland – see Sunday Times in National newspapers UK and Ireland, page 3

Superbike
Link House Magazines Ltd, Link House,
Dingwall Avenue, Croydon CR9 2TA
tel 0181-686 2599 *fax* 0181-781 6042
Editor Grant Leonard
Monthly £2.50

Sports and high performance motorcycling, tests, reviews of related products,
tuning and motorcycle sport. Payment:
by arrangement. Illustrations: colour.

The Tablet
1 King Street Cloisters, Clifton Walk,
London W6 0QZ
tel 0181-748 8484 *fax* 0181-748 1550
Editor John Wilkins
Weekly £1.35

The senior Catholic weekly. Religion, philosophy, politics, society, books and arts.
International coverage. Freelance work

welcomed. Length: 1500 words.
Illustrations: cartoons. Payment: by
arrangement. Founded 1840.

Take a Break
25-27 Camden Road, London NW1 9LL
tel 0171-284 0909 *fax* 0171-284 3778
Editor John Dale
Weekly 46p

Lively, tabloid women's weekly. True life
features, celebrities, health and beauty,
family, travel; short stories (up to 1500
words); lots of puzzles. Payment: by
arrangement. Illustrated. Founded 1990.

tate: The Art Magazine
Blueprint Media Ltd, Christ Church,
Cosway Street, London NW1 5NJ
tel 0171-706 4596 *fax* 0171-479 8515
e-mail cmullins@aspenmags.co.uk
Editor Tim Marlow
3 p.a. £2.95

Independent visual arts magazine: features, news, interviews, reviews, previews and opinion pieces. Length: up to
5000 words but usually commissioned.
Illustrations: colour and b&w photos.
Payment: negotiable. Founded 1993.

The Tatler
Vogue House, Hanover Square, London W1R 0AD
tel 0171-499 9080 *fax* 0171-409 0451
Editor Jane Procter
Monthly £2.60

Smart society magazine favouring sharp
articles, profiles, fashion and the arts.
Illustrations: colour, b&w, but all commissioned. Founded 1709.

Technology Ireland
Forbairt (Irish Science and Technology Agency),
Glasnevin, Dublin 9, Republic of Ireland
tel (01) 8082345 *fax* (01) 8367122
Editors Mary Mulvihill and Tom Kennedy
Monthly £25.00 p.a.

Articles, features, reviews and news on
current science and technology. Length:
1500-2000 words. Illustrations: line, half-
tone, colour. Payment: varies. Founded
1969.

The Teacher
National Union of Teachers, Hamilton House,
Mabledon Place, London WC1H 9BD
tel 0171-380 4708 *fax* 0171-387 8458
Editor Mitch Howard
8 p.a. Free to NUT members

Articles, features and news of interest to
all those involved in the teaching profes-

sion. Length: 750 words. Payment: NUJ rates to NUJ members. Founded 1872.

Telegraph Magazine – see Daily Telegraph in National newspapers UK and Ireland, page 3

Television
Reed Business Information Ltd, Quadrant House, The Quadrant, Sutton, Surrey SM2 5AS
tel 0181-652 8120 *fax* 0181-652 8956
Monthly £2.50

Articles on the technical aspects of domestic TV and video equipment, especially servicing, long-distance television, constructional projects, satellite TV, video recording, teletext and viewdata, test equipment, monitors. Payment: by arrangement. Illustrations: photos and line drawings for litho. Founded 1950.

Tempo
Boosey & Hawkes, Music Publishers, Ltd, 295 Regent Street, London W1R 8JH
tel 0171-580 2060 *fax* 0171-436 5675
Editor Calum MacDonald
Quarterly £3.00 (£15.00 p.a.)

Authoritative articles about 2000-4000 words on contemporary music. Payment: by arrangement. Illustrations: music type, occasional photographic or musical supplements.

Tennis World
Presswatch Ltd, The Spendlove Centre, Enstone Road, Charlbury, Oxford OX7 3PQ
tel (01608) 811446 *fax* (01608) 811380
Editor Alastair McIver
Monthly £2.50

Tournament reports, topical features, personality profiles, instructional articles. Length: 600-1500 words. Payment: by arrangement. Illustrations: line, half-tone, colour.

TGO (The Great Outdoors) Magazine
Caledonian Magazines Ltd, 7th Floor, The Plaza Tower, East Kilbride, Glasgow G74 1LW
tel (01355) 246444 *fax* (01355) 263013
Editor Cameron McNeish
Monthly £2.25 (£26.00 p.a.)

Articles on walking or lightweight camping in specific areas, preferably illustrated. Length: 1200-1800 words. Payment: by arrangement. Illustrations: colour, cartoons. Founded 1978.

that's life!
H. Bauer Publishing, 2nd Floor, 1-5 Maple Place, London W1P 5FX
tel 0171-462 4700 *Mercury* 19059412
fax 0171-636 1824
Editor Janice Turner
Weekly 47p

Dramatic true life stories about women. Length: average 1000 words. Illustrations: colour photos and cartoons. Payment: £650. Founded 1995.

The Mag!
Specialist Publications (UK) Ltd, Clifton Heights, Triangle West, Clifton, Bristol BS8 1EJ
tel (0117) 9251696 *fax* (0117) 9251808
Editor Karen Ellison
Quarterly 45p

Short features on health, beauty, gardening, home improvements; celebrity interviews and human interest stories; short fiction. Length: approx. 800 words. Illustrations: colour transparencies, artwork and cartoons. Payment: £200 per feature; £200 for illustrations. Founded 1995.

Theology
SPCK, Holy Trinity Church, Marylebone Road, London NW1 4DU
tel 0171-387 5282 *fax* 0171-388 2352
Editor William Jacob
Bi-monthly £3.25

Articles and reviews on theology, ethics, Church and Society. Length: up to 3500 words. Payment: none. Founded 1920.

Therapy Weekly
Macmillan Magazines Ltd, Porters South, 4-6 Crinan Street, London N1 9SQ
tel 0171-843 4730 *fax* 0171-843 4744
Editor Carol Harris
Weekly Free to NHS and local authority therapists (£42.50 p.a.)

Articles of interest to chartered physiotherapists, occupational therapists and speech and language therapists. Guidelines to contributors available. Send proposals only initially. Length: up to 1000 words. Illustrations: colour and b&w photos, line, cartoons. Payment: by arrangement. Founded 1974 as *Therapy*.

Third Way
St Peter's, Sumner Road, Harrow, Middlesex HA2 4BX
tel 0181-423 8494 *fax* 0181-423 5367
e-mail editor@thirdway.org.uk
10 p.a. £2.90

Aims to present biblical perspectives on the political, social and cultural issues of the day. Payment: by arrangement on publication. Founded 1977.

This Caring Business

1 St Thomas' Road, Hastings,
East Sussex TN34 3LG
tel (01424) 718406 *fax* (01424) 718460
Editor Michael J. Monk
Monthly £50.00 p a

Specialist contributions relating to the commercial aspects of nursing and residential care, including hospitals. Payment: £75 per 1000 words. Illustrations: line, half-tone. Founded 1985.

This England

PO Box 52, Cheltenham, Glos. GL50 1YQ
tel (01242) 577775
Editor Roy Faiers
Quarterly £3.20

Articles on towns, villages, traditions, customs, legends, crafts of England; stories of people. Length: 250-2000 words. Payment: £25 per page and pro rata. Illustrations: line, half-tone, colour. Founded 1968.

The Times Magazine – **see The Times in National newspapers UK and Ireland, page 3**

The Times Educational Supplement

Admiral House, 66-68 East Smithfield,
London E1 9XY
tel 0171-782 3000 *fax* 0171-782 3200
e-mail copy@tesl.demon.co.uk
web site http://www.tes.co.uk
Editor Caroline St John-Brooks
Weekly £1.00

Articles on education written with special knowledge or experience; news items; books, arts and equipment reviews. Advisable to check with features, news or picture editor before submitting. Illustrations: suitable photos and drawings of educational interest, cartoons. Payment: standard rates, or by arrangement.

Times Educational Supplement Scotland

37 George Street, Edinburgh EH2 2HN
tel 0131-220 1100 *fax* 0131-220 1616
Editor Willis Pickard
Weekly 90p

Articles on education, preferably 800-1200 words, written with special knowl-edge or experience. News items about Scottish educational affairs. Illustrations: line, half-tone. Payment: by arrangement. Founded 1965.

Times Higher Education Supplement

Admiral House, 66-68 East Smithfield,
London E1 9XY
tel 0171-782 3000 *fax* 0171-782 3300
Editor Auriol Stevens
Weekly £1.10

Articles on higher education written with special knowledge or experience, or articles dealing with academic topics. Also news items. Illustrations: suitable photos and drawings of educational interest. Payment: by arrangement. Founded 1971.

The Times Literary Supplement

Admiral House, 66-68 East Smithfield,
London E1 9XY
tel 0171-782 3000 *fax* 0171-782 3100
Editor Ferdinand Mount
Weekly £2.00

Will consider poems for publication, literary discoveries and articles, particularly of an opinionated kind, on literary and cultural affairs. Payment: by arrangement.

Titbits

Caversham Communications, 2 Caversham Street,
London SW3 4AH
tel/fax 0171-351 4995
Editor James Hughes
Monthly £1.50

Men's interest articles; also show business, pop stars and medical. No fiction. Illustrations: colour transparencies and photos, cartoons. No b&w. Payment: details on application. Founded 1881.

Today's Golfer

EMAP Pursuit Publishing Ltd, Bretton Court, Bretton, Peterborough PE3 8DZ
tel (01733) 264666 *fax* (01733) 465221
Editor Neil Pope
Monthly £2.60

Specialist features and articles on golf instruction and equipment. Founded 1988.

Today's Runner

EMAP Pursuit Publishing, Bretton Court, Bretton, Peterborough PE3 8DZ
tel (01733) 264666 *fax* (01733) 267198
Editor Victoria Tebbs
Monthly £2.20

Practical articles on all aspects of running lifestyle, especially road running training and events, and advice on health, fitness and injury. Illustrations: colour photos, cartoons. Payment: by negotiation. Founded 1985.

Together with Children
The National Society, Church House, Great Smith Street, London SW1P 3NZ
tel 0171-222 1672 *fax* 0171-233 2592
Editor Pam Macnaughton
Monthly £1.50 (£13.50 p.a.)

Short, practical or topical articles and resources dealing with all forms of children's Christian education and all-age learning and worship. Length: up to 1200 words. Payment: by arrangement. Founded 1956.

Top of the Pops Magazine
BBC Worldwide, 80 Wood Lane, London W12 0TT
tel 0181-576 3254 *fax* 0181-576 3267
Editor Peter Loraine
Monthly £1.35

Fun, lively and humorous articles on pop music aimed at fans of the TV show aged 12-17 – mostly commissioned. Length: 700-1000 words (features). Payment: £200 per 1000 words. Founded 1995.

Top Santé Health & Beauty
Presse Publishing Ltd, Endeavour House, 189 Shaftesbury Avenue, London WC2H 8JG
tel 0171-938 3033 *fax* 0171-938 5464
Monthly £1.95

Articles, features and news on all aspects of health and beauty. Ideas welcome. Length: 1-2 pages. Illustrations: colour photos and drawings. Payment: £200 per 1000 words; illustrations by arrangement. Founded 1993.

Total Football
Future Publishing Ltd, 30 Monmouth Street, Bath BA1 2BW
tel (01225) 442244 *fax* (01225) 732248
e-mail rjones@futurenet.co.uk
Editor Richard Jones
Monthly £2.40

News, features and reviews of domestic and international football events and related stories. Illustrations: colour and b&w. Payment: 12-15p a word/variable page rate. Founded 1995.

Total Sport
Emap Metro, Mappin House, 4 Winsley Street, London W1N 7AR
tel 0171-312 8933 *fax* 0171-312 8936
Editor Danny Kelly
Monthly £2.40

For people who enjoy watching and talking about sport, in particular football, cricket, rugby, athletics and car racing. Features, photofeatures, profiles and news: the angle is entertainment and popular culture, rather than traditional. Founded 1995.

Toy Trader
Trade Media, Brookmead House, Thorney Leys Business Park, Witney, Oxon OX8 7GE
tel (01993) 775545 *fax* (01993) 778884
Editor Oscar Henderson
Monthly £54.00 p.a.

Trade journal specialising in anything to do with games and toys, circulated to manufacturers and retailers. Length: by negotiation. Illustrations: cartoons. Payment: by negotiation. Founded 1908.

Traveller
Wexas Ltd, 45 Brompton Road, London SW3 1DE
tel 0171-581 4130 *fax* 0171-581 1357
e-mail miranda@wexas.com
Editor Miranda Haines
Quarterly £39.58 p.a.

Features usually based on long-haul and offbeat destinations, with a particular emphasis on cultural or anthropological angles. Recent features include: Mask-making in Mali; The Skeleton Coast of Namibia; New Year in Laos. Length: 1000-2000 words. Illustrations: first-class transparencies. Payment: £125 per 1000 words; colour £25 (£50 cover). Founded 1970.

The Trefoil
C.H.Q., The Guide Association, 17-19 Buckingham Palace Road, London SW1W 0PT
tel 0171-834 6242 *fax* 0171-828 8317
Editor Gillian Ellis
Quarterly

Official Journal of The Trefoil Guild. Articles on the activities of the Guild in the UK and overseas and on the work of voluntary organisations. Length: not more than 500 words. No fiction. Illustrations: photos. No payment.

Tribune

308 Gray's Inn Road, London WC1X 8DY
tel 0171-278 0911
Editor Mark Seddon, *Reviews Editor* Caroline Rees
Weekly £1.00

Political, literary, with Socialist outlook. Informative articles (about 700 words), news stories (250-300 words). No unsolicited reviews or fiction. Payment: by arrangement. Illustrations: cartoons and photos.

Trout and Salmon

EMAP Pursuit Publishing Ltd, Bretton Court, Bretton Centre, Peterborough PE3 8DZ
tel (01733) 264666 *fax* (01733) 465436
Editor Sandy Leventon
Monthly £2.30

Articles of good quality with strong trout or salmon angling interest. Length: 400-2000 words, accompanied if possible by colour transparencies or good-quality colour prints. Payment: by arrangement. Illustrations: line, colour transparencies and prints, cartoons. Founded 1955.

Truck & Driver

Reed Business Information, Quadrant House, The Quadrant, Sutton, Surrey SM2 5AS
tel 0171-652 3682 *fax* 0171-652 8988
e-mail truckmag@cityscape.co.uk
Editor Dave Young
Monthly £1.80

News, articles on truck personalities and features of interest to truck drivers. Words (on disk) and picture packages preferred. Length: approx. 2000 words. Illustrations: colour transparencies and artwork, cartoons. Payment: negotiable. Founded 1984.

Trucking International

A & S Publishing, Messenger House, 35 St Michael's Square, Gloucester GL1 1HX
tel (01452) 307181 *fax* (01452) 307170
Editor Richard Simpson
Monthly £1.80

For truck drivers, owner-drivers and small fleet operators: news, articles, features and technical advice. Length: 750-2500 words. Illustrations: mostly 35 mm colour transparencies. Payment: by negotiation. Founded 1983.

TV Quick

25-27 Camden Road, London NW1 9LL
tel 0171-284 0909 *fax* 0171-284 0593
Editor Lori Miles
Weekly 60p

Real life features, readers' tips and letters. No fiction. Illustrations: colour. Payment: £250 (real life stories). Founded 1991.

TV Times

IPC Magazines Ltd, 10th Floor, King's Reach Tower, Stamford Street, London SE1 9LS
tel 0171-261 7000 *fax* 0171-261 7777
Editor Liz Murphy
Weekly 62p

Features with an affinity to ITV, BBC1, BBC2, Channel 4, satellite and radio personalities and television generally. Length: by arrangement. Photographs: commissioned only. Payment: by arrangement.

Twinkle

D.C. Thomson & Co. Ltd, Albert Square, Dundee DD1 9QJ
tel (01382) 223131 *fax* (01382) 322214
185 Fleet Street, London EC4A 2HS
tel 0171-242 5086 *fax* 0171-404 5694
Weekly 55p

Picture stories, features and comic strips. Drawings in colour for gravure. Special encouragement to promising writers and artists. Payment: on acceptance.

U magazine

Smurfit Publications Ltd, 126 Lower Baggot Street, Dublin 2, Republic of Ireland
tel (01) 6623158 *fax* (01) 6610767
Editor Annette O'Meara, *Assistant Editor* Lucy Tayler
Monthly £1.75

Ireland's review for women today. Special reports, interviews, analysis, fashion, humour, travel, health, arts. Material mostly commissioned. Length: 1000 words. Illustrations: line, half-tone, colour. Payment: varies. Founded 1978.

Ulster Grocer

Greer Publications, 151 University Street, Belfast BT7 1HR
tel (01232) 231634 *fax* (01232) 325736
Editor Brian McCalden
Monthly Controlled circulation

Topical features (500-1000 words) on agribusiness – retail and manufacturing – and exhibitions; news (200 words) with a Northern Ireland bias. All features commissioned; no speculative articles accepted. Illustrations: colour and b&w photos. Payment: features £75, news £30; photos £40. Founded 1972.

The Universe
1st Floor, St James's Buildings, Oxford Street, Manchester M1 6FP
tel 0161-236 8856 *fax* 0161-236 8530
Editor Joe Kelly
Weekly 50p

Catholic Sunday newspaper. News stories, features and photos on all aspects of Catholic life required; also cartoons. MSS should not be submitted without sae. Payment: by arrangement. Founded 1860.

Vanity Fair
The Condé Nast Publications Ltd, Vogue House, Hanover Square, London W1R 0AD
tel 0171-499 9080 *fax* 0171-499 4415
International Editor Henry Porter
tel 0171-221 6228 *fax* 0171-221 6269
Monthly £2.00

Media, glamour and politics for grown-up readers. No unsolicited material. Payment: by arrangement. Illustrated.

The Vegan
The Vegan Society, Donald Watson House, 7 Battle Road, St Leonards-on-Sea, East Sussex TN37 7AA
tel (01424) 427393 *fax* (01424) 717064
Editor Richard Farhall
Quarterly £1.75

Articles on animal rights, nutrition, cookery, agriculture, Third World, health. Length: approx. 1500 words. Payment: by arrangement. Illustrations: photos, cartoons, line drawings – foods, animals, livestock systems, crops, people, events; colour for cover. Founded 1944.

The Veterinary Review
John C. Alborough Ltd, Battisford Road, Ringshall, Suffolk IP14 2JA
tel (01473) 658006 *fax* (01473) 658922
e-mail 100762.1214@compuserve.com
Editor Tim Wesley
6 p.a. £30 p.a.

News, articles – both topical and general – and product listings for veterinarians. Articles and illustrations are both negotiable.

Farm & Country Retailer
News, articles and product listings for the agricultural supply trade.

Video Camera
W.V. Publications & Exhibitions, 57-59 Rochester Place, London NW1 9JU
tel 0171-485 0011 *fax* 0171-482 6249
Editor Philip Lattimore
Monthly. £2.50

Technique articles on how to use camcorders and equipment tests. Material mostly commissioned. Length: 800-1000 words. Illustrations: colour photos, cartoons, diagrams. Payment: £90 per 1000 words; £90 per page for illustrations. Founded 1989.

Viz
House of Viz, PO Box 1PT, Newcastle upon Tyne NE99 1PT
fax (0191) 2819048
e-mail web@johnbrown.co.uk
web site www.viz.co.uk
Editor Chris Donald
6 p.a. £1.50

Cartoons, cartoon scripts, articles. Illustrations: half-tone, line, cartoons. Payment: £300 per page (cartoons). Founded 1979.

Vogue
Vogue House, Hanover Square, London W1R 0AD
tel 0171-499 9080 *fax* 0171-408 0559
Editor Alexandra Shulman
Monthly £2.80

Fashion, beauty, health, decorating, art, theatre, films, literature, music, travel, food and wine. Length: articles from 1000 words. Illustrated.

The Voice
370 Coldharbour Lane, London SW9 8PL
tel 0171-737 7377 *fax* 0171-274 8994
e-mail veeteeay@gn.apc.org
Editor Annie Stewart
Weekly 65p

News, general and arts features of interest to black readers. Illustrations: colour and b&w photos, cartoons. Payment: £100 per 1000 words; £20-£35 for illustrations. Founded 1982.

Voice Intelligence Report
15A Lowndes Street, London SW1X 9EY
tel 0171-235 5966 *fax* 0171-259 6694
Editor Ann Morris
Quarterly £18.00 (£60.00 p.a.)

Background intelligence reports on the Press, media, Parliament, European Parliament, banking, diplomats, Saudi Arabia and the Arab Gulf countries, with specific reference to Middle East. All material commissioned. Write for specimen copy. Illustrations: none. Founded 1972.

Vox

IPC Magazines Ltd, 25th Floor, King's Reach
Tower, Stamford Street, London SE1 9LS
tel 0171-261 6312 *fax* 0171-261 5627
Editor Steve Sutherland
Monthly £2.40

Music and movies, aimed at 18-35 market – interviews, non-interview features,
reviews. Illustrations: colour and b&w
photos; commissioned illustrations and
cartoons. Payment: by negotiation.
Founded 1990.

Wanderlust

PO Box 1832, Windsor SL4 6YP
tel (01753) 620426
Editor Lyn Hughes
Bi-monthly £2.50

Features on independent and special-interest travel. Send sae for 'Guidelines
for contributors'. Length: up to 2500
words. Illustrations: colour (send stocklist first). Payment: by arrangement.
Founded 1993.

War Cry

101 Queen Victoria Street, London EC4P 4EP
tel 0171-236 5222 *fax* 0171-236 3491
e-mail wcry@globalnet.co.uk
Editor Captain Charles King
Weekly 20p (£25.54 p.a. UK)

Voluntary contributions; puzzles.
Illustrations: line and photos, cartoons.
Published by The Salvation Army.
Founded 1879.

Wasafiri

Queen Mary & Westfield College, English
Department, Mile End Road, London E1 4NS
tel 0171-775 3120
e-mail wasafiri@qmw.ac.uk
web site www.qmw.ac.uk/~english/wasafiri.html
Managing Editor Anthony Ilona, *Editor* Susheila
Nasta
Bi-Annual £12.00 p.a. (£16.00 p.a. institutions)

Published at University of London. Short
stories, poetry, reviews, essays on literature and film. Submit MSS in duplicate,
with an sae. Illustrations: b&w photos.
Payment: none. Founded 1984.

Waterways World

Waterways World Ltd, The Well House,
High Street, Burton-on-Trent, Staffs. DE14 1JQ
tel (01283) 742951
Managing Editor Anthony Ilona, *Editor* Hugh
Potter
Monthly £2.20

Feature articles on all aspects of inland
waterways in Britain and abroad,
including historical material; factual
and technical articles preferred. No
short stories or poetry. Send sae for
'Notes for WW Contributors'. Payment:
£37 per 1000 words. Illustrations:
colour transparencies or prints, line.
Founded 1972.

Wedding and Home

IPC Magazines Ltd, King's Reach Tower,
Stamford Street, London SE1 9LS
tel 0171-261 7471 *fax* 0171-261 7459
Bi-monthly £3.25

Bridal fashion and beauty, home and
style, financial, travel, emotional, real
life. Approach in writing. Length: 500-1500 words. Illustrations: colour and
b&w photos. Payment: by negotiation.
Founded 1985.

Weekend – see The Guardian in National newspapers UK and Ireland, page 3

The Weekly Journal

Positive Time & Space Ltd, 36 Skylines,
London E14 9TS
tel 0171-537 3222 *fax* 0171-537 2288
Editor Barbara Campbell
Weekly 60p

Features, news, interviews, arts, society,
business from an African Caribbean,
multicultural perspective. Length: 300-3000 words. Illustrations: half-tone, cartoons. Payment: negotiable. Founded
1992.

The Weekly News

D.C. Thomson & Co. Ltd, Albert Square,
Dundee DD1 9QJ
tel (01382) 223131
137 Chapel Street, Manchester M3 6AA
tel 0161-834 5122
144 Port Dundas Road, Glasgow G4 0HZ
tel 0141-332 9933
185 Fleet Street, London EC4A 2HS
tel 0171-242 5086
Weekly 40p

Real-life dramas of around 2000 words
told in the first person. Non-fiction series
with lively themes or about interesting
people. Keynote throughout is strong
human interest. Joke sketches.
Illustrations: cartoons. Payment: on
acceptance.

Weight Watchers Magazine

Bloomsbury House Ltd, The Old School
House, East Lodge Lane, Enfield,
Middlesex EN2 8AS
tel/fax 0181-366 9501
8 p.a. £1.70

Features page – health, beauty, news,
astrology; food-orientated articles; success stories. All material commissioned.
Length: 1/2-3 pages. Illustrations: colour
photos and cartoons. Payment: by
arrangement.

West Africa

43-45 Coldharbour Lane,
London SE5 9NR
tel 0171-737 2946 *fax* 0171-978 8334
Managing Editor Maxwell Nwagboso
Weekly £1.70

Weekly summary of West African news,
with articles on political, economic and
commercial matters, and on all matters
of general interest affecting Africa; also
book reviews. Length: articles about 1200
words. Payment: as arranged.
Illustrations: half-tone.

West Lothian Life

Ballencrieff Cottage, Ballencrieff Toll, Bathgate,
West Lothian EH48 4LD
tel/fax (01506) 632728
Editor Susan Coon
Quarterly £2.00

Articles, profiles etc with a West Lothian
angle. Length: 800-3000 words.
Illustrations: colour and b&w photos,
b&w artwork and cartoons. Payment: £10
per 1000 words. Founded 1995.

What Car?

Haymarket Motoring Magazines Ltd,
38-42 Hampton Road, Teddington,
Middlesex TW11 0JE
tel 0181-943 5044 *fax* 0181-943 5959
Editor Mark Payton
Monthly £2.95

Road tests, buying guide, consumer stories and used car features. No unsolicited
material. Illustrations: colour and b&w
photos, line drawings. Payment: by negotiation. Founded 1973.

What's on TV

IPC Magazines Ltd, 10th Floor, King's Reach
Tower, Stamford Street, London SE1 9LS
tel 0171-261 7769 *fax* 0171-261 7739
Editor Mike Hollingsworth
Weekly 47p

Features on TV programmes and personalities. All material commissioned.
Length: up to 500 words. Illustrations:
colour and b&w photos, cartoons.
Payment: by agreement. Founded 1991.

When Saturday Comes

When Saturday Comes Ltd, 4th Floor,
2 Pear Tree Court, London EC1R 0DS
tel 0171-251 8595 *fax* 0171-490 1598
e-mail editorial@wsc.co.uk
web site http://www.wsc.cp/uk/wsc/
Editor Andy Lyons
Monthly £1.40

Features on football from the fans' perspective. Read the magazine for style
first. Length: 500-2000 words.
Illustrations: colour and b&w photos,
occasional illustrations. Payment: £50-
£100 for words; £50-£75 for illustrations.
Founded 1986.

Wine

Quest Magazines Ltd, Publishing House,
652 Victoria Road, South Ruislip,
Middlesex HA4 0SX
tel 0181-842 1010 *fax* 0181-841 2557
Editor Susan Vumback Low
11 p.a. £2.95

Articles, features and news on new
developments in wine; travelogues, tastings and profiles. Illustrations: colour.
Payment: £125 per 1000 words. Founded
1983.

Wisden Cricket Monthly

25 Down Road, Merrow, Guildford,
Surrey GU12 2PY
tel (01483) 570358 *fax* (01483) 533153
Editor Tim de Lisle
Monthly £2.50

Cricket articles of exceptional interest
(unsolicited pieces seldom used). Length:
up to 3000 words. Payment: by arrangement. Illustrations: half-tone, colour.
Founded 1979.

Woman

IPC Magazines Ltd, King's Reach Tower,
Stamford Street, London SE1 9LS
tel 0171-261 5000 *fax* 0171-261 5997
Editor Carole Russell
Weekly 57p

Practical articles of varying length on all
subjects of interest to women. No unsolicited fiction. Payment: by arrangement.
Illustrations: colour transparencies, photos, sketches, cartoons. Founded 1937.

Woman Alive

(formerly Christian Woman)
Herald House Ltd, 96 Dominion Road, Worthing,
West Sussex BN14 8JP
tel (01903) 821082 *fax* (01903) 821081
Editor Elizabeth Proctor
Monthly £1.60

Aimed at women aged 25 upwards.
Celebrity interviews, topical features,
Christian issues, 'Day in the life of' profiles of women in interesting occupations, Christian testimonies, fashion,
beauty, health, crafts. Unsolicited material should include colour slides or b&w
photos. Length: 'Day in the life of'/testimonies 750 words, interviews/features
1300 words. Payment: £50 per 1000
words published. Founded 1982.

Woman and Home

(incorporating Living)
IPC Magazines Ltd, King's Reach Tower,
Stamford Street, London SE1 9LS
tel 0171-261 5000 *fax* 0171-261 7346
Editor Jan Henderson
Monthly £1.50

Centres on the personal and home interests of the lively-minded woman with or
without career and family. Articles dealing with fashion, beauty, leisure pursuits,
gardening; things to buy and make for
the home; features on people and places.
Fiction: complete stories from 1000-5000
words in length. Illustrations: commissioned colour photos and sketches.
Please note: non-commissioned work is
rarely accepted and regrettably cannot be
returned. Founded 1926.

The Woman Journalist

59 Grace Avenue, Maidstone, Kent ME16 0BS
Editor Barbara Haynes
3 p.a. Free to members

Periodical of the Society of Women
Writers and Journalists. Short articles of
interest to professional writers. Payment:
none. Founded 1894.

Woman's Journal

IPC Magazines Ltd, King's Reach Tower,
Stamford Street, London SE1 9LS
tel 0171-261 6622 *fax* 0171-261 7061
Editor Deirdre Vine
Monthly £2.00

Magazine devoted to the looks and lives
of intelligent women aged 30 plus: interviews and articles (1000-2000 words)
dealing with topical subjects and personalities; fashion, beauty and health, food
and houses. No fiction accepted.
Illustrations: full colour, line and wash,
first-rate photos. Payment: by arrangement. Founded 1927.

Woman's Own

IPC Magazines Ltd, King's Reach Tower,
Stamford Street, London SE1 9LS
tel 0171-261 5474
Editor Keith McNeill
Weekly 57p

Modern women's magazine aimed at the
20-35 age group. No unsolicited features
or fiction. Illustrations: colour and b&w:
interior decorating and furnishing, fashion. Address work to relevant department editor. Payment: by arrangement.

Woman's Realm

IPC Magazines Ltd, King's Reach Tower,
Stamford Street, London SE1 9LS
tel 0171-261 5000
Weekly 55p

Lively general interest weekly magazine.
Articles on celebrities, topical subjects,
cookery, fashion, beauty, home. Human
interest real-life features; dramatic emotional stories. (Regretfully, no unsolicited
features or fiction accepted.) Payment: by
arrangement. Illustrated. Founded 1958.

Woman's Way

Smurfit Publications Ltd, 126 Lower Baggot
Street, Dublin 2, Republic of Ireland
tel (01) 6623158 *fax* (01) 6619757
Editor Celine Naughton
Weekly 75p

Short stories, personality interviews,
general features. Length: 1000-1500
words. Payment: £25-£100 approx.
Illustrations: line, half-tone, colour.
Founded 1963.

Woman's Weekly

IPC Magazines Ltd, King's Reach Tower,
Stamford Street, London SE1 9LS
tel 0171-261 5000 *fax* 0171-261 6322
Editor Olwen Rice
Weekly 52p

Lively, family-interest magazine. One
serial, averaging 4000 words, each instalment of strong romantic interest, and
several short stories of 1000- 2500 words
of general emotional interest. Celebrity
and strong human interest features; also
inspirational and entertaining personal
stories. Payment: by arrangement.

Illustrations: full colour fiction illustrations, small sketches and photos. Founded 1911.

The Woodworker
Nexus Special Interests Ltd, Nexus House, Boundary Way, Hemel Hempstead, Herts. HP2 7ST
tel (01442) 66551 *fax* (01442) 66998
Editor Mark Ramuz
Monthly £2.35
For the craft and professional woodworker. Practical illustrated articles on cabinet work, carpentry, wood polishing, wood turning, wood carving, rural crafts, craft history, antique and period furniture; also wooden toys and models, musical instruments; timber procurement, conditioning, seasoning; tool, machinery and equipment reviews. Payment: by arrangement. Illustrations: line drawings and photos.

The Word
Divine Word Missionaries, Donamon, Roscommon, Republic of Ireland
tel/fax (0903) 62608
Editor Fr Tom Cahill SVD
Monthly 50p
General interest magazine with religious emphasis. Illustrated articles up to 2000 words and good picture features. Payment: by arrangement. Illustrations: photos and large colour transparencies, cartoons. Founded 1936.

Work Study
Leeds Metropolitan University Learning Support Services, Calverley Street, Leeds LS1 3HE
tel (0113) 283 2600 *fax* (0113) 283 3123
Editor John Heap
7 p.a. £349.00
Authoritative articles on all aspects of work study including work measurement, method study, O&M, industrial engineering, payment systems. Length: 2000-4000 words. Payment: by arrangement. Illustrations: line, half-tone.

Workbox
Ebony, Trevithick House, Moorswater, Liskeard, Cornwall PL14 4LH
tel (01579) 340100 *fax* (01579) 340200
Bi-monthly £1.60
Features, of any length, on all aspects of needlecrafts. No 'how-to' articles. Send sae with enquiries and submissions. Illustrations: good colour transparencies. Payment: by agreement. Founded 1984.

World Fishing
Nexus Media Ltd, Nexus House, Azalea Drive, Swanley, Kent BR8 8HY
tel (01322) 660070 *fax* (01322) 667633
Editor Martin Gill
Monthly £35.00 p.a.
International journal of commercial fishing. Technical and management emphasis on catching, processing, farming and marketing of fish and related products; fishery operations and vessels covered worldwide. Length: 1000-2000 words. Payment: by arrangement. Illustrations: photos and diagrams for litho reproduction. Founded 1952.

World Bowls
44 Oak Street, Southport, Lanc. PR8 6DD
tel (01704) 549054 *fax* (01704) 548900
Editor Keith Hale
Monthly £1.95
The official magazine of The English Bowling Association, The English Indoor Bowling Association, The English Women's Bowling Association and The English Women's Indoor Bowling Association. Bowls related stories and features relating to indoor and outdoor bowls. Illustrations: colour transparencies and photos. Payment: by negotiation.

The World of Embroidery
The Embroiderers' Guild, PO Box 42B, East Molesey, Surrey KT8 9BB
tel 0181-943 1229
6 p.a. £3.75 (£22.50 p.a.)
Articles on historical and contemporary embroidery by curators, artists and craftsmen; exhibition and book reviews; saleroom report; diary of events. Illustrations: line, half-tone, colour. Payment: by arrangement.

The World of Interiors
The Condé Nast Publications Ltd, Vogue House, Hanover Square, London W1R 0AD
tel 0171-499 9080 *fax* 0171-493 4013
Editor Min Hogg
Monthly £3.00
All material commissioned: send synopsis/visual reference for article ideas. Length: 1000-1500 words. Illustrations: colour photos. Payment: £400 per 1000 words; photos from £100. Founded 1981.

World Soccer
IPC Magazines Ltd, King's Reach Tower,
Stamford Street, London SE1 9LS
tel 0171-261 5737 *fax* 0171-261 7474
Editor Keir Radnedge
Monthly £2.20

Articles, features, news concerning football, its personalities and worldwide development. Length: 600-2000 words. Illustrations: colour and b&w photos, cartoons. Payment: by arrangement. Founded 1960.

The World Today
The Royal Institute of International Affairs,
Chatham House, 10 St James's Square,
London SW1Y 4LE
tel 0171-957 5700 *fax* 0171-957 5710
Editor Graham Walker
Monthly £2.50

Analysis of international issues and current events by journalists, diplomats, politicians and academics. Length: 1700-3000 words. Payment: nominal. Founded 1945.

World's Children
Save the Children, 17 Grove Lane,
London SE5 8RD
tel 0171-703 5400 *fax* 0171-708 2508
Editor Lotte Hughes
Quarterly Sent free to regular donors

The magazine of Save the Children. Articles on child welfare and rights, related to Save the Children's work overseas and in the UK. No unsolicited features. Length: 500 words. Payment: by arrangement. Illustrations: colour and b&w photos. Founded 1920.

Writers' Forum
21 Belle Vue Street, Filey,
North Yorkshire YO14 9HZ
Editor Morgan Kenney
Quarterly £14.50 p.a.

Welcomes fillers and articles on any aspect of the craft and business of writing. Length: 300-1000 words. Payment: by arrangement. Administers 2 annual prizes: the Petra Kenney Memorial Poetry Prize (total £1750), and a Short Story Competition (total £300). Founded 1993.

Writers' Guide
(incorporating Fiction and Freelance Magazine and Poetry News)
11 Shirley Street, Hove, East Sussex BN3 3WJ
Editor Geoff Carroll
Bi-monthly £2.00 (by post)

News and articles about markets and opportunities for freelance writers and authors. Length: 300-900 words. Payment: from £1 per 100 words. Founded 1991.

Writers News
PO Box 4, Nairn IV12 4HU
tel (01667) 454441 *fax* (01667) 454401
Editor Richard Bell
Monthly £42.90 p.a. (£37.90 p.a. CC/DD)

News, competitions and articles on all aspects of writing. Length: 800-1500 words. Illustrations: line, half-tone. Payment: by arrangement. Founded 1989.

Writing Magazine
PO Box 4, Nairn IV12 4HU
tel (01667) 454441 *fax* (01667) 454401
Editor Richard Bell
Bi-monthly £2.50 (free to subscribers of *Writers News*)

Articles on all aspects of writing. Length: 800-1500 words. Illustrations: line, half-tone. Payment: by arrangement. Founded 1992.

Yachting Monthly
IPC Magazines Ltd, King's Reach Tower,
Stamford Street, London SE1 9LS
tel 0171 261 6040 *fax* 0171 261 7555
Editor Geoff Pack
Monthly £2.65

Technical articles, up to 2250 words, on all aspects of seamanship, navigation, the handling of sailing craft, and their design, construction and equipment. Well-written narrative accounts, up to 2500 words, of cruises in yachts. Payment: quoted on acceptance. Illustrations: b&w, colour transparencies, line or wash drawings, cartoons. Founded 1906.

Yachting World
IPC Magazines Ltd, King's Reach Tower,
Stamford Street, London SE1 9LS
tel 0171-261 6800 *fax* 0171-261 6818
e-mail yachting_world@ipc.co.uk
Editor Andrew Bray
Monthly £2.75

Practical articles of an original nature, dealing with sailing and boats. Length: 1500-2000 words. Payment: varies. Illustrations: colour transparencies, drawings, cartoons. Founded 1894.

Yachts and Yachting

196 Eastern Esplanade, Southend-on-Sea,
Essex SS1 3AB
tel (01702) 582245 *fax* (01702) 588434
Editor Frazer Clark
Fortnightly £2.35

Short articles which should be technically correct. Payment: by arrangement. Illustrations: line, half-tone, colour. Founded 1947.

Yes! – see The People in National newspapers UK and Ireland, page 3

Yorkshire Ridings Magazine

33 Beverley Road, Driffield,
Yorkshire YO25 7SD
tel/fax (01377) 253232
Editor Winston Halstead
Bi-monthly £1.00

Articles exclusively about people, life and character of the 3 Ridings of Yorkshire. Length: up to 1500 words. Payment: approx. £30-£35 per published page. Illustrations: line, half-tone, colour. Founded 1964.

You – see Mail on Sunday in National newspapers UK and Ireland, page 3

You and Your Wedding

You and Your Wedding Publications Ltd,
Silver House, 31-35 Beak Street,
London W1R 3LD
tel 0171-437 2998 *fax* 0171-287 8655
Editor Carole Hamilton
Bi-monthly £3.25

Articles, features and news covering all aspects of planning a wedding. Illustrations: colour. Payment: £200 per 1000 words. Founded 1985.

Young People Now

National Youth Agency,
17-23 Albion Street,
Leicester LE1 6GD
tel (0116) 285 6789 *fax* (0116) 247 1043
Editor Mary Durkin
Monthly £2.00 (£22.80 p.a.)

Informative articles, highlighting issues of concern to all those who work with young people – including youth work-, probation and social services, teach- and volunteers. Guidelines for con- ators available on request. Founded

Young Writer

Glebe House, Weobley, Herefordshire HR4 8SD
tel (01544) 318901 *fax* (01544) 318901
e-mail youngwriter@enterprise.net
web site http://www.mystworld.com/youngwriter
Editor Kate Jones
3 p.a. £2.50 (£6.50 for 3 issues)

Specialist magazine for young writers aged about 7-15 years: ideas for them and writing by them. Includes interviews of famous writers by children, fiction and non-fiction pieces, poetry; also explores words and grammar, issues related to writing (e.g. dyslexia), plus competitions with prizes. Length: 750 or 1500 words (features), up to 400 words (news), 750 words (short stories – unless specified otherwise in a competition), poetry of any length. Illustrations: colour – drawings by children, snapshots to accompany features. Payment: most children's material is published without payment; £25-£100 (features); £25 (cover cartoon). Founded 1995.

Your Dog

EMAP Apex Publications, Oundle Road,
Peterborough PE2 9NP
tel (01733) 898100 *fax* (01733) 898487
Editor Sarah Wright
Monthly £2.10

Articles and information of interest to dog lovers; features on all aspects of pet dogs. Length: approx. 1200 words. Illustrations: colour transparencies, prints and line drawings. Payment: £60 per 1000 words. Founded 1994.

Your Garden

IPC Magazines Ltd, Westover House,
West Quay Road, Poole, Dorset BH15 1JG
tel (01202) 680603 *fax* (01202) 674335
Editor Michael Pilcher
Monthly £2.10

Anything on gardening for the enthusiastic beginner. Commissioned material only; send brief synopsis of ideas. Length: 800-2000 words. Illustrations: colour photos and line. Payment: £100 per published 1000 words. Founded 1993.

Yours

Apex House, Oundle Road,
Peterborough PE2 9NP
tel (01733) 555123 *fax* (01733) 898487
Editor Neil Patrick
Monthly 75p

Features and news about and /or of interest to the over-60s age group including nostalgia and short stories. Study of magazine essential; approach in writing in first instance. Length: articles up to 1000 words, short stories up to 1800 words. Illustrations: preferably colour transparencies/prints but will consider good b&w prints/line drawings, cartoons. Payment: at editor's discretion or by agreement. Founded 1973.

Zest

National Magazine House, 72 Broadwick Street, London W1V 2BP
tel 0171-439 5000 *fax* 0171-439 5632
Editor Eve Cameron
Monthly £? 10

Health and beauty magazine. Commissioned material only! Health, fitness and beauty, features, news and sports, Length: 50-2000 words. Illustrations: colour and b&w photos and line. Payment: £250 per 1000 words. Founded 1994.

Newspapers and magazines overseas

Listings are given for newspapers and magazines in Australia (below), Canada (page 113), New Zealand (page 116) and South Africa (page 118). For information on submitting material to the USA, see page 120. Newspapers are listed under the towns in which they are published.

Australia

(Adelaide) Advertiser
121 King William Street, Adelaide, SA 5000
tel (08) 8206 2000 *fax* (08) 8206 3669
London office PO Box 481, 1 Virginia Street,
London E1 9BD
tel 0171-702 1355 *fax* 0171-702 1384
Editor Steve Howard
Daily Mon-Fri 70c, Sat$1.00
Descriptive and news background material, 400-800 words, preferably with pictures; also cartoons. Founded 1858.

(Adelaide) Sunday Mail
121 King William Street, Adelaide, SA 5000
postal address GPO Box 339, Adelaide, SA 5001
tel (08) 206 2796 *fax* (08) 206 3646
Editor K. Sullivan
Weekly $1.20
Founded 1912.

Australasian Sporting Shooter
Yaffa Publishing Group, 17-21 Bellevue Street,
Surry Hills, NSW 2010
tel (02) 281 2333 *fax* (02) 281 2750
Editor Ray Galea
Monthly $3.70
All aspects of game shooting, collecting, antiques, archery (associated with hunting), pistol shooting, clay target shooting, reloading, ballistics and articles of a technical nature. Payment: by arrangement.

Australian Bookseller & Publisher
18 Salmon Street, Port Melbourne, Victoria 3207
tel (03) 245 7370 *fax* (03) 245 7395
Editors Kim Hutchins and D.W. Thorpe
Monthly $55.00 p.a. ($82.00 p.a. NZ/Asia; $93.00 p.a. USA/Canada; $99.00 p.a. UK/Europe)
Founded 1921.

The Australian Financial Review
IBM Building, Level 25, 201 Sussex Street,
Sydney 2001
tel (02) 282 2512 *fax* (02) 282 3137
London office 95 Fetter Lane,
London EC4A 1HE
tel 0171-242 0044 *fax* 0171-242 0066
New York office Suite 1002, 1500 Broadway,
NY 10036
tel 212-398-9494
Editor Gregory Hywood
Daily Mon-Fri $1.50
Investment business and economic news and reviews; government and politics, production, banking, commercial, and Stock Exchange statistics; company analysis. General features in Friday *Weekend Review* supplement.

Australian Flying
Yaffa Publishing Group, 17-21 Bellevue Street,
Surry Hills, NSW 2010
tel (02) 281 2333 *fax* (02) 281 2750
e-mail yaffa@yaffa.com.au
Editor James Ostinga
London office 64 The Mall,
London W5 5LS
tel 0181-579 4836
Editor Robert Logan
6 p.a. $5.25
Covers the Australian aviation industry, from light aircraft to airliners. Payment: by arrangement.

Australian Geographic
PO Box 321, Terrey Hills, NSW 2084
tel (02) 9450 2344 *fax* (02) 9450 2990
e-mail www.ausgeo.com.au
Editor Howard Whelan
Quarterly $39.60 p.a. .
Short articles and features about Australia, particularly life, technology and natural history in remote parts of the country. Material mostly commissioned. Length: articles, 300-800 words, features, 2000-3000 words. Illustrations: all commissioned. Payment: $500 per 1000 words; illustrations by negotiation. Founded 1986.

108　Newspapers and magazines

Australian Home Beautiful
32 Walsh Street, West Melbourne, Victoria 3003
tel (03) 9320 7000 fax (03) 9320 7410
Editor W. Buttner
Monthly $4.40
Deals with home building, interior decoration, furnishing, gardening, cookery, etc. Short articles with accompanying photos with Australian slant accepted. Preliminary letter advisable. Payment: Australian average. Founded 1913.

Australian House and Garden
54 Park Street, Sydney, NSW 2000
tel (02) 282 8456 fax (02) 267 4912
Editor Stephanie King
Monthly $4.50
Factual articles dealing with interior decorating, home design, gardening, wine, food. Preliminary letter essential. Payment: by arrangement. Illustrations: line, half-tone, colour. Founded 1948.

Australian Journal of International Affairs
Department of International Relations, RSPAS, Australian National University, Canberra, ACT 0200
tel (06) 249 2169 fax (06) 279 8010
Editor Dr Stephanie Lawson
3 p.a. Personal rate A$60.00 p.a., institutions A$112.00 p.a. (Australia); other rates on application
Scholarly articles on international affairs. Length: 3000-7000 words. Payment: none.

The Australian Journal of Politics and History
Department of History, University of Queensland, St Lucia, Queensland 4067
tel (07) 3365 3163 fax (07) 3365 1388
Editors Geoff Stokes and Ross Johnston
3 p.a. $60.00 (US $58.00, UK £33.00)
Australian, Commonwealth, Asian, SW Pacific and international articles. Special feature: regular surveys of Australian Foreign Policy and State and Commonwealth politics. Length: 8000 words max. Illustrations: line, only when necessary. Payment: none.

Australian Photography
Yaffa Publishing Group, 17-21 Bellevue Street, Surry Hills, NSW 2010
tel (02) 9281 2333 fax (02) 9281 2750
Editor Robin Nichols
Monthly $4.95
Illustrated articles – picture-taking techniques, technical. Length/illustrations: 1000 words/colour and b&w prints or slides. Payment: $80 per page. Founded 1950.

Australasian Post
32 Walsh Street, Melbourne, Victoria 3003
tel (03) 320 7000 fax (03) 320 7409
Editor Graeme Johnstone
Weekly $2.20
Feature stories about Australia and Australians, both urban and rural; characters and achievers, known and unknown; short stories and poems. Material mostly commissioned. Length: 750-1000 words. Illustrations: colour transparencies. Payment: $300-500 per feature/illustration. Founded 1864.

Australian Powerboat
Yaffa Publishing Group, GPO Box 606, Sydney, NSW 1041
tel (02) 9213 8257 fax (02) 9281 2750
Editor Graham Lloyd
Bi-monthly $5.20
Articles and news on boats and boating, racing, water skiing and products. Length: 1500 words (articles), 200 words (news). Illustrations: colour (transparencies preferred). Payment: $100 per 1000 words; from $30. Founded 1976.

The Australian Quarterly
Australian Institute of Political Science, PO Box 145, Balmain, NSW 2041
tel (02) 810 5642 fax (02) 810 2406
Editors Damian Grace and Ian Marsh
Quarterly $55.00 p.a. individuals, $95.00 p.a. institutions ($65/$105 overseas)
Peer-reviewed articles for the informed non-specialist on politics, law, economics, social issues, etc. Length: 3500 words preferred. Payment: none. Founded 1929.

Australian Short Stories
Pascoe Publishing Pty Ltd, PO Box 42, Apollo Bay, Victoria 3233
tel (03) 523 76311 fax (03) 523 76559
Editors Bruce Pascoe and Lyn Harwood
Quarterly $9.95
Contemporary short stories from around the world. Length: 500-5000 words. Illustrations: b&w artwork. Payment $90 per 1000 words; $70. Founded 1983.

The Australian Way
BRW Media, Level 2, 469 Latrobe Street, Melbourne, Victoria 3000
postal address GPO Box 257C, Melbourne, Victoria 3001

tel (03) 9603 3888 *fax* (03) 9642 0852
Editor Mike Dobbie
Monthly Free

Inflight magazine for Qantas Airways. Articles of international interest; profiles, third-person stories that use locations as a backdrop, pictorial essays and features on prominent Australians. Length: 800-1500 words. Illustrations: colour transparencies. Payment: by negotiation. Founded 1986.

The Australian Women's Weekly
Australian Consolidated Press Ltd, 54 Park Street, Sydney, NSW 2000
postal address GPO Box 4178, Sydney, NSW 1028
tel (02) 9282 8000 *fax* (02) 9267 4459
Editor Suzanne Monks
Monthly $3.60

Fiction and features. Length: fiction 1000-5000 words; features 750-1500 words plus colour or b&w photos. Payment: according to length and merit. Fiction illustrations: sketches by own artists and freelances.

(Brisbane) The Courier-Mail
Queensland Newspapers Pty Ltd, Campbell Street, Bowen Hills, Brisbane, Queensland 4006
tel (07) 3252 6011 *fax* (07) 3252 6696
Editor C. Mitchell
Daily 70c

Occasional topical special articles required. Length: 1000 words.

(Brisbane) Sunday Mail
Queensland Newspapers Pty Ltd, PO Box 130, Campbell Street, Bowen Hills, Brisbane, Queensland 4006
tel (07) 252 6011
Editor Michael Prain
Weekly $1.30

Anything of general interest. Length: up to 1500 words. Illustrations: line, photos, b&w and colour, cartoons. Payment: by arrangement. Rejected MSS returned if postage enclosed.

The Bulletin with Newsweek
54 Park Street, Sydney, NSW 2000
tel (02) 282 8200 *fax* (02) 267 4359
Editor Lyndall Crisp
Weekly $3.30

General interest articles, features; humour. Length: 750 words per page, max. 2100 words. Illustrations: colour photos and cartoons. Payment: $450 per 1000 words published; $100 colour cartoons and photos, according to size used.

Cleo
Level 4, 54 Park Street, Sydney, NSW 1028
tel (02) 9282 8617 *fax* (02) 9267 4368
Editor Gina Johnson
Monthly $4.80

Articles (relationship, emotional, self-help) up to 3000 words, short quizzes. Payment: by negotiation. Founded 1972.

Countryman
219 St Georges Terrace, Perth, Western Australia 6000
tel (09) 482 3322 *fax* (09) 482 3324
Editor John Dare
Weekly 70c

Agriculture, farming or country interest features and service columns. Payment: standard rates. Illustrations: line, half-tone, colour, cartoons.

Current Affairs Bulletin
CAB, 72 Bathurst Street, Sydney, NSW 2000
tel (02) 264 5726 *fax* (02) 267 7900
Managing Editor Sue Phillips
6 p.a. $6.50 ($40.00 p.a., $57.00 p.a. overseas)

Authoritative well-documented articles on all national and international affairs: politics, economics, science, the arts, business and social questions. Length: 3000-5000 words. Illustrations: line, half-tone. Payment: none. Founded 1942.

Dance Australia
Yaffa Publishing Group, Box 606, GPO Sydney, NSW 2001
tel (02) 281 2333 *fax* (02) 281 2750
e-mail yaffa@yaffa.com.au
Editor Karen van Ulzen
Bi-Monthly $5.50

Articles and features on all aspects of dance in Australia. Material mostly commissioned, but will consider unsolicited contributions. Length: as appropriate. Illustrations: b&w photos, line drawings, cartoons. Payment: $200 per 1000 words; illustrations by negotiation. Founded 1980.

Dolly
54 Park Street, Sydney, NSW 1028
tel (02) 9282 8437 *fax* (02) 9267 4911
Editor Susie Pitts
Monthly $3.60

Features on fashion, health and beauty, personalities, music, social issues and how to cope with growing up, etc. Length: not less than 1000 words. Illustrations: colour, b&w, line, cartoons. Payment: by arrangement. Founded 1970.

Electronics Australia with ETI
PO Box 199, Alexandria, NSW 2015
tel (02) 9353 0620 *fax* (02) 9353 0613
Editor Jamieson Rowe
Monthly $5.50
Articles on technical television and
radio, hi-fi, popular electronics, micro-
computers and avionics. Length: up to
2000 words. Payment: by arrangement.
Illustrations: line, half-tone, cartoons.

Elle (Australia)
54 Park Street, Sydney, 2000
tel 61 2 282 8790 *fax* 61 2 267 4375
Editor Deborah Thomas
Monthly $4.95
Profiles, news reports, cultural essays,
fashion stories. Length: 300-3000 words.
Payment: varies. Founded 1990.

Fishing World Magazine
Yaffa Publishing Group, 17-21 Bellevue Street,
Surry Hills, NSW 2010
tel (02) 9281 2333 *fax* (02) 9281 2750
telex AA 121887
Editor Jim Harnwell
Monthly $4.95
Rock, surf, stream, deep sea and game
fishing, with comprehensive sections on
gear, equipment and boats. Payment: by
arrangement.

Geo Australasia
Geo Productions Pty Ltd, PO Box 1390,
Chatswood, NSW 2057
tel (02) 9411 1766 *fax* (02) 9413 2689
Editor Michael Hohensee
Bi-Monthly $7.95 ($55.00 p.a. surface mail,
$85.00 p.a. airmail)
Non-fiction articles on wildlife, adven-
ture, culture and lifestyles, natural histo-
ry and the environment in Australia,
New Zealand, the Pacific and SE Asia.
Length: 1500-3000 words. Payment:
$600-$1500 by arrangement. Illustrations:
photos, colour transparencies. Founded
1978.

Guns Australia
Yaffa Publishing Group Pty Ltd,
17-21 Bellevue Street, Surry Hills, NSW 2010
tel (02) 281 2333 *fax* (02) 281 2750
Editor Ray Galea
Bi-Monthly $3.90
Articles, features, technical pieces, news.
All material commissioned. Length: 2000
words. Illustrations: colour slides, b&w
photos. Payment: $50 per page.

Herald of the South
GPO Box 283, Canberra, ACT 2601
tel/fax (02) 970 6710
Quarterly $28.00 p.a.
Baha'i magazine with emphasis on reli-
gious approach to unity. Features, fiction
and non-fiction. Length: up to 3500 words.
Illustrations: colour and b&w photos.
Payment: by negotiation. Founded 1925.

HQ Magazine
54 Park Street, Sydney, NSW 2000
tel (02) 9282 8260 *fax* (02) 9267 3616
Editor Fenella Souter
Bi-Monthly $5.95
General interest features and profiles for a
literate readership. Length: 1500-5000
words. Illustrations: colour and b&w photos. Payment: by negotiation. Founded
1989.

(Launceston) Examiner
Box 99A, PO Launceston, Tasmania 7250
tel (03) 633 15111 *fax* (03) 633 47328
Editor Rod Scott
Daily 75c
Accepts freelance material. Payment: by
arrangement.

(Melbourne) Age
David Syme & Co. Ltd, 250 Spencer Street,
Melbourne, Victoria 3000
tel (03) 9600 4211 *fax* (03) 9670 7514
Editor Bruce Guthrie
London office 95 Fetter Lane, London EC4A 1HE
Daily Mon-Fri 90c Sat $1.30
Independent liberal morning daily; room
occasionally for outside matter. An illus-
trated weekend magazine and literary
review is published on Saturday; accepts
occasional freelance material.

(Melbourne) Australasian Post
Pacific Publications Pty Ltd, 32 Walsh Street,
GPO Box 501H, Melbourne, Victoria 3003
tel (03) 9320 7000
Deputy Editor Peter Mayer
Weekly $2.50
Opening for casual contributions of topi-
cal factual illustrated articles of
Australian interest. General appeal.
Payment: by arrangement.

(Melbourne) Herald Sun
HWT Tower, 40 City Road, Southbank,
Victoria 3006
tel (03) 9292 1816 *fax* (03) 9292 1776
Editor Peter Blunden
Daily Mon-Fri 70c Sat 90c Sun $1.20

Accepts freelance articles, preferably with illustrations. Length: up to 750 words. Illustrations: half-tone, line, cartoons. Payment: on merit.

(Melbourne) The Sunday Age
250 Spencer Street, Melbourne, Victoria 3000
tel (03) 600 4211 *fax* (03) 602 1856
e-mail sunacre@theage.com.au
Editor Jill Baker
London office 95 Fetter Lane, London EC4A 1HE
tel 0171-242 0044 *fax* 0171-242 0066
Weekly 70c

Features. Length: 500-2000 words. Payment: by arrangement. Founded 1989.

(Melbourne) Sunday Herald Sun
HWT Tower, 40 City Road, Southbank, Victoria 3006
tel (03) 9292 2000 *fax* (03) 9292 2080
Editor Alan Howe
Weekly $1.20

Accepts freelance articles, preferably with illustrations. Length: up to 2000 words. Illustrations: colour. Payment: on merit.

Mode Australia
ACP Publishing Pty Ltd, 54 Park Street, Sydney, NSW 2001
tel (02) 282 8703 *fax* (02) 267 4456
Editor Karin Upton Baker
Bi-Monthly $5.50

Fashion, health and beauty, celebrity news. Length: 3000 words. Illustrations: colour and b&w photos. Payment: $500 per 1000 words; $150. Founded 1973.

Modern Boating
180 Bourke Road, Alexandria, NSW 2015
tel (02) 693 6666 *fax* (02) 317 4615
Editor Mark Rothfield
Monthly $5.95

Articles on all types of boats and boating. Payment: $130-$200 per 1000 words. Illustrations: half-tone, colour. Founded 1965.

New Idea
32 Walsh Street, PO Box 1292K GPO, Melbourne, Victoria 3001
tel (03) 320 7000 *fax* (03) 320 7439
Editor F. Wingett
Weekly $2.50

General interest women's magazine; news stories, features, fashion, services, short stories of general interest to women of all ages. Length: stories, 500-4000 words: articles, 500-2000 words. Payment: on acceptance. Founded 1902.

New Weekly
54 Park Street, Sydney, NSW 2000
tel (02) 282 8285 *fax* (02) 264 6005
Editor Juliet Ashworth
Weekly $2.70

News and features on celebrities, food, new products, fashion and astrology. Illustrated. Payment: by negotiation. Founded 1993.

New Woman
Level 16, 213 Miller Street, North Sydney, NSW 2060
tel (02) 9956 1000 *fax* (02) 9956 1088
Editor Cyndi Tebbel
Monthly $4.50

Self-development for the thirty-something woman: articles, features, fashion, beauty, health, reviews and book excerpts. Material mostly commissioned. Length: average 1200 words. Payment: 55c a word. Illustrated. Founded 1989.

Overland
PO Box 14146, Melbourne, Victoria 8001
tel (03) 9380 1152 *fax* (03) 9380 2586
Editor Iam Syson
Quarterly $32.00 p.a.

Literary and cultural. Australian material preferred. Payment: by arrangement. Illustrations: line, half-tone, cartoons.

People Magazine
54 Park Street, Sydney, NSW 2000
tel (02) 282 8743 *fax* (02) 267 4365
Editor D. Naylor
Weekly $2.80

National weekly news-pictorial. Mainly people stories. Photos depicting exciting happenings, glamour, show business, unusual occupations, rites, customs. Payment: $300 per page, text and photos.

(Perth) Sunday Times
34-50 Stirling Street, Perth, Western Australia 6000
tel (09) 326 8326 *fax* (09) 221 1121
Managing Editor Don Smith
Weekly $1.30

Topical articles to 800 words. Payment: on acceptance. Founded 1897.

(Perth) The West Australian
219 St Georges Terrace, Perth, Western Australia 6000
tel (09) 482 3111 *fax* (09) 324 1416
Editor Paul Murray
Daily Mon-Fri 70c Sat $1.20

Articles and sketches about people and events in Australia and abroad. Length: 300-700 words. Payment: Award rates or better. Illustrations: line, half-tone. Founded 1833.

Poetry Australia
South Head Press, The Market Place, Berrima, NSW 2577
tel (048) 771 421
Editor John Millett
Quarterly $40 p.a.
Previously unpublished new poetry, and criticism. Payment: copy of magazine. Founded 1964.

Quadrant
46 George Street, Fitzroy, Victoria 3065
postal address PO Box 1495, Collingwood, Victoria 3066
tel (03) 9417 6855 *fax* (03) 9416 2980
Editor Robert Manne
Monthly $5.50
Articles, short stories, verse, etc. Prose length: 2000-5000 words. Illustrations: cartoons. Payment: minimum $90 articles/stories, $60 reviews, $40 poems; illustrations by arrangement.

Reader's Digest
26-32 Waterloo Street, Surry Hills, NSW 2010
tel (02) 600 6111 *fax* (02) 600 8165
Editor Bruce Heilbuth
Monthly $3.95
Articles on Australian subjects by commission only. No unsolicited MSS accepted. Length: 2500-5000 words. Payment: up to $5000 per article; brief filler paragraphs, $50-$250. Illustrations: half-tone, colour.

Redoubt
Faculty of Communication, University of Canberra, PO Box 1, Belconnen, ACT 2616
tel (06) 201 2945 *fax* (06) 201 5300
e-mail redoubt@comserver.canberra.edu.au
web site http://services.canberra.edu.au/uc/comm /schiflgcs/profwr/redoubt/redoubt.html
Managing Editor Jeff Doyle
Bi-Annual $8.50
Literary magazine: mainly short stories, poetry, reviews, articles and profiles of writers. Length: short poetry; prose up to 3000 words; reviews up to 600 words. Illustrations: b&w photos and line drawings. Payment: copy of magazine. Founded 1988.

Scuba Diver
Yaffa Publishing Group, 17-21 Bellevue Street, Surry Hills, NSW 2010
tel (02) 9281 2333 *fax* (02) 9281 2750
e-mail yaffa@yaffa.com.au
Editor Sue Crowe
Bi-monthly $5.75
News, features, articles and short stories on scuba diving. Length: 1500 words (articles/features), 300-800 words (news), 800-1000 (short stories). Illustrations: colour. Payment: $70 per page, negotiable (words and pictures).

She
ACP Publishing Pty Ltd, 54 Park Street, Sydney, NSW 2000
tel (02) 9282 8585 *fax* (02) 9267 4457
Editor-in-Chief Pat Ingram
Monthly $4.50
Lifestyle magazine for young women. Length: 2000 words, variable (articles/features). Illustrations: colour and b&w. Founded 1993.

The Sun-Herald
GPO Box 506, Sydney, NSW 2001
tel (02) 9282 2822 *fax* (02) 9282 2151
Editor Andrew Clark
London office John Fairfax (UK) Ltd, 93 Fetter Lane, London EC4A 1HE
tel 0171-242 0044
Weekly $1.00
Topical articles to 1000 words; sections on politics, social issues, show business, finance and fashion. Payment: by arrangement.

The Sunday Telegraph
News Ltd, 2 Holt Street, Surry Hills, Sydney, NSW 2010
tel (02) 9288 3305 *fax* (02) 9288 2300
Editor Roy Miller
Weekly $1.00
News and features. Illustrations: colour transparencies. Payment: varies. Founded 1935.

(Sydney) The Daily Telegraph
News Limited, 2 Holt Street, Surry Hills, NSW 2010
tel (02) 9288 3000 *fax* (02) 9288 3481
Editor-in-Chief John Hartigan
Daily Mon-Fri 80c Sat $1.00
Modern feature articles and series of Australian or world interest. Length: 1000-2000 words. Payment: according to merit/length.

The Sydney Morning Herald
PO Box 506, Sydney, NSW 2001
tel (02) 9282 2858
Editor-in-Chief John Alexander
London office 95 Fetter Lane, London EC4A 1HE
tel 0171-242 0044 *fax* 0171-242 0066
Daily 90c

Saturday edition has pages of literary criticism and also magazine articles, plus glossy colour magazine. Topical articles 600-4000 words. Payment: varies, but minimum $100 per 1000 words. Illustrations: all types. Founded 1831.

Woman's Day
54-58 Park Street, Sydney, NSW 2000
tel (02) 9282 8000 *fax* (02) 9267 4360
Editor Buntie Avieson
Weekly $2.60

National women's magazine; news, show business, fiction, fashion, general articles, cookery, home economy.

Canada

ArtsAtlantic
Confederation Centre of the Arts,
145 Richmond Street, Charlottetown,
Prince Edward Island C1A 1J1
tel 902-628-6138 *fax* 902-566-4648
e-mail artsatlantic@isn.net
web site www.isn.net/artsatlantic
Editor Joseph Sherman
3 p.a. $29.95 for 4 issues ($45.95 for 8 issues)

Features and reviews on the art history of Atlantic Canada, the work of contemporary artists and the ideas and issues affecting Canadian culture. No fiction or poetry. All material commissioned; send enquiries (plus CV and samples of published work). Length: reviews, 300-900 words, features, 1000-3000 words. Illustrations: colour and b&w. Payment: $75 per review, features 15c per word to $250 maximum; illustrations by negotiation. Founded 1977.

The Beaver: Exploring Canada's History
Canada's National History Society, Suite 478,
167 Lombard Avenue, Winnipeg,
Manitoba R3B 0T6
tel 204-988-9300 *fax* 204-988-9309
Editor Christopher Dafoe
Bi-Monthly $27.50 p.a. ($34.50 p.a. elsewhere)

Articles, historical and modern, on Canadian history. Length: 1500-5000

words, with illustrations. Payment: on acceptance, approx. 10c per word. Illustrations: b&w and colour photos or drawings.

Books in Canada
427 Mount Pleasant Road, Toronto,
Ontario M4S 2L8
tel 416-489-4755 *fax* 416-489-6045
Editor Norman Doidge
9 p.a. $3.95

Commissioned reviews, informed criticism and articles on Canadian literary scene. Query first – do not send unsolicited material. Payment: 12c per word. Founded 1971.

C Magazine
PO Box 5, Station B, Toronto, Ontario M5T 2T2
tel 416-539-9495 *fax* 416-539-9903
e-mail cmag@istar.ca
Editor Joyce Mason
Quarterly US$8.25

Arts and artists' projects, features, reviews. Accept submissions. Length: features, varies; reviews, 500 words. Illustrations: b&w photos. Payment: $250-$500 features, $100 reviews. Founded 1972.

Canadian Author
PO Box 419, Campbellford, Ontario K0L 1L0
tel 705-653-0323 *fax* 705-653-0593
Editor Doug Bale
Quarterly $18.00 p.a. individual, $30.00 p.a. corporate (add $10.00 p.a. outside Canada)

Published by Canadian Authors Association. Interested in an international view on writing techniques, profiles, interviews, freelance opportunities for Canadian writers. Query only. Payment: $30 per printed page.

The Canadian Forum
251 Laurier Avenue W, Suite 804, Ottawa,
Ontario K1P 5J6
tel 613-230-3078 *fax* 613-233-1458
Editor Duncan Cameron
10 p.a. $3.50 ($29.96 p.a.)

Articles on public affairs and the arts; book reviews. Length: up to 2500 words. Payment: varies. Illustrations: line and photos.

Canadian Interiors
Crailer Communications, 360 Dupont Street,
Toronto, Ontario M5R 1V9
tel 416-966-9944 *fax* 416-966-9946
Editor Sheri Craig
8 p.a. $34.24 p.a. (US$75.00 p.a. elsewhere)

Articles on all aspects of the interior design industry. Illustrations: half-tone, colour.

Canadian Literature

1855 West Mall, University of British Columbia, Vancouver, BC V6T 1Z2
tel 604-882-2780 *fax* 604-822-9452
Editor E.M. Kröller
Quarterly $15.00 plus postage

Articles on Canadian writers and writing in English and French. Length: up to 5000 words. Payment: $5 per printed page. Founded 1959.

Canadian Theatre Review (CTR)

Dept of Drama, University of Guelph, Guelph, Ontario N1G 2W1
Contact Editorial Committee
Quarterly $9.50 ($32.00 p.a.)

Feature and review articles on Canadian theatre aimed at theatre professionals; book and play reviews. Send MSS accompanied by PC compatible disk. Length: 2000-3000 words. Illustrations: b&w. Payment: $200-275 (features/articles), $50 (book/play reviews). Founded 1974.

Canadian Yachting

Kerrwil Publications Ltd, 395 Matheson Boulevard East, Mississauga, Ontario L4Z 2H2
tel 905-890-1846 *fax* 905-890-5769
Editor Heather Ormerod
6 p.a. $3.95

Features, news and views. Query letters preferred. Length: regulars, 1000-2000 words; features, 1800-2700 words. Illustrations: line, half-tone, colour, cartoons. Payment: up to $350 regulars, up to $350 features; $50-$250 line, $30-$100 photos, $200 cover shots. Founded 1974.

Chatelaine

777 Bay Street, Toronto, Ontario M5W 1A7
tel 416-596-5425
Editor Rona Maynard
Monthly $2.99

Women's interest articles; Canadian angle preferred. Payment: on acceptance; from $1000.

Chickadee

Owl Communications Inc., PO Box 53, 370 King Street, Suite 300, Toronto, Ontario M5V 1J9
tel (416) 971 5275 *fax* (416) 971 5294
web site http://www.owl.on.ca
Editor Susan Petersiel Berg
9 p.a. $2.95 ($24.00 p.a. Canada, US$14.95 USA, $34.00 rest of world)

Highly illustrated mix of stories and activities on the theme of the world around kids; aimed at children aged 6-9. Length: 10-100 words (articles), 800-900 words (fiction). Illustrations: colour. Payment: $250 (fiction). Founded 1979.

The Dalhousie Review

Dalhousie University Press Ltd, Sir James Dunn Building, Suite 314, Halifax, NS B3H 3J5
tel 902-494-2541
Editor Dr Alan Andrews
Quarterly $8.50 (plus postage) ($30.00 p.a., $80.00 for 3 years; $40.00/$100.00 outside Canada)

Articles on literary, political, historical, philosophical and social topics; fiction; verse; book reviews. Length: prose, normally not more than 5000 words; verse, preferably less than 40 words. Payment: $1 per printed page for fiction; $3 for 1st poem, $2 for each subsequent poem (per issue). Contributors receive 2 copies of issue and 15 offprints of their work. Usually not more than 2 stories and about 10 or 12 poems in any one issue.

Equinox

11450 Albert-Hudon Blvd, Montreal, Montreal, QC H1G 3J9
tel 514-327-4464 *fax* 514-327-0514
e-mail amokantz@limestone.kosone.com
Editor Alan Morantz
Bi-Monthly ($22.95 p.a. Canada; Can.$29.00 p.a. USA; Can.$35.00 elsewhere)

Magazine of discovery in science, human cultures, technology and geography. Accepts articles on hard science topics (length: 100-500 words); welcomes queries (2-3-page outline) for specific assignments. No phone queries please. Illustrations: colour transparencies. Payment: by arrangement. Founded 1982.

The Fiddlehead

Campus House, University of New Brunswick, PO Box 4400, Fredericton, NB E3B 5A3
tel 506-453-3501
Editor Bill Gaston
Quarterly $9.00

Reviews, poetry, short stories. Payment: approx. $10-$12 per printed page. Founded 1945.

(Hamilton) The Spectator

44 Frid Street, Hamilton, Ontario L8N 3G3
tel 905-526-3333
Publisher Patrick J. Collins
Daily Mon-Fri 75c Sat $1.75

Articles of general interest, political analysis and background; interviews, stories of Canadians abroad. Length: 800 words maximum. Payment: rate varies. Founded 1846.

Inuit Art Quarterly

2081 Merivale Road, Nepean, Ontario K2G 1G9
tel 613-224-8189 *fax* 613-224-2907
e-mail iaf@inuitart.org
web site www.inuitart.org
Editor Marybelle Mitchell
Quarterly $6.25

Features, news and reviews on the Inuit art world. Freelance contributors are expected to have a thorough knowledge of the arts. Length: varies. Illustrations: colour and b&w photos and line. Payment: by arrangement; illustrations $50. Founded 1986.

Journal of Canadian Studies

Trent University, Peterborough, Ontario K9J 7B8
tel 705-748-1279 *fax* 705-748-1655
e-mail jcs_rec@trentu.ca
Editors Michèle Lacombe, James Conley, Kerry Cannon
Quarterly US$35.00 p.a. (US$55.00 p.a. institutions)

Major academic review of Canadian studies. Articles of general as well as scholarly interest on history, politics, literature, society, arts. Length: 7000-10,000 words.

The Malahat Review

University of Victoria, PO Box 1700, Victoria, BC V8W 2Y2
tel 604-721-8524
Editor Derk Wynand
Quarterly $25.00 p.a. ($35.00 p.a. overseas)

Short stories, poetry, short plays, reviews, some graphics. Payment: $25 per magazine page. Illustrations: half-tone. Founded 1967.

Performing Arts & Entertainment in Canada (PA&E)

104 Glenrose Avenue, Toronto, Ontario M4T 1K8
tel 416-484-4534 *fax* 416-484-6214
Editor Karen Bell
Quarterly $8.00 p.a. ($14.00 p.a. elsewhere)

Feature articles on Canadian theatre, music, dance and film artists and organisations; technical articles on scenery, lighting, make-up, costumes, etc. Length: 800-1500 words. Payment: $150-$250, one month after publication. Illustrations: b&w photos, colour slides. Founded 1961.

Photo Life

Toronto-Dominion Centre, Suite 2550, Box 77, Toronto, Ontario M5K 1E7
tel 800-905-7468 *fax* 800-664-2739
e-mail apex@photolife.com
web site http://www.photolife.com
Editor Jacques Thibault
8 p.a. $3.95

Covers all aspects of photography of interest to amateur and professional photographers. Length: 1500-2500 words. Illustrations: colour and b&w photos. Payment: by arrangement. Founded 1976.

Quebec Chronicle Telegraph

Quebec Chronicle-Telegraph Inc., 3484 chemin Ste-Foy, Quebec City, Quebec G1X 1S8
tel 418-650-1764
Editor Karen Macdonald
Weekly 40c

Covers local events within English community in Quebec City. Some feature articles. Founded 1764.

Quill & Quire

70 The Esplanade, Suite 210, Toronto, Ontario M5E 1R2
tel 416-360-0044 *fax* 416-955-0794
e-mail quill@hookup.net
Editor Scott Anderson
12 p.a. $45.00 p.a. (outside Canada $75p.a.)

Articles of interest about the Canadian book trade. Payment: from $100. Illustrations: line, half-tone. Subscription includes Canadian Publishers Directory (2 p.a.). Founded 1935.

Reader's Digest

215 Redfern Avenue, Montreal, Quebec H3Z 2V9
tel 514-934-0751
Editor Alexander Farrell
Monthly $2.49

Original articles on all subjects of broad general appeal, thoroughly researched and professionally written. Outline or query only. Length: 3000 words approx. Payment: from $2700. Also previously published material. Illustrations: line, half-tone, colour.

(Toronto) The Globe and Mail

444 Front Street West, Toronto, Ontario M5V 2S9
Publisher Roger Parkinson, *Editor-in-Chief* William Thorsell
Daily 60c

Unsolicited material considered. Payment: by arrangement. Founded 1844.

Toronto Life

59 Front Street East, Toronto, Ontario M5E 1B3
tel 416-364-3333 *fax* 416-861-1169
Editor John Macfarlane
Monthly $3.95

Articles, profiles on Toronto and
Torontonians. Illustrations: line, half-
tone, colour. Founded 1967.

Toronto Star

One Yonge Street, Toronto, Ontario M5E 1E6
tel 416-367-2000
London office Level 4A, PO Box 495,
Virginia Street, London E1 9XY
tel 0171-833 0791
Daily Mon-Fri 30c Sat$1.00 Sun 75c

Features, life, world/national politics.
Payment: by arrangement. Founded 1892.

(Vancouver) Province

2250 Granville Street, Vancouver, BC V6H 3G2
tel 604-732-2007 *fax* 604-732-2378
Editor-in-Chief Michael Cooke
Daily Mon-Fri 60c Sun $1.00

Founded 1898.

Vancouver Sun

2250 Granville Street, Vancouver, BC V6H 3G2
tel 604-732-2318 *fax* 604-732-2323
e-mail jcruickshank@pacpress.southam.ca
web site www.vancouversun.com
Editor-in-Chief John Cruickshank
London office Southam News, 4th Floor,
8 Bouverie Street, London EC4Y 8AX
tel 0171-583 7322
Daily Mon-Thu 60c Fri, Sat $1.25

Saturday Review, arts magazine, accepts
contributions. Travel, Op-Ed pieces considered. Payment: by arrangement.

Wascana Review of Contemporary Poetry & Short Fiction

c/o English Department, University of Regina,
Regina, Sask. S4S 0A2
tel 306-585-4311 *fax* 306-585-4827
Editor Kathleen Wall
Bi-Annual $7.00 p.a. ($8.00 p.a. outside Canada)

Criticism, short stories, poetry, reviews.
Manuscripts from freelance writers welcome. Length: prose, not more than 6000
words; verse, up to 100 lines. Payment:
$3 per page for prose; $10 per printed
page for verse; $3 per page for reviews.
Contributors also receive 2 free copies
and a year's subscription. Founded 1966.

Windspeaker

15001-112 Ave NW, Edmonton, Alberta T5M 2V6
tel 403-455-2700 *fax* 403-455-7639
Editor Debora Lockyer
Monthly ($36.00 p.a.)

National newspaper by and about
Aboriginal people: articles, features,
news, guest editorials. Write for
'Freelancer's guidelines'. Length: 300-800
words. Illustrations: prefer colour prints.
Payment: $3.00 per published column
inch; $15-$50 per photo. Founded 1983.

Winnipeg Free Press

PO Box 9500, Winnipeg, Manitoba R2X 3A2
tel 204-694-2022
Editor John Dafoe
Daily Mon-Fri 25c Sat $1.25 Sun 35c

Some freelance articles. Payment: $100.
Founded 1872.

New Zealand

(Auckland) New Zealand Herald

PO Box 32, Auckland
tel (09) 379-5050 *fax* (09) 366-1568
Editor Gavin Ellis
Daily 70c

Topical and informative articles 800-
1100 words. Payment: minimum $150-
$300. Illustrations: colour negatives or
prints. Founded 1863.

(Auckland) Sunday News

155 New North Road, Auckland
tel (09) 302-1300 *fax* (09) 358-3003
Editor Suzanne Chetwin
Weekly $1.00

Will consider anything. Length: varies.
Illustrations: colour and b&w photos and
line. Payment: depends on quality.
Founded 1963.

(Auckland) Sunday Star-Times

News Media Auckland Ltd, PO Box 1327,
Auckland 1
tel (09) 302-1300 *fax* (09) 309-0258
Editor Michael Forbes
Sun $1.30

(Christchurch) The Press

Private Bag 4722, Christchurch
tel (03) 379-0940 *fax* (03) 364-8238
Editor Bruce Baskett
Daily 40c

Articles of general interest not more than
1000 words. Illustrations: photos and
line drawings, cartoons. Payment: by
arrangement.

Christchurch Star

Tuam Street, Christchurch
tel (03) 379-7100 *fax* (03) 366-0180
Editor Mike Fletcher
Bi-weekly Free

Will consider freelance material, excluding travel; also cartoons. Founded 1868.

(Dunedin) Otago Daily Times

PO Box 181, Dunedin
tel (03) 477-4760 *fax* (03) 477-1313
Editor R.L. Charteris
Daily 60c

Any articles of general interest up to 1000 words, but preference is given to NZ writers. Topical illustrations and personalities. Payment: current NZ rates. Founded 1861.

The Gisborne Herald

PO Box 1143, 64 Gladstone Road, Gisborne
tel (06) 867-2099
Editor Iain Gillies
Daily 12c

Topical features of local interest. Length: 1000-1500 words. Payment: by arrangement. Illustrations: bromides. Founded 1874.

Hawke's Bay Herald Tribune

PO Box 180, Karamu Road North, Hastings
tel (06) 878-5155 *fax* (06) 876-0655
Editor J.E. Morgan
Daily 65c

Limited requirements. Payment: $30 upwards for articles, $10 upwards for photos. Illustrations: web offset.

(Invercargill) The Southland Times

PO Box 805, Invercargill
tel (03) 218-1909 *fax* (03) 214-9905
e-mail editor@sh.co.nz
Editor C.A. Lind
Daily 70c

Articles of up to 800 words on topics of Southland interest. Payment: by arrangement. Illustrations: line, half-tone, colour, cartoons. Founded 1862.

Management

Profile Publishing, PO Box 5544, Auckland
tel (09) 630-8940 *fax* (09) 630-1046
e-mail sprofile@iconz.co.nz
Editor Carroll du Chateau
Monthly $5.95

Articles on the practice of management skills and techniques, individual and company profiles, coverage of business trends and topics. A NZ/Australian angle or application preferred. Length: 2000 words. Payment: by arrangement; minimum 23c per word. Illustrations: photos, line drawings.

(Napier) The Daily Telegraph

PO Box 343, Napier
tel (06) 835-4488 *fax* (06) 835-1129
Editor H. Pierard
Daily 70c

Limited market for features. Illustrations: line, half-tone, colour. Payment: $50 upwards per 1000 words; $20 a picture. Founded 1871.

The Nelson Mail

PO Box 244, 15 Bridge Street, Nelson
tel (03) 548-7079 *fax* (03) 546-2802
Editor David Mitchell
Daily 70c

Features, articles on NZ subjects. Length: 500-1000 words. Payment: up to $100 per 1000 words. Illustrations: half-tone, colour.

(New Plymouth) The Daily News

PO Box 444, Currie Street, New Plymouth
tel (06) 758-0559 *fax* (06) 758-6849
Editor Murray Goston
Daily 70c

Articles preferably with a Taranaki connection. Payment: by negotiation. Illustrations: half-tone, cartoons. Founded 1857.

New Truth and TV Extra

News Media Auckland Ltd, 155 New North Road, Auckland, PO Box 1074
tel (09) 302-1300 *fax* (09) 309-2279
Editor Mike Smith
Weekly $1.50

Bold investigative reporting, exposés. Length: 500-1000 words, preferably accompanied by photos. Payment: about $150 per 500 words, extra for photos.

New Zealand Farmer

NZ Rural Press Ltd, PO Box 4233, 300 Great South Road, Greenlane, Auckland 5
tel (09) 520-9451 *fax* (09) 520-9459
Editor Hugh Stringleman
Fortnightly

Authoritative, simply written articles on new developments in livestock husbandry, grassland farming, cropping, farm machinery, marketing. Length: 500 words. Payment: $200 per 1000 words.

New Zealand Woman's Day

Private Bag 92512, Wellesley Street, Auckland
tel (09) 373-5408 *fax* (09) 357-0978
Editor Louise Wright
Weekly $3.10

Celebrity interviews, exclusive news stories, short stories, gossip. Length: 1000

words. Illustrations: colour transparencies; payment according to use. Payment: £400. Founded 1989.

She & More

Private Bag 92512, Wellesley Street,
Auckland 1036
tel (09) 308 2735 *fax* (09) 309 8718
Editor Jane Binsley
Monthly $5.95

Lifestyle magazine for young women. Length: 1000-2000 words (features), 300 words (profiles). Illustrations: colour. Payment: negotiable. Founded 1996.

Straight Furrow

PO Box 715, Wellington
tel (04) 473-7269 *fax* (04) 473-1081
Editor Susan Grant
Fortnightly $1.60

Factual news and features of interest to the farming/rural sector. Length: 500 words news, 1000 words features. Illustrations: colour and b&w photos. Payment: 25c per published word; $20 per published photo. Founded 1933.

Takahe

Takahe Collective Trust, PO Box 13335,
Christchurch 8001
tel (03) 359-8133
Quarterly $32 p.a. international/$24 p.a. domestic
Quality short fiction and poetry by both new and established writers. Payment: approx. $30 per issue. Founded 1989.

The Timaru Herald

PO Box 46, Bank Street, Timaru
tel (03) 684-4129 *fax* (03) 688-1042
Editor D.H. Wood
Daily 50c

Topical articles. Payment: by arrangement. Illustrations: colour or b&w prints, cartoons.

(Wellington) The Evening Post

PO Box 3740, 40 Boulcott Street, Wellington
tel (04) 474-0444 *fax* (04) 474-0237 *Editor's fax*
(04) 474-0536
Editor S.L. Carty
Daily Mon-Sat 70c

General topical articles, 600 words. Payment: NZ current rates or by arrangement. News illustrations, cartoons. Founded 1865.

Your Home and Garden

Australian Consolidated Press (New Zealand) Ltd,
Private Bag 92512, Wellesley Street, Auckland
tel (09) 308-2700 *fax* (09) 377 6725

Editor Sharon Newey
Monthly $5.25

Advice, ideas and projects for homeowners – interiors and gardens. Length: 1000 words. Illustrations: good quality colour transparencies. Payment: 30c per word/ $75 per transparency. Founded 1991.

South Africa

(Cape Town) Cape Times

Newspaper House, 122 St George's Street,
Cape Town 8001
tel (021) 488-4911
postal address PO Box 11, Cape Town 8000
Editor J.C. Viviers
London office 1st Floor, 32-33 Hatton Garden,
London EC1N 8DL
tel 0171-405 3742
Daily R1.20

Contributions must be suitable for a daily newspaper and must not exceed 800 words. Illustrations: photos of outstanding South African interest. Founded 1876.

Car

PO Box 180, Howard Place 7450
tel (021) 531-1391 *fax* (021) 531-3333
e-mail car@rsp.co.za
web site http://www.carmag.com
Editor John Wright
Monthly R7.50

New car announcements with pictures and full colour features of motoring interest. Payment: by arrangement. Illustrations: colour, cartoons. Founded 1957.

(Durban) The Mercury

Natal Newspapers Ltd, 18 Osborne Street,
Greyville 4001
tel (031) 308-2300 *fax* (031) 308-2333
Editor J.M. Patten
Daily Mon-Fri R2.00

Serious background news and inside details of world events. Length: 700-900 words. Illustrations: photos of general interest. Founded 1852.

Fair Lady

National Magazines, PO Box 1802,
Cape Town 8000
tel (021) 406-2204
Editor Roz Wrottesley
London office tel 0171-404 3216
Fortnightly R6.95

Fashion, beauty, articles and stories for women including showbiz, travel, humour. Length: articles up to 2000 words, short

stories approx. 3000 words; short novels and serialisation of book material. Illustrations: cartoons. Payment: on quality rather than length – by arrangement.

Femina Magazine

Associated Magazines, Box 3647, Cape Town 8000
tel (021) 462-3070
Editor Jane Raphaely
Monthly R6.95

For busy young professionals, often with families. Humour, good fiction, personalities, real-life drama, medical breakthroughs, popular science. Payment: by arrangement. Illustrations: line, half-tone, colour.

Independent Newspapers Holdings Ltd

Cape Town **Argus,** Daily R1.70
Weekend Argus Sat R3.90
Cape Times R2.00
Durban **Daily News** R1.60
The Saturday Paper R2.20
Ilanga, R1.20
Post (Natal) R2.50
Natal Mercury R2.20
Sunday Tribune R4.00
Johannesburg **The Star** R2.00
Saturday Star R2.50
Sunday Star R2.50
Sunday Independent R5.50
Sowetan, R1.30
Pretoria **Pretoria News** R1.70
web site http://www.star.co.za

Accepts articles of general and South African interest; also cartoons. Payment: in accordance with an editor's assessment. Contributions should be addressed to PO Box 1014, Johannesburg 2000.

(Johannesburg) Sunday Times

PO Box 1742, Saxonwold 2132
tel (011) 280-5105 *fax* (011) 280 5150
e-mail suntimes@tml.co.za
Editor B.C. Pottinger
London office South African Morning Newspapers Ltd, 63-66 Hatton Garden, London EC1N 8LE
tel 0171-405 3742
Sun R3.95

Illustrated articles of political or human interest, from a South African angle if possible. Maximum 1000 words long and 2 or 3 photos. Shorter essays, stories and articles of a light nature from 500-750 words. Payment: average rate £100 a column. Illustrations: photos (colour or b&w) and line.

Natal Witness

244 Longmarket Street, Pieter- maritzburg, KwaZulu-Natal 3201
tel (0331) 551-111 *fax* (0331) 551-122
e-mail nw.subs@alpha.futurenet.co.za
Editor J.H. Conyngham
Daily R1.60

Accepts topical articles. All material should be submitted direct to the editor in Pietermaritzburg. Length: 500-1000 words. Payment: average of R200 per 1000 words. Founded 1846.

Republican Press

PO Box 32083, Mobeni 4060, Natal
tel (031) 422-041
UK office Suite 15-17, The Outer Temple, 222-225 Strand, London WC2R 1BA
tel 0171-353 2580 *fax* 0171-353 2578

Bona

Monthly R4.35

Articles on fashion, cookery, sport, music of interest to black people. Length: up to 3000 words. Payment: by arrangement. Illustrations: line, half-tone, colour, cartoons.

Farmer's Weekly

Editor C. Venter
Weekly R6.00

Articles, generally illustrated, up to 1000 words, on all aspects of practical farming and research with particular reference to conditions in Southern Africa. Includes women's section which accepts suitable, illustrated articles. Illustrations: line, half-tone, colour, cartoons. Payment: according to merit. Founded 1911.

Garden and Home

Editor Margaret Wasserfall
Monthly R9.85

Well-illustrated articles on gardening, suitable for southern hemisphere. Articles for home section on furnishings, flower arrangement, food. Payment: by arrangement. Illustrations: half-tone, colour, cartoons.

Living and Loving

Editor Fiona Wayman
Monthly R6.80

Romantic fiction, 1500-4000 words. Articles dealing with first-person experiences; baby, family and marriage, medical articles up to 3000 words. Payment: by merit. Illustrations: line, half-tone, colour, cartoons. Founded 1970.

Personality
Editor D. Mullany
Weekly R5.50
Illustrated. Primarily an entertainment-oriented magazine but also a market for articles about people and places, preferably with South African angle. Strong news features and/or photojournalism, 1000-4000 words, with b&w and colour photos. Short stories 1500-5000 words; also cartoons. Payment: by arrangement. Illustrations: usually commissioned.

Your Family
Editor Angela Waller-Paton
Monthly R7.00
Cookery, knitting, crochet and home-crafts. Family drama, happy ending. Payment: by arrangement. Illustrations: continuous tone, colour and line, cartoons.

South African Yachting
Neil Rusch, PO Box 3473, Cape Town 8000
tel (021) 461-7472 *fax* (021) 461-3758
e-mail 10077,260
Monthly R5.80
Articles on yachting, boating or allied subjects. Payment: R12 per 100 words. Illustrations: line, half-tone, cartoons; colour covers. Founded 1957.

Southern Cross
PO Box 2372, Cape Town 8000
tel (021) 455-007 *fax* (021) 453-850
e-mail scross@iafrica.com
Editor Michael Shackleton
Weekly R1.80
National English-language Catholic weekly. Catholic news reports, world and South African. Length: 700-word articles. Illustrations: cartoons of Catholic interest acceptable from freelance contributors. Payment: 10c per word; illustrations R23.10.

The Star & SA Times online
web site http://wwwsatimes.press.net/

World Airnews
PO Box 35082, Northway, Durban 4065
tel (031) 84-1319 *fax* (031) 83-7115
Editor Tom Chalmers
Monthly £36.00 p.a.
Aviation news and features with an African angle. Payment: by negotiation.

USA

The Yearbook does not contain a detailed list of US magazines and journals. The Overseas volume of Willings Press Guide is the most useful general reference guide to US publications, available in most reference libraries. For readers with a particular interest in the US market, the publications listed here will be helpful (please make any payments in US funds).

American Markets Newsletter
175 Westland Drive, Glasgow G14 9JQ
e-mail foconnor@iee.org
Editor Sheila O'Connor
10 p.a. £29.00 p.a. (£53 for 2 years)
Editorial guidelines for US, Canadian and other overseas markets, plus information on press trips, non-fiction/fiction markets and writers' tips. Sample issue £2.95 (payable to S. O'Connor).

Freelance Market News
Sevendale House, 7 Dale Street, Manchester M1 1JB
tel 0161-237 1827 *fax* 0161-228 3533
Editor Angela Cox
A helpful newsletter which can provide details of availability of the above publications in the UK.

Willings Press Guide
Hollis Directories Ltd, 7 High Street, Teddington, Middlesex TW11 8EL
tel 0181-977 7711 *fax* 0181-977 1133

The Writer
The Writer Inc., 120 Boylston Street, Boston, MA 02116
Monthly ($35.00 p.a., must be in US funds)
Contains articles of instruction on all writing fields, lists of markets for MSS and special features of interest to free-lance writers everywhere.

The Writer Inc. also publishes books on writing fiction, non-fiction, poetry, articles, plays, etc.

Writer's Digest
Writer's Digest Books (address below)
($27.00 plus $10 surface post, $56.00 airmail p.a.)
Monthly handbook for writers who want to write better and sell more; aims to inform, instruct and inspire the freelance.

Writer's Digest Books
Writer's Digest Books, 1507 Dana Avenue, Cincinnati, OH 45207

Also publishes *Novel and Short Story Writer's Market, Children's Writer's and Illustrator's Market, Poet's Market, Artist's & Graphic Designer's Market, Guide to Literary Agents* and many other books on creating and selling writing and illustrations.

The Writer's Handbook

The Writer Inc. (address above)
($29.95 plus $17.34 airmail, $3.97 surface mail)

A substantial volume containing 110 chapters, each written by an authority, giving practical instruction on a wide variety of aspects of freelance writing and includes details of 3000 markets, payment rates and addresses.

Writer's Market

Writer's Digest Books (address below)
($27.99 plus $4.00 p&p)

An annual guidebook giving editorial requirements and other details of over 4000 US markets for freelance writing.

Submitting manuscripts

When submitting material to US journals, include a covering letter, together with return postage in the form of International Reply Coupons (IRC). IRCs can be exchanged in any foreign country for stamps representing the minimum postage payable on a letter sent from one country to another. Make it clear what rights are being offered for sale as some editors like to purchase MSS outright, thus securing world copyright, i.e. the traditional British market as well as the US market. Send the MSS direct to the US office of the journal and not to any London office.

In many cases it is best to send a preliminary letter giving a rough outline of your article or story (enclose IRCs for a reply). Most magazines will send a leaflet giving guidance to authors.

Magazines by subject area

These lists can be only a broad classification. They should be regarded as a pointer to possible markets and should be used with discrimination. Addresses for magazines start on page 20.

Fiction (see also Literary)

The following take short stories, unless otherwise stated. 'Long' refers to long complete stories, from 35,000 words upwards.

Active Life
Ambit
Australian Short Stories
The Australian Women's Weekly
Bella
Best
Bike
Chat
Cosmopolitan
Fair Lady (SA) (also serials)
Femina (SA)
The Fiddlehead (Can.)
Fly-Fishing & Fly-Tying
Girl Talk
Granta
HU (The Honest Ulsterman) (Ire.)

IMAGE (Ire.)
Interzone
Ireland's Eye
Ireland's Own
IT (Ire.)
Living and Loving (SA)
London Magazine
The Malahat Review (Can.)
More!
My Weekly (also serials)
My Weekly Story Library (long only)
New Idea (Aus.)
New Impact
Peninsular Magazine
People's Friend (also serials)
People's Friend Library (long only)
Personality (SA)
Prospect
Punch
Quadrant (Aus.)
QWF

Redoubt (Aus.)
Reality (Ire.)
Scots Magazine
Songwriting and Composing
Springboard
Stand
Staple New Writing
Takahe (NZ)
Take a Break
The Mag!
Wascana Review (Can.)
Woman and Home (also serials)
Woman's Day (Aus.)
Woman's Own
Woman's Way (Ire.)
Woman's Weekly (also serials)
Yours

Letters to the Editor

Art & Craft
The Australian Woman's Weekly
Babycare and Your Pregnancy
BBC Gardeners' World Magazine
Bella
Best
The Big Issue
Buster
Chat
Child Education
Choice
Control & Instrumentation
Dolly (Aus.)
Electrical Times
Fair Lady (SA)
Family Circle
Femina (SA)
Freelance Market News
The Furrow (Ire.)
Garden News
Goldlife for 50-Forward
Ideal Home
Junior Education
M&J
Mobile & Holiday Homes
Modern Painters
Moneywise
Mother & Baby
Motor Caravan Magazine
My Weekly
Our Baby
Penthouse
Police Journal
Practical Householder
Practical Parenting
Practical Photography
Practical Woodworking
Prima
Right Start
Saga Magazine
She
Shout
Slimming Magazine
Take a Break
Television
that's life!
True Story
TV Quick
The Weekly News
What's on TV
Woman
Woman's Day (Aus.)
Woman's Own
Woman's Realm
Woman's Way (Ire.)
Woman's Weekly
Writers' Forum
Yours

Gossip paragraphs

Aeroplane Monthly
African Business
Amateur Gardening
The Architects' Journal
Art Business Today
Art Monthly
Auto Express
Babycare and Your Pregnancy
BBC Music Magazine
Big!
The Big Issue
Bike
Bliss
Blueprint
Boards
Bowls International
Broadcast
Building Design
Cage and Aviary Birds
Campaign
Canadian Yachting
Car
Caravan Magazine
Carers World
Cat World
Catholic Pictorial
Classic Boat
Classic Cars
Classical Music
Climber
Country Life
Cycling Weekly
Dirt Bike Rider
Drapers Record
Electrical Times
Eventing
Farming News
Film Review
Flicks
FW (Fashion Weekly)
Financial Weekly
FourFourTwo
Freelance Market News
Fresh Produce Journal
Garden News
Geographical Magazine
Gibbons Stamp Monthly
Gifts International
Goldlife for 50-Forward
Golf World
Horse and Hound
Hotel and Catering Review (Ire.)
Inuit Art Quarterly (Can.)
Irish Farmers Journal
Irish Medical Times
Irish Printer
Jewish Chronicle
Journalist
Justice of the Peace and Local
  Government Law

The Lawyer
Marketing Week
Men Only
Mode Australia
Mojo
Music Week
New Statesman
The New Welsh Review
Nursing Times and Nursing
  Mirror
The Oldie
Opera Now
Organic Gardening
PC Review
Photo Life (Can.)
Pilot
The Pink Paper
Police Review
Practical Fishkeeping
The Press and Journal
Private Eye
Radio Times
Red Pepper
Rugby World
Runner's World
The Scottish Farmer
Sea Breezes
Shoot
Shout
South African Yachting
The Squash Player
The Stage
Success Now
The Tablet
tate: The Art Magazine
that's life!
Therapy Weekly
Titbits
Today's Runner
Woman
Woman's Realm
Woman's Way (Ire.)
World Soccer
Writers' Forum
Yachts and Yachting

Brief filler paragraphs

Accountancy Age
Active Life
Aeroplane Monthly
Africa Confidential
African Business
Air Pictorial International
Amateur Gardening
American Markets Newsletter
Angler's Mail
The Architects' Journal
Art Monthly
Athletics Weekly
Auto Express

Babycare and Your Pregnancy
BBC Music Magazine
Bella
Best of British
Big!
The Big Issue
Bike
Black Beauty & Hair
Blueprint
Boards
Bowls International
Broadcast
Buses
Cage and Aviary Birds
Canadian Yachting
Car
Caravan Magazine
Carers World
Cat World
The Catholic Herald
Catholic Pictorial
Classic Boat
Classic Cars
Climber
Communicate
Country Garden & Smallholding
Country Life
The Countryman
Cycling Weekly
Dorset Life – The Dorset Magazine
Drapers Record
East Lothian Life
Electrical Times
Eventing
Family Circle
Farming News
The Field
Film Review
Fire
Flight International
Fly-Fishing & Fly-Tying
FourFourTwo
FRANCE Magazine
Freelance Market News
Fresh Produce Journal
FW (Fashion Weekly)
Garden News
Geographical Magazine
Gibbons Stamp Monthly
Gifts International
Goldlife for 50-Forward
Golf Illustrated Weekly
Golf World
Greetings Magazine
Health & Fitness
Heritage
Hi-Fi News & Record Review
Horse and Hound
Horticulture Week
Hortus
Hotel and Catering Review (Ire.)

The Illustrated London News
IMAGE (Ire.)
Insurance Age
Inuit Art Quarterly (Can.)
Ireland's Own
Irish Farmers Journal
Irish Medical Times
Irish Printer
Jane's Defence Weekly
Jewish Chronicle
Journalist
Justice of the Peace and Local Government Law
The Lawyer
Marketing Week
Men Only
Mode Australia
Model Engineer
Motor Boat and Yachting
Motor Boats Monthly
My Weekly
Nautical Magazine
New Christian Herald
New Scientist
The New Welsh Review
Nursing Times and Nursing Mirror
The Oldie
Opera Now
Organic Gardening
Parents and Computers
Park Home & Holiday Caravan
Pig Farming
Pilot
The Pink Paper
Police Review
Post Magazine
Practical Caravan
Practical Fishkeeping
Practical Woodworking
The Press and Journal
Priests and People
Printing World
Private Eye
Radio Times
Railway Gazette
Railway Magazine
Reader's Digest
Reader's Digest (Aus.)
Red Pepper
Runner's World
Saga Magazine
The Scottish Farmer
Sea Breezes
Shoot
Somerset Magazine
Songwriter (Ire.)
South African Yachting
Southern Cross (SA)
Squash Player
The Stage
Staple New Writing
Steam Classic

Studio Sound
Success Now
The Tablet
tate: The Art Magazine
Technology Ireland
TGO
Therapy Weekly
This England
Titbits
Today's Runner
Total Football
Trucking International
TV Quick
Waterways World
Weight Watchers Magazine
Woman
Woman's Realm
The Woodworker
World Airnews (SA)
World Fishing
World Soccer
Writers' Forum
Writers' Guide
Yachts and Yachting
Yours

Puzzles and quizzes

The following take puzzles and/ or quizzes on an occasional or, in some cases, regular basis. Ideas must be tailored to suit each publication; approach in writing in the first instance.

Art Business Today
Athletics Weekly
Baptist Times
Best of British
Bike
Bird Watching
Bliss
Bowls International
Brownie
Cage and Aviary Birds
Canadian Yachting
Carers World
Cat World
Catholic Gazette
The Catholic Herald
Catholic Pictorial
Choice
Church of England Newspaper
Cleo (Aus.)
Country Life
Country-Side
The Cricketer International
The Dandy
Darts World
Dirt Bike Rider
Disability Now
Dolly (Aus.)

East Lothian Life
Electrical Times
Essentials
Everyday with Practical
  Electronics
Fair Lady (SA)
Farmers Weekly (SA)
Film Review
Financial Adviser
Football Picture Story Library
Fore!
Garden and Home (SA)
Garden News
Gifts International
Golf Monthly
Golf World
Guiding
Health & Efficiency International
Here's Health
Hertfordshire Countryside
Horse and Hound
Horse & Pony
Hospital Doctor
Hotel and Catering Review (Ire.)
HouseBuilder
The Illustrated London News
Ireland's Eye
Ireland's Own
Irish Medical Times
Journalist
Just Seventeen
Kids Alive!
Living and Loving (SA)
M&J
Men Only
Methodist Recorder
My Weekly Puzzle Time
New Christian Herald
New Idea (Aus.)
New Impact
New Scientist
The New Welsh Review
New Woman (Aus.)
New World
19
Nursing Times and Nursing
  Mirror
Opera
Opera Now
Parents and Computers
Park Home & Holiday Caravan
Personality (SA)
Pilot
Pony
Practical Motorist
Practical Photography
The Practitioner
Prospect
Publishing News
Reality (Ire.)
Red Pepper
Red Tape
Runner's World

The Scottish Farmer
Scottish Homes and Country
She
Shoot
The Short Wave Magazine
Shout
South African Yachting
Southern Cross (SA)
The Spectator
The Stage
Stamp Lover
The Tablet
Take a Break
TGO
The Mag!
Therapy Weekly
The Times Educational
  Supplement
Titbits
Today's Runner
Total Football
Total Sport
Trout and Salmon
TV Quick
Twinkle
The Universe
Vox
War Cry
Waterways World
Woman
The Woodworker
The Word (Ire.)
World Soccer
Your Family (SA)
Yours

UK ethnic weekly newspapers

Asian Times
Caribbean Times
Eastern Eye
The Voice
The Weekly Journal

Women's interest magazines (see also Health and home)

The Australian Women's Weekly
Bella
Best
Black Beauty & Hair
Bliss
Bona (SA)
Chat
Chatelaine (Can.)
Chic
Clothes Show Magazine
Company

Cosmopolitan
Country Living
Elle (Australia)
Elle (UK)
Essentials
Eva
Executive PA
Executive Woman
Fair Lady (SA)
Family Circle
Femina (SA)
For Women
Girl About Town
Good Housekeeping
Hairflair
Harpers & Queen
Hello!
Home and Country
Home Words
HQ (Aus.)
IMAGE (Ire.)
IT (Ire.)
Just Seventeen
Lady
Living and Loving (SA)
Looks Magazine
Marie Claire
Mode Australia
Modern Woman (Ire.)
More!
Mother & Baby
Ms London
My Weekly
My Weekly Puzzle Time
New Idea (Aus.)
New Woman
New Woman (Aus.)
New Zealand Woman's Day
New Zealand Woman's
  Weekly
19
Nursery World
Office Secretary
OK! Magazine
Options
People's Friend
The Pink Paper
Pride
Prima
Right Start
She
She (Aus.)
She & More (NZ)
Sugar
Take a Break
The Tatler
that's life!
The Mag!
U magazine (Ire.)
Vanity Fair
Vogue
Wedding and Home
Woman

Woman Alive
Woman and Home
Woman's Day (Aus.)
Woman's Journal
Woman's Own
Woman's Realm
Woman's Way (Ire.)
Woman's Weekly
World's Children
Your Family (SA)
You and Your Wedding

Men's interest magazines

Arena
Attitude
Country
Esquire
FHM (For Him Magazine)
Gay Times
GQ
Loaded
Masonic Square
Mayfair
Men Only
Men's Health
The Pink Paper
Titbits

Children's and young adult magazines

The Beano
Beano Comic Library
Big!
Brownie
Bunty
Bunty Library
Buster
Chickadee (Can.)
Commando
The Dandy
Dandy Comic Library
Dolly (Aus.)
Football Picture Story Library
Girl Talk
Horse & Pony
Hot Press (Ire.)
i-D Magazine
Just Seventeen
Live & Kicking Magazine
Looks Magazine
M&J
Mandy Library
Mizz
Playdays
Pony
Scouting
Shoot
Shout
Sky Magazine

Smash Hits
Top of the Pops Magazine
Twinkle
Vox
Young Writer

Subject articles

Advertising, design, printing and publishing
(see also Literary)

Arena
Australian Bookseller & Publisher
Blueprint
The Bookseller
British Journalism Review
British Printer
Building Design
Campaign
Canadian Interiors
The Face
Freelance Market News
Greetings Magazine
Indexer
InterMedia
Irish Printer
Journalist
Learned Publishing
Market Newsletter
Media Week
New Media Age
PR Week
Printing World
Publishing News
The World of Interiors
Young Writer

Agriculture, farming and horticulture

Country Garden & Smallholding
Country Life
The Countryman
Countryman (Aus.)
Country-Side
Dairy Farmer
Farmer's Weekly
Farmer's Weekly (SA)
Farming News
The Field
Fresh Produce Journal
The Grower
Horticulture Week
Irish Farmers Journal
New Zealand Farmer
Pig Farming
Poultry World
Scottish Farmer

Smallholder
Straight Furrow (NZ)
Town and Country Planning

Architecture and building

The Architects' Journal
Architectural Design
Architectural Review
Architecture Today
Blueprint
Building
Building Design
Built Environment
Burlington Magazine
Construction Europe
Contemporary Review
Country Homes & Interiors
Country Life
Education
Estates Gazette
Homes and Gardens
House & Garden
HouseBuilder
Ideal Home
International Construction
Local Historian
Mortgage Finance Gazette
Museums Journal
Perspectives on Architecture
Property Week

Art and collecting

The Antique Dealer & Collectors Guide
Apollo
Art & Design
Art Business Today
Art Monthly
The Art Newspaper
Art Review
The Artist
Artists and Illustrators
AN (Artists Newsletter)
ArtsAtlantic (Can.)
BBC Homes & Antiques
Book and Magazine Collector
Burlington Magazine
C Magazine (Can.)
Clocks
Coin News
Contemporary Review
contemporary visual arts
Country Life
Creative Camera
Eastern Art Report
Gibbons Stamp Monthly
The Illustrated London News
Inuit Art Quarterly (Can.)

Leisure Painter
Medal News
Modern Painters
Museums Journal
Numismatic Chronicle
RA Magazine
Stamp Lover
Stamp Magazine
tate: The Art Magazine
Make: the magazine of women's art
The World of Embroidery
The World of Interiors

Aviation

Aeromodeller
Aeroplane Monthly
Air International
Air Pictorial International
Australian Flying
Flight International
FlyPast
Pilot
Transport
World Airnews (SA)

Blind and partially sighted

Published by the Royal National Institute for the Blind in braille unless otherwise stated (see under Book publishers UK and Ireland)

3-FM
Absolutely Boys
Absolutely Girls
Access IT (also disk)
After Hours
Aphra
BBC on Air
Blast Off!
Braille Chess Magazine
Braille Journal of Physiotherapy
Braille at Bedtime
Braille Music Magazine (also disk)
Braille Radio Times
Braille TV Times (5 regions)
Broadcast Times (disk)
Busy Solicitor's Digest
Channels of Blessing (also abridged in Moon)
Come Gardening
Compute IT (also disk)
Contention
Conundrum
Daily Bread
Diane (Moon)

Eye Contact (also print)
Good Vibrations (also disk)
High Browse (also print, tape and disk)
Light of the Moon (Moon)
The Moon Magazine (Moon)
Money Matters
New Beacon (also print, tape and disk)
News to You? (also print, tape and disk)
Physiotherapists' Quarterly
Piano Tuners' Quarterly
Progress (also disk)
Rhetoric
Scientific Enquiry (also disk)
Shaping Up
Shop Window
Slugs and Snails
Spotlight (also print, tape and disk)
Sugar and Spice
Theological Times (also tape)
Upbeat (also disk)
The Weekender (also Moon)
You & Your Child
ViaAbility (also print)
Welcome to a World of ... (also disk)

Business, industry and management

Achievement
The Bank of Scotland Magazine
Brewing & Distilling International
Business Life
Business Scotland
BusinessMatters
Chartered Secretary
Communicate
Contemporary Review
Cosmetic World News
CWU Voice
Dairy Industries International
Director
Enterprise
European Chemical News
European Drinks Buyer
European Frozen Food Buyer
European Plastic News
Executive PA
Executive Woman
Fashion Forecast International
Financial Director
Fire
Fishing News
FW (Fashion Weekly)
Information and Software Technology

IPA magazine
Land & Liberty
Leisureweek
Management (NZ)
Management Today
Mobile and Cellular Magazine
Nationwide Magazine
New Impact
Office Secretary
People Management
The Political Quarterly
Success Now
The Sunday Business Post (Ire.)
The Woodworker
Work Study

Cinema and films

Campaign
Empire
Film Review
Flicks
New Statesman
Screen International
Sight and Sound
Stand
Studio Sound

Computers

Computer Weekly
Computing
Internet
.net The Internet Magazine
New Media Age
Parents and Computers
PC Direct
PC Review
Personal Computer World
Scientific Computing World

Economics, accountancy and finance

Accountancy
Accountancy Age
Active Life
Africa Confidential
African Business
The Australian Financial Review
The Banker
Business Scotland
Certified Accountant
Choice
Contemporary Review
Dairy Industries International
Economica
The Economist
Enterprise
Financial Accountant

Financial Adviser
Financial Director
The Grower
Insurance Age
Insurance Brokers' Monthly
Investors Chronicle
The Journal
Land & Liberty
Local Government Chronicle
MoneyMarketing
Moneywise
Mortgage Finance Gazette
New Statesman
Pensions World
Personal Finance
Post Magazine
Studies (Ire.)
Tribune
West Africa

Education

Amateur Stage
Art & Craft
BBC English
British Journal of Special
  Education
Child Education
Education
Guiding
Infant Projects
Junior Education
Junior Focus
Linguist
Local Historian
Modern Language Review
Modus
Month
Museums Journal
Music Teacher
New Blackfriars
New Impact
New Statesman
Nursery World
Parents
Practical Parenting
Prep School
Reality (Ire.)
Report
Right Start
Safety Education
School Librarian
Scottish Educational Journal
Spoken English
The Teacher
Theology
The Times Educational
  Supplement
Times Educational Supplement
  Scotland
Times Higher Education
  Supplement

Together With Children
Tribune
World's Children
Young People Now

Engineering and mechanics (see also Architecture, Aviation, Business, Motor transport, Nautical, Radio, Sciences)

Buses
Car Mechanics
Control & Instrumentation
Electrical Review
Electrical Times
Electronics Australia
Electronics Times
The Engineer
Engineering
European Chemical News
Everyday with Practical
  Electronics
Fire
International Construction
Mobile and Cellular Magazine
Model Engineer
New Electronics
Petroleum Economist
Practical Woodworking
Rail
Railway Gazette International
Railway Magazine
Transport

Gardening

Amateur Gardening
BBC Gardeners' World Magazine
Country
Country Garden &
  Smallholding
Country Life
The Field
The Garden
Garden and Home (SA)
Garden Answers
Garden News
Gardens Illustrated
Homestyle
Hortus
House and Garden
Organic Gardening
Your Garden

Health and home (see also Women's interest magazines)

Active Life
The Asda Magazine
Australian Home Beautiful
Australian House and Garden
Babycare and Your Pregnancy
The Bank of Scotland Magazine
BBC GoodFood
BBC Homes & Antiques
BBC Vegetarian GoodFood
Canadian Interiors
Choice
Classic Stitches
Country Homes & Interiors
Cycling Today
Garden and Home (SA)
Goldlife for 50-Forward
Health & Efficiency International
Health & Fitness
Healthy Eating
Here's Health
Home and Family
Homes and Gardens
Homes and Ideas
HomeFlair Magazine
Homestyle
Hospitality
House & Garden
House Beautiful
Ideal Home
Inspirations
Jewish Telegraph
Modus
Nationwide Magazine
Our Baby
Parents
Parents and Computers
Perfect Home
Period Living & Traditional Homes
Practical Householder
Practical Parenting
Running Magazine
Safety Education
Saga
Sainsbury's: The Magazine
Scottish Home and Country
Slimmer Magazine
Slimming Magazine
The Mag!
Today's Runner
Vegan
Weight Watchers Magazine
Wine
The World of Embroidery
The World of Interiors
Your Family (SA)
Your Home and Garden (NZ)
Yours
Zest

History and archaeology

Best of British
Coin News
Contemporary Review
Country Quest
English Historical Review
Geographical Magazine
History
History Today
Illustrated London News
In Britain
Local Historian
Museums Journal
The National Trust Magazine
New Blackfriars
Picture Postcard Monthly
Studies (Ire.)

Hotel, catering and leisure

Caterer & Hotelkeeper
European Drinks Buyer
European Frozen Food Buyer
Health Club Management
Hospitality
Hotel and Catering Review (Ire.)
The Leisure Manager
Leisureweek

Humour and satire

Private Eye
Punch
Viz

Inflight magazines

The Australian Way
Business Life
Hot Air

Legal and police

The Criminologist
Family Law
Justice of the Peace and Local
   Government Law
The Lawyer
New Law Journal
Police Journal
Police Review
Solicitors Journal

Leisure interests, pets
(see also Nautical, Sports)

Aeromodeller
Astronomy Now
Bird Keeper
Bird Watching
Birdwatch
Boards
British Birds
Camping Magazine
Caravan Magazine
Classic Stitches
Climber
Country Walking
Dogs Today
Family Tree Magazine
The Field
Gibbons Stamp Monthly
Guiding
In Britain
Military Modelling
Model Boats
Model Engineer
Motor Caravan Magazine
Motorcaravan and Motorhome
   Monthly
Needlecraft
Our Dogs
Park Home & Holiday Caravan
Popular Crafts
Practical Caravan
Radio Control Models
Rambling Today
Scale Models International
Scottish Field
Scouting
Scuba Diver (Aus.)
Stamp Lover
Stamp Magazine
Steam Classic
Wine
The Woodworker
Workbox
Your Dog

Literary *(see also Poetry)*

American Markets Newsletter
Australian Bookseller &
   Publisher
Australian Short Stories
Author
The Book Collector
Books in Canada
Books Ireland
Books Magazine
The Bookseller
British Journalism Review
Canadian Author
The Canadian Forum

Canadian Literature
Cencrastus
Chapman
Contemporary Review
Critical Quarterly
The Dalhousie Review (Can.)
The Dickensian
Edinburgh Review
European Bookseller
Fiddlehead (Can.)
Freelance Market News
Granta
The Illustrated London News
Index on Censorship
The Indexer
Journal of Canadian Studies
Journalist
Learned Publishing
The Library
The Literary Review
Llais Llyfrau
LOGOS
London Magazine
London Review of Books
The Malahat Review (Can.)
Modern Languages
New Library World
New Statesman
The New Welsh Review
The Oldie
Orbis
Outposts Poetry Quarterly
Overland (Aus.)
Peninsular Magazine
Planet
Prospect
Publishing News
Quadrant (Aus.)
Quill & Quire (Can.)
QWF
Reality (Ire.)
Redoubt (Aus.)
Scottish Book Collector
Signal
The Spectator
Springboard
Stand
Studies (Ire.)
Takahe (NZ)
TGO
The Times Literary Supplement
Tribune
Wasafiri
Wascana Review (Can.)
Woman Journalist
Writers' Forum
Writers' Guide
Writers News
Writing Magazine
Young Writer

Local government and civil service

Justice of the Peace and Local
  Government Law
Local Government Chronicle
Public Service & Local
  Government
Red Tape

Marketing and retailing

CTN
Drapers Record
FW (Fashion Weekly)
Gifts International
Greetings Magazine
The Grocer
Marketing Week
Off Licence News
Retail Week
Toy Trader
Ulster Grocer

Medicine and nursing

Balance
BMA New Review
The British Deaf News
British Journal of General
  Practice
British Medical Journal
Carers World
Chemist & Druggist
Community Care
Dental Update
Disability Now
Doctor
Hospital Doctor
Irish Journal of Medical Science
Irish Medical Times
Journal of Alternative and
  Complementary Medicine
Lancet
Nursery World
Nursing Times
Occupational Health
The Pharmaceutical Journal
The Practitioner
Professional Nurse
Pulse
Therapy Weekly
This Caring Business
The Veterinary Review
Young People Now

Military

Army Quarterly & Defence
  Journal
Guns Australia
Jane's Defence Weekly
RUSI Journal

Motor transport and cycling

AA Magazine
Auto Express
Autocar
Back Street Heroes
BBC Top Gear Magazine
Bike
Buses
Car
Car (SA)
Car Mechanics
Classic & Sportscar
Classic Cars
Commercial Motor
Custom Car
Cycling Today
Cycling Weekly
Dirt Bike Rider
Motor Cycle News
Motorcycle International
Performance Car
Practical Motorist
Ride
Scootering
Superbike
Truck & Driver
Trucking International
What Car?

Music and recording

Arena
BBC Music Magazine
Classic CD
Classical Music
Early Music
The Face
Gramophone
Hi-Fi News
i-D Magazine
Jazz Journal International
Kerrang!
Keyboard Review
Making Music
Melody Maker
Mojo
Music and Letters
The Music Review
Music Teacher
Music Week
Musical Opinion

Musical Times
New Musical Express
Opera
Opera Now
The Organ
Q Magazine
Select Magazine
Sky Magazine
Smash Hits
Songwriter (Ire.)
Songwriting and Composing
Studio Sound
Tempo
Top of the Pops Magazine
Vox

Natural history (see also Agriculture, Rural life)

The Aquarist and Pondkeeper
BBC Wildlife Magazine
Bird Keeper
Bird Watching
Birdwatch
British Birds
Budgerigar World
Cage and Aviary Birds
Cat World
Chickadee (Can.)
Dalesman
Dogs Today
The Ecologist
Equinox (Can.)
Geo Australasia
Geographical Magazine
Glaucus
Guiding
Horse & Pony
The National Trust Magazine
Natural World
Naturalist
Nature
Our Dogs
Pony
Practical Fishkeeping

Nautical and marine

Australian Powerboat
Canadian Yachting
Classic Boat
Diver
Modern Boating (Aus.)
Motor Boat and Yachting
Motor Boats Monthly
Nautical Magazine
Practical Boat Owner
Sea Breezes
Ship & Boat International
Ships Monthly
South African Yachting

Transport
Yachting Monthly
Yachting World
Yachts and Yachting

Photography

Amateur Photographer
Australian Photography
The British Journal of
  Photography
Camcorder User
Creative Camera
Photo Answers
Photo Life (Can.)
Photon
Photo Technique
Practical Photography
Professional Photographer
Video Camera

Poetry

*Magazines that only take the
occasional poem; check with
the editor before submitting.*

Acumen
Agenda
Ambit
Best of British
Cencrastus
Chapman
The Countryman*
Critical Quarterly
Cyphers (Ire.)
The Dalhousie Review (Can.)
Day by Day*
Edinburgh Review
Envoi
The Fiddlehead (Can.)
Fortnight (Ire.)
Helicon Poetry Magazine
HQ: The Haiku Quarterly
  Poetry Magazine
HU (The Honest Ulsterman) (Ire.)
Jewish Quarterly*
Krino (Ire.)
Life & Work*
The Literary Review
London Magazine
London Review of Books
The Malahat Review (Can.)
New Statesman
The New Welsh Review
Orbis
Outposts Poetry Quarterly
Oxford Poetry
Planet
PN Review

Poetry Australia
Poetry Ireland Review/Éigse
  Éireann
Poetry London Newsletter
Poetry Nottingham International
Poetry Review
Poetry Wales
Quadrant (Aus.)
Quaker Monthly*
Redoubt (Aus.)
The Rialto
The Scots Magazine*
Springboard
Stand Magazine
Staple New Writing
Takahe (NZ)
The Times Literary Supplement*
Tribune*
Wasafiri
Wascana Review (Can.)
Young Writer

Politics

Africa Confidential
Australian Journal of
  International Affairs
The Australian Journal of
  Politics and History
The Australian Quarterly
The China Quarterly
The Big Issues (Ire.)
Contemporary Review
Current Affairs Bulletin (Aus.)
Fortnight (Ire.)
The Illustrated London News
International Affairs
Justice of the Peace
Local Government Chronicle
Middle East International
New Blackfriars
New Christian Herald
New Internationalist
New Statesman
Peace News
The Political Quarterly
Prospect
Red Pepper
Studies (Ire.)
Tribune
Voice Intelligence Report
West Africa
The World Today

Radio, TV and video

BBC English
Broadcast
Campaign
Electronics Australia
Empire
Film Review
Flicks
Gramophone
Hi-Fi News
InterMedia
New Statesman
Opera Now
Practical Wireless
Radio Times
Satellite Times
Short-Wave Magazine
The Stage
Studio Sound
Television
Tribune
TV Quick
TV Times
What's on TV

Religion, philosophy and New Age

Baptist Times
Catholic Gazette
The Catholic Herald
Catholic Pictorial
Catholic Times
Church of England Newspaper
Church of Ireland Gazette
Church Times
Contemporary Review
Day by Day
The Downside Review
Fortean Times
Friend
The Furrow (Ire.)
Herald of the South (Aus.)
Home and Family
Home Words
Inquirer
Jewish Chronicle
Jewish Quarterly
Jewish Telegraph
Kids Alive!
Life & Work
Methodist Recorder
Mind
Modern Believing
Month
New Blackfriars
New Christian Herald
New Humanist
Priests & People
Quaker Monthly

Reality (Ire.)
Reform
Sign
Southern Cross (SA)
Studies (Ire.)
Tablet
Theology
Third Way
Together with Children
Universe
War Cry
West Africa
Woman Alive
Word (Ire.)

Rural life and country (see also Natural history)

Australasian Post
Country
Country Life
Country Quest
The Countryman
Country-Side
County
Cumbria and Lake District Magazine
Dalesman
Derbyshire Life and Countryside
Dorset Life – The Dorset Magazine
East Lothian Life
Essex Countryside
The Field
Hampshire
Heritage
Hertfordshire Countryside
In Britain
Ireland's Eye
The Lady
Lancashire Magazine
Lincolnshire Life
The Local Historian
The National Trust Magazine
New Buckinghamshire Countryside
Rambling Today
The Scots Magazine
Scottish Field
Scottish Home and Country
Shooting Times and Country Magazine
The Shropshire Magazine
Somerset Magazine
This England
Waterways World
West Lothian Life
Yorkshire Ridings Magazine

Sciences

The Criminologist
Equinox (Can.)
Geological Magazine
Mind
Nature
New Scientist
Science Progress
Scientific Computing World
Technology Ireland

Sports and games (see also Leisure interests, Motoring, Nautical)

Anglers' Mail
Angling Times
Athletics Weekly
Australasian Sporting Shooter
Australian Powerboat
Bowls International
Bridge International
British Chess Magazine
Chess Monthly
The Cricketer International
Darts World
Eventing
The Field
Fishing World Magazine (Aus.)
Fly-Fishing & Fly-Tying
Fore!
FourFourTwo
Golf Monthly
Golf Weekly
Golf World
Guns Australia
Horse and Hound
Horse and Rider
Inside Edge
Our Dogs
Rugby World
Runner's World
Scottish Field
Scuba Diver (Aus.)
Sea Angler
Shoot
Shooting Times
The Skier and The Snowboarder
Snooker Scene
The Sporting Life
The Squash Player
Tennis World
Today's Golfer
Today's Runner
Total Football
Total Sport
Trout and Salmon

When Saturday Comes
Wisden Cricket Monthly
Word (Ire.)
World Bowls
World Fishing
World Soccer

Theatre, drama and dancing (see also Cinema, Music)

Amateur Stage
Ballroom Dancing Times
Canadian Forum
Contemporary Review
CTR (Canadian Theatre Review)
Dance & Dancers
Dance Australia
Dancing Times
The Illustrated London News
In Britain
New Statesman
New Theatre Quarterly
Performing Arts & Entertainment in Canada
Plays & Players
Radio Times
Reality (Ire.)
Speech and Drama
The Stage
Tribune
TV Quick
TV Times

Travel and geography

Australian Geographic
Australian Skiing
Caravan Magazine
Contemporary Review
Equinox (Can.)
FRANCE Magazine
Geo Australasia
Geographical Journal
Geographical Magazine
Heritage
The Illustrated London News
In Britain
In Dublin (Ire.)
Ireland of the Welcomes
The Local Historian
Natal Witness (SA)
Traveller
Wanderlust

Newspapers and magazines on the Internet

E-zines are the electronic equivalent on the Internet of newspapers and magazines in printed format. See main listings starting on pages 3 and 20 for web site addresses.

Balance
BBC Top Gear Magazine
Bridge Magazine
British Medical Journal
Chess Monthly
Daily Record (Glasgow)
Electronic Telegraph
The European
Evening Times (Glasgow)
Financial Director
The Financial Times
Flicks
Fortean Times

Guardian Online
The Herald (Glasgow)
Insurance Brokers' Monthly
Internet
The Irish Times on the Web
Lancashire Evening Telegraph
Making Music
Marketing Week
Moneywise
Nature
New Scientist
PC Direct
Pensions World

Personal Computer World
Radio Times
Reader's Digest
The Sporting Life
The Star & SA Times online
 (South Africa)
Sunday Mail (Glasgow)
Sunday Times
The Observer Online
The Times
The Sunderland Echo
Viz
When Saturday Comes

Recent changes to newspapers and magazines

The following changes have taken place since the last edition of the Yearbook.

Changes of name and mergers

Administrator *now* Chartered Secretary
Artists Newsletter *now* AN
Contemporary Art *now* contemporary visual arts
The Cork Examiner *now* The Examiner
Cumbria *now* Cumbria and Lake District Magazine
The Daily Express *now* The Express
The Dalesman *now* Dalesman
The Echo *now* Sunderland Echo
Fashion Weekly *now* FW
First Steps *now* Babycare and Your Pregnancy
Fishkeeping Answers *now* merged with Practical Fishkeeping
Gas World International *now* Petroleum Economist

The Haiku Quarterly *now* HQ: The Haiku Quarterly Poetry Magazine
Involvement *now* IPA Magazine
Mandy/Judy *now* M&J
New Statesman & Society *now* New Statesman
90 Minutes *now* incorporated into Shoot
OK! Weekly *now* OK! Magazine
photo pro *now* Photon
Poetry Ireland *now* Poetry Ireland Review
Practical Gardening *now* incorporated into Gardening Answers
Staple *now* Staple New Writing
Sunday Express *now* Express on Sunday
West Lancashire Evening Gazette *now* The Gazette
Women's Art Magazine *now* Make: the magazine of women's art
Yorkshire Evening Press *now* The Evening Press

Your Home *now* Your Home and Garden

Titles ceased publication

The Antique Collector
Bedfordshire Magazine
Business Age
Catch
Combat & Militaria
Critical Wave: The European Science Fiction & Fantasy Review
The Good Society Review
Fourth World Review
Iron
Love Story
Simply Crafts
Sport
Today's Horse
Woman's Story
Writers' Monthly
YX (Youth Express)

Writing for newspapers

Newspaper editors now commission more freelance work than ever before. Editors are looking for contributors who identify with the readers and understand what they want. Such contributors are never short of work, and they enjoy great personal satisfaction. **Jill Dick** *looks at newspapers from the freelance's point of view.*

Imagine looking at a white space the size of a tennis court and knowing you have to fill it with words and pictures. This is the task editors of newspapers face regularly and it's a wonder any can sleep at night for worrying about how they're going to do it. Not only must the space be filled, it must be temptingly – irresistibly – filled, if existing readers are to be kept happy and new ones attracted.

There have been great changes in the newspaper world in recent times and because staff have been reduced on many newspapers, more freelance work is being accepted than ever before. Although competition is tough, with former staff members now among the competitors, today's freelance writers have many advantages over their predecessors, including being able to benefit from the use of modern technology. But nobody would claim that modern technology makes a good journalist; there is still no substitute for good writing – and never will be.

Use of freelance copy on the Internet without the copyright owners' permission is one of the less welcome changes to the working scene. More and more publishers are asking writers to sign over all rights, i.e. copyright, before freelance work is accepted. There have been many legal cases over allegedly 'stolen' copy appearing elsewhere without extra payment and the battle rumbles on. Copyright is a valuable asset and writers should think very seriously before signing agreements robbing them of it.

Ideas

Newspapers' needs change from day to day or week to week according to the frequency of publication and to provide a list of topics to write about would not be helpful. Furthermore, mere lists of ideas can encourage stultified thinking. Countless writers have stared at similar lists and tried to wrench inspiration from them; countless editors have seen (and rejected) the results. More is needed than an idea. A unique slant on one may be the pointer to a worthwhile venture but an idea is most likely to be successful when it arrives in your head jockeying for priority, albeit loosely at first, with a notion of how you're going to write it.

Fishermen bait their hooks not with what they like, but with what fish like. There are many hard lessons to learn about freelancing and one of the toughest is that you have to write not just the stories that appeal to you, but the stories that will sell.

Reporting

News writing can be dramatic but frequently it is writing about something quite prosaic: a report of a local council meeting, for instance, where an important decision is awaited affecting a keenly felt local issue. Suddenly, perhaps, someone accuses councillors of rigging the ballot on the issue in question – and you will find yourself in the position of not just writing a report but filing a news story. If

there is a paper coming out the next morning you, as a freelance, could be the only person able to write it.

Local reporters are hard-working folk at the very root of a paper's activities. They are likely to be out and about collecting information from tip-offs supplied by the office, waiting to file the latest news on a 'running' story or they might be engaged on any one of a dozen duties in the circulation area. A local newspaper is where many a leading journalist began learning the craft. Reporters carry considerable responsibility in a challenging job that should not be undertaken without careful consideration. Being committed to maintaining a flow of news from a small town or village or district can be a chore when you want to go on holiday, or if you are ill, or if you suddenly don't feel like doing it. But the first rule of the job is not to let your community down.

Doing the 'calls' will be a regular task. This means calling on the people or organisations likely to tell you what's going on: the police and fire stations, local hospitals, the town hall, the Citizens Advice Bureau, the morgue, the courts, schools, health clinics, community centres – anywhere and everywhere in the locality where a spokesperson is able and willing to give you news or the basis of a news story to pass on to readers of the paper. Being a reporter will almost certainly bring you more rewards than cash. Your writing skills will benefit by making quick decisions about your copy, learning how to present it clearly in print and over the phone; you will develop an increasing awareness of what is and what is not newsworthy and your confidence will grow.

Market study

What we need to study is not newspapers but readers. Are they treated as serious-minded thinkers or light-heartedly? What are their main interests – domestic, political, adventurous, romantic, creative? Is the language used appropriate for immature youngsters or for folk with more experience of life? Above all, do you

know how to talk to them? Picture the very readers the paper is trying to reach and think of someone you know who might be one. For thoughtful market evaluation read newspaper advertisements carefully. Advertisers don't spend large sums of money without precise reader targeting and freelances can benefit from trying to see the readers through the same eyes.

There is no better way of finding out who the readers are and how they think and live than making a close, regular and up-to-date study of the papers you'd like to write for. Analyse their content, their page layout and format and discover why they print what they do. Even such attention to detail isn't infallible, for at best it can only reveal what they printed and were interested in yesterday or last week. As for what they'll want tomorrow and next week …

No matter where you live or work, whom you meet, how you spend your time or what your hobbies and interests may be, you'll find a story. Feature, filler, news item, article, review, regular series, specialist column, interview, diary item, letter, anecdote, profile, preview; there is always something to be written. In buying a paper readers instinctively ask themselves, 'What's in it for me?' You are providing the answer.

There are several well-established market guides, the best being *Writers' & Artists' Yearbook*, *Willings Press Guide* and *The Media Guide* (see further reading, page 141).

Page-stoppers

Written work submitted to editors or features editors may be referred to as a feature, an article, a piece or just 'copy'. Call it what you wish, it needs to stop them in their tracks or at least intrigue them sufficiently to contact you about development of a point here or getting a picture there. So important is this 'must have' factor that such features are called 'page-stoppers' in newspaper offices. A feature is often tagged to a news event. It may, for instance, give background information on

a running story about the progress of hospitalised casualties following a local coach crash, highlight the warnings about a nearby crumbling cliff or reveal some awkward facts following the disappearance of funds from a charity's coffers. Whatever its theme, always be careful your story is not out of date, having been overtaken by more recent events.

Features may be based entirely on facts but it is their relevance to people that makes them viable. Make yourself the bringer of comfort, an inspiration, an instructor or a wallower in nostalgia. Give readers information about education, medical services, local transport, job opportunities – they are all important to people. Above all, be sure not to fill your piece with little more than your own opinion and personal experiences; unless you are famous or well known in the locality, such views are unlikely to be required.

It pays to look ahead, particularly in ways other writers may not. This is not always easy to do and you will have to work hard on an article before ever writing a word. Research can never be skimped. A thinly researched piece quickly lands on the reject pile if another author has taken more time and trouble to delve into the subject than you have. The real value of research lies not in the facts and figures you have unearthed but in the greater understanding you can give your readers from what you have yourself understood.

Reference libraries offer extensive facilities for researching anything and everything, particularly with the aid of highly specialised on-line search engines, but the most comprehensive single volume to help you is *Research for Writers* by Ann Hoffmann (see further reading, page 141). As your pile of researched material grows so will your interest and enthusiasm. To write well you have to be interested in what you're writing, or at least make yourself interested. If you're not, why should anyone else be?

Original freelance copy on an editor's desk is more welcome than a tea-break. A good feature writer can write about virtually anything. When you do so make it strong; make them laugh, cry, want to know more, swear, feel encouraged, understand something or someone better, agree, disagree – or whatever you choose – but make sure they do or feel something.

Specialist spots

The many freelances who write a regular page/half page/column/corner know it's not a commission won without effort, often over a number of years. Editors need to know you will be able to sustain an unlimited time at the job, that your copy will constantly be fresh and innovative and, most importantly, that it will always arrive on time. But when satisfied about these criteria, most are only too glad to hand over responsibility for a portion of the paper and know it is being handled efficiently. Making editors aware of your worth by selling them copy is a good basis for seeking a regular column for yourself.

The golden rule that applies for all copy is that (short of real and rare emergencies) it must never be late. To be calm about accepting deadlines you need to plan ahead carefully, to accept your own limits in terms of the research needed for a particular job of work and the time it is likely to take you to write it, and (the best and only true safety net) to have plenty of copy ready in your private store.

What types of regular columns are popular with readers? Their themes are boundless: nature, profiles of famous people, chess, horoscopes, crosswords, competitions, children's and women's pages, young mothers, pop music, pets, food – anything that interests people will make a good column. As a column will get you known and your work constantly read you should be prepared for the feedback from readers. This can be one of the most rewarding aspects of column-running if you don't let it take up too much of your writing time. And at the end of every month you are guaranteed a pre-negotiated fee without having to invoice anyone.

A few topics fall into a separate category: travel, sport, motoring, business and finance among them. These are nearly

always covered by staff writers and contributions to these sections have to be exceptional, if not unique.

Reviews

The distinctive task of reviewing books, drama, films, videos, radio and television programmes is seldom work for beginners. Sometimes a person who is not even thought of as a writer but who is famous in another sphere might be invited to contribute – a politician or a top sportsperson, perhaps – to attract readers with the name of the reviewer rather than the quality of the review, but the established papers have their own trained and experienced staff reviewers.

How, then, do you gain experience? For all categories of reviewing it is at the discretion of editors (or features editors) that you may be given a chance. And the only way to build up a solid reputation is to keep writing the copy they want when (or preferably just before) they want it.

Letters, fillers, anecdotes and humour

Writers may complain that computerised page layout leaves fewer spaces for small items but (as in all marketing) it is a matter of finding your own openings. It is sometimes worthwhile amassing a good collection of fillers and filing them to an editor as a single package. Fillers, be they Letters to the Editor, snippets to make readers laugh or small pieces of general interest, are covered by the same copyright protection as their weightier brothers: the original copy belongs to the writer and only an exact copy of it by an unauthorised person infringes that copyright. Other people taking up the ideas in themes or fillers are quite free to develop them as they wish – in fact Letters to the Editor are generally chosen with just this in mind: that the original may generate sufficient interest for other readers to write more letters with their views.

To a freelance writer nothing observed or overheard is ever wasted. Humour is nearly always welcome and the newspaper world is full of surprises: a writer friend persuaded the editor of her evening paper that a 'funny' corner would give readers at least one thing to laugh at every day. That's her column now; it's been running for several years and the readers love it. It's easy to laugh at humour, not easy to write it and virtually impossible to teach someone how to do it. If you can, you're lucky.

Business

Never be deterred by the thought that a freelance writer must also be a seller – or afraid to discuss what you will be paid for work accepted. Bona fide freelances have to deal with tax self-assessment but with this status you can claim many benefits, setting some of your expenses against tax and even working at a tax loss. To satisfy the Inland Revenue you must demonstrate that you are a professional writer, that you are trying to make a profit and that you are eligible to be taxed under Schedule D (see *Income tax* on page 641). This means your taxable income from writing will be the amount you receive in fees less expenses wholly and exclusively incurred in the pursuit of your writing. If you hold another full-time job it may not be easy to substantiate your writing credentials, but being able to produce genuine records and receipts and to demonstrate a proper businesslike approach to your writing work will be to your advantage.

Freelances sometimes fear their work will not be accepted because there is not enough room in the paper after the staff have filled all the editorial space available for each edition. Write what editors want – that's the simple recipe for success; do that and space will always be found. Perhaps that last sentence sums up all we writers need to know.

Jill Dick has spent many years working for national, regional and local newspapers as a feature writer, columnist, reviewer and departmental editor. Her published books include *Freelance Writing for Newspapers* and *Writing for Magazines*, both published by A & C Black.

Writing magazine articles

For the would-be writer there can be little doubt that magazine articles offer the easiest way to get into print. **John Hines** *offers guidance to potential contributors.*

The magazine market is vast and is growing steadily. *Willings Press Guide 1997* recorded no less than 12,238 UK periodicals, excluding newspapers and annuals, and the majority of these rely on freelance contributions to fill their pages. New magazines appear almost daily and, although some founder, most of them survive. The subject material covered by these magazines is so varied that few writers would find their special interests not included.

The magazines range from the modest budget publications to the expensive glossies. Beginners can cut their teeth on the lower end of the market, knowing that, although the fees are modest, the competition is small. These publications provide an excellent start for building skills, self-confidence and credibility. The opportunity for steadily moving up-market is there for the taking, until the writer reaches the level which fulfils his or her ambitions.

The idea

Established article writers usually have files bulging with ideas. They will include newspaper and magazine clippings, jottings from television and radio programmes and personal observations. Almost anything which intrigues the writer or fires the imagination is worth a place in the ideas file. There is an adage in the writing world that it pays to write about what you know. Certainly this is a good idea, for you write more comfortably and competently on a familiar subject, but the wise diversify as well.

In selecting subjects, it is most rewarding to pick those which interest you or, better still, fascinate you. They provide absorbing research and can result in articles rich in original thought with your enthusiasm showing through. As a freelance, you have the luxury of being able to pick and choose, so why not select those articles which are a pleasure to write?

Market study

Successful writers know that effective market study is vital. Any editor will tell you that the vast majority of unsolicited material which lands on their desk is quite unsuitable. The material may be wrong in length, style or choice of subject. Yet studying a copy of the magazine could have helped to avoid these mistakes.

Try to read at least two recent copies of the magazine for which you are aiming to write. Analyse it carefully. Check the number of articles which are staff written (the staff are usually listed in the front of the magazine). By studying several issues you may also discover that there are contributors with regular slots and so deduce the opportunities which exist for the freelance.

The pathway to successful article writing

- have a good idea for a subject;
- find a suitable market;
- produce an interesting and well-written article for that market;
- submit a professional-looking typescript;
- have a sound sales strategy throughout.

If the magazine looks promising, study the type of subject which the editor favours. Check the approximate length of the average article. Ask yourself if the magazine's style is one with which you would be comfortable or to which you could adapt.

Few writers seem to study the advertisements and this is a big mistake. Advertising agencies spend a great deal of money on painstaking expert research, aimed at identifying the typical reader. By studying the advertisements you can benefit from this valuable information which can be most helpful when slanting your article to the readers' interests.

Studying the *Writers' & Artists' Yearbook* can give you a good insight into the requirements of many magazines, even including the fees they pay.

Freelance Market News is the best market newsletter for the freelance writer (see further reading, page 141). However, the finest market information is that which freelances compile for themselves from personal experience. A card filing system is useful here but, like all market information, its value depends on its being kept up to date.

Research and accuracy

Although some articles can be written from personal experience or knowledge, most articles require some sound current research. Public libraries can be very helpful, particularly if you enlist the help of a qualified librarian rather than a library assistant. The copyright libraries, of which the British Library is the best known, are superb. Would-be researchers must establish their bona fides before being issued with a ticket. (See also *Books, research and reference* on page 571.)

All facts should be checked for accuracy, going back to the source wherever possible. The books of others are not infallible, even reference books. Errors can be embarrassing and inevitably attract unwelcome letters from readers. File your researched material away for future use; an effective filing system is essential. The best book on the subject is *Research for Writers* by Ann Hoffmann (see further reading, page 141).

The Internet can offer a vast amount of research material, particularly in the form of published articles. As some Internet sources may include information of dubious quality, your routine check for accuracy should be made conscientiously. Research may entail interviewing people and this is a skill which the freelance should consider developing. For effective interviews, sound preparation is important. Research in advance as much as possible about the interviewee and their field of interest. Make a list of important questions in logical sequence. But be prepared to divert from your questions and follow any unexpected revelations. If you use a tape recorder, test it beforehand and always carry spare batteries and tapes. It is essential to have a notebook as a back-up and to carry spare pens.

Sensitivity and courtesy should be the criteria for all interviewing for normal articles. Start with easy general questions. Guide the interview gently, but firmly. Wind up the interview as you began, on an easy note. The interviewee should be left with the feeling that it has been an enjoyable experience. Some interviewees ask if they can vet the finished article. You should always politely refuse, but do offer to allow them to withdraw anything they may regret saying.

For more information on interviewing technique, see *Tape-recording interviews* on page 142, and *Freelance Writing for Newspapers* and *The Way to Write Magazine Articles* in the further reading list on page 141.

Non-linear thinking

A stumbling block for many inexperienced writers is beginning their article, particularly when faced with a daunting mass of notes, clippings and research references. Related research material must be associated and the various aspects considered in order of importance. However, when marshalling material, we often tend to arrange it in a linear fashion, rather like a shopping list. This tends to restrict our thinking on each point.

It has been found that non-linear thinking stimulates ideas and their logical development. I use this method as a framework for my articles, particularly those which are complex. Non-linear flow-of-thought patterns are easy to compile and to use. The subject is written in the centre of a large sheet of paper with the major aspects to be covered radiating from it. From these, further spurs are drawn, filling in other important material. Less significant points are added on minor spurs until all aspects are covered. Never discard these patterns; file them away for future use as a valuable concise reference to your research material.

A detailed explanation of this method, together with illustrations of typical non-linear patterns, is given in *The Way to Write Magazine Articles*; and more general coverage can be found in *Use Your Head* (see further reading, page 141).

The article structure

We all develop our own style, but it is important to learn to modify it to suit the requirements of our market. The majority of articles are relatively short and must put over their story crisply without wasting words. Often this can best be done with fairly short sentences and relatively short paragraphs. Never write long convoluted sentences which require reading more than once to understand.

The opening

The first paragraph of an article has special importance. It must grip the editor's attention immediately, its purpose being to force the editor to read on. You can often make your opening irresistible by selecting a point from your article which is intriguing, startling or even audacious.

The body

You will not sell an article on the strength of its opening. The body of the article must fulfil the promise of that good first paragraph. It is here that the main text or message of your article will be unfolded.

Your thought patterns will help you to move logically from one aspect to the next in a smooth progression and ensure that nothing important is left out.

The end

The poor article appears to finish when the writer runs out of ideas. A good ending must aim to tie up any loose ends positively. The way it does this depends a great deal on the subject. It can be speculative – a look into the future, perhaps. It might go back to answer a question posed in the beginning. Avoid a mere recap of the main text for this gives a weak ending. Try to set aside some 'meat' to include in the ending; this could leave the reader with a strong point to ponder over.

Dialogue

Dialogue can breathe life into an article and give it sparkle. It must be used judiciously, for over-use may unbalance the article. It is often effective when used appropriately as the first sentence of an article.

The typescript

The conventional layout of a typescript is described in *Preparing and submitting a manuscript* on page 527. However, an article for the British magazine market needs the addition of a typed cover sheet with the writer's name and address in the top right-hand corner, the article's title centred halfway down the page followed by the writer's name. If you are using a pseudonym it goes here, not at the top.

About two-thirds down the page on the left should be the number of words in the article and two or three lines' space below, the rights which you are offering the editor. For normal practical purposes this would be First British Serial Rights, usually abbreviated to 'FBSR offered' – see below. The cover sheet is not used for USA markets.

An increasing number of editors are asking writers to submit their articles on disk. It pays you to provide this facility if

you can. You should always verify with the editor that your system and theirs are compatible before submission. You will find that most editors also require a hard copy (printout) in addition to the disk. For more information, see *The Professional Typescript for Magazine Articles* (further reading, page 141).

Illustrations

Good illustrations enhance an article, making it more saleable. The writer/illustrator also receives an extra fee. It is self-evident that all article writers should try to produce that editors' delight – the words and pictures package. If you are a reasonable photographer, you are halfway there. If you are not, there is little excuse for not trying with one of the fully automatic cameras which are available today.

Study magazines to see, not only whether they use black and white or colour, but also the way they use illustrations. Do they tend to be small and plentiful to assist in the understanding of the text? Does the editor favour large dramatic pictures, sometimes covering as much as a whole page or even two? Finally, can your pictures match those in the magazine?

Your pictures must be pin-sharp and properly exposed. They must avoid all the basic mistakes of composition which are outlined in any photographic primer. For black and white you should submit glossy, borderless prints, 254 x 203mm (10 x 8in). Transparencies are demanded by most quality magazines for their colour illustrations, although a small but growing number of periodicals will consider colour prints. You must always confirm that a magazine uses colour prints before submitting them. For covers, most magazines use 35mm transparencies, but many prefer a larger format. Illustrations are covered in depth in *The Way to Write Magazine Articles* (see further reading, page 141.)

Writers who turn to supplementing their writing with photography rarely look back. They report better sales and increased earnings. (See also *Pictures into print* on page 252.)

Rights

By offering First British Serial Rights you are inviting the magazine to publish your article once and for the first time in Britain. You are retaining the right to sell it elsewhere in the world. Some editors will try to wring all rights from you. Do not give way as it leaves the magazine free to sell your article worldwide and pocket the proceeds.

Second British Serial Rights are rarely sold, but a magazine may ask to buy them if they see your article in print and wish to reproduce it themselves. You would normally accept, but as Second Rights earn lower fees than First Rights, it is not worth making a particular effort to sell them. It pays to rewrite the original article, reslanting it to suit the new market and possibly introducing some new material. This effectively makes it a new article for which the First Rights may be legitimately offered.

The sales strategy

Probably the most common reason for good articles failing to get published is lack of a sound sales strategy. A surprisingly large number of writers complete a good article and then peddle it hopefully around the markets. This is quite the wrong way. Your article must always be written specifically for the market you have in mind. Your sales strategy should begin the moment you look at your material and can say: 'Yes, there is enough here for a good article.' You then use your market study to find a number of likely magazines which might publish such an article.

Query letters

The sound query letter is essential for sustained success in the article-writing field. Examine your list of possible magazines and arrange them in order of your preference. Select the top one and write your query letter to its editor. Keep it brief and state your idea for the article, mentioning any special slant you have in mind. If you

are qualified in any way to write such an article or if you have a 'track-record' of writing in that field, you should say so. Also mention if you have suitable illustrations.

Ask the editor how many words he or she would like to see. It is particularly important to ask for the magazine's rates for contributors. Always enclose an sae. The query letter is your initial shop-window and its quality should be the best of which you are capable. If the editor turns down the idea, write immediately to the next magazine on your list and so on.

If the editor likes your idea, you may get a commission, but if you are unknown it is more likely that you will be asked to submit the article on spec. Some editors try to side-step divulging their rates in advance, but you must be professional and insist on knowing them.

An acceptance is the usual outcome from an editor's expression of interest. As you become better at matching subject to magazine, writing shrewd query letters and producing sound articles, your rejections should drop to virtually nil.

On acceptance, the professional freelance looks around for another outlet. Writing is easy, it is the research which takes the time. Make sure you get the maximum from your research (see above).

Payment

Some magazines pay on acceptance, but the majority pay on publication. Avoid those magazines which hold your material on spec with no guarantee of ultimate publication. They are not worthy of consideration. Never be afraid to question offers of low rates, for many editors will negotiate. If low rates are not improved upon, be professional and withdraw the offer of your article.

Fresh fields

When you have written articles extensively on a subject, it may be worth considering whether the subject is suitable for a non-fiction book (see *The Way to Write Non-fiction*, further reading, below). If so, your articles could be valuable as evidence of your writing skills, your knowledge of the subject and the wide interest the subject can generate. Many writers have used their published articles as a means of gaining an advance contract for a non-fiction book.

John Hines is a freelance writer and lecturer covering a wide range of interests, but specialises in health and the environment. He lectures extensively on writing, both in the UK and abroad.

Further reading

Buzan, Tony, *Use Your Head*, BBC, revised edn, 1995

Dick, Jill, *Freelance Writing for Newspapers*, A & C Black, 1991, 2nd edn due March 1998

Dick, Jill, *Writing for Magazines*, A & C Black, 2nd edn, 1996

Freelance Market News, Sevendale House, 7 Dale Street, Manchester M1 1JB (on subscription)

Hines, John, *The Professional Typescript for Magazine Articles*, Tanglewood, 1995

Hines, John, *The Way to Write Magazine Articles*, Hamish Hamilton, repr. 1995

Hines, John, *The Way to Write Non-fiction*, Hamish Hamilton, 1990. o.p.

Hoffmann, Ann, *Research for Writers*, A & C Black, 5th edn, 1996

Howard, Godfrey, *The Good English Guide*, Pan Macmillan, 1994

Legat, Michael, *The Nuts and Bolts of Writing*, Robert Hale, repr. 1993

Peak, Steve (ed.), *The Media Guide*, Fourth Estate, annual

The Oxford Writers' Dictionary, Oxford Reference, 1990

Willings Press Guide, Hollis Directories Ltd, annual

Tape-recording interviews

Tape-recording interviews can both liberate and protect journalists in their craft. Freed of the notepad, they can engage more directly with the interviewee and come away with a fuller and more interesting interview. And having a recording of what was said can solve disputes which may arise at a later date. **John Crace** *describes how to use a tape recorder for successful interviewing.*

Ask any journalist to name his or her most important item of equipment – word processor excepted – and the chances are that the answer will be a tape recorder. Few writers, save for some hard-nosed old pros on the news desk, are familiar with speedwriting or shorthand techniques and, in any case, most interviews these days are better conducted using a tape machine. For the aspiring writer, a tape recorder is an absolute must. Almost every commission will involve talking to someone, be it a celebrity, an expert or an ordinary member of the public. Don't panic about the expense, though. You don't need broadcast quality – something cheap, cheerful and audible will do fine, and will solve most of your interviewing problems. Just don't imagine that it will solve them all.

Using a tape recorder

The first thing to remember about tape recorders is that they can go wrong. Sometimes this will be the machine's fault; most of the time it will be yours. My first-ever interview was with a woman whose son was in prison for murder. While pouring her heart out she cried frequently over the course of our 30-minute conversation, and it was only as we were winding to a close that I noticed I had left the pause button on. So, I guiltily blamed the machine and asked if she would start again. Fortunately, she agreed. Not everybody will be so considerate or have the time, and a few precautionary checks

before each interview will avert most potential disasters.

More than anything else, journalists fear their batteries running out on them. So it is not a bad idea always to use fresh ones when starting an interview. This isn't necessary if you're only planning a short chat and you know that your last interview took only 15 minutes. If you know the interview will take a long time, the most practical solution is to test the machine before you start, to see if there is any sign of the machine running slow. If not, you will probably be OK, but have a spare set of batteries in reserve, just in case.

Positioning the recorder is vital. Try to find a quiet spot, where there are few outside disturbances, and place the machine as near to the subject as possible. Get your interviewee to say a few words into the microphone, and play them back to make sure you can hear clearly what has been said. I always find that no matter how well I position the machine I can always hear myself far better than the other person, but as long as I can understand my subject I don't worry too much.

Never use unfamiliar and untried equipment for an interview. I once bought a gadget that would enable me to record telephone conversations. I carefully followed the instructions for setting it up but when I came to play back the interview I couldn't hear anything. I've never dared to use it again. So, the message is: never use any item you haven't tested at home first, and only then if you feel confident with it.

The benefits of a tape recorder

Conducting an interview involves far more than the mere asking of questions and the writing down or recording of replies. It's about the facial expressions and body language of the subject. Most interviews and profiles depend on the journalist picking up nuances of behaviour to give the article colour and depth. So if you have your head buried in a notepad as you struggle to jot down your subject's *bons mots* word for word, you will end up with a one-dimensional piece of writing. It will probably be factual and accurate, but it will also be excruciatingly dull.

A good interview should flow like a normal conversation. This can be tricky when your subject is on his or her fourth interview of the day or when time is tight, but at least a tape recorder allows an approximation of it. Before starting, make a list of questions to ask, but do not be too dogmatic about sticking to it. Watch your interviewee for signs of interest, boredom or discomfort and follow up appropriately. Sometimes, the conversation can flow into other more interesting areas, and allowing your interviewee to wander off the point can help to put him or her at ease, and may even engender more honest answers to difficult questions. As long as you make sure you cover the ground you had planned, just let your subject speak.

Interviews and the law

Occasionally, an interviewee may let something slip in an unguarded moment, or give a surprisingly candid answer. What you do with this is up to you. A tape recorder can be a powerful tool, and it can present you with some moral dilemmas. Do you use a quote that is certain to upset and humiliate your interviewee later? I try to respect the spirit in which the inter-view has been given. If it has been antagonistic, I feel that anything is fair game. If not, I attempt to allude to the sense of what has been said, but in an inoffensive and unembarrassing manner. Most importantly, if someone says something that they ask me not to use, I never do so.

If you do decide to use what has been said, a taped interview can be a formidable ally against libel threats that may arise – providing you have quoted the person verbatim. With written notes it is your word against that of the interviewee, but a tape can deter even the most eager litigant. I once interviewed a person about the Hillsborough disaster who bitterly regretted having been so outspoken about his feelings. On the day the piece was published he phoned, threatening to sue me. I was able to play back to him the relevant passage to prove I had not misquoted, and he was pacified – if not entirely happy. Remember, though, just because someone says he won't sue doesn't mean that he may not change his mind. Legal proceedings can be started at any time up to seven years from the date of publication. So always use a new tape when you are interviewing, and keep your old ones safely stored away.

And finally ...

Above all, try not to get over-anxious about an interview. Come well prepared, and concentrate on enjoying it. The more relaxed you are, the more relaxed your subject will be, and the better the conversation will go. Remember – doing the interview should be the fun part of the process. The really hard work starts with the writing.

John Crace is a feature writer regularly working for *The Guardian*, *The Independent* and the *Evening Standard*. He also contributes to many magazines, including the *New Statesman* and *GQ*, and has written five books.

Syndicates, news and press agencies

Before submitting material, you are strongly advised to make preliminary enquiries and to ascertain terms of work. Strictly speaking, syndication is the selling and reselling of previously published work although some news and press agencies handle original material.

Academic File

Eastern Art Publishing Group, 27 Wallorton Gardens, London SW14 8DX
tel 0181-392 1122 *fax* 0181-392 1422
e-mail easternart@compuserve.com
Managing Editor Sajid Rizvi, *Executive Editor* Shirley Rizvi

Feature and photo syndication with special reference to the developing world and immigrant communities in the West. Founded 1985.

Advance Features

Stubbs Wood Cottage, Hammerwood, East Grinstead, West Sussex RH19 3QE
tel/fax (01342) 850480
Managing Editor Peter Norman

Supplies text and visual services to the national and regional press in Britain and newspapers overseas. Instructional graphic panels on a variety of subjects. Text services (weekly); stars, nature and royalty articles. Crosswords: daily, weekly and theme; general puzzles. Daily and weekly cartoons for the regional and national press (not single cartoons).

ALI Press Agency Ltd

Boulevard Anspach 111-115, Bte 9, B9-1000 Brussels, Belgium
tel 02 512 73 94 *fax* 02 512 03 30
Director George Lans

All types of feature services except information and news: cartoons, puzzles, strips, comics, illustrations, picture stories, transparencies, articles of general interest, etc. for magazines, newspapers and books, especially illustrated books for children and adults. Syndication in all major countries. Commissions: 35%. Syndication: 50%. Founded 1948.

The Associated Press Ltd

(News Department), The Associated Press House, 12 Norwich Street, London EC4A 1BP
tel 0171-353 1515 *fax* 0171-353 8118
Australian Associated Press
12 Norwich Street, London EC4A 1EJ
tel 0171-353 0153 *fax* 0171-583 3563

News service to the Australian, New Zealand and Pacific Island press, radio and TV. Founded 1935.

BIPS

(Bernsen's International Press Service Ltd)
9 Paradise Close, Eastbourne, East Sussex BN20 8BT
tel (01323) 728760
Editor Harry Gresty

Specialise in photo-features, both b&w and colour. Seek human interest, oddity, glamour, pin-ups, scientific, medical, etc., material suitable for marketing through own branches in London, San Francisco, Paris, Hamburg, Milan, Stockholm, Amsterdam (for Benelux), Helsinki.

Neil Bradley Puzzles

Linden House, 34 Hardy Barn, Shipley, Derbyshire DE75 7JA
tel/fax (01773) 768960
Director Neil Bradley

Supplies visual puzzles to national and regional press; emphasis placed on variety and topicality with work based on current media listings. Work supplied on disk or prints to Mac or PC. Daily single frame and strip cartoons. Contact for free booklet and disk demo. Founded 1981.

Bulls Presstjänst AB

Tulegatan 39, Box 6519, S-11383 Stockholm, Sweden
tel (08) 23 40 20 *fax* (08) 15 80 10

Bulls Pressedienst GmbH
Eysseneckstrasse 50, D-60322 Frankfurt am Main, Germany
tel (069) 959 270 *fax* (069) 959 27111

Bulls Pressetjeneste A/S
Ebbells Gate 3, N-0183 Oslo, Norway
tel 22 20 56 01 *fax* 22 20 49 78

Bulls Pressetjeneste
Östbanegade 9, 1th, DK-2100 Copenhagen, Denmark
tel 31 38 90 99 *fax* 31 38 25 16

Bulls Finska Försäljnings AB
Isonniitynkatu 7, Box 180, FIN-00521, Helsinki, Finland
tel (09) 757 13 11 *fax* (09) 757 06 34

Bulls Press, ul.
Chocimska 28, Pokoj 509, 00-791 Warsawa, Poland
tel/fax (22) 49 80 18

Bulls Press
Pikk 29 A, EE 0001 Tallinn, Estonia
tel (2) 501 84 85 *fax* (2) 631 41 65

Market newspapers, magazines, weeklies and advertising agencies in Sweden, Denmark, Norway, Finland, Iceland, Poland, The Baltic States, Germany, Austria and German-speaking Switzerland.

Syndicates human interest picture stories; topical and well-illustrated background articles and series; photographic features dealing with science, people, personalities, glamour; genre pictures for advertising; condensations and serialisations of best-selling fiction and non-fiction; cartoons, comic strips, film and TV rights, merchandising and newspaper graphics on-line via modem or ISDN.

The Canadian Press

Associated Press House, 12 Norwich Street, London EC4A 1EJ
tel 0171-353 6355 *fax* 0171-583 4238
Chief Correspondent Helen Branswell

London Bureau of the national news agency of Canada. Founded 1919.

Capital Press Service

2 Long Cottage, Church Street, Leatherhead, Surrey KT22 8EJ
tel (01372) 377451
Directors M. Stone, E.W. Stone, *News Editor* Mark Stone

Stories of trade, commerce and industry for trade papers in this country and abroad. Interested in air-cargo affairs and business travel (including hotels, luggage, guides, new routes via air, sea, road and train) for UK and US journals.

Central Press Features

20 Spectrum House, 32-34 Gordon House Road, London NW5 1LP
tel 0171-284 1433 *fax* 0171-284 4494

Supplies every type of feature to newspapers and other publications in 50 countries. Included in over 100 daily and weekly services are columns on international affairs, politics, sports, medicine, law, finance, computers, video, motoring, science, gardening, fashion, house and home, health and beauty, women's and children's features, strips, crosswords, cartoons and regular 6-12 article illustrated series of international human interest; also editorial material for advertising features.

J.W. Crabtree and Son

36 Sunbridge Road, Bradford BD1 2AA
tel (01274) 732937 (office), (01535) 655288 (home)

News, general, trade and sport; information and research for features undertaken. Founded 1919.

Daily & Sunday Telegraph Syndication

Ewan MacNaughton Associates, Alexandra Chambers, 6 Alexandra Road, Tonbridge, Kent TN9 2AA
tel (01732) 771116 *fax* (01732) 771160
e-mail ema@dial.pipex.com

News, features, photography; worldwide distribution and representation.

Environmental & Occupational Health Research Foundation

PenroseHouse, Birtles Road, Whirley, Cheshire SK10 3JQ
tel/fax (01625) 615323
e-mail eoh@msn.com
Managing Editor Peggy Bentham

Undertakes individual commissions and syndicates articles to both diverse scientific journals and general consumer media – from peer reviewed and accredited contributors from academia and professional institutions.

Europa-Press

Saltmätargatan 8, 1st Floor, Box 6410, S-113 82,
Stockholm, Sweden
tel 8-34 94 35 *fax* 8-34 80 79
e-mail red.led@europapress.se
Managing Director Sven Berlin
Market: newspapers, magazines and
weeklies in Sweden, Denmark, Norway
and Finland. Syndicates high quality features of international appeal such as topical articles, photo-features – b&w and
colour, women's features, short stories,
serial novels, non-fiction stories and serials with strong human interest, crime articles, popular science, cartoons, comic
strips.

Europress Features (UK)

18 St Chads Road, Didsbury,
Nr Manchester M20 9WH
tel 0161-445 2945
Representation of newspapers and magazines in Europe, Australia, United States.
Syndication of top-flight features with
exclusive illustrations – human interest
stories – showbusiness personalities. 30-
35% commission on sales of material
successfully accepted; 40% on exclusive
illustrations.

Express Enterprises

(division of Express Newspapers plc)
Ludgate House, 245 Blackfriars Road,
London SE1 9UX
tel 0171-922 7902 *fax* 0171-922 7871
Text and pictures from all Express titles.
Archive from 1900. Numerous strips and
political cartoons. Material handled
worldwide for freelance journalists.

Features International

Tolland, Lydeard St Lawrence,
Taunton TA4 3PS
tel (01984) 623014 *fax* (01984) 623901
Editorial Director Anthony Sharrock
Syndicates features to magazines and
newspapers throughout the world. The
agency produces a wide range of material
– mainly from freelance sources –
including topical articles, women's features and weekly columns. Distributes
directly to all English-language countries. Agents throughout the Common
Market countries, Japan, the Americas
and Eastern Europe. Buys copy outright
and welcomes story ideas. Sae essential.

Frontline Photo Press Agency

18 Wall Street, Norwood, Australia 5067
postal address PO Box 162, Kent Town,
Australia 5071
tel (08) 8333 2691 *fax* (08) 8364 0604
e-mail fppa@tne.net.au
web site http://www.tne.net.au/fppa
Director Carlo Irlitti
Photographic press agency specialising
in sports coverage. Services provided:
news, interviews, features, articles and
photos for newspapers, magazines and
other media. Digital photo wire services.

Syndicates sports, celebrity, travel,
women's and general interest features
and articles with photos. Welcomes
approaches from individuals and organisations abroad. Assignments undertaken.
Rates negotiable. Founded 1988.

Gemini News Service

9 White Lion Street, London N1 9PD
tel 0171-833 4141 *fax* 0171-837 5118
e-mail Gemini@gn.apc.org
Editor Daniel Nelson, *Managing Director* Bethel
Njoku
Network of freelance contributors and
specialist writers all over the world.
Specialists in news-features of interna-
tional, topical and development interest.
Preferred length 800-1200 words.

Global Syndication & Literary Agency, Limited

120 Westmont, Hemet, CA 00510, USA
President A.D. Fowler
Interested in previously published books
for possible syndication and placement
of subsidiary rights. Our book reviewers
always looking for non-fiction titles. US
postage or International Reply Coupons
required for return of material.

Graphic Syndication

4 Reyntiens View, Odiham,
Hants RG29 1AF
tel (01256) 703004
e-mail flanagan@argonet.co.uk
web site www.argonet.co.uk/users/mike.flanagan
Manager M. Flanagan
Cartoon strips and single frames sup-
plied to newspapers and magazines in
Britain and overseas. Terms: 50%.
Founded 1981.

India-International News Service
Head office Jute House, 12 India Exchange Place, Calcutta 700001, India
tel 2209563, 4791009
Proprietor Ing H. Kothari BSc, DWP(Lond), FIMechE, FIE, FVI. FInstD
'Calcutta Letters' and Air Mail news service from Calcutta. Specialists in industrial and technical news.

INS (International News Service)/ Irish International News Service
7 King's Avenue, Minnis Bay, Birchington-on-Sea, East Kent CT7 9QL
tel (01843) 845022
Editor and Managing Director Barry J. Hardy PC, *Photo Editor* Jan Vanek
News, sport, book and magazine reviews (please forward copies), TV, radio, photographic department; also equipment for TV films, etc.

International Fashion Press Agency
PenroseHouse, Birtles Road, Whirley, Cheshire SK10 3JQ
tel/fax (01625) 615323
e-mail ifpa@msn.com
Directors P. Bentham (managing), P. Dyson, S. Fagette, L.C. Mottershead, L.B. Fell
Monitors and photographs international fashion collections and developments in textile and fashion industry. Specialist writers on health, fitness, beauty and personalities. Undertakes individual commissioned features. Supplies syndicated columns/pages to press, radio and TV (NUJ staff writers and photographers).

International Feature Service
104 rue de Laeken, 1000 Brussels, Belgium
tel 217-03-42 *fax* 217-03-42
Managing Director Max S. Kleiter
Feature articles, serial rights, tests, cartoons, comic strips and illustrations. Handles English TV-features and books; also production of articles for merchandising.

International Press Agency (Pty) Ltd
PO Box 67, Howard Place 7450, South Africa
tel (021) 531 1926 *fax* (021) 531 8789
e-mail inpra@iafrika.com
Manager Mrs T. Temple
UK office 19 Avenue South, Surbiton, Surrey KT5 8PJ
tel/fax 0181-390 4414
Managing Editor Mrs U.A. Barnett PhD

South African agents for many leading British, American and continental press firms for the syndication of comic strips, cartoons, jokes, feature articles, short stories, serials, press photos for the South African market. Founded 1934.

ITAR-Tass Agency
Suite 12-20, Morley House, 314-320 Regent Street, London W1R 5AB
tel 0171-580 5543 *fax* 0171-580 5547
General, economic and commercial news service to Russia and the CIS.

Joker Feature Service (JFS)
PO Box 253, 6040 AG, Roermond, The Netherlands
tel (0475) 337338 *fax* (0475) 315663
e-mail j.f.s@tip.nl
Managing Director Ruud Kerstens
Feature articles, serial rights, tests, cartoons, comic strips and illustrations, puzzles. Handles TV-features and books; also production for merchandising.

Knight Features
20 Crescent Grove, London SW4 7AH
tel 0171-622 1467 *fax* 0171-622 1522
Director Peter Knight, *Associates* Ann King-Hall, Gaby Martin, Andrew Knight, Giovanna Farrell-Vinay
Worldwide selling of strip cartoons and major features and serialisations. Exclusive agent in UK and Republic of Ireland for United Feature Syndicate and Newspaper Enterprise Association of New York. Founded 1985.

London News Service
63 Gee Street, London EC1V 3RS
tel 0171-336 0632 *fax* 0171-253 8419
Editor John Rodgers
Worldwide syndication of features and photos.

Maharaja Features Pvt. Ltd
5-226 Sion Road East, Bombay 400022, India
tel 22-4097951 *fax* 22-4097801
e-mail mahafeat@bom2.vsnl.net.in
Editor K.R.N. Swamy, *Managing Editor* K.R. Padmanabhan
Syndicates feature and pictorial material, of interest to Asian readers, to newspapers and magazines in India, UK and abroad. Specialists in well-researched articles on India by eminent authorities for publication in prestige journals

throughout the world. Also topical features 1000-1500 words. Illustrations: b&w prints and colour transparencies.

Mirror Syndication International

Unique House, 21-31 Woodfield Road, London W9 2BA
tel 0171-266 1133 *fax* 0171-266 2563
Supplies publishing material and international rights for news text and pictures from Mirror Group Newspapers and other large publishing houses. Extensive picture library of all subjects.

National Association of Press Agencies (NAPA)

41 Lansdowne Crescent, Leamington Spa, Warwickshire CV32 4PR
tel (01926) 424181 *fax* (01926) 424760
Directors Denis Cassidy, Chris Johnson, Barrie Tracey, Peter Steele, John Quinn, Richard Reed
NAPA is a network of independent, established and experienced press agencies serving newspapers, magazines, TV and radio networks. Founded 1980.

New Zealand Press Association

12 Norwich Street, London EC4A 1EJ
tel 0171-353 7040 *fax* 0171-583 3563

News Blitz International

Via Guido Danti 34,
00191 Rome, Italy
tel 333 26 41, 333 02 52 *fax* 333 26 51
President Vinicio Congiu, *Sales Manager* Gianni Piccione, *Graphic, Literary and Television Depts* Giovanni Congiu
Syndicates cartoons, comic strips, humorous books with drawings, feature and pictorial material, environment, travels, throughout the world. Average rates of commission 60-40%, monthly report of sales, payment 60 days after the date of monthly report.

Outdoor Press Agency

6A Kenton Park Centre, Gosforth, Newcastle upon Tyne NE3 4NN
tel 0191-2132058 *fax* 0191-2132052
e-mail carlton@cix.compulink.co.uk
web site http://ds.dial.pipex.com/cycling/
Director Carlton Reid
Supplies newspapers and magazines with articles from specialist freelances on all aspects of the outdoors, especially active and adventurous outdoor sports. Commissions undertaken. Founded 1995.

PA News Ltd

292 Vauxhall Bridge Road, London SW1V 1AE
tel 0171-963 7000
Chief Executive Robert Simpson, *Editor* Paul Potts, *Sales Director* Clive Marshall
PA News National news agency for the UK and Republic of Ireland. Comprehensive news, photo and information services, as well as extensive news cuttings and photo libraries.
PA Sport Full coverage of national sport plus fast results service.
PA Data Design Page-ready information – formatted sports results, TV listings, stocklists, racecards and weather reports. Founded 1868.

Chandra S. Perera

Cinetra, 437 Pethiyagoda, Kelaniya-11600, Sri Lanka
tel 94-1-911885 *fax* 94-1-541414/332867 ATTN CHANDRA PERERA
Press and TV news, news films on Sri Lanka and Maldives, colour and b&w photo news and features, photographic and film coverages, screenplays and scripts for TV and films, press clippings. Broadcasting, TV and newspapers; journalistic features, news, broadcasting and TV interviews.

Pixfeatures

5 Latimer Road, Barnet, Herts. EN5 5NU
tel 0181-449 9946 *fax* 0181-441 2725
Contact Peter Wickman
Spanish office tel 884 74932
Contact Roy Wickman
News agency and picture library. Specialises in selling Spanish pictures and features to British and European press.

Christopher Rann & Associates Pty Ltd

7th Floor, NZI House, 117 King William Street, Adelaide, SA 5000, Australia
postal address GPO Box 958, Adelaide, SA 5001
tel (08) 211 7771 *fax* (08) 212 2272
Proprietors C.F. Rann, J.M. Jose
Full range of professional PR, press releases, special newsletters, commercial intelligence, media monitoring. Welcomes approaches from organisations requiring PR representation or press release distribution. Founded 1977.

Republican Press (London)

Suite 15-17, The Outer Temple, 222-225 Strand,
London WC2R 1BA
tel 0171-353 2580 *fax* 0171-353 2578

Acquire material for publication in South
Africa.

Reuters Limited

85 Fleet Street, London EC4P 4AJ
tel 0171-250 1122

Singer Media Corporation

Seaview Business Park, 1030 Calle Cordillera,
Unit 106, San Clemente, CA 92673, USA
tel 714-498-7227
Vice-President Helen J. Lee

Features (celebrity interviews and profiles, business, health, fitness, beauty,
diet, self-help, how-to, etc.), cartoons,
puzzles and quizzes of international
appeal for international and domestic
syndication. Represented in most countries abroad. No local or national material; no comic strips. Query first.

Solo Syndication Ltd

49-53 Kensington High Street, London W8 5ED
tel 0171-376 2166 *fax* 0171-938 3165
Chairman Don Short

Worldwide syndication of newspaper
features, photos, cartoons, strips and
book serialisations. Professional journalists only. Commission: 50/50. Agency
represents the international syndication
of Associated Newspapers (*Daily Mail,
Mail on Sunday, Evening Standard*), IPC
Magazines (*Woman, Woman's Own,
Woman's Realm, Woman's Weekly*), *The
European, The Guinness Book of
Records*, Guinness Publishing, News Ltd
of Australia, *New Idea* and *TV Week*,
Australia. Founded 1978.

Southern Media Services

(division of Maximedia Pty Ltd)
PO Box 268, Springwood, NSW 2777, Australia
tel (047) 514 967 *fax* (047) 515 545
Directors Nic van Oudtshoorn, Daphne van
Oudtshoorn

Illustrated features (colour and b&w) to
newspapers and magazines in Australasia
and many parts of the world. Also stock
colour library. Assignments (news and
feature stories, photos) accepted at mod-
erate rates. Syndicates freelance features
and photo features in Australia and
abroad, but query before submitting.
Commission: 50% or by arrangement.

Syndicated International Network (SIN)

Unit 4, 2 Somerset Road, London N17 9EJ
tel 0181-808 8660 *fax* 0181-808 1821
e-mail 101457.1516@compuserve.com
Managing Director Marianne Lassen

Worldwide syndication of interview texts
and photos, primarily of music and cinema
artists. Unsolicited material always considered. Commission: 50%. Founded 1984.

Peter Tauber Press Agency

94 East End Road, London N3 2SX
tel 0181-346 4165

UK and worldwide syndication of
unpublished exclusive big name celebrity interviews, especially interviews with
their associates or ex-associates. Also
unique human interest features.
Commission: 25%. Founded 1950.

TEXT Syndication

26 Ingelow Road, London SW8 3QA
tel 0171-978 2116 *fax* 0171-627 0746
e-mail features@textsynd.co.uk
Contact Amanda McKee

Specialises in syndicating previously published material worldwide for freelance
journalists. Require high quality features
of international appeal (including human
interest, health, beauty, relationships,
celebrity interviews, general features).
Please enquire before submitting MSS.
Commission: 50%. Founded 1993.

TransAtlantic News Service

7100 Hillside Avenue, Suite 304, Hollywood,
CA 90046, USA
tel 213-874-1284

News and photo agency serving the
British and foreign press, TANS supplies
entertainment news, features and
columns from Hollywood, and topical
news in general from California. Covers
all Hollywood events and undertakes
commissions and assignments in all
fields. Candid photos of stars at major
Hollywood events a speciality.

United Press International

408 Strand, London WC2R 0NG
tel 0171-333 0999 (news), 0171-468 1600 (admin),
0171-333 1666 (sports) *fax* 0171-333 1670

Universal Pictorial Press & Agency Ltd

29-31 Saffron Hill, London EC1N 8FH
tel 0171-421 6000 *fax* 0171-421 6006
Managing Director T.R. Smith

Syndication of daily press and library photo service to the national and provincial press, periodicals and TV companies in the British Isles and overseas. Founded 1929.

Visual Humour

5 Greymouth Close, Stockton-on-Tees TS18 5LF
tel (01642) 581847/0121-429 5861
fax (01642) 581847
Contact Peter Dodsworth

Daily and weekly humorous cartoon strips; also single panel cartoon features (not single cartoons) for possible syndication in the UK and abroad. Picture puzzles also considered. Submit photocopy samples only initially, with sae. Founded 1984.

Worldwide Media Ltd

PO Box 3821, London NW2 4DQ
tel 0181-452 6241 *fax* 0181-452 7258
e-mail wm@icr1.demon.co.uk
Director Robert Wallis

Specialises in unusual, often bizarre, features for the international magazine market. Purchases outright text and photos. Write or fax ideas first. Founded 1995.

Yaffa Newspaper Service of New Zealand

29 Queens Avenue, Balmoral, Auckland 4, New Zealand
tel (09) 631 5225 *fax* (09) 631 0040

Books

Submitting material

Each year, thousands of manuscripts are submitted to publishers by hopeful authors but only a small proportion are accepted for publication. Some manuscripts are needlessly rejected either because they were sent to the wrong publisher, or because the publisher's submission procedure was not followed. We give here some guidelines to consider before submitting a manuscript.

First of all, choose the right publisher. It is a waste of time and money to send the manuscript of a novel to a publisher who publishes no fiction, or poetry to one who publishes no verse. By studying the entries in the *Yearbook*, examining publishers' lists of publications, or by looking for the names of suitable publishers in the relevant sections in libraries and bookshops, you will find the names of several publishers which might be interested in seeing your material.

Secondly, approach the publisher in the way they prefer. Many publishers will not accept unsolicited material – you must enquire first if they would be willing to read the whole manuscript. A few publishers are prepared to speak on the telephone, allowing you to describe, briefly, the work on offer. Most prefer a preliminary letter; and many publishers, particularly of fiction, will only see material submitted through a literary agent. It has to be said that some publishing houses, the larger ones in particular, may well employ all three methods!

Enclose a synopsis of the work, and two or three sample chapters, with your preliminary letter, plus return postage (International Reply Coupons if you are writing from outside the country). Writers have been known to send out such letters in duplicated form, an approach unlikely to stimulate a publisher's interest. Remember, also, that whilst every reasonable care will be taken of material in the publishers' possession, responsibility cannot be accepted if material is lost or damaged. Never send your only copy of the manuscript. For more information, see *Preparing and submitting a manuscript* on page 527. An alphabetical listing of publishers' names and addresses follows on page 153. For classified lists, see below.

Fiction

See page 222 for a list of *Publishers of fiction*, by fiction genre. A full list of *Literary agents* starts on page 334.

Poetry

Publishers which consider poetry for adults are listed in *Publishers of poetry* on page 280. See also the article *Poetry into print* on page 269 and *Poetry organisations* on page 274.

Children's books

The market for children's books is considered in *Writing and illustrating children's books* on page 245 and is followed by a list of *Children's book publishers and packagers* on page 249, which includes publishers of poetry for children. A list of *Literary agents for children's books* is on page 352.

Small presses

It is beyond the scope of the *Yearbook* to list all the many smaller publishers which have either a limited output, or that spe-

cialise in poetry, avant-garde or other fringe publishing. We include details of some of the better-known small poetry houses but for a comprehensive listing refer to *Small Presses & Little Magazines in the UK and Ireland* (available from the Stationery Office Oriel Bookshop, The Friary, Cardiff CF1 4AA *tel* (01222) 395548.

Self-publishing

Authors are strongly advised not to pay for the publication of their work. A reputable firm of publishers will undertake publication at its own expense, except possibly for works of an academic nature.

See *Doing it on your own* on page 255 for an introduction to self-publishing, *Vanity publishing* on page 259, and *Publishing agreements* on page 599.

See also ...

- *Book publishers* in *Australia*, page 225; in *Canada*, page 228; in *New Zealand*, page 231; in *South Africa*, page 233; and in the *USA*, page 234
- *Literary agents*, page 333
- *Top hundred chart of 1996 paperback fast-sellers*, page 261
- *Book packagers*, page 216
- *Publishers of multimedia*, page 224
- *Publishers of plays*, page 332
- *Pictures into print*, page 252

Book publishers UK and Ireland

*Member of the Publishers Association or Scottish Publishers Association
†Member of the Irish Book Publishers' Association

AA Publishing*
Automobile Association, Fanum House,
Basingstoke, Hants RG21 2EA
tel (01256) 20123 *fax* (01256) 22575
Managing Director John Howard, *Marketing and International Sales Director* S.J. Mesquita,
Editorial Manager Michael Buttler

Travel, atlases, maps, leisure interests, including Baedeker, Essential, Thomas Cook and Explorer Travel Guides. Founded 1979.

Abacus – see Little, Brown and Company (UK)*

ABC, All Books for Children
33 Museum Street, London WC1A 1LD
tel 0171-436 6300 *fax* 0171-240 6923
Managing Director and Publisher Susan Tarsky,
Chairman Timothy Chadwick, *Financial Director* Michael Raine

Children's picture books up to age 7; non-fiction for 7-11. Submit MSS with sae if return required to Carol Mackenzie. Division of The All Children's Co. Ltd. Founded 1990.

ABC-Clio Ltd
(formerly Clio Press Ltd)
Old Clarendon Ironworks, 35A Great Clarendon Street, Oxford OX2 6AT
tel (01865) 311350 *fax* (01865) 311358
e-mail 100433.3535@compuserve.com
Directors Tony Sloggett (managing), Bob Neville (UK editorial and production)

General and academic reference: history, art, photography, mythology, literature, ethnic studies; bibliography. Publishes *World Bibliographical Series* (comprehensive guides to individual countries), *World Photographers Reference Series*, *The Clio Montessori Series*, *International Organisations Series* (annotated bibliographies), *Electronic Library* (CD-Roms of abstracting services in modern art,

American studies and history). Subsidiary of ABC-CLIO Inc. Founded 1971.

Absolute Press
Scarborough House, 29 James Street West,
Bath BA1 2BT
tel (01225) 316013 *fax* (01225) 445836
Publisher Jon Croft, *Directors* Amanda Hawkins (sales), Bronwen Douglas (marketing)

General list: cookery, food-related topics, wine, lifestyle, travel. Streetwise maps, accordian fold, and laminated city maps. No fiction. *Out Lines* is a series of monographs on gay and lesbian artists. No unsolicited MSS. Founded 1979.

Academic Press – see Harcourt Brace & Co. Ltd*

Academy Editions – acquired by John Wiley & Sons Ltd

Access Press – see HarperCollins Publishers*

Ace Books – see Age Concern Books

Acorn Editions – see James Clarke & Co. Ltd*

Actinic Press – see Cressrelles Publishing Co. Ltd

Addison Wesley Longman Ltd*
Edinburgh Gate, Harlow, Essex CM20 2JE
tel (01279) 623623 *fax* (01279) 431059
e-mail enq.order@awl.co.uk
web site http://www.awl.co.uk
Directors J. Larry Jones (USA), D. Smith (USA), T.C. Davy, J.E. Robinson

Addison Wesley Longman was established in 1995 with the merger of Longman and Addison-Wesley, both Pearson companies. It publishes materials for pupils and students from nursery-school to post-graduate level in virtually every country.

Adlard Coles Nautical – see A & C Black (Publishers) Ltd*

Adlib – see Scholastic Children's Books*

Age Concern Books
(formerly Ace Books)
Age Concern England, 1268 London Road, London SW16 4ER
tel 0181-679 8000 *fax* 0181-679 6069
e-mail books@ace.org.uk
Publisher Richard Holloway, *Marketing* Michael Addison
Health and care, advice, finance, gerontology. Founded 1973.

Airlife Publishing Ltd
101 Longden Road, Shrewsbury, Shropshire SY3 9EB
tel (01743) 235651 *fax* (01743) 232944
Directors Alastair Simpson (chairman and managing), Robert Pooley, Andrew Johnston (sales), John Gibbs, Peter Holmes (finance)
Aviation, technical and general, military. Founded 1976.
Swan Hill Press (imprint)
Managing Editor P. Coles
Natural history, wildlife, arts, travel, equestrian, fishing, country sports and pursuits.
Waterline Books (imprint)
Managing Editor P. Coles
Sailing.

Aladdin/Watts – see The Watts Publishing Group*

Ian Allan Ltd
Coombelands House, Coombelands Lane, Addlestone, Surrey KT15 1HY
tel (01932) 855909 *fax* (01932) 854750
Publishing Manager Peter Waller
Transport: railways, aircraft, shipping, road; naval and military history; reference books and magazines; sport and walking guides; no fiction.

George Allen & Unwin Publishers Ltd – acquired by HarperCollins Publishers*

J.A. Allen & Co. Ltd
1 Lower Grosvenor Place, Buckingham Palace Road, London SW1W 0EL
tel 0171-834 0090/5606 *fax* 0171-976 5836
Executive Director Caroline Burt
Specialist publishers of books on the horse and equestrianism including bloodstock breeding, racing, polo, dressage, horse care, carriage driving, breeds, veterinary and farriery. Technical books usually commissioned but willing to consider any serious, specialist MSS on the horse and related subjects. No fiction or autobiography. Founded 1926.

W.H. Allen – acquired by Virgin Publishing Ltd

Allen Lane The Penguin Press – see Penguin Books Ltd*

Allison & Busby Ltd
114 New Cavendish Street, London W1M 7FD
tel 0171-636 2942 *fax* 0171-323 2023
e-mail aandbuk@aol.com
Publisher Peter Day, *Publicity and Marketing* Susan Herbert, *Editorial* Vanessa Unwin, Jason Beckford-Ball
Biography and memoirs, and new crime, fiction, translations, writers' guides. Unsolicited MSS welcome (synopsis and 2 sample chapters initially) but sae essential.

The Alpha Press – see Sussex Academic Press

AN Publications
PO Box 23, Sunderland SR4 6DG
tel 0191-507 0509 *fax* 0101-564 1600
e-mail anpubs@anpubs.demon.co.uk
Editorial Coordinator Hannah Firth, *Publisher* Richard Padwick
Information for the visual arts, including critical reviews, issues and news and practical advice. Founded 1980.

Anchor – see Transworld Publishers Ltd*

Andersen Press Ltd
20 Vauxhall Bridge Road, London SW1V 2SA
tel 0171-973 9720 *fax* 0171-233 6263
e-mail 101370.533@compuserve.com
Managing Director/Publisher Klaus Flugge, *Directors* Philip Durrance, Janice Thomson (editorial), Joëlle Flugge (company secretary)
Children's picture books, novelties and fiction (send synopsis and full MS with sae); no short stories. International co-productions. Founded 1976.

Andromeda Oxford Ltd
11-15 The Vineyard, Abingdon, Oxon OX14 3PX
tel (01235) 550296 *fax* (01235) 550330
e-mail books@andromeda.co.uk
web site www.andromeda.co.uk

Directors Mark Ritchie (managing), Graham Bateman (adult books), Derek Hall (children's books), Clive Sparling (production)

Publishes adult and junior reference books: history, science, natural history, medicine; children's information and activity books. Founded 1986.

Anness Publishing
88-89 Blackfriars Road, London SE1 8HP
tel 0171-401 2077 *fax* 0171-633 9499
Managing Director Paul Anness, *Publisher* Joanna Lorenz

Practical illustrated books on crafts, cookery and gardening, and children's non-fiction. Founded 1989.

Hermes House (imprint)
Illustrated promotional and bargain books on practical subjects.

Lorenz Books (imprint)
Lifestyle, cookery, crafts, gardening, and all practical illustrated subjects.

Antique Collectors' Club
5 Church Street, Woodbridge, Suffolk IP12 1DS
tel (01394) 385501 *fax* (01394) 384434
Managing Director Diana Steel

Fine art, antiques, gardening and garden history, architecture. Founded 1966.

Anvil Books/The Children's Press†
45 Palmerston Road, Dublin 6, Republic of Ireland
tel (01) 4973628 *fax* (01) 4968263
Directors Rena Dardis (managing), Margaret Dardis (editorial)

Anvil: history, biography; Children's Press: adventure, humour, fantasy. Founded 1964.

Anvil Press Poetry
Neptune House, 70 Royal Hill,
London SE10 8RT
tel 0181-469 3033 *fax* 0181-469 3363
e-mail anvil@cix.co.uk
Director Peter Jay

Poetry. Submissions only with sae. Founded 1968.

Apple Press
The Old Brewery, 6 Blundell Street,
London N7 9BH
tel 0171-700 6700 *fax* 0171-700 4191
Publisher Oliver Salzmann, *Sales Director* Stuart Henderson

Imprint of **Quarto Publishing plc**, book packagers. Leisure, domestic and craft pursuits; cookery, gardening, sport, transport, militaria, fine and decorative art, children's. Founded 1984.

Appletree Press Ltd†
19-21 Alfred Street, Belfast BT2 8DL
tel (01232) 243074 *fax* (01232) 246756
e-mail frontdesk@appletree.ie
web site www.appletree.ie
Director John Murphy

Gift books, biography, cookery, guidebooks, history, Irish interest, literary criticism, music, photographic, social studies, sport, travel. Founded 1974.

Arc Publications
Nanholme Mill, Shaw Wood Road, Todmorden, Lancs. OL14 6DA
tel (01706) 812338 *fax* (01706) 818948
Partners Rosemary Jones, Tony Ward (general editor), Angela Jarman, *Associate Editors* Michael Hulse (international), David Morley (UK)

Poetry. Manuscripts with sae only.

Arcadia Books Ltd
6-9 Cynthia Street, London N1 9JF
tel 0171-278 2586 *fax* 0171-833 4804
Directors Gary Pulsifer (managing), J.M. Bull (editorial)

Original paperback fiction, fiction in translation, autobiography, biography, travel, gender studies, gay books. Founded 1996.

Architectural Press – see Reed Educational and Professional Publishing Ltd

Arden Shakespeare – see Thomas Nelson & Sons Ltd*

Arkana – see Penguin Books Ltd*

Arms & Armour Press – see Cassell plc

E.J. Arnold Publishing Division – acquired by Thomas Nelson & Sons Ltd*

Edward Arnold – see Hodder Headline plc

Arrow Books Ltd – see Random House UK Ltd*

Art Trade Press Ltd
9 Brockhampton Road, Havant,
Hants PO9 1NU
tel (01705) 484943
Editorial Director J.M. Curley

Publishers of *Who's Who in Art*.

Ashgate Publishing Ltd

Gower House, Croft Road, Aldershot,
Hants GU11 3HR
tel (01252) 331551 *fax* (01252) 344405
e-mail gower@cityscape.co.uk
Chairman Nigel Farrow
Editors Sarah Markham (social sciences), Jo
Gooderham (social work and public service),
John Hindley (aviation management), Alec
MacAulay (history, economic and general),
Pamela Edwardes (art and art history), Rachel
Lynch (music and literary studies)

Publishes a wide range of academic
research in the social sciences and
humanities, and professional practice in
the management of business and public
services. Founded 1967.

Dartmouth (imprint)
Editor John Irwin
Law and legal studies.

Gower (imprint)
Editor Julia Scott
Business and management.

Variorum (imprint)
Editor John Smedley
History.

Ashmolean Museum Publications

Beaumont Street, Oxford OX1 2PH
tel (01865) 278009/278010 *fax* (01865) 278018
web site http://www.ashmol.ox.ac.uk/
Publications Officer Ian Charlton
Fine and applied art, archaeology, history, numismatics. Founded 1972.

Aslib

(The Association for Information Management)
20-24 Old Street, London EC1V 9AP
tel 0171-253 4488 *fax* 0171-430 01514
e-mail pubs@aslib.co.uk
web site http://www.aslib.co.uk/
Head of Publications Sarah Blair

Information management, librarianship,
information science, general reference,
computing. Founded 1924.

Associated University Presses – see
Golden Cockerel Press

The Athlone Press Ltd

1 Park Drive, London NW11 7SG
tel 0181-458 0888 *fax* 0181-201 8115
Directors Brian Southam (editorial), Doris
Southam, Gill Davies

Anthropology, archaeology, architecture,
art, economics, film studies, history,
Japan, language, law, literature, medical,
music, oriental, philosophy, politics, psychology, religion, science, sociology, cultural studies. Founded 1949.

Atlantic Europe Publishing Co. Ltd

Greys Court Farm, Greys Court, Henley on
Thames, Oxon RG4 4PG
tel (01491) 628188 *fax* (01491) 628189
e-mail info@aepublish.com
Directors Dr B.J. Knapp, D.L.R. McCrae

Children's colour information books: science, geography, history, design and
technology. Associate company:
Earthscape Editions (see Book
Packagers). Founded 1989.

Attic Press[†]

29 Upper Mount Street, Dublin 2,
Republic of Ireland
tel (01) 6616128 *fax* (01) 6616176
e-mail atticirl@iol.ie
web site http://www.iol.ie/~atticirl/
Directors Róisín Conroy, Maeve Kneafsey, Ann
Harper

Books by and about women in the areas
of social and political comment, fiction,
women's studies, humour, reference
guides and handbooks. Founded 1984.

Basement Press (imprint)
Fiction and non-fiction by men and
women.

Aureus Publishing

144 Marlborough Road, Cardiff CF2 5BZ
tel/fax (01222) 455200
e-mail meurynhughes@aureus.co.uk
web site http://aureus.co.uk
Proprietor Meuryn Hughes

Fiction, education, fine art, autobiography, sport, religion; also publishes
music. Founded 1993.

Aurum Press Ltd

25 Bedford Avenue, London WC1B 3AT
tel 0171-637 3225 *fax* 0171-580 2469
Directors André Deutsch (chairman), Bill
McCreadie (managing), Piers Burnett (editorial),
Sheila Murphy (editorial), Ken Banerji

General, illustrated and non-illustrated
adult non-fiction: biography and memoirs, visual arts, film, home interest, travel. Founded 1977.

Award Publications Ltd

1st Floor, 27 Longford Street, London NW1 3DZ
tel 0171-388 7800 *fax* 0171-388 7887
Managing Director Ron Wilkinson

Children's books: full colour picture
story books; early learning, information
and activity books. Founded 1954.

Bernard Babani (Publishing) Ltd

The Grampians, Shepherds Bush Road,
London W6 7NF
tel 0171-603 2581/7296 *fax* 0171-603 8203
Directors S. Babani, M.H. Babani BSc(Eng)

Practical handbooks on radio, electronics and computing.

Baillière Tindall Ltd – see Harcourt Brace & Co. Ltd*

Duncan Baird Publishers

Sixth Floor, Castle House, 75-76 Wells Street,
London W1P 3RE
tel 0171-323 2229 *fax* 0171-580 5692
Directors Duncan Baird (managing), Bob Saxton (editorial), Roger Walton (art), Alex Mitchell (international sales), Nick Foster (financial)

Non-fiction, illustrated reference. Founded 1994.

The Bankers' Almanac – see Reed Information Services

Bantam – see Transworld Publishers Ltd*

Barefoot Books Ltd

PO Box 95, Kingswood, Bristol BS15 5BH
tel (0117) 932 8885 *fax* (0117) 932 8881
Publisher Tessa Strickland

Children's picture books: myth, legend, fairytale. No unsolicited MSS. Founded 1993.

Barrie & Jenkins – see Random House UK Ltd*

Bartholomew – see HarperCollins Publishers*

Basement Press – see Attic Press†

B.T. Batsford Ltd

583 Fulham Road, London SW6 5BY
tel 0171-471 1100 *fax* 0171-471 1101
web site http://www.batsford.com
Chairman Gerard Mizrahi, *Chief Executive* Jules Perel
Directors R.E. Huggins (managing director of Batsford Distribution), Chris Gill (marketing), Alan Ritchie (sales), John Andrews (finance)

Archaeology, architecture, bridge, building, art techniques, film, chess, fashion, costume, equestrian, country sports, craft, pottery, needlecraft, lace, embroidery, horticulture, junior reference, technical/professional, graphic design, woodworking. Founded 1843.

BBC Worldwide Ltd*

Woodlands, 80 Wood Lane, London W12 0TT
tel 0181-576 2000

Founded 1843.

BBC Books

fax 0181-576 2858
Editorial Manager Tracey Smith

Books tied in to BBC television and radio programmes of all subjects.

BBC Radio Collection

tel 0181-576 2567 *fax* 0181-576 3851
Head of Spoken Word Jan Paterson

Audio cassettes and CDs of BBC Radio and Television comedy, readings and dramatised serials for adults and children.

Network Books (imprint of BBC Books)
Range of non-fiction titles tied in to non-BBC television programmes.

BBC Children's Publishing

Head of Children's Publishing Rona Selby

Range of fiction and non-fiction titles tied in to BBC television programmes.

Bedford Square Press – see NCVO Publications

Belitha Press

London House, Great Eastern Wharf,
Parkgate Road, London SW11 4NQ
tel 0171-978 6330 *fax* 0171-223 4936
Contact Peter Osborn

Illustrated children's non-fiction for international co-editions: art, atlases, geography, history, natural history, reference, science. Imprint of **Collins & Brown**. Founded 1980.

Bell & Hyman Ltd – acquired by HarperCollins Publishers*

Bellew Publishing Co. Ltd

The Nightingale Centre, 8 Balham Hill,
London SW12 9EA
tcl 0181-673 5611 *fax* 0181-675 2142
Chairman Ian McCorquodale, *Managing Director* Ib Bellew

Sociology, religion, politics, art and art criticism, some fiction, poetry. Founded 1983.

David Bennett Books Ltd

15 High Street, St Albans, Herts. AL3 4ED
tel (01727) 855878 *fax* (01727) 864085
Managing Director David Bennett

Highly illustrated children's fiction and non-fiction; baby books, interactive play books and gift books for the young. Founded 1989.

Berg Publishers

150 Cowley Road, Oxford OX4 1JJ
tel (01865) 245104 *fax* (01865) 791165
Editorial Director Kathryn Earle

Social anthropology, European studies, politics and economics, literature. Founded 1983.

Berkswell Publishing Co. Ltd

PO Box 420, Warminster, Wilts. BA12 9XB
tel/fax (01985) 840189
Directors J.N.G. Stidolph, S.A. Abbott

Books of local interest in Wessex, field sports, royalty. Ideas and MSS welcome. Also provide editorial, design, research, picture research, exhibition organisation and design.

Berlitz Publishing Co. Ltd

Berlitz House, Peterley Road,
Oxford OX4 2TX
tel (01865) 747033 *fax* (01865) 779700
Managing Director Roger Kirkpatrick

Travel, language and related multimedia. Founded 1960.

Bible Society

Stonehill Green, Westlea, Swindon,
Wilts. SN5 7DG
tel (01793) 418100 *fax* (01793) 418118
e-mail corpcom.bfbs.org.uk

Bibles, testaments, portions and selections in English and over 2000 other languages; also books and audiovisual material on use of Bible for personal, education and church groups.

Clive Bingley Ltd – see Library Association Publishing Ltd*

Birnbaum – see HarperCollins Publishers*

A & C Black (Publishers) Ltd*

35 Bedford Row, London WC1R 4JH
tel 0171-242 0946 *fax* 0171-831 8478
e-mail enquiries@acblack.co.uk
Chairman and Joint Managing Director Charles Black, *Joint Managing Director* Jill Coleman, *Directors* Paul Langridge (rights), Janet Murphy (Adlard Coles Nautical), Terry Rouelett (distribution), Oscar Heini (production), Robert Kirk (Christopher Helm, ornithology), Susan Kodicek (sales)

Children's and educational books (including music) for 3-15 years (preliminary enquiry appreciated – fiction guidelines available on request); ceramics, calligraphy, drama (*New Mermaid* series),
fishing, ornithology, reference (*Who's Who*), sport, theatre, travel (*Blue Guides*), books for writers. Subsidiary of A & C Black plc. Founded 1807.

Adlard Coles Nautical (imprint)
Editorial Director Janet Murphy
Nautical.

Christopher Helm (imprint)
Editorial Director Robert Kirk
Ornithology.

The Herbert Press (imprint)
Visual arts.

Black Ace Books*

PO Box 6557, Forfar DD8 2YS
tel (01307) 465096 *fax* (01307) 465494
Publisher Hunter Steele, *Art, Publicity and Sales* Boo Wood

New fiction, Scottish and general; new editions of outstanding recent fiction. Non-fiction: biography, history, psychology and philosophy. No unsolicited MSS. Send A4 sae for current requirements. Imprints: Black Ace Books, Black Ace Paperbacks. Founded 1991.

Black Butterfly – see Writers & Readers Ltd*

Black Lace – see Virgin Publishing Ltd

Black Swan – see Transworld Publishers Ltd*

Blackie Academic and Professional – see Thomson Science & Professional*

Blackstaff Press Ltd[+]

3 Galway Park, Dundonald BT16 0AN
tel (01232) 487161 *fax* (01232) 489552
e-mail books@blkstaff.dnet.co.uk
Managing Director Anne Tannahill

Fiction, poetry, biography, history, politics, art, natural history, sport, education, fine limited editions. Founded 1971.

Blackstone Press Ltd

9-15 Aldine Street, London W12 8AW
tel 0181-740 2277 *fax* 0181-743 2292
Directors Alistair MacQueen (managing), Heather Saward (editorial), Jeremy Stein (sales and marketing)

Law books for practitioners and students. Contact Alistair MacQueen with ideas, or send MSS. Founded 1988.

The Blackwater Press[+] – see Folens Publishing Company

Blackwell Publishers*
(Basil Blackwell Ltd)
108 Cowley Road, Oxford OX4 1JF
tel (01865) 791100 *fax* (01865) 791347
Directors Nigel Blackwell (chairman), René
Olivieri (managing), Philip Carpenter, Sue
Corbett, Mark Houlton, John Davey, Stephan
Chambers, Carolyn Dougherty

Economics, education (academic), geography, history, industrial relations, linguistics, literature and criticism, politics, psychology, social anthropology, social policy and administration, sociology, theology, business studies, professional, law, reference, feminism, information technology, philosophy. Founded 1922.

InfoSource International (division)
InfoSource House, 54 Marston Street,
Oxford OX4 1JU
tel (01865) 244068 *fax* (01865) 791347
Directors René Olivieri, Mark Houlton

Computer-based training, skills assessment and instructor manuals. Specialist areas include: PC applications (e.g. Microsoft Excel, WordPerfect, Lotus 1-2-3), networks and Internet.

NCC Blackwell (imprint)
fax (01865) 798210
Director Stephan Chambers

Professional and student books in computing/information technology. Specialist areas include: systems analysis and design, SSADM, PRINCE, security, open systems, communications and networking.

Shakespeare Head Press (imprint)
Finely printed books; scholarly works.

Blackwell Science Ltd*
Osney Mead, Oxford OX2 0EL
tel (01865) 206206 *fax* (01865) 721205
web site http://www.blacksci.co.uk
Chairman Nigel Blackwell, *Managing Director*
Robert Campbell, *Directors* Jonathan Conibear,
Peter Saugman (editorial), Martin Wilkinson
(finance), John Strange (production), Bill Gibson
(Boston)

Medicine, nursing, dentistry, veterinary medicine, life sciences, earth sciences, chemistry, professional including construction, allied health. Founded 1939.

Blake Publishing
3 Bramber Court, 2 Bramber Road,
London W14 9PB
tel 0171-381 0666 *fax* 0171-381 6868
Chairman David Blake, *Managing Director* John
Blake, *Deputy Managing Director* Rosie Ries,
Production Editor Sadie Mayne

Popular fiction and non-fiction, including biographies and true crime. No unsolicited fiction. Founded 1991.

Blandford Press – see Cassell plc

Bloodaxe Books Ltd
PO Box 1SN, Newcastle upon Tyne NE99 1SN
tel (01434) 684855 *fax* (01434) 684862
e-mail editor@bloodaxebooks.demon.co.uk
Directors Neil Astley, Simon Thirsk

Poetry, literary criticism, literary biography. Founded 1978.

Bloodlines – see The Do-Not Press

Bloomsbury Publishing plc*
38 Soho Square, London W1V 5DF
tel 0171-494 2111 *fax* 0171-434 0151
Chairman and Managing Director Nigel Newton,
Directors David Reynolds (deputy managing and
publishing), Liz Calder (publishing), Alan Wherry
(publishing), Kathy Rooney (reference), Emma
Kirby (sales), Sarah Beal (marketing), Becky Shaw
(publicity), Ruth Logan (rights), Penny Edwards
(production), Matthew Hamilton (paperbacks),
Noni Ware (paperbacks marketing), Sarah
Odedina (children's), Colin Adams (finance)

Fiction, biography, illustrated, reference, travel, trade paperback and mass market paperback. Founded 1986.

Bodley Head – see Random House UK Ltd*

Bodley Head Children's – see Random House UK Ltd*

Bounty – see Reed Books

Bowker-Saur
Maypole House, Maypole Road, East Grinstead,
West Sussex RH19 1HU
tel (01342) 330100 *fax* (01342) 330191
Directors Gerard Dummett (publishing), Charles
Halpin (managing)

Bibliographies, trade and reference directories, library and information science, electronic publishing, abstracts and indexes.

Headland Business Information (imprint)
Business information newsletters, journals and directories.

Hans Zell Publishers (imprint)
PO Box 56, Oxford OX1 2SJ
tel (01865) 511428 *fax* (01865) 311534/793298

Bibliographies, directories and other reference works; African studies, African literature (criticism only); development studies; studies on publishing and book development.

Boxtree Ltd*
25 Eccleston Place, London SW1W 9NF
tel 0171-881 8000 *fax* 0171-881 8001
Directors Adrian Sington (publishing), Susanna Wadeson (editorial)

TV and film tie-ins (adult and children's non-fiction); illustrated and general non-fiction; mass market paperbacks linked to TV, film, rock and sporting events; humour. Imprint of **Macmillan Publishers Ltd**. Founded 1986.

Marion Boyars Publishers Ltd*
24 Lacy Road, London SW15 1NL
tel 0181-788 9522 *fax* 0181-789 8122
Directors Marion Boyars, Arthur Boyars

Belles-lettres and criticism, fiction, sociology, psychology, feminism, history of ideas, music, drama, cinema, dance, biography.

Boydell & Brewer Ltd
PO Box 9, Woodbridge, Suffolk IP12 3DF

Medieval studies, history, literature, archaeology, art history. No unsolicited MSS. Founded 1969.

BPP (Letts Educational) Ltd
(trading as Letts Educational)
Aldine House, Aldine Place, London W12 8AW
tel 0181-743 7514 *fax* 0181-743 8451
Managing Director Jonathan Harris, *Publishing Directors* Richard Carr, Edward Peppitt, *Editorial Production Director* Catherine Tilley

Revision and exam preparation, and course books for the school, college and home study markets. Founded 1979.

Brandon Book Publishers Ltd†
Cooleen, Dingle, Co. Kerry, Republic of Ireland
tel (066) 51463 *fax* (066) 51234
Directors Steve MacDonogh, Bernard Goggin

Biography, literature, politics, fiction, travel (Ireland), history, children's folklore. Founded 1982.

Brassey's (UK) Ltd
33 John Street, London WC1N 2AT
tel 0171-753 7777 *fax* 0171-753 7794
Managing Director Jenny Shaw BSc(Econ), MA

Defence and national security, international relations, weapons technology, military affairs, military biography, military history, reference. Publisher to the Centre for Defence Studies. Founded 1886.

Conway Maritime Press (imprint)
Maritime and naval history, ship modelling.

Putnam Aeronautical Books (imprint)
Technical and historical aviation reference.

Nicholas Brealey Publishing Ltd*
36 John Street, London WC1N 2AT
tel 0171-430 0224 *fax* 0171-404 8311
web site http://www.nbrealey-books.com
Managing Director Nicholas Brealey

Business, management, training, employment law, international affairs. Founded 1992.

Breedon Books Publishing Co. Ltd
44 Friar Gate, Derby DE1 1DA
tel (01332) 384235 *fax* (01332) 292755
Directors Anton Rippon (chairman and editorial), Patricia Rippon, Graham Hales

Autobiographies, biographies, sports, heritage, local history. No unsolicited MSS; preliminary letter essential. Founded 1981.

Brewin Books
Doric House, 56 Alcester Road, Studley, Warks. B80 7LG
tel (01527) 854228/853624 *fax* (01527) 852746
Publishing Director K.A.F. Brewin

Non-fiction: Midland regional history (Birmingham, Warwickshire, Worcs.), transport history, biography (with Midlands connection). Founded 1976.

Brilliant Publications
The Old School Yard, Leighton Road, Northall, Dunstable, Beds. LU6 2HA
tel (01525) 222844 *fax* (01525) 221250
e-mail brilliantpublications@compuserve.com
Managing Director Priscilla Hannaford

Books for primary school teachers, focusing on English, maths, science and history. Founded 1993.

Brimax Books – see Reed Books

Bristol Classical Press – see Gerald Duckworth & Co. Ltd

British Academic Press – see I.B. Tauris & Co. Ltd

The British Library (Publications)*
Marketing & Publishing Office, Public Affairs, 41 Russell Square, London WC1B 3DG
tel 0171-412 7704 *fax* 0171-412 7768
Director Jane Carr, *Managers* David Way (publishing), Anne Young (product development), Jenny McKinley (marketing)

Bibliography, book arts, music, maps, oriental, manuscript studies, history, literature, facsimiles, audio-visual, and multimedia CD-Rom. Founded 1973.

British Museum Press*
46 Bloomsbury Street, London WC1B 3QQ
tel 0171-323 1234 *fax* 0171-436 7315
Managing Director Patrick Wright, *Head of Publishing* Emma Way
Art history, archaeology, numismatics, history, oriental art and archaeology, horology. A division of The British Museum Company Ltd. Founded 1973.

Brockhampton Press – see Hodder Headline plc

Brown, Son & Ferguson, Ltd*
4-10 Darnley Street, Glasgow G41 2SD
tel 0141-429 1234 (24 hours) *fax* 0141-420 1694.
Editorial Director L. Ingram-Brown
Nautical books; Scottish poetry and plays; Scout, Cub Scout, Brownie Guide and Guide story books. Founded 1860.

Brown Wells & Jacobs Ltd
Foresters Hall, 25-27 Westow Street,
London SE19 3RY
tel 0181-771 5115 *fax* 0181-771 9994
Managing Director Graham Brown
Children's non-fiction novelty and pop-ups. Founded 1970.

Bryntirion Press
(formerly Evangelical Press of Wales)
Bryntirion, Bridgend, Mid Glamorgan CF31 4DX
tel (01656) 655886 *fax* (01656) 656095
Chief Executive David Kingdon
Theology and religion (in English and Welsh). Founded 1955.

Burns & Oates Ltd
(Publishers to the Holy See)
Wellwood, North Farm Road, Tunbridge Wells,
Kent TN2 3DR
tel (01892) 510850 *fax* (01892) 515903
Directors Charlotte de la Bedoyere, Hans Küpfer
Theology, philosophy, spirituality, church history, Catholic interest, craft books with religious themes. Founded 1847.

Butterworth & Co. (Publishers) Ltd
Halsbury House, 35 Chancery Lane,
London WC2A 1EL
tel 0171-400 2500 *fax* 0171-400 2842
e-mail neville.cusworth@butterworths.co.uk
Chairman and Chief Executive Neville Cusworth
Law, tax and accountancy publishing. Division of Reed Elsevier (UK) Ltd.
British and Irish Legal Division
Legal books, journals, loose leaf and electronic services; tax and accountancy books, journals and loose leaf and electronic services.

Butterworth Heinemann UK – see Reed Educational and Professional Publishing Ltd

Cadogan Books plc
(now incorporating Everyman's Library and David Campbell Publishers Ltd)
3rd Floor, 27-29 Berwick Street,
London W1V 3RF
tel 0171-287 6555 *fax* 0171-734 1733
Chairman Alewyn Birch, *Managing Director* William Colegrave, *Publisher* David Campbell, *Finance Director* Mark Bicknell, *Publisher (Cadogan Guides and Chess)* Rachel Fielding
Cadogan Travel Guides; Cadogan Chess.

Calder Publications Ltd*
126 Cornwall Road, London SE1 8TQ
tel 0171-633 0599
Director John Calder
European, international and British fiction and plays, art, literary, music and social criticism, biography and autobiography, essays, humanities and social sciences, European classics. No unsolicited MSS. Inquiry letters must include an sae. Series include: *English National Opera Guides, New Paris Editions, Scottish Library, New Writing and Writers, Platform Books, Opera Library, Historical Perspectives.*

Calmann and King Ltd – see Laurence King Publishing*

Cambridge University Press*
The Edinburgh Building, Shaftesbury Road,
Cambridge CB2 2RU
tel (01223) 312393 *fax* (01223) 315052
e-mail information@cup.cam.ac.uk
web site http://www.cup.cam.ac.uk
Chief Executive of the Press and University Printer Anthony K. Wilson MA, *Deputy Chief Executive and Managing Director (Publishing Division)* Jeremy Mynott MA, PhD
Anthropology and archaeology, art and architecture, classical studies, computer science, educational (primary, secondary, tertiary), educational software, English language teaching, history, journals (humanities, technology, social sciences and sciences), language and literature, law, mathematics, medicine, music, oriental, philosophy, politics, psychology, reference, science (physical and biological), technology, social sciences, theology, religion. The Bible and Prayer Book. Founded 1534.

Canongate Books Ltd*
14 High Street, Edinburgh EH1 1TE
tel 0131-557 5111 *fax* 0131-557 5211
e-mail info@canongate.co.uk
web site http://www.canongate.co.uk/
Directors Jamie Byng, Hugh Andrew, Ronnie Shanks, Neville Moir

Adult general non-fiction and fiction: Canongate Classics, Kelpie Paperbacks (children's fiction), art, travel, Canongate Audio (audio books). Founded 1973.

Payback Press (imprint)
Publishing Director Jamie Byng, *Chief Editor* Lloyd Bradley
e-mail payback@canongate.co.uk
Afro-American and Jamaican culture: non-fiction, fiction, music, poetry, biography.

Rebel Inc. (imprint)
Publishing Director Jamie Byng, *Chief Editor* Kevin Williamson
e-mail rebelinc@canongate.co.uk
Counter cultural fiction and non-fiction translation.

The Canterbury Press Norwich
St Mary's Works, St Mary's Plain, Norwich, Norfolk NR3 3BH
tel (01603) 616563/612914 *fax* (01603) 624483
Publisher G.A. Knights

Book publishing imprint of **Hymns Ancient and Modern Ltd**, music publishers. C of E doctrine, theology, history and associated topics, music and liturgy.

Jonathan Cape – see Random House UK Ltd*

Jonathan Cape Children's Books – see Random House UK Ltd*

Carcanet Press Ltd
4th Floor, Conavon Court, 12-16 Blackfriars Street, Manchester M3 5BQ
tel 0161-834 8730 *fax* 0161-832 0084
e-mail pnr@carcanet.u-net.com
Director Michael Schmidt

Poetry, *Fyfield* series, translations. Founded 1969.

Carlton Books
20 St Anne's Court, Wardour Street, London W1V 3AW
tel 0171-734 7338 *fax* 0171-434 1196
e-mail sales @carltonbooks.co.uk
Directors Jonathan Goodman (managing), John Maynard (operations), Piers Murray Hill (editorial), Russell Porter (design), Adrian Whitton (finance), Keith Allen-Jones (international sales)

Popular music, sport, games, film, video, popular science, lifestyle, New Age, TV tie-ins, criminology. Founded 1992.

Cartermill International – see Pearson Professional Ltd*

Frank Cass & Co. Ltd
Newbury House, 890-900 Eastern Avenue, Newbury Park, Ilford, Essex IG2 7HH
tel 0181-599 8866 *fax* 0181-599 0984
Directors Frank Cass (managing), Stewart Cass, A.E. Cass, M.P. Zaidner

History, economic and social history, military and strategic studies, politics, international affairs, development studies, African studies, Middle East studies, law, business management and academic journals in all of these fields.

Vallentine Mitchell (imprint)
Jewish interest. Founded 1958.

Woburn Press (imprint)
Educational.

Cassell plc
Wellington House, 125 Strand, London WC2R 0BB
tel 0171-420 5555 *fax* 0171-240 7261
Chairman and Chief Executive Philip Sturrock

Founded 1848.

Arms & Armour Press (imprint)
Director Rod Dymott
Military history (land, sea, air, weaponry), military reference, military adventure non-fiction, modern defence/intelligence.

Blandford Press (imprint)
Director Rod Dymott
Aviculture, history, hobbies, music, natural history, practical handbooks, sport, New Age/mind, body, spirit.

Cassell (general imprint)
Editorial Director Alison Goff
Cookery, poetry, lifestyle, gardening, word reference, art and craft, popular science, current affairs.

Cassell (general reference list)
Commissioning Editor Nigel Wilcockson
General interest reference.

Cassell (academic reference list)
Director Janet Joyce
Foreign language, humanities, social science reference.

Cassell (professional lists)
Director Naomi Roth
Education, hotel and catering management, psychology and counselling, business and professional reference.

Cassell (contemporary studies lists)
Director Janet Joyce
Gender studies, global issues, film studies.
Geoffrey Chapman (imprint)
Publisher Gillian Paterson
Religion and theology, particularly
Roman Catholic.
Victor Gollancz Ltd (imprint)
Director Jane Blackstock
Biography and autobiography, current
affairs, history, humour, sociology, travel;
fiction, crime fiction, science fiction, fantasy. In association with Peter Crawley:
Master Bridge Series. No unsolicited submissions.
Indigo (imprint)
Editorial Director Mike Petty
Literary fiction and general non-fiction.
No unsolicited submissions.
Leicester University Press (imprint)
Director Janet Joyce
Academic books, especially medieval
history, museum studies, political
theory.
Mansell Publishing (imprint)
Director Janet Joyce
Bibliographies in all academic subject
areas and monographs in urban and
regional planning, Islamic studies,
librarianship, history.
Mowbray (imprint)
Publisher Gillian Paterson
Religion and theology, both Anglican and
non-denominational.
New Orchard Editions (imprint)
Director Kevin Bristow
Antiques and collecting, children's,
cookery, wines and spirits, gardening,
history and antiquarian, illustrated and
fine editions, military and war, natural
history, reference and dictionaries, transport, travel and topography.
Pinter (imprint)
Director Janet Joyce
Academic and professional publishers
specialising in social sciences including
international relations, politics, economics, new technology, linguistics, communications and religious studies.
Studio Vista (imprint)
Commissioning Editor Barry Holmes
Art, antiques and collecting, architecture
and design, decorative arts, film books,
practical art.

Vista (imprint)
Editorial Director Humphrey Price
Popular fiction and commercial non-fiction. No unsolicited submissions.
Ward Lock (imprint)
Director Alison Goff
Cookery, gardening, equestrian and outdoor pursuits, popular reference books,
DIY, health.
Wisley Handbooks (imprint)
Trade Publisher Barry Holmes
Gardening.

Castle House Publications Ltd
28-30 Church Road, Tunbridge Wells, Kent TN1 1JP
tel (01892) 539606 *fax* (01892) 517773
Director D. Reinders
Medical. Founded 1973.

Kyle Cathie Ltd
20 Vauxhall Bridge Road, London SW1V 2SA
tel 0171-973 9710 *fax* 0171-821 9258
Publisher and Managing Director Kyle Cathie
Natural history, health, beauty, food and
drink; craft; gardening; reference.
Founded 1990.

Catholic Truth Society
192 Vauxhall Bridge Road, London SW1V 1PD
tel 0171-834 4392 *fax* 0171-630 1124
Chairman Rt Rev. Peter Smith DCL, LLB, *General
Secretary* Fergal Martin LLB, LLM
General books of Roman Catholic and
Christian interest, bibles, prayer books
and pamphlets of doctrinal, historical,
devotional or social interest. MSS of
11,000-15,000 words with up to 6 illustrations considered for publication as
pamphlets. Founded 1868.

Causeway Press Ltd
PO Box 13, 129 New Court Way, Ormskirk,
Lancs. L39 5HP
tel (01695) 576048/577360 *fax* (01695) 570714
Directors Mike Haralambos (chairman and
editorial), Pauline Haralambos, Dave Gray
(company secretary), David Alcorn
School textbooks: mathematics, history,
economics, business studies, sociology,
politics, geography, technology. Founded
1982.

Cavendish Publishing Ltd*
The Glass House, Wharton Street,
London WC1X 9PX
tel 0171-278 8000 *fax* 0171-278 8080
e-mail info@cavendishpublishing.com
web site http://www.cavendishpublishing.com
Publishing Director Sonny Leong, *Managing
Editor* Jo Reddy

A wide range of legal and medico-legal books and journals. Founded 1990.

CBD Research Ltd
15 Wickham Road, Beckenham, Kent BR3 5JS
tel 0181-650 7745 *fax* 0181-650 0768
e-mail 100702.32@compuserv.com
Directors G.P. Henderson, S.P.A. Henderson, C.A.P. Henderson, A.J.W. Henderson
Directories, reference books, bibliographies, guides to business and statistical information. Founded 1961.
Chancery House Press (imprint)
Unusual non-fiction/reference works. Preliminary letter and synopsis with return postage essential.

Centaur Press
Fontwell, Arundel, West Sussex BN18 0TA
tel (01243) 543302
Directors Jon Wynne-Tyson, Jennifer M. Wynne-Tyson
Philosophy, environment, humane education, biography. Principal series: *The Kinship Library.* Send a preliminary letter with sae before submitting MS. Founded 1954.

Century – see Random House UK Ltd*

Chadwyck-Healey Ltd*
The Quorum, Barnwell Road, Cambridge CB5 8SW
tel (01223) 215512 *fax* (01223) 215514
e-mail marketing @chadwyck.co.uk
Chairman Sir Charles Chadwyck-Healey, *Directors* Steven Hall (managing), Michael Healy (editorial), Alison Moss (publishing)
CD-Roms: News and business information, bibliographies and reference works, literature, arts, statistics, cartography and climate. Founded 1971.

Chambers – see Larousse plc*

Chameleon – see André Deutsch Ltd*

Chancery House Press – see CBD Research Ltd

Chansitor Publications Ltd
St Mary's Works, St Mary's Plain, Norwich, Norfolk NR3 3BH
tel (01603) 615995 *fax* (01603) 624483
Publisher G.A. Knights
Church Pulpit Year Book.
Religious and Moral Education Press (RMEP) (imprint)
Books for teachers, primary and secondary schools on religious, moral, personal and social education.

Chapman – now incorporated into The Orion Publishing Group Ltd

Chapman & Hall – see Thomson Science & Professional*

Geoffrey Chapman – see Cassell plc

Paul Chapman Publishing Ltd
144 Liverpool Road, London N1 1LA
tel 0171-609 5315/6 *fax* 0171-700 1057
Directors P.R. Chapman (managing), Marianne Lagrange (editorial)
Business, management, accounting, finance, economics, geography, environment, planning, education. Founded 1987.

Chart Books Ltd
Chart Warren, Seal, Sevenoaks, Kent TW15 OEJ
tel (01732) 465515 *fax* (01732) 465595
Executive Directors Christine Pedersen (editorial/rights), Stephen Kirby (financial), Jenny Wilmot-Smith (editorial/publicity)
Children's picture books; novelty books; children's fiction. Founded 1995.

Chatham Publishing – see Gerald Duckworth & Co. Ltd

Chatto & Windus – see Random House UK Ltd*

Child's Play (International) Ltd
Ashworth Road, Bridgemead, Swindon, Wilts. SN5 7YD
tel (01793) 616286 *fax* (01793) 512795
Chairman and Publishing Director Michael Twinn
Children's educational books: board, activity and play books, fiction and non-fiction. Founded 1972.

Churchill Communications Europe – see Pearson Professional Ltd*

Churchill Livingstone – see Pearson Professional Ltd*

Cicerone Press
2 Police Square, Milnthorpe, Cumbria LA7 7PY
tel (015395) 62069 *fax* (015395) 63417
Directors Dorothy Unsworth (managing and sales), Walt Unsworth (editorial), R.B. Evans (production)
Guidebooks to the great outdoors – walking, climbing, etc – Britain, Europe, and

worldwide; general books about the North of England. No fiction or poetry. Founded 1969.

Clarendon Press – see Oxford University Press*

Robin Clark Ltd
27 Goodge Street, London W1P 2LD
tel 0171-636 3992 *fax* 0171-637 1866
Chairman and Director N.I. Attallah
Fiction, biography, social history in paperback. Member of the Namara Group. Founded 1976.

T. & T. Clark
59 George Street, Edinburgh EH2 2LQ
tel 0131-225 4703 *fax* 0131-220 4260
Managing Director Geoffrey F. Green MA, PhD
Theology, philosophy, law. Founded 1821.

James Clarke & Co. Ltd*
PO Box 60, Cambridge CB1 2NT
tel (01223) 350865 *fax* (01223) 366951
e-mail lutterworth.pr@dial.pipex.com
web site http://dialspace.dial.pipex.com/butterworth.pr/
Managing Director Adrian Brink
Theology, academic, reference books. Founded 1859.

Acorn Editions (imprint)
Sponsored books.

Patrick Hardy Books (imprint of Lutterworth Press)
Children's fiction.

Lutterworth Press (subsidiary)
The arts, biography, children's books (fiction, non-fiction, picture, rewards), educational, environmental, general, history, leisure, philosophy, science, sociology, theology and religion.

Cló Iar-Chonnachta Teo.†
Indreabhán, Conamara, Co. Galway, Republic of Ireland
tel (091) 593307 *fax* (091) 593362
e-mail cic@iol.ie
web site http://www.wombat.ie/cic
Director Micheál Ó Conghaile, *Editor* Nóirín Ní Ghrádaigh, *General Manager* Deirdre O'Toole
Mostly Irish-language publications – novels, short stories, plays, poetry, songs, history; cassettes (writers reading from their works in Irish and English). Promotes the translation of contemporary Irish fiction and poetry into other languages. Founded 1985.

Richard Cohen Books
Basement Offices, 7 Manchester Square, London W1M 5RE
tel 0171-935 2099 *fax* 0171-935 2199
Directors Richard Cohen (managing), Peter Heydon (USA), H. Stuart Hughes (company secretary), *Managing Editor* Patricia Chetwyn
Fiction, biography, current affairs, travel, history, politics, the arts, sport. Founded 1995.

Collins – see HarperCollins Publishers*

Collins & Brown
London House, Great Eastern Wharf, Parkgate Road, London SW11 4NQ
tel 0171-924 2575 *fax* 0171-924 7725
Publisher Mark Collins, *Chief Executive* Cameron Brown, *Art Director* Roger Bristow, *Editorial Directors* Susan Berry, Sarah Hoggett, Cindy Richards, Colin Ziegler
Lifestyle and interiors, gardening, photography, practical arts, health and beauty, hobbies and crafts, natural history, history, ancient civilisation and astrology, fantasy art and general interest. Founded 1989.

Belitha Press (imprint)
Contact Peter Osborn
Children's educational (see page 157).

Paper Tiger (imprint)
Contact Cameron Brown, Mark Collins
Fantasy art.

Parkgate Books (imprint)
tel 0171-924 6678
Publisher Ken Webb
Promotional books.

Pavilion Books (imprint)
See page 193.

The Collins Press
Carey's Lane, The Huguenot Quarter, Cork, Republic of Ireland
tel 021 271346 *fax* 021 275489
e-mail info@collins-bookshop.ie
Managing Director Con Collins, *Editor* Maria O'Donovan
Archaeology, biography, fiction, general non-fiction, health, history, mind, body and spirit, poetry, photographic and travel guides. Unsolicited MSS, synopses and ideas for books welcome.

The Columba Press†
55A Spruce Avenue, Stillorgan Industrial Park, Blackrock, Co. Dublin, Republic of Ireland
tel (1) 2942556 *fax* (1) 2942564
e-mail columba@indigo.ie
Publisher and Managing Director Seán O'Boyle

Religion (Roman Catholic and Anglican) including pastoral handbooks, spirituality, theology, liturgy and prayer; counselling and self-help. Founded 1985.

Condé Nast Books – see Random House UK Ltd*

Conran Octopus – see Reed Books

Conservative Political Centre
32 Smith Square, London SW1P 3HH
tel 0171-896 4161 *fax* 0171-896 4163
Politics, current affairs. Founded 1945.

Constable & Co. Ltd*
3 The Lanchesters, 162 Fulham Palace Road, London W6 9ER
tel 0181-741 3663 *fax* 0181-748 7562
Chairman and Managing Director Benjamin Glazebrook, *Directors* Richard Dodman, Richard Tomkins, Jeremy Potter, Carol O'Brien
Fiction: general, crime and suspense; general non-fiction: literature, biography, memoirs, history, politics, current affairs, food, travel and guidebooks, social sciences, psychology and psychiatry, counselling, social work, sociology, mass media. Founded 1890.

Consumers' Association – see Which? Ltd*

Conway Maritime Press – see Brassey's (UK) Ltd

Leo Cooper – see Pen & Sword Books Ltd

Corgi – see Transworld Publishers Ltd*

Cork University Press†
Crawford Business Park, Crosses Green, Cork, Republic of Ireland
tel (021) 902980 *fax* (021) 315329
e-mail corkunip@www.ucc.ie
Publisher Sara Wilbourne
Irish literature, history, cultural studies, medieval studies, English literature, poetry and translations. Founded 1925.

Cornwall Books – see Golden Cockerel Press

Coronet – see Hodder Headline plc

Council for British Archaeology
Bowes Morrell House, 111 Walmgate, York YO1 2UA
tel (01904) 671417 *fax* (01904) 671384
e-mail archaeology@compuserve.com
web site http://britac3.britac.ac.uk/cba
Director Richard Morris, *Managing Editor* Christine Pietrowski
British archaeology – academic; practical handbooks; no general books. Founded 1944.

Countryside Books
2 Highfield Avenue, Newbury, Berks. RG14 5DS
tel (01635) 43816 *fax* (01635) 551004
Partners Nicholas Battle, Suzanne Battle
Books of local or regional interest, usually on a county basis, walking, outdoor activity, local history; genealogy. Founded 1976.

Cressrelles Publishing Co. Ltd
10 Station Road Industrial Estate, Colwall, Malvern, Worcs. WR13 6RN
tel (01684) 540154 *fax* (01684) 540154
Directors Leslie Smith, Simon Smith
General publishing. Founded 1973.
Actinic Press (imprint)
Chiropody.
Kenyon-Deane (imprint)
Plays and drama textbooks, especially for amateur dramatic societies. Specialists in plays for women.

Crime & Passion – see Virgin Publishing Ltd

The Crowood Press
The Stable Block, Ramsbury, Marlborough, Wilts. SN8 2HR
tel (01672) 520320 *fax* (01672) 520280
Directors John Dennis (chairman), Ken Hathaway (managing)
Sport, motoring, climbing and walking, fishing, country sports, farming, natural history, gardening, DIY, crafts, dogs, equestrian, games. Founded 1982.
Helmsman (imprint)
Nautical.

Current Science Group
34-42 Cleveland Street, London W1P 6LB
tel 0171-323 0323 *fax* 0171-580 1938
Chairman Vitek Tracz, *Chief Executive* Richard Charkin, *Group Managing Director* Anne Greenwood
Biological sciences, medicine, chemistry, pharmaceutical science, general science, law, Internet communities, electronic publishing.

James Currey Ltd
73 Botley Road, Oxford OX2 0BS
tel (01865) 244111 *fax* (01865) 246454
Directors James Currey (editorial), Clare Currey,
Keith Sambrook, Douglas H. Johnson

Academic studies of Africa, Caribbean, Third World: history, archaeology, economics, agriculture, politics, literary criticism, sociology. Founded 1985.

Curzon Press Ltd
15 The Quadrant, Richmond, Surrey TW9 1BP
tel 0181-948 4660 *fax* 0181-332 6735
e-mail publish@curzonpress.demon.co.uk
web site http://nias.ku.dk/curzonpress.html
Managing Director/Publisher Malcolm Campbell

Academic/scholarly books on humanities and social sciences in the context of Asia. Imprints: Japan Library, Caucasus World. Founded 1970.

Cygnus Arts – see Golden Cockerel Press

Dalesman Publishing Co. Ltd
Stable Courtyard, Broughton Hall, Skipton,
North Yorkshire BD23 3AE
tel (01756) 701381 *fax* (01756) 701326
Chairman T.J. Benn, *Managing Director* C.G.
Benn, *General Manager* R. Flanagan

Countryside books and magazines covering the North of England. Founded 1939.

Terence Dalton Ltd
Water Street, Lavenham, Sudbury,
Suffolk CO10 9RN
tel (01787) 247572 *fax* (01787) 248267
Directors T.A.J. Dalton, E.H. Whitehair (managing)

Maritime and aeronautical history, East Anglian interest and history. Founded 1966.

The C.W. Daniel Company Ltd
1 Church Path, Saffron Walden, Essex CB10 1JP
tel (01799) 521909 *fax* (01799) 513462
Directors Ian Miller, Jane Miller

Natural healing, Bach Flower Remedies, homoeopathy, aromatherapy, mysticism. Founded 1902.

Health Science Press (imprint)
Directors Ian Miller, Jane Miller

Homeopathy.

Neville Spearman Publishers (imprint)
Editorial Director Sebastian Hobnut

Mysticism, metaphysical.

Dartmouth Publishing Co. Ltd –
subsidiary of Ashgate Publishing Ltd

Darton, Longman & Todd Ltd*
1 Spencer Court, 140-142 Wandsworth High
Street, London SW18 4JJ
tel 0181-875 0155 *fax* 0181-875 0133
Editorial Director Morag Reeve

Religious books and bibles, including the following themes: bible study, spirituality, prayer and meditation, anthologies, daily readings, healing, counselling and pastoral care, bereavement, personal growth, mission, political, environmental and social issues, biography/autobiography, theological and historical studies. Founded 1959.

Darwen Finlayson Ltd – see Phillimore & Co. Ltd

David & Charles plc
Brunel House, Newton Abbot,
Devon TQ12 4PU
tel (01626) 61121 *fax* (01626) 334998
Directors Neil A. Page (managing), Piers Spence
(publishing), John Allgrove (sales and marketing)

High quality illustrated non-fiction specialising in crafts, hobbies, art techniques, cookery, gardening, natural history, equestrian, DIY. Founded 1960.

Christopher Davies Publishers Ltd
PO Box 403, Swansea SA1 4YF
tel (01792) 648825 *fax* (01792) 648825
Directors Christopher Talfan Davies (editorial),
K.E.T. Colayera, D.M. Davies

History, leisure books, sport and general of Welsh interest, Welsh dictionaries, *Triskele Books*. Founded 1949.

Dedalus Ltd
24 St Judith's Lane, Sawtry,
Cambs. PE17 5XE
tel/fax (01487) 832382
e-mail dedaluslimited@compuserve.com
Chairman Juri Gabriel, *Directors* Eric Lane
(managing), Robert Irwin (editorial), Lindsay
Thomas (marketing), Mike Mitchell
(translations)

Original fiction in English and in translation; Empire of the Senses, Dedalus European Classics, Surrealism and Literary Fantasy Anthologies. Founded 1983.

Delta – see Hodder Headline plc

J.M. Dent – now incorporated into The Orion Publishing Group Ltd

André Deutsch Ltd*

106 Great Russell Street, London WC1B 3LJ
tel 0171-580 2746 *fax* 0171-631-3253
Managing Director Tim Forrester, *Editorial Manager* Louise Dixon

A subsidiary of VCI Plc. Founded 1950.

Chameleon (imprint)
Film, TV tie-ins, music, comedy, sport.

André Deutsch (imprint)
Hardback fiction, biography, politics, current affairs, photography and music.

André Deutsch Classics (imprint)
Children's hardback classic books.

Madcap (imprint)
Innovative, fun and accessible children's titles.

Manchester United Books (imprint)
Publishing interests of Manchester United Football Club.

André Deutsch Children's Books – see Scholastic Children's Books*

Dial – see Reed Information Services

diehard

3 Spittal Street, Edinburgh EH3 9DY
tel (0131) 229 7252
Directors Ian William King (managing), Sally Evans King (marketing)

Contemporary drama; literature and historic reprints. Founded 1993.

Discovery Walking Guides Ltd

10 Tennyson Close, Dallington, Northampton NN5 7HJ
tel/fax (01604) 752576
Chairman Rosamund C. Brawn

'Warm island' walking guides and plant and flower guides to European holiday destinations. Founded 1994.

Eric Dobby Publishing Ltd

12 Warnford Road, Orpington, Kent BR6 6LW
tel/fax (01622) 718962 *fax* (01622) 717089
Managing Director E.R. Dobby

Biography, true crime, antiques (especially wristwatches), sport, dictionaries. Founded 1992.

The Do-Not Press

PO Box 4215, London SE23 2QD
tel 0181-291 7733 *fax* 0181-244 6815
e-mail j-j-jim@private.nethead.co.uk
web site http://www.thedonotpress.co.uk
Publisher Jim Driver

'Fiercely independent publishing'. Contemporary fiction, humour, music, non-fiction. Write in the first instance with outline, synopsis or sample chapter. Nothing unusual is ruled out. Founded 1995.

Bloodlines (imprint)
Crime fiction.

John Donald Publishers Ltd

138 St Stephen Street, Edinburgh EH3 5AA
tel 0131-225 1146 *fax* 0131-220 0567
Directors Gordon Angus, D.L. Morrison, J. Elder

British history, archaeology, ethnology, local history, vernacular architecture, general non-fiction. Founded 1973.

Dorling Kindersley Ltd

9 Henrietta Street, London WC2E 8PS
tel 0171-836 5411 *fax* 0171-836 7570
web site www.dk.com
Chairman Peter Kindersley, *Deputy Chairman and Publisher* Christopher Davis, *Group Directors* Rod Hare (managing), Peter Gill (finance), Anita Fulton (legal), *Subsidiary Directors* Stuart Jackman (group design), Martyn Longly (group production), David Holmes (managing, UK publishing), Daphne Razazan, David Lamb, Jackie Douglas (adult editorial), Anne-Marie Bulat, Linda Cole, Peter Luff (adult art), Ruth Sandys (managing, children's), Linda Davis, Ingrid Selberg (children's fiction), Roger Priddy, Miranda Kennedy (children's art), Sue Unstead, Sophie Mitchell (children's editorial), Katharine Thompson (managing, Vision), Alan Buckingham, Jonathan Reed (managing, Multimedia), Peter Cartwright (managing, DKFL-Int.), Mike Ward (managing, DKFL-UK)

High quality illustrated books on non-fiction subjects, including health, atlases, travel, cookery, gardening, crafts and reference; also children's non-fiction, picture books and fiction. Specialists in international co-editions, CD-Rom and television/video creation. Founded 1974.

Doubleday (UK) – see Transworld Publishers Ltd*

Doubleday Children's Books – see Transworld Publishers Ltd*

Dragon's World Ltd – acquired by Collins & Brown

Dryden Press – see Harcourt Brace & Co. Ltd*

Dublar Scripts

204 Mercer Way, Romsey, Hants SO51 7QJ
tel/fax (01794) 501377
Managing Director Robert Heather

Pantomine scripts, one-act and full-length plays. Founded 1994.

Gerald Duckworth & Co. Ltd
48 Hoxton Square, London N1 6PB
tel 0171-729 5986 *fax* 0171-729 0015
Directors Stephen Hill (chairman), Robin Baird-Smith (publisher and managing), Deborah Blake (editorial), John Betts (academic)
General trade publishers with a strong academic division. Imprints: Bristol Classical Press and Chatham Publishing; naval and maritime history. Founded 1898.

Martin Dunitz Ltd
The Livery House, 7-9 Pratt Street, London NW1 0AE
tel 0171-482 2202 *fax* 0171-267 0159
e-mail info@dunitz.co.uk
web site http://www.dunitz.co.uk
Directors Martin Dunitz, Ruth Dunitz, John Slaytor, Rosemary Allen
Books, journals and slide atlases in: cardiology, dentistry, dermatology, gastroenterology, haematology, metabolic bone disease, neurology, oncology, ophthalmology, orthopaedics, otorhinolaryngology, pathology, plastic surgery, psychiatry, radiology, respiratory medicine, sports medicine, urology. Founded 1978.

Earthscan Publications Ltd – see Kogan Page Ltd*

East-West Publications (UK) Ltd
8 Caledonia Street, London N1 9DZ
tel 0171-837 5061 *fax* 0171-278 4429
Chairman L.W. Carp, *Editor* B. Thompson
General non-fiction, travel, Eastern studies, sufism. No unsolicited MSS; please write first. Founded 1977.
Gallery Children's Books (imprint)
Quality children's books.

Ebury Press – see Random House UK Ltd*

Edinburgh University Press*
22 George Square, Edinburgh EH8 9LF
tel 0131-650 4218 *fax* 0131-662 0053
Chairman David Martin, *Editorial Director* Ms Jackie Jones
Academic and general publishers. Archaeology, botany, cultural studies, Islamic studies, history, linguistics, literature (criticism), philosophy, politics, Scottish studies, theology, women's studies.

Keele University Press Ltd (imprint)
American studies, politics, literature, history.
Polygon (imprint)
tel 0131-650 4689
New international fiction, including translations, oral history, general, Scottish, social and political (*Determinations* series).

The Educational Company of Ireland
PO Box 43A, Ballymount Road, Walkinstown, Dublin 12, Republic of Ireland
tel (01) 4500611 *fax* (01) 4500993
Executive Directors F.J. Maguire (chief executive), O. Mulcahy, R. McLoughlin
Trading unit of Smurfit Services Ltd. Educational MSS on all subjects in English or Gaelic.

Educational Explorers
11 Crown Street, Reading, Berks. RG1 2TQ
tel (01734) 873101 *fax* (01734) 873103
Directors M.J. Hollyfield, D.M. Gattegno
Educational, mathematics: *Numbers in colour with Cuisenaire Rods*, languages: *The Silent Way*, literacy, reading: *Words in Colour*; educational films. Founded 1962.

Eel Pie – see Plexus Publishing Ltd

Element Books
The Old School House, The Courtyard, Bell Street, Shaftesbury, Dorset SP7 8BP
tel (01747) 851448 *fax* (01747) 855721
Directors Michael Mann (chairman and publisher), David Alexander (chief executive), Julia McCutchen (editorial and managing), Roger Lane (production), Barry Cunningham (children's books, managing), Elinor Bagenal (children's books, editorial)
Complementary health, personal development, self-help, psychology, philosophy, religion, colour illustrated books. Children's non-fiction, fiction, picture books and board books. Founded 1978.

Edward Elgar Publishing Ltd
8 Lansdown Place, Cheltenham, Glos. GL50 2HU
tel (01242) 226934 *fax* (01242) 262111
e-mail info @e-elgar.co.uk
web site http://www.e-elgar.co.uk
Managing Director Edward Elgar
Economics and other social sciences. Founded 1986.

Elliot Right Way Books

Kingswood Buildings, Brighton Road,
Lower Kingswood, Tadworth,
Surrey KT20 6TD
tel (01737) 832202 *fax* (01737) 830311
Managing Directors Clive Elliot, Malcolm Elliot

Independent publishers of practical non-fiction 'how to' paperbacks. The low-price *Right Way* series includes games, pastimes, horses, pets, motoring, sport, health, business, public speaking and jokes, financial and legal, cookery and etiquette. Similar subjects are covered in the *Clarion* series of large-format paperbacks, sold in supermarkets and bargain bookshops. Welcomes new ideas. Founded 1946.

Aidan Ellis Publishing

Whinfield, Herbert Road, Salcombe,
Devon TQ8 8HN
tel (01548) 842755 *fax* (01548) 844356
e-mail aidan@aepub.demon.co.uk
web site http://www.demon.co.uk/aepub
Publisher Aidan Ellis

Non-fiction: gardening, maritime, art, general. Founded 1971.

ELM Publications

Seaton House, Kings Ripton, Huntingdon,
Cambs. PE17 2NJ
tel (01487) 773238 *fax* (01487) 773359
Managing Director Sheila Ritchie

Educational books and resources; books and training aids (tutor's packs and software) for business and management; software simulations; library and information studies. Telephone in the first instance, rather than send MSS. Please note: we publish mainly to curricula and course syllabi. Founded 1977.

Elm Tree Books – see Penguin Books Ltd*

Elsevier Science Ltd

The Boulevard, Langford Lane, Kidlington,
Oxford OX5 1GB
tel (01865) 843000 *fax* (01865) 843010
Managing Director C. Blake, *Editorial Director (Primary and Reference)* B. Barret, *Publishing Director (Magazines and Newsletters)* D. Bousfield

Journal, magazine and book publishers in science, technology and medicine.
Imprints: Pergamon, Elsevier Applied Science, Elsevier Trends Journals, Butterworth Heinemann Journals.

Encyclopaedia Britannica International Ltd

Chancery House, St Nicholas Way, Sutton,
Surrey SM1 1JB
tel 0181-770 7766 *fax* 0181-642 9090
Managing Director Richard D. Anderson

Enitharmon Press

36 St George's Avenue, London N7 0HD
tel 0171-607 7194 *fax* 0171-607 8694
Director Stephen Stuart-Smith

Poetry, literary criticism, translations, artists' books. No unsolicited MSS. Founded 1968.

Epworth Press

c/o Methodist Publishing House, 20 Ivatt Way,
Peterborough PE3 7PG
tel (01733) 332202 *fax* (01733) 331201
Editorial Committee Rev. Gerald Burt (hon. secretary), Dr Valerie Edden, Dr E. Dorothy Graham, Rev. Dr Ivor H. Jones, Rev. Dr John A. Newton (chairman), Rev. Dr Cyril S. Rodd, Rev. Michael J. Townsend

Religion, theology, church history.

Eros Plus – see Titan Books Ltd

Eurobook Ltd – see Peter Lowe (Eurobook Ltd)

Euromonitor plc

60-61 Britton Street, London EC1M 5NA
tel 0171-251 8024 *fax* 0171-608 3149
e-mail info@euromonitor.com
web site http://www.euromonitor.com
Directors T.J. Fenwick (managing), R.N. Senior (chairman)

Business and commercial reference, marketing information, European and International Surveys, directories. Founded 1972.

Europa Publications Ltd

18 Bedford Square, London WC1B 3JN
tel 0171-580 8236 *fax* 0171-636 1664
Directors C.H. Martin (chairman), P.A. McGinley (managing), J.P. Desmond, R.M. Hughes, P.G.C. Jackson, M.R. Milton

Directories, international relations, reference, yearbooks.

Evangelical Press of Wales – see Bryntirion Press

Evans Brothers Ltd*

2A Portman Mansions, Chiltern Street,
London W1M 1LE
tel 0171-935 7160 *fax* 0171-487 5034
Directors S.T. Pawley (managing), Brian D. Jones (international publishing), A.O. Ojora (Nigeria), A.E. Solly, J.D. Solly, *Editorial Manager* Su Swallow

Educational books, particularly pre-school, school library and teachers' books for the UK, including the Rainbows series of graded information books for 5-8-year-olds; primary and secondary for Africa, the Caribbean and Hong Kong. Founded 1908.

Everyman – see The Orion Publishing Group Ltd

Everyman's Library
(now merged with Cadogan Books plc)
79 Berwick Street, London W1V 3PF
tel 0171-287 0035 *fax* 0171-287 0038
Publisher David Campbell, *Finance Director* Mark Bicknell
Clothbound reprints of the classics; *Everyman's Children's Classics*; *Everyman's Travel Guides*; *Pocket Poets*; *Everyman-EMI Music Companions.*

Exley Publications Ltd
16 Chalk Hill, Watford, Herts. WD1 4BN
tel (01923) 250505 *fax* (01923) 818733/800440
Directors Dalton Exley, Helen Exley (editorial), Lincoln Exley, Richard Exley
Popular colour gift books for an international market. 60 new titles a year. No unsolicited MSS. Creative gift book series ideas needed. Founded 1976.

Faber & Faber Ltd*
3 Queen Square, London WC1N 3AU
tel 0171-465 0045 *fax* 0171-465 0034
Chairman and Managing Director Matthew Evans, *Directors* John Bodley, Dennis Crutcher, Patrick Curran, Giles de la Mare, Valerie Eliot, T.E. Faber, Tom Kelleher, Joanna Mackle, Peter Simpson (company secretary)
High quality general fiction and non-fiction; all forms of creative writing, including plays. Write to Sales Department for current lists. For information on submission procedure ring 0171-465 0189. For practical and security reasons submissions by fax or on disk cannot be accepted, except by special arrangement. Please allow 6-8 weeks for a response. Freelance readers and proofreaders without in-house experience need not apply.

Fabian Society
11 Dartmouth Street, London SW1H 9BN
tel 0171-222 8877 *fax* 0171-976 7153
e-mail fabian-society@geo2.poptel.org.uk
Research and Publications Officer Ian Corfield
Current affairs, economics, educational,

environment, political economy, social policy. Also controls NCLC Publishing Society Ltd. Founded 1884.

Facts on File
c/o Roundhouse Publishing Group, PO Box 140, Oxford OX2 7FF
tel (01865) 512682 *fax* (01865) 559594
e-mail 100637.3571@compuserve.com
Contact Alan Goodworth
Non-fiction reference and information books in a broad range of disciplines.

J.B. Fairfax Press Ltd – see Merehurst Ltd/J.B. Fairfax Press Ltd

C.J. Fallon
Lucan Road, Palmerstown, Dublin 20, Republic of Ireland
tel (01) 6265777 *fax* (01) 6268225
Directors H.J. McNicholas (managing), P. Tolan (financial), N. White (editorial)
Educational text books. Founded 1927.

Farming Press
2 Wharfedale Road, Ipswich, Suffolk IP1 4LG
tel (01473) 241122 *fax* (01473) 240501
e-mail farmingpress@dotfarming.com
web site http://www.dotfarming.com
Manager Roger Smith
Agriculture, humour, veterinary; videos; audio. Founded 1951.

Fernhurst Books
Duke's Path, High Street, Arundel, West Sussex BN18 9AJ
tel (01903) 882277 *fax* (01903) 882715
Publisher Tim Davison
Sailing, watersports. Founded 1979.

First and Best in Education Ltd*
(incorporating Hamilton House Publishing)
32 Nene Valley Business Park, Oundle, Peterborough PE8 4HJ
tel (01832) 274716 *fax* (01832) 275281
e-mail main.schools@pop3.hiway.co.uk
Directors Tony Attwood, Philippa Attwood
Contacts Clare Dowd, Kirsty Meadows (editors)
Education-related books. Currently actively recruiting new writers for schools; ideas welcome. Sae must accompany submissions. Founded 1992.

Fishing News Books Ltd
Osney Mead, Oxford OX2 0EL
tel (01865) 206206 *fax* (01865) 206096
Manager Philip Saugman
Commercial fisheries, aquaculture and allied subjects. Founded 1953.

Fitzroy Dearborn Publishers
11 Rathbone Place, London W1P 1DE
tel 0171-636 6627 *fax* 0171-636 6982
e-mail Fitzroy Dearborn
100420.3277@compuserve.com
Managing Director Daniel Kirkpatrick, *Senior Commissioning Editor* Lesley Henderson, *Publishers* Roda Morrison, Kate Berney
Reference books: history, design, art, literature, gender, business, science. Founded 1994.

Flamingo – see HarperCollins Publishers*

Flicks Books
29 Bradford Road, Trowbridge, Wilts. BA14 9AN
tel (01225) 767728 *fax* (01225) 760418
Partners Matthew Stevens (publisher), Aletta Stevens
Cinema, TV, related media. Founded 1986.

Flint River – see Philip Wilson Publishers Ltd

Floris Books*
15 Harrison Gardens, Edinburgh EH11 1SH
tel 0131-337 2372 *fax* 0131-346 7516
Editor Christopher Moore
Religion, science, Celtic studies, craft; children's books: picture and board books, fiction, activity books. Founded 1978.

Focal Press – see Reed Educational and Professional Publishing Ltd

Fodor Guides – see Random House UK Ltd*

Folens Ltd
Albert House, Apex Business Centre, Boscombe Road, Dunstable LU5 4RL
tel (01582) 472788 *fax* (01582) 472575
e-mail folens@folens.com
Managing Director Malcolm Watson
Primary and secondary educational books, learn at home books. Founded 1987.

Folens Publishing Company
Unit 8, Broomhill Business Park, Broomhill Road, Tallaght, Dublin 24, Republic of Ireland
tel (01) 4515311 *fax* (01) 4515306
Chairman Dirk Folens, Directors John O'Connor (managing), Anna O'Donovan (secondary), Deirdre Whelan (primary)
Educational (primary, secondary, comprehensive, technical, in English and Irish), educational children's magazines.

The Blackwater Press[†] (imprint)
General non-fiction, Irish interest.

Fontana – now HarperCollins Paperbacks*

Fontana Press – see HarperCollins Publishers*

Forest Books
20 Forest View, Chingford, London E4 7AY
tel 0181-529 8470 *fax* 0181-524 7890
Managing Director Brenda Walker
Only international literature in English translation; poetry, plays, novels and short stories, especially East European literature. No unsolicited material please. Founded 1984.

G.T. Foulis & Co. – see Haynes Publishing

W. Foulsham & Co. Ltd
The Publishing House, Bennetts Close, Slough, Berks. SL1 5AP
tel (01753) 526769 *fax* (01753) 535003
Managing Director B.A.R. Belasco, *Editorial Director* W. Hobson
General know-how, cookery, health and alternative therapies, hobbies and games, gardening, sport, travel guides, DIY, collectibles, popular new age. Founded 1819.

Quantum (imprint)
Editor Ian Fenton
Mind, body and spirit, popular philosophy and practical psychology.

Raphael's (imprint)
Editor Ian Fenton
Astrology.

The Foundational Book Company
(for The John W. Doorly Trust)
PO Box 659, London SW3 6SJ
tel 0171-584 1053
Trustee for Publications Mrs Peggy M. Brook
Spiritual Science.

Foundery Press – see Methodist Publishing House

Fount – see HarperCollins Publishers*

Four Courts Press[†]
55 Prussia Street, Dublin 7, Republic of Ireland
tel (01) 8388960 *fax* (01) 8388951
e-mail fcp@indigo.ie
Managing Director Michael Adams

Academic books in the humanities, especially history and Celtic and medieval studies. Founded 1969.

Fourmat Publishing – see Tolley Publishing Co. Ltd

Fourth Estate Ltd
6 Salem Road, London W2 4BU
tel 0171-727 8993 *fax* 0171-792 3176
Directors Victoria Barnsley (managing), Patric Duffy (financial), Christopher Potter (publishing), Joanna Prior (publicity and marketing), Stephen Page (sales and deputy managing)

Current affairs, literature, popular culture, fiction, humour, politics, science, popular reference, TV tie-ins. No unsolicited MSS. Founded 1984.

Fourth Estate Paperbacks (imprint)
Publishes paperback editions of Fourth Estate hardback titles.

Guardian Books (imprint)
Books stemming from *The Guardian* newspaper.

Framework Press Educational Publishers Ltd*
Albert House, Apex Business Centre, Boscombe Road, Dunstable LU5 4RL
tel (01582) 478110 *fax* (01582) 475524
Commissioning Editor Colin Forbes

School and college management, staff development, vocational, English, PSE. Founded 1983.

Franklin Watts – see the Watts Publishing Group*

Free Association Books
57 Warren Street, London W1P 5PA
tel 0171-388 3182 *fax* 0171-388 3187
e-mail fab@melmoth.demon.co.uk
Managing Director T.E. Brown, *Publisher* Gill Davies

Psychoanalysis, psychotherapy, counselling, cultural studies, social sciences, social welfare. Founded 1984.

W.H. Freeman
Macmillan Press Ltd, Houndmills, Basingstoke, Hants RG21 6XS
tel (01256) 332807 *fax* (01256) 330688
Sales Director E. Warner

Science, technical, medicine, economics, psychology, archaeology.

Freeway – see Transworld Publishers Ltd*

Samuel French Ltd*
52 Fitzroy Street, London W1P 6JR
tel 0171-387 9373 *fax* 0171-387 2161
Directors Charles Van Nostrand (chairman), John Bedding (managing), Amanda Smith, Paul Taylor

Publishers of plays and agents for the collection of royalties. Founded 1830.

FT Law & Tax – see Pearson Professional Ltd*

David Fulton Publishers Ltd*
Ormond House, 26-27 Boswell Street, London WC1N 3JD
tel 0171-405 5606 *fax* 0171-831 4840
e-mail fultonbooks@mail.easynet.co.uk
Managing Director David Fulton, *Editorial Director* John Owens, *Marketing Director* Pamela Fulton

Initial and continuing teacher education (special needs, primary and secondary), educational management and psychology, geography (for undergraduates). Unsolicited MSS not returned. Founded 1987.

Gaia Books Ltd
66 Charlotte Street, London W1P 1LR
tel 0171-323 4010 *fax* 0171-323 0435 and
20 High Street, Stroud, Glos. GL5 1AS
tel (01453) 752985 *fax* (01453) 752987
Directors Joss Pearson (managing), David Pearson, Lars Kjeldsen, Tor Svensson

Illustrated reference books on ecology, natural living, health, mind. Submissions (outline and sample chapter) to managing director.

Gairm Publications
(incorporating Alex MacLaren & Sons)
29 Waterloo Street, Glasgow G2 6BZ
tel/fax 0141-221 1971
Editorial Director Derick Thomson

(Gaelic and Gaelic-related only) dictionaries, language books, novels, poetry, music, children's books, quarterly magazine. Founded 1875.

Gallery Children's Books – see East-West Publications (UK) Ltd

The Gallery Press
Loughcrew, Oldcastle, Co. Meath, Republic of Ireland
tel/fax (049) 41779
e-mail gallery@indigo.ie
Editor/Publisher Peter Fallon

Poetry, drama, occasionally fiction, by Irish authors. Also, hand-printed limited

editions poetry. Allied company: Deerfield Publications Inc., Massachusetts. Founded 1970.

Garnet Publishing Ltd
8 Southern Court, South Street, Reading RG1 4QS
tel (01189) 597847 *fax* (01189) 597356
Managing Director Kenneth Banerji

Art, architecture, photography, fiction religious studies and general, mainly on Middle and Far East, and Islam. Founded 1991.

Ithaca Press (imprint)
Post-graduate academic works, especially on the Middle East.

Gateway Books
The Hollies, Wellow, Nr Bath BA2 8QJ
tel (01225) 835127 *fax* (01225) 840012
e-mail info@gatewaybooks.com
web site http://www.gatewaybooks.com
Publisher Alick Bartholomew

Popular psychology, spirituality, health and healing, earth mysteries, ecology, self help, metaphysics and alternative science. Please do not send unsolicited MSS – outline and sample welcome. Founded 1982.

The Gay Men's Press – see GMP Publishers Ltd

Geddes & Grosset Ltd*
David Dale House, New Lanark ML11 9DJ
tel (01555) 665000 *fax* (01555) 665694
Directors Ron Grosset, Mike Miller, David Geddes

Popular reference including cookery; children's picture books, non-fiction and activity books. Founded 1988.

Gee & Son (Denbigh) Ltd
Chapel Street, Denbigh, Denbighshire LL16 3SW
tel (01745) 812020 *fax* (01745) 812825
Directors E. Evans, E.M. Evans

Oldest Welsh publishers. Books of interest to Wales, in Welsh and English. Founded 1808.

Geographia – now Bartholomew – see HarperCollins Publishers*

GeoInformation International – see Pearson Professional Ltd*

Stanley Gibbons Publications*
Parkside, Christchurch Road, Ringwood, Hants BH24 3SH
tel (01425) 472363 *fax* (01425) 470247
Chairman P.I. Fraser

Philatelic handbooks, stamp catalogues and albums, *Gibbons Stamp Monthly*. Founded 1856.

Robert Gibson & Sons Glasgow Ltd
17 Fitzroy Place, Glasgow G3 7SF
tel 0141-248 5674 *fax* 0141-221 8219
web site robert.gibsonsons@btinternet.com
Directors R.G.C. Gibson, M. Pinkerton, H.C. Crawford, N.J. Crawford (editorial)

Bibliography and library science; educational and textbooks. Founded 1885.

Gill & Macmillan Ltd†
Goldenbridge, Inchicore, Dublin 8, Republic of Ireland
tel (01) 4531005 *fax* (01) 4541688

Biography or memoirs, educational (secondary, university), history, sociology, theology and religion, popular psychology, literature, cookery, current affairs, guidebooks, professional (law, accountancy, tax). Founded 1968.

Ginn & Co. – see Reed Educational and Professional Publishing Ltd

Mary Glasgow Publications – now incorporated into Stanley Thornes (Publishers) Ltd

GMP Publishers Ltd
PO Box 247, Swaffham, Norfolk PE37 8PA
tel (01366) 328101 *fax* (01366) 328102
e-mail gmppubs.co.uk
Publishers Aubrey Walter, David Fernbach
Founded 1979.

The Gay Men's Press (imprint)
Modern, popular, historical/literary fiction, including translations from European languages, biography and memoir, history, drama, health, social and political questions, literary criticism. *Gay Modern Classics* – reprints of gay fiction/non-fiction from the past 100 years.

Éditions Aubrey Walter (imprint)
Male photography both art and glamour, fine art editions of gay artists.

Heretic Books (imprint)
Ecology, animal liberation, green politics, Third World.

Godsfield Press Ltd
Laurel House, Station Approach, New Alresford, Hants SO24 9AT
tel (01962) 735633 *fax* (01962) 735320
Directors John Hunt, Debbie Thorpe

Adult and children's books for international co-editions. Specialises in books on spirituality, across traditional faiths and contemporary developments in spiritual growth. Associate company of **Hunt & Thorpe Ltd**. Founded 1994.

Golden Age Editions – see **New Cavendish Books**

Golden Cockerel Press
16 Barter Street, London WC1A 2AH
tel 0171-405 7979 *fax* 0171-404 3598
e-mail lindesay@ibm.net
Contact Tamar Lindesay
Academic.

Associated University Presses (imprint)
Literary criticism, art, music, history, film, theology, philosophy, Jewish studies, politics, sociology.

Cornwall Books (imprint)
Antiques, history, film.

Cygnus Arts (imprint)
The arts.

The Goldsmith Press
Newbridge, Co. Kildare, Republic of Ireland
tel (045) 433613 *fax* (045) 434648
Directors D. Egan, V. Abbott, *Secretary* Bernadette Smyth
Literature, art, Irish interest, poetry. Founded 1972.

Victor Gollancz Ltd – see **Cassell plc**

Gomer Press
Llandysul, Dyfed SA44 4BQ
tel (01559) 362371 *fax* (01559) 363758
Directors Jonathan Lewis, John H. Lewis, Dyfed Elis-Gruffydd, *Editors* Mairwen Prys Jones, Gordon Jones
Literature and non-fiction with a Welsh background or relevance: biography, history, aspects of Welsh culture, children's books. No unsolicited MSS; preliminary letter essential. Founded 1892.

Government Supplies Agency
Publications Division, 4-5 Harcourt Road, Dublin 2, Republic of Ireland
tel (01) 6613111 *fax* (01) 4752760
Parliamentary publications.

Gower Publishing Ltd – subsidiary of **Ashgate Publishing Ltd**

Grafton – now **HarperCollins Paperbacks***

Graham & Whiteside Ltd
Tuition House, 5-6 Francis Grove, London SW19 4DT
tel 0181-947 1011 *fax* 0181-947 1163
e-mail sales@major-co-data.com
Directors A.M.W. Graham, H.C.H. Whiteside, R.M. Whiteside, P.L. Murphy
Directories for international business and professional markets. Founded 1995.

Granta Publications
2-3 Hanover Yard, Noel Road, London N1 8BE
tel 0171-704 9776 *fax* 0171-704 0474
Book Publisher Frances Coady, *Publishing Director* Neil Belton, *Magazine Editor* Ian Jack
Fiction, autobiography, political non-fiction. Founded 1982.

Green Books
Foxhole, Dartington, Totnes, Devon TQ9 6EB
tel/fax (01803) 863843
Managing Director John Elford
Environment (practical and philosophical). No fiction or children's books. No MSS; synopsis and covering letter please. Founded 1987.

Green Print – see **Merlin Press Ltd**

Greenhill Books/Lionel Leventhal Ltd
Park House, 1 Russell Gardens, London NW11 9NN
tel 0181-458 6314 *fax* 0181-905 5245
Managing Director Lionel Leventhal
Military history. Founded 1984.

Gresham Books Ltd
The Gresham Press, PO Box 61, Henley-on-Thames, Oxon RG9 3LQ
tel/fax (01189) 403789
Chief Executive Mrs M.V. Green
Hymn books, Prayer books, and Service books.

Grub Street
The Basement, 10 Chivalry Road, London SW11 1HT
tel 0171-924 3966/738 1008 *fax* 0171-738 1009
Principals John B. Davies, Anne Dolamore
Adult non-fiction: aviation history, cookery, health and reference. Founded 1989.

Guardian Books – see **Fourth Estate Ltd**

Guild of Master Craftsman Publications Ltd
Castle Place, 166 High Street, Lewes, East Sussex BN7 1XU
tel (01273) 477374/478449 *fax* (01273) 486300
Managing Director Alan Phillips

Practical, illustrated crafts, including needlecrafts, dolls' houses, woodworking and other leisure and hobby subjects. Founded 1979.

Guinness Publishing Ltd*

338 Euston Road, London NW1 3BD
tel 0181-367 4567 *fax* 0181-367 5912
Joint Publishing Directors Michael Feldman, Ian Castello-Cortes

The Guinness Book of Records, general reference, music and sports reference. Founded 1954.

Gwasg Bryntirion Press – see Bryntirion Press

Gwasg Gee – see Gee & Son (Denbigh) Ltd

Peter Halban Publishers Ltd

42 South Molton Street, London W1Y 1HB
tel 0171-491 1582 *fax* 0171-629 5381
Directors Martine Halban, Peter Halban

General non-fiction; history and biography; Jewish subjects and Middle East. No unsolicited MSS considered; preliminary letter essential. Founded 1986.

Robert Hale Ltd

Clerkenwell House, 45-47 Clerkenwell Green, London EC1R 0HT
tel 0171-251 2661 *fax* 0171-490 4958
Directors John Hale (managing and editorial), Robert Kynaston (financial), Martin Kendall (marketing), Betty Weston (rights)

Adult general non-fiction and fiction. Founded 1936.

Hamish Hamilton Ltd – see Penguin Books Ltd*

Hamish Hamilton Children's Books – see Penguin Books Ltd*

Hamilton House Publishing – see First and Best in Education Ltd*

Hamlyn – see Reed Books

Hamlyn Children's Non-fiction – see Reed Books

Harcourt Brace & Co. Ltd*

24-28 Oval Road, London NW1 7DX
tel 0171-267 4466 *fax* 0171-482 2293/485 4752
Managing Director Peter H. Lengemann

Scientific and medical.

Academic Press (division)
Managing Director Jan Velterop

Academic and reference.

Baillière Tindall Ltd (division)
Editorial Director Sean Duggan

Medical, veterinary, nursing, pharmaceutical books and journals.

Dryden Press (division)
Managing Director Peter H. Lengemann

Educational books (college, university), economics, business.

W.B. Saunders Co. Ltd (division)
Editorial Director Sean Duggan

Medical and scientific.

Patrick Hardy Books – see James Clarke & Co. Ltd*

Harlem River Press – see Writers & Readers Ltd*

Harlequin Mills & Boon Ltd*

Eton House, 18-24 Paradise Road, Richmond, Surrey TW9 1SR
tel 0181-948 0444 *fax* 0181-288 2899
Directors R. Guzner (managing), A. Meredith (production), D. Elliott (direct marketing), A.W. Boon, S. Cummings (finance), K. Stoecker (editorial), H. O'Neil (retail marketing and exports), J. Oldham (human resources)

Founded 1908.

Medical & Historical (series)
Senior Editor E. Johnson

Romance fiction.

Mills & Boon (imprint)
Senior Editors T. Shapcott, S. Hodgson

Contemporary romance fiction in paperback and hardback.

Mira Books (imprint)
Senior Editor L. Fildew

Women's fiction.

Silhouette (imprint)
Senior Editor L. Stonehouse

Popular romantic women's fiction.

HarperCollins Publishers*

77-85 Fulham Palace Road, London W6 8JB
tel 0181-741 7070 *fax* 0181-307 4440
Executive Chairman and Publisher Eddie Bell, *Divisional Managing Directors* Adrian Bourne (trade), Eileen Campbell (Thorsons/religious), Stephen Bray (cartographic), Robin Wood (reference/dictionaries), Kate Harris (education/children's), *Publishers* Stuart Proffitt (trade)

All fiction and trade non-fiction must be submitted through an agent. Unsolicited submissions should be made in the form of a typewritten synopsis. Founded 1819.

Access Press (imprint)

Travel guides.

Bartholomew (imprint)
Maps, atlases, electronic products.
Birnbaum (imprint)
Travel guides.
Collins (imprints)
Collins Crime, Collins Classics, Collins
Educational, Collins bibles, Collins
Liturgical Books, Collins Dictionaries,
Collins Cobuild, Collins Gems, Collins
New Naturalist Library, Collins Willow,
Collins Longman.
Collins (children's imprint)
Publishing Directors Gail Penston, Domenica de
Rosa
Includes Jets, Yellow Storybooks, Red
Storybooks, fiction for older children and
toddler books.
Collins Children's Audio (imprint)
Collins Children's Books (imprint)
Collins Picture Lions (imprint)
Children's picture paperbacks.
Collins Tracks (imprint)
Young adult books.
Flamingo (imprint)
Editorial Director Philip Gwyn Jones
Literary fiction in hardback and paperback.
Fontana Press (imprint)
Editorial Director Philip Gwyn Jones
Paperback intellectual non-fiction.
Fount (imprint)
Managing Director Eileen Campbell
Religious.
HarperCollins (imprints)
Audiobooks, hardbacks (fiction and non-
fiction), paperbacks (fiction and non-fic-
tion), religious.
HarperCollins Broadcasting Consultancy
Contact Cresta Norris
Exploits TV and film rights across the
company.
HarperCollins Electronic Products
Managing Director Kate Harris
CD-Rom, floppy disk and on-line.
Specialises in special interest, children's,
reference and interactive fiction.
HarperCollins World
Managing Director Robin Wood
General trade titles imported into the UK
market.
Lions (imprint)
Publishing Director Gail Penston
Children's books.

Marshall Pickering (imprint)
Managing Director Eileen Campbell
Theology, music, popular religion, illus-
trated children's, wide range of Christian
books.
Nicholson (imprint)
Managing Director Stephen Bray
London maps, atlases and guidebooks.
Waterways maps and guidebooks.
Pandora Press (imprint)
Managing Director Eileen Campbell
Feminist press publishing. General non-
fiction: biography, arts, media, health, cur-
rent affairs, reference and sexual politics.
Thorsons (imprint)
Managing Director Eileen Campbell
Complementary medicine, health and
nutrition, business and management,
self-help and positive thinking, popular
psychology, parenting and childcare,
astrology, tarot and divination, mytholo-
gy and psychic awareness.
Times Books (imprint)
Managing Director Stephen Bray
World atlases and maps, thematic atlases,
reference, guides and crosswords.
Tolkien (imprint)
Projects Director David Brawn, *Editorial Director*
Jane Johnson
Voyager (imprint)
Editorial Director Jane Johnson
Science fiction, fantasy fiction and media
tie-ins.

Harrap*
7 Hopetoun Crescent, Edinburgh EH7 4AY
tel 0131-557 4571 *fax* 0131-556 5313
Chairman John Clement, *Sales Director* Robert
Snuggs, *Publishing Manager* Patrick White
Bilingual dictionaries. Subsidiary of
Larousse plc.

Harvard University Press – see under
USA in Overseas book publishers, page
225

Harvester Wheatsheaf – see Prentice
Hall Europe/Academic***

The Harvill Press
84 Thornhill Road, London N1 1RD
tel 0171-609 1119 *fax* 0171-609 2019
e-mail harvill@harvill-press.com
Publisher and Chairman Christopher MacLehose,
Directors John Mitchinson (managing), Guido
Waldman (editorial), Rachael Kerr (marketing),
Rights Manager Katharina Bielenberg

English-language and world literature in translation (mainly literary fiction, but including non-fiction and some first-class narrative thrillers); monographs in the fields of ethnography, art, horticulture and natural history. Unsolicited MSS only accepted with sae. Founded 1946.

Hawk Books
Suite 309, Canalot Studios, 222 Kensal Road, London W10 5BN
tel 0181-969 8091 *fax* 0181-968 9012
Director Patrick Hawkey

Comics, nostalgia, juveniles, art. Founded 1986.

Haynes Publishing
Sparkford, Yeovil, Somerset BA22 7JJ
tel (01963) 440635 *fax* (01963) 440023
Directors J.H. Haynes (chairman), A.C. Haynes, I.P. Mauger, D.J. Reach (editorial), A.J. Sperring, K.C. Fullman (managing), C. Davies, D.J. Hermelin, C.G. Magnus

Car and motorcycle owners workshop manuals, car handbooks/servicing guides, do-it-yourself books, aircraft, trains, nautical.

G.T. Foulis & Co. (imprint)
Editor Darryl Reach

Motoring/motorcycling, marque and model history, practical maintenance and renovation, related biographies, aircraft, nautical, aviation.

Haynes (imprint)
Home DIY and leisure activities (e.g. cycling).

Oxford Illustrated Press (imprint)
Editor Darryl Reach

Well-illustrated non-fiction books, sport, leisure and travel guides, car books, art books, general.

Oxford Publishing Company (OPC Railbooks) (imprint)
Editor Peter Nicholson

Railway transport.

Patrick Stephens Ltd (imprint)
Editorial Director Darryl Reach

Aviation, biography, maritime, military and wargaming, model making, motorcycling, motoring and motor racing, railways and railway modelling.

Hazar Publishing Ltd
147 Chiswick High Road, London W4 2DT
tel 0181-742 8578 *fax* 0181-994 1407
Managing Director Greg Hill, *Editor* Marie Clayton

Children's picture and novelty books; adult non-fiction: architecture and design. Founded 1992.

Headland Business Information – see Bowker-Saur

Headland Publications
Editorial office Tyˆ Coch, Galltegfa, Llanfwrog, Ruthin, Clwyd LL15 2AR
and 38 York Avenue, West Kirby, Wirral, Merseyside L48 3JF
Director and Editor Gladys Mary Coles

Poetry, anthologies of poetry and prose. No unsolicited MSS. Founded 1970.

Headline Book Publishing Ltd – see Hodder Headline plc

Headway – see Hodder Headline plc

Health Science Press – see The C.W. Daniel Company Ltd

William Heinemann – see Random House UK Ltd*

Heinemann Educational – see Reed Educational and Professional Publishing Ltd

Heinemann English Language Teaching – see Reed Educational and Professional Publishing Ltd

Heinemann Young Books – see Reed Books

Helicon Publishing Ltd
42 Hythe Bridge Street, Oxford OX1 2EP
tel (01865) 204204 *fax* (01865) 204205
e-mail 7477.3250@compuserve.com
Directors David Attwooll (managing), Michael Upshall (publishing), Edward Knighton (finance), Anne-Lucie Norton (editorial, subject reference), Hilary McGlynn (associate editorial, general reference), Tony Ballsdon (production), Brigid Macleod (sales and marketing), Clare Painter (associate rights)

General trade reference, hardback and paperback: *Hutchinson Encyclopedias*, history, science, the arts and current affairs; electronic reference. Founded 1992.

Christopher Helm – see A & C Black (Publishers) Ltd*

Helmsman – see The Crowood Press

Henderson Publishing Ltd
Marsh House, Tide Mill Way, Woodbridge,
Suffolk IP12 1AN
tel (01394) 380622 *fax* (01394) 380618
Managing Director Barrie Henderson, *Managing Editor* Lucy Bater
Children's books: picture books, activity, novelty, non-fiction. Acquired by Dorling Kindersley Ltd. Founded 1990.

The Herbert Press – see A & C Black (Publishers) Ltd*

Heretic Books – see GMP Publishers Ltd

Hermes House – see Anness Publishing

Nick Hern Books Ltd
14 Larden Road, London W3 7ST
tel 0181-740 9539 *fax* 0181-746 2006
Publisher Nick Hern
Theatre, professionally produced plays. Initial letter required. Founded 1988.

Hilmarton Manor Press
Calne, Wilts. SN11 8SB
tel (01249) 760208 *fax* (01249) 760379
Editorial Director Charles Baile de Laperriere
Fine art, photography, antiques, visual arts. Founded 1964.

Hippo – see Scholastic Children's Books*

Hippopotamus Press
22 Whitewell Road, Frome, Somerset BA11 4EL
tel/fax (01373) 466653
Editors Roland John, Anna Martin
Poetry, essays, criticism. Publishes *Outposts Poetry Quarterly*. Poetry submissions from new writers welcome. Founded 1974.

HMSO Books – see The Stationery Office/National Publishing*

Hobsons Publishing plc
Bateman Street, Cambridge CB2 1LZ
tel (01223) 460366 *fax* (01223) 323154
Non-executive Director Charles Sinclair, *Chairman* Martin Morgan, *Directors* Chris Letcher, Frances Halliwell, Robert Baker
Database publisher of educational and careers information under licence to CRAC (Careers Research and Advisory Centre). Also publishes accommodation guides under Johansens brand. Founded 1974.

Hodder Headline plc
338 Euston Road, London NW1 3BH
tel 0171-873 6000 *fax* 0171-873 6024
Chairman Christopher Weston (non-executive), *Group Chief Executive* Tim Hely Hutchinson, *Deputy Chief Executive* Mark Opzoomer CA Canada, MBA, *Directors* Martin Neild (managing, Hodder & Stoughton General), Sue Fletcher (deputy managing, Hodder & Stoughton General), John Lloyd (non-executive), Mary Tapissier (managing, Children's; chairman, Religious), Amanda Ridout (managing, Headline), Malcolm Edwards (managing, Australia and New Zealand), Philip Walker (managing, Educational), Richard Stileman (managing, Edward Arnold), Mandy Warnford-Davis (non-executive), Richard Adam (finance)
Founded 1986.

Edward Arnold (division)
Managing Director Richard Stileman, *Humanities* Chris Wheeler, *Medical, Science and Engineering* Nicki Dennis
Academic and professional books and journals.

Brockhampton Press (division)
Managing Director John Maxwell, *Sales Director* Jack Cooper
Promotional books.

Headline Book Publishing Ltd (division)
Managing Director Amanda Ridout, *Non-fiction* Heather Holden-Brown, *Fiction* Jane Morpeth
Publishes under **Headline, Headline Feature, Headline Review**.
Publishers Bill Massey (Feature), Geraldine Cook (Review)
Commercial fiction (hardback and paperback); popular non-fiction including: biography, cinema, design and film, food and wine, countryside, TV tie-ins and sports yearbooks.

Headline Delta (imprint of Headline Book Publishing)
Associate Publisher Mike Bailey
General erotica.

Headline Liaison (imprint of Headline Book Publishing)
Associate Publisher Mike Bailey
Erotica for both sexes, to be read separately, or with a partner.

Hodder Children's Books (division)
Managing Director Mary Tapissier, *Editorial Director* Margaret Conroy
Publishes under **Hodder & Stoughton, Knight**. Picture books, fiction and non-fiction.

Hodder & Stoughton Educational (division)
Managing Director Philip Walters, *Humanities, Science and Mathematics* Elisabeth Tribe, *Languages, Business and Psychology* Tim Gregson-Williams

Publishes under **Hodder & Stoughton Educational**, **Teach Yourself**, **Headway**. Textbooks for the primary, secondary, tertiary and further education sectors and for self-improvement.

Hodder & Stoughton General (division)
Managing Director Martin Neild, *Deputy Managing Director* Sue Fletcher, *Non-fiction* Roland Philipps, *Horror* Nick Austin, *Sceptre* Carole Welch, *Fiction* Carolyn Mays, Carolyn Caughey, *Audio* Rupert Lancaster

Publishes under **Hodder & Stoughton**, **Coronet**, **New English Library**, **Sceptre**. Commercial and literary fiction; biography, autobiography, history, self-help, humour, travel and other general interest non-fiction; audio.

Hodder & Stoughton Religious (division)
Managing Director Charles Nettleton, *Editorial Directors* Emma Sealey (bibles and liturgical), Judith Longman (religious trade)

Publishes under **New International Version of the Bible**, **Hodder Christian** paperbacks. Bibles, commentaries, liturgical works (both printed and software), wide range of Christian paperbacks.

Hodder & Stoughton – see Hodder Headline plc

Hogarth Press – see Random House UK Ltd*

Hollis Directories Ltd
Harlequin House, 7 High Street, Teddington, Middlesex TW11 8EL
tel 0181-977 7711 *fax* 0181-977 1133
web site www.hollis-pr.co.uk
Managing Director Gary Zabel

Media, public relations and sponsorship directories, including *Willings Press Guide*

Honno Ltd
Pen Roc, Rhodfa'r Môr, Aberystwyth, Ceredigion SY23 2AZ
tel (01222) 515014 and (01970) 623150
Secretary Rosanne Reeves

Books written by women in Wales or with a Welsh connection. All subjects considered – fiction, non-fiction, poetry, autobiographies. Honno is a collective. Founded 1986.

Ellis Horwood – see Prentice Hall Europe/Academic*

How To Books Ltd
3 Newtec Place, Magdalen Road, Oxford OX4 1RE
Managing Director Giles Lewis, *Secretary* Derek Phillips

How To series of personal achievement paperbacks covering student life, careers, employment and expatriate topics, practical business skills, creative/ media skills, education, family reference and personal development. Founded 1991.

Hugo's Language Books Ltd
9 Henrietta Street, London WC2E 8PS
tel 0171-753 3587 *fax* 0171-753 7561
Editorial Director Robin Batchelor-Smith

Hugo's language books and courses. Acquired by Dorling Kindersley Ltd. Founded 1864.

Hunt & Thorpe
Laurel House, Station Approach, New Alresford, Hants SO24 9JH
tel (01962) 735633 *fax* (01962) 735320
Partners John Hunt, Debbie Thorpe

Children's and adult religious, full colour books for the international market. MSS welcome; send sae. Founded 1989.

C. Hurst & Co. (Publishers) Ltd*
38 King Street, London WC2E 8JZ
tel 0171-240 2666, (night) 0181-852 9021
fax 0171-240 2667
e-mail hurst@atlas.co.uk
Directors Christopher Hurst, Michael Dwyer

Scholarly 'area studies' covering contemporary history, politics, social studies and the religions of Asia and Africa. Founded 1967.

Hutchinson – see Random House UK Ltd*

Hutchinson Children's – see Random House UK Ltd*

ICSA Publishing
Campus 400, Maylands Avenue, Hemel Hempstead, Herts. HP2 7EZ
tel (01442) 881900 *fax* (01442) 252544
e-mail rachel_frost@prenhall.co.uk
Marketing Manager Rachel Frost

Professional business books for the private, public and voluntary sectors. Publish titles for The Institute of Chartered Secretaries and Administrators. Founded 1981.

Idol – see Virgin Publishing Ltd

Impact Books Ltd
Axe and Bottle Court, 70 Newcomen Street,
London SE1 1YT
tel 0171-403 3541 *fax* 0171-407 6437
Chairman Jean-Luc Barbanneau (publisher),
Directors David Skinner, David Collins, Roy
Greenslade
Travel writing, illustrated country books,
practical guides and reference. No unso-
licited MSS. Send synopsis and sample
first. Founded 1985.

In Print Publishing Ltd
Coleridge House, 4-5 Coleridge Gardens,
London NW6 3QH
tel 0171-372 2600 *fax* 0171-372 2253
e-mail jedmondip @aol.com
Directors Alastair Dingwall, John Edmondson
Special interest travel (including literary
guides), Japan, Southeast Asia, guides to
teaching English. Founded 1990.

Indigo – see Cassell plc

InfoSource International – see
Blackwell Publishers*

**Institute of Personnel and
Development**
IPD House, 35 Camp Road,
London SW19 4UX
tel 0181-971 9000 *fax* 0181-263 3333
e-mail publish@ipd.co.uk
Head of Publishing Judith Dennett
Personnel management, training and
development.

Institute of Physics Publishing*
Dirac House, Temple Back, Bristol BS1 6BE
tel (0117) 929 7481 *fax* (0117) 930 1186
e-mail margaret.ogorman@ioppublishing.co.uk
web site http://www.iop.org
Books and Reference Works Publisher Margaret
O'Gorman
Monographs, graduate texts, conference
proceedings and reference works in
physics and physics-related science and
technology; also popular science titles.

Institute of Public Administration†
Vergemount Hall, Clonskeagh, Dublin 6,
Republic of Ireland
tel (01) 2697011 *fax* (01) 2698644
e-mail tmcnamara@ipa.ie
Head of Publishing Tony McNamara
Government, economics, politics, law,
social policy and administrative history.
Founded 1957.

Inter-Varsity Press*
38 De Montfort Street, Leicester LE1 7GP
tel (0116) 255 1754 *fax* (0116) 254 2044
e-mail ivp@uccf.org.uk
Managing Editor Mrs S.J. Heald
Theology and religion.

Irish Academic Press Ltd†
44 Northumberland Road, Balesbridge, Dublin 4,
Republic of Ireland
tel (01) 6688244 *fax* (01) 6601610
Directors Stewart Cass, Frank Cass, Michael
Philip Zaidner
Publishes under the imprints **Irish
University Press** and **Irish Academic
Press**. Scholarly books especially in 19th
and 20th century history and literature.
Founded 1974.

Ithaca Press – see Garnet Publishing Ltd

Arthur James Ltd
70 Cross Oak Road, Berkhampsted,
Herts. HP4 3HZ
tel (01442) 877511 *fax* (01442) 873019
e-mail 101666.2033@compuserve.com
Editorial Director John Hunt, *Managing Director*
Ian Carlile
Religion, sociology, psychology, meditation. Founded 1935.

Jane's Information Group
163 Brighton Road, Coulsdon, Surrey CR5 2NH
tel 0181-700 3701 *fax* 0181-700 3704
web site http://www.janes.co.uk/janes.html
Managing Director Alfred Rolington
Military, aviation, naval, defence, non-
fiction, reference, fiction, police, geo-
political; CD-Rom games in association
with Electronic Arts.

Jarrold Publishing
Whitefriars, Norwich NR3 1TR
tel (01603) 763300 *fax* (01603) 662748
Managing Director Antony Jarrold, *Publishing
Director* Caroline Jarrold
UK travel guidebooks, pictorial books
and calendars. About 30 titles a year.
Unsolicited MSS, synopses and ideas
welcome but approach in writing before
submitting to Donald Greig, Managing
Editor. Division of Jarrold & Sons Ltd.
Founded 1770.

Jewish Chronicle Publications
c/o Vallentine Mitchell, Newbury House,
900 Eastern Avenue, Ilford, Essex IG2 7HH
tel 0181-599 8866 *fax* 0171-405 9040
e-mail vm@frankcass.com
web site http://www.frankcass.com/um

Theology and religion, reference; *Jewish Year Book, Jewish Travel Guide*.

Johnson Publications Ltd
130 Wigmore Street, London W1H 0AT
tel 0171-486 6757 *fax* 0171-487 5436
Directors M.A. Murray-Pearce, Z.M. Pauncefort

Perfume, aromachology, cosmetics, beauty culture, aromatherapy and essential oils, including dictionaries, *objets d'art*, advertising, marketing, biography and memoirs. Send return postage with unsolicited MSS. Founded 1946.

Jordan Publishing Ltd
21 St Thomas Street, Bristol BS1 6JS
tel (0117) 923 0600 *fax* (0117) 925 0486
web site http://www.jordans.co.uk
Managing Director Richard Hudson

Law and business administration. Also specialist Family Law imprint (including the *Family Law Journal*). Books, looseleaf services, serials, CD-Roms and on-line.

Michael Joseph Ltd – see Penguin Books Ltd*

The Journeyman Press – see Pluto Press

Karnak House
300 Westbourne Park Road, London W11 1EH
tel/fax 0171-221 6490
Directors Dimela Yekwai (chairman), Amon Saba Saakana (editorial), Gloria Flaxman (administration), Seheri Sujai (art)

Specialists in African/Caribbean studies worldwide: anthropology, education, Egyptology, fiction, history, language, linguistics, literary criticism, music, parapsychology, philosophy, prehistory. Founded 1979.

Keele University Press Ltd – see Edinburgh University Press*

Kelly's – see Reed Information Services

The Kenilworth Press Ltd
Addington, Buckingham MK18 2JR
tel (0129 671) 5101 *fax* (0129 671) 5148
Directors David Blunt, Deirdre Blunt

Equestrian, including official publications for the British Horse Society. Founded 1989. Incorporates Threshold Books; founded 1970.

Kenyon-Deane – see Cressrelles Publishing Co. Ltd

Laurence King Publishing*
71 Great Russell Street, London WC1B 3BN
tel 0171-831 6351 *fax* 0171-831 8356
e-mail 101456.1525@compuserve.com
Directors Robin Hyman (chairman), Laurence King (managing), Lesley Ripley Greenfield (editorial: college and fine arts), Judith Rasmussen (production)

Imprint of **Calmann and King Ltd**, book packagers. Art, design, decorative art. Founded 1991.

Kingfisher – see Larousse plc*

Jessica Kingsley Publishers*
116 Pentonville Road, London N1 9JB
tel 0171-833 2307 *fax* 0171-837 2917
e-mail post@jkp.com
Director Jessica Kingsley

Psychology, psychotherapy, therapy, arts therapies, social work, higher education policy, regional studies, education, law. Founded 1987.

Kingsway Publications*
Lottbridge Drove, Eastbourne, East Sussex BN23 6NT
tel (01323) 410930 *fax* (01323) 411970
Joint Managing Directors John Paculabo, Brian Davies, *Director of Publishing* Richard Herkes

Christian theology for the lay person. No poetry. Submissions must have Evangelical Christian content. Please send synopsis/2 sample chapters only with return postage.

Kluwer Publishing
Croner House, London Road, Kingston-upon-Thames, Surrey KT2 6SR
tel 0181-547 3333 *fax* 0181-547 2637
Managing Director Hans Staal

Law, taxation, finance, insurance, looseleaf information services. Subsidiary of Croner Publications Ltd. Founded 1972.

Knight – see Hodder Headline plc

Charles Knight Publishing – see Tolley Publishing Co. Ltd

Knockabout Comics
10 Acklam Road, London W10 5QZ
tel 0181-969 2945 *fax* 0181-968 7614
Editors Tony Bennett, Carol Bennett

Humorous and satirical comic strips for an adult readership. Founded 1975.

Kogan Page Ltd*

120 Pentonville Road, London N1 9JN
tel 0171-278 0433 *fax* 0171-837 6348
Managing Director Philip Kogan, *Directors*
Pauline Goodwin (editorial), Peter Chadwick
(production and editorial), Gordon Watts
(financial), Philip Mudd (editorial), Jonathan
Sinclair-Wilson (Earthscan, editorial), Julie
McNair (sales)

Education, training, educational and
training technology, journals, business
and management, human resource management, transport and distribution, marketing, sales, advertising and PR, finance
and accounting, directories, small business, careers and vocational, personal
finance, environment. Founded 1967.

Earthscan Publications Ltd (subsidiary)
Directors Philip Kogan, Jonathan Sinclair-Wilson
(editorial)

Third World and environmental issues
including politics, sociology, environment, economics, current events, geography, health.

Kompass – see Reed Information Services

Ladybird Books Ltd*

Beeches Road, Loughborough, Leics. LE11 2NQ
tel (01509) 268021 *fax* (01509) 234672
Managing Director Laurence James

Children's books for 0-10 year-olds –
babies, toddlers, preschoolers, general
and home educational (infants, primary,
junior and secondary). A subsidiary of
The Penguin Group. Founded 1924.

Lampada Press – see The University of Hull Press

Larousse plc*

London office Elsley House, 24-30 Great
Titchfield Street, London W1P 7AD
tel 0171-631 0878 *fax* 0171-323 4694
Edinburgh office 7 Hopetoun Crescent,
Edinburgh EH7 4AY
tel 0131-557 4571 *fax* 0131-557 2936
Chairman Bertil Hessel, *Directors* Marc Zagar
(finance), Robert Snuggs (sales and marketing),
John Richards (production)

See also Harrap.

Chambers (imprint)
Publishing Manager Elaine Higgleton

Dictionaries, reference and local interest.

Kingfisher (imprint)
Publishing Directors Ann Davies (non-fiction),
Ann-Janine Murtagh (fiction)

Children's books.

Larousse (imprint)

Reference books and bilingual dictionaries.

Lawrence & Wishart Ltd

99A Wallis Road, London E9 5LN
tel 0181-533 2506 *fax* 0181-533 7369
e-mail lw@l-w-bks.demon.co.uk
Directors S. Davison (editorial), J. Rodrigues, B.
Kirsch, M. Seaton, M. Perryman, A. Greenaway

Cultural studies, current affairs, history,
socialism and Marxism, political philosophy, politics, popular culture.

Legend – see Random House UK Ltd*

Leicester University Press – see
Cassell plc

Lennard Publishing

Windmill Cottage, Mackerye End, Harpenden,
Herts. AL5 5DR
tel (01582) 715866 *fax* (01582) 715121
e-mail lennard@lenqap.demon.co.uk
Directors K.A.A. Stephenson, R.H. Stephenson

Media tie-ins, sponsored books, special
commissions. No unsolicited MSS.
Division of Lennard Associates Ltd.

Letts Educational – see BPP (Letts
Educational) Ltd

Levinson Books Ltd

Greenland Place, 115-123 Bayham Street,
London NW1 0AG
tel 0171-424 0488 *fax* 0171-424 0499
Managing Director Joanna Levinson, *Art Director*
Paula Burgess

Picture books, novelty books, toy books,
activity books for under-7 age group.
Founded 1994.

Lewis Masonic

Coombelands House, Coombelands Lane,
Addlestone, Surrey KT15 1HY
tel (01932) 820560 *fax* (01932) 821258

Masonic books; *Masonic Square
Magazine*. Founded 1870.

Liaison – see Hodder Headline plc

John Libbey & Co. Ltd

13 Smiths Yard, Summerley Street,
London SW18 4HR
tel 0181-947 2777 *fax* 0181-947 2664
e-mail libbey@earlsfield.win.uk.net
Directors John Libbey, G. Cahn

Medical: nutrition, obesity, epilepsy,
neurology, nuclear medicine, oncology.
Film/cinema. Founded 1979.

Library Association Publishing*
7 Ridgmount Street, London WC1E 7AE
tel 0171-636 7543 *fax* 0171-636 3627
e-mail lapublishing@la-hq.org.uk
Managing Director Janet Liebster
Library and information science, information technology, reference works, directories, bibliographies.

Clive Bingley Ltd (imprint)
Library and information science, reference works.

Libris Ltd
10 Burghley Road, London NW5 1UE
tel 0171-482 2390 *fax* 0171-485 4220
Directors Nicholas Jacobs, S.A. Kitzinger
Literature, literary biography, German studies, bilingual poetry. Founded 1986.

The Lilliput Press Ltd†
62-63 Sitric Road, Dublin 7, Republic of Ireland
tel/fax (01) 6711647
Managing Director Antony T. Farrell
General and Irish literature: essays, biography/autobiography, fiction, criticism; Irish history; philosophy; contemporary culture; nature and environment. Founded 1984.

Frances Lincoln Ltd
4 Torriano Mews, Torriano Avenue, London NW5 2RZ
tel 0171-284 4009 *fax* 0171-485 0490
Directors Frances Lincoln (managing), Erica Hunningher (editorial, adult books), Janetta Otter-Barry (editorial, children's books)
Illustrated, international co-editions: gardening, interiors, health, cookery, art, gift, children's books. Founded 1977.

Lion Publishing plc*
Peter's Way, Sandy Lane West, Oxford OX4 5HG
tel (01865) 747550 *fax* (01865) 747568
Directors David Alexander, Pat Alexander, Tony Wales, Paul Clifford, Denis Cole, Rebecca Winter (editorial), Dy Leyland, Peter Young
Reference, paperbacks, illustrated children's books, educational, gift books, multimedia, religion and theology; all reflecting a Christian position. Founded 1971.

Lions – see HarperCollins Publishers*

Little, Brown and Company (UK)*
Brettenham House, Lancaster Place, London WC2E 7EN
tel 0171-911 8000 *fax* 0171-911 8100
Chief Executive and Publisher Philippa Harrison, *Directors* David Young (managing), B. Boote (editorial), A. Samson (editorial), David Kent (home sales), Nigel Batt (financial), Charles Viney (export sales), Terry Jackson (marketing)
Hardback and paperback fiction, general non-fiction and illustrated books. No unsolicited MSS. Founded 1988.

Abacus (division)
Editorial Director Richard Beswick
Trade paperbacks.

Illustrated (division)
Editorial Director Julia Charles
Hardback photographic and art books.

Orbit (imprint)
Editorial Director Tim Holman
Science fiction and fantasy paperbacks.

Virago (division)
Publisher Lennie Goodings, *Senior Editor* Sally Abbey
Fiction, including Modern Classics Series, biography, autobiography and general non-fiction which highlight all aspects of women's lives.

Warner (division)
Editorial Directors Barbara Boote, Alan Samson, Hilary Hale, Imogen Taylor
Paperbacks: original fiction and non-fiction; reprints.

X Libris (imprint)
Editor Helen Goodwin
Erotic fiction for women.

Liverpool University Press*
Senate House, Abercromby Square, Liverpool L69 3BX
tel 0151-794 2233/7 *fax* 0151-794 2235
e-mail sandrob@liverpool.ac.uk
Publisher Robin Bloxsidge
Academic and scholarly books in a range of disciplines. Special interests: art history, education, European and American literature, science fiction criticism, social, political, economic and ancient history, archaeology, veterinary science, urban and regional planning. Major new series, *Modern French Writers*, established 1997. Founded 1901.

Y Lolfa Cyf.
Talybont, Ceredigion SY24 5HE
tel (01970) 832304 *fax* (01970) 832782
e-mail ylolfa@netwales.co.uk
web site http://www. ylolfa.wales.com
Directors Robat Gruffudd, Enid Gruffudd, *Editor* Lefi Gruffudd
Welsh-language popular fiction and non-fiction, music, children's books; Welsh-

language tutors; English-language political books and a range of Welsh-interest books for the tourist market. Founded 1967.

Lonely Planet Publications

The Barley Mow Centre, 10 Barley Mow Passage, London W4 4PH
tel 0181-742 3161 *fax* 0181-742 2772
e-mail 100413.3551@compuserve.com
web site lonelyplanet.com
Directors Tony Wheeler, Jim Hart, Maureen Wheeler, *General Manager UK* Charlotte Hindle
Travel guidebooks, atlases, phrasebooks, language-learning audio packs, travel literature. Founded 1973.

Longman Group – see Addison Wesley Longman Ltd*

Longman Training – now Training Direct – see Pearson Professional Ltd*

Lorenz Books – see Anness Publishing

Peter Lowe (Eurobook Ltd)

PO Box 52, Wallingford, Oxon OX10 0XU
tel (01865) 858333 *fax* (01865) 858263
Director P.S. Lowe
Publishers of popular science and related subjects (including natural history) as illustrated non-fiction. Age 12+ but no general fiction or teen fiction. Founded 1968.

Lund Humphries Publishers Ltd

Park House, 1 Russell Gardens,
London NW11 9NN
tel 0181-458 6314 *fax* 0181-905 5245
Managing Director Lionel Leventhal, *Editorial Director* Lucy Myers
Art, architecture, graphic art and design.

Lutterworth Press – see James Clarke & Co. Ltd*

Macdonald Young Books

61 Western Road, Hove, East Sussex BN3 1JD
tel (01273) 722561 *fax* (01273) 329314
e-mail wayland1@fastnet.co.uk
Publishing Director Stephen White-Thomson
Fiction, non-fiction, picture books and story books for children from pre-school to teenage. Founded 1994.

McGraw-Hill Book Company Europe*

McGraw-Hill House, Shoppenhangers Road, Maidenhead, Berks. SL6 2QL
tel (01628) 23432 *fax* (01628) 770224
Group Vice President, UK Fred J. Perkins,

Directors Andrew Phillips (editorial), Peter Kitley (financial)
Technical, scientific, professional reference.

Macmillan Interactive Publishing – see Macmillan Publishers Ltd*

Macmillan Press Ltd – see Macmillan Publishers Ltd*

Macmillan Publishers Ltd*

25 Eccleston Place, London SW1W 9NF
tel 0171- 881 8000
Chairman N.G. Byam Shaw, *Directors* R. Barker, M. Barnard, The Hon. D. Macmillan, C.J. Paterson, A. Soar, A.J. Sutherland, G.R.U. Todd

Macmillan Children's Books Ltd (division)

Publisher Kate Wilson, *Editorial Director (Picture Books and Properties)* Alison Green, *Editorial Director* Marion Lloyd
Publishes under **Macmillan, Pan, Campbell Books**. Picture books, fiction, poetry, non-fiction, early learning, pop-up, novelty. No unsolicited material.

Macmillan Education (division)

Houndmills, Basingstoke, Hants RG21 6XS
tel (01256) 329242 *fax* (01256) 479985
Managing Director Christopher Harrison, *Publishing Director* Alison Hubert, *Sales Director* John G. Watson, *Director (Latin America)* Christopher West
International School and College books in all subjects for all ages, including English Language Teaching.

Macmillan General Books (division)

Managing Director Ian S. Chapman, *Editor-in-Chief* Clare Alexander
Publishes under **Macmillan, Pan, Papermac, Sidgwick & Jackson**.
Boxtree
See page 160.
Macmillan
Executive Editorial Director (Fiction) Suzanne Baboneau
Novels, detective fiction, sci-fi, fantasy and horror.
Editorial Directors (Non-fiction) Georgina Morley, Catherine Hurley
Autobiography, biography, business and industry, crafts and hobbies, economics, gift books, health and beauty, history, humour, natural history, travel, philosophy, politics and world affairs, psychology, theatre and drama, gardening and cookery, encyclopedias. Founded 1865.

Pan
Publisher Peter Lavery
Fiction: novels, detective fiction, sci-fi, fantasy and horror. Non-fiction: sports and games, theatre and drama, travel, gardening and cookery, encyclopaedias. Founded 1947.

Papermac
Publisher Jon Riley, *Editor* Tanya Stobbs
Series non-fiction: history, biography, science, political economy, cultural criticism and art history. Founded 1965.

Picador
Publisher Jon Riley, *Editorial Director* Ursula Doyle
Literary international fiction and non-fiction. Founded 1972.

Sidgwick & Jackson
Editorial Director Georgina Morley
Military and war, music, pop and rock. MSS, synopses and ideas welcome. Send to submissions editor, with return postage. Founded 1908.

Macmillan Interactive Publishing (division)
New Media Development Director Michael Barnard
CD-Rom and on-line.

Macmillan Press Ltd (division)
Houndmills, Brunel Road, Basingstoke, Hants RG21 6XS
tel (01256) 329242 *fax* (01256) 479476
Managing Director D. Knight, *Publishing Directors* J. Marks (journals), T.M. Farmiloe (scholarly), S. Kennedy (higher education), J. Winkler (further education)
Textbooks, monographs and works of reference in academic, professional and vocational subjects; medical and scientific journals; directories.

Julia MacRae Books – see **Random House UK Ltd***

Madcap – see **André Deutsch Ltd***

Magi Publications
22 Manchester Street, London W1M 5PG
tel 0171-486 0925 *fax* 0171-486 0926
Publisher Monty Bhatia, *Editor* Linda Jennings
Quality children's picture books. New material will be considered from authors and illustrators, but please enquire first. Founded 1987.

Mainstream Publishing Co. (Edinburgh) Ltd*
7 Albany Street, Edinburgh EH1 3UG
tel 0131-557 2959 *fax* 0131-556 8720
Directors Bill Campbell, Peter MacKenzie
Biography, autobiography, art, photography, sport, health, guidebooks, humour, literature, current affairs, history, politics. Founded 1978.

Mammoth – see **Reed Books**

Management Books 2000 Ltd
(incorporating Mercury Books)
Cowcombe House, Cowcombe Hill, Chalford, Glos. GL6 8HP
tel (01285) 760722 *fax* (01285) 760708
e-mail mb2000@compuserve.com
Directors N. Dale-Harris (publisher), R. Hartman
Business books.

Manchester United Books – see **André Deutsch Ltd***

Manchester University Press*
Oxford Road, Manchester M13 9NR
tel 0161-273 5539 *fax* 0161-274 3346
e-mail mup@man.ac.uk
Editorial Director Vanessa Graham
Works of academic scholarship: literary criticism, cultural studies, media studies, art history, design, architecture, history, politics, economics, international law, modern language texts. Textbooks and monographs. Founded 1912.

Mandarin – acquired by **Random House UK Ltd**

Mandrake of Oxford
PO Box 250, Oxford OX1 1AP
tel (01865) 243671 *fax* (01865) 432929
e-mail krm@mandrake.compulink.co.uk
web site http://www.compulink.co.uk/~mandrake/welcome.htm
Directors Kris Morgan, Shantidevi Nath
Occult and bizarre. Founded 1986.

Mansell Publishing – see **Cassell plc**

Manson Publishing Ltd*
73 Corringham Road, London NW11 7DL
tel 0181-905 5150 *fax* 0181-201 9233
e-mail manson@man-pub.demon.co.uk
Managing Director Michael Manson
Medical, scientific, veterinary. Founded 1992.

Mantra Publishing
5 Alexandra Grove, London N12 8NU
tel 0181-445 5123 *fax* 0181-446 7745
e-mail mantrapub@aol.com
web site http://www.mantrapublish.com
Managing Director M. Chatterji
Children's multicultural picture books; dual language books/cassettes; South Asian literature/teenage fiction; CD-Roms and videos. Founded 1984.

Marino Books – see The Mercier Press†

Marshall Editions Ltd
170 Piccadilly, London W1V 9DD
tel 0171-629 0079 *fax* 0171-834 8844
e-mail info@mediakey.u-net.com
web site www.marshallmedia.com
Directors Richard Harman (chairman), Barry Baker (managing), Barbara Anderson Marshall, Ed Day (creative), John Christmas, Belinda Ioni Rasmussen, David Rivers, Sophie Collins (editorial, adult), Sean Keogh, Cynthia O'Brien (editorial, children's), Janice Storr, Avril Farley
Highly illustrated non-fiction, for the adult and children's co-edition markets, including science and natural history, fitness and well-being, lifestyle and leisure interests. Founded 1977.

Marshall Pickering – see HarperCollins Publishers*

Martin Books
Grafton House, 64 Maids Causeway, Cambridge CB5 8DD
tel (01223) 366733 *fax* (01223) 461428
Editorial Director Janet Copleston
Imprint of Simon & Schuster Consumer Group. Cookery, gardening, illustrated non-fiction and sponsored publishing.

Kenneth Mason Publications Ltd*
Dudley House, 12 North Street, Emsworth, Hants PO10 7DQ
tel (01243) 377977 *fax* (01243) 379136
Directors Kenneth Mason (chairman), Piers Mason (managing), Michael Mason, Anthea Mason
Nautical, slimming, health, fitness; technical journals. Founded 1958.

Kevin Mayhew Ltd
Buxhall, Suffolk IP14 3DJ
tel (01449) 737978 *fax* (01449) 737834
e-mail kevinmayhewltd@msn.com
Directors Kevin Mayhew (chairman), Gordon Carter (managing) Ray Gilbert (production), Jonathan Bugden (sales)

Christianity: prayer and spirituality, pastoral care, preaching, liturgy worship, *Springboard* series, children's, instant art. Music: hymns, organ and choral, piano and instrumental. Contact Editorial Dept before sending MSS/synopses. Founded 1976.

Meadowfield Press Ltd
22 Abbey Road, Darlington, Co. Durham DL3 8LR
tel (01325) 351661
Directors Dr J.G. Cook (editorial), M. Cook, J.A. Verdon, A.M. Creasey
Microbiology, zoology, archaeology, botany, biology. Founded 1976.

Medical & Historical – see Harlequin Mills & Boon Ltd*

Medici Society Ltd
34-42 Pentonville Road, London N1 9HG
tel 0171-837 7099 *fax* 0171-837 9152
Publishers of Medici Prints, greetings cards and other colour reproductions. Art and children's books. Preliminary letter with brief details of the work requested; mark for the attention of The Art Dept.

Melrose Press Ltd
3 Regal Lane, Soham, Ely, Cambs. CB7 5BA
tel (01353) 721091 *fax* (01353) 721839
Directors R.A. Kay, J.M. Kay, B.J. Wilson, N.S. Law (editorial), C. Emmett FCA, V.A. Kay, J.E. Pearson
International biographical reference works, including *International Authors & Writers Who's Who, International Who's Who in Poetry* and *Poets' Encyclopedia*. Founded 1969.

The Mercat Press*
James Thin Ltd, 53-59 South Bridge, Edinburgh EH1 1YS
tel 0131-556 6743 *fax* 0131-557 8149
e-mail james.thin.ltd @almac.co.uk
web site http://www.jthin.co.uk
Chairman D. Ainslie Thin, *Editorial Managers* Tom Johnstone, Seán Costello
Scottish books of general and academic interest. No fiction. Founded 1970.

The Mercier Press†
PO Box 5, 5 French Church Street, Cork, Republic of Ireland
tel (021) 275040 *fax* (021) 274969
e-mail books@mercier.ie
web site http://www.mercier.ie/mercier
Directors G. Eaton (chairman), J.F. Spillane (managing), M.P. Feehan, D.J. Keily, A. O'Donnell, J. O'Donoghue

Irish literature, folklore, history, politics, humour, ballads, education, theology, law. Founded 1944.

Marino Books (imprint)
16 Hume Street, Dublin 2, Republic of Ireland
tel (01) 6615299 *fax* (01) 6618583
e-mail books@marino.ie
Publisher Jo O'Donoghue
Fiction, children's fiction, current affairs, health, mind and spirit, general non-fiction.

Merehurst Ltd/J.B. Fairfax Press Ltd
Ferry House, 51-57 Lacy Road,
London SW15 1PR
tel 0181-355 1480 *fax* 0181-355 1499
Directors Debbie Kent (sales and marketing), Shirley Patton (publishing), Kirsten Schlesinger (rights), Roger Potter (finance)
Crafts and hobbies, cake decorating, cookery, homes and interiors, children's non-fiction, gardening.

Merlin Press Ltd
2 Rendlesham Mews, Rendlesham,
Nr Woodbridge, Suffolk IP2 2SZ
tel (01394) 461313 *fax* (01394) 461314
Directors M.W. Eve, P.M. Eve
Radical history and social studies. Letters/synopses only please.

Green Print (imprint)
Green politics and the environment.

Seafarer Books (imprint)
Commissioning Editor Martin Eve
Books on traditional sailing, mainly narrative; also travel literature.

Merrell Holberton Publishers Ltd
Willcox House, 42 Southwark Street,
London SE1 1UN
tel 0171-403 2047 *fax* 0171-407 1333
e-mail merrholb@dircon.co.uk
Publishing Director Hugh Merrell, *Editorial Director* Paul Holberton
Illustrated fine art books. Founded 1993.

Merrow Publishing Co. Ltd
22 Abbey Road, Darlington,
Co. Durham DL3 8LR
tel (01325) 351661 *fax* (01325) 774888
Directors Dr J.G. Cook (editorial), M. Cook, J.A. Verdon, A.M. Creasey
Textiles, plastics, popular science, scientific. Founded 1951.

Methodist Publishing House
20 Ivatt Way, Peterborough PE3 7PG
tel (01733) 332202 *fax* (01733) 331201

Hymn and service books, general religious titles, church supplies. Founded 1773.

Foundery Press (imprint)
Ecumenical titles.

Methuen – see Random House UK Ltd*

Methuen Academic – now incorporated into Routledge*

Methuen Children's Books – see Reed Books*

Metro Publishing Ltd
19 Gerrard Street, London W1V 7LA
tel 0171-734 1411 *fax* 0171-734 1811
e-mail susannemcdadd@metrobooks.co.uk
Managing Director Susanne McDadd

Metro Books (imprint)
'Books to help you get the most out of life.' Non-fiction: popular psychology, childcare, self-help, health, cookery, travel, leisure, biography, autobiography. Founded 1995.

Michelin Tyre plc
Tourism Department, The Edward Hyde Building, 38 Clarendon Road, Watford, Herts. WD1 1SX
tel (01923) 415000 *fax* (01923) 415052
Head of Tourism Department J. Lewis
Tourist guides, maps and atlases, hotel and restaurant guides; children's activity books. Founded 1989.

Milestone Publications
62 Murray Road, Horndean,
Waterlooville PO8 9SL
tel (01705) 597440 *fax* (01705) 591975
Managing Director Nicholas J. Pine
Heraldic china, antique porcelain, business, economics. Founded 1967.

Millennium – see The Orion Publishing Group Ltd

J. Garnet Miller Ltd
10 Station Road Industrial Estate, Colwall,
Malvern, Worcs. WR13 6RN
tel (01684) 540154 *fax* (01684) 540154
Directors Leslie Smith, Simon Smith
Drama, theatre, plays. Founded 1951.

Harvey Miller Publishers*
197 Knightsbridge, London SW7 1RB
tel 0171-584 7676 *fax* 0171-823 7969
Editor-in-Chief Elly Miller
Imprint of G+B Arts International. Art history.

Miller Freeman Information Services

Riverbank House, Angel Lane, Tonbridge, Kent TN9 1SE
tel (01732) 362666 *fax* (01732) 367301

Over 35 directories for business and industry, including *Benn's Media* and *The Knowledge*, guides for the media and film and TV markets respectively.

Millers – see Reed Books

Mills & Boon (Publishers) Ltd – now Harlequin Mills & Boon Ltd*

Minerva – acquired by Random House UK Ltd

Mira Books – see Harlequin Mills & Boon Ltd*

The MIT Press – see under USA in Overseas book publishers, page 225

Mitchell Beazley – see Reed Books

Monarch Publications

Broadway House, The Broadway, Crowborough, East Sussex TN6 1HQ
tel (01892) 652364 *fax* (01892) 663329
e-mail imonarch@dial.pipex.com
Publisher Tony Collins, Jane Collins

Christian books: (Monarch) issues of faith and society; (MARC) leadership, mission, evangelism. Submit synopsis/2 sample chapters only with return postage please.

Mosby International

5th Floor, Lynton House, 7-12 Tavistock Square, London WC1H 9LB
tel 0171-388 7676 *fax* 0171-391 6555

Mosby (imprint)
International student textbooks and post-graduate works of reference in full colour in medicine, nursing and bio-medical sciences.

Mosby Wolfe (imprint)
International colour atlases in medicine, biomedical science, dentistry and veterinary medical.

Mosby Wolfe Medical Communications (division)
Managing Director Derrick Holman

Supplies the global pharmaceutical industry with medically relevant educational and promotional programmes in support of ethical drugs. Produces books, ideas, slides and multimedia programmes for the clinical and consumer health markets. Also runs the co-editions and translation rights businesses.

The Mothers' Union

24 Tufton Street, London SW1P 3RB
tel 0171-222 5533 *fax* 0171-222 1591

Religious, educational and social subjects connected with marriage and the family; religious books for adults and children; quarterly magazine *Home and Family*. Founded 1876.

Mowbray – see Cassell plc

MQ Publications Ltd

254-258 Goswell Road, London EC1V 7EB
tel 0171-490 7732 *fax* 0171-253 7358
Chief Executive Officer Susan Jenkins

Craft, style and gift books. Founded 1993.

Multimedia Books – see Prion Books

John Murray (Publishers) Ltd*

50 Albemarle Street, London W1X 4BD
tel 0171-493 4361 *fax* 0171-499 1792
Chairman John R. Murray (general books marketing), *Managing Director* Nicholas Perren, *Directors* Grant McIntyre (general editorial), Judith Reinhold (educational marketing), *Company Secretary* Philip Carter

General: art and architecture, biography and autobiography, letters and diaries, travel, exploration and guidebooks, Middle East, Asia, India and sub-continent, general history, health education, aviation, craft and practical. No unsolicited MSS please.

Educational: biology, chemistry, physics, business studies, economics, management and law, English, geography and environmental studies, history and social studies, mathematics, modern languages, special educational needs, technical subjects. Also self teaching in all subjects in *Success Studybook* series. Founded 1768.

National Christian Education Council*

(incorporating International Bible Reading Association)
1020 Bristol Road, Selly Oak, Birmingham B26 6LB
tel 0121-472 4242 *fax* 0121-472 7575
e-mail ncec@netlink.co.uk
web site http://www.netlink.co.uk/users.ncec/

Resource materials for worship and learning in Church. Training material for children and youth workers in the Church. Worship resources for use in primary schools. Christian drama and musicals, Activity Club material and Bible reading resources.

National Poetry Foundation
27 Mill Road, Fareham, Hants PO16 0TH
tel (01329) 822218
Founder/Trustee Johnathon Clifford
Poetry. Founded 1981.

The National Trust
36 Queen Anne's Gate, London SW1H 9AS
tel 0171-222 9251 *fax* 0171-222 5097
Publisher Margaret Willes
History, cookery, architecture, gardening, guidebooks, children's non-fiction. No unsolicited MSS. Founded 1895.

The Natural History Museum Publications
Cromwell Road, London SW7 5BD
tel 0171-938 9048 *fax* 0171-938 8709
e-mail j.hogg@nhm.ac.uk
Head of Publishing Jane Hogg
Natural sciences; entomology, botany, geology, palaeontology, zoology. Founded 1881.

Nautical Books – now Adlard Coles
Nautical – see A & C Black (Publishers) Ltd*

NCC Blackwell – see Blackwell Publishers*

NCVO Publications
(incorporating Bedford Square Press)
Regent's Wharf, 8 All Saints Street, London N1 9RL
tel 0171-713 6161 *fax* 0171-713 6300
Imprint of the National Council for Voluntary Organisations. Practical guides, reference books, directories and policy studies on voluntary sector concerns including management and trustee development, legal, finance and fundraising, self-help and Europe.

Thomas Nelson & Sons Ltd*
Nelson House, Mayfield Road, Walton-on-Thames, Surrey KT12 5PL
tel (01932) 252211 *fax* (01932) 246109
e-mail nelinfo@nelson.co.uk
Directors Rod E. Gauvin (managing), David Fothergill, Nick White

Print and electronic publishers for educational market (primary, secondary and college). Imprint: Arden Shakespeare. Founded 1798.

Network Books – see BBC Worldwide Ltd*

New Adventures – see Virgin Publishing Ltd

New Beacon Books
76 Stroud Green Road, London N4 3EN
tel 0171-272 4889
Directors John La Rose, Sarah White, Michael La Rose, Janice Durham
Small specialist publishers: general non-fiction, fiction, poetry, critical writings, mainly concerning the Caribbean, Africa, African-America, Black Britain and Europe. No unsolicited MSS. Founded 1966.

New Cavendish Books
3 Denbigh Road, London W11 2SJ
tel 0171-229 6765/792 9984 *fax* 0171-792 01027
e-mail narisa@new-cav.demon.co.uk
Specialist books for the collector; art reference, Thai guidebooks. Founded 1973.
White Mouse Editions Ltd (imprint)
Contact Chris Shelley
Transport.
Golden Age Editions (imprint)
Contact Chris Shelley
Limited edition books on fine toys.

New English Library – see Hodder Headline plc

New Holland (Publishers) Ltd*
Chapel House, 24 Nutford Place, London W1H 6DQ
tel 0171-724 7773 *fax* 0171-724 6184
e-mail vobis@nhpub.u-net.com
Managing Director John Beaufoy, *Publishing Directors* Charlotte Parry-Crooke, Yvonne McFarlane (lifestyle)
Illustrated books on natural history, travel, cookery, needlecrafts and handicrafts, interior design, DIY, gardening.

New Orchard Editions – see Cassell plc

New Playwrights' Network
Flat 4, Brocklehurst Manor, 25 Brocklehurst Avenue, Macclesfield, Cheshire SK10 2RX
tel/fax (01625) 425312
Publishing Director J.C.F. Gray
General plays for the amateur, one-act and full length.

Nexus – see Virgin Publishing Ltd

Nexus Special Interests Ltd
Nexus House, Boundary Way, Hemel Hempstead, Herts. HP2 7ST
tel (01442) 66551 *fax* (01442) 66998
Manager B. Laughlin
Modelling, model engineering, woodworking, aviation, railways, military, crafts, electronics, home brewing and winemaking.

NFER-NELSON Publishing Co. Ltd*
Darville House, 2 Oxford Road East, Windsor, Berks. SL4 1DF
tel (01753) 858961 *fax* (01753) 856830
Business Development Director Ian Florance

Testing, assessment and management publications and services for education, business and health care. Founded 1981.

Nia – see the X Press

Nicholson – see HarperCollins Publishers*

James Nisbet & Co. Ltd
78 Tilehouse Street, Hitchin, Herts. SG5 2DY
tel (01462) 438331 *fax* (01462) 431528
Directors Miss E.M. Mackenzie-Wood, Mrs A.A.C. Bierrum

Dictionaries, educational (infants, primary, secondary), business management. Founded 1810.

Northcote House Publishers Ltd
Plymbridge House, Estover Road, Plymouth, Devon PL6 7PY
tel (01752) 202368 *fax* (01752) 202330
Directors B.R.W. Hulme, A.V. Hulme (secretary)

Careers, education and education management, educational dance and drama, English literature (*Writers and their Work*). Founded 1985.

W.W. Norton & Company
10 Coptic Street, London WC1A 1PU
tel 0171-323 1579 *fax* 0171-436 4553
Managing Director Alan Cameron

History, biography, current affairs, sailing, English and American literature, economics, music, psychology, science. Founded 1980.

Notting Hill Electronic Publishers
31 Brunswick Gardens, London W8 4AW
tel 0171-229 0591 *fax* 0171-727 6641
e-mail 100444.232 @compuserve.com
Chairman Andreas Whittam Smith, *Directors* Ben Whittam Smith, Rachael Broughton (sales and marketing)

Electronic publishing on-line and off-line on CD-Rom platform: food and wine, sport, popular science, music, art and biography. Founded 1995.

Oak Tree Press⁺
Merrion Building, Lower Merrion Street, Dublin 2, Republic of Ireland
tel (01) 6761600 *fax* (01) 6761644
e-mail oaktreep@iol.ie
Directors Brian O'Kane, Rita O'Kane, *General Manager* David Givens

Law, accountancy, business management. Founded 1991.

O'Brien Educational
20 Victoria Road, Rathgar, Dublin 6, Republic of Ireland
tel (01) 4923333 *fax* (01) 4922777
Directors Michael O'Brien, Bride Rosney

Humanities, science, environmental studies, history, geography, English, Irish, art, commerce, music, careers, media studies. Founded 1976.

The O'Brien Press Ltd⁺
20 Victoria Road, Rathgar, Dublin 6, Republic of Ireland
tel (01) 4923333 *fax* (01) 4922777
e-mail books@obrien.ie
Directors Michael O'Brien, Ide Ni Laoghaire, Ivan O'Brien

Folklore, nature, fiction, architecture, topography, history, general, illustrated books, sport, true crime, music, anthropology, children's (fiction and non-fiction), biography; tapes for children. Series include *Lucky Tree Books*, *Junior Biography Library*, *Urban Heritage*, *Other World* Series (science fiction/fantasy/horror for juveniles). Founded 1974.

The Octagon Press Ltd
PO Box 227, London N6 4EW
tel 0181-348 9392 *fax* 0181-341 5971
e-mail octagon@schredds.demon.co.uk
web site http://www.clearlight.com/octagon/
Managing Director George R. Schrager

Psychology, philosophy, Eastern religion. Unsolicited MSS not accepted. Founded 1972.

The Oleander Press
17 Stansgate Avenue, Cambridge CB2 2QZ
tel (01223) 244688
Managing Director P. Ward

Travel, language, literature, Libya, Arabia and Middle East, Cambridgeshire, humour, reference. Preliminary letter

required before submitting MSS; please send sae for reply. Founded 1960.

Michael O'Mara Books Ltd
9 Lion Yard, Tremadoc Road, London SW4 7NQ
tel 0171-720 8643 *fax* 0171-627 8953
Chairman Michael O'Mara, *Managing Director* Lesley O'Mara

General non-fiction: Royal books, history, ancient history, humour, anthologies and biography. Founded 1985.

Omnibus Press/Music Sales Ltd*
8-9 Frith Street, London W1V 5TZ
tel 0171-434 0066 *fax* 0171-439 2848
Sales and Marketing Manager Hilary Power

Rock music biographies, books about music. Founded 1976.

On Stream Publications Ltd
Currabaha, Cloghroe, Blarney, Co. Cork, Republic of Ireland
tel/fax (021) 385798
e-mail onstream@indigo.ie
Owner Rosalind Crowley

Cookery, wine, travel, human interest non-fiction, local history, academic and practical books. Founded 1986.

Oneworld Publications
185 Banbury Road, Oxford, Oxon OX2 7AR
tel (01865) 310597 *fax* (01865) 310598
e-mail oneworld@cix.co.uk
web site http://www.oneworld-publications.com
Directors Juliet Mabey (editorial), Novin Doostdar (marketing)

Social issues, psychology, self-help, religion, world religion, inter-religious dialogue, Islamic studies, philosophy. Founded 1984.

Onlywomen Press Ltd
40 St Lawrence Terrace, London W10 5ST
tel 0181-960 7122 *fax* 0181-960 2817
e-mail 100756.1242@compuserve.com
Managing Director Lilian Mohin

Lesbian feminist: theory, fiction, poetry, crime fiction and cultural criticism. Founded 1974.

Open Books Publishing Ltd
Beaumont House, New Street, Wells, Somerset BA5 2LD
tel (01749) 677276 *fax* (01749) 670760
Directors P. Taylor (managing), C. Taylor

Books on gardening. Founded 1974.

Open University Press*
Celtic Court, 22 Ballmoor, Buckingham MK18 1XW
tel (01280) 823388 *fax* (01280) 823233

e-mail enquiries@openup.co.uk
Directors John Skelton (managing), Jacinta Evans (editorial), Sue Hadden (production), Barry Clarke (financial)

Education, management, psychology, sociology, criminology, counselling, health and social welfare, women's studies. Founded 1977.

Optima – see Random House UK Ltd*

Orbit – see Little, Brown and Company (UK)*

Orchard Books – see The Watts Publishing Group*

The Orion Publishing Group Ltd
Orion House, 5 Upper St Martin's Lane, London WC2H 9EA
tel 0171-240 3444 *fax* 0171-240 4822
Directors Nicholas Barber (chairman), Anthony Cheetham (chief executive), Peter Roche (managing)

No unsolicited MSS; approach in writing in the first instance. Founded 1992.

Illustrated (division)
Contact Michael Dover

Illustrated non-fiction: design, cookery, wine, gardening, art and architecture, natural history and personality based books.

Mass Market (division)
Contact Susan Lamb

Mass market fiction and non-fiction under **Everyman**, **Orion** and **Phoenix** imprints.

Millennium (imprint of Orion)
Contact Caroline Oakley

Science fiction and fantasy.

Orion (division)
Directors Rosemary Cheetham, Jane Wood

Hardcover fiction and non-fiction.

Orion Children's Books (division)
fax 0171-240 4823
Managing Director and Publisher Judith Elliott

Children's fiction and non-fiction.

Phoenix House (imprint of Weidenfeld & Nicolson)
Director Maggie McKernan

Literary fiction.

Weidenfeld & Nicolson (division)
Managing Director Ion Trewin

General non-fiction, biography, autobiography, history and travel.

Osprey – see Reed Books

Peter Owen Ltd
73 Kenway Road, London SW5 0RE
tel 0171-373 5628/370 6093 *fax* 0171-373 6760
Managing Director Peter L. Owen
Art, belles-lettres, biography and memoirs, fiction, general, theatre.

Oxford Illustrated Press – see Haynes Publishing

Oxford Publishing Company (OPC Railbooks) – see Haynes Publishing

Oxford University Press*
Great Clarendon Street, Oxford OX2 6DP
tel (01865) 556767 *fax* (01865) 556646
Chief Executive and Secretary to the Delegates
James Arnold-Baker, *Group Finance Director*
Roger Boning, *Academic Division Managing
Director* Ivon Asquith, *Educational Division
Managing Director* Peter Mothersole, *ELT
Division Managing Director* Bill Andrewes,
Group Personnel Director Martin Havelock
Anthropology, archaeology, architecture, art, belles-lettres, bibles, bibliography, children's books (fiction, non-fiction, picture), commerce, current affairs, dictionaries, drama, economics, educational (infants, primary, secondary, technical, university), English language teaching, electronic publishing, essays, general history, hymn and service books, journals, law, maps and atlases, medical, music, oriental, philosophy, poetry, political economy, prayer books, reference, science, sociology, theology and religion, educational software. Academic books published under the imprint **Clarendon Press**. Trade paperbacks published under the imprint of **Oxford Paperbacks**. Founded 1478.

Paladin – now Flamingo – see HarperCollins Publishers*

Pan – see Macmillan Publishers Ltd*

Pan Macmillan Ltd – now Macmillan General Books*

Pan Macmillan Children's Books Ltd – now Macmillan Children's Books Ltd*

Pandora Press – see HarperCollins Publishers*

Paper Tiger – see Collins & Brown

Papermac – see Macmillan Publishers Ltd*

Parkgate Books – see Collins & Brown

Partridge Press – see Transworld Publishers Ltd*

Paternoster Publishing*
PO Box 300, Carlisle, Cumbria CA3 0QS
tel (01228) 512512 *fax* (01228) 593388
e-mail patprod@aol.com
Managing Director Pieter Kwant
Biblical studies, Christian theology, ethics, history, mission. Imprints: Paternoster Press, Partnership, Regnum, Rutherford House, W.E.F., OM Publishing, Solway, Hunt & Thorpe (co-publishing partners), Challenge, Paternoster Periodicals.

Stanley Paul – see Random House UK Ltd*

Pavilion Books
London House, Great Eastern Wharf, Parkgate Road, London SW11 4NQ
tel 0171-924 2575 *fax* 0171-924 7725
Directors Cameron Brown, Mark Collins, Colin Webb, Pamela Webb
Cookery, gardening, travel, humour, sport, art, children's. Acquired by **Collins & Brown**. Founded 1980.

Payback Press – see Canongate Books Ltd*

Pearson Professional Ltd*
Maple House, 149 Tottenham Court Road, London W1P 9LL
tel 0171-896 2000 *fax* 0171-896 2099
Chief Executive Peter Warwick

Cartermill International (division)
Technology Centre, St Andrews, Fife KY16 9EA
tel (01334) 477660 *fax* (01334) 477180
Managing Director M. Campbell
Print and electronic research and information management products and services on science, technology and industry; health and social care reference; business intelligence and current affairs.

Churchill Communications Europe (division)
Maple House, 149 Tottenham Court Road, London W1P 9LL
tel 0171-896 2111 *fax* 0171-896 2112
Managing Director M. Freris, *Directors* A. Dryburgh, D. Riding
Full-service medical communications for pharmaceutical companies – i.e. sponsored publishing, drug registration, patient education, etc.

Churchill Livingstone (division)
Robert Stevenson House, 1-3 Baxter's Place,
Leith Walk, Edinburgh EH1 3AF
tel 0131-556 2424 *fax* 0131-558 1278
Divisional Directors Andrew Stevenson, Peter
Shepherd (nursing and allied health), John
Richardson (publishing services), Mary Law
(nursing and allied health), Timothy Wright (sales)

Medical books and journals for students,
trainees and practitioners; books and journals in nursing, midwifery, physiotherapy,
complementary medicine, and other allied
health disciplines. Note: preliminary letter
recommended before submitting MSS.

FT Law & Tax (division)
21-27 Lamb's Conduit Street, London WC1N 3NJ
tel 0171-242 2548 *fax* 0171-831 8119
Managing Director C. Stibbs, *Divisional Directors*
A.R. Wells, M. Staunton

Books and professional journals on law,
business, taxation, pensions, insurance,
government contracting, finance and
accountancy. Formerly Longman Law
Tax and Finance.

GeoInformation International (division)
307 Cambridge Science Park, Milton Road,
Cambridge CB4 4ZD
tel (01223) 423020 *fax* (01223) 425787
Managing Director Seppe Cassettari

Digital geographical information.
Publishes *GIS Europe*, *Mapping
Awareness* magazines.

Pitman Publishing (division)
128 Long Acre, London WC2E 9AN
tel 0171-447 2000 *fax* 0171-240 5771
Managing Director Rod Bristow, *Publishing
Directors* Simon Lake (educational), Mark Allin
(professional)

Business education, management, professional studies, M & E Handbooks.

Training Direct (imprint)
(formerly Longman Training)
Edinburgh Gate, Harlow, Essex CM20 2JE
tel (01279) 623850 *fax* (01279) 623795
Managing Director Mike Smith

Video and technology-based multimedia
interactive training resources for use in
business and industry.

Pelham Books – see Penguin Books Ltd*

Pen & Sword Books Ltd
47 Church Street, Barnsley,
South Yorkshire S70 2AS
tel (01226) 734222 *fax* (01226) 734438
web site www.yorkshire-web.co.uk/ps/
Chairman Sir Nicholas Hewitt, Bt, *Director and
Company Secretary* T.G. Hewitt

Military history. Imprints: Leo Cooper,
Pen & Sword Paperbacks.

Wharncliffe* (imprint)
Local history.

Penguin Books Ltd*
Bath Road, Harmondsworth, Middlesex UB7 0DA
tel 0181-899 4000 *fax* 0181-899 4099
London office 27 Wrights Lane,
London W8 5TZ
tel 0171-416 3000 *fax* 0171-416 3099
Founder Sir Allen Lane, *Chief Executive* Michael
Lynton, *Directors* Peter Carson, Roger Clarke,
Stephen Hall, Tony Lacey, Max Adam, Helen
Fraser, Jonathan Yglesias, Sally Floyer, Susan
Watt, Duncan Campbell Smith, Alastair Rolfe,
Cecily Engle, Andrew Welham, Pat McCarthy,
Philippa Milnes-Smith, Peter Haley, Anthony
Forbes Watson (managing)

Allen Lane The Penguin Press (imprint)
fax 0171-416 3274
Publishing Director Alastair Rolfe

Hardback non-fiction titles of academic
and intellectual interest, principally but
not exclusively the humanities.
Unsolicited MSS and poetry discouraged.

Arkana (imprint)
Publishing Director Alastair Rolfe

'Mind, body and spirit' list. Please do not
submit unsolicited proposals.

Elm Tree Books (imprint of **Hamish
Hamilton Ltd**)

'How-to' books on the media.

Hamish Hamilton Ltd (subsidiary)
tel 0171-416 3000 *fax* 0171-416 3274
Editorial Director Kate Jones

Fiction, belles-lettres, biography and
memoirs, current affairs, general, history,
literature, politics, travel. Synopses and
non-fiction ideas welcome; unsolicited
fiction MSS discouraged.

Hamish Hamilton Children's Books
(imprint)
Associate Publisher Jane Nissen

Children's fiction and picture books.
Unsolicited MSS, synopses and ideas
welcome.

Michael Joseph Ltd (subsidiary)
tel 0171-416 3000 *fax* 0171-416 3293
Publishing Director Tom Weldon

Biography and memoirs, current affairs,
fiction, history, humour, travel, crafts,
sports, handbooks, general leisure, illustrated books. Unsolicited MSS discouraged; synopses and ideas welcome.

Pelham Books (imprint of **Michael Joseph Ltd**)
tel 0171-416 3000 *fax* 0171-416 3293
Contact Susan Watt
Pears Cyclopaedia, Junior Pears Encyclopaedia. Autobiographies of men and women in sport, sports handbooks, hobbies, crafts and pastimes, practical handbooks on dogs and other pets, country pursuits.

Penguin (imprint)
fax 0171-416 3193
Publishing Director Tony Lacey
Adult paperback books – wide range of fiction, non-fiction, classics, TV and film tie-ins. No unsolicited fiction or poetry.

Penguin Audiobooks
Contact Anna Hopkins

Puffin (imprint)
fax 0171-416 3086
Publisher Philippa Milnes-Smith
Children's paperback books – mainly reprints: fiction, poetry, picture books, limited non-fiction, film and TV tie-ins. Unsolicited MSS discouraged; ideas and synopses are welcome.

Ventura Publishing Ltd (subsidiary)
fax 0171-416 3199
Publisher Sally Floyer
Eric Hill's *Spot.*

Viking (imprint)
fax 0171-416 3274
Publishing Director Juliet Annan
Fiction, general non-fiction; literature, biography, autobiography, current affairs, popular science, travel, popular culture and reference. Please do not submit unsolicited MSS for fiction; approach in writing only.

Viking Children's Books (imprint)
fax 0171-416 3086
Publisher Philippa Milnes-Smith
Fiction, poetry, picture books. Unsolicited MSS discouraged; synopses and ideas welcome.

Frederick Warne & Co. Ltd (subsidiary)
fax 0171-416 3199
Publisher Sally Floyer
Beatrix Potter, Flower Fairies, Orlando.

Pergamon – see Elsevier Science Ltd

Peterloo Poets
2 Kelly Gardens, Calstock, Cornwall PL18 9SA
tel (01822) 833473
Publishing Director Harry Chambers, *Trustees*
Rosemarie Bailey, Linda Squire, David Selzer, *Honorary President* Charles Causley CBE
Poetry. Founded 1976.

Phaidon Press Ltd
Regent's Wharf, All Saints Street, London N1 9PA
tel 0171-843 1000 *fax* 0171-843 1010
Chairman Richard Schlagman, *Directors* Paula Kahn (managing), Andrew Price (financial), Neil Palfreyman (production), David Jenkins (editorial), David Graham (sales), Amanda Renshaw (international editions)
Fine art, architecture, design, decorative arts, photography, music.

Philips – see Reed Books

Phillimore & Co. Ltd
(incorporating Darwen Finlayson Ltd)
Shopwyke Manor Barn, Chichester, West Sussex PO20 6BG
tel (01243) 787636 *fax* (01243) 787639
Directors Philip Harris JP (chairman), Noel Osborne MA, FSA (managing), Hilary Clifford Brown (marketing)
Local and family history; architectural history, archaeology, genealogy and heraldry; also Darwen County History series and History from the Sources series. Founded 1870.

Phoenix House – see The Orion Publishing Group Ltd

Piatkus Books
5 Windmill Street, London W1P 1HF
tel 0171-631 0710 *fax* 0171-436 7137
e-mail piatkus.books@dial.pipex.com
Managing Director Judy Piatkus, *Directors* Philip Cotterell (marketing), Gill Cormode (editorial)
Self-help, health, mind, body and spirit, business, careers, women's interest, fiction, how-to and practical, popular psychology, cookery, parenting and childcare, biography and paranormal. Founded 1979.

Picador – see Macmillan Publishers Ltd*

Piccadilly Press
5 Castle Road, London NW1 8PR
tel 0171-267 4492 *fax* 0171-267 4493
Directors Brenda Gardner (chairman and managing), Philip Durrance (secretary)
Children's hardback books and parents' interest trade paperbacks; trade paperback teenage information, fiction and humour books. Founded 1983.

Pimlico – see Random House UK Ltd*

Pinter – see Cassell plc

Pitkin Guides – see Reed Books

Pitman Publishing – see Pearson Professional Ltd*

The Playwrights Publishing Company
70 Nottingham Road, Burton Joyce, Notts. NG14 5AL
tel (0115) 931 3356
Proprietor Liz Breeze, Consultant Tony Breeze
One-act and full-length drama: serious work and comedies, for mixed cast, all women or schools. Reading fee and sae required. Founded 1990.

Plexus Publishing Ltd
55A Clapham Common Southside, London SW4 9BX
tel 0171-622 2440 *fax* 0171-622 2441
Directors Terence Porter (managing), Sandra Wake (editorial)
Film, music, biography, popular culture, fashion. Founded 1973.
Eel Pie (imprint)
Film, music, biography, popular culture, fashion.

Pluto Press
345 Archway Road, London N6 5AA
tel 0181 348 2724 *fax* 0181 348 0133
e-mail pluto@plutobks.demon.co.uk
web site http://www.leevalley.co.uk/plutopress
Directors Roger van Zwanenberg (managing), Anne Beech (editorial)
Sociology, social and political science including economics, history; cultural, international, women's studies, legal studies, Irish studies, Black studies, Third World and development, anthropology, media studies. Founded 1968.
The Journeyman Press (trade imprint)
Feminist, biography, social history, media handbooks.

Pocket Books – see Simon & Schuster*

Point – see Scholastic Children's Books*

The Policy Press
(incorporating SAUS Publications)
University of Bristol, Rodney Lodge, Grange Road, Bristol BS8 4EA
tel (0117) 9738797 *fax* (0117) 9737308
e-mail tpp@bris.ac.uk
Publishing Manager Alison Shaw, *Editorial Manager* Dawn Louise Pudney, *Marketing and Sales Manager* Julia Mortimer, *Journals Manager/Book Editor* Sue Hayman

Community care; public policy, social policy; family policy and child welfare; health, housing, employment and urban studies; governance. Founded 1996.

Polity Press
65 Bridge Street, Cambridge CB2 1UR
tel (01223) 324315 *fax* (01223) 461385
Directors Anthony Giddens, David Held, John Thompson
Social and political theory, politics, sociology, history, economics, psychology, media and cultural studies, philosophy, theology, literary theory, feminism, human geography, anthropology. Founded 1983.

Polygon – see Edinburgh University Press*

Poolbeg Press Ltd†
123 Baldoyle Industrial Estate, Baldoyle, Dublin 13, Republic of Ireland
tel (01) 8321477 *fax* (01) 8321430
Directors Philip MacDermott (managing), Kieran Devlin
Fiction, public interest, women's interest, history, politics, current affairs. Imprints: Business Poolbeg, Children's Poolbeg, Beachwood. Founded 1976.

Prentice Hall Europe/Academic*
Campus 400, Maylands Avenue, Hemel Hempstead, Herts. HP2 7EZ
tel (01442) 881900 *fax* (01442) 882099
Acting President John Isley (President, Simon & Schuster Europe), *Sales Director* Simon Allen, *Editorial Director* Clare Grist, *Marketing Director* Jane Mackarell, *Rights & Permissions* Jean Spurr
Business and economics, computer science, engineering, physics, mathematics, politics, sociology and social policy, psychology, health studies, literature, trade computing. Imprints: Allyn & Bacon, Appleton & Lange, Ellis Horwood, Prentice Hall, Prentice Hall Europe, Prentice Hall/Harvester Wheatsheaf, Woodhead-Faulkner.

Prentice Hall Europe/CPTR*
(Computer Professional Trade Reference)
Campus 400, Maylands Avenue, Hemel Hempstead, Herts. HP2 7EZ
tel (01442) 881900 *fax* (01442) 882099
President Jim Donohue, *Director of Marketing* Alan Bower, *Trade Sales Manager* Neil Broomfield, *Trade Editor* Jason Dunne
Divisions: Macmillan Computer Publishing (USA), Prentice Hall PTR (Professional Technical Reference),

Jossey-Bass Publishers, ICSA Publishing, New York Institute of Finance, Prentice Hall Direct, Prentice Hall Europe.

Prion Books
(formerly Multimedia Books Ltd)
Unit L, 32-34 Gordon House Road,
London NW5 1LP
tel 0171-482 4248 *fax* 0171-482 4203
e-mail books@prion.co.uk
Managing Director Barry Winkleman

Food and drink, travel guides, humour, popular culture, psychology and health. Founded 1986.

Prism Press
The Thatched Cottage, Partway Lane, Hazelbury Bryan, Sturminster Newton, Dorset DT10 2DP
tel (01258) 817164 *fax* (01258) 817635
Directors Julian King, Diana King

Non-fiction, including health, food, psychology, politics, ecology. Synopses and ideas welcome, but no complete MSS. Founded 1974.

Profile Books
62 Queen Anne Street, London W1M 9LA
tel 0171-486 6010 *fax* 0171-486 6012
e-mail profilebooks@compuserve.com
Publisher and Managing Director Andrew Franklin, *Editorial Director* Stephen Brough

Non-fiction: current affairs, politics, social sciences, history, psychology, business and management; *The Economist* books. No unsolicited MSS; phone or send preliminary letter. Founded 1996.

PSI
(Policy Studies Institute)
100 Park Village East, London NW1 3SR
tel 0171-468 0468 *fax* 0171-388 0914
e-mail postmaster@psi.org.uk
Director Pamela Meadows, *Head of Publications* Jo O'Driscoll

Economic, industrial and social policy, political institutions, social sciences, arts and cultural industries.

Puffin – see Penguin Books Ltd*

Putnam Aeronautical Books – see Brassey's (UK) Ltd

Quadrille Publishing
3rd Floor, 9 Irving Street, London WC2H 7AT
tel 0171-839 7117 *fax* 0171-839 7118
Directors Alison Cathie (managing), Anne Furniss (publishing), Jane O'Shea (editorial), Mary Evans (art), Marlis Ironmonger (commercial), Vincent Smith (production)

Illustrated non-fiction: cookery, craft, health and medical, gardening and interiors. Founded 1994.

Quantum – see W. Foulsham & Co. Ltd

Quartet Books Ltd
27 Goodge Street, London W1P 2LD
tel 0171-636 3992 *fax* 0171-637 1866
e-mail quartetbooks@easynet.co.uk
Chairman N.I. Attallah, *Managing Director* Jeremy Beale

General fiction and non-fiction, foreign literature in translation, classical music, jazz, contemporary music, biography. Member of the Namara Group. Founded 1972.

Queen Anne Press
Windmill Cottage, Mackerye End, Harpenden, Herts. AL5 5DR
tel (01582) 715866 *fax* (01582) 715121
e-mail queenanne@lenqap.demon.co.uk
Directors K.A.A. Stephenson, R.H. Stephenson

Sport and leisure activities. No unsolicited MSS. Division of Lennard Associates Ltd.

Quiller Press Ltd
46 Lillie Road, London SW6 1TN
tel 0171-499 6529 *fax* 0171-381 8941
e-mail quiller@premier.services.demon.co.uk
Directors J.J. Greenwood, A.E. Carlile

Publishers of sponsored books: guidebooks, history, industry, humour, architecture, cookery, collectables, country sports.

Radcliffe Medical Press Ltd
18 Marcham Road, Abingdon, Oxon OX14 1AA
tel (01235) 528820 *fax* (01235) 528830
e-mail medical@radpress.win.uk.net
Directors Andrew Bax (managing), Gill Nineham (editorial), Margaret McKeown (financial), *Head of Marketing* Gregory Moxon

Medicine: management in primary care; management in secondary care; health service development; palliative and cancer care; clinical management. Dentistry: practice management. Pharmacy. Founded 1987.

Ragged Bears Ltd
Ragged Appleshaw, Andover, Hants SP11 9HX
tel (01264) 772269 *fax* (01264) 772391
e-mail book@ragged-bears.co.uk
web site http://www.ragged-bears.co.uk
Managing Director Mrs C. Shirley, *Rights and Editorial Director* Henrietta Stickland

Publisher and distributor of children's fiction and non-fiction. Imprints: Ragged Bears, Spindlewood. Founded 1984.

Random House UK Ltd*

20 Vauxhall Bridge Road, London SW1V 2SA
tel 0171-840 8400 *fax* 0171-233 6058
Chairman and Chief Executive Gail Rebuck,
Directors Simon Master (deputy chairman),
Simon King (publishing), Piet Snyman
(chairman, Children's Division), Amelia Thorpe
(managing, Ebury Press), Mike Broderick (UK
sales), Anthony McConnell (finance), David
Pemberton (operations), Susan Sandon (publicity
and marketing), Katherine Mulders (rights),
Stephen Esson (production), Joanna Page
(personnel)

Arrow Books Ltd (imprint)

tel 0171-973 9700 *fax* 0171-233 6127
Directors Simon King (managing), Andy
McKillop (publishing), Kate Farquhar-Thomson
(publicity)

Fiction, non-fiction, science fiction, fantasy, crime, humour, film tie-ins.

Barrie & Jenkins (imprint of Ebury Press)

tel 0171-973 9710/9670 *fax* 0171-233 6057
Managing Director Julian Shuckburgh

Art, antiques and collecting, architecture, decorative and applied arts

Jonathan Cape (imprint)

tel 0171-973 9730 *fax* 0171-233 6117
Directors Dan Franklin, Robin Robertson, Tom
Maschler, Tony Colwell, Gail Lynch (publicity)

Archaeology, biography and memoirs, current affairs, drama, economics, fiction, history, philosophy, poetry, sociology, travel. Imprint: **Bodley Head**.

Century (imprint)

tel 0171-973 9680 *fax* 0171-233 6127
Directors Simon King (managing), Kate Parkin
(publishing), Mark Booth, Oliver Johnson, Katie
White (publicity)

Fiction, classics, romance, biography, autobiography, general non-fiction, film tie-ins; *Century Business Books*.

Chatto & Windus (imprint)

tel 0171-973 9740 *fax* 0171-233 6123
Directors Jonathan Burnham (publishing)

Art, belles-lettres, biography and memoirs, cookery, crime/thrillers, current affairs, drama, essays, fiction, history, illustrated books, poetry, politics, psychoanalysis, translations, travel, hardbacks and paperbacks. No unsolicited MSS. Imprint: Hogarth Press.

Condé Nast Books (imprint of Ebury Press)

Editorial Director Julian Shuckburgh

Highly illustrated home interest books, fashion and beauty, food.

Ebury Press Special Books (division)

Cookery, health, beauty, photography, crafts, biography, antiques, hobbies, gardening, natural history, DIY, diaries, stationery. Publishes books from *Good Housekeeping, Cosmopolitan, Harpers & Queen, She, Esquire, Country Living, House Beautiful* magazines.

Fodor Guides (imprint of Ebury Press)

Worldwide annual travel guides.

William Heinemann (imprint)

tel 0171-840 8517
Publishing Director Maria Rejt

Fiction and general non-fiction. No unsolicited MSS and synopses considered.

Hutchinson (imprint)

tel 0171-973 9680 *fax* 0171-233 6129
Directors Simon King (managing), Sue Freestone
(publishing), Anthony Whittome, Paul Sidey
(editorial), Alex Hippisley-Cox (publicity)

Belles-lettres, biography, memoirs, thrillers, crime, current affairs, general history, politics, translations, travel, film tie-ins.

Legend (imprint of Arrow Books Ltd)

Science fiction and fantasy.

Methuen (imprint)

tel 0171-840 8629
Publishing Director Michael Earle

Drama, humour, fiction, music, arts, plays. No unsolicited MSS or synopses considered.

Optima – see Vermilion

Stanley Paul (imprint of Ebury Press)

tel 0171-973 9690 *fax* 0171-233 6057
Publishing Director Julian Shuckburgh

Sport, games, hobbies and handicrafts, sporting biographies, practical books on breeding, care, training and general management of dogs.

Pimlico (imprint)

tel 0171-973 9730 *fax* 0171-828 7213
Publishing Director Will Sulkin

History, biography, literature.

Random House Audio Books

tel 0171-973 9700

Random House Children's Books (division)

tel 0171-973 9750
Directors Piet Snyman (chairman), Ian Hudson
(managing), Caroline Roberts (publishing,
Hutchinson), Tom Maschler (publishing,
Jonathan Cape), Pilar Jenkins (publishing, Red
Fox), Linda Summers (rights)

Publishes under **Bodley Head Children's**, **Jonathan Cape Children's Books**, **Hutchinson Children's**, **Julia MacRae Books**, **Red Fox**, **Tellastory**. Picture books, fiction, poetry, music, non-fiction, audio cassettes.

Rider (imprint of **Ebury Press**)
Publishing Director Fiona MacIntyre, *Editorial Consultant* Judith Kendra

Buddhism, religion and philosophy, psychology, ecology, health and healing, mysticism, meditation and yoga.

Random House New Media
fax 0171-233 6129

Interactive multimedia, education and entertainment.

Secker and Warburg (imprint)
tel 0171-840 8649
Directors Geoff Mulligan (editorial), Kate Harbinson (publicity)

Literary fiction, general non-fiction. No unsolicited MSS/synopses.

Sinclair-Stevenson (imprint)
tel 0171-840 8643
Editorial Director Penny Hoare, *Publicity Manager* Jemima Burrill

Fiction and general non-fiction. No unsolicited MSS or synopses considered.

Studio (imprint of **Ebury Press**)
Art and design, history, cartography, Victoriana and nostalgia, music, mythology, military and aviation.

Studio Editions (imprint of **Ebury Press**)
Social stationery.

Vermilion (imprint of **Ebury Press**)
Editorial Director Fiona MacIntyre, *Senior Editor* Sarah Sutton

Paperback practical self-help, health, fitness, guidebooks, practical parenting.

Vintage (imprint)
Publisher Caroline Michel, *Associate Publishing Director* Will Sulkin

Quality fiction and non-fiction.

Raphael's – see W. Foulsham & Co. Ltd

Rapid Science – see Thomson Science & Professional*

The Reader's Digest Association Ltd*
11 Westferry Circus, Canary Wharf, London E14 4HE
tel 0171-715 8000 *fax* 0171-715 8181
Managing Director S.N. McRae, *Editorial Directors* R.G. Twisk (magazine editor), Cortina Butler (general books)

Monthly magazine, condensed and series books; also DIY, car maintenance, gardening, medical, handicrafts, law, touring guides, encyclopedias, dictionaries, nature, folklore, atlases, cookery, music; videos; merchandise catalogue.

Reader's Digest Children's Books
King's Court, Parsonage Lane, Bath BA1 1ER
tel (01225) 463401 *fax* (01225) 460942

Publishers of mass market novelty and children's information books. A division of **Victoria House Publishing Ltd** (fully owned subsidiary of Reader's Digest Association Inc.). Founded 1996.

Reaktion Books
11 Rathbone Place, London W1P 1DE
tel 0171-580 9928 *fax* 0171-580 9935
e-mail 101473@compuserve.com
General Editor Michael R. Leaman

Art history, design, architecture, history, cultural studies, Asian studies, travel and photography. Founded 1985.

Rebel Inc. – see Canongate Books Ltd*

Red Fox – see Random House UK Ltd*

Reed Books
Michelin House, 81 Fulham Road, London SW3 6RB
tel 0171-581 9393 *fax* 0171-225 9424
e-mail name@reedbooks.co.uk
Chief Executive John Holloran, *Executive Directors* Derek Freeman, Peter Murphy, John Philbin, Ross Clayton

Consumer book publishing subsidiary of Reed Elsevier (UK) Ltd.

Bounty (imprint)
fax 0171-225 9031
Publishing Director Laura Bamford

Promotional publishing, children's and adult's books.

Brimax Books (imprint)
Units 4-5, Studland Park Industrial Estate, Exning Road, Newmarket, Suffolk CB8 7AU
tel (01638) 664611 *fax* (01638) 665220
Managing Director Patricia Gillette

Mass market picture books for children.

Conran Octopus (imprint)
37 Shelton Street, London WC2H 9HN
tel 0171-240 6961 *fax* 0171-836 9951
Publishing Director John Wallace

Quality illustrated books, particularly lifestyle, cookery, gardening.

Hamlyn (imprint)
fax 0171-225 9458
Publishing Director Laura Bamford

Popular illustrated non-fiction, particularly cookery, gardening, craft, sport, film tie-ins, rock'n'roll.

Hamlyn Children's Non-Fiction (imprint)
fax 0171-225 9731
Managing Director Jane Winterbotham

Illustrated non-fiction and reference books for children.

Heinemann Young Books (imprint)
fax 0171-225 9731
Managing Director Jane Winterbotham

Books for children including quality picture books, novels, anthologies.

Mammoth (imprint)
fax 0171-225 9731
Managing Director Jane Winterbotham

Children's paperbacks, licensed characters and tie-ins.

Methuen Children's Books (imprint)
fax 0171-225 9731
Managing Director Jane Winterbotham

Books for children including picture books and fiction for babies to early teens.

Millers (imprint)
The Cellars, High Street, Tenterden, Kent TN30 6DN
tel (01580) 766411 *fax* (01580) 766100
Publishing Director Jane Aspden

Quality illustrated books on antiques and collectibles.

Mitchell Beazley (imprint)
fax 0171-225 9458
Publishing Director Jane Aspden

Quality illustrated books, particularly antiques, gardening, craft and interiors, wine.

Osprey (imprint)
fax 0171-225 9458
Managing Director Jonathan Parker

Militaria, aviation, automotive.

Philips (imprint)
fax 0171-225 9458
Publishing Director John Gaisford

Atlases, maps, astronomy, encyclopaedias, globes.

Pitkin Guides (imprint)
Healey House, Dene Road, Andover, Hants SP10 2AA
tel (01264) 334303 *fax* (01264) 334110
Managing Director Ian Corsie

Illustrated souvenir guides.

William Reed Directories
Broadfield Park, Crawley, West Sussex RH11 9RT
tel (01293) 613400 *fax* (01293) 610322
e-mail online@foodanddrink.co.uk
web site www.foodanddrink.co.uk
Managing Director Maria Atkin, *Editorial Manager* Helen Turner

Publishers of leading business-to-business directories and reports, including *The Grocer Marketing Directory* and *The Grocer Food & Drink Directory*.

Reed Educational and Professional Publishing Ltd
Halley Court, Jordan Hill, Oxford OX2 8EJ
tel (01865) 311366 *fax* (01865) 314641
Chief Executive William Shepherd

Architectural Press (imprint)
Editorial Director Peter Dixon, *Publisher* Neil Warnock-Smith

Architecture, the environment, planning, townscape, building technology; general.

Butterworth Heinemann UK (imprint)
Linacre House, Jordan Hill, Oxford OX2 8EJ
tel (01865) 311366 *fax* (01865) 310898
Managing Director Philip Shaw

Books and electronic products across business, technical, medical and open learning fields for students and professionals.

Focal Press (imprint)
fax (01865) 314572
Publishing Director Peter Dixon, *Senior Commissioning Editor* Margaret Riley

Professional, technical and academic books on photography, broadcasting, film, television, radio, audiovisual and communication media.

Ginn & Co. (imprint)
Prebendal House, Parson's Fee, Aylesbury, Bucks. HP20 2QY
tel (01296) 394442 *fax* (01296) 393433
Managing Director Nigel Hall

Textbook/other educational resources for primary and secondary schools.

Heinemann Educational (imprint)
fax (01865) 314140
Managing Director Bob Osborne

Textbooks/literature/other educational resources for all levels.

Heinemann English Language Teaching (imprint)
fax (01865) 314193
Managing Director Mike Esplon

English language teaching books and materials.

See also **Butterworth & Co. (Publishers) Ltd.**

Reed Information Services
(part of Reed Business Information)
Windsor Court, East Grinstead House,
East Grinstead, West Sussex RH19 1XA
tel (01342) 326972 *fax* (01342) 335612
e-mail ssmart@reedinfo.co.uk
web site http://www.reedinfo.co.uk
Chief Executive Keith Jones, *Joint Managing Directors* John Minch and Charles Halpin

Directories and reference books covering professional and industrial sectors, including *Kompass*, *Kelly's*, *Dial* and *The Bankers' Almanac*. Part of Reed Elsevier plc. Founded 1983.

Religious and Moral Education Press (RMEP) – see Chansitor Publications Ltd

Rider – see Random House UK Ltd*

Rivelin Grapheme Press
Merlin House, Church Street, Hungerford,
Berks. RG17 0JG
tel (01488) 684645 *fax* (01488) 683018
Director Snowdon Barnett

Poetry. No unsolicited MSS. Founded 1984.

Rivers Oram Press
144 Hemingford Road, London N1 1DE
tel 0171-607 0823 *fax* 0171-609 2776
Directors Elizabeth Rivers Fidlon (managing),
Anthony Harris

Non-ficton: social and political science, current affairs, social history, gender studies, sexual politics, cultural studies and photography. Founded 1991.

Robinson Publishing Ltd
7 Kensington Church Court, London W8 4SP
tel 0171-938 3830 *fax* 0171-938 4214
e-mail 100560.3511 @compuserve.com
Publisher Nicholas Robinson

Fiction: anthologies; general non-fiction includes health, self-help, psychology, true crime, puzzles, military history. Children's: anthologies, fiction, humour, games. Do not send MSS; letters/synopses only. No unsolicited fiction. Founded 1983.

Scarlet (imprint)
Editor Sue Curran

Women's fiction: 100,000-word MSS with a strong central romance. Contemporary (present day) setting. Will look at Regency and medical romances, provided they are sensuous in tone. Guidelines are available.

Robson Books
Bolsover House, 5-6 Clipstone Street,
London W1P 8LE
tel 0171-323 1223/637 5937 *fax* 0171-636 0798
Managing Director Jeremy Robson

General, biography, music, humour, sport. Founded 1973.

George Ronald
46 High Street, Kidlington, Oxon OX5 2DN
tel (01865) 841515 *fax* (01865) 841230
e-mail sales@grpubl.demon.co.uk
Managers W. Momen, E. Leith

Religion, specialising in the Baha'i Faith. Founded 1939.

Barry Rose Law Publishers Ltd
Little London, Chichester, West Sussex PO19 1PG
tel (01243) 775552/779174 *fax* (01243) 779278
e-mail jp@barry-rose-law.co.uk

Law, local government, police, legal history. Founded 1972.

Rosendale Press Ltd
Premier House, 10 Greycoat Place,
London SW1P 1SB
tel 0171-222 8866 *fax* 0171-799 1416
Chairman Timothy S. Green, *Editorial Director* Maureen P. Green

Food and drink, gourmet guides/travel, business and investment, health and lifestyle. Founded 1987.

Round Hall Sweet & Maxwell
Brehon House, 4 Upper Ormond Quay, Dublin 7,
Republic of Ireland
tel (01) 8730101 *fax* (01) 8720078
Chairman Anthony Kinahan, *Editorial Manager* Michael Divney

Law.

Roundhouse Publishing Ltd
PO Box 140, Oxford OX2 7FF
tel (01865) 512682 *fax* (01865) 559594
e-mail 100637.3571@compuserve.com
Publisher Alan T. Goodworth

Film, cinema, and performing arts; reference books. No unsolicited MSS. Founded 1991.

Routledge*
11 New Fetter Lane, London EC4P 4EE
tel 0171-583 9855 *fax* 0171-842 2298
Directors David Hill (managing), Peter Sowden (publishing), David Tebbutt (finance)

Addiction, anthropology, archaeology, Asian studies, business, classical studies,

counselling, criminology, development and environment, dictionaries, economics, education, geography, health, history, Japanese studies, library science, language, linguistics, literary criticism, media and culture, nursing, performance studies, philosophy, politics, psychiatry, psychology, reference, social administration, social studies/sociology, women's studies. Routledge is an independent company.

Royal National Institute for the Blind

PO Box 173, Peterborough, Cambs. PE2 6WS
tel (0345) 023153 *fax* (01733) 371555
textphone (0345) 585 691

Magazines and books for blind and partially sighted people, to support daily living, leisure, learning and employment reading needs. Produced in braille, audio, large/legible print, disk and Moon. For complete list of magazines see page 126. Founded 1868.

Ryland Peters & Small

Cavendish House, 51-55 Mortimer Street, London W1N 7TD
tel 0171-436 9090 *fax* 0171-436 9790
e-mail louise.sherwin-stark@rps.co.uk
Directors David Peters (managing), Anne Ryland (publishing), Jacqui Small (art)

Highly illustrated books on cookery, craft, interiors and gardening. Founded 1995.

Sage Publications Ltd*

6 Bonhill Street, London EC2A 4PU
tel 0171-374 0645 *fax* 0171-374 8741
e-mail info@sagepub.co.uk
web site http://www.sagepub.co.uk
Directors Stephen Barr (managing), Lynn Adams, Ian Eastment, Mike Birch, Matt Jackson, Ziyad Marar, David F. McCune (USA), Sara Miller McCune (USA)

Social sciences, behavioural sciences, humanities, software. Founded 1971.

The Saint Andrew Press*

121 George Street, Edinburgh EH2 4YN
tel 0131-225 5722 *fax* 0131-220 3113
Publishing Manager Lesley A. Taylor

Theology and religion, church and local history. Section of Church of Scotland Board of Communication.

St Pauls

St Pauls (Publishing Sector), Morpeth Terrace, London SW1P 1EP
tel 0171-828 5582 *fax* 0171-828 3329

Theology, ethics, spirituality, biography, education, general books of Roman Catholic and Christian interest. Founded 1948.

St Paul's Bibliographies

West End House, 1 Step Terrace, Winchester, Hants SO22 5BW
tel (01962) 860524 *fax* (01962) 842409
e-mail stpaul-b@winterb.demon.co.uk
Managing Director Robert S. Cross

Bibliography and scholarly works on the history of the Book and the book trade. Founded 1974.

Salamander Books Ltd

129-137 York Way, London N7 9LG
tel 0171-267 4447 *fax* 0171-267 5112
Directors Jef Proost (chairman), David Spence (managing), Richard Collins (editorial), Vincent Proost (commercial), Colin Gower (sales)

Cookery, crafts, children's, military, natural history, music, gardening, hobbies, pets, transport, sports. Imprint: Vega. Founded 1973.

Salvationist Publishing and Supplies Ltd

117-121 Judd Street, London WC1H 9NN
tel 0171-387 1656 *fax* 0171-383 3420
Managing Director Lt.-Col. Michael Williams

Devotional books, theology, biography, worldwide Christian and social service, children's books, music.

W.B. Saunders Co. Ltd – see Harcourt Brace & Co. Ltd*

SAUS Publications – see The Policy Press

S.B. Publications

c/o 19 Grove Road, Seaford, East Sussex BN25 1TP
tel (01323) 893498. *Proprietor* Stephen Benz

Local history (illustrated by postcards/old photographs), local themes (e.g. walking books, guides), maritime history, transport, specific themes. Founded 1987.

Scala – see Philip Wilson Publishers Ltd

Scarlet – see Robinson Publishing Ltd

Scarlet Press

5 Montague Road, London E8 2HN
tel 0171-241 3702 *fax* 0171-275 0031
Editorial Director Avis Lewallen

Women's studies, lesbian, cultural studies, history, politics, health. Founded 1990.

Sceptre – see Hodder Headline plc

Schofield & Sims Ltd
Dogley Mill, Fenay Bridge, Huddersfield HD8 0NQ
tel (01484) 607080 *fax* (01484) 606815
e-mail 100641.252@compuserve.com
Directors John S. Nesbitt (chairman), J. Stephen
Platts (managing), J. Brierley (sales), M.S. Nesbitt
Educational: infants, primary, secondary,
children's books and posters. Founded
1901.

Scholastic Children's Books*
Commonwealth House, 1-19 New Oxford Street,
London WC1A 1NU
tel 0171-421 9000 *fax* 0171-421 9001
Publishing Director David Fickling, *Character
and Preschool Publisher* Penny Morris
Imprint of **Scholastic Ltd**.

Adlib (imprint)
Publishing Director David Fickling
Quality teenage fiction.

André Deutsch Children's Books (imprint)
Publishing Director David Fickling
Children's fiction and non-fiction.

Hippo (imprint)
Editorial Director, Fiction Editor Anne Finnis
Children's paperbacks – fiction and non-
fiction. No unsolicited MSS.

Point (imprint)
Commissioning Editor Julia Moffatt
Fiction for 11+: horror, crime, romance,
fantasy, science fiction.

Scholastic Ltd*
Villiers House, Clarendon Avenue,
Leamington Spa, Warks. CV32 5PR
tel (01926) 887799 *fax* (01926) 883331
London office Commonwealth House,
1-19 New Oxford Street, London WC1A 1NU
tel 0171-421 9000 *fax* 0171-421 9001
Directors D.M.R. Kewley (managing), M.R.
Robinson (USA), R.M. Spaulding (USA), D.J.
Walsh (USA)

Children's Division
Publishing Director David Fickling
See **Scholastic Children's Books***

Direct Marketing
Managing Director, Book Fair Division Will
Oldham, *Managing Director, School Book Clubs
and Continuities* Victoria Birkett, *Managing
Director, Consumer Book Clubs and Party Plan*
David Teale, *Sales and Marketing Director* Gavin
Lang
Children's book clubs and school book
fairs.

Educational Division
Publishing Director Anne Peel

Publishers of books for teachers (*Bright
Ideas* and other series), primary classroom resources and magazines for teachers (*Child Education, Junior Education*
and others). Founded 1964.

Science Museum Publications
Science Museum, Exhibition Road,
London SW7 2DD
tel 0171-938 8211 *fax* 0171-938 8169
e-mail g.day@ic.ac.uk
Publications Officer Giskin Day
History of science and technology, public
understanding of science, including
books for children.

SCM Press Ltd*
9-17 St Albans Place, London N1 0NX
tel 0171-359 8033 *fax* 0171-359 0049
Managing Director and Editor John Bowden,
Directors Margaret Lydamore (associate editor
and company secretary), Roger Pygram
(finance)
Theological books with special emphasis
on biblical, philosophical and modern
theology; books on sociology of religion
and religious aspects of current issues.
Founded 1929.

Scottish Academic Press
56 Hanover Street, Edinburgh EH2 2DX
tel 0131-225 7483 *fax* 0131-225 7662
Editor Dr Douglas Grant
All types of academic books and books of
Scottish interest. Founded 1969.

Scottish Cultural Press*
Unit 14, Leith Walk Business Centre,
130 Leith Walk, Edinburgh EH6 5DT
tel 0131-555 5950 *fax* 0131-555 5018
e-mail scp@sol.co.uk
web site http://www.taynet.co.uk/users/scp
Director Jill Dick
Literature, poetry, history, archaeology,
biography and environmental history.
Founded 1992.

Scottish Children's Press (imprint)
Children's Administrator Avril Gray
Scottish fiction, Scottish non-fiction and
Scots language, children's writing.

The Scout Association
Baden-Powell House, Queen's Gate,
London SW7 5JS
tel 0171-584 7030 *fax* 0171-590 5103
General Editor David Easton
Technical books dealing with all subjects
relevant to Scouting and monthly journal
Scouting.

Scripture Union*

207-209 Queensway, Bletchley, Milton Keynes, Bucks. MK2 2EB
tel (01908) 856000 *fax* (01908) 856111
e-mail postmaster@scriptureunion.org.uk

Christian books and Bible reading materials for people of all ages; educational and worship resources for churches; children's fiction and non-fiction; adult non-fiction. Founded 1867.

Seafarer Books – see Merlin Press Ltd

Search Press Ltd

Wellwood, North Farm Road, Tunbridge Wells, Kent TN2 3DR
tel (01892) 510850 *fax* (01892) 515903
Directors Rosalind Dale (editorial), Martin de la Bedoyere, The Hon. G.E. Noel, Ruth B. Saunders

Arts, crafts, leisure, organic gardening. Founded 1962.

Secker and Warburg – see Random House UK Ltd*

Seren Books

First Floor, 2 Wyndham Street, Bridgend CF31 1EF
tel/fax (01656) 767834
Director Mick Felton

Poetry, fiction, drama, history, film, literary criticism, biography, art – mostly with relevance to Wales. Founded 1981.

Serif

47 Strahan Road, London E3 5DA
tel/fax 0181-981 3990
e-mail threshold.demon.co.uk
Editorial Director Stephen Hayward

Politics, history, Irish studies, cookery. No unsolicited MSS. Founded 1993.

Serpent's Tail

4 Blackstock Mews, London N4 2BT
tel 0171-354 1949 *fax* 0171-704 6467
e-mail info@serpentstail.com
Director Peter Ayrton

Modern fiction in paperback: literary and experimental work, and work in translation. Approach with query letter please; do not send complete MSS. Sae essential as is familiarity with list. Founded 1986.

Settle Press

10 Boyne Terrace Mews, London W11 3LR
tel 0171-243 0695
Directors D. Settle (managing), M. Carter (editorial)

Travel guidebooks. Founded 1983.

Severn House Publishers

9-15 High Street, Sutton, Surrey SM1 1DF
tel 0181-770 3930 *fax* 0181-770 3850
Chairman Edwin Buckhalter, *Managing Editor* Sara Short

Adult fiction: romances, thrillers, detective, adventure, war, science fiction; film and TV tie-ins. No unsolicited MSS.

Shakespeare Head Press – see Blackwell Publishers*

Sheed & Ward Ltd

14 Coopers Row, London EC3N 2BH
tel 0171-702 9799 *fax* 0171-702 3583
Directors M.T. Redfern, K.G. Darke, A.M. Redfern

Publishers of books, mostly by Catholics. History, philosophy, theology, catechetics, scripture and religion. Founded 1926.

Sheldon Press – see Society for Promoting Christian Knowledge*

Sheldrake Press

188 Cavendish Road, London SW12 0DA
tel 0181-675 1767 *fax* 0181-675 7736
Publisher J.S. Rigge

History, travel, architecture, cookery, music; stationery. Founded 1979.

Shepheard-Walwyn (Publishers) Ltd

Suite 34, 26 Charing Cross Road, London WC2H 0DH
tel 0171-240 5992 *fax* 0171-379 5770
Directors A.R.A. Werner, M.M. Werner

History, political economy, philosophy; illustrated gift books, some originated in calligraphy; Scottish interest. Founded 1971.

John Sherratt & Son Ltd

Hotspur House, 2 Gloucester Street, Manchester M1 5QR
tel 0161-236 9963 *fax* 0161-236 2026
Managing Director P.A. Westaway

Educational (primary, secondary, technical, university), medical, practical handbooks, collectors' books.

Shire Publications Ltd

Cromwell House, Church Street, Princes Risborough, Bucks. HP27 9AA
tel (01844) 344301 *fax* (01844) 347080
Director J.W. Rotheroe

Discovering paperbacks, Shire Albums, Shire Archaeology, Shire Natural History, Shire Ethnography, Shire Egyptology, Shire Garden History. Founded 1966.

Sidgwick & Jackson – see Macmillan
Publishers Ltd*

Sigma Press
1 South Oak Lane, Wilmslow,
Cheshire SK9 6AR
tel (01625) 531035 *fax* (01625) 536800
e-mail sigma.press@zetnet.co.uk
web site http://www.sigmapress.co.uk
Partners Graham Beech, Diana Beech
Leisure (country walking, cycling,
regional heritage, sport, cookery, folklore); popular science. Founded 1979.

Silhouette – see Harlequin Mills &
Boon Ltd*

Simon & Schuster*
West Garden Place, Kendal Street,
London W2 2AQ
tel 0171-316 1900 *fax* 0171-402 0639
Directors Nick Webb (managing), Jo Frank
(editorial, fiction), Martin Fletcher (editorial,
mass-market fiction and Touchstone), Diane
Spivey (rights), Helen Gummer (editorial, non-
fiction), Bob Kelly (international sales and
marketing)
Fiction; non-fiction: reference, music,
travel, mass-market paperbacks. Founded
1986.
Pocket Books (imprint)
Mass-market fiction and non-fiction
paperbacks.
Touchstone (imprint)
Quality upmarket fiction and non-fiction
paperbacks.

Sinclair-Stevenson – see Random
House UK Ltd*

Skoob Books Ltd
76A Oldfield Road, London N16 0RS
tel/fax 0171-275 9811
e-mail books@skoob.demon.co.uk
Director I.K. Ong, *Editorial* M. Lovell
Literary guides, cultural studies, esoteri-
ca/occult, oriental literature. Unsolicited
summaries and samples with sae only;
no MSS. Founded 1979.

Slow Dancer Press
Flat 2, 59 Parliament Hill, London NW3 2TB
Director John Harvey
Poetry and short prose, especially associated with jazz. Study writings published by Slow Dancer first; send letter
before submitting material. Founded
1977.

Smith Gryphon Ltd
12 Bridge Wharf, 156 Caledonian Road,
London N1 9UU
tel 0171-278 2444 *fax* 0171-833 5680
Chairman and Managing Director Robert Smith
Biography, autobiography, rock music,
cinema, true crime, topical issues,
finance and business, wine, food and
cookery, health and fitness, illustrated
books. Founded 1990.

Colin Smythe Ltd*
PO Box 6, Gerrards Cross, Bucks. SL9 8XA
tel (01753) 886000 *fax* (01753) 886469
Directors Colin Smythe (managing and editorial),
Peter Bander van Duren, A. Norman Jeffares, Ann
Saddlemyer, Leslie Hayward
Biography, phaleristics, literary criticism,
folklore, Irish interest and Anglo-Irish lit-
erature. Founded 1966.

**Society for Promoting Christian
Knowledge***
Holy Trinity Church, Marylebone Road,
London NW1 4DU
tel 0171-387 5282 *fax* 0171-388 2352
e-mail publishing@spck.co.uk
Director of Publishing Simon Kingston
Founded 1698.
Sheldon Press (imprint)
Editorial Director Joanna Moriarty
Popular medicine, health, self-help, psy-
chology, business.
SPCK (imprint)
Editorial Director Joanna Moriarty
Theology and academic, liturgy, prayer,
spirituality, biblical studies, educational
resources, mission, gospel and culture.
Triangle (imprint)
Editorial Director Joanna Moriarty
Popular Christian paperbacks.

Sotheby's Publications – see Philip
Wilson Publishers Ltd

Souvenir Press Ltd
43 Great Russell Street, London WC1B 3PA
tel 0171-580 9307-8 and 637 5711/2/3
fax 0171-580 5064
Managing Director Ernest Hecht BSc(Econ), BCom,
Executive Director Jeanne Manchee
Archaeology, biography and memoirs,
educational (secondary, technical), fiction,
general, humour, practical handbooks,
psychiatry, psychology, sociology, sports,
games and hobbies, travel, supernatural,
parapsychology, illustrated books.

SPCK – see **Society for Promoting Christian Knowledge***

Neville Spearman Publishers – see **The C.W. Daniel Company Ltd**

Specialist Crafts Ltd
(formerly Dryad)
PO Box 247, Leicester LE1 9QS
tel (0116) 251 0405 *fax* (0116) 251 5015
e-mail post@speccrafts.demon.co.uk
web site www.speccrafts.demon.co.uk
Joint Managing Director P.A. Crick

'How to' booklets on various art and craft skills. *Specialist Crafts 500* series full colour craft booklets and patterns. Suppliers of over 8000 art and craft items.

Spellmount Ltd*
The Old Rectory, Staplehurst,
Kent TN12 0AZ
tel (01580) 893730 *fax* (01580) 893731
Proprietor Jamie A.G. Wilson

Ancient, 15th-20th century history/military history. Send sae with submissions please. Founded 1984.

Spindlewood – see **Ragged Bears Ltd**

Spon – see **Thomson Science & Professional***

Springboard Fiction – see **Yorkshire Art Circus**

Springer-Verlag London Ltd*
Sweetapple House, Catteshall Road, Godalming, Surrey GU7 3DJ
tel (01483) 418800 *fax* (01483) 415151
e-mail postmaster@svl.co.uk
web site http://www.springer.co.uk
Managing Director John Watson, *Executive Directors* C. Michaletz, D. Goetz

Medicine, computing, engineering, astronomy, mathematics. Founded 1972.

Stacey International
128 Kensington Church Street,
London W8 4BH
tel 0171-221 7166 *fax* 0171-792 9288
e-mail 106463.424@compuserve.com
Directors Tom Stacey (managing), C.S. Stacey, *Publishing Executive* Kitty Carruthers

Illustrated non-fiction, encyclopedic books on regions and countries, Islamic and Arab subjects, world affairs, art, travel, belles-lettres. Founded 1974.

Stainer & Bell Ltd
PO Box 110, Victoria House, 23 Gruneisen Road,
London N3 1DZ
tel 0181-343 3303 *fax* 0181-343 3024
e-mail post@stainer.demon.co.uk
Directors Bernard Braley ACIS (chairman), Keith Wakefield (joint managing), Carol Wakefield (joint managing and secretary), Joan Braley, John Hosier CBE, Antony Kearns

Books on music, religious communication. Founded 1907.

Harold Starke Publishers Ltd*
Pixey Green, Stradbroke, Eye, Suffolk IP21 5NG
tel (01379) 388334 *fax* (01379) 388335
203 Bunyan Court, Barbican, London EC2Y 8DH
tel 0171-588 5195
Directors Harold K. Starke, Naomi Galinski (editorial)

Specialist, scientific, medical, reference.

The Stationery Office/National Publishing*
Head Office St Crispins, Duke Street,
Norwich NR3 1PD
tel (01003) 095532 *fax* (01003) 695317
Distribution and Order Point The Stationery Office Publication Centre, PO Box 276,
London SW8 5DT
tel 0171-873 0011
Chief Executive, National Publishing Fred Perkins, *Managing Director, Publishing* Robert McKay, *Business Development Director* Kevan Lawton

Archaeology, architecture, art, business, current affairs, directories and guidebooks, educational (primary, secondary, technical, university), general, heritage, history, naval and military, medical, pharmaceutical, professional, practical handbooks, reference, science, sociology, year books.

Stationery Office (Ireland) – see **Government Supplies Agency**

Patrick Stephens Ltd – see **Haynes Publishing**

Sterling Publishing Group plc
PO Box 839, 86-88 Edgware Road,
London W2 2YW
tel 0171-258 0066 *fax* 0171-723 5766
Chairman Christopher Haines, *Chief Executive* Simone Kessler, *Directors* R. Harrison, D. Watson, L.S. Garman, C. Gillings, R. Panton Corbett

International business-to-business publishing. Reference, management and technology directories, leisure,

commemorative publishing, exhibition organising. Founded 1978.

Stride Publications
11 Sylvan Road, Exeter, Devon EX4 6EW
e-mail rml@madbear.demon.co.uk
Managing Editor Rupert M. Loydell
Poetry, short story collections, literary experimental novels, contemporary music and visual arts, theology of arts. Submissions in writing only. Founded 1980.

Studio – see Random House UK Ltd*

Studio Editions – see Random House UK Ltd*

Studio Vista – see Cassell plc

Summersdale Publishers
46 West Street, Chichester, West Sussex PO19 1RP
tel (01243) 771107 *fax* (01243) 786300
Editors Alastair Williams, Stewart Ferris
Cookery, biography, sport, humour, popular psychology, business and travel. Founded 1990.

Sunflower Books
12 Kendrick Mews, London SW7 3HG
tel 0171-589 1862 *fax* 0171-589 1862
web site http://www.sunflowerbooks.co.uk/
Directors P.A. Underwood (editorial), J.G. Underwood, S.J. Seccombe
Travel guidebooks.

Sussex Academic Press
18 Chichester Place, Brighton BN2 1FF
tel (01273) 699533 *fax* (01273) 621262
e-mail 100101.377@compuserve.com
Editorial Director Anthony Grahame
British history and Middle East studies. Founded 1994.
The Alpha Press (imprint)
Religion and sport.

Sutton Publishing Ltd
Phoenix Mill, Thrupp, Stroud,
Glos. GL5 2BU
tel (01453) 731114 *fax* (01453) 731117
Directors David Prigent, Peter Clifford (publishing), Christopher Sackett, Alan Plank, David Hogg, Nick Carter
General and academic publishers of high quality illustrated books, including history, military, regional interest, local history, literature, biography, archaeology. Founded 1978.

Swan Hill Press – see Airlife Publishing Ltd

Swedenborg Society
20-21 Bloomsbury Way, London WC1A 2TH
tel 0171-405 7986 *fax* 0171-831 5848
e-mail swed.soc@netmatters.co.uk
The Writings of Swedenborg.

Sweet & Maxwell Ltd*
100 Avenue Road, London NW3 3PF
tel 0171-393 7000 *fax* 0171-393 7010
Directors M. Boswood, I. Drane, P. Riddle, B. Grandage, S. Leach, D. Lane, J. Rhodes, S. Andrews, A. Lourie, A. Foster, A. Kinahan
Law. Founded 1799; incorporated 1889.

Take That Ltd
PO Box 200, Harrogate, North Yorkshire HG1 4XB
tel (01423) 507545 *fax* (01423) 526035
e-mail sales@takethat.co.uk
Managing Director Chris Brown
Internet/computing, business, finance, gambling, illustrated humour. Send sae with synopsis/samples. Founded 1986.

Tamarind Ltd
PO Box 296, Camberley, Surrey GU15 4WD
tel (01276) 683979 *fax* (01276) 685365
Managing Director Verna Wilkins
Multicultural children's picture books and educational material. Publications give a high positive profile to black children. Unsolicited material welcome with return postage. Founded 1987.

Tango Books – imprint of Sadie Fields Productions Ltd, book packagers

Tarquin Publications
Stradbroke, Diss, Norfolk IP21 5JP
tel (01379) 384218 *fax* (01379) 384289
Partners Gerald Jenkins, Margaret Jenkins
Mathematics and mathematical models; paper cutting, paper engineering and pop-up books for intelligent children. No unsolicited MSS; send suggestion or synopsis in first instance. Founded 1970.

Tate Gallery Publishing Ltd
Millbank, London SW1P 4RG
tel 0171-887 8869/70 *fax* 0171-887 8878
Managing Director Celia Clear, *Senior Manager* Brian McGahon, *Retail Manager* Rosemary Bennett, *Marketing Manager* Mark Eastment, *Production Manager* Tim Holton
Publishers for the Tate Gallery in London, Liverpool and St Ives. Exhibition catalogues, general and educational books, diaries, calendars, posters and stationery in the field of British and modern art. Founded 1996.

I.B. Tauris & Co. Ltd
Victoria House, Bloomsbury Square,
London WC1B 4DZ
tel 0171-916 1069 *fax* 0171-916 1068
e-mail mail@ibtauris.com
Directors I. Bagherzade (chairman and publisher),
Jonathan McDonnell (managing)

History, politics, international relations,
economics, current affairs, Middle East,
cultural and media studies. Founded 1983.

British Academic Press (imprint)
Academic monographs and research dissertations in history, political science
and social sciences.

Tauris Academic Studies (imprint)
Academic monographs on history, politics, international relations, economics,
international law.

Tauris Parke Books (imprint)
Illustrated books on architecture, design,
cultural history and travel.

Taylor & Francis Group Ltd*
1 Gunpowder Square, London EC4A 3DE
tel 0171-583 0490 *fax* 0171-583 0581
Group Publishing Director (Editorial) Stephen
Neal

Educational (university), science: physics,
mathematics, chemistry, electronics, natural history, pharmacology and drug
metabolism, toxicology, technology, history of science, ergonomics, production
engineering, remote sensing, geographic
information systems, psychology.

Teach Yourself – see Hodder Headline
plc

Telegraph Books
The Daily Telegraph, 1 Canada Square,
Canary Wharf, London E14 5DT
tel 0171-538 6826 *fax* 0171-538 6064
Manager Susannah Charlton

Business, personal finance, crosswords,
sport, travel and guides, cookery and
wine, general, gardening, history – all by
Telegraph journalists and contributors,
and co-published with major publishing
houses. Founded 1920.

Tellastory – see Random House UK Ltd*

The Templar Company plc
Pippbrook Mill, London Road, Dorking,
Surrey RH4 1JE
tel (01306) 876361 *fax* (01306) 889097
Directors Amanda Wood, Ruth Huddleston,
Graeme East, Richard Carlisle

Children's novelty and gift books; picture books; illustrated educational, particularly natural history; marketing and
communications literature. Founded
1980.

Thames and Hudson Ltd*
30-34 Bloomsbury Street, London WC1B 3QP
tel 0171-636 5488 *fax* 0171-636 4799
e-mail mail@thbooks.demon.co.uk
Chairman E.U. Neurath, *Managing Director*
T.M. Neurath, *Directors* E. Bates (company
secretary), J.R. Camplin (editorial), T.L. Evans
(sales and marketing), C.A. Ferguson
(production), W. Guttmann, C.M. Kaine (design),
N. Stangos (editorial), T.J. Flood (finance), P.
Hughes CBE

Illustrated non-fiction for an international audience, especially art, architecture,
graphic design, garden and landscape
design, archaeology, cultural history, historical reference, fashion, photography,
ethnic arts, mythology and religion.

Thames Publishing
14 Barlby Road, London W10 6AR
tel 0181-969 3579 *fax* 0181-969 1465
Publishing Manager John Bishop

Books about music (not pop), particularly British composers and musicians. Preliminary letter essential. Founded 1970.

D.C. Thomson & Co. Ltd – Publications
Dundee DD1 9QJ
tel (01382) 223131　*fax* (01382) 322214
London office 185 Fleet Street, London EC4A 2HS
tel 0171-242 5086 *fax* 0171-404 5694

Publishers of newspapers and periodicals. Children's books (annuals), based
on weekly magazine characters; fiction.

Thomson Science & Professional*
2-6 Boundary Row, London SE1 8HN
tel 0171-865 0066 *fax* 0171-522 9623

A division of International Thomson
Publishing.

Thomson Science (division)
Chief Executive Officer Geoffrey Burn, *Managing
Director* Michael Dixon, *Senior Personnel* A.
Bisztyga (rights), D. Cox (human resources), A.
Davis (finance), A. Gresford (special sales), P.
McKay (marketing), D. Vaugan (publishing), J.
Lavender (electronic), A. Watkinson (intellectual
property)

Scientific, technical and medical publisher. Imprints: Chapman & Hall, Rapid
Science, Blackie Academic &
Professional.

Thomson Professional (division)
Chief Executive Officer Geoffrey Burn, *President*
Marianne Russell, *Senior Personnel* A. Bisztyga
(rights), D. Cox (human resources), R. Creffield
(marketing), A. Davis (finance), R. Read
(publishing)
Professional publisher. Imprints: Spon,
VNR.

Stanley Thornes (Publishers) Ltd
(incorporating Mary Glasgow Publications)
Ellenborough House, Wellington Street,
Cheltenham, Glos. GL50 1YW
tel (01242) 228888 *fax* (01242) 221914
Directors David Smith (managing), Brian Carvell,
Paul Vinson, Dominic Richardson
Educational: primary, secondary, further
education books, higher education, pro-
fessional.

Thorsons – see HarperCollins
Publishers*

Times Books – see HarperCollins
Publishers*

**Times Mirror International
Publishers Ltd (TMIP Ltd)** – see
Mosby International

Titan Books Ltd
42-44 Dolben Street, London SE1 0UP
tel 0171-620 0200 *fax* 0171-620 0032
e-mail 101447.2455@compuserve.com
Publisher and Managing Director Nick Landau,
Editorial Director Katy Wild
Graphic novels, including Aliens and
Batman, featuring comic strip material;
film and TV tie-ins and reference books,
including *Star Wars* and *Star Trek*. Erotic
fiction under the Eros Plus imprint. No
fiction or children's proposals and no
unsolicited material without preliminary
letter please; send large sae for current
author guidelines. Founded 1981.

Tolkien – see HarperCollins Publishers***

Tolley Publishing Co. Ltd
Tolley House, 2 Addiscombe Road, Croydon,
Surrey CR9 5AF
tel 0181-686 9141 *fax* 0181-681 7986
e-mail sales@tolley.co.uk
Directors Nigel Stapleton (chairman), Christine
Durman (managing), Gareth Taylor (editorial, tax/
accountancy), Carol Doyle-Linden (editorial,
legal/business), Jill Howis (finance and
operations)
Law, taxation, accountancy, business.
Founded 1916.

Fourmat Publishing (division)
Director Carol Doyle-Linden, *Commissioning
Editor* Irene Kaplan
Books and legal forms for lawyers, busi-
ness and the professions.

Charles Knight Publishing (division)
Director Carol Doyle-Linden, *Managing Editor*
S.C. Cotter
Looseleaf legal works and periodicals on
local government law, construction law
and technical subjects.

Touchstone – see Simon & Schuster***

Town House and Country House†
Trinity House, Charleston Road, Ranelagh,
Dublin 6, Republic of Ireland
tel (01) 4972399 *fax* (01) 4970927
e-mail books@townhouse.ie
Directors Treasa Coady, Jim Coady
General illustrated non-fiction, popular
fiction, art, archaeology and biography.
Founded 1981.

Training Direct – see Pearson
Professional Ltd*

Transworld Publishers Ltd*
61-63 Uxbridge Road, London W5 5SA
tel 0181- 579 2652 *fax* 0181-579 5479
Chairman Stephen Rubin, *Managing Director*
Mark Barty-King, *Deputy Managing Director*
Barry Hempstead (operations), *Publishers* Patrick
Janson-Smith (adult trade books), Ursula
Mackenzie (hardbacks), Larry Finlay (paperbacks)
Subsidiary of Bertelsmann AG.

Anchor (division)
Publisher John Saddler
Literary fiction and non-fiction.

Bantam (imprint)
Publishing Director Francesca Liversidge
Paperback general fiction and non-fiction.

Bantam Press (imprint)
Publishing Director Sally Gaminara
Fiction, general, cookery, business,
crime, health and diet, history, humour,
military, music, paranormal, self-help,
science, travel and adventure, biography
and autobiography.

Bantam Children's Books (division)
Publisher Philippa Dickinson
Paperback young adult books and series.

Black Swan (imprint)
Editorial Director Bill Scott-Kerr
Paperback quality fiction.

Corgi (imprint)
Editorial Director Bill Scott-Kerr
Paperback general fiction and non-fiction.

Corgi Children's Books (division)
Publisher Philippa Dickinson
Children's paperback picture books, fiction and poetry.

Doubleday (UK) (imprint)
Publisher Marianne Velmans
General fiction and non-fiction.

Doubleday Children's Books (imprint)
Publisher Philippa Dickinson
Hardback picture books, fiction and poetry for children.

Freeway (imprint)
Editorial Director Philippa Dickinson
Paperback young adult books.

Partridge Press (imprint)
Publishing Manager Alison Barrow
Sport and leisure.
Also: **IDG Computer Books** and **Expert Gardening Books**.

Treehouse Children's Books Ltd
Page Farm, Newtown, West Pennard,
Glastonbury, Somerset BA6 8NN
tel (01405) 035757 *fax* (01405) 035758
Editorial Director Richard Powell
Pre-school children's books and novelty books. Founded 1989.

Trentham Books Ltd*
Westview House, 734 London Road, Oakhill,
Stoke-on-Trent, Staffs. ST4 5NP
tel (01782) 745567/844699 *fax* (01782) 745553
e-mail tb@trentham.books.co.uk
web site http://www.trentham-books.co.uk
Directors Prof S.J. Eggleston (managing), Gillian Klein (editorial), Barbara Wiggins (executive)
Editorial office 28 Hillside Gardens,
London N6 5ST
tel 0181-348 2174
Education (including specialist fields – multicultural issues, equal opportunities, bullying, design and technology, early years), social policy, sociology of education, European education. Does not publish books for use by children or fiction, biography and poetry. Founded 1968.

Triangle – see Society for Promoting Christian Knowledge*

Trotman & Company Ltd
12 Hill Rise, Richmond, Surrey TW10 6UA
tel 0181-940 5668 *fax* 0181-948 9267
Chairman A.F. Trotman, *Publishing Director* Morfydd Jones
Higher education guidance, careers, classroom resources. Founded 1970.

Two Heads Publishing
9 Whitehall Park, London N19 3TS
tel 0171-561 1606 *fax* 0171-561 1607
e-mail twoheads.demon.co.uk
Publisher Charles Frewin
Sport, especially cricket and football.
Founded 1992.

Two-Can Publishing*
346 Old Street, London EC1V 9NQ
tel 0171-684 4000 *fax* 0171-613 3371
e-mail info@two-can.co.uk
Directors Andrew Jarvis (chairman), Ian Grant (marketing), Sara Lynn (creative)
Children's: reference and non-fiction books, magazines, video and multimedia products. Founded 1987.

Twocan/Watts – see The Watts Publishing Group*

UCL Press Ltd
1 Gunpowder Square, London EC4A 3DE
tel 0171-583 0490 *fax* 0171-583 0581
Publisher Steven Gerrard
Art, architecture, archaeology, history, language, literature and literary theory, philosophy, politics, cultural studies, planning and geography, social research methods, sociology. A member of the Taylor & Francis Group. Founded 1991.

Unicorn Books
16 Laxton Gardens, Paddock Wood, Kent TN12 6BB
tel (01892) 833648 *fax* (01892) 833577
Director R. Green
Militaria, music, transport

University of Exeter Press*
Reed Hall, Streatham Drive, Exeter, Devon EX4 4QR
tel (01392) 263066 *fax* (01392) 263064
e-mail uep @exeter.ac.uk
web site http://www.ex.ac.uk/uep/
Publisher Simon Baker
Academic and scholarly books on history, local history (Exeter and the South West), archaeology, classical studies, English literature, film history, medieval English, linguistics, modern languages, European studies, maritime studies, mining history, politics, Arabic studies, American studies. Founded 1958.

The University of Hull Press & Lampada Press
Cottingham Road, Hull,
North Humberside HU6 7RX
tel (01482) 465322 *fax* (01482) 466857
Publisher Glen Innes

General interest: economic and social history, history, local history, modern languages, English, geography, law, music, literature, poetry, art history. Founded 1983/1991.

University of Wales Press
6 Gwennyth Street, Cathays, Cardiff CF2 4YD
tel (01222) 231919 *fax* (01222) 230908
e-mail press@press.wales.ac.uk
web site http://www.swan.ac.uk/uwp/home.htm
Editorial Director Ned Thomas

Academic and educational (Welsh and English). Publishers of *Welsh History Review, Studia Celtica, Llên Cymru, Delta, Y Gwyddonydd, Efrydiau Athronyddol, Contemporary Wales, Welsh Journal of Education, Journal of Celtic Linguistics, ALT-J (Association for Learning Technology Journal), Borderlines.* Founded 1922.

Merlin Unwin Books
Palmers House, 7 Corve Street, Ludlow, Shropshire SY8 1DB
tel (01584) 877456 *fax* (01584) 877457
Proprietor Merlin Unwin

Fishing. Founded 1990.

Unwin Hyman Ltd – acquired by HarperCollins Publishers*

Unwin Hyman Academic – now incorporated into Routledge*

Usborne Publishing*
Usborne House, 83-85 Saffron Hill, London EC1N 8RT
tel 0171-430 2800 *fax* 0171-430 1562
Directors Peter Usborne, Jenny Tyler (editorial), Robert Jones, David Lowe, Keith Ball, David Harte, Lorna Hunt

Children's books: reference, practical, craft, natural history, science, languages, history, geography, fiction. Founded 1973.

V&A Publications
160 Brompton Road, London SW3 1HW
tel 0171-938 9663 *fax* 0171-938 8370
web site http://www.vam.ac.uk
Head of Publications Mary Butler

Popular and scholarly books on fine and decorative arts, architecture, contemporary design, fashion and photography. Founded 1980.

Vallentine Mitchell – see Frank Cass & Co. Ltd

Variorum – see Ashgate Publishing Ltd

Ventura Publishing Ltd – see Penguin Books Ltd*

Veritas Publications†
Veritas House, 7-8 Lower Abbey Street, Dublin 1, Republic of Ireland
tel (01) 8788177 *fax* (01) 8786507
UK Veritas Book & Video Distribution Ltd, Lower Avenue, Leamington Spa, Warks. CV31 3NP
tel (0926) 451 730 *fax* (0926) 451 733

Religion, including social and educational works, and material relating to the media of communication. Division of the Catholic Communications Institute of Ireland, Inc.

Vermilion – see Random House UK Ltd*

Verso Ltd
6 Meard Street, London W1V 3HR
tel 0171-437 3546 *fax* 0171-734 0059
e-mail verso@verso.co.uk
Directors Lucy Heller (executive chairman), Colin Robinson, Robin Blackburn, Tony Stevenson, Mike Sprinker, Mike Davis, Tariq Ali, Perry Anderson

Politics, sociology, economics, history, philosophy, cultural studies. Founded 1970.

Viking – see Penguin Books Ltd*

Viking Children's Books – see Penguin Books Ltd*

Vintage – see Random House UK Ltd*

Virago – see Little, Brown and Company (UK)*

Virgin Publishing Ltd
332 Ladbroke Grove, London W10 5AH
tel 0181-968 7554 *fax* 0181-968 0929
Chairman Robert Devereux, *Directors* Robert Shreeve (managing), Richard Branson, *Management* Peter Darvill-Evans (publisher, fiction), Carolyn Price (publisher, illustrated), K.T. Forster (international sales), Amy Nelson-Bennett (marketing), Susan Atkinson (publicity), Ray Mudie (sales), Nigel Williams (financial), Rod Green (senior editor, general)

Black Lace (imprint)
Editor Kerri Sharp

Erotic fiction by women for women.

Crime & Passion (imprint)
Publisher Peter Darvill-Evans

Crime fiction with erotic content.

Idol (imprint)
Editor Rebecca Levene
Homerotic fiction for men.
New Adventures (imprint)
Editor Simon Winstone
Science fiction.
Nexus (imprint)
Publisher Peter Darvill-Evans
Erotic fiction.
Virgin (imprint)
Editorial Carolyn Price (illustrated), Rod Green (general, film and TV tie-ins, humour), Peter Darvill-Evans (fiction)
Popular culture: entertainment, showbiz, arts, film and TV, music, humour, biography and autobiography, popular reference, true crime, children's books, mainly juvenile fiction.

Virtue Books Ltd
Edward House, Tenter Street, Rotherham S60 1LB
tel (01709) 365005 *fax* (01709) 829982
Directors Peter E. Russum, Margaret H. Russum, Michael G. Virtue (editorial)
Books for the professional chef, catering and drink.

Vista – see Cassell plc

VNR – see Thomson Science & Professional*

Voyager – see HarperCollins Publishers*

Walker Books Ltd
87 Vauxhall Walk, London SE11 5HJ
tel 0171-793 0909 *fax* 0171-587 1123
Directors David Heatherwick, Wendy Boase, David Lloyd, Amelia Edwards, Judy Burdsall, Harold G. Gould OBE, Henryk Wesolowski, Sarah Foster, Gary Gentel
Children's – mainly picture books; junior and teenage fiction. Founded 1979.

Éditions Aubrey Walter – see GMP Publishers Ltd

Warburg Institute
University of London, Woburn Square, London WC1H 0AB
tel 0171-580 9663 *fax* 0171-436 2852
Cultural and intellectual history, with special reference to the history of the classical tradition.

Ward Lock – see Cassell plc

Ward Lock Educational Co. Ltd
BIC Ling Kee House, 1 Christopher Road, East Grinstead, West Sussex RH19 3BT

tel (01342) 318980 *fax* (01342) 410980
Directors Au Bak Ling (chairman, Hong Kong), Au King Kwok (Hong Kong), Au Wai Kwok (Hong Kong), Albert Kw Au (Hong Kong), Au Chun Kwok (Hong Kong), *General Manager* Penny Kitchenham
Primary and secondary pupil materials, Kent Mathematics Project: KMP BASC for primary and KMP Main for secondary, Reading Workshops, Take Part Series and Take Part Starters, teachers' books, music books, Target Series for the National Curriculum: Target Science and Target Geography, religious education, environmental studies. Founded 1952.

Frederick Warne & Co. Ltd – see **Penguin Books Ltd***

Warner – see **Little, Brown and Company (UK)***

Warner/Chappell Plays Ltd
129 Park Street, London W1Y 3FA
tel 0171-514 5236 *fax* 0171-514 5201
e-mail warner.chappell@dial.pipex.com
Editorial Director Michael Callahan
Stage plays only, in both acting and trade editions. Preliminary letter essential.

Waterline Books – see **Airlife Publishing Ltd**

The Watts Publishing Group*
96 Leonard Street, London EC2A 4RH
tel 0171-739 2929 *fax* 0171-739 2318
Directors Francesca Dow (publishing, Orchard), Philippa Stewart (publishing, Franklin Watts), Marlene Johnson (managing), George Spicer (sales)
Division of Grolier Ltd.
Franklin Watts (division)
Publishing Director Philippa Stewart
Children's illustrated non-fiction, reference, education. Imprints: Aladdin/Watts, Twocan/Watts.
Orchard Books (division)
Publishing Director Francesca Dow
Children's picture books, fiction, poetry, novelty books, board books.

Wayland Publishers Ltd*
61-61A Western Road, Hove, East Sussex BN3 1JD
tel (01273) 722561 *fax* (01273) 329314
Managing Director D.J. Smith, *Directors* R. Bailey (general manager), S. White-Thompson (product development), N. Padbury (finance), M. McWhinnie (sales)
Children's information books for ages 4–18. Founded 1969.

Websters International Publishers Ltd

2nd Floor, Axe & Bottle Court,
70 Newcomen Street, London SE1 1YT
tel 0171-407 2846 *fax* 0171-407 6437
Chairman and Publisher Adrian Webster,
Managing Director Jean-Luc Barbanneau,
Publishing Director Susannah Webster
Wine, food, travel, health. Founded 1983.

Weidenfeld & Nicolson – see The Orion Publishing Group Ltd

Wharncliffe* – see Pen & Sword Books Ltd

Which? Ltd*

2 Marylebone Road, London NW1 4DF
tel 0171-830 6000 *fax* 0171-830 7660
e-mail books@which.net
Chief Executive Sheila McKechnie, *Assistant Director* Kim Lavely, *Head of Publishing* Gill Rowley
Part of Consumers' Association. Founded 1957.

Which? Books (imprint)
Travel, restaurant, hotel and wine guides, medicine, law and personal finance for the layman, gardening, education, DIY – all branded *Which?* books.

J. Whitaker & Sons Ltd*

12 Dyott Street, London WC1A 1DF
tel 0171-420 6000 *fax* 0171-836 2909
Directors Peter Allsop, Robin Baum (non-executive chairman), John Lycett, Jonathan Nowell, Chris Ostrom, Paul Pounsford, Tom Sweetman, Sally Whitaker (deputy chairman), Martin Whitaker (managing)
Reference including *Whitaker's Almanack* (founded 1869), *The Bookseller* (1858), *Whitaker's Books in Print* (1874), and other book trade directories.

White Mouse Editions Ltd – see New Cavendish Books

Whittet Books Ltd

18 Anley Road, London W14 0BY
tel 0171-603 1139 *fax* 0171-603 8154
Directors Annabel Whittet, John Whittet
Natural history, countryside, transport, pets, horses. Founded 1976.

Whurr Publishers Ltd*

19B Compton Terrace, London N1 2UN
tel 0171-359 5979 *fax* 0171-226 5290
Managing Director Colin Whurr
Disorders of human communication, medicine, psychology, psychiatry, occupational therapy, physiotherapy, business. Founded 1987.

John Wiley & Sons Ltd*

(incorporating Interscience Publishers)
Baffins Lane, Chichester,
West Sussex PO19 1UD
tel (01243) 779777 *fax* (01243) 775878
e-mail europe@wiley.co.uk
Chairman The Duke of Richmond, *Managing Director* J.H. Jarvis, *Publishing Director* S. Mair
Physics, chemistry, mathematics, statistics, engineering, architecture, computer science, biology, medicine, earth science, psychology, business, economics, finance, law.

Neil Wilson Publishing Ltd*

303A The Pentagon Centre, 36 Washington Street,
Glasgow G3 8AZ
tel 0141-221 1117 *fax* 0141-221 5363
e-mail nwp@cqm.co.uk
web site http://www.nwp.co.uk
Managing Director Neil Wilson
Scottish interest, biography, history, food and drink, hill walking, travel, humour, true crime, whisk(e)y and real ale. Founded 1992.

Philip Wilson Publishers Ltd

143-149 Great Portland Street,
London W1N 5FB
tel 0171-436 4490 *fax* 0171-436 4403
Chairman P. Wilson, *Managing Director* A. White, *Publishing Director* A. Jackson
Fine and applied art, architecture, museums. Founded 1975.

Flint River (imprint)
Countries.

Scala (imprint)
Museums.

Sotheby's Publications (imprint)
Art, art history, architecture, collectables.

The Windrush Press

Little Window, High Street, Moreton-in-Marsh,
Glos. GL56 0LL
tel (01608) 652012/652025 *fax* (01608) 652125
e-mail 106570.2715@compuserve.com
Managing Director Geoffrey Smith, *Publishing Director* Victoria Huxley
History, military history, travel, biography, humour. Founded 1987.

Wisley Handbooks – see Cassell plc

Woburn Press – see Frank Cass & Co. Ltd

Wolfhound Press†

68 Mountjoy Square, Dublin 1, Republic of Ireland
tel (01) 8740354 *fax* 8720207
Publisher Seamus Cashman, *Editor* Susan
Houlden

Literary studies and criticism, fiction, art,
biography, history, young readers, children's and teenage fiction, law, gift titles,
cookery, general non-fiction. Founded
1974.

The Women's Press

34 Great Sutton Street, London EC1V 0DX
tel 0171-251 3007 *fax* 0171-608 1938
Directors Kathy Gale (publishing), Mary
Hemming (sales)

Books by women in the areas of literary
fiction, crime novels, biography and
autobiography, health, politics, handbooks, literary criticism, psychology and
self-help, the arts. Founded 1978.

Livewire (imprint)

Books for young women.

Woodhead Publishing Ltd

Abington Hall, Abington, Cambridge CB1 6AH
tel (01223) 891358 *fax* (01223) 893694
e-mail woodhead @dial.pipex.com
Managing Director Martin Woodhead

Materials engineering, welding, textiles,
finance, investment, banking, business,
food science and technology. Founded
1989.

Woodhead-Faulkner – see Prentice Hall Europe/Academic*

Wordsworth Editions Ltd

6 London Street, London W2 1HL
tel 0171-706 8822 *fax* 0171-706 8833
e-mail 100434.276@compuserve.com
Directors Michael Trayler (managing), Helen
Trayler (operations), Marcus Clapham (editorial),
Clive Reynard (sales and company secretary)

Reprints of classic books: literary, children's, American, women's, military,
erotica, poetry; reference. Founded 1987.

World International Ltd

Deanway Technology Centre, Wilmslow Road,
Handforth, Cheshire SK9 3FB
tel (01625) 650011 *fax* (01625) 650040
Directors Ian Findlay (managing), David
Sheldrake (production), Michael Herridge
(editorial), Peter Hey, Andrew Maddock

Books for children of all ages; early
learning, activity, annuals; character publishing including *Mr Men*.

Writers & Readers Ltd*

6-9 Cynthia Street, London N1 9JF
tel 0171-713 0386 *fax* 0171-833 4804
e-mail faye@writersandreaders.com/
web site http://www.writersandreaders.com
Publisher Glenn Thompson

African/Black studies, architecture, performing arts, media, history, music, philosophy, photography, poetry, political studies, psychology, religion, science, social
issues, spirit and body, US studies, women/
gender studies, *For Beginners* documentary comic book series. Founded 1974.

Black Butterfly (imprint)

Children's books.

Harlem River Press (imprint)

Poetry anthologies and spiritual writing
by Black women writers, Black political
studies.

X Libris – see Little, Brown and Company (UK)*

The X Press

6 Hoxton Square, London N1 6NU
tel 0171-729 1199 *fax* 0171-729 1771
e-mail x@xpress.co.uk
Editorial Director Dotun Adebayo, *Marketing
Director* Steve Pope

Black interest popular novels, particularly reflecting contemporary ethnic experiences. *Black Classics* series: reprints of
American classic novels by black writers.
Founded 1992.

Nia (imprint)

Literary black fiction.

Yale University Press London*

23 Pond Street, London NW3 2PN
tel 0171-431 4422 *fax* 0171-431 3755
Managing Director John Nicoll

Art, architecture, history, economics, political science, literary criticism, Asian and
African studies, religion, philosophy, psychology, history of science. Founded 1961.

Yorkshire Art Circus

School Lane, Glass Houghton, Castleford,
West Yorkshire WF10 4QH
tel (01977) 550401 *fax* (01977) 512819
e-mail books@artcircus.demon.co.uk
Contact Clare Conlon

Specialises in new writing by first-time
authors. Publishes autobiography, community books and local interest
(Yorkshire/Humberside). No local history, children's, reference or nostalgia.

Unsolicited MSS discouraged; send for fact sheet first. Founded 1986.

Springboard Fiction (imprint)

Novels of a contemporary nature by first-time authors (Yorkshire/Humberside). Send for fact sheet. Founded 1993.

Young Library (Assetpulse Ltd)
PO Box 2231, Reading RG4 9YP
tel (01734) 722805 *fax* (01734) 722544
Director Roger Bonnett

Highly illustrated non-fiction for children's libraries, including geography, history, natural history, social and urban studies, science and technology, comparative religion. Founded 1982.

Zed Books Ltd*
7 Cynthia Street, London N1 9JF
tel 0171-837 4014 (general), 0171-837 0384 (editorial) *fax* 0171-833 3960
e-mail zed @ zedbooks.demon.co.uk
web site http://www.zedbooks.demon.co.uk
Editors Robert Molteno, Louise Murray

Social sciences on international issues; women's studies, cultural studies, development and environmental studies; area studies (Africa, Asia, Caribbean, Latin America, Middle East and the Pacific). Founded 1976.

Hans Zell Publishers – see Bowker-Saur

Zoë Books Ltd
15 Worthy Lane, Winchester, Hants SO23 7AB
tel (01962) 851318 *fax* (01962) 843015
Directors I.Z. Dawson (managing publishing), A.R. Davidson

Publishers of children's information books for the school and library markets in the UK; specialists in co-editions for world markets. Founded 1990.

Book packagers

Many modern illustrated books are created by book packagers, whose special skills are in the areas of book design and graphic content. In-house desk editors and art editors match up the expertise of specialist writers, artists and photographers who usually work on a freelance basis.

Packaged books are often expensive to produce, beyond the cost parameters set by traditional publishers for their own markets. The packager recoups the expense by pre-selling titles to publishers in various countries. The usual subject areas are children's interests and informational how-to, such as crafts and cookery. Thus packaged books are usually international in content and approach, avoiding local interests such as cricket or Cornish cream teas.

The working style in most packagers' offices is more akin to magazine publishing than to traditional book publishing, with creative groups concentrating on the complexities of integrating words and pictures for individual titles rather than merely manuscript editing for a broad publishing list.

The many opportunities for freelance writers, specialist contributors and consultants, photographers and illustrators will usually be short-term and high pressure; packagers rarely spend more than a year on any title.

Payment

As packaged books are frequently the work of more than one 'author' and because of the complications of the overseas rights deals that will be made and the formulae for a packager's earnings, which are obviously only a proportion of a book's retail price, flat fees are often suggested rather than royalty agreements. Where royalties are appropriate, they will be based on the packager's receipts but the expectation is that there will be more foreign language editions than a traditional publisher can achieve.

The Book Packagers Association
93A Blenheim Crescent, London W11 2EQ
Secretary Rosemary Pettit
tel 0171-221 9089
The forum for the exchange of creative and commercial experience in this branch of the publishing industry. The BPA has devised standard contracts to cover members' relationships with contributors and customers.

*Member of the Book Packagers Association

Aladdin Books Ltd
28 Percy Street, London W1P 0LD
tel 0171-323 3319 *fax* 0171-323 4829
Directors Charles Nicholas, Bibby Whittaker
Full design and book packaging facility specialising in children's non-fiction and reference. Founded 1980.

Albion Press Ltd
Spring Hill, Idbury, Oxon OX7 6RU
tel (01993) 831094 *fax* (01993) 831982
Directors Emma Bradford, Neil Philip

Quality integrated illustrated titles. Specialises in children's books. Supply finished books. Publishers' commissions undertaken. Founded 1984.

Alphabet & Image Ltd
Marston House, Marston Magna, Yeovil, Somerset BA22 8DH
tel/fax (01935) 851331
Directors Anthony Birks-Hay, Leslie Birks-Hay
Complete editorial, picture research, photographic, design and production service

for illustrated books on ceramics, fine art, horticulture, architecture, history, etc. Imprint: Marston House. Founded 1972.

Andromeda Oxford Ltd
11-15 The Vineyard, Abingdon, Oxon OX14 3PX
tel (01235) 550296 *fax* (01235) 550330
e-mail books@andromeda.co.uk
web site http://www.andromeda.co.uk
Directors M. Ritchie (managing), A. Flatt, J.G. Bateman, C. Sparling, D. Hall

Illustrated reference titles for the international market for children and adults. Its subsidiary Andromeda Interactive Ltd publishes CD-Roms. Founded 1986.

BCS Publishing Ltd
1 Bignell Park Barns, Kirtlington Road, Chesterton, Bicester, Oxon OX6 8TD
tel (01869) 324423 *fax* (01869) 324385
e-mail bcs-publishing@dial.pipex.com
Managing and Art Director Steve McCurdy, *Head of Marketing* Robert Gwyn Palmer, *Managing Editor* Jo Newson

Specialises in the preparation of illustrated general interest books; provides a full creative, design, editorial and production service. Opportunities for freelances. Founded 1993.

Bellew Publishing Co. Ltd
The Nightingale Centre, 8 Balham Hill, London SW12 9EA
tel 0181-675 2142 *fax* 0181-675 2142
Chairman Ian McCorquodale, *Managing Director* Ib Bellew

Adult and children's illustrated titles from origination of idea through concept and design to production. Founded 1983.

Bender Richardson White
PO Box 266, Uxbridge, Middlesex UB9 5NX
tel (01895) 832444 *fax* (01895) 835213
Partners Lionel Bender, Kim Richardson, Ben White

Book and multimedia packaging, specialising in children's natural history, science and family information. Opportunities for freelances. See also **Lionheart Books**. Founded 1990.

BLA Publishing Ltd
BIC Ling Kee House, 1 Christopher Road, East Grinstead, West Sussex RH19 3BT
tel (01342) 318980 *fax* (01342) 410980
Directors Au Bak Ling (chairman, Hong Kong), Au King Kwok (Hong Kong), Au Chun Kwok (Hong Kong), Albert Kw Au (Hong Kong), Au Wai Kwok (Hong Kong). *Contact* Penny Kitchenham

High quality illustrated reference books, particularly science dictionaries and

encyclopedias, for the international market. Founded 1981.

Book Packaging and Marketing*
3 Murswell Lane, Silverstone, Towcester, Northants. NN12 8UT
tel/fax (01327) 858380
Proprietor Martin F. Marix Evans

Illustrated general and informational non-fiction and reference for adults, especially travel, military history, countryside, health and fitness. Product development and project management; editorial and marketing consultancy. Opportunities for freelances. Founded 1990.

Breslich & Foss*
20 Wells Mews, London W1P 3FJ
tel 0171-580 8774 *fax* 0171-580 8784
Directors Paula G. Breslich, K.B. Dunning

Books produced from MS to bound copy stage from in-house ideas. Specialising in the arts, crafts, gardening, gift and novelty, children's. Founded 1978.

Brown Packaging Books Ltd*
Bradley's Close, 74-77 White Lion Street, London N1 9PF
tel 0171-520 7600 *fax* 0171-520 7606/7607
Managing Director Stasz Gnych, *Rights and Operations Director* Sara Ballard

Book, partwork and continuity set packaging services for trade, promotional and international publishers. Subject areas include military, aviation, gardening, music, sport and craft. Opportunities for freelances. Imprints: Brown Books Ltd and Amber Books Ltd. Founded 1989.

Brown Partworks Ltd
255-257 Liverpool Road, London N1 1LX
tel 0171-607 9039 *fax* 0171-700 5673
Director Sharon Hutton

Book, partwork and continuity set packaging services for trade, promotional and international publishers. Opportunities for freelances. Founded 1989.

Brown Wells & Jacobs Ltd
Foresters Hall, 25-27 Westow Street, London SE19 3RY
tel 0181-771 5115 *fax* 0181-771 9994
Director Graham Brown

Design, editorial, illustration and production of high quality non-fiction illustrated children's books. Specialities include pop-ups and novelties. Opportunities for freelances. Founded 1981.

Calmann and King Ltd
71 Great Russell Street, London WC1B 3BN
tel 0171-831 6351 *fax* 0171-831 8356
e-mail 101456.1525@compuserve.com
Directors Robin Hyman, Laurence King, Judy
Rasmussen, Lesley Ripley Greenfield
Illustrated books on design, art, history,
carpets and textiles, and architecture for
international co-editions. Imprint:
Laurence King. Founded 1976.

Cambridge Language Services Ltd
64 Baldock Street, Ware, Herts. SG12 9DT
tel/fax (01920) 486526
e-mail name@oakleaf.demon.co.uk
Managing Director Paul Procter
Suppliers to publishers, societies and
other organisations of customised database management systems, with
advanced retrieval mechanisms, and
electronic publishing systems for the
preparation of dictionaries, reference
books, encyclopedias, catalogues, journals, archives. PC (windows) based.
Founded 1902.

Cameron Books
PO Box 1, Moffat, Dumfriesshire DG10 9SU
tel (01683) 220808 *fax* (01683) 220012
Directors Ian A. Cameron, Jill Hollis
Illustrated non-fiction including architecture, design, fine arts (including environmental and land art), the decorative arts
and crafts, antiques, collecting, natural
history, environmental studies, social
history, film, food. Founded 1976.
Edition
Design, editing, typesetting, production
work from concept to finished book for
other publishers. Founded 1975.

Carroll & Brown Ltd*
5 Lonsdale Road, London NW6 6RA
tel 0171-372 0900 *fax* 0171-372 0460
e-mail 100675.1470@compuserve.com
Directors Amy Carroll (managing), Denise Brown
(creative)
Editorial and design through to final film
and printing of cookery, health, craft and
lifestyle titles. Opportunities for freelances. Founded 1989.

Philip Clark Ltd*
53 Calton Avenue, London SE21 7DF
tel 0181-693 5605 *fax* 0181-299 4647
Director Philip Clark
Illustrated non-fiction for the international co-edition market. Titles include the

Travellers Wine Guides series; consultancy service; sponsored publications.
Founded 1981.

Roger Coote Publishing
Gissing's Farm, Fressingfield, Eye,
Suffolk IP21 5SH
tel (01379) 588044 *fax* (01379) 588055
e-mail 101577.1530@compuserve.com
Director Roger Goddard-Coote
High quality illustrated children's non-
fiction titles for trade, institutional and
international markets. Commissions
undertaken. Freelance opportunities for
editors and designers. Founded 1989.

D & N Publishing
Membury Business Park, Lambourn Woodlands,
Hungerford, Berks. RG17 7TJ
tel (01488) 71210 *fax* (01488) 71220
Partners David and Namrita Price-Goodfellow
Production from MS to printed book.
Specialises in taking raw MS and doing
all necessary liaison, editorial, design
and production work up to when book is
ready to print, but can also organise
printing. Opportunities for freelances.
Founded 1991.

Diagram Visual Information Ltd
195 Kentish Town Road, London NW5 2JU
tel 0171-482 3633 *fax* 0171-482 4932
Director Bruce Robertson
Research, writing, design and illustration
of reference books, supplied as film,
computer disks or manufactured copies.
Opportunities for freelances. Founded
1967.

Earthscape Editions
Greys Court Farm, Greys Court,
Henley on Thames, Oxon RG9 4PG
tel (01491) 628188 *fax* (01491) 628189
Partners B.J. Knapp, D.L.R. McCrae
High quality, full colour, illustrated chil-
dren's books, including co-editions, for
education and library market. Also mul-
timedia productions. Sae with MSS
essential. Opportunities for freelances.
Associate company: Atlantic Europe
Publishing Co. Ltd. Founded 1987.

Eddison Sadd Editions Ltd*
St Chad's House, 148 King's Cross Road,
London WC1X 9DH
tel 0171-837 1968 *fax* 0171-837 2025
Directors Nick Eddison, Ian Jackson, David
Owen, Elaine Partington, Charles James
Illustrated non-fiction books for the inter-

national co-edition market. Founded 1982.

Equinox (Oxford) Ltd – acquired by Andromeda Oxford Ltd

First Rank Publishing
23 Ditchling Rise, Brighton, East Sussex BN1 4QL
tel (01273) 279934 *fax* (01273) 297128
e-mail 100772.3566@compuserve.com
web site www.netivity.co.uk/firstrank
Partners Byron Jacobs and Andrew Kinsman

Packager and publisher of sports, games and leisure books. No unsolicited MSS but ideas and synopses welcome. Payment usually fees. Also provides editorial, production and typesetting services. Founded 1996.

Gardenhouse Editions
15 Grafton Square, London SW4 0DQ
tel 0171-622 1720 *fax* 0171-720 9114
Managing Director Lorraine Johnson

Practical and art-related books on gardening, cookery, interior design, fashion, architecture. Founded 1980.

Geddes & Grosset Ltd
David Dale House, New Lanark ML11 9DJ
tel (01555) 665000 *fax* (01555) 665694
Directors R. Michael Miller, Ron Grosset, David Geddes

Complete packaging service to bound books, production, editorial project and joint venture management. Publishers of children's and mass market books and popular reference books. Opportunities for freelances. Founded 1988.

Graham-Cameron Publishing
The Studio, 23 Holt Road, Sheringham, Norfolk NR26 8NB
tel (01263) 821333 *fax* (01263) 821334
Directors Mike Graham-Cameron, Helen Graham-Cameron

Educational and children's books; sponsored publications. Illustration agency, editorial and production services. No unsolicited MSS please. Founded 1984.

Haldane Mason Ltd*
59 Chepstow Road, London W2 5BP
tel 0171-702 2123 *fax* 0171-221 3965
e-mail haldane.mason@dial.pipex.com
Directors Ron Samuels, Sydney Francis

Illustrated and reference books for the international market, for both trade and promotional publishers. Opportunities for freelances. Founded 1992.

Angus Hudson Ltd
Concorde House, Grenville Place, London NW7 3SA
tel 0181-959 3668 *fax* 0181-959 3678
Directors Angus Hudson (chairman), Nicholas Jones (managing), Stephen Price (production), Geoffrey Benge, William Brooks

Children's and religious international co-editions, from concept to finished copies. Publishing imprints: Candle Books and Concorde House Books. Founded 1971.

Lennard Books
Windmill Cottage, Mackerye End, Harpenden, Herts. AL5 5DR
tel (01582) 715866 *fax* (01582) 715121
e-mail lennard@lenqap.demon.co.uk
Directors K.A.A. Stephenson, R.H. Stephenson

Sport, personalities, TV tie-ins, humour. Division of Lennard Associates Ltd.

Lexus Ltd
13 Newton Terrace, Glasgow G3 7PJ
tel 0141-221 5266 *fax* 0141-226 3139
e-mail pt@lexus.win-uk.net
Director P.M. Terrell

Reference book publishing (especially bilingual dictionaries) as contractor, packager, consultant; translation. Founded 1980.

Lionheart Books
10 Chelmsford Square, London NW10 3AR
tel 0181-459 0453 *fax* 0181-451 3681
Partners Lionel Bender (editorial), Madeleine Bender (editorial), Ben White (design)

Handle all aspects of editorial and design packaging of, mostly, children's illustrated science, natural history and history projects. See also **Bender Richardson White**. Founded 1985.

Market House Books Ltd*
2 Market House, Market Square, Aylesbury, Bucks. HP20 1TN
tel (01296) 84911 *fax* (01296) 437073
e-mail mhb_aylesbury@compuserve.com
Directors Dr Alan Isaacs, Dr John Daintith, P.C. Sapsed

Compilation of dictionaries, encyclopedias, and reference books. Founded 1981.

Marshall Cavendish Books*
119 Wardour Street, London W1V 3TD
tel 0171-734 6710 *fax* 0171-439 1423
Head of Books Ellen Dupont

Cookery, crafts, gardening, do-it-yourself, general illustrated non-fiction. Founded 1969.

Marshall Editions Ltd*

170 Piccadilly, London W1V 9DD
tel 0171-629 0079 *fax* 0171-834 8844
e-mail info@mediakey.u-net.com
web site www.marshallmedia.com
Directors Richard Harman (chairman),
Barry Baker (managing), Barbara Anderson
Marshall, Ed Day (creative), John Christmas,
Belinda Ioni Rasmussen, David Rivers,
Sophie Collins (editorial, adult), Sean Keogh,
Cynthia O'Brien (editorial, children's), Janice
Storr, Avril Farley

Highly illustrated non-fiction, for the
adult and children's co-edition markets,
including science and natural history, fitness and well-being, lifestyle and leisure
interests. Founded 1977.

Orpheus Books Ltd

2 Church Green, Witney, Oxon OX8 6AW
tel (01993) 774949 *fax* (01993) 700330
Executive Directors Nicholas Harris (editorial,
design and marketing), Joanna Turner
(production and administration)

Children's illustrated non-fiction/refer-
ence. Opportunities for freelance artists.
Founded 1992.

Oyster Books

Unit 4, Kirklea Farm, Badgworth, Axbridge,
Somerset BS26 2QH
tel (01934) 732251 *fax* (01934) 732514
Directors Jenny Wood, Tim Wood, Ali Brooks,
Donna Webber

Specialises in high-quality children's
books and book/toy gift items. Founded
1985.

Playne Books Ltd

Chapel House, Trefin, Haverfordwest,
Pembrokeshire SA62 5AU
tel (01348) 837073 *fax* (01348) 837063
Design and Production David Playne, *Editor* Gill
Davies

Specialises in highly illustrated adult
non-fiction and books for very young
children. All stages of production undertaken from initial concept (editorial,
design and manufacture) to delivery of
completed books. Founded 1987.

Mathew Price Ltd

The Old Glove Factory, Bristol Road, Sherborne,
Dorset DT9 4HP
tel (01935) 816010 *fax* (01935) 816310
Chairman Mathew Price

Illustrated fiction and non-fiction children's books for all ages for the international market. Founded 1983.

Quarto Children's Books Ltd

3rd Floor, The Fitzpatrick Building,
188-194 York Way, London N7 9QP
tel 0171-607 3322 *fax* 0171-700 2951
Publisher Roberta Butler

Highly illustrated non-fiction children's
books.

Quarto Publishing plc/Quintet Publishing Ltd

The Old Brewery, 6 Blundell Street,
London N7 9BH
tel 0171-700 6700 *fax* 0171-700 4191
Directors L.F. Orbach, R.J. Morley, M.J. Mousley

International co-editions. Founded
1976/1984.

Sadie Fields Productions Ltd

3D West Point, 36-37 Warple Way,
London W3 0RG
tel 0181-746 1171 *fax* 0181-746 1170
e-mail sadiefields@compuserve.com
Directors Sheri Safran, David Fielder

Creates and produces international co-
productions of pop-up, novelty and picture and board books for children.
Founded 1983.

Savitri Books Ltd*

115J Cleveland Street, London W1P 5PN
tel 0171-436 9932 *fax* 0171-580 6330
Director Mrinalini S. Srivastava

Packaging, design, production. Founded
1983.

Signpost Books Ltd

25 Eden Drive, Headington, Oxford OX3 0AB
tel (01865) 760444 *fax* (01865) 751399
Directors Dorothy Wood, Sally Wood

Project development, editorial, design
and production through to finished
books, film or CRC. Specialises in children's fiction, non-fiction and novelty.
Opportunities for freelances. Founded
1988.

The Templar Company plc

Pippbrook Mill, London Road, Dorking,
Surrey RH4 1JE
tel (01306) 876361 *fax* (01306) 889097
Directors Richard Carlisle, Amanda Wood, Ruth
Huddleston, Graeme East

Children's gift, novelty, picture and illustrated information books; most titles
aimed at international co-edition market.
Established links with major co-publish-
ers in USA, Australia and throughout
Europe.

Toucan Books Ltd*

Fourth Floor, 32-38 Saffron Hill,
London EC1M 8BS
tel 0171-404 8181 *fax* 0171-404 8282
Directors Robert Sackville West, Adam Nicolson,
Jane MacAndrew

International co-editions; editorial, design
and production services. Founded 1985.

Touchstone Publishing Ltd

Gissing's Farm, Fressingfield, Eye,
Suffolk IP21 5SH
tel (01379) 588044 *fax* (01379) 588055
Directors Roger Goddard-Coote (managing),
Edwina Conner (publishing)

High quality, illustrated children's non-
fiction for trade and institutional markets
worldwide. Supply CRC, film or finished
books. Publishers' commissions undertaken. Founded 1989.

Tucker Slingsby

5th Floor, Berkeley House, 73 Upper Richmond
Road, London SW15 2RZ
tel 0181-874 3400 *fax* 0181-874 3004
Directors Janet Slingsby, Del Tucker

Creation, editorial and design to disk, film
or finished copy of children's books, magazines and general interest adult books.
Commissioned work undertaken. Opportunities for freelances. Founded 1993.

Ventura Publishing Ltd

27 Wrights Lane, London W8 5TZ
tel 0171-416 3000 *fax* 0171-416 3070
Publisher Sally Floyer

Specialises in production of the *Spot*
books by Eric Hill.

Victoria House Publishing Ltd

King's Court, Parsonage Lane, Bath BA1 1EF
tel (01225) 463401 *fax* (01225) 460942
Managing Director Clyde Hunter

Packagers of mass market children's and
novelty information books under
Reader's Digest Children's Books
imprint. Fully owned subsidiary of
Reader's Digest Association Inc. Founded
1980.

Webb & Bower (Publishers) Ltd

9 Duke Street, Dartmouth, Devon TQ6 9PY
tel (01803) 835525 *fax* (01803) 835552
Director Richard Webb

Specialises in licensing illustrated non-
fiction books. Founded 1975.

Wordwright Books*

25 Oakford Road, London NW5 1AJ
tel 0171-284 0056 *fax* 0171-284 0041
Director Charles Perkins

Full packaging/production service – from
original concept to delivery of film or finished copies. Produces illustrated non-
fiction. Also assesses and prepares MSS
for the US market. Founded 1987.

Zigzag Multimedia Ltd

The Old Parlour, Randolph's Farm, Brighton
Road, Hurstpierpoint, West Sussex BN6 9EL
tel (01273) 832777 *fax* (01273) 835511
Directors Dr T.C. Potter, B. Austin, G. Sutton

Children's books and multimedia.
Opportunities for freelances. Founded
1989.

Publishers of fiction

Addresses for Book publishers UK and Ireland start on page 153.

Adventure/thrillers

Bantam
Bantam Press
Black Swan
Blake Publishing
Bloomsbury Publishing
Brandon Book Publishers
Chatto & Windus
Richard Cohen Books
Corgi
Coronet
André Deutsch
Doubleday (UK)
Fourth Estate
Gairm Publications
Victor Gollancz
HarperCollins Publishers
Headline Book Publishing
William Heinemann
Hodder & Stoughton
Hutchinson Books
Jane's Information Group
Michael Joseph
Little, Brown
New English Library
Orion
Pan
Penguin Books
Piatkus Books
Random House UK
Sceptre
Severn House Publishers
Simon & Schuster
Sinclair-Stevenson
Souvenir Press
Vintage
Virago Press
Warner
The Women's Press

Crime/mystery/suspense

Allison & Busby Ltd
Arrow Books
Bantam
Bantam Press
Bellew
Black Swan

Blake Publishing
Bloomsbury Publishing
Chatto & Windus
Richard Cohen Books
Constable & Co.
Corgi
Coronet
Crime & Passion
André Deutsch
The Do-Not Press
Faber & Faber
Fourth Estate
Gairm Publications
Victor Gollancz
Hamish Hamilton
HarperCollins Publishers
Headline Book Publishing
William Heinemann
Hodder & Stoughton
Hutchinson Books
Michael Joseph
Little, Brown
Macmillan
New English Library
Orion
Pan
Penguin Books
Piatkus Books
Random House UK
Sceptre
Serpent's Tail
Severn House Publishers
Sinclair-Stevenson
Souvenir Press
Titan Books
Viking
Vintage
Virago Press
Warner – Futura
The Women's Press

Gay/lesbian

Bantam
Black Swan
Marion Boyars Publishers
Richard Cohen Books
Corgi
Faber & Faber

Fourth Estate
GMP Publishers
Victor Gollancz
Hamish Hamilton
Onlywomen Press
Peter Owen
Penguin Books
Polygon
Serpent's Tail
Vintage
Virago Press
The Women's Press

General

Allison & Busby Ltd
Arcadia Books Ltd
Aureus Publishing
Bantam
Bantam Press
Basement Press (Ire.)
Bellew
Black Ace Books
Black Swan
Blackstaff Press Ltd (Ire.)
Blake Publishing
Bloomsbury Publishing
Marion Boyars Publishers
Brandon Book Publishers Ltd
  (Ire.)
Canongate Books
Jonathan Cape
Century
Chatto & Windus
Cló Iar-Chonnachta Teo. (Ire.)
Richard Cohen Books
The Collins Press (Ire.)
Constable & Co.
Corgi
André Deutsch
Doubleday (UK)
Gerald Duckworth & Co.
Faber & Faber
Fourth Estate
Gairm Publications
The Gallery Press (Ire.)
Garnet Publishing
Victor Gollancz
Granta Publications

Robert Hale
Hamish Hamilton
HarperCollins Publishers
Headline Book Publishing
William Heinemann
Hodder & Stoughton
Honno Ltd
Hutchinson Books
Michael Joseph
Karnak House
The Lilliput Press (Ire.)
Little, Brown
Y Lolfa Cyf. (Welsh language)
Macmillan
Marino Books (Ire.)
The Mercier Press
Methuen
New English Library
The O'Brien Press (Ire.)
Orion
Peter Owen
Pan Books
Penguin Books
Piatkus Books
Piccadilly Press
Pimlico
Pocket Books
Poolbeg Press (Ire.)
Quartet Books
Random House UK
Sceptre
Secker and Warburg
Serpent's Tail
Simon & Schuster
Sinclair-Stevenson
Souvenir Press
Touchstone
Town House and Country
  House (Ire.)
Viking
Vintage
Virago Press
Warner
Wolfhound Press (Ire.)
Worldwide Books
Yorkshire Art Circus

Historical

Bantam
Bantam Press
Bellew
Black Ace Books
Marion Boyars Publishers
Canongate Books
Jonathan Cape
Robin Clark
Richard Cohen Books
Constable & Co.
André Deutsch
diehard
Doubleday (UK)

Fourth Estate
Victor Gollancz
Robert Hale
HarperCollins Publishers
Headline Book Publishing
William Heinemann
Hodder & Stoughton
Hutchinson Books
Michael Joseph
Karnak House
Little, Brown
Orion
Peter Owen
Pan
Penguin Books
Piatkus Books
Pimlico
Random House UK
Sceptre
Simon & Schuster
Sinclair-Stevenson
Souvenir Press
Vintage
Virago Press
Warner

Literary

Abacus
Anchor
Bantam
Bantam Press
Black Ace Books
Black Swan
Bloomsbury Publishing
Marion Boyars Publishers
Calder Publications
Canongate Books
Jonathan Cape
Chatto & Windus
Robin Clark
Richard Cohen Books
Constable & Co.
Corgi
Dedalus
André Deutsch
diehard
Doubleday (UK)
Faber & Faber
Flamingo
Forest Books
Fourth Estate
Gairm Publications
Victor Gollancz
Granta Publications
Robert Hale
Hamish Hamilton
HarperCollins Publishers
Harvill
William Heinemann
Hodder & Stoughton
Hutchinson Books

Karnak House
The Lilliput Press (Ire.)
Little, Brown
Macmillan
Methuen
Orion
Peter Owen
Pan
Penguin Books
Phoenix
Picador
Pimlico
Polygon
Random House UK
Sceptre
Scottish Cultural Press
Secker and Warburg
Serpent's Tail
Sinclair-Stevenson
Skoob Books
Souvenir Press
Stride Publications
Viking
Vintage
Virago Press
The Women's Press

Romantic

Bantam
Bantam Press
Black Swan
Blake Publishing
Corgi
Coronet
Doubleday (UK)
Robert Hale
Harlequin Mills & Boon
Headline Book Publishing
William Heinemann
Hodder & Stoughton
Little, Brown
Macmillan
Monarch Publications
Orion
Pan
Piatkus Books
Random House UK
Scarlet
Silhouette
Souvenir Press
Warner

Science fiction/fantasy

Arrow Books
Bantam
Bantam Press
Black Swan
Blake Publishing
Corgi

Coronet
Victor Gollancz
HarperCollins Publishers
Headline Book Publishing
Hodder & Stoughton
Legend
Little, Brown
Millennium
New Adventures
New English Library
Orbit
Orion
Pan
Penguin Books
Random House UK
Severn House Publishers
Titan Books
The Women's Press

Short stories

Bellew
Bloomsbury Publishing
Marion Boyars Publishers
Jonathan Cape
Chatto & Windus
Constable & Co.
Forest Books
Fourth Estate
Gairm Publications
Granta Publications
Hamish Hamilton
William Heinemann
Hodder & Stoughton

Karnak House
Little, Brown
Peter Owen
Pan
Penguin Books
Polygon
Random House UK
Robinson Publishing
Secker and Warburg
Serpent's Tail
Severn House Publishers
Sinclair-Stevenson
Stride Publications
Yorkshire Art Circus

Other

Ethnic

The X Press

Erotic

Black Lace
Crime & Passion
Delta
Eros Plus
Idol
Liaison
Nexus

Graphic

Titan Books

Horror

Chapman
Warner

Humour

Black Swan
Corgi
Victor Gollancz
Warner

New/experimental

Serpent's Tail
Stride Publications

Translations

Arcadia Books Ltd
Marion Boyars Publishers
Dedalus
The Harvill Press
Quartet Books
Serpent's Tail

War

Severn House Publishers

Westerns

Robert Hale
Severn House Publishers

Publishers of multimedia

Addresses for Book publishers UK and Ireland start on page 153 and for Book packagers on page 216.

ABC-Clio Ltd
Addison Wesley Longman
BBC Worldwide Ltd
Berlitz Publishing
Blackwell Publishers
(InfoSource International)
The British Library
(Publications)
Butterworth & Co. (Publishers)
Ltd
Chadwyck-Healey Ltd
Current Science Group
Dorling Kindersley Multimedia
Harcourt Brace & Co. Ltd

(Academic Press)
Helicon Publishing
Hodder Headline
Jane's Information Group
Lion Publishing plc
McGraw Hill
Macmillan Interactive
Publishing
Mosby Wolfe Medical
Communications
Thomas Nelson
Notting Hill Electronic
Publishers
Oxford University Press

Random House New Media
Reed Educational Electronic
Publishing
Thames & Hudson
Training Direct (Pearson
Professional Ltd)
Two-Can Publishing
Usborne Publishing
The Watts Publishing Group
Wayland Publishers
Zigzag Multimedia Ltd

Book publishers overseas

Listings are given for book publishers in Australia (below), Canada (page 228), New Zealand (page 231), South Africa (page 233) and the USA (page 234).

Australia

Member of the Australian Publishers Association

Access Press
35 Stuart Street, Northbridge, Western Australia 6003
postal address PO Box 132, Northbridge, Western Australia 6865
tel (09) 328 9188 *fax* (09) 328 4605
e-mail ctomlins@omen.com.au
Managing Editor Helen Weller
Australiana, poetry, children's, history, general. Privately financed books published and distributed. Founded 1979.

Addison Wesley Longman Australia Pty Ltd*
95 Coventry Street, South Melbourne, Victoria 3205
tel (03) 9697 0666 *fax* (03) 9699 2041
e-mail robertf@awl.com.au
Managing Director Robert W. Fisher
Educational, academic and trade publishers.

Allen & Unwin Pty Ltd*
9 Atchison Street, PO Box 8500, St Leonards, NSW 2065
tel (02) 9901 4088 *fax* (02) 9906 2218
e-mail frontdesk@allen.unwin.com.au
web site www.allen-unwin.com.au
General trade, including fiction and children's books, academic, especially social science and history.

The Australian Council for Educational Research Ltd*
19 Prospect Hill Road, Private Bag 55, Camberwell, Victoria 3124
tel (03) 9277 5555 *fax* (03) 9277 5500
e-mail info@acer.edu.au
Range of books and kits: for teachers, trainee teachers, parents, psychologists, counsellors, students of education, researchers.

Blackwell Science*
54 University Street, Carlton, Victoria 3053
tel (03) 9347 0300 *fax* (03) 9347 5001
e-mail 100231.1015@compuserve.com
Editorial Director Mark Robertson
Medical, healthcare, life, earth sciences, professional.

Butterworths*
271-273 Lane Cove Road, North Ryde, NSW 2113
tel (02) 9335 4444 *fax* (02) 9335 4655
web site www.butterworths.com.au
Managing Director Murray Hamilton, *Editorial/Deputy Managing Director* J. Broadfoot
Legal, tax and commercial. Division of Reed International Books Australia Pty Ltd.

Cambridge University Press Australian Branch*
10 Stamford Road, Oakleigh, Melbourne, Victoria 3166
tel (03) 9568 0322 *fax* (03) 9563 1517
Director Kim W. Harris
Academic, educational, reference, English as a second language.

Craftsman House*
Level 1, Tower A, 112 Talavera Road, North Ryde, NSW 2113
tel (02) 9878 8222 *fax* (02) 9878 8122
Directors Nevill Drury (publishing), Martin Gordon, Nichola Dyson Walker (marketing manager)
Australian and European fine arts. Founded 1981.

Dominie Pty Ltd
Drama Department, 8 Cross Street, Brookvale, NSW 2100
tel (02) 9905 0201 *fax* (02) 9905 5209
Australian representatives of publishers

of plays and agents for the collection of royalties for Samuel French Ltd, incorporating Evans Plays and Samuel French Inc., The Society of Authors, ACTAC, and Bakers Plays of Boston.

Elephas Books
1-18 Mooney Street, Bayswater, WA 6053
tel (09) 370 1461 *fax* (09) 341 8952
Principals Alan J. Falkson, Rune Karlson
How-to and informational subjects. Founded 1989.

Samuel French Ltd – see Dominie Pty Ltd

HarperCollins Publishers (Australia) Pty Limited Group*
25-31 Ryde Road, Pymble, NSW 2073
postal address PO Box 321, Pymble, NSW 2073
tel (02) 9952 5000 *fax* (02) 9952 5555
Managing Director Barrie Hitchon
Literary fiction and non-fiction, popular fiction, reference, biography, autobiography, current affairs, sport, lifestyle, health/self-help, humour, true crime, travel, Australiana, history, business, gift/stationery, religion.

Hill of Content Publishing Co. Pty Ltd*
86 Bourke Street, Melbourne, Victoria 3000
tel (03) 9662 2282 *fax* (03) 9662 2527
Directors M. Slamen, M.G. Zifcak, Michelle Anderson
Health, general, lifestyle. Founded 1965.

Hodder Headline Australia Pty Ltd*
10-16 South Street, (Locked Bag 386), Rydalmere, NSW 2116
tel (02) 9841 2800 *fax* (02) 9841 2810
e-mail hsales@hha.com.au
Directors Malcolm Edwards (managing), Tim Hely Hutchinson, Lisa Highton, Mary Howell, Michael Burge, David Cocking, Mark Opzoomer
General, illustrated non-fiction, children's, religious, educational books.

Jacaranda Wiley Ltd*
33 Park Road, Milton, Queensland 4064
tel (07) 3859 9755 *fax* (07) 3859 9715 and
184-186 Glenferrie Road, Malvern, Victoria 3144
tel (03) 9576 1011 *fax* (03) 9576 1132 and
Suite 4A, 113 Wicks Road, North Ryde, NSW 2113
tel (02) 9805 1100 *fax* (02) 9805 1597
e-mail headoffice @jacwiley.com.au
Managing Director P. Donoughue
Educational, technical, atlases, professional, reference, trade.

Kangaroo Press
3 Whitehall Road, Kenthurst, NSW 2156
postal address PO Box 6125, Dural Delivery Centre, Dural, NSW 2158
tel (02) 9654 1502 *fax* (02) 9654 1338
e-mail kangaroo@parramatta.starway.net.au
Publisher David Rosenberg, *Publicist* Priscilla Rosenberg
Gardening, craft, Australian history and natural history, collecting, fitness, transport, children's non-fiction. An imprint of Simon & Schuster Australia. Founded 1980.

The Law Book Company Ltd*
50 Waterloo Road, North Ryde, NSW 2113
tel (02) 936 6444 *fax* (02) 888 9706

Lonely Planet Publications*
PO Box 617, Hawthorn, Victoria 3122
tel (03) 9819 1877 *fax* (03) 9819 6459
e-mail talk2us@lonelyplanet.com.au
web site http://www.lonelyplanet.com
Publisher Tony Wheeler
Travel guidebooks, walking guides, travel atlases, phrasebooks, travel literature and audio packs. Founded 1973.

Thomas C. Lothian Pty Ltd*
11 Munro Street, Port Melbourne, Victoria 3207
tel (03) 9645 1544 *fax* (03) 9646 4882
Chairman/Managing Director P. Lothian,
Directors E. McDonald, G. Matthews, B. Hilliard
Juveniles, health, gardening, general literature, craft, educational, reference, Australian history, business.

Macmillan Education Australia Pty Ltd*
Melbourne office 107 Moray Street, South Melbourne, Victoria 3205
tel (03) 9699 8922 *fax* (03) 9690 6938
e-mail meapl@macmillan.com.au
Sydney office Suite 310, Henry Lawson Business Centre, Birkenhead Point, Carey Street, Drummoyne, NSW 2047
tel (02) 9719 8944 *fax* (02) 9719 8613
e-mail measyd@macmillan.com.au
Directors N. Byam Shaw (UK), Brian Stonier (executive chairman), John Rolfe (managing), Margaret Brownie (primary publishing), Peter Debus (tertiary publishing), Peter Huntley (sales), Rex Parry (secondary publishing), George Smith (production), Kay Watts (marketing), *Company Secretary/Financial Controller* Terry White
Educational books.

Melbourne University Press*
268 Drummond Street, Carlton, Victoria 3053
postal address PO Box 278, Carlton South, Victoria 3053

tel (03) 9347 3455 fax (03) 9349 2527
Chairman Prof Barry Sheeham, *Director* John Meckan

Academic, scholastic and cultural; educational textbooks and books of reference.

Mimosa Publications Pty Ltd – see Weldon International Pty Ltd*

Nelson ITP*

102 Dodds Street, South Melbourne, Victoria 3205
tel (03) 9685 4111 fax (03) 9685 4199

Educational books.

Oxford University Press, Australia*

253 Normanby Road, South Melbourne, Victoria 3205
postal address GPO Box 2784Y, Melbourne, Victoria 3001
tel (03) 9934 9123 fax (03) 9934 9100
Managing Director Marek Palka

Australian history, biography, literary criticism, general, but excluding fiction; school books in all subjects.

Pan Macmillan Australia Pty Ltd*

Level 18, 31 Market Street, Sydney, NSW 2000
tel (02) 9261 5611 fax (02) 9261 5047
Directors Ross Gibb (managing), James Fraser (publishing), Roxarne Burns (publishing), Siv Toigo (finance), Peter Phillips (sales), Jeannine Fowler (publicity)

Fiction, non-fiction, children's.

Pearson Professional (Australia) Pty Ltd

King's Gardens, 95 Coventry Street, South Melbourne, Victoria 3205
tel (03) 9699 5400 fax (03) 9696 5205
Managing Director Peter Hylands

Medical, legal and business and professional publishers.

Penguin Books Australia Ltd*

(PO Box 257), 487 Maroondah Highway, Ringwood, Victoria 3134
tel (03) 9871 2400 fax (03) 9870 9618
Managing Director P.J. Field, *Publishing Director* R.P. Sessions

Fiction, general non-fiction, current affairs, sociology, economics, environmental, travel guides, anthropology, politics, children's, health, cookery, gardening, pictorial and general books relating to Australia under Penguin Books and Viking imprints. Founded 1946.

Random House Australia Pty Ltd*

20 Alfred Street, Milsons Point, NSW 2061
tel (02) 9954 9966 fax (02) 9954 4562

e-mail random@randomhouse.com.au
Managing Director E.F. Mason

General, non-fiction, fiction, children's.

Reed Books Pty Ltd*

35 Cotham Road, Kew, Victoria 3101
tel (03) 9261 5555 fax (03) 9261 5566
Managing Director Stewart Gill

Children's books and illustrated books.

Reed Education & Professional Publishing Australia*

22 Salmon Street, Port Melbourne, Victoria 3207
tel (03) 9245 7111 fax (03) 9245 7333
Managing Director Jack Mulcahy

Art, chemistry, chemical engineering, environmental studies, geography, geology, health, nutrition, history, mathematics, physics, languages. Primary and Secondary. Division of Reed Books. Founded 1982.

Reeve Books

35 Stuart Street, Northbridge, Western Australia 6003
postal address PO Box 132, Northbridge, Western Australia 6865
tel (09) 328 9188 fax (09) 328 4605
e-mail ctomlins@omen.com.au
Managing Director/Editor Helen Weller

Biography, local history, general non-fiction. Commissioned works only. Founded 1987.

Rigby Heinemann – see Reed Education & Professional Publishing Australia*

Scholastic Australia Pty Ltd*

PO Box 579, Gosford, NSW 2250
tel (043) 283555 fax (043) 233827
Managing Director Ken Jolly

Children's fiction/non-fiction; educational materials for elementary schools, teacher reference. Founded 1968.

Transworld Publishers (Aust) Pty Ltd*

Ground Floor, 40 Yeo Street, Neutral Bay, NSW 2089
tel (02) 9908 4366 fax (02) 9953 8563
Managing Director Geoffrey Rumpf, *Publisher* Shona Martyn

Bio, self-help, personal awareness, health, parenting and childcare, sports, current affairs, social history, popular culture, fiction. Founded 1981.

University of Queensland Press
PO Box 42, St Lucia, Queensland 4067
tel (07) 3365 2127 *fax* (07) 3365 7579
e-mail uqpbris@peg.apc.org.au
General Manager L.C. Muller

Scholarly works, tertiary texts, Australian fiction, young adult fiction, poetry, history, general interest. Founded 1948.

University of Western Australia Press
Tuart House, Nedlands 6907, Western Australia
tel (09) 380 3670 *fax* (09) 380 1027
e-mail uwap@cyllene.uwa.edu.au
web site http://www.uwa.edu.au/cyllene/uwap

History, natural history, literary criticism, Asian studies, Aboriginal studies, biography, children's picture books. Imprint: Cygnet Books. Founded 1954.

Viking – see Penguin Books*

Weldon International Pty Ltd*
107 Union Street, North Sydney, NSW 2060
tel (02) 9955 0091 *fax* (02) 9955 9390
Chairman Kevin Weldon

Mimosa Publications Pty Ltd (division)
Primary school education.

Weldon Owen (division)
Cookery, natural science, aerial photography, encyclopedic reference works, young readers' non-fiction.

Weldon Russell (division)
Illustrated non-fiction including natural history, cookery, gardening, ancient history, general reference books and gift books.

Wild & Woolley P*
PO Box 41, Glebe, NSW 2037
tel (02) 692 0166 *fax* (02) 552 4320
web site http://www.fastbooks.com.au
Director Pat Woolley

Offers short-run paperback printing for self-publishing writers. Founded 1974.

Canada

*Member of the Canadian Publishers' Council
†Member of the Association of Canadian Publishers

Annick Press Ltd
15 Patricia Avenue, Willowdale, Ontario M2M 1H9
tel 416-221-4802 *fax* 416-221-8400
e-mail annickpress@powerwindows.ca
Co-editors Anne Millyard, Rick Wilks

Juvenile fiction. Founded 1975.

Butterworths Canada Ltd
75 Clegg Road, Markham, Ontario L6G 1A1
tel 905-479-2665 *fax* 905-479-2826
e-mail name@butterworths.ca

Canada Publishing Corporation
164 Commander Boulevard, Scarborough, Ontario M1S 3C7
tel 416-293-8141 *fax* 416-293-9009

Publishers of elementary and secondary school textbooks; general trade/consumer publications including cookbooks, business, sport and fiction; professional and reference materials; annual publications, including *Canadian Global Almanac* and *Who's Who in Canada*. Founded 1844.

Canadian Stage and Arts Publications Ltd
104 Glenrose Avenue, Toronto, Ontario M4T 1K8
tel 416-484-4534 *fax* 416-484-6214
President/Publisher George Hencz

Primarily interested in children's books of an educational nature, art books. Also publishes quarterly *Performing Arts & Entertainment in Canada*, (Editor: Karen Bell).

Carswell, Thomson Professional Publishing
Corporate Plaza, 2075 Kennedy Road, Scarborough, Ontario M1T 3V4
tel 416-609-8000 *fax* 416-298-5094
Chairman/ceo Ross M. Inkpen

Law, tax, business reference.

The Charlton Press
2040 Yonge Street, Suite 208, Toronto, Ontario M4S 1Z9
tel 416-488-1418 *fax* 416-488-4656
e-mail chpress@charltonpress.com
web site www.charltonpress.com
President W.K. Cross

Collectibles, numismatics, Sportscard price catalogues. Founded 1952.

Copp Clark Ltd*
2775 Matheson Boulevard East, Mississauga, Ontario L4W 4P7
tel 905-238-6074 *fax* 905-238-6075
President Robert F. Gurnham

Professional publishers. Preliminary letter required before submitting MSS.

Doubleday Canada Ltd
105 Bond Street, Toronto, Ontario M5B 1Y3
tel 416-340-0777 *fax* 416-340-1069
Chairman Abraham Simkin, *President* John Neale

General trade non-fiction: current affairs,

politics; fiction; children's fiction and illustrated. Founded 1942.

Douglas & McIntyre Ltd[†]
1615 Venables Street, Vancouver, BC V5L 2H1
tel 604-254-7191 *fax* 604-254-9099
e-mail dm@douglas-mcintyre.com
General list, including Greystone Books imprint: Canadian biography, art and architecture, natural history, history, native studies, Canadian fiction. Children's division (Groundwood Books) specialises in fiction and illustrated flats. No unsolicited MSS. Founded 1964.

ECW Press[†]
2120 Queen Street E, Toronto, Ontario M4E 1E2
tel 416-694-3348 *fax* 416-698-9906
e-mail ecw@sympatico.ca
President Jack David, *Secretary-Treasurer* Robert Lecker
Literary criticism, general trade books, biographies, guidebooks. Founded 1979.

Fitzhenry & Whiteside Limited
195 Allstate Parkway, Markham, Ontario L3R 4T8
tel 905-477-9700 *fax* 905-477-9179
toll free 1-800-387-9776
Director Sharon Fitzhenry
Trade, educational, college books. Founded 1966.

Gage Educational Publishing Company – see Canada Publishing Corporation*

Gold Eagle Books – see Harlequin Enterprises Ltd*

Harcourt Brace & Company Canada, Ltd
55 Horner Avenue, Toronto, Ontario M8Z 4X6
tel 416-255-4491 *fax* 416-255-4046

Harlequin Enterprises Ltd*
225 Duncan Mill Road, Don Mills, Ontario M3B 3K9
tel 416-445-5860 *fax* 416-445-8655
President/ceo Brian E. Hickey
Romance, action adventure, mystery. Founded 1949.

Gold Eagle Books (imprint)
Senior Editor/Editorial Co-ordinator Feroze Mohammed
Series action adventure fiction.

Harlequin Books (imprint)
Editorial Director Randall Toye
Contemporary and historical romance fiction in series.

Mira Books (imprint)
Senior Editor/Editorial Co-ordinator Dianne Moggy
Women's fiction: contemporary and historical dramas, family sagas, romantic suspense and relationship novels.

Silhouette Books (imprint)
Editorial Director Isabel Swift
Contemporary romance fiction in series.

Worldwide Library (imprint)
Senior Editor/Editorial Co-ordinator Feroze Mohammed
Contemporary mystery fiction. Reprints only.

HarperCollins Canada
Markham Road, Scarborough, Ontario M1B 5M8
tel 416-321-2241 *fax* 416-321-3033

HarperCollins Publishers Ltd
Suite 2900, Hazelton Lanes, 55 Avenue Road, Toronto, Ontario M5R 3L2
tel 416-975-9334 *fax* 416-975-9884
Publishers of general literature, trade and reference, religious, mass market paperbacks, children's books. Founded 1989.

Irwin Publishing
1800 Steeles Avenue W, Concord, Ontario L4K 2P3
tel 905-660-0611 *fax* 905-660-0676
e-mail irwin@irwin-pub.com
President Brian O'Donnell, *Chairman* Jack Stoddart
Educational books at the elementary, high school and college levels. Division of General Publishing Co. Ltd.

ITP Nelson
(formerly Nelson Canada)
1120 Birchmount Road, Scarborough, Ontario M1K 5G4
tel 416-752-9100 *fax* 416-752-9646
Directors Herb Hilderley (president), Wilena White, Loren Darroch, Jim Black, Ken Proctor, Lynn Fisher, David Morrow
School (K-12), college and university, career education, measurement and guidance, professional and reference, and ESL titles. Founded 1914.

Kids Can Press Ltd[†]
29 Birch Avenue, Toronto, Ontario M4V 1E2
tel 416-925-5437 *fax* 416-960-5437
Publisher Valerie Hussey
Juvenile/young adult books.

Alfred A. Knopf Canada
33 Yonge Street, Suite 210, Toronto, Ontario M5E 1G4

tel 416-777-9477 *fax* 416-777-9470
web site http://www.randomhouse.com
Publisher, Vice-President Louise Dennys
Literary fiction and non-fiction. A division of **Random House of Canada Ltd.** Founded 1991.

Lester Publishing Ltd[t]
Key Porter Books Ltd, 70 The Esplanade, Toronto, Ontario M5E 1R2
tel 416-862-7777 *fax* 416-862-2304
President/Publisher Malcolm Lester
Biography, history, fiction, children's. An imprint of Key Porter Books Ltd. Founded 1991.

Lone Pine Publishing
206, 10426-81 Avenue, Edmonton, Alberta T6E 1X5
tel 403-433-9333 *fax* 403-433-9646
Publisher and Founder Grant Kennedy, *President* Shane Kennedy
Natural history, recreation and wildlife guidebooks, gardening, popular history. Founded 1980.

McClelland & Stewart Inc.[t]
481 University Avenue, Suite 900, Toronto, Ontario M5G 2E9
tel 416-598-1114 *fax* 416-598-7764
Chairman/President/ceo Avie Bennett
General. Founded 1906.

McGill-Queen's University Press[t]
3430 McTavish Street, Montreal, Quebec H3A 1X9
tel 514-398-3750 *fax* 514-398-4333
e-mail mqup@printing.lan.mcgill.ca and
Queen's University, Kingston, Ontario K7L 3N6
tel 613-545-2155 *fax* 613-545-6822
e-mail mqup@qucdn.queensu.ca
Academic. Founded 1969.

McGraw-Hill Ryerson Ltd*
300 Water Street, Whitby, Ontario L1N 9B6
tel 905-430-5000 *fax* 905-430-5020
Educational and trade books.

Macmillan Canada[t]
29 Birch Avenue, Toronto, Ontario M4V 1E2
tel 416-963-8830 *fax* 416-923-4821
Trade book publishers. Division of Canada Publishing Corporation. Founded 1905.

Maxwell Macmillan Canada –
acquired by Prentice Hall Canada Inc.*

Mira Books – see Harlequin
Enterprises Ltd

Nelson Canada – see ITP Nelson

Oberon Press[t]
400-350 Sparks Street, Ottawa, Ontario K1R 7S8
tel/fax 613-238-3275
General.

Oxford University Press, Canada
70 Wynford Drive, Don Mills, Ontario M3C 1J9
tel 416-441-2941 *fax* 416-444-0427
web site http://www.oupcan.com
Managing Director Susan Froud
General, educational and academic.

Pippin Publishing Corporation
Suite 232, 85 Ellesmere Road, Scarborough, Ontario M1R 4B9
tel 416-510-2918 *fax* 416-510-3359
President/Editorial Director Jonathan Lovat Dickson
ESL/EFL, teacher reference, adult basic education, school texts (all subjects).

Prentice Hall Canada Inc.*
1870 Birchmount Road, Scarborough, Ontario M1P 2J7
tel 416-293-3621 *fax* 416-299-2529
President Brian Heer
Academic, technical, educational, children's and adult, trade. Founded 1960.

Quarry Press[t]
PO Box 1061, Kingston, Ontario K7L 4Y5
tel 613-548-8429 *fax* 613-548-1556
Publisher Bob Hilderley
Fiction, poetry, children's, biography, historical non-fiction, travel, folk stories. Founded 1965.

Random House of Canada Ltd
33 Yonge Street, Suite 210, Toronto, Ontario M5E 1G4
tel 416-777-9477 *fax* 416-777-9470
web site http://www.randomhouse.com
President and Publisher David Kent
Imprints: Ballantine Canada, Knopf Canada, Random House Canada, Vintage Canada. Subsidiary of **Random House, Inc.** Founded 1944.

Silhouette Books – see Harlequin
Enterprises Ltd*

Stoddart Publishing Co. Ltd
34 Lesmill Road, Don Mills, Ontario M3B 2T6
tel 416-445-3333 *fax* 416-445-5967
e-mail stoddart@genpub.com
Fiction and non-fiction.

Tundra Books Inc.
481 University Avenue, Suite 802, Toronto, Ontario M5G 2E9
tel 416-598-4786 *fax* 416-598-0247

High quality children's picture books.

University of Toronto Press Inc.†
10 St Mary Street, Suite 700, Toronto,
Ontario M4Y 2W8
tel 416-978-2239 *fax* 416-978-4738
President/Publisher George L. Meadows

**Worldwide Library – see Harlequin
Enterprises Ltd***

New Zealand

**Member of the New Zealand Book
Publishers' Association*

Addison Wesley Longman*
Private Bag 102908, North Shore Mail Centre,
Glenfield, Auckland 10
tel (09) 444-4968 *fax* (09) 444-4957
e-mail rosemary.stagg@awl.co.nz
NZ educational books.

**Ashton Scholastic Ltd – see Scholastic
New Zealand Ltd**

Auckland University Press*
University of Auckland, Private Bag 92019,
Auckland
tel (09) 373-7528 *fax* (09) 373-7465
e-mail aup@auckland.ac.nz
Director Elizabeth Caffin
NZ history, NZ poetry, Maori and Pacific
studies, politics, sociology, literary criticism, art history, biography, media studies, women's studies. Founded 1966.

David Bateman Ltd*
Tarndale Grove, Albany Business Park,
Bush Road, Albany, Auckland
postal address PO Box 100242, North Shore Mail
Centre, Auckland 10
tel (09) 415-7664 *fax* (09) 415-8892
Chairman/Publisher David L. Bateman, *Directors*
Janet Bateman, Paul Bateman (joint managing),
Paul Parkinson (joint managing)
Natural history, gardening, encyclope-
dias, sport, art, cookery, historical, juve-
nile, travel, motoring, maritime history,
business. Founded 1979.

Bush Press Communications Ltd
4 Bayview Road, Hauraki Corner, Takapuna,
Auckland 1309
postal address PO Box 33-029, Takapuna,
Auckland 1309
tel/fax (09) 486-2667
Governing Director/Publisher Gordon Ell
NZ non-fiction, particularly outdoor,
nature, travel, architecture, crafts, Maori,

popular history; children's non-fiction.
Founded 1979.

Butterworths of New Zealand Ltd*
203-207 Victoria Street, Wellington
tel (04) 385-1479 *fax* (04) 385-1598
Publishing Director James Clarke
Law, accountancy.

The Caxton Press*
113 Victoria Street, Christchurch, PO Box 25-088
tel (03) 366-8516 *fax* (03) 365-7840
Director E.B. Bascand
Fine printers and publishers since 1935
of NZ books of many kinds, including
biography, history, natural history, travel,
gardening.

Dunmore Press Ltd*
PO Box 5115, Palmerston North
tel (06) 358-7169 *fax* (06) 357-9242
e-mail dunmore@xtra.co.nz
Directors Murray Gatenby, Sharmian Firth
Education, history, sociology, business
studies, general non-fiction. Founded 1970.

Godwit Publishing Ltd*
PO Box 34-683, Birkenhead, Auckland
tel (09) 480-5410 *fax* (09) 480-5930
e-mail godwit@godwit.co.nz
Publisher Jane Connor, *Executive Director* Brian
Phillips
Art, gardening, lifestyle, literature and
natural history. Founded 1994.

Grantham House Publishing
PO Box 17-256, Wellington 6033
tel (04) 476-4625 *fax* (04) 476-3048
Publisher/Chief Executive Graham C. Stewart,
Editorial Anna Rogers, Lorraine Olphert
Antiques and collecting, architecture and
design, aviation, gardening, history and
antiquarian, illustrated and fine editions,
military and war, nautical, transport, railways, tramways. Founded 1984.

**HarperCollins Publishers (New
Zealand) Ltd***
PO Box 1, Auckland
tel (09) 443-9400 *fax* (09) 443-9403
Publishers of general literature, teen fiction, non-fiction, reference books, trade
paperbacks.

Hodder Moa Beckett Publishers Ltd*
PO Box 100-749, North Shore Mail Centre,
Auckland 1330
tel (09) 478-1000 *fax* (09) 478-1010
Managing Director Neil Aston, *Publisher* Sarah
Beresford

Sport, gardening, cooking, travel, atlases, general, fiction, children's.

Mallinson Rendel Publishers Ltd
7 Grass Street, PO Box 9409, Wellington
tel (04) 385-7340 *fax* (04) 385-4235
Directors Ann Mallinson, David Rendel
Children's, general NZ books. Founded 1980.

Nelson Price Milburn Ltd*
PO Box 38-945, Wellington Mail Centre, Wellington
located at 1 Te Puni Street, Petone
tel (04) 568-7179 *fax* (04) 568-2115
Children's fiction, primary school texts, especially school readers and maths, secondary educational.

New Zealand Council for Educational Research
Box 3237, Education House,
178-182 Willis Street, Wellington 1
tel (04) 384-7939 *fax* (04) 384-7933
Director Anne Meade, *Publisher* Peter Ridder
Education, including educational policy and institutions, early childhood education, higher education, educational achievement tests, Maori education, curriculum and assessment, etc. Founded 1933.

Oxford University Press*
PO Box 11-149, Ellerslie, Auckland 5
tel (09) 525-8020 *fax* (09) 525-1072
NZ Academic/Trade Publisher Linda Cassells

Random House New Zealand Ltd*
Private Bag 102950, North Shore Mail Centre, Auckland 10
tel (09) 444-7197 *fax* (09) 444-7524
Managing Director J. Rogers
Fiction, general non-fiction, gardening, business, health. Founded 1977.

Reed Publishing (New Zealand) Ltd*
(incorporating Reed Consumer Books and Heinemann Education)
39 Rawene Road, Private Bag 34901, Birkenhead, Auckland 10
tel (09) 480-4950 *fax* (09) 480-4999
Chairman John Holloran, *Managing Director* Alan Smith
NZ literature, specialist and general titles, primary, secondary and tertiary textbooks. Imprints: George Philip, Conran Octopus, Mitchell Beazley, Reed Publishing Group Australia Pty Ltd, Heinemann Young Books, Secker & Warburg, Hamlyn, Bounty, Dean, Buzz, Minerva, Mandarin, Cedar, Methuen Drama, Brimax, Budget Books, Octopus Publishing Group, Ginn & Company, Heinemann Education Books, Rigby Heinemann (Australia), Rigby (USA), Heinemann Education Books Inc. (USA).

Scholastic New Zealand Ltd*
21 Lady Ruby Drive, East Tamaki, Auckland
postal address Private Bag 94407, Greenmount, Auckland
tel (09) 274-8112 *fax* (09) 274-8114
Managing Director/Publisher Joan Baker, *Finance and Operations Director* David Peagram
Children's books. Founded 1962.

Shortland Publications Ltd*
2B Cawley Street, Ellerslie, Auckland 5
tel (09) 526 6200 *fax* (09) 526 4499
Managing Director Avelyn Davidson
Children's educational books: reading material (ages 5-12), science/non-fiction (ages 5-14). Founded 1984.

University of Otago Press*
University of Otago, PO Box 56, Dunedin
tel/fax (03) 479-8807 *fax* (03) 479-8385
e-mail university.press@otago.ac.nz
Managing Editor Wendy Harrex
Student texts and scholarly works in all disciplines and general books, including Maori and women's studies, natural history and environmental studies, health and fiction. Also publishes journals including *Landfall* and the *Women's Studies Journal*. Founded 1958.

Victoria University Press*
Victoria University of Wellington, PO Box 600, Wellington
tel (04) 496-6580 *fax* (04) 496-6581
Publisher Fergus Barrowman
Academic, scholarly books on NZ history, sociology, environment, law, biology; Maori language; fiction, plays, poetry. Founded 1974.

Viking Sevenseas Ltd
23B Ihakara Street, Paraparaumu
tel (04) 297-1990 *fax* (04) 297-1990
Managing Director M.B. Riley
Factual books on New Zealand only.

South Africa

**Member of the South African
Publishers' Association publisher*

Jonathan Ball Publishers (Pty) Ltd*
10-14 Watkins Street, Denver Ext. 4,
Johannesburg
postal address Box 33977, Jeppestown 2043
tel (011) 622 2900 *fax* (011) 622 3553
Ad Donker (division)
Africana, literature, history, academic.
Jonathan Ball/HarperCollins (division)
General publications, reference books,
business, history, politics.
Delta Books (division)
General non-fiction.

Cambridge University Press
1 The Moorings, Portswood Ridge,
Victoria & Alfred Waterfront, Cape Town 8001
tel (021) 419-8414
Director Tony Seddon
Educational, ELT and academic publishers serving primary and secondary
schools, further education, technikons
and universities.

Ad Donker (Pty) Ltd – see Jonathan Ball Publishers (Pty) Ltd

HarperCollins Publishers (SA) (Pty) Ltd – see Jonathan Ball Publishers (Pty) Ltd

Juta & Company Ltd*
PO Box 14373, Kenwyn 7790, Cape Town
tel (021) 797-5101 *fax* (021) 762-7424
e-mail books@juta.co.za
School, academic, professional, law and
electronic publishers. Founded 1853.

Knowledge Unlimited (Pty) Ltd
Private Bag 16, Centurion 0046
tel (011) 652-1800 *fax* (011) 314-2984
Managing Director M.A.C. Jacklin, *Production
Manager* H.B.C. Mason, *Head of Editorial* Dr
H.J.M. Retief
Children's fiction and non-fiction;
Afrikaans large print books. Subjects
include aviation, natural history,
romance, general science, technology
and transportation. Imprints: Knowledge
Unlimited, Mike Jacklin, Kennis
Onbeperk, Daan Retief. A subsidiary of
Time Life Books BV. Founded 1992.

Lovedale Press
Private Bag X1346, Alice 5700, Eastern Cape
tel (0404) 31-135 *fax* (0404) 31-871
Educational, religious and general book
publications for African and overseas
market.

Maskew Miller Longman (Pty) Ltd*
Howard Drive, Pinelands 7405
postal address PO Box 396, Cape Town 8000
tel (021) 531-7750 *fax* (021) 531-4049
Educational and general publishers.

Oxford University Press (Southern African Branch)*
Vasco Boulevard, NI City, Goodwood 7460
postal address PO Box 12119, Goodwood 7463
tel (021) 595 4400
e-mail oxford@oup.co.za
Managing Director Kate McCallum

David Philip Publishers (Pty) Ltd*
PO Box 23408, Claremont 7735, Western Cape
tel (21) 644-136 *fax* (21) 643-358
e-mail dpp@iafrica.com
Managing Directors David Philip, Marie Philip,
Directors Russell Martin, Bridget Impey
Academic, history, social sciences, politics, theology, biography, belles-lettres,
reference books, fiction, educational,
children's books. Founded 1971.

Ravan Press (Pty) Ltd*
4th Floor, Randhill, 104 Bordeaux Drive,
Randburg
postal address PO Box 145, Randburg 2125
tel (011) 789-7636 *fax* (011) 789-7653
Executive Chairman G.E. de Villiers
South African studies: history, politics,
social studies; fiction, literature, children's, educational. Founded 1972.

Shuter and Shooter (Pty) Ltd*
230 Church Street and 199 Pietermaritz Street,
Pietermaritzburg 3201, Natal
postal address PO Box 109, Pietermaritzburg 3200
tel (0331) 946-830/948-881
fax (0331) 943-096/427-419
Publishing Director D.F. Ryder
Primary and secondary educational, science, biology, history, maths, geography,
English, Afrikaans, biblical studies,
music, teacher training, agriculture,
accounting, school readiness, dictionaries, African languages. Founded 1925.

Southern Book Publishers (Pty) Ltd*
PO Box 3103, Halfway House, Gauteng 1685
tel (011) 315-3633/7 *fax* (011) 315-3810

Publishers of general non-fiction books, especially natural history, as well as those of South African interest.

Struik Publishers (Pty) Ltd*
PO Box 1144, Cape Town 8000
tel (021) 462-4360 *fax* (021) 461-9378/462-4379
Managing Director Dick Wilkins

General illustrated non-fiction. Division of The Struik Publishing Group (Pty) Ltd.

Struik Winchester Publishers*
PO Box 3755, Cape Town 8000
tel (021) 462-4360 *fax* (021) 462-4379/461-9378
e-mail sms@struik.co.za
Managing Director Nick Pryte

Natural history, cultural history. Division of The Struik Publishing Group (Pty) Ltd.

Unisa Press*
PO Box 392, Pretoria 0003
tel (012) 429-3051 *fax* (012) 429-3221
e-mail unisa-press@unisa.ac.za
web site http://www.unisa.ac.za/0/
Head Mrs P. Van Der Walt

Theology and all academic disciplines. Publishers of University of South Africa. Imprint: UNISA. Founded 1957.

J.L. Van Schaik Publishers*
PO Box 12681, Hatfield, Pretoria 0028
tel (012) 342-2765 *fax* (012) 433-563
e-mail mbotha@nbh.naspers.co.za
web site http://www.naspers.co.za

Publishers of books in English, Afrikaans and African languages. Specialists in non-fiction, religion, textbooks and fiction in eleven official languages. Founded 1914.

William Waterman Publications Pty Ltd*
(incorporating Ashanti Publishing, Justified Press, Justified Press for Juniors)
PO Box 5091, Rivonia 2128
tel (011) 882-1408 *fax* (011) 882-1559
Directors Murray J. Bolton, Nicholas W. Combrinck (managing)

General non-fiction, military history, literature, poetry, children's educational.

Witwatersrand University Press*
PO Wits, 2050
tel (011) 484-5910 *fax* (011) 484-5971
e-mail wup@iafrica.com

USA

Member of the Association of American Publishers, Inc.

Abbeville Press
488 Madison Avenue, 23rd Floor, New York, NY 10022
tel 212-888-1969 *fax* 212-644-5085
Publisher/President Robert Abrams

Art and illustrated books. Founded 1977.

Abingdon Press
PO Box 801, Nashville, TN 37202-0801
tel 615-749-6404 *fax* 615-749-6512
Editorial office for academic books 2495 Lawrenceville Highway, Decatur, GA 30033-3240
tel 404-636-6001 *fax* 404-636-5894
Editorial Director Harriett Jane Olson

General interest, professional, academic and reference – primarily directed to the religious market.

Academy Chicago Publishers
363 West Erie Street, Chicago, IL 60610
tel 312-751-7300 *fax* 312-751-7306
Directors Anita Miller, Jordan Miller

Fiction, mystery, biography, travel, books of interest to women; quality reprints. Founded 1975.

Andrews McMeel Publishing
4520 Main Street, Kansas City, MO 64111
tel 816-932-6700 *fax* 816-932-6706
Vice-President/Editorial Director Christine Schillig

General trade publishing, with emphasis on humour, how-to, self-help, women's issues.

Arcade Publishing
141 Fifth Avenue, New York, NY 10010
tel 212-475-2633 *fax* 212-353-8148
President/Publisher Richard Seaver, *Associate Publisher/Marketing Director* Jeannette Seaver, *General Manager* Cal Barksdale

General, including adult hard cover and paperbacks.

Atlantic Monthly Press – see Grove/Atlantic, Inc.

Avon Books*
The Hearst Corporation, 1350 Avenue of the Americas, New York, NY 10019
tel 212-261-6800 *fax* 212-261-6895
Senior Vice-President/Publisher Lou Aronica

All subjects, fiction and non-fiction. Founded 1941.

Walter H. Baker Company

100 Chauncy Street, Boston, MA 02111
tel 617-482-1280 *fax* 617-482-7613
President Charles Van Nostrand, *Editor* John B. Welch
UK Agent Samuel French Ltd, 52 Fitzroy Street, London W1P 6JR

Plays and books on the theatre. Also agents for plays. Founded 1845.

Bantam Doubleday Dell Publishing Group Inc.*

1540 Broadway, New York, NY 10036
tel 212-354-6500 *fax* 212-782-9597
Chairman, President/ceo Jack Hoeft

Fiction, classics, biography, health, business, general non-fiction, social sciences, religion, sports, science, audio tapes.

Barron's Educational Series, Inc.

250 Wireless Boulevard, Hauppage, NY 11788
tel 516-434-3311 *fax* 516-434-3723
President Manuel H. Barron, *Executive Vice President* Ellen Sibley

Test preparation, juvenile, cookbooks, crafts, business, pets, gardening, family and health, art, study guides, school guides. Founded 1941.

Beacon Press*

25 Beacon Street, Boston, MA 02108
tel 617-742-2110 *fax* 617-723-3097
Director Helene Atwan

General non-fiction in fields of religion, ethics, philosophy, current affairs, gender studies, environmental concerns, African-American studies, anthropology and women's studies, nature.

R.R. Bowker*

121 Chanlon Road, New Providence, NJ 07974
tel 908-464-6800 *fax* 908-464-3553
President Ira T. Siegel

A Reed Reference Publishing company. Bibliographies and reference tools for the book trade and literary and library worlds, available in hardcopy, on microfiche, on-line and CD-Rom. Reference books for music, art, business, computer industry, cable industry and information industry.

Boyds Mills Press

815 Church Street, Honesdale, PA 18431
tel 717-253-1164 *fax* 717-253-0179
Publisher Kent Brown Jr, *President* Clay Winters, *Editorial Director* Larry Rosler, *Art Director* Tim Gillner

Fiction, non-fiction, and poetry trade books for children. Founded 1990.

Brassey's, Inc.

22883 Quicksilver Drive, Dulles, VA 20166
tel 703-260-0602
Managing Director Jim Sutton

Foreign policy, defence, national and international affairs, military history, intelligence, biography, sports. Founded 1984.

George Braziller Inc.

171 Madison Avenue, New York, NY 10016
tel 212-889-0909 *fax* 212-689-5405
Publisher George Braziller, *Assistant to the Publisher* Mary Taveras

Art, architecture, history, biography, fiction, poetry, science. Founded 1955.

Cambridge University Press (North American branch)*

40 West 20th Street, New York, NY 10011
tel 212-924-3900 *fax* 212-691-3239
Director Barbara Colson

Candlewick Press

2067 Massachusetts Avenue, Cambridge, MA 02140
tel 617-661-3330 *fax* 617-661-0565
Editor-in-Chief Liz Bicknell, *Senior Editor* Mary Lee Donovan, *Editors* Gale Pryor, Susan Halperin, *Consulting Editor* Amy Ehrlich

Children's books – 6 months to 14 years: board books, picture books, novels, non-fiction, novelty books. Submit material through a literary agent. Founded 1991.

Capra Press

PO Box 2068, Santa Barbara, CA 93120
tel 805-966-4590 *fax* 805-965-8020
Publisher Noel Young

Fiction, natural history, animals. Founded 1969.

Carroll & Graf Publishers, Inc.

19 West 21st Street, Suite 601, New York, NY 10010
tel 212-889-8772
President Herman Graf, *Publisher* Kent Carroll, *Subrights* Adam Dunn, *Foreign Rights* Henry Lincoln

Mystery and science fiction, popular fiction, history, biography, literature, business, sports. Founded 1983.

Chilton Book Company – acquired by Krause Publications

Chronicle Books

85 Second Street, San Francisco, CA 94105
tel 415-777-7240 *fax* 415-777-2289
web site www.chronbooks.com
Publisher Jack Jensen, *Associates* Christine
Carswell, Caroline Herter, Nion McEvoy, Victoria
Rock

Cooking, art, fiction, general, children's,
gift, new media, gardening, regional,
nature. Founded 1967.

Coffee House Press

27 N 4th Street, Suite 400, Minneapolis,
MN 55401
tel 612-338-0125 *fax* 612-338-4004
Publisher Allan Kornblum
UK agent Patrick Walsh, Christopher Little Agency

Literary fiction and poetry; collectors'
editions. Founded 1984.

Columbia University Press*

562 West 113th Street, New York, NY 10025
tel 212-666-1000 *fax* 212-316-3100
Editor-in-Chief Kate Wittenberg
UK 1 Oldlands Way, Bognor Regis,
West Sussex PO22 9SA
tel (0243) 042165 *fax* (0243) 842167

General reference works in print and
electronic formats, translations and
serious non-fiction of more general
interest.

Concordia Publishing House

3558 S Jefferson Avenue, St Louis, MO 63118
tel 314-268-1000 *fax* 314-268-1329
Executive Vice-President, Editorial Dr Earl Gaulke

Religious books, Lutheran perspective.
Few freelance MSS accepted; query first.
Founded 1869.

NTC/Contemporary Publishing Company

4255 West Touhy Avenue, Lincolnwood, IL 60646
tel 847-679-5500 *fax* 847-679-2494
Vice President/Publisher Christine Albritton,
Editorial Director John Nolan

Non-fiction.

The Continuum Publishing Company, Inc.*

370 Lexington Avenue, New York, NY 10017-6503
tel 212-953-5858 *fax* 212-953-5944
e-mail contin@tiac.net
web site http://www.continuum-books.com
Chairman/Publisher Werner Mark Linz

General non-fiction, education, literature,
psychology, politics, sociology, literary
criticism, religious studies. Founded
1980.

Cornell University Press*

(including ILR Press and Comstock Publishing
Associates)
Sage House, 512 East State Street, Ithaca,
NY 14850
tel 607-277-2338 *fax* 607-277-2374
Director John G. Ackerman.

Scholarly books. Founded 1869.

Council Oak Books

1350 East 15th Street, Tulsa, OK 74120-5801
tel 918-587-6454 *fax* 918-583-4995
e-mail oakie@ionet.net
Chief Operating Officer David Kanbar, *Publishers*
Sally Dennison PhD, Paulette Millichap

Non-fiction: native American, multicultural, life skills, life accounts, Earth
awareness, meditation. Founded 1984.

The Countryman Press, Inc.

PO Box 748, Rte 12N, Mount Tom, Woodstock,
VT 05091
tel 802-457-4826 *fax* 802-457-1678
Editor-in-Chief Helen Whybrow

Outdoor recreation guides for anglers,
hikers, cyclists, canoeists and skiers, US
travel guides, New England non-fiction,
how-to books, country living books,
books on nature and the environment,
classic reprints and general non-fiction.
No unsolicited MSS. Founded 1973.

Crown Publishing Group

201 East 50th Street, New York, NY 10022
tel 212-572-2408 *fax* 212-940-7408
President/Publisher Chip Gibson

General fiction, non-fiction, illustrated
books.

Devin-Adair Publishers, Inc.

PO Box A, Old Greenwich, CT 06830
tel 203-531-7755

Conservative politics, health and ecology,
Irish topics, gardening and travel, homeopathy and holistic health books, original
photography publications. Founded 1911.

Doubleday – see Bantam Doubleday Dell Publishing Group Inc.*

Dover Publications, Inc.

31 E 2nd Street, Mineola, NY 11501
tel 516-294-7000 *fax* 516-873 1401
Vice-President, Editorial Paul Negri

Art, architecture, antiques, crafts, juvenile, food, history, folklore, literary classics, mystery, language, music, math and
science, nature, design and ready-to-use
art. Founded 1941.

Dryden Press
City Center Tower II, 301 Commerce Street,
Suite 3700, Fort Worth, TX 76102
tel 817-334-7711 *fax* 817-334-0878
Publisher George E. Provol
College textbooks.

Dutton/Signet*
375 Hudson Street, New York, NY 10014
tel 212-366-2000 *fax* 212-366-2666
General publishers. General non-fiction,
including biographies, adventure, history,
travel, fiction, mysteries, juveniles, quality paperbacks. Division of Penguin USA.

Dutton Children's Books*
375 Hudson Street, 3rd Floor, New York,
NY 10014
tel 212-366-2600 *fax* 212-366-2011
President/Publisher Christopher Franceschelli,
Editor-in-Chief Lucia Monfried, *Executive Editor*
Donna Brooks, *Director of Operations* Karen Lotz
Picture books, young adult novels, non-
fiction photographic books.

Faber and Faber, Inc.
53 Shore Road, Winchester, MA 01890
tel 617-721-1427 *fax* 617-729-2783
Publisher Tom Kelleher, *Senior Editors* Valerie J.
Cimino, Dan Weaver
Adult non-fiction: biographies, popular
history, film, popular music, ethnic and
cultural works, travelogues, anthologies,
literary novels, popular science, women's
issues, gay and lesbian fiction and non-
fiction. Founded 1976.

Facts On File, Inc.
11 Penn Plaza, 15th Floor, New York,
NY 10001-2006
tel 212-967 8800 *fax* 212-967 9196
Chairman Mark McDonnell, *President* Beverly
Balaz
General reference books and services for
colleges, libraries, schools and general
public. Founded 1940.

Farrar, Straus & Giroux Inc.
19 Union Square West, New York, NY 10003
tel 212-741-6900 *fax* 212-633-9385
Executive Vice-President/Editor-in-Chief Jonathan
Galassi
General publishers.

Firebrand Books
141 The Commons, Ithaca, NY 14850
tel 607-272-0000
Editor/Publisher Nancy K. Bereano
Feminist and lesbian fiction and non-fiction. Founded 1986.

Four Walls Eight Windows
39 West 14th Street, Room 503, New York,
NY 10011
tel 212-206-8965 *fax* 212-206-8799
e-mail eightwind@aol.com
web site http://www.fourwallseightwindows.com
Publisher John Oakes
Fiction, graphic works, novels, memoirs,
art, African-American studies, current
affairs, biography, environment, health.
No unsolicited submissions accepted.
Founded 1987.

Samuel French Inc.
45 West 25th Street, New York, NY 10010
tel 212-206-8990 *fax* 212-206-1429
Play publishers and authors' representatives (dramatic).

David R. Godine, Publisher Inc.
PO Box 9103, Lincoln, MA 01773
President David R. Godine, *Editorial Director*
Mark Polizzotti
Fiction, photography, poetry, art, biography, children's, essays, history, typography, architecture, nature and gardening,
music, cooking, words and writing, and
mysteries. Founded 1970.

Greenwillow Books
1350 Avenue of the Americas, New York,
NY 10019
tel 212-261-6500 *fax* 212-261-6619
Senior Vice-President/Editor-in-Chief Susan
Hirschman
Children's books. Division of William
Morrow & Co., Inc.

Grosset & Dunlap, Inc.
200 Madison Avenue, New York, NY 10016
tel 212-951-8700
President/Publisher Jane O'Connor
Children's mass market: easy-to-reads,
series books, activity books, board
books.

Grove/Atlantic, Inc.
841 Broadway, New York, NY 10003-4793
tel 212-614-7850 *fax* 212-614-7886
Publisher Morgan Entrekin
MSS of permanent interest, fiction, biography, autobiography, history, current
affairs, social science, belles-lettres, natural history. Imprints: **Atlantic Monthly
Press**, **Grove Press**.

Grove Press – see Grove/Atlantic, Inc.

Harcourt Brace & Company*
525 B Street, Suite 1900, San Diego, CA 92101
tel 619-231-6616 *fax* 619-699-6320
President Rubin Pfeffer, *Vice President/Publisher, Children's Books* Louise Pelan, *Vice President/ Publisher, Adult Books* Dan Farley
General publishers. Fiction, history, biography, etc.

HarperCollins Publishers*
10 East 53rd Street, New York, NY 10022
tel 212-207-7000
President/Chief Executive Officer Anthea Disney
HarperCollins San Francisco 1160 Battery Street, San Francisco, CA 94111
tel 415-477-4400 *fax* 415-477-4444
London HarperCollins Publishers, 77-85 Fulham Palace Road, London W6 8JB
Fiction, history, biography, poetry, science, travel, juvenile, educational, business, technical and religious. No unsolicited material; all submissions must come through a literary agent. Founded 1817.

Harvard University Press*
79 Garden Street, Cambridge, MA 02138-1499
tel 617-495 2600 *fax* 617-495-5898
web site http://www.hup.harvard.edu
Director William P. Sisler, *Editor-in-Chief/ Assistant Director* Aida D. Donald
History, philosophy, literary criticism, politics, economics, sociology, music, science, classics, social sciences.

Hastings House
50 Washington Street, Norwalk, CT 06854
tel 803-838-4083 *fax* 803-838 4084
Publisher Henno Lohmeyer, *Editor-in-Chief* Hy Steirman
Non-fiction, general, consumer, travel, cooking, controversy and how-to.

D.C. Heath and Co. – acquired by Houghton Mifflin Company*

Hill & Wang
19 Union Square West, New York, NY 10003
tel 212-741-6900 *fax* 212-633-9385
Publisher Elisabeth Sifton, *Editor* Lauren M. Osborne, *Consulting Editor* Arthur W. Wang
General non-fiction, history, drama. Division of Farrar, Straus & Giroux Inc. Founded 1956.

Hippocrene Books, Inc.
171 Madison Avenue, New York, NY 10016
tel 212-685-4371 *fax* 212-779-9338
President/Editorial Director George Blagowidow, *Publisher/Director of Marketing* Jacek Galazka
Foreign language books, foreign language dictionaries, travel, military history, Polonia, general trade. Founded 1971.

Holiday House
425 Madison Avenue, New York, NY 10017
tel 212-688-0085 *fax* 212-421-6134
President John Briggs, *Vice-President/Editor-in-Chief* Regina Griffin
General children's books. Founded 1935.

Holmes & Meier Publishers Inc.
160 Broadway, New York, NY 10038
tel 212-374-0100 *fax* 212-374-1313
Executive Editor Katharine Turok
History, biography, political science, art, costume, Jewish studies, international affairs, Latin American studies, sociology, theatre (history), women's studies, fiction in translation, Africana publishing. Founded 1969.

Henry Holt and Company, Inc.*
115 West 18th Street, New York, NY 10011
tel 212-886-9200 *fax* 212-633-0748
Associate Publisher, Editor-in-Chief Adult Books William Strachan, *Associate Publisher, Editor-in-Chief Books for Young Readers* Marjorie Cuyler, *Associate Publisher, Editorial Director Reference Books* Ken Wright, *Publisher, Twenty-First Century Books* Jeanne Vestal, *Editorial Director MIS Press and M&T Books* Paul Farrell, *Associate Publisher, Editorial Director Metropolitan Books* Sara Bershtel, *Associate Publisher, Editorial Director Owl Books* Gregory Hamlin
History, biography, nature, science, self-help, novels, mysteries; books for young readers; trade paperback line, computer books. Founded 1866.

Houghton Mifflin Company*
222 Berkeley Street, Boston, MA 02116
tel 617-351-5000
Executive Vice-President/Publisher, Trade and Reference Division Wendy J. Strothman
Fiction and non-fiction – history, political science, biography, travel, nature (Peterson Guides), and gardening guides; both adult and juvenile. Imprints: Mariner (original and reprint paperbacks); Chapters (cookbooks). Best length: 60,000-180,000 words; juveniles, any reasonable length. Founded 1832.

Indiana University Press
601 North Morton Street, Bloomington, IN 47404-3797
tel 812-855-4203 *fax* 812-855-7931
Director John Gallman

African studies, Russian and East European studies, semiotics, literary criticism, music, history, women's studies, Jewish studies, African-American studies, film, folklore, philosophy, medical ethics, archaeology, anthropology. Founded 1950.

The Johns Hopkins University Press*
2715 North Charles Street, Baltimore, MD 21218-4319
tel 410-516-6971 *fax* 410-516-6968
Director Dr Willis Regier

History, literary criticism, classics, politics, economic development, environmental studies, biology, medical genetics, consumer health. Founded 1878.

Keats Publishing Inc.
27 Pine Street, PO Box 876, New Canaan, CT 06840
tel 203-966-8721
President/Publisher Norman Goldfind

Natural health, alternative medicine, nutrition and medical books. Founded 1971.

Alfred A. Knopf Inc.
201 East 50th Street, New York, NY 10022
tel 212-751-2600 *fax* 212-572-2593
web site http://www.randomhouse.com

General literature, fiction, belles-lettres, sociology, politics, history, nature, science, etc. Subsidiary of Random House, Inc. Founded 1915.

Krause Publications
700 East State Street, Iola, WI 54990-0001
tel 715-445-2214 *fax* 715-445-4087
Acquisitions Editor Deborah Faupel

Antiques and collectibles, sewing and crafts, ceramics.

Lippincott-Raven Publishers
227 East Washington Square, Philadelphia, PA 19106
tel 215-238-4200
President/ceo Mary M. Rogers, *President* J.W. Lippincott, III, *Publishers* Kathey Alexander (medical), Donna Hilton (nursing)

Medical and nursing books and journals. A Wolters Kluwer company. Founded 1792.

Little, Brown & Company*
34 Beacon Street, Boston, MA 02108
tel 617-227-0730

General literature, especially fiction, non-fiction, biography, history, trade paperbacks, books for boys and girls. Art and photography books under the Bulfinch Press imprint.

Lothrop, Lee & Shepard Books
1350 Avenue of the Americas, New York, NY 10019
tel 212-261-6641 *fax* 212-261-6648
Vice-President/Editor-in-Chief Susan Pearson

Children's books only. Division of William Morrow & Co., Inc. Founded 1904.

Lyons & Burford, Publishers
31 West 21st Street, New York, NY 10010
tel 212-620-9580 *fax* 212-929-1836
Publishers Nick Lyons, Peter Burford

Outdoor sport, natural history, general sports, art.

McGraw-Hill Co.*
1221 Avenue of the Americas, New York, NY 10020
tel 212-512-2000
Professional and Reference Books Theodore Nardin

Professional and reference: engineering, scientific, business, architecture, encyclopedias; college textbooks; high school and vocational textbooks: business, secretarial, career; trade books; training materials for industry.

Macmillan Publishing USA – reference imprint of Simon & Schuster*

McPherson & Company
PO Box 1126, Kingston, NY 12402
tel/fax 914-331-5807
e-mail bmcpher@mhv.net
web site www.mcphersonco.com
Publisher Bruce R. McPherson

Literary fiction; non-fiction: art criticism, writings by artists, filmmaking, etc; occasional general titles (e.g. anthropology). No poetry. No unsolicited MSS; query first. Founded 1974.

Mercury House
785 Market Street, Suite 1500, San Francisco, CA 94103
tel 415-974-0729 *fax* 415-974-0832
web site http://www.wenet.net/~mercury/
Executive Editor Thomas Christensen

Fiction; non-fiction: biography/memoirs, contemporary issues, translations, nature/environment, literary travel, women's issues, philosophy and personal growth. Material only accepted through agents. Founded 1985.

Milkweed Editions

430 First Avenue North, Suite 400, Minneapolis,
MN 55401
tel 612-332-3192 *fax* 612-332-6248
Publisher/Editor Emilie Buchwald

Fiction, poetry, essays, literature, children's novels and biographies (ages 8-14). Founded 1979.

The MIT Press*

5 Cambridge Center, Cambridge, MA 02142-1493
tel 617-253-5646 *fax* 617-258-6779
web site http://mitpress.mit.edu
Director Frank Urbanowski, *Editor-in-Chief*
Laurence Cohen

Architecture, art and design, cognitive sciences, neuroscience, linguistics, computer science and artificial intelligence, economics, philosophy, environment and ecology, natural history. Founded 1961.

Morehouse Publishing Co.

PO Box 1321, Harrisburg, PA 17105
tel 717-541-8130 *fax* 717-541-8128
President Kenneth Quigley, *Publisher* Harold Rast

Religious books, religious education, texts, seminary texts, children's books.

Morrow Jr. Books

1350 Avenue of the Americas, New York, NY 10019
tel 212-261-6500 *fax* 212-261-6689
Vice-President/Editor-in-Chief David Reuther

Children's books only. No unsolicited material accepted. Division of William Morrow & Co., Inc.

William Morrow & Co., Inc.

1350 Avenue of the Americas, New York,
NY 10019
tel 212-261-6500 *fax* 212-261-6595
Senior Vice-President/Editor-in-Chief William
Schwalbe

General literature, fiction and juveniles. Imprints: Greenwillow Books, Lothrop, Lee & Shepard, Morrow Jr Books, Tambourine Books, Mulberry/Beech Tree/Tupelo.

The Naiad Press, Inc.

PO Box 10543, Tallahassee, FL 32302
tel 904-539-5965 *fax* 904-539-9731
Ceo Barbara Grier

Lesbian fiction; non-fiction: bibliographies, biographies, essays. Founded 1973.

Thomas Nelson, Inc.*

Nelson Place at Elm Hill Pike, PO Box 141000,
Nashville, TN 37214-1000
tel 615-889-9000 *fax* 615-391-5225
President of Publishing Byron Williamson

Bibles, religious, non-fiction and fiction

general trade, stationery gift items. Founded 1798.

W.W. Norton & Company, Inc.

500 Fifth Avenue, New York, NY 10110
tel 212-354-5500 *fax* 212-869-0856
e-mail ftp@wwnorton.com
web site http://www.wwnorton.com

General fiction and non-fiction, music, boating, psychiatry, economics, family therapy, social work, reprints, college texts, science.

Orchard Books

95 Madison Avenue, New York, NY 10016
tel 212-951-2600 *fax* 212-213-6435
President/Publisher Judy V. Wilson

Books for children and young adults; picture books, fiction. Founded 1987.

Ottenheimer Publishers Inc.

10 Church Lane, Baltimore, MD 21208
tel 410-484-2100 *fax* 410-486-8301
Directors Allan T. Hirsh, Jr, Allan T. Hirsh, III

Juvenile and adult non-fiction, reference. Founded 1890.

The Overlook Press*

386 West Broadway, 4th Floor, New York,
NY 10012
tel 212-965-8400 *fax* 212-965-9834
Editorial Director Tracy Carns

Non-fiction, fiction, children's books.

Oxford University Press, Inc.*

198 Madison Avenue, New York, NY 10016
tel 212-726-6000 *fax* 212-726-6455
web site www.oup-usa.org

Scholarly, professional, reference, bibles, college textbooks, religion, medicals, music.

Pantheon Books*

201 East 50th Street, New York, NY 10022
tel 212-572-2838 *fax* 212-572-6030
web site http://www.randomhouse.com

Fiction, mysteries, belles-lettres, translations, philosophy, history and art, sociology, psychology. Division of Random House, Inc.

Peachtree Publishers Ltd

494 Armour Circle NE, Atlanta, GA 30324-4088
tel 404-876-8761 *fax* 404-875-2578
President and Publisher Margaret Quinlin,
Editorial Director Kathy Landwehr

Children's picture books and novels. Non-fiction subjects include self-help, the American South, cookbooks and gardening; also gift books and fiction. Founded 1977.

Pelican Publishing Company*

PO Box 3110, Gretna, LA 70054
tel 504-368-1175 *fax* 504-368-1195
e-mail sales@pelicanpub.com
Publisher/President Milburn Calhoun

Art and architecture, cookbooks, travel, music, business, children's. Founded 1926.

The Penguin Group*

375 Hudson Street, New York, NY 10014
tel 212-366-2000 *fax* 212-366-2666
Chairman/ceo Michael Lynton, *President* Marvin Brown

General books, fiction, non-fiction, biography, sociology, poetry, art, travel, children's books.

Penn State University Press*

820 North University Drive, USB1, Suite C, University Park, PA 16802
tel 814-865-1327 *fax* 814-863-1408
web site www.psu.edu/psupress
Senior Editor, Humanities Philip Winsor, *Editor, History and Social Science* Peter Potter

Art history, literary criticism, religious studies, philosophy, political science, sociology, history, Russian and East European studies, Latin American studies and medieval studies. Founded 1956.

The Permanent Press and Second Chance Press

4170 Noyac Road, Sag Harbor, NY 11963
tel 516-725-1101
Directors Martin Shepard, Judith Shepard

Quality fiction. Founded 1978.

Praeger Publishers

Greenwood Publishing Group, Inc., 88 Post Road West, Westport, CT 06881
tel 203-226-3571 *fax* 203-222-1502

Non-fiction on international relations, social sciences, economics, contemporary issues, urban affairs, psychology, education.

Prentice Hall – imprint of Simon & Schuster*

Price Stern Sloan, Inc.

(a division of Putnam & Grosset, NY)
200 Madison Avenue, New York, NY 10016
Editorial Director Lisa Rojany

Children's books: novelty/lift-flaps, activity books, middle-grade fiction, midgrade and YA non-fiction, cutting-edge graphic readers, picture books, books plus. Founded 1963.

The Putnam Berkley Group Inc.

200 Madison Avenue, New York, NY 10016
tel 212-951-8400

All types of literature; history, economics, political science, natural science, and standard literature; fiction; children's books.

Rand McNally

PO Box 7600, Chicago, IL 60680
tel 847-329-8100
Chairman Andrew McNally IV, *Executive Ceo* John Bakalar

Maps, guides, atlases, educational publications, globes and children's geographical titles and atlases.

Random House, Inc.*

201 East 50th Street, New York, NY 10022
tel 212-751-2600

General publishers.

Rawson Associates

1230 Avenue of the Americas, New York, NY 10020
tel 212-632-4941 *fax* 212-632-4918
Publisher Eleanor S. Rawson

Adult non-fiction of wide general interest.

Rizzoli International Publications, Inc.

300 Park Avenue South, New York, NY 10010
tel 212-387-3400 *fax* 212-387-3535
Publisher Solveig Williams

Art, architecture, photography, fashion, gardening, design, gift books, cookbooks. Founded 1976.

Rodale Press, Inc.

33 East Minor Street, Emmaus, PA 18098
tel 610-967-5171 *fax* 610-967-8961
President, Book Division Pat Corpora, *Editor-in-Chief, Book Division* Bill Gottlieb

Health, women's health, men's health, fitness, gardening, woodworking, do-it-yourself, quilting, crafts, healthy cooking, psychological self-help. Founded 1930.

Ronin Publishing Inc.

Box 1035, Berkeley, CA 94701
tel 510-540 6278 *fax* 510-548-7326
e-mail roninpub@dnai.com
web site www.roninpub.com

New Age business, psychedelics, marijuana, visionary, underground comix. Preliminary letter essential; no unsolicited MSS or artwork.

Routledge, Inc.
29 West 35th Street, New York, NY 10001
tel 212-244-3336 *fax* 212-563-2269
President and Publisher Colin Jones, *Vice-President and Associate Publisher* Kenneth Wright

Literary criticism, history, philosophy, psychology and psychiatry, politics, women's studies, education, anthropology, religion, lesbian and gay studies, classical studies.

Running Press Book Publishers
125 S 22 St, Philadelphia, Pennsylvania 19103
tel 215-567-5080 *fax* 215-568 2919
Publisher Nancy Steele, *Editorial Director* Jeff Day, *Design Director* Ken Newbaker, *Production Director* Richard Conklin

Art, craft/how-to, general non-fiction, children's books. Imprints: Courage Books, Running Press Miniature Editions. Founded 1972.

Rutledge Hill Press
211 Seventh Avenue North, Nashville, TN 37219
tel 615-244-2700 *fax* 615-244-2978
e-mail bjayne@compuserve.com
President William E. Jayne, *Publisher* Lawrence M. Stone

Regional books, cookbooks, books on quilts, gift books. Founded 1982.

St Martin's Press, Inc.*
175 Fifth Avenue, New York, NY 10010
tel 212-674-5151 *fax* 212-420-9314

Trade, reference, college.

Saunders College Publishing
The Public Ledger Building, 150 South Independence Mall West, Suite 1250, Philadelphia, PA 19106
tel 215-238-5500 *fax* 215-238-5660

College textbooks.

Scribner – imprint of Simon & Schuster*

Simon & Schuster*
1230 Avenue of the Americas, New York, NY 10020
tel 212-698-7000
President/ceo Jonathan Newcomb

General fiction, non-fiction, children's and young adult books, CD-Rom and multimedia products, travel guides, reference books; educational books, multimedia materials and integrated learning systems; English-as-a-Second Language and English Language Teaching materials; computer-use books, business and professional books, audio-visual products, health care journals, training programs and computer-based learning systems.

Soho Press Inc.
853 Broadway, New York, NY 10003
tel 212-260-1900 *fax* 212-260-1902
Publisher Juris Jurjevics, *Associate Publisher* Laura Hruska

Literary fiction, commercial fiction, mystery, thrillers, travel, memoir, general non-fiction. Founded 1986.

Stanford University Press*
Stanford, CA 94305-2235
tel 415-723-9434 *fax* 415-725-3457
Director Norris Pope

Scholarly non-fiction.

Strawberry Hill Press
3848 SE Division Street, Portland, OR 97202
tel 503-235-5989
President Jean-Louis Brindamour PhD, *Executive Vice-President/Art Director* Ku Fu-Sheng, *Treasurer* Edward E. Serres

Health, self help, cookbooks, philosophy, religion, history, drama, science and technology, biography, mystery, Third World. No unsolicited MSS; preliminary letter and return postage essential. Founded 1973.

Theatre Arts Books
29 West 35th Street, New York, NY 10001
tel 212-244-3336
President Colin Jones, *Publishing Director* William Germano

Successor to the book publishing department of Theatre Arts (1921-1948). Theatre, performance, dance and allied books – acting techniques, costume, tailoring, etc.; a few plays. Division of Routledge, Inc.

Time Life Inc.
2000 Duke Street, Alexandria, VA 22314
tel 703-838-7000 *fax* 703-838-7225
President, Chairman/ceo George Artandi

Non-fiction: art, cooking, crafts, food, gardening, health, history, home maintenance, nature, photography, science. A subsidiary of Time Warner Inc. Founded 1961.

Tor Books
175 Fifth Avenue, 14th Floor, New York, NY 10010
tel 212-388-0100 *fax* 212-388-0191
President/Publisher Tom Doherty

Fiction: general, historical, western, suspense, mystery, horror, science fiction, fantasy, humour, juvenile, classics (English language); non-fiction: adult and juvenile. Subsidiary of St Martin's Press, Inc. Founded 1980.

Charles E. Tuttle Co., Inc.*
153 Milk Street, Boston, MA 02109
tel 617-951-4080 *fax* 617-951-4045
Suido I-chome, 2-6 Bunkyo-ku, Tokyo 112, Japan
tel 813-3811-7741 *fax* 813-5689 4926
President Eric Oey

Oriental art, culture, Eastern philosophy, martial arts, health. Founded 1948.

The University of Alabama Press
Box 870380, Tuscaloosa, AL 35487
tel 205-348-5180 *fax* 205-348-9201
Director Nicole Mitchell, *Managing Editor* Elizabeth May

American and Southern history, rhetoric and speech communication, Judaic studies, linguistics, literary criticism, anthropology and archaeology, history of American science and technology. Founded 1945.

The University of Arkansas Press
The University of Arkansas, 201 Ozark Street, Fayetteville, AR 72701
tel 501-575-3246 *fax* 501-575-6044
Director John Coghlan

History, literary criticism, biography, poetry, fiction. Founded 1980.

University of California Press
2120 Berkeley Way, Berkeley, CA 94720
tel 510-642-4247 *fax* 510-643-7127
Director James H. Clark
UK office University Presses of California, Columbia, and Princeton, 1 Oldlands Way, Bognor Regis, West Sussex PO22 9SA
tel (01243) 842165 *fax* (01243) 842167

Publishes scholarly books, books of general interest, series of scholarly monographs and scholarly journals.

University of Chicago Press*
5801 South Ellis Avenue, Chicago, IL 60637
tel 773-702-7700 *fax* 773-702-9756
Director Morris Philipson

Scholarly books and monographs, religious and scientific books, general trade books, and 54 scholarly journals.

University of Illinois Press
1325 South Oak Street, Champaign, IL 61820
tel 217-333-0950 *fax* 217-244-8082
Director Richard L. Wentworth

American studies (history, music, literature), poetry, working-class and ethnic studies, communications, regional studies, architecture, philosophy and women's studies. Founded 1918.

The University of Massachussetts Press
PO Box 429, Amherst, MA 01004-0429
tel 413-545-2217 *fax* 413-545-1226
Director Bruce G. Wilcox

Scholarly books and works of general interest: American studies and history, black and ethnic studies, women's studies, cultural criticism, architecture and environmental design, literary criticism, poetry, fiction, philosophy, political science, sociology, books of regional interest. Founded 1964.

The University of Michigan Press
839 Greene Street, PO Box 1104, Ann Arbor, MI 48106
tel 313-764-4388 *fax* 313-936-0456
e-mail um.press@umich.edu
web site www.press.umich.edu/
Director Colin Day, *Assistant Director* Mary Erwin, *Executive Editor* LeAnn Fields, *Managing Editor* Christina Milton

Scholarly works in literature, classics, history, theatre, women's studies, political science, law, anthropology, economics, archaeology; textbooks in English as a second language; regional trade titles, health policy and management. Founded 1930.

University of Missouri Press
2910 LeMone Boulevard, Columbia, MO 65201
tel 573-882-7641 *fax* 573-884-4498
Director/Editor-in-Chief Beverly Jarrett, *Acquisitions Editor* Clair Willcox

American and European history, American, British and Latin American literary criticism, journalism, political philosophy, art history, regional studies; short fiction. Founded 1958.

University of New Mexico Press
1720 Lomas Boulevard NE, Albuquerque, NM 87131-1591
tel 505-277-2346 *fax* 505-277-9270
Director Elizabeth C. Hadas

Western history, anthropology and archaeology, Latin American studies, photography, multicultural literature. Founded 1929.

The University of North Carolina Press*

PO Box 2288, 116 South Boundary Street, Chapel Hill, NC 27514
tel 919-966-3561 fax 919-966-3829
Director Kate Douglas Torrey

American history, American studies, Southern studies, European history, women's studies, Latin American studies, political science, anthropology and folklore, classics, regional trade. Founded 1922.

University of Oklahoma Press*

1005 Asp Avenue, Norman, OK 73019-0445
tel 405-325-5111 fax 405-325-4000
Director George Bauer

History of American West, American Indian studies, Mesoamerican studies, classical studies, women's studies, natural history, political science. Founded 1928.

University of Pennsylvania Press

4200 Pine Street, Philadelphia, PA 19104-4090
tel 215-898-6261 fax 215-898-0404
Director Eric Halpern

American and British history, anthropology, art, architecture, business, cultural studies, economics, folklore, ancient studies, human rights, law, literature, medicine, Pennsylvania regional studies, women's studies. Founded 1890.

University of Texas Press

PO Box 7819, Austin, TX 78713-7819
tel 512-471-7233 fax 512-320-0668
e-mail utpress@uts.cc.utexas.edu
web site http://www.utexas.edu/utpress/
Director Joanna Hitchcock, *Assistant Director and Executive Editor* Theresa May, *Assistant Director and Financial Officer* Joyce Lewandowski

Scholarly non-fiction: anthropology, classics and the Ancient World, conservation and the environment, film and media studies, geography, Latin American and Latino studies, Middle Eastern studies, natural history, ornithology, Texas and Western studies. Founded 1950.

University of Washington Press

PO Box 50096, Seattle, WA 98145-5096
tel 206-543-4050 fax 206-543-3932
Director Patrick Soden, *Associate Director/Editor-in-Chief* Naomi B. Pascal

Anthropology, Asian-American studies, Asian studies, art and art history, aviation history, environmental studies, forest history, Jewish studies, literary criticism, marine sciences, Middle East studies, music, regional studies, including history and culture of the Pacific Northwest and Alaska, Native American studies, resource management and public policy, Russian and East European studies, Scandinavian studies. Founded 1909.

University Press of Kansas

2501 West 15th Street, Lawrence, Kansas 66049-3904
tel 913-864-4155 fax 913-864-4586
e-mail upkansas@kuhub.cc.ukans.edu
Director Fred Woodward, *Editor-in-Chief* Michael Briggs, *Senior Production Editor* Melinda Wirkus

American history, military history, American political thought, American presidency studies, law and constitutional history, political science and philosophy. Founded 1946.

Van Nostrand Reinhold

115 Fifth Avenue, New York, NY 10003
tel 212-254-3232 fax 212-475-2548
President Marianne J. Russell

Professional and reference publisher of information products for culinary arts/hospitality, architecture/design, environmental sciences and business technology. A division of International Thomson Publishing. Founded 1848.

Viking – see Penguin USA*

Walker & Co.

435 Hudson Street, New York, NY 10014
tel 212-727-8300 fax 212-727-0984
Publisher George Gibson, *Mystery* Michael Seidman, *Juvenile* Emily Easton

General publishers, biography, popular science, health, business, mystery/suspense, history, juveniles, early childhood education, parenting, self-help. Founded 1960.

Warner Books Inc.*

1271 Avenue of the Americas, 9th Floor, New York, NY 10020
tel 212-522-7200 fax 212-522-7991
President Laurence J. Kirshbaum

Fiction and non-fiction, hardcovers, trade paperbacks, mass market paperbacks. Founded 1973.

Franklin Watts

Sherman Turnpike, Danbury, CT 06813
tel 203-797-3500 fax 203-797-6986

School and library books for grades K-12.

Westminster John Knox Press
100 Witherspoon Street, Louisville,
KY 40202-1396
tel 502-569-5043 *fax* 502-569-5113
Editorial Manager Stephanie Egnotovich
Religious, academic, reference, general.

Whispering Coyote Press, Inc.
300 Crescent Court, Suite 850, Dallas, TX 75201
tel 214-871-5599 *fax* 214-871-5577
President Lou Alpert
Children's picture books. Founded 1989.

Workman Publishing Co.
708 Broadway, New York, NY 10003
tel 212-254-5900 *fax* 212-254-8098
President Peter Workman
General non-fiction, calendars. Founded
1968.

Writer's Digest Books
1507 Dana Avenue, Cincinnati, OH 45207
tel 513-531-2690 *fax* 513-531-7107
Market Directories, books for writers,
photographers and songwriters.

North Light Books (imprint)
Fine art and graphic arts instruction
books.

Betterway Books (imprint)
How-to in home building, remodelling,
woodworking, sports, home organisation,
theatre.

Yale University Press*
302 Temple Street, New Haven, CT 06511
postal address PO Box 209040, New Haven,
CT 06520
tel 203-432-0960 *fax* 203-432-0948/2394
Director John G. Ryden
London office 23 Pond Street, London NW3 2PN
tel 0171-431 4422 *fax* 0171-431 3755
Scholarly books and art books.

Zoland Books, Inc.
384 Huron Avenue, Cambridge, MA 02138
tel 617-864-6252 *fax* 617-661-4998
Publisher Roland F. Pease Jr., *Managing Editor*
Michael Lindgren
Fiction, poetry, art criticism, memoirs.
Founded 1987.

Writing and illustrating children's books

Sammy the Squirrel, Cyril the Slug, Teddy the Traffic Light ... mention such titles to a group of children's book editors and they all recognise yesterday's pile of rejected manuscripts. Editors are looking for something with more originality and punch. **Caroline Sheldon** *guides the potential children's author and/or illustrator in the direction of success.*

The best way to get a feel of what children's publishers are publishing today is to read a large range of children's books published now and over the last 30 years. They cover an enormous spectrum in length and content – from simple, highly illustrated picture book stories to full length novels for teenagers, and most children's publishers' lists cover the whole range.

Writing children's books

Observe all the rules of submitting any other manuscript – a doubled-spaced,

attractively presented manuscript; a covering letter giving information about yourself and your writing; return postage; no bulky ring binders that burst open in the post. Mention any experience you have had of working with children.

Picture books

There is limited opportunity for authors to get involved in bath books or board books, and therefore picture books are generally the youngest end of the age range for writers.

The high cost of printing in full colour necessitates a long print run of copies to keep the unit cost down. To achieve this, collaboration with an American, European or other foreign publisher is essential. Thus a publisher has to believe a book is really going to make its mark in the international market before taking it on. It is a very competitive field but, when asked what they are short of, most publishers will say good picture book texts – which just proves how difficult they are to write successfully.

Almost all picture books are 32 pages long with 12-14 spreads (i.e. double pages) of full colour illustration. The number of words varies from none (it has been done; the author provided the storyline to which the artist worked) to a maximum of about 2500. The book has to encompass a big enough idea to make it something of an event, yet not deal with issues too wide to resolve within the limits of the page size and design. A narrative with a strong beginning, middle and end is needed to encourage the reader to turn the pages. Even some successful authors in the area find their publisher or agent may reject five stories before one magically slips into place. So be warned, it's tough ...

Picture book manuscripts should be typed as a series of numbered pages each with its own text. Detailed descriptions of the illustrations and instructions to the illustrator are almost always a mistake. However, if there is something that should be included in the picture, but it is not clear from the text, it should be pointed out.

Younger fiction

This area of publishing is designed for children who are reading their first whole novels. Texts tend to be anything from 1500 to 7500 words long; in many cases the books will be illustrated with line illustrations to break up the words on the page. Generally, publishers don't want a use of restricted vocabulary, but writers should remember that, particularly at the bottom end of the age range, they are writing for children who have just learnt to read. Novels for this age range can be published as individual books but often publishers put them out under an umbrella series name. Investigate a series before approaching the publisher and check that your book fits in to that series in terms of length and interest level. You can indicate in a covering letter that you have planned that it will be illustrated, but don't give illustration notes in the manuscript.

The table oppposite shows some currently published series with the approximate word length of the manuscript and the age group at which the books are aimed.

General fiction

Children's novels for the over nine age group are mainly published as individual books. Generally, they are shorter than children's books read by previous generations. Any books over 40,000 words will have to face the problems of a higher price than the publisher would like. Each book stands on its own merits and publishers are looking for authors whose work they like and whom they believe will go on to write a number of books for their list.

There are also a number of extremely successful fiction series for older children that have recently become established. For example, Scholastic commission books for their *Point* series with genres including horror, romance, crime and science fiction. Sample material submitted to a publisher should consist of the first three chapters, a brief synopsis and a covering letter.

Non-fiction

Non-fiction is an area almost exclusively covered by specialists. Some publishers have much of their non-fiction written by their own staff. If you are interested in this area, nothing can replace a research trip to a good children's library or bookshop to establish who is publishing what, and how your work or field of interest could fit in.

Publisher	Series name	Word length	Age group	Comments
Andersen Press	Tigers	3000-5000	6-9	B&w illustrations on every page
A & C Black	Jets	2500	6-8	B&w illustrations on every page
	Graffix	4000	9-12	B&w illustrations on every page
	Chillers	4000-5000	7-9	B&w illustrations on every page
Hamish Hamilton	Cartwheels	1000	4-8	Full colour illustrations
	Gazelles	4000	5-8	B&w illustrations on every page
	Antelopes	7500	6-9	B&w illustrations on every page
	Surfers	10,000-12,000	9-12	B&w illustrations
HarperCollins	Colour Jets	2500	6-9	Colour illustrations on every page
	Yellow Storybooks	2000-3000	6-8	B&w illustrations on every page
	Red Storybooks	6000-8000	6-8	B&w illustrations
Heinemann	Blue Bananas	1000-1500	3-5	Full colour illustrations
	Yellow Bananas	3000	6-9	Full colour illustrations
Hodder	Read Alone	2000-4000	6-8	B&w illustrations on every page
	Story Book	8000-12,000	7-9	B&w illustrations
Kingfisher	Beginners	1000-1500	5-7	Full colour illustrations
Macdonald Young Books	Story Books	2000-3000	6-9	Colour and b&w illustrations
	Shivery Storybooks	2000-2500	6-9	Colour and b&w illustrations
Methuen	Read Aloud	8000	5-7	B&w line illustrations
Orchard	Beginners	1000	5-7	B&w illustrations on every page
	Read Alone	2000-4000	7-9	B&w illustrations on every page
Puffin	Ready, Steady, Read	1500	5-7	B&w illustrations on every page
Red Fox	Read Alone	3000 or 7000	6-9	B&w illustrations on every page
Transworld	Corgi Pups	2000-2500	5-8	B&w illustrations on every page
	Young Corgi	3000-7000	6-8	B&w illustrations
Viking	Read Alone	2500	6-8	B&w illustrations on every page
	Kites	6000	7-9	B&w illustrations
Walker	Sprinters	3000-4000	6-8	B&w illustrations on every page

Illustrating children's books

Illustrating children's books is a highly professional field but one in which there is always room for new talent. Most illustrators working in children's books have an art school background but there are also those who have come to it without formal training. The work available varies from illustrations for full-colour picture books, to jackets and black and white line illustrations for novels, to non-fiction illustration.

Illustrators looking for work in this area should try to make appointments to show their portfolios to either the Art Director or Children's Book Editor at a publishing house and to show their work to suitable agents. A portfolio should show as wide a range of work as possible – it is well worth working up some black and white line illustrations for children's novels for the 6-10 age range since so much bread-and-butter work is commissioned in this area. Once you have achieved this, people are more likely to be interested in spending time with you developing your special picture book project. The main complaints of those who look at prospective illustrators' portfolios is that the work shown is too stylised and sophisticated, and there is not an obvious application to children's book illustration.

If you find it difficult to get an appointment, send in a folder of photocopied samples of your work together with a letter outlining the type of work for which you are looking. Always send photocopies of work, never the original artwork; even if the photocopies don't do full justice to the colour, publishers are experienced at spotting the sort of quality that makes them want to see more.

Words/pictures – which come first?

Unless you are best buddies with a best-selling illustrator or writer, it is best to present your work individually. It is an unwanted complication to have wonderful artwork tied in to an amateurish text, or a nice text illustrated by an artist whose work won't stand up in the very competitive picture book market. Publishers are experienced in matching the work of writers and artists, and the individual work should stand on its own. Having said that, at the younger end of children's publishing, life is much simpler if you are a writer/illustrator.

Caroline Sheldon is an established literary agent who represents writers and artists working in children's books and adult fiction.

Children's book publishers and packagers

A quick reference guide to children's book publishers and packagers by subject area. Listings for Book publishers UK and Ireland start on page 153 and listings for Book packagers start on page 216.

Picture books

Book publishers
ABC, All Books for Children
Andersen Press
Award Publications
Bantam
Barefoot Books
BBC Books
David Bennett Books
A & C Black
Bloomsbury Children's Books
Bodley Head Children's Books
Brimax Books
Jonathan Cape Children's Books
Chart Books
Child's Play International
J.M. Dent
André Deutsch Children's Books
Dorling Kindersley
Element Books
Floris Books
Gairm Publications (Gaelic)
Gallery Children's Books
Victor Gollancz
Hamish Hamilton Children's Books
HarperCollins Publishers
Hawk Books
Hazar Publishing
Heinemann Young Books
Henderson Publishing
Hippo Books
Hodder & Stoughton
Hunt & Thorpe
Hutchinson Children's Books
Kingfisher
Ladybird Books
Levinson Books
Frances Lincoln
Lion Publishing
Little, Brown and Company (UK)

Peter Lowe (Eurobook Ltd)
Lutterworth Press
Macdonald Young Books
Macmillan Children's Books
Julia MacRae Books
Magi Publications
Mammoth
Mantra Publishing
Medici Society
Methuen Children's Books
Michael O'Mara Books
Orchard Books
Orion Children's Books
Oxford University Press
Pavilion Books
Piccadilly Press
Puffin
Ragged Bears
Red Fox
Scripture Union
Tamarind
Tango Books
The Templar Company
Transworld Publishers
Usborne Publishing
Ventura Publishing
Viking Children's Books
Walker Books
Frederick Warne
World International

Book packagers
Aladdin Books
Albion Press
Andromeda Oxford
Breslich & Foss
Geddes & Grosset
Graham-Cameron Publishing
Angus Hudson
Marshall Editions
Playne Books
Mathew Price
Sadie Fields Productions
The Templar Company
Tucker Slingsby

Ventura Publishing (Spot books by Eric Hill)
Victoria House Publishing
Zigzag Multimedia

Fiction

Book publishers
Adlib
Andersen Press
Anvil Books/The Children's Press (Ire.)
Bantam
Barefoot Books
BBC Children's Books
David Bennett Books
A & C Black
Bloomsbury Children's Books
Bodley Head Children's Books
Brimax Books
Brown, Son & Ferguson (Scout/Guide)
Canongate Books
Jonathan Cape Children's Books
Chart Books
Child's Play (International)
J.M. Dent
André Deutsch Children's Books
Dorling Kindersley
Element Books
Faber & Faber
Floris Books
Gairm Publications (Gaelic)
Victor Gollancz
Gomer Press
Hamish Hamilton Children's Books
Patrick Hardy Books
HarperCollins Publishers
Hawk Books
Heinemann Young Books
Hippo
Hodder & Stoughton

Hutchinson Children's Books
Kingfisher
Ladybird Books
Frances Lincoln
Lion Publishing
Y Lolfa Cyf. (Welsh)
Peter Lowe (Eurobook Ltd)
Lutterworth Press
Macdonald Young Books
Macmillan Children's Books
Julia MacRae Books
Mammoth
Mantra Publishing
Marino Books (Ire.)
Methuen Children's Books
Michael O'Mara Books
The O'Brien Press (Ire.)
Orchard Books
Orion Children's Books
Oxford University Press
Pavilion Books
Piccadilly Press
Point
Puffin
Ragged Bears
Red Fox
Robinson Publishing
Schofield & Sims
Scottish Children's Press
Scripture Union
Tango Books
D.C. Thomson & Co. Ltd – Publications
Titan Books (film/TV tie-ins)
Transworld Publishers
Usborne Publishing
Viking Children's Books
Virgin
Walker Books
Wolfhound Press (Ire.)
World International

Book packagers

Albion Press
Oyster Books
Mathew Price
Signpost Books
Victoria House Publishing

Non-fiction

Book publishers

ABC, All Books for Children
Aladdin/Watts
Anness Publishing
Apple Press
Atlantic Europe Publishing Co.
Bantam
BBC Children's Books
Belitha Press

David Bennett Books
A & C Black
Boxtree (film/TV tie-ins)
Brandon Book Publishers (Ire.)
Brimax Books
Brown Wells & Jacobs
Child's Play International
J.M. Dent
André Deutsch Children's Books
Dorling Kindersley
Element Books
Evans Brothers
Exley Publications
Folens (Ire.)
Geddes & Grosset
Hamlyn Children's Non-Fiction
HarperCollins Publishers
Heinemann Young Books
Henderson Publishing
Hippo
Hodder & Stoughton
Kingfisher
Ladybird Books
Levinson Books
Frances Lincoln
Lion Publishing
Little, Brown and Company (UK)
Y Lolfa Cyf. (Welsh)
Peter Lowe (Eurobook Ltd)
Lutterworth Press
Macdonald Young Books
Macmillan Children's Books
Julia MacRae Books
Madcap
Mantra Publishing
Medici Society
Morehurst
Michelin Tyre
The National Trust
New Orchard Editions
The O'Brien Press (Ire.)
Oxford University Press
Pavilion Books
Piccadilly Press
Puffin
Ragged Bears
Salamander Books
Science Museum Publications
Schofield & Sims
Scottish Children's Press
Scripture Union
Studio Editions
Tango Books
The Templar Company
Transworld Publishers
Two-Can Publishing
Twocan/Watts
Usborne Publishing
Walker Books
Frederick Warne

Wayland
World International
Young Library

Book packagers

Aladdin Books
Albion Press
Bender Richardson White
Breslich & Foss
Brown Wells & Jacobs
Philip Clark
Earthscape Editions
Geddes & Grosset
Graham-Cameron Publishing
Lionheart Books
Marshall Editions
Orpheus Books
Oyster Books
Mathew Price
Signpost Books
The Templar Company
Touchstone Publishing
Tucker Slingsby
Victoria House Publishing
Zigzag Multimedia
Zoe Books

Other

Activity and novelty

Book publishers

Andersen Press
Apple Press
Atlantic Europe Publishing Co.
Award Publications
BBC Books
Belitha Press
David Bennett Books
Bloomsbury Children's Books
Brimax Books
Brown Wells & Jacobs
Chart Books
Child's Play International
Dorling Kindersley
Exley Publications
Floris Books
Geddes & Grosset
Hamlyn Children's Non-Fiction
Hazar Publishing
Heinemann Young Books
Henderson Publishing
Hippo
Kingfisher
Ladybird Books
Levinson Books
Frances Lincoln
Lion Publishing
Macmillan Children's Books
Mammoth

Methuen Children's Books
Michelin Tyre
Michael O'Mara Books
Orchard Books
Orion Children's Books
Oxford University Press
Pavilion Books
Piccadilly Press
Puffin
Salamander Books
Scripture Union
Studio Editions
Tango Books
The Templar Company
Transworld Publishers
Two-Can Publishing
Usborne Publishing
Walker Books
Frederick Warne
World International

Book packagers
Aladdin Books
Andromeda Oxford
Bellew Publishing
Breslich & Foss
Brown Wells & Jacobs
Earthscape Editions
Geddes & Grosset
Graham-Cameron Publishing
Angus Hudson
Oyster Books
Mathew Price
Sadie Fields Productions
Signpost Books
The Templar Company
Tucker Slingsby
Victoria House Publishing
Zigzag Multimedia
Zoe Books

Audiobooks

Book publishers
BBC Books
Canongate Books
HarperCollins Publishers
Henderson Publishing
Hodder Headline
Ladybird Books
Frances Lincoln
Mantra Publishing
The O'Brien Press (Ire.)
Random House Audio Books
Tellastory
Transworld Audio Books
Usborne Publishing

Multimedia

Book publishers
BBC Books
Dorling Kindersley
Ginn
HarperCollins
Heinemann Educational
Hodder Headline
Macmillan
Oxford University Press
Puffin
Random House
Thomas Nelson
Two-Can Publishing
Usborne Publishing
Frederick Warne
Wayland Publishers

Book packagers
Bender Richardson White
Earthscape Editions
Zigzag Multimedia

Music

Book publishers
A & C Black
Canongate Books
Child's Play International
Exley Publications
Gallery Children's Books
Henderson Publishing
Mantra Publishing
Scripture Union
Usborne Publishing

Poetry

Book publishers
Andersen Press
Bantam
A & C Black
Bloomsbury Children's Books
Bodley Head Children's Books
Jonathan Cape Children's Books
André Deutsch Children's
  Books
Faber & Faber
HarperCollins Publishers
Heinemann Young Books
Hutchinson Children's Books
Kingfisher
Lutterworth Press
Macmillan Children's Books

Mammoth
Methuen Children's Books
Orchard Books
Oxford University Press
Puffin
Red Fox
Transworld Publishers
Usborne Publishing
Viking Children's Books
Walker Books

Book packagers
Albion Press

Religion

Book publishers
Gallery Children's Books
Hamlyn Children's Non-Fiction
HarperCollins Publishers
Angus Hudson
Hunt & Thorpe
Lion Publishing
Lutterworth Press
Marshall Pickering
Medici Society
The Mothers' Union
National Christian Education
  Council
Oxford University Press
Salvationist Publishing and
  Supplies
Scripture Union Publishing

Book packagers
Albion Press
Graham-Cameron Publishing
Angus Hudson
Marshall Editions
Oyster Books
Victoria House Publishing

Pictures into print

*More and more writers wish to supply their own photographs to illustrate their written work, and in many cases they are well placed to do so. The requirements of a publisher must be understood to avoid basic mistakes. **David Askham** gives some useful pointers for starting out.*

Imagine completing a book-length manuscript, accompanied by a fine selection of your own photographs, only to discover that the publisher requires colour transparencies, whereas your illustrations are in the form of colour prints!

To an author such a setback can be highly demoralising. Apart from the frustrations of lost time and opportunities, there is the daunting prospect of a major re-shoot of the photography, a costly conversion of negatives into transparencies, or facing up to hiring photographs from a picture library at a cost probably not included in the original budget.

Interestingly, had our author produced a short article for a popular consumer magazine, colour prints may well have been an acceptable alternative to colour transparencies. This is where a photographer experienced in producing pictures for the media would have either known what was required or would have clarified the requirement with the editor. Increasingly, more and more writers are undertaking the provision of their own photographs to illustrate their written work. And why not? Modern cameras are well-endowed with automatic features to simplify the task and are quite capable of yielding results perfectly acceptable for reproduction.

It should be stressed, however, that you should know and respect the upper limits of your photographic capabilities. A publisher will not thank you for second-rate results. If in doubt, consider engaging a talented colleague, though your agreement needs to take account of the ulti-

mate division of labour. At all times be honest with your editor about the degree of confidence you have in providing acceptable photography. It is sensible to submit samples of your best photographic work so that your commissioning editor can consider its standard and suitability and advise you accordingly.

On the positive side, many authors have acquired and developed photographic skills to the point where their work is highly accomplished in its own right. But first – back to basics.

Basic requirements

Before embarking on any photography it is essential first to elicit a publisher's or editor's requirements. In the case of a book-length project the contract should set out, precisely, what the author accepts and is obliged to produce in terms of numbers of pictures and their breakdown, where appropriate, into colour and monochrome images. Check also whether colour pictures are required in the form of colour transparencies (slides) or colour prints. With illustrated features, it is less usual to have a written contract prior to production. Nevertheless, a letter should spell out the salient facts concerning the provision of pictures.

The question of fees and reproduction rights should also be addressed, not only for text but also for the illustrations. Publishers have budgets for their editorial needs and prior agreement on fees is essential if the contributing author is not to finish the commitment unwittingly

well out of pocket. While photographic film may appear a relatively inexpensive item, travel to distant locations can inflate overall costs. Thought, therefore, must be given to the question of expenses.

Where colour is concerned, transparencies (derived from colour reversal or slide film) provide the better source for high quality reproduction than do colour prints. Gradually this situation may change as reproduction techniques continue to develop. To be safe, however, always check with your publisher before deviating from industry standards. If in any doubt when, for example, you are producing pilot material to form the basis of a book proposal, do use colour slide film. Then, if the proposal is accepted, you have already made a valuable start with your photography.

Editors rarely influence the choice of pictorial content of images produced by authors, provided the pictures offered meet certain criteria and accepted standards. So, while the author would appear to enjoy unbridled freedom in deciding what pictures to take and supply to the publisher, the editor will only be satisfied if your pictures are truly relevant to the manuscript and the aim of your work, and are also of a satisfactory quality. Let us now look at these aspects in more detail.

Picture relevance

Images should complement and help to clarify the text. In addition, they can beautify and add interest. Picture subjects often suggest themselves. However, there is a potential trap in sacrificing relevance when the most appropriate pictures are unavailable or difficult to acquire.

Take an example of a non-fiction book about London Midland and Scottish Railway locomotives which would clearly require illustrations of some, if not all, of the models described. It would be quite misleading to intermix pictures of the London and North Western Railway locomotives unless a specific point of comparison or contrast was being made. Without such justification, readers could become confused, misled and eventually lose

interest in the book. The author's credibility would suffer. Fortunately, such lack of relevance should be spotted at the editorial stage and the author would be required to rectify the error.

A biographer seeking to illustrate the boyhood home environment of an historical figure would be lucky indeed to find the actual dwelling, let alone the atmosphere of the period, unless immortalised in a museum. In the absence of contemporary artwork, it becomes acceptable to show the current locale provided captions clearly account for the time-shift.

Occasionally a publisher will have preferences or fixed ideas on the need for certain illustrations. Provided these ideas are feasible and reasonable they should be respected and added to the author's list of picture requirements.

Picture quality

Picture quality is vitally important; photographs should be sharp and clear. Modern cameras are capable of yielding high definition results provided the lens is correctly focused on the principal subject and the camera is held steady at the time of exposure. The latter calls for practice and suggestions for success appear in instruction manuals and books.

Paradoxically, a photograph may appear to be sharp but at the same time suffer from lack of clarity. Why should this be? Usually the cause of such obfuscation is conflict and confusion in the picture area, caused by lack of thought at the time of exposure. Remedies lie in isolating the main subject by using certain simple techniques such as careful framing, differential focus or employing contrasting tones or colour.

It should be realised that no amount of camera automation will substitute for skill on the part of the photographer. Only the photographer can compose the picture in such a way as to communicate his or her ideas clearly and unambiguously to the reader.

Quality results also depend on reliable equipment, films, processing and presentation. Avoid skimping in any of these

areas. It is not necessary to invest a small fortune in photographic equipment. A modern 35mm camera of a reputable make will serve an author well. Choose wisely, taking counsel from a learned colleague or trusted dealer. Use fresh films and have them processed by a professional laboratory rather than a cut-price corner shop.

While the emphasis has been on colour photography, most of the principles apply equally to monochrome pictures. Black and white photography will continue to be an important source of illustration in publishing.

It is becoming more and more difficult to find good processors of black and white films so many photographers print their own 10 x 8in or whole plate (6½ x 8½in) enlargements. However, impressive black and white illustrations can be derived from colour transparency originals, albeit at a cost.

Administration

Once you start producing your own pictures for publication, it is important to consider their administration.

Each picture should be presented in such a way that your name, address, telephone number, reference and caption is clearly related to the subject. Captions should include all relevant information and answer the classic journalistic questions such as who? what? where? when? and why? Records should be kept of pictures stored in your library and of those held by publishers. Despite all reasonable care losses will occasionally occur. Depending on circumstances, compensation should be claimed.

Colour transparencies need to be mounted, handled and stored with extreme care if damage is to be avoided. Never mount colour transparencies in glass if they are intended for publication.

Depending on urgency, pictures can be dispatched by post or courier services. In all cases they should be carefully packed and insured, if so inclined, according to their value.

In general, an author retains copyright both of his or her literary and artistic works unless these are assigned to a publisher. It is customary to assign only limited rights – e.g. First British Serial Rights for an article, or Single Reproduction Rights (qualified by territory and time if appropriate) – for pictures unless special circumstances prevail. See *British copyright law* on page 615 for more detail.

Occasionally problems arise in the reproduction of historic photographs, such as those produced, for example, by Henry Fox Talbot and other pioneering practitioners. By any definition these old pictures would be out of copyright by virtue of the time elapsed since the photographer's death. However, trustees or independent commercial libraries often levy hire charges if material in their possession is subsequently reproduced.

In summary, authors are well placed to produce their own photography to illustrate their literary works. With sensible understanding of publishers' requirements and thoughtful application with the camera, writers will derive extra pleasure and profit from seeing their pictures, as well as words, in print.

David Askham is author of *Photo Libraries and Agencies* (BFP Books) and has been illustrating his written work for over 35 years. His photographs have been published worldwide in books, brochures, magazines and newspapers, many through international agencies.

Doing it on your own

Reasons for self-publishing are varied. Many highly respected comtemporary and past authors have published their own works. **Peter Finch** *introduces the concept and outlines the implications of such an undertaking.*

Why bother?

You've tried all the usual channels and been turned down; your work is uncommercial, specialised, technical, out of fashion; you are concerned with art while everyone else is obsessed with cash; you need a book out quickly; you want to take up small publishing as a hobby; you've heard that publishers make a lot of money out of their authors and you'd like a slice – all reason enough. But be sure you understand what you are doing before you begin.

But isn't this cheating? It can't be real publishing – where is the critical judgement? Publishing is a respectable activity carried out by firms of specialists. Writers of any ability never get involved.

But they do. Start self-publishing and you'll be in good historical company: Horace Walpole, Balzac, Walt Whitman, Virginia Woolf, Gertrude Stein, John Galsworthy, Rudyard Kipling, Beatrix Potter, Lord Byron, Thomas Paine, Mark Twain, Upton Sinclair, W.H. Davies, Zane Grey, Ezra Pound, D.H. Lawrence, William Carlos Williams, Alexander Pope, Robbie Burns, James Joyce, Anaïs Nin and Lawrence Stern. All these at some time in their careers dabbled in doing it themselves. William Blake did nothing else. He even made his own ink, handprinted his pages and got Mrs Blake to sew on the covers.

But today it's different?

Not necessarily. This is not vanity publishing we're talking about although if all you want to do is produce a pamphlet of poems to give away to friends then self-publishing will be the cheapest way. Doing it yourself today can be a valid form of business enterprise. Being twice shortlisted for the Booker Prize sharpened Timothy Mo's acumen. Turning his back on mass-market paperbacks, he published *Brownout on Breadfruit Boulevard* on his own. Michael Tod's badger trilogy, *The Silver Tide*, has been paperbacked by Orion, Susan Hill self-produced her short stories, *Listening to the Orchestra*, and as an example to us all Jill Paton Walsh's self-published *Knowledge of Angels* was shortlisted for the Booker Prize.

Can anyone do it?

Certainly. If you are a writer then a fair number of the required qualities will already be in hand. If, in addition, you can put up a shelf then the manufacture of the book to go on it will not be beyond you. The more able and practical you are then the cheaper the process will be. The utterly inept will need to pay others to help them, but it will still be self-publishing in the end.

Where do I start?

With research. Read up on the subject. Make sure you know what the parts of a book are. Terms like *verso*, *recto*, prelims, typeface and point size all have to lose their mystery. You will not need to become an expert but you will need a certain familiarity. Don't rush. Learn.

What about ISBN numbers?

International Standard Book Numbers – a standard bibliographic code, individual to each book published, are used by book-

sellers and librarians alike. They are issued free of charge by the Standard Book Numbering Agency, 12 Dyott Street, London WC1A 1DF. Write giving the basic details of your proposed book and, if appropriate, you will receive an ISBN by return.

Next?

Put your book together – be it the typed pages of your novel, your selected poems or your story of how it was in the war – and see how large a volume it will make. See *Preparing and submitting a manuscript* on page 527 for guidelines on how to lay out the text.

No real idea of what your book should look like? Anything will not do. Go to your local bookshop and hunt out a few contemporary examples of volumes produced in a style you would like to emulate. Ask the manager for advice. Take your manuscript and your examples round to a number of local printers (find these through *Yellow Pages*) and ask for a quote. This costs nothing and will give you an idea of what the enterprise is likely to involve. Some examples of printers who are specialists in low print runs are given in the box above. A number of others advertise their services in the writers' magazines. Many are worth a look but tread with care. Don't rush.

How much?

It depends. How long is a piece of string? You will not get a pamphlet of poems out for less than a few hundred pounds while a hardbacked work of prose will cost several thousand. Unit cost is important. The larger the number of copies you have printed the less each will cost. Print too many and the total bill will be enormous. Books are no longer cheap; perhaps they never were.

Can I make it cost less?

Yes. Do some of the work yourself. If you want to publish poems and you are prepared to use a text set by a home word processor, you will make a considerable saving. Many word processing programs today have desktop publishing (DTP) facilities which will enhance the look of

---

Low print run printers

Start by asking a few local printers for quotes. It is also worth trying:

Anthony Rowe Ltd
Bumper's Way, Bristol Road,
Chippenham SN14 6LM
Specialist in low print runs from camera ready copy.

Book-in-Hand Ltd
20 Shepherds Hill, London N6 5AH

Evergreen Graphics
Meadow Lane, West Wittering, Chichester,
West Sussex PO20 8LR

---

your text. See *Desktop publishing* on page 535. Could you accept home production, run the pages off on an office photocopier, then staple the sheets? Editions made this way can be very presentable. For longer texts keyed in on a word processor, savings can be made by supplying the work on disk to an operator of a more sophisticated DTP program. They can import your text into their program without the need for any retyping.

Home binding, if your abilities lie in that direction, can save a fair bit. What it all comes down to is the standard of production you want and indeed at whom your book is aimed. Books for the commercial marketplace need to look like their fellows; specialist publications can afford to be more eccentric.

Who decides how it looks?

You do. No one should ever ask a printer simply to produce a book. You should plan the design of your publication with as much care as you would a house extension. Books which sell are those which stand out in the bookshop. Spend as much time and money as you can on the cover. It is the part of the book your buyer will see first. Look at the volumes in bookshop displays, especially those in the window. Imitate British paperback design – it's the best in the world.

How many copies should I produce?

Small press poetry pamphlets sell about 300 copies, new novels sometimes man-

age 1000, literary paperbacks 10,000, mass-market blockbusters over a million. But that is generally where there is a sales team and whole distribution organisation behind the book. You are an individual. You must do everything yourself. Do not, on the one hand, end up with a prohibitively high unit cost by ordering too few copies. One hundred of anything is usually a waste of time. On the other hand can you really sell 3000? Will shops buy in dozens? They will probably only want twos and threes. Take care. Research your market first.

How do I sell it?
With all your might. This is perhaps the hardest part of publishing. It is certainly as time consuming as both the writing of the work and the printing of it put together. To succeed here you need a certain flair and you should definitely not be of a retiring nature. If you intend selling through the trade (and even if you don't you are bound to come into contact with bookshop orders at some stage), your costing must be correct and worked out in advance. Shops will want at least 33% of the selling price as discount. You'll need about the same again to cover your distribution, promotion and other overheads, leaving the final third to cover production costs and any profit you may wish to make. Multiply your unit production cost by at least four. Commerical publishers often multiply by as much as nine.

Do not expect the trade to pay your carriage costs. Your terms should be 33% post free on everything bar single copy orders. Penalise these by reducing your discount to 25%. Some shops will suggest that you sell copies to them on sale or return. This means that they only pay you for what they sell and then only after they've sold it. This is a common practice with certain categories of publications and often the only way to get independent books into certain shops; but from the self-publisher's point of view it should be avoided if at all possible. Cash in hand is best but expect to have your invoices paid by cheque at a later date. Buy a duplicate pad in order to keep track of what's going

on. Phone the shops you have decided should take your book or turn up in person and ask to see the buyer. Letters and sample copies sent by post will get ignored. Get a freelance distributor to handle all of this for you if you can. Check the trade section of Cassell's *Directory of Publishing* or advertise for one in *The Bookseller*. If you can contract one they will want another 12% or so commission on top of the shops' discount – but expect to have to go it alone.

What about promotion?
A vital aspect often overlooked by beginners. Send out as many review copies as you can, all accompanied by slips quoting selling price and name and address of the publisher. Never admit to being that person yourself. Invent a name: it will give your operation a professional feel. Ring up newspapers and local radio stations ostensibly to check that your copy has arrived but really to see if they are prepared to give your book space. Try to think of an angle for them, anything around which they can write a story. Buying advertising space rarely pays for itself but good local promotion with 100% effort will generate dividends.

What about depositing copies at the British Library?
Under the Copyright Acts the British Library, the Bodleian Library, Oxford, The University Library, Cambridge, The National Library of Scotland, the Library of Trinity College Dublin and the National Library of Wales are all entitled to a free copy of your book which must be sent to them within one month of publication. One copy should go direct to the Legal Deposit Office at The British Library, Boston Spa, Wetherby, West Yorkshire LS23 7BY. The other libraries use an agent, Mr A.T. Smail, at 100 Euston Street, London NW1 2HQ *tel* 0171-388 5061. Contact him directly to find out how many copies he requires. Many self-publishers object to sending books out for nothing but there are advantages. Data on your title will be used by the libraries as part of their bibliographic services and

the book itself will eventually form part of a comprehensive national archive and be made available to the public.

What if I can't manage all this myself?

You can employ others to do it for you. If you are a novelist and you opt for a package covering everything, it could set you back more than £10,000. A number of publishers and associations advertise such services in writers' journals and in the Sunday classifieds. 'Authors. Publish with us.' is a typical ploy. They will do a competent job for you, certainly, but you will still end up having to do the bulk of the selling yourself. It is a costly route, fraught with difficulty. Do the job on your own if you possibly can.

And what if it goes wrong?

Put all the unsolds under the bed or give them away. It has happened to lots of us. Even the big companies who are experienced at these things have their regular flops. It was an adventure and you did get your book published. On the other hand you may be so successful that you'll be at the London Book Fair selling the film rights and wondering if you've reprinted enough. Whichever way it goes – good luck.

Can the Internet help?

Certainly. The World Wide Web, with which many authors are now dabbling, offers unrivalled opportunity for self-promulgation. This rapidly developing and highly flexible medium enables participants to promote themselves and their work internationally for as little as £10 per month. Initial investment may be high – you need a decent computer, a modem and a set of software – but the benefits can

Useful organisations

Association of Little Presses (ALP)
Chairperson Lawrence Upton, 25 St Benedict's Close, Church Lane, London SW17 9NX
web site http://www.melloworld.com/alp
Offers advice, publishes a catalogue of small independent publications, produces a newsletter, organises book fairs. Publishes a booklet: *Self-Publishing: Not So Difficult After All.* Membership £12.50.

Password (Books) Ltd
23 New Mount Street, Manchester M4 4DE
tel 0161-953 4009
Runs publishing training courses for small and self-publishers.

Author-Publisher Network
6 Kelvinbrook, West Molesey, Surrey KT8 1R2
tel 0181-979 3060
A self-publishers' self-help organisation. Runs courses and lectures; publishes *Write to Publish*, an essential self-publisher's newsletter; compiles a catalogue of members' publications; and a directory of services. Self-publishers should certainly join the A-PE. Membership £15.

be enormous. And it's fun. Some authors are happy simply to advertise their books while others produce complete on-line electronic versions for the world to read. The process may at first appear difficult but it is actually no more complex than traditional publishing. If you'd like to try then read up before investing.

Peter Finch is a poet, bookseller and former small publisher. His best-selling *How to Publish Yourself* (Allison & Busby) has just gone into a third, completely revised edition.

Further reading

Bride, Mac, *Teach Yourself the Internet*, Hodder & Stoughton, 2nd edn, 1997

Finch, Peter, *How To Publish Yourself*, Allison & Busby, 3rd edn, 1997

Foster, Charles, *Editing, Design and Book Production*, Journeyman, 1993

Godber, Bill, Webb, Robert, and Smith, Keith, *Marketing For Small Publishers*, Journeyman, 1992

Kennedy, Angus J., *The Internet & World Wide Web: The Rough Guide*, Rough Guides Ltd, 1995

Ross, Tom and Marilyn, *The Complete Guide to Self-Publishing*, Writer's Digest Books, 1994

Spicer, Robert, *How To Publish A Book*, How To Books, 1993

Zeitlyn, Jonathan, *Print: How You Can Do It Yourself!*, Journeyman, 1992

Vanity publishing

Vanity publishers produce copies of a book in return for a fee paid by its author. The job they undertake is very different from that carried out by a publisher, which invests its own money in the whole publishing process. Authors considering vanity publishing should exercise caution.

Publishers very rarely ask authors to pay for the production of their work, to contribute to its cost, or to undertake purchase of copies. Exceptions may be a book of an extremely specialised nature with a very limited market, or perhaps the first book of poems by a talented new writer. In such cases, especially if the book makes a significant contribution to its subject, an established and reliable publisher may be prepared to accept a subvention from the author to make publication possible, and such financial grants often come from scientific or other academic foundations or funds. This is a very different procedure from that of the vanity publisher who claims to perform, for a fee to be paid by the author, all the many functions involved in publishing a book.

Manufacture *v.* publication

Some vanity publishers clearly state the services they provide and are open in all their dealings. However, the promotional material sent out by many vanity publishers makes claims which prove to be lacking in substance and foundation. The Advertising Standards Authority, with the support of the Committee of Advertising Practice, has issued revised guidelines to advertisers in an endeavour to reduce misleading claims made by some vanity publishers in their follow-up material. In their effort to secure business, vanity publishers may give exaggerated praise to an author's work and arouse equally unrealistic hopes of its commercial success. True publishers

invest their own money in the whole publishing process: editorial, design, manufacturing, selling and distribution. The vanity publisher usually invests the author's money in but one part of this process: manufacture.

The distressing reports the *Writers' & Artists' Yearbook* office has received from embittered victims of vanity publishers underlines the importance of reading with extreme care the contracts offered by such publishers. It is worth asking a solicitor to check over this paperwork. The Publishers Association (see page 469) may also be able to provide useful advice. Often, these contacts will provide for the

---

Vanity publishing considerations

Any author who wants to use their money to publish their own books through a vanity publisher should:
- not immediately believe all the claims of a vanity publisher's promotional material
- treat with caution enthusiastic praise by a vanity publisher of a manuscript submitted
- take any contract to a solicitor to be read
- not sign anything without first consulting a solicitor
- ask to see examples of reviews which they have obtained in the national press
- ask to see a sample of a book published by them to assess the standard of publication
- make sure that the vanity publisher is connected with a distributor
- remember that the publishing business in general is risky, so never part with more money than he or she can afford to lose.

printing of, say, 2000 copies of the book, usually at a quite exorbitant cost to the author, but will leave the 'publisher' under no obligation to bind more than a very limited number. Alternatively, the vanity publisher may promise to print any number of copies for an author, but actually print only 100 copies or fewer.

Frequently, too, the author will be expected to pay extra for the cost of any effective advertising, while the 'publisher' makes little or no effort to promote the distribution and sale of the book. The names and imprints of vanity publishers are well known to literary editors and, with some worthy exceptions, their productions are rarely reviewed in any important periodical. Such books are unlikely to be stocked by major booksellers.

Mainstream publishers receive a very large number of unsolicited manuscripts, only a small percentage of which are published. Manuscripts may be rejected because they are not of an acceptable standard, because they do not fit in with the kind of books the publisher normally produces or because the market for them is too small or too local. In any case, getting a manuscript accepted by a mainstream publisher requires careful targeting and perseverance (see Michael Ridpath's *Foreword*).

If you are unable to persuade a mainstream publisher to take your manuscript and decide to publish at your own expense, you could consider the possibility of self-publishing (see page 255). If you decide to approach a vanity publisher do so with caution and do not expect any commercial gain from your investment.

Having checked that the sum asked for is a reasonable one, and the publisher will provide the services you require, take the attitude that you are paying simply for the pleasure of seeing your work in print. You are less likely to be disappointed.

Top hundred chart of 1996 paperback fastsellers

*Every year since 1979, **Alex Hamilton** has compiled for The Guardian an annual survey comprising a table of the 100 topselling paperbacks published for the first time during that year by British publishers. For readers new to the chart he describes here its terms of reference and indicates certain limitations.*

Bestsellers and fastsellers

An important distinction has first to be made between 'bestsellers' and the term used here – 'fastsellers'. Bestsellers have the real commercial pedigree. Sometimes, but not always, they have made a very visible showing in the fastseller lane, but among bestselling authors there are hundreds whose books have made a slow start and only through the cumulative sales over many years vindicate the faith of the original publisher. Among many examples of those whose sales in their lifetimes were modest but the posthumous interest spectacular, two durable cases are D.H. Lawrence and George Orwell.

Poetry

While serious poets never repeat Lord Byron's success in becoming a bestseller and 'famous overnight', and the only two works with short lines in a decade of fastsellers were collections of comic verse, a poet such as T.S. Eliot – not to mention Shakespeare and Chaucer – will over the long haul rack up sales in millions. And an outside event, such as the award of the Nobel Prize to Seamus Heaney in 1995, produces an immediate selling bonanza.

Fiction and non-fiction

The bread and butter of publishing has long been Bibles, classic authors, cookbooks, dictionaries and other reference books, and these are also the bridge for the trade into CD-Roms. Although the larger bulk of counter sales, and of library borrowings, consists of fiction, the topselling individual titles for this century, with figures of over 20 million copies, include most of these categories. However, the gross figures worldwide for hardcover and paperback, with translations, of prolific authors such as Agatha Christie, Alistair MacLean, Mickey Spillane, Stephen King and Catherine Cookson are claimed to be between 50 million and 300 million copies.

Individual titles of such popular authors would generally show up in topical bestseller lists, but not always. Dennis Wheatley, for instance, had a big following in Britain, but the 'British' quality he prided himself on did not travel; overseas he was hardly read. Something like it happens also with Barbara Cartland who, with more than 500 titles, is so prolific as to compete with herself: her individual books are never bestsellers but all together they do loom large.

The fastselling list which follows is limited to paperbacks which have appeared for the first time in that year from British publishers (regardless of their hardcover provenance). It is tempting to include old titles revived to synchronise with film releases and television serials, because these tie-ins have a strong influence (a good example for 1996 is John Grisham's *A Time To Kill*, which sold 226,760 more) but except when the figure is very large, I try to exclude them.

Looking at the figures

Since 1979 there were always, until the 1990s, recession, between 102 and 125 titles which passed the 100,000 mark – a convenient round figure for those who like to make comparisons. (This year there were 124.) While publishers inevitably highlight the performances of their own authors, it was never my aim to make the list look like a competition. Nor should it be seen as a yardstick of publishing efficiency, or solvency. The high-profile books which achieve six-figure sales are a vital part of the trade, but the list has little significance in the assessment of quality, policy and financial acumen in any one publishing house. It is possible to go broke with a runaway fast-seller – on more than one occasion the success of a single book has led to an unrealistic expansion – but on the other hand, there are many attractive and profitable imprints which never come within hailing distance of having a title in this list. The best way to look at it is as a reflection of popular taste accentuated by aggressive marketing.

A distortion for titles published at the end of the period may naturally be suspected but in actual fact it rarely makes much difference. The widespread use of electronic stock control by booksellers now enables them to more closely match their ordering to demand. The significant sale of new paperbacks, particularly by authors with a regular following, takes place within a few weeks of their appearance on the racks. Having said this, however, a few do enter the magic circle of bestsellers: during the 1980s the highest cumulative sales were for books by Sue Townsend and Jeffrey Archer, each passing five million, having sold 400,000 and a million respectively in their first year.

The authors

Surveyed over a period, the fastseller lists indicate a rather conservative attitude on the part of buyers. It is not very common for a book to appear in the top 20 (which earn between them much the same as the rest of the list put together) which has not appeared somewhere on the list in previous years. (1996 is an exception to the rule in providing three newcomers.) Once established on the list, an author has only to turn in a regular supply of similar works to stay on it. Being comfortable with a formula is therefore a psychological asset for those wanting to compete in this market; however, like actors who are typecast, authors may find too late that the market will then not allow them to escape. One among several stories of authors corralled in their own fantasies relates that thriller writer Peter Cheyney gave his publisher a book unlike the rest of his oeuvre and was told to bury it, lest its publication confuse his loyal following.

The dominant figures of the 1980s were Wilbur Smith (now with more than 20 novels past the million), Barbara Taylor Bradford, Dick Francis, Len Deighton, Stephen King, Catherine Cookson, Jeffrey Archer, Danielle Steel and Victoria Holt, with Jilly Cooper coming through at the end, particularly in the UK market. The 1990s have not seen any very significant shift, save the introduction as front-runners of John Grisham and Maeve Binchy. It is the author's name that matters most, as shown by the fact that of 1800 titles only six have been volumes of short stories, two with sales over 750,000 copies, because they were by Frederick Forsyth and Jeffrey Archer, and two with 500,000 (Archer again, and Rosamund Pilcher).

More than half the buyers of books have always been women but for most of the 1980s hardly more than a quarter of the authors were women. However, in the 1990s they have had a steadily increasing presence, from 25% rising to settle at a new level between 35% and 40%.

Genres

Some 80% of the bulk is usually fiction. The regular elements of the non-fiction remainder are diet books, the horoscope division of astrology, joke books, showbiz lives and exploitations based on big movies (anything by Spielberg, for instance). Of fiction, genres take up most

of the slots, particularly adventure yarns, thrillers, horror stories, family sagas and a mixed bag of romances, from historical to 'Gothic' to the now faded bodice-rippers and 'sex'n'shopping' (which has dropped the shopping), and career-conflict stories under the vague umbrella of 'women's fiction'. There seems to be no overt category of 'men's fiction' that might once have included authors like Mickey Spillane and Harold Robbins, or today would correspond to the focus and tone of laddish magazines. Perhaps there is a slight hint of this in the popularity of heroics by SAS men, war commanders and pilots who have been shot down, but it is not yet a developed genre, and has run into a problem with the Ministry of Defence objecting to the revelation of secret techniques.

Science fantasy is more likely to show than science fiction of a harder, more experimental kind. Westerns have never featured at all, despite the sometime fame of authors such as Zane Grey, Louis L'Amour and J.T. Edson. Travellers' tales have had no significant presence until this year, when the American Bill Bryson's flattering farewell journey around Britain sold more copies in one year than any other travelogue has in 20.

Heavyweight to juvenile

There are rarely more than 10-12 titles in any list that could count on reviews from serious book pages, and most of these appear some way down. However, in recent years, broadly since the television focus on it, the Booker Prize has taken winners into the fastseller list. When it does happen, this award seems to establish the book rather than the author, and the only winners to keep a place with subsequent books are Anita Brookner and Roddy Doyle. No other literary award has yet resulted in a 100,000 paperback sale for the author.

The highest selling title for the 1980s happens to have been a juvenile, *The Secret Diary of Adrian Mole Aged 13¾*, whose author Sue Townsend is said to have been embarrassed when she heard that the publishers had a print run of 70,000 in hand, and begged them to reduce it because she could not bear to think of them risking so much on her behalf. With this and a sequel she very nearly equals the total sale for 11 titles of the best known author in children's fiction, the late Roald Dahl. The latter's death left the role of natural market leader vacant, a position apparently now being being filled by Terry Pratchett. Horror books that can be racked at children's eye level, such as Scholastic's *Point Horror* series, are examples of a perennially popular genre.

The year 1996

On the whole, 1996 was a difficult year for children's books, though the film *Babe* lifted the sales of its source book, *The Sheep-Pig* by Dick King-Smith (published in 1986) to half a million.

The new element for the trade over the past two years has been its adaptation to the price flexibility resulting from the collapse of the Net Book Agreement (whereby booksellers maintained the cover price fixed by the publisher). At present, although one major chain does reduce prices on some paperbacks, it seems that discounting is felt more among about 200 top hardcover titles. Indeed the fastsellers list is one feature that remains almost eerily stable, as if these books had an independent orbit. The most common price point is now £5.99 (61 examples), and the average price paid by the buyer appears to have risen from £5.87 to £5.96. However the rest of the book business may have fared, the fastsellers' performance grows ever stronger, showing an aggregate rise of 26 million to 30 million units, with an increase in turnover from £151 million to £178.8 million (the first 25 titles accounting for 16 million books and £86 million). Export turnover was also up though its relative share fell from 32% to 30.5%.

Casting about for evidence of those genres which have been spoken of optimistically in recent times, it seems few fulfil their promise. Those that do are new subdivisions in the major categories of

No	Title	Genre	Author	Imprint
1	The Green Mile (6 titles)	Horror	Stephen King (US)	Penguin
2	The Rainmaker	Thriller	John Grisham (US)	Arrow
3	The Horse Whisperer	Novel	Nicholas Evans (Br)	Corgi
4	Highway Code (revised)	Handbook	DoT (Br)	HMSO
5	The Seventh Scroll	Adventure	Wilbur Smith (SA)	Pan
6	Sophie's World	Juvenile	Jostein Gaarder (Nor)	Phoenix
7	A Ruthless Need	Saga	Catherine Cookson (Br)	Corgi
8	Come to Grief	Thriller	Dick Francis (Br)	Pan
9	Coming Home	Romance	Rosamunde Pilcher (Br)	Coronet
10	From Potter's Field	Crime	Patricia Cornwell (US)	Warner
11	The Obsession	Saga	Catherine Cookson (Br)	Corgi
12	The Lost World	Adventure	Michael Crichton (US)	Arrow
13	Immediate Action	Action	Andy McNab (Br)	Corgi
14	Morning, Noon and Night	Thriller	Sidney Sheldon (US)	HarperCollins
15	Lightning	Romance	Danielle Steel (US)	Corgi
16	Enigma	Thriller	Robert Harris (Br)	Arrow
17	Notes from a Small Island	Travel	Bill Bryson (US)	Black Swan
18	Rose Madder	Horror	Stephen King (US)	NEL
19	Five Days in Paris	Romance	Danielle Steel (US)	Corgi
20	The Best of Friends	Novel	Joanna Trollope (Br)	Black Swan
21	Dangerous to Know	Romance	Barbara T. Bradford (Br)	HarperCollins
22	Wings	Romance	Danielle Steel (US)	Corgi
23	Our Game	Thriller	John le Carré (Br)	Coronet
24	The Apocalypse Watch	Thriller	Robert Ludlum (US)	HarperCollins
25	Original Sin	Crime	P.D. James (Br)	Penguin
26	Sleepers	Autobiog	Lorenzo Carcaterra (US)	Arrow
27	High Fidelity	Novel	Nick Hornby (Br)	Indigo
28	Forbidden Places	Romance	Penny Vincenzi (Br)	Orion
29	Grantchester Grind	Humour	Tom Sharpe (Br)	Pan
30	Complete Theory Test	Handbook	Driving Standards (Br)	HMSO
31	The Juror	Thriller	George D. Green (US)	Bantam
32	A Place Called Freedom	Adventure	Ken Follett (Br)	Pan
33	Maskerade	Fantasy	Terry Pratchett (Br)	Corgi
34	Games of State	Thriller	Clancy & Pieczenik (US)	HarperCollins
35	Behind the Scenes at the Museum	Novel	Kate Atkinson (Br)	Black Swan
36	Ground Zero	X-Files	Kevin J. Anderson (US)	Voyager
37	The Truth is Out There	X-Files	Brian Lowry (US)	Voyager
38	Intensity	Thriller	Dean Koontz (US)	Headline
39	Love in Another Town	Novel	Barbara T. Badford (Br)	HarperCollins
40	Ready Steady Cook	Cookery	Turner & Thompson (Br)	BBC
41	Betrayal	Thriller	Clare Francis (Br)	Pan
42	The One That Got Away	Action	Chris Ryan (Br)	Arrow
43	Dark Room	Crime	Minette Walters (Br)	Pan
44	Living a Lie	Saga	Josephine Cox (Br)	Headline
45	Angel of Death	Thriller	Jack Higgins (Br)	Signet
46	The Winter King	Novel	Bernard Cornwell (Br)	Penguin
47	Precipice	Thriller	Colin Forbes (Br)	Pan
48	The Devil You Know	Saga	Josephine Cox (Br)	Headline
49	Strange Highways	Stories	Dean Koontz (US)	Headline
50	Unofficial X-Files I	X-Files	N.E. Genge (US)	Pan

Price £	Month	Home	Export	Total	Gross £	No
1.99	Mar	1,308,084	934,255	2,242,339	4,462,255	1
5.99	Jan	616,964	409,589	1,026,553	6,149,052	2
5.99	July	555,095	354,517	909,612	5,448,576	3
0.99	July	781,747	0	781,747	773,930	4
6.99	Oct	331,438	394,748	726,186	5,076,040	5
6.99	Mar	442,812	254,400	697,212	4,873,512	6
5.99	Mar	561,973	130,686	692,659	4,149,027	7
5.99	Nov	458,569	211,122	669,691	4,011,449	8
6.99	April	433,789	176,385	610,174	4,265,116	9
5.99	June	440,537	169,482	610,019	3,654,014	10
5.99	Sept	454,285	124,151	578,436	3,464,832	11
5.99	July	302,937	227,398	530,335	3,176,707	12
5.99	Oct	402,752	120,274	523,026	3,132,926	13
5.99	May	248,968	268,390	517,358	3,098,974	14
5.99	July	388,400	124,214	512,614	3,070,558	15
5.99	May	288,709	218,646	507,355	3,039,056	16
6.99	Aug	445,404	55,967	501,371	3,504,583	17
6.99	June	322,134	147,347	469,481	3,281,672	18
5.99	Nov	345,424	105,229	450,653	2,699,411	19
6.99	May	352,709	70,505	423,214	2,958,266	20
5.99	Aug	298,944	117,348	416,292	2,493,589	21
5.99	April	284,747	116,366	401,113	2,402,667	22
5.99	Mar	267,478	125,389	392,867	2,353,273	23
5.99	Mar	162,013	223,576	385,589	2,309,678	24
5.99	Mar	199,408	182,961	382,369	2,290,390	25
6.99	April	239,701	135,595	375,296	2,623,319	26
5.99	April	321,319	21,554	342,873	2,053,809	27
5.99	July	224,309	116,926	341,235	2,043,998	28
5.99	June	275,107	65,254	340,361	2,038,762	29
9.99	Mar	339,645	0	339,645	3,393,054	30
5.99	Jan	225,142	105,819	330,961	1,982,456	31
5.99	Aug	181,847	143,508	325,355	1,948,876	32
5.99	Nov	264,606	59,966	324,572	1,944,186	33
5.99	June	158,939	152,601	311,540	1,866,125	34
6.99	Jan	275,903	30,813	306,716	2,143,945	35
5.99	June	195,058	111,304	306,362	1,835,108	36
9.99	Jan	221,865	65,492	287,357	2,870,696	37
5.99	Oct	151,327	110,991	262,318	1,571,285	38
4.99	Dec	171,646	78,735	250,381	1,249,401	39
4.99	Feb	241,388	240	241,628	1,205,724	40
5.99	July	160,561	79,399	239,960	1,437,360	41
5.99	June	176,755	59,159	235,914	1,413,125	42
5.99	May	169,467	47,660	217,127	1,300,591	43
5.99	Mar	192,285	21,666	213,951	1,281,566	44
5.99	May	144,804	65,942	210,746	1,262,369	45
5.99	Sept	165,224	43,155	208,379	1,248,190	46
5.99	Dec	139,452	66,821	206,273	1,235,575	47
5.99	Sept	165,676	35,719	201,395	1,206,356	48
5.99	April	119,686	80,255	199,941	1,197,647	49
9.99	Jan	168,458	29,074	197,532	1,973,345	50

No	Title	Genre	Author	Imprint
51	Ecstasy	Stories	Irvine Welsh (Br)	Cape
52	In the Presence of Enemy	Crime	Elizabeth George (US)	Bantam
53	Escape	Adventure	James Clavell Jr	Coronet
54	Backwards	Red Dwarf	Rob Grant (Br)	Penguin
55	Kiss the Girls	Thriller	James Patterson (US)	HarperCollins
56	A Simple Life	Romance	Rosie Thomas (Br)	Minerva
57	There's Treasure Everywhere	Humour	Bill Watterson (US)	Warner
58	Therapy	Novel	David Lodge (Br)	Penguin
59	The Moor's Last Sigh	Novel	Salman Rushdie (Br)	Vintage
60	Complete Flat Stomach	Health	Rosemary Conley (Br)	Arrow
61	Belgarath the Sorcerer	Fantasy	D. & L. Eddings (US)	Voyager
62	World of Difference	Saga	Audrey Howard (Br)	Coronet
63	The Ghost Road	Novel	Pat Barker (Br)	Penguin
64	Emotional Intelligence	Psychol	Daniel Goleman (US)	Bloomsbury
65	Memnoch the Devil	Thriller	Anne Rice (US)	Arrow
66	Tangled Web	Romance	Judith Michael (US)	Warner
67	Cause of Death	Crime	Patricia Cornwell (US)	Little, Brown
68	Return of the Stranger	Saga	Reay Tannahill (Br)	Orion
69	Hope	Thriller	Len Deighton (Br)	HarperCollins
70	The Runaway Jury	Thriller	John Grisham (US)	Arrow
71	Fingerprints of the Gods	History	Graham Hancock (Br)	Mandarin
72	X Marks the Spot	X-Files	Les Martin (US)	Voyager
73	Bloodlines	Stories	Ruth Rendell (Br)	Arrow
74	Whit	Novel	Iain Banks (Br)	Abacus
75	Last Chapter and Worse	Humour	Gary Larson (US)	Warner
76	Primary Colors	Novel	Anon (US)	Vintage
77	The State We're In	Economics	Will Hutton (Br)	Vintage
78	The 100 Secret Senses	Novel	Amy Tan (US)	Flamingo
79	The Steps of the Sun	Saga	Caroline Harvey (Br)	Corgi
80	The Jump	Thriller	Martina Cole (Br)	Headline
81	Ready Steady Cook 2	Cookery	Anthony & Cawley (Br)	BBC
82	The Web	Thriller	Jonathan Kellerman (US)	Warner
83	True Crime	Thriller	Andrew Klavan (US)	Warner
84	Out of the Sun	Novel	Robert Goddard (Br)	Corgi
85	House of Echoes	Thriller	Barbara Erskine (Br)	HarperCollins
86	Superplonk	Wine guide	Malcolm Gluck (Br)	Coronet
87	Easy Care Gardening	Garden	D.G. Hessayon (Br)	Expert
88	A Woman's Place	Saga	Edwina Currie (Br)	Coronet
89	Promises Lost	Saga	Audrey Howard (Br)	Coronet
90	The Cry of the Halidon	Thriller	Robert Ludlum (US)	HarperCollins
91	Unofficial X-Files II	X-Files	N.E. Genge (US)	Pan
92	Rise of the Merchant Prince	Fantasy	Raymond Feist (US)	Voyager
93	Kiss Chase	Romance	Fiona Walker (Br)	Coronet
94	The Information	Novel	Martin Amis (Br)	Flamingo
95	Walking in Darkness	Thriller	Charlotte Lamb (Br)	Signet
96	The Nightingale Sings	Saga	Charlotte Bingham (Br)	Bantam
97	Trust No One	X-Files	Brian Lowry (US)	Voyager
98	Spencerville	Thriller	Nelson DeMille (US)	HarperCollins
99	Darkness Falls	X-Files	Les Martin (US)	Voyager
100	X-Files Confidential	X-Files	Ted Edwards (US)	Little, Brown

Price £	Month	Home	Export	Total	Gross £	No
9.99	May	170,112	26,074	196,186	1,959,898	**51**
5.99	Nov	122,186	68,941	191,127	1,144,851	**52**
5.99	Feb	114,496	72,611	187,107	1,120,771	**53**
5.99	Nov	147,651	37,250	184,901	1,107,557	**54**
5.99	Feb	107,803	75,800	183,603	1,099,782	**55**
5.99	Mar	144,545	34,640	179,185	1,073,318	**56**
8.99	Sept	128,916	46,073	174,989	1,573,151	**57**
6.99	May	127,912	46,382	174,294	1,218,315	**58**
6.99	July	80,421	91,982	172,403	1,205,097	**59**
4.99	Jan	161,609	9,204	170,813	852,357	**60**
6.99	July	80,710	87,256	167,966	1,174,082	**61**
5.99	May	144,937	22,971	167,908	1,005,769	**62**
6.99	July	128,963	35,218	164,181	1,147,625	**63**
7.99	Sept	135,023	28,333	163,356	1,305,214	**64**
5.99	Aug	83,994	76,974	160,968	964,198	**65**
5.99	Mar	100,527	58,043	158,570	949,834	**66**
9.99	Oct	17,709	139,707	157,416	1,572,586	**67**
5.99	Feb	113,672	37,718	151,390	906,826	**68**
5.99	Sept	94,800	56,513	151,313	906,365	**69**
9.99	Nov	149,993	0	149,993	1,498,430	**70**
6.99	Feb	94,293	53,791	148,084	1,035,107	**71**
3.99	Feb	99,142	47,779	146,921	586,215	**72**
4.99	Sept	106,938	38,481	145,419	725,641	**73**
6.99	Sept	122,956	21,943	144,899	1,012,844	**74**
6.99	Nov	119,797	22,719	142,516	996,187	**75**
6.99	Sept	90,326	50,011	140,337	980,956	**76**
7.99	Jan	134,890	4,482	139,372	1,113,582	**77**
6.99	Nov	49,780	87,852	137,632	962,048	**78**
5.99	Mar	110,380	23,652	134,032	802,852	**79**
5.99	July	104,583	28,778	133,361	798,832	**80**
4.99	Sept	128,795	120	128,915	643,286	**81**
5.99	June	72,151	56,247	128,398	769,104	**82**
5.99	May	71,257	56,811	128,068	767,127	**83**
5.99	Dec	96,031	31,528	127,559	764,078	**84**
5.99	Nov	92,884	34,059	126,943	760,389	**85**
5.99	Nov	126,250	0	126,250	756,238	**86**
5.99	April	112,693	13,364	126,057	755,081	**87**
5.99	Oct	106,549	19,208	125,757	753,284	**88**
5.99	Nov	98,697	23,723	122,420	733,296	**89**
5.99	Dec	3,485	116,431	119,916	718,297	**90**
9.99	Nov	104,463	13,718	118,181	1,180,628	**91**
5.99	Oct	53,429	64,664	118,093	707,377	**92**
5.99	June	98,201	19,220	117,421	703,352	**93**
6.99	June	87,389	28,863	116,252	812,601	**94**
5.99	Aug	66,208	49,665	115,873	694,079	**95**
5.99	Aug	78,766	36,493	115,259	690,401	**96**
9.99	Dec	72,145	42,750	114,895	1,147,801	**97**
5.99	May	40,085	73,543	113,628	680,632	**98**
3.99	Feb	69,452	44,147	113,599	453,260	**99**
9.99	Oct	101,012	12,161	113,173	1,130,598	**100**

thriller, horror and romance. The Western has disappeared into the sunset; the modest flutter in travel writing in the late 1980s subsided; fantasy now does better than hardcore science fiction; and 'green books', after looking as if they would be as uplifting commercially as sermons in the late 19th century, have not much expanded their original niche market. The current vogue for courtroom drama stems from the success of American lawyer John Grisham, and *X-Files* novelisations are having a run of sorts. Looking at incipient genres, and the way that some are being fuelled with many varieties of religious speculation, it is to be feared that enough millennial books will appear to form a road block.

Alex Hamilton is a journalist and award-winning travel writer, and the author of several novels and volumes of short stories.

Poetry

Poetry into print

John Whitworth has submitted hundreds of poems and has had dealings with a number of publishers of poetry. He gives advice here 'from the handle end of the long spoon that poets use to sup with those they would persuade or bamboozle into printing, even paying for, their work.'

There are two things to say at the outset. Do not expect to make more than pin money *directly* from publication of your work. You may, in the fullness of time, make quite a tidy sum *indirectly* – I mean you get work because you are a published poet: readings, workshops, reviewing and so forth, if you like any of that sort of thing. But if you get £50 for a poem from a national magazine you may feel very satisfied, and as for your published slim volumes – they will not sell in four figures, nor do the publishers, except in a very few instances, expect them to. In a sense, nearly all poetry publishing is vanity publishing. Nobody is in it for the money.

And, secondly, as one poet put it to me, do not have too much respect for the taste of individual literary editors. She is right. An editor is not God (whatever he or she thinks). Remember that, though it can be hard if you are diffident (and most poets are). But this person is just like you; the fact that he or she (nearly always he) is warming an editorial chair may mean many things. It certainly does not mean papal infallibility. If Snooks of the *Review* sends back your work, despatch it immediately to Snurd of the *Supplement*. And if Snurd concurs with Snooks, they may both be wrong, indeed neither may actually have read through (or at all) what you sent. Grit your teeth and send to Snarl and then to Snivel. Do not be discouraged by rejection. If your poems are as good as you can make them and have been submitted in as professional a way as you can manage, then just keep on sending them out. I

started writing poems in 1968, wrote my first good one in 1972, and was paid my first proper money (£40 from the Arts Council) in 1976. The first book was published in 1980. So patience and a thick skin are big advantages.

It does help, of course, to have read the magazine you are making submissions to. This will prevent you sending your bawdy ballad to *The Times Literary Supplement (TLS)* or concrete poetry to *The Literary Review*. And I am assuming that you actually are interested in the craft of poetry and the names of, say, Milton, Tennyson and Eliot mean something to you. You will also be interested to know what Heaney, Hughes, Harrison and Hannah actually do. You don't have to like it, but you ought to want to know about it. If no one is writing anything remotely like your work, perhaps you should ask yourself why that might be. On the other hand, remember the words of Charlie Coburn, the old music-hall singer: 'I sang my song to them, and they didn't like it. So I sang it again, and they still didn't like it. So I sang it a third time and one of them thought he might just get to like it if I changed the tune and altered the words. So I sang it again, just exactly the same way, and after a bit they all liked it.'

Submitting your work to magazines

I asked a number of poets about this. Some of them said they never submitted to magazines at all, because they disliked being rejected. I must say I think that a rather craven attitude, but you *can* carve

out a poetic reputation through work-shops and readings. You must be good at putting yourself about in public and have the time and energy to expend on it. All who did submit work regularly agreed on a number of basics:
• Submit your poem on an A4 sheet, typed or printed out from a word proces-sor. One poet, David Phillips, reckoned his percentage of successful submissions had gone up appreciably since he bought his word processor, and he assumed it was because his work now looked much more professional. It might be, of course, that it has just got better. Do not type it in italic, capitals or mock cursive. Keep it simple.
• Put your name and address at the bot-tom of each poem. Editors, reasonably, do not keep your letters, only the poems that interest them. You might consider one of those rubber stamps. I know a number of poets who have them, though I don't myself.
• Fold the poem once and put it into the sort of envelope designed to take A4 folded once. I don't know why poets like to scrunch their verses into tiny envelopes, but don't do it. Don't go to the other extreme either and send it dec-orated with admonitions not to bend, etcetera. Include a stamped, self-addressed envelope of the same size. This really is important. Shakespeare himself would be consigned to the wpb without an appropriate sae.
• Do not send just one poem. Do not send 20 poems. Send enough to give a reasonable flavour of your work – say about four or five. Long poems are less likely to be accepted than short poems. If you write different kinds of things, then make sure your selection covers a fair few of these kinds. Send what you think of as your best work, but do not be surprised if what is finally accepted is the one you put in at the last minute, 'to make the others look better' as Larkin lugubriously puts it. And if an editor says he or she likes your work and would like to see more, then send more as soon as possible. The editor wasn't just being polite. Editors aren't.

Submitting poems
• Submit poems on an A4 sheet, simply typed.
• Put your name and addess at the bot-tom of each sheet.
• Fold the sheet only once and use an A5 envelope.
• Send about four or five poems.
• Consider whether to submit the same poem simultaneously to more than one editor.
• Always keep copies of your poems.
• Include a short covering letter.

It was said because it was meant.
• At this point there is generally some po-faced stuff about never sending the same poem to more than one editor simultaneously. As it happens, I don't do this, but some well-known poets do. And indeed, if Snurd of the *Supplement* sits on your poems for six months, what are you supposed to do, since the polite fol-low-up letter recommended will, almost certainly, have no effect at all, except to waste your time and your stamps? The real reason for not making multiple sub-missions is the embarrassment of having to make grovelling noises when the same poem is accepted by two editors at once. I once, inadvertently, won two micro-scopic prizes in poetry competitions for the same poem. What did I do? I kept my mouth shut and cashed the cheques, that's what I did.
• You wouldn't have been daft enough to send off your *only* copies of poems to Snurd, would you? *Of course* he lost them and it's all your own silly fault. No you can't sue him through the civil courts, but you'll know better next time. Send photocopies and keep your origi-nals. No, editors don't mind photocopies. Why should they? They look a lot better than the original all covered in Tippex anyway.
• Keep your covering letter short, but if you have been published in reputable places then it will do no harm to say so. This advice comes from Duncan Forbes. Selling poems is very like selling any-

thing else, so blow your own trumpet, but don't blow for too long. Don't ask the editor for help in the advancement of your poetic career. Editors don't care, and anyway, what do they know? Being rude won't help either. I know artists are supposed to be rude and a lot of them are, too, but it hasn't actually helped them to anything except an ulcer or a punch on the nose.

Which magazines?

You could start with the *TLS* but I wouldn't advise it. One editor (not from the *TLS*) said honestly that he tended to reject, more or less unread, poems from anyone he had never heard of. Before you play with the big boys perhaps you ought to have some sort of a record in the little magazines. Some of these pay and some do not. The size of the cheque seems to depend on the size of the Arts Council grant rather than the quality of the magazine. What matters is not the cash but whether you feel proud or ashamed to be seen in the thing. The Poetry Library at the South Bank Centre (Royal Festival Hall, London SE1 8XX) publishes a list of poetry magazines, and if you can get along there (very convenient for Waterloo Station and open 11am-8pm except Mondays), you can nose around among the back numbers and see what is appealing to you. If you can't do that, then a letter with an sae will get you the list (see also page 275).

Judge where you think you will fit in, and buy yourself a big sheet of second-class stamps. Send off your work and be prepared to be reasonably patient. Most editors reply in the end. Little magazines have a high mortality rate, so be prepared for a particularly crushing form of disappointment – having your work accepted by a magazine which promptly ceases publication. It happens to us all; it goes on happening to me. The Poetry Library also sends out for an sae of 75p a satisfying wodge of bumph about poetry publishing in general. Worth the money.

Some inexperienced poets seem very worried that editors will filch their 'ideas' and pay them nothing, but poems are not made up of ideas; they are made up of words, and if anyone prints your poem without permission they are infringing your copyright and you can threaten them with all sorts of horrible things. But, honestly, this is a buyer's market, and even the editor of that badly photocopied rag has more material than can be used.

There seems to be a new kind of organisation that solicits poems. Often with names like Global or International, they don't ask for money up front, so are not exactly vanity presses. But they encourage you in marketers' prose to buy superduper anthologies for £40 or so. Harmless, I suppose, but I'd rather appear in something less pretentious along with some poets I had actually heard of.

Subscribe to *Poetry Review,* the magazine of the Poetry Society. It's quarterly, expensive and the best poetry magazine. *Poetry Wales* and *The New Welsh Review* are both beautifully produced, though they lack *PR's* bite and attack, and there is a certain amount of relentless celticity. *HU (The Honest Ulsterman)* is unpretentious to look at, but consistently interesting and intelligent – you don't have to be at all Irish to contribute either. *Ambit* is lively with good artwork; the editors take ages to look at submissions. *Iron* is run by a relic of the Sixties (Peter Mortimer who has a little boy called Dylan). The quality of the work has steadily improved along with the quality of the production. Mortimer is a most conscientious editor too, and replies promptly and individually. *Stand* has a wide distribution – a rather *Guardian*-y feel to the poems and opinions. *London Magazine* is as good as ever – Alan Ross scribbles cryptic encouragement on poems that don't quite make it. *PN Review* is a Leavisite dinosaur with very rude reviewers, an offshoot of the publisher Carcanet (or the other way round) and prints a wide range of poems. *Edinburgh Review* also has rude reviewers. *The Rialto* is well spoken of. This is a personal list – magazines I read from time to time. (See the list on page 130 for the poetry magazines listed in this *Yearbook*.)

The two literary heavyweights are *The*

Times Literary Supplement and *The London Review of Books*, and both publish poetry. The *TLS* does not publish Fiona Pitt-Kethley's ruderies.

Book publication

Every poet wants to get a book out. How do you do it? One pretty sure way is to win a big prize in a competition, the National or the biennial Arvon or Harry Chambers' Peterloo. Otherwise, you wait until you have reached the stage of having had two or three dozen poems published in reputable places; then you type out enough poems for a collection, traditionally 64pp but collections seem to be getting longer, and send them out, keeping your own copy and including return postage. I suppose you do. I first got published by talking to Anthony Thwaite in a pub; everybody needs a slice of luck. I know some excellent poets who are still trying to place their first book and, contrariwise, there are books ... Poetry, like most things, goes in fashions. But don't be in a hurry. Wait until you have a reputation in the magazines and small presses. Neil Astley at Bloodaxe reckons more than 90% of what comes through his letterbox he sends back, and he has usually had an eye on the successful ones before they got around to submitting.

Who do you send out to? Faber are still out in front (though they did turn down Larkin's *The Less Deceived*, the most influential book of English poems in the last 50 years). It is not that their poets are better, but Faber promote them heavily and care about them. And being a Faber poet puts you in the company of Eliot and Larkin. Penguin have revived their excellent *Modern Poets* series and have 12 titles so far. Most other big publishers do poetry – fortunes wax and wane with the person, often a poet, nearly always a man, in the editorial chair.

But being published by a household name does not mean selling thousands – hundreds are more common. Publishers like to have poetry on their list as a badge of virtue, but often they don't want to know much about it, they don't promote

Small press information

Association of Little Presses (ALP)
Chairperson Lawrence Upton, 25 St Benedict's Close, Church Lane, London SW17 9NX
web site http://www.melloworld.com.alp
They put out a newsletter and a catalogue for £3.00 plus 75p p&p.

The Stationery Office Oriel Bookshop
The Friary, Cardiff CF1 4AA
Publishes *Small Presses and Little Magazines of the UK and Ireland*.

The National Small Press Centre
BM BOZO, London WC1N 3XX
Publishes *Small Press Listings* quarterly.

Photon Press
The Light House, 29 Longfield Road, Tring, Herts. HP23 4DG
Light's List is a list of over 600 small press magazines. It costs £1.25 plus A5 sae.

The Poetry Library
Royal Festival Hall, South Bank Centre, London SE1 8XX
tel 0171-921 0943/0664 *fax* 0171-921 0939
Lists of poetry magazines, poetry bookshops, current competitions, etc. See also page 275.

it and they don't persist with it. The book sinks or swims, and usually it sinks. (Publishers that consider poetry for adults are listed in *Publishers of poetry* on page 280; *Children's book publishers and packagers* on page 249 includes publishers of poetry for children.)

Specialist poetry presses (some, though not all of which, publish nothing but poetry) produce books that look every bit as good and, in most cases, sell every bit as well (or badly). Bloodaxe, Peterloo and Carcanet, none of them London-based, are leaders in the field.

Bloodaxe sounds fearsomely dismissive, but the name is from a Viking who conquered Northumbria. They have more titles and possibly better poets than Faber but they still fail the railway bookstall test. 'From traditional formalists to postmodernists', says Neil Astley. Half the

poets on his list are women – good if you are a woman. Carcanet publish both Elizabeth Jennings and John Ashberry, which indicates Michael Schmidt's catholicity and willingness to go outside this country. He sees them as extending the Wordsworthian tradition of the common voice and welcomes manuscripts, though he wishes people would read some of the books on his list first. This is good advice; every publisher has a style, just as every magazine has. His latest find is Sophie Hannah, the infant phenomenon. If infancy is long past, then Harry Chambers at Peterloo is worth a try. He published a first book by Kirkpatrick Dobie in the poet's 84th year. Dana Gioia, the American 'new formalist' and Ursula Fanthorpe are his biggest guns.

Anvil are based in London and do a lot of poetry in translation. Enitharmon have Duncan Forbes, the most underrated poet now writing, Seren is Welsh, Peepal Tree is ethnic and the Women's Press is women. There are a lot more excellent small presses and information on them can be obtained through the organisations listed in the box.

Competitions

Some poets are snooty about these. Of course they are popular because they make money for the organisers: a biggish competition may attract 10,000 entries paying £3 a time. That gives an income of £30,000, enough to pay for some good prizes, a fair bit of promotion, fees for the judges and running costs, and still leave a nice bit in the kitty. But, from the poet's end, it is a good deal too. Though unknowns (everybody starts as an unknown, don't they?) only occasionally win the big prizes, they do pick up the smaller ones quite often, and that can be a great encouragement when you need it. If you are just starting out, then enter the competitions with first prizes of hundreds rather than thousands of pounds. The big guns probably won't enter these.

For more information on current competitions, see page 276 and *Prizes and awards* on page 488.

Getting on radio

Michael Conaghan, who has had many poems broadcast, says BBC local radio – more talk than its commercial equivalent – is the place to start. Find out who is responsible for Arts programming and contact them. 'Short punchy, topical work is probably what they want, and events/festivals concentrate their minds wonderfully. Nationally, Radio 1's Mark Radcliffe is a notable friend to poets.'

Poetry on the Internet

To get on the Internet you need a computer (PC or Mac, not an Amstrad word processor), a modem and a phone line. Any of the service providers are eager to give you an Internet connection for a few pounds per month. You can then e-mail anywhere or surf the World Wide Web.

The poet Peter Howard writes an Internet column for *Poetry Review* and suggests you can submit to electronic magazines or set up your own site and get people to visit it. You can even set up your own magazine – there's no extra charge. 'Everything's up for grabs – there are no real reputations yet, though they're forming', he says.

Poetry for children

Not (repeat *not*) a dustbin for grow-up rejects. The publishing grapevine says there is a shortage of good poetry for children, and schools pay poets (some with more brass-neck than talent) to perform in book weeks. Poet Lindsay MacRae thinks it helps to be young and a woman. But Roger McGough is oldish and a man. Write, enclosing a sae, to the Poetry Library for further information. (See also page 277.)

Vanity/subsidy publishing

Never give a publisher money. That is what they give to you. If you want your work in print and nobody will do it for you without a cheque, then do it yourself. See *Doing it on your own* on page 255. You

could probably buy yourself a second-hand word processor with the money you save by not answering that advertisement!

A last word

Invest some time, invest some money. Buy yourself, if not a word processor, at least a decent typewriter and some nice paper. Buy some books of poetry and try to see how your favourites do it. If you're a joiner, join a local group. Your local Regional Arts Board (see page 470) will know who they are. The Muse chooses her favourites, but be a bit welcoming.

John Whitworth has published six books of poetry, including *Landscape With Small Humans* (Peterloo) and, for children, *The Complete Poetical Works of Phoebe Flood* (Hodder). He has been a Faber anthologist, both judge and prize-winner in national poetry competitions, and has been published in national newspapers and on radio and television.

Poetry organisations

Britain probably has more publicly funded poetry organisations than any other country. These are all committed to helping poets and poetry in different ways and are useful ports of call for the aspiring poet. **Mary Enright**, *Chair of the Poetry Society, introduces the most important of these organisations.*

Societies

The Poetry Society
22 Betterton Street, London WC2H 9BU
tel 0171-240 4810 *fax* 0171-240 4818
e-mail poetrysoc@dial.pipex.com
web site http://www.poetrysoc.com
The Poetry Society has been operating for over 80 years and works to help poets and poetry thrive in Britain today. Its principal activities include the publication of *Poetry Review* and *Poetry News*; involvement in promotions such as National Poetry Day; running an information and training service; administration of the W.H. Smith-sponsored Poets-in-Schools scheme and the annual National Poetry Competition; provision of 'The Script' critical service; and 'the Poetry Surgery', offering immediate one-to-one feedback on work.

Its new centre – the Poetry Place – includes a café, reading room, meeting space and access to the Internet. It is also a venue for a wide variety of readings, workshops and other poetry events, and is open to members and friends of the Society, which is open to all. You can also visit the Place via the Society's web site, 'the Poetry Map'.

Poetry Ireland
Bermingham Tower, Upper Yard, Dublin Castle, Dublin 2, Republic of Ireland
tel (01) 6714632 *fax* (01) 6714634
Poetry Ireland acts as the Irish Poetry Society and also runs the Austin Clarke Library, a reference library of over 10,000 titles. It publishes *Poetry Ireland Review*, a quarterly magazine, organises readings in Dublin and nationally, and runs the Writers in Schools scheme.

European Association for the Promotion of Poetry
European Poetry Centre, 'The Seven Sleepers', J.P. Minckelersstraat 168, B-3000 Louvain, Belgium
tel (16) 235351

Regional Arts Boards (RABs)
Information Service, The Arts Council of England, 14 Great Peter Street, London SW1P 3NQ
The officers responsible for literature in the Regional Arts Boards can provide information on local poetry groups, workshops and societies. Many RABs give grant aid to local publishers and magazines and help fund festivals and readings, etc; some run critical services. A list of the relevant officers is available on receipt of an sae. See also page 470.

The Poetry Book Society
Book House, 45 East Hill, London SW18 2RX
tel 0181-870 8403 *fax* 0181-874 6361

The Poetry Book Society (PBS) is a unique book club for readers of poetry, founded in 1953 by T.S. Eliot, and funded by the Arts Council of England. Every quarter, selectors choose one outstanding publication (the PBS Choice), and make four recommendations. Members can receive some or all of these books free and are also offered substantial discounts on other poetry books. The PBS also runs the T.S. Eliot Prize (see page 496). Write for details of membership packages.

Libraries

The Poetry Library
Royal Festival Hall, South Bank Centre,
London SE1 8XX
tel 0171-921 0943/0664 *fax* 0171-921 0939

The Poetry Library was founded in 1953 by the Arts Council of Great Britain. It is situated on Level 5 of the Royal Festival Hall. Its two principal roles are to collect and preserve all poetry published in the UK in this century, and to act as a public lending library. Two copies of all titles are purchased, allowing one to be available for consultation and the other to go out on loan. Books may be borrowed by those outside London through the national Inter-Library Lending network. The collection of about 35,000 titles is all in the English language, although it includes translations from all over the world. There is a large children's section, as well as poetry on cassette, record and video.

As well as the normal functions of all libraries, the Poetry Library also runs an active information service on all poetry-related activities, and offers advice to the new poet. Current awareness lists are produced and are available by post on receipt of a large sae. They include lists of magazines, competitions, bookshops, groups and workshops, evening classes, festivals, etc and are updated regularly. The Library also stocks the full range of British poetry magazines as well as a large selection from abroad.

Membership of the Library is free, and is open to all on production of proof of identity and current address.

The Scottish Poetry Library
Tweeddale Court, 14 High Street,
Edinburgh EH1 1TE
tel 0131-557 2876
e-mail spl_queries@presence.co.uk

Founded in 1984, the Scottish Poetry Library is run along similar lines to the Poetry Library in London, specialising in 20th-century poetry written in Scotland, in Scots, Gaelic and English. It also collects some pre-20th century poetry and contemporary poetry from all over the world. Information and advice on all poets is given and visits by individuals, groups and schools are welcome. Borrowing is free of charge and there is a membership scheme at £10.00 p.a., which includes use of the members' reading room and a regular newsletter. It has branches in libraries and arts centres throughout Scotland and also runs a mobile library service. Readings and exhibitions are regularly organised, particularly during the Edinburgh Festival.

Northern Poetry Library
County Library, The Willows, Morpeth,
Northumberland NE61 1TA
tel (01670) 512385 *fax* (01670) 518012

Founded in 1968, the Northern Poetry Library serves the area covered by the Northern Arts Regional Board, i.e. Tyne and Wear, Durham, Northumberland, Cumbria and Cleveland. Its collection contains over 14,000 titles of mostly British material and includes magazines and poetry in translation. There is a full information service, access to a database of pre-20th-century poetry, and a postal lending service to members. Full membership is free to those living in the region and associate membership is free to those outside. It is run by Northumberland County Library as one of its special services.

The British Haiku Society Library
27 Park Street, Westcliff-on-Sea, Essex SS0 7PA

The BHS Library is a collection of books, magazines and cassettes in haiku and related forms. It is a mail-order, members-only lending library. Write for membership details.

Public libraries

Public libraries can be an invaluable source of information on writing activities in the area in addition to having collections of modern poetry for loan. Some also have literature field workers or writers-in-residence, who can be very helpful to beginners.

Competitions and awards

There are literally hundreds of poetry competitions going on throughout the year, varying widely in quality and quantity of entries and prizes. The two most important are the National Poetry Competition run by the Poetry Society and the biennial Arvon Foundation International Poetry Competition. Details of these and other competitions can be found under *Prizes and awards* (page 488). The Poetry Library produces a free list, updated monthly, of these and other competitions, and is available on receipt of a large sae.

There are several prestigious awards for poetry, most awarded annually to published poets, and therefore non-competitive. A complete list of prizes is included in the *Guide to Literary Prizes 1997*, published by Book Trust at £3.99 (which also produces a free leaflet on grants and awards).

Bookshops

Not all general bookshops have a strong modern poetry section but there are some which specialise in poetry. The principal ones are listed below. These and other good bookshops stocking a range of poetry are listed by the Poetry Library; this list is divided into London and outside London areas and can be obtained by sending a large sae.

The Poetry Bookshop/Alan Halsey
22 Broad Street, Hay-on-Wye,
Herefordshire HR3 5DB
tel (01497) 820305

The Stationery Office Oriel Bookshop
The Friary, Cardiff CF1 4AA
tel (01222) 395548

Peter Riley
27 Sturton Street, Cambridge CB1 2QG
tel (01223) 576422

Festivals

Literature festivals have become increasingly popular and prestigious in the past few years and are now held in almost every part of the country. Information on what is happening in your area should be readily available from your local library and Regional Arts Board. A selection of literature festivals is listed on page 521.

The British Council
Information Officer, Literature Department, British Council, 11 Portland Place,
London W1N 4EJ
web site http://www.britcoun.org/literature/litfest.htm

For a list of forthcoming literature festivals, send an A4 or A5 size sae or visit the web site. See also page 445

Performance venues

In London the best way to keep up to date with readings and poetry events is through the weekly listing magazines, *Time Out* and *What's On in London*. The main London venues are given below.

Outside London, local listings magazines should be helpful and Regional Arts Boards and public libraries will have details of all literature events happening in their area.

Voice Box
Level 5, Royal Festival Hall, London SE1 8XX
tel 0171-921 0906 (information), 0171-960 4242 (tickets)

The Poetry Place
The Poetry Society, 22 Betterton Street,
London WC2H 9BU
tel 0171-240 2133 (tickets and information)

Apples and Snakes Performance Poetry
Battersea Arts Centre, Lavender Hill,
London SW11
tel 0171-692 0393 (information), 0181-223 2223 (tickets)

Blue Nose Poetry
tel (0958) 402657
1997 venue Golden Square Books,
16 Golden Square, London W1R 3AR
Phone for details of 1998 venue.

Terrible Beauty
Troubadour Coffee House,
265 Old Brompton Road, London SW5
Alternate Mondays 8pm-10pm.

Poetry groups and workshops

Joining a poetry group can be an excellent way to get useful help and advice on writing and publishing. Groups vary enormously; if possible, try a few in your area to find the one most congenial to your style. They tend to wax and wane, but your Regional Arts Board and local library should have up-to-date information on those currently active, or you could consult *Poetry Groups Register*, published by Blaxland Family Press.

The Poetry Library compiles a list of groups and workshops for the Greater London area; this is updated regularly and available on receipt of a large sae.

Poetry Groups Register
Blaxland Family Press, 12 Matthews Road,
Taunton, Somerset TA1 4NH
tel (01823) 257634

Writing courses

There is currently much more available than ever before in the area of short-term creative writing courses, as writers-in-residence are appointed by Regional Arts Boards, and by libraries, colleges, prisons, etc. There is also a choice of residential writing courses, of which the long established ones are run by the Arvon Foundation and the Ty Newydd. All areas of writing are covered, as well as poetry.

Information on other courses not listed here can be obtained from the Regional Arts Borads, local libraries or the Poetry Library.

The Arvon Foundation
The Arvon Foundation at Lumb Bank
Hebden Bridge, West Yorkshire HX7 6DF
The Arvon Foundation at Totleigh Barton
Sheepwash, Beaworthy, Devon EX21 5NS
The Arvon Foundation at Moniack Mhor
Teavarran, Kiltarlity, Beauly,
Inverness-shire IV4 7HT

Runs three centres and has wide experience of residential writing courses. Most last for about five days and offer tuition by working writers.

Ty Newydd
Taliesin, Ty Newydd, Llanystumdwy, Criccieth,
Gwynedd LL52 0LW
Courses here are run along similar lines to the Arvon Houses with a wide variety of courses offered. Some of the tutors used are Welsh writers though there is a good mix.

Write Away, East Midlands Arts
Mountfields House, Epinal Way, Loughborough,
Leics. LE11 0QE
East Midlands Arts runs five residential writing courses from April 1997 to April 1998 located at Leicester University. A variety of types of writing is covered.

The Poets' House/Teach na hÉigse
Clonbarra, Falcarragh, Co. Donegal, Ireland
tel (74) 65470 *fax* (74) 65471
The Poets' House runs courses in poetry only. Three two-week courses are offered over the summer months; an MA in creative writing is also available.

Poetry for children and young adults

Poetry Society Education
The Poetry Society, 22 Betterton Street,
London WC2H 9BU
tel 0171-240 4810
Poetry Society Education promotes poetry throughout the formal education sector and beyond. It offers a wide range of services and facilities to teachers, young people and students, running activities such as the W.H. Smith Poets-in-Schools scheme and Poets in Hospitals. In addition to publishing a range of materials including the Teachers' Poetry Resources File, poetry posters and the Young Poetry Pack, Poetry Society Education also produces teaching resources for Education members of the Poetry Society. Other services include training courses and events for students, teachers, readers and writers. These occur both on-site at the Poetry Place and at selected venues around the country. INSET is also available – along with an Advice and Information Service which puts schools in touch with poets and works to keep young writers informed about competitions, magazines and ways to develop their creative writing. Publications may

be obtained via the Publications Officer. Further information about educational services can be obtained from the Education Development Officer.

Children's Section, The Poetry Library
Royal Festival Hall, London SE1 8XX
The Poetry Library has a large children's section of about 4000 books incorporating the SIGNAL Collection of Children's Poetry. It runs an education service for teachers and schools, which includes class visits and poet-led workshops. A teachers' information pack covering all aspects of poetry in education is available, as are selected reading lists for different age groups. There is a special collection of books and materials for teachers and poets involved in education; the teachers' membership scheme offers special loan facilities to use books in the classroom.

Young Book Trust
Book House, 45 East Hill, London SW18 2QZ
The children's division of Book Trust, the aims of Young Book Trust are to promote reading and offer advice and information on all aspects of children's reading and books. It runs a library of all children's books published over the last two years. It organises Children's Book Week, held usually in October, co-ordinating national activities throughout the week. It also offers an information service, including information on authors (Authorbank), and publishes a newsletter. A subscription service is available for schools, libraries, colleges, bookshops and publishers.

National Association of Writers in Education (NAWE)
PO Box 1, Sheriff Hutton, York YO6 7YU
tel/fax (01653) 618429
NAWE is a national organisation which aims to widen the scope of writing in education, and co-ordinate activities between writers, teachers and funding bodies. It publishes a magazine, *Writing in Education*, and a national directory of writers who work in schools, colleges and the community. Write for membership details.

Competitions

The number of good poetry competitions for children are limited. The main annual ones are:

W.H. Smith Young Writers Competition
Strand House, 7 Holbein Place, Sloane Square, London SW1W 8NR
An open competition for original writing – poems, stories, plays or articles – by children aged 16 and under.

Welsh Academy Young Writers Competition
PO Box 328, Cardiff CF2 4XL
A national competition in which poetry and prose are acceptable in three categories, the upper limit being 18. The closing date is usually July.

BBC Radio 4 Young Poetry Competition
BBC Broadcasting House, Whiteladies Road, Bristol BS8 2LR
First launched in 1994, there are three age categories between 8 and 21 years for poems written for radio.

The Roald Dahl Foundation Poetry Competition
PO Box 1375, 20 Vauxhall Bridge Road, London SW1V 2SA
Competition divided into four age groups, between 7 and 17 years.

Mary Enright has been Librarian at the Poetry Library, London, since 1988 and is Chair of the Poetry Society.

Further reading

ALP, *Catalogue of Little Press Books in Print*, Association of Little Presses, 1997

Baldwin, Michael, *The Way to Write Poetry*, Elm Tree Books, 1982

Bolton, Marjorie, *The Anatomy of Poetry*, Routledge, 1990

Chisholm, Alison, *The Craft of Writing Poetry*, Allison & Busby, 1992

Chisholm, Alison, *A Practical Poetry*

Course, Allison & Busby, 1994

Clifford, Johnathon, *Metric Feet and Other Gang Members*, Johnathon Clifford, 1993

Clifford, Johnathon, *Vanity Press & The Proper Poetry Publishers*, Johnathon Clifford, 1994

Corti, Doris, *Writing Poetry*, Thomas & Lochar, 1994

Fairfax, John and Moat, John, *The Way to Write*, Elm Tree Books, 1981

Fergusson, Rosalind, *The Penguin Rhyming Dictionary*, Penguin Books, 1992

Finch, Peter, *How to Publish Your Poetry*, Allison & Busby, o.p. 2nd edn due 1998

Finch, Peter, *The Poetry Business*, Seren Books, 1994

Finch, Peter, *Small Presses and Little Magazines of the UK and Ireland: an address list*, Oriel

Fulton, Len, *Directory of Poetry Publishers*, 10th edn, Dustbooks, USA

Fulton, Len, *The International Directory of Little Magazines and Small Presses*, 30th edn, Dustbooks, USA

Gortschacher, Wolfgang, *Little Magazines Profiles*, University of Salzburg, 1993

Guide to Literary Prizes 1997, Book Trust, 45 East Hill, London SW18 2QZ, 9th edn, 1997

Hamilton, Ian, *The Oxford Companion to Twentieth-Century Poetry in English*, Oxford University Press, 1994

Hyland, Paul, *Getting into Poetry*, Bloodaxe, 2nd edn, 1996

Jerome, Judson, *1997 Poet's Market: Where and How to Publish Your Poetry*, Writer's Digest Books, USA

Lendennie, Jessie, *The Salmon Guide to Poetry Publishing in Ireland*, Salmon Publishing, 1989

Livingstone, Dinah, *Poetry Handbook for Readers & Writers*, Macmillan, 1992

Myers, Jack and Simms, Michael, *Longman Dictionary and Handbook of Poetry*, Longman, o.p.

PALPI Poetry and Little Press Information, Association of Little Presses

Preminger, Alex, *New Princeton Encyclopedia of Poetry and Poetics*, Princeton University Press, USA, 3rd rev. edn, 1993

Riggs, Thomas (ed.), *Contemporary Poets*, St James Press, 6th edn, 1996

Roberts, Philip Davies, *How Poetry Works: the Elements of English Poetry*, Penguin Books, 1991

Sansom, Peter, *Writing Poems*, Bloodaxe, 1994, repr. 1997

Scannell, Vernon, *How to Enjoy Poetry*, Piatkus, 1987, o.p.

Sweeney, Matthew and Williams, John Hartley, *Teach Yourself Writing Poetry*, Hodder & Stoughton, 1997

Publishers of poetry

Addresses for Book publishers UK and Ireland start on page 153. See Children's book publishers and packagers on page 249 for publishers of poetry for children.

Anvil Press Poetry
Arc Publications
Bellew Publishing
Blackstaff Press Ltd (Ire.)
Bloodaxe Books
Jonathan Cape
Carcanet Press
Cassell plc
Chatto & Windus
Cló Iar-Chonnachta Teo. (Ire.)
The Collins Press (Ire.)
Enitharmon Press
Faber & Faber

Forest Books
Gairm Publications
The Gallery Press (Ire.)
The Goldsmith Press (Ire.)
Headland Publications
Hippopotamus Press
Honno Ltd
Libris Ltd
National Poetry Foundation
New Beacon Books
Onlywomen Press
Oxford University Press
Payback Press

Penguin Books
Peterloo Poets
Random House UK
Rivelin Grapheme Press
Scottish Cultural Press
Seren Books
Slow Dancer Press
Stride Publications
The University of Hull Press &
   Lampada Press
Writers & Readers Ltd

Television and film

Writing for television

'Television drama' is a generic term which covers several varied and specialist areas of writing for the domestic screen. Each differs from the others in terms of requirements and rewards and each is definable in copyright terms. **Bill Craig** *explains.*

The television play is a one-off creation of a single mind and talent and absolutely the property of its author. As a form it is the vehicle for the talents of the newest and least-experienced writers in the medium as well as for those who are held in the highest regard. It is (for practical reasons) the traditional point of entry for the tyro.

There has been a reduction in the number of plays produced annually but the BBC and certain ITV companies are still in the market for 30-, 60- and 90-minute slot-length works. If the bad news is that they get several thousand unsolicited manuscripts every year, the good news is that they are all read. No script unit will risk missing out on an undiscovered genius.

The same observations (with some modification) would apply to the original series or serial: that is, a multi-part work of sole authorship and of finite length. They tend to be written by established television writers who have a proven ability to go the necessary distance, but a new writer with an attractive idea can come in through this door.

What's the procedure?

Invest some time and talent and write the play. A commission on a synopsis is unlikely without some evidence that you can write interesting action, dialogue and characters. For the finite series/serial, write the first episode and synopsise the rest.

The situation comedy is the most highly paid area of television writing – and understandably so. It calls for a quirky and idiosyncratic mind, and its overriding imperative – to make the viewer laugh – subordinates all of the other dramatic tools to this end. If it's difficult to play Beethoven's *Ninth* on a one-stringed fiddle, then it's Hell to do it for a run of six episodes. The sit-com is unique in screen drama in so far as most of them are played before live studio audiences. Once upon a time, they were constructed around individual comedians. Some still are, but for several years now the practice has been to cast according to the script with actors who can play comedy. And that's not a bad thing, is it?

Again, this form is an original in copyright terms, though dual authorships are not uncommon. A synopsis is pretty useless (ever tried to explain a joke?), so write the pilot-script and briefly indicate where you can go with other episodes.

Copyright

We now come to a significant point of departure and go into those areas where the copyright is split with another party.

First, the drama-series: *Bramwell, The Bill, Casualty*, et al. These are definable as a series of original and self-contained scripts using the same characters and backgrounds throughout. The format – i.e., the characters and general ambience – will be owned or leased by the production organisation. They represent a substantial part of television drama, but it is rare for a writer without previous screen experience to be commissioned to write for them. It is quite pointless to submit a speculative script or synopsis: the series you are see-

ing now was recorded months ago.

Serials, such as *Coronation Street*, *Brookside*, *Take the High Road* and *Emmerdale*, will occasionally try out new writers, but the production pressures on reliability and deadline delivery dates don't allow for too many risks to be taken outside what is usually an established and pretty permanent writing team.

Dramatisation and adaptation

'Dramatisation' and 'adaptation' are terms which are interchanged in an ignorantly casual manner; they are not the same thing. A dramatisation is the conversion of a prose work to a screenplay. An adaptation is a similar conversion of a dramatic work. The difference is considerable, and the screen credit should reflect this fact.

There has been a great increase in the number of dramatisations made from novels. Again, these are usually written by writers with a track record in television but occasionally the author of the book to be dramatised will be approached to write the screenplay. If you don't come under either of those headings, then you probably wouldn't get very far by simply suggesting that you'd like to dramatise this or that novel. Adaptations are usually 'in-house' works.

All of this leaves uncovered an odd and often lucrative area – the format. It is possible to sell an idea for a series without ever having written a script. But make sure that your submission is as detailed as it possibly can be in terms of background, main characters and development. Doing it the simple way in this instance can mean finding out that 50 other people have had the same simple idea. And selling an idea carries no guarantee that you'll be asked to write the scripts.

See *Presenting scripts for television and film* on page 293.

Contracts and payments

Given success to your efforts, you will be contracted under the terms of the relevant agreement between the British Broadcasting Corporation or the ITV Network Centre and the Writers' Guild of Great Britain. The Guild has sole bargaining rights in the television drama rates, its agreements are complex and comprehensive and several of the rights and benefits contained in them are available to Guild members only (see page 485).

Payments are made in stages: the BBC pays half on commission, half on acceptance; ITV Network Centre pays half on commission, a quarter on delivery, a quarter on acceptance. A new system of part-networking has come into being. The initial fee is lower than that paid for a full network transmission, but increments are payable for each franchise area that transmits the programme.

Independent producers

The foregoing comments apply mainly to programmes produced by the British Broadcasting Corporation or the ITV companies. The increasingly important independent production sector should not, however, be ignored, since many of their

Useful information

Producers Alliance for Cinema and Television (PACT)

45 Mortimer Street, London W1N 7TD
tel 0171-331 6000 *fax* 0171-331 6700
Contacts John Woodward (Chief Executive), David Alan Mills (Membership Officer

PACT serves the feature film and independent television production sector and is the UK contact point for co-production, co-finance partners and distributors.

The Writers' Guild of Great Britain

430 Edgware Road, London W2 1EH
tel 0171-723 8074 *fax* 0171-706 2413
For detailed information see page 485.

The Spotlight

7 Leicester Place, London WC2H 7BP
tel 0171-437 7631
Publishes a book called *Contacts*, which contains useful information and addresses. The 1997-98 edition is available from October.

productions are primarily intended for television screening (see page 296). If the television play shows signs of becoming an endangered species, its position on the schedules is being replaced by the made-for-TV movie which is shot in such a manner as to allow theatrical release. These programmes are made by either entirely independent production organisations or subsidiaries of the ITV companies (e.g. Meridian).

The procedures described above for submitting unsolicited work should be observed. There are several dozen independents and most are listed in the relevant handbooks. The Writers' Guild of Great Britain maintains a list which can be purchased for a small sum. The independents, however, tend to operate in specialist fields and a pragmatic method would be to note the production house end credit on a filmed drama.

Contracts should conform to the terms laid down by the agreement between the Writers' Guild of Great Britain and the Producers Alliance for Cinema and Television (PACT). Again, the agreement is comprehensive and covers all forms and aspects of screen drama. Payment is made in four stages: treatment, first draft, second draft and principal photography. Further exploitation is also covered.

Bill Craig has been a professional screen writer for more than 40 years, during which time he has written over 500 scripts. He is a past President of the Writers' Guild of Great Britain.

Further reading

Kelsey, Gerald, *Writing for Television*, A & C Black, 2nd edn, 1995

Wolfe, Ronald, *Writing Comedy,* Robert Hale, 2nd edn, 1996

BBC national television

The BBC continues to be in a state of reorganisation. It commissions from both BBC Production and independent producers (page 296), as well as from BBC regional centres.

BBC Broadcast

BBC Broadcast, Television Centre, Wood Lane, London W12 7RJ
tel 0181-743 8000

In April 1997 BBC Broadcast came into being as the commissioning, scheduling, marketing and broadcast directorate of the BBC – for both TV and radio. Almost 14,000 hours of TV programmes are broadcast each year on its two current channels, BBC1 and BBC2.

The great majority of programmes are commissioned from BBC Production, but BBC Broadcast has a statutory obligation to ensure that 25% of its network programmes are made by independent producers and, further, that a significant proportion are made in the regions outside London.

Chief Executive Will Wyatt
Director of Television and Controller, BBC1 Alan Yentob
Controller, BBC2 Mark Thompson
Director of Regional Broadcasting Mark Byford
Controller, Programme Acquisition Alan Howden
Head of Purchased Programmes June Dromgoole
Head of Independent Commissioning Group Jane Root
Head of Children's Commissioning Roy Thompson
Head of Daytime Commissioning Liz Barron
Head of Commissioning, Education for Adults Glenwyn Benson
Head of Commissioning, Schools and Colleges Frank Flynn

BBC Production

BBC Production, Television Centre, Wood Lane, London W12 7RJ
tel 0181-743 8000

BBC Production is the largest single programme maker in Europe. There are 20 bi-media programme departments based in London and the English regions, including BBC Sport, the Natural History Unit, Music, Drama, Features, Religion, Education, Children's, Entertainment, Consumer and Leisure, Science, Documentaries and History, and the Arts. Addresses are given for individual departments if they are different from above.
Chief Executive, Production Ronald Neil
Production Controller Colin Adams

Drama

Centre House, 56 Wood Lane, London W12 7SB
tel 0181-743 8000
Controller of Drama Production Colin Adams
Head of Films and Single Drama David Thompson
Head of Serials Michael Wearing
Head of Series Jo Wright

Television Drama Group

There are a number of initiatives within BBC Television Drama to encourage new writers. The schemes are run by producers and development executives working in London and at drama centres in Birmingham, Belfast, Cardiff and Glasgow, who encourage the submission of original dramas for film. These vary in length from 10-minute shorts to 75- and 90-minute screenplays, often for special seasons such as *Black Screen* (London), *Tartan Shorts* (Glasgow), *Northern Lights* (Belfast) and *Brief Encounters* (with Channel 4). Contact the relevant drama head for more information on current schemes.

In single drama, series and serials, competition is fierce and all unsolicited scripts are rigorously reviewed, as they have to compete with regularly commissioned work for BBC1 and BBC2.

Scripts should be submitted to the relevant drama head in London or at the appropriate regional centre.

Entertainment

fax 0181-743 9459
Head of Entertainment Group Paul Jackson
Head of Comedy Geoffrey Perkins
Head of Light Entertainment Michael Leggo
Head of Comedy Entertainment Jon Plowman
Head of Independent Commissioning Entertainment Kevin Lygo
Senior Script Editor, Bi-media Development Unit Bill Dare

Entertainment Group

Room 4006
Contact The Script Editors

The Comedy Department Script Development Unit welcomes new 30-minute comedy series. Only original formats, preferably mainly studio based, are required. The script editors prefer to see a completed half-hour script rather than an idea or outline, novel or treatment, etc. They do not read sketch material but they will read and respond to all comedy script submissions, although it is a highly competitive market. For brief sitcom writing guidelines send an A4 sae.

Arts

Head of BBC Arts Kim Evans
Editor, Arts Features Keith Alexander
Editor, Omnibus Gillian Greenwood
Editor, Arena Anthony Wall
Editor, Home Front/The Bookworm Daisy Goodwin
Editor, One Foot in the Past Basil Comely
Editor, The Works/Late Review Michael Poole

Music

Head of Classical Music (TV and radio) Roger Wright
Head of Music Entertainment (TV and radio) Trevor Dann
Head of Music (TV) Avril MacRory
Editor, Music (TV) Peter Maniura
Executive Producer, Dance Bob Lockyer

Documentaries

White City, 201 Wood Lane, London W12 7TS
tel 0181-752 5252 *fax* 0181-752 6060
Head of Documentaries Paul Hamman
Executive Producers Clare Paterson, Edward Mirzoeff
Editor, Inside Story Olivia Lichenstein
Editor, Modern Times Stephen Lambert
Editor, Reputations Janice Hadlow
Editor, Timewatch Laurence Rees
Head of Community and Disability Programmes Giles Oakley

Science

201 Wood Lane, London W12 7RJ
tel 0181-752 6178
Head of Science and Features Jana Bennett
Editor, Tomorrow's World Saul Nasse
Editor, Horizon John Lynch
Editor, QED Lorraine Heggessey
Editor, Animal Hospital Sarah Hargreaves

Consumer and Leisure

White City, 201 Wood Lane, London W12 7TS
tel 0181-752 5252
Head of Consumer and Leisure Anne Morrison
Deputy Head and Editor, Holiday Jane Lush
Series Producer, Crimewatch UK Seetha Kumar
Series Editor, Esther Patsy Newey
Series Editor, Watchdog Steve Anderson
Series Editor, Film '97 Bruce Thompson
Series Producer, Jobs for the Boys Nick Handel
Producer, Points of View Penny Lewis
Editor, Sky at Night Pieter Morpurgo
Editor, Food & Drink Tim Hinks (Bazal
  Productions *tel* 0171-637 0137)
Executive Producer, Ready Steady Cook Linda
  Clifford

Children's Programmes

Head of Children's Programmes Anna Home
Executive Producer, Drama Richard Langridge
Executive Producer, Entertainment Chris
  Pilkington
Executive Producer, Factual Programmes Eric
  Rowan
Editor, Blue Peter Oliver Macfarlane
Producer, Grange Hill Stephen Andrew
Editor, Live & Kicking Christopher Bellinger
Editor, Newsround Susie Staples

Sport and Events

Head of Television Sport Brian Barwick
Head of Events Philip Gilbert
Editor, Grandstand Dave Gordon
Editor, Sport Philip Bernie
*Editor, Match of the Day and Sports
  Documentaries* Niall Sloane

News

tel 0181-743 8000
Chief Executive, BBC News Tony Hall
Head of Weekly Programmes Mark Damazer
Managing Editor, Weekly Programmes Tim Suter
Head of News Programmes Peter Bell
Managing Editor, News Programmes John
  Morrison
Head of Political Programmes Samir Shah
Head of News Gathering Richard Sambrook
Editor, Foreign Affairs Unit John Simpson
Editor, Business and Economics Unit Peter Jay
News Editor, Breakfast News Tim Orchard
News Editor, One O'Clock News Jon Barton
News Editor, Six O'Clock News Nikki Clarke
News Editor, Nine O'Clock News Malcolm Balen

News Editor, Newsnight Peter Horrocks
Editor, Public Eye Mark Wakefield
Editor, Panorama Steve Hewlett
Editor, The Money Programme Jane Ellison
Editor, On the Record David Jordan

Ceefax

Room 7013
tel 0181-576 1801
Editor Peter Clifton

The BBC's main news and information service, broadcasting hundreds of pages on both BBC1 and BBC2. It is on the air at all times when transmitters are broadcasting.

Subtitling

Room 1468, BBC White City, 201 Wood Lane,
London W12 7TS
tel 0181-752 7054, 0141-330 2345 ext 2128
Head of Subtitling Ruth Griffiths

A rapidly expanding service, available via Ceefax page 888. Units based in both London and Glasgow.

Education

BBC White City, 201 Wood Lane,
London W12 7TS
tel 0181-752 5252 *fax* 0181-752 4398

BBC Education works across all media (TV, radio, audio, print, digital media) to provide a range of resources for all learning opportunities. It offers learning for life for everyone from early childhood to retirement. Over 2000 hours of education and training programmes for schools and adults, on radio and TV, are broadcast each year.

Director of Education Jane Drabble
*Chief Adviser, Education Policy and Corporate
  Affairs* Lucia Jones
Head of Strategy and Planning tba
Head of Commissioning, Schools and Colleges
  Frank Flynn
Head of Commissioning, Education for Adults
  Glenwyn Benson
Head of Marketing Dafna Israeli
*Head of Commissioning, Open University
  Production Centre* Paul Gerhardt
Head of Digital Media Jonathan Drori
Head of Learning Support Steve Pollock

BBC regional television

The regions are responsible for producing both television and radio programmes.

BBC regions

BBC Northern Ireland
Broadcasting House, Belfast BT2 8HQ
tel (01232) 338000

Regular programmes include *Country Times, Newsline 6.30, Home Truths, Hearts and Minds, Sportsnight from Northern Ireland, Spotlight* and *Ballykissangel*. All programme-making departments are bi-media.
Controller Patrick Loughrey
Head of Broadcast Anna Carragher
Head of Production Paul Evans
Head of News and Current Affairs Tony Maddox
Editor, Current Affairs Andrew Colman
Head of Drama Robert Cooper
Political Editor Jim Dougal
Chief Producer, Agriculture Veronica Hughes
Chief Producer, Education Michael McGowan
Chief Producer, Entertainment Charlie Warmington
Chief Producer, Magazines Kathleen Carragher
Chief Producer, Music and Arts tba
Chief Producer, Documentaries Bruce Batten
Chief Producer, Religion Rev. Bert Tosh
Chief Producer, Music Sequences tba
Chief Producer, Sport Terry Smith
News Intake Editor Tim Cooke
Editor Newsline 6.30 Iain Webster

BBC Scotland
Broadcasting House, Queen Margaret Drive, Glasgow G12 8DG
tel 0141-339 8844

Headquarters of BBC Scotland with opt-out stations based in Aberdeen, Dundee, Edinburgh and Inverness. Regular programmes include the nightly *Reporting Scotland* plus *Friday Sportscene, Frontline Scotland* and *Landward* (bi-monthly farming news).
Controller John McCormick
Head of Production Colin Cameron
Head of Broadcast Ken McQuarrie

Head of News and Current Affairs Ken Cargill
Head of Arts and Entertainment Mike Bolland
Head of Drama Andrea Calderwood
Head of Sport and Leisure Neil Fraser
Head of Children's and Features Liz Scott
Head of Education and Religion Andrew Barr

Aberdeen
Broadcasting House, Beechgrove Terrace, Aberdeen AB9 2ZT
tel (01224) 625233

News, plus some features, but most programmes are made in Glasgow.

Dundee
Nethergate Centre, 66 Nethergate, Dundee DD1 4ER
tel (01382) 202481

News only.

Edinburgh
Broadcasting House, Queen Street, Edinburgh EH2 1JF
tel 0131-469 4200

Education, religion and news.

Inverness
7 Culduthel Road, Inverness IV2 4AD
tel (01463) 221711

News only.

BBC Wales
Broadcasting House, Llandaff, Cardiff CF5 2YQ
tel (01222) 322000 *fax* (01222) 552973

Headquarters of BBC Wales, with regional TV centres in Bangor and Swansea. All Welsh language programmes are transmitted by S4C and produced in Cardiff or Swansea. Regular programmes include *Wales Today, Wales on Saturday* and *Pobol y Cwm* (Welsh language drama series).
Controller Geraint Talfan Davies
Head of Broadcast (Welsh Language) Gwynn Pritchard
Head of Broadcast (English Language) Dai Smith
Head of Production John Geraint
Head of News and Current Affairs Aled Eirug
Head of Drama Pedr James

Head of Sport Arthur Emyr
Head of Entertainment Geraint Evans
Head of Arts, Music and Features Phil George
Commissioning Editor, Radio Wales Nick Evans
Commissioning Editor, Radio Cymru Aled
  Glynne Davies
Series Editor, Pobol y Cwm William Gwyn

Bangor
Broadcasting House, Meirion Road, Bangor,
Gwynedd LL57 2BY
tel (01248) 370880 *fax* (01248) 351443
Head of Production Marian Wyn Jones

News only.

Swansea
Broadcasting House, 32 Alexandra Road,
Swansea, West Glamorgan SA1 5DZ
Senior Producer Geraint Davies

BBC English regions

BBC Birmingham
Broadcasting Centre, Pebble Mill Road,
Birmingham B5 7QQ
tel 0121-414 8888

Regular programmes include *The Clothes
Show, Telly Addicts, Top Gear, East,
Network East, Gardener's World,
Countryfile, The Really Useful Show,
Can't Cook, Won't Cook, Kilroy* (TV); *The
Archers, Folk on Two, Jazz Notes,
Farming Today, Costing the Earth* (radio).
   Local news programmes include
Midlands Today, Midlands Report and
Out and About.

Network Production
Head of Network Production Rod Natkiel
Head of Television Drama Tony Virgo
Executive Editor, Radio Owen Bentley
Editor, Asian Programmes Paresh Solanki
Editor, Consumer Affairs and Features Huw Marks
Editor, Entertainment Richard Lewis
Editor, Leisure and Lifestyle Roger Casstles
Editor, Motoring and Leisure Sports Jon Bentley
Editor, Music Geoffrey Hewitt
Editor, Rural Affairs Paul Cannon
Production and Development Executives Tony
  Steyger, Stephanie Silk
Head of Regional and Local Programmes Laura
  Dalgleish
Editor, News and Current Affairs Peter Lowe

BBC East Midlands (Nottingham)
East Midlands Broadcasting Centre, York House,
Mansfield Road, Nottingham NG1 3JA
tel 0115-9550500
Head of Local Programmes Richard Lucas

Local news programmes such as *East
Midlands Today.*

BBC East (Norwich)
St Catherine's Close, All Saint's Green, Norwich,
Norfolk NR1 3ND
tel (01603) 619331

Regular programmes include *Look East*
and *Matter of Fact.*
Head of Centre Arnold Miller
Editor, News and Current Affairs Adam
Bullimore

BBC Manchester
New Broadcasting House, Oxford Road,
Manchester M60 1SJ
tel 0161-200 2020

Also headquarters of BBC North West's
local and regional programmes operation.

Regular programmes include *Rough
Guides, The Travel Show, Red Dwarf,
The Sunday Show; Songs of Praise,
Everyman, Heart of the Matter.*
Head of Entertainment and Features John
  Whiston
Head of Religious Broadcasting Rev. Ernest Rea
*Head of Regional and Local Programmes (BBC
  North West)* David Holdsworth
*Editor, News and Current Affairs (BBC North
  West)* Colin Philpott

Leeds
Broadcasting Centre, Woodhouse Lane,
Leeds LS2 9PX
tel (01132) 441188

Also headquarters of local and regional
programme operations for the North.
*Head of Regional and Local Programmes (BBC
  North)* Martin Brooks
Acting Editor, News and Current Affairs John
  Lilley
Regional Political Editor Geoff Talbott
Series Producer, Close Up North Ian Cundall

Newcastle upon Tyne
Broadcasting Centre, Barrack Road,
Newcastle upon Tyne NE99 2NE
tel 0191-232 1313

Also headquarters of local and regional
programme operations for the North East
and Cumbria.
*Head of Regional and Local Programmes (BBC
  North East and Cumbria)* Olwyn Hocking
*Acting Editor, News and Current Affairs/News
  Editor, Look North* Michael Wild
Producers, Look North Iain Williams, Brid
  Fitzpatrick, Andrew Lambert

BBC Bristol

Broadcasting House, Whiteladies Road,
Bristol BS8 2LR
tel 0117-9732211

The home of the BBC's Natural History Unit, which produces regular programmes like *Wildlife On One*, *The Natural World* and *The Really Wild Show*. The Bristol features department produces a wide range of regular TV programmes, such as *Antiques Roadshow*, *999*, *Picture This*, *Under the Sun*, *Great Antiques Hunt* and *Rick Stein*.

Head of Features Jeremy Gibson
Head of Natural History Unit Alastair Fothergill
Head of Regional and Local Programmes John Conway

BBC West

Broadcasting House, Whiteladies Road,
Bristol BS8 2LR
tel 0117-9732211

Bristol is also the home of BBC West, which produces nearly 300 hours of TV each year, including the nightly news magazine *News West*, news bulletins throughout the day, the 30-minute local current affairs programme *Close Up West*, the leisure strand *Out and About*, and the weekly parliamentary programme *Out of Westminster*.

Head of Regional and Local Programmes John Conway
Editor, News and Current Affairs Ian Cameron

BBC South (Southampton)

Broadcasting House, Havelock Road,
Southampton, Hants SO14 7PU
tel (01703) 226201

Produces nearly 300 hours of TV each year, including the nightly news magazine *South Today*, news bulletins throughout the day, the 30-minute local current affairs programme *Southern Eye*, the leisure strand *Out and About*, and the weekly parliamentary programme *South of Westminster*.

Acting Head of Regional and Local Programmes Andy Griffee
Acting Editor, News and Current Affairs Craig Henderson

BBC South West (Plymouth)

Broadcasting House, Mannamead, Plymouth,
Devon PL3 5BD
tel (01752) 229201

Produces nearly 300 hours of TV each year, including the nightly news magazine *Spotlight*, news bulletins throughout the day, the 30-minute local current affairs programme *Close Up*, the leisure strand *Out and About*, and the weekly parliamentary programme *Spotlight on Westminster*.

Head of Regional and Local Programmes Roy Roberts
Editor, News Roger Clark
Editor, Current Affairs Simon Willis

BBC South East (Elstree)

Elstree Centre, Clarendon Road, Borehamwood,
Herts. WD6 1JF
tel 0181-953 6100

Produces nearly 300 hours of TV each year, including the nightly news magazine *Newsroom South East*, news bulletins throughout the day, the 30-minute local current affairs programme *First Sight*, the leisure strand *Out and About*, and the weekly parliamentary programme *Around Westminster*.

Head of Regional and Local Programmes tba
Editor, News and Current Affairs Jane Mote

BBC broadcasting rights and terms

Contributors are advised to check latest details of fees with the BBC.

Rights and terms

Specially written material

Fees for submitted material are paid on acceptance. For commissioned material, half the fee is paid on commissioning and half on acceptance as being suitable for television. All fees are subject to negotiation above the minima.
• Rates for one performance of a 60-minute original television play are a minimum of £4728 for a play written by a beginner and a 'going rate' of £7450 for an established writer, or *pro rata* for shorter or longer timings.
• Fees for a 50-minute episode in a series during the same period are a minimum of £3900 for a beginner and a 'going rate' of £5634 for an established writer.
• Fees for a 50-minute dramatisation are a minimum of £2721 for a beginner and a 'going rate' of £4010 for an established writer.
• Fees for a 50-minute adaptation of an existing stage play or other dramatic work are a minimum of £1640 for a beginner and a 'going rate' of £2403 for an established writer.

Specially written light entertainment sketch material

• The rates for sketch material range from £31.31 per minute for beginners with a 'going rate' of £62.62 for established writers.
• The fee for a quickie or news item is half the amount of the writer's per minute rate.
• Fees for submitted material are payable on acceptance and for commissioned material half on signature and half on acceptance.

Published prose and poems

• Prose works: £17.21 per minute.
• Poems: £19.97 per half minute. ·

Stage plays and source material for television

• Fees for stage plays and source novels are negotiable.

Repeats in BBC programmes

• Further proportionate fees are payable for repeats.

Use abroad of recordings of BBC programmes

If the BBC sends abroad recordings of its programmes for use by overseas broadcasting organisations on their own networks or stations, further payments accrue to the author, usually in the form of additional percentages of the basic fee paid for the initial performance or a royalty based on the percentage of the distributors' receipts. This can apply to both sound and television programmes.

Value Added Tax

A self-billing system for VAT was introduced in January 1978 for programmes made in London. This now covers radio, external services and television.

Talks

Contributors to talks will be offered the standard television talks contract which provides the BBC certain rights to broadcast the material in a complete, abridged and/or translated manner, and which provides for the payment of further fees for additional usage of the material whether by television, domestic radio or external broadcasting. The contract also covers the assignment of material and limited publication rights. Alternatively, a contract taking in all standard rights may be negotiated. Fees are arranged by the contract authorities in London and the Regions.

Independent national, satellite and cable television

BSkyB

Grant Way, Isleworth, Middlesex TW7 5QD
tel 0171-705 3000 *fax* 0171-705 3030/3113
web site http://www.sky.co.uk

Channel 5 Broadcasting Ltd

22 Long Acre, London WC2E 9LY
tel 0171-497 5225 *fax* 0171-497 5222

The fifth and last national 'free to air' terrestrial 24-hour TV channel. Commissions a wide range of programmes to suit all tastes.

Channel 4 Television Corporation

124 Horseferry Road, London SW1P 2TX
tel 0171-396 4444 *fax* 0171-306 8347

Commissions and purchases programmes (it does not make them) for broadcast during the whole week throughout the United Kingdom (except Wales).

GMTV

London Television Centre, Upper Ground, London SE1 9TT
tel 0171-827 7000 *fax* 0171-827 7001

ITV's national breakfast TV service, 6.00-9.25am, seven days a week.

Independent Television Commission (ITC)

33 Foley Street, London W1P 7LB
tel 0171-255 3000 *fax* 0171-306 7800

Licenses and regulates all commercially funded TV services in the UK, including cable and satellite services as well as terrestrial services.

ITN

200 Gray's Inn Road, London WC1X 8XZ
tel 0171-833 3000

Provides the national and international news programmes for ITV, Channel 4 and Channel 5.

ITV Network Centre

200 Gray's Inn Road, London WC1X 8HF
tel 0171-843 8000 *fax* 0171-843 8158

ON TV

NTL National Media, Bristol House,
1 Lakeside Road, Farnborough, Hants GU14 6XP
tel (01252) 402675 *fax* (01252) 402679
e-mail ontv@cabletel.co.uk
National Producer Sally Allen

Operates 24-hour cable TV service, broadcasting to West Scotland, Northern Ireland, Huddersfield/Kirklees, South Wales, Bedfordshire, Hertfordshire, East Hampshire/West Surrey. Caters for all age groups and interests – reviews, interviews, product testing. Ideas for potential programming material welcome.

Teletext Ltd

101 Farm Lane, London SW6 1QJ
tel 0171-386 5000 *fax* 0171-386 5002

Independent regional television

It is advisable to check before submitting any ideas/material – in all cases, scripts are preferred to synopses. Programmes should be planned with natural breaks for the insertion of advertisements. These companies also provide some programmes for Channel 4.

Anglia Television Ltd
Anglia House, Norwich NR1 3JG
tel (01603) 615151 *fax* (01603) 631032
48 Leicester Square, London WC2H 7FB
tel 0171-389 8555 *fax* 0171-930 8499
Provides programmes for the East of England, daytime discussion programmes, drama and Survival natural history programmes for the ITV Network. Drama submissions only through an accredited agency or similar source.

Border Television plc
The Television Centre, Carlisle CA1 3NT
tel (01228) 25101
Provides programmes for The Borders and the Isle of Man, during the whole week. Ideas for programmes, but not drama programmes, are considered from outside sources. Suggestions should be sent to Neil Robinson, Controller of Programmes.

Carlton Broadcasting
101 St Martin's Lane, London WC2N 4AZ
tel 0171-240 4000 *fax* 0171-240 4171
Provides ITV programmes for London and the South East from Monday to Friday.

Central Broadcasting
Central House, Broad Street, Birmingham B1 2JP
tel 0121-643 9898 *fax* 0121-643 4897
The Television House, Lenton Lane, Nottingham NG7 2NA
tel (0115) 986 3322 *fax* (0115) 964 5552
Unit 9, Windrush Court, Abingdon Business Park, Abingdon, Oxon OX1 1SA
tel (01235) 554123 *fax* (01235) 524024
Provides ITV programmes for the East, West and South Midlands seven days a week.

Channel Television
The Television Centre, St Helier, Jersey JE2 3ZD
tel (01534) 816816 *fax* (01534) 816817
Provides programmes for the Channel Islands during the whole week relating mainly to Channel Islands news and current affairs.

Grampian Television plc
Queens Cross, Aberdeen AB15 4XJ
tel (01224) 846846 *fax* (01224) 846800
e-mail gtv@grampiantv.co.uk
Albany House, 68 Albany Road, West Ferry, Dundee DD5 1NW
tel (01382) 739363
23-25 Huntly Street, Inverness IV3 5PR
tel (01463) 242624
Seaforth House, 54 Seaforth Road, Stornoway HS1 2SD
tel (01851) 704433 *fax* (01851) 706406
Provides programmes for North Scotland during the whole week.

Granada Television Ltd
Granada Television Centre, Manchester M60 9EA
tel 0161-832 7211 and
36 Golden Square, London W1R 4AH
tel 0171-734 8080
The ITV franchise holder for the North West of England. Produces programmes across a broad range for both its region and the ITV Network. Writers are advised to make their approach through agents who would have some knowledge of Granada's current requirements.

HTV Ltd
HTV Wales, The Television Centre, Culverhouse Cross, Cardiff CF5 6XJ
tel (01222) 590590 and
HTV West, The Television Centre, Bristol BS4 3HG
tel (0117) 977 8366

Provides programmes for Wales and West of England during the whole week. Produces programmes for home and international sales.

LWT

The London Television Centre, London SE1 9LT
tel 0171-620 1620

Provides programmes for Greater London and much of the Home Counties area from Friday 5.15pm to Monday 6.00am (excluding 6.00-9.25am on Sat/Sun).

Meridian Broadcasting

Television Centre, Southampton, Hants SO14 0PZ
tel (01703) 222555 *fax* (01703) 335050
web site www.meridian.tv.co.uk

The ITV franchise holder for the South and South East. Meridian produces quality drama, factual and children's programming for the ITV network.

Scottish Television Enterprises

Cowcaddens, Glasgow G2 3PR
tel 0141-300 3000 *fax* 0141 300 3030

Wholly owned subsidiary of Scottish Television, making drama and other programmes for the ITV network. Material: ideas and formats for long-form series with or without a Scottish flavour. Approach in the first instance to the Controller of Drama, Robert Love.

Tyne Tees Television Ltd

The Television Centre, City Road, Newcastle upon Tyne NE1 2AL
tel 0191-261 0181 *fax* 0191-261 2302

15 Bloomsbury Square, London WC1A 2LJ
tel 0171-312 3700

Serving the North of England seven days a week, 24 hours a day.

Ulster Television plc

Havelock House, Ormeau Road, Belfast, Northern Ireland BT7 1EB
tel (01232) 328122 *fax* (01232) 246695

Provides programmes for Northern Ireland during the whole week.

Westcountry Television Ltd

Langage Science Park, Plymouth PL7 5BG
tel (01752) 333333 *fax* (01752) 333444

Provides programmes for South West England throughout the week. In-house production mainly news, regional current affairs and topical features; other regional features commissioned from independent producers. Conduit to the Network for independent production packages.

Yorkshire Television Ltd

The Television Centre, Leeds LS3 1JS
tel (0113) 243 8283 *fax* (0113) 244 5107
Television House, 15 Bloomsbury Square, London WC1A 2LJ
tel 0171-312 3700

Yorkshire Television is a Network Company which produces many programmes for the ITV Network and the Yorkshire area seven days a week. Material preferred submitted through agents.

Presenting scripts for television and film

*There is an old saying that the plot of the best movie can be written on a post-card. However, whether your aim is to write a big feature film or a television play to be made on film (as most are nowadays), you must be prepared to write the full screenplay. **Jean McConnell** describes how to lay out your manuscript and how to submit it for consideration.*

Film-making is on a roll

The good news is that over the next few years, lottery money is to be channelled into British films by the Arts Council. Better still, distributing them will also be taken into account: too many British movies moulder on the unshown shelf. And the July 1997 Budget gave a generous incentive to film production companies.

What is a screenplay?

A screenplay should tell a story in terms of visual action and dialogue spoken by the characters. A script for a full-length feature film running about one and a half hours will be about 100-130 pages long. Whether it is a feature film, a short film for children, say, or a documentary, it is better to present a version which is too short rather than too long.

Elaborate camera directions are not necessary as a shooting script will be made at a later stage. Your job is to write the master scenes, clearly broken down into each incident and location.

Layout

Individual companies may vary slightly in their house style but the general layout of a screenplay, either for a feature film or television film, is illustrated on page 295. The following points should be noted.
• Each scene should be numbered on the left and given a title which indicates whether the scene is an interior or an exterior, where it takes place, and the lighting conditions, i.e. day or night. The situation of each scene should be standardised; don't call your 'sitting room' a 'lounge' the next time you come to it, or people will think you mean a different place.
• Note that the dialogue is spaced out, with the qualifying directions such as '(frowning)' on a separate line, slightly inset from the dialogue. Double space each speech from the previous one.
• Always put the names of the characters in CAPITALS, except when they occur in the actual dialogue. Double space the stage directions from the dialogue, but single space the lines of the stage directions themselves.
• Use A4 size paper. Leave at least a 4cm margin on the left and a reasonably wide right-hand margin. It is false economy to cram the page. Use one side of the sheet only.
• Only give the camera directions when you feel it to be essential. For instance, if you want to show something from a particular character's point of view, or if you think you need it to make a point, i.e. 'HARRY approaches the cliff edge and looks down. LONG SHOT – HARRY'S POINT OF VIEW. ALICE fully clad is walking into the sea. CUT TO: CLOSE UP OF HARRY'S HORRIFIED FACE.' Note the camera directions are put in capital letters on a separate line, as in the specimen page.
• Character sketches should appear in the body of the screenplay, e.g. PETE enters. He is a man you wouldn't want to meet in a dark alley.

Preparation of manuscript

The title page should give the name and nature of your piece. Also include your (or your agent's) address. The second page should give a list of the main characters.

Add a front and back cover and bind your screenplay, securing the pages firmly. Make sure you have saved it on disk or retain a master copy. Never part with the only copy you possess. If you do, it will surely get lost.

Submission

Try to get an agent. A good agent will give you a fair opinion of your work and, if your work is worthwhile, he or she will know the particular film company which will want to buy it. Remember that if film companies state that they will only consider material sent through an agent, they definitely mean it.

If you are sending your manuscript to a company direct, it is advisable to first check as far as possible in case it is already working on a similar idea.

Attach a stamped, addressed envelope to your manuscript whether sending it through an agent or direct. Most companies have a story department, to which you should address your material. As story editors are very busy people, you can make their life easier by complying with the submission notes listed in the box.

Accept that this is really a tough market, namely because:
• films cost so much to make today that the decision to go ahead is only taken after a great many important factors have been satisfied and an even greater number of important people are happy about it;
• writing a screenplay calls for knowledge and appreciation of the technicalities of film-making, as well as the ability to combine dialogue, action and pictures, throughout in the language of a visual medium.

The treatment

If a producer likes the idea of your screenplay, he or she may ask to see a treatment.

Submission notes

If you have based your screenplay on someone else's published work you should make the fact clear in a covering letter, stating that:
• the material is no longer in copyright, or
• you yourself own the copyright, or at least an option on it, or
• you have not obtained the copyright but have reason to believe that there would be no difficulty in doing so.

Apart from a note of any relevant credits you may already possess, do not regale the editor with your personal details, unless they bear a direct relation to the material submitted. For instance, if your story concerns a brain surgeon, then it would be relevant for the editor to know that you actually are one. Otherwise, trust your work to stand on its own merit.

There is no need to mention if your work has been turned down by other companies, however regretfully. The comments of others will not influence a story editor one way or the other.

Do not suggest actors or actresses you would like to play your characters. This decision is entirely out of your hands.

Don't pester the company if you don't get a reply, or even an acknowledgement, for some weeks. Most companies will formally acknowledge receipt and then leave you in limbo for at least six weeks. However, after about three months or so, a brief letter politely asking what has happened is in order. A telephone call is unlikely to be helpful. It is possible the company may have liked your work enough to have sent it to America, or to be getting further readers' opinions on it. This all takes time. If they don't like it, you will certainly get your manuscript back in due course.

A treatment can range from a basic outline through to a synopsis of the story with a breakdown of the main characters and some of the key scenes written in detail. Its aim is to demonstrate the style and general flavour of the piece and may be wanted before the whole script is read and/or in order to interest his or her colleagues. It may be no more than half a dozen pages but it is likely to be your major selling document. So do your best to thrill the producer to the core in a couple of minutes flat.

13.   INT.   BARN   DAY

ALAN regards ELIZABETH anxiously. ELIZABETH is staring at the large wine vat. She backs away from it and crosses to the door, where she turns.

> ELIZABETH
> I still think the police ought to know.

She goes out. ALAN listens as her footsteps retreat. the he crosses quickly to the vat, climbs up and heaves at the lid.

> CUT TO:

14.   EXT.   FARMYARD   DAY

DONALD intercepts ELIZABETH as she crosses the yard.

> DONALD
> What does he say?

> ELIZABETH
> Nothing.

> DONALD
> (frowning)
> Right. Now it's my turn.

He starts for the barn. ELIZABETH watches him go.

> CUT TO:

15.   INT.   BARN   DAY

DONALD'S shadow falls across the threshold. He hesitates, his eyes getting used to the gloom.

> DONALD
> Alan?

ALAN lets the lid of the vat fall. He jumps down. He stands quite still as DONALD crosses to him. The two men eye each other silently. ALAN turns away.

> DONALD
> (with sudden realisation)
> You knew it was there ... didn't you?

> CUT TO:

CLOSE-UP OF ALAN'S FACE: IT IS HAGGARD

> ALAN
> I hoped to God it wouldn't be.

Television and film producers

Jean McConnell advises on submitting a screenplay for consideration.

The recommended approach for placing material is through a recognised literary agent. Most film companies have a story department to which material can be sent for consideration by its editors. If you choose to submit material direct, first check with the company to make sure it is worth your while.

It is a fact that many of the feature films these days are based on already best-selling books. However, there are some companies, particularly those with a television outlet, which will sometimes accept unsolicited material if it seems to be exceptionally original.

When a writer submits material direct to a company, some of the larger ones — usually those based in the United States — may request that a Release Form be signed before they are prepared to read it. This document is ostensibly designed to absolve the company from any charge of plagiarism if they should be working on a similar idea; and also to limit their liability in the event of any legal action. Writers must make up their own minds whether they wish to sign this but, in principle, it is not highly recommended.

It should be noted that there are a number of independent companies making films specifically for television presentation. These are included in the list below of companies currently in active production.

Jean McConnell is a founder member of the Writers' Guild of Great Britain. She has written screenplays, radio and stage plays, and books. She is a member of the Crime Writers' Association and the Society of Women Writers and Journalists.

Aardman Animations
Gas Ferry Road, Bristol BS1 6UN
tel (0117) 984 8485 *fax* (0117) 984 8486
web site http://www.aardman.com
Producer, Broadcast/Features Michael Rose
Specialists in model animation, looking for screenplays for adults and families for cinema and TV. Founded 1972.

Agran Barton Television Ltd
The Yacht Club, Chelsea Harbour,
London SW10 0XA
tel 0171-351 7070 *fax* 0171-352 3528
Contact Development Executive
Screenplays for cinema; drama and factual TV programmes. Founded 1993.

British Lion Screen Entertainment
Pinewood Studios, Iver, Bucks. SL0 0NH
tel (01753) 651700 *fax* (01753) 656391
Contact Peter Snell
Screenplays and treatments for cinema; TV drama and sitcoms. No unsolicited material. Founded 1927.

Brook Associates Ltd
21-24 Bruges Place, Randolph Street,
London NW1 0TF
tel 0171-482 6111 *fax* 0171-284 0626
Development Executives Anne Lapping, Phillip Whitehead, Udi Eichler
TV documentaries and current affairs.

Carlton Productions
35-38 Portman Square,
London W1H 0NU
tel 0171-486 6688 *fax* 0171-486 1132
Director of Programmes Andy Allan
Makes and commissions programmes for Central Broadcasting and Carlton Broadcasting to supply ITV.

Catalyst Television Ltd
Brook Green Studios, 186 Shepherds Bush Road,
London W6 7LL
tel 0171-603 7030 *fax* 0171-603 9519
Contact Head of Drama Development
Screenplays/novels for adaptation for TV. Will only consider material submitted

through an agent or publisher. Founded 1991.

Celador Productions Ltd
39 Long Acre, London WC2E 9JT
tel 0171-240 8101 *fax* 0171-836 1117
Contacts Paul Smith (game shows), Nic Phillips (sitcoms)

Entertainment TV programmes: comedy, entertainment, game show productions, 'people show' ideas, light documentary, drama. Founded 1982.

Chatsworth Television Ltd
97-99 Dean Street, London W1V 5RA
tel 0171-734 4302 *fax* 0171-437 3301
e-mail 106035,663@compuserve.com
Head of Drama Development Stephen Jeffery-Poulter (film and TV drama scripts)
Head of Entertainment Justin Scroggie (infotainment, entertainment and game show formats)

No sitcoms. Founded 1980.

Children's Film and Television Foundation Ltd
Elstree Studios, Borehamwood, Herts. WD6 1JG
tel 0181-953 0844 *fax* 0181-207 0860

Not a production company; finances script development, especially for feature films (principally TV) aimed at children between 5 and 12 years old.

Childsplay Productions Ltd
8 Lonsdale Road, London NW6 6RD
tel 0171-328 1429 *fax* 0171-328 1416
Contact Kim Burke

Children's (not pre-school) and family TV programming; chiefly drama. Founded 1984.

The Comic Strip Ltd
8-10 Great Titchfield Street, London W1P 7AA
tel 0171-462 6006 *fax* 0171-436 0632
Contact Rebecca Jeffrey, Peter Richardson

Screenplays for cinema and TV; ½-hour comedy and drama series. Founded 1980.

The Walt Disney Company Ltd
Beaumont House, Kensington Village, Avonmore, London W14 8TS
tel 0181-222 1000 *fax* 0181-222 2795

Screenplays not accepted by London office. Must be submitted by an agent to The Walt Disney Studios in Burbank, California.

Diverse Fiction Ltd
Gorleston Street, London W14 8XS
tel 0171-603 4567 *fax* 0171-603 2148
Drama Producer Laurence Bowen

Film and TV drama. Founded 1982.

Fairwater Films Ltd
68 Vista Rise, Llandaff, Cardiff CF5 2SD
tel/fax (01222) 578488
e-mail 100756,3440 @compuserve.com
Managing Director Tony Barnes

Animation for cinema and TV; live action entertainment. All material should be submitted through an agent. Founded 1982.

The First Film Company Ltd
38 Great Windmill Street, London W1V 7PA
tel 0171-439 1640 *fax* 0171-437 2062
Producers Roger Randall-Cutler, Simon Flind, Bob Cheek

Screenplays for cinema. All material should be submitted through an agent. Founded 1984.

Focus Films Ltd
The Rotunda Studios, rear of 116-118 Finchley Road, London NW3 5HT
tel 0171-435 9004 *fax* 0171-431 3562
Contact Head of Development

Screenplays for cinema. Will only consider material submitted through an agent. Founded 1982.

Mark Forstater Productions Ltd
27 Lonsdale Road, London NW6 6RA
tel 0171-624 1123 *fax* 0171-624 1124
Contact Rosie Homan

Film and TV production. No unsolicited scripts, please.

Front Page Films
23 West Smithfield, London EC1A 9HY
tel 0171-329 6866 *fax* 0171-329 6844
Contact Script Editor

Screenplays for cinema. Material only accepted through agents. Founded 1985.

Gaia Communictions
Sanctuary House, 35 Harding Avenue, Eastbourne, East Sussex BN22 8PL
tel (01323) 727183 *tel/fax* (01323) 734809
Director Robert Armstrong, *Script Editor* Loni von Gruner

Specialises in Southeast regional documentary programmes, particularly historical and tourist; can include documentary/drama. Expanding operation into programmes for the new multiple satellite stations. MSS 16,000-21,000 words. Send synopsis in first instance with sae for return of material. Founded 1987.

Noel Gay Television
1 Albion Court, Albion Place, Galena Road, London W6 0QT

tel 0181-600 5200 *fax* 0181-600 5222
Contact Head of Development
Screenplays for cinema and TV; entertainment and drama. Founded 1987.

Granada Film
The London TV Centre, Upper Ground,
London SE1 9LT
tel 0171-737 8681 *fax* 0171-737 8682
Head of Film Pippa Cross
Screenplays for cinema: major commercial feature films and smaller UK-based films. No unsolicited material. Founded 1989.

Hammer Film Production Ltd
Elstree Studios, Borehamwood,
Herts. WD6 1JG
tel 0181-207 4011 *fax* 0181-905 1127
Contact Roy Skeggs
Completed screenplays and published books for cinema and TV development: drama/mystery/horror/ghost. No unsolicited material.

Hartswood Films
Twickenham Studios, The Barons, St Margaret's,
Twickenham, Middlesex TW1 2AW
tel 0181-607 8736 *fax* 0181-607 8744
Producer Beryl Vertue, *Development* Elaine Cameron
Screenplays for cinema and TV; comedy and drama. No unsolicited material. Founded 1981.

Hat Trick Productions Ltd
10 Livonia Street, London W1V 3PH
tel 0171-434 2451 *fax* 0171-287 9791
Contact Denise O'Donoghue
Situation and drama comedy series and light entertainment shows. Founded 1986.

Jim Henson Productions Ltd
30 Oval Road, London NW1 7DE
tel 0171-428 4000 *fax* 0171-428 4001
Contact Angus Fletcher
Screenplays for cinema and TV; fantasy, family and children's programmes – usually involving puppetry or animatronics. All material should be submitted through an agent. Founded 1979.

Hightimes Productions
5 Anglers Lane, London NW5 3DG
tel 0171-482 5202 *fax* 0171-485 4254
Production Executive Tony Humphreys
Screenplays for TV; light entertainment, comedy and drama. Founded 1981.

Illuminations
19-20 Rheidol Mews, Rheidol Terrace,
London N1 8NU
tel 0171-226 0266 *fax* 0171-359 1151
web site http://www.illumin.co.uk
Contact Linda Zuck
Screenplays for TV; cultural documentaries, arts and entertainment for broadcast TV. All material should be submitted through an agent. Founded 1982.

Kensington Films and Television Ltd
60 Charlotte Street, London W1P 2AX
tel 0171-927 8458 *fax* 0171-927 8444
Screenplays for cinema and TV drama. Send material to Margot Gavan Duffy. Founded 1993.

Brian Lapping Associates
21 Bruges Place, Randolph Street,
London NW1 0TF
tel 0171-482 5855 *fax* 0171-284 0626
Contact Brian Lapping
Screenplays for TV; documentary series, studio programmes. Founded 1988.

Little Bird Company Ltd
7 Lower James Street, London W1R 3PL
tel 0171-434 1131 *fax* 0171-434 1803
Development Executives J. Cavendish, M. Pope
Screenplays for cinema and TV. Founded 1982.

Little Dancer Ltd
Avonway, 3 Naseby Road, London SE19 3JJ
tel 0181-653 9343
Producer Robert Smith
Screenplays for cinema and TV; drama. Founded 1992.

London Film Productions Ltd
35 Davies Street, London W1Y 1FN
tel 0171-499 7800 *fax* 0171-499 7994
Chairman J. Eliasch
No unsolicited material considered.

Malone Gill Productions Ltd
Canaletto House, 39 Beak Street,
London W1R 3LD
tel 0171-287 3970 *fax* 0171-287 8146
e-mail ikonic@compuserve.com
Contact Georgina Denison
TV programmes. Founded 1978.

Maya Vision Ltd
43 New Oxford Street, London WC1A 1BH
tel 0171-836 1113 *fax* 0171-838 5169
Producer/Director Rebecca Dobbs
Features, TV dramas and documentaries. No unsolicited scripts. Founded 1982/3.

Monogram Productions Ltd
27-29 Berwick Street, London W1V 3RF
tel 0171-734 9873 *fax* 0171-734 9874
Managing Director Eileen Quinn

Screenplays for cinema and TV; drama series and serials only. All material should be submitted through an agent. Founded 1997.

New Blitz TV
Via Guido Banti 34, 00191 Rome, Italy
tel 333 26 41 *fax* 333 26 51
Television Department Giovanni A. Congiu

Importation and dubbing TV series, documentaries, educational films and video for schools. Material from freelance sources required.

Oxford Scientific Films Ltd
Lower Road, Long Hanborough,
Oxon OX8 8LL
tel (01993) 881881 *fax* (01993) 882808
Managing Director Karen Goldie-Morrison

Natural history and science-based programmes for broadcast, multimedia, educational and advertising markets. See also entry in picture agencies and libraries section. Founded 1968.

Penumbra Productions Ltd
80 Brondesbury Road, London NW6 6RX
tel 0171-328 4550 *fax* 0171-328 3844
e-mail 101621.3135@compuserve.com
Contact H.O. Nazareth

Drama for feature films and TV; documentaries for TV; non-broadcast videos to commissions. Founded 1981.

Picture Palace Films Ltd
53A Brewer Street, Soho, London W1R 3FD
tel 0171-734 6630 *fax* 0171-734 8574
Contact Malcolm Craddock

Screenplays for cinema and TV; low budget films; TV drama series. Material only considered if submitted through an agent. Founded 1971.

Planet 24
The Planet Building, 195 Marsh Wall,
Thames Quay, London E14 9SG
tel 0171-345 2424 *fax* 0171-345 9400
Contact Development Department

Screenplays for cinema and TV; drama and comedy for TV and radio. Founded 1992.

Portman Productions Ltd
167 Wardour Street, London W1V 3TA
tel 0171-468 3400 *fax* 0171-468 3499
Head of Development Katherine Butler

TV drama. Founded 1944.

Portobello Pictures Ltd
42 Tavistock Road, London W11 1AW
tel 0171-379 5566 *fax* 0171-379 5599
Contact Eric Abraham

Screenplays for cinema. Founded 1987.

Primetime Television Associates
Seymour Mews House, Seymour Mews,
Wigmore Street, London W1H 9PE
tel 0171-935 9000 *fax* 0171-935 1992 or
0171-487 3975
Contact Victoria Hull

Screenplays for TV and TV programmes of international interest, especially drama and documentary series. No unsolicited scripts. Founded 1968.

Red Rooster Film & Television Entertainment Ltd
29 Floral Street, London WC2E 9DP
tel 0171-379 7727 *fax* 0171-379 5756
Contacts Jill Green (managing director), Linda James, Julia Ouston

Screenplays for cinema and TV; drama. All material should be submitted through an agent. Founded 1982.

Regent Productions Ltd
The Mews, 6 Putney Common, London SW15 1HL
tel 0181-789 5350 *fax* 0181-789 5332
Contact William G. Stewart

Screenplays for TV; drama, situation comedies. Founded 1982.

RM Associates Ltd
46 Great Marlborough Street, London W1V 1DB
tel 0171-439 2637 *fax* 0171-439 2316
Contact Meckie Offermanns

Music and arts programmes: opera, dance, music, arts features and documentary series. Founded 1982.

Specific Films
25 Rathbone Street, London W1P 1AG
tel 0171-580 7476 *fax* 0171-494 2676
Contact Clare Wise

Feature-length screenplays.

Spitting Image Productions Ltd
Cairo Studios, 4 Nile Street, London N1 7ZZ
tel 0171-251 2626 *fax* 0171-251 2066
Head of Development Roger Law, *Managing Director* Richard Bennett

Projects for puppets and animation. Founded 1983.

Talisman Films Ltd
5 Addison Place, London W11 4RJ
tel 0171-603 7474 *fax* 0171-602 7422
e-mail talisman_films@dial.pipex.com
Contact Alan Shallcross

Screenplays for cinema and TV. Material only considered if submitted through an agent. Founded 1991.

TalkBack Productions
36 Percy Street, London W1P 0LN
tel 0171-323 9777 *fax* 0171-637 5105

TV situation comedies and comedy dramas. Send unsolicited material to PA to Managing Director; material through an agent to Peter Fincham. Founded 1989.

Tiger Aspect Productions Ltd
5 Soho Square, London W1V 5DE
tel 0171-434 0672 *fax* 0171-287 1448
Contact Lucy Kenwright

TV comedy drama and sitcoms. All material should be submitted through an agent. Founded 1993.

Triple Vision Ltd
Folly Lodge, Folly Lane, North Wooton,
Somerset BA4 4ER
tel/fax (01749) 890610
Contact Terry Flaxton

Screenplays for cinema and TV; arts/drama and documentaries, plays. Material only accepted through agents. Founded 1983.

Twentieth Century Fox Productions Ltd
Twentieth Century House, 31-32 Soho Square,
London W1V 6AP
tel 0171-437 7766 *fax* 0171-434 2170

Will not consider unsolicited material.

Twenty Twenty Television
20 Kentish Town Road, London NW1 9NX
tel 0171-284 2020 *fax* 0171-284 1810
Executive Producer Claudia Milne

Current affairs, documentaries, travel films, science and educational programmes, drama documentaries. Founded 1982.

UBA Ltd
21 Alderville Road, London SW6 3RL
tel 0171-371 0160 *fax* (01984) 623733
Contact Peter Shaw

Screenplays for cinema and TV of international interest. All material should be submitted through an agent. Founded 1983.

United Film and Television Productions
48 Leicester Square, London WC2H 7FB
tel 0171-389 8555 *fax* 0171-930 8499
Managing Director Vernon Lawrence

Synopses for TV drama or mini-series, non-factual programme ideas. Founded 1996.

Warner Bros. Productions Ltd
135 Wardour Street, London W1V 4AP
tel 0171-437 5600

Screenplays for cinema. Will only consider material submitted through an agent.

Warner Sisters Film & TV Ltd
Canalot Studios, 222 Kensal Road,
London W10 5BN
tel 0181-960 3550 *fax* 0181-960 3880

Screenplays for cinema and TV; TV programmes. All material should be submitted through an agent. Founded 1984.

Michael White
48 Dean Street, London W1V 5HL
tel 0171-734 7707 *fax* 0171-734 7727

Screenplays for cinema and TV. No unsolicited scripts. Founded 1963.

Working Title Films
76 Oxford Street, London W1N 9FD
tel 0171-307 3000 *fax* 0171-307 3001/2/3
Head of Development Debra Hayward (Films),
Simon Wright (TV)

Screenplays for film and TV – drama and comedy. Founded 1984.

World Productions Ltd
17 Golden Square, London W1R 4BB
tel 0171-734 3536 *fax* 0171-734 3585
Head of Development Serena Cullen

Screenplays for TV; TV drama series and serials.

Zenith Productions Ltd
43-45 Dorset Street, London W1H 4AB
tel 0171-224 2440 *fax* 0171-224 3194

Screenplays for cinema; TV drama. No unsolicited scripts.

Television and radio companies overseas

Opportunities are outlined here for submitting material to television and radio companies in Australia, Canada, Republic of Ireland, New Zealand and South Africa.

Australia

Australian Broadcasting Corporation
Box 9994, Sydney, NSW 2001
web site http://www.abc.net.au
Manager for Europe Australian Broadcasting Corporation, 54 Portland Place, London W1N 4DY

Provides TV and radio programmes in the national broadcasting service; operates Radio Australia; operates the international TV service, Australia Television; and co-ordinates a network of six symphony orchestras and stages concerts throughout Australia.

ABC TV restricts its production resources to work closely related to the Australian environment. ABC radio also looks principally to Australian writers for the basis of its drama output. However, ABC radio is interested in reading or auditioning new creative material of a high quality from overseas sources and this may be submitted in script or taped form. No journalistic material is required. Talks on international affairs are commissioned.

ATN Channel 7
Australian Television Network, Amalgamated Television Services Pty Ltd, Television Centre, Epping, NSW 2121
tel (02) 9877 7777 *fax* (02) 9877 7886

Unsolicited material not accepted.

BTQ Channel 7
Brisbane TV Limited, Sir Samuel Griffith Drive, Mt Coot-tha, GPO Box 604, Brisbane 4001
tel (07) 3369 7777 *fax* (07) 3368 2970
Network Director, Children's Programs Dina Browne

Children's educational-type series, children's entertainment programmes. Writers should have a thorough understanding of Australian culture.

HSV Channel 7 Melbourne
HSV Channel 7 Pty Ltd, 119 Wells Street, South Melbourne, Victoria 3205
tel (03) 96 97 7777
web site http://7.con.au

No unsolicited material accepted.

National Nine Network
(TCN-9 Sydney, GTV-9 Melbourne, QTQ-9 Brisbane, NWS-9 Adelaide, STW-9 Perth)
c/o 24 Artarmon Road, Willoughby, NSW 2068
tel (02) 9906 9999 *fax* (02) 9958 2279
Network Program Director John Stephens, *Network Director of Drama* Kris Noble, *Network Director Program Development* David Lyle

Interested in receiving material from freelance writers strictly on the basis of payment for material or ideas used. No necessity for writers to be Australian-based, but membership of the Australian Writers' Guild is helpful.

Canada

Canadian Broadcasting Corporation
250 Lanark Avenue, PO Box 3220, Stn. 'C', Ottawa, Ontario K1Y 1E4
tel 613-724-1200

Republic of Ireland

Radio Telefis Eireann
Donnybrook, Dublin 4
tel (01) 2083111 *fax* (01) 2083080
web site http://www.rte.ie

The Irish national broadcasting service operating radio and TV.

Television Ongoing production of both a rural and an urban drama serial. Treatments and character profiles accepted for one-off drama productions, drama series and situation comedies, preferably set in Ireland or of strong Irish interest, with preferred durations of commercial half hour or hour length. Forwarding of fully dialogued submissions not encouraged. Before submitting material to Current Affairs, Drama, Features or Young People's programmes, authors are advised to write to the department in question.

Radio Short stories (length 13-14 minutes) in Irish or English suitable for broadcasting; plays (running 30, 60 or 90 minutes) are welcomed and paid for according to merit. Guidelines on writing for radio drama are available from the RTE Radio Drama Department, Radio Centre, Donnybrook, Dublin 4.

Independent Radio and Television Commission (IRTC)
Marine House, Clanwilliam Place, Dublin 2, Republic of Ireland
tel (01) 6760966 *fax* (01) 6760948
e-mail info@irtc.ie

Statutory body with responsibility for independent broadcasting. At present there are 21 local radio stations operating in Ireland, in addition to one special interest/community station and one Irish language station. A further 11 community and community of interest radio stations are currently on air as part of a community radio pilot project.

The IRTC launched a new national radio station, Radio Ireland on 17 March 1997 and negotiations are currently under way for the establishment of a national independent television service.

New Zealand

The Radio Network of New Zealand Ltd
PO Box 3526, Auckland
tel (09) 377-6199 *fax* (09) 367-4619
Chief Executive Joan Withers

A 24-hour radio enterprise, with editorial and programming independence, controlling a NZ-wide group of over 56 commercial radio stations in metropolitan and provincial markets.

Television New Zealand Ltd
PO Box 3819, Auckland
tel (09) 377-0630 *fax* (09) 375-0918
Chairman Norman Geary, *Group Chief Executive* Chris Anderson

TVNZ is a state-owned enterprise with production facilities in all four main centres. It owns and operates TV ONE, TV2 and subsidiary companies, South Pacific Pictures Ltd, Avalon Studios Ltd, Broadcast Communications Ltd and Horizon Pacific Television, which operates five regional TV stations.

South Africa

South African Broadcasting Corporation
Private Bag XI, Auckland Park 2006
tel (011) 714-9111 *fax* (011) 714-3106
web site http://www.sabc.co.za

Operates 16 internal radio networks, one external radio service and three TV services.

Radio

Writing drama for radio

Writing drama for radio allows a freedom which none of the other performing arts can give. **Lee Hall** *guides the radio drama writer to submit a script which will be both well received and merit production.*

With upwards of 300 hours of radio drama commissioned each year, radio is an insatiable medium and, therefore, one which is constantly seeking new blood. It is no surprise to find that many of our most eminent dramatists, such as Pinter and Stoppard, did important radio work early in their careers.

Although the centrality of radio has been eclipsed somewhat by television and fringe theatre, it continues to launch new writers, and its products often find popular recognition in other media (for example, the film version of Anthony Mingella's *Truly Madly Deeply*). Because radio is often cited as the discoverer and springboard of so many talents, this should not obscure the fact that many writers make a living primarily out of their radio writing and the work itself is massively popular, with plays regularly getting audiences of over 500,000 people.

For the dramatist, the medium offers a variety of work which is difficult to find anywhere else: serials, dramatisations, new commissions of various lengths (from a couple of minutes to several hours), musicals, soap operas, adaptations of the classics, as well as a real enthusiasm to examine new forms.

Because it is no more expensive to be in the Hindu Kush than to be in a laundrette in Deptford, the scope of the world is only limited by the imagination of the writer. However, though radio drama in the 'Fifties and 'Sixties was an important conduit for absurdism, there is a perceived notion that radio drama on the BBC is domestic, Home Counties and endlessly trotting out psychological trauma in a rather naturalistic fash-

ion. This is not a fair assessment of the true range of work presented. The BBC itself is anxious to challenge this idea and as the face of broadcasting changes, there is a conscious move to attract new audiences with new kinds of work.

Get to know the form

Listen to as many plays as possible, read plays that are in print, and try to analyse what works, what doesn't and why. This may seem obvious, but it is easy to fall back on your preconceived notions of what radio plays are. The more you hear other people's successes and failures, the more tools you will have to discriminate when it comes to your own work.

Plays on radio tend to fit into specific time slots: 30, 60, 75, 90 minutes, and each slot will have a different feel – an afternoon play will be targeted at a different audience from one at 10.30pm.

A radio play will be chosen on artistic grounds but nevertheless a writer should be familiar with the market. This should not be seen as an invitation merely to copy forms or to try to make your play 'fit', but an opportunity to gain some sense of what the producers are dealing with. Producers are looking for new and fresh voices, ones which are unique, open new areas or challenge certain preconceptions. This is not to suggest you should be wilfully idiosyncratic but to be aware that it is the individuality of your 'voice' that people will notice.

Write what you feel strongly about, in the way that most attracts you. It should be bold, personal, entertaining, challeng-

ing and stimulating. Radio has the scope to explore drama that wouldn't get produced in theatres or on television, so treat it as the most radical forum for new writing. How many times have you listened to the radio with the sense that you've heard it all before? Never feel limited by what exists but be aware how your voice can enrich the possibilities of the future.

Who to approach

Opportunities for writing for radio in the UK are dominated by the BBC. Whilst there are increasing opportunities with independent stations, BBC Radio Drama overwhelms the field. Its output is huge. The variety of the work – from soaps to the classics – makes it the true national repertory for drama in its broadest sense. However, the BBC is increasingly commissioning productions from independent producers, so you can:

• send your unsolicited script to the Editor, Plays or Series and Serials, BBC Radio Drama (see page 306) where it will be assessed by a reader. If they find it of interest they will put you in contact with a suitable producer.

• approach a producer directly. This may be a producer at the BBC or at an independent company (see page 319). Both will give a personal response based on their own taste, rather than an institutional one.

Producers have a broad role: they find new writers, develop projects, edit the script, cast the actors, record and edit the play, and even write up the blurb for the *Radio Times*. Because of this intense involvement, the producer needs to have a strong personal interest in the writer or writing when they take on a project.

The system of commissioning programmes at the BBC is such that staff producers or independent production companies offer projects to commissioning editors to decide upon. Thus, a writer must be linked to a producer in the first instance to either get their play produced or get a commission for a new piece of work. Therefore, going direct to a producer can be a convenient short cut, but it requires more preparation.

Approaching a producer

Discovering and developing the work of new writers is only a small part of a producer's responsibilities, so be selective. Do your homework – there is little point in sending your sci-fi series to a producer who exclusively produces one-off period comedies.

To help decide which producer will be the most receptive to your work, become familiar with the work of each producer you are intersted in and the type of writers they work with. Use the *Radio Times* to help with your research and listen to as many of their plays as possible. It is well worth the effort in order to be sure to send your play to the right person. If you can quote the reasons why you've chosen them in particular, it can only help to get a congenial reception. It will also give you confidence in their response, as the comments – good or bad – will be from someone you respect.

Submitting your work

Don't stuff your manuscript into an envelope as soon as you've written 'The End'. You owe it to yourself to get the script into the best possible state before anyone sees it. First impressions matter and time spent refining will pay dividends in attracting attention.

Ask a person you trust to give you some feedback. Try to edit the work yourself, cutting things that don't work and spending time revising and reinventing anything which you think could be better. Make sure that what you send is the best you can possibly do.

Producers have mountains of scripts to read. The more bulky your tome the less enthusiastically it will be received. (It's better to send a sparkling 10-page sample than your whole 300-page masterpiece.) Try to make the first scene excellent. The more you can surprise, engage or delight in the first few pages, the more chance the rest will be carefully read. The adage that a reader can tell whether a play is any good after the first three pages might be wholly inaccurate but it reflects a cyni-

cism versed by the practice of script reading. The reader will probably approach your script with the expectation that it is unsuitable, and part of getting noticed is jolting them out of their complacency.

Have your script presentably typed. Make sure your letter of introduction is well informed and shows that you haven't just picked a name at random. Do not send it to more than one producer at a time, as this is considered bad etiquette. And don't expect an instantaneous response – it may take a couple of months before you receive a reply. Don't be afraid of calling up if they keep you waiting for an unreasonable length of time, but don't badger people as this will inevitably be counterproductive.

Finally

Don't be discouraged by rejection and *don't* assume that because one person has rejected your script that it is no good. It is all a question of taste. Use the criticism positively to help your work, not as a personal attack.

Lee Hall's first radio play, *I Luv U, Jimmy Spud*, won the Alfred Bradley Bursary Award, The Richard Imison Award, and the Society of Authors/Sony Award in 1996. He has written several other plays for BBC Radio, as well as the series *God's Country* and a serial dramatisation of Mario Vargas Llosa's *Aunt Julia and the Scriptwriter*.

BBC national radio

The BBC continues to be in a state of reorganisation. It commissions from both BBC Production and independent producers (see page 319), as well as from BBC regional centres.

BBC Broadcast

BBC Broadcast, Broadcasting House, London W1A 1AA
tel 0171-580 4468

In April 1997 BBC Broadcast came into being as the commissioning, scheduling, marketing and broadcast directorate of the BBC – for both radio and TV.

The BBC has five national radio networks – Radio 1, Radio 2, Radio 3, Radio 4 and Radio 5 Live – broadcasting approximately 41,000 hours of music, comedy, drama, features, news and sport each year.

In 1995-96, BBC Radio commissioned over 2000 hours of output from independent radio producers. On every network key programmes are now being made independently. Some outstanding examples include the *Chris Evans Breakfast Show* on Radio 1, *The Jamesons* on Radio 2, *Morning Collection* on Radio 3,

Gardeners' Question Time on Radio 4, and the *Entertainment News* service on Radio 5 Live.

Director of Radio/Controller, Radio 1 Matthew Bannister
Controller, Radio 2 James Moir
Controller, Radio 3 Nicholas Kenyon
Controller, Radio 4 James Boyle
Controller, Radio 5 Live Roger Mosey
Deputy Controller, Radio 1 Andy Parfitt
Deputy Controller, Radio 5 Live/Controller, Sports Rights, Radio Mike Lewis
Head of Music Policy, Radio 1 Jeff Smith
Head of Music Policy, Radio 2 Geoff Mullins
Managing Editor, Radio 1 Ian Parkinson
Managing Editor, Radio 2 Lesley Douglas
Managing Editor, Radio 3 Brian Barfield
Commissioning Editor, Music (Policy), Radio 3 Hilary Boulding
Commissioning Editor, Music (Live), Radio 3 Martyn Westerman
Commissioning Editors, Radio 4 Elizabeth Burke, Andrew Caspari, Fiona Cooper, Jane Ellison, Caroline Raphael, Mary Sharp
Commissioning Editor, News, Radio 5 Live Martin Cox

BBC Production

BBC Production, Broadcasting House,
London W1A 1AA
tel 0171-580 4468

BBC Production is the largest single programme maker in Europe. There are 20 bi-media programme departments based in London and the English regions, including (for radio) BBC Sport, the Natural History Unit, Music, Drama, Topical Features, Religion, Education, Light Entertainment, Consumer and Leisure, Science, History and the Arts. Addresses are given for individual departments if they are different from above.

Radio Drama

(part of Bi-media Drama Dept)
Room 6058

The Drama Department broadcasts 400 hours of new plays and adaptations every year, in addition to readings. There is therefore a very large market regularly available to the freelance writer. A free leaflet, *Writing Plays for Radio*, giving basic guidance on the technique of radio writing and also on the market is available from the Chief Producer, Plays (Radio Drama); see also *Writing drama for radio* on page 303. Submissions should be addressed to the Editor, Plays or Series and Serials. Allow up to two months for a reply.

Short stories specially written for broadcasting will be considered for the 'short story' slot on Radio 4. A story written for a 15-minute broadcasting space should be between 2000 and 2300 words in length. Unsolicited material is considered but it has to compete with regularly commissioned work. Submissions should be addressed to the Editor, Readings (Radio Drama).

Head of Drama, Radio Kate Rowland
Editor, Single Plays Jeremy Mortimer
Editor, Series and Serials Marylin Imrie
Editor, Readings Paul Kent

Radio Light Entertainment

(part of Bi-media Entertainment Dept)
Head, Light Entertainment, Radio Jonathan James-Moore

Light Entertainment is interested in receiving scripts or ideas for series of half-hour sitcoms or panel games, principally for Radio 4. Before submitting material, send for the writers' guidelines – available from the Senior Producer, Scripts, Light Entertainment Radio (enclose an A4 sae).

Two programmes, *Week Ending* and *The News Huddlines*, are interested in using unsolicited topical sketches during the course of their run. *Week Ending* holds a weekly writers' meeting at which anyone is welcome, at the above address. Details (and times of deadlines) can be obtained by phoning and asking for the production office of the programme concerned. All fees are a matter for negotiation with the Corporation's Copyright Department.

Radio Arts

(part of Bi-media Arts Dept)
Editor, Arts, Radio John Boundy
Editor, Kadeidoscope (Radio 4) John Boundy
Editor, Night Waves (Radio 3) Abigail Appleton

Radio Music

(part of Bi-media Music Dept)
Head, Radio 3 Music Dr John Evans

At the heart of the BBC's music policy is a commitment to high-quality, live music making in all its forms and across the full range of styles and periods. Audition sessions for professional soloists and ensembles are held twice a year in May and November, with an outside professional assessor on the listening panel. The BBC also regularly commissions new works from a wide range of composers both nationally and internationally for all its house orchestras and the BBC Singers as well as for other groups and special occasions. Their range includes jazz, electronic and radiophonic media.

The BBC makes best endeavours to consider all unsolicited scores and tapes for broadcast. This is carried out chiefly by the Music Department's New Music Unit, and where further opinions are sought, they are put before the Readers on the New Music Panel, who provide objective advice to the production teams without bias or prejudice.

Radio Science

(part of Bi-media Science Dept)
Editor, Science, Radio Deborah Cohen

Radio Consumer and Leisure

(part of Bi-media Consumer and Leisure Dept)
Editor, Face the Facts (Radio 4) Graham Ellis
Editor, You and Yours (Radio 4) Chris Burns
Series Producer, The Food Programme (Radio 4)
  Sheila Dillon
Series Producer, Breakaway (Radio 4) Eleanor
  Garland

Radio Sport

(part of Bi-media Sport Dept)
Head of Sport, Radio Bob Shennan
Controller, Sports Rights, Radio Mike Lewis
Editor, Sports Newsgathering Charles Runcie
Editor, Sport Gordon Turnbull
Editor, Magazines and Documentaries Alison
  Rusted

Topical Features

Head, Topical Features Anne Winder
Managing Editor, Daily Programmes (inc.
  Woman's Hour, Afternoon Shift – Radio 4)
  Nadine Grieve
Editor, Documentaries Richard Bannerman
Editor, Features (inc. Any Questions? – Radio 4)
  Sharon Banoff
Editor, Factual Entertainment (inc. Loose Ends,
  Start the Week, Desert Island Discs – Radio 4)
  Ian Guardhouse

Education – see Television section, page 285

BBC international radio

BBC World Service

Bush House, Strand, London WC2B 4PH
tel 0171-240 3456 *fax* 0171-257 8258
e-mail worldservice.letters@bbc.co.uk
web site http://www.bbc.co.uk/worldservice
Provides radio services in English and 44
other languages. Its key aims are:
• To deliver objective information
• To help meet the need for education
and English language teaching
• To give access to the best of British
culture and entertainment.

BBC World Service reports and analy-
ses world events around the clock, every
day of the year. On-the-spot coverage
comes from the full network of 250 BBC
correspondents and 50 news bureaux
worldwide. In addition to news and
analysis, there is a wide choice of other
radio programmes in the larger language
services. In English, the range includes:
the arts, features, religious affairs, drama,
music, education, science, entertainment
and sport. BBC World Service has the
biggest global audience.
Managing Director Sam Younger
Director of News and Programme Commissioning
  Bob Jobbins
Commissioning Editor (with responsibility for
  independent productions) Tim Dean
Controller, English Network Penny Tuerk
Head of Resources Commissioning Chris Gill
Head of Region, Africa and Middle East Barry
  Langridge
Head of Region, Americas Jerry Timmins
Head of Region, Asia-Pacific Elizabeth Wright
Head of Region, Europe Benny Ammar
*Head of Region, Former Soviet Union and SW
  Asia* David Morton
Regional Director Andrew Taussig

BBC regional radio

The regions are responsible for producing both television and radio programmes. For addresses, see BBC Regional television section on page 286.

The regions produce a total of over 7250 hours of radio broadcasting on all five networks. BBC Pebble Mill in Birmingham is the source of almost half this output – music for broadcast on Radio 2 and Radio 3, farming and environment programmes for Radio 4, and Asian and motoring magazines for Radio 5 Live. It also produces a wide range of drama, from *The Archers* to Sony award-winning Radio 3 drama *Albion Tower*.

BBC North in Manchester provides religious programmes for all five networks, features such as *Mediumwave* and regular editions of *Kaleidoscope*, Radio 1's *Roadshow* and the *Mark Radcliffe Show*, and is also home to the BBC Philharmonic Orchestra. BBC Bristol specialises in history, travel, literature and human interest features, mainly for Radio 4, including *Poetry Please* and *With Great Pleasure*.

BBC Scotland contributes programmes to all the networks, including BBC Scottish Symphony Orchestra concerts (Radio 3), *Sherlock Holmes* and *'P' Division 41* (Radio 4), and *Night Moves* and *Five Live at the Fringe* (Radio 5 Live).

BBC Wales and BBC Northern Ireland have both increased their commissions for Network Radio. Programme highlights have included Sony award winner *The Fly* and *Wales Night* – part of Radio 3's Fairest Isle season (Wales) and dramas such as *Firefly Summer* and *Drumcree* (Northern Ireland).

BBC local radio

There are opportunities for writers to submit short stories, plays and poetry to local radio. A number of stations hold play-writing or short story competitions and the winners have their work broadcast. Others consider original work from local writers. Material should be submitted to the Assistant Editor.

South region

BBC Radio Bristol
PO Box 194, Bristol BS99 7QT
tel 0117-974 1111

BBC Radio Cornwall
Phoenix Wharf, Truro, Cornwall TR1 1UA
tel (01872) 75421

BBC Radio Devon
Broadcasting House, Seymour Road, Mannamead,
Plymouth, Devon PL3 5BD
tel (01752) 260323

BBC Radio Gloucestershire
London Road, Gloucester GL1 1SW
tel (01452) 308585

BBC GLR
(London)
35c Marylebone High Street, London W1A 4LG
tel 0171-224 2424

BBC Radio Guernsey
Commerce House, Les Banques, St Peter Port,
Guernsey, Channel Islands
tel (01481) 728977

BBC Radio Jersey
18 Parade Road, St Helier, Jersey,
Channel Islands
tel (01534) 870000

BBC Radio Kent
Sun Pier, Chatham, Kent ME4 4EZ
tel (01634) 830505

BBC Radio Solent
Broadcasting House, Havelock Road,
Southampton SO14 7PW
tel (01703) 631311

BBC Somerset Sound
14-15 Paul Street, Taunton,
Somerset TA1 3PF
tel (01823) 252437

BBC Southern Counties Radio
(Sussex and Surrey)
Broadcasting House, Guildford, Surrey GU2 5AP
tel (01483) 306306

BBC Thames Valley FM
(Oxfordshire and Berkshire)
PO Box 952, Oxford OX2 7YL
PO Box 954, Slough SL1 1BA
PO Box 1044, Reading RG30 1PL

BBC Wiltshire Sound
Broadcasting House, Prospect Place, Swindon,
Wilts. SN1 3RW
tel (01793) 513626

Midlands and East region

BBC Asian Network
Epic House, Charles Street, Leicester LE1 3SH
tel 0116-251 6688
Pebble Mill Road, Birmingham B5 7SD
tel 0121-414 8484

BBC Radio Cambridgeshire
Broadcasting House, 104 Hills Road,
Cambridge CB2 1LD
tel (01223) 259696

BBC Coventry and Warwickshire
25 Warwick Road, Coventry CV1 2WR
tel (01203) 559911

BBC Radio Derby
56 St Helen's Street, Derby DE1 3HY
tel (01332) 361111

BBC Essex
PO Box 765, Chelmsford, Essex CM2 9XB
tel (01245) 262393

BBC Hereford and Worcester
Hylton Road, Worcester WR2 5WW
tel (01905) 748485
43 Broad Street, Hereford HR4 9HH
tel (01432) 355252

BBC Radio Leicester
Epic House, Charles Street, Leicester LE1 3SH
tel 0116-251 6688

BBC Radio Lincolnshire
PO Box 219, Newport, Lincoln LN1 3XY
tel (01522) 511411

BBC Radio Norfolk
Norfolk Tower, Surrey Street, Norwich NR1 3PA
tel (01603) 617411

BBC Radio Northampton
PO Box 1107, Abington Street,
Northampton NN1 2BE
tel (01604) 239100

BBC Radio Nottingham
York House, Mansfield Road, Nottingham NG1 3JB
tel 0115-955 0500

BBC Radio Shropshire
PO Box 397, Shrewsbury, Shropshire SY1 3TT
tel (01743) 248484

BBC Radio Stoke
Cheapside, Hanley, Stoke-on-Trent, Staffs. ST1 1JJ
tel (01782) 208080

BBC Radio Suffolk
Broadcasting House, St Matthews Street,
Ipswich, Suffolk IP1 3EP
tel (01473) 250000

BBC Three Counties Radio
(Bedfordshire, Hertfordshire and Buckinghamshire)
PO Box 476, Hastings Street, Luton, Beds. LU1 5BA
tel (01582) 459111

BBC Radio WM
(West Midlands)
PO Box 206, Birmingham B5 7QQ
tel 0121-414 8484

North region

BBC Radio Cleveland
PO Box 95FM, Broadcasting House,
Newport Road, Middlesbrough, Cleveland TS1 5DG
tel (01642) 225211

BBC Radio Cumbria
Annetwell Street, Carlisle, Cumbria CA3 8BB
tel (01228) 592444

BBC GMR
(Manchester)
New Broadcasting House, Oxford Road,
Manchester M60 1SJ
tel 0161-200 2000

BBC Radio Humberside
9 Chapel Street, Hull, North Humberside HU1 3NU
tel (01482) 23232

BBC Radio Lancashire
20-26 Darwen Street, Blackburn, Lancs. BB2 2EA
tel (01254) 262411

BBC Radio Leeds
Broadcasting House, Woodhouse Lane,
Leeds LS2 9PN
tel 0113-244 2131

BBC Radio Merseyside
55 Paradise Street, Liverpool L1 3BP
tel 0151-708 5500

BBC Radio Newcastle
Barrack Road, Newcastle upon Tyne NE99 1RN
tel 0191-232 4141

BBC Radio Sheffield
Ashdell Grove, 60 Westbourne Road,
Sheffield S10 2QU
tel 0114-268 6785

BBC Radio York
20 Bootham Row, York YO3 7BR
tel (01904) 641351

Scotland, Wales and Ireland

BBC Radio Scotland
Broadcasting House, Queen Margaret Drive,
Glasgow G12 8DG
tel 0141-338 2000 *fax* 0141-334 0614
Castle Street, Kirkwall, Orkney KW15 1DF
tel (01856) 873939 *fax* (01856) 872908
Municipal Buildings, High Street, Selkirk TD7 4BU
tel (01750) 21884 *fax* (01750) 22400
Brentham House, Lerwick, Shetland ZE1 0LR
tel (01595) 694747 *fax* (01595) 694307
'Elmbank', Lovers' Walk, Dumfries DG1 1NZ
tel (01387) 268008 *fax* (01387) 252568

BBC Radio Nan Gaidheal
7 Culduthel Road, Inverness IV2 4AD
tel (01463) 720720 *fax* (01463) 236125
Rosebank, Church Street, Stornoway,
Isle of Lewis PA87 2LS
tel (01851) 705000 *fax* (01851) 704633

BBC Radio Wales/Cymru
Broadcasting House, Llantrisant Road, Llandaff,
Cardiff CF5 2YQ
tel (01222) 572888 *fax* (01222) 552973

BBC Radio Ulster
Broadcasting House, Ormeau Avenue,
Belfast BT2 8HQ
tel (01232) 338000 *fax* (01232) 338800

BBC Radio Foyle
8 Northland Road, Londonderry BT48 7NE
tel (01504) 262244 *fax* (01504) 378666

BBC broadcasting rights and terms

Contributors are advised to check latest details of fees with the BBC.

Rights and terms

Specially written material

Fees are assessed on the basis of the type of material, its length, the author's status and experience in writing for radio. Fees for submitted material are paid on acceptance. For commissioned material, half the fee is paid on commissioning and half on acceptance as being suitable for broadcasting.
* Rates for specially written radio dramas in English (other than educational programmes) are £37.82 a minute for beginners and a 'going rate' of £57.58 a minute for established writers. This rate covers two broadcasts.

Specially written short stories

* Fees range from £117.00 for 15 minutes.

Published material

Domestic radio
* Dramatic works: £11.36 per minute.
* Prose works: £11.36 per minute.
* Prose works required for dramatisation: £8.86 per minute.
* Poems: £11.36 per half minute.

World Service Radio (English)
* Dramatic works: £5.69 per minute for broadcasts within a seven-day period.
* Prose works: £5.69 per minute for broadcasts within a seven-day period.
* Prose works required for dramatisation: £4.43 per minute for broadcasts

within a seven-day period.
* Poems: £5.69 per half minute for broadcasts within a seven-day period.
* Foreign Language Services are approximately one-fifth of the rate for English Language Services.

Repeats in BBC programmes

* Further proportionate fees are payable for repeats.

Use abroad of recordings of BBC programmes

If the BBC sends abroad recordings of its programmes for use by overseas broadcasting organisations on their own networks or stations, further payments accrue to the author, usually in the form of additional percentages of the basic fee paid for the initial performance or a royalty based on the percentage of the distributors' receipts. This can apply to both sound and television programmes.

Value Added Tax

There is a self-billing system for VAT which covers radio, external services and television for programmes made in London.

Talks

Contributors to talks for domestic Radio and World Service broadcasting may be offered either:
* the standard talks contract which takes rights and provides for residual pay-

ments, as does the television standard contract; or
• an STC (Short Talks Contract) which takes all rights except print publication rights where the airtime of the contribution does not exceed five minutes and which

has set fees or disturbance money payable; or
• an NFC (No Fee Contract) where no payment is made which provides an acknowledgement that a contribution may be used by the BBC.

Independent national radio

Commercial Radio Companies Association (CRCA)
(formerly Association of Independent Radio Companies – AIRC)
77 Shaftesbury Avenue, London W1V 7AD
tel 0171-306 2603 *fax* 0171-470 0062
CRCA is the trade body for UK commerical radio. It represents commercial radio to Government, the Radio Authority, copyright societies and other organisations concerned with radio. CRCA is a source of advice to members and acts as a clearing house for radio information.
CRCA runs the Radio Advertising Clearance Centre. It jointly owns Radio Joint Audience Research Ltd (RAJAR) with the BBC, and also owns the Network Chart Show, sponsored by Pepsi.
CRCA is a founder member of the Association of European Radios (AER), which lobbies European institutions on behalf of commercial radio.

Classic FM
Academic House, 24-28 Oval Road, London NW1 7DQ
tel 0171-284 3000 *fax* 0171-713 2630
web site http://www.classicnet.co.uk

IRN (Independent Radio News)
6th Floor, 200 Gray's Inn Road, London WC1X 8XZ
tel 0171-430 4090 *fax* 0171-430 4092
e-mail news@irn.co.uk
National news provider to all UK commercial radio stations, including live news bulletins, sport and financial news, and coverage of the House of Commons.

The Radio Authority
Holbrook House, 14 Great Queen Street, London WC2B 5DG
tel 0171-430 2724 *fax* 0171-405 7062
Licenses and regulates Independent Radio. Plans frequencies, awards licences, regulates programming and radio advertising, and plays an active role in the discussion and formulation of policies which affect the Independent Radio industry and its listeners.

Talk Radio
76 Oxford Street, London W1N 0TR
tel 0171-636 1089 *fax* 0171-636 1053

Virgin Radio
1 Golden Square, London W1R 4DJ
tel 0171-434 1215 *fax* 0171-434 1197
e-mail virgin@radio.co.uk
web site http://www.virginradio.co.uk/

Independent local radio

Many of the local radio stations listed here broadcast music and/or chat shows only. However, some do accept ideas and material for programmes. Phone to ascertain a station's requirements.

Aberdeen
Northsound One and Northsound Two,
45 King's Gate, Aberdeen AB15 4EL
tel (01224) 632234

Alton
Wey Valley Radio, Prospect Place, Mill Lane,
Alton, Hants GU34 2SY
tel (01420) 544444 *fax* (01420) 544044

Aylesbury
MIX 96, Friars Square Studios,
11 Bourbon Street, Aylesbury,
Bucks. HP20 2PZ
tel (01296) 399396 *fax* (01296) 398988

Ayr
West Sound AM/West FM, Radio House,
54A Holmston Road, Ayr KA7 3BE
tel (01292) 283662 *fax* (01292) 283665
e-mail westsound@srh.co.uk

Bedford
B97 and Classic Gold 792, 55 Goldington Road,
Bedford MK40 3LS
tel (01234) 272400 *fax* (01234) 218580

Belfast
96.7 BCR, Russell Court, Claremont Street,
Lisburn Road, Belfast,
Northern Ireland BT9 6JX
tel (01232) 438500 *fax* (01232) 230505

Belfast
Downtown Radio/Cool FM,
Kiltonga Industrial Estate, Newtownards,
Co. Down, Northern Ireland BT23 4ES
tel (01247) 815555 *fax* (01247) 818913

Birmingham
96.4FM BRMB/1152 Xtra AM, Radio House,
Aston Road North, Birmingham B6 4BX
tel 0121-359 4481 *fax* 0121-359 1117

Birmingham
Choice FM, 95 Broad Street,
Birmingham B15 1AU
tel 0121-616 1000 *fax* 0121-616 1011

Birmingham
Radio XL 1296 AM, KMS House, Bradford Street,
Birmingham B12 0JD
tel 0121-753 5353 *fax* 0121-753 3111

Blackpool
Radio Wave, 965 Mowbray Drive, Blackpool,
Lancs. FY3 7JR
tel (01253) 304965 *fax* (01253) 301965

Borders
Radio Borders, Tweedside Park,
Galashiels TD1 3TD
tel (01896) 759444 *fax* (01896) 759494

Bournemouth
Two Counties Radio, 5-7 Southcote Road,
Bournemouth, Hants BH1 3LR
tel (01202) 259259 *fax* (01202) 255244
web site http://www.2crfm.co.uk

Bradford
Sunrise FM, 30 Chapel Street, Little Germany,
Bradford BD1 5DN
tel (01274) 735043 *fax* (01274) 728534

Bradford/Huddersfield & Halifax
The Pulse, Forster Square, Bradford BD1 5NE
tel (01274) 731521 *fax* (01274) 392031

Brighton, Eastbourne/Hastings
South Coast Radio/Southern FM, Radio House,
PO Box 2000, Brighton, East Sussex BN14 2SS
tel (01273) 430111 *fax* (01273) 430098
e-mail info@southernradio.co.uk

Bristol
GWR Radio, PO Box 2000, Bristol BS99 7SN
tel (0117) 984 3200 *fax* (0117) 984 3202

Bury St Edmunds
SGR-FM, PO Box 250, Bury St Edmunds,
Suffolk IP33 1AD
tel (01284) 702622 *fax* (01473) 741200

Cambridge & Newmarket
Q 103 FM, PO Box 103, The Vision Park,
Chivers Way, Histon, Cambridge CB4 4WW
tel (01223) 235255 *fax* (01223) 235161

Cardiff & Newport
Red Dragon FM, West Canal Wharf,
Cardiff CF1 5XJ
tel (01222) 384041 *fax* (01222) 384014

Cardiff & Newport
Touch Radio, West Canal Wharf, Cardiff CF1 5YJ
tel (01222) 237878 *fax* (01222) 384014

Carlisle
CFM, PO Box 964, Carlisle, Cumbria CA1 3NG
tel (01228) 818964

Central Scotland
SCOT FM, 1 Albert Quay, Leith,
Edinburgh EH6 7DN
tel 0131-554 2266 *fax* 0131-554 2266

Ceredigion
Radio Ceredigion, Yr Hen Ysgol Cymraeg,
Ffordd Alecsandra, Aberystwyth,
Ceredigion SY23 1LF
tel (01970) 627999 *fax* (01970) 627206

Channel Tunnel
Channel Travel Radio, Eurotunnel, UK Terminal,
Main Control Building, PO Box 2000,
Folkestone, Kent CT18 8XY
tel (01303) 283873 *fax* (01303) 283874

Cheltenham
Cheltenham Radio, Regent Arcade, Cheltenham,
Glos. GL50 1JZ
tel (01242) 699555 *fax* (01242) 699666

Chichester, Bognor Regis & Littlehampton
Spirit FM, 9-10 Dukes Court, Bognor Road,
Chichester, West Sussex PO19 2FX
tel (01243) 773600 *fax* (01243) 786464

Colchester
SGR Colchester, Abbeygate Two,
9 Whitewell Road, Colchester, Essex CO2 7DE
tel (01206) 575859 *fax* (01206) 561199

Colchester & North East Essex
Mellow 1557, The Media Centre, 2 St John's
Wynd, Culver Square, Colchester, Essex CO1 1WQ
tel (01206) 764466 *fax* (01206) 764672
e-mail mellow@enterprise.net

Cornwall/Plymouth/West Devon
Pirate FM102·2/8, Carn Brea Studios,
Wilson Way, Redruth, Cornwall TR15 3XX
tel (01209) 314400 *fax* (01209) 314345
Plymouth office Foot & Bowden Building,
19 The Crescent, Plymouth PL1 3AD
tel (01752) 675179 *fax* (01752) 675185

Coventry
Mercia FM and Classic Gold 1359,
Hertford Place, Coventry CV1 3TT
tel (01203) 868200 *fax* (01203) 868202

Coventry
KIX 96, St Mark's Church Annexe, Bird Street,
Stoney Stanton Road, Coventry CV1 4FH
tel (01203) 525656 *fax* (01203) 551744

Darlington, Aycliffe & Sedgefield
Alpha 103.2, 11 Woodland Road, Darlington,
Co. Durham DL3 7BJ
tel (01325) 255552 *fax* (01325) 255551

Derby
Ram FM, The Market Place, Derby DE1 3AA
tel (01332) 292945 *fax* (01332) 292229

Dumfries
South West Sound/West Sound, Campbell House,
Bankend Road, Dumfries DG1 4TH
e-mail wsradio@aol.com
tel (01387) 250999 *fax* (01387) 265629

Dundee/Perth
Radio Tay AM (PO Box 123), Tay FM (PO Box
1028), 6 North Isla Street, Dundee DD1 9UF
tel (01382) 200800 *fax* (01382) 593252
e-mail tayam@srh.co.uk, tayfm@srh.co.uk

Edinburgh
Forth AM/Forth FM, Forth House, Forth Street,
Edinburgh EH1 3LF
tel 0131-556 9255 *fax* 0131-558 3277

Exeter/Torbay
Gemini Radio, Hawthorn House,
Exeter Business Park, Exeter, Devon EX1 3QS
tel (01392) 444444 *fax* (01392) 444433

Fort William
Nevis Radio, Inverlochy, Fort William,
Inverness-shire PH33 6LU
tel (01397) 700007 *fax* (01397) 701007
e-mail nevisradio@lochaber.co.uk

Glasgow
Clyde 1 FM and Clyde 2, Clydebank Business
Park, Clydebank, Glasgow G81 2RX
tel 0141-306 2272 *fax* 0141-306 2295

Gloucester & Cheltenham
Severn Sound, Old Talbot House,
Southgate Street, Gloucester GL1 2DQ
tel (01452) 423791 *fax* (01452) 529446

Guernsey
Island FM, 12 Westerbrook, St Sampson,
Guernsey GY2 4QQ, Channel Islands
tel (01481) 42000 *fax* (01481) 49676

Guildford, Haslemere, Reigate & Crawley
Mercury Extra AM/Radio Mercury FM East,
Broadfield House, Brighton Road, Crawley,
West Sussex RH11 9TT
tel (01293) 519161 *fax* (01293) 565663

Harlow
Ten 17, Latton Bush Centre, Southern Way,
Harlow, Essex CM18 7BU
tel (01279) 431017 *fax* (01279) 445289
e-mail ten 17@netforce.net
web site www.ten 17.netforce.net

Harrogate
97.2 Stray FM, Stray Studios, PO Box 972,
Station Parade, Harrogate HG1 5YF
tel (01423) 522972 *fax* (01423) 522922
e-mail yourradio@972strayfm.co.uk

Hereford/Worcester
Radio Wyvern, 5-6 Barbourne Terrace,
Worcester WR1 3JZ
tel (01905) 612212 *fax* (01905) 612849

High Wycombe
elevenSEVENTY, PO Box 1170, High Wycombe,
Bucks HP13 6YT
tel (01494) 446611 *fax* (01494) 445400
news fax (01494) 447272

Humberside
Viking FM, Commercial Road, Hull HU1 2SG
tel (01482) 325141 *fax* (01482) 587067

Inverness
Moray Firth Radio, Scorguie Place,
Inverness IV3 6SF
tel (01463) 224433 *fax* (01463) 243224/227714
e-mail moray_firth_radio@cali.co.uk

Inverurie
North East Community Radio, Town House,
Inverurie, Aberdeenshire AB51 0US
tel (01467) 632878 *fax* (01467) 632969

Ipswich
SGR·FM, Radio House, Alpha Business Park,
Whitehouse Road, Ipswich IP1 5LT
tel (01473) 461000 *fax* (01473) 741200

Isle of Wight
Isle of Wight Radio, Dodnor Park, Newport,
Isle of Wight PO30 5XE
tel (01983) 822557 *news tel* (01933) 821777
fax (01983) 822109

Jersey
Channel 103, 6 Tunnell Street, St Helier,
Jersey JE2 4LU, Channel Islands
tel (01534) 888103 *fax* (01534) 887799

Kettering
KCBC Radio, Unit One, Centre 2000, Robinson
Close, Kettering, Northants. NN16 8PU
tel (01536) 412413 *fax* (01536) 517390

King's Lynn
KL·FM96·7, PO Box 77, 18 Blackfriars Street,
King's Lynn, Norfolk PE30 1NN
tel (01553) 772777 *fax* (01553) 766453

Leeds
Kiss 105, Josephs Well, Westgate, Leeds LS3 1AB

Leeds/Wakefield/West Yorkshire
Radio Aire FM/Magic 828, PO Box 2000,
51 Burley Road, Leeds LS3 1LR
tel (0113) 245 2299 *fax* (0113) 242 1380
news fax (0113) 242 3985

Leicester
Leicester Sound FM, Granville House,
Granville Road, Leicester LE1 7RW
tel (0116) 256 1300 *fax* (0116) 256 1303

Leicester
Sabras Sound, Radio House, 63 Melton Road,
Leicester LE4 6PN
tel (0116) 261 0666 *fax* (0116) 266 7776

Lincoln
Lincs FM, Witham Park, Waterside South,
Lincoln LN5 7JN
tel (01522) 549900 *fax* (01522) 549911

Liverpool
Radio City 1548 AM/96·7 City FM,
8-10 Stanley Street, Liverpool L1 6AF
tel 0151-227 5100 newsdesk *tel* 0151-471 0216
fax 0151-471 0333

London (General and Entertainment Service)
Capital Radio, 30 Leicester Square,
London WC2H 7LA
tel 0171-766 6000 *fax* 0171-766 6100

London (Brixton)
Choice FM, 16-18 Trinity Gardens,
London SW9 8DP
tel 0171-738 7969 *fax* 0171-738 6619

London (Haringey)
London Greek Radio, Florentia Village,
Vale Road, London N4 1TD
tel 0181-800 8001 *fax* 0181-800 8005

London, Greater
Festival Radio, Universal House,
251 Tottenham Court Road,
London W1P 9AD
tel 0171-580 5668 *fax* 0171-580 5669

London, Greater
Heart 106·2, The Chrysalis Building,
Bramley Road, London W10 6SP
tel 0171-468 1062 *fax* 0171-470 1062

London, Greater
jazzfm, 26-27 Castlereagh Street,
London W1H 6DJ
tel 0171-706 4100 *fax* 0171-723 9742
web site http://www.jazzfm.co.uk

London, Greater
Kiss 100 FM, Kiss House, 80 Holloway Road,
London N7 8JG
tel 0171-700 6100 *fax* 0171-700 3979

London, Greater
963 Liberty Radio, Golden Rose House,
26- 27 Castlereagh Street, London W1H 6DJ
tel 0171-706 9963 *fax* 0171-723 9742

London, Greater
LBC 1152AM and News Direct 97·3FM
200 Gray's Inn Road, London WC1X 8XZ
tel 0171-973 1152 *fax* 0171-973 8833

London, Greater
Melody FM, 180 Brompton Road,
London SW3 1HF
tel 0171-581 1054 *fax* 0171-581 7000

London, Greater
Millennium FM, Thamesmead Town Offices,
Harrow Manorway, London SE2 9UG
tel 0181-311 3112 *fax* 0181-312 1930
web site rtm.greenwich.uk.com

London, Greater
Premier Radio, Glen House, Stag Place,
London SW1E 5AG
tel 0171-233 6705 *fax* 0171-233 6706

London, Greater
RTL Country 1035 AM, PO Box 1035,
London W1
tel 0171-540 1010 *fax* 0171-540 1020

London, Greater
Spectrum Radio, 204-206 Queenstown Road,
London SW8 3NR
tel 0171-627 4433 *fax* 0171-627 3409

London, Greater
Sunrise Radio London 1458AM,
Sunrise House, Sunrise Road, Southall,
Middlesex UB2 4AU
tel 0181-574 6666 *fax* 0181-813 9800

London, Greater
Virgin Radio London, 1 Golden Square,
London W1R 4DJ
tel 0171-434 1215 *fax* 0171-434 1197

Londonderry
Q102·9 FM, The Old Waterside, Railway Station,
Duke Street, Waterside, Londonderry,
Northern Ireland BT47 1DH
tel (01504) 44449

Ludlow
Sunshine 855, Sunshine House, Waterside,
Ludlow, Shropshire SY8 1GS
tel (01584) 873795 *fax* (01584) 875900

Luton/Bedford
Chiltern Radio, Chiltern Road, Dunstable,
Beds. LU6 1HQ
tel (01582) 676200 *fax* (01582) 676201

Maidstone & Medway/East Kent
Invicta FM and Invicta SuperGold,
Radio House, John Wilson Business Park,
Whitstable, Kent CT5 3QX
tel (01227) 772004 *fax* (01227) 771558

Manchester
Fortune 1458, PO Box 1458, Quay West,
Trafford Park, Manchester M17 1FL
tel 0161-872 1458 *fax* 0161-872 0206

Manchester
Kiss 102, Kiss House, PO Box 102,
Manchester M60 1GJ
tel 0161-228 0102 *fax* 0161-228 1020

Manchester
Piccadilly Radio, Castle Quay,
Manchester M1 4AW
tel 0161-288 5000 *fax* 0161-288 5001

Mid Ulster
Townland Radio 828 AM, PO Box 828
Cookstown, Co. Tyrone BT80 9LQ
tel (016487) 64828 *fax* (016487) 63828

Milton Keynes
FM 103 Horizon, Broadcast Centre,
Crownhill Industry, Milton Keynes MK8 0AB
tel (01908) 269111 *fax* (01908) 564093

Montgomeryshire
Radio Maldwyn (The Magic 756), The Park,
Newtown, Powys SY16 2NZ
tel (01686) 623555 phone-in *tel* (01686) 624756
fax (01686) 623666

North Devon
Lantern FM, The Light House, 17 Market Place,
Bideford, Devon EX39 2DR
tel (01237) 424444 *fax* (01237) 423333
e-mail info@lantern.romgroup.co.uk
web site http://www.rom.net/lantern/

North East
Century Radio, PO Box 100, Gateshead NE8 2YY
tel 0191-477 6666

North Lancashire/South Cumbria
The Bay 96·9 FM, PO Box 969, St George's Quay,
Lancaster LA1 3LD
tel (01524) 848747 *fax* (01524) 848787

North Wales Coast
Marcher Coast FM, 41 Conway Road,
Colwyn Bay, Clwyd LL28 5AB
tel (01492) 534555 *fax* (01492) 535248

North West
jazzfm 100.4, The World Trade Centre,
Exchange Quay, Manchester M5 3EJ
tel 0161-877 1004 *fax* 0161-877 1005

Northampton
Northants 96, 19-21 St Edmunds Road,
Northampton NN1 5DY
tel (01604) 795690 *fax* (01604) 795601
e-mail reception@northants96.musicradio.com

Norwich & Great Yarmouth
Amber Radio, PO Box 4000,
Norwich NR3 1DB
tel (01603) 630621 *fax* (01603) 666353
e-mail sales@broadland102.co.uk

Norwich & Great Yarmouth
Broadland 102·4 FM, St George's Plain,
47-49 Colegate, Norwich NR3 1DB
tel (01603) 630621 *fax* (01603) 666353

Nottingham
TRENT FM, 29-31 Castle Gate,
Nottingham NG1 7AP
tel 0115-952 7000 *fax* 0115-912 9302
e-mail director@trentfm.musicradio.com

Nottingham & Derby
GEM AM, 29-31 Castle Gate, Nottingham NG1 7AP
tel (0115) 952 7000 *fax* 0115-912 9302
e-mail director@gemam.musicradio.com

Oxford/Banbury
Fox FM, Brush House, Pony Road,
Oxford OX4 2XR
tel (01865) 871000 *fax* (01865) 871036

Paisley
96.3 QFM, 26 Lady Lane, Paisley PA1 2LG
tel 0141-887 9630 *fax* 0141-887 0963

Peterborough
Classic Gold 1332 AM, PO Box 225,
Queensgate Centre, Peterborough PE1 1XJ
tel (01733) 460460 *fax* (01733) 281444

Peterborough
102·7 Hereward FM, PO Box 225, Queensgate
Centre, Peterborough, Cambs. PE1 1XJ
tel (01733) 460460 *fax* (01733) 281444

Pitlochry & Aberfeldy
Heartland FM, Atholl Curling Rink, Lower
Oakfield, Pitlochry, Perthshire PH16 5HQ
tel (01796) 474040 *fax* (01796) 474007

Plymouth
Plymouth Sound, Earl's Acre, Plymouth PL3 4HX
tel (01752) 227272 *fax* (01752) 670730

Portsmouth & Southampton
South Coast Radio, Radio House, Fareham,
Hants PO15 5SH
tel (01489) 589911 *fax* (01489) 589453

Portsmouth, Southampton & Winchester
Ocean FM/Power FM, Radio House,
Whittle Avenue, Segensworth West, Fareham,
Hants PO15 5SH
tel (01489) 589911 *fax* (01489) 589453

Preston, Blackpool & Lancashire
Red Rose 999, PO Box 999, Preston,
Lancs. PR1 1XR
tel (01772) 556301 *fax* (01772) 201917

Reading/Basingstoke
Classic Gold, PO Box 2020, Reading RG31 7RZ
tel 0118-925 4400 *fax* 0118-925 4456

Reading/Basingstoke & Andover
2-TEN FM, PO Box 2020, Reading,
Berks. RG31 7FG
tel 0118-925 4400 *fax* 0118-925 4456

St Albans/Watford
Oasis Radio, Broadcast Centre, 7 Hatfield Road,
St Albans, Herts. AL1 3RS
tel (01727) 831966 *fax* (01727) 834456

Salisbury
Spire FM, City Hall Studios, Malthouse Lane,
Salisbury, Wilts. SP2 7QQ
tel (01722) 416644 *fax* (01722) 415102

Scarborough
Yorkshire Coast Radio, PO Box 962,
62 Falsgrave Road, Scarborough,
North Yorkshire YO12 5AX
tel (01723) 500962 *fax* (01723) 501050

Severn Estuary
Galaxy 101, Broadcast Centre, Portland Square,
Bristol BS2 8RZ
tel (0117) 924 0111 *fax* (0117) 924 5589
e-mail addressee@galaxy101.co.uk

Shaftesbury
Gold Radio, Longmead, Shaftesbury,
Dorset SP7 8QQ
tel (01747) 855711 *fax* (01747) 855722

Sheffield & Rotherham/Barnsley/ Doncaster
Hallam FM and Great Yorkshire Gold,
Radio House, 900 Herries Road, Hillsborough,
Sheffield S6 1RH
tel (0114) 285 3333 *fax* (0114) 285 3159

Shetland Islands
SIBC, Market Street, Lerwick,
Shetland ZE1 0JN
tel (01595) 695299 *fax* (01595) 695696

Somerset
Orchard FM, Haygrove House, Shoreditch,
Taunton, Somerset TA3 7BT
tel (01823) 338448
web site http://rhwww.richuish.ac.uk/ext/orchard

Southend

Essex FM and Breeze, Radio House, Clifftown
Road, Southend-on-Sea, Essex SS1 1SX
tel (01702) 333711 *fax* (01702) 345224
e-mail (Essex FM) essexfm@netforce.net
web site www.essexfm.netforce.net
e-mail (The Breeze) breeze@netforce.net
web site www.breeze.netforce.net

Staffordshire & Cheshire

Signal 105 Radio, Regent House, Heaton Lane,
Stockport SK4 1BX
tel 0161-285 4545 *fax* 0161-285 1050

Stirling

Central 103·1 FM, John Player Building,
Stirling Enterprise Park, Stirling FK7 7YJ
tel (01786) 451188 *fax* (01786) 461883

Sunderland

Sun FM 103·4, PO Box 1034, Sunderland,
Tyne and Wear SR1 3YZ
tel 0191-567 3333 *fax* 0191-567 0888

Surrey & NE Hampshire

County South Radio Network, Dolphin House,
Worth Street, Guildford, Surrey GU1 4AA
tel (01483) 300964 *fax* (01483) 531612

Swansea

Sound Wave 96·4 FM, Victoria Road, Gowerton,
Swansea, West Glamorgan SA4 3AB
tel (01792) 511964 *fax* (01792) 511965

Swansea

Swansea Sound 1170 MW, Victoria Road,
Gowerton, Swansea, West Glamorgan SA4 3AB
tel (01792) 511170 *fax* (01792) 511171

Swindon/West Wiltshire

GWR Radio, PO Box 2345, Westlea,
Wilts. SN5 7HF
tel 0118-928 4313 *fax* 0118-928 4310

Teesside

TFM Radio, Yale Crescent, Stockton-on-Tees,
Cleveland TS17 6AA
tel (01642) 888222 *fax* (01642) 868288

Tonbridge, Tunbridge Wells & Sevenoaks

KFM, 1 East Street, Tonbridge, Kent TN9 1AR
tel (01732) 369200 *fax* (01732) 369201

Tyne and Wear

Metro FM, Long Rigg, Swalwell,
Newcastle upon Tyne NE99 1BB
tel 0191-420 0971 *fax* 0191-488 9222

West Cumbria

CFM, PO Box 964, Carlisle CA1 3NG
tel (01228) 818964 *fax* (01228) 819444

West Midlands

100·7 Heart FM, PO Box 1007, 1 The Square,
111 Broad Street, Edgbaston, Birmingham B15 1AS
tel 0121-626 1007 *fax* 0121-696 1007

Weymouth & Dorchester

Wessex FM, Radio House, Trinity Street,
Dorchester, Dorset DT1 1DJ
tel (01305) 250333 *fax* (01305) 250052

Whitstable

Invicta Radio, PO Box 100, Whitstable,
Kent CT5 3YR
tel (01227) 772004 *fax* (01227) 771558

Windsor, Slough & Maidenhead

106·6 Star FM, The Observatory Shopping
Centre, Slough, Berks. SL1 1LH
tel (01753) 551066 *fax* (01753) 512277

Wolverhampton & the Black Country/Shrewsbury & Telford

Beacon Radio, 267 Tettenhall Road,
Wolverhampton WV6 0DQ
tel (01902) 838383 and
28 Castle Street, Shrewsbury SY1 2BQ
tel (01743) 232271

Wolverhampton & the Black Country/Shrewsbury & Telford

WABC, 267 Tettenhall Road,
Wolverhampton WV6 0DQ
tel (01902) 838383 *fax* (01902) 755163 or 838266

Wrexham, Chester & Deeside, Wirral and North Wales

Marcher Radio Group, The Studios, Mold Road,
Wrexham, Clwyd LL11 4AF
tel (01978) 752202 *fax* (01978) 759701
e-mail mfm.radio@ukonline.co.uk

York

Minster FM, PO Box 123, Dunnington,
York YO1 5ZX
tel (01904) 488 888 *fax* (01904) 488 811

Yorkshire/Lincolnshire

Great Yorkshire Gold, Radio House,
900 Herries Road, Sheffield S6 1RH
tel (0114) 285 2121 *fax* (0114) 285 3159
Forster Square, Bradford BD1 5NE
tel (01274) 731521 *fax* (01274) 392031
Commercial Road, Hull HU1 2SG
tel (01482) 325141 *fax* (01482) 587067

Independent radio producers

Many writers approach independent production companies direct and, increasingly, BBC Radio is commissioning independent producers to make programmes.

Boom Media Ltd
25 Market Place, Halesworth, Suffolk IP19 8DA
tel (01986) 875000 *fax* (01986) 875050
Director Nick Patrick

Features and docs with an East Anglian bias, sports' features, popular culture, East Anglian drama. Founded 1993.

Business Sound Ltd
Unit 9, Bramley Business Centre, Station Road, Bramley, Surrey GU5 0AZ
tel (01483) 898868 *fax* (01483) 894056
Managing Director Michael Bartlett

Ideas and synopses for packages for the corporate training market; docs. No unsolicited material; initial approach by phone, please. Founded 1989.

Fast Forward Productions
A132, Riverside Business Centre, Bendon Valley, London SW18 4LZ
tel 0181-875 9999 *fax* 0181-875 0344
Producer Adrian Quine

Aviation. Founded 1994.

Festival Radio Productions (Level Broadcast Ltd)
6B Steine Gardens, Brighton,
East Sussex BN2 1WB
tel (01273) 628688 *fax* (01273) 628689
Director Daniel Nathan

Plays, docs and features. Founded 1989.

The Fiction Factory
201 Greenwich High Road, London SE10 8NB
tel 0181-853 5100 *fax* 0181-293 3001
e-mail drama@mill.cityscape.co.uk
Creative Director John Taylor

Plays, dramatisations, readings, documentaries, arts features and children's drama mainly for BBC radio (R4, R2, World Service, etc). Original radio drama scripts and ideas for all radio genres considered. Founded 1993.

The Flying Dutchman Company
5-7 Hughes Mews, 143 Chatham Road,
London SW11 6HJ
tel 0171-223 9067 *fax* 0171-585 0459
Partner Michael Cameron

Plays, docs and other programmes on all topics. Founded 1988.

GRF Christian Radio
342 Argyle Street, Glasgow G2 8LY
tel 0141-221 9447 *fax* 0141-332 9187
e-mail grf.radio@scet.org.uk
Programme Controller Brian W. Muir

Docs on ethical/moral/religious issues; mini-dramas (up to four minutes) on religious themes; one-minute scripts; children's programmes (religious/educational). Founded 1948.

Heavy Entertainment Ltd
208-209 Canalot Studios, 222 Kensal Road,
London W10 5BN
tel 0181-960 9001/2 *fax* 0181-960 9003
e-mail scripts@heavyentertainment.co.uk
Company Directors David Roper, Nick St George

Full-length plays, docs and comedy programmes. Founded 1992.

Mike Hopwood Productions Ltd
Conway House, Cheapside, Hanley,
Stoke-on-Trent, Staffs. ST1 1JJ
tel (01782) 201319 *fax* (01782) 289115
Editor Mike Hopwood

Plays, docs, comedy, soaps, light entertainment. Founded 1991.

Independent Productions Ltd
46A Willowtree Road, Hale, Altrincham,
Cheshire WA14 2EG
tel 0161-928 6105 *fax* 0161-928 6105
Director Tony Hawkins

Scripts and ideas for commercials and promotions for independent radio. Founded 1990.

IRDP
PO Box 518, Manningtree,
Essex CO11 1XD
tel (01206) 299088
web site http://www.irdp.co.uk/

New writing schemes for radio and theatre, and professional independent productions.

Mediatracks
93 Columbia Way, Blackburn, Lancs. BB2 7EA
tel/fax (01254) 691197
Contact Steve Johnson

Pop-music and general interest docs for BBC local radio network. Founded 1987.

Mr Punch Productions
4 Hughes Mews, 143 Chatham Road,
London SW11 6HJ
tel 0171-924 7767 *fax* 0171-924 7775
Director Stewart Richards

Plays and dramatisations for broadcast on BBC Radio 4 and for audiobooks. Founded 1993.

Partners in Sound Ltd
The Tower, Church Studios, North Villas,
London NW1 9AY
tel 0171-485 0873 *mobile* (0973) 221 479
fax 0171-428 0541
e-mail 101641.2726@compuserve.com
Director Ian Willox

Scripts for plays, docs and other programmes.

Penumbra Productions Ltd
80 Brondesbury Road, London NW6 6RX
tel 0171-328 4550 *fax* 0171-328 3844
e-mail 101621.3135@compuserve.com
Contact R. Elsgood

Drama and documentaries for Radio 3 and 4. Founded 1981.

Planet 24
Norex Court, Thames Quay, 195 Marsh Wall,
London E14 9SG
tel 0171-345 2424 *fax* 0171-345 9400
Managing Director Alex Connock

Scripts, synopses and ideas for plays, docs and other programmes. Founded 1991.

Quantam Radio Syndications Ltd
A132, Riverside Business Centre, Haldane Place,
London SW18 4UQ
tel 0181-875 9999 *fax* 0181-875 0344
Producer Adrian Quine

Sponsored syndicated radio programmes.

Rewind Productions Ltd
The Media Centre, 131-151 Great Titchfield
Street, London W1P 8AE
tel 0171-577 7770 *fax* 0171-577 7771
Managing Director Chris Parry-Davies

Plays, docs, popular and classical music, comedy and game shows. Founded 1989.

ScreenPlay Ltd
25 Cleveland Road, Brighton,
East Sussex BN1 6FF
tel (01273) 708610 *fax* (01273) 708611
e-mail screenplay@dial.pipex.com
Managing Director Robert J. Shepherd

Scripts for drama and comedy, particularly series and serials. Unsolicited material not considered. Write with synopsis in first instance; sae essential for return of material. Founded 1987.

SH Radio
Robert Symes, Green Dene Cottage, Honeysuckle
Bottom, East Horsley, Surrey KT24 5TD
tel/fax (01483) 283223
Mary-Jean Hasler
22 Carew Road, London W13 9QL
tel 0181-567 2100

Music series, documentary features and broadcast/non-broadcast commercial material, voice over for films. Founded 1988.

Smooth Operations
PO Box 286, Cambridge CB1 4TW
tel (01223) 880835 *fax* (01223) 881647
e-mail smoothops@cix.compulink.co.uk
Executive Producers Nick Barraclough, John
Leonard

Scripts and ideas for docs and series. Founded 1992.

Soundbite Productions Ltd
55 Tasman Road, London SW9 9LZ
tel/fax 0171-274 1349
Managing Director Lizzie Jackson

Well-thought-out ideas and research for series and programmes for BBC Radio and World Service. Material only accepted from those with a proven track record in radio or TV. Founded 1991.

Testbed Productions
10 Margaret Street, London W1N 7LF
tel 0171-436 0555 *fax* 0171-436 2800
Directors Viv Black, Nick Baker

Docs and other programmes; ideas for interviews, feature series, magazine, plays and panel/quiz games. Founded 1992.

Theatre

Marketing a stage play

Despite the financial problems facing many subsidised theatres and the mounting costs of commercial productions, there are still plenty of companies interested in producing new plays and supporting new writers. Indeed, the sheer number and variety of such companies can be daunting. **Ben Jancovich** *examines the options.*

Selecting the theatre

Given the financial costs of submitting a play and the emotional strain in waiting for a response, it is important to take the time to research where a submission is most likely to gain a positive response. Start by recognising the disparate nature of contemporary outlets for new plays. Study the box (right) and decide on which kind of theatre company you should concentrate your efforts.

Clearly, the sheer volume of plays submitted to certain companies and the specific requirements of others make a blanket marketing campaign likely to be neither practical nor successful. An in-depth examination is needed on how to give your submission a head start.

Submitting your play

If the subject matter, form or the references in the play are specific enough, start by submitting your play to a theatre company which is likely to be predisposed towards those aspects of your play. For instance, if your play is about disability, you will want to be aware that the *raison d'etre* of the Graeae Theatre Company is to explore this theme. Likewise, if you have written a play for children you should know about the Polka Theatre for Children in Wimbledon. There is a danger of compartmentalising both writers and companies but, if your play has a distinct selling point, do the research and work to that strength.

Similarly, if your play details the life or history of a specific locale or region, send a copy of your script to the repertory theatre for that area – they may well have an interest in plays with a local appeal.

If a character in your play has a specific and discernible quality for which you think a particular actor may be uniquely suitable, it may be worth contacting them

---

Types of theatre companies

- **Metropolitan new writing theatre companies:** Largely London-based theatres which specialise in new writing, such as Hampstead Theatre, Royal Court, Bush Theatre, Soho Theatre, etc.
- **Regional repertory theatre companies:** Theatres based in towns and cities across the country which may do new plays as part of their repertoire.
- **Commercial producing managements:** Unsubsidised profit-making theatre producers who may occasionally be interested in new plays to take on tour or to present in the West End.
- **Small and/or middle-scale touring companies:** Companies – mostly touring – which exist to explore or promote specific themes or are geared towards specific kinds of audiences.
- **Independent theatre practitioners:** For example, actors who may be looking for interesting plays in which to appear.
- **Independent theatre producers:** For example, young directors or producers who are looking for plays to produce at the onset of their career.
- **Drama schools and amateur dramatics companies.**

through their agent. Of course, there is no point in contacting an actor merely because they are famous – they will already receive many more scripts than they could ever read. Therefore, only consider doing this if there is genuinely something specific about the play that demands their attention.

Further options

If your play does not obviously fit any such niche, there are still plenty of companies which are keen to read exciting new writing irrespective of subject matter.

Metropolitan new writing companies, the regional repertory theatres and commercial producers are all, to different degrees, in the market for new plays. Additionally, and often most successfully, are the plethora of young directors and other practitioners who institute productions under the aegis of their own independent theatre companies. An all-inclusive list of these latter organisations would be daunting, so research their interests and be selective. Reading reviews in the national and local press and listings magazines, such as *Time Out*, will give you some idea of which are the most productive and successful companies and practitioners.

Choosing which company to approach can be difficult as past productions and achievements rarely give precise indications of the way a company wants to move forward. Likewise, the notion of a successful 'commercial' company or play is not straightforward. For example, recent new plays with youthful, urban and often violent content have proved big commercial hits despite appearing anathema to the cliché of a well-made West End play.

Amateur companies/drama schools

Two other avenues to consider are amateur theatres and drama schools. Certain amateur theatre companies, such as Questors Theatre in Ealing, have premiered plays by both new and established writers. The Leisure Department of your local council should be able to give information on groups which exist in your area.

One good reason for approaching such a company is that they are often the only organisations (apart from the RSC and RNT) which can afford to mount large cast plays. It is a reality of modern theatre that, if you write a play requiring a cast of more than 10, it will prove financially problematic for many companies.

Similar considerations are at work regarding drama schools, with the added incentive that the people involved – directors and actors – may form an attachment to the play and want to work on it professionally elsewhere. The publication *Contacts* lists and gives contact details of the drama schools which are recognised by and accredited to the Conference of Drama Schools.

How to approach a company

Although some details may be obvious, they are worth noting and of course much depends on who you are approaching. At the very least, only ever submit a script which is legible, typed and bound, and always include a stamped addressed envelope large enough for its return. Find out the name and position of the best person to receive and assess your script. Do this not only a matter of courtesy but also because it will help if you need to follow up anything at a later date.

Do your best to ensure that you are happy with the script as it stands. Mistakes are inevitable but it is unprofessional to send rewrites before the original draft has even been read. Obviously, always keep a copy of your play.

Some theatres employ a literary manager or dramaturg whose job is specifically to facilitate the passage of plays through the administrative and artistic channels. In such cases, submissions should be simple and, under their management, the theatre should always be willing and ready to read plays by writers previously unknown to them (although some may not be interested in musicals, revues or translations and adaptations).

Useful addresses

The Arts Council of England
14 Great Peter Street,
London SW1P 3NQ
Contact The Drama Director

Publishes a brochure, *Schemes for Writers & Theatre Companies*, which gives details of various forms of assistance available to playwrights and to theatres wishing to commission new plays. The Council awards Bursaries (e.g. the John Whiting Award) and helps writers who are being commissioned or encouraged by a theatre company. A number of Resident Dramatists' Attachment Awards are available. See also page 439.

New Playwrights Trust
Interchange Studios, Dalby Street,
London NW5 3NQ

A useful organisation which provides members with the fruits of its extensive knowledge of the industry through publications, forums and databases.

The Spotlight
7 Leicester Place, London WC2H 7BP
tel 0171-437 7631

Publishes a book, *Contacts*, which contains all the addresses for professional organisations and theatre companies listed in the article. The 1997-98 edition is available from October.

However, in the majority of cases there will be no one person whose main function is to deal with writers and their plays. Therefore, you will need to be particularly rigorous in finding out the theatre's policy (remember that due to the pressure of work, dealing with writers may not be the highest of priorities).

Some companies may only accept submission of scripts through agents or with some sort of recommendation. Others may want a brief description of the play so they can decide whether it is worth their time looking at it. They may want this either sent by post, or they may prefer a brief telephone conversation.

What to expect

Since working practices vary from organisation to organisation, the response you can expect and how long before you get it will also vary. After submitting your script, do not expect any response for two to three months. If you have heard nothing from the company after six months, make a gentle inquiry. Obviously, badgering the company for a response is unlikely to work to your advantage.

The company is likely to give one or more of the following responses:
• an explanation for the rejection of the play;
• the offer of a 'getting to know you' meeting;
• a more formal dramaturgical meeting to discuss possible textual changes or clarifications;
• a reading or workshop on the play;
• advice on where else to send the play;
• an offer of a more formal recommendation for the play to colleagues working elsewhere.

Agents

When you enter into any kind of contractual relationship with a theatre company you should find an agent. An agent can help you on all the legal aspects of selling a play and ensure that your rights are protected. He or she will also help to promote you and your work and in guiding your career. As the relationship between you and your agent is crucial to the long-term development of you as a writer, meet as many agents as possible to seek out someone with whom you feel at ease and have an affinity. See *Literary agents for television, film, radio and theatre* on page 368.

New writing support agencies

Aside from theatre companies and practitioners, there is a burgeoning industry of organisations which exist to help writers develop their craft, their contacts and their appreciation of the industry. One cross-over organisation is the National

Theatre Studio, which is part of the Royal National Theatre but exists more as a service to theatre artists and the industry at large rather than directly for the scheduling of the company's three theatres. The national New Playwrights Trust exists as an information and research organisation.

Attached and supported by most of the Regional Arts Boards are regional forums, such as Stage Coach for the Midlands and North West Playwrights for the north of England. It is worth making contact with these organisations, especially if you are based outside one of the metropolitan areas as they can act on your behalf. Some are very good at the national promotion of the work of their local writers, while others are more active in putting writers and directors in contact with each other. Contact your local Regional Arts Board (see page 470) or repertory theatre for more information.

Bursaries and prizes

There are various schemes run by theatre companies, arts boards, television companies and independent organisations to financially assist writers. These fall into two categories: bursaries and prizes. Bursaries relate to the writer rather than their work, and can sometimes include an attachment to a theatre or arts organisation. Some writers can apply for themselves (e.g. The Arts Council's Writers Bursaries), while for other awards a theatre company applies on the writer's behalf. Prizes usually (though not always) relate to the judging of a play. Because the prize for such a scheme may be either a production or sufficient money to encourage one to happen, it is worth familiarising yourself with the various schemes and their deadlines. This is best done either through membership of New Playwrights Trust or by being in contact with the regional forums, mentioned above. Also, watch out for announcements in the Press, especially *The Observer*, *The Author*, *Amateur Stage* and *The Stage*. A list of magazines dealing with the theatre is on page 131; see also *Prizes and awards* on page 488.

Ben Jancovich is Literary Manager of Hampstead Theatre. Previously Literary Assistant at the Royal Shakespeare Company, he has directed plays in the London fringe and has worked as a freelance theatre critic with *City Limits*.

Theatre producers

This list is divided into London theatres (below), provincial theatres (page 326) and touring companies (page 330). See also Marketing a stage play on page 321.

London

Bush Theatre
Shepherd's Bush Green, London W12 8QD
tel 0171-602 3703 *fax* 0171-602 7614
Literary Manager Joanne Reardon
Welcomes unsolicited full-length scripts (plus one small and one large sae); commissions writers at an early stage in their career; produces 6 premieres a year.

Michael Codron Plays Ltd
Aldwych Theatre Offices, Aldwych, London WC2B 4DF
tel 0171-240 8291 *fax* 0171-240 8467

Ray Cooney Presentations Ltd
Hollowfield Cottage, Littleton, Surrey GU3 1HN
tel (01483) 440 443 *fax* (01483) 532068
Contact H.S. Udwin

English Stage Company Ltd
Royal Court Theatre, Sloane Square, London SW1W 8AS
tel 0171-730 5174 *fax* 0171-730 4705
Literary Manager Graham Whybrow
New plays.

Greenwich Theatre Ltd
Greenwich Theatre, Crooms Hill, London SE10 8ES
tel 0181-858 4447 *fax* 0181-858 8042
Contact Artistic Director

Hampstead Theatre
Swiss Cottage Centre, Avenue Road,
London NW3 3EX
tel 0171-722 9224 *fax* 0171-722 3860
Contact Ben Jancovich

New plays and the occasional modern
classic. After initial assessment, promising
scripts are then read by the literary manager and/or artistic director. It can therefore
take 2-3 months to reach a decision.

Bill Kenwright Ltd
59 Shaftesbury Avenue, London W1V 8JA
tel 0171-439 4466 *fax* 0171-437 8370
Chief Executive Brett Finnigan

King's Head Theatre
115 Upper Street, London N1 1QN
tel 0171-226 8561 *fax* 0171-226 8507
Contact General Manager

Brian Kirk Associates
3 Wigton Place, London SE11 4AN
tel 0171-820 0077 *fax* 0171-820 1237

Commerical producing management.

Knightsbridge Theatrical Productions Ltd
21 New Fetter Lane, London EC4A 1JJ
tel 0171-583 8687 *fax* 0171-583 1040
Contact Mrs Sheila H. Gray

Lyric Theatre Hammersmith
King Street, London W6 0QL
tel 0181-741 0824 *fax* 0181-741 7694
Chief Executive Sue Storr, *Artistic Director* Neil
Bartlett, *Administrative Producer* Simon Mellor

A producing theatre as well as a receiving venue for work by new writers, translators, performers and composers.

Man in the Moon Theatre
392 King's Road, London SW3 5UZ
tel 0171-351 5701 *fax* 0171-351 1873
Associate Director Genene Cooper

Theatre and studio space; medium-scale
company. Broad range of plays produced
in-house (24-40 a year), including new
writing; scripts from new writers considered.

The Old Red Lion Theatre
418 St John Street, London EC1V 4QE
tel 0171-833 3053 *fax* 0171-833 3053
Artistic Director Ken McClymont

Interested in contemporary pieces, especially from unproduced writers. No funding: incoming production company pays
to rent the theatre. Sae essential with
enquiries. Founded 1977.

Orange Tree Theatre
1 Clarence Street, Richmond, Surrey TW9 2SA
tel 0181-940 0141 *fax* 0181-332 0369

Polka Theatre for Children
240 The Broadway, London SW19 1SB
tel 0181-542 4258 *fax* 0181-542 7723
Artistic Director Vicky Ireland

Exclusively for children, the Main
Theatre seats 300 and The Adventure
Theatre seats 80. Programmed for 18
months to 2 years in advance. Theatre of
new writing, with targeted commissions.
Founded 1967.

Questors Theatre
Mattock Lane, London W5 5BQ
tel 0181-567 0011 *fax* 0181-567 8736
Theatre Manager Elaine Orchard, *Marketing
Manager* Sonja Garsvo

Student Playwriting Competition with
£1000 prize.

Royal National Theatre
South Bank, London SE1 9PX
tel 0171-928 2033 *fax* 0171-620 1197

Little opportunity for the production of
unsolicited material, but submissions
welcomed. Send to Jack Bradley, Literary
Manager, together with an sae.

Royal Shakespeare Company
Barbican Theatre, Barbican, London EC2Y 8BQ
tel 0171-628 3351 *fax* 0171-374 0818
Literary Manager Colin Chambers

Soho Theatre Company
21 Dean Street, London W1V 6NE
tel 0171-287 5060 *fax* 0171-287 5061
e-mail sohotheatre.co.uk
Artistic Director Abigail Morris, *Literary Manager*
Paul Sirett

Always on the look out for new plays
and playwrights and welcome unsolicited scripts. These are read by a professional panel who write a detailed critical
report. Also offer various levels of workshop facilities, including rehearsed reading and platform performances, for
promising playwrights, and in-depth
script development with the Artistic
Director and Literary Manager. See also
the Verity Bargate Award on page 490.

The Steam Industry
Finborough Theatre, 118 Finborough Road,
London SW10 9ED
tel 0171-244 7439 *fax* 0171-835 1853
Contact Phil Willmoh

Creates and develops large cast productions which deal with 'big' subjects in an ambitious and innovative way. Founded 1994.

Stoll Moss Theatres
Manor House, 21 Soho Square, London W1V 5FD
tel 0171-494 5200 *fax* 0171-434 1217
Production Director Nica Burns

Owns 10 West End theatres: Apollo, Cambridge, Duchess, Garrick, Gielgud, Her Majesty's, London Palladium, Lyric Shaftesbury Avenue, Queens and Theatre Royal Drury Lane. Now commissions new plays from both established writers and new talent. Founded 1978.

Tabard Theatre
2 Bath Road, Turnham Green, London W4 1LW
tel 0181-995 6035 *fax* 0181-747 8256
Contact Artistic Director

Produces a number of shows each year from contemporary world theatre.

Theatre Royal, Stratford East
Gerry Raffles Square, London E15 1BN
tel 0181-534 7374 *fax* 0181-534 8381
Assistant Director Mr Kerry Michael

The Tricycle Theatre Company
Tricycle Theatre, 269 Kilburn High Road, London NW6 7JR
tel 0171-372 6611 *fax* 0171-328 0795
Contact Nicolas Kent

Metropolitan new writing theatre company.

Triumph Proscenium Productions Ltd
Suite 4, Waldorf Chambers, 11 Aldwych, London WC2B 4DA
tel 0171-836 0186 *fax* 0171-240 7511

Unicorn Theatre for Children
Arts Theatre, 6-7 Great Newport Street, London WC2H 7JB
tel 0171-379 3280 *fax* 0171-836 5366
Administrative Director Christopher Moxon, *Artistic Director* Tony Graham

Six productions a year, in repertoire, for children aged 4-12 – new writing and adaptations.

Warehouse Theatre
Dingwall Road, Croydon CR0 2NF
tel 0181-681 1257 *fax* 0181-688 6699
Artistic Director Ted Craig

New playwriting theatre producing up to 6 in-house productions each year.

Submit new scripts via the International Playwriting Festival (see page 524).

Michael White
48 Dean Street, London W1V 5HL
tel 0171-734 7707 *fax* 0171-734 7727

No unsolicited scripts.

Provincial

Abbey Theatre
Lower Abbey Street, Dublin 1, Republic of Ireland
tel (01) 8748741 *fax* (01) 8729177
Artistic Director Patrick Mason, *General Manager* Martin Fahy

Mainly produces plays written by Irish authors or on Irish subjects. Foreign plays are however regularly produced.

Yvonne Arnaud Theatre Management Ltd
Millbrook, Guildford, Surrey GU1 3UX
tel (01483) 440077 *fax* (01483) 564071

Receives and produces Number One touring and pre-West End product.

Belgrade Theatre
Belgrade Square, Coventry CV1 1GS
tel (01203) 256431 *fax* (01203) 550680
Contact Julie Evans

Produces new plays both in the main house and studio.

Birmingham Repertory Theatre Ltd
Broad Street, Birmingham B1 2EP
tel 0121-236 6771 *fax* 0121-236 7883
Artistic Director Bill Alexander, *Literary Manager* Ben Payne

Aims to provide a platform for the best work from new writers from both within and beyond the West Midlands region. The development, commissioning and production of new writing takes place across the full range of the theatre's programme including: the Main House (capacity 900); the Studio, a space dedicated to new work; and its biannual Community tours. Unsolicited submissions are welcome largely from the point of view of beginning a relationship with a writer. Priority in such development work is given to writers from the region.

Bristol Old Vic Company
Theatre Royal, King Street, Bristol BS1 4ED
tel (0117) 949 3993 *fax* (0117) 949 3996
Director's Office Hilary Davis, *Artistic Director* Andy Hay

Programme includes classical and new plays. New writing encouraged. New scripts read by experienced reader for a fee, currently £10.

The Byre Theatre of St Andrews Ltd
Abbey Street, St Andrews KY16 9LA
tel (01334) 476288 *fax* (01334) 475370
Artistic Director Ken Alexander

Currently involved in a major rebuilding programme. On reopening (scheduled for the end of 1998), the theatre will continue to operate a blend of in-house productions and touring productions. The Byre Theatre Company meanwhile maintains a policy of producing a wide variety of new and established work, theatre-in-education projects, youth theatre and community work in Fife. The company also offers support for new writing through the Byre Writers, a well-established and successful playwrights group.

Chester Gateway Theatre Trust Ltd
Hamilton Place, Chester CH1 2BH
tel (01244) 344238 *fax* (01244) 317277
Administrative Director Katy Spicer

Chichester Festival Theatre Productions Company Ltd
Chichester Festival Theatre, Oaklands Park, Chichester, West Sussex PO19 4AP
tel (01243) 784437 *fax* (01243) 787288
e-mail admin@cftplay.demon.co.uk
Director Duncan C. Weldon, *General Manager* Paul Rogerson, *Administrator* David Bownes

Festival season Apr-Oct in Festival Theatre and Minerva Theatre; rest of year seasons of touring plays, opera, ballet, dance, jazz, orchestral concerts and Minerva Movies.

Churchill Theatre
High Street, Bromley, Kent BR1 1HA
tel 0181-464 7131 *fax* 0181-290 6968
Contact General Manager

Full-length plays; comedies, thrillers, dramas, new plays considered.

Theatr Clwyd
Mold, Flintshire CH7 1YA
tel (01352) 756331 *fax* (01352) 758323
e-mail drama@celtic.co.uk

Colchester Mercury Theatre Ltd
Balkerne Gate, Colchester, Essex CO1 1PT
tel (01206) 577006 *fax* (01206) 769607
Artistic Director and Chief Executive Pat Trueman

The Coliseum Theatre
Fairbottom Street, Oldham OL1 3SW
tel 0161-624 1731 *fax* 0161-624 5318
Chief Executive Kenneth Alan Taylor

Special interest in northern plays. Contact by letter initially.

Contact Theatre Company
Oxford Road, Manchester M15 6JA
tel 0161-274 3434 *fax* 0161-273 6286
Artistic Director Benjamin Twist

Interested in exciting, theatrical plays for a younger (under 25) audience.

Derby Playhouse Ltd
Theatre Walk, Eagle Centre, Derby DE1 2NF
tel (01332) 363271 *fax* (01332) 294412

Druid Theatre Company
Druid Lane Theatre, Chapel Lane, Galway, Republic of Ireland
tel (091) 568617/568660 *fax* (091) 563109
e-mail druid@iol.ie
General Manager Louise Donlon, *Artistic Director* Garry Hynes

The Duke's Playhouse
Moor Lane, Lancaster LA1 1QE
tel (01524) 67461 *fax* (01524) 846817
Artistic Director Ewan Marshall

Dundee Repertory Theatre
Tay Square, Dundee DD1 1PB
tel (01382) 227684
Artistic Director Hamish Glen

Everyman Theatre
5-9 Hope Street, Liverpool L1 9BH
tel 0151-708 0338 *fax* 0151-709 0398
Executive Producer Kevin Fearon, *General Manager* Sharon Duckworth

Regional repertory theatre company.

Everyman Theatre
Regent Street, Cheltenham, Glos. GL50 1HQ
tel (01242) 512515 *fax* (01242) 224305
Chief Executive Richard Hogger

Grand Theatre
Singleton Street, Swansea SA1 3QJ
tel (01792) 475242 *fax* (01792) 475379
General Manager Gary Iles

Regional receiving theatre.

Haymarket Theatre Company
The Haymarket Theatre, Wote Street, Basingstoke, Hants RG21 7NW
tel (01256) 355844 *fax* (01256) 357130
Theatre Director Adrian Reynolds

Mounts seasons of plays, many of which are designed for co-production with London managements.

Leicester Haymarket Theatre
Belgrave Gate, Leicester LE1 3YQ
tel (0116) 253 0021 *fax* (0116) 251 3310
web site http://ourworld.compuserve.com/
homepages/htl

Library Theatre Company
St Peter's Square, Manchester M2 5PD
tel (0161) 234 1913 *fax* (0161) 228 6481
Contact Artistic Director

Contemporary drama, classics, plays for
children. Aims to produce drama which
illuminates the contemporary world;
scripts from new writers considered.

Liverpool Repertory Theatre Ltd
Liverpool Playhouse, Williamson Square,
Liverpool L1 1EL
tel 0151-709 8478 *fax* 0151-709 7113
Theatre Manager Caroline Parry

New Victoria Theatre
Etruria Road, Newcastle under Lyme ST5 0JG
tel (01782) 717954 *fax* (01782) 712885
Theatre Director Peter Cheeseman

Europe's first purpose built theatre in the
round, presenting major classics, adaptations, contemporary plays, documentaries. New plays limited.

New Victoria Theatre
Peacocks Arts & Entertainment Centre, Woking,
Surrey GU21 1GQ
tel (01483) 747422 *fax* (01483) 740477
Contact Robert Cogo-Fawcett, Beaufort Cottage,
Grosvenor, Bath BA1 6PZ
tel (01225) 311248

Large-scale touring house. Interested to
co-produce or produce.

Northampton Repertory Players Ltd
The Royal Theatre, Guildhall Road,
Northampton NN1 1EA
tel (01604) 38343 *fax* (01604) 602408

Presents plays for main house, studio,
theatre-in-education, community touring
and youth theatre. Please send scripts,
indicating which area of work they are
for, to Michael Napier Brown, Artistic
Director.

Northcott Theatre
Stocker Road, Exeter, Devon EX4 4QB
tel (01392) 256182
Artistic Director John Durnin

Northern Stage Company
Newcastle Playhouse, Barras Bridge,
Newcastle upon Tyne NE1 1RH
tel 0191-232 3366 *fax* 0191-261 8093
Artistic Director Alan Lyddiard

Nottingham Playhouse
Nottingham Theatre Trust Ltd, Wellington Circus,
Nottingham NG1 5AF
tel (0115) 947 4361 *fax* (0115) 947 5759
Artistic Director Martin Duncan

Works closely with communities of Nottingham and Nottinghamshire; presents
best of innovative and world theatre.
Takes 6 months to read unsolicited MSS.

Nuffield Theatre
University Road, Southampton SO17 1TR
tel (01703) 315500 *fax* (01703) 315511
Script Executive Penny Gold

Octagon Theatre
Howell Croft South, Bolton BL1 1SB
tel (01204) 529407 *fax* (01204) 380110
Administrative Director Amanda Belcham,
Artistic Director Lawrence Till

Repertory season Sept-June, including
new plays and contemporary theatre.

Oxford Stage Company
15-19 George Street, Oxford OX1 2AU
tel (01865) 245781 *fax* (01865) 790025
Contact Marketing Manager

Palace Theatre
Clarendon Road, Watford, Herts. WD1 1JZ
tel (01923) 235455 *fax* (01923) 819664
Contact Giles Croft

Palace Theatre Trust Ltd
London Road, Westcliff-on-Sea, Essex SS0 9LA
tel (01702) 347816 *fax* (01702) 435031
Theatre Secretary Iris Stewart

Subsidised repertory theatre producing a
programme of predominantly modern
British drama with some foreign writers,
particularly American. Most new work is
done in small, 100-seater studio.

Peacock Theatre
The Abbey Theatre, Lower Abbey Street,
Dublin 1, Republic of Ireland
tel (01) 8748741 *fax* (01) 8729177
Artistic Director Patrick Mason, *General Manager*
Martin Fahy

Experimental theatre associated with the
Abbey Theatre; presents mostly new
writing as well as exploring the entire
canon of world drama.

Perth Theatre Ltd
185 High Street, Perth PH1 5UW
tel (01738) 472700 *fax* (01738) 624576
e-mail theatre@perth.org.uk
web site www.perth.org.uk/perth/theatre.htm
Artistic Director Michael Winter, *General
Manager* Paul McLennan

Three-weekly repertory programme Aug-May of plays, musicals, revivals and new writing; also studio and theatre-in-education work.

Plymouth Theatre Royal
Theatre Royal, Royal Parade, Plymouth, Devon PL1 2TR
tel (01752) 668282 *fax* (01752) 671179
Chief Executive Adrian Vinken, *Producer* Grahame Morris

Queen's Theatre Hornchurch
(Havering Theatre Trust Ltd)
Billet Lane, Hornchurch, Essex RM11 1QT
tel (01708) 456118 *fax* (01708) 452348
Contact Tony Hill

Medium scale regional repertory company producing popular comedy, drama and musicals. Scripts from new writers welcome especially as co-productions with commercial producer or additional funding.

Royal Exchange Theatre Company Ltd
St Ann's Square, Manchester M2 7DH
tel 0161-833 9333 *fax* 0161-832 0881
General Manager Patricia Weller

Provides a varied programme of major classics, new plays, musicals, contemporary British and European drama; also explores the creative work of diverse cultures.

Royal Lyceum Theatre Company Ltd
Royal Lyceum Theatre, Grindlay Street, Edinburgh EH3 9AX
tel 0131-229 7404 *fax* 0131-228 3955
e-mail lyceum@infoser.com
web sites http://www.infoser.com/infotheatre/lyceum
http://www.infoser.com/infotheatre/vtour
Artistic Director Kenny Ireland, *Associate Literary Director* Tom McGrath

Salisbury Playhouse
Malthouse Lane, Salisbury, Wilts. SP2 7RA
tel (01722) 320117 *fax* (01722) 421991
Artistic Director Jonathan Church

Regional repertory theatre producing a broad programme of classical and modern plays.

Scarborough Theatre Trust Ltd
Stephen Joseph Theatre, Westborough, Scarborough, North Yorkshire YO11 1JW
tel (01723) 370540 *fax* (01723) 360506
Literary Manager Connal Orton

Sheffield Theatres
(Crucible, Crucible Studio & Lyceum),
55 Norfolk Street, Sheffield S1 1DA
tel 0114-2760621 *fax* 0114-2701532
Artistic Director Deborah Paige

Large-scale producing house with distinctive thrust stage; smallish studio; Victorian proscenium arch theatre used mainly for touring productions.

Sherman Theatre
Senghennydd Road, Cardiff CF2 4YE
tel (01222) 396844 *fax* (01222) 665581
General Manager Margaret Jones

Plays mainly for 15-25 age range. Founded 1974.

Show of Strength Theatre Company Ltd
Hebron House, Sion Road, Bedminster, Bristol BS3 3BD
tel 0117-987 9444 ext. 239 *fax* 0117-963 1770
Administrator Sheila Hannon

Small-scale company committed to producing new and unperformed work. Theatre season: Oct-Jan. Send sae for return of MSS. Founded 1986.

Swan Theatre
The Moors, Worcester WR1 3EF
tel (01905) 726969 *fax* (01905) 723738
Artistic Director Jenny Stephens

Theatre Royal
Windsor, Berks. SL4 1PS
tel (01753) 863444 *fax* (01753) 831673
Executive Producer Bill Kenwright, *Executive Director* Mark Piper

Thorndike Theatre
Church Street, Leatherhead, Surrey KT22 8DF
tel (01372) 376211 *fax* (01372) 362595
Contact Theatre Manager

Traverse Theatre
10 Cambridge Street, Edinburgh EH1 2ED
tel 0131-228 3223 *fax* 0131-229 8443
Literary Director John Tiffany, *Literary Associate* Ella Wildridge

Scotland's new writing theatre.

Watermill Theatre Ltd
Bagnor, Newbury, Berks. RG20 8AE
tel (01635) 45834
Contact Jill Fraser

Small professional theatre. Interested in all types of new work, including drama and musicals, suitable for small stage and auditorium.

The West Yorkshire Playhouse
Playhouse Square, Quarry Hill,
Leeds LS2 7UP
tel (0113) 244 2141 *fax* (0113) 244 8252
Artistic Director Jude Kelly, *Literary Co-ordinator*
Alfred Hickling
Twin auditoria complex – with a policy of encouraging new writing; community theatre; Young People's Theatre programme.

The Wolsey Theatre
Civic Drive, Ipswich, Suffolk IP1 2AS
tel (01473) 218911 *fax* (01473) 212946
Administrative Director Lorna Anderson, *Artistic Director* Antony Tuckey

York Citizens' Theatre Trust Ltd
Theatre Royal, St Leonard's Place,
York YO1 2HD
tel (01904) 658162 *fax* (01904) 611534
Executive Director Elizabeth Jones, *Artistic Director* John Doyle
Repertory productions, tours.

Touring companies

Actors Touring Company
Alford House, Aveline Street, London SE11 5DQ
tel 0171-735 8311 *fax* 0171-735 1031
Executive Producer Hetty Shand
Small to medium-scale company producing new theatre from old stories, myths and legends.

Black Theatre Co-Operative Ltd
Unit 3P, Leroy House, 436 Essex Road,
London N1 3QP
tel 0171-226 1225 *fax* 0171-226 0223
Artistic Director Felix Cross, *Marketing Officer* Gillian Christie
Interested in Black plays, especially those that relate to the experiences of Black people both in Britain and outside Britain.

Bristol Express Theatre Company
Flat 1, Stepney Green Court,
London E1 3LJ
tel 0171-423 9453
Artistic Director Andy Jordan
Most productions are new plays; scripts from new writers considered.

Compass Theatre Company
Carver Street Institute, 24 Rockingham Lane,
Sheffield S1 4FW
tel (0114) 275 5328 *fax* (0114) 278 6931
General Manager William Jones

Gay Sweatshop
The Holborn Centre, Three Cups Yard,
Sandland Street, London WC1R 4PZ
tel 0171-242 1168 *fax* 0171-242 3143
e-mail 100255.2725@compuserve.com
Artistic Director Lois Weaver
Interested in developing (often commissioning) scripts into full production of new plays by lesbian and gay writers.

Graeae Theatre Company
Interchange Studios, Dalby Street,
London NW5 3NQ
tel 0171 267 1959 *fax* 0171-267 2703
Contact Kevin Dunn
Small-scale company. Welcomes scripts from new writers. Founded 1980.

The Hiss & Boo Company
24 West Grove, Walton-on-Thames,
Surrey KT12 5NX
tel (01932) 248931 *fax* (01932) 248946
e-mail 100547.1656 @compuserve.com
Not much scope for new plays, but will consider comedy thrillers/chillers and plays/musicals for children. Send synopsis first. Plays/synopses will be returned only if accompanied by an sae.

Hull Truck Theatre Co. Ltd
Hull Truck Theatre, Spring Street, Hull HU2 8RW
tel (01482) 224800 *fax* (01482) 581182
General Manager Simon Stallworthy

Live Theatre
8 Trinity Chare, Quayside,
Newcastle upon Tyne NE1 3DF
tel 0191-261 2694 *fax* 0191-232 2224
Artistic Director Max Roberts
Interested in new plays which relate to the present and/or history, culture and concerns of the region and which are accessible to a wide audience.

The London Bubble
(Bubble Theatre Company)
3-5 Elephant Lane, London SE16 4JD
tel 0171-237 4434 *fax* 0171-231 2366
e-mail londonbubble@gn.apc.org

M6 Theatre Company
Hamer C.P. School, Albert Royds Street,
Rochdale, Lancs. OL16 2SU
tel (01706) 355898 *fax* (01706) 711700
Contact Jane Milne
Theatre-in-education company providing high quality, educational, innovative and relevant live theatre for children and for audiences who may not normally have access to theatre.

Made in Wales

Chapter, Market Road, Canton, Cardiff CF5 1QE
tel (01222) 484017 *fax* (01222) 484016
Artistic Director Jeff Teare

Three productions per year of new plays relevant to Wales; scripts from new writers always welcome.

New Perspectives Company

The Old Library, Leeming Street, Mansfield,
Notts. NG18 1NG
tel (01623) 635225 *fax* (01623) 635240
e-mail art@nperspex.demon.co.uk
Artistic Director Gavin Stride

Has a policy of employing writers for new work. Regret unsolicited scripts returned, unless writers are local to the East Midlands region.

NTC Touring Theatre Company

The Playhouse, Bondgate Without, Alnwick,
Northumberland NE66 1PQ
tel (01665) 602586 *fax* (01665) 605837
Artistic Director Gillian Hambleton

Performs a wide cross-section of work: new plays, extant scripts, classics and theatre for young people. Particularly interested in non-naturalism, physical theatre and plays with direct relevance to rural audiences. Formerly Northumberland Theatre Company.

Orchard Theatre Company

108 Newport Road, Barnstaple,
North Devon EX32 9BA
tel (01271) 71475 *fax* (01271) 71825
Administrator Frederica Notley

Paines Plough

4th Floor, 43 Aldwych, London WC2B 4DA
tel 0171-240 4533 *fax* 0171-240 4534
Artistic Director Vicky Featherstone, *Literary Director* Mark Ravenhill

Tours new plays by British writers to a national audience and is increasingly developing an international profile. The company believes that the playwright's voice should be at the centre of contemporary theatre and works with new and experienced writers. A programme of workshops and readings develops new work and approx. 4 playwrights a year are commissioned by the company. A new programme seeks to develop the company's relationship with writers outside London. For script-reading service send 2 saes, one for acknowledgement, and one for return of script with reader's report.

Proteus Theatre Company

Fairfields Arts Centre, Council Road, Basingstoke,
Hants RG21 3DH
tel (01256) 354541
Administrative Director Katherine Ives, *Artistic Director* Chris Baldwin, *Associate Director (Community and Education)* Amanda Wilde

Small-scale touring company committed to new writing and new work, education and internationalism. Presents 2-3 touring plays per year plus 2-3 main projects, all of which may include new commissions. Founded 1981.

Quicksilver Theatre

4 Enfield Road, London N1 5AZ
tel 0171-241 2942 *fax* 0171-254 3119
Artistic Director Guy Holland

A professional touring theatre company which brings live theatre to schools all over the country. Delivers good stories, original music, kaleidoscopic design and humorous, poignant writing to entertain and make children think. Three new plays a year for 3-5 year-olds, 7-11 year-olds and 6+ years and families. Founded 1978.

Red Ladder Theatre Co.

Cobden Avenue, Lower Wortley,
Leeds LS12 5PB
tel (0113) 279 2228 *fax* (0113) 231 0660
e-mail red-ladder@geo2.poptel.org.uk
Artistic Director Kully Thiarai

Theatre performances for young people (14-25) in youth clubs and small-scale theatre venues. Commissions at least two new plays each year. Training/residentials for youth workers/young people.

Red Shift Theatre Company

9 The Leathermarket, Weston Street,
London SE1 3ER
tel 0171-378 9787 *fax* 0171-378 9789
Artistic Director Jonathan Holloway

Solent Peoples Theatre

The Heathfield Centre, Valentine Avenue,
Sholing, Southampton SO19 0EQ
tel (01703) 443943 *fax* (01703) 440752
Administrative Director Caroline Routh

The Sphinx Theatre Co. Ltd

25 Short Street, London SE1 8LJ
tel 0171-401 9993/4 *fax* 0171-401 9995
Artistic Director Sue Parrish

Women writers only.

Stage One Theatre Company

34 Jasmine Grove, London SE20 8JW
tel 0181-778 5213 *fax* 0181-778 1756
Scripts address Buddy Dalton,
c/o 11 Cannon Place, London NW3 1EH

Scripts from new writers considered.

Talawa Theatre Company

3rd Floor, 23-25 Great Sutton Street,
London EC1V 0DN
tel 0171-251 6644 *fax* 0171-251 5969
Contact Oscar Watson

Scripts from new writers considered.
Particularly interested in scripts from
black writers and plays portraying a
black experience.

Theatre Centre

Toynbee Workshops, 3 Gunthorpe Street,
London E1 7RQ
tel 0171-377 0379 *fax* 0171-377 1376
Contact Jackie Alexis

National touring theatre for young people
– schools, art centres, venues.

Theatre Workshop Company

34 Hamilton Place, Edinburgh EH3 5AX
tel (0131) 225 7942 *fax* (0131) 220 0112
Contact Robert Rae

Plays include new writing/community/
children's/disabled. Scripts from new
writers considered.

Publishers of plays

Playwrights are reminded that it is unusual for a publisher of trade editions of plays to publish plays which have not had at least reasonably successful, usually professional, productions on stage first. See listings beginning on page 153 for addresses.

Cló Iar-Chonnachta Teo
Dublar Scripts
Faber & Faber Ltd
Samuel French Ltd

Nick Hern Books Ltd
Kenyon-Deane
Methuen, Random House
J. Garnet Miller Ltd

New Playwrights' Network
The Playwrights Publishing
Company
Warner/Chappell Plays Ltd

Literary agents

The role of the literary agent

The primary task of a literary agent is to look after a writer's commercial interests and to exploit fully the rights in the material he or she handles. This can mean anything from placing work with a British publisher to the sale of US, translation, dramatic, film, television, audio, electronic or other rights.

Agents can supply editorial guidance, advise on career strategy, and – in the increasingly fluid and unpredictable world of modern publishing – provide the author with a degree of continuity.

What agents cannot be expected to do is comment at length on unsuitable work or sell the unsaleable. Nor can they guarantee that the writer's life is without disappointments.

Approaching an agent

Try to define your needs and choose an agent who seems most likely to meet them. Work from an up-to-date edition of this *Yearbook* and either ring (but check the entry first as some smaller agencies prefer initial contact by letter) or write a preliminary letter to the agent(s) of your choice to ascertain whether the agent is taking on new clients. Describe as succinctly as possible the nature of your work, your future plans, and give any biographical information that might be relevant to your writing.

Enquire about the agent's terms. Some of this information will be given in the listings that follow, but make sure you understand how the agency operates. Does it use associates for the sale of subsidiary rights, and how does this affect commission? Does it have a letter of agreement for its clients which details its terms of business?

When submitting your work, make sure the manuscript is well presented (see *Preparing and submitting a manuscript*, page 527) and enclose return postage. Bear in mind that it is not good practice to send work to more than one agent at the same time.

Code of practice

The Association of Authors' Agents (see page 441) is the trade association of British agents. Members, designated with an asterisk in the following list, meet regularly and are committed to a code of practice. They do not charge authors a reading fee. Agents that do charge a reading fee usually refund the fee (which covers a report on the manuscript) on acceptance of the material by a publisher. This fee is not to be confused with commission, which is the agreed percentage charged by the agent to the author and deducted by the agent from publishers' advances, royalties earned and any other monies paid to the author.

The listings

All the agents listed on the following pages have been sent a *Writers' & Artists' Yearbook* questionnaire designed to provide pertinent information. Each one is asked regularly to update this information. The list is not exhaustive. If any literary agents who are not included would like to receive a copy of the questionnaire and to be considered for inclusion, please contact the publishers.

Literary agents UK and Ireland

*Full member of the Association of Authors' Agents

A & B Personal Management Ltd
5th Floor, Plaza Suite, 114 Jermyn Street,
London SW1Y 6HJ
tel 0171-839 4433 *fax* 0171-930 5738
Directors K.W. Ellis, R. Ellis

Full-length MSS. Scripts for TV, theatre, cinema; also novels, fiction and non-fiction (home 12.5%, overseas 15%), performance rights (12.5%). Synopsis required initially from writers submitting work for first time. No reading fee for synopsis, plays or screenplays, but fee charged for full-length MSS. Return postage required. Founded 1982.

The Agency (London) Ltd*
(incorporating Lemon Unna & Durbridge Ltd)
24 Pottery Lane, London W11 4LZ
tol 0171-727 1346 *fax* 0171-727 9037
Directors Stephen Durbridge, Leah Schmidt, Sebastian Born, Julia Kreitman, Girsha Reid, Bethan Evans, Wendy Gresser, Hilary Delamere

Represents writers for theatre, film, TV, radio and children's writers and illustrators. Also film and TV rights in novels and non-fiction. Adult novels represented only for existing clients. Commission: 10% unless sub-agents employed overseas; works in conjunction with agents in USA and overseas. No unsolicited MSS. Preliminary letter including publishing/production history and sae essential. Founded 1995.

Aitken & Stone Ltd*
(and Hughes Massie Ltd)
29 Fernshaw Road, London SW10 0TG
tel 0171-351 7561 *fax* 0171-376 3594
e-mail 100303.1765@compuserve.com
Directors Gillon Aitken, Brian Stone, Sally Riley, Antony Harwood

Full-length MSS (home 10%, USA 15%, translations 20%). Preliminary letter and return postage essential.

Authors include Pat Barker, Agatha

Christie Estate, Sebastian Faulks, Germaine Greer, Alan Hollinghurst, Susan Howatch, A.L. Kennedy, V.S. Naipaul, Caryl Phillips, Paul Theroux.

Jacintha Alexander Associates – see Lucas Alexander Whitley*

Darley Anderson Literary, TV and Film Agency*
Estelle House, 11 Eustace Road, London SW6 1JB
tel 0171-385 6652 *fax* 0171-386 5571
Proprietor Darley Anderson, *Associates* Gabi Chase (film/TV), Elizabeth Wright (crime/contemporary women's fiction), Kerith Biggs (foreign rights)

Full-length MSS. Popular, commercial fiction and non-fiction (home 15%, US/translation 20%, film/TV/radio 20%). Special fiction interests: all types of thrillers and crime (cosy/hard boiled/historical); women's fiction including contemporary, 20th century romantic sagas, love stories, erotica and women in jeopardy; thrillers, horror; comedy (TV and books); and Irish novels.

Special non-fiction interests: investigative books, TV tie-ins, celebrity autobiographies, true life women in jeopardy, diet, beauty, health, cookery, popular psychology, self-improvement, inspirational, popular religion and supernatural. No poetry, plays or academic books. Can arrange PR and author publicity and specialist financial advice; editorial guidance on selected MSS. Preliminary letter, synopsis and first 3 chapters. Return postage/sae must accompany submission. No reading fee. Overseas associates: Renaissance-Swanson Film Agency (LA/Hollywood) and leading foreign agents worldwide.

Authors include Tessa Barclay, Paul Carson, Lee Child, Martina Cole, Joseph

Corvo, Debbie Frank, Martica Heaner, Beryl Kingston, Frank Lean, Deborah McKinlay, Lesley Pearse, Allan Pease, Adrian Plass, Ben Richards, Fred Secombe, Jane Walmsley.

Artellus Ltd
30 Dorset House, Gloucester Place, London NW1 5AD
tel 0171-935 6972 *fax* 0171-487 5957
Director Leslie Gardner, *Chairman* Gabriele Pantucci
Full-length and short MSS; scripts for films (home 10%, overseas 12.5-20%). Crime, science fiction, historical, contemporary and literary fiction; non-fiction: science, art history, current affairs, biography, general history. Works directly in USA and with agencies in Europe, Japan and Russia. Will suggest revision. No reading fee. Founded 1986.

Associated Publicity Holdings Ltd
5-7 Young Street, London W8 5EH
tel 0171-937 5277 *fax* 0171-937 2833
Managing Director Jonathan G. Harris
Full-length and short MSS. Fiction and non-fiction, particularly sport, history, archaeology, biographies, thrillers and crime novels (home 10%, overseas 20%), performance, film and TV rights (15%). Send outline, 2 sample chapters and sae. Will suggest revision. Works with foreign agencies. No reading fee. Founded 1987.

Yvonne Baker Associates
8 Temple Fortune Lane, London NW11 7UD
tel 0181-455 8687 *fax* 0181-458 3143
Television, film, theatre, radio (10%). Particularly interested in contemporary drama and TV comedy drama series. No books, short stories, articles, poetry. No reading fee but preliminary letter essential with full information and sae. Founded 1987.

Blake Friedmann Literary, TV & Film Agency Ltd*
37-41 Gower Street, London WC1E 6HH
tel 0171-631 4331 *fax* 0171-323 1274
Directors Carole Blake, Julian Friedmann, Barbara Jones, Conrad Williams
Full-length MSS. Fiction: thrillers, women's novels and literary fiction; non-fiction: investigative books, biography, travel; no poetry or plays (home 15%, overseas 20%). Specialises in film and

TV rights; place journalism and short stories for existing clients only. Represented worldwide in 26 markets. Preliminary letter, synopsis and first 2 chapters preferred. No reading fee.

Authors include Gilbert Adair, Ted Allbeury, Jane Asher, Teresa Crane, Barbara Erskine, Maeve Haran, John Harvey, Ken Hom, Glenn Meade, Lawrence Norfolk, Joseph O'Connor, Michael Ridpath, Tim Sebastian, Robyn Sisman. Founded 1977.

David Bolt Associates
12 Heath Drive, Send, Surrey GU23 7EP
tel/fax (01483) 721118
Specialises in biography, fiction, theology. Full-length MSS (home 10%, overseas 19%; all other rights including film, video and TV 10%). No unsolicited short stories or play scripts. Will sometimes suggest revision. Works in association with overseas agencies worldwide. Preliminary letter essential. Reading fee terms on application.

Authors include Chinua Achebe, David Bret, Arthur Jacobs, Nicci Mackay, James Purdy, Joseph Rhymer, Colin Wilson.

BookBlast Ltd
21 Chesterton Road, London W10 5LY
tel 0181-968 3089 *fax* 0181-932 4087
Director G. de Chamberet
Full-length MSS (home 10%, overseas 20%). Fiction and non-fiction; traditional and underground literature. Also authors from the African diaspora, Asia, Europe. No unsolicited material. Preliminary letter, biographical information and sae essential. No reading fee. Will suggest revisions. Founded 1997.

Alan Brodie Representation Ltd
(incorporating Michael Imison Playwrights)
211 Piccadilly, London W1V 9LD
tel 0171-917 2871 *fax* 0171-917 2872
e-mail alanbrodie@aol.com
Directors Alan Brodie, Caroline Brodie, Sarah McNair
Consultant Michael Imison
Specialises in stage plays, radio, TV, film, stage/film directors (home 10%, overseas 15%); no fiction or general MSS. Represented in all major countries. No unsolicited scripts; recommendation from known professional required.

Rosemary Bromley Literary Agency

Avington, Winchester, Hants SO21 1DB
tel/fax (01962) 779656

Specialises in biography, travel, leisure, cookery, health (home 10%, overseas from 15%.) No poetry. No reading fee. No unsolicited MSS; enquiries unaccompanied by return postage will not be answered. For children's books see **Juvenilia**.

Felicity Bryan*

2A North Parade, Banbury Road, Oxford OX2 6PE
tel (01865) 513816 *fax* (01865) 310055

Fiction and general non-fiction; no light romance, science fiction, short stories, plays or children's (home 10%, overseas 20%). Translation rights handled by Andrew Nurnberg Associates; works in conjunction with US agents. Return postage essential.

Peter Bryant (Writers)

94 Adelaide Avenue, London SE4 1YR
tel 0181-691 9085 *fax* 0181-692 9107

Special interests: animation, children's fiction and TV comedy; also handles drama scripts for theatre, radio and TV (home/USA 10%). Overseas associate: Hartmann and Stauffacher, Germany. No reading fee for the above categories, but sae essential for all submissions.

Authors include Isabelle Amyes, Roy Apps, Joe Boyle, Andrew Brenner, Lucy Daniel, Jimmy Hibbert, Jan Page, Ruth Silvestre, Peter Symonds, George Tarry. Founded 1980.

Bycornute Books

76A Ashford Road, Eastbourne, East Sussex BN21 3TE
tel (01323) 726819 *fax* (01323) 649053
Director Asia Haleem

Specialises in illustrated books on sacred art, comparative religion, mythology, cosmology, astrology, iconography, symbolism, metaphysics, art history and popular archaeology/ancient history (not fiction, poetry, children's, psychic studies or psychology) (home 10%, overseas 15%). No unsolicited MSS.

Authors include Gordon Strachan, Asia Shepsut, Peter Clough, Robertson of Strathloch, Anne Macaulay, George Hart.

Campbell Thomson & McLaughlin Ltd*

1 King's Mews, London WC1N 2JA
tel 0171-242 0958 *fax* 0171-242 2408
Directors John McLaughlin, Charlotte Bruton, Hal Cheetham

Full-length book MSS (home 10%, overseas up to 20% including commission to foreign agent). No poetry, plays or TV scripts, short stories or children's books. USA agents represented: Raines & Raines, The Fox Chase Agency, Inc. Representatives in most European countries. Preliminary letter with synopsis and sae first, please. No reading fee, but return postage required. Subsidiary company: Peter Janson-Smith Ltd.

Casarotto Ramsay Ltd

National House, 60-66 Wardour Street, London W1V 3HP
tel 0171-287 4450 *fax* 0171-287 9128
Directors Tom Erhardt, Jenne Casarotto

MSS – theatre, films, TV, sound broadcasting only (10%). Works in conjunction with agents in USA and in all foreign countries. Preliminary letter essential. No reading fee.

Authors include Alan Ayckbourn, Peter Barnes, Edward Bond, Caryl Churchill, Christopher Hampton, David Hare, Larry Kramer, Willy Russell, Martin Sherman, David Wood. Founded 1992; formerly Margaret Ramsay Ltd, 1953.

Celia Catchpole

56 Gilpin Avenue, London SW14 8QY
tel 0181-255 7200 *fax* 0181-878 0594

Specialises as agent for children's writers and illustrators (home 10% writers, 15% illustrators; overseas 20%). Phone before sending scripts or artwork. Founded 1996.

Chapman & Vincent

(formerly Media House)
The Mount, Sun Hill, Royston, Herts. SG8 9AT
tel (01763) 247474 *fax* (01763) 243033
Directors Jennifer Chapman, Gilly Vincent

Original non-fiction, quality fiction, works with film or TV potential (but no scripts). Home 15%; overseas 20%. No reading fee. Will help with a revision as appropriate. Most clients come from personal recommendation. For fiction, send synopsis and 2 sample chapters with sae. Associates in Stockholm and Zurich.

Authors include Leslie Geddes-Brown, Sara George, Rowley Leigh, Dorit Peleg. Founded 1995.

Mic Cheetham Literary Agency
138 Buckingham Palace Road, London SW1W 9SA
tel 0171-730 3027 *fax* 0171-259 9706
Director Mic Cheetham

General and literary fiction, science fiction, general non-fiction (home 10%, overseas 20%); film, TV and radio rights (10-15%); will suggest revision. Works with The Marsh Agency for foreign rights. No unsolicited MSS. Founded 1994.

Judith Chilcote*
8 Wentworth Mansions, Keats Grove, London NW3 2RL
tel 0171-794 3717 *fax* 0171-794 7431
e-mail judybks@aol.com

Commercial fiction, non-fiction – sports, self-help and health, autobiography and biography, cinema, current affairs, TV tie-ins (home 15%, overseas 20-25%). No short stories, science fiction, children's, poetry. Works in conjunction with overseas agents and New York affiliate. No reading fee but preliminary letter with 3 chapters only, CV and sae essential.

Authors include Jane Alexander, David Emery, Dr Patricia Macnair, Maureen Paton, Douglas Thompson. Founded 1990.

Teresa Chris Literary Agency
43 Musard Road, London W6 8NR
tel 0171-386 0633
Director Teresa Chris

All fiction, especially crime, women's commercial, general and literary fiction; all non-fiction, especially health, cooking, arts and crafts. No science fiction, horror, fantasy, short stories, poetry, academic books (home 10%, USA 15%, rest 20%). Own US office: Thompson & Chris Literary Agency. No reading fee. No unsolicited MSS. Send introductory letter describing work, sample chapter and sae. Founded 1988.

Christy & Moore Ltd – see Sheil Land Associates Ltd*

Serafina Clarke*
98 Tunis Road, London W12 7EY
tel 0181-749 6979 *fax* 0181-740 6862

Full-length MSS (home 15%, overseas 20%). Works in conjunction with agents overseas. No reading fee, but preliminary letter, 2 sample chapters and return postage essential. Founded 1980.

Mary Clemmey*
6 Dunollie Road, London NW5 2XP
tel/fax 0171-267 1290

High quality fiction and non-fiction with an international market (home 10%, overseas 20%), performance rights (15%). No children's books, science fiction or fantasy. Works in conjunction with US agent. No reading fee. Small exclusive agency, approach by letter (including sae) first. Founded 1992.

Jonathan Clowes Ltd*
10 Iron Bridge House, Bridge Approach, London NW1 8BD
tel 0171-722 7674 *fax* 0171-722 7677
Directors Jonathan Clowes, Ann Evans, Brie Burkeman

Full-length MSS fiction and non-fiction; no academic or text books (home/USA 15%, translation 19%). Television, film, theatre and radio. Works in association with agents in most foreign countries. Founded 1960.

Elspeth Cochrane Agency
11-13 Orlando Road, London SW4 0LE
tel 0171-622 0314, 0171-622 4279
fax 0171-622 5815
Contacts Elspeth Cochrane, Nicholas Turrell

Send synopsis with covering letter in first instance (home and overseas 12.5%), performance rights (12.5%). No reading fee.

Authors include Robert Tanitch, David Pinner, Royce Ryton. Founded 1960.

Rosica Colin Ltd
1 Clareville Grove Mews, London SW7 5AH
tel 0171-370 1080 *fax* 0171-244 6441
Directors Sylvie Marston, Joanna Marston

All full-length MSS (excluding sci-fi and poetry); also theatre, film and sound broadcasting (home 10%, overseas 10-20%). No reading fee, but may take 3-4 months to consider full MSS. Send synopsis only in first instance, with letter outlining writing credits and whether MS has been previously submitted, plus return postage.

Authors include Richard Aldington, Simone de Beauvoir (in UK), Samuel Beckett (publication rights), Steven Berkoff, Alan Brownjohn, Donald

Campbell, Nick Dear, J.T. Edson, Bernard Farrell, Rainer Werner Fassbinder (in UK), Jean Genet, Franz Xaver Kroetz, Heiner Müller (in UK), Graham Reid, Botho Strauss (in UK), Wim Wenders (in UK). Founded 1949.

Jane Conway-Gordon*

(in association with Andrew Mann Ltd)
1 Old Compton Street, London W1V 5PH
tel 0171-494 0148 *fax* 0171-287 9264
Full length MSS, performance rights (home 10%, overseas 20%). Represented in all foreign countries. No reading fee but preliminary letter and return postage essential. Founded 1982.

Coombs Moylett Literary Agency

222 Dalling Road, London W6 0ER
tel 0181-748 5599 *fax* 0181-563 0164
Partners Georgina Coombs and Lisa Moylett
Specialises in crime, thrillers, women's fiction and literary fiction (home 10%; overseas 15%). Will help with a revision as appropriate. Return postage essential.

Rupert Crew Ltd*

1A King's Mews, London WC1N 2JA
tel 0171-242 8586 *fax* 0171-831 7914
e-mail rupertcrew@compuserve.com
Directors Kathleen A. Crew, Doreen Montgomery, Caroline Montgomery
International representation, handling volume and subsidiary rights in fiction and non-fiction properties (home 10-15%, elsewhere 20%); no plays, poetry, journalism or short stories. No reading fee, but preliminary letter and sae essential. Also acts independently as publishers' consultants. Founded 1927 by F. Rupert Crew.

Cruickshank Cazenove Ltd

97 Old South Lambeth Road, London SW8 1XU
tel 0171-735 2933 *fax* 0171-820 1081
Director Harriet Cruickshank
Film, TV and theatre scripts only (home 10%, overseas varies). Works with agents abroad. No reading fee but preliminary letter essential with sae. Also agent for directors and designers. Founded 1983.

Curtis Brown*

Haymarket House, 28-29 Haymarket, London SW1Y 4SP
tel 0171-396 6600 *fax* 0171-396 0110
Chairman Paul Scherer, *Managing Director* Jonathan Lloyd, *Directors* Jane Bradish-Ellames, Mark Collingbourne (finance), Tim Curnow (Australia), Sue Freathy, Jonny Geller, Giles Gordon, Diana Mackay, Nick Marston, Anthea Morton-Saner, Peter Murphy, Peter Robinson, Vivienne Schuster, Michael Shaw, Elizabeth Stevens
Agents for the negotiation in all markets of novels, general non-fiction, children's books and associated rights (home 10%, overseas 20%). Preliminary letter required; no reading fee. MSS for films, theatre, TV and radio. Also agents for directors and designers. Return postage essential.

Judy Daish Associates Ltd

2 St Charles Place, London W10 6EG
tel 0181-964 8811 *fax* 0181-964 8966
Agents Judy Daish, Sara Stroud, Deborah Harwood
Theatre, film, TV, radio (rates by negotiation). No unsolicited MSS. Founded 1978.

The Caroline Davidson Literary Agency

5 Queen Anne's Gardens, London W4 1TU
tel 0181-995 5768 *fax* 0181-994 2770
Specialises in literary fiction and non-fiction of all kinds, including highly illustrated books, academic and reference works (12.5%); will suggest revision and edit if necessary. No reading fee, but preliminary letter with book proposal and/or sample text, CV and sae required.

Authors include Robert Baldock, Maggie Black, John Brackenbury, Elizabeth Bradley, Lynda Brown, Andrew Dalby, Emma Donoghue, Willi Elsener, Hazel Evans, David Grove, Anissa Helou, Paul Hillyard, Tom Jaine, Guy Johnson, Bernard Lavery, J.P. McEvoy, Simon Maginn, Huon Mallalieu, Rena Salaman, Roland Vernon, Florence and Kenneth Wood. Founded 1988.

Merric Davidson Literary Agency

12 Priors Heath, Goudhurst, Cranbrook, Kent TN17 2RE
tel/fax (01580) 212041
Specialising in contemporary adult fiction (home 10%, overseas 20%). No unsolicited MSS. Preliminary letter with synopsis, author information and sae, though very few new clients taken on. No initial reading fee, may suggest revision, subsequent editorial advice by arrangement.

Authors include Valerie Blumenthal,

Louise Doughty, Alison Habens, Elizabeth Harris, Alison MacLeod, Mark Pepper. Founded 1990.

Felix De Wolfe

Manfield House, 1 Southampton Street, London WC2R 0LR
tel 0171-379 5767 fax 0171-836 0337

Theatre, films, TV, sound broadcasting, fiction (home 10-12.5%, overseas 20%). Works in conjunction with many foreign agencies.

Dorian Literary Agency

Upper Thornehill, 27 Church Road, St Marychurch, Torquay, Devon TQ1 4QY
tel/fax (01803) 312095
Proprietor Mrs D. Lumley

Full-length MSS. Specialises in women's fiction, science fiction, fantasy and horror, crime, thrillers and mainstream (home 10%, USA 15%, translations 20-25%), performance rights (10%). No poetry, children's or short stories. Works in conjunction with agencies in most countries; negotiates direct with USA. No reading fee; preliminary letter with sample material essential; return postage essential.

Authors include Brian Lumley, Dee Williams, Amy Myers, Stephen Jones. Founded 1986.

Anne Drexl

8 Roland Gardens, London SW7 3PH
tel 0171-244 9645

Special interest in women's fiction, glitzy, family sagas, crime fiction and non-fiction. Also illustrated books for young readers, activity titles, and juvenile fiction (home 12.5%, overseas 20-25%). Works in conjunction with foreign agencies and negotiates direct with foreign publishers. No reading fee, but no unsolicited MSS; return postage and preliminary letter essential. Founded 1988.

Toby Eady Associates Ltd

3rd Floor, 9 Orme Court, London W2 4RL
tel 0171-792 0092 fax 0171-792 0879
e-mail 100571.2263@compuserve.com
Directors Toby Eady, Alexandra Pringle

Books on Africa, the Middle East, China, fiction, non-fiction (home 10%, overseas 20%), performance rights (10%). Works with overseas associates. No reading fee, but return postage essential.

Authors include Jung Chang, Bernard Cornwell, Julia Blackburn, Barbara Trapido, Esther Freud, Tim Pears. Founded 1968.

Eddison Pearson

44 Inverness Terrace, London W2 3JA
tel 0171-727 9113 fax 0171-727 9143
Partners Clare Pearson and Tom Eddison

Literary fiction, non-fiction and poetry; children's fiction and picture books; screenplays; theatre, TV and radio scripts (home 10%, overseas 15%). Unsolicited MSS welcome with sae; send sample chapters if a work is very long. No reading fee. Will suggest revision.

Authors include Michael Catchpool, Beverley Cato, Gordon Fleming, A.J. Khan.

Edwards Fuglewicz*

49 Great Ormond Street, London WC1N 3HZ
tel 0171-405 6725 fax 0171-405 6726
e-mail efla@ftech.co.uk
Partners Ros Edwards and Helenka Fuglewicz

Full-length MSS. Fiction: adult (literary and commercial). Non-fiction: quality general interest including music and film. Home 10%, overseas 20%. No reading fee but sae essential. Founded 1996.

Faith Evans Associates*

27 Park Avenue North, London N8 7RU
tel 0181-340 9920 fax 0181-340 9410

Small select agency (home 15%, overseas 20%). Sub-agents in most countries. No phone calls, scripts or unsolicited MSS.

Authors include Melissa Benn, Eleanor Bron, Saeed Jaffrey, Helena Kennedy, Seumas Milne, Christine Purkis, Sheila Rowbotham, Lorna Sage, Hwee Hwee Tan, Marion Urch, Andrea Weiss, Elizabeth Wilson. Founded 1987.

Fact & Fiction Agency Ltd

16 Greenway Close, London NW9 5AZ
tel 0181-205 5716
Directors Roy Lomax, Vera Lomax

Television and radio – comedy only (home 10%, overseas 15%). By introduction only.

John Farquharson Ltd* – see Curtis Brown*

Film Rights Ltd

483 Southbank House, Black Prince Road, Albert Embankment, London SE1 7SJ
tel 0171-735 8171
Directors Brendan Davis, Joan Potts

Theatre, films, TV and sound broadcasting (10%). Represented in USA and abroad. Founded 1932.

Laurence Fitch Ltd

(incorporating The London Play Company 1922)
483 Southbank House, Black Prince Road,
Albert Embankment, London SE1 7SJ
tel 0171-735 8171
Directors F.H.L. Fitch, Joan Potts, Brendan Davis

Theatre, films, TV and sound broadcasting. Also works with several agencies in New York and in Europe.

Authors include The Estate of the Late Dodie Smith, Ray Coony, John Chapman, Carlo Ardito, John Graham, Edward Taylor, Judy Allen, Dawn Lowe-Watson, Peter Coke, Glyn Robbins. Founded 1952.

Jill Foster Ltd

9 Barb Mews, Brook Green, London W6 7PA
tel 0171-602 1263 *fax* 0171-602 9336

Theatre, films, TV, sound broadcasting (12.5%). Particularly interested in film and TV comedy and drama. No novels or short stories. No reading fee. Preliminary letter essential. Founded 1978.

Fox & Howard Literary Agency

4 Bramerton Street, London SW3 5JX
tel 0171-352 8691 *fax* 0171-352 8691
Partners Chelsey Fox, Charlotte Howard

Full-length MSS. General non-fiction: biography, popular history, current affairs, reference, business, self-help, health and mind, body and spirit (home 10%, overseas 20%); will suggest revision where appropriate. No poetry, plays, short stories, children's, science fiction, fantasy or horror. No reading fee, but preliminary letter and synopsis with sae essential.

Authors include Sir Rhodes Boyson, Tony Clayton Lea, Betty Parsons, Jane Struthers. Founded 1992.

Fraser & Dunlop Ltd, Fraser & Dunlop Scripts Ltd – see The Peters Fraser & Dunlop Group Ltd*

French's

9 Elgin Mews South, London W9 1JZ
tel 0171-266 3321 *fax* 0171-286 6716
Director John French

All MSS; specialises in novels and screenplays (home/overseas 10%); the-

atre, films, TV, radio (10%). Reading service available, details on application. Sae must be enclosed with all MSS.

Vernon Futerman Associates*

159 Goldhurst Terrace,
London NW6 3EU
tel/fax 0171-625 9601
Submissions address 17 Deanhill Road,
London SW14 7DQ
Contacts Vernon Futerman (academic/politics/current affairs), Alexandra Groom (education/art), Guy Rose (fiction/show business/TV, film & theatre scripts)

Fiction and non-fiction, including academic, art/educational, politics, history, current affairs, show business; also scripts for film, TV and theatre. No short stories, science fiction, crafts or hobbies. No unsolicited MSS; send preliminary letter with detailed synopsis and sae. No reading fee. Literature (home 12.5-17.5%, overseas 17.5-22.5%); drama, screenplays (home 15-17.5%, overseas 20-22.5%), translations (20-22.5%). Overseas associates: USA, South Africa, France (Lora Fountain), Germany/ Scandinavia (Brigitte Axter).

Authors include Stephen Lowe, Valerie Grosvenor Myer, Sir Martin Ewans KCMG, Susan George, Ernie Wise, Judy Upton, Prof Wu Ningkun, Russell Warren Howe. Founded 1984.

Jüri Gabriel

35 Camberwell Grove, London SE5 8JA
tel/fax 0171-703 6186

Quality fiction and non-fiction (current specialisations: medical, military, practical art, popular academic); radio, TV and film. Full-length MSS (home 10%, overseas 20%), performance rights (10%); will suggest revision where appropriate. No short stories, articles, verse or books for children. No reading fee; return postage essential. Jüri Gabriel is the chairman of Dedalus (publishers) and was a writer/translator for 20 years.

Authors include Nigel Cawthorne, Diana Constance, Stephen Dunn, Pat Gray, James Hawes, Robert Irwin, 'David Madsen', 'Mark Lloyd', David Miller, Prof Cedric Mims, John Outram, Ewen Southby-Tailyour, Dr Terence White, Herbert Williams, John Wyatt, Dr Robert Youngson.

Eric Glass Ltd
28 Berkeley Square, London W1X 6HD
tel 0171-629 7162 *fax* 0171-499 6780
Director Janet Glass

Full-length MSS only; also theatre, films, TV, and sound broadcasting. No unsolicited MSS. No reading fee. Sole representatives of the French Society of Authors (Societé des Auteurs et Compositeurs Dramatiques). Founded 1932.

David Godwin Associates
14 Goodwins Court, London WC2N 4LL
tel 0171-240 9992 *fax* 0171-240 3007
Director David Godwin

Literary fiction and general non-fiction (home 10%, overseas 20%). No reading fee; send sae for return of MSS. Founded 1996.

Christine Green Authors' Agent*
40 Doughty Street, London WC1N 2LF
tel 0171-831 4956 *fax* 0171-405 3935

Fiction and general non-fiction. Full-length MSS (home 10%, overseas 20%). Works in conjunction with agencies in Europe and Scandinavia. No reading fee, but preliminary letter and return postage essential. Founded 1984.

Greene & Heaton Ltd*
37 Goldhawk Road, London W12 8QQ
tel 0181-749 0315 *fax* 0181-749 0318
Directors Carol Heaton, Judith Murray, Charles Elliott, *Junior Agent* Antony Topping

Full-length MSS, fiction and non-fiction (home 10%, overseas 20%, translation 20%). No plays, TV or film scripts, or children's books. Works in conjunction with agencies in most countries. No reading fee. Preliminary letter and return postage required. Founded 1962.

Gregory & Radice Authors' Agents*
3 Barb Mews, London W6 7PA
tel 0171-610 4676 *fax* 0171-610 4686
Partners Jane Gregory, Dr Lisanne Radice (editorial), Pippa Dyson (film and TV rights)

Full-length MSS; fiction and non-fiction. Specialises in crime fiction, commercial and literary fiction, thrillers and politics. Particularly interested in books with potential for sales abroad and/or to film and TV (home 15%, articles, USA and translation 20%, film/TV rights 15%). No short stories, plays, film scripts, science fiction, fantasy, poetry, academic or children's books. Represented in all foreign markets. No reading fee, editorial advice given to own authors. No unsolicited MSS: preliminary letter, synopsis and first 3 chapters essential plus return postage. Founded 1987.

David Grossman Literary Agency Ltd
118B Holland Park Avenue, London W11 4UA
tel 0171-221 2770 *fax* 0171-221 1445

Full-length MSS (home 10-15%, overseas 20% including foreign agent's commission), performance rights (15%). Works in conjunction with agents in New York, Los Angeles, Europe, Japan. No reading fee, but preliminary letter required. Founded 1976.

The Guidelines Partnership
4 Shelton Park, Shrewsbury SY3 8BL
tel (01743) 340559 *fax* (01743) 340619
e-mail 101662.2120@compuserve.com
Partners Geoff Black, Stuart Wall, Linda Black, Eleanor Wall

Specialises in educational texts and exam-related study guides for most ages and most subject areas (home 15%, overseas 20%); will suggest revision where appropriate. No fiction. Works with overseas educational publishers. No reading fee. Preliminary letter or fax essential. Founded 1986.

Richard Hatton Ltd
29 Roehampton Gate, London SW15 5JR
tel 0181-876 6699 *fax* 0181-876 8278
Director Richard Hatton

Stage plays; TV, cinema and radio scripts (15%). No reading fee; will suggest a revision. Send sae for return of MSS. Founded 1954.

A.M. Heath & Co. Ltd*
79 St Martin's Lane, London WC2N 4AA
tel 0171-836 4271 *fax* 0171-497 2561
Directors Michael Thomas, William Hamilton, Sara Fisher, Sarah Molloy

Full-length MSS (home 10-15%, USA 20%, translation 20%), performance rights (15%). Agents in USA and all European countries and Japan. No reading fee. Founded 1919.

David Higham Associates Ltd*

(incorporating Murray Pollinger)
5-8 Lower John Street, Golden Square,
London W1R 4HA
tel 0171-437 7888 *fax* 0171-437 1072
Directors Bruce Hunter, Jacqueline Korn,
Anthony Crouch, Elizabeth Cree, Anthony Goff,
Ania Corless

Agents for the negotiation of all rights in
fiction, general non-fiction, children's fiction and picture books, plays, film and
TV scripts (home 10%, USA/translation
20%). USA associate agency: Harold
Ober Associates Inc. Represented in all
foreign markets. Preliminary letter and
return postage essential. No reading fee.
Founded 1935.

Vanessa Holt Ltd*

59 Crescent Road, Leigh-on-Sea,
Essex SS9 2PF
tel (01702) 73787 *fax* (01702) 471890

General adult fiction and non-fiction
(home 10%, overseas 20%). Works in
conjunction with many foreign agencies.
No reading fee, but preliminary letter
and sae essential. Founded 1989.

Valerie Hoskins Associates

20 Charlotte Street, London W1P 1HJ
tel 0171-637 4490 *fax* 0171-637 4493
e-mail 101654.616@compuserve.com
Proprietor Valerie Hoskins

Film, TV and radio only (12.5% home
and maximum 20% overseas). No reading fee, but sae appreciated. Works in
conjunction with overseas agents. No
unsolicited MSS; preliminary letter
essential.

Tanja Howarth Literary Agency*

19 New Row, London WC2N 4LA
tel 0171-240 5553/836 4142 *fax* 0171-379 0969

Full-length MSS. General fiction and
non-fiction, thrillers, contemporary and
historical women's novels and sagas
(home 15%, USA/translation 20%).
Represented in the USA by various
agents. Please submit preliminary letter,
synopsis and 3 sample chapters with
return postage. No reading fee. Founded
1970.

ICM Ltd

Oxford House, 76 Oxford Street,
London W1N 0AX
tel 0171-636 6565 *fax* 0171-323 0101
Directors Duncan Heath, Susan Rodgers, Michael

Foster, Ian Amos, Paul Lyon-Maris
Literary Agents Jessica Sykes, Catherine King,
Amanda Davis

Specialises in scripts for film, theatre,
TV, radio (home 10%, overseas 10%).
Part of International Creative
Management Inc., Los Angeles and New
York. No reading fee.

Intercontinental Literary Agency*

The Chambers, Chelsea Harbour, Lots Road,
London SW10 0XF
tel 0171-351 4763 *fax* 0171-351 4809
Contacts Anthony Guest Gornall, Nicki Kennedy,
Jessica Buckman

Represents translation rights for The
Peters Fraser & Dunlop Group Ltd,
London and Harold Matson Company,
Inc., New York. Founded 1965.

International Copyright Bureau Ltd

22A Aubrey House, Maida Avenue,
London W2 1TQ
tel 0171-724 8034 *fax* 0171-724 7662
Directors Joy Westendarp, J.C.H. Hadfield

Theatre, films, TV, radio (home 10%,
overseas 19%). Works in conjunction
with agents in New York and most foreign countries. Preliminary letter essential. Founded 1905.

International Management Group

Pier House, Strand on the Green,
London W4 3NN
tel 0181-233 5000 *fax* 0181-233 5001
Chairman Mark H. McCormack, *Agents* Jean
Cooke (UK), Julian Bach, David Chalfant, Mark
Reiter (US), Fumiko Matsuki (Japan)

Represents sports celebrities, classical
musicians and broadcasting personalities
(home/US 15%, elsewhere 25%). No
reading fee. Please send synopsis, 3 sample chapters and sae.

International Scripts

1 Norland Square, London W11 4PX
tel 0171-229 0736 *fax* 0171-792 3287
Directors H.P. Tanner, J. Lawson

Specialises in full-length contemporary
and women's fiction, horror, general non-
fiction (home 15%, overseas 20-25%),
performance rights (15-20%); no poetry
or short stories. Works with overseas
agents worldwide. Preliminary letter
required. Return postage required for
MSS plus a £30.00 reading fee (for which
a report will be provided).

Authors include Richard Laymon,

Anna Jacobs, Mary Ryan, Ed Gorman, Julie Harris, Peter Haining, Graham Masterton, Zita Adamson, Simon Clark, John and Anne Spencer. Founded 1979.

Mary Irvine
11 Upland Park Road, Oxford OX2 7RU
tel (01865) 513570
Specialises in women's fiction and family sagas. No plays, scripts, children's books, short stories or poetry (home 10%, USA 15%, translations 20%). Works with agents in USA, Europe, Japan. No unsolicited MSS. Preliminary letter essential and return postage required. No reading fee. Founded 1974.

John Johnson (Authors' Agent) Ltd*
Clerkenwell House, 45-47 Clerkenwell Green, London EC1R 0HT
tel 0171-251 0125 *fax* 0171-251 2172
Full-length MSS (home 10%, overseas direct 15%, with subagent maximum of 20%). Works in conjunction with agents in USA and many European countries. No unsolicited MSS. Founded 1956.

Jane Judd Literary Agency*
18 Belitha Villas, London N1 1PD
tel 0171-607 0273 *fax* 0171-607 0623
Full-length MSS only (home 10%, overseas 20%). Works with agents in USA and most foreign countries. No reading fee, but preliminary letter with synopsis and sae essential. Founded 1986.

Juvenilia
Avington, Winchester, Hants SO21 1DB
tel/fax (01962) 779656
Proprietor Mrs Rosemary Bromley
Full-length MSS for the children's market, fiction and non-fiction (home 10%, overseas from 15%), illustration (20%), performance rights (10%). Short stories only if specifically for picture books, radio or TV. No verse. No unsolicited MSS; preliminary letter with sae and full details essential. No reading fee. Postage for acknowledgement and return of material imperative. Founded 1973.

Michelle Kass Associates*
36-38 Glasshouse Street, London W1R 5RH
tel 0171-439 1624 *fax* 0171-734 3394
e-mail 106435.1024@compuserve.com
Proprietor Michelle Kass
Full-length MSS. Fiction and drama (screen and stage) (home 10%, overseas 15-20%), performance rights (10%); will suggest revision where appropriate. Works with agents overseas. No reading fee. Preliminary letter and return postage required. Founded 1991.

Frances Kelly Agency*
111 Clifton Road, Kingston-upon-Thames, Surrey KT2 6PL
tel 0181-549 7830 *fax* 0181-547 0051
Full-length MSS. Non-fiction: general and academic, reference and professional books, all subjects (home 10%, overseas 20%), TV, radio (10%). No reading fee, but no unsolicited MSS; preliminary letter with synopsis, CV and return postage essential. Founded 1978.

Peter Knight Agency
20 Crescent Grove, London SW4 7AH
tel 0171-622 1467 *fax* 0171-622 1522
Director Peter Knight, *Associates* Ann King-Hall, Gaby Martin, Andrew Knight, Giovanna Farrell-Vinay
Motor sports, cartoon books for both adults and children, and factual and biographical material (commission dependent upon authors and territories). No poetry, science fiction or cookery. Overseas associates: United Media (USA), Auspac Media (Australia). No unsolicited MSS. Send letter accompanied by CV and sae with synopsis of proposed work. Founded 1985.

Cat Ledger Literary Agency*
33 Percy Street, London W1P 9FG
tel 0171-436 5030 *fax* 0171-631 4273
General non-fiction and fiction (home 10%, overseas 20%). No reading fee.
Authors include Pauline Collins, Lenny Henry, Stan Hey, Mark Lawson, John Peel, Griff Rhys Jones, Alexei Sayle, Jim White, British School of Motoring.

Lemon Unna & Durbridge Ltd – see The Agency (London) Ltd*

Barbara Levy Literary Agency*
64 Greenhill, Hampstead High Street, London NW3 5TZ
tel 0171-435 9046 *fax* 0171-431 2063
Director Barbara Levy, *Associate* John Selby (solicitor)
Full-length MSS only; also films, TV and radio (home 10%, overseas by arrangement). No reading fee, but informative

preliminary letter and return postage essential. Founded 1986.

Limelight Management

54 Marshall Street, London WC1V 1LR
tel 0171-734 1218 *fax* 0171-287 1998
Directors Fiona Lindsay, Linda Shanks

Full-length and short MSS. Food, wine, health, crafts, gardening (home 15%, overseas 20%), TV and radio rights (10-20%); will suggest revision where appropriate. No reading fee. Founded 1991.

The Christopher Little Literary Agency*

48 Walham Grove, London SW6 1QR
tel 0171-386 1800 *fax* 0171-381 2248
e-mail 100555.3137 @compuserve.com
Contacts Christopher Little, Patrick Walsh (fiction, non-fiction), *Office Manager* Emma Bowles

Commercial and literary full-length fiction and non-fiction and film/TV scripts. Special interests: crime, thrillers, autobiographies, popular science and narrative and investigative non-fiction. Also makes a particular speciality out of packaging celebrities for the book market and representing book projects for journalists. Rights representative in the UK for 6 US literary agencies (home 15%; US, translation, motion picture 20%). No reading fee. No unsolicited submissions.

Authors include Felice Arena, Simon Beckett, Marcus Berkmann, Colin Cameron, Harriet Castor, Linford Christie, Storm Constantine, Michael Cordy, Mike Dash, Frankie Dettori, Ginny Elliot, Simon Gandolfi, Brian Hall, Paula Hamilton, Damon Hill, Tom Holland, Carol Hughes, Clare Latimer, Alistair MacNeill, Sanjida O'Connell, Samantha Phillips, A.J. Quinnell, Alvin Rakoff, Candace Robb, Peter Rosenberg, Joanne Rowling, Vivienne Savory, John Spurling, David Thomas, Laura Thompson, John Watson, James Whitaker, John Wilson. Founded 1979.

London Independent Books

26 Chalcot Crescent, London NW1 8YD
tel 0171-706 0486 *fax* 0171-724 3122
Proprietor Carolyn Whitaker

Specialises in commercial and fantasy fiction, cinema, jazz, show business, travel. Full-length MSS (home 15%, overseas 20%), films, TV and sound broadcasting (15%). Will suggest revision of promising MSS. No reading fee.

Authors include Bruce Crowther, Nigel Frith, Keith Grey, Andre Launay, Glenn Mitchell, Connie Monk, Emma Sinclair. Founded 1971.

Andrew Lownie Literary Agency*

122 Bedford Court Mansions, Bedford Square, London WC1B 3AH
tel 0171-636 4917 *fax* 436 1898
Director Andrew Lownie

Full-length MSS. Biography, history, reference, current affairs and thrillers (worldwide 15%). No reading fee; will suggest a revision.

Authors include Juliet Barker, Timothy Good, Norma Major, Nick Pope; *The Oxford Classical Dictionary*, *The Cambridge Guide to Literature in English*. Founded 1988.

Lucas Alexander Whitley*

Elsinore House, 77 Fulham Palace Road, London W6 8JA
tel 0181-600 3800 *fax* 0181-600 3810
Directors Mark Lucas, Julian Alexander, Araminta Whitley, Robert Houghton

Full length MSS. Fiction and general non-fiction (home 15%, overseas 20%). No poetry, plays, textbooks or children's books. Film or TV scripts for established clients only. Works with agents and publishers worldwide. Preliminary letter, synopsis and 2 chapters with sae preferred. No reading fee. Founded 1996.

Jennifer Luithlen Agency

88 Holmfield Road, Leicester LE2 1SB
tel (0116) 273 8863 *fax* (0116) 273 5697
Agent Jennifer Luithlen

Children's books; adult fiction: crime, historical, saga (home 10%, overseas 20%), performance rights (15%); will suggest revision where appropriate. Handles translation sales direct. No reading fee. Not looking for new clients. Founded 1986.

Lutyens & Rubinstein*

231 Westbourne Park Road, London W11 1EB
tel 0171-792 4855 *fax* 0171-792 4833
Directors Sarah Lutyens, Felicity Rubinstein

Fiction and non-fiction, commercial and literary (home 10%, overseas 20%). Send outline/two sample chapters and sae. No reading fee. Founded 1993.

Duncan McAra

28 Beresford Gardens, Edinburgh EH5 3ES
tel/fax 0131-552 1558

Thrillers and literary fiction; non-fiction: art, architecture, archaeology, biography, film, military, travel (home 10%, overseas by arrangement). Preliminary letter with sae essential. No reading fee. Founded 1988.

McLean & Slora Literary Agents

20A Eildon Street, Edinburgh EH3 5JU
tel 0131-556 3368 *fax* 0131-443 9118
Partners Barbara McLean and Annie Slora

Full-length MSS. Literary fiction, biography, cookery, poetry, Scottish interest (home 10%, overseas 20%). No reading fee; will suggest a revision and undertake for a fee.

Authors include Tom Bryan, John Herdman, Ruari McLean.

Eunice McMullen Children's Literary Agent Ltd

38 Clewer Hill Road, Windsor, Berks. SL4 4BW
tel (01753) 830348 *fax* (01753) 833459
Director Eunice McMullen

All types of children's books, particularly picture books (home 10%, overseas 15%). No unsolicited scripts.

Authors include Wayne Anderson, Reg Cartwright, Richard Fowler, Charles Fuge, Simon James, Moira Maclean, Graham Oakley, Sue Porter, Jim Riordan, Carol Thompson, David Wood. Founded 1992.

Andrew Mann Ltd*

(in association with Jane Conway-Gordon)
1 Old Compton Street, London W1V 5PH
tel 0171-734 4751 *fax* 0171-287 9264
Directors Anne Dewe, Tina Betts

Full-length MSS. Scripts for TV, cinema, radio and theatre (home 10%, USA 19%, Europe 19%). Associated with agents worldwide. No reading fee, but no unsolicited MSS without preliminary enquiry and sae. Founded 1974.

Manuscript ReSearch

PO Box 33, Bicester, Oxon OX6 7PP
tel (01869) 323447 *fax* (01869) 324096
Proprietor T.G. Jenkins

Full-length MSS. Specialises in crime/thrillers, biographies (home 10%, overseas 20%, performance rights 15%); short MSS only from established clients. No reading fee, but sae for script return essential.

Authors include Tom Barrat, Kay Williams, Roscoe Howells, Val Manning, Peter Pook, Kev Shannon, Duncan Noble, John MacDonald Smith. Founded 1988.

The Marsh Agency*

138 Buckingham Palace Road, London SW1W 9SA
tel 0171-730 1124 *fax* 0171-730 0037
e-mail 100614.1702 @compuserve.com
Partners Paul Marsh, Susanna Nicklin

Specialisation: translation rights (10%). Founded 1994.

Judy Martin

94 Goldhurst Terrace, London NW6 3HS
tel 0171-372 8422 *fax* 0171-372 8423

Fiction, non-fiction, humour, film and TV scripts (home 15%, overseas 20%; dramatic rights 15%). No plays, poetry, cookery, gardening or children's stories. Translation rights handled by The Marsh Agency. No reading fee, but sae required for all unsolicited MSS, together with details of publishing history. Founded 1990.

M.C. Martinez Literary Agency

60 Oakwood Avenue, London N14 6QL
tel 0181-886 5829
Proprietor Mary Caroline Martinez

Fiction, children's books, arts and crafts, interior design, alternative health and complementary medicine, cookery, travel, autobiographies and biographies, popular music, sport and business. Also scripts for TV and radio. Specialises in fiction, children's and alternative health. No unsolicited typescripts. No reading fee but an admin fee may be charged where appropriate. DTP service available. Preliminary letter with synopsis and sae required (home 15%; US, overseas and translation 20%; performance rights 20%). Telephone first, possible change of address.

Authors include Faustin Charles, Carol Donockley, Alan Fisk, David Holbrook, Nina Milton, Dorothy Thompson, Carol Turner, Roger Stevens, Sylvia Wickham. Founded 1988.

Blanche Marvin

21A St John's Wood High Street, London NW8 7NG
tel/fax 0171-722 2313

Full-length MSS (home 12.5% + 12.5% overseas), performance rights. No reading fee but return postage essential.

Authors include Christopher Bond.

MBA Literary Agents Ltd*

62 Grafton Way, London W1P 5LD
tel 0171-387 2076/4785 *fax* 0171-387 2042
e-mail 101572.353@compuserve.com
Directors Diana Tyler, John Richard Parker, Meg
Davis, Ruth Needham, Timothy Webb

Full-length MSS; no poetry (home 10%, overseas 20%), theatre, TV, radio (10%), films (10-15%). Works in conjunction with agents in most countries. No reading fee. No unsolicited material.

Authors include Jeffrey Caine, Glenn Chandler, Campbell Armstrong, Maggie Furey, Valerie Georgson, Andrew Hodges, Roy Lancaster, Paul J. McAuley, Anne McCaffrey, Anne Perry, Iain Sinclair, Tom Vernon, Douglas Watkinson, Fred Warrington, Sir Roger Penrose, Richard Weston, Valerie Windsor, Elspeth Sandys and the estate of B.S. Johnson. Founded 1971.

Richard Milne Ltd

15 Summerlee Gardens, London N2 9QN
tel 0181-883 3987
Directors R.M. Sharples, K.N. Sharples

Specialises in scripts for films, TV, sound broadcasting (10%). Unable to represent any additional authors at present. Founded 1956.

Jay Morris & Co. Authors' Agents

PO Box 70, Blackpool FY1 2GE
Directors Jay Morris (managing), Dr Phillida Kanta, *Assistant Director* Toby Tillyard-Burrows

Full-length MSS (home 10%, overseas 15%). Mainstream commercial adult fiction: racy sagas, gay erotica, horror, children's fantasy, women in power (not women's issues), thrillers and crime. No reading fee; will suggest a revision. Send preliminary letter with synopsis and sae.

Authors include Jonathan Douglas, Saxon Hollis, Hon. Joy Parker-Dixon, Elika Rise, Piers de Villias. Founded 1994.

William Morris Agency (UK) Ltd*

31-32 Soho Square, London W1V 6HH
tel 0171-434 2191 *fax* 0171-437 0238
e-mail adl@wma.com
Contacts Stephen Kenis, Jane Annakin, Alan Radcliffe (film and TV); Alan Radcliffe (stage); Stephanie Cabot (books)

Worldwide theatrical and literary agency with offices in New York, Beverly Hills and Nashville, and associates in Munich and Sydney. Handles film, TV, stage and radio scripts; fiction and general non-fiction (film/TV/theatre/UK books 10%, US books and translation 20%). No unsolicited material without a preliminary letter. No reading fee. Founded 1965.

MS-S

Julia MacRae, 13 Pattison Road, London NW2 2HL
tel/fax 0171-435 7882 and
Christopher Sinclair-Stevenson, 3 South Terrace, London SW7 2TB
tel/fax 0171-581 2550

Julia MacRae: children's fiction and picture books, music, history and the arts. Christopher Sinclair-Stevenson: general. Worldwide 10%. Will suggest a revision (see page 557). Founded 1996.

Judith Murdoch Literary Agency

19 Chalcot Square, London NW1 8YA
tel 0171-722 4197

Full-length fiction only (home 15%, overseas 20%). No genre novels, science fiction/fantasy, poetry, short stories or children's. Don't phone – write! Send first 2 chapters and synopsis with preliminary letter. Return postage/sae essential. Editorial advice given; no reading fee. Translation rights handled by The Marsh Agency. Founded 1993.

Negotiate Ltd

Gavin Kennedy, 22 Braid Avenue, Edinburgh EH10 6EE
tel 0131-452 8404 *fax* 0131-452 8388
e-mail gavin@neg1.demon.co.uk

Specialises in the negotiation of author's contracts and subsidiary rights. Established authors only or new authors with draft contract from a publisher. Preliminary letter or fax please. Founded 1986.

Maggie Noach Literary Agency*

21 Redan Street, London W14 0AB
tel 0171-602 2451 *fax* 0171-603 4712

General fiction and non-fiction; non-illustrated children's books. Full-length MSS (home 15%, US/translation 20%). No scientific, academic or specialist non-fiction; no poetry, plays, short stories or books for the very young. Encourages promising young writers but very few new clients taken on as it is considered vital to give individual attention to each author's work. Unsolicited MSS not welcome. Approach by letter (not by telephone), giving a brief description of the

book and enclosing a few sample pages. Return postage essential. No reading fee. Founded 1982.

Andrew Nurnberg Associates Ltd*
Clerkenwell House, 45-47 Clerkenwell Green, London EC1R 0HT
tel 0171-417 8800 *fax* 0171-417 8812
e-mail 100663.727@compuserve.com

Specialises in the sale of translation rights of English and American authors into European languages.

Alexandra Nye, Writers & Agents
Cauldhame Cottage, Sheriffmuir, Dunblane, Perthshire FK15 0LN
tel (01786) 825114
Director Alexandra Nye

Literary fiction, historical, biographies; no poetry or plays (home 10%, overseas 20%, translation 15%). Will suggest revision where appropriate. Send preliminary letter and synopsis in first instance; sae essential for return. No reading fee. Critical service available for a fee. Founded 1991.

David O'Leary Literary Agency
10 Lansdowne Court, Lansdowne Rise, London W11 2NR
tel 0171-229 1623 *fax* 0171-727 9624

Popular and literary fiction and non-fiction: special interests Russia, Ireland, history, science (home 10%, overseas 20%), performance rights (15%). Will suggest revision; no reading fee. Write or call before submitting MSS; please enclose sae.

Authors include Alexander Cordell, Jim Lusby, Alex Keegan, James Kennedy, Edward Toman. Founded 1988.

Deborah Owen Ltd*
78 Narrow Street, Limehouse, London E14 8BP
tel 0171-987 5119/5441 *fax* 0171-538 4004
Contact Deborah Owen

Full-length MSS (home 10%, overseas 15%). All types of literary material except plays, scripts, children's books, short stories or poetry. No unsolicited MSS. No new authors at present.

Authors include Ellis Peters, Amos Oz, Delia Smith. Founded 1971.

Mark Paterson & Associates*
10 Brook Street, Wivenhoe, Colchester, Essex CO7 9DS
tel (01206) 825433/4 *fax* (01206) 822990

Book-length MSS; general but with special experience in psychoanalysis, psychotherapy, history, copyright and education (20% worldwide including sub-agents' commission). No articles or short stories except for existing clients. Preliminary letter with synopsis, sample material and sae essential.

Authors include Sigmund Freud, Anna Freud, Hugh Brogan, Donald Winnicott, Peter Moss, Sir Arthur Evans, Dorothy Richardson, Hugh Schonfield, Georg Groddeck, Patrick Casement. Founded 1955.

John Pawsey
60 High Street, Tarring, Worthing, West Sussex BN14 7NR
tel (01903) 205167 *fax* (01903) 205167

Full-length popular fiction and non-fiction MSS (home 10-15%, overseas 19%). No unsolicited material, poetry, short stories, journalism or original film and stage scripts. Preliminary letter and return postage with all correspondence essential. Works in association with agencies in the USA, Europe and the Far East. Will suggest revision if MS sufficiently promising. No reading fee.

Authors include Jonathan Agnew, Dr David Lewis, Peter Hobday, Jon Silverman. Founded 1981.

Maggie Pearlstine Associates Ltd*
31 Ashley Gardens, Ambrosden Avenue, London SW1P 1QE
tel 0171-828 4212 *fax* 0171-834 5546

Full-length MSS, fiction and non-fiction. Special interests: commercial fiction, illustrated non-fiction, home and leisure, health, biography, history and politics (home 10-12.5%, overseas, journalism and media 20%). Translation rights handled by Aitken & Stone Ltd. No children's or poetry; only deals with scripts and short stories by authors already on its books. No unsolicited MSS. Preliminary letter required and sae. No reading fee.

Authors include David Aaronovitch, John Biffen, Matthew Baylis, Kate Bingham, James Cox, John Drews, Glorafilia, Prof Roger Gosden, Roy Hattersley, Prof Lisa Jardine, Charles Kennedy, Prof Nicholas Lowe, Sara Morrison, Prof Lesley Regan, Jackie

Rowley, Polly Sellar, Lady Henrietta Spencer-Churchill, Jack Straw, Dr Thomas Stuttaford, Brian Wilson, Prof the Lord Winston, Tony Wright. Founded 1989.

The Peters Fraser & Dunlop Group Ltd*

(incorporating A.D. Peters & Co. Ltd, Fraser & Dunlop Scripts Ltd, Fraser & Dunlop Ltd, June Hall Literary Agency Ltd)
503-4 The Chambers, Chelsea Harbour, Lots Road, London SW10 0XF
tel 0171-344 1000 *fax* 0171-352 7356/351 1756
e-mail rscoular@pfd.co.uk
Directors Michael Sissons (joint chairman), Anthony Jones (joint chairman), Anthony Baring (managing director), Kenneth Ewing, Pat Kavanagh, Tim Corrie, Maureen Vincent, Norman North, Caroline Dawnay, Ginette Chalmers
Associated agencies Intercontinental Literary Agency, Sterling Lord Literistic (New York), Chelsea West Inc. (New York)

Specialists in the negotiation of all rights in general fiction and non-fiction, film and TV scripts, plays, and certain specialist and academic works. Children's MSS and illustrations to Peters Fraser & Dunlop Children's List, Rosemary Canter (home/overseas 10-20%). No unsolicited MSS accepted. We ask for an introductory letter from the author describing the work offered, with sae. No reading fee.

Laurence Pollinger Ltd

18 Maddox Street, London W1R 0EU
tel 0171-629 9761 *fax* 0171-629 9765
e-mail 106225.3645@compuserve.com
Directors Gerald J. Pollinger, Heather Chalcroft, Lesley Hadcroft, Juliet Burton, Secretary Denzil De Silva, *Dramatic Associate* Micheline Steinberg

All material except original film stories, poetry and freelance journalistic articles. Commission: 15%, except for translation (20%), which may include commission to the associate in the territory concerned. No reading fee. An editorial contribution may be requested.

Murray Pollinger – see David Higham Associates Ltd*

Shelley Power Literary Agency Ltd*

Le Montaud, 24220 Berbiguières, France
tel 53 29 62 52 *fax* 53 29 62 54

General fiction and non-fiction. Full-length MSS (home 10%, USA and translations 19%). No children's books, poetry

or plays. Works in conjunction with agents abroad. No reading fee, but preliminary letter with sae for return from UK or France essential.

Authors include Madge Swindells, William Gibson, Elizabeth Hand, Michael Swanwick, Richard Stern, Peter Lambley and Roger Wilkes. Also based in the UK. Founded 1976.

PVA Management Ltd

Hallow Park, Worcester WR2 6PG
tel (01905) 640663 *fax* (01905) 641842
Managing Director Paul Vaughan

Full-length MSS (home 15%, overseas 20%), performance rights (15%). Please send synopsis and sample chapters together with return postage.

Radala & Associates

17 Avenue Mansions, Finchley Road, London NW3 7AX
tel 0171-794 4495 *fax* 0171-431 7636
Director Richard Gollner, *Associates* Neil Hornick, Anna Swan, Andy Marino

Full-length MSS (home 10%, overseas 15%). Fiction and non-fiction. Books, TV, sound broadcasting. Submit synopsis in first instance; evaluation of MSS charged (£50 upwards); outlines, proposals, etc at no charge. Founded 1970.

Margaret Ramsay Ltd – now Casarotto Ramsay Ltd

Rogers, Coleridge & White Ltd*

20 Powis Mews, London W11 1JN
tel 0171-221 3717 *fax* 0171-229 9084
Directors Deborah Rogers, Gill Coleridge, Patricia White (USA), *Consultant* Ann Warnford-Davis
USA Associate International Creative Management, Inc.

Full-length book MSS, including children's books (home 10%, USA 15%, translations 20%). No unsolicited MSS please, and no submissions by fax. No reading fee. Founded 1967.

Elizabeth Roy Literary Agency

White Cottage, Greatford, Nr Stamford, Lincs. PE9 4PR
tel/fax (01778) 560672

Women's fiction, crime fiction, children's books – writers and illustrators (home 10-15%, overseas 20%). Will suggest revision. Preliminary letter, synopsis and sample chapters essential with names of publishers and agents previously con-

tacted. Return postage essential. No reading fee. Founded 1990.

Hilary Rubinstein Books
32 Ladbroke Grove, London W11 3BQ
tel 0171-792 4282 *fax* 0171-221 5291
Director Hilary Rubinstein

Full-length MSS. Fiction and non-fiction (home 10%, overseas 20%); will suggest revision where appropriate. No plays, scripts, children's books or poetry. No reading fee, but no unsolicited MSS without preliminary letter or call.

Authors include Eric Lomax, Donna Williams. Founded 1992.

Uli Rushby-Smith and Shirley Stewart
72 Plimsoll Road, London N4 2EE
tel/fax 0171-354 2718
Directors Uli Rushby-Smith, Shirley Stewart

Full length MSS only. Fiction and non-fiction, literary and commercial (home 10%, USA/foreign 20%). Work in conjunction with foreign sub-agents in some countries. UK representatives of Curtis Brown Ltd, New York and Henry Holt & Co, Inc., New York. Send outline, sample chapters and sae; no reading fee. Founded 1993.

Rosemary Sandberg Ltd
6 Bayley Street, London WC1B 3HB
tel 0171-304 4110 *fax* 0171-304 4109
Directors Rosemary Sandberg, Ed Victor, Graham Greene CBE

Children's – writers and illustrators, general fiction and non-fiction (home 10-15%, overseas 20%). Absolutely no unsolicited MSS: client list is full. Founded 1991.

Tessa Sayle Agency*
11 Jubilee Place, London SW3 3TE
tel 0171-823 3883 (5 lines) *fax* 0171-823 3363
Publishing Rachel Calder, *Film, TV, Theatre,* Jane Villiers

Full-length MSS (home 10%, overseas 20%), film, TV, theatre (home 10%, overseas 15-20%). USA Associates: Darhansoff & Verrill, 1220 Park Avenue, New York, NY 10128. Represented in all foreign countries. No reading fee, but preliminary letter and return postage essential.

The Sharland Organisation Ltd
9 Marlborough Crescent, Bedford Park, London W4 1HE
tel 0181-742 1919 *fax* 0181-995 7688
Directors Mike Sharland, Alice Sharland

Specialises in film, TV, stage and radio rights throughout the world (home 15%, overseas 20%); also negotiates multimedia, interactive TV deals and computer game contracts. Works in conjunction with overseas agents. Preliminary letter and return postage is essential. Founded 1988.

Sheil Land Associates Ltd*
(incorporating Christy & Moore Ltd 1912 and Richard Scott Simon Ltd 1971)
43 Doughty Street, London WC1N 2LF
tel 0171-405 9351 *fax* 0171-831 2127
Agents Anthony Sheil, Sonia Land, Vivien Green, Simon Trewin, John Rush (film/drama/TV), Laura Susiju (foreign rights department)

Full-length general and literary fiction, biography, travel, cookery, humour (home 10%, USA/translations 20%); theatre, film, radio and TV scripts (home 10%, overseas 20%). Preliminary letter and return postage essential.

Authors include Peter Ackroyd, Melvyn Bragg, John Banville, Catherine Cookson, Josephine Cox, Seamus Deane, Nick Fisher, John Fowles, Susan Hill, HRH The Prince of Wales, Michael Ignatieff, John Keegan, Tom Sharpe, Rose Tremain, John Wilsher. Founded 1962.

Foreign Rights Department
19 John Street, London WC1N 2DL
tel 0171-405 7473 *fax* 0171-405 5239
Contacts Laura Susiju, Anthony Sheil, Sonia Land, Talya Boston

Translation rights only. Founded 1985.

Caroline Sheldon Literary Agency*
71 Hillgate Place, London W8 7SS
tel 0171-727 9102
Proprietor Caroline Sheldon

Full-length MSS. General fiction, women's fiction, and children's books (home 10%, overseas 20%). No reading fee. Synopsis and first 3 chapters with large sae in case of return required initially. Founded 1985.

Jeffrey Simmons
10 Lowndes Square, London SW1X 9HA
tel 0171-235 8852 *fax* 0171-235 9733

Specialises in fiction (no sci-fi, horror or fantasy), biography, autobiography, show business, personality books, law, crime, politics, world affairs. Full-length MSS (home from 10%, overseas from 15%). Will suggest revision. No reading fee, but

preliminary letter essential.

Authors include Billy Boy, Clive Collins, Margaret Crosland, Euphrosyne Doxiadis, Fred Lawrence Guiles, James Haskins, Keith Wright.

Richard Scott Simon Ltd – see Sheil Land Associates Ltd*

Simpson Fox Associates*
52 Shaftesbury Avenue, London W1V 7DE
tel 0171-434 9167 *fax* 0171-494 2887
Directors David Watson, Angela Fox, John Simpson, Anita Land, Georgina Capel, Robert Fox

General fiction and non-fiction, scripts (worldwide 15%). No reading fee. Write to Georgina Capel with synopsis and sample chapter.

Authors include Julie Burchill, Niall Ferguson, Suzanne Moore, Andrew Roberts.

Sinclair-Stevenson
3 South Terrace, London SW7 2TB
tel/fax 0171-581 2550
Directors Christopher Sinclair-Stevenson, Deborah Sinclair-Stevenson

Full-length MSS (worldwide 10%). General – no children's books. No reading fee; will suggest a revision. Founded 1995.

The Carol Smith Literary Agency
22 Adam and Eve Mews,
London W8 6UJ
tel 0171-937 4874 *fax* 0171-938 5323
e-mail 100067,1643

Full-length fiction and non-fiction. Specialises in contemporary commercial and literary novels (home 10%, overseas/translation 20%). Please write rather than phone. Send first 3-4 chapters and synopsis with preliminary letter. Return postage essential. No reading fee. MSS submissions by invitation only.

Solo Literary Agency Ltd
49-53 Kensington High Street, London W8 5ED
tel 0171-376 2166 *fax* 0171-938 3165
Directors Don Short (managing), Wendy Short (secretary)

Specialises in celebrity and autobiographical books. Fiction from established authors only (home 15%, overseas 20%). No reading fee.

Authors include Peter Essex, Rosemary Kingsland, Edward Vale. Founded 1978.

Abner Stein*
10 Roland Gardens, London SW7 3PH
tel 0171-373 0456 *fax* 0171-370 6316

Full-length and short MSS (home 10%, overseas 20%). No reading fee, but no unsolicited MSS; preliminary letter and return postage required.

Micheline Steinberg Playwrights' Agent
409 Triumph House, 187-191 Regent Street, London W1R 7WF
tel 0171-287 4383 *fax* 0171-287 4384

Full-length MSS – theatre, films, TV, radio (home 10%, overseas 15%). Dramatic Associate for Laurence Pollinger Ltd; works in conjunction with agents in USA and other countries. No reading fee, but preliminary letter essential and return postage with MSS. Founded 1987.

Rochelle Stevens & Co.
2 Terretts Place, Upper Street, London N1 1QZ
tel 0171-359 3900 *fax* 0171-354 5729
Proprietor Rochelle Stevens, *Associate* Frances Grannum

Drama scripts for film, TV, theatre and radio (10%); will suggest revision where appropriate. No reading fee, but preliminary letter and return postage essential. Founded 1984.

Peter Tauber Press Agency
94 East End Road, London N3 2SX
tel 0181-346 4165
Director Robert Tauber

Non-fiction: auto/biographies of the famous; innovative, provable diet books; solutions to important historical or scientific mysteries. Fiction: high quality contemporary women's fiction; horror and thrillers. Prefer new fiction authors to have some writing background, e.g. press, media, advertising. No poetry, short stories, plays, children's or foreign books. Send letter, synopsis, author CV, copies of all previous rejections, a fully stamped addressed envelope. Replies only on these terms. Commission: 20%. Founded 1950.

J.M. Thurley Management
213 Linen Hall, 162-168 Regent Street, London W1R 5TA
tel 0171-437 9545/6 *fax* 0171-287 9208
Associates Jon Thurley, Patricia Preece

Specialises in commercial and literary full-length fiction and commercial work for film and TV. No plays, poetry, short stories, articles or fantasy. No reading fee but preliminary letter and sae essential. Editorial/creative advice provided to clients (home 15%, overseas 20%). Links with leading US and European agents. Founded 1976.

Lavinia Trevor*
7 The Glasshouse, 49A Goldhawk Road, London W12 8QP
tel 0181-749 8481 *fax* 0181-749 7377
Fiction and non-fiction for the general trade market. No reading fee. Founded 1993.

Jane Turnbull*
13 Wendell Road, London W12 9RS
tel 0181-743 9580 *fax* 0181-749 6079
Fiction and non-fiction (home 10%, USA 15%, translation 20%), performance rights (15%). No science fiction, romantic fiction, children's or short stories. Works in conjunction with Aitken & Stone for sale of translation rights. No reading fee but preliminary letter and sae essential. Founded 1986.

Harvey Unna & Stephen Durbridge Ltd – see The Agency (London) Ltd*

Ed Victor Ltd*
6 Bayley Street, Bedford Square, London WC1B 3HB
tel 0171-304 4100 *fax* 0171-304 4111
Directors Ed Victor, Graham C. Greene cbe, Carol Ryan, Leon Morgan, Margaret Phillips, Sophie Hicks (children's writers and illustrators)
Full-length MSS, fiction and non-fiction, but no short stories, film/TV scripts, poetry or plays (home 15%, USA 15%, translation 20%), performance rights (15%). Represented in all foreign markets. No unsolicited MSS.
Authors include Douglas Adams, Sir Ranulph Fiennes, Josephine Hart, Jack Higgins, Erica Jong, Kathy Lette, Iris Murdoch, Nigel Nicolson, Erich Segal, Will Self, and the estates of Irving Wallace, Raymond Chandler, Sir Stephen Spender. Founded 1976.

Warner Chappell Plays Ltd
129 Park Street, London W1Y 3FA
tel 0171-514 5236 *fax* 0171-514 5201

Specialises in stage plays. Works in conjunction with overseas agents. Preliminary letter essential. Formerly English Theatre Guild Ltd; part of Warner Chappell Music Ltd. Founded 1938.

Watson, Little Ltd*
Capo Di Monte, Windmill Hill, London NW3 6RJ
tel 0171-431 0770 *fax* 0171-431 7225
Directors Sheila Watson, Amanda Little, Sugra Zaman
Full-length MSS. Special interests: business books, popular science, psychology, all leisure activities, popular culture, fiction; no short stories or play scripts (home 10%, serial 15%, overseas 19%; electronic rights 20%; all other rights including film, video and TV 10%). Works in association with US agencies and many foreign agencies. Preliminary letter please.

A.P. Watt Ltd*
20 John Street, London WC1N 2DR
tel 0171-405 6774 *fax* 0171-831 2154 (books)/0171-430 1952 (drama)
Directors Caradoc King, Linda Shaughnessy, Derek Johns
Full-length MSS; dramatic works for all media (home 10%, US and foreign 20% including commission to US or foreign agent). No poetry. Works in conjunction with agents in USA and most European countries and Japan. No reading fee. No unsolicited MSS. Founded 1875.

WCA Licensing
18 Beckwith Road, London SE24 9LG
tel 0171-274 6263 *fax* 0171-274 1509
e-mail wca@pro-net.co.uk
Partners Elaine Collins and Arabella Woods
TV tie-ins, thrillers, science fiction; no poetry (home 15%, overseas 20%). No reading fee; will suggest a revision. Founded 1993.

Dinah Wiener Ltd*
27 Arlington Road, London NW1 7ER
tel 0171-388 2577 *fax* 0171-388 7559
Full-length MSS only, fiction and general non-fiction (home 15%, overseas 20%), film and TV in association (15%). No plays, scripts, poetry, short stories or children's books. No reading fee, but preliminary letter and return postage essential.

Jonathan Williams Literary Agency

2 Mews, 10 Sandycove Avenue West, Sandycove,
Co. Dublin, Republic of Ireland
tel/fax (01) 2803482
Director Jonathan Williams

General fiction and non-fiction, preferably
by Irish authors (home 10%). Will suggest
revision; usually no reading fee. Return
postage appreciated. Founded 1981.

Elisabeth Wilson

24 Thornhill Square, London N1 1BQ
fax 0171-609 6045

Rights agent and consultant on illustrated books. Founded 1979.

The Wylie Agency (UK) Ltd

36 Parkside, 52 Knightsbridge, London SW1X 3JP
tel 0171-235 6394 *fax* 0171-838 9030
Directors Andrew Wylie (president), Georgia
Garrett, Victoria Scott, Benita Edzard

Literary fiction and non-fiction (home
10%, overseas 20%, USA 15%). No
unsolicited MSS; send preliminary letter
with 2 sample chapters and sae in the
first instance. Founded 1996.

Literary agents for children's books

*The following literary agents will consider work suitable for children's books,
from both authors and illustrators. See also Writing and illustrating children's
books on page 245 and Art agents and commercial art studios on page 375.*

The Agency (London) Ltd
Peter Bryant (Writers)
Curtis Brown
Darley Anderson Literary, TV
  and Film Agency
Celia Catchpole
Anne Drexl
Eddison Pearson
Edwards Fuglewicz

A.M. Heath & Co Ltd (Michael
  Thomas)
David Higham Associates Ltd
Juvenilia
Jennifer Luithlen Agency
Eunice McMullen Children's
  Literary Agent Ltd
M.C. Martinez Literary Agency
MS-S (Julia MacRae)

Maggie Noach Literary Agency
The Peters, Fraser & Dunlop
  Group Ltd (Rosemary Canter)
Rogers, Coleridge & White Ltd
Elizabeth Roy Literary Agency
Rosemary Sandberg Ltd
Caroline Sheldon Literary
  Agency
Ed Victor Ltd (Sophie Hicks)

Literary agents overseas

Before submitting material, writers are advised to send a preliminary letter with an sae (or an International Reply Coupon) and to ascertain terms. Listings for overseas literary agents other than in the USA start on page 362.

*Member of the Association of Authors' Representatives

USA

American Play Company Inc.
19 West 44th Street, Suite 1204, New York, NY 10036
tel 212-921-0545 *fax* 212-869-4032
President Sheldon Abend

The Axelrod Agency*
54 Church Street, Lenox, MA 01240
tel 413-637-2000 *fax* 413-637-4725
President Steven Axelrod
Full-length MSS. Fiction and non-fiction, software (home 10%, overseas 20%), film and TV rights (10%); will suggest revision where appropriate. Works with overseas agents. No reading fee. Founded 1983.

The Balkin Agency Inc.*
PO Box 222, Amherst, MA 01004
tel 413-548-9835 *fax* 413-548-9836
e-mail balkin@crocker.com
Director Richard Balkin
European and British Representative Christopher Little Agency
Full-length MSS – adult non-fiction only (home 15%, overseas 20%). Query first. May suggest revision. No reading fee.

Virginia Barber Literary Agency, Inc.*
101 Fifth Avenue, New York, NY 10003
tel 212-255-6515 *fax* 212-691-9418
President Virginia Barber, *Contacts* Jennifer Rudolph Walsh, Jay Mandel, Claire Tisne, Cornelius Howland
General fiction and non-fiction (home 15%, overseas 20%), performance rights (15%); will suggest revision. Has co-agents in all major countries; Abner Stein handles UK rights. No reading fee. Founded 1974.

Berman, Boals & Flynn, Inc.*
225 Lafayette Street, Suite 1207, New York, NY 10012
tel 212-966-0339 *fax* 212-966-0389
Agents Lois Berman, Judy Boals, Jim Flynn
Dramatic writing only (and only by recommendation).

Georges Borchardt Inc.*
136 East 57th Street, New York, NY 10022
tel 212-753-5785 *fax* 212-838-6518
Directors Georges Borchardt, Anne Borchardt
Full-length and short MSS (home/British/performance 15%, translations 20%). Agents in most foreign countries. No unsolicited MSS. No reading fee. Founded 1967.

Brandt & Brandt Literary Agents Inc.*
1501 Broadway, New York, NY 10036
tel 212-840-5760 *fax* 212-840-5776
British Representative A.M. Heath & Co. Ltd
Full-length and short MSS (home 15%, overseas 20%), performance rights (10%). No reading fee.

The Helen Brann Agency Inc.*
94 Curtis Road, Bridgewater, CT 06752
tel 203-354-9580 *fax* 203-355-2572

Maria Carvainis Agency, Inc.*
235 West End Avenue, New York, NY 10023
tel 212-580-1559 *fax* 212-877-3486
President Maria Carvainis
Fiction: all categories (except science fiction), especially general fiction/literary and mainstream; mystery, thrillers and suspense; fantasy; young adult and children's; historical, Regency and category romance. Non-fiction: political and film biographies; medicine and women's

health; business, finance, psychology and popular science (home 15%, overseas 20%). Maria Carvainis views the author's editorial needs and career development as integral components of the literary agent's role, in addition to the negotiation of intricate contracts. Works in conjunction with foreign, TV and movie agents. No reading fee. Query first; no unsolicited MSS.

Martha Casselman, Literary Agent*
PO Box 342, Calistoga, CA 94515-0342
tel 707-942-4341 *fax* 707-942-4358
Food and cookbook, other adult non-fiction (combined home/overseas 25%); will suggest revision where appropriate. No fiction, poetry or textbooks; no MSS; include return postage with query. Works with overseas agents. No reading fee. Founded 1978.

Faith Childs Literary Agency, Inc.*
132 West 22nd Street, 4th Floor, New York, NY 10011
tel 212-645 4600 *fax* 212-645 4644
Director Faith Hampton Childs, *Associates* Emily E. Bernard, Arlene T. Stoltz
Literary fiction; non-fiction (home 15%, overseas 20%). Works in conjunction with overseas agents. Will suggest revision. No reading fee. Founded 1990.

Ruth Cohen, Inc. Literary Agency*
PO Box 7626, Menlo Park, CA 94025
tel 415-854-2054
Requires quality writing: women's contemporary fiction; mysteries; juvenile – picture books to middle grade novels (home 15%, overseas 20%), film, TV rights (15%); will suggest revision. Works in conjunction with overseas agents. Send query letter and 25 opening pages; must include sae. No reading fee. Founded 1982.

Frances Collin Literary Agent*
PO Box 33, Wayne, PA 19087-0033
tel 610-254-0555
Full-length MSS (specialisations of interest to UK writers: mysteries, women's fiction, history, biography, science fiction, fantasy) (home 15%, overseas 20%), performance rights (20%). No screenplays. Works in conjunction with agents worldwide. No reading fee. No unsolicited MSS please. Letter queries must include

sufficient international postage response coupons. Founded 1948; successor to Marie Rodell-Frances Collin Literary Agency.

Don Congdon Associates, Inc.*
156 Fifth Avenue, Suite 625, New York, NY 10010
tel 212-645-1229 *fax* 212-727-2688
e-mail doncongdon@aol.com
Agents Don Congdon, Michael Congdon, Susan Ramer
Full-length and short MSS. General fiction and non-fiction (home 10%, overseas 19%), performance rights (10%); will sometimes suggest revision. Works with co-agents overseas. No reading fee, but no unsolicited MSS – query first. Founded 1983.

Richard Curtis Associates Inc.*
171 East 74th Street, New York, NY 10021
tel 212-772-7363 *fax* 212-772-7393
President Richard Curtis, *Associates* Amy Victoria Moo, Laura Tucker
All types of commercial fiction; also non-fiction (home 15%P overseas 20%), multimedia, film, TV rights (15%). Works in conjunction with overseas agents. Will suggest revision. No reading fee. Founded 1970.

Curtis Brown Ltd*
10 Astor Place, New York, NY 10003
tel 212-473-5400
Chairman Perry Knowlton
1750 Montgomery Street, San Francisco, CA 94111
tel 415-954-8566
Contact Peter Ginsberg
Fiction and non-fiction, juvenile, film and TV rights. No unsolicited MSS; query first with sae. No reading fee; handling fees.

Joan Daves Agency*
67 Clinton Road, Bedford Hills, NY 10507
tel 212-685-2663 *fax* 212-685-1781
Director Jennifer Lyons, *Assistant* Edward Lee
Full-length MSS or a detailed outline of non-fiction projects (home 15%, overseas 20%). No reading fee. No unpublished writers. Subsidiary of **Writers House Inc.** Founded in 1952 by Joan Daves.

Elaine Davie Literary Agency
620 Park Avenue, Rochester, NY 14607
tel 716-442-0830
President Elaine Davie

Full-length MSS. Specialises in books by and for women, especially genre romance (home 15%, overseas 20%); will sometimes suggest revision. Works with overseas agents. No reading fee, but preliminary letter with sae essential. Query or first 100 pages/synopsis. Founded 1986.

Sandra Dijkstra Literary Agency*

1155 Camino del Mar, Suite 515, Del Mar, CA 92014
tel 619-755-3115
President Sandra Dijkstra

Adult fiction, especially literary/contemporary, mystery/suspense; non-fiction: current affairs, memoir/biography, science, health, history and psychology/self-help, business, how-to; selected children's projects (home 15%, overseas 20%). Works in conjunction with foreign agents. Will suggest revision. No reading fee. Send first 50 pages and sae for response/return. No faxed queries accepted. Response period 2-8 weeks; do not call to enquire. Founded 1981.

Donadio & Ashworth, Inc.*

121 West 27th Street, Suite 704, New York, NY 10001
tel 212-691-8077 *fax* 212-633-2837

Literary book agents, fiction and non-fiction.

Dorese Agency

37965 Palo Verde Drive, Cathedral City, CA 92234
tel 619-321-1115 *fax* 619-321-1049
Contact Alyss Barlow Dorese

Specialises in true crime, non-fiction.

Peter Elek Associates

PO Box 223, Canal Street Station, New York, NY 10013
tel 212-431-9368/9371 *fax* 212-966-5768
e-mail 73174.2515 @compuserve.com
Directors Peter Elek, Helene W. Elek

Full-length and short MSS. Adult and illustrated adult non-fiction: style, culture, popular history, popular science, current affairs; juvenile picture books (home 15%, overseas 20%), performance rights (20%); will sometimes suggest revision. Works with overseas agents. No reading fee. Experienced in licensing for multimedia, on-line and off-line. Founded 1979.

Ann Elmo Agency, Inc.*

60 East 42nd Street, New York, NY 10165
tel 212-661-2880 *fax* 212-661-2883
Director Lettie Lee

Full-length fiction and non-fiction MSS (home 15%, overseas 20%), theatre, films, TV (15%). Will suggest revision when MSS is promising. Works with foreign agencies. No reading fee.

Frieda Fishbein Associates

PO Box 723, Bedford, NY 10506
tel 914-234-7232 *fax* 914-234-4196
e-mail fishbein@juno.com
Contacts Heidi Carlson, Douglas Michael

TV, plays, books, screenplays, film and TV rights. No unsolicited MSS; query first. Reading fee for new writers, or published writers in a new genre.

Forthwrite Literary Agency

3579 E Foothill Boulevard, Suite 327, Pasadena, CA 91107
tel 818-795 2646 *fax* 818-795 5311
e-mail literaryag@aol.com
Owner Wendy Keller

Only non-fiction: business, self-help popular psychology, how-to. Subjects include: animals, art, horticulture/gardening, archaeology, European history (especially English), biography, health (especially homeopathy and alternative medicines), parenting, coffee table (illustrated) books, crafts (bobbin lace, handicrafts, etc), nature, psychology. Send IRC with query. Response in 8 weeks. Founded 1988.

The Fox Chase Agency Inc.*

The Public Ledger Building, Room 930, Independence Square, Philadelphia, PA 19106
tel 215-625-2450 *fax* 215-574-9190

Jeanne Fredericks Literary Agency, Inc.

221 Benedict Hill Road, New Canaan, CT 06840
tel/fax 203-972-3011
e-mail phi@idt.net

Quality non-fiction, especially health, science, women's issues, gardening, antiques and decorative arts, biography, cookbooks, popular reference, business, natural history (home 15%, overseas 20%). No reading fee. Query first, enclosing sae. Founded 1997.

Robert A. Freedman Dramatic Agency, Inc.*

1501 Broadway, Suite 2310, New York, NY 10036
tel 212-840-5760

Plays, motion picture and TV scripts. Send letter of enquiry first, with sae. Formerly Harold Freedman Brandt & Brandt Dramatic Dept., Inc.

Samuel French Inc.*

45 West 25th Street, New York, NY 10010
tel 212-206-8990 *fax* 212-206-1429
President Charles R. Van Nostrand

Play publishers and authors' representatives.

Jay Garon-Brooke Associates Inc.* – see Pinder, Lane & Garon-Brooke Associates Ltd

Gelfman Schneider Literary Agents, Inc.*

250 West 57th Street, Suite 2515, New York, NY 10107
tel 212-245-1993 *fax* 212-245-8678
Directors Jane Gelfman, Deborah Schneider

General adult fiction and non-fiction (home 15%, overseas 20%). Works in conjunction with Curtis Brown, London. Will suggest revision. No reading fee but please send sae for return of material.

Goodman Associates, Literary Agents*

500 West End Avenue, New York, NY 10024
tel 212-873-4806 *fax* 212-580-3278
Partners Arnold P. Goodman, Elise Simon Goodman

Adult book length fiction and non-fiction (home 15%, overseas 20%). No reading fee. Founded 1976.

Sanford J. Greenburger Associates, Inc.*

55 Fifth Avenue, New York, NY 10003
tel 212-206-5600 *fax* 212-463-8718
Contacts Heide Lange, Faith Hamlin, Beth Vesel, Theresa Park, Elyse Cheney

Fiction and non-fiction, film and TV rights. No unsolicited MSS; query first. No reading fee.

The Joy Harris Literary Agency, Inc.*

156 Fifth Avenue, Suite 617, New York, NY 10010-7002
tel 212-924-6269 *fax* 212-924-6609
e-mail jhlitagent@aol.com
President Joy Harris

John Hawkins & Associates, Inc.*

(formerly Paul R. Reynolds, Inc.)
71 West 23rd Street, Suite 1600, New York, NY 10010
tel 212-807-7040 *fax* 212-807-9555
President John Hawkins, *Vice-President* William Reiss, *Foreign Rights* Moses Cardona, *Permissions* Gladys Guadalupe, *Other Agents* Elinor B. Sidel, J. Warren Frazier

Fiction, non-fiction, juvenile. Founded 1893.

Heacock Literary Agency, Inc.*

1523 Sixth Street, Suite 14, Santa Monica, CA 90401
tel 310-393-6277
President Rosalie G. Heacock, *Associate Agent* Robin Henning

Adult non-fiction: self-help, health/medicine, science/technology, philosophy/ psychology, art, women's studies, biography. Fiction including mystery/suspense, action/adventure, mainstream (home 15%, overseas 15%-25%). Will suggest revision; no reading fee but charges for expenses. Works in conjunction with overseas agents. No unsolicited MSS or facsimile submissions. Send synopsis, say why you wrote the book, include bio and 1-2 sample chapters plus sae. Founded 1978.

The Jeff Herman Agency, Inc.*

104 Charles Street, Suite 15A, New York, NY 10014
tel 212-941-0540

Business, reference, popular psychology, computers, health and beauty, spirituality, general non-fiction (home/overseas 15%); will suggest revision where appropriate. Works with overseas agents. No reading fee. Founded 1986.

Frederick Hill Associates

1842 Union Street, San Francisco, CA 94123
tel 415-921-2910 *fax* 415-921-2802
Branch office 8446½ Melrose Place, Los Angeles, CA 90069
tel 213-852-0830 *fax* 213-852-0426

Full-length fiction and non-fiction (home 15%, overseas 20%). Will suggest revision. Works in conjunction with agents in Scandinavia, France, Germany, Holland, Japan, Spain. No reading fee. Founded 1979.

IMG Bach Literary*

22 East 71st Street, New York, NY 10021
tel 212-772-8900 *fax* 212-772-2617

Fiction (no science fiction) and non-fiction. Send query letter with sae for response.

InterLicense, Ltd
200 Gate Five Road, Suite 207, Sausalito, CA 94965
tel 415-331-7460 *fax* 415-331-6940
Executive Director Manfred Mroczkowski

International administration of creative rights in non-fiction, self-help and esoterica, children's books (home/overseas 15%-33%). No reading fee. Founded 1982.

International Creative Management, Inc.*
40 West 57th Street, New York, NY 10019
tel 212-556-5600 *fax* 212-556-5665

No unsolicited MSS, please; send query letters.

JCA Literary Agency Inc.*
27 West 20th Street, Suite 1103, New York, NY 10011
tel 212-807-0888
Contacts Jane Cushman, Jeff Gerecke, Tony Outhwaite

Adult fiction and non-fiction. No unsolicited MSS; query first.

Ben F. Kamsler Ltd
5501 Noble Avenue, Sherman Oaks, CA 91411
tel 818-785-4167 *fax* 818-988-8304
Directors Ben Kamsler, Irene Kamsler

Full-length novel MSS, plays, TV specials, screenplays (home 10%, overseas 20%), performance rights (10%). Will suggest revision on promising MSS. No reading fee, but preliminary letter with sae essential. Founded 1990.

Barbara S. Kouts, Literary Agent*
PO Box 560, Bellport, NY 11713
tel 516-286-1278 *fax* 516-286-1538

Full-length MSS. Fiction and non-fiction, children's and adult (home 10%, overseas 20%); will suggest revision. Works with overseas agents. No reading fee. Query first. Founded 1980.

The Lazear Agency Inc.
430 First Avenue North, Suite 416, Minneapolis, MN 55401
tel 612-332-8640 *fax* 612-332-4648
Contacts Jonathon Lazear, Christi Cardenas-Roen, Cheryl Kissel, Susanne Moncur

Fiction: full-length MSS; non-fiction: proposals. Adult fiction and non-fiction; film and TV rights; foreign language rights; audio, video and electronic rights (home 15%, overseas 20%). No reading fee. No unsolicited MSS; 2-3 page query first with sae for response. No faxed queries. Founded 1984.

Lescher & Lescher Ltd*
67 Irving Place, New York, NY 10003
tel 212-529-1790 *fax* 212-529-2716
Directors Robert Lescher, Susan Lescher

Full-length and short MSS (home 15%, overseas 25%). No unsolicited MSS; query first with sae. No reading fee. Founded 1966.

Ellen Levine Literary Agency Inc.*
Suite 1801, 15 East 26th Street, New York, NY 10010
tel 212-899-0620 *fax* 212-725-4501
Contacts Elizabeth Kaplan, Diana Finch, Louise Quayle
UK Representative A.M. Heath

Full-length MSS: biography, contemporary affairs, women's issues, history, science, literary and commercial fiction (home 15%, overseas 20%); in conjunction with co-agents, theatre, films, TV (15%). Will suggest revision. Works in conjunction with agents in Europe, Japan, Israel, Brazil, Argentina, Australia, Far East. No reading fee; preliminary letter and sae essential. Founded 1980.

Margret McBride Literary Agency*
7744 Fay Avenue, Suite 201, La Jolla, CA 92037
tel 619-454-1550 *fax* 619-454-2156
11684 Ventura Blvd., Suite 956, Studio City, CA 91604
tel 818-508-0031 *fax* 818-508-0039
President Margret McBride, *Vice-President, Associate Agent* Winifred Golden, *Associate Agent (LA office)* Kim Sauer, *Manager of Submissions* Mindy Riesenberg

Full-length and short MSS. Mainstream fiction and non-fiction; no poetry or children's books (home 15%, overseas 25%). No reading fee. Submit query letter with sae to Mindy Riesenberg. Founded 1981.

Gerard McCauley Agency, Inc.*
PO Box 844, Katonah, NY 10536
tel 914-232-5700

Specialises in history, biography, science for general reader.

Anita D. McClellan Associates*
50 Stearns Street, Cambridge, MA 02138
tel 617-576-6950
Director Anita D. McClellan

General fiction and non-fiction. Full-length MSS (home 15%, overseas 20%). Will suggest revision for agency clients. No unsolicited MSS. Send preliminary letter and sae bearing US postage or IRC.

McIntosh & Otis Inc.*
310 Madison Avenue, New York, NY 10017
tel 212-687-7400 *fax* 212-687-6894
Adult Eugene H. Winick, Samuel L. Pinkus, *Adult, Subsidiary Rights* Jakki Spicer, *Juvenile* Dorothy Markinko, Renée Cho, *Film and TV* Evva Joan Pryor

Adult and juvenile literary fiction and non-fiction, film and TV rights. No unsolicited MSS; query first with outline, sample chapters and sae. No reading fee. Founded 1928.

Carol Mann Agency*
55 Fifth Avenue, New York, NY 10003
tel 212-206-5635 *fax* 212-675-4809
Associates Carol Mann, Gareth Esersky, *Rights* Gail Feinberg

Psychology, popular history, biography, general non-fiction; fiction (home 15%, overseas 20%). Works in conjunction with foreign agents. No reading fee. Founded 1977.

Elaine Markson Literary Agency*
44 Greenwich Avenue, New York, NY 10011
tel 212-243-8480 *fax* 212-691-9014
Directors Elaine Markson, Geri Thoma, Sally Wofford-Girand

Full-length MSS. Literary and mainstream commercial fiction (no genre); biography, sociology, history, popular culture, feminism (home 15%, overseas 20%), performance rights (10%); will suggest revision. Works with overseas agents. No reading fee. Founded 1973.

Mildred Marmur Associates Ltd*
2005 Palmer Avenue, Suite 127, Larchmont, NY 10538-2469
tel 212-949-6055 *fax* 212-949-0329
President Mildred Marmur, *Associate* Jane Lebowitz

Serious non-fiction, literary fiction, juveniles. Full-length and short MSS (home licences 15%, overseas licences 20%), performance rights (15%). Works with co-agents in all major countries. No reading fee. Queries must include sae or International Reply Coupons. Founded 1987.

The Evan Marshall Agency
6 Tristam Place, Pine Brook, NJ 07058-9445
tel 201-882-1122 *fax* 201-882-3099
e-mail esmarshall@juno.com
President Evan Marshall

General fiction and non-fiction (home 15%, overseas 20%); screenplays, teleplays (20%). Works in conjunction with overseas agents. Will suggest revision; no reading fee but $38 handling fee for unpublished writers. Founded 1987.

Elisabeth Marton Agency*
1 Union Square, Suite 612, New York, NY 10003-3303
tel 212-255-1908 *fax* 212-691-9061
Owner Tonda Marton

Stage plays only.

Harold Matson Company, Inc.*
276 Fifth Avenue, New York, NY 10001
tel 212-679-4490 *fax* 212-545-1224

Full-length MSS (home 10%, UK 19%, translation 19%). No unsolicited MSS. No reading fee. Founded 1937.

Scott Meredith Literary Agency LP
845 Third Avenue, New York, NY 10022
tel 212-751-4545 *fax* 212-755-2972
President Arthur Klebanoff, *Vice-President* Lisa J. Edwards, *Director, Subsidiary Rights* Barry N. Malzberg
London office A.M. Heath & Co. Ltd

Full-length and short MSS. General fiction and non-fiction, books and magazines, juveniles, plays, TV scripts, motion picture rights and properties (home 10%, overseas 20%), performance rights (10%). Will read unsolicited MSS, queries, outlines. Single fee charged for readings, criticism and assistance in revision. Founded 1946.

Helen Merrill Ltd*
425 West 23rd Street, Suite 1F, New York, NY 10011
tel 212-691-5326 *fax* 212-727-0545

William Morris Agency Inc.*
1325 Avenue of the Americas, New York, NY 10019
tel 212-586-5100

Multimedia Product Development Inc.*
410 South Michigan Avenue, Suite 724, Chicago, IL 60605
tel 312-922-3063 *fax* 312-922-1905
Contact Jane Jordan Browne

General fiction and non-fiction (home 15%, overseas 20%), performance rights (15%). Works in conjunction with foreign agents. Will suggest revision; no reading fee. Founded 1971.

Jean V. Naggar Literary Agency*
216 East 75th Street, Suite 1E, New York, NY 10021
tel 212-794-1082
President Jean V. Naggar, *Agents* Anne Engel, Frances Kuffel

Mainstream commercial and literary fiction (no formula fiction); non-fiction: psychology, science, biography (home 15%, overseas 20%), performance rights (15%). Works in conjunction with foreign agents. No reading fee. Founded 1978.

Ruth Nathan Agency
53 East 34th Street, Suite 207, New York, NY 10016
tel/fax 212-481-1185
Director Ruth Nathan

Fine art, decorative arts, show biz, biographies pertaining to those areas; fiction (Middle Ages only) and true crime (home 15%, overseas 10-15%). No reading fee. Founded 1981.

New England Publishing Associates, Inc.*
PO Box 5, Chester, CT 06412
tel 860-345-READ *fax* 860-345-3660
Directors Elizabeth Frost Knappman, Edward W. Knappman
London Representative Scott Ferris

Serious non-fiction for the adult market (home 15%, overseas varies), performance rights (varies). Works in conjunction with foreign publishers. No reading fee; will suggest revision – if undertaken; 15% fee for placing MSS. Founded 1982.

Harold Ober Associates Inc.*
425 Madison Avenue, New York, NY 10017
tel 212-759-8600 *fax* 212-759-9428
Directors Phyllis Westberg, Henry Dunow, Wendy Schmalz

Full-length MSS (home 15%, British 20%, overseas 20%), performance rights (15%). Will suggest revision. No reading fee. Founded 1929.

Fifi Oscard Agency Inc.*
24 West 40th Street, New York, NY 10018
tel 212-764-1100 *fax* 212-840 5019
President Fifi Oscard, *Agents* Ivy Fischer Stone, Kevin McShane, Nancy Murray

Full-length MSS (home 15%, overseas 20%), performance rights (15%). Will suggest revision. Works in conjunction with many foreign agencies. No reading fee, but no unsolicited submissions.

James Peter Associates, Inc.*
151 Sunset Lane, PO Box 772, Tenafly, NJ 07670
tel 201-568-0760 *fax* 201-568 2959
e-mail bholtje@attmail.com
Contact Bert Holtje

Non-fiction, especially history, politics, popular culture, health, psychology, reference, biography (home 15%, overseas 20%). Foreign rights handled by: Bobbe Siegel, 41 West 83rd Street, New York, NY 10024. Will suggest revision. No reading fee. Founded 1981.

The Pimlico Agency Inc.
Box 20447, Cherokee Station, New York, NY 10021
tel 212-628-9729 *fax* 212-535-7861
Contact Christopher Shepard, *Directors* Kay McCauley, Kirby McCauley

Specialise in general non-fiction and science fiction, horror and fantasy.

Pinder, Lane & Garon-Brooke Associates Ltd
159 West 53rd Street, Suite 14, New York, NY 10019
tel 212-489 0880 *fax* 212-586 9346
London Representative Abner Stein
tel 0171-373 0456

Specialises in fiction. Writer must be referred by an editor or a client. Will not read unsolicited MSS

PMA Literary and Film Management, Inc.
132 West 22nd Street – 12th Floor, New York, NY 10011
tel 212-929-1222 *fax* 212-206-0238
e-mail pmalitfilm@aol.com
President Peter Miller

Full-length MSS, specialising in commercial fiction (especially thrillers), true crime, non-fiction of all types, and all books with global publishing and film and TV production potential (home 15%, overseas 25%), films, TV (10-20%). Works in conjunction with agents worldwide. Preliminary enquiry with career goals, synopsis and resumé essential. Founded 1976.

Raines & Raines*

71 Park Avenue, New York, NY 10016
tel 212-684-5160
Directors Theron Raines, Joan Raines, Keith
Korman
Full-length MSS (home 15%, overseas
20%). Works in conjunction with over-
seas agents. No unsolicited MSS.
Founded 1961.

Renaissance–A Literary Talent Agency

8523 Sunset Boulevard, Los Angeles, CA 90069
tel 310-289-3636 *fax* 310 289-3637
Partners Joel Gotler, Alan Nevins, Irv Schwarz,
Agents Steve Fisher, Brian Lipson
Full-length MSS. Fiction and non-fiction,
plays (home 15%, overseas 20%), film
and TV rights (home 10%, overseas
20%), performance rights. No unsolicited
MSS; query first, submit outline. No
reading fee. Founded 1934.

Helen Rees Literary Agency*

300 Commonwealth Avenue, Boston, MA 02115
tel 617-262-2401 *fax* 617-236-0133
Contact Joan Mazmanian
Business books, self-help, biography,
autobiography, political, literary fiction
(home 15%). Works with foreign agent.
No reading fee. Submit query letter with
sae. Founded 1982.

Mitchell Rose Literary Agency

688 Avenue of the Americas, Suite 303,
New York, NY 10010
tel 212-929-1401 *fax* 212-929-9819
e-mail 71324,1413@compuserve.com
President Mitchell Rose
Popular culture, health, history, general-
non-fiction, distinctive fiction, ethnic
issues (home 15%, overseas 20%); will
suggest revision. No reading fee.
Founded 1987.

Rosenstone/Wender*

3 East 48th Street, New York, NY 10017
tel 212-832-8330 *fax* 212-759-4524
Contacts Phyllis Wender, Susan Perlman Cohen,
Hannah Wallace
Fiction, non-fiction, film and TV rights.
No unsolicited MSS; query first. No read-
ing fee.

Robin Rue*

310 Madison Avenue, New York, NY 10017
tel 212-687-1122 *fax* 212-972-1756
Fiction, non-technical non-fiction.

Russell & Volkening Inc.*

50 West 29th Street, Suite 7E, New York,
NY 10001
tel 212-684-6050 *fax* 212-889-3206
Contacts Jennie Dunham, Timothy Seldes, Joseph
Regal
General fiction and non-fiction, film and
TV rights. No screenplays. No unsolicit-
ed MSS; query first with letter and sae.
No reading fee.

Susan Schulman Literary & Dramatic Agents Inc.*

454 West 44th Street, New York, NY 10036
tel 212-713-1633 *fax* 212-581-8830
Agents for negotiation in all markets
(with co-agents) of fiction, general non-
fiction, children's books, academic and
professional works, and associated subsidiary rights including plays, film and
TV (home 15%, UK 7.5%, overseas
20%). Return postage required.

Charlotte Sheedy Literary Agency, Inc.*

65 Bleecker Street, New York, NY 10012
tel 212-780-9800 *fax* 212-780-0308
Contact Charlotte Sheedy
Fiction and non-fiction, film and TV
rights. No unsolicited MSS; query first
with outline and sample chapters. No
reading fee.

The Shukat Company Ltd*

340 West 55th Street, Suite 1A, New York,
NY 10019
tel 212-582-7614 *fax* 212-315-3752
e-mail staff@shukat.com
President Scott Shukat, *Contact* Patricia
McLaughlin, Maribel Rivas
Theatre, films, novels, TV, radio (15%).
No reading fee. No unsolicited material
accepted.

Singer Media Corporation

Seaview Business Park, 1030 Calle Cordillera,
Unit 106, San Clemente, CA 92673
tel 714-498-7227
Vice-president Helen J. Lee
Interested in foreign language reprint
rights and syndication rights of published non-fiction and fiction.
Represented in most countries abroad
(home 15%, overseas 20%). Published
authors only. No unsolicited MSS; query
first with sae.

The Spieler Agency
154 West 57th Street, Room 135, New York, NY 10019
tel 212-757-4439 *fax* 212-333-2019
Directors F. Joseph Spieler, Lisa M. Ross, John F. Thornton
West Coast office 1328 6th Avenue, Berkeley, CA 94710
tel 510-528-2616 *fax* 510-528-8117
Principal agent Victoria Shoemaker

Full- and short-length MSS. History, politics, ecology, business, consumer reference, some fiction (home 15%, overseas 20%). No reading fee. Founded 1982.

Philip G. Spitzer Literary Agency*
50 Talmage Farm Lane, East Hampton, NY 11937
tel 516-329-3650 *fax* 516-329-3651

General fiction and non-fiction; specialises in mystery/suspense, sports, politics, biography, social issues.

Stepping Stone Literary Agency*
59 West 71st Street, Suite 9B, New York, NY 10023
tel 212-362-9277 *fax* 212-501-8240
President Sarah Jane Freymann, *Associate* Katharine Sands

Fiction and non-fiction, especially commercial and mainstream fiction (home/ overseas 15%). Works in conjunction with Abner Stein and Marsh & Sheil in London. No reading fee. Founded 1974.

Sterling Lord Literistic, Inc.
65 Bleecker Street, New York, NY 10012
tel 212-780-6050 *fax* 212-780-6095
Directors Peter Matson, Sterling Lord, Philippa Brophy, Jody Hotchkiss

Full-length and short MSS (home 15%, overseas 20%), performance rights (15%). Will suggest revision. No reading fee.

Gloria Stern Agency*
12535 Chandler Boulevard, Suite 3, North Hollywood, CA 91607-1934
tel 818-508-6296 *fax* 818-508-6296
Director Gloria Stern

Fiction and films, electronics and multimedia (home 10%, overseas 15%). Reading fee; consultation fee for revisions; some author expenses for placing MSS. Founded 1984.

Roslyn Targ Literary Agency, Inc.*
105 West 13th Street, New York, NY 10011
tel 212-206-9390 *fax* 212-989-6233
e-mail roslyntarg@aol.com

Non-fiction: query with outline, publication history and CV. Fiction: query with approx. 50 pages of MS, synopsis or outline, and CV. All submissions require sae. No phone or fax queries. Affiliates in most foreign countries. No reading fee.

Ralph M. Vicinanza Ltd*
111 8th Avenue, Suite 1501, New York, NY 10011
tel 212-924-7090
Contact Ralph Vicinanza, Chris Lotts, Sharon Friedman

Fiction: literary, women's, 'multicultural', popular (especially science fiction, fantasy and thrillers), children's. Non-fiction (history, business, science, biography, popular culture). Foreign rights specialists. No unsolicited MSS.

Austin Wahl Agency Ltd
1820 North 76th Court, Elmwood Park, IL 60707-3631
tel 708-456-2301 *fax* 708-456-2031
President Thomas Wahl

Full-length and short MSS (home 15%, overseas 20%), theatre, films, TV (10%). No reading fee; professional writers only. Founded 1935.

Wallace Literary Agency, Inc.*
177 East 70th Street, New York, NY 10021
tel 212-570-9090 *fax* 212-772-8979
Directors Lois Wallace, Thomas C. Wallace

Full-length MSS; no cookery, humour, how-to; film, TV, theatre for agency clients. Will suggest revision. No unsolicited MSS; no faxed queries. Founded 1988.

Watkins/Loomis Agency, Inc.
133 East 35th Street, New York, NY 10016
tel 212-532-0080 *fax* 212-889-0506
e-mail watkloomis@aol.com
President Gloria Loomis, *Associate* Nicole Aragi, *Contact* Stacy Schwandt
Representatives Abner Stein (UK), The Marsh Agency (foreign)

Fiction and non-fiction, art, film and TV rights. No unsolicited MSS; query first with sae. No reading fee.

Sandra Watt and Associates
8033 Sunset Boulevard, Suite 4053, Hollywood, CA 90046
tel 213-653-2339
Owner Sandra Watt

Lead women's fiction, suspense, mysteries, New Age, cyber-punk; psychological

self-help, gardening, single-volume reference works; screenplays (home 15%, overseas 25%), films (10%). Works in conjunction with foreign agents. Will suggest revision; no reading fee; $100 marketing fee for unpublished authors. Founded 1978.

Wecksler-Incomco
170 West End Avenue, New York, NY 10023
tel 212-787-2239 *fax* 212-496-7035
President Sally Wecksler, *Associate* Joann Amparan
Illustrated books, non-fiction, some literary fiction, children's books (home 12-15%, overseas 20%); will suggest revision where appropriate. No reading fee. Founded 1971.

Rhoda Weyr Agency*
151 Bergen Street, Brooklyn, NY 11217
tel 718-522-0480 *fax* 718-522-0410
General non-fiction and fiction with particular interest in science, history, biography. Full length MSS for fiction; proposal for n-f (home 15%, overseas 20%), performance rights (15%). Co-agents in all foreign markets. Sae required. Founded 1983.

Writers House Inc.*
21 West 26th Street, New York, NY 10010
tel 212-685-2400 *fax* 212-685-1781
President Albert Zuckerman, *Executive Vice-President* Amy Berkower
Fiction and non-fiction, including all rights; film and TV rights. Original CD-Rom and computer game projects. No screenplays or software. Query first; no reading fee. Founded 1974.

The Wylie Agency, Inc.
250 West 57th Street, Suite 2114, New York, NY 10107
tel 212-246-0069 *fax* 212-586-8953
Directors Andrew Wylie (president), Sarah Chalfant, Bridget Love
London office The Wylie Agency UK Ltd
Literary fiction/non-fiction (home 10%, overseas 20%). No unsolicited MSS accepted.

Mary Yost Associates, Inc.*
59 East 54th Street, Suite 72, New York, NY 10022
tel 212-980-4988
Full-length and short MSS (home and overseas 10%). Works with individual agents in all foreign countries. Will suggest revision. No reading fee. Founded 1958.

Susan Zeckendorf Associates Inc.*
171 West 57th Street, New York, NY 10019
tel 212-245-2928
President Susan Zeckendorf
Literary fiction, women's commercial fiction, mysteries, thrillers, science, music (home 15%, overseas 20%), film, TV rights (15%). Works in conjunction with overseas agents. Will suggest revision. No reading fee. Founded 1978.

Overseas literary agents – other

Most of the agents listed here work in association with an agent in London. Before submitting a manuscript, writers are advised to send a preliminary letter and to ascertain terms.

Argentina

International Editors Co.
Avenida Cabildo 1156, 1426 Buenos Aires
tel 541-786-0888/788-2992
fax 541-786-0888/552-5833

The Nancy H. Smith Literary Agency
(formerly Lawrence Smith Agency)
Avenida de los Incas 3110, Buenos Aires 1426
tel/fax 552-5012
Founded 1938.

Australia

Curtis Brown (Australia) Pty Ltd
27 Union Street, Paddington, Sydney, NSW 2021
tel (02) 9331 5301/9361 6161 *fax* (02) 9360 3935

Literary Resources
6/88A Kurraba Road, Neutral Bay, NSW 2089
fax (02) 9909 3752
Principal Doug Nancarrow
Full-length and short MSS, adult fiction and non-fiction (home 10%, overseas 20%), performance rights (10%); will suggest revision. Works with overseas agents. One-off reading fee for unpublished authors only. Founded 1992.

Brazil

Agencia Literária Balcells Mello e Souza Riff
Rua Visconde de Pirajá, 414 s1 1108 Ipanema, 22410-002 Rio de Janeiro, RJ
tel (55-21) 287-6299 fax (55-21) 267-6393
e-mail lriff@mtec.com.br
Contact Lucia de Mello e Souza Riff

Karin Schindler, Rights Representative
(formerly Dr J.E. Bloch Literary Agency)
Caixa Postal 19051, 04505-970 São Paulo, SP
tel 241-9177 fax 241-9077

Canada

Acacia House Publishing Services Ltd
51 Acacia Road, Toronto, Ontario M4S 2K6
tel/fax 416-484-8356
Managing Director Mrs Frances A. Hanna
Literary fiction and non-fiction, quality commercial fiction, most non-fiction, except business books; selective quality children's list, mainly fiction (15% English language worldwide, 30% translation), performance rights (15-30%). No science fiction, horror or occult. Works with overseas agents. Reading fee on MS over 200pp, where an evaluation is also provided. Founded 1985.

Authors' Marketing Services Ltd
200 Simpson Avenue, Toronto, M4K 1A6
tel 416-463-7200 fax 416-469-4494
e-mail 102047.111@compuserve.com
Director Larry Hoffman
Adult fiction, biography and autobiography (home 15%, overseas 20%). Reading fee charged for unpublished writers; will suggest a revision. Founded 1978.

Eastern Europe

Artisjus
Mészáros u. 15-17, 1016 Budapest, Hungary
postal address H-1538 Budapest, Pf. 593, Hungary
tel 1-212-15-53 fax 1-212-15-52
e-mail artisjus@datanet.hu
Agency for Theatre and Literature of the Hungarian Bureau for the Protection of Authors' Rights.

Aura-Pont, Theatrical and Literary Agency Ltd
Radlická 99, Prague 5, Czech Republic
tel/fax (0422) 53 99 09, 53 63 51
Director Zuzana Jezková
Handles authors' rights in books, theatre, film, TV, radio software – both Czech and foreign, literary scouting for Czech publishers (home 10%, overseas 15%). Founded 1990.

Dilia
Krátkého 1, Prague 9, 190 03, Czech Republic
tel (02) 82 68 41/8 fax (0422) 82 40 09
Theatrical and Literary Agency.

Interlit Services Ltd
PO Box 125, 130 00 Prague 3, Czech Republic
tel (02) 78 19 324 tel/fax 78 10 327
Directors Klaus Flugge, Otakar Bozejowski, Manager Alena Smídová
Sells rights to Czech and Slovak publishers, including fiction, sci-fi, popular science and esoteric (home 10%). Founded 1993.

Lex Copyright
Szemere utca 21, 1054 Budapest, Hungary
tel (1) 332 9340 fax (1) 131 6181
Director Dr Gyorgy Tibor Szanto
Specialises in representing American and British authors in Hungary. Founded 1991.

Lita
Partizánska 21, 815 30 Bratislava, Slovakia
tel/fax 42 7 313645
Slovak Literary Agency.

Andrew Nurnberg Associates Prague, s.r.o
Seifertova 81, Prague 3, Czech Republic
tel/fax (42) 2278 2041 fax (42) 2278 2308
e-mail nurnprg@mbox.vol.cz
Contact Petra Tobisková

Prava i Prevodi
Koste Jovanovica 18, 11000 Belgrade, Yugoslavia
tel (11) 460 290 fax (11) 472 146
e-mail pipbelyu@eunet.yu
Director Ana Milenkovic
Specialises in representing American and British authors in former Eastern Europe (15 languages). Founded 1983.

France

Bureau Littéraire International Marguerite Scialtiel
14 rue Chanoinesse, 75004 Paris
tel (1) 43 54 71 16
Contact Geneviéve Ulmann

Agence Hoffman
77 boulevard Saint-Michel, 75005 Paris
tel (1) 43 26 56 94 *fax* (1) 43 26 34 07

Mme Michelle Lapautre
6 rue Jean Carriès, 75007 Paris
tel (1) 47 34 82 41 *fax* (1) 47 34 00 90

La Nouvelle Agence
7 rue Corneille, 75006 Paris
tel (1) 43 25 85 60 *fax* (1) 43 25 47 98
Contact Mary Kling

Germany (see also Switzerland)

Brigitte Axster
Dreieichstr. 43, D-60594 Frankfurt/Main
tel 069-629856 *fax* 069-623526

Agence Hoffman
Bechsteinstrasse 2, 80804 Munich
tel 089-308 48 07 *fax* 089-308 21 08

Michael Meller Literary Agency
PO Box 400 323, 80703 Munich
tel (089) 366371 *fax* (089) 366372
Full-length MSS. Fiction and non-fiction, screenplays for films and TV (home 15%, overseas 20%). Own US office. No reading fee. Founded 1988.

Thomas Schlück
Literary Agency, Hinter der Worth 12, 30827 Garbsen
tel 05131-93053 *fax* 05131-93045

India

Ajanta Books International
1 U.B. Jawahar Nagar, Bungalow Road, Delhi 110007
tel 2926182, 7258630 *fax* 91-11-7132908/7213076
Proprietor S. Balwant
Full-length MSS in social sciences and humanities (commission varies according to market – Indian books in Indian and foreign languages, foreign books into Indian languages). Will suggest revision; charges made if agency undertakes revision; reading fee. Founded 1975.

Israel

I. Pikarski Ltd Literary Agency
200 Hayarkon Street, PO Box 4006, Tel Aviv 61040
tel 03-5270159/5231880 *fax* 03-5270160
Director Ilana Pikarski
General trade publishing and merchandising rights. Founded 1977.

Italy

Eulama SRL
Via Guido de Ruggiero 28, 00142 Rome
tel (06) 540 73 09 *fax* (06) 540 87 72
Directors Harald Kahnemann, Karin von Prellwitz, Norbert von Prellwitz, Pina Ocello von Prellwitz
Quality fiction and non-fiction, social sciences, politics, philosophy, religion, psychology, education, linguistics, architecture, urban studies (home 15%, overseas 20%); will suggest revision where appropriate. Works with overseas agents. No reading fee. Founded 1962.

Grandi Associati SRL
Via Caradosso 12, 20123 Milan
tel (02) 469 55 41/481 89 62 *fax* (02) 481 95108
e-mail lgest@mbox.vol.it
Directors Laura Grandi, Stefano Tettamanti
Provides publicity and foreign rights consultation for publishers and authors as well as sub-agent services; will suggest revision where appropriate. Reading fee. Founded 1988.

ILA – International Literary Agency – USA
I-18010 Terzorie-IM
tel (0184) 48 40 48 *fax* (0184) 48 72 92
e-mail libri.ggadmw.it
Publishers' and authors' agent, interested only in series of best-selling and mass market books by proven, published authors with a track record. Also interested in published books on antiques and collectibles. Founded 1969.

Agenzia Letteraria Internazionale SRL
Via Fratelli Gabba 3, 20121 Milan
tel (02) 86 54 45/86 46 34 18/86 15 72 *fax* (02) 87 62 22

News Blitz International
Via Guido Banti 34, 00191 Rome
tel (06) 33 32 641/33 30 252 *fax* (06) 33 32 651
Literary Department Giovanni A. Congiu

Japan

The English Agency (Japan) Ltd
Sakuragi Building 4F, 6-7-3 Minami Aoyama,
Minato-ku, Tokyo 107
tel 03-3406 5385 *fax* 03-3406 5387
Managing Director William Miller
Handles work by English-language writers living in Japan; arranges Japanese translations for internationally established publishers, agents and authors; arranges Japanese localisations for CD-Rom. Standard commission: 10%. Own representatives in New York and London. No reading fee. Founded 1979.

Orion Literary Agency
1-3-5-3F Kanda-Jimbocho, Chiyoda-ku, Tokyo 101
tel 03-3295-1405 *fax* 03-3295-4366

Netherlands

Auteursbureau Greta Baars-Jelgersma
Clingelbeeck, Utrechtseweg 131-6, NL-6812,
AA Arnhem
tel (026) 446 24 31 *fax* (026) 446 21 97
Literature; illustrated co-productions, including children's, art, handicraft, hobby and nature (home/overseas 20%). Works with overseas agents. Occasionally charges a reading fee. Founded 1951.

Internationaal Literatuur Bureau B.V.
Postbus 10014, 1201 DA, Hilversum
tel (035) 621 35 00 *fax* (035) 621 57 71
e-mail mkohn@worldaccess.nl
Contact Menno Kohn

New Zealand

Glenys Bean Literary Agency
PO Box 47-098, Auckland 2
tel/fax (09) 378-6287
Adult and children's fiction, educational, non-fiction, film, TV, radio (home, UK 15%, foreign rights 20%). Represented by Sanford Greenburger (USA); translations – Sheil Land (UK). Preliminary letter, synopsis and sae required. Founded 1989.

Richards Literary Agency
3-49 Aberdeen Road, Castor Bay, Auckland 9
postal address PO Box 31240, Milford, Auckland 9
tel (09) 410-5681 *fax* (09) 410-6389
Partners Ray Richards, Barbara Richards
Full-length MSS, fiction, non-fiction, juvenile, educational, academic books; films, TV, radio (home 10%, overseas 10-20%). Preliminary letter, synopsis with sae required. No reading fee. Founded 1977.

Nigeria

Joe-Tolalu & Associates (Nigeria) Ltd
Plot 14, Block A, Surulere Industrial Road, Ogba,
PO Box 7031, Ikeja, Lagos
tel 01-4925078, 059-412041
Directors Joseph Omosade Awolalu, Tosin Awolalu, Foluke Awolalu, Dimeji Popoola
Full-length MSS: fiction and non-fiction; Christian literature; short MSS: picture books only (home 10-15%, overseas 15-20%; translation 15%, performance/film/ TV 10%); will suggest revision. Works with overseas agents. Preliminary letter essential; no reading fee. Founded 1983.

Portugal

Ilidio da Fonseca Matos
Avenida Gomes Pereira, 105-3¬-B, 1500 Lisbon
tel 716 29 88 *fax* 715 44 45

Russia

Permissions & Rights Ltd, Moscow
14-12 Sadovaya Triumfalnaya, 103006 Moscow,
Russia
tel (095) 209 2263 *fax* (095) 883 6050
Director Konstantin Palchikov
Specialises in representing American and British authors in Russia, Latvia, Lithuania, Estonia and Ukraine. Founded 1993.

Scandinavia, including Finland and Iceland

A/S Bookman
Nørregade 45, DK-1165 Copenhagen K, Denmark
tel 33 14 57 20 *fax* 33 12 00 07
Handles rights in Denmark, Sweden, Norway, Finland and Iceland for foreign authors.

Gösta Dahl & Son, AB
Aladdinsvägan 14, S-167 61 Bromma, Sweden
tel 08 25 62 35 *fax* 08 25 11 18

Lennart Sane Agency AB
Holländareplan 9, S-374 34 Karlshamm, Sweden
tel 0454 123 56 *fax* 0454 149 20
Directors Lennart Sane, Elisabeth Sane, Ulf Töregård
Fiction, non-fiction, children's books. Founded 1969.

Leonhardt & Høier Literary Agency aps
Studiostræude 35, DK-1455 Copenhagen K, Denmark
tel 33 13 25 23 *fax* 33 13 49 92

Gustaf von Sydow
Lorensbergsvägen 76, S 136 69 Haninge, Sweden
tel/fax 08 776 10 54
Directors Gustaf von Sydow, Elisabeth von Sydow
Handles TV, film, celebrity and news features in Sweden, Norway, Denmark and Finland. Literary agent working in Sweden, Norway, Denmark and Finland. Founded 1988.

Sane Töregård Agency
Holländareplan 9, S-374 34 Karlshamn, Sweden
tel (46) 454 12356 *fax* (46) 454 14920
e-mail toregard@algonet.se
Directors Lennart Sane, Elisabeth Sane, Ulf Töregård
Represents authors, agents and publishers in Scandinavia and Holland for rights in fiction, non-fiction and children's books. Founded 1995.

Singapore

Susan Wakeford Literary Agency
11 Malcolm Road, Singapore 308254
tel/fax (65) 252-0391
Director Susan Wakeford
General fiction and non-fiction. No reading fee. Founded 1996.

South Africa

Frances Bond Literary Services
32B Stanley Teale Road, Westville North 3630, KwaZulu-Natal
postal address PO Box 223, Westville 3630
tel (031) 824532 *fax* (031) 822620
Managing Editor Frances Bond, *Chief Editor* Eileen Molver
Full length MSS. Fiction and non-fiction; juvenile and children's literature. Consultancy service on contracts and copyright. Preliminary phone call or letter and sae required. Founded 1985.

International Press Agency (Pty) Ltd
PO Box 67, Howard Place 7450
tel (021) 5311926 *fax* (021) 5318789
Manager Terry Temple
UK office Ursula A. Barnett, 19 Avenue South, Surbiton, Surrey KT5 8PJ
tel/fax 0181- 390 4414

Literary Dynamics
PO Box 51037, Musgrave 4002
tel/fax (031) 222139/3092913
Managing Editor Isabel Cooke
Full-length MSS, fiction and non-fiction, screenplays; public speaking consultant, literary consultant to industry; reading fee for in-depth evaluation. Founded 1985.

Sandton Literary Agency
PO Box 785799, Sandton 2146
tel (011) 4428624
Directors J. Victoria Canning, M. Sutherland
Full-length MSS and screenplays; lecture agents. Professional editing. Write or phone first. Works in conjunction with Renaissance-Swan Film Agency, Inc., Los Angeles, USA. Founded 1982.

Spain

A.C.E.R. Literary Agency
Amor de Dios 1, 28014 Madrid
tel 1-369-2061 *fax* 1-369-2052
Directors Elizabeth Atkins, Laure Merle d'Aubigné
Represents UK, US, French and German publishers for Spanish and Portuguese translation rights; represents Spanish- and Portuguese-language authors (home/overseas 10%); will suggest revision where appropriate. £20 reading fee. Founded 1959.

Miss Carmen Balcells
Agencia Literaria Carmen Balcells, Diagonal 580, Barcelona 08021
tel 200-89-33, 200-85-65 *fax* 200-70-41

Mercedes Casanovas Literary Agency
Iradier 24, 08017 Barcelona
tel 212-47-91 *fax* 417-90-37
Literature, non-fiction, children's books (home 10%, overseas 20%). Works with overseas agents. No reading fee. Founded 1980.

Raquel de la Concha
Plaza de las Salesas 9, 1°B-28004 Madrid
tel 308-55-85 *fax* 308-56-00
Director Raquel de la Concha
Representing foreign fiction, non-fiction, children's books and Spanish authors. No reading fee.

International Editors Co., S.A.
Rambla Cataluña 63, 3°-1ª, 08007 Barcelona
tel 215-88-12 *fax* 487-35-83

Lennart Sane Agency AB
Paseo de Mejico 65, Las Cumbres-Elviria, E-29600 Marbella (Malaga)
tel (9) 52 83 41 80 *fax* (9) 52 83 31 96
Fiction, non-fiction, children's books, film and TV scripts; will suggest revision where appropriate. No reading fee. Founded 1965.

Julio F. Yañez
Agencia Literaria, Via Augusta 139, 6°-2ª, 08021 Barcelona
tel 200-71-07 *fax* 209-48-65

Switzerland

Paul & Peter Fritz AG Literary Agency
Jupiterstrasse 1, CH-8032 Zürich
postal address Postfach 1773, CH-8032 Zürich
tel (01) 388 41 40 *fax* (01) 388 41 30

Represents authors, agents and publishers in German-language areas.

Liepman AG
Maienburgweg 23, CH-8044 Zürich
tel (01) 261 76 60 *fax* (01) 261 01 24
Contacts Eva Koralnik, Ruth Weibel
Represents authors, agents and publishers from all over the world for German translation rights, and selected authors for world rights.

Mohrbooks AG, Literary Agency
Klosbachstrasse 110, CH-8032 Zürich
tel (01) 251 16 10 *fax* (01) 262 52 13
Contact Sabine Ibach

Niedieck Linder AG
Zollikerstrasse 87, Postbox, CH-8034 Zürich
tel (01) 381 65 92 *fax* (01) 381 65 13
Represents German-language authors and Italian-language authors on the German market.

West Indies

CMS Literary Services
PO Box 993, Road Town, Tortola, British Virgin Islands
tel/fax 809-495-9202
e-mail maczero@caribsurf.com
Directors Ginger Hodge, George Graham
Children's and adult fiction; Caribbean literature and poetry (10%). Will suggest revision; no reading fee. Willing to work with other agencies in publishing Caribbean writers. Founded 1994.

Literary agents for television, film, radio and theatre

Listings for these and other literary agents start on page 334.
*US literary agents

A & B Personal Management Ltd
American Play Company Inc.*
Artellus Ltd
Yvonne Baker Associates
Berman, Boals & Flynn, Inc.*
Blake Friedman Literary, TV & Film Agency Ltd
Alan Brodie Representation Ltd
Rosemary Bromley Literary Agency
Peter Bryant (Writers)
Casarotto Ramsay Ltd
Jonathan Clowes
Elspeth Cochrane Agency
Rosica Colin Ltd
Jane Conway-Gordon
Cruickshank Cazenove Ltd
Curtis Brown
Curtis Brown Ltd*
Judy Daish Associates Ltd
Felix De Wolfe
Eddison Pearson
Ann Elmo Agency*
Fact & Fiction Agency Ltd
Film Rights Ltd
Frieda Fishbein Ltd*
Laurence Fitch Ltd
Jill Foster Ltd
Robert A. Freedman Dramatic Agency, Inc.*
French's

Vernon Futerman Associates
Jüri Gabriel
Eric Glass
Gregory & Radice Authors' Agents*
Richard Hatton Ltd
David Higham Associates Ltd
Valerie Hoskins
ICM Ltd
International Copyright Bureau Ltd
Harry Joyce Ltd
Juvenilia
Ben F. Kamsler Ltd*
The Lazear Agency Inc.*
Lemon Unna & Durbridge Ltd
Ellen Levine Literary Agency, Inc.*
Barbara Levy Literary Agency
Christopher Little Literary Agent
Andrew Mann Ltd
The Evan Marshall Agency*
Judy Martin
Elisabeth Marton Agency*
Blanche Marvin
MBA Literary Agents
Scott Meredith Literary Agency Inc.*
Helen Merrill Ltd*
Richard Milne

William Morris Agency Inc.*
William Morris Agency (UK) Ltd
Fifi Oscard Associates, Inc.*
The Peters Fraser & Dunlop Group Ltd
PMA Literary and Film Management, Inc.*
PVA Management Ltd
Radala & Associates
Renaissance-Swanson Film Agency, Inc.*
Tessa Sayle Agency
Susan F. Schulman Literary & Dramatic Agents Inc.*
The Sharland Organisation Ltd
Sheil Land Associates Ltd
Caroline Sheldon Literary Agency
The Shukat Company Ltd*
Singer Media Corporation*
Micheline Steinberg Playwrights' Agent
Sterling Lord Literistic, Inc.*
Gloria Stern Agency*
Jon Thurley
Austin Wahl Agency, Inc.*
Wallace Literary Agency, Inc.*
Warner Chappell Plays Ltd
A.P. Watt Ltd
Sandra Watt and Associates*

Merchandising agents

A number of agents specialise in the exploitation of characters derived from books, films, television programmes, and so on. This can include selling properties to production companies as well as the handling and developing of any merchandise related to the characters concerned. What follows is a selective listing, both of agents and of properties handled.

BBC Licensing, BBC Worldwide Ltd
Woodlands, 80 Wood Lane, London W12 0TT
tel 0181-576 2725 *fax* 0181-743 0393
Representing BBC TV and Radio and a selection of copyright owners. Properties: *Animal Hospital, Animals of Farthing Wood, Antiques Roadshow, The Archers, BBC News & Current Affairs, BBC Sport, Big Break, Blue Peter, The Busy World of Richard Scarry, Clothes Show, Dad's Army, Doctor Who, EastEnders, Every Second Counts, Fireman Sam, Food & Drink, Gardeners' World, The Generation Game, Grandstand, Hairy Jeremy, Heartbreak High, Keeping Up Appearances, Live & Kicking, Mastermind, Match of the Day, Monty – the Dog Who Wears Glasses!, Morag the Cow, Mr Blobby, Noddy, Noel's House Party, Oakie Doke, One Foot in the Grave, One Man & his Dog, Only Fools & Horses, Otis the Aardvark, People's Century, Pingu, Plasmo, The Prince of Atlantis, A Question of Sport, Radio 1, Radio 2, Radio 3, Radio 4, Radio 5 Live, Reeves & Mortimer, The Silver Brumby, Songs of Praise, Spider, Teletubbies, Telly Addicts, Top Gear, Top of the Pops, Wallace & Gromit, William's Wish Wellingtons.*

Copyright Promotions Ltd
12th Floor, Metropolis House, 22 Percy Street, London W1P 0DN
tel 0171-580 7431 *fax* 0171-631 1147
Managing Director Richard Culley, *Publicity Manager* Jane Garner
Properties: *Star Wars, Indiana Jones, Young Indiana Jones, Spider-Man, Fantastic Four, Ironman, The Incredible Hulk, Mask Animation, Sky Dancers,*

Dragon Flyz, Test and County Cricket Club, Story Store, Judge Dredd, Judge Dredd the Movie, Mr Men and *Little Miss, Pink Panther, Sonic the Hedgehog* (Sega); Kate Veal originals: *Oliver Otter & Friends, Cherished Teddies, Reboot, Wind in the Willows, Willows in Winter, Manga Video, Cosmopolitan* (Hearst Magazines), *Boyzone, Dennis the Menace, Desperate Dan, Minnie the Minx, Bash Street Kids, Zig and Zag, X Files, Tank Girl, Mighty Morphin Power Rangers Movie.* Founded 1974.

The Copyrights Company (UK) Ltd
Manor Barn, Milton, Nr Banbury, Oxon OX15 4HH
tel (01295) 721188 *fax* (01295) 720145
London office 7 Square Rigger Row, Plantation Wharf, York Road, London SW11 3TZ
tel 0171-924 3292 *fax* 0171-924 3208
Directors Nicholas Durbridge (Managing), Linda Pooley, Mark Robinson, Julie Nellthorp, Karen Addison
Properties include *Beatrix Potter, Paddington Bear, Brambly Hedge, Postman Pat, Flower Fairies,* and other book-related properties for merchandise licensing.

Hawk Books
309 Canalot Studios, 222 Kensal Road, London W10 5BN
tel 0181-969 8091 *fax* 0181-968 9012
Director Patrick Hawkey
Properties: *Billy Bunter, Dopey Dinosaur.*

Link Licensing Ltd
7 Baron's Gate, 33-35 Rothschild Road, London W4 5HT
tel 0181-996 4800 *fax* 0181-747 9452
Directors Claire Derry, David Hamilton, Gordon Power

Properties: *Asterix*, *Barbie*, *Bug Alert*, *Camberwick Green*, *Caribou Kitchen*, *Christopher Crocodile*, *Creature Comforts*, *The Forgotten Toys*, *Goosebumps*, *The Magic Roundabout*, *The Magic School Bus*, The Natural History Museum, *Noah's Island*, *Jane Hissey's Old Bear & Friends*, *Percy the Park Keeper*, *The Slow Norris*, *The Very Hungry Caterpillar*, *The Wind in the Willows*, *What-a-Mess*. Founded 1986.

Patrick, Sinfield (PSL)

95 White Lion Street, London N1 9PF
tel 0171 837 5440 *fax* 0171-837 5334
e-mail psluk@dircon.co.uk
Directors Christopher Patrick, John Sinfield

Represents properties of: *Rugrats*, *Clarissa Explains It All*, *The Ren & Stimpy Show*, *Rocko's Modern Life*, *Hey Arnold!*, *Aaahh!! Real Monsters*; *Fido Dido*, *Snoopy*, *Dilbert*; *World of Bears*, *Planet Happy*; *MTV logo*; *Beavis and Butt-Head*; *Garfield*; *Face Offs*; *The Mask of Zorro*, *Zorro – The animated TV series*; *Crayola*; *Love Letters*. Founded 1980.

WCA Licensing

18 Beckwith Road, London SE24 9LG
tel 0171-274 6263 *fax* 0171-274 1509
e-mail wca@pro-net.co.uk
Partners Elaine collins and Arabella Woods

Properties include *Coronation Street*, *Lexx*, *Tom & Vicky*, *The Grand*, *Cracker*, *Mrs Merton*, *This Morning* plus a range of celebrity chefs and comedians. Founded 1993.

Michael Woodward Creations

Parlington Hall, Aberford,
West Yorkshire LS25 3EG
tel (0113) 281 3913 *fax* (0113) 281 3911
Contacts Michael Woodward, Janet Woodward (Licensing Director), Rebecca Sheavyn (Licensing Manager)

International licensing company with own US office and associated offices in Holland, Japan and Australia. Artist management, licensing of design and character merchandise worldwide. Current properties include: *Teddy Tum Tum*, *Rambling Ted*, *Wild Ones*, *Best Bunny Company*, *Ragamuffins*, John Seerey-Lester, Alan Hunt, Debbie Cook, Sarah Jane Szikora, Richard Henson, Christine Jopling. New artists and concepts considered. Send sae with synopsis/illustrations; scripts only not accepted. Founded 1979.

Art and illustration

Freelancing for beginners

*Full-time posts for illustrators are not only highly specialised but, sadly, very rare. Because the needs of those who commission illustration tend to change on a regular basis, most artists have little choice but to offer their skills to a variety of clients in order to make a living. **Fig Taylor** describes the opportunities open to the freelance illustrator.*

As a freelance illustrator you will be entering a hugely competitive arena and a professional attitude towards targeting, presenting, promoting and delivering your work will be vital to your success. Equally crucial is a realistic understanding of how the illustration industry works and of your place within the scheme of things. Without adequate research into your chosen field of interest it is all too easy to approach inappropriate clients – a frustrating and disheartening experience for both parties, to say nothing of its being both expensive and time-consuming.

Who commissions illustration?

Magazines and newspapers

Whatever your eventual career goals, your first stop for research should be your largest local newsagent. Most illustrators receive their first commissions from editorial clients who, whilst offering comparatively modest fees, are actively keen to try out fresh talent. Briefs are by and large fairly loose, though deadlines can be short, particularly in the case of daily and weekly publications. However, fast turnover also ensures a swift appearance in print – positive proof of your professional status to clients in other, more lucrative, spheres. Given then that it is possible to use the editorial field as a springboard, it is essential to appreciate its breadth when seeking to identify your own individual market. Between them, magazines and newspapers accommodate an infinite variety of illustrative styles and techniques. Don't limit your horizons by approaching only the most obvious titles and/or those you would read yourself. Consider also trade and professional journals, free publications and those available on subscription from membership organisations or charities. Remember, the more potential clients you uncover, the brighter your future will be.

Greetings cards

Many decorative, humorous and fine art-biased illustrators are interested in providing designs for greetings cards and giftwrap, where there is a definite market for their skills. As with editorial, fees are unlikely to be high but many small card companies are keen to use new or lesser known artists. You may be expected to produce samples of artwork on a speculative basis prior to receiving a definite commission – therefore it makes sense to target those companies who are likely to be most responsive (see *Card sense*, page 379).

In addition to card shops and the gift departments of larger stores (many of whom employ commissioning buyers for their own ranges), you may find trade fairs such as London's bi-annual Top Drawer and Birmingham's International Spring and Autumn Shows yield the best results for your research. Geared primarily towards buyers, trade fairs offer you the

opportunity to check out the forthcoming ranges of numerous card, stationery and giftware manufacturers as well as enabling you to make contacts.

Be warned, however, that most exhibitors will be far too busy selling to go through your work there and then. It is best to make a separate appointment to do this after the fair has ended. For further details, contact Top Drawer organisers, P&O Events, or Trade Promotion Services Ltd, which organise the International Shows.

Book publishing

With the exception of adult illustrated non-fiction, where the emphasis is on decorative, specialist and technical illustration, the majority of publishers are interested in full-colour figurative work for use on paperback and hardback book covers. Strong, realistic work which shows the figure in a narrative context is invaluable to those who commission massmarket fiction, which includes such genres as historical and contemporary romance, thrillers, family sagas, horror, science fiction and fantasy. On the whole, publishing deadlines are civilised and massmarket covers well paid. Illustrators whose work is more stylised or experimental would be better advised to approach those smaller imprints and independent publishing houses which deal with more literary, upmarket fiction. Although fees are significantly lower and commissions less frequent, briefs are less restrictive and a wider range of styles can be accommodated.

Children's publishers use a diversity of styles, covering the gamut from baby books, activity and early learning through to full-colour picture books, older children's novels with black and white spot illustrations and teenage fiction and non-fiction. Author/illustrators are particularly welcomed by picture book publishers – though, whatever your style, you must be able to draw children well and to sustain a character throughout a narrative. See *Writing and illustrating children's books* on page 245.

Design

It is unnecessary for you to have design training in order to approach a design group for illustration work. However, it is advisable that you be in print. Both designers and their clients – who are largely uncreative and will ultimately be footing the bill – will be impressed and reassured by relevant, published work. Although fees are higher than those in editorial and publishing, this third-party involvement generally means a more restrictive brief. Deadlines may vary while styles favoured range from conceptual through to realistic, decorative, humorous and technical.

For research purposes, look at *Design Week* or the monthly *Creative Review* (both published by Centaur Communications), or the monthly *Graphics International* (published by Market Link Publishing). Design groups have different biases and specialities – for instance, some might concentrate on packaging while others may deal exclusively with corporate and financial literature.

The Creative Handbook (published by Variety Media Publications), available at some reference libraries, carries many listings. Individual contact names are also available at a price from File FX, which specialises in providing creative suppliers with up-to-date information on commissioning clients in all spheres.

Advertising

As with design, you should ideally be quite well established before seeking commissions in advertising. Fees can be high, deadlines short and clients extremely demanding. Advertising agencies currently use significantly less illustration than clients in other areas and have a tendency to 'play safe' stylistically. What little illustration they do commission might be incorporated into direct mail or press advertising, hoardings or, very occasionally, animated for television – fees will vary depending on whether a campaign is locally or nationally based.

Most agencies employ an art buyer to

look at portfolios. A good one will know what each creative team is working on at any given time and may refer you to specific art directors. Agency listings and client details may be found in the *BRAD Agencies & Advertisers* (published by Emap Media) and *ALF* (Account List File, published by Register Information Services), available at reference libraries. File FX can supply individual contact names. Magazines such as *Creative Review* and Haymarket's weekly, *Campaign*, also carry agency news.

Portfolio presentation

Obviously, the more outlets you can find for your talents the better. However, do not be tempted to develop a myriad of styles in an attempt to please every client you see. Firstly it's unlikely that you will and secondly, in the UK market, you'll stand a better chance of being remembered for one strong, consistent style. You'll also get far more commissions that way. Thus, when assembling your professional portfolio, try to exclude samples which are, in your own eyes, weak, irrelevant, uncharacteristic or simply unenjoyable to do – it is worth noting that even published work counts for little if the content is substandard. For maximum impact, aim to focus solely on your strengths. Should you be one of those rare, multi-talented individuals who find it hard to limit themselves stylistically, try splitting conflicting media or subject matter into separate portfolios geared towards different types of clients.

Having no formal illustrative training need not be a handicap providing your portfolio accurately reflects the needs of potential clients. With this is mind, some find it useful to assemble 'mock-ups' using existing magazine layouts. By responding to the copy, working in proportion to original images and replacing them with your own illustrations, both you and the client will be able to see how your work will look in context. Eventually, as you become more established, you'll be able to augment these with published pieces.

Ideally, your folder should be of the zip-up, ringbound variety and never any bigger than A2 as clients usually have very little desk space. Complexity of style and diversity of subject matter will be key elements in deciding how many pieces to include but all should be neatly, consistently mounted on lightweight paper or card and placed inside protective plastic leaves. Professional photographs of originals are acceptable to clients, as are good quality lasercopies or bubblejet prints. However, tacky, out-of-focus snapshots are not. Also avoid including too many sketchbooks and academic studies – particularly life drawings, which are anathema to clients. It will be taken for granted that you know how to draw from observation.

Interviews and beyond

Making appointments can be hard work but clients take a dim view of spontaneous visits from passing illustrators. Having identified the most relevant person to see (either from a written source or by asking the company directly), clients are best approached by letter or telephone call. Most magazines and publishing houses are happy to see freelances, though portfolio 'drop-offs' are becoming increasingly common within the industry. Some clients will automatically take photocopies of your work for their files. However, it is always advisable to have some form of self-promotional material to leave behind – for instance, a full-colour A6 postcard is ideal for this purpose. In the case of larger companies, it is also worth asking your contact if others might be interested in your work. An introduction by word of mouth has a distinct advantage over cold-calling.

Cleanliness, punctuality and enthusiasm are more important to clients than the kind of clothes you wear – as is a professional attitude towards taking and fulfilling a brief. A thorough understanding of what a job entails is paramount from the outset. You will need to know all your client's requirements regarding roughs; format, size and flexibility of artwork; pre-

Useful addresses

Centaur Communications
49-50 Poland Street, London W1V 4AX
tel 0171-439 4222
Publishes *Design Week* and *Creative Review*.

Emap Media
Emap Business Communications,
33-39 Bowling Green Lane, London EC1R 0DA
tel 0171-505 8000
Publishes *BRAD Agencies & Advertisers*.

File FX
Unit 14, 83-93 Shepperton Road,
London N1 3DF
tel 0171-226 6646
Specialises in providing creative suppliers with up-to-date information on commissioning clients in all spheres.

Association of Illustrators
1st Floor, 32-38 Saffron Hill, London EC1N 8FH
tel 0171-831 7377
Publishes *Survive – the Illustrators Guide to a Professional Career* and *Rights – the Illustrators Guide to Professional Practice*.

Market Link Publishing
The Mill, Dearwalden Business Park,
Wendens Ambo, Saffrom Walden,
Essex CB11 4JX
tel (01799) 544200
Publishes *Graphics International*.

P&O Events Ltd
Earls Court Exhibition Centre, Warwick Road,
London SW5 9TA
tel 0171-370 8185
Top Drawer organisers.

Register Information Services
2 Holford Yard, Cruikshank Street,
London WC1X 9HF
tel 0171-833 3883
Publishes *ALF* (Account List File).

Trade Promotion Services Ltd
Exhibition House, 6 Warren Lane,
London SE18 6BW
tel 0181-855 9201

Variety Media Publications
34-35 Newman Street, London W1P 3RD
tel 0171-637 3663
Publishes *The Creative Handbook*.

ferred medium and whether the image is to be executed in colour or black and white. You will also need to know when the deadline is. Never, under any circumstances, agree to undertake a commission unless you are certain you can deliver on time and always work within your limitations. Talent is nothing without reliability.

Be organised!

Once your career is off the ground it is imperative to keep organised records of all your commissions. Contracts can be verbal as well as written, though details – financial and otherwise – should always be confirmed in writing and duplicated for your files. Likewise, file away corresponding client faxes, letters and order forms. *Survive – the Illustrators Guide to a Professional Career* and *Rights – the Illustrators Guide to Professional Practice* (both published by the Association of Illustrators) offer artists a wealth of practical, legal and ethical information. Subjects covered include contracts, licences, royalties, copyright and ownership of artwork.

Money

Try not to undertake a commission before agreeing on a fee, although this may not always prove practicable in the case of rush jobs. Most publishing and editorial fees are fixed and, unfortunately, there are no hard and fast rules for negotiation where design and advertising are concerned. As a pointer, however, take into consideration the type of client involved and the distribution of the final printed product – obviously a national 48-sheet poster advertising a well-known supermarket chain is likely to pay better than a local press advertisement for a poodle parlour! Some illustrators find it helpful to work out a daily rate incorporating various overheads such as the cost of computer equipment, rent, heating, materials, travel and telephone charges – while others prefer to negotiate on a flat fee basis. Some clients will actually tell you if they have a specific figure in mind, though you

may have to put them on the spot. Certainly, as you become more established, you'll be able to use comparable jobs as benchmarks when negotiating a fee.

Basic book-keeping – making a simple, legible record of all your financial transactions, both incoming and outgoing – will be vital to your sanity once the tax inspector starts to loom. It will also make your accountant's job easier, thereby saving you money. If your annual turnover is less than £15,000, it is unnecessary to provide the Inland Revenue with detailed accounts of your earnings. Information regarding your turnover, allowable expenses and net profit may simply be entered on your tax return. Although an accountant is not integral to this process, many find it advantageous to employ one. The tax system is complicated and deal-ing with the Inland Revenue can be stressful, intimidating and time-consuming – not least since the introduction of changes regarding 'self-assessment', which applies to the 1996-1997 tax year onwards. Accountants offer invaluable advice on tax allowances, National Insurance and tax assessments as well as dealing expertly with the Revenue on your behalf – thereby enabling you to attend to the business of illustrating. See *Income tax* on page 641, *Social security contributions* on page 651 and *Social security benefits* on page 659.

Fig Taylor began her career as an illustrators' agent in 1983. For 12 years she has been resident 'portfolio surgeon' at the Association of Illustrators and also operates as a private consultant to non-AOI member artists. In addition, she lectures extensively in Business Awareness to BA and HND illustration students.

Art agents and commercial art studios

Before submitting work, artists are advised to make preliminary enquiries and to ascertain terms of work. Commission varies but averages 25-30%. The Association of Illustrators (see page 458) provides a valuable service for illustrators, agents and clients.

*Member of The Society of Artists Agents

A.L.I. Press Agency Ltd
Boulevard Anspach 111-115, B9–1000 Brussels, Belgium
tel 02 512 73 94 *fax* 02 512 03 30
Director G. Lans

Cartoons, comics, strips, puzzles, entertainment features, illustrations for covers. All feature material for newspapers and magazines. Large choice of picture stories for children and adults. Market for transparencies: paintings, portraits, nudes, landscapes, handicrafts. Interest in video productions.

Allied Artists Ltd
31 Harcourt Street, London W1H 1DT
tel 0171-724 8809 *fax* 0171-262 8526
Director Gary Mills

Represents over 35 artists specialising in highly finished realistic figure illustra-tion for magazines, books, video, plates, prints and advertising. Also offers extensive library of second rights illustrations for syndication.

Arena*
144 Royal College Street, London NW1 0TA
tel 0171-267 9661 *fax* 0171-284 0486
Contacts Tamlyn Hennessey, Valerie Paine, Alison Eldred and Charlotte Phillips

Represents 45 artists working mostly for book covers, children's books and design groups. Average commission 30%. Founded 1970.

Art Solutions
4 Granville Road, Sevenoaks, Kent TN13 1ER
tel/fax (01732) 458917
e-mail buky@centrenet.co.uk
Director Anne Buky

Unusually varied and versatile artwork suitable for reproduction on greetings cards, giftwrap, stationery, ceramics, gifts of all kinds; children's and adult's publishing. Commission: 30%. Founded 1992.

Aspect Art

Courtyard Unit E5, The Old Imperial Laundry, 71-73 Warriner Gardens, London SW11 4XW
tel/fax 0171-720 5439
Partners Lady Vanessa Brown and M.T.G. O'Donovan

Architectural art in any medium to sell, commission or exhibit; also publish original prints. Commission: 30%. Founded 1994.

Associated Freelance Artists Ltd

124 Elm Park Mansions, Park Walk, London SW10 0AR
tel 0171-352 6890 *fax* 0171-352 8125
Directors Eva Morris, Doug FitzMaurice

Freelance illustrators mainly in children's and educational fields; and lots of greetings cards.

Sarah Brown Agency

10 The Avenue, London W13 8PH
tel 0181-998 0390 *fax* 0181-843 1175
Contact Brian Fennelly

Illustrations for publishing and advertising. Sae essential for unsolicited material. Commission: 25% UK, 33.3% USA. Founded 1977.

Beint & Beint*

3 Richborne Terrace, London SW8 1AR
tel 0171-793 7000 *fax* 0171-735 2565

Illustrations in a variety of styles for advertising, design groups and publishing. Founded 1976.

Central Illustration Agency*

36 Wellington Street, London WC2E 7BD
tel 0171-240 8925/836 1106 *fax* 0171-836 1177
e-mail c.illustration.a@dial.pipex.comm.
Director Brian Grimwood

Illustrations for design, publishing and advertising. Commission: 30%. Founded 1983.

Barry Everitt Associates

23 Mill Road, Stock, Essex CM4 9LJ
tel (01277) 840639 *fax* (01277) 841223
Director Barry M. Everitt

UK/international representation for artists, illustrators and designers seeking high quality markets for their work. Greetings cards, fine art prints, calendars, collectors' ceramics, giftware, books, etc. Sae required for return of work.

Jacqui Figgis*

The Glasshouse, 11 Lettice Street, London SW6 4EH
tel 0171-610 9933 *fax* 0171-610 9944
Director Jacqui Figgis

Illustrations for advertising, design, publishing and editorial. Commission: 30%. Founded 1995.

Folio Illustrators' & Designers' Agents*

10 Gate Street, Lincoln's Inn Fields, London WC2A 3HP
tel 0171-242 9562 *fax* 0171-242 1816

All areas of illustration. Founded 1976.

Simon Girling & Associates

61D High Street, Hadleigh, Suffolk IP7 5DY
tel (01473) 824083 *fax* (01473) 827846
e-mail info@sga.keme.co.uk

Representing over 50 illustrators, accepting commissions for book publishing (children's and adult), encyclopaedias, magazines, dust jackets, as well as a portfolio of licensed characters. Commission: 30%. Founded 1985.

Graham-Cameron Illustration

The Studio, 23 Holt Road, Sheringham, Norfolk NR26 8NB
tel (01263) 821333 *fax* (01263) 821334
Partners Mike Graham-Cameron, Helen Graham-Cameron

All forms of illustration for publishing, communications and advertising. Specialises in children's books and educational materials. Founded 1988.

The Guild of Aviation Artists

Unit 4.18, Bondway Business Centre, 71 Bondway, London SW8 1SQ
tel/fax 0171-735 0634
President Michael Turner PGAVA, *Secretary* Hugo Trotter DFC

Professional body of 350 artists specialising in aviation art in all mediums. The Guild sells, commissions and exhibits members' work. Commission: 25%. Founded 1971.

Hambleside Ltd

Winton Road, Petersfield, Hants GU32 3HA
tel (01730) 231010 *fax* (01730) 231117
e-mail hambleside@compuserve.com
web site hambleside@btinternet.com
Directors D.R. Yellop, R.A. Jeffery, M.G.W. Goodman, W.J.Cumper, R.B. Gamble (USA)

Design studio specialising in all forms of promotional graphics, advertising and marketing. Enquiries from technical illustrators and special effect photographers welcome. Founded 1990.

John Hodgson Agency*

38 Westminster Palace Gardens, Artillery Row, London SW1P 1RR
tel 0171-580 3773 *fax* 0171-222 4468

Illustrations for publishing, advertising, design. Sae with samples please. Commission: 25%. Founded 1965.

Image by Design

Lydford Farm, Highbury Street, Coleford, Bath BA3 5NS
tel/fax (01373) 812393
Partners John R. Brown, Burniece M. Brown

Artwork for prints, greetings cards, calendars, posters, stationery, book publishing, jigsaw puzzles, tableware, ceramics. Commission: negotiable. Founded 1987.

Kathy Jakeman Illustration*

20 Trefoil Road, London SW18 2EQ
tel 0181-875 9525 *fax* 0181-874 4874

Illustration for publishing – especially children's; also design, editorial and advertising. Please send sae with samples. Commission: 25%.

Libba Jones Associates

Hopton Manor, Hopton, Nr Wirksworth, Derbyshire DE4 4DF
tel (01629) 540353 *fax* (01629) 540577
Contacts Libba Jones, Ieuan Jones

High quality artwork and design for china, greetings cards and giftwrap, jigsaw puzzles, calendars, prints, posters, stationery, book illustration, fabric design. Submission of samples required for consideration. Founded 1983.

John Martin & Artists Ltd*

26 Danbury Street, London N1 8JU
tel 0171-734 9000 *fax* 0171-226 6069
Directors W. Bowen-Davies, C.M. Bowen-Davies, B.L. Bowen-Davies, L.A. Bowen-Davies

Illustrations for children (educational and fictional), dust jackets, paperbacks, magazines, encyclopedias, advertising. Return postage with any artwork sent please. Founded 1956.

Meiklejohn Illustration

28 Shelton Street, London WC2H 9HP
tel 0171-240 2077 *fax* 0171-836 0199

Contacts Chris Meiklejohn, Paul Meiklejohn, Malcolm Sanders

All types of illustration. Founded 1971.

N.E. Middleton

20 Trefoil Road, London SW18 2EQ
tel 0181-875 9525 *fax* 0181-874 4874

Designs for greetings cards, stationery, prints, calendars and china. Sae with samples, please.

Maggie Mundy Illustrators' Agency*

14 Ravenscourt Park Mansions, Dalling Road, London W6 0HG
tel 0181-748 2029 *fax* 0181-748 0353
e-mail 106206.1417@compuserve.com

Represents 25 artists in varying styles of illustration for children's books. Return postage must be included with submissions.

The Organisation*

The Basement, 69 Caledonian Road, London N1 9BT
tel 0171-833 8268 *fax* 0171-833 8269
e-mail organise@easynet.co.uk
Partners Jane Buxton and Lorraine Owen

All aspects of illustration from advertising campaigns, book covers, print, packaging, editorial work through to working directly with clients both in the UK and abroad. Commission: 30%. Founded 1986.

Oxford Illustrators Ltd

Aristotle Lane, Oxford OX2 6TR
tel (01865) 512331 *fax* (01865) 512408
e-mail oxford_illust@compuserve.com

Studio of 25 full-time illustrators working for publishers, business and industry. All types of artwork including science, technical, airbrush, graphic, medical, biological, botanical, natural history, figure, cartoon, maps, diagrams, and charts. Artwork supplied as PMT, bromide, film, Syquest, Zip, optical disk, Mac or PC, with both b&w and colour proofs. Plus ISDN line. Not an agency. Founded 1968.

Pennant Illustration*

Studio Crown Reach, 149A Grosvenor Road, London SW1V 3JY
tel 0171-630 8914 *fax* 0171 834 9470
Director Matthew Doyle

Illustrations for publishing, design and advertising. Samples must be accompanied by an sae. Commission: 25%. Founded 1992.

Specs Art

93 London Road, Cheltenham, Glos. GL52 6HL
tel (01242) 515951 *fax* (01242) 518862
e-mail roland@specsart.co.uk
web site www.specsart.co.uk
Partners Roland Berry and Stephanie Prosser

High quality illustration work for advertisers, publishers and all other forms of visual communication.

Summer Lane Pictures Ltd

Lower Tower Street, Birmingham B19 3NE
tel 0121-359 6269 *fax* 0121-333 5366
Managing Director Malcolm McGivan

Design-led licensing agency offering a wide variety of images, linking artists and illustrators with manufacturers in the gift and publishing industries; in-house reproduction facilities available. Sae with samples essential. Founded 1993.

Temple Rogers Artists' Agency

120 Crofton Road, Orpington, Kent BR6 8HZ
tel (01689) 826249 *fax* (01689) 896312
Contact Patrick Kelleher

Illustrations for children's educational books, picture strips and magazine illustrations. Commission: by arrangement.

2D Illustration Agency

114 Ladbroke Grove, London W10 5NE
tel 0171-727 5243/8685 *fax* 0171-727 9680
Proprietors Brian Whitehead, Mair Ellis

Stylised, contemporary illustrations for advertising, design and publishing, Europe-wide. Sae with samples please. Commission: 30% UK, 35% overseas. Founded 1986.

Vicki Thomas Associates

19 Hickman Close, Fulmer Road,
London E16 3TA
tel 0171-511 5767 *fax* 0171-473 5177
Consultant Vicki Thomas

Considers the work of illustrators and designers working in greetings and gift industries, and promotes such work to gift, toy, publishing and related industries. Written application and b&w photocopies required. Commission: 30%. Founded 1985.

Wildlife Art Agency

Studio 16 Muspole Workshops,
25-27 Muspole Street, Norwich, Norfolk NR3 1DJ
tel (01603) 617868 *fax* (01603) 219017
e-mail wildlife@paston.co.uk
Contact Sarah Whittley

Illustrations of all things natural, including gardening and food. Clients range from children's/adults' books, greetings cards, design and advertising agencies. Sae must be included with work submitted for consideration. Commission: 30%. Founded 1992.

Michael Woodward Creations

Parlington Hall, Aberford,
West Yorkshire LS25 3EG
tel (0113) 281 3913 *fax* (0113) 281 3911
Proprietor Michael R. Woodward

International art licensing agency with offices in the USA and subsidiary offices in Holland, Japan and Australia. Licenses artists' work for greetings cards, stationery, posters, fine art prints, gift products, etc. Specialist character merchandise division. Freelance artists please send samples with sae. Founded 1979.

Michael Woodward Fine Art

Parlington Hall, Aberford,
West Yorkshire LS25 3EG
tel (0113) 281 3913 *fax* (0113) 281 3911
Proprietor Michael R. Woodward

Artist management. Represents: Mackenzie Thorpe, Sarah Jane Szikora, John Holt. Artists wanting representation in the fine art field should send transparencies of work with biography, plus sae. Founded 1996.

Card sense

Finding the right outlet for greetings card designs is easier once the market is explained. **William Shone** *describes the differences between the two types of greetings card publishers and how to identify which to submit work to.*

Greetings card publishers have a voracious appetite for fresh design ideas but they are not the sort to win the Turner Prize. The sitting room mantlepiece is traditionally the home of a greetings card, so the more mantlepiece-friendly a design is, the more a publisher is likely to accept and print it. Warm, bright sunflowers and tubby, baroque cherubs have been highly popular in their time as cards, but never anatomical cross sections of farm animals.

The market

There are currently around 800 publishers of greetings cards, from multi-million pound organisations such as Hallmark to small-time sole traders operating at home. Publishers used to produce their own distinct ranges of cards with a common style or design theme but today intense competition has led to poaching of publishing territories in both the designs of cards and the retail outlets where they are sold. However, the market for artists remains clear: there are two types of publisher – wholesale and direct-to-retail. Wholesale publishers produce the cards sold in corner shops, post offices and newsagents. Direct-to-retail publishers produce cards sold in specialist card shops.

The wholesale publisher

Wholesale cards are purchased by retailers from a warehouse or cash-and-carry shop. This type of card is for an occasion such as a birthday or Mother's Day, and carries a message or verse inside. The designs of wholesale cards fall into five main categories:

- 'traditional' – typically a vase of flowers or a country scene
- 'juvenile' – ponies and racing cars
- 'cute characters' – teddy bears
- 'whimsical' – boozy Christmas parties
- 'cute and whimsical' – boozy teddy bears.

Wholesale publishers have recently started to print commissioned contemporary art cards, i.e. cards which do not fit in to any of the above categories, but these represent a minority of their designs. Wholesale cards need to have mass market, as opposed to a 'cutting edge,' appeal. Because they are cheaper to buy than direct-to-retail cards, wholesale publishers rely on a high volume of sales to recoup satisfactory returns. There is also a high turnover of designs so artists working in the wholesale sector can expect a steady flow of new commissions.

Since wholesale sector cards are designed for a captioned occasion such as Mother's Day, the more occasions a design will fit the better its chances of being published. A teddy bear design for Father's Day might, if suitably executed, be republished at a later date with a 'Happy Birthday Son' caption. Republishing the same design with a new caption will bring the artist a repeat fee.

When wholesale cards are displayed in shops, only the top third of each card can be seen because of the way they are stacked. Therefore the message and the most striking features of the artwork needs to be in this part of the card and

arranged in as eye-catching a way as possible – a card only has seconds to attract customers' attention.

Direct-to-retail publishers

Direct-to-retail publishers produce more innovative, some say more creative, ranges of cards than those from the wholesale sector. Each range is identified by a common design theme with a minimum of about eight designs per range. There may be some occasions cards but most of the ranges are blank. Categories of direct-to-retail cards include 'fine art', 'humour', 'children's', 'handmade,' 'contemporary' and 'photographic.' Specialist card shops buy the cards from publishers via agents or representatives.

The commissioned art cards found in the wholesale trade usually mimic trends created by direct-to-retail publishers. Cards produced by direct-to-retail publishers have a contemporary feel drawn from trends in illustration, design, photography and fashion. At the time of writing the same bright colours fashionable for clothes are also in fashion for cards. The most commercial card designs are original and exciting and ahead of their time, but only by about five minutes – anything too off-beat won't sell. There are some peculiar ranges of humour cards for the under 35's, but original cards that are successful tend also to be uncomplicated and warm.

Targeting

Too much good artwork boomerangs home because artists target unsuitable publishers. Before submitting work, look around card shops to see which card publishers might best suit your designs. The publisher's name, address and telephone number is printed on the back of every card. There is no standard procedure for presenting work so you will need to find out from publishers individually what they expect to see. First of all, telephone and ask if they will look at freelance work. Some of the larger wholesale publishers only employ in-house designers.

Trade magazines

Two trade magazines that cover the industry are useful to the artist for their updates on card art trends.

Progressive Greetings
Max Publishing Ltd, United House, North Road, London N7 9DP
tel 0171-700 6740
Editor Jacqueline Brown
Monthly £30 p.a.

Includes names and addresses of publishers; the editor is keen to tailor the magazine more for artists. Also publishes a directory of services twice a year with some relevant information on agents and copyright consultants and a special supplement on art cards. The editor organises seminars for artists who want to publish their work as greetings cards and she welcomes queries from artists about the greetings industry.

Greetings Magazine
Lema Publishing, Unit No. 1, Queen Mary's Avenue, Watford, Herts. WD1 7JR
tel (01923) 250909 *fax* (01923) 250995
10 p.a. £30 p.a.

Official journal of the Greeting Card Association. Articles, features and news related to the greetings card and giftwrap industry. A new artists' directory lists artists' names, contact details, medium and subject matter with up to 3 colour samples of work reproduced for each. It costs £120 p.a. to advertise in the directory.

The wider your portfolio of styles the better, but ask whether the publisher prefers to see a range of finished work, some sketches or both. Remember that most designs will need to be in portrait because of the way cards are stacked in shops.

If you are sending work to a wholesale publisher, each design must be organised around a caption. It is usual to leave a blank space on the finished design for your suggested caption because, in the event of publication, the caption will be overprinted on the design. Check with the publisher for their requirements.

The majority of direct-to-retail cards are blank but there is a trend now toward captioning. Whereas a wholesale card caption is an overprinted and generally replaceable message, the caption of a direct-to-retail card is integral to the style and feel of that design – a part of the total artwork.

Always include a stamped addressed envelope with work. A colour laser copy, photograph or slide is perfectly adequate for assessment purposes – it is never a good idea to send originals.

The Greeting Card Association has a list of 45 of their members willing to receive freelance work (see also pages 382 and 429). A thoroughly concentrated search can be carried out at the various card and gift fairs which take place throughout the year. The major forthcoming shows are: the Spring Fair at the NEC, Birmingham, Top Drawer at Earls Court, London and the Harrogate Gift Trade Fair. The advantage of visiting trade fairs is that artists can meet the publishers face to face. It is useful to have a supply of business cards at hand. If publishers are too busy with buyers to see your portfolio, you can exchange cards and make an appointment after the fair has ended.

The Internet

There are a number of art directories springing up on the Internet. At the time of writing, the on-line directory with the strongest link to the greetings industry is probably Redbox. The Internet is still finding its virtual feet, but the potential advantage of an on-line service is that it can offer freelances the chance to market their portfolios worldwide to card publishers and many other creative buyers.

Copyright

Most publishers will pay freelance artists a one-off flat fee of between £175 and £300 per design. Royalties are generally only paid to artists with a long and successful track record in greetings card design. When you make an agreement with a publisher, it is important to have a

Further information

The Greeting Card Association
41 Links Drive, Elstree WD6 3PP
tel/fax 0181-236 0024
Contact Leslie Grace
Publishes a list of members, available by sending an A5 sae.

AN Publications
PO Box 23, Sunderland SR4 6DG
tel 0191-567 3589 *fax* 0191-564 1600
e-mail anpubs@anpubs.demon.co.uk
Publish *Licensing Reproductions* and *Commissioning Contracts*. Price: £3 each.

Illustrators, The Association of
First Floor, 32-38 Saffron Hill,
London EC1N 8FN
tel 0171-831 7377 *fax* 0171-831 6277
Publishes *Rights* by Simon Stern, a comprehensive guide to commissioning. Price: £25 plus £1 p&p (non-members); £15 plus £1 p&p (members).

Trade fairs

The Spring Fair at the NEC
tel 0181-855 9201

Top Drawer at Earls Court, London
tel (01923) 244555

Harrogate Gift Trade Fair
tel 0171-370 8360

The Internet

Redbox
web site http://www.redbox.onthevine.com

signed written contract, a copy for each party. In all circumstances artists should retain the copyright of their designs and the ownership of the physical artwork. The licence agreement should specify this and other essential 'ground rules' concerning what a publishing company intends to use the design for (e.g. for only greetings cards or for other merchandise as well), where it will be used (in the UK, Europe, USA, or worldwide) and for how long it will be used. Defining the use and area leaves the artist free to exploit for-

eign rights without having to ask permission from the client (i.e. the card publisher). For further information on licensing agreements, see *British copyright law* on page 615.

In brief

Before submitting work, decide if you want to target the wholesale or direct-to-retail market, or both. Find out which publishers are suitable for your style(s)/designs and ask how they like work to be presented. If your artwork is accepted for publication or you are offered a commission, be clear about the terms of any proposed agreements.

William Shone has published a range of greetings cards and is now working on projects to develop links between artists and greetings card publishers.

Card and stationery publishers which accept illustrations and verses

Before submitting work, artists are advised to write giving details of the work they have to offer, and asking for requirements.

*Member of the Greeting Card Association

Abacus Cards Ltd*
Gazeley Road, Kentford, Newmarket, Suffolk CB8 7QB
tel (01638) 552399 *fax* (01638) 552103
Partners Jeff Fothergill and Brian Carey, *Art Director* Bev Cunningham
Quality greetings cards and giftwrap. Most subjects considered; submit artwork or transparencies. Will consider copy/ideas/jokes for humour cards. Founded 1991.

Arcadian Publications Ltd
Foster House, Maxwell Road, Borhamwood, Herts. WD6 1JB
tel 0181-381 5000 *fax* 0181-953 3674
Directors Susan Gregg, Adrian Neil Cantrill
Traditional fine art images; 5 x 4in transparencies. No verses. Founded 1994.

The Andrew Brownsword Collection*
Kelston Park, Kelston, Bath BA1 9AE
Senior Design Manager Nick Adsett
Contemporary and traditional imagery for greetings cards, giftwrap and social stationery. Submit transparencies of original artwork, or original artwork. Will consider verses. Founded 1975.

The Bucentaur Gallery Ltd*
Eastway, Fulwood, Preston PR2 9WS
tel (01772) 662967 *fax* (01772) 002909
Contact Range Co-ordinator
Fine art, traditional greetings cards: florals, animals, wildlife, cottages, etc., plus traditional Christmas subjects. All submissions to be accompanied by an sae; original artwork, or minimum 5 x 4in transparencies, photographs or laser copies of originals. No verses please. Founded 1977.

Card Connection Ltd*
Park House, South Street, Farnham, Surrey GU9 7QQ
tel (01252) 733177 *fax* (01252) 735644
e-mail ho@cardconnection.co.uk
Managing Director Adrian Atkinson, *Product Director* Jonathan Waterson
Cute, humour, traditional, floral, contemporary, sport. Submit artwork, colour copies or 5 x 4in transparencies of originals. No verses. Founded 1992.

Carlton Cards Ltd
Mill Street East, Dewsbury, West Yorkshire WF12 9AW
tel (01924) 465200
Marketing Director Keith Auty, *Creative Director for Alternative Ranges* Ged Backland

All types of artwork, any size; submit as colour roughs, colour copies or transparencies. Especially interested in humorous artwork and ideas.

Caspari Ltd*
9 Shire Hill, Saffron Walden, Essex CB11 3AP
tel (01799) 513010 *fax* (01799) 513101
Managing Director Keith Entwisle

Traditional fine art/classic images; 5 x 4in transparencies. No verses. Founded 1990.

C.C.A. Stationery Ltd
Eastway, Fulwood, Preston PR2 9WS
tel (01772) 662800

Publishers of personalised wedding stationery and Christmas cards. Pleased to consider original artwork, preferably of relevant subject matter; Christmas verses considered.

The Classic Card Company Ltd – Classic/Valentines*
James Street West, Bath BA1 2BS
tel (01225) 444228 *fax* (01225) 444214

Greetings cards for all occasions; giftwrap, artwork in colour; sentimental and humorous editorial verses considered.

J. Arthur Dixon
Forest Side, Newport, Isle of Wight PO30 5QW
tel (01983) 523381 *fax* (01983) 529719
Managing Director Andy McGarrick, *Head of Design* Carlton Knight

All subjects considered – artwork and photographs (transparencies 35mm or larger). Verses considered. Founded 1930.

Gallery Five Ltd*
121 King Street, London W6 9JG
tel 0181-741 8394 *fax* 0181-741 4444
Contact D.J. Walser (art director)

Send samples which give an idea of style; or phone for an appointment on the day (i.e. no forward appointments). No verses. Founded 1960.

Gibson Greetings International Ltd
Gibson House, Hortonwood 30, Telford, Shropshire TF1 4ET
tel (01952) 608333 *fax* (01952) 608363
Product Director Jan Duncan

Everyday, wedding and all seasonal illustrations: cute, humorous, juvenile age, traditional landscapes and subjects;

giftwrap and calendars. Greeting card traditional and humorous verse. Founded 1991.

Giesen & Wolff (UK) Ltd
Kaygee House, Rothersthorpe Crescent, Northampton NN4 9JD
tel (01604) 709499 *fax* (01604) 709399
Contact Studio Manager

Illustrations: cute characters, wedding, sympathy, juvenile age subjects, traditional landscapes, humour – anything suitable for everyday and all seasonal occasions. Will consider verses. Founded 1908.

The Gift Business
Lower Tower Street, Birmingham B19 3NE
tel 0121-359 7088 *fax* 0121-333 5366
Managing Director Trevor Jones, *Sales and Marketing Director* Sue Hammond

Commercial decorative art with broad appeal – especially classic and contemporary floral imagery, William Morris designs, fine art – for greetings cards and gift stationery. Founded 1986.

Graphic Humour Ltd
4 Britannia House, Point Pleasant, Wallsend, Tyne and Wear NE28 6HQ
tel 0191-295 4200 *fax* 0191-295 3916

Risqué and everyday artwork ideas for greetings cards; short, humorous copy. Also unusual and Victorian photos/illustrations for use as humorous greetings cards. Founded 1984.

Greetings Cards By Noel Tatt Ltd
Appledown House, Barton Business Park, Appledown Way, New Dover Road, Canterbury, Kent CT1 3AA
tel (01227) 455540 *fax* (01227) 458976
Directors Noel Tatt, Vencke Tatt, Jarle Tatt, Diane Tatt, Richard Parsons

Greetings cards and giftwrap. Founded 1954/1988.

Hallmark Cards Ltd*
Hallmark House, Station Road, Henley-on-Thames, Oxon RG9 1LQ
tel (01491) 578383 *fax* (01491) 578817
Chairman and Chief Executive A. Brownsword, *Managing Director UK* Ian Bant, *Product Director* B. Arganbright

Humorous editorial ideas considered, including short jokes and punchlines. Submit all ideas to the Editorial Department. No traditional verse.

Hambledon Studios Ltd

Metcalf Drive, Altham Industrial Estate, Altham,
Accrington, Lancs. BB5 5SS
tel (01282) 687300 *fax* (01282) 687404
Art Managers D. Jaundrell, J. Ashton, D. Fuller,
N. Harrison, K. Ellis, *Creative Director* M. Smith

Designs suitable for reproduction as
greetings cards. *Brands* Arnold Barton,
Donny Mac, Reflections, New Image.

Hammond Gower Publications*

14 Tideway Yard, Mortlake High Street,
London SW14 8SN
tel 0181-878 5210 *fax* 0181-876 1487
Directors Alan Daly, Nicci Gower

Greetings cards and giftwrap: children's,
contemporary, occasions, blank cards.
All types of artwork considered: paintings, silk, line drawing, embroidery, etc.
Founded 1985.

Hanson White

9th Floor, Wettern House, 56 Dingwall Road,
Croydon, Surrey CR0 0XH
tel 0181-260 1200 *fax* 0181-260 1212
Product Development Manager Sarah Garratt

Artwork for greetings cards, giftwrap and
related stationery items: cute, humorous,
contemporary, fine art. Humorous copy
lines, including rude jokes, poems and
punchlines; occasionally accept non-
humorous verses. Founded 1958.

Images & Editions*

Bourne Road, Essendine, Nr Stamford,
Lincs. PE9 4UW
tel (01780) 57118 *fax* (01780) 54620
Directors Lesley Forrow, Maurice Miller

Greetings card artwork: cute, floral, animals. Founded 1984.

Jodds

PO Box 353, Kidlington, Oxon OX5 2UU
tel (01865) 331437 *fax* (01865) 331007
Partners M. Payne and J.S. Payne

Bright contemporary art style greetings
cards which include humour; must give
out a warm feel. Submit colour photocopies with sae. No verses. Founded 1988.

Jooles Ltd*

Unit 5, St Margaret's Business Centre,
Drummond Place, Moor Mead Road,
Twickenham, Middlesex TW1 1JN
tel 0181-744 1333 *fax* 0181-891 4295
Product Manager Maggie Waller

Write with sae for submission of artwork.
Artwork for greetings cards: humorous,
traditional, cute. Founded 1988.

Thomas Leach Ltd

54 Ock Street, Abingdon,
Oxon OX14 5DE
tel (01235) 520444 *fax* (01235) 554270
Contact David Leach

Line drawings of religious subjects suitable for reproduction as Christmas or
Easter cards.

Henry Ling & Son (London) Ltd*

14-20 Eldon Way, Paddock Wood,
Kent TN12 6BE
tel (01892) 838574 *fax* (01892) 838676
Contact Head of Publishing

Artwork for greetings cards; no verses.

M.G. Media

22 Maze Street, Bolton,
Lancs. BL3 1SB
tel (01204) 384768
Proprietor Marcia J. Galley

Consultant to writers, publishers and
artists in the greetings card market.
Researches publishers' requirements and
helps find a suitable outlet for creative
work. All styles and occasions represented. Founded 1995.

Medici Society Ltd

34-42 Pentonville Road, London N1 9HG
tel 0171-837 7099 *fax* 0171-837 9152
Contact The Art Department

Requirements: full colour paintings suitable for reproduction as greetings cards.
Send preliminary letter with brief details
of work.

The Paper House Group plc*

Shepherd Road, Gloucester,
Glos. GL2 6EL
tel (01452) 423451 *fax* (01452) 410312
Publishing Director Graham Foster

Publishers of greetings cards, humorous
and fine art. Brands: Elgin Court,
Parnassus Gallery, Aries Design, The
Humour Factory, Royle Publications.
Submit original artwork, or transparen-
cies or photographs of originals.

Paperlink Ltd*

356 Kennington Road, London SE11 4LD
tel 0171-582 8244 *fax* 0171-587 5212
Directors Louise Tighe, Jo Townsend, Tim Porte,
Tim Purcell

Publishers of ranges of humorous and
contemporary art greetings cards,
giftwrap, calendars, notelets, mugs, T-
shirts, prints. Produce products under
licence for charities. Founded 1986.

Pomegranate Europe Ltd
Fullbridge House, Fullbridge, Maldon,
Essex CM9 4LE
tel (01621) 851646 *fax* (01621) 852426
Sales Director Dave Harris

Contemporary art for cards, calendars
and gift stationery. Will consider original
artwork or transparencies of originals.
Founded 1993.

postLEEDS
4 Granby Road, Leeds LS6 3AS
tel/fax 0113-278 7540
Contact Christine Hankinson

Publishers of postcards and distributor
for mail order, and overseas agent for
card distribution. Cards to subvert the
dominant paradigm, preferably with
humour and style. Founded 1979.

Nigel Quiney Publications Ltd*
Cloudesley House, Shire Hill, Saffron Walden,
Essex CB11 3FB
tel (01799) 520200 *fax* (01799) 520100
Contact Ms J. Arkinstall

Everyday and seasonal greetings cards
(sizes: 7 x 5in, 9 x 6in and 12 x 9in) and
giftwrap. Submit original artwork or
5 x 4in transparencies of originals.

Rainbow Cards Ltd*
Albrighton Business Park, Newport Road,
Albrighton, Wolverhampton,
West Midlands WV7 3ET
tel (01902) 374347
Directors M. Whitehouse, R. Fellows, J.
Whitehouse, I. Mackintosh

Artwork for greetings cards and verses.
Founded 1977.

The Really Good Card Company Ltd*
Osney Mead, Oxford OX2 0ES
tel (01865) 246888 *fax* (01865) 246999
Director David Hicks

Do not send original artwork; send photocopies or snapshots with sae. No verses. Founded 1987.

Felix Rosenstiel's Widow & Son Ltd
Fine Art Publishers, 33-35 Markham Street,
London SW3 3NR
tel 0171-352 3551

Invites offers of original oil paintings and
strong watercolours of a professional
standard for reproduction as picture
prints for the picture framing trade. Any
type of subject considered; send photographs of work.

Royle Publications Ltd
Royle House, Wenlock Road, London N1 7ST
tel 0171-253 7654
Creative Director Richard D'Arcy

Greetings cards, calendars, fine art reproductions and social stationery.

Santoro Graphics Ltd
342-344 London Road, Mitcham Cricket Green,
Mitcham, Surrey CR4 3ND
tel 0181-640 9777 *fax* 0181-640 2888
Directors Lucio Santoro, Meera Santoro (art)

Publishers of innovative and contemporary images for greetings cards, giftwrap
and gift stationery. Subjects covered:
humorous, florals, gardens, landscapes,
animals, still life. Submit artwork or
colour photocopies. Founded 1985.

Scandecor Ltd
3 The Ermine Centre, Hurricane Close,
Huntingdon, Cambs. PE18 6XX
tel (01480) 456395 *fax* (01480) 456269
Director G. Huldtgren

Drawings all sizes. Founded 1967.

Second Nature Ltd*
10 Malton Road, London W10 5UP
tel 0181-960 0212 *fax* 0181-960 8700
Marketing/Publishing Director Rod Schragger

Contemporary artwork for greetings
cards; jokes for humorous range; short
modern sentiment; verses. Founded 1981.

W.N. Sharpe Ltd – now The Classic Card Company Ltd

Solomon & Whitehead Ltd
Lynn Lane, Shenstone, Staffs. WS14 0DX
tel (01543) 480696 *fax* (01543) 481619

Fine art prints and limited editions,
framed and unframed.

Noel Tatt Ltd
Coombe House, Coombe Valley Road, Dover,
Kent CT17 0EU
tel (01304) 211644 *fax* (01304) 240470
Directors Noel Tatt, Vencke Tatt, Derek Bates,
Anthony Sharpe, Paul Tatt, Robert Dixon

Greetings cards, prints, postcards.
Founded 1954.

Valentines – see The Classic Card Company Ltd*

Waverley 1770*
Godalming Business Centre, Woolsack Way,
Godalming, Surrey GU7 1XW
tel (01483) 426277 *fax* (01483) 426947

e-mail info@waverley.com
Publishing Director Rosemary French, *Design Manager* Debbie Granger
Gift stationery (calendars, notecards, gift-wrap). Colour illustrations; cute/traditional/floral. Submit original artwork or 5 x 4in transparencies. No verses. Founded 1770.

Webb Ivory (Burton) Ltd
Queen Street, Burton-on-Trent, Staffs. DE14 3LP
tel (01283) 566311
High quality Christmas cards and paper products.

A serious look at marketing cartoons

There are many freelance opportunities for comic artists and illustrators. **John Byrne** *explores potential markets and offers guidance for success.*

Although in the business of being funny, cartoonists can be quite a morose bunch, bemoaning the passing of the original *Punch* and complaining that the market for general cartoons is growing smaller. Yet many of the most lucrative merchandising properties in recent years, from *Garfield* to *Judge Dredd*, started life as cartoons. Freelance cartooning has its share of ups and downs, but there are still many opportunities for comic artists and for illustrators and writers, too. Many cartoonists are certainly accomplished artists, but today funny ideas and sharp captions are just as important as the visuals. Writers with comic flair may consider collaborating with an artist or even trying their own simple drawings.

Research and presentation

See page 389 for *Newspapers and magazines which accept cartoons.*

Study the publication you are planning to submit to. What cartoon subjects feature most frequently, especially for joke or 'gag' cartoons (see 'Markets', below): married couples? children? animals? Are all the cartoons domestic or office based, or is there a mixture? Are the characters drawn in semi-realistic or more distorted styles? Are the jokes mainly in the captions or is the humour visual?

Be aware of changing fashions in

humour. Thanks to Gary Larson's *The Far Side* the pun, formerly derided as a low form of wit, is currently very much in vogue. Consider technical details: Are the cartoons colour or black and white? What shape are they? It is pointless sending portrait-shaped cartoons to publications that only use landscape ones.

While most magazines still typeset cartoon captions, some now accept hand-drawn captions or balloons. Avoid spelling mistakes for which cartoonists are notorious and which often result in rejection of otherwise saleable drawings. This can also happen if a clever cartoon becomes illegible when reduced to printed size. Editors often squeeze cartoons into very small spaces – be sure your drawings are simple and bold enough to survive reduction.

It is useful to have a knowledge of copyright and libel. See *British copyright law* on page 615, *US copyright law* on page 625 and *Libel* on page 633.

Submitting cartoons

A preliminary letter saves wasted effort and can yield useful information. Busy editors find unsolicited phone calls very unamusing – but one call you will need to make is to check exactly who to address your letter to: full-time cartoon editors are rare and the person who chooses cartoons

can be anyone from the art director to the person in charge of the puzzle page. Sending a number of cartoons together increases the chance of at least one being accepted, but quality is better than quantity. A few good jokes will get a better response when the editor doesn't have to extract them from a mountain of 'fillers'.

Rejections

While current fashions in cartoons encompass a wide range of styles, both visual and in terms of being funny, humour is still very subjective. Rejections are a fact of life for even the most successful cartoonists, but one editor's rejected cartoon may be snapped up by another publication.

One way to lessen the sting is to have several submissions on the go at once. A strong pre-paid envelope will ensure that work comes back in one piece, ready for its next expedition. (Put your name and address on the back of each cartoon in case it gets detached from the main bundle.) If you are sending lots of cartoons back and forth to different publications it is wise to create a filing system. Otherwise you'll inevitably receive the dreaded response 'You've sent this one before ... and it wasn't funny the first time'.

Markets

General gag cartoons

The demise of *The Cartoonist*, *Squib* and other brave attempts to launch cartoon magazines in the wake of *Punch* may suggest that the traditional gag cartoon is an endangered species. However, *Punch* has been resurrected and magazines like *Private Eye* and *The Spectator* still publish joke or gag cartoons alongside more topical items, and new cartoon magazines continue to appear.

Topical cartoons

Topical cartoons are a good market for the quick-witted artist. Remember that the cartoon must still be topical on the day it is published. This is (relatively) easy if the

---

Useful organisations

For specialist advice, and to meet other members of what can be a solitary profession, make contact with:

Cartoon Art Trust
67-68 Hatton Gardens, London EC1N 8JY
tel 0171-405 9717

The Cartoonists' Guild and The Cartoonists' Club of Great Britain
46 Strawberry Vale, Twickenham TW1 4SE
tel 0181-892 3621

Comics Creators Guild
171 Oldfield Grove, Surrey Quays,
London SE16 2NE
tel 0171-232 0703

---

cartoon is for a newspaper coming out the next day, but a topical cartoon can become very outdated in the time it takes a weekly or fortnightly magazine to publish. Faxing roughs to the editor can save time. If accepted, you may need to produce finished artwork to very tight deadlines.

Try to get your cartoons back after publication – people featured in topical cartoons sometimes ask to buy the original artwork.

Specialist and trade publications

This is an under-exploited market for cartoonists who are able to tailor jokes to particular subjects – but remember you are dealing with an expert audience. A stereotypical cartoon chef may suffice for general cartoons, but you'd better get the terminology and different uniforms right for *Bakery World* or *Catering*.

Try creating your own markets. Think about jobs you've had, past or present, or your particular sports, hobbies and interests. No matter how obscure, there may be a related publication just waiting to be brightened up by your combination of cartoon skills and specialist knowledge.

Regular comic strips and syndication

For regular comic strips or cartoon features, editors need to see that you can pro-

duce not only funny material but that you can maintain a consistent output. Submit a good supply of roughs along with examples of finished cartoons to show that you can sustain the idea. The same applies when approaching a syndicate with your strip and feature ideas (see *Syndicates, news and press agencies* on page 144). Cartoons may be in syndication for a long time, and in different countries, so very topical humour and local references are best avoided. If cartoons are syndicated in other languages humour based on verbal puns may not translate very well.

Other

Card and stationery publishers which accept illustrations and verses on page 382 and *Merchandising agents* on page 369 should suggest other markets for cartoons. Cartoons are often used to illustrate books for both adults and children (list-ings of *Book publishers UK and Ireland* start on page 153 and *Book packagers* start on page 216). Some of the *Art agents and commercial art studios* listed on page 375 represent cartoonists.

Cartoon sites on the Internet are some of the most frequently visited and cartoonists selling their wares through this new medium have reported very good responses.

Finally ...

The life of a full-time funny person can be precarious, but properly researching and tailoring work to specific markets and adopting an organised approach to submissions should greatly reduce your rejection collection.

John Byrne combines his own writing and drawing career with internationally acclaimed training workshops on cartooning and comedy writing.

Further reading

John Byrne, *Drawing Cartoons that Sell*, HarperCollins, 1997
John Byrne, *Learn to Draw Cartoons*, HarperCollins, 1995

Hall, Robin, *The Cartoonist's Workbook*, A & C Black, 1995
Steve Whitaker, *The Encyclopaedia of Cartooning Techniques*, Headline, 1994

Newspapers and magazines which accept cartoons

Listed below are newspapers and magazines which take cartoons – either occasionally, or on a regular basis. Approach in writing in first instance (see listings starting on pages 3, 12 and 20 for addresses) to ascertain the editor's requirements.

Newspapers and colour supplements

Aberdeen Evening Express
Birmingham Evening Mail
Daily Mail
Daily Mirror
Daily Sport
The European
Evening Echo
Evening Gazette
The Evening Press
Glasgow Evening Times
Grimsby Evening Telegraph
The Guardian Weekend
Hartlepool Mail
The Herald
The Independent Magazine
Independent on Sunday
The Journal
Lancashire Evening Post
Liverpool Echo
Mail on Sunday
The News, Portsmouth
Nottingham Evening Post
The Scotsman
South Wales Echo
The Star
The Sun
Sunday Mail
Sunday Mercury
The Sunday Sun
The Sunday Times
Telegraph Magazine
The Times
The Weekly News
Western Daily Press
The Western Mail
Yorkshire Evening Post
Yorkshire Post
Young Telegraph

Consumer and special interest magazines

Aeroplane Monthly
Air International
Amateur Photographer
The Aquarist and Pondkeeper
Athletics Weekly
The Author
Back Street Heroes
Baptist Times
BBC Vegetarian GoodFood
Bella
Best
Big!
Bike
Bird Watching
Boards
Bowls International
British Chess Magazine
Bunty
Buster
Cage and Aviary Birds
Cat World
Catholic Gazette
The Catholic Herald
Catholic Pictorial
Chapman
Church of England Newspaper
Classic Cars
Classic CD
Computer Weekly
Computing
Country Life
The Countryman
Country-Side
The Cricketer International
Cycling Weekly
The Dandy
Darts World
Dirt Bike Rider
Disability Now
Dogs Today
East Lothian Life

The Economist
Everyday with Practical
  Electronics
Financial Adviser
Football Picture Story Library
Fore!
Fortean Times
Garden News
Gay Times
Geographical Magazine
Golf Monthly
Golf World
Guiding
Health & Efficiency
  International
Here's Health
Hertfordshire Countryside
Home and Country
Home Words
Horse and Hound
Horse & Pony
Index on Censorship
Jewish Telegraph
Just Seventeen
Kids Alive!
Life and Work
Live & Kicking Magazine
M&J
Men Only
Modus
Motor Boat and Yachting
Motor Caravan Magazine
Musical Opinion
My Weekly Puzzle Time
New Christian Herald
New Internationalist
New Musical Express
New Scientist
New Statesman
The New Welsh Review
New World
Office Secretary
The Oldie
Opera Now
Organic Gardening

Park Home & Holiday Caravan
Performance Car
Pilot
Planet
Poetry Review
Pony
Practical Fishkeeping
Practical Householder
Practical Photography
Priests & People
Private Eye
Punch
Red Pepper
Reform
Runner's World
Scootering
The Scots Magazine
Scottish Home and Country
Scouting
She
The Short Wave Magazine
Sight and Sound
Smallholder
The Spectator
The Squash Player
The Tablet
Take a Break
TGO (The Great Outdoors)
Magazine
The Times Educational
Supplement

Titbits
Today's Runner
Tribune
Trout and Salmon
Twinkle
The Universe
The Vegan
Viz
The Voice
Vox
War Cry
The Weekly Journal
Weight Watchers Magazine
What's on TV
Woman
World Soccer
Yachting Monthly
Yachting World
Yours

Business and professional magazines

Accountancy
Art Business Today
British Printer
Broadcast
Building Design
Carers World
Certified Accountant

Child Education
Control & Instrumentation
CTN
Drapers Record
Education
Electrical Review
Electrical Times
Hospitality
HouseBuilder
International Construction
Journalist
Local Government Chronicle
Marketing Week
Mobile and Cellular Magazine
Museums Journal
Music Teacher
Nursing Times and Nursing
Mirror
Pig Farming
Police Review
Post Magazine
Printing World
Publishing News
Red Tape
Solicitors Journal
Therapy Weekly
Toy Trader
Waterways World

Photography and picture research

The freelance and the agent

Photographic agencies and libraries have a dual role in the service they provide. They meet the needs and demands of picture editors, picture researchers and art buyers and, at the same time, provide a service to the freelance photographer. **Bruce Coleman** *describes the relationship between the freelance photographer and the agent.*

The enterprising photographer wishing to penetrate the publishing market would do well to consider employing the services of an agent. Their knowledge of current trends and client contact will gear the photographer's output to the requirements of the markets. The complexities of reproduction rights are also best left to an agent to deal with – that's if you wish to protect the copyright of your work!

Selecting the right agent very much depends on your type of work and you should, therefore, look at several agencies before choosing the one you think is best for you. Some agents, for example, work in the syndication area, selling news and topical pictures to the world's press; others are in the stock business maintaining a library of photographers' work orientated to the editorial market.

Agents normally do not sell pictures outright but lease them for a specific use and fee from which they deduct a commission. A good photograph in the hands of a good agent can be published several times over and bring in royalties for many years.

Before submitting your work to an agent, write a letter to enquire whether the agent is accepting new photographers and to ask for details of their specific needs.

The agent will wish to see an initial presentation of at least 200 photographs and photographers should indicate the number of photographs they plan to submit in the course of a year. Agents are keen to encourage the active photographer who can supply a regular stream of good quality work.

Serious attention should be given to the caption of every picture as this can often mean the difference between a sale or a rejection. A caption should be brief and legible and an example of a good nature caption is:

> Spotted Hyena (*C. crocuta*)
> Serengeti
> Aggressive behaviour

or, a geographical caption:

> Canada: Northwest Territories
> Inuit fur trappers and dogsled

Some time spent on the presentation of your work, editing for composition, content, sharpness and, in the case of transparencies, colour saturation, will help to create a favourable impression. When submitting original colour transparencies, to ensure they are protected from damage and also to facilitate easy examination, place them in clear plastic sleeves, never between glass. Do not submit transparencies which you may require for personal use as it is impossible for an agent to

recall pictures at short notice from a client.

Never supply similar photographs to more than one agent as the problems created by almost identical pictures appearing, say, on a calendar or a greetings card can be embarrassing and costly to rectify.

Indeed, for this reason, many agents insist on an exclusive arrangement between themselves and their photographers.

Bruce Coleman is Managing Director of the Bruce Coleman Collection and past President of the British Association of Pictures Libraries.

How to run your own picture library

One way for photographers to market their work themselves is to set up a specialist library. **John Feltwell** *offers guidelines on how to run a picture library.*

Terms of business

It is important to draw up strict Terms & Conditions to cover items such as search fee, holding fee, and loss of or damage to prints and transparencies.

Guarding against loss or damage

The photographer's transparencies are treasured possessions. Unfortunately some publishing and magazine personnel do not see it like that and treat them as dispensable and with some irreverence. You can be sure that picture researchers who are members of the Picture Research Association (formerly SPREd, see page 435) know all about looking after transparencies responsibly. Beware of supplying private individuals who are naive to procedures. Some libraries ask for an official letter of request from the publisher before despatching anything.

In the event of an original transparency being lost or damaged in any way, make a charge of £635 or more. Ensure that this is included in your Terms & Conditions and remember that the loss/damage fee is subject to tax as earnings. See also *Picture research* on page 430.

Holding and search fees

A month is a reasonable time for transparencies to be reviewed. Thereafter, a holding fee charged weekly per transparency is recommended. Decide if search fees are to be waived if transparencies are accepted for reproduction.

Beware of and budget for use of transparencies by editors, and especially design studios, for preparation of 'dummies'; pictures used may not be accounted for in-house by the resident picture researcher if acquired by editors, sub editors, etc.

Once accepted, transparencies may lie for several months waiting to be used. This can run on to a year, unless strictly controlled. To look after your own interests, arrange for payment to be made three months after acceptance or on publication, whichever happens first. Otherwise, you will be without both transparencies and payment until publication, possibly way into the future, or never.

Reproduction rights

Reproduction rights should be calculated according to territorial limitations, whether one-time one-edition non-exclusive UK only, English speaking countries, world rights, etc, as well as size (small 'editorial' size to front cover). Work out sliding scales and bulk discount rates. Agree fees, including repeat fees, before publication. Restrict all electronic rights.

Useful contacts

Picture Search
No 3, 81-83 Surbiton Road,
Surbiton KT1 2HW
tel 0181-541 5147 *fax* 0181-541 1979
e-mail chris@picturesearch.demon.co.uk
web site http://www.picture-search.demon.co.uk
Contact Chris Barton
Search this site for the latest requests put on-line by picture researchers (a free service to them). Requests tend to be the more demanding ones. Useful source of opportunities and contacts.

The Specialist Source
Skyscan
tel (01242) 621357 *fax* (01242) 621343
Ecoscene
tel (01428) 751056 *fax* (01428) 751057
Leslie Garland Photo Library
tel/fax 0191-281 3442
A group of specialist libraries which recommend each other when a picture request is received. Currently about 40 participants, rising to a planned ceiling of 50. A single search and service fee is charged (from the source or contact library) to the picture researcher, yet the images may arrive from several other libraries at no extra charge. The aim is to fulfil all picture requests on a single telephone call to the contact library. Prices are then harmonised within the group. Picture librarians with specialist collections may find this scheme advantageous. Contact Skyscan, Ecoscene or the Leslie Garland Photo Library. Established 1996.

BAPLA (British Association of Picture Libraries and Agencies)
18 Vine Hill, London EC1R 5DX
tel 0171-713 1780 *fax* 0171-713 1211
e-mail sarah@bapla.org.uk
web site http://www.bapla.org.uk
Contact Sarah Saunders
Mostly represents commercial and institutional libraries. Smaller libraries, which are perhaps more vulnerable to disputes, can only be assisted (the right is reserved) by BAPLA after first year of membership. Publishes the *BAPLA Directory* and *Light Box* (quarterly). Annual membership £440 inc. VAT.

VOICE of the Specialist Libraries
Details Lupe Cunha, Photo-Arte Gallery,
19 Ashfield Parade, London N14 5EH
tel 0181-882 6441 *fax* 0181-882 6303
e-mail lupe.cunha@btinternet.com
A monthly magazine which aims to increase communication between libraries, photographers, researchers and those involved in the stock industry. Includes useful marketing information, forthright comment, survey results. Publishes *Specialist Directory*. Founded 1995. Annual subscription £30 inc. VAT new members; £25 inc. VAT renewals.

Dispatch and liability

Dispatch securely transparencies in sleeves and use security labels. Send them in a reliable way, e.g. by messenger/courier or by Registered Plus post with Consequential Loss Insurance, and make sure they are adequately insured. Buy transit insurance.

Make sure that the recipient knows when his or her liability starts and finishes. This includes transit to printers away from publishers' premises. Specify that transparencies must be returned from printers in a clean condition without any printers' solvents but with their original mounts.

Artists and designers

Be wary of how artists and designers use transparencies. If they are borrowed in order to derive ideas from, this should be pre-arranged with you. Similarly, publicity and advertising companies may use transparencies to generate computer models and logos, in which case invoice accordingly. Forbid any slide projection of transparencies.

John Feltwell is the proprietor of Garden Matters and Wildlife Matters Photographic Library.

Picture agencies and libraries

As well as supplying images to picture editors, picture researchers and others who use pictures, picture agencies and libraries provide a service to the freelance photographer as one way of selling their work. Most of the picture agencies and libraries listed in this section take work from other photographers.

Before submitting examples of work, photographers should first telephone or write to ascertain the terms and conditions of a picture agency or library. Colour transparencies are most commonly required: medium and large format are preferred to 35mm. Only top quality transparencies are considered; inferior work is never accepted.

To find agencies and libraries which cover specific subjects, start by referring to the *Picture agencies and libraries by subject area* on page 422.

See also ...

• *Card and stationery publishers which accept photographs* on page 429
• *Syndicates, news and press agencies* on page 144
• *The freelance and the agent* on page 391
• *How to run your own picture library* on page 392
• *Pictures into print* on page 252
• *National newspapers UK and Ireland* on page 3
• *Magazines by subject area* on page 121
• *Children's book publishers and packagers* on page 249.

*Member of the British Association of Picture Libraries and Agencies

A.A. & A. Ancient Art & Architecture Collection*

Suite 7, 2nd Floor, 410-420 Rayners Lane, Pinner, Middlesex HA5 5DY
tel 0181-429 3131 *fax* 0181-429 4646
Specialises in the history of civilisations of the Middle East, Mediterranean countries, Europe, Asia, Americas, from ancient times to recent past, their arts, architecture, beliefs and peoples.

A-Z Botanical Collection Ltd*

82-84 Clerkenwell Road, London EC1M 5RJ
tel 0171-336 7942 *fax* 0171-336 7943
e-mail a-z@image-data.com
web site www.a-z.picture-library.com
Contact Robin McGeever
Colour transparencies of plant life worldwide, including named gardens, habitats, gardening, still life, romantic seasonal shots, fungi, pests and diseases, etc (6 x 6cm, 35mm, 5 x 4in).

Abode Interiors Photographic Library*

Albion Court, 1 Pierce Street, Macclesfield, Cheshire SK11 6ER
tel (01625) 500070 *fax* (01625) 500910
Contact Mary Jarvis or Judi Goodwin
Colour photo library specialising in English and Scottish house interiors of all styles, types and periods. High quality material only; terms by agreement. Founded 1993.

Academic File News Photos

Eastern Art Publishing Group, 27 Wallorton Gardens, London SW14 8DX
tel 0181-392 1122 *fax* 0181-392 1422
e-mail easternart@compuserve.com
Director Sajid Rizvi
Daily news coverage in UK and general library of arts, cultures, people and places, with special reference to the Middle East, North Africa and Asia. New photographers welcomed to cover UK

and abroad. Pictures accepted in TIFF over e-mail. Founded 1985.

Ace Photo Agency*

Satellite House, 2 Salisbury Road,
London SW19 4EZ
tel 0181-944 9944 *fax* 0181-944 9940

General library: people, industry, business, travel, commerce, skies, sport, music and natural history. Worldwide syndication. Sae for enquiries. Very selective editing policy. Terms: 50%. Founded 1980.

Action Plus*

54-58 Tanner Street, London SE1 3PH
tel 0171-403 1558 *fax* 0171-403 1526

Specialist sports and action picture library. Comprehensive collection of creative images, including all aspects of 130 professional and amateur sports worldwide. Covers all age groups, all ethnic groups and all levels of ability. 35mm colour stock and on-line digital archive accessible by ISDN or modem. Terms: 50%. Founded 1986.

Lesley and Roy Adkins Picture Library

Longstone Lodge, Aller, Langport,
Somerset TA10 0QT
tel (01458) 250075 *fax* (01458) 250858
web site http://ourworld.compuserve.com/homepages/adkins_archaeology

Colour library covering archaeology and heritage; prehistoric, Roman, Greek and medieval sites and monuments; landscape, countryside, architecture, towns, villages and religious monuments. Catalogue available. Founded 1989.

Aerofilms

Hunting Aerofilms Ltd, Gate Studios,
Station Road, Borehamwood, Herts. WD6 1EJ
tel 0181-207 0666 *fax* 0181-207 5433
e-mail aerofilms@compuserve.com

Comprehensive library – over 1.5 million photos going back to 1919 – of vertical and oblique aerial photographs of UK; large areas with complete cover. Founded 1919.

Air Photo Supply

42 Sunningvale Avenue, Biggin Hill,
Kent TN16 3BX
tel (01959) 574872

Aircraft and associated subjects, South-East England, colour and monochrome.

No other photographers' material required. Founded 1963.

AKG London*

(Arts and History Picture Library)
10 Plato Place, 72-74 St Dionis Road,
London SW6 4TU
tel 0171-610 6103 *fax* 0171-610 6125

Principal subjects covered: art, archaeology and history. Exclusive UK and US representative for the Archiv für Kunst und Geschichte (AKG) with full access to the 9 million images held by AKG Berlin. Also exclusively represents the Erich Lessing Culture and Fine Art Archives in the UK. Founded 1994.

Bryan and Cherry Alexander Photography*

Higher Cottage, Manston, Sturminster Newton,
Dorset DT10 1EZ
tel (01258) 473006 *fax* (01258) 473333
e-mail arcticfoto@aol.com
web site http://members.aol.com/arcticfoto/

Polar regions with emphasis on Eskimos, Lapps and the modern Arctic, Antarctica. Founded 1973.

Rev. J. Catling Allen

St Giles House, Little Torrington,
Devon EX38 8PS
tel (01805) 622497

Library of colour transparencies (35mm) and b&w photos of Bible Lands, including archaeological sites and the religions of Christianity, Islam and Judaism. Medieval abbeys and priories, cathedrals and churches in Britain. Also historic, rural and scenic Britain. (Not an agent or buyer.)

Allied Artists Ltd

31 Harcourt Street, London W1H 1DT
tel 0171-724 8809 *fax* 0171-262 8526
Contact Gary Mills

Agency for illustrators specialising in realistic figure illustration. Large colour library of illustrations for syndication. Founded 1983.

Allsport Photographic Ltd*

3 Greenlea Park, Prince George's Road,
London SW19 2JD
tel 0181-685 1010 *fax* 0181-648 5240

International sport and leisure. Founded 1972.

American History Picture Library

3 Barton Buildings, Bath BA1 2JR
tel (01225) 334213

Photographs, engravings, colour transparencies covering the exploration, social, political and military history of North America from 15th to 20th century. Conquistadores, Civil War, gangsters, Moon landings, etc.

AMIS
(Atlas Mountains Information Services)
26 Kirkcaldy Road, Burntisland,
Fife KY3 9HQ
tel (01592) 873546
Proprietor Hamish Brown
Picture library on Moroccan sites, topography, mountains, travel. Illustration service. Commissions undertaken. No pictures purchased.

Andalucía Slide Library
Apto 499, Estepona, Málaga 29680, Spain
tel/fax (34) 52-793647
e-mail library@andalucia.com
web site http://www.andalucia.com
Contact Chris Chaplow
Colour transparencies (35mm and medium format) covering all aspects of Andalucía and Spain, principally its geography and culture. Digitised images available by ISDN or modem. Commissions undertaken. Founded 1991.

Andes Press Agency*
26 Padbury Court, London E2 7EH
tel 0171-613 5417 *fax* 0171-739 3159
e-mail photos@andespress.demon.co.uk
Director Carlos Reyes
Social, political and economic aspects of Latin America, Africa, Asia, Middle East, Europe and Britain; specialises in Latin America and contemporary world religions. Founded 1983.

Heather Angel/Biofotos*
Highways, 6 Vicarage Hill, Farnham,
Surrey GU9 8HJ
tel (01252) 716700 *fax* (01252) 727464
Colour transparencies (35mm and 2¹/₄in square) with worldwide coverage of natural history and biological subjects including animals, plants, natural habitats (deserts, polar regions, rainforests, wetlands, etc), landscapes, gardens, close-ups and underwater images; also man's impact on the environment – pollution, acid rain, urban wildlife, etc. Large China file. Detailed catalogues on request by *bona fide* picture researchers.

Animal Photography*
4 Marylebone Mews, New Cavendish Street,
London W1M 7LF
tel 0171-935 0503 *fax* 0171-487 3038
Horses, dogs, cats, small pets, East Africa, Galapagos. Founded 1955.

Aquarius Picture Library*
PO Box 5, Hastings, East Sussex TN34 1IIR
tel (01424) 721196 *fax* (01424) 717704
Contact David Corkill
Showbusiness specialist library with over one million colour and b&w images: film stills, classic portraiture, candids, archive material to present. New material added every week. Archival situation stills for advertising and magazine illustration use. Also television, vintage pop, opera, ballet and stage. Worldwide representation and direct sales. Collections considered, either outright purchase or 50%-50% marketing.

Aquila Photographics*
PO Box 1, Studley, Warks. B80 7JG
tel (01527) 852357 *fax* (01527) 857507
e-mail interbirdnet @dial.pipex.com
Specialists in ornithological subjects, but covering all aspects of natural history, also pets and landscapes, in both colour and b&w.

Arcaid Architectural Photography and Picture Library*
The Factory, 2 Acre Road, Kingston,
Surrey KT2 6EF
tel 0181-546 4352 *fax* 0181-541 5230
web site http://www.arcaid.co.uk
'The built environment' – international collection: architecture, interior design, gardens, travel, museums, historic and contemporary. Terms: 50%.

Archivio Veneziano – see Venice Picture Library*

Arctic Camera
66 Ashburnham Grove, London SE10 8UJ
tel/fax 0181-692 7651
Contact Derek Fordham
Colour transparencies of all aspects of Arctic life and environment. Founded 1978.

Ardea London Ltd*
35 Brodrick Road, London SW17 7DX
tel 0181-672 2067 *fax* 0181-672 8787

Su Gooders. Specialist worldwide natural history photographic library of animals, birds, plants, fish, insects, reptiles, worldwide scenics.

Aspect Picture Library Ltd*
40 Rostrevor Road, London SW6 5AD
tel 0171-736 1998/731 7362 *fax* 0171-731 7362
General library including wildlife, tribes, cities, industry, science, Space. Founded 1971.

The Associated Press Ltd
News Photo Department, The Associated Press House, 12 Norwich Street, London EC4A 1BP
tel 0171-353 1390 (colour and b&w request), 0171-353 1515 ext 4264 (library manager)
fax 0171-353 0836
News, features, sports.

Attard Photolibrary
5 Brewer Street, London W1R 3FN
tel 0171-434 4444 *fax* 0171-287 3977
Director Nigel Attard
Specialises in people: lifestyle, romance, contemporary themes. Terms: 50%. Founded 1992.

Australia Pictures
28 Sheen Common Drive, Richmond, London TW10 5BN
tel/fax 0181-898 0150 *fax* 0181-876 3637
Contact John Miles
Comprehensive library covering Australia, Aboriginals and their art, indigenous peoples, underwater, Tibet, Peru, Bolivia, Iran, Irian Jaya, Pakistan, Yemen. Founded 1988.

Aviation Photographs International
15 Downs View Road, Swindon, Wilts. SN3 1NS
tel (01793) 497179 *fax* (01793) 434030
All types of aviation and military subjects. Assignments undertaken. Founded 1970.

Aviation Picture Library* (Austin J. Brown)
35 Kingsley Avenue, London W13 0EQ
tel 0181-566 7712 *fax* 0181-566 7714
cellphone (01860) 670073
Worldwide aviation photographic library, including dynamic views of aircraft. Aerial and travel library including Europe, Caribbean, USA, and East and West Africa. Material taken since 1960. Specialising in air-to-air and air-to-ground commissions. Chief photographers for *Flyer* magazine. Founded 1970.

B. & B. Photographs
Prospect House, Clifford Chambers, Stratford upon Avon, Warks. CV37 8HX
tel (01789) 298106 *fax* (01789) 292450
35mm/medium format colour library of horticulture (especially pests and diseases) and biogeography (worldwide), natural history (especially Britain) and biological education. Other photographers' work not represented. Founded 1974.

Bandphoto Agency
(division of UPPA Ltd)
29-31 Saffron Hill, London EC1N 8FH
tel 0171-421 6000 *fax* 0171-421 6006
International news and feature picture service for British and overseas publishers.

Barnaby's Picture Library*
19 Rathbone Street, London W1P 1AF
tel 0171-636 6128/9 *fax* 0171-637 4317
General library of 4 million photos, colour and b&w, illustrating yesterday, today and tomorrow. Requires photographs for advertising and editorial publication. Photographs not purchased, sender retains copyright.

Barnardo's Photographic Archive*
Tanners Lane, Barkingside, Ilford, Essex IG6 1QG
tel 0181-550 8822 *fax* 0181-550 0429
Extensive collection of b&w and colour images dating from 1874 to the present day covering social history with the emphasis on children and child care. Also 300 films dating from 1905. Founded 1874.

BBC Hulton Picture Library – see Getty Images Ltd*

BBC Natural History Unit Picture Library*
BBC Broadcasting House, Whiteladies Road, Bristol BS8 2LR
tel 0117-9746720 *fax* 0117-9238166
e-mail nhu.picture.library@bbc.co.uk
Holds photographs relating to the Unit's film-making activities and represents the work of top wildlife photographers from around the world. Also has a unique collection of archive photographs relating to the history of film-making in the Unit. Founded 1995.

Dr Alan Beaumont
52 Squires Walk, Lowestoft, Suffolk NR32 4LA
tel (01502) 560126
Worldwide collection of monochrome prints and colour transparencies (35mm and 6 x 7cm) of natural history, countryside, windmills and aircraft. Subject lists available. No other photographers required.

Bee Photographs – see Heritage & Natural History Photography

Stephen Benson Slide Bureau
45 Sugden Road, London SW11 5EB
tel 0171-223 8635
World: agriculture, archaeology, architecture, commerce, everyday life, culture, environment, geography, science, tourism. Speciality: South America, the Caribbean, Australasia, Nepal, Turkey, Israel and Egypt. Assignments undertaken.

BIPS
(Bernsen's International Press Service Ltd)
9 Paradise Close, Eastbourne,
East Sussex BN20 8BT
tel (01323) 728760
For full details see page 144.

Bird Images
28 Carousel Walk, Sherburn in Elmet,
North Yorkshire LS25 6LP
tel/fax (01977) 684666
Principal P. Doherty
Specialist in the birds of Britain and Europe. Expert captioning service available. Founded 1989.

John Birdsall Photography*
75 Raleigh Street, Nottingham NG7 4DL
tel (0115) 978 2645 *fax* (0115) 978 5546
e-mail birdsall@innotts.co.uk
Contact Clare Marsh
Contemporary social documentary library covering children, youth, old age, health, disability, education, housing, work; also Nottingham and surrounding area; Spain – commissions and stock pictures. Founded 1980.

The Anthony Blake Photo Library*
54 Hill Rise, Richmond, Surrey TW10 6UB
tel 0181-940 7583 *fax* 0181-948 1224
Food and wine images from around the world, including raw ingredients, finished dishes, shops, restaurants, markets, agriculture and viticulture. Commissions undertaken. Contributors welcome. Brochure available.

John Blake Picture Library
74 South Ealing Road, London W5 4QB
tel 0181-840 4141 *fax* 0181-566 2568
Manager Alan Denny
General topography of England, Europe and the rest of the world. Landscapes, architecture, churches, gardens, countryside, towns and villages. Horse trials covered including Badminton and Gatcombe Park. Terms: 50%. Founded 1975.

Blitz International News & Photo Agency
Stubcroft Studios, Stubcroft Farm, Stubcroft Lane, East Wittering, Nr Chichester,
West Sussex PO20 8PJ
tel (01243) 671469
Contact Simon Green
Comprehensive library of colour transparencies and monochrome prints (35mm, medium and large formats). Action and sports photography (especially yachting and motorsport, including Le Mans 24hr race), travel, natural history, landscapes and aerial, agriculture, reportage, personalities, news, advertising shots, general. Commissions undertaken and photographers accepted. Catalogue on request. Terms: 50%. Founded 1988.

Bodleian Library
Oxford OX1 3BG
tel (01865) 277153/277214 *fax* (01865) 277182
Photographic library of 32,000 35mm colour transparencies, of subjects mostly from medieval manuscripts with iconographical index to illuminations; 35mm filmstrips available for immediate sale (not hire); other formats to order.

Bookart Architecture Picture Library
1 Woodcock Lodge, Epping Green,
Hertford SG13 8ND
tel (01707) 875253 *fax* (01707) 875286
Modern and historic buildings, landscapes, works of named architects in Great Britain, Europe, Scandinavia, North America, India, South-East Asia, Japan, North and East Africa; modern sculpture. Listed under style, place and personality. Founded 1991.

Boxing Picture Library

3 Barton Buildings, Bath BA1 2JR
tel (01225) 334213

Prints, engravings and photos of famous boxers, boxing personalities and famous fights from 18th century to recent years.

Bridgeman Art Library*

17-19 Garway Road, London W2 4PH
tel 0171-727 4065 *fax* 0171-792 8509
e-mail info@bridgeman.co.uk

Comprehensive source of fine art images for publication, acting as an agent for over 650 museums, galleries and private collections around the world. Large format colour transparencies. Currently holds more than 85,000 different images and is growing by 500 every week. Fully computerised, the image database runs on a custom-written free text keyword search system. CD-Rom catalogues. Founded 1971.

Britain on View Photographic Library*

Design, BTA, Thames Tower, Black's Road, London W6 9EL
tel 0181-846 9000 *fax* 0181-563 0302

Official photographic library for British Tourist Authority and English Tourist Board. Encompasses all aspects of Britain: coast, countryside, villages, towns, pageantry, landmarks, historic houses and the British people. For details of b&w, contact the Manager.

David Broadbent/Peak District Pictures

66 Norfolk Street, Glossop, Derbyshire SK13 9RA
tel/fax (01457) 862997

The Peak District fully covered, landscape, natural history, birds a speciality; sports. Commissions undertaken. New material welcome. Terms: 50%. Founded 1989.

Hamish Brown, Scottish Photographic

26 Kirkcaldy Road, Burntisland, Fife KY3 9HQ
tel (01592) 873546

Picture library on Scottish sites, topography, mountains, travel. Book illustrations. Commissions undertaken. No pictures purchased.

Butterflies

27 Lucastes Lane, Haywards Heath, West Sussex RH16 1LE
tel (01444) 454254
Proprietors Dr J. Tampion, Mrs M.D. Tampion

Worldwide: butterflies, silkmoths, hawkmoths, adults, larvae, pupae, their food-plants, poisonous plants, wild, garden and greenhouse plants, botanical and gardening science, ecology, environment. Articles and line illustrations also available; commissions undertaken. Terms: 50%. Founded 1990.

Camera Press Ltd*

21 Queen Elizabeth Street, London SE1 2PD
tel 0171-378 1300 *fax* 0171-278 5126

B&w prints and colour transparencies covering British Royalty, portraits of world statesmen, politicians, entertainers, reportage, humour, nature, pop, features. Terms: 50%. Founded 1947.

Camerapix – see C.P.L. (Camerapix Picture Library)

J. Allan Cash Photolibrary (J. Allan Cash Ltd)*

74 South Ealing Road, London W5 4QB
tel 0181-840 4141 *fax* 0181-566 2568
Manager Alan Denny

Worldwide photographic library: travel, landscape, natural history, sport, industry, agriculture. Details available for photographers interested in contributing.

The Central Press Photos Ltd – see Getty Images Ltd*

Cephas Picture Library*

Hurst House, 157 Walton Road, East Molesey, Surrey KT8 0DX
tel 0181-979 8647 *fax* 0181-224 8095
e-mail mickrock@cephas.co.uk
web site www.cephas.co.uk

Food and drink picture archive. Over 60,000 images of wine and vineyards of the world, mainly 6 x 7cm originals, covering virtually every aspect of the subject. Also spirits, beer and cider. Free catalogue available. Terms: 50%.

City Syndication Ltd* – see Monitor Syndication

Michael Cole Camerawork*

The Coach House, 27 The Avenue, Beckenham, Kent BR3 2DP
tel/fax 0181-658 6120

Probably the largest and most comprehensive tennis library in the world. Includes over 50 years of the Wimbledon Championships. All grand slam and major events covered. Founded 1945.

Bruce Coleman Inc.

117 East 24th Street, New York,
NY 10010-2919, USA
tel 212-979-6252 *fax* 212-979-5468
e-mail 72757,1343@compuserve.com,
norman@bciusa.com
President Norman Owen Tomalin

Specialising exclusively in colour transparencies. All formats from 35mm
acceptable. All subjects required.

Bruce Coleman Collection*

16 Chiltern Business Village, Arundel Road,
Uxbridge, Middlesex UB8 2SN
tel (01895) 257094 *fax* (01895) 272357

Colour transparencies on natural history,
ecology, environment, geography, archaeology, anthropology, agriculture, science,
scenics and travel.

Collections*

13 Woodberry Crescent, London N10 1PJ
tel 0181-883 0083 *fax* 0181-883 9215

The British Isles only; places, people,
buildings, industry, leisure; specialist
collections on customs, castles, bridges,
London, emergency services; also family
life from pregnancy through birth, childhood, education to being grown up.
Founded 1990.

Colorific Photo Library*

The Innovation Centre, 225 Marsh Wall,
London E14 9FX
tel 0171-515 3000 *fax* 0171-538 3555

Handles the work of top international
photographers, most subjects currently
on file, upwards of 250,000 images.
Represents the following agencies: Black
Star (New York), Contact Press Images
(New York/Paris), Visages (Los Angeles),
Icone (Paris), Regards (Paris), ANA Press
(Paris). Also represents *Sports
Illustrated*.

Sylvia Cordaiy Photo Library

72 East Ham Road, Littlehampton,
West Sussex BN17 7BQ
tel/fax (01903) 715297
e-mail sylvia_cordaiy@photosource.co.uk
web site http://www.photosource.co.uk/
photosource/sylvia-cordaiy.htm

Worldwide travel and architecture, global environmental topics, wildlife and
domestic animals, veterinary, comprehensive UK files, ocean racing. Terms:
50%. Founded 1990.

C.P.L. (Camerapix Picture Library)

8 Ruston Mews, London W11 1RB
tel 0171-221 0077 *fax* 0171-792 8105
e-mail camerapixuk@btinternet.com
and PO Box 45048 Nairobi, Kenya
tel 448923 *fax* 448926
e-mail camerapix@form-net.com

Kenya, Tanzania, Pakistan, Jordan,
Namibia, Nepal, Maldives, Mauritius,
Seychelles, Zimbabwe; portraits, agriculture, industry, tribal cultures, landscapes;
wildlife including rare species; extensive
collection on Aldabra Island; Islamic
portfolio: Mecca, Medina, Muslim pilgrimage. News material available and
special assignments arranged. Further
material available from collection held in
Nairobi.

Crafts Council Picture Library

44A Pentonville Road, London N1 9BY
tel 0171-806 2503 or 0171-278 7700 ext. 503
fax 0171-837 6891

Large, medium and small format transparencies. Coverage includes ceramics,
jewellery, textiles, metal and silver, furniture, wood, glass, knitting, weaving,
bookbinding, fashion accessories, toys
and musical instruments supplied by
selected makers and from *Crafts* magazine. Founded 1973.

Peter Cumberlidge Photo Library

Sunways, Slapton, Kingsbridge, Devon TQ7 2PR
tel (01584) 580461 *fax* (01584) 580588
Contact Jane Cumberlidge

Nautical, travel and coastal colour transparencies 35mm and 6 x 6cm.
Specialities: boats, harbours, marinas,
inland waterways. Travel and holiday
subjects in Northern Europe and the
Mediterranean. No other photographers'
material required. Founded 1982.

Cumbria Picture Library*

PO Box 33, Kendal, Cumbria LA9 4SU
tel (015394) 48894 *fax* (015394) 48294
Contact Eric Whitehead

Specialist picture library with over 40,000
images covering every aspect of Cumbria
and The Lake District. Subjects include:
places, people, events, customs, outdoor
pursuits and landscapes; snooker photos
by Eric Whitehead. The library holds
work from many photographers and commissions are accepted. Founded 1990.

Lupe Cunha
Photo-Arte Gallery, 19 Ashfield Parade,
London N14 5EH
tel 0181-882 6441 *fax* 0181-882 6303
e-mail lupe.cunha@btinternet.com
Specialist library on all aspects of childhood from pregnancy to school age, also women's interest and health/medical with focus on the patient and nursing care. Commissioned photography undertaken. Also represents collection on Brazil for Brazil Photo Agency. Terms: 50%. Founded 1987.

Sue Cunningham Photographic*
56 Chatham Road, Kingston-upon-Thames,
Surrey KT1 3AA
tel 0181-541 3024 *fax* 0181-541 5388
e-mail scphotographic@btinternet
International coverage on many subjects: Latin America, East Africa and Eastern Europe. Also Western Europe, London (including aerial) and Cornwall.

The Dance Library
12 Southwick Mews, London W2 1JG
tel 0171-262 6300 *fax* 0171-262 6400
Contemporary and historical dance: classical ballet, jazz, tap, disco, popping, ice dancing, musicals, variety, folk, tribal rites and rituals. Founded 1983.

Das Photo
Chalet le Pin, Domaine de Bellevue 181,
6940 Septon, Belgium
tel/fax (086) 322426
c/o Old School House, Llanfilo, Brecon,
Powys LD3 0RH
tel (01874) 711953
Arab countries, Americas, Europe, SE Asia, Amazon, world festivals, archaeology, people, biblical, motor bikes, education, schools, modern languages. Founded 1975.

Barry Davies
Dyffryn, Bolahaul Road, Cwmffrwd, Carmarthen,
Ceredigion SA31 2LP
tel/fax (01267) 233625
Natural history, landscape (especially waterfalls), Egypt, children, outdoor activities and general subjects. Formats 35mm, 6 x 6cm, 6 x 7cm, 5 x 4in. Other photographers' work not accepted. Founded 1983.

Dennis Davis Photography
9 Great Burrow Rise, Northam, Bideford,
Devon EX39 1TB
tel (01237) 475165

Gardens, wild and garden flowers, domestic livestock including rare breeds and poultry, agricultural landscapes, architecture – interiors and exteriors, landscape, coastal, rural life. Commissions welcomed. No other photographers required. Founded 1984.

James Davis Travel Photography*
65 Brighton Road, Shoreham,
West Sussex BN43 6RE
tel (01273) 452252 *fax* (01273) 440116
Proprietor Paul Seheult
Stock transparency library specialising in worldwide travel photos. Suppliers to publishers, advertising agents, etc.

Peter Dazeley*
The Studios, 5 Heathmans Road, London SW6 4TJ
tel 0171-736 3171 *fax* 0171-371 8876
Extensive golf library dating from 1970. Colour and b&w coverage of major tournaments. Constantly updated, with over 250,000 images of players (male and female), courses worldwide, action shots, portraits, trophies, including miscellaneous images: clubs, balls and teaching shots.

George A. Dey
'Drumcairn', Aberdeen Road, Laurencekirk,
Kincardineshire AB30 1AJ
tel (01561 37) 8845
Scottish Highland landscapes, Highland Games, forestry, seabirds, castles of NE Scotland, gardens, spring, autumn, winter scenes, veteran cars, North Holland, New Zealand (North Island). Founded 1986.

Douglas Dickins Photo Library
2 Wessex Gardens, London NW11 9RT
tel 0181-455 6221
Worldwide collection of colour transparencies (mostly 6 x 6cm, some 35mm) and b&w prints (10 x 8in originals), specialising in Asia, particularly India and Indonesia; also, USA, Canada, France, Austria and Switzerland, Japan, China, Burma. Founded 1946.

Gordon Dickson
Flagstones, 72 Catisfield Lane, Fareham,
Hants PO15 5NS
tel (01329) 842131
Colour transparencies of fungi, in natural habitat; also wildflowers, butterflies, moths, beetles. No other photographers required. Founded 1975.

C.M. Dixon*

The Orchard, Marley Lane, Kingston, Canterbury,
Kent CT4 6JH
tel (01227) 830075 fax (01227) 831135
Europe and Ethiopia, Iceland, Jordan, Sri
Lanka, Tunisia, Turkey, former USSR.
Main subjects include agriculture,
ancient art, archaeology, architecture,
clouds, geography, geology, history, horses, industry, meteorology, mosaics, mountains, mythology, occupations, people.

Earth Images Picture Library

PO Box 43, Keynsham, Bristol BS18 2TH
tel/fax (0117) 986 1144/(01275) 839643
Director Richard Arthur
Earth from Space (satellite remote sensing); earth science and art-in-science
imagery – from cosmic to sub-atomic.
Founded 1989.

Ecoscene*

The Oasts, Headley Lane, Passfield, Liphook,
Hants GU30 7RX
tel (01428) 751056 fax (01428) 751057
e-mail ecoscene@photosource.co.uk
web site http://www.photosource.co.uk/
photosource/ecoscene.htm
Contact Sally Morgan
Specialists in environment and ecology.
Subjects include agriculture, conservation, energy, industry, pollution, habitats
and habitat loss, sustainability, wildlife;
worldwide coverage. Terms: 55% to photographer. Founded 1987.

English Heritage Photographic Library*

23 Savile Row, London W1X 1AB
tel 0171-973 3338/3339 fax 0171-973 3330
Wide range of high quality, large format
colour transparencies, ranging from
ancient monuments to artefacts, leg-
endary castles to stone circles, elegant
interiors to industrial architecture and
post-war listed buildings. Founded 1984.

Environmental Investigation Agency

15 Bowling Green Lane, London EC1R 0BD
tel 0171-490 7040 fax 0171-490 0436
e-mail eiauk@gn.apc.org
Photograph Co-ordinators Ben Rogers, Liz
Maisonpierre
Specialist library covering animal abuse,
trade in endangered species, abuse of the
environment; also animals in their natural environment. Founded 1985.

Greg Evans International Photo Library*

Chilston Cottages, North Street, Windsor,
Berks. SL4 4TH
tel 0171-636 8238 fax 0171-637 1439
e-mail greg@geipl.demon.co.uk
web site http://www.geipl.demon.co.uk
Comprehensive, general colour library
with over 300,000 transparencies.
Subjects include: abstract, aircraft, arts,
animals, beaches, business, children,
computers, couples, families,
food/restaurant, women, industry, skies,
sports (action and leisure), UK scenics,
worldwide travel. Visitors welcome;
combined commissions undertaken;
first search fee. Photographers' submissions welcome. Free brochure. Founded
1979.

Mary Evans Picture Library*

59 Tranquil Vale, London SE3 0BS
tel 0181-318 0034 fax 0181-852 5040
e-mail lib@mepl.co.uk
Millions of historical illustrations docu-
menting social, political, cultural, technical, geographical and biographical themes
from ancient times to the mid 20th century. Photographs, original prints, and
ephemera backed by a large international
book and magazine collection. Special
collections include Sigmund Freud, the
Fawcett Library (women's rights), the
Meledin Collection (20th-century Russian
history) and individual photographers
active from the 1930s to the 1970s.
Colour brochure available.

Eyeline Photography

259 London Road, Cheltenham,
Glos. GL52 6YG
tel/fax (01242) 513567
Watersports, particularly sailing; wind-
vanes; sheepdog trials. Founded 1979.

Famous*

Studio 4, Limehouse Cut, 46 Morris Road,
London E14 6NQ
tel 0171-537 7055 fax 0171-537 7056
e-mail famous@compuserve.com
Colour pictures and features library covering music, film and TV personalities.
Terms: 50%. Founded 1990.

Feature-Pix Colour Library – see World Pictures*

Financial Times Pictures*

Number One, Southwark Bridge,
London SE1 9HL
tel 0171-873 3671 *fax* 0171-873 4606
e-mail suzie.kew@ft.com

Colour and b&w library serving *The Financial Times*. Specialises in world business, industry and commerce; world politicians and statespeople; cities and countries; plus many other subjects. Also *FT* maps and graphics. All material available in colour and b&w, print and electronic formats. Library updated daily.

Fine Art Photographic Library*

Rawlings House, 2A Milner Street,
London SW3 2PU
tel 0171- 589 3127 *fax* 0171-584 1944
web site http://www.picture-library.com

Holds over 25,000 transparencies of paintings by British and European artists, from Old Masters to contemporary. Free brochure. Founded 1980.

FirePix International*

68 Arkles Lane, Anfield, Liverpool L4 2SP
tel/fax 0151-260 0111
web site http://www.merseyworld.com/firepix/
Contact Tony Myers ARPS, GIFireE

Holds 15,000 images of fire and firefighters at work in the UK, USA and Japan. Also covers other emergency services. Established by photographer Tony Myers after 28 years in service with the British Fire Service. Many images are stored digitally. Founded 1993.

Fogden Natural History Photographs*

Mid Cambushinnie Cottage, Kinbuck, Dunblane,
Perthshire FK15 9JU
tel/fax (01786) 822069
Library Manager Susan Fogden

Wide natural history coverage, including camouflage, warning coloration, mimicry, breeding strategies, feeding, animal/plant relationships, environmental studies, especially in rain forests and deserts. Founded 1980.

Ron and Christine Foord

155B City Way, Rochester, Kent ME1 2BE
tel/fax (01634) 847348

Colour picture library of over 1000 species of wild flowers. Also British insects, garden flowers, pests and diseases, lichen, mosses and cacti.

Footprints Colour Picture Library*

Goldfin Cottage, Maidlands Farm, Broad Oak,
Rye, East Sussex TN31 6BJ
tel/fax (01424) 883078
Proprietor Paula Leaver

Specialises in underwater and above water coverage of holiday destinations in the tropics; also food and flowers by Debbie Patterson. Founded 1991.

Forest Life Picture Library*

Forestry Commission, 231 Corstorphine Road,
Edinburgh EH12 7AT
Picture Researcher Neill Campbell
tel 0131-314 6411
e-mail n.campbell@forestry.gov.uk
Business Manager Douglas Green
tel 0131-314 6200 *fax* 0131-314 6285
e-mail d.green@forestry.gov.uk

Tree species, forest and woodland management, employment, landscapes, wildlife, flora and fauna, conservation, sport and leisure. Founded 1983.

Werner Forman Archive*

36 Camden Square, London NW1 9XA
tel 0171-267 1034 *fax* 0171-267 6026

Art, architecture, archaeology, history and peoples of ancient, oriental and primitive cultures. Founded 1975.

Fortean Picture Library*

Henblas, Mwrog Street, Ruthin LL15 1LG
tel (01824) 707278 *fax* (01824) 705324

Library of colour and b&w pictures covering all strange phenomena: UFOs, Loch Ness Monster, ghosts, Bigfoot, witchcraft, etc; also antiquities (especially in Britain – prehistoric and Roman sites, castles, churches).

Fotoccompli–The Picture Library

11 Ampton Road, Edgbaston,
Birmingham B15 2UH
tel 0121-454 3305 *fax* 0121-454 9257

Comprehensive library, ranging from abstracts to zoology, serving all of Britain, especially the Birmingham and West Midlands areas. Terms: 50%; minimum retention period – 3 years. Founded 1989.

Fotomas Index

12 Pickhurst Rise, West Wickham, Kent BR4 0AL
tel/fax 0181-776 2772

Specialises in supplying pre-20th century (mostly pre-Victorian) illustrative material to publishing and academic

worlds, and for television and advertising. Complete production back-up for interior décor, exhibitions and locations.

Fox Photos – see Getty Images Ltd*

Freelance Focus
7 King Edward Terrace, Brough,
East Yorkshire HU15 1EE
tel/fax (01482) 666036
Contact Gary Hicks

UK/international network of photographers. Over 2 million stock pictures available, covering all subjects, worldwide, at competitive rates. Assignments undertaken for all types of clients. Further details/subject list available on request. Also publishes directory of photographers and photo libraries/agencies. Founded 1988.

Frontline Photo Press Agency
18 Wall Street, Norwood, Australia 5067
postal address PO Box 162, Kent Town,
Australia 5071
tel (08) 8333 2691 *fax* (08) 8364 0604
e-mail fppa@tne.net.au
web site http://www.tne.net.au/fppa
Director Carlo Irlitti

Stock photo agency, picture library and photographic press agency with 350,000 images. Covers sport, people, personalities, travel, scenics, environmental, agricultural, industrial, natural history, concepts, science, medicine, social documentary and press images. Seeking worldwide stock contributors. Assignments undertaken. Write, fax or e-mail for submission guidelines, photo requirements and other details. Terms: 60% to photographer (stock); assignment rates negotiable. Founded 1988.

Frost Historical Newspaper Collection
8 Monks Avenue, New Barnet, Herts. EN5 1DB
tel/fax 0181-440 3159

Headline stories from 60,000 British and overseas newspapers reporting major events since 1850.

Brian Gadsby Picture Library
Route des Pyrénées, Labatut-Riviere 65700,
Hautes Pyrénées, France
tel 05 62 96 38 44

Colour (6 x 6cm, 6 x 4.5cm, 35mm) and b&w prints. Wide range of subjects but emphasis on travel, natural history, children. Catalogue on request by picture researchers. No other photographers' material required.

Galaxy Picture Library*
1 Milverton Drive, Ickenham, Uxbridge,
Middlesex UB10 8PP
tel (01895) 637463 *fax* (01895) 623277
e-mail galaxypix@compuserve.com
web site http://ourworld.compuserve.com/
homepages/galaxypix
Contact Robin Scagell

Astronomy: specialities include the night sky, amateur astronomy, astronomers and observatories. Founded 1992.

Garden Matters Photographic Library*
Marlham, Henley's Down, Battle,
East Sussex TN33 9BN
tel (01424) 830566 *fax* (01424) 830224
e-mail gardens@ftech.co.uk, gardenpics@aol.com
web site http://web.ftech.net/~gardens
Contact Dr John Feltwell

Plant 6000 Over 6000 scientifically named species of garden flowers, wild plants, trees (over 800 species), grasses, crops, herbs, spices, houseplants, carnivorous plants, climbers, roses and pests.

General gardening How-to, gardening techniques, garden design and embellishments, cottage gardens, USA designer-gardens, 200 garden portfolios from 16 states in the USA, 100 portfolios from 12 European countries. Several photographers now represented. Founded 1993.

Leslie Garland Picture Library
69 Fern Avenue, Jesmond,
Newcastle upon Tyne NE2 2QU
tel 0191-281 3442 *fax* 0191-281 3442

All subjects in the geographic areas of North Yorkshire, Cleveland, Cumbria, Durham, Tyne & Wear, Northumberland, Borders, Dumfries and Galloway, Norway and Sweden – major cities, sites and scenes, heritage, industry, etc. Applied science and engineering – bridges, cranes, ship building, chemical plants, industrial processes, etc. Also miscellaneous subjects – e.g. light bulbs, hydraulic rams, soap powders. Colour transparencies only, medium format preferred; please send sae for guidelines. Terms: 50%. Founded 1985.

Colin Garratt – see Railways –
Milepost 92½*

Genesis Space Photo Library*
Greenbanks, Robins Hill, Raleigh, Bideford,
Devon EX39 3PA
tel (01237) 471960 *fax* (01237) 472060
e-mail tim@space.romgroup.co.uk
web site http://www.rom.net/spaceport
Contact Tim Furniss
Specialises in rockets, spacecraft, space-
men, Earth, Moon, planets. Founded 1990.

Geo Aerial Photography*
4 Christian Fields, London SW16 3JZ
tel/fax 0181-764 6292, (0115) 981 5474 or
(0115) 981 9418
Director J.F.J. Douglas
Air-to-air and air-to-ground colour
library: natural and cultural/man-made
landscapes and individual features.
Commissions undertaken. Terms: 50%.
Founded 1992.

GeoScience Features*
(incorporates K.S.F. and R.I.D.A. photolibraries)
6 Orchard Drive, Wye, Kent TN25 5AU
tel (01233) 812707 *fax* (01233) 812707
e-mail gsf@geoscience.demon.co.uk
web site http://www.geoscience.demon.co.uk
Director Dr Basil Booth
Colour library (35mm to 5 x 4in).
Animals, biology, birds, botany, chemistry, earth science, ecology, environment, geology, geography, habitats, landscapes, macro/micro, peoples, plants,
travel, sky, weather, wildlife and zoology; Americas, Africa, Australasia,
Europe, India, South-East Asia. Over one
third million colour images available.

Geoslides*
4 Christian Fields, London SW16 3JZ
tel/fax 0181-764 6292 or (0115) 981 9418
Library Director John Douglas
Broadly based and substantial collections
from Africa, Asia, Antarctic, Arctic and
sub-Arctic areas, Australia (Blackwood
Collection). Worldwide commissions
undertaken. Photographs for all types of
publications, television, advertising.
Terms: 50% on UK sales. Founded 1968.

Mark Gerson Photography
3 Regal Lane, Regents Park Road,
London NW1 7TH
tel 0171-286 5894 *fax* 0171-267 9246
Portrait photographs of personalities,
mainly literary, in colour and b&w from
1950 to the present. No other photographers' material required.

Getty Images Ltd*
Unique House, 21-31 Woodfield Road,
London W9 2BA
tel 0171-266 2662 *fax* 0171-289 6392
web site http://www.hultongetty.com
One of the largest picture resources in
Europe, with over 15 million b&w and
colour images. Specialises in social his-
tory, Royalty, transport, war, fashion,
sport, entertainment, people, places and
early photography. Collections include
Picture Post, Express, Evening Standard,
Keystone, Fox and Topical Press.
Manages Syndication International; only
London agents for the Reuter News
Picture Service; publisher of CD-Roms
for creative image access.

Global Syndications
Chartwood Towers, Punchbowl Lane, Dorking,
Surrey RH5 4ED
tel (01306) 741213 *fax* (01306) 875347
e-mail globalsynd@aol.com
web site http://www.surreyad.co.uk/globalsynd/
homepage.html
Managing Editor Sam Hall
Colour transparencies of all aspects of
Arctic life and environment, particularly
Eskimo (Inuit) and Lapps (Sami);
Scandinavia and UK (landscapes, people,
etc). Assignments undertaken. No other
photographers required. Founded 1990.

John Glover Photography
Fairfield, Hale House Lane, Churt, Farnham,
Surrey GU10 2NQ
tel (01428) 717196 *mobile* (0973) 307078
fax (01428) 717129
e-mail john@glovphot.demon.co.uk
Gardens and gardening, from overall
views of gardens to plant portraits with
Latin names; UK landscapes including
ancient sites, Stonehenge, etc. Founded
1979.

Martin and Dorothy Grace*
40 Clipstone Avenue, Mapperley,
Nottingham NG3 5JZ
tel (0115) 920 8248 *fax* (0115) 962 6802
General British natural history, specialising in native trees, shrubs, flowers, ferns,
habitats and ecology. Founded 1984.

Tim Graham Picture Library
31 Ferncroft Avenue, London NW3 7PG
tel 0171-435 7693 *fax* 0171-431 4312
Royal Family in this country and on
tours; background pictures on royal

homes, staff, hobbies, sports, cars, etc; English and foreign country scenes; international heads of state, VIPs and celebrities. Founded 1978.

Greater London Record Office – see London Metropolitan Archives

Robert Harding Picture Library*
58-59 Great Marlborough Street, London W1V 1DD
tel 0171-287 5414 *fax* 0171-631 1070
Photographic library. Require photographs of outstanding quality for advertising and editorial use, all subjects considered particularly lifestyle.

Harper Horticultural Slide Library
219 Robanna Drive, Seaford, VA 23696, USA
tel 757-898-6453 *fax* 757-890-9378
160,000 35mm slides of plants, gardens and native habitats.

Heritage & Natural History Photography
37 Plainwood Close, Summersdale, Chichester, West Sussex PO19 4YB
tel (01243) 533822
Contact Dr John B. Free
Archaeology, history, agriculture: Arabia, China, India, Iran, Ireland, Japan, Kenya, Mediterranean countries, Mexico, Nepal, North America, Oman, Russia, Thailand, UK. Bees and bee keeping, insects and small invertebrates, tropical crops and flowers.

Historical Picture Service
3 Barton Buildings, Bath BA1 2JR
tel (01225) 334213
Engravings, prints and photos on all aspects of history from ancient times to 1920. Special collection Old London: buildings, inns, theatres, many of which no longer exist.

Pat Hodgson Library & Picture Research Agency
Jasmine Cottage, Spring Grove Road, Richmond, Surrey TW10 6EH
tel 0181-940 5986
Small collection of b&w historical engravings, book illustrations, ephemera, etc; some colour and modern photos. Subjects include history, Victoriana, ancient civilisations, occult, travel. Text written and research undertaken on any subject. Of special interest to educational

publishers, film makers and exhibition designers.

Holt Studios International Ltd*
The Courtyard, 24 High Street, Hungerford, Berks. RG17 0NF
tel (01488) 683523 *fax* (01488) 683511
e-mail library@holt-studios.co.uk
web site http://www.holt-studios.co.uk/library
50,000 pictures on worldwide agriculture, horticulture, crops and associated pests (and their predators), diseases and deficiencies, farming people and practices, livestock, machinery, landscapes, diverse environments, natural flora and fauna. Founded 1981.

Horizon International Creative Images
Horizon International, St Anne's House, 3 St Anne's Walk, Alderney GY9 3HF, Channel Islands
tel (01481) 822587 *fax* (01481) 823880
Picture research and UK sales enquiries Images Colour Library Ltd, 12 14 Argyll Street, London W1V 1AB
tel 0171-734 7344 *fax* 0171-287 3933
General stock library covering travel, people, sport, business, industry, etc. Founded 1978.

David Hosking FRPS*
Pages Green House, Wetheringsett, Stowmarket, Suffolk IP14 5QA
tel (01728) 861113 *fax* (01728) 860222
Natural history subjects, especially birds covering whole world. Also Dr D.P. Wilson's unique collection of marine photos.

Houses & Interiors Photographic Features Agency*
82-84 Clerkenwell Road, London EC1M 5RJ
tel 0171-336 7942 *fax* 0171-336 7943
Contact Victoria Norman
Stylish house interiors and exteriors, home dossiers, renovations, architectural details, interior design, gardens and houseplants. Also step-by-step photographic sequences of DIY subjects, fresh and dried flower arrangements and gardening techniques. Food. Colour only. Commissions undertaken. Terms: 50%, negotiable. Founded 1985.

Hulton Getty Picture Collection – see Getty Images Ltd*

The Hutchison Library*

118B Holland Park Avenue, London W11 4UA
tel 0171-229 2743 fax 0171-792 0259

General colour library; worldwide subjects: agriculture, environments, festivals, human relationships, industry, landscape, peoples, religion, towns, travel. Founded 1976.

The Illustrated London News Picture Library*

20 Upper Ground, London SE1 9PF
tel 0171-805 5585 fax 0171-805 5905

Engravings, photos, illustrations in b&w and colour from 1842 to present day, especially 19th and 20th century social history, wars, portraits, Royalty. Travel archive including The Thomas Cook collection.

The Image Bank*

17 Conway Street, London W1P 6EE
tel 0171-312 0300 fax 0171-391 9111
web site http://www.imagebank.co.uk

Image Bank Scotland

14 Alva Street, Edinburgh EH2 4QG
tel 0131-225 1770 fax 0131-225 1660

Image Bank Manchester

4 Jordan Street, Manchester M15 4PY
tel 0161-236 9226 fax 0161-236 8723

General library of still and moving imagery from the world's top artists. Digital search facilities and CD catalogues. Founded 1979.

Image Diggers

618B Finchley Road, London NW11 7RR
tel/fax 0181-455 4564
Contact Neil Hornick

Stills archive covering performing arts, popular culture, human interest, natural history, architecture, nautical, children and people, strange phenomena, religions and other. Also audio and video for research purposes and ephemera including magazines, books, comic books, sheet music, postcards. Founded 1980.

Images Colour Library Ltd*

Leeds Office Manager Jess Diebel
15-17 High Court Lane, The Calls, Leeds LS2 7EU
tel (0113) 243 3389 fax (0113) 242 5605
London Office Manager Cara Botting
12-14 Argyll Street, London W1V 1AB
tel 0171-734 7344 fax 0171-287 3933

General, contemporary stock library including people, business, UK and world travel, industry and sport. Terms: 50%. Founded 1983.

Images of Africa Photobank*

11 The Windings, Lichfield, Staffs. WS13 7EX
tel (01543) 262898 fax (01543) 417154
Contact Jacquie Shipton, Library Manager
Proprietor David Keith Jones, ABIPP, FRPS

135,000 images covering 14 African countries: Botswana, Egypt, Ethiopia, Kenya, Malawi, Namibia, Rwanda, South Africa, Swaziland, Tanzania, Uganda, Zaire, Zambia and Zimbabwe. Specialities: wildlife, people, landscapes, tourism, hotels and lodges, National Parks and Reserves. Colour brochure available. Terms: 50%. Founded 1983.

Imperial War Museum*

Photograph Archive, Lambeth Road, London SE1 6HZ
tel 0171-416 5000 fax 0171-416 5379

National archive of over 5 million photos, dealing with war in the 20th century involving the armed forces of Britain and the Commonwealth countries. Visitors' Room (IWM All Saints Annexe, Austral Street, SE11 – 5 minutes walk from main building) open by appointment Mon-Fri. Enquiries should be as specific as possible; prints made to order. Founded 1917.

International Press Agency (Pty) Ltd

PO Box 67, Howard Place 7450, South Africa
tel (021) 531 1926 fax (021) 531 8789
e-mail inpra@iafrica.com

Press photos for South African market. Founded 1934.

Isle of Wight Photo Library

The Old Rectory, Calbourne, Isle of Wight PO30 4JE
tel (01983) 531575 fax (01983) 531253

Specialist library of colour transparencies of the Isle of Wight: landscapes, seascapes, architecture, gardens, flora and boats. In association with **S. & O. Mathews**. Founded 1995.

Isle of Wight Pictures

60 York Street, Cowes, Isle of Wight PO31 7BS
tel (01983) 290366 fax (01983) 297282
Proprietor Patrick Eden

Covers all aspects of the Isle of Wight, including Cowes Week, sailing events, nautical aspects. Any picture not on file can be shot on request. Founded 1985.

Japan Archive

9 Victoria Drive, Horsforth, Leeds LS18 4PN
tel (0113) 258 3244
Contact S.R. Turnbull

Japan: modern, daily life, architecture, religion, history, personalities, gardens, natural world. Founded 1993.

Jazz Index*

26 Fosse Way, London W13 0BZ
tel/fax 0181-998 1232
e-mail 106400.1300@compuserve.com

Photo library of jazz, blues and contemporary musicians. Also photos of instruments, clubs, crowds at concerts. Photos sold on behalf of photographers. Terms: 50%. Founded 1979.

Joe Filmbase Studios

107 Oakfield Road, London N17 5RL
tel 0171-523 0400 *fax* 0171-523 1117
e-mail 106310.231@compuserve.com

General library. Terms: 3-year contract. Transparencies only; 35mm, 6 x 7cm etc formats. Founded 1991.

JS Library International

101A Brondesbury Park, London NW2 5JL
tel 0181-451 2668 *fax* 0181-459 0223
e-mail jslibraryinternational@ukbusiness.com
web site http://www.ukbusiness.com/jslibraryinternational

The Royal Family, worldwide travel pictures, particularly the African continent, stage and screen celebrities, authors, worldwide general material. New material on any subject, in any quantity, always urgently required; features also required. Assignments undertaken. Founded 1979.

Just Europe

50 Basingfield Road, Thames Ditton, Surrey KT7 0PD
tel/fax 0181-398 2468

Specialises in Europe – major cities, towns, people and customs. Assignments undertaken; background information available; advice and research service. Founded 1989.

Keystone Collection – see Getty Images Ltd*

Lakeland Life Picture Library

Langsett, Lyndene Drive, Grange-over-Sands, Cumbria LA11 6QP
tel (015395) 33565 (answerphone)

English Lake District: industries, crafts, sports, shows, customs, architecture, people. Also provides colour and b&w, illustrated articles. Not an agency. Catalogue available on request. Founded 1979.

Landscape Only*

c/o Images Colour Library Ltd,
12-14 Argyll Street, London W1V 1AB
tel 0171-734 7344 *fax* 0171-287 3933

Outdoor landscapes of villages and countryside worldwide by some of the world's leading landscape photographers. Terms: 50%. Founded 1986.

Frank Lane Picture Agency Ltd*

Pages Green House, Wetheringsett, Stowmarket, Suffolk IP14 5QA
tel (01728) 860789 *fax* (01728) 860222
e-mail flpa@compuserve.com

Natural history, ecology, environment, farming, geography, trees and weather.

Michael Leach

Brookside, Kinnerley, Oswestry SY10 8DB
tel/fax (01691) 682639

General worldwide wildlife and natural history subjects, with particular emphasis on mammals and urban wildlife. Comprehensive collection of owls from all over the world. No other photographers required.

Dave Lewis Nostalgia Collection

20 The Avenue, Starbeck, Harrogate, North Yorkshire NG1 4QD
tel/fax (01423) 888642

A collection in 2 and 3 dimensions of social and commercial history 1800s-1960s. Many images are on transparency and individual commissions are readily undertaken. Founded 1995.

Link Picture Library*

33 Greyhound Road, London W6 8NH
tel 0171-381 2261/2433 *fax* 0171-385 6244
e-mail lib@linkpics.demon.co.uk
Proprietor Orde Eliason

Specialist archives on Southern Africa, Asia, Southeast Asia, Israel and music. Electronic images on Photo CD Disc. Commissions accepted. Terms: 50%. Founded 1982.

London Metropolitan Archives

(formerly Greater London Record Office)
40 Northampton Road, London EC1R 0HB
tel 0171-332 3820 *fax* 0171-833 9136

Over 350,000 photographic prints and 1,500,000 negatives of London and the London area from c.1860 to 1986. Especially strong on local authority projects, including schools, public housing and open spaces.

The Billie Love Historical Collection

Reflections, 3 Winton Street, Ryde,
Isle of Wight PO33 2BX
tel (01983) 812572 *fax* (01983) 811164
Proprietor Billie Love

Photos (late 19th century-1930s), engravings, coloured lithographs, covering subjects from earliest times, people, places and events up to the Second World War; also more recent material. Founded 1969.

Ludvigsen Library Ltd*

73 Collier Street, London N1 9BE
tel 0171-837 1700 *fax* 0171-837 1776
e-mail ludvigsen@mail.bogo.co.uk
Photographic resources Paul Parker

Specialist automotive and motor racing photo library. Includes much rare and unpublished material from Edward Eves, Max le Grand, Karl Ludvigsen, Rodolfo Mailander, Stanley Rosenthall and others. Founded 1984.

The MacQuitty International Collection*

7 Elm Lodge, River Gardens, Stevenage Road,
London SW6 6NZ
tel 0171-385 6031 *tel/fax* 0171-384 1781

300,000 photos covering aspects of life in 70 countries: archaeology, art, buildings, flora and fauna, gardens, museums, people and occupations, scenery, religions, methods of transport, surgery, acupuncture, funeral customs, fishing, farming, dancing, music, crafts, sports, weddings, carnivals, food, drink, jewellery and oriental subjects. Period: 1920 to present day.

Mander & Mitchenson Theatre Collection*

The Mansion, Beckenham Place Park,
Beckenham, Kent BR3 2BP
tel 0181-658 7725 *fax* 0181-663 0313

Prints, drawings, photos, programmes, etc, theatre, opera, ballet, music hall, and other allied subjects including composers, playwrights, etc. All periods. Available for books, magazines, TV.

Mansell Collection Ltd

42 Linden Gardens, London W2 4ER
tel 0171-229 5475 *fax* 0171-792 0469

General historical material up to the 1920s, 1930s.

John Massey Stewart

20 Hillway, London N6 6QA
tel 0181-341 3544 *fax* 0181-341 5292

Large collection Russia/USSR, including topography, people, culture, Siberia, plus Russian and Soviet history, 3000 pre-revolutionary PCs, etc. Also Britain, Europe, Asia, Alaska, USA, Israel, Sinai desert, etc.

S. & O. Mathews*

The Old Rectory, Calbourne,
Isle of Wight PO30 4JE
tel (01983) 531247 *fax* (01983) 531253

Gardens, flowers and landscapes.

Chris Mattison

138 Dalewood Road, Sheffield S8 0EF
tel/fax (0114) 236 4433
e-mail chris.mattison@btinternet.com

Colour library specialising in reptiles and amphibians; other natural history subjects; habitats and landscapes in Africa, SE Asia, South America, USA, Mexico, Mediterranean. Captions or detailed copy supplied if required. No other photographers' material required.

Medimage

32 Brooklyn Road, Coventry CV1 4JT
tel/fax (01203) 668562
Contact Anthony King

Specialist library of 12,000 medium format transparencies of subjects in Mediterranean countries: agriculture, architecture, crafts, festivals, flora, industry, landscape, markets, portraits, recreation, seascapes, sport and transport. Commissions undertaken. Other photographers' work not accepted. Founded 1992.

Merseyside Photo Library

Suite 1, Egerton House, Tower Road, Birkenhead,
Wirral L41 1FN
tel 0151-650 6975 *fax* 0151-650 6976
Operated by Ron Jones Associates

Library specialising in images of Liverpool and Merseyside but includes other destinations. Founded 1989.

Microscopix

Middle Travelly, Beguildy, Nr Knighton,
Powys LD7 1UW
tel (01547) 510242 *fax* (01547) 510317
e-mail mik@micropix.demon.co.uk

Scientific photo library specialising in scanning electron micrographs and photomicrographs for technical and aesthetic purposes. Commissioned work, both biological and non-biological, undertaken offering a wide variety of applicable microscopical techniques. Founded 1986.

Military History Picture Library
3 Barton Buildings, Bath BA1 2JR
tel (01225) 334213

Prints, engravings, photos, colour transparencies covering all aspects of warfare and uniforms from ancient times to the present.

Mirror Syndication International*
One Canada Square, Canary Wharf,
London E14 5AP
tel 0171-293 3700 *fax* 0171-293 2712
e-mail desk@mirpix.com

Specialises in current affairs, personalities, royalty, sport, cinema and travel. Agents for Mirror Group Newspapers.

Monitor Syndication
(incorporates the City Syndication library)
17 Old Street, London EC1V 9HL
tel 0171-253 7071 *fax* 0171-250 0966
Contact Stewart White

Specialists in portrait photos of leading national and international personalities from politics, trade unions, entertainment, sport, Royalty and well-known buildings in London. Founded 1960.

Motorcycles Unlimited
48 Lemsford Road, St Albans, Herts. AL1 3PR
tel (01727) 869001 *fax* (01727) 869014
e-mail rolandbrown@motobike.demon.co.uk
Owner Roland Brown

Bikes of all kinds, from latest roadsters to classics, racers to tourers. Detailed information available on all machines pictured. Founded 1993.

Mountain Dynamics
Heathcourt, Morven Way, Monaltrie,
Ballater AB35 5SF
tel (013397) 55081 *fax* (013397) 55526
Proprietor Graham P. Adams

Scottish and European mountains – from ground to summits – in panoramic (6 x 17cm), 5 x 4in and medium format. Commissions undertaken. Terms: 50%. Founded 1990.

Mountain Visions
25 The Mallards, Langstone, Havant,
Hants PO9 1SS
tel (01705) 478441
Contact Graham Elson and Roslyn Elson

Colour transparencies of mountaineering, skiing, and tourism in Europe, Africa, Himalayas, Arctic, Far East, South America and Australia. Does not act as agent for other photographers. Founded 1984.

David Muscroft Photography and David Muscroft Picture Library
16 Broadfield Road, Heeley,
Sheffield S8 0XJ
tel (0114) 258 9299 *fax* (0114) 255 0113

Large, varied and expanding library on babyhood, family, pregnancy, supplying all the UK's baby magazines. Founded 1977.

The Mustograph Agency
19 Rathbone Street, London W1P 1AF
tel 0171-636 6128/9 *fax* 0171-637 4317

Britain only: b&w general subjects of countryside life, work, history and scenery.

National Maritime Museum Picture Library*
National Maritime Museum, Park Row,
London SE10 9NF
tel 0181-312 6631 *fax* 0181-312 6722
Picture Library Manager Christopher Gray

Maritime, transport, time and space and historic photographs.

National Motor Museum, Beaulieu
Motoring Picture Library, Beaulieu,
Hants SO42 7ZN
tel (01590) 612345 *fax* (01590) 612655

All aspects of motoring, cars, commercial vehicles, motor cycles, personalities, etc. Illustrations of period scenes and motor sport. Also large library of 5 x 4in and smaller colour transparencies of veteran, vintage and modern cars, commercial vehicles and motor cycles. Over 700,000 images in total.

Natural History Photographic Agency – see NHPA*

Natural Image
31 Shaftesbury Road, Poole,
Dorset BH15 2LT
tel (01202) 675916 *fax* (01202) 242944
Contact Dr Bob Gibbons

Colour library covering natural history, habitats, countryside and gardening (UK and worldwide); special emphasis on conservation. Commissions undertaken. Terms: 50%. Founded 1982.

News Blitz International
Via Guido Banti 34, 00191 Rome, Italy
tel 333 26 41/333 02 52 *fax* 333 26 51
Contact Giovanni A. Congiu

News and general library.

NHPA*
(Natural History Photographic Agency)
57 High Street, Ardingly, West Sussex RH17 6TB
tel (01444) 892514 *fax* (01444) 892168
Represents more than 100 of the world's leading natural history photographers covering a wide range of wildlife, marine life, domestic animals and pets, plants, landscapes and environmental subjects. Specialisations include the unique high-speed photography of Stephen Dalton, comprehensive coverage on North America and Africa, and the ANT collection of Australasian material (for which NHPA is UK agent). Recent additions to the files include strong coverage from China, Russia, Romania, Vietnam and Peru. Pictures are generally supplied to companies and institutions only, and are sent to freelance writers and artists by agreement with their publisher or commissioning company.

The Northern Picture Library*
Greenheys Business Centre, 10 Pencroft Way, Manchester M15 6JJ
tel 0161-226 2007 *fax* 0161-226 2022
Proprietor Roy Conchie
General library covering Britain, the world, industry, sport, leisure, etc. Submissions considered from photographers.

Operation Raleigh – see Raleigh International*

Orion Press
1-13 Kanda Jimbocho, Chiyoda-ku, Tokyo 101, Japan
tel (03) 3295-1400 *fax* (03) 3295-0227
e-mail orionprs@po.iijnet.or.jp
All subjects in all formats.

Christine Osborne/Middle East Pictures Inc.*
53A Crimsworth Road, London SW8 4RJ
tel/fax 0171-720 6951
Specialises in the Arab World/Middle East, Indian subcontinent, Africa and Southeast Asia. Stock from 28 Islamic countries. Special files on environment, women in society, architecture, agriculture and food production, crafts and religions. Other pictures relate to assignments by photojournalist Osbourne in more than 50 countries – family life, people at work, city management, Eastern foods. Founded 1984.

Oxford Scientific Films Ltd, Photo Library*
(incorporating the Survival Anglia Photo Library)
Lower Road, Long Hanborough, Oxon OX8 8LL
tel (01993) 881881 *fax* (01993) 882808
e-mail 101573.163@compuserve.com
300,000 colour transparencies of wildlife, natural science and environmental images supplied by over 300 photographers worldwide. UK agents for *Animals Animals* and *Photo Researchers*, New York and *Okapia*, Frankfurt.

PA News Photo Library*
292 Vauxhall Bridge Road, London SW1V 1AE
tel 0171-963 7032/34/35 *fax* 0171-963 7066
Over 5 million photos dating from the turn of the century, covering news, sport, royalty and showbiz. Library updated daily. Searches undertaken, or customers are welcome to visit. Founded 1902.

Panos Pictures*
1 Chapel Court, Borough High Street, London SE1 1HH
tel 0171-234 0010 *fax* 0171-357 0094
e-mail panospics@corporate.nethead.co.uk
Third World and Eastern European documentary photos focusing on social, political and economic issues with a special emphasis on environment and development. Files on agriculture, conflict, education, energy, environment, family life, festivals, food, health, industry, landscape, people, politics, pollution, refugees, religions, rural life, transport, urban life, water, weather. Terms: 50%. Founded 1986.

Papilio Natural History & Travel Library*
44 Palestine Grove, London SW19 2QN
tel/fax 0181-687 2202 *mobile* (0973) 310072
Contacts Robert Pickett, Justine Bowler
Worldwide coverage of natural history and environmental subjects including travel section; commissions undertaken. Founded 1988.

Ann & Bury Peerless*
22 King's Avenue, Minnis Bay, Birchington-on-Sea, Kent CT7 9QL
tel (01843) 841428 *fax* (01843) 848321
Art, craft (including textiles), archaeology, architecture, dance, iconography, miniature paintings, manuscripts, museum artefacts, social, cultural, agricultur-

al, industrial, historical, political, educational, geographical subjects and travel in India, Pakistan, Bangladesh, Afghanistan, Burma, Cambodia, China, Egypt, Iran, Israel, Kenya, Libya, Malta, Malaysia, Morocco, Nepal, Russia (Moscow, St Petersburg, Samarkand and Bukhara, Uzbekistan), Sri Lanka, Spain, Sudan, Taiwan, Thailand, Tunisia, Uganda, Zambia and Zimbabwe. Specialist material on historical and world religions: Hinduism, Buddhism, Jainism, Judaism, Christianity, Confucianism, Islam, Sikhism, Taoism, Zoroastrianism (Parsees of India).

Chandra S. Perera Cinetra
437 Pethiyagoda, Kelaniya-11600, Sri Lanka
tel (94) 1-911885 *fax* (94) 1-541414/332867
B&w and colour library including news, wildlife, religious, social, political, sports, adventure, environmental, forestry, nature and tourism. Photographic and journalistic features on any subject. Founded 1958.

Performing Arts Library*
52 Agate Road, London W6 0AH
tel 0181-748 2002 *fax* 0181-563 0538
e mail 100546 507@compuserve.com
Specialist library with an international portfolio including: actors, actresses, singers, musicians, conductors, opera, ballet, plays and musical instruments. Originally based on the work of Clive Barda, the library now covers all aspects of the performing arts and holds over 100,000 images. Founded 1992.

Photo Flora*
46 Jacoby Place, Priory Road, Birmingham B5 7UN
tel/fax 0121-471 3300
Comprehensive collection of British wild plants; Mediterranean wild plants and travel; Egypt, India, Tibet, China, Nepal, Thailand, Mexico. Founded 1982.

Photo Library International
PO Box 75, Leeds LS7 3NZ
tel (0113) 262 3005 *fax* (0113) 262 5366
Colour transparencies only. Most subjects. New material always welcome.

Photo Link
126 Quarry Lane, Northfield, Birmingham B31 2QD
tel/fax 0121-475 8712
Contact Mike Vines

Colour and b&w aviation library, covering subjects from 1909 to the present day. Specialises in air-to-air photography. Assignments undertaken; can also research and write aviation press releases. Founded 1990.

Photo Resources*
The Orchard, Marley Lane, Kingston, Canterbury, Kent CT4 6JH
tel (01227) 830075 *fax* (01227) 831135
Ancient civilisations, art, archaeology, world religions, myth, and museum objects covering the period from 30,000 BC to AD 1900. European birds, butterflies, trees.

Photofusion*
17A Electric Lane, London SW9 8LA
tel 0171-738 5774 *fax* 0171-738 5509
web site http://www.photosource.co.uk/photosource/photofusion.htm
Collection of 50,000 b&w photos and 15,000 colour transparencies on contemporary social issues, including disability, education, family, health, homelessness and work.

The Photographers' Library*
81A Endell Street, London WC2H 9AJ
tel 0171-836 5591 *fax* 0171-379 4650
Requires transparency material on worldwide travel, industry, agriculture, commerce, sport, people, leisure, girls, scenic. Colour only. Terms: 50%. Founded 1978.

Pictor International Ltd*
Lymehouse Studios, 30-31 Lyme Street, London NW1 0EE
tel 0171-482 0478 *fax* 0171-267 1396
e-mail postmaster@pictor.demon.co.uk
web site http://www.pictor.co.uk
Offices in 18 countries. All subjects. Terms: 50%.

The Picture Company
3 Barley Rise, Baldock, Herts. SG7 6RT
tel (01462) 894742 *Mobile* 0850 971491
fax (01438) 726969
Contact Chris Bonass
Colour transparencies ($2^{1}/_{4}$ x $2^{1}/_{4}$in and 35mm) of people and places worldwide. Taken by award-winning film and TV cameraman and largely unseen and unpublished. Also aviation pictures old and new, including air-to-air photography and a unique archive on 16mm film and broadcast videotape. Used by BBC,

C4, etc. Assignments undertaken. Founded 1993.

Picture Research Service
Rich Research, One Bradby, 77 Carlton Hill, London NW8 9XE
tel/fax 0171-624 7755
Contact Diane Rich

Visuals found for all sectors of the media and publishing. Artwork and photography commissioned. Rights and permissions negotiated. Established 1978.

Picturepoint Ltd – see Topham Picturepoint*

Sylvia Pitcher
75 Bristol Road, London E7 8HG
tel/fax 0181-552 8308

Specialist in blues, jazz, old-time country and bluegrass, cajun and zydeco musicians; also towns, rural scenes, details, record labels, and still life etc. relevant to the music. Founded 1968.

Pixfeatures
5 Latimer Road, Barnet, Herts. EN5 5NU
tel 0181-449 9946 *fax* 0181-441 2725
Contact Peter Wickman

Pictures and features covering big news events, royalty, showbiz and travel (all countries). National newspapers' extensive collection of people in the news to 1970. *Stern* magazine features (before 1985). Documentary and historical photos. Special collections: Dukes of Windsor and Kent, Kennedys, Beatles, Keeler/Levy, trainrobbers. Terms: 50%.

Planet Earth Pictures*
The Innovation Centre, 225 Marsh Wall, London E14 9FX
tel 0171-293 2999 *fax* 0171-293 2998

All aspects of natural history and the natural environment, farming, fishing, pollution and conservation. Founded 1969.

POPPERFOTO (Paul Popper Ltd)*
The Old Mill, Overstone Farm, Overstone, Northampton NN6 0AB
tel (01604) 670670 *fax* (01604) 670635

Over 13 million images, covering 150 years of photographic history. Unrivalled archival material, world-famous sports library and extensive stock photography. Credit line includes Reuters, Bob Thomas Sports Photography, UPI, AFP and EPA, Acme, INP, Planet, Paul Popper, Exclusive News Agency, Victory Archive, Odhams Periodicals Library, *Illustrated*, Harris Picture Agency, and H.G. Ponting which holds the Scott 1910-12 Antarctic expedition material.

Colour from 1940, b&w from 1870 to present. Major subjects covered worldwide include: events, personalities, wars, royalty, sport, politics, transport, crime, history and social conditions. POPPERFOTO policy is to make material available, same day, to clients throughout the world. Mac-desk accessible. Researchers welcome by appointment. Free catalogue available.

Power Pix International Picture Library – see S. & I. Williams, Power Pix International Picture Library

Premaphotos Wildlife
Amberstone, 1 Kirland Road, Bodmin, Cornwall PL30 5JQ
tel (01208) 78258 *fax* (01208) 72302
e-mail 106153.1070@compuserve.com

Library of 35mm transparencies; wide range of natural history subjects from around the world. Invertebrate behaviour a speciality.

Press Association Photos – see PA News Photo Library*

Profile Photo Library
2B Winner Commercial Building, 401-403 Lockhart Road, Hong Kong
tel (852) 2574 7788 *fax* (852) 2574 8884
e-mail profile@hk.linkage.net
web site http://www.profilephoto.com.hk
Singapore office
62A Smith Street, Chinatown, Singapore 058964
tel (65) 324 3747 *fax* (65) 324 3748
e-mail profile@singnet.comsg
Director Neil Farrin
Thailand office
Room 406, 4th Floor Kitpanit Building, 18 Patpong Soi 1, Suriwonges Road, Bangrak, Bangkok 10500
tel (662) 634 3065 *fax* (662) 634 3066
e-mail winyou@ksc9.th.com

General photo library. Film footage available. Terms: 50%. Founded 1982.

Public Record Office Image Library*
Public Record Office, Ruskin Avenue, Kew, Surrey TW9 4DU
tel 0181-392 5225 *fax* 0181-392 5266
e-mail enterprises.pro.kew@gtnet.gov.uk
web site http://www.open.gov.uk/pro/imagelib.htp

Unique collection of millions of historical documents on a wide range of formats from 1066 to 1960s. Special collections include: Victorian and Edwardian advertisements and photographs, World War Two propaganda, military history, maps, decorative and technical designs and medieval illuminations. Founded 1995.

Punch Cartoon Library*

100 Brompton Road, London SW3 1ER
tel 0171-225 6711/6710 *fax* 0171-225 6712
e-mail edit@punch.co.uk

Comprehensive collection of cartoons and illustrations, indexed under subject categories: humour, historical events, politics, fashion, sport, personalities, etc. Founded 1841.

Railways – Milepost 92½*

Milepost 92½, Newton Harcourt,
Leics. LE8 9FH
tel (0116) 259 2068 *fax* (0116) 259 3001
e-mail michael@milepost.demon.co.uk

Comprehensive collection of all aspects of modern railway operations, and scenic pictures from the UK and abroad. Includes Colin Garratt's collection of world steam trains as well as archive b&w photos. Founded 1969.

Raleigh International Picture Library*

Raleigh House, 27 Parson's Green Lane,
London SW6 4HS
tel 0171-371 8585 *fax* 0171-371 5116
Contact Sophia Wilson

Source of stock colour images from locations around the world: the 100,000-plus images are updated 8 times a year. Open to researchers by appointment, 9.30 a.m.-5.30 p.m. Mon-Fri. Founded 1978.

Retna Pictures Ltd*

1 Fitzroy Mews, Cleveland Street,
London W1P 5DQ
tel 0171-209 0200 *fax* 0171-383 7151

Library of colour transparencies and b&w prints of rock and pop performers, show business personalities, celebrities, actors and actresses. Also extensive lifestyle and stock library. Founded 1984.

Retrograph Nostalgia Archive Ltd*

164 Kensington Park Road, London W11 2ER
tel 0171-727 9378 *answerphone* (outside office hours) 0171-727 9426 *fax* 0171-229 3395
e-mail mbreese999@aol.com

Worldwide advertising, packaging, posters, postcards, decorative and fine art illustrations from 1880-1970. Special collections include Victoriana illustrations and scraps (1860-1901), fashion and beauty (1880-1975), RetroTravel Archive: travel and tourism, RetroGourmet Archive: food and drink (1890-1950). Research service and Image Consultancy services; Retro-Montages: Victoriana montage design service. Free colour leaflets. Founded 1984.

Ann Ronan at Image Select*

19 Radnor Road, Harrow, Middlesex HA1 1RY
tel 0181-861 1122 *fax* 0181-861 4755

Woodcuts, engravings, etc, social and political history plus history of science and technology, including military and space, literature and music.

Roundhouse Ornithology Collection

c/o John Stewart-Smith, 24 Carneton Close,
Crantock, Newquay, Cornwall TR8 5RY
tel/fax (01637) 830546

Colour library specialising in birds of UK, Europe, Middle East (especially), North Africa, Far East and South America. Founded 1991.

Royal Geographical Society Picture Library*

1 Kensington Gore, London SW7 2AR
tel 0171-591 3060 *fax* 0171-591 3061
e-mail pictures@rgs.org
Contact Picture Library Manager

Worldwide coverage of geography, travel, exploration, expeditions and cultural environment from 1870s to the present. Founded 1830.

The Royal Photographic Society*

The Octagon, Milsom Street, Bath BA1 1DN
tel (01225) 462841 *fax* (01225) 448688

Exhibitions; library of books, photos and photographic equipment. Founded 1853.

Royal Society for Asian Affairs

2 Belgrave Square, London SW1X 8PJ
tel 0171-235 5122

Archive library of original 19th and 20th century b&w photos, glass slides, etc, of Asia. Publishes *Asian Affairs* 3 p.a.

Royal Society of Chemistry Library and Information Centre*

Burlington House, Piccadilly,
London W1V 0BN
tel 0171-437 8656 *fax* 0171-287 9798

Covers all aspects of chemistry information. Images collection dating from 1538 includes prints and photographs of famous chemists, *Vanity Fair* cartoons, scenes, lantern slides of similar subjects and colour photomicrographs of crystal structures. Founded 1841.

RSPCA Photolibrary*

RSPCA Trading Ltd, Causeway, Horsham, West Sussex RH12 1HG
tel (01403) 223150 *fax* (01403) 241048
e-mail photolibrary@rspca.org.uk
Manager Andrew Forsyth

A comprehensive collection of natural history pictures representing the work of over 300 photographers, and a unique record of the work of the RSPCA. Its specialist collection covers: animal hospitals, veterinary treatment, wildlife rehabilitation work, cruelty to animals, animal welfare education, RSPCA inspectors at work and other animal welfare issues such as environmental problems and cruel sports. Founded 1993.

Dawn Runnals Photographic Library

5 St Marys Terrace, Kenwyn Road, Truro, Cornwall TR1 3SW
tel (01872) 79353

General library: land and seascapes, flora and fauna, sport, animals, people, buildings, boats, harbours, miscellaneous section and some specialised subjects – details on application. Other photographers' work not accepted. Sae appreciated with enquiries. Founded 1985.

The Russia and Republics Photo Library*

Conifers House, Cheapside Lane, Denham, Uxbridge, Middlesex UB9 5AE
tel (01895) 834814 *fax* (01895) 834028
Library Manager Mark Wadlow

Colour photo library specialising in cities, towns, famous landmarks and people. Do not accept other photographers' work. Founded 1988.

Salamander Picture Library

129-137 York Way, London N7 9LG
tel 0171-267 4447 *fax* 0171-267 5112
Picture Manager Terry Forshaw

General collection including American history, collectables, cookery, crafts, military, natural history, space and transport. Founded 1996.

Peter Sanders Photography*

24 Meades Lane, Chesham, Bucks. HP5 1ND
tel/fax (01494) 773674

Specialises in Islamic world, but now expanding into other world religions, beliefs, cultures, architecture and industry. Founded 1987.

Steffi Schubert, Wildlife Conservation Collection Photographic Library

Avondale Farm, Southwold Road, Holton, Nr Halesworth, Suffolk IP19 8PW
tel/fax (01986) 872777

All aspects of British wildlife and fauna. Founded 1990.

Science Photo Library*

112 Westbourne Grove, London W2 5RU
tel 0171-727 4712 *fax* 0171-727 6041
e-mail andy@sciencephoto.co.uk

Scientific photography of all kinds – medicine, technology, Space, nature. 100,000 different images. Founded 1979.

Science & Society Picture Library*

Science Museum, Exhibition Road, London SW7 2DD
tel 0171-938 9750 *fax* 0171-938 9751
e-mail piclib@nmsi.ac.uk
web site http://www.nmsi.ac.uk/piclib/

Subjects include: science and technology, medicine, industry, transport, social documentary and the media. Extensive collection; images drawn from the Science Museum in London, the National Railway Museum in York and the National Museum of Photography, Film and Television in Bradford. Free brochure available on request. Founded 1993.

Scotland in Focus Picture Library

22 Fleming Place, Fountainhall, Galashiels, Selkirkshire TD1 2TA
tel/fax (01578 760) 256
e-mail scotfocus@taynet.co.uk
web site www.scotland.net/scotfocus

Library specialising in all aspects of Scotland, including British wildlife and natural history subjects. All Scottish material required on 35mm and upwards, medium format preferred. Photographers must enclose return postage. Terms: 50%. Founded 1988.

SCR Photo Library

Society for Co-operation in Russian and Soviet Studies, 320 Brixton Road, London SW9 6AB
tel 0171-274 2282 *fax* 0171-274 3230

Russian and Soviet life and history. Comprehensive coverage of cultural subjects: art, theatre, folk art, costume, music; agriculture and industry, architecture, armed forces, education, history, places, politics, science, sport. Also posters and theatre props, artistic reference, advice. Research by appointment only. Founded 1943.

Seaco Picture Library*

Sea Containers House, 20 Upper Ground, London SE1 9PF
tel 0171-805 5831/5834 *fax* 0171-805 5926

Stills and video footage of: container shipping; fast ferries and ports; produce and fruit farming – India and Africa; hotels and resorts in Botswana, South Africa, Portugal, USA, Brazil, Italy and Australia. Railways, including the Venice-Simplon-Orient-Express and Oriental Express luxury tourist train services and the recently launched Road to Mandalay cruiseship in Burma. Founded 1995.

Sealand Aerial Photography Ltd*

Goodwood Airfield, Goodwood, Chichester, West Sussex PO18 0PH
tel (01243) 781025 *fax* (01243) 531422

Aerial photo coverage of any subject that can be photographed from the air in the UK. Most stock on 2¼in format colour negative/transparency. Subjects constantly updated from new flying. Founded 1976.

S & G Press Agency Ltd*

63 Gee Street, London EC1V 3RS
tel 0171-336 0632 *fax* 0171-253 8419

Press photos and vast photo library. Send photos, but negatives preferred.

Mick Sharp

Eithinog, Waun, Penisarwaun, Caernarfon, Gwynedd LL55 3PW
tel/fax (01286) 872425

Archaeology, ancient monuments, buildings, churches, countryside, environment, history, landscape, past cultures and topography. Emphasis on British Isles, but material from many other countries including France, Iraq, Morocco and USA. Access to other similar photo collections. B&w prints from 5 x 4in nega-

tives, and 35mm and 6 x 4.5cm colour transparencies. Founded 1981.

Shout Picture Library*

Rowan House, Aston-le-Walls, Northants. NN11 6UF
tel (01295) 660374 *fax* (01295) 660518
e-mail john@shout-pictures.demon.co.uk
web site http://www.shout-pictures.demon.co.uk
Contact John Callan

Specialises in the emergency services: fires, road traffic accidents, surgery, various police and hospital units. Commissions accepted; terms as recommended by BAPLA. Founded 1994.

Brian and Sal Shuel – see Collections*

Sites, Sights and Cities

2 Godsons Piece, High Street, Lower Brailes, Banbury, Oxon OX15 5AQ
tel/fax (01608) 685119
e-mail devereuxp@aol.com
Director Paul Devereux

Ancient monuments, mainly in Britain, Egypt, Greece and USA; city features in UK, Europe and USA; general nature shots. Founded 1990.

Skishoot – Offshoot*

Hall Place, Upper Woodcott, Whitchurch, Hants RG28 7PY
tel (01635) 255527 *fax* (01635) 255528
e-mail skishoot@surfersparadise.net
Librarian Fiona Foote

Library specialising in all aspects of skiing and snowboarding. Also travel (especially France). Assignments undertaken. Terms: 50%. Founded 1986.

Skyscan Photolibrary*

Oak House, Toddington, Cheltenham, Glos. GL54 5BY
tel (01242) 621357 *fax* (01242) 621343

Based on a unique collection of aerial images of British landscapes, cities, heritage sites, patterns, etc, taken from a tethered balloon which produces unusual viewpoints and very high definition photos. Now expanding to include other aerial collections i.e. air-to-ground, air-to-air, balloons, etc. Terms: 50%. Founded 1984.

The Slide File*

79 Merrion Square South, Dublin 2, Republic of Ireland
tel (01) 6766850 *fax* (01) 6624476

Specialises in Eire and Northern Ireland: landscapes, Irish natural history, agricul-

ture and industry, Irish people and their traditions, Celtic heritage. Founded 1978.

Patrick Smith Associates

Gloucester House, High Street, Borth, Dyfed SY24 5HZ
tel/fax (01970) 871296

South London 1950-1977, mid-Wales, aviation; also The Patrick Smith Collection of London photos, now in The Museum of London. Founded 1964.

Society for Anglo-Chinese Understanding

Sally & Richard Greenhill Photo Library, 357A Liverpool Road, London N1 1NL
tel 0171-607 8549 *fax* 0171-607 7151

Colour and b&w prints of China, late 1960s-1989. Founded 1965.

Society for Co-operation in Russian and Soviet Studies – see SCR Photo Library

Source Photographic Archives

66 Claremont Road, Sandymount, Dublin 4, Republic of Ireland
tel (01) 6607090
Director Thomas Kennedy

Mostly recent photos by living photographers on many different subjects. Founded 1974.

Spectrum Colour Library*

41-42 Berners Street, London W1P 3AA
tel 0171-637 1587 *fax* 0171-637 3681

Extensive general library of high-quality transparencies, for worldwide marketing, including electronically. Photographer's information pack available. Purchases photos and collections of photos.

Sporting Pictures (UK) Ltd*

7A Lambs Conduit Passage, London WC1R 4RG
tel 0171-405 4500 *fax* 0171-831 7991
e-mail photos@sportingpictures.demon.co.uk
Director Crispin J. Thruston, *Librarian* Justin Downing

Specialises in sports, sporting events, sportsmen.

Peter Stiles Picture Library

49 Palmerston Avenue, Goring-by-Sea, West Sussex BN12 4RN
tel/fax (01903) 503147 *mobile* (0976) 351369

Specialises in horticulture, plus natural history, pictorial views. Sequences and illustrated features. Own pictures only. Commissions undertaken.

The Still Moving Picture Company*

67A Logie Green Road, Edinburgh EH7 4HF
tel 0131-557 9697 *fax* 0131-557 9699
e-mail 101320.3322@compuserve.com

250,000 pictures of Scotland and all things Scottish; sport (Allsport agent for Scotland). Founded 1991.

STILL Pictures Whole Earth Photo Library*

199 Shooters Hill Road, London SE3 8UL
tel 0181-858 8307 *fax* 0181-858 2049
Proprietor Mark Edwards

Specialises in people and the environment; the Third World; wildlife and habitats. Includes industry, agriculture, indigenous peoples and cultures, nature and endangered species. Terms: 50%. Founded 1970.

Tony Stone Images*

101 Bayham Street, London NW1 0AG
tel 0171-267 8988 *fax* 0171-722 9305
Contact Creative Dept

International photo library. Subjects required: travel, people, natural history, commerce, industry, technology, sport, etc. Terms: 50%.

Survival Anglia Photo Library – see Oxford Scientific Films Ltd*

Sutcliffe Gallery

1 Flowergate, Whitby, North Yorkshire YO21 3BA
tel (01947) 602239 *fax* (01947) 820287

Collection of 19th century photography, all by Frank M. Sutcliffe Hon. FRPS (1853-1941), especially inshore fishing boats and fishing community; also farming interests. Period covered 1872 to 1910.

Charles Tait Photo Library

Kelton, St Ola, Orkney KW15 1TR
tel (01856) 873738/875003 *fax* (01856) 875313
e-mail charles @velvia.demon.co.uk
web site www.orkneyislands.com/charlestait

Colour photo library specialising in islands: Orkney, Shetland and Western Isles (including St Kilda, North Rona, Sula Sgeir), as well as many parts of Scotland and France; also Venice. Subjects include archaeology, landscapes, transport, industry, seascapes, events, people and wildlife, especially seabirds and seals. Panoramic landscapes using Alpa Rotocam a speciality. Publisher of postcards, calendars, guidebooks. All transparencies with detailed captions and bar coded. Founded 1978.

The Tank Museum Photo Library & Archive
The Tank Museum, Bovington,
Dorset BH20 6JG
tel (01929) 403463 *fax* (01929) 405360
International collection, from 1900 to present, of armoured fighting vehicles and military transport, including tanks, armoured cars, personnel carriers, self-propelled artillery carriers, missile launchers, cars, lorries and tractors. Founded *c*.1946.

Telegraph Colour Library*
The Innovation Centre, 225 Marsh Wall,
London E14 9FX
tel 0171-987 1212 *fax* 0171-538 3309
Stock photography agency covering a wide subject range: business, sport, people, industry, animals, medical, nature, space, travel and graphics. Sameday service for all UK clients. Free catalogues available upon request.

Theatre Museum
National Museum of the Performing Arts,
1E Tavistock Street, London WC2E 7PA
tel 0171-836 7891 *fax* 0171-836 5148
In addition to extensive public displays on live entertainment, the Museum has an unrivalled collection of programmes, playbills, prints, photos, videos, texts and press cuttings relating to performers and productions from the 17th century onwards. Available by appointment, free of charge through the Study Room. Open Tues-Fri 10.30am-4.30pm. Reprographic services available.

3rd Millennium Music Ltd
22 Avon, Hockley, Tamworth, Staffs. B77 5QA
tel/fax (01827) 286086
Contact Neil Williams (Managing Director)
Specialises in classical music ephemera, including portraits of composers, musicians, conductors and opera singers. Old and sometimes rare photographs, postcards, prints, cigarette cards, stamps, concert programmes, Victorian newspapers, etc. Also modern photographs of composer references such as museums, statues, memorials etc.

Other subjects: ballet and dance, musical instruments, concert halls and other music venues, manuscripts, church organs, ethnic music, jazz and other music groups. Founded 1996.

Three Lions – see Getty Images Ltd*

Topham Picturepoint*
PO Box 33, Edenbridge, Kent TN8 5PB
tel (01342) 850313 *fax* (01342) 850244
e-mail pictures@topham.demon.co.uk
web site http://www.topham.co.uk/topham/
Contact Bernice Fairchild
Eight million contemporary and historical images, including the United Nations Environment Programme (UNEP) library. Delivery on-line if requested. New photographers – sample submission of 50 transparencies; 5-year contract, 50% commission.

B.M. Totterdell Photography*
Constable Cottage, Burlings Lane, Knockholt,
Kent TN14 7PE
tel/fax (01959) 532001
Specialist volleyball library, covering all aspects of the sport. Founded 1989.

Transworld/Scope
26 St Cross Street, London EC1N 8UH
tel 0171-405 2997 *fax* 0171-831 4549
Contact Valerie Dobson
Colour: situations/beauty pictures.

Travel Images
4 Lewisham Hill, London SE13 7EJ
tel 0181-318 4824
Sales and Marketing Manager Frances Allen
Comprehensive travel library, covering over 80 countries. Founded 1990.

Travel Ink Photo & Feature Library*
The Old Coach House, 14 High Street,
Goring-on-Thames, Nr Reading, Berks. RG8 9AT
tel (01491) 873011 *fax* (01491) 875558
e-mail abbie@travink.demon.co.uk
web site http://www.photosource.co.uk/
photosource/travink.htm
Travel, tourism and lifestyles covering around 150 countries – including the UK. Specialist sections include Hong Kong (including construction of the Tsing Ma Bridge), North Wales and Greece. Founded 1988.

Travel Photo International
8 Delph Common Road, Aughton, Ormskirk,
Lancs. L39 5DW
tel/fax (01695) 423720
Touristic interest including scenery, towns, monuments, historic buildings, archaeological sites, local people. Specialises in travel brochures and books. Terms: 50%.

Tropix Photographic Library*
156 Meols Parade, Meols, Wirral,
Merseyside L47 6AN
tel/fax 0151-632 1698

All human and environmental aspects of tropics, sub-tropics and non-tropical developing countries. Environmental issues are accepted from locations worldwide. New collections welcome but preliminary enquiry in writing essential; send 4 first class stamps for details. Terms: 50%. Founded 1973.

Ulster Folk and Transport Museum
153 Bangor Road, Cultra, Holywood,
Co. Down BT18 0EU, Northern Ireland
tel (01232) 428428 *fax* (01232) 428728
Head of Dept of Photography T.K. Anderson

Photographs from 1850s to the present day, including the work of W.A. Green, Rose Shaw and R.J. Welsh while he was under contract to Harland and Wolf Ltd. Subjects include Belfast shipbuilding (80,000 photographs, including 70 original negatives of the *Titanic*), road and rail transport, folk life, agriculture and the linen industry. B&w and colour (35mm, medium and large format). Founded 1962.

Ulster Photographic Agency
22 Casaeldona Park, Belfast BT6 9RB
tel (01232) 795738

Motoring and motorsport. Terms: 50% or outright purchase. Founded 1985.

Universal Pictorial Press & Agency Ltd (UPPA)*
29-31 Saffron Hill, London EC1N 8FH
tel 0171-421 6000 *fax* 0171-421 6006

Notable Royal, political, company, academic, legal, diplomatic, church, military, pop, arts, entertainment and sports personalities and well-known views and buildings. Commercial, industrial, corporate and public relations photo assignments undertaken. Founded 1929.

Venice Picture Library*
(formerly Archivio Veneziano)
Rawlings House, 2A Milner Street,
London SW3 2PU
tel 0171-589 3127 *fax* 0171-584 1944
e-mail vpl@idsukltd.demon.co.uk
web site http://www.a-z.tecc.co.uk
Contact Michelle Wood

Specialises in Venice, covering most aspects of the city, islands and lagoon, especially architecture and the environ-

ment. Commissions undertaken; visitors welcome by appointment. Founded 1990.

John Vickers Theatre Collection
27 Shorrolds Road, London SW6 7TR
tel 0171-385 5774

Archives of British theatre and portraits of actors, writers and musicians by John Vickers from 1938-1974.

Vidocq Photo Library
162 Burwell Meadow, Witney, Oxon OX8 7GD
tel/fax (01993) 778518

Specialist in photographs for language and educational text books. Detailed coverage of France. Assignments undertaken. Founded 1983.

Viewfinder Colour Photo Library*
3 Northload Street, Glastonbury, Somerset BA6 9JJ
tel (01458) 832600 *fax* (01458) 832850

Colour library covering industry, agriculture, transport, people, worldwide travel and the British Isles in detail; also world religions. Terms: 50%. Founded 1984.

The Charles Walker Collection*
c/o Images Colour Library Ltd,
12-14 Argyll Street, London W1V 1AB
tel 0171-734 7344 *fax* 0171-287 3933
London Office Manager Cara Botting

World's largest archive of colour pictures relating to the occult, magical, esoteric, mystical and mythological traditions. Founded 1983.

Simon Warner
Whitestone Farm, Stanbury, Keighley,
West Yorkshire BD22 0JW
tel/fax (01535) 644644

Landscape photographer with own stock pictures of northern England, North Wales and Northwest Scotland.

Waterways Photo Library*
39 Manor Court Road, London W7 3EJ
tel 0181-840 1659 *fax* 0181-567 0605
Contact Derek Pratt

British inland waterways; canals, rivers; bridges, aqueducts, locks and all waterside architectural features; watersports; waterway holidays, boats, fishing; town and countryside scenes. No other photographers' work required. Founded 1976.

Weimar Archive
8-9 The Incline, Coalport, Telford,
Shropshire TF8 7HR
tel (01952) 680050 *fax* (01952) 587184

Germany, specialising in First World War, Weimar Republic and Third Reich; but all aspects of social, political and cultural life in central Europe from Middle Ages until 1945; plus a comprehensive collection of German painting and sculpture, Soviet posters and cartoons 1917-1945, and GDR. Founded 1983.

Welfare History Picture Library
Heatherbank Museum of Social Work, Caledonian University, Park Campus, 1 Park Drive, Glasgow G3 6LP
tel 0141-337 4402 *fax* 0141-337 4500
e-mail a.ramage@gcal.ac.uk

Social history and social work, especially child welfare, poorhouses, prisons, hospitals, slum clearance, women's movement, social reformers and their work. Catalogue on request. Founded 1975.

Richard Welsby Photography
37 Grieveship Brae, Stromness, Orkney Islands KW16 3BG
tel/fax (01856) 850910
Contact Richard Welsby

Specialist library of the Orkney Islands: business and industry, scenics, geology, archaeology and historic; wide coverage of flowers, plants and other natural history subjects; aerials. Founded 1984.

Westcountry Pictures
23 Southernhay West, Exeter, Devon EX1 1PR
tel (01392) 426640 *fax* (01392) 51745
Contact Peter Cooper

All aspects of Devon and Cornwall. Founded 1989.

Western Americana Picture Library
3 Barton Buildings, Bath BA1 2JR
tel (01225) 334213

Prints, engravings, photos and colour transparencies on the American West, cowboys, gunfighters, Indians, including pictures by Frederic Remington and Charles Russell, etc. Interested in buying pictures on American West.

Roy J. Westlake ARPS
West Country Photo Library, 31 Redwood Drive, Plympton, Plymouth PL7 2FS
tel/fax (01752) 336444

Landscapes, seascapes, architecture, leisure activities, etc, for tourist brochures, advertising, books, magazines, calendars, etc. Also camping, caravanning and inland waterways subjects in Britain, including rivers and canals. Some world travel. Other photographers' work not accepted.

Eric Whitehead Picture Agency and Library – see Cumbria Picture Library*

Derek G. Widdicombe
Worldwide Photographic Library, 'Oldfield', High Street, Clayton West, Huddersfield HD8 9NS
tel/fax (01484) 862638 *pager* (0839) 764024

Landscapes, seascapes, architecture, human interest of Britain and abroad. Moods and seasons, buildings and natural features. Holds copyright of Noel Habgood FRPS Collection.

Wilderness Photographic Library*
Mill Barn, Broad Raine, Sedbergh, Cumbria LA10 5ED
tel (015396) 20196 *fax* (015396) 21293
Director John Noble FRGS

Specialist library in mountain and wilderness regions, especially polar. Associated aspects of people, places, natural history, geographical features, exploration and mountaineering, adventure sports, travel.

Wildlife Matters Photographic Library*
Marlham, Henley's Down, Battle, East Sussex TN33 9BN
tel (01424) 830566 *fax* (01424) 830224
e-mail gardens@ftech.co.uk, jfeltwell@aol.com
web site http://web.ftech.net/~gardens
Contact Dr John Feltwell

Ecology, conservation and environment; habitats and pollution; agriculture and horticulture; general natural history, entomology; Mediterranean wildlife; rainforests (Central America and Indonesia); aerial pics of countryside UK, Europe, USA. Founded 1980.

David Williams Picture Library*
50 Burlington Avenue, Glasgow G12 0LH
tel 0141-339 7823 *fax* 0141-337 3031

Specialises in colour transparencies of Scotland and Iceland (2¹/₄in and 35mm). Subjects include landscapes, towns, villages, buildings, antiquities, geology and physical geography. Smaller collections include many European countries and Western USA. Catalogue available. Commissions undertaken. Founded 1989.

S. & I. Williams, Power Pix International Picture Library
Castle Lodge, Wenvoe, Cardiff CF5 6AD
tel (01222) 595163 *fax* (01222) 593905
Worldwide travel, people and views, girl and 'mood-pix', sub-aqua, aircraft, flora, fauna, agriculture, children. Agents worldwide. Founded 1968.

Windrush Photos*
99 Noah's Ark, Kemsing, Sevenoaks, Kent TN15 6PD
tel (01732) 763486 *fax* (01732) 763285
Owner David Tipling
Birds are a speciality. Strong coverage of British wildlife and landscapes. Ornothological consultancy. Photographic and features commissions undertaken. Terms: 50%. Founded 1991.

Timothy Woodcock
45 Lyewater, Crewkerne, Somerset TA18 8BB
tel (01460) 74488 *fax* (01460) 74988
e-mail timwoodc@aol.com
British and Eire landscape, seascape, architecture and heritage; children, parenthood, adults and education; gardens and containers; mountain biking. Location commissions undertaken. Terms: 50%. Founded 1983.

Woodmansterne Publications Ltd*
1 The Boulevard, Blackmoor Lane, Watford, Herts. WD1 8YW
tel (01923) 228236 *fax* (01923) 245788
Britain, Europe, Holy Land; architecture, cathedral and stately home interiors; general art subjects; museum collections; natural history, butterflies, geography, volcanoes, transport, Space; opera and ballet; major state occasions; British heritage.

World Pictures*
(formerly Feature-Pix Colour Library)
85A Great Portland Street, London W1N 5RA
tel 0171-437 2121/436 0440 *fax* 0171-439 1307
Directors Joan Brenes, David Brenes
Over 600,000 medium and large format colour transparencies aimed at travel and travel-related markets. Extensive coverage of cities, countries and specific resort areas, together with material of an emotive nature, i.e. children, couples and families on holiday, all types of winter and summer sporting activities, motoring abroad, etc. Terms: 50%; major contributing photographers 60%.

Murray Wren Picture Library
3 Hallgate, London SE3 9SG
tel 0181-852 7556
Outdoor nudes; nudist holiday resorts and activities in Europe and elsewhere; historic and erotic art of the nude through the ages. Media enquiries only; no new photographers required.

The Allan Wright Photo Library
t/a Cauldron Press Ltd, The Stables, Parton, Castle Douglas, Kirkcudbrightshire DG7 3NB
tel (016444) 70260 *fax* (016444) 70202
North Sea oil, offshore life 'on the rigs', Dumfries and Galloway, Argyll and Scottish highlands, scenic and environmental. Founded 1986.

Yemen Pictures
38 Camac Road, Twickenham TW2 6NU
tel/fax 0181-898 0150 or 0181-876 3637
Contact John Miles
Specialist colour library of Yemen, covering all aspects of culture, people, architecture, dance, qat and music. Also Africa, Australia, Middle East and Asia. Founded 1995.

York Archaeological Trust Picture Library
Cromwell House, 13 Ogleforth, York YO1 2JG
tel (01904) 663044/663000 *fax* (01904) 640029
Picture Librarian H. Dawson
York archaeology covering Romans, Dark Ages, Vikings and Middle Ages; traditional crafts; scenes of York and Yorkshire. Founded 1987.

Yorkshire in Focus
75A Selby Road, Garforth, Leeds LS25 1LR
tel (0113) 286 3016
Transparencies, 35mm/6 x 9cm. Landscapes, rivers, buildings, tourist attractions in Yorkshire and the north. Camping and caravanning subjects: sites, caravans, motor caravans, tents and all equipment. Large collection of touristy stock subjects. Assignments undertaken.

Zoological Society of London
Regent's Park, London NW1 4RY
tel 0171-449 6293 *fax* 0171-586 5743
Librarian Ann Sylph
Archive collection of photographs, paintings and prints, from the 16th century onwards, covering almost all vertebrate animals, many now extinct or rare, plus invertebrates. Founded 1826.

Picture agencies and libraries by subject area

This index gives the major subject area(s) only of each entry in the main listing which begins on page 394, and should be used with discrimination.

Aerial photography

Aerofilms Ltd
Aviation Picture Library
Geo Aerial Photography
The Picture Company
Sealand Aerial Photography
Skyscan Photolibrary

Africa

Academic File News Agency
Animal Photography
Hamish Brown, Scottish
  Photographic
Sue Cunningham Photographic
  (East)
David Hosking (animals)
Images of Africa Photobank
Joe Filmbase Studios
Link Picture Library (Southern
  Africa)
Panos Pictures
Tropix Photographic Library
Yemen Pictures

Agriculture and farming

The Anthony Blake Photo
  Library
Blitz International News &
  Photo Agency
Dennis Davis Photography
Frontline Photo Press Agency
Heritage & Natural History
  Photography
Frank Lane Picture Agency Ltd
Holt Studios International
Planet Earth Pictures
Sutcliffe Gallery

Aircraft and aviation

Air Photo Supply
Aviation Photographs
  International
Aviation Picture Library
Dr Alan Beaumont
Photo Link
The Picture Company
Patrick Smith Associates

Archaeology, antiquities, ancient monuments and heritage

A.A. and A. Ancient Art &
  Architecture Collection
Lesley and Roy Adkins Picture
  Library
AKG London
Rev. J. Catling Allen
C.M. Dixon
English Heritage Photo Library
Werner Forman Archive
Fortean Picture Library
Heritage & Natural History
  Photography
Pat Hodgson Library
Chandra S. Perera Cinetra
Mick Sharp
Sites, Sights and Cities
Skyscan Balloon Photography
Woodmansterne Publications Ltd
York Archaeological Trust
  Picture Library

Architecture, houses and interiors

A.A. & A. Ancient Art and
  Architecture Collection
Abode Interiors
ARCAID Architectural

Photography and Picture
  Library
Bookart Architecture Picture
  Library
Dennis Davis Photography
English Heritage Photo Library
Houses & Interiors
  Photographic Features Agency
The Venice Picture Library
Woodmansterne Publications Ltd

Art, sculpture and crafts

A.A. & A. Ancient Art and
  Architecture Collection
Abode Interiors Photographic
  Library
Academic File News Agency
AKG London
Bodleian Library
Bookart Architecture Picture
  Library
Bridgeman Art Library
Crafts Council Picture Library
Fine Art Photographic Library
Werner Forman Archive
Photo Resources
Retrograph Nostalgia Archive Ltd
The Venice Picture Library

Asia

Academic File News Agency
Douglas Dickins Photo Library
Japan Archive
Link Picture Library
Ann & Bury Peerless
Photo Flora
Royal Society for Asian Affairs
Society for Anglo-Chinese
  Understanding
Travel Ink Photo & Feature
  Library (Hong Kong)
Yemen Pictures

Australia and New Zealand

Australia Pictures
George A. Dey
Yemen Pictures

Britain (see also Ireland, Scotland, Wales)

Rev. J. Catling Allen
John Blake Picture Library
Britain on View Photographic
Library
David Broadbent/Peak District
Pictures
Collections
Cumbria Picture Library
English Heritage Photo Library
Fotoccompli – The Picture
Libraryy
Leslie Garland Picture Library
(North England)
Global Syndications
Isle of Wight Photo Library
Isle of Wight Pictures
Just Europe
Lakeland Life Picture Library
(Lake District)
Landscape Only
Merseyside Photo Library
The Mustograph Agency
Spectrum Colour Library
Viewfinder Colour Photo
Library
Simon Warner (North England)
Westcountry Pictures (Devon,
Cornwall)
Roy J. Westlake
Derek G. Widdicombe
Timothy Woodcock
Woodmansterne Publications
Ltd
York Archaeological Trust
Picture Library
Yorkshire in Focus

Business, industry and commerce

Financial Times Pictures

Camping and caravanning

Roy J. Westlake
Yorkshire in Focus

Children and people (see also Social issues)

Attard Photolibrary
Barnardo's Photographic
Archive
Collections
Lupe Cunha
Brian Gadsby Picture Library
The Hutchinson Library
David Muscroft Picture Library
Photofusion
Telegraph Colour Library
Timothy Woodcock

Cities and towns (see also London)

Lesley and Roy Adkins Picture
Library
Financial Times Pictures
Sites, Sights and Cities
Skyscan Photolibrary
Waterways Photo Library

Civilisations, cultures and way of life

Bryan and Cherry Alexander
Photography
Andalucía Slide Library (Spain)
Werner Forman Archive
Medimage (Mediterranean)
Christine Osborne/Middle East
Pictures Inc.
Photo Resources
Peter Sanders Photography
Mick Sharp
STILL Pictures Whole Earth
Photo Library

Countryside and rural life (see also Landscapes)

Andalucía Slide Library (Spain)
Dr Alan Beaumont
Ron and Christine Foord
Forest Life Picture Library
Tim Graham
Isle of Wight Pictures
Lakeland Life Picture Library
Sutcliffe Gallery
Ulster Folk and Transport
Museum
Waterways Photo Library
Wildlife Matters Photographic
Library

Developing countries

Geoslides
Christine Osborne/Middle East
Pictures Inc.
Panos Pictures
STILL Pictures Whole Earth
Photo Library
Tropix Photographic Library

Environment, conservation, ecology and habitats

Heather Angel
Aquila Photographics
Ardea London Ltd
Dr Alan Beaumont
Butterflies
Bruce Coleman Ltd
George A. Dey (forestry, natural
history)
Ecoscene
Environmental Investigation
Agency
Fogden Natural History
Photographs
Forest Life Picture Library
Martin and Dorothy Grace
Harper Horticultural Slide
Library
Holt Studios International
Frank Lane Picture Agency Ltd
Chris Mattison
Natural Image
NHPA
Papilio Natural History &
Travel Library
Planet Earth Pictures
Premaphotos Wildlife
STILL Pictures Whole Earth
Photo Library
Tropix Photographic Library
Wildlife Matters Photographic
Library
Windrush Photos

Europe and Eastern Europe (excluding UK/Ireland)

Andalucía Slide Library (Spain)
Sue Cunningham Photographic
Das Photo
James Davis Travel Photography
Douglas Dickins Photo Library
C.M. Dixon
Lesley Garland Picture Library (Norway)
Global Syndications (Scandinavia)
Joe Filmbase Studios
Just Europe
Medimage (Mediterranean)
Panos Pictures (Eastern Europe)
Russia & Republics Photolibrary
The Venice Picture Library
Vidocq Photo Library (France)
Weimar Archive (Germany)
David Williams Picture Library (Iceland)

Food and drink

The Anthony Blake Photo Library
Cephas Picture Library
Footprints Colour Picture Library
Retrograph Nostalgia Archive

Gardens, gardening and horticulture (see also Plant life)

A-Z Botanical Collection
Ardea London Ltd
B. & B. Photographs
Butterflies
Collections
Dennis Davis Photography
Forest Life Picture Library
Garden Matters Photographic Library
John Glover Photography
Harper Horticultural Slide Library
Holt Studios International
Houses & Interiors Photographic Features Agency
S. & O. Mathews
Natural Image
Peter Stiles Picture Library
Timothy Woodcock

General and stock libraries

Ace Photo Agency
Aspect Picture Library Ltd
Bandphoto Agency
Barnaby's Picture Library
Stephen Benson Slide Bureau
Blitz International News & Photo Agency
J. Allan Cash Photolibrary
Bruce Coleman Inc.
Bruce Coleman Ltd
Colorific Photo Library
Sylvia Cordaiy Photo Library
C.P.L. (Camerapix Picture Library)
Barry Davies
C.M. Dixon
Greg Evans International Photo Library
Fotoccompli – The Picture Libraryy
Freelance Focus
Frontline Photo Press Agency
Geo Aerial Photography
GeoScience Features
Geoslides
Getty Images Ltd
Robert Harding Picture Library
Horizon International Creative Images
The Hutchison Library
The Image Bank
Images Colour Library
Joe Filmbase Studios
Lears Magical Lanterns Museum
The MacQuitty International Collection
News Blitz International
The Northern Picture Library
Orion Press
Photo Library International
Photofusion
The Photographers' Library
Pictor International Ltd
Picture Research Service
POPPERFOTO (Paul Popper Ltd)
Pro-file Photo Library
Raleigh International Picture Library
Retna Pictures Ltd
Royal Geographical Society Picture Library
The Royal Photographic Society
Dawn Runnals Photographic Library
S & G Press Agency Ltd
Source Photographic Archives

Spectrum Colour Library
Tony Stone Images
Telegraph Colour Library
Universal Pictorial Press & Agency Ltd (UPPA)
Vidocq Photo Library
Viewfinder Colour Photo Library
Derek G. Widdicombe
S. & I. Williams, Power Pix International Picture Library
Yorkshire in Focus

Geography, biogeography and topography

Arctic Camera
B. & B. Photographs
John Blake Picture Library
Geoslides

Glamour, moods and nudes

Attard Photolibrary
The Photographers' Library
Transworld/Scope
S. & I. Williams, Power Pix International Picture Library
Murray Wren Picture Library

Health and medicine

Lupe Cunha
Science & Society Picture Library
Shout Picture Library

High-tech, high-speed, macro/micro, special effects and step-by-step

Earth Images Picture Library (high-tech)
Houses & Interiors Photographic Features Agency (step-by-step)
The Image Bank (high-tech, special effects)
Microscopix
NHPA (high-speed)
Oxford Scientific Films Ltd, Photo Library (special effects)

History

AKG London
Barnardo's Photographic Archive
Bodleian Library
Mary Evans Picture Library
Frost Historical Newspaper
  Collection
Historical Picture Service
Pat Hodgson Library
Dave Lewis Nostalgia Collection
The Billie Love Historical
  Collection
Mansell Collection Ltd
Public Record Office Image
  Library
The Royal Photographic Society
Royal Society of Chemistry
  Library
Salamander Books Picture
  Archive
Science & Society Picture
  Library
Topham Picturepoint
Weimar Archive (Europe)

Illustrations, prints, engravings, lithographs and cartoons

Allied Artists Ltd
Bodleian Library
Mary Evans Picture Library
The Illustrated London News
  Picture Library
The Billie Love Historical
  Collection
Public Record Office Image
  Library
Punch Cartoon Library
Royal Society of Chemistry
  Library
Zoological Society of London

Ireland

Picturepoint
The Slide File
Source Photographic Archives
Heritage & Natural History
  Photography

Landscapes and scenics

Bookart Architecture Picture
  Library
Cumbria Picture Library
Barry Davies
James Davis Travel Photography
George A. Dey (Scottish)
Eyeline Photography
Geo Aerial Photography
John Glover Photography
Isle of Wight Photo Library
Isle of Wight Pictures
Landscape Only
S. & O. Mathews
Chris Mattison
Medimage (Mediterranean)
The Picture Company
Scotland in Focus Picture
  Library
Mick Sharp
Skyscan Photolibrary
Peter Stiles Picture Library
The Still Moving Picture
  Company
Charles Tait Photo Library
Simon Warner
Richard Welsby Photography
  (Orkney Islands)
Roy J. Westlake
Derek G. Widdicombe
Windrush Photos
The Allan Wright Photo Library

Latin America

Andes Press Agency
Das Photo
Fogden Natural History
  Photographs

London

ARCAID Architectural
  Photographic and Picture
  Library
Greater London Record Office
Historical Picture Service
The Illustrated London News
  Picture Library
Monitor Syndication
Skyscan Photolibrary
Patrick Smith Associates

Middle East

Academic File News Agency
Stephen Benson Slide Bureau
Das Photo
Christine Osborne/Middle East
  Pictures Inc.
Ann & Bury Peerless
Yemen Pictures

Military and armed forces

Air Photo Supply
Aviation Photographs
  International
Imperial War Museum
Military History Picture Library
Public Record Office Image
  Library
Salamander Books Picture
  Archive
The Tank Museum Photo
  Library & Archive

Mountains

AMIS
Hamish Brown, Scottish
  Photographic
Mountain Dynamics
Mountain Visions
Royal Geographical Society
  Picture Library
Wilderness Photographic
  Library

Natural history (see also Environment, Plant life)

A-Z Botanical Collection
Heather Angel
Animal Photography
Aquila Photographics
Ardea London Ltd
B. & B. Photographs
BBC Natural History Unit
  Picture Library
Dr Alan Beaumont
Bird Images
David Broadbent/Peak District
  Pictures (birds)
Butterflies
Bruce Coleman Ltd
Sylvia Cordaiy Photo Library
Barry Davies
Gordon Dickson (fungi, insects)
Ecoscene
Environmental Investigation
  Agency

Fogden Natural History
Photographs
Ron and Christine Foord
(insects)
Footprints Colour Picture
Library
Brian Gadsby Picture Library
Geoscience Features
Martin and Dorothy Grace
Heritage & Natural History
Photography (insects, espe-
cially bees)
David Hosking (birds)
Image Diggers
Michael Leach (owls)
Chris Mattison (reptiles,
amphibians)
Natural Image
NHPA
Oxford Scientific Films Ltd,
Photo Library
Papilio Natural History &
Travel Library
Planet Earth Pictures
Premaphotos Wildlife
Roundhouse Ornithology
Collection
RSPCA Photolibrary
Salamander Books Picture
Archive
Steffi Schubert, Wildlife
Conservation Collection
Photographic Library
Scotland in Focus Picture
Library
Peter Stiles Picture Library
STILL Pictures Whole Earth
Photo Library
Richard Welsby Photography
(Orkney Islands)
Wildlife Matters Photographic
Agency
Windrush Photos (birds)
Zoological Society of London

Nautical and maritime

Peter Cumberlidge Photo
Library
National Maritime Museum
Picture Library
Seaco Picture Library
Ulster Folk and Transport
Museum

News, features and photo features

Academic File News Photos
The Associated Press Ltd
Bandphoto Agency
BIPS
Blitz International News &
Photo Agency
Financial Times Pictures
Frost Historical Newspaper
Collection
International Press Agency
(Pty) Ltd
News Blitz International
PA News Photo Library
Chandra S. Perera Cinetra
Pixfeatures
S & G Press Agency Ltd
Topham Picturepoint

North America

American History Picture
Library
Douglas Dickins Photo Library
Western Americana Picture
Library

Nostalgia, ephemera and advertising

Fotomas Index
Dave Lewis Nostalgia Collection
Retrograph Nostalgia Archive
Ltd

Performing arts (theatre, dance, music)

Aquarius Picture Library
Camera Press Ltd
The Dance Library
Famous
Image Diggers
Jazz I°ndex
Link Picture Library (music)
Mander & Mitchenson Theatre
Collection
Performing Arts Library
Sylvia Pitcher
Theatre Museum
John Vickers Theatre Collection

Personalities and portraits (see also Royalty)

Aquarius Picture Library
Camera Press Ltd
Famous
Financial Times Pictures
Mark Gerson Photography
Tim Graham
Pat Hodgson Library (historical)
JS Library International
Mander & Mitchenson Theatre
Collection
Monitor Syndication
Performing Arts Library
Pixfeatures
POPPERFOTO (Paul Popper
Ltd)
Punch Cartoon Library
Retna Pictures Ltd
The Royal Photographic Society
Royal Society of Chemistry
Library
Syndication International Ltd
Topham Picturepoint
Universal Pictorial Press &
Agency Ltd (UPPA)
John Vickers Theatre Collection

Plant life (see also Gardens)

A-Z Botanical Collection Ltd
Heather Angel
Aquila Photographics
Ron and Christine Foord
Garden Matters Photographic
Library
John Glover Photography
Martin and Dorothy Grace
Harper Horticultural Slide
Library
Photo Flora
Premaphotos Wildlife
Source Photographic Archives
Richard Welsby Photography
(Orkney Islands)

Polar and Arctic

Bryan and Cherry Alexander
Photography
Arctic Camera
Global Syndications
POPPERFOTO (Paul Popper Ltd)
Royal Geographical Society
Picture Library
Wilderness Photographic Library

Religions and religious monuments

Lesley and Roy Adkins Picture
  Library
Rev. J. Catling Allen
Andes Press Agency
Ann & Bury Peerless
Photo Resources
Peter Sanders Photography

Royalty

Camera Press Ltd
Tim Graham
JS Library International
Monitor Syndication
Pixfeatures
Syndication International Ltd

Russia

John Massey Stewart
The Russia and Republics
  Photo Library
SCR Photo Library

Science, technology and meteorology

Ace Photo Agency
Earth Images Picture Library
Leslie Garland Picture Library
GeoScience Features
Frank Lane Picture Agency Ltd
Microscopix
Ann Ronan at Image Select
Royal Society of Chemistry
  Library
Science Photo Library
Science & Society Picture
  Library

Scotland

Hamish Brown, Scottish
  Photographic
George A. Dey (castles,
  Highland Games)
Scotland in Focus Picture
  Library
The Still Moving Picture
  Company
Charles Tait Photo Library
Simon Warner
David Williams Picture Library
The Allan Wright Photo Library

Social issues and social history

Andes Press Agency
Barnardo's Photographic
  Archive
John Birdsall Photography
Mary Evans Picture Library
FirePix
Greater London Record Office
Imperial War Museum
Photofusion
RSPCA Photolibrary
Ann Ronan at Image Select
Shout Picture Library
Welfare History Picture Library

South America

Animal Photography
  (Galapagos)
Australia Pictures
Stephen Benson Slide Bureau
Lupe Cunha (Brazil)
Sue Cunningham Photographic
David Hosking (Falklands)

Space and astronomy

Aspect Picture Library
Earth Images Picture Library
Galaxy Picture Library
Genesis Space Photo Library
National Maritime Museum
  Picture Library
Salamander Books Picture
  Archive
Science Photo Library

Sport and leisure

Action Plus
Allsport Photographic Ltd
The Associated Press Ltd
John Blake Photo Library
  (equestrian)
Boxing Picture Library
Michael Cole Camerawork
Cumbria Picture Library
  (snooker)
Peter Dazeley (golf)
Eyeline Photography (water-
  sports, sheepdog trials)
Frontline Photo Press Agency
Mountain Visions (moun-
  taineering, skiing)
POPPERFOTO (Paul Popper Ltd)
Skishoot – Offshoot
Sporting Pictures (UK) Ltd
The Still Moving Picture
  Company
B.M. Totterdell Photography
  (volleyball)
Ulster Photography Agency
  (motorsport)
Universal Pictorial Press &
  Agency Ltd (UPPA)
World Pictures

Strange phenomena, occult and mystical

Fortean Picture Library
Image Diggers
Sites, Sights and Cities
The Charles Walker Collection

Transport (cars and motoring, railways)

Ludvigsen Library
Motorcycles Unlimited
National Maritime Museum
  Picture Library
National Motor Museum,
  Beaulieu
Railways – Milepost $9\frac{1}{2}$
Science & Society Picture
  Library
Seaco Picture Library
Ulster Folk and Transport
  Museum
Ulster Photographic Agency

Travel and tourism

Ace Photo Agency
Air Photo Supply
ARCAID Architectural
  Photography and Picture
  Library
Aspect Picture Library
Aviation Picture Library
Bandphoto Agency
The Anthony Blake Photo
  Library
Britain on View Photographic
  Library
Sylvia Cordaiy Picture Library
Peter Cumberlidge Photo
  Library
James Davis Travel Photography
Ecoscene
Greg Evans International Photo
  Library
Footprints Colour Picture
  Library
Fotoccompli – The Picture
  Libraryy
Brian Gadsby Picture Library
The Hutchinson Library
The Illustrated London News

Picture Library
JS Library International
Just Europe
Landscape Only
Mountain Visions
Papilio Natural History &
  Travel Library
Photo Flora
The Photographers' Library
The Picture Company
Raleigh International Picture
  Library
Peter Sanders Photography
Seaco Picture Library
Skishoot – Offshoot
Spectrum Colour Library
Charles Tait Photo Library
Telegraph Colour Library
Travel Images
Travel Ink Photo & Feature
  Library
Travel Photo International
Viewfinder Colour Photo
  Library
Wilderness Photographic
  Library
World Pictures

Wales

Patrick Smith Associates
Travel Ink Photo & Feature
  Library

Waterways

Peter Cumberlidge Photo
  Library
Waterways Photo Library
Roy J. Westlake

Card and stationery publishers which accept photographs

Before submitting work, photographers are advised to ascertain requirements, including terms and conditions. Only top quality material should be submitted; inferior work is never accepted. Postage for return of material should be enclosed.

*Member of the Greeting Card Association

Abacus Cards Ltd*
Gazeley Road, Kentford, Newmarket,
Suffolk CB8 7QB
tel (01638) 552399 *fax* (01638) 552103
Partners Jeff Fothergill and Brian Carey, *Art Director* Bev Cunningham
Quality greetings cards. Florals, garden scenes, still lifes etc.; submit 35mm transparencies or larger formats. Founded 1991.

Caspari Ltd*
9 Shire Hill, Saffron Walden, Essex CB11 3AP
tel (01799) 513010 *fax* (01799) 513101
Managing Director Keith Entwisle
Traditional fine art/classic images; 5 x 4in transparencies. No verses. Founded 1990.

Chapter and Verse*
Granta House, 96 High Street, Linton,
Cambs. CB1 6JT
tel (01223) 891951 *fax* (01223) 894137
Buildings, animals, flowers, scenic, or domestic subjects in series, suitable for greetings cards and postcards. All sizes of transparency. No verses. Founded 1981.

Dennis Print and Publishing
Printing House Square, Melrose Street,
Scarborough, North Yorkshire YO12 7SJ
tel (01723) 500555 *fax* (01723) 501488/500545
e-mail dennis@etwltd.demon.co.uk
web site www.dennisprint.com
Interested in first-class transparencies for reproduction as local view postcards and calendars. 3¹/4 x 2¹/4in or 35mm transparencies ideal for postcard reproduction.

J. Arthur Dixon
Forest Side, Newport,
Isle of Wight PO30 5QW
tel (01983) 523381 *fax* (01983) 529719
Managing Director Andy McGarrick, *Head of Design* Carlton Knight
All subjects considered; transparencies 35mm or larger. Verses considered. Founded 1930.

Giesen & Wolff (UK) Ltd
Kaygee House, Rothersthorpe Crescent,
Northampton NN4 9JD
tel (01604) 709499 *fax* (01604) 709399
Contact Art Manager
Transparencies, 2¹/4in sq minimum: floral studies, still life. Founded 1908.

Hambledon Studios Ltd
Metcalf Drive, Altham Industrial Estate, Altham,
Accrington, Lancs. BB5 5SS
tel (01282) 687300 *fax* (01282) 687404
Art Managers D. Jaundrell, J. Ashton, D. Fuller, N. Harrison, K. Ellis
Photos for reproduction as greetings cards. *Brands* Arnold Barton, Donny Mac, Reflections, New Image.

Images & Editions*
Metcalf Drive, Altham Industrial Estate, Altham,
Accrington, Lancs. BB5 5SS
tel (01282) 687300 *fax* (01282) 687404
Directors Lesley Forrow, Maurice Miller
Greetings cards, giftwrap, gift products and social stationery: flowers, gardens and landscape, animals, especially cats and teddy bears. Any format accepted; transparencies preferred. Founded 1984.

Jane's Information Group

Sentinel House, 163 Brighton Road, Coulsdon,
Surrey CR5 2NH
tel 0181-700 3700 *fax* 0181-700 1006

Considers defence, aerospace and transportation transparencies.

Jarrold Publishing

Whitefriars, Norwich NR3 1TR
tel (01603) 763300 *fax* (01603) 662748
Managing Director Antony Jarrold, *Publishing Director* Caroline Jarrold
Contact Vivienne Buckingham *tel* (01603) 227325

Transparencies (35mm or larger) for calendars. Verses not required. Founded 1770.

Pomegranate Europe Ltd

Fullbridge House, Fullbridge, Maldon,
Essex CM9 4LE
tel (01621) 851646 *fax* (01621) 852426
Sales Director Dave Harris

Photographs or transparencies (any size) for cards, calendars, postcards and posters: art, architecture, the environment, Third World issues and art, history, politics and photography. Founded 1993.

J. Salmon Ltd

100 London Road, Sevenoaks, Kent TN13 1BB
tel (01732) 452381 *fax* (01732) 450951

Picture postcards, calendars and local view booklets.

Santoro Graphics Ltd

342-344 London Road, Mitcham Cricket Green,
Mitcham, Surrey CR4 3ND
tel 0181-640 9777 *fax* 0181-640 2888
Directors L. Santoro, M. Santoro

Publishers of innovative and contemporary images for greetings cards, giftwrap and gift stationery. Subjects covered: humorous, florals, gardens, landscapes, animals, still life. All formats accepted in both b&w and colour; transparencies ideally 5 x 4in but will accept 35mm. No verses. Founded 1985.

Scandecor Ltd

3 The Ermine Centre, Hurricane Close,
Huntingdon, Cambs. PE18 6XX
tel (01480) 456395 *fax* (01480) 456269
Director G. Huldtgren

Transparencies all sizes. Founded 1967.

Picture research

*A multitude of pictures are reproduced in the media and their images consumed by the viewer as part of daily life. The role of the picture researcher is to obtain these pictures and to be conversant with the legal implications concerning their reproduction. **Jennie Karrach** explains.*

Picture research is the art of obtaining pictures – photos and illustrations – suitable for reproduction, which suit the project's brief, budget and deadline. It also includes the clearance of permissions, copyright, the negotiation of rights and fees, and the eventual return of pictures to their owners at the end of the project.

Picture researchers are responsible for supplying a vast range of clients: in the book and magazine industry – both publishers and packagers – advertising agencies, film, television and video companies, newspapers and exhibition organisers. Although the skills involved in picture research are relevant in all these contexts, the type of pictures required varies enormously. Consequently, researchers tend to specialise in the type of work they undertake, and they may well have a specialist knowledge of one particular area, such as science and technology.

Picture researchers are employed either as staff members or on a freelance basis, paid by the hour or day, or for the duration of a project, as appropriate. An employee working full time on a long-running project may have time to carry out extensive research, but freelance work is often constrained by the client's budget and schedule. It is here that experience counts. Knowing where to find material quickly to suit the brief saves time and therefore money.

The researcher's fees are often included in the total budget, so that although the final deadline for delivery of pictures to the client may be a month away, the total allowed for picture research amounts to three days' work. It may be that this is unrealistic, and that the job will require five days. These details all need to be clarified at the outset and some sort of agreement listing the picture brief, deadlines, budget and invoicing particulars needs to be drawn up. It is important to put everything in writing so that in the event of dispute both parties can refer back to the agreement. Pictures are often worth large amounts of money, and in the event of loss it will become difficult to agree who will pay compensation unless this has been pre-arranged. It can also prove difficult to collect payment for work completed, so it may be advisable to agree upon regular payments and an advance to cover expenses such as travel, postage and telephone, etc.

The brief

It is important to clarify the brief so that both parties, the picture researcher and the editor/design team, are agreed upon the image required. It may be that the picture requested needs no further description – a work of art, by a well-known artist, e.g. *The Mona Lisa* by Leonardo da Vinci, to be used in colour. Or it may be that the picture is to depict an historical event which occurred long before the advent of photography. What is required? A photo of a contemporary manuscript which describes the incident, or perhaps a contemporary illumination exists. Or does the client have in mind an illustration executed by a more recent artist, perhaps a nineteenth-century engraving? Or a photograph of the remains of an historic site? It may be that the client has no one image in mind, but rather needs to evoke a specific mood, or provoke a reaction. This is often the case in advertising campaigns. Pictures are highly subjective, and what is evocative to some will appear bleak to others. A good picture researcher is able to capture the image conjured up

in a picture meeting, responding to the ideas of an art director or editor.

It may be that the picture required must be a specific shape – portrait (upright) or landscape (horizontal), or it may need to have an area lacking in detail, such as sky, into which text can fit. Or a dark area suitable for text reversal. If there are too many design constraints it may be cost effective to commission a photographer, rather than to search for a non-existent 'existing' photo.

The budget, rights and deadline

Once the brief has been agreed, the budget, rights and deadline must be confirmed. These are interdependent. Picture fees increase according to the size and use made of the image; for instance, a picture used at quarter-page size in a school textbook will cost less than one used quarter-page size in a glossy, adult non-fiction book. Fees vary according to the media: books, magazines, television, video, CD-Rom, etc. The print run/circulation of a book/magazine also affects the price charged for use. Fees are calculated also according to the rights requested. The larger the territory, the larger the fee, although the percentage increase between the various categories will vary from agency to agency. The territories sold are usually:

- UK only
- UK and first foreign edition
- English language, world rights, excluding US
- English language, world rights, including US
- world rights, all languages.

It may well be that, as the European Union attempts to remove trade barriers, the rights available will change.

Other fees will need to be budgeted for. Many commercial picture agencies charge 'research' or 'service' fees. These may be linked to the amount of material they are loaning or there may be a fixed charge levied. In both cases the source should advise of this at the initial enquiry stage. Some will only charge if a personal visit is not possible and pictures are despatched by a member of their staff.

The levying of these fees can erode the total picture budget quickly. It is not unusual to receive a service fee of £30, which may be acceptable if this is the only source used, and the pictures obtained are accepted by the client. However, on projects where a selection of pictures to cover a wider range of topics is required, many sources will have to be approached. It is worth discussing service fees at the outset. It is not unknown for agencies to waive or reduce them if it increases the likelihood of a sale. Some only charge the service fee if all pictures are returned and none selected for use. Other sources do not loan out material but instead sell copy transparencies or prints. This is usually the case with museums who can supply a transparency of a particular object or manuscript, but are unable to respond to a vague request for a selection of pictures for possible use. Museums often charge a monthly hire fee as well as the final reproduction fee.

Most commercial picture libraries or agencies operate on a loan system. Pictures are selected and loaned for an agreed period, usually a month. After this time material not required should be returned and some indication given as to the fate of the pictures still held. Is a subsequent picture selection to be made, or are those retained going to be used? If material is kept longer than the agreed loan period, then holding fees may be charged. These should only be levied if a reminder sent fails to elicit news of the pictures or return. (Freelance picture researchers need to make sure that such reminders are forwarded to them either by the source or sent on by the client.) Holding fees are charged per picture, per week over the deadline, and are usually waived over the deadline, and are usually waived if a reasonable extension to the free loan period is requested.

Picture sources

Sources are many and various. They include government departments, institutions, companies, libraries, commercial picture libraries and agencies, individual collectors, and individual photographers.

Some of these sources supply pictures without charge, but that is not to say that they are necessarily easy to obtain, or that no copyright pertains. Many sources are not primarily concerned with the supply of pictures and give it low priority. Access to the collection may be limited to research students and those who hold a reader's card. Enquiries may have to be made in writing, and the idea of urgency is an alien one. Or lack of resources may prevent an efficient service.

There is no one source book which lists all picture sources and if one existed it would run to many volumes and be in need of constant updating. Commercial libraries and agencies maintain a high profile, advertising by mail shots to prospective clients. The larger ones produce glossy catalogues, usually free, which include a selection of their images, enough to give a flavour of the type of stock held.

New technology is affecting picture storage and use. Some large agencies produce CD-Roms which clients can purchase for future reference. These discs allow rapid viewing of thousands of images. On-line facilities at news agencies allow quick transmission of pictures to clients and use of the World Wide Web via the Internet enables subscribers to browse and download high resolution images for use. There are serious implications for copyright control resulting from electronic storage, e.g. unauthorised use or manipulation of photographs.

General stock libraries

'General stock libraries' hold pictures which fall into broad categories, namely: travel, architecture, food, business, science/medicine, people, sport, nature, animals, transport, etc. They would almost certainly hold pictures of famous foreign landmarks, e.g. the Eiffel Tower, photographed from the ground, the air, by night, by day, with lovers ... It is much more difficult to find pictures of less glamorous sites. Street furniture, cars and pedestrians date quickly, and some agencies, keen to keep pictures saleable for as

Useful directories

Picture Sources UK
by Rosemary Eakins, Macdonald, 1985

Now out of print but may be available through a library.

Picture Researcher's Handbook
by Hilary and Mary Evans, 6th edn, Blueprint Routledge, £39.00 (£42.50 inc. p&p)

Available from bookshops and:
The Mary Evans Picture Library
59 Tranquil Vale, London SE3 0BS
tel 0181-318 0034 *fax* 0181-852 7211

BAPLA Directory
18 Vine Hill, London EC1R 5DX
tel 0171-713 1780 *fax* 0171-713 1211

Lists all the current members of the British Association of Picture Libraries and Agencies (BAPLA), at present totalling around 300. Copies available (£10) from Sarah Saunders at BAPLA.

1995 Directory of Photographers
GHP Publishing, Freepost (HU593),
Brough HU15 1BR
tel (01482) 666036

Fully indexed source book, with over 430 entries of advertising, editorial and commercial photographers, picture libraries and agencies. Cost: £12.95 inc. p&p.

---

long as possible, will attempt to keep such features to a minimum. The result is strange; London, peopled only by bobbies and red buses, Venice reduced to St Mark's Square and gondoliers on the Grand Canal, Los Angeles depicted by traffic on freeways. This problem extends to the 'people' pictures, which tend to be stereotypes posed by models. It is not impossible to find pictures of 'real' people going about everyday activities, but it can be time-consuming. Directories cannot hope to express the nuances of photographic collections, and it is only over time, after visits to many sources, that an overview of the range available will emerge. Specialist picture libraries are usually one-subject libraries, and cover the whole range of picture needs. The level of captioning is usually higher in specialist sources as the photographer has expert knowledge. It can be the case that a good quality photograph badly captioned is rendered useless. A photo filed in the 'elderly people' category of a general stock agency showed a woman standing in a slight depression in the desert somewhere. The woman was actually a famous anthropologist, but her name meant nothing to the library so she had been miscaptioned and then wrongly filed. It may be that for certain purposes any train, boat, car, etc will be acceptable, but if the picture required is of a specific model then it is frustrating to find insubstantial captions and undated pictures.

Use of photos

Permission

Once pictures have been found which fit the brief, the next stage is clearance for use. Permission must be sought from the copyright holder for use of particular photos in set contexts. The supply of photos does not automatically guarantee permission to reproduce. It may be that the agency or picture source is not the copyright holder, and permission has to be sought elsewhere. This is often the case with photos of works of art still in copyright. The artist, or the artist's estate, may be represented by a copyright protection society such as DACS (Design and Artists Copyright Society – see page 452), which will approach the estate or artist on behalf of a picture researcher and, if permission is granted, often subject to conditions, issue a licence. Conditions could include the right to approve colour proofs. The production department or designer of the project would therefore need to be informed to allow time in the schedule. DACS has reciprocal representation agreements with similar copyright protection societies in some 26 countries. This simplifies a copyright enquiry considerably but sufficient time should be allowed for clearance. It may take a day or several weeks. If the copyright holder and the supplier of the photograph are not one and the same, then a fee may be due to both parties.

Context

It may be that the context in which the photo is to appear is a sensitive one, perhaps an article about child abuse, divorce, AIDS, or that the caption is to make some derogatory statement about the subject. If this is the case it is important to be honest about the context with the supplier of the photo. If the article is educational and positive in its approach, then the photo will play a different role from one appearing in an exposé of shameful goings on. It is prudent to enquire whether the photographer has obtained 'model release' from the subject in the photo. In return for a sum of money the model grants the photographer the right to sell the photos taken. This is standard procedure at photo sessions, where a particular shot has been commissioned by a client, or a personality has granted a shoot. The release may have certain riders attached as to use, precisely to avoid certain contexts.

An agency may grant permission to use the photo in a sensitive area, but insist on a declaration appearing with it or with the photo credits 'all photos posed by models'. Or it may be that the agency or photographer do not have model release for the photo. At present in the UK, if a person is photographed in public they cannot prevent that photo being published. Hence the breed of paparazzi photographers. There is as yet no law protecting against the invasion of privacy. (The situation is different in the USA.) As a result many British photo libraries hold photos of members of the public, taken 'in the public domain' for which they hold no model release. Most agencies reproduce the following or similar statement in their Terms & Conditions: 'although the agency takes all reasonable care, the agency shall not be liable for any loss or damage suffered by the client or by any third party arising from any defect in the picture or its caption, or in any way from its reproduction.' The onus is put onto the picture user. It is fair to say that if the context of the photo is an innocent one, most members of the public are pleased to be in the spotlight, and require no more than a complimentary copy of the book, magazine, or whatever.

Captions

It is important for picture researchers to make caption writers aware that litigation may result from derogatory or inappropriate captions. Staff researchers should attempt to prevent pictures which were obtained for one project, e.g. a book on health care, being transferred to another, such as a booklet on safe sex. Freelance researchers would be well advised to include a paragraph in the agreement mentioned above which would disclaim responsibility for use by the client of pictures supplied in any use other than that stated in the brief, and any subsequent copyright infringement by the client. It is not unknown for clients to withhold information or mislead picture researchers as to the length of the print run, or the production of foreign language editions.

Picture researchers do not generally write captions themselves but may be asked to provide information for captions. This can be very time-consuming if the pictures do not already have a reasonable amount of caption information attached, supplied by the source or photographer.

Credits and copyright

Once pictures have been selected, captioned, and sized for the project in hand, the credit or acknowledgement list will need to be drawn up. This usually includes a courtesy line thanking the various picture sources for permission to reproduce photographs. Sources are either listed alphabetically, with page numbers as to where their pictures appear, or the name of the source appears next to the picture.

Copyright

Under the provisions of the Copyright, Designs and Patents Act 1988, photographers have 'moral rights' which include the right to be identified as the author of a

photograph (see *British copyright law*, page 615). Newspapers, magazines, encyclopedias, and other works of reference, are exempt from crediting contributors but most will include credits as a matter of course. Under the terms of the 1988 Act photography is copyright for the same duration and in the same way as other works of art. This was for 50 years after the death of the photographer until 1 January 1996, when 'the Term Directive' was implemented. The Term Directive harmonised copyright laws throughout the European Union and it extends the term of copyright in the UK to 70 years after the death of the photographer. Commissioned work, where previously the copyright belonged to the commissioner, is now the property of the photographer. This means that photos can only be kept for a limited period after a photo session, and rights must be agreed in the same way as for stock library images. All photos, used and unused, must be returned to the photographer. Staff photographers as employees do not own copyright on their photos.

A short booklet produced by the British Photographers Liaison Committee (BPLC), *The ABC Guide to UK Photographic Copyright*, summarises the changes in copyright relevant to photographers brought about by the 1988 Act. This is available from the Association of Photographers.

Last stages

When the pictures are ready to go off to the printer, a final check should be made to see that they have not been damaged by any of the people who have handled them – editors, designers, etc. If the printer returns photos damaged it will be easier to refute claims that pictures were already scratched if everything is checked as a matter of course. If prints or transparencies are damaged, a fee to compensate the agency or photographer is due. This will vary in amount according to whether the picture was an original or a duplicate. Some photographs are irreplaceable. The amount due for loss is stated in the Terms &

Useful organisations

BAPLA (British Association of Picture Libraries and Agencies)
18 Vine Hill, London EC1R 5DX
tel 0171-713 1780 *fax* 0171-713 1211
e-mail sarah@bapla.org.uk
web site http://www.bapla.org.uk
Contact Sarah Saunders
See page 442.

DACS (Design and Artists Copyright Society)
13 Northburgh Street, London EC1V 0AH
tel 0171-336 8811 *fax* 0171-336 8822
See page 452.

Association of Photographers
9-10 Domingo Street, London EC1Y 01TA
tel 0171-608 1441 *fax* 0171-253 3007
Includes fashion and advertising photographers amongst its members.

The Picture Research Association
(formerly SPREd)
455 Finchley Road, London NW3 6HN
tel 0171-431 9886 *fax* 0171-431 9887
e-mail pra@pictures.demon.co.uk
Contact Emma Krikler (General Secretary)
A professional body for picture researchers, managers, picture editors and all those involved in the research, management and supply of visual material to all forms of the media.

The Association's main aims are to promote the interests and specific skills of its members internationally; to bring together those involved in the research and publication of visual material; to provide a forum for the exchange of information and to provide guidance to its members. It offers a free advisory service for members, regular meetings, a quarterly magazine, a monthly newsletter and Freelance Register. Founded in 1977 as the Society of Picture Researchers & Editors (SPREd).

Conditions listed on the reverse of most delivery notes. This may be in the region of £400 for an original. Sometimes pictures are not damaged irreparably but are returned by the printer with torn mounts,

or still sticky from origination. It is best to return such pictures to the printer for cleaning, in case any damage occurs during a DIY cleaning session. Pictures should then be returned to their owners and one or two copies of the book or proofs supplied as evidence of use, as stated in the Terms & Conditions of the source.

Getting into picture research

This can be difficult as employers are loath to employ people without experience, and some picture sources are nervous about loaning pictures. A job with a picture library would give an insight into that particular source and might lead into a job as a picture researcher. Jobs in picture libraries, and picture research work, are advertised in the Creative, Media and Sales section of *The Guardian* on Saturdays and Mondays and in *The Independent* on Mondays. Sometimes such ads appear in *The Bookseller*, the weekly publishing journal, and *Campaign*, the weekly advertising magazine. These may all be available to read at your local library. Salaries tend to be low initially as one learns the skills involved. The idea of working freelance may appeal but it is difficult to obtain enough freelance work without the contacts amassed over a period of time.

Many picture researchers build up experience working for an employer full time, and then go freelance. This is not without risks. Getting enough work, being

Picture research courses

Book House Training Centre
45 East Hill, London SW18 2QZ
tel 0181-874 2718/4608 *fax* 0181-870 8985
Offers a 2-day course in picture research, designed for people working in book publishing. Its objectives are to give a professional approach to the search for and use of suitable sources; to make picture researchers aware of all the implications of their task: suitability for reproduction, legal and financial aspects, and efficient administration. Held in June and in December.

The London School of Publishing
David Game House, 69 Notting Hill Gate, London W11 3JS
tel 0171-221 3399
e-mail isp@easynet.co.uk
Course Director John Dalton
Offers a 10-week course in picture research 4 times a year. Each course takes place between 6.30-8.30pm, one evening per week. On successful completion a certificate in picture research is awarded. NUJ approved.

paid for work completed, sorting out tax and National Insurance to be paid, motivation, and loneliness are some of the problems which may arise.

Jennie Karrach is a freelance picture researcher and former chair of SPREd, who has worked with major national and international clients.

Societies, prizes and festivals

Societies, associations and clubs

The societies, associations and clubs listed here will be of interest to both writers and artists. They include appreciation societies devoted to specific authors, professional bodies and national institutions. Some also offer prizes and awards (see page 488); open exhibitions for artists are listed on page 519.

Yr Academi Gymreig (Welsh Academy)
3rd Floor, Mount Stuart House, Mount Stuart Square, The Docks, Cardiff CF1 6DQ
tel (01222) 492064
President Prof J.E. Caerwyn Williams, *Chairman* Nesta Wyn Jones, *Director* Dafydd Rogers

Founded to promote creative writing in the Welsh language, existing members elect new members on the basis of their contribution to Welsh literature or criticism. Publishes a literary magazine, *Taliesin*, books on Welsh literature and translations of modern European classics into Welsh; has recently published a new English/Welsh Dictionary. Founded 1959.

English Language Section
tel (01222) 492025 *fax* (01222) 492930
President Dannie Abse, *Chairman* Sally Roberts Jones, *Director* Kevin Thomas

Founded to provide a meeting point for writers in the English language who are of Welsh origin and/or take Wales as a main theme of their work. Membership open to all those deemed to have made a contribution to the literature of Wales, whether as writers, editors or critics. Associate membership is open to all interested individuals or organisations. Founded 1968.

Acrylic Painters' Association, National (NAPA)
President Alwyn Crawshaw, *Vice-President* Dr Sally A. Bulgin
Director/Founder Kenneth J. Hodgson, 134 Rake Lane, Wallasey, Wirral, Merseyside L45 1JW
tel 0151-639 2980

Promotes interest in, and encourages excellence and innovation in, the work of painters in acrylic. Holds an annual exhibition at the Royal Birmingham Society of Artists Gallery; publishes an annual journal and a newsletter.
Membership: £16 p.a. (full), £8 p.a. (associate). Founded 1985.

Agricultural Journalists, Guild of
President Drew Sloan, *Chairman* Arthur Anderson, *Hon. General Secretary* Don Gomery, Charmwood, 47 Court Meadow, Rotherfield, East Sussex TN6 3LQ
tel (01892) 853187

Established to promote a high standard among journalists who specialise in agricultural matters and to assist them to increase their sources of information and technical knowledge.

Amateur Artists, Society of
PO Box 50, Newark, Notts. NG23 5GY
tel (01949) 844050 *fax* (01949) 844051

To inform, encourage and inspire everyone, whatever their ability, who wants to paint, and to promote friendship and companionship amongst fellow artists. Holds meetings and events at local level, organises painting holidays, workshops, local exhibitions and competitions, publishes newsletter *Paint* (quarterly). Initial membership fee: £17.50, overseas £27.50. Founded 1992.

American Correspondents, Association of
President Karen Curry
Secretary Sandra Marshall, Associated Press, 12 Norwich Street, London EC4A 1BP
tel 0171-353 1515 oxt 4202 *fax* 0171-936 2229

American Publishers, Association of, Inc.
71 Fifth Avenue, New York, NY 10003, USA
tel 212-255-0200 *fax* 212-255-7007
President Patricia S. Schroeder, *Executive Vice-President* Thomas D. McKee
Founded 1970.

American Society of Composers, Authors and Publishers

One Lincoln Plaza, New York, NY 10023
tel 212-621-6000 *fax* 212-721-0955
President Marilyn Bergman

ASCAP is a membership association of over 50,000 writers and publishers, which protects its members' rights and those of affiliated foreign societies. It licenses and collects royalties for public performance of copyrighted music. Annual membership: $10.00 (writers), $50.00(publishers). Founded 1914.

American Society of Indexers

PO Box 48267, Seattle, WA 98148-0267, USA
tel 206-241-9196 *fax* 206-727-6430
e-mail asi@well.com
web site http://www.well.com/user/asi

Aims to improve the quality and standards of indexing and related areas of information science; acts as an advisory board on renumeration and qualifications of indexers and abstractors; defends and safeguards the professional interests of indexers. Holds meetings, seminars, workshops; provides *The Indexer* (bi-annual) and *Key Words* newsletter (6 p.a.). Annual membership: $65, $35 (student), $150 (corporate) Founded 1968.

Art and Design, National Society for Education in

The Gatehouse, Corsham Court, Corsham, Wilts. SN13 0BZ
tel (01249) 714825 *fax* (01249) 716138
General Secretary Dr John Steers NDD, ATC, DAE, PhD

Professional association of principals and lecturers in colleges and schools of art and of specialist art, craft and design teachers in other schools and colleges. Has representatives on National and Regional Committees concerned with Art and Design Education. Publication: *Journal of Art and Design Education* (3 p.a.), (Blackwells). Founded 1888.

Art Club, New English

17 Carlton House Terrace,
London SW1Y 5BD
tel 0171-930 6844 *fax* 0171-839 7830
Hon. Secretary William Bowyer RA, RWS, RP

For all those interested in the art of painting, and the promotion of fine arts. Open Annual Exhibition at the Mall Galleries, The Mall, London SW1.

Art Historians, Association of (AAH)

Cowcross Court, 77 Cowcross Street,
London EC1M 6BP
tel 0171-490 3211 *fax* 0171-490 3277
Hon. Secretary Dr Fintan Cullen, Dept. of Art History, The Art Centre, University of Nottingham, University Park, Nottingham NG7 2RO

Formed to promote the study of art history, the AAH has become a large and lively organisation for professional art historians, researchers and teachers in the field. The history of art itself is a broad and constantly evolving subject enlivened by cross-fertilisation with many other disciplines. The association is keen not only to extend its promotion of all activities in the visual arts but to ensure a wider public recognition of the field's rich diversity. There are 3 options for personal membership, depending upon the choice of publications; special rates for students/unwaged; corporate membership available. Founded 1974.

Artists, Federation of British

17 Carlton House Terrace, London SW1Y 5BD
tel 0171-930 6844 *fax* 0171-930 7830

Administers 9 major National Art Societies at The Mall Galleries, The Mall, London SW1.

Artists, International Guild of

Ralston House, 41 Lister Street, Riverside Gardens, Ilkley, West Yorkshire LS29 9ET
tel (01943) 609073
Director Leslie Simpson FRSA

Organises 4 seasonal exhibitions per year for three national societies: Society of Miniaturists, British Society of Painters in Oils, Pastels & Acrylics and British Watercolour Society. Promotes these 3 societies in countries outside the British Isles.

Artists Agents, Society of

144 Royal College Street, London NW1 0TA
tel 0171-267 9661
Contact Alison Eldred

Formed to promote professionalism in the industry and to forge closer links between clients and artists through an agreed set of guidelines. The Society believes in an ethical approach through proper terms and conditions, thereby protecting the interests of the artists and clients. Founded 1992.

Artists in Ireland, Association of
Arthouse, Temple Bar, Dublin 2,
Republic of Ireland
tel (01) 8740529 *fax* (01) 6771585
e-mail artists_ireland@connect.ie
Director Stella Coffey
To support and advise professional visu-
al artists in Ireland, to promote the visual
arts, to develop international exchanges
of artists. Publishes *Art Bulletin* (6 p.a.).
Published (1994) *Irish Visual Artists'
Handbook*, available by mail £14 (inc.
p&p). Annual membership: £25.
Founded 1981.

Artists, Royal Birmingham Society of
69A New Street, Birmingham B2 4DU
tel 0121-643 3768 *fax* 0121-644 5298
Society has its own galleries and rooms
in the city centre. Members (RBSA) and
Associates (ARBSA) are elected annually.
Holds 3 Open Exhibitions: Oil &
Sculpture (February), Watercolour &
Crafts (May), Pastel & Drawing
(November) – send sae for schedules,
available 6 weeks prior to Exhibition. A
further Open £1000 First Prize
Exhibition is held (June/July) for works
in any media. Other substantial money
prizes can be won with no preference
given to Members and Associates. Also
an Exhibition of Printmakers (February),
an Autumn Exhibition open to Members
and Associates, and 2 Friends
Exhibitions (January and August).
Friends of the RBSA pay an annual subscription of £14, which entitles them to
attend various functions and to submit
work for the Annual Exhibitions.

Artists, Royal Society of British
17 Carlton House Terrace, London SW1Y 5BD
tel 0171-930 6844 *fax* 0171-839 7830
President Colin Hayes RA, *Keeper* Alfred Daniels
Incorporated by Royal Charter for the
purpose of encouraging the study and
practice of the arts of painting, sculpture
and architectural designs. Annual Open
Exhibition at the Mall Galleries, The
Mall, London SW1.

Arts Boards – see Regional Arts Boards

Arts Club
40 Dover Street, London W1X 3RB
tel 0171-499 8581 *fax* 0171-409 0913
Secretary Jackie Downing

For all those connected with or interested in the arts, literature and science.
Founded 1863.

**The Arts Council/An Chomhairle
Ealáion**
Literature Officer, 70 Merrion Square, Dublin 2,
Republic of Ireland
tel (01) 6611840 *fax* (01) 6761302
Literature Officer Laurence Cassidy, *Visual Arts
Officer* Oliver Dowling
The national development agency for the
arts in Ireland, including literature in
English and Irish. Founded 1951.

Arts Council of England
14 Great Peter Street, London SW1P 3NQ
tel 0171-333 0100 *fax* 0171-973 6590
web site artscouncil.org.uk/
Chairman Lord Gowrie, *Secretary-General* Mary
Allen, *Director of Literature* Gary McKeone,
Director of Visual Arts Marjorie Allthorpe-Guyton
To develop and improve the knowledge,
understanding and practice of the arts,
and to increase their accessibility to the
public throughout England. The arts with
which the Council is mainly concerned
are dance, drama, mime, literature,
music and opera, the visual arts, including photography and documentary films
and videos on the arts.
  Within literature, 15 annual writers'
awards are awarded competitively (see
also page 489). Subsidies are provided to
literary organisations and magazines, and
schemes include support for translation,
writers' residencies in prisons, tours by
authors and the promotion of literature
in libraries and education.
  The Visual Arts Department is committed to the long-term improvement of visual artists' economic standing and working
conditions in England. In collaboration
with the Regional Arts Boards it supports
a number of national artists' agencies,
provides grants for the benefit of individual practitioners and promotes artists'
professional development initiatives.

Arts Council of Northern Ireland
185 Stranmillis Road, Belfast BT9 5DU
tel (01232) 381591 *fax* (01232) 661715
Chief Executive Brian Ferran, *Literature Officer*
Ciaran Carson, *Visual Arts Officer* Paula
Campbell
Promotes and encourages the arts
throughout Northern Ireland. Artists in

drama, dance, music and jazz, literature, the visual arts, traditional arts and community arts, can apply for support for specific schemes and projects. The value of the grant will be set according to the aims of the application. Applicants must have contributed regularly to the artistic activities of the community, with residency of at least one year in Northern Ireland.

Arts Council of Wales
9 Museum Place, Cardiff CF1 3NX
tel (01222) 394711 *fax* (01222) 221447
Chairman Sir Richard Lloyd Jones KCB, *Chief Executive* Emyr Jenkins

National organisation with specific responsibility for the funding and development of the arts in Wales. ACW receives grants from central and local government; also distributes the National Lottery funds in Wales. From these resources, ACW makes grants to support arts activity and facilities. Some of the funds are allocated in the form of annual revenue grants to full-time arts organisations; also operates schemes which provide financial and other forms of support for individual activities or projects. Undertakes this work in both the English and Welsh languages.

North Wales Regional Office
10 Wellfield House, Bangor, Gwynedd LL57 1ER
tel (01248) 353248 *fax* (01248) 351077

South East Wales Regional Office
Victoria Street, Cwmbrân NP44 3YT
tel (01633) 875075 *fax* (01633) 875389

West Wales Regional Office
6 Gardd Llydaw, Carmarthen SA31 1QD
tel (01267) 234248 *fax* (01267) 233084

Arts, Manufactures and Commerce, Royal Society for the encouragement of (RSA)
8 John Adam Street, London WC2N 6EZ
tel 0171-930 5115 *fax* 0171-839 5805
e-mail rsa@rsa.ftech.co.uk
web site http://www.cs.mdx.ac.uk/rsa/
Chairman of Council Richard Onians

With 20,000 Fellows, the RSA sustains a forum for people from all walks of life to come together to address issues, shape new ideas and stimulate action. It works through projects, award schemes and its lecture programme, the proceedings of which are recorded in *RSA Journal*. Founded 1754.

Asian Affairs, Royal Society for
2 Belgrave Square, London SW1X 8PJ
tel 0171-235 5122 *fax* 0171-259 6771
President The Lord Denman CBE, MC, TD,
Chairman of Council Sir Donald Hawley KCMG, MBE, *Secretary* Mrs Helen McKeag

For the study of all Asia past and present; fortnightly lectures, etc; library. Publishes *Asian Affairs* (3 p.a.), free to members. Subscription: £45 London, £35 more than 60 miles from London; other rates on application. Founded 1901.

Aslib (The Association for Information Management)
Information House, 20-24 Old Street, London EC1V 9AP
tel 0171-253 4488 *fax* 0171-430 0514
e-mail aslib@aslib.co.uk
web site http://www.aslib.co.uk/
Membership Manager Helen Rebera

Actively promotes best practice in the management of information resources. It represents its members and lobbies on all aspects of the management of and legislation concerning information at local, national and international levels. Aslib provides consultancy and information services, professional development training, conferences, specialist recruitment, and publishes primary and secondary journals, conference proceedings, Directories and monographs. Founded 1924.

The Jane Austen Society
Secretary Mrs Susan McCartan, Carton House, Redwood Lane, Medstead, Alton, Hants GU34 5PE
tel (01705) 475855 *fax* (01705) 788842
e-mail rosemary@sndc.demon.co.uk

Founded in 1940 to promote interest in, and enjoyment of, Jane Austen's novels and letters. Eight branches in UK. Membership: UK £10, life £150; overseas £12, life £180.

Australia Council
PO Box 788, Strawberry Hills, NSW 2012, Australia
located at 181 Lawson Street, Redfern, NSW 2016
tel (02) 9950 9000 *fax* (02) 9950 9111
Chairperson Dr Margaret Seares

Provides a broad range of support for the arts in Australia, embracing music, theatre, literature, visual arts, crafts, Aboriginal arts, community and new media arts. It has 8 major Funds: Literature, Visual Arts/Craft, Music, Theatre, Dance, New Media, Community

Cultural Development, Major Organisations, as well as the Aboriginal and Torres Strait Islander Arts Board.

The Literature Fund
Australia Council, PO Box 788, Strawberry Hills, NSW 2012, Australia
tel (02) 9950 9000 *fax* (02) 9950 9111
Because of its size and isolation and the competition its literature meets from other English-speaking countries, Australia has always needed to subsidise writing of creative and cultural significance. The Fund's chief objective is the support of the writing of all forms of creative literature – novels, short stories, poetry, plays and literary non-fiction. It also assists with the publication of literary magazines, has a publishing subsidies programme, and initiates and supports projects of many kinds designed to promote Australian literature both within Australia and abroad.

Australian Library and Information Association
PO Box E441, Kingston, ACT 2604, Australia
tel (06) 285 1877 *fax* (06) 282 2249
e-mail enquiry@alia.org.au
web site http://www.alia.org.au/
Executive Director Virginia Walsh
Aims to promote and improve the services of libraries and other information agencies; to improve the standard of library and information personnel and foster their professional interests; to represent the interests of members to governments, other organisations and the community; and to encourage people to contribute to the improvement of library and information services by supporting the association.

Australian Publishers Association (APA)
89 Jones Street, Ultimo, NSW 2007, Australia
tel (02) 9281 9788 *fax* (02) 9281 1073
e-mail apa@magna.com.au
web site http://www.publishers.asn.au

The Australian Society of Authors
PO Box 1566, Strawberry Hills, NSW 2012, Australia
located at 98 Pitt Street, Redfern, NSW 2016, Australia
tel (02) 9318 0877 *fax* (02) 9318 0530
e-mail asauthors@peg.pegasus.oz.au
web site http://www.peg.apc.org/~asauthors
Executive Director Lynne Spender

Aims to represent and enhance author rights and interests, through providing information, contract advice, publications (newsletters and journals), representation in disputes. Also seminars, research and information on new issues and new directions in writing and publishing. Annual membership: $110 (full/associate), $70 (affiliate); joining fee: $20.

Australian Writers' Guild Ltd
60 Kellett Street, Kings Cross, NSW 2011, Australia
tel (02) 9357 7888 *fax* (02) 9357 7776
e-mail awgsyd@ozemail.com.au
Executive Officer Simon Lake
Professional association dedicated to promoting and protecting the professional interests of writers for stage, screen, TV and radio. Full membership: entrance fee $150, annual fee $165-$600 dependent on income from writing; associate membership: entrance fee $75, annual fee $95. Founded 1962.

Authors, The Society of
84 Drayton Gardens, London SW10 9SB
tel 0171-373 6642
e-mail authorsoc@writers.org.uk
web site http://www.writers.org.uk
Chairman Simon Brett, *General Secretary* Mark Le Fanu
Founded in 1884 by Sir Walter Besant with the object of representing, assisting and protecting authors. A limited company and independent trade union, the Society's scope has been continuously extended; specialist associations have been created for translators, broadcasters, educational, medical and children's writers and illustrators (details are elsewhere in this *Yearbook*). Members are entitled to legal as well as general advice in connection with their work, their contracts, their choice of a publisher, problems with publishers, broadcasting organisations, etc. Annual subscription: £70 (£65 by direct debit) with reductions available to authors under 35 or over 65. Full particulars of membership from the Society's offices (see also page 482).

Authors' Agents, The Association of
President Vivien Green, *Vice President* Jonathan Lloyd, *Treasurer* David Miller
Secretary Carol Heaton, 37 Goldhawk Road, London W12 8QQ
tel 0181-749 0315 *fax* 0181-749 0318

Maintains a code of professional practice to which all members of the Association commit themselves; holds regular meetings to discuss matters of common professional interest; and provides a vehicle for representing the view of authors' agents in discussion of matters of common interest with other professional bodies. Founded 1974.

Authors' Club (at the Arts Club)

40 Dover Street, London W1X 3RB
tel 0171-499 8581 *fax* 0171-409 0913
Secretary Ann Carter

Founded by Sir Walter Besant, the Authors' Club welcomes as members writers, publishers, critics, journalists, academics and anyone involved with literature. Administers the Authors' Club Best First Novel Award, Sir Banister Fletcher Award, Marsh Biography Award and the Marsh Award for Children's Literature in Translation. Membership: apply to Secretary. Founded 1891.

The Authors League of America, Inc.

330 West 42nd Street, New York, NY 10036, USA
tel 212-564-8350 *fax* 212-564-8363

National membership organisation to promote the professional interest of authors and dramatists, procure satisfactory copyright legislation and treaties, guard freedom of expression and support fair tax treatment for writers. Founded 1912.

Authors' Licensing and Collecting Society Ltd (ALCS)

Isis House, 74 New Oxford Street, London WC1A 1EF
tel 0171-255 2034 *fax* 0171-323 0486
e-mail alcs@alcs.co.uk
web site http://www.alcs.co.uk

Independent collecting society for the collective administration of literary and dramatic rights in the spheres of photocopying, rental and lending right, off-air and private recording and cable retransmission. Annual membership: £5.88 (inc. VAT) for UK residents, £5 for other EU residents, £7 for residents outside EU; open to authors, successor membership to authors' heirs. Free membership to members of the Society of Authors and the Writers' Guild of Great Britain. See also page 604.

Authors' Representatives, Inc., Association of

Ten Astor Place, 3rd Floor, New York, NY 10003, USA
tel 212-353-3709

Founded 1991.

Aviation Artists, The Guild of

(incorporating the Society of Aviation Artists)
The Bondway Business Centre, 71 Bondway, Vauxhall Cross, London SW8 1SQ
tel/fax 0171-735 0634
President Michael Turner PGAvA, *Secretary* Hugo Trotter DFC

Formed in 1971 to promote aviation art through the organisation of exhibitions and meetings. Holds annual open exhibition in July in London; £1000 for 'Aviation Painting of the Year'. quarterly members' journal. Associates £40, Members £55 (by invitation), non-exhibiting artists and friends £15.

AXIS

Visual Arts Information Service, Room H301, Leeds Metropolitan University, Calverley Street, Leeds LS1 3HE
tel 0113-283 3125 *fax* 0113-283 5938
e-mail axis@gn.apc.org
web site http://www.lmu.ac.uk/ces/axis/

A unique arts information service which promotes the work of contemporary visual artists through the AXIS Database, a sophisticated multimedia database which records and displays comprehensive information about each artist, including a full CV and high quality colour images. Over 2000 practising artists are represented on the Database, which is used by commissions agents, curators, journalists, researchers, architects and other interested parties.

AXIS offers a telephone and written enquiry service, providing information on artists. It also operates a public access point network where visitors can personally use the Database, currently located in Leeds, Newcastle, Glasgow and Inverness. Founded 1991.

BAPLA (British Association of Picture Libraries and Agencies)

18 Vine Hill, London EC1R 5DX
tel 0171-713 1780 *fax* 0171-713 1211
e-mail sarah@bapla.org.uk
web site http://www.bapla.org.uk
Chief Executive Sarah Saunders

BAPLA is the trade organisation representing the British picture library and agency industry, offering an impressive 300 million pictures. With 310 members, it is the largest organisation of its kind in the world, and offers a unique pool of material and expertise. The Association promotes the highest standards of professionalism and service in the loan and reproduction of pictures. No library or agency is admitted to membership unless it undertakes to abide by the code of practice. BAPLA is active in lobbying to protect intellectual property rights both in the UK and internationally. Founded 1975.

BASCA (British Academy of Songwriters, Composers and Authors)
The Penthouse, 4 Brook Street, London W1Y 1AA
tel 0171-629 0992 *fax* 0171-629 0993
e-mail basca@basca.org.uk
Contact Guy Fletcher (Chairman)

Europe's largest composer body. Represented on PRS and MCPS boards. Competitions. Quarterly magazine. Song for Europe. Presents Ivor Novello Awards.

The Beckford Society
President James Lees-Milne
Secretary Sidney Blackmore, 15 Healey Street, London NW1 8SR
tel 0171-267 7750 *fax* (01985) 213195

Aims to promote an interest in the life and works of William Beckford of Fonthill (1760-1844) and his circle. Encourages Beckford studies and scholarship through exhibitions, lectures and publications, including *The Beckford Journal* (annual) and occasional newsletters. Annual subscription: £10 minimum. Founded 1995.

Thomas Lovell Beddoes Society
11 Laund Nook, Belper, Derbyshire DE56 1GY
tel (01773) 828066

Aims to promote an interest in the life and works of Thomas Lovell Beddoes (1803-1849). The Society promotes and undertakes Beddoes studies, and disseminates and publishes useful research. Founded 1994.

The E.F. Benson Society
The Old Coach House, High Street, Rye, East Sussex TN31 7JF
tel (01797) 223114
Secretary Allan Downend

To promote interest in the author E.F. Benson and the Benson family. Arranges annual literary evening, annual outing to Rye (July), talks on the Bensons and exhibitions. Archive includes the Austin Seckersen Collection, transcriptions of the Benson diaries and letters. Publishes postcards, anthologies of Benson's works and an annual journal, *The Dodo*. Annual subscription: £7.50 single, £8.50 2 people at same address, £12.50 overseas. Founded 1984.

E.F. Benson: The Tilling Society
5 Friars Bank, Pett Road, Guestling, East Sussex TN35 4ET
tel (01797) 222242 *fax* (01797) 227335
Secretaries Cynthia and Tony Reavell

To bring together enthusiasts for E.F. Benson and his Mapp & Lucia novels; annual gathering in Rye. Publishes 2 lengthy newsletters p.a. Annual subscription: £8, overseas £10; full starters membership (including all back newsletters) £20, overseas £24. Founded 1982.

Bibliographical Society
c/o Wellcome Institute, 183 Euston Road, London NW1 2BE
tel 0171-611 7244 *fax* 0171-611 8703
e-mail jm93@dial.pipex.com
President R. Myers, *Hon. Secretary* D. Pearson

Acquisition and dissemination of information upon subjects connected with historical bibliography. Founded 1892.

The Blackpool Art Society
The Studio, Wilkinson Avenue, Blackpool FY3 9HB
President Eileen Potter
Hon. Secretary Denise Fergyson, 29 Stafford Avenue, Poulton-le-Fylde, Lancs. FY6 8BJ
tel (01253) 884645

Summer and autumn exhibition (members' work only). Studio meetings, practicals, lectures, etc, out-of-door sketching, workshops. Founded 1884.

Book Packagers Association
93A Blenheim Crescent, London W11 2EQ
tel 0171-221 9089
Secretary Rosemary Pettit

Aims to represent the interests of book packagers; to exchange information at meetings and seminars; to provide services such as standard contracts and display/meeting facilities at book fairs. Annual subscription: £75-£150. Founded 1985.

Book Trust

Book House, 45 East Hill, London SW18 2QZ
tel 0181-870 9055 *fax* 0181-874-4790
Patron HRH Prince Philip, Duke of Edinburgh,
Chairman Prof Eric Bolton, *Director* Brian
Perman

Book Trust exists to open up the world of
books and reading to people of all ages
and cultures. Its services include the
Book Information Service, a unique, specialist information and research service
for all queries on books and reading
(business callers are charged via a premi-
um rate telephone service and should
phone 0897-161193; calls are charged at
£1.50 per minute). Book Trust administers a number of literary prizes, including the Booker Prize and produces a
wide range of books, pamphlets and
leaflets designed to make books more
easily accessible to the public. Founded
1925 as the National Book Council.

Young Book Trust
Provides practical help and advice on all
aspects of children's books and reading.
The Children's Library houses a unique
collection of every children's title published in the UK during the last 2 years.
On joining, subscribers receive a welcome
pack containing free copies of all Young
Book Trust publications, information,
posters, etc, plus author information,
Book Week material and book lists. Young
Book Trust produces a termly newsletter
for its subscribers, which include publishers, schools, libraries and booksellers.
Annual subscription: £30 plus VAT.

Book Trust Scotland

The Scottish Book Centre, 137 Dundee Street,
Edinburgh EH11 1BG
tel 0131-229 3663 *fax* 0131-228 4293
With a particular responsibility towards
Scottish writing, and especially active in
the field of children's writing, the Trust
exists to promote literature and reading,
and aims to reach (and create) a wider
reading public than has existed before. It
also organises exhibitions, readings and
storytellings, operates an extensive children's reference library available to
everyone and administers literary prizes.
The Trust also publishes short biographies, literary guides and Directories and
advises other relevant art organisations.

In addition, the Trust administers the
Writers in Schools/Writers in Public
schemes which support writers' visits
throughout Scotland. Readiscovery
Touring, the Trust's touring arm, runs the
Readiscovery Book Bus and publishes
the literary *Touring Co-ordination
Newsletter* (quarterly). Founded 1960.

Books Across the Sea

The English-Speaking Union of the
Commonwealth, Dartmouth House,
37 Charles Street, London W1X 8AB
tel 0171-493 3328 *fax* 0171-495 6108
e-mail esu@mailbox.ulcc.ac.uk
The English Speaking Union of the United States,
16 East 69th Street, New York, NY 10021, USA
tel 212-879-6800 *fax* 212-772-2886

World voluntary organisation devoted to
the promotion of international understanding and friendship. Exchanges books
with its corresponding BAS Committees
in New York, Russia and Australia. The
books are selected to reflect the life and
culture of each country and the best of its
recent publishing and writing. New selections are announced by bulletin, *The
Ambassador Booklist.*

Booksellers Association of Great Britain and Ireland

272 Vauxhall Bridge Road, London SW1V 1BA
tel 0171-834 5477 *fax* 0171-834 8812
e-mail 100437.2261@compuserve.com
Chief Executive T.E. Godfray
Founded 1895.

The George Borrow Society

Hon. Secretary Dr James H. Reading, The Gables,
112 Irchester Road, Rushden,
Northants. NN10 9XQ
tel/fax (01933) 312965
Promotes knowledge of the life and works
of George Borrow (1803-81), traveller and
author. Publishes *Bulletin* (bi-annual).
Annual membership: £8. Founded 1991.

Botanical Artists, Society of

Founder President Suzanne Lucas FLS, PRMS,
FPSBA, *Hon. Treasurer* Pamela Davis, *Hon.
Secretary* Margaret Stevens
Executive Secretary Mrs Pam Henderson, 1 Knapp
Cottages, Wyke, Gillingham, Dorset SP8 4NQ
tel (01747) 825718 (0171-222 2723 during
exhibitions)
Aims to encourage the art of botanical
painting. Membership through selection.
Annual Open Exhibition held, around
Easter time, at The Westminster Gallery,

Westminster Central Hall, Storey's Gate, London SW1H 9NH. Information and entrance forms available from the Executive Secretary from October, on receipt of sae. Membership: £90; lay members £20. Founded 1985.

British Academy
20-21 Cornwall Terrace, London NW1 4QP
tel 0171-487 5966 *fax* 0171-224 3807
e-mail basec@britac.ac.uk
web site http://britac3.britac.ac.uk
President Sir Tony Wrigley, *Vice-President* Prof M.M. McGowan, *Treasurer* Mr J.S. Flemming, *Foreign Secretary* Prof B.E. Supple, *Publications Secretary* Prof F.G.B. Millar, *Secretary* P.W.H. Brown CBE

The British Academy is the national Academy for the humanities and social sciences. It is an independent and self-governing fellowship of scholars, elected for distinction and achievement in one or more branches of the academic disciplines that make up the humanities and social sciences. In the absence of a research council with responsibility for the humanities, the British Academy is now the principal channel outside the universities for the Government's support of advanced research in the humanities, and it receives a Parliamentary grant-in-aid to support its activities. These include a wide range of grant schemes for research at postdoctoral level, and the organisation of the national scheme for postgraduate awards in the humanities. Founded 1901.

British Amateur Press Association (BAPA)
Secretary Mr L.E. Linford, Flat 36, Priory Park, Botanical Way, St Osyth, Essex CO16 8TE

A non-profit making, non-sectarian hobby organisation to 'promote the fellowship of amateur writers, artists, editors, printers, publishers and others, and to encourage them to edit, print and publish, *as a hobby*, magazines and newsletters, etc' by letterpress and other processes, including photocopiers and DTP/word-processors. Not an outlet for placing work commercially, only with other members in their private publications circulated within the association and friends. A fraternity providing contacts between amateur writers, poets, editors, artists, etc. Postal enquiries only, please send first class stamp. Founded 1890.

British American Arts Association (BAAA)
118 Commercial Street, London E1 6NF
tel 0171-247 5385 *fax* 0171-247 5256
e-mail baaa@easynet.co.uk
Director Jennifer Williams

A non-profit-making organisation working in the field of arts and education. BAAA conducts research, organises conferences, produces a quarterly newsletter and is part of an international network of arts and education organisations. As well as a specialised arts and education library, BAAA has a more general library holding information on opportunities for artists and performers both in the UK and abroad. BAAA is not a grant-giving organisation.

The British Council
10 Spring Gardens, London SW1A 2BN
tel 0171-930 8466 *fax* 0171-839 6347
web site http://www.britcoun.org/
Chairman Sir Martin Jacomb, *Director-General* Sir John Hanson KCMG, CBE

The British Council promotes Britain abroad, by providing access to British ideas, talent and experience in education and training, books and the English language, information, the arts, the sciences and technology. The Council is an authority on teaching English as a second or foreign language and gives advice and information on curriculum, methodology, materials and testing. It also promotes British literature overseas through writers' tours, academic visits, seminars and exhibitions. The Council works in 109 countries where it runs 200 libraries and resource centres and 118 teaching centres.

The Council's lending and reference libraries throughout the world stock material appropriate to the Council's priorities in individual countries. Where appropriate the libraries act as showcases for the latest British publications. They vary in size from small reference collections and information centres to comprehensive libraries equipped with reference works, CD-Rom, on-line facilities and a selection of British periodicals. Bibliographies of British books on special subjects are prepared on request.

The Council organises book and elec-

tronic publishing exhibitions for showing overseas, ranging from small specialist displays to larger exhibitions at major international book fairs such as Frankfurt.

The Council publishes *New Writing*, an annual anthology; a series of literary bibliographies, including *The Novel in Britain since 1970*; *Contemporary Writers*, a series of over 30 pamphlets on modern British writers; and exhibitions on literary topics such as *Writers Abroad British Travel Writing*. A catalogue is available on request, as is a catalogue of other publications, covering the arts, books, libraries and publishing, education and training, English language teaching and information for and about overseas students.

The Visual Arts Department, part of the Council's Arts Division, develops and enlarges overseas knowledge and appreciation of British achievement in the fields of painting, sculpture, printmaking, design, photography, the crafts and architecture, working closely with the Council's overseas offices and with professional colleagues in Britain and abroad.

The Council acts as an agent of the Overseas Development Administration for book aid projects for developing countries. In 1995/96 the Council also supported over 2000 events in the visual arts, film and TV, drama, literature, dance and music, ranging from the classical to the contemporary.

Further information about the work of the British Council is available from the Press and Public Relations Department at the headquarters in London or from British Council offices and libraries overseas.

British Film Institute (BFI)

21 Stephen Street, London W1P 2LN
tel 0171-255 1444 *fax* 0171-436 7950
Director Wilf Stevenson, *Head of Press and Corporate Affairs* Tony Slaughter

Set up in 1933 and now established by Royal Charter, the BFI is the UK national agency with responsibility for encouraging and preserving the arts of film and TV. The BFI's aim is to ensure that the many audiences in the UK are offered access to the widest possible choice of cinema and TV, so that their enjoyment is enhanced through a deeper understanding of the history and potential of these vital and popular art forms. The BFI's Library and Information Service contains the world's largest collection of published and unpublished material relating to film and TV. Annual membership: £11.95; includes NFT monthly programmes. Library passes: £17.50 (members); £30 (non-members). Concessionary rates are available.

British Interactive Multimedia Association (BIMA)

61 Ravenscourt Road, London W6 0UJ
tel 0181-741 5522 *fax* 0181-563 9443
e-mail 100624.1420@compuserve.com
web site www.bima.co.uk
Secretary Norma Hughes

BIMA was established to promote a wider understanding of the benefits of interactive multimedia to industry, government and education and to provide a regular forum for the exchange of views amongst members. Members come from the fields of application development, computer manufacturing, publishing, disk pressing, hardware distribution, programming and consultancy. Membership is open to any organisation or individual with an interest in multimedia. As well as regular monthly meetings, BIMA publishes a quarterly newsletter. Membership: commercial £650; institutional £300; individual £150. Founded 1984.

Broadcasting Entertainment Cinematograph and Theatre Union (BECTU), Writers Section

111 Wardour Street, London W1V 4AY
tel 0171-437 8506 *fax* 0171-437 8268
Supervisory Official Marilyn Goodman, *General Secretary* R. Bolton

To defend the interests of writers in film, TV and radio. By virtue of its industrial strength, the Union is able to help its writer members to secure favourable terms and conditions. In cases of disputes with employers, the Union can intervene in order to ensure an equitable settlement. Its production agreement with PACT lays down minimum terms for writers working in the documentary area. Founded 1946.

Broadcasting Group
84 Drayton Gardens, London SW10 9SB
tel 0171-373 6642

Specialist group within the Society of Authors (see page 482) for radio and TV writers and others involved in broadcasting.

The Brontë Society
Membership Secretary, The Brontë Parsonage Museum, Haworth, Keighley, West Yorkshire BD22 8DR
tel (01535) 642323 fax (01535) 647131
web site http://www.virtual-pc.com/bpmweb

Examination, preservation, illustration of the memoirs and literary remains of the Brontë family; exhibitions of MSS and other subjects. Publishes *The Transactions of the Brontë Society* (annual) and *The Brontë Gazette* (bi-annual).

The Browning Society
Secretary Ralph Ensz, 468 Russell Court, Woburn Place, London WC1H 0NL
tel 0171-278 8033

Aims to widen the appreciation and understanding of the lives and poetry of Robert Browning and Elizabeth Barrett Browning, and other Victorian writers and poets. Membership: £15. Founded 1881; refounded 1969.

The John Buchan Society
Hon. Secretary Russell Paterson, Limpsfield, 16 Ranfurly Road, Bridge of Weir, Renfrewshire PA11 3EL
tel (01505) 613116

Promotes a wider understanding and appreciation of the life and works of John Buchan. Encourages publication of a complete annotated edition of Buchan's works, and supports the John Buchan Centre and Museum at Broughton, Borders. Holds regular meetings and social gatherings; produces a Newsletter and a Journal. Annual subscription: £10.00 full/overseas; other rates on application. Founded 1979.

Byron Society (International)
Byron House, 6 Gertrude Street, London SW10 0JN
tel 0171-352 5112 fax 0171-352 1226
Hon. Director Mrs Elma Dangerfield OBE

To promote research into the life and works of Lord Byron by seminars, discussions, lectures and readings. Publishes *The Byron Journal* (annual, £5 plus postage). Annual subscription: £18. Founded 1971.

The Cable Communications Association
Fifth Floor, Artillery House, Artillery Row, London SW1P 1RT
tel 0171-222 2900 fax 0171-799 1471

Founded 1934.

Randolph Caldecott Society
Secretary Kenn Oultram, Clatterwick Hall, Little Leigh, Northwich, Cheshire CW8 4RJ
tel (01606) 891303 (office hours)

To encourage an interest in the life and works of Randolph Caldecott, the Victorian artist, illustrator and sculptor. Meetings held in Chester and London. Annual subscription: £7-£10. Founded 1983.

Canada, Periodical Writers Association of
54 Wolseley Street, Toronto, Ontario M5T 1A5, Canada
tel 416-504-1645 fax 416-703-0059
e-mail pwac@cycor.ca
web site http://www.cycor.ca/pwac
Executive Director Ruth Biderman.

Founded 1976.

Canada, Writers Guild of
35 McCaul Street, 3rd Floor, Toronto, Ontario M5T 1V7, Canada
tel 416-979-7907 toll free 1-800-567-9974
fax 416-979-9273
Executive Director Maureen Parker

To further the professional, creative and economic rights and interests of writers in radio, TV, film, video and all recorded media; to promote full freedom of expression and communication, and to oppose censorship unequivocally. Annual membership: $150, plus 2% of fees earned in the Guild's jurisdiction.

Canada, The Writers' Union of
24 Ryerson Avenue, Toronto, Ontario M5T 2P3, Canada
tel 416-703-8982 fax 416-703-0826
Chair Paul Quarrington

Canadian Authors Association
PO Box 419, 27 Doxsee Avenue North, Campbellford, Ontario K0L 1L0, Canada
tel 705-653-0323 fax 705-653-0593
President Murphy Shewchuk, Administrator Alec McEachern

Canadian Magazine Publishers Association
130 Spadina Avenue, Suite 202, Toronto, Ontario M5V 2L4, Canada
tel 416-504-0274 fax 416-504-0437
President Catherine Keachie

Founded 1989.

Canadian Poets, League of

54 Wolseley Street, 3rd Floor, Toronto,
Ontario M5T 1A5, Canada
tel 416-504-1657 *fax* 416-703-0059
e-mail league@ican.net
web site http://www.swifty.com/lc/
Executive Director Edita Petrauskaite

To promote the interests of poets and to advance Canadian poetry in Canada and abroad. Administers 2 annual awards; runs an annual poetry competition and a Canadian chapbook manuscript competition; publishes a newsletter and *Poetry Markets for Canadians*, *Who's Who in The League of Canadian Poets*, *Poets in the Classroom* (teaching guide), *Vintage 96* (contest anthology). Promotes and sells members' poetry books. Organises poetry book exhibitions. Founded 1966.

Canadian Publishers, Association of

2 Gloucester Street, Suite 301, Toronto,
Ontario M4Y 1L5, Canada
tel 416-413-4929 *fax* 416-413-4920
Director Paul Davidson

Founded 1976; formerly Independent Publishers Association, 1971.

Canadian Publishers' Council

250 Merton Street, Suite 203, Toronto,
Ontario M4S 1B1, Canada
tel 416-322-7011 *fax* 416-322-6999
e-mail pubadmin@pubcouncil.ca
web site www.pubcouncil.ca
Executive Director Jacqueline Hushion

Careers Writers' Association

Membership Secretary Barbara Button,
71 Wimborne Road, Colehill, Wimborne,
Doreset BH21 2RP
tel (01202) 880320)

Society for established writers on the inter-related topics of education, training and careers. Holds occasional meetings on subjects of interest to members, and circulates details of members to information providers. Annual membership: £15. Founded 1980.

(Daresbury) Lewis Carroll Society

Secretary Kenn Oultram, Clatterwick Hall,
Little Leigh, Northwich, Cheshire CW8 4RJ
tel (01606) 891303 (office hours)

To encourage an interest in the life and works of Lewis Carroll, author of *Alice's Adventures*. Meetings at Carroll's birth village (Daresbury, Cheshire). Elects an annual 'Alice'. Annual subscription: £5. Founded 1970.

The Lewis Carroll Society

Secretary Sarah Stanfield, Acorns, Dargate,
Nr Faversham, Kent ME13 9HG

To promote interest in the life and works of Lewis Carroll (Revd Charles Lutwidge Dodgson) and to encourage research. Activities include regular meetings and publication of *Jabberwocky* (quarterly) and newsletter *Bandersnatch*. Annual subscription: £13 (UK), £15 (Europe), £17 (elsewhere); apply for special rates for retired and institutions. Founded 1969.

Cartoonists Club of Great Britain

Secretary Terry Christien, 46 Strawberry Vale,
Twickenham TW1 4SE
tel 0181-892 3621 *fax* 0181-891 5946

Aims to encourage social contact between members and endeavours to promote the professional standing and prestige of cartoonists. Fee on joining: full, provisional, or associate £35; thereafter annual fee £25.

The Chesterton Society

Hon. Secretary Robert Hughes, 11 Lawrence Leys,
Bloxham, Nr Banbury, Oxon OX15 4NU
tel (01295) 720869

To promote interest in the life and work of G.K. Chesterton and those associated with him or influenced by his writings. Annual subscription: £20, including journal *The Chesterton Review* (quarterly) and newsletters. Founded 1974.

Children's Book Circle

c/o Naomi Cooper, Transworld Children's Books,
61-63 Uxbridge Road, London W5 5SA
tel 0181-231 6648 *fax* 0181-231 6727
Membership Secretary Gaby Morgan
tel 0171-881 8199

Provides a discussion forum for anybody involved with children's books. Monthly meetings are addressed by a panel of invited speakers and topics focus on current and controversial issues. Holds the annual Patrick Hardy lecture and administers the Eleanor Farjeon Award. Annual membership: £15 if working inside M25; outside £12. Founded 1962.

Children's Book Foundation – now Young Book Trust; see Book Trust

Children's Writers and Illustrators Group

84 Drayton Gardens, London SW10 9SB
tel 0171-373 6642

Subsidiary group for writers and illustrators of children's books, who are mem-

bers of the Society of Authors (see page 482).

Christian Literature, United Society for
Robertson House, Leas Road, Guildford, Surrey GU1 4QW
tel (01483) 577877 *fax* (01483) 301387
Chairman John Clark, *General Secretary* Dr Alwyn Marriage

To aid Christian literature principally in developing countries and Eastern Europe. Founded 1799.

Christian Writers, Fellowship of
Chairman Juliet Hughes, 74 Longleaze, Wootton Bassett, Swindon, Wilts. SN4 8AS
tel (01793) 852296

Aims to see the quality of writing in every area of the media, either overtly Christian or shaped by a Christian perspective, reaching the widest range of people across the UK and beyond. To inspire and equip people to use their talents and skills with integrity to devise, write and market excellent material which comes from a Christian world view. Annual membership: individual £10; couples/overseas £12.50. Founded 1971.

Agatha Christie Society
PO Box 985, London SW1X 9XA
e-mail agathachristie@dial.pipex.com
Secretary Elaine Z. Wiltshire

To promote communication between the fans of Agatha Christie and the various media who bring her works to the public. Publishes newsletters (4 p.a.). Annual subscription: £12.50 (UK), £15 (Europe), $30 (USA), £15 (rest of world). Founded 1993.

Civil Service Authors, Society of
Secretary Mrs J.M. Hykin, 4 Top Street, Wing, Nr Oakham, Rutland, Leics. LE15 8SE

Aims to encourage authorship by present and past members of the Civil Service (and some other public service bodies). Holds annual competitions for poetry, short stories, etc, open to members only, and annual 'Writer of the Year' award. Publishes *The Civil Service Author* magazine; £12 p.a., free to members. Poetry Workshop offers newletter, weekend, anthology; subscription additional £3.

The John Clare Society
The Stables, 1A West Street, Helpston, Peterborough PE6 7DU
tel (01733) 252678

Promotes a wider appreciation of the life and works of the poet John Clare. Annual subscription: £9.50 (UK individual); other rates (including overseas) on application. Founded 1981.

Classical Association
Secretary (Council) Dr M. Schofield, St John's College, Cambridge CB2 1TP
Publictiy Officer Dr J. March, PO Box 38, Alresford, Hants SO24 0ZQ

To promote and sustain interest in classical studies, to maintain their rightful position in universities and schools, and to give scholars and teachers opportunities for meeting and discussing their problems. Organises an annual conference lasting 3-4 days, in a university centre, and sponsors over 20 branches, which arrange programmes, lectures and discussions. Annual subscription: £5; life membership £105 (individuals only).

The William Cobbett Society
Chairman Molly Townsend, Johnsons Farm, Sheet, Petersfield, Hants GU32 2BY
tel (01730) 262060

To make the life and work of William Cobbett better known. Annual subscription: £8. Founded 1976.

The Wilkie Collins Society
Membership Secretary Paul Lewis, 47 Hereford Road, London W3 9JW
Chairman Andrew Gasson

To promote interest in the life and works of Wilkie Collins. Publishes a newsletter, an occasional scholarly journal and reprints of Collins's lesser known works. Annual subscription: £8.50, $12.50 (USA). Founded 1981.

Comedy Writers Association of Great Britain
Ken Rock, 61 Parry Road, Wolverhampton WV11 2PS
tel/fax (01902) 722729

Aims to develop and promote comedy writing in a professional and friendly way. Annual membership: £40. Founded 1981.

Comhairle nan Leabhraichean (The Gaelic Books Council)
22 Mansfield Street, Glasgow G11 5QP
tel 0141-337 6211
Chairman Boyd Robertson

Stimulates Scottish Gaelic publishing by awarding publication grants for new

books, commissioning authors and providing editorial services and general assistance to writers and readers. Founded 1968.

Comics Creators Guild
(formerly Society for Strip Illustration)
171 Oldfield Grove, Surrey Quays,
London SE16 2NE
tel 0171-232 0703 *fax* 0171-237 6364

Open to all those concerned with, or interested in, professional comics creation. Holds monthly meetings and publishes *Comics Forum* newsletter (monthly), a Directory of Members' Work, Submission Guidelines for the major comics publishers, sample scripts for artists, a 'Guide to Contracts' and 'Getting Started in Comics', a beginners' guide to working in the industry.

The Commonwealth Institute
Kensington High Street, London W8 6NQ
tel 0171-603 4535 *fax* 0171-602 7374
e-mail info@commonwealth.org.uk
web site http://www.commonwealth.org.uk/

Promotes Commonwealth education and culture in Britain. The Commonwealth Galleries are being renamed 'The Commonwealth Experience' and open to the public on 24 May 1997. The Education Centre and Resource Centre continue to offer services to teachers and school groups, and facilities for commercial hire continue to be available. Founded 1893.

Communicators in Business, The British Association of
Bolsover House, 5-6 Clipstone Street,
London W1P 7EB
tel 0171-436 2545 *fax* 0171-436 2565

Aims to be the market leader for those involved in corporate media management and practice by providing professional, authoritative, dynamic, supportive and innovative services. Founded 1949.

Composers, The Association of Professional
The Penthouse, 4 Brook Street, London W1Y 1AA
tel 0171-629 4828 *fax* 0171-629 0993
e-mail a.p.c@dial.pipex.com
Administrator Rosemary Dixson

Furthers the collective interest of its members and informs and advises them on professional and artistic matters.

Holds 4 general meetings p.a., and arranges a number of seminars and workshops. Publishes *The Composer's Guide to Music Publishing*, *Professional Composing* and a Newsletter (3 p.a.). Annual subscription: £30, plus 2% levy on PRS royalties amounting to c.£170. Founded 1980.

The Composers' Guild of Great Britain
The Penthouse, 4 Brook Street, London W1Y 1AA
tel 0171-629 4828 *fax* 0171-629 0993

Aims to represent and protect the professional interests of composers and to nurture the art of composition. It provides copyright and commissioning advice. Publications include *Composer News* and *First Performances*. Annual subscription: £30.00, associate membership: £22.50. Further particulars obtainable from the General Secretary.

The Joseph Conrad Society (UK)
Chairman Keith Carabine, *President* Philip Conrad, *Secretary* Hugh Epstein
The Conradian, Dept. of English,
St Mary's University College, Twickenham,
Middlesex TW1 4SX
Editor Allan Simmons

Maintains close and friendly links with the Conrad family. Activities include an annual international conference; publication of *The Conradian* and a series of pamphlets; and maintenance of a study centre at the Polish Cultural Centre, 238-246 King Street, London W6 0RF. Administers the Juliet McLauchlan Prize: £100 annual award for the winner of an essay competition. Founded 1973.

Contemporary Art Society (CAS)
17 Bloomsbury Square, London WC1A 1LP
tel 0171-831 7311 *fax* 0171-831 7345

Aims to increase the support and appreciation of contemporary art. As a charity, the CAS acquires paintings, sculpture, photographs, videos, installation work and applied art and crafts by contemporary artists to give to public museums. Annual membership: single £30.00; 2 people at same address £35.00; students £22.50. Founded 1910.

Contemporary Arts, Institute of
The Mall, London SW1Y 5AH
tel 0171-930 0493 *fax* 0171-873 0051
web site http://www.illumin.co.uk/ica

Encourages collaboration between art-forms, promotes experimental work and the mutual interchange of ideas and cultural practice at a national and international level. Produces diverse monthly programme of exhibitions, theatre, dance, music, literature, cinema, video, lectures, conferences, discussions. Open 1200-0100 Mon-Sat, 1200-2300 Sun. Various levels of membership available; open to the public with daypass £1.50.

Copyright Clearance Center, Inc.
222 Rosewood Drive, Danvers, MA 01923, USA
tel 508-750-8400 *fax* 508-750-4250
web site http://www.copyright.com
Operates a centralised photocopy authorisations and payment system in the US, serving photocopy users in their efforts to comply with the law, and foreign and domestic copyright owners in their efforts to protect their printed works. Free registration to rights holders. Founded 1978.

Copyright Council, The British
Copyright House, 29-33 Berners Street, London W1P 4AA
tel/fax 0181-371 9993
President Denis de Freitas OBE, *Vice-President* Geoffrey Adams, *Chairman* Maureen Duffy, *Vice Chairmen* Rachel Duffield, Mark Le Fanu, Robert Montgomery, *Secretary* Heather Rosenblatt, *Treasurer* Lord Brain
Aims to defend and foster the true principles of creators' copyright and their acceptance throughout the world, to bring together bodies representing all who are interested in the protection of such copyright, and to keep watch on any legal or other changes which may require an amendment of the law.

The Copyright Licensing Agency Ltd (CLA)
90 Tottenham Court Road, London W1P 0LP
tel 0171-436 5931 *fax* 0171-436 3986
Secretary Colin P. Hadley
The CLA administers collectively photocopying and other copying rights that it is uneconomic for writers and publishers to administer for themselves. The Agency issues collective and transactional licences, and the fees it collects, after the deduction of its operating costs, are distributed at regular intervals to authors

and publishers via their respective societies. See also page 606. Founded 1983.

Crime Writers' Association
60 Drayton Road, Kings Heath, Brimingham B14 7LR
Secretary Judith Cutler
For professional writers of crime novels, short stories, plays for stage, TV and sound radio, or of serious works on crime. Associate membership open to publishers, journalists, booksellers specialising in crime literature. Publishes *Red Herrings* (monthly), available to members only. Founded 1953.

The Critics' Circle
President Allen Robertson, *Hon. General Secretary* Charles Hedges
Contact Catherine Cooper, 47 Bermondsey Street, London SE1 3XT
tel 0171-403 1818 Ext. 106
Aims to promote the art of criticism, to uphold its integrity in practice, to foster and safeguard the professional interests of its members, to provide opportunities for social intercourse among them, and to support the advancement of the arts. Membership is by invitation of the Council. Such invitations are issued only to persons engaged professionally, regularly and substantially in the writing or broadcasting of criticism of drama, music, films, dance and the visual arts. Founded 1913.

The Cromwell Association
Press Liaison Officer B. Denton, 10 Melrose Avenue, off Bants Lane, Northampton NN5 5PB
tel/fax (01604) 582516 (office hours)
Encourages the study of Oliver Cromwell and his times. Holds academic lectures and meetings, publishes annual journal *Cromwelliana*. Annual subscription: £15. Founded 1935.

Cultural Desk, International
6 Belmont Crescent, Glasgow G12 8ES
tel 0141-339 0090 *fax* 0141-337 2271
e-mail icd@dial.pipex.com
web site http://dspace.dial.pipex.com/icd/
Development Manager Hilde Bollen, *Information Officer* Anne Robb
Aims to assist Scottish artists and arts organisations to take up international opportunities by providing timely and targeted information and advice. The Desk provides information and advice on fund-

ing sources, European cultural policy development, international cultural networks, basic data on international opportunities, and contact and partner finding as a starting point for international collaborations. Publishes *Communication* (bi-monthly) and *InFocus*, a new series of specialised guides with an international focus. Founded 1994.

Cyngor Llyfrau Cymru – see Welsh Books Council

The De Vere Society

8 Western Road, Henley-on-Thames, Oxon RG9 1JL
tel (01491) 576662 *fax* (01491) 579111
e-mail 100644.3717@compuserve.com
web site http://www.shakespeare-oxford.com
Secretary Christopher H. Dams

Aims to seek, and if possible to establish, the truth concerning the authorship of the Shakespeare plays and poems and, in addition, to promote research into the life of Edward de Vere, 17th Earl of Oxford. Founded 1986.

Deaf Broadcasting Council

70 Blacketts Wood Drive, Chorleywood, Rickmansworth, Herts. WD3 5QQ
tel/fax (01923) 283127 (text phone only)
e-mail dmyers@cix.co.uk
Secretary Ruth Myers

Aims to ensure that TV and radio are accessible to deaf, deafened and hard of hearing people and that access is of suitable quality. Annual membership: £3. Founded 1980.

Design and Artists Copyright Society Ltd (DACS)

Parchment House, 13 Northburgh Street, London EC1V 0AH
tel 0171-336 8811 *fax* 0171-336 8822
e-mail info@dacs.co.uk
Chief Executive Rachel Duffield, *Deputy Chief Executive* Janet Ibbotson, *Administrator* Janet Tod

DACS is the British copyright and collecting society for the visual arts. It aims to protect and administer visual artists' copyright both nationally and internationally. DACS provides individual and blanket licences to users of artistic works in the UK. The Society also advises about copyright for visual creators, and pursues infringements where appropriate. Life membership: £25 (inc. VAT). Founded 1983.

Designers, The Chartered Society of

First Floor, 32-38 Saffron Hill, London EC1N 8FH
tel 0171-831 9777 *fax* 0171-831 6277
Director Brian Lymbery

Works to promote and regulate standards of competence, professional conduct and integrity, including representation on government and official bodies, design education and competitions. The services to members include general information, publications, guidance on copyright and other professional issues, access to professional indemnity insurance and a credit-checking/debt collection service. Activities in the regions are included in an extensive annual programme of events and training courses. The Society publishes a Code of Conduct, and has developed a Business and Design Programme to strengthen the links between designers and clients in business and industry.

Designers in Ireland, Institute of

8 Merrion Square, Dublin 2, Republic of Ireland
tel/fax (01) 2841477

Irish design profession's representative body, covering every field of design. Details from the honorary secretary. Annual membership: £130 (full), £45 (licentiate). Founded 1972.

Dickens Fellowship

The Dickens House, 48 Doughty Street, London WC1N 2LF
tel 0171-405 2127 *fax* 0171-831 5175
Hon. Secretary Edward G. Preston

Based in house occupied by Dickens 1837-9; publishes *The Dickensian* (3 p.a.). Membership rates and particulars on application. Founded 1902.

Directory Publishers Association

Secretary Rosemary Pettit, 93A Blenheim Crescent, London W11 2EQ
tel 0171-221 9089

Maintains a code of professional practice; aims to raise the standard and professional status of UK directory publishing and to protect (and promote) the legal, statutory and common interests of directory publishers; provides for the exchange of technical, commercial and management information between members. Annual subscription: £110-£1100. Founded 1970.

Sean Dorman Manuscript Society
Cherry Trees, Crosemere Road, Cockshutt,
Ellesmere, Shropshire SY12 0JP
tel (01939) 270293
Director Mary Driver
Aims to provide mutual help among part-
time writers in England, Scotland and
Wales. Members regularly receive circulating manuscript parcels affording constructive criticism of their work and providing
opportunities for technical and general
discussion. Annual subscription: £6.50.
Send sae for full details. Founded 1957.

The Arthur Conan Doyle Society
Organisers Christopher and Barbara Roden,
PO Box 1360, Ashcroft, B.C., Canada V0K 1A0
tel 250-453-2045 *fax* 250-453-2075
e-mail ashtree@mail.netshop.net
Promotes the study of the life and works
of Sir Arthur Conan Doyle. Publishes
ACD journal (annual), *The Parish
Magazine* newsletter (bi-annual) and
occasional reprints of Conan Doyle material. Major annual convention. Annual
subscription: £15, overseas £16 (airmail
extra). Founded 1989.

Early English Text Society
Christ Church, Oxford OX1 1DP
Hon. Director Prof John Burrow
Executive Secretary R.F.S. Hamer
To bring unprinted early English literature
within the reach of students in sound texts.
Annual subscription: £15. Founded 1864.

The Eckhart Society
Summa, 22 Tippings Lane, Woodley, Reading,
Berks. RG5 4RX
tel/fax (01189) 690118
web site http://www.op.org/eckhart
Secretary Ashley Young
Aims to promote the understanding and
appreciation of Eckhart's writings and
their importance for Christian thought
and practice; to facilitate scholarly
research into Eckhart's life and works;
and to promote the study of Eckhart's
teaching as a contribution to inter-religious dialogue. Membership: £14 p.a.;
£7.50 p.a. OAPs/students. Founded 1987.

Edinburgh Bibliographical Society
c/o Dept. of Special Collections, Edinburgh
University Library, George Square,
Edinburgh EH8 9LJ
tel 0131-650 3412 *fax* 0131-650 6863
Secretary M.C.T. Simpson, *Treasurer* K. Thomson

Encourages bibliographical activity
through organising talks for members,
particularly on bibliographical topics
relating to Scotland, and visits to
libraries. Also publishes *Transactions*
(bi-annual, free to members) and other
occasional publications. Membership:
£10 p.a. (£15 p.a. institutions; £5 full-
time students). Founded 1890.

Editors, Association of British
Executive Director Jock Gallagher, Broadvision,
49 Frederick Road, Edgbaston,
Birmingham B15 1HN
tel 0121-455 7949 *fax* 0121-454 6187
Independent organisation set up to study
and enhance the practice of journalism
in all media; to protect and promote the
freedom of the media, in the UK and
throughout the world; to consider common problems independent of any individual, group or interest. Publishes
British Editor journal (quarterly). Annual
subscription: £50. Founded 1985.

Educational Writers Group
84 Drayton Gardens, London SW10 9SB
tel 0171-373 6642
Specialist group within the membership
of the Society of Authors (see page 482).

The Eighteen Nineties Society
Patron HRH Princess Michael of Kent, *President*
Countess of Longford CBE, *Chairman* Martyn Goff
OBE, *Secretary* Dr G. Krishnamurti
Hon. Secretary 97D Brixton Road,
London SW9 6EE
tel 0171-582 4690
Founded in 1963 as The Francis
Thompson Society, it now embraces the
entire artistic and literary scene of the
1890 decade. Holds exhibitions, lectures,
poetry readings; publishes biographies of
neglected authors and artists of the period; also check lists, bibliographies, etc.
Its Journal appears periodically, and
includes biographical, bibliographical
and critical articles and book reviews.

The George Eliot Fellowship
President Jonathan G. Ouvry
Secretary Mrs K.M. Adams, 71 Stepping Stones
Road, Coventry CV5 8JT
tel (01203) 592231
Promotes an interest in the life and work
of George Eliot and helps to extend her
influence; arranges meetings; produces
an annual magazine and a quarterly

newsletter. Annual subscription: £8. Founded 1930.

English Association
University of Leicester, University Road, Leicester LE1 7RH
tel (0116) 252 3982 *fax* (0116) 252 2301
Chairman Roger Knight, *Secretary* Helen Lucas

Aims to further knowledge, understanding and enjoyment of English literature and the English language, by working towards a fuller recognition of English as an essential element in education and in the community at large; by encouraging the study of English literature and language by means of conferences, lectures and publications; by fostering the discussion of methods of teaching English of all kinds; and by the establishment of local groups for the exchange of views and to work to further the status of English literature and language in the community.

English Regional Arts Boards – see Regional Arts Boards

English Speaking Board (International) Ltd
26A Princes Street, Southport PR8 1EQ
tel (01704) 501730
e-mail admin@esbuk.demon.co.uk
President Christabel Burniston MBE, *Chairman* Richard Ellis

Aims to foster all activities concerned with oral communication. The Board conducts examinations and training courses for teachers and students in schools and colleges where stress is on individual oral expression; also for those engaged in technical or industrial concerns, and for those using English as an acquired language. Members receive *Spoken English* (Mar/Sept); articles are invited on any special aspect of spoken English. Members can purchase other ESB publications at reduced rates. Conference and AGM in the spring. Membership: individuals, £20 p.a., corporate £35 p.a.

The English-Speaking Union
Dartmouth House, 37 Charles Street, London W1X 8AB
tel 0171-493 3328 *fax* 0171-495 6108
e-mail esu@mailbox.ulcc.ac.uk
Director-General Mrs Valerie Mitchell

Aims to promote international understanding and human achievement through the widening use of the English language throughout the world. The ESU is an educational charity which sponsors scholarships and exchanges, educational programmes promoting the effective use of English, and a wide range of international and cultural events. Members contribute to our work across the world. Annual membership: various categories. See also **Books Across the Sea**. Founded 1918.

European Broadcasting Union
Ancienne Route 17, Case Postale 67, CH-1218 Grand Saconnex (Geneva), Switzerland
tel (22) 7172111 *fax* (22) 7172481
e-mail ebu@ebu.ch
Secretary-General Dr Jean-Bernard Münch

Supports and promotes co-operation between its members and broadcasting organisations worldwide; represents the interests of its members in programme, legal, technical and other fields. Annual membership: fee according to number of broadcasting licences or households equipped with radio and/or TV receivers. Founded 1950.

European Publishers, Federation of
President John Clement
Secretary Mechthild von Alemann, 204 avenue de Tervuren, 1150 Brussels, Belgium
tel (2) 770 11 10 *fax* (2) 771 20 71
e-mail fep.vonalemann@linkline

Represents the interests of European publishers on EU affairs; informs members on the development of EU policies which could affect the publishing industry. Founded 1967.

Fabian Society
11 Dartmouth Street, London SW1H 9BN
tel 0171-222 8877 *fax* 0171-976 7153

Membership organisation which serves as a forum for the discussion on the Centre-Left. Holds conferences and publishes pamphlets and *Fabian Review* journal (quarterly). Individual membership: £25 (£10.50 reduced rate), library subscription: £60.

Fantasy Society, The British
2 Harwood Street, Heaton Norris, Stockport SK4 1JJ
tel 0161-476 5368 (after 6pm)
e-mail howe@which.net
web site http://www.personal.u-net.com/~djb/
President Ramsey Campbell, *Secretary* Robert Parkinson

For devotees of fantasy, horror and related fields, in literature, art and the cinema. Publications include *British Fantasy Newsletter* (bi-monthly) featuring news and reviews and several annual booklets, including: *Dark Horizons*; *Masters of Fantasy* on individual authors. There is a small-press library and an annual convention and fantasy awards sponsored by the Society. Annual membership: £17. Founded 1971.

Federation Against Copyright Theft Ltd (FACT)

7 Victory Business Centre, Worton Road, Isleworth, Middlesex TW7 6DB
tel 0181-568 6646 *fax* 0181-560 6364
Director General Reg Dixon, *Company Secretary* David Lowe

FACT aims to protect the interests of its members and others against infringement in the UK of copyright in cinematograph films, TV programmes and all forms of audio-visual recording. Founded 1982.

The Fine Art Trade Guild

16-18 Empress Place, London SW6 1TT
tel 0171-381 6616 *fax* 0171-381 2596
e-mail information@fineart.co.uk
web site http://www.fineart.co.uk
Managing Director Rosie Sumner

Promotes the sale of fine art prints and picture framing in the UK and overseas markets; establishes and raises standards amongst members and communicates these to the buying public. The Guild publishes *The Directory* and *Art Business Today*, the trade's longest established magazine and various specialist books. Founded 1910.

FOCAL (Federation of Commercial AudioVisual Libraries Ltd)

PO Box 422, Harrow, Middlesex HA1 3YN
tel/fax 0181-423 5853
e-mail anne@focalltd.demon.co.uk
web site http://www.focalltd.demon.co.uk
Administrator/Secretariat Anne Johnson

Founded 1985.

The Folklore Society

University College, Gower Street, London WC1E 6BT
tel 0171-387 5894
Hon. Secretary Dr Jacqueline Simpson

Collection, recording and study of folklore. Founded 1878.

Foreign Press Association in London

Registered Office 11 Carlton House Terrace, London SW1Y 5AJ
tel 0171-930 0445 *fax* 0171-925 0469
President Barbara Kollmeyer, *Secretaries* Davina Crole and Catherine Flury

Aims to promote the professional interests of its members. Full Membership open to overseas professional journalists residing in the UK; Associate Membership available for British press and freelance journalists. Entrance fee: £139.23; annual subscription: £117.50. Founded 1888.

Free Painters & Sculptors

Loggia Gallery and Sculpture Garden, 15 Buckingham Gate, London SW1E 6LB
tel 0171-828 5963

Exhibits progressive work of all artistic allegiances and provides opportunities for FPS members to meet and discuss their work in either one-person or group shows.Gallery hours: Mon-Fri 6-8pm, Sat-Sun 2-6pm.

Freelance Editors and Proofreaders, Society of (SFEP)

Office Mermaid House, 1 Mermaid Court, London SE1 1HR
tel 0171-403 5141

Aims to promote high editorial standards and achieve recognition of its members' professional status, through local and national meetings, an annual conference, a monthly newsletter and a programme of reasonably priced workshops/training sessions. These sessions help newcomers to acquire basic skills, enable experienced editors to update their skills or broaden their competence, and also cover aspects of professional practice or business for the self-employed. An annual Directory of members' services is available to publishers. The Society supports moves towards recognised standards of training and accreditation for editors and proofreaders; its own system of accreditation will come into operation during 1996. It has close links with Book House Training Centre and the Society of Indexers, is represented on the BSI Technical Committee dealing with copy preparation and proof correction (BS 5261), and works to foster good relations with all relevant bodies and organisations in the UK and worldwide. Founded 1988.

Freelance Photographers, Bureau of

Focus House, 497 Green Lanes, London N13 4BP
tel 0181-882 3315 *fax* 0181-886 5174
Chief Executive John Tracy

To help the freelance photographer by providing information on markets, and free advisory service. Publishes *Market Newsletter* (monthly). Annual membership: £40. Founded 1965.

French Publishers' Association

(Syndicat National de l'Edition)
115 Blvd St Germain, 75006 Paris, France
tel (1) 44 41 40 50 *fax* (1) 44 41 40 77

The Gaelic Books Council – see Comhairle nan Leabhraichean

The Gaskell Society

Far Yew Tree House, Over Tabley, Knutsford, Cheshire WA16 0HN
tel (01565) 634668
Hon. Secretary Mrs Joan Leach

Promotes and encourages the study and appreciation of the work and life of Elizabeth Cleghorn Gaskell. Holds regular meetings in Knutsford, London and Manchester, visits and residential conferences; produces an annual Journal and bi-annual Newsletters. Annual subscription: £8. Founded 1985.

Gay Authors Workshop

Kathryn Byrd, BM Box 5700, London WC1N 3XX
tel 0181-520 5223

To encourage writers who are lesbian, gay or bisexual. Quarterly newsletter. Membership: £5.00; unwaged £2.00. Founded 1978.

General Practitioners Writers Association

President Dr Robin Hull, West Carnliath, Strathtay, Pitlochry, Perthshire PH9 0PG
tel (01887) 840380

Aims to improve the writing by, for, from or about general medical practice. Publishes *The GP Writer* (2 p.a.); register of members' writing interests is sent to medical editors and publishers. Founded 1985.

German Publishers' and Booksellers' Association

(Börsenverein des Deutschen Buchhandels e.V.)
Postfach 100442, 60004 Frankfurt am Main, Germany
tel (069) 13060 *fax* (069) 1306201
web site http://www.buchhandel.de
General Manager Dr Hans-Karl von Kupsch

The Ghost Story Society

Organisers Barbara and Christopher Roden, Flat One, 36 Hamilton Street, Hoole, Chester CH2 3JQ

Devoted mainly to supernatural fiction in the literary tradition of M.R. James, Walter de la Mare, Arthur Machen, Algernon Blackwood, etc. Produces magazine (3 p.a.). Membership: £15 (£16/$26 overseas). Founded 1988.

Gothic Association, The International

Dept. of English Studies, University of Stirling, Stirling FK9 4LA
e-mail gs1@stirling.ac.uk
Secretary Treasurer Glennis Byron

Promotes scholarly research into Gothic fiction, drama, poetry, art, film and other forms from 18th century on. Publishes *The Monk* newsletter (quarterly) and a journal, *Gothic Studies*. Annual subscription: £25/US$40; student/unwaged £12.50/US$20. Founded 1991.

The Gothic Society

Chatham House, Gosshill Road, Chislehurst, Kent BR7 5NS
tel 0181-467 8475 *fax* 0181-295 1967

For the study of morbid, macabre and black-hued themes: Mrs Radcliffe, Monk Lewis, Mary Shelley, Sheridan Le Fanu, the Brontës, Bram Stoker, and many other writers and artists in the horror-romance genre. Also publish new art and literature in the same mood. Books, monographs and a quarterly newsletter and glossy magazine, *Udolpho*. Annual subscription: £22.50, overseas £26. Founded 1990.

Graphic Fine Art, Society of

15 Willow Way, Hatfield, Herts AL10 9QD
President Jean Canter

A fine art society holding an annual open exhibition. Membership by election, requires work of high quality with an emphasis on good drawing, whether by pen, pencil (with our without wash), watercolour, pastel or any of the forms of print making. Founded 1919.

Graphical, Paper & Media Union

Keys House, 63-67 Bromham Road, Bedford MK40 2AG
tel (01234) 351521 *fax* (01234) 270580
General Secretary Tony Dubbins

Trade union representing the interests of employees in the printing, paper, publishing and allied industries.

The Greeting Card Association
41 Links Drive, Elstree, Herts. WD6 3PP
tel/fax 0181-236 0024
web site http://greeting-card.assoc.co.uk
Publishes *Greetings* (10 p.a.).

Guernsey Arts Council
St James Concert and Assembly Hall,
St Peter Port, Guernsey, CI
tel (01481) 721902
Secretary Angela Simon
Co-ordinates the organisations under the
council's umbrella, presents artistic
events, sponsors reports, aims to bring
about the creation of an arts centre in
Guernsey and to encourage all the arts in
Guernsey, Alderney and Sark. Member-
ship: £5, under 18 £2. Founded 1981.

The Neil Gunn Society
Secretary Mrs J. Campbell, 25 Newton Avenue,
Wick, Caithness KW1 5LJ
tel (01955) 602607
To promote the works of the Scottish
novelist, Neil Gunn; to research into the
background of, and to encourage discussion on and evaluation of, Gunn's work;
to collect material related to his life and
work; to provide a focal point for and
help with any Gunn-related activity.
Annual membership: £5.00, students
£2.00. Founded 1985.

Hakluyt Society
c/o The Map Library, The British Library,
Great Russell Street, London WC1B 3DG
tel (01986) 788359 *fax* (01986) 788181
e-mail haksoc@paston.co.uk
President Sarah Tyacke, *Hon. Secretary* Anthony
P. Payne
Publication of original narratives of voy-
ages, travels, naval expeditions, and other
geographical records. Founded 1846.

The Thomas Hardy Society Ltd
PO Box 1438, Dorchester, Dorset DT1 1YH
tel (01305) 251501
Publishes *The Thomas Hardy Journal* (3
p.a.). Biennial conference in Dorchester,
1998. Annual subscription: £12.00
(£15.00 overseas). Founded 1967.

Harleian Society
College of Arms, Queen Victoria Street,
London EC4V 4BT
Chairman J. Brooke-Little CVO, MA, FSA, *Hon.
Secretary* T.H.S. Duke, Chester Herald of Arms
Instituted for transcribing, printing and
publishing the heraldic visitations of

Counties, Parish Registers and any manuscripts relating to genealogy, family history and heraldry. Founded 1869.

Heraldic Arts, Society of
46 Reigate Road, Reigate, Surrey RH2 0QN
tel (01737) 242945
Secretary John Ferguson ARCA, SHA, FRSA, DFACH
Aims to serve the interests of heraldic
artists, craftsmen, designers and writers, to
provide a 'shop window' for their work, to
obtain commissions on their behalf and to
act as a forum for the exchange of information and ideas. Also offers an information
service to the public. Candidates for
admission as craft members should be
artists or craftsmen whose work comprises
a substantial element of heraldry and is of
a sufficiently high standard to satisfy the
requirements of the society's advisory
council.Annual membership: £12 (associate); £17 (craft). Founded 1987.

The Sherlock Holmes Society of London
President A.D. Howlett MA, LLB, *Chairman*
Richard Lancelyn-Green
General enquiries H.C. Owen, 64 Graham Road,
London SW19 3SS
tel/fax 0181-540 7657
e-mail 100616.1332@compuserve.com
Membership R.J. Ellis, 13 Crofton Avenue,
Orpington, Kent BA6 8DU
tel/fax (01689) 811314
Aims to bring together those who have a
common interest as readers and students
of the literature of Sherlock Holmes, and
to encourage the pursuit of knowledge of
the public and private lives of Sherlock
Holmes and Dr Watson. Annual sub-
scription: £14.00 (UK/Europe), £18.00
(Far East), US$30.50 (USA), including
The Sherlock Holmes Journal (2 p.a.).
Founded 1951.

Hopkins Society
c/o The Secretary, Arts Council of Wales,
Library, Museum & Gallery, Earl Road,
Mold CH7 1AP
tel (01352) 758403 *fax* (01352) 700236
To promote and celebrate the work of the
poet, Gerard Manley Hopkins, to inform
members about the latest publications
about Hopkins and to support educational projects concerning his work. Annual
lecture held in North Wales in the
spring; publishes Newsletter (2 p.a.)
Annual subscription: £5. Founded 1990.

Housman Society
80 New Road, Bromsgrove, Worcs. B60 2LA
tel (01527) 874136 *fax* (01527) 837274
Chairman Jim Page
Aims to foster interest in and promote knowledge of A.E. Housman, his sister Clemence and their brother Laurence. Membership: £7.50 p.a. Founded 1973.

Hesketh Hubbard Art Society
17 Carlton House Terrace, London SW1Y 5BD
tel 0171-930 6844 *fax* 0171-839 7830
President Simon Whittle
Weekly drawing workshops open to all.

Illustrators, The Association of
First Floor, 32-38 Saffron Hill,
London EC1N 8FN
tel 0171-831 7377 *fax* 0171-831 6277
Contact Stephanie Smith
To support illustrators, promote illustration and encourage professional standards in the industry. Publishes monthly magazine; presents an annual programme of events; annual competition, Images – the Best of British Illustration: call for entries March/April. Founded 1973.

Illustrators, Society of Architectural
PO Box 22, Stroud, Glos. GL5 3DH
tel/fax (01453) 882563
Administrator Eric Monk
Professional body to represent all who practise architectural illustration, including the related fields of model making and photography. Founded 1975.

Independent Literary Agents Association, Inc. – merged in 1991 with Society of Authors' Representatives, Inc., to become Authors' Representatives, Inc., Association of

Independent Programme Producers Association – see PACT

Indexers, Society of
Secretary Mrs C. Shuttleworth, Mermaid House, 1 Mermaid Court, London SE1 1HR
tel 0171-403 4947
Aims to improve the standard of indexing, and to raise the status of indexers and to safeguard their interests. Maintains a Register of Indexers; acts as an advisory body on the qualifications and remuneration of indexers; publishes or communicates books, papers and notes on the subject of indexing; publishes and runs an open-learning indexing course, 'Training in Indexing'. The Society's journal, *The Indexer*, is sent free to members. Annual subscription: £40 UK/Europe (£52 overseas), corporate £60 (£80 overseas).

Indian Publishers, The Federation of
18/1-C Institutional Area, J.N.U. Road,
New Delhi 110067, India
tel 6964847, 6852263 *fax* 91-11-6864054

Irish Book Publishers Association (Clé)
Irish Writers' Centre, 19 Parnell Square, Dublin 1, Republic of Ireland
tel (01) 8729090 *fax* (01) 8722035
President Michael Gill, *Administrator* Orla Martin

The Irish Copyright Licensing Agency
19 Parnell Square, Dublin 1, Republic of Ireland
tel (01) 8729202 *fax* (01) 8722035
Administrator Orla O'Sullivan
Licences schools and other users of copyright material to photocopy extracts of such material, and distributes the monies collected to the authors and publishers whose works have been copied. Founded 1992.

Irish Playwrights, Society of
(Cumann Drámadóirí na hÉireann)
Irish Writers' Centre, 19 Parnell Square, Dublin 1, Republic of Ireland
tel (01) 8721302 *fax* (01) 8726282
Secretary Sean Moffatt
To safeguard the rights of Irish playwrights and to foster and promote Irish playwriting. Annual subscription: IR£25. Founded 1969.

Irish Translators' Association
Irish Writers' Centre, 19 Parnell Square, Dublin 1, Republic of Ireland
tel (01) 8721302 *fax* (01) 8726282
web site http://infomatique.iol.ie/ita/
Secretary Miriam Lee
Promotes translation in Ireland, the translation of Irish authors abroad and the practical training of translators, and promotes the interests of translators. Catalogues the works of translators in areas of Irish interest; secures the awarding of prizes and bursaries for translators; and maintains a detailed register of translators. Annual membership: £15 (member), £30 (professional member). Founded 1986.

Irish Writers' Union/Comhar na Scríbhneoirí
Irish Writers' Centre, 19 Parnell Square, Dublin 1, Republic of Ireland
tel (01) 8721302 *fax* (01) 8726282
Secretary Mara Rainwater

The Union aims to advance the cause of writing as a profession, to achieve better remuneration and more favourable conditions for writers and to provide a means for the expression of the collective opinion of writers on matters affecting their profession. Founded 1986.

The Richard Jefferies Society
President Richard Mabey
Hon. Secretary Phyllis Treitel, Eidsvoll, Bedwells Heath, Boars Hill, Oxford OX1 5JE
tel (01865) 735678

Worldwide membership. Promotes interest in the life, works and associations of the naturalist and novelist, Richard Jefferies; helps to preserve buildings and memorials, and co-operates in the development of a Museum in his birthplace. Arranges regular meetings in Swindon, and occasionally elsewhere; organises outings and displays; publishes a Journal and Newsletter in spring and an Annual Report in September. Annual subscription: £7. Founded 1950.

The Johnson Society
Johnson Birthplace Museum, Breadmarket Street, Lichfield, Staffs. WS13 6LG
tel (01543) 264972
Hon. General Secretary Norma Hooper

To encourage the study of the life and works of Dr Samuel Johnson; to preserve the memorials, associations, books, manuscripts, letters of Dr Johnson and his contemporaries; preservation of his birthplace.

Johnson Society of London
President The Revd Dr E.F. Carpenter KCVO
Secretary Mrs Zandra O'Donnell MA, 255 Baring Road, London SE12 0BQ
tel 0181-851 0173

To study the life and works of Dr Johnson, and to perpetuate his memory in the city of his adoption. Founded 1928.

Journalists, The Chartered Institute of
General Secretary Christopher Underwood FCIJ, 2 Dock Offices, Surrey Quays Road, London SE16 2XU
tel 0171-252 1187 *fax* 0171-232 2302
e-mail cioj@dircon.co.uk

The senior organisation of the profession, founded in 1884 and incorporated by Royal Charter in 1890. The Chartered Institute maintains an employment register and has accumulated funds for the assistance of members. A Freelance Division links editors and publishers with freelances and a Directory is published of freelance writers, with their specialisations. There are special sections for broadcasters, motoring correspondents and public relations practitioners. Occasional contributors to the media may qualify for election as Affiliates. Annual subscription: related to earnings – maximum £150, minimum £75; affiliate £100.

Journalists, National Council for the Training of
Latton Bush Centre, Southern Way, Harlow, Essex CM18 7BL
tel (01279) 430009 *fax* (01279) 438008
e-mail nctj@itecharlow.co.uk
web site http://www.itecharlow.co.uk.nctj/
Chief Executive Rob Selwood

A registered charity which aims to advance the education and training of trainee journalists, including press photographers. Founded 1952.

Keats-Shelley Memorial Association
Hon. Treasurer R.E. Cavaliero, 10 Lansdowne Road, Tunbridge Wells, Kent TN1 2NJ
tel (01892) 533452 *fax* (01892) 519142
Patron HM Queen Elizabeth the Queen Mother, *Chairman* Hon. Mrs H. Cullen, *Hon. Secretary* D.R. Leigh-Hunt

Owns and supports house in Rome where John Keats died, and celebrates the poets Keats, Shelley and Leigh Hunt. Occasional meetings; annual *Review* and progress reports. Subscription to 'Friends of the Keats-Shelley Memorial', minimum £10 p.a. Founded 1903.

Kent and Sussex Poetry Society
President Laurence Lerner, *Chairman* Clive Eastwood
Hon. Secretary Mrs Doriel Hulse, Costens, Carpenters Lane, Hadlow, Kent TN11 0EY
tel (01732) 851404

Based in Tunbridge Wells, the society was formed in 1946 to create a greater interest in Poetry. Well-known poets address the Society, a Folio of members' work is produced and a full programme of recitals, discussions, competitions and

readings is provided. See page 500 for details of Open Poetry Competition. Annual subscription: attending members £6, country members £3, students £1.

Kinematograph, Sound and Television Society, British

63-71 Victoria House, Vernon Place, London WC1B 4DB
tel 0171-242 8400 *fax* 0171-405 3560
Executive Director Anne Fenton, *Hon. Secretary* Wendy Laybourn

Aims to encourage technical and scientific progress in the industries of its title. Publishes technical information, arranges international conferences and exhibitions, lectures and demonstrations, and encourages the exchange of ideas. Journals: *Image Technology* (monthly), *Images* (monthly), *Cinema Technology* (quarterly). Founded 1931, incorporated 1946.

The Kipling Society

Secretary Michael Smith, 2 Brownleaf Road, Brighton, East Sussex BN2 6LB
tel (01273) 303719
web site http://www.kipling.org.uk

Aims to honour and extend the influence of Kipling, to assist in the study of his writings, to hold discussion-meetings, to publish a quarterly journal and to maintain a Kipling Reference Library. Membership details on application.

The Lancashire Authors' Association

President Frank Sunderland
General Secretary Eric Holt, 5 Quakerfields, Westhoughton, Bolton BL5 2BJ
tel (01942) 791390

'For writers and lovers of Lancashire literature and history.' Publishes *The Record* (quarterly). Annual subscription: £9.00. Founded 1909.

The T.E. Lawrence Society

PO Box 728, Oxford OX2 6YP

Promotes the memory of T.E. Lawrence and furthers knowledge by research into his life; publishes *Journal* (bi-annual) and *Newsletter* (quarterly). Annual subscription: £14, overseas £18. Founded 1985.

Learned and Professional Society Publishers, The Association of

Secretary-General Prof B.T. Donovan, 48 Kelsey Lane, Beckenham, Kent BR3 3NE
tel 0181-658 0459

Aims to promote and develop the publishing activities of learned and professional organisations. Membership is open to professional and learned societies and allied organisations. Founded 1972.

Librarians, Association of Assistant

c/o The Library Association, 7 Ridgmount Street, London WC1E 7AE
President Peter Loewenstein BA, MSc, ALA, *Hon. Secretary* Jean Bennett BA

Publishes bibliographical aids, the journal *Assistant Librarian*, works on librarianship; and runs educational courses. Founded 1895.

The Library Association

7 Ridgmount Street, London WC1E 7AE
tel 0171-636 7543 *fax* 0171-436 7218
e-mail info@la-hq.org.uk
web site http://www.la-hq.org.uk
Chief Executive R. Shimmon FLA

For over a century, the Library Association has promoted and defended the interests of the Library and Information Service profession, those working within it and the people who use the services. The journal *The Library Association Record* (monthly), is distributed free to all members. Subscription: varies according to income. Founded 1877.

Limners, The Society of

Founder/President Elizabeth Davys Wood PSLM, SWA
Executive Secretary Mrs C. Melmore, 104 Poverest Road, Orpington, Kent BR5 2DQ

Aims to promote an interest in miniature painting (in any medium), calligraphy and heraldry and encourage their development to a high standard. New members are elected after the submission of 4 works of acceptable standard and guidelines are provided for new artists. Members receive up to 4 newsletters a year and 2 annual exhibitions are arranged. Annual membership: £20; Friends (£12). Friends membership is open to non-exhibitors and includes newsletters and invitations to exhibitions and seminar. Founded 1986.

Linguists, Institute of

Saxon House, 48 Southwark Street, London SE1 1UN
tel 0171-940 3100 *fax* 0171-940 3101

To provide language qualifications; to encourage Government and industry to develop the use of modern languages and

encourage recognition of the status of professional linguists in all occupations; to promote the exchange and dissemination of information on matters of concern to linguists.

Literary Societies, Alliance of

Secretary Bill Adams, 71 Stepping Stones Road, Coventry CV5 8JT
tel (01203) 592231
e-mail http://www.sndc.demon.co.uk
Chapter One, Clatterwick Hall, Little Leigh, Northwich, Cheshire CW8 4RJ
tel (01606) 891303 (office hours)
Editor Kenn Oultram

Any literary society may affiliate and may attend the annual convention and receive an allocation of the official publication *Chapter One*. Some financial assistance may be granted to small societies. Subscription: graded dependent upon size of society.

Literature, Royal Society of

1 Hyde Park Gardens, London W2 2LT
tel 0171-723 5104 *fax* 0171-402 0199
Chairman of Council John Mortimer CBE, QC, FRSL,
Secretary Maggie Fergusson

For the advancement of literature by the holding of lectures, discussions, readings, and by publications. Administers the Royal Society of Literature Award under the W.H. Heinemann Bequest and the Royal Society of Literature Award under the Winifred Holtby Memorial Bequest. Annual subscription: £30. Founded 1823.

Little Presses, Association of (ALP)

Chairperson Lawrence Upton, 25 St Benedict's Close, Church Lane, London SW17 9NX
web site http://www.melloworld.com/alp

Loosely-knit association of individuals running little presses who have grouped together for mutual self-help, while retaining their right to operate autonomously. Publications include: Newsletter, *Poetry and Little Press Information*, *Catalogue of Little Press Books in Print*, *Getting Your Poetry Published*, *Publishing Yourself*. It does not publish any creative writing. Annual membership: £12.50. Founded 1966.

Little Theatre Guild of Great Britain

Public Relations Officer Marjorie Havard, 19 Abbey Park Road, Great Grimsby DN32 0HJ
tel (01472) 343424

Aims to promote closer co-operation amongst the little theatres constituting its membership; to act as co-ordinating and representative body on behalf of the little theatres; to maintain and advance the highest standards in the art of theatre; and to assist in encouraging the establishment of other little theatres. Yearbook available to non-members £5.00.

The Arthur Machen Society

5 Birch Terrace, Hangingbirch Lane, Horam, East Sussex TN21 0PA
tel (01435) 813224
Patron Julian Lloyd Webber, *President* Barry Humphries, *Secretary* Ray Russell

Provides a forum for the exchange of ideas and information about Arthur Machen, novelist, and aims to bring his work before a new generation of readers. Publishes *Avallaunius* journal (bi-annual) and newsletter *The Silurist* (bi-annual); hardback books, by and about Machen and his circle, and an audio-cassette tape. Relevant second-hand and small press booklist available. Annual subscription: £15 (UK), £18 (overseas and libraries), US$ account. Founded 1986.

Marine Artists, Royal Society of

17 Carlton House Terrace, London SW1Y 5BD
tel 0171-930 6844 *fax* 0171-839 7830
President Mark Myers

To promote and encourage marine painting. Open Annual Exhibition at the Mall Galleries, London.

The Marlowe Society

Secretary Miss C.M. Barford, c/o Alleyn's School, Dulwich, London SE22 8SO
tel 0181-693 3422

To extend appreciation and widen recognition of Christopher Marlowe (1564-93) as the foremost poet and dramatist preceding Shakespeare, whose development he influenced. Holds meetings, and visits Tudor stately homes, yeomen houses and farms, etc. Annual subscription: £7.50, concessions £5. Founded 1955.

The John Masefield Society

Secretary Peter J.R. Carter, The Frith, Ledbury, Herefordshire HR8 1LW
tel (01531) 633800

To stimulate interest in and public awareness and enjoyment of the life and works of the poet John Masefield. Holds

a 2-day annual festival, annual lecture and other, less formal, readings and gatherings; publishes an annual Journal and quarterly Newsletters. Annual membership: £5, overseas £10, family/institutions £8. Founded 1992.

Mechanical-Copyright Protection Society Ltd (MCPS)
Elgar House, 41 Streatham High Road, London SW16 1ER
tel 0181-664 4400 *fax* 0181-769 8792
e-mail corpcomms@mcps.co.uk
Chief Executive John Hutchinson, *Contact* Corporate Communications Department

Founded in 1910, the Society grants licences for the use of copyright material by mechanical reproduction, be it sound, film, radio and TV recordings, magnetic tape or videocassettes. Protection is worldwide, by virtue of its affiliations with other similar organisations and agencies. Membership of the Society is open to all music copyright owners, composers, lyric writers and publishers. No entrance fee or subscription.

The Media Society
Secretary Peter Dannheisser, 56 Roseneath Road, London SW11 6AQ
tel/fax 0171-223 5031

To promote and encourage collective and independent research into the standards, performance, organisation and economics of the media and hold regular discussions, debates, etc. on subjects of topical or special interest and concern to print and broadcast journalists and others working in or with the media. Annual subscription: £25. Founded 1973.

Medical Journalists Association
Barley Mow, 185 High Street, Stony Stratford, Milton Keynes MK11 1AP
tel (01908) 564623
Chairman John Illman, *Hon. Secretary* Gwen Yates

Aims to improve the quality and practice of health and medical journalism. Administers major awards for health and medical journalism and broadcasting. Publishes The *MJA Directory* and *MJA News* newsletter. Annual membership: £30. Founded 1966.

Medical Writers Group
84 Drayton Gardens, London SW10 9SB
tel 0171-373 6642

Specialist group within the membership of the Society of Authors (see page 482) giving contractual and legal advice. Also organises talks, day seminars covering many aspects of medical writing, and administers the medical prizes sponsored by the Royal Society of Medicine.

Miniature Painters, Sculptors and Gravers, Royal Society of
President Suzanne Lucas FLS, PRMS, FPSBA, *Treasurer* Alastair MacDonald, *Hon. Secretary* Pauline Gyles
Executive Secretary Mrs Pam Henderson, 1 Knapp Cottages, Wyke, Gillingham, Dorset SP8 4NQ
tel (01747) 825718; 0171-222 2723 (during exhibitions)

Membership is by selection and standard of work over a period of years (ARMS associate, RMS full member). Annual Open Exhibition in November in London, hand-in Sept/Oct; schedules available in July (send sae). Applications and enquiries to the Executive Secretary. Founded 1895.

Miniaturists, British Society of
Director Leslie Simpson FRSA, Ralston House, 41 Lister Street, Riverside Gardens, Ilkley, West Yorkshire LS29 9ET
tel (01943) 609075

'The world's oldest miniature society.' Holds 2 open exhibitions p.a. Membership by selection. Founded 1895.

Miniaturists, The Hilliard Society of
The Executive Officer Mrs S.M. Burton, 15 Union Street, Wells, Somerset BA5 2PU
tel (01749) 674472 *fax* (01749) 672918
President Com. G.W.G. Hunt, RMS, HS, MASF, RN

International society with approx. 300 members. Founded to increase knowledge and promote the art of miniature painting. Annual Exhibition held in May/June at Wells; seminars; Young People's Awards (11-19 years). Encourages Patron membership to keep collectors in touch with artists. Informative Newsletter includes technical section and news from miniature societies around the world. Membership: from £20. Founded 1982.

William Morris Society
Kelmscott House, 26 Upper Mall, London W6 9TA
tel 0181-741 3735
Secretary Derek Baker

To spread knowledge of the life, work and ideas of William Morris; publishes *Newsletter* (quarterly) and *Journal* (2 p.a.). Library and collections open to the public Thu and Sat, 2-5pm. Founded 1955.

Motoring Artists, The Guild of
Administrator David Purvis, 71 Brook Court, Watling Street, Radlett, Herts. WD7 7JA
tel (01923) 853803

To promote, publicise and develop motoring fine art; to build a recognised group of artists interested in motoring art, holding events and exchanging ideas and support; to hold motoring art exhibitions. Annual membership: £27.50, associate £22.50, friend £18. Founded 1986.

Motoring Writers, The Guild of
Contact General Secretary, 30 The Cravens, Smallfield, Surrey RH6 9QS
tel (01342) 843294 *fax* (01342) 844093

To raise the standard of motoring journalism. For writers, broadcasters, photographers on matters of motoring, but who are not connected with the motor industry.

Music Publishers Association Ltd
3rd Floor, Strandgate, 18-20 York Buildings, London WC2N 6JU
tel 0171-839 7779 *fax* 0171-839 7776
e-mail mpa@mcps.co.uk
Chief Executive Sarah Faulder, *Executive Adviser* Peter Dadswell

The only trade organisation representing the UK music publishing industry; protects and promotes its members' interests in copyright, trade and related matters. A number of sub-committees and groups deal with particular interests. Details of subscriptions available on written request. Founded 1881.

Musical Association, The Royal
Contact Dr Jonathan Stock, Music School, Palace Green, Durham DH1 3RL
fax 0191-374 3219
e-mail j.p.j.stock@durham.ac.uk

Musicians, Incorporated Society of
10 Stratford Place, London W1N 9AE
tel 0171-629 4413 *fax* 0171-408 1538
President 1997-8: Prof George Pratt, *Chief Executive* Neil Hoyle

Professional body for musicians. Aims to promote the art of music; protect the interests and raise the standards of the musical profession; provide services,

support and advice for its members. Publishes *Music Journal* (12 p.a.); Yearbook and 3 Registers of Specialists annually. Annual subscription: £85.

Musicians, The Worshipful Company of
1st Floor, 74-75 Watling Street, London EC4M 9BL
tel 0171-489 8888 *fax* 0171-489 1614
Clerk S.F.N. Waley
Founded 1500.

Name Studies in Britain and Ireland, Society for
Hon. Secretary Miss Jennifer Scherr, c/o Queen's Building Library, University of Bristol, University Walk, Bristol BS8 1TR
Membership Secretary Dr M. Higham, 22 Peel Park Avenue, Clitheroe, Lancs. BB7 1ET

Aims to advance, promote and support research into the place-names and personal names of Britain and Ireland and related regions by the collection, documentation and interpretation of such names; the publication of the material and the results of such research; the exchange of information between the various regions. Acts as a consultative body on Name Studies; holds annual conferences; publishes an annual journal, *Nomina*, and an occasional newsletter. Annual subscription: £15.

National Campaign for the Arts (NCA)
Francis House, Francis Street, London SW1P 1DE
tel 0171-828 4448 *fax* 0171-931 9959
e-mail nca@ecna.org
web site http://www.ecna.org/nca/
Secretary Laverne Layland

Aims to be a strong advocate for all art forms on the national stage; to fight government funding cuts; to seek recognition for the value of the arts in a civilised society; to represent the diverse views and wishes of its members. Membership: £19.50; unwaged £13.50; special rates for organisations. Founded 1985.

The National Small Press Centre
BM BOZO, London WC1N 3XX
Director John Nicholson, *Press Officer* Cecilia Doggis, *Liaison Officer* John Dench, *Treasurer* Andy Hopton

Provides a focus for small presses and independent self-publishers and actively promotes them by collecting and disseminating information in the form of exhibitions, talks, courses, workshops, confer-

ences and fairs. Publishes *News from the Centre* (bi-monthly) and *Small Press Listings* (quarterly) – joint subscription: £12 p.a.; *Handbook* £12 plus £1.50 p&p.

Small Press Fairs are held annually in the Royal Festival Hall, London. The Centre is twinned with the Mainz Mini-Press Archive in Mainz, Germany and the New York Small Press Center. Founded 1992.

National Union of Journalists

Head Office Acorn House, 314-320 Gray's Inn Road, London WC1X 8DP
tel 0171-278 7916 *fax* 0171-837 8143
e-mail nuj@mcr1.poptel.org.uk

Trade union for working journalists with 28,000 members and 147 branches throughout the UK and the Republic of Ireland, and in Paris, Brussels, Geneva and the Netherlands. It covers the newspaper press, news agencies and broadcasting, the major part of periodical and book publishing, and a number of public relations departments and consultancies, information services and Prestel-Viewdata services. Administers disputes, unemployment, benevolent and provident benefits. Official publications: *The Journalist, Freelance Directory, Freelance Fees Guide* and policy pamphlets.

The Edith Nesbit Society

73 Brookehowse Road, London SE6 3TH
tel 0181-698 8907

Aims to promote an interest in the life and works of Edith Nesbit (1858-1924) by means of talks, a regular newsletter and and other publications, and visits to relevant places. Annual membership: £5; organisations/overseas £10. Founded 1996.

New Science Fiction Alliance (NSFA)

Chris Reed, BBR, PO Box 625, Sheffield S1 3GY
web site http://www.syspace.co.uk/bbr/nsfa-cat.html
Publicity Officer Chris Reed

The NSFA is committed to supporting the work of new writers and artists by promoting independent and small press publications worldwide. It was founded by a group of independent publishers to give writers the opportunity to explore the small press and find the right market for their material. It offers a mail order service for magazines. Founded 1989.

New Zealand, Book Publishers Association of, Inc.

Box 36477, Northcote, Auckland, New Zealand
tel (09) 480-2711 *fax* (09) 480-1130
President Wendy Harrex

New Zealand Copyright Council Inc.

PO Box 5028, Wellington, New Zealand
tel (04) 472-4430 *fax* (04) 471-0765
Chairman Bernard Darby, *Secretary* Tony Chance

Newspaper Press Fund

Dickens House, 35 Wathen Road, Dorking, Surrey RH4 1JY
tel (01306) 887511 *fax* (01306) 876104
Secretary P.W. Evans

For the relief of hardship amongst member journalists, their widows and dependants. Financial assistance and retirement housing are provided. Limited help is available for non-member journalists and their dependants.

The Newspaper Publishers Association Ltd

34 Southwark Bridge Road, London SE1 9EU
tel 0171-928 6928 *fax* 0171-928 2067

Newspaper Society

Bloomsbury House, 74-77 Great Russell Street, London WC1B 3DA
tel 0171-636 7014 *fax* 0171-631 5119
ᴀᴜᴅᴜᴏ ᴅᴀᴊᴇ.ᴏᴜ ᴜᴀᴀᴍᴀᴏᴜᴜʏ
e-mail ns@newspapersoc.org.uk
Director David Newell

Oil Painters, Royal Institute of

17 Carlton House Terrace, London SW1Y 5BD
tel 0171-930 6844 *fax* 0171-839 7830
President Frederick Beckett Hon. RI

Promotes and encourages the art of painting in oils. Open Annual Exhibition at the Mall Galleries, London.

Oils, Pastels and Acrylics, British Society of Painters in

Ralston House, 41 Lister Street, Riverside Gardens, Ilkley, West Yorkshire LS29 9ET
tel (01943) 609075
Director Leslie Simpson FRSA

Promotes interest and encourages high quality in the work of painters in these media. Holds 2 open exhibitions per annum. Membership by selection. Founded 1988.

The Orton Society

21 Brockenhurst Road, Croydon, Surrey CR0 7DR
President Sue Townsend, *Chairman* Bill Kelly

Aims to promote the life and work of Joe Orton and to draw him to the attention of future generations. Membership: £5.00 p.a. Founded 1994.

Outdoor Writers' Guild
Secretary Terry Marsh, PO Box 520, Bamber Bridge, Preston, Lancs. PR5 8LF
tel/fax (01772) 696732
e-mail 101551.2323@compuserve.com
web site http://ourworld.compuserve.com/homepages/owg
Aims to promote and maintain a high professional standard among writers and photographers who specialise in outdoor activities; represents members' interests to representative bodies in the outdoor leisure industry; circulates members with news of media opportunities; provides a forum for members to meet colleagues and others in the outdoor leisure industry. Presents annual literary and photographic awards. Annual membership: £35 plus £20 joining fee. Founded 1980.

Wilfred Owen Association
17 Belmont, Shrewsbury SY1 1TE
tel/fax (01743) 235904
To commemorate the life and work of Wilfred Owen, and to encourage and enhance appreciation of his work through visits, public events and a newsletter. Annual subscription: £4 (£6 overseas), groups/institutions £10, senior citizens/students/unemployed £2. Founded 1989.

PACT (Producers Alliance for Cinema and Television)
45 Mortimer Street, London W1N 7TD
tel 0171-331 6000 *fax* 0171-331 6700
Chief Executive John Woodward
Membership Officer David Alan Mills
PACT serves the feature film and independent TV production sector and is the UK contact point for co-production, co-finance partners and distributors.

Painter-Printmakers, Royal Society of
Bankside Gallery, 48 Hopton Street, London SE1 9JH
tel 0171-928 7521
President Prof David L. Carpanini Hon. RWS, RBA, RWA, NEAC
Membership (RE) open to British and overseas artists. An election of Associates is held annually, and applica-

tions for the necesssary forms and particulars should be addressed to the Secretary. The Society organises workshops and lectures on original printmaking; holds one members' exhibition per year. Friends of the RE open to all those interested in artists' original printmaking. Founded 1880.

Painters, Sculptors and Printmakers, National Society of
President Denis Baxter PNS, UA, FRSA
Hon. Secretary Gwen Spencer, 122 Copse Hill, London SW20 0NL
tel 0181-946 7878
An annual exhibition in London representing all aspects of art for artists of every creed and outlook. Newsletter (2 p.a.) for members. Founded 1930

The Pastel Society
17 Carlton House Terrace, London SW1Y 5BD
tel 0171-930 6844 *fax* 0171-839 7830
President Thomas Coates
Pastel and drawings in pencil or chalk. Annual Exhibition open to all artists working in dry media held at the Mall Galleries, London. Members elected from approved candidates' list. Founded 1899.

The Mervyn Peake Society
Hon. President Sebastian Peake, *Chairman* Brian Sibley
Secretary Frank Surry, 2 Mount Park Road, London W5 2RP
Devoted to recording the life and works of Mervyn Peake; publishes a journal and newsletter. Annual subscription: £12 (UK and Europe), £10 (students), £14 (all other countries). Founded 1975.

PEN, International
International President Ronald Harwood
International Secretary Alexandre Blokh, 9-10 Charterhouse Buildings, Goswell Road, London EC1M 7AT
tel 0171-253 4308 *fax* 0171-253 5711

English PEN Centre
President Josephine Pullein-Thompson MBE
General Secretary Gillian Vincent, 7 Dilke Street, London SW3 4JE
tel 0171-352 6303 *fax* 0171-351 0220

Scottish PEN Centre
President Paul H. Scott
Secretary Laura Fiorentini, 33 Drumsheugh Gardens, Edinburgh EH3 7RN
tel 0131-225 1038

Welsh PEN Centre
President Ned Thomas, University of Wales
Press, Gwynneth Street, Cathays,
Cardiff CF2 4YD
tel (01222) 231919

A world association of writers. PEN was
founded in 1921 by C.A. Dawson Scott
under the presidency of John
Galsworthy, to promote friendship and
understanding between writers and to
defend freedom of expression within and
between all nations. The initials PEN
stand for Poets, Playwrights, Editors,
Essayists, Novelists – but membership is
open to all writers of standing (including
translators), whether men or women,
without distinction of creed or race, who
subscribe to these fundamental principles. PEN takes no part in state or party
politics. The International PEN Writers
in Prison Committee works on behalf of
writers imprisoned for exercising their
right to freedom of expression, a right
implicit in the PEN Charter to which all
members subscribe. The International
PEN Translations and Linguistic Rights
Committee strives to promote the translations of works by writers in the lesser-
known languages and to defend those
languages. The Writers for Peace
Committee exists to find ways in which
writers can work for peaceful co-exis-
tence in the world. The Women Writers'
Committee works to promote women's
writing and publishing in developing
countries. International Congresses are
held most years. The 62nd Congress was
held in Fremantle, Western Australia in
October 1995; the 63rd Congress will be
held in Guadalajara, Mexico in
November 1996.

Membership of any one Centre
implies membership of all Centres; at
present 126 autonomous Centres exist
throughout the world. Membership of
the English Centre is £30 p.a. for country and overseas members, £35 for
London members. Associate membership is available for writers not yet eligible for full membership and for persons connected with literature. The
English Centre has a programme of literary lectures, discussion, dinners and
parties. A yearly Writers' Day is open to
the public as are some literary lectures.

Please apply to the Scottish and Welsh
Centres for information about their membership fees and activities.

The Penman Club
Secretary Mark Sorrell, 185 Daws Heath Road,
Benfleet, Essex SS7 2TF
tel (01702) 557431

Writers' society offering criticism of
members' work and general advice. Send
sae for prospectus. Annual membership:
£15 for first year, £8.25 thereafter.
Founded 1950.

Performing Right Society Ltd
29-33 Berners Street, London W1P 4AA
tel 0171-580 5544 *fax* 0171-306 4050
Contact Corporate Communications

An association of composers, authors
and publishers of copyright musical
works, established in 1914, to grant
licences and collect royalties for the public performance, broadcasting and diffusion by cable of such works; also to
restrain unauthorised use thereof. The
Society is affiliated to the national societies of more than 30 other countries. All
composers of musical works and authors
of lyrics or poems which have been set
to music are eligible for membership. An
initial admission fee only is payable.
Founded 1914.

Periodical Publishers Association
Queens House, 28 Kingsway,
London WC2B 6UN
tel 0171-404 4166 *fax* 0171-404 4167
e-mail info1@ppa.co.uk
web site http://www.ppa.co.uk
Chief Executive Ian Locks

The Personal Managers' Association Ltd
Liaison Secretary Angela Adler, 1 Summer Road,
East Molesey, Surrey KT8 9LX
tel/fax 0181-398 9796

Association of theatrical agents in the
theatre, film and entertainment world
generally.

Photographers, The Association of
Co-Secretary Gwen Thomas, 9-10 Domingo
Street, London EC1Y 0TA
tel 0171-608 1441 *fax* 0171-253 3007

To protect and promote the interests of
fashion advertising and editorial photographers. Annual subscription: £72-£355,
depending on turnover. Founded 1969.

Photographers Association, Master
Hallmark House, 2 Beaumont Street, Darlington,
Co. Durham DL1 5SZ
tel (01325) 356555 *fax* (01325) 357813
e-mail generalenquiries@mpauk.demon.co.uk
To promote and protect professional photographers. Members qualify for awards of Licentiate, Associate and Fellowship. Annual subscription: £87.00.

Photographic Society, The Royal
The Octagon, Milsom Street, Bath BA1 1DN
tel (01225) 462841 *fax* (01225) 448688
e-mail info@rpsbath.demon.co.uk
web site http://www.rps.org
Aims to promote the general advancement of photography and its applications; publishes *The Photographic Journal* (monthly), £75 p.a., overseas £67 p.a. and *The Journal of Photographic Science* (bi-monthly), £94 p.a., overseas £104. Founded 1853.

Photography, British Institute of Professional
Amwell End, Ware, Herts. SG12 9HN
tel (01920) 464011
To represent all who practise photography as a profession in any field; to improve the quality of photography; establish recognised examination qualifications and a high standard of conduct; to safeguard the interests of the public and the profession. Admission can be obtained either via examinations, or by submission of work and other information to the appropriate examining board. Fellows, Associates and Licentiates are entitled to the designation Incorporated Photographer or Incorporated Photographic Technician. Organises numerous meetings and conferences in various parts of the country throughout the year; publishes *The Photographer* journal (monthly), and an annual Register of Members and *Guide to Buyers of Photography*, plus various pamphlets and leaflets on professional photography. Founded 1901, incorporated 1921.

Picture Libraries and Agencies, British Association of – see BAPLA

The Picture Research Association
(formerly SPREd)
455 Finchley Road, London NW3 6HN
tel 0171-431 9886 *fax* 0171-431 9887
Generel Secretary Emma Krikler

Professional organisation of picture researchers and picture editors. See page 435.

Player-Playwrights
Secretary Peter Thompson, 9 Hillfield Park, London N10 3QT
tel 0181-883 0371
Meets on Monday evenings at St Augustine's Church Hall, Queen's Gate, London SW1. The society reads, performs and discusses plays and scripts submitted by members, with a view to assisting the writers in improving and marketing their work. Newcomers and new acting members are always welcome. Annual membership: £7.50 (and £1 per attendance). Founded 1948.

Playwrights Trust, New
Interchange Studios, Dalby Street, London NW5 3NQ
tel 0171-284 2818 *fax* 0171-482 5292
e-mail npt@easynet.co.uk
Executive Director Jonathan Meth, *Information & Research Officer* Angela Kelly
Research and development organisation for playwrights and aspiring playwrights, and those interested in developing and producing new work. Services include scriptreading; information guides; writer/company Link Service; 6-weekly *Newsletter*. Subscription: rates on application.

Poetry Book Society
Book House, 45 East Hill, London SW18 2QZ
tel 0181-870 8403 *fax* 0181-877 1615
Chairman Martyn Goff, *Director* Clare Brown
Foremost in getting books of new poetry to readers through quarterly selections, special offers, and 300-strong backlist which it sells at favourable rates to members. Publishes *Bulletin* (quarterly) and holds quarterly readings at the Royal Festival Hall. Runs the annual T.S. Eliot Prize for the best collection of new poetry. Operates as a charitable Book Club with annual membership (£10, £30, £120) open to all.

Poetry Foundation, National
27 Mill Road, Fareham, Hants PO16 0TH
tel (01329) 822218
Aims to provide a truly national poetry organisation which in turn provides free advice on publishing, information and a magazine, all for a single low-cost fee, and to help poets have a book of their own poetry published at no additional

cost, once they have sufficient poetry of a high enough standard. The Foundation also gives grants to deserving causes directly related to poetry and gives free advice on problems relating to book publication. Founded 1981.

The Poetry Society

22 Betterton Street, London WC2H 9BU
tel 0171-240 4810 *fax* 0171-240 4818
Chairman Mary Enright, *Director* Chris Meade

National membership body, open to all, to help poets and poetry thrive in Britain today. Publishes *Poetry Review* (quarterly) and *Poetry News* (quarterly), has an information and imagination service, runs promotions and educational projects, helps co-ordinate National Poetry Day, and administers the annual National Poetry Competition and the biennial European Poetry Translation Prize. Founded 1909.

The Polidori Society

Contact The Secretary, Ebenezer House, 31 Ebenezer Street, Langley Mill, Notts. NG16 4DA
tel 0181-994 5902 *fax* 0181-995 3275
President Franklin Bishop

To promote appreciation of the life and works of John William Polidori MD (1795–1821), romantic poet, novelist, diarist, traveller, philosopher, essayist and tragedian. Author of the seminal *The Vampyre – A tale* (1819), thereby introducing into English literature the icon of the vampyre portrayed as an aristocrat and seducer. Polidori was an intimate of the leading figures of the Romantic Movement in the early 19th century, including Byron, Percy and Mary Shelley. The Society celebrates the life of Polidori by way of an annual grand dinner and members receive newsletters, book offers and the opportunity to attend social events. International membership. Membership: contact the Secretary. Founded 1990.

Portrait Painters, Royal Society of

17 Carlton House Terrace, London SW1Y 5BD
tel 0171-930 6844 *fax* 0171-839 7830
President Daphne Todd

Annual Exhibition at the Mall Galleries, London, when work may be submitted by non-members with a view to exhibition. Founded 1891.

Portuguese Association of Publishers and Booksellers

(Associação Portuguesa de Editores e Livreiros)
Av. Estados Unidos da América, 97-6° Esq., Lisboa 1700, Portugal (1)
tel 8489136 *fax* (1) 8489377

Beatrix Potter Society

Chairman Judy Taylor
Secretary Marian Werner, 32 Etchingham Park Road, London N3 2DT

Promotes the study and appreciation of the life and works of Beatrix Potter as author, artist, diarist, farmer and conservationist. Annual subscription: UK £10, overseas US$25/Can$30/Aus$30. Founded 1980.

Press Agencies, National Association of

The Administrator, 41 Lansdowne Crescent, Leamington Spa, Warks. CV32 4PR
tel (01926) 424181 *fax* (01926) 424760

Trade association representing the interests of the leading national news and photographic agencies. Annual subscription: £250. Founded 1983.

The Press Complaints Commission

Chairman The Rt Hon Lord Wakeham
Director Guy Black, 1 Salisbury Square, London EC4Y 8AE
tel 0171-353 1248 *Helpline tel* 0171-353 3733
fax 0171-353 8355

Independent body founded to oversee self-regulation of the Press. Deals with complaints by the public about the contents and conduct of British newspapers and magazines and advises editors on journalistic ethics. Complaints must be about the failure of newspapers or magazines to follow the letter or spirit of a Code of Practice, drafted by newspaper and magazine editors, adopted by the industry and supervised by the Commission. Founded 1991.

Printmakers Council

Clerkenwell Workshops, 31 Clerkenwell Close, London EC1R 0AT
tel 0171-250 1927 *fax* 0171-608 3848
President Stanley Jones, *Chair* Sheila Sloss

Artist-led group which aims 'to promote the use of both traditional and innovative printmaking techniques by:
• holding exhibitions of prints;
• providing information on prints and printmaking to both its membership and the public;

• encouraging co-operation and exchanges between members, other associations and interested individuals.' Annual membership: £45; students £22.50. Founded 1965.

Private Libraries Association

Ravelston, South View Road, Pinner, Middlesex HA5 3YD
President Robin de Beaumont, *Hon. Editors* David Chambers and Paul W. Nash, *Hon. Secretary* Frank Broomhead

International society of book collectors and private libraries. Publications include *Private Library* (quarterly), annual *Private Press Books*, and other books on book collecting. Annual subscription: £25. Founded 1956.

The Producers Association – see PACT

Public Art Commissions Agency

Studio 6, Victoria Works, Vittoria Street, Birmingham B1 3PE
tel 0121-212 4454 *fax* 0121-212 4426
Director Vivien Lovell, *Administrators* Maureen Gaynor, Caron Wright

A charity and non-profit consultancy for public art commissions throughout the UK and Europe. Advice is given to developers, government departments, local authorities, transport and health authorities, private sector clients, artists, architects, landscape architects, etc. Holds lectures and workshops, and has a commissioning service. Founded 1987.

The Publishers Association

1 Kingsway, London WC2B 6XF
tel 0171-565 7474 *fax* 0171-836 4543
e-mail mail@publishers.org.uk
Chief Executive Clive Bradley, *Director of International and Trade Divisions (BDC)* Ian Taylor, *Director of Educational and Academic and Professional Publishing* John Davies
Founded 1896.

Publishers Association, International

3 avenue de Miremont, CH-1206 Geneva, Switzerland
tel (022) 346-30-18 *fax* (022) 347-57-17
e-mail secretariat@ipa-uie.org
President Alain Gründ, *Secretary-General* J. Alexis Koutchoumow
Founded 1896.

Publishers Guild, Independent

25 Cambridge Road, Hampton, Middlesex TW12 2JL
tel 0181-979 0250 *fax* 0181-979 6393

Full membership is open to new and established publishers and book packagers; supplier membership is available to specialists in fields allied to publishing (but not printers and binders). The Guild offers a forum for the exchange of ideas and information and represents the interests of its members. Annual membership: £75 (plus VAT). Founded 1962.

Publishers Licensing Society Limited

5 Dryden Street, London WC2E 9NW
tel 0171-829 8486 *fax* 0171-829 8488
Chairman Maurice Long, *Manager* Caroline Elmslie

Aims to exercise and enforce on behalf of publishers the rights of copyright and other rights of a similar nature; to authorise the granting of licences for the making of reprographic copies of copyright works; and to receive and distribute to publisher copyright owners the sums received from licensed use. PLS intends to increase the range and repertoire of those mandated publishers including, specifically, seeking their authorisation for electro-storage of information and digital copying. Founded 1981.

Publishers Publicity Circle

Secretary Christina Thomas, 48 Crabtree Lane, London SW6 6LW
tel/fax 0171-385 3708

Enables all book publicists to meet and share information regularly. Monthly meetings provide a forum for press journalists, TV and radio researchers and producers to meet publicists collectively. In conjunction with *Publishing News*, awards are presented for the best PR campaigns. Monthly newsletter includes recruitment advertising. Founded 1955.

Puzzle Writers, International Association of

Secretary Dr Jeremy Sims, 42 Brigstocke Terrace, Ryde, Isle of Wight PO33 2PD
tel (01983) 811688

Aims to bring puzzle writers and games designers worldwide, both amateur and professional, closer together and to provide support and information. Promotes the art of puzzle writing and games design to publishers, games manufacturers and the general public. Membership is free but send 6 stamps or IRCs to cover postage of bi-monthly newsletter. Founded 1996.

The Radclyffe International Philosophical Association

BM-RIPhA, Old Gloucester Street, London WC1N 3XX
President William Mann FRIPhA, *Secretary General* John Khasseyan FRIPhA

Aims to dignify those achievements which might otherwise escape formal recognition; to promote the interests and talent of its members; to encourage their good fellowship; and to form a medium for the exchange of ideas between members. Annual subscription: £25.00 (Fellows, Members and Associates). Published authors and artists usually enter at Fellowship level. Founded 1955.

RADIO

(formerly Independent Association of Radio Producers – IARP)
PO Box 14880, London NW1 9ZD
tel 0171-485 0873 *fax* 0171-428 0541
Chair Ian Willox

The trade association for independent producers in radio and audio. Annual membership: student £30, full £50. Founded 1993.

The Radio Academy

PO Box 4SZ, London W1A 4SZ
tel 0171-255 2010 *fax* 0171-255 2029
e-mail info@radacad.demon.co.uk
Director John Bradford

The Radio Academy is the professional association for those engaged in the UK radio industry with over 1200 individual members and 30 corporate patrons. It organises conferences, seminars, debates, the annual UK Radio Festival and social events for members; publishes newsletter *Off Air* (monthly), and an annual *Yearbook*. The Academy also has a number of Collegiate members and offers some practical training opportunities for students of radio.

Railway Artists, Guild of

Chief Executive Officer F.P. Hodges, 45 Dickins Road, Warwick CV34 5NS
tel (01926) 499246

Aims to forge a link between artists depicting railway subjects and to give members a corporate identity; also stages railway art exhibitions and members' meetings. Founded 1979.

Regional Arts Boards (RABs)

web site http://www.poptel.org.uk/arts

Following a process of restructuring in 1990/91, a network of 10 Regional Arts Boards now covers England. The RABs are autonomous, strategic bodies which work in partnership with local authorities and a wide variety of other sectors and organisations and are policy led. Legally, they are limited companies with charitable status. They are concerned with all the arts and crafts – visual, performing, media, published – and work at regional level as partners of the 3 national agencies which provide most of their funds: the Arts Council, the British Film Institute, the Crafts Council.

The Arts Council retains the national responsibility for funding and assessing the 'national companies', the symphony orchestras and a handful of other high profile clients. The building-based drama companies are mostly funded by the RABs. The overall planning system is becoming more 'integrated' with the principle of subsidiarity being increasingly applied to project and development work. The resources available to the RABs during 1997/98 total over £60 million.

The Welsh Regional Arts Associations have been integrated with the Arts Council of Wales (see page 440). There are no regional arts boards in Scotland and all enquiries should be addressed to the Scottish Arts Council (see page 473).

English Regional Arts Boards

5 City Road, Winchester, Hants SO23 8SD
tel (01962) 851063 *fax* (01962) 842033
e-mail info.erab@artsfb.org.uk
Chief Executive Christopher Gordon, *Assistant* Carolyn Nixson

The representative body for the 10 Regional Arts Boards in England. Its secretariat provides project management, services and information for the members and acts on their behalf in appropriate circumstances.

Eastern Arts Board

Cherry Hinton Hall, Cherry Hinton Road, Cambridge CB1 4DW
tel (01223) 215355 *fax* (01223) 248075
Chief Executive Lou Stein, *Literature Officer* Emma Drew, *Visual Arts Officer* Niki Braithwaite

Bedfordshire, Cambridgeshire, Essex, Hertfordshire, Lincolnshire, Norfolk and Suffolk. Founded 1971.

East Midlands Arts Board
Mountfields House, Epinal Way, Loughborough, Leics. LE11 0QE
tel (01509) 218292 *fax* (01509) 262214
Chief Executive John Buston, *Literature Officer* Sue Stewart, *Visual Arts Officer* Janet Currie

Derbyshire (excluding High Peak District), Leicestershire, Northamptonshire and Nottinghamshire. Founded 1969.

London Arts Board
Elme House, 133 Long Acre,
London WC2E 9AF
Helpline 0171-249 7690
tel 0171-240 1313 *fax* 0171-240 4580
Principal Literature Officer John Hampson, *Principal Visual Arts and Crafts Officer* Holly Tebbutt

The area of the 32 London Boroughs and the City of London. Founded 1991.

North West Arts Board
Manchester House, 22 Bridge Street,
Manchester M3 3AB
tel 0161-834 6644 *fax* 0161-834 6969
Chief Executive Sue Harrison, *Director Visual Arts & Media* Aileen McEvoy, *Media Officer, Literature* Bronwen Williams

Greater Manchester, Merseyside, High Peak District of Derbyshire, Lancashire and Cheshire. Founded 1966.

Northern Arts
9-10 Osborne Terrace,
Newcastle upon Tyne NE2 1NZ
tel 0191-281 6334 *fax* 0191-281 3276
Chief Executive Andrew Dixon, *Head of Published and Broadcast Arts* Catriona Ferguson, *Visual Arts Officer* James Bustard

Cleveland, Cumbria, Durham, Northumberland, Metropolitan Districts of Newcastle, Gateshead, Sunderland and Tyneside. Founded 1961.

South East Arts Board
10 Mount Ephraim, Tunbridge Wells,
Kent TN4 8AS
tel (01892) 515210 *Information Dept. ext.* 205/206 *fax* (01892) 549383

Chief Executive Felicity Harvest, *Literature Officer* Anne Downes (*ext.* 210/211), *Visual Arts Officer* Jim Shea (*ext.* 213)

Kent, Surrey, East Sussex and West Sussex. Information and publications list available. Founded 1973.

South West Arts
Bradninch Place, Gandy Street, Exeter,
Devon EX4 3LS
tel (01392) 218188 *fax* (01392) 413554
Chief Executive Graham Long, *Director, Visual Arts & Crafts* Mrs Val Millington, *Director, Media & Published Arts* David Drake

Bath and North-East Somerset, Cornwall, Devon, Dorset (except Districts of Bournemouth, Christchurch and Poole), Gloucestershire, Somerset. Founded 1956.

Southern Arts Board
13 St Clement Street, Winchester,
Hants SO23 9DQ
tel (01962) 855099 *fax* (01962) 861186
Chief Executive Robert Hutchison, *Literature Officer* Keiran Phelan, *Visual Arts Officer* Philip Smith

Berkshire, Buckinghamshire, Hampshire, Isle of Wight, Oxfordshire, Wiltshire and South East Dorset. Founded 1968.

West Midlands Arts Board
82 Granville Street, Birmingham B1 2LH
tel 0121-631 3121 *fax* 0121-643 7239
Chief Executive Sally Luton, *Director, Visual Arts, Crafts & Media* Caroline Foxhall

County of Hereford and Worcester, Shropshire, Staffordshire, Warwickshire and the Metropolitan West Midlands. Founded 1971.

Yorkshire and Humberside Arts
21 Bond Street, Dewsbury,
West Yorkshire WF13 1AX
tel (01924) 455555 *fax* (01924) 466522
Chief Executive Roger Lancaster, *Literature Officer* Steve Dearden

Barnsley, Bradford, Calderdale, Doncaster, Kirklees, Leeds, Rotherham, Sheffield, Wakefield and North, South, and East Yorkshire. Funds schemes and projects for the promotion of contemporary literature and writing activities. Provides grants for festivals, events, courses, residencies, publishing. Offers advice and information on various aspects of literature. Preliminary enquiry advised. Founded 1991.

Ridley Art Society
37 James Street, Hounslow, Middlesex TW3 1SP
tel 0181-570 6419
President Carel Weight CH, CBE, RA, *Chairman* Ernie Donagh
Represents a wide variety of attitudes towards the making of art. In recent years

has sought to encourage young artists. At least one central London exhibition annually. Founded 1889.

The Romantic Novelists' Association

Chairman Angela Arney, 43 Wilton Gardens, Shirley, Southampton SO1 2QS

To raise the prestige of Romantic Authorship. Open to romantic and historical novelists. See also under Literary Awards.

Royal Academy of Arts

Piccadilly, London W1V 0DS
tel 0171-439 7438 *fax* 0171-434 0837
President Sir Philip Dowson CBE, *Keeper* Leonard McComb RA, *Treasurer* Michael Kenny RA, *Secretary* David Gordon

Academicians (RA) are elected from the most distinguished artists in the UK. Major loan exhibitions throughout the year with the Annual Summer Exhibition, June to August. Also runs art schools for 60 post-graduate students in painting and sculpture.

The Royal Literary Fund

144 Temple Chambers, Temple Avenue, London EC4Y 0DA
tel 0171-353 7150
President His Honour Sir Stephen Tumim, *Secretary* Fiona Clark

Founded in 1790, the Fund is the oldest and largest charity serving literature, set up to help writers and their families who face hardship. It does not offer grants to writers who can earn their living in other ways, nor does it provide financial support for writing projects. But it sustains authors who have for one reason or another fallen on hard times – illness, family misfortune, or sheer loss of writing form. Applicants must have published work of approved literary merit, which may include important contributions to periodicals. The literary claim of every new applicant must be accepted by the General Committee before the question of need can be considered.

The Royal Society

6 Carlton House Terrace, London SW1Y 5AG
tel 0171-839 5561 *fax* 0171-930 2170
President Sir Aaron Klug OM, PRS, *Treasurer* Sir John H. Horlock FRS, F.Eng, *Biological Secretary* Prof P. Lachmann FRS, *Physical Secretary* Prof J.S. Rowlinson FRS, F.Eng, *Foreign Secretary* Prof B. Heap CBE, FRS, *Executive Secretary* Mrs S. Cox

Promotion of the natural sciences (pure and applied). Founded 1660.

The Ruskin Society of London

Hon. Secretary Miss O.E. Forbes-Madden, 351 Woodstock Road, Oxford OX2 7NX
tel (01865) 310987

To promote literary and biographical interest in John Ruskin and his contemporaries. The Society issues an annual *Ruskin Gazette* free to members. Annual subscription: £10. Founded 1985.

The Dorothy L. Sayers Society

Chairman Christopher J. Dean, Rose Cottage, Malthouse Lane, Hurstpierpoint, West Sussex BN6 9JY
tel (01273) 833444 *fax* (01273) 835988
Secretaries Lenelle Davis, Jasmine Simeone

To promote and encourage the study of the works of Dorothy L. Sayers; to collect relics and reminiscences about her and make them available to students and biographers; to hold an annual seminar and other meetings; to publish proceedings, pamphlets and a bi-monthly bulletin. Annual subscription: £10. Founded 1976.

Science Fiction Association Ltd, The British

President Arthur C. Clarke
Membership Secretary Paul Billinger, 1 Long Row Close, Everdon, Daventry, Northants. NN11 3BE
e-mail billinger@enterprise.net

For authors, publishers, booksellers and readers of science fiction, fantasy and allied genres. Publishes *Matrix*, an informal magazine of news and information; *Focus*, an amateur writers' magazine; *Vector*, a critical magazine and The Orbiter Service, a network of postal writers workshops. Founded 1958.

Science Writers, Association of British

c/o British Association for the Advancement of Science, 23 Savile Row, London W1X 2NB
tel 0171-439 1205 *fax* 0171 973 3051
e-mail absw@absw-demon.co.uk
Chairman Richard Stevenson, *Administrator* Barbara Drillsma

Association of science writers, editors, and radio, film and TV producers concerned with the presentation and communication of science, technology and medicine. Aims to improve the standard of science writing and to assist its members in their work.

Scientific and Technical Communicators, The Institute of

Kings Court, 2-16 Goodge Street,
London W1P 1FF
tel 0171-436 4425 *fax* 0171-580 0747
President Gerry Gentle, *Executive Secretary* Carol Battson

Professional body for those engaged in the communication of scientific and technical information. Aims to establish and maintain professional standards, to encourage and co-operate in professional training and to provide a source of information on, and to encourage research and development in, all aspects of scientific and technical communication. Publishes *The Communicator* (4 p.a.), the official journal of the Institute. Founded 1972.

Scottish Academy, Royal

The Mound, Edinburgh EH2 2EL
tel 0131-225 6671 *fax* 0131-225 2349
President William J.L. Baillie PRSA, *Secretary* Ian McKenzie Smith RSA, *Treasurer* James Morris RSA

Academicians (RSA) and Associates (ARSA) and non-members may exhibit in the Annual Exhibition of Painting, Sculpture and Architecture, held approximately mid April to July; Festival Exhibition August/September. Other artists' societies' annual exhibitions, normally between October and January. Royal Scottish Academy Student Competition held in March. Founded 1826.

Scottish Arts

24 Rutland Square, Edinburgh EH1 2BW
tel 0131-229 1076
Hon. Secretary Colin J.M. Sutherland
tel 0131-229 8157

Art, literature, music. Annual subscription: £275 (full); reductions available.

Scottish Arts Council

12 Manor Place, Edinburgh EH3 7DD
tel 0131-226 6051
Chairman Magnus Linklater, *Director* Seona Reid, *Literature Director* Jenny Brown, *Visual Arts Director* tba

Principal channel for government funding of the arts in Scotland, the Scottish Arts Council is funded by the Scottish Office. It aims to develop and improve the knowledge, understanding and practice of the arts, and to increase their accessibility throughout Scotland. It offers about 1300 grants a year to artists and arts organisations concerned with the visual arts, drama, dance and mime, literature, music, festivals, and traditional, ethnic and community arts. It is also the distributor of National Lottery funds to the arts in Scotland.

Scottish Book Marketing Group

Scottish Book Centre, 137 Dundee Street, Edinburgh EH11 1BG
tel 0131-228 6866 *fax* 0131-228 3220
Co-ordinator Joanna Mattinson

Co-operative venture set up by the Scottish Publishers Association and the Booksellers Association (Scottish Branch) which aims to promote Scottish books through member booksellers. Founded 1986.

Scottish Daily Newspaper Society

48 Palmerston Place, Edinburgh EH12 5DE
tel 0131-220 4353 *fax* 0131-220 4344
Director J.B. Raeburn FCIS

Scottish History Society

Dept of History and Economic History, University of Aberdeen, King's College, Old Aberdeen AB24 3FX
tel/fax (01224) 273885
Hon. Secretary Steve Boardman PhD

The Society exists to publish documents illustrating the history of Scotland. Founded 1886.

Scottish Literary Studies, Association for (ASLS)

c/o Dept of Scottish History, 9 University Gardens, University of Glasgow G12 8QH
tel 0141-330 5309
e-mail cmc@arts.gla.ac.uk
Hon. President Dr David Robb, *Hon. Secretary* Jim Alison, *Hon. Treasurer* Dr Elaine Petrie, *Publishing Manager* Catherine McInerney

Promotes the study, teaching and writing of Scottish literature and furthers the study of the languages of Scotland. Publishes annually an edited text of Scottish literature, an anthology of new Scottish writing and a series of academic journals, and a twice-yearly Newsletter and a schools supplement. Also publishes *Scotnotes* – comprehensive study guides to major Scottish writers, and literary texts and commentary cassettes designed to assist the classroom teacher, and a series of occasional papers. The ASLS organises 3 conferences a year.

Annual membership: individuals/schools £28, UK students £14, corporate £56. Founded 1970.

Scottish Newspaper Publishers' Association

48 Palmerston Place, Edinburgh EH12 5DE
tel 0131-220 4353 *fax* 0131-220 4344
President A. Lumsden
Director J.B. Raeburn FCIS

Scottish Publishers Association

Scottish Book Centre, 137 Dundee Street, Edinburgh EH11 1BG
tel 0131-228 6866 *fax* 0131-228 3220
Director Lorraine Fannin, *Administrator* Davinder Bedi, *Marketing Manager* Susanne Gilmour, *Scottish Book Marketing Group Coordinator* Joanna Mattinson

Founded 1974.

Screenwriters Workshop, London

Holborn Centre for the Performing Arts, Sandland Street, London WC1R 4PZ
tel 0171-242 2134
web site http://dspace.dial.pipex.com/town/square/gh91/lsw.htm
Contact Alan Denman, Paul Gallagher

Forum for contact, information and tuition, the LSW helps new and established writers work successfully in the film and TV industry, and organises a continuous programme of activities, events, courses and seminars, many of which are free/reduced to members and open to non-members at reasonable rates. The largest screenwriting organisation in Europe, now receiving Media II funding from the EC. Annual subscription: £25. Founded 1983.

SCRIBO

Contact K. & P. Sylvester, Flat 1, 31 Hamilton Road, Bournemouth BH1 4EQ

A postal forum for novelists (published and unpublished), SCRIBO aims to give friendly, informed encouragement and help, to discuss all matters of interest to novelists and to offer criticism via MSS folios: crime/thrillers, fantasy/sci-fi, mainstream, aga-saga/popular women's fiction, 2 literary folios (mostly graduates writing serious fiction). A new MSS folio for Gothic suspense/women in jeopardy novels is being formed. Porn is not accepted. No subscription but a £5 joining fee is required. Founded 1971.

Sculptors, Royal Society of British (RBS)

108 Old Brompton Road, London SW7 3RA
tel 0171-373 8615 or 0171-244 8431
fax 0171-370 3721
President Maurice Blik

Established to promote and advance the art and practice of sculpture, the RBS is now assisted in its endeavours by The Sculpture Company, its commissioning and event management arm. The Sculpture Company has a resource centre to assist corporate, municipal or private patrons to commission or purchase sculpture. The Sculpture Company also organises exhibitions, lectures and awards on behalf of the RBS and supports the RBS education policy and *Sculpture 108*, the RBS publication. Founded 1904.

The Shaw Society

Secretary Barbara Smoker, 51 Farmfield Road, Downham, Bromley, Kent BR1 4NF
tel 0181-697 3619

Improvement and diffusion of knowledge of the life and works of Bernard Shaw and his circle. Meetings in London; annual festival at Ayot St Lawrence in July; publishes *The Shavian*. Annual membership: £10/$20.

Society of Authors – see Authors, The Society of, and page 482

Songwriters & Composers, The Guild of International

Sovereign House, 12 Trewartha Road, Praa Sands, Penzance, Cornwall TR20 9ST
tel (01736) 762826 *fax* (01736) 763328
e-mail songmag@aol.com
web site http://www.icn.co.uk/gisc.html
Secretary Carole Ann Jones

Gives advice to members on contractual and copyright matters; assists with protection of members rights; assists with analysis of members' works; international collaboration register free to members; outlines requirements to record companies, publishers, artists. Publishes *Songwriting & Composing* (quarterly). Annual subscription: £35 (UK), £45 (EU/overseas).

Songwriters, Composers and Authors, British Academy of – see BASCA

South Africa, Publishers' Association of (PASA)
PO Box 116, St James, 7946 Cape Town,
South Africa
tel (021) 788-6470 *fax* (021) 788-6469
e-mail pasa@iafrica.com

South African Writers' Circle
Secretary Pat Lister, PO Box 10558, Marine
Parade, Durban 4056, South Africa
tel (031) 251-769

Aims to help and encourage all writers,
new and experienced, in the art of writing. Publishes a monthly *Newsletter*, and
runs competitions with prizes for the
winners. Annual subscription: R60
(local), R90 (overseas). Founded 1960.

Southwest Scriptwriters
149 St Andrew's Road, Montpelier,
Bristol BS6 5EL
tel 0117-944 5424 *fax* 0117-944 5413
e-mail 100621.2037@compuserve.com
Secretary John Colborn

Aims to promote the work of people
writing for the stage, screen, radio and
TV in the region. The group focuses on
script development through workshop
sessions and rehearsed readings, supported by talks on scriptwriting technique and visits from established writers.
Provides a friendly, informal forum
where dramatists can meet and discuss
their work. Newsletter subscription £5
p.a. Founded 1994.

**Spanish Publishers' Association,
Federation of**
(Federación de Gremios de Editores de España)
Juan Ramón Jiménez 45 9° Izda., 28036 Madrid,
Spain
tel 350 91 05/03 *fax* 345 43 51
President Juan Isasa, *Secretary* Ana Moltó Blasco

**SPREd (Society of Picture Researchers
and Editors) – see The Picture Research
Association**

**Stationers and Newspaper Makers,
Worshipful Company of**
Stationers' Hall, London EC4M 7DD
tel 0171-248 2934 *fax* 0171-489 1975
Master Alderman Clive H. Martin OBE, TD, DL,
Clerk Brig. Denzil Sharp, AFC

One of the Livery Companies of the City
of London. Connected with the printing,
publishing, bookselling, newspaper and
allied trades. Operates a Registry for
those requiring proof of ownership of
copyright. Written works or those on
tape, record, video or computer disk can
be registered. Founded 1557.

**Strip Illustration, Society for – now
Comics Creators Guild**

Sussex Authors, The Society of
Secretary Michael Legat, Bookends, Lewes Road,
Horsted Keynes, Haywards Heath,
West Sussex RH17 7DP
tel/fax (01825) 790755

Aims to encourage social contact
between members, and to promote interest in literature and authors. Membership
open to writers living in Sussex who
have had at least one book commercially
published or who have worked extensively in journalism, radio, TV or the
theatre. Annual subscription: £8.
Founded 1969.

Sussex Playwrights' Club
Hon. Secretary, Sussex Playwrights' Club,
2 Princes Avenue, Hove, East Sussex BN3 4GD

Members' plays are read by local actors
before an audience of Club members.
The Club from time to time sponsors productions of members' plays by local
drama companies. Non-writing members
welcome. Founded 1935.

Swedish Publishers' Association
(Svenska Förläggareföreningen)
Drottninggaten 97, 2 tr., 113 60 Stockholm,
Sweden
tel 08-736 19 40 *fax* 08-736 19 44
Director Kristina Ahlinder

Founded 1843.

Television Society, Royal
Holborn Hall, 100 Gray's Inn Road,
London WC1X 8AL
tel 0171-430 1000 *fax* 0171-430 0924
Executive Director Michael Bunce, *Membership
Secretary* Lynda Gooderson

The Society is a unique, central, independent forum to debate the art, science
and politics of TV. Holds awards, conferences, dinners, lectures and workshops.
Annual membership: £55. Founded
1927.

The Tennyson Society
Secretary Kathleen Jefferson, Brayford House,
Lucy Tower Street, Lincoln LN1 1XN
tel (01522) 552851 *fax* (01522) 552858
e-mail lincs.lib@dial.pipex.com

Promotes the study and understanding of the life and work of the poet Alfred, Lord Tennyson and supports the Tennyson Research Centre in Lincoln; holds lectures, visits and seminars; publishes the *Tennyson Research Bulletin* (annual), Monographs and Occasional Papers; tapes/recordings available. Annual membership: £8, family £10, institutions £15. Founded 1960.

Theatre Exchange, International
Secretariat 19 Abbey Park Road,
Grimsby DN32 0HJ
tel (01472) 343424

To encourage, foster and promote exchanges of theatre; student, educational, adult, puppet theatre activities at international level. To organise international seminars, workshops, courses and conferences, and to collect and collate information of all types for national and international dissemination.

Theatre Research, The Society for
c/o The Theatre Museum, 1E Tavistock Street, London WC2E 7PA
Hon. Secretaries Eileen Cottis and Frances Dann

Publishes annual volumes and journal, *Theatre Notebook*, holds lectures, runs enquiry service and makes annual research grants (current total sum approx. £4000). Starting in 1998, the Society's 50th anniversary, it will award an annual prize, initially £400, for the best book published in English on the historical or current practice of the British theatre.

Theatre Writers' Union
c/o GFTU, Central House, Upper Woburn Place, London WC1H 0HY
tel 0181-365 3850
Chair David Edgar, *Administrator* Sheelah Sloane

The only union devoted to the specific needs of those who write for live performance, and responsible for national standard agreements with management associations covering minimum pay and conditions for theatre writers. Members receive a quarterly newsletter, and are eligible for free professional and legal advice, support in disputes and copies of standard contracts; there is an active regional branch network. Annual subscription: based on writing income. Founded 1975.

Angela Thirkell Society
Chairman Mrs J.E. Self, Mayfair, Hamstreet Road, Shadoxhurst, Ashford, Kent TN26 1NL
tel (01233) 733445
Secretary Mrs I.J. Cox, 32 Murvagh Close, Cheltenham, Glos. GL53 7QY
tel (01242) 251604

Aims 'to honour the memory of Angela Thirkell (1890-1960) as a writer, and to make her works available to new generations'. Publishes an *Annual Journal*, and encourages Thirkell studies. Annual membership: £5. Founded 1980.

The Edward Thomas Fellowship
Butler's Cottage, Halswell House, Goathurst, Nr Bridgwater, Somerset TA5 2DH
tel (01278) 662856
Hon. Secretary Richard N. Emeny

To perpetuate the memory of Edward Thomas, poet and nature writer, foster an interest in his life and work, to assist in the preservation of places associated with him and to arrange events which extend fellowship amongst his admirers. Annual subscription: £5. Founded 1980.

The Francis Thompson Society – now incorporated in The Eighteen Nineties Society

The Tolkien Society
Secretary Annie Haward, Flat 6,
8 Staverton Road, Oxford, Oxon OX2 6XJ
e-mail anniehoward@spc.ox.ac.uk
Membership Secretary Trevor Reynolds,
Caer Lao, 16 Gibbons Green, Hoolands, Milton Keynes MK13 7NII
e-mail trevor@caerlas.demon.co.uk
web site http://www.tolkiensociety.org

Dedicated to promoting research into and educating the public in the life and works of Prof J.R.R. Tolkien. Annual subscription: UK £15; overseas rates on application. Founded 1969.

Translation & Interpreting, The Institute of (ITI)
Contact The Secretary, 377 City Road,
London EC1V 1NA
tel 0171-713 7600 *fax* 0171-713 7650
e-mail iti@compuserve.com

The ITI is a professional association of translators and interpreters which aims to promote the highest standards in translating and interpreting. It has a strong corporate membership and runs professional development courses and

conferences, sometimes in conjunction with its language, regional and subject networks. Membership is open to those with a genuine and proven involvement in translation and interpreting. As a full and active member of the International Federation of Translators, it maintains good contacts with translators and interpreters worldwide. ITI's directory of members and its bi-monthly bulletin are available from the Secretariat.

Translations Centre, International
Schuttersveld 2, 2611 WE Delft, Netherlands
tel (015) 214-22-42 *fax* (015) 215-85-35
e-mail itc@library.tudelft.nl
Director M. Risseeuw

A non-profit-making international awareness centre facilitating access to existing translations of scientific and technical literature in Western and other languages. ITC does not translate or commission translations of documents. Founded 1961.

The Translators Association
84 Drayton Gardens, London SW10 9SB
tel 0171-373 6642

Specialist unit within the membership of the Society of Authors (see page 482), exclusively concerned with the interests and special problems of translators into English whose work is published or performed commercially in Great Britain and English-speaking countries overseas. Members are entitled to general and legal advice on all questions connected with their work, including remuneration and contractual arrangements with publishers, editors, broadcasting organisations. Administers a range of translation prizes (see page 512). Annual subscription: £65 by direct debit, £70 by cheque – includes membership of the Society of Authors. Founded 1958.

Travel Writers, The British Guild of
Hon. Secretary John Harrison, 90 Corringway, London W5 3HA
tel 0181-998 2223

Arranges meetings, discussions and visits for its 170 members (who are all professional travel journalists) to help them encourage the public's interest in travel. Publishes a monthly newsletter (for members only) and an annual *Yearbook*, which contains details of members and lists travel industry PRs and contacts.

The Trollope Society
9A North Street, London SW4 0HN
tel 0171-720 6789
Chairman John Letts

Aims to produce the first ever complete edition of the novels of Anthony Trollope (28 vols now available). Membership: £24 p.a., £240 (life). Founded 1987.

The Turner Society
BCM Box Turner, London WC1N 3XX
Chairman Evelyn Joll

To foster a wider appreciation of all facets of Turner's work; to encourage exhibitions of his paintings, drawings and engravings. Publishes *Turner Society News* (3 p.a.). Annual subscription: £10; other rates on application. Founded 1975.

Typographic Designers, Society of
President John Harrison FSTD, *Chair* David Quay FSTD/Freda Sack FSTD
Hon. Secretary Helen Cornish, Chapelfield Cottage, Randwick, Stroud, Glos. GL6 6HS
tel (01453) 759311 *fax* (01453) 759311

Advises and acts on matters of professional practice, provides a better understanding of the typographic craft and the rapidly changing technology in the graphic industries by lectures, discussions and through the journal *Typographic* and the Newsletter. Typographic students are encouraged to gain Licentiate membership of the Society, by entering the annual student assessment project. Founded 1928.

Undeb Awduron Cymru
(Union of Welsh Writers)
Botacho Wyn, Nefyn, Gwynedd LL53 6HA
tel (01758) 720430

Aims to provide practical and inspirational help to writers in the Welsh language. Produces a newsletter/magazine (3 p.a.); meets at Aberystwyth (2 or 3 p.a.) and annually at the National Eisteddfod. Annual subscription: £5. Founded 1975.

Visiting Arts Office of Great Britain and Northern Ireland
11 Portland Place, London W1N 4EJ
tel 0171-389 3015 *fax* 0171-389 3016
web site http://www.britcoun.org/visitingarts/
Director T. Sandell

A joint venture of the 4 UK arts councils, the Crafts Council, the Foreign Office

and the British Council. It promotes and facilitates the flow of foreign arts into the UK in the context of the contribution they can make to cultural relations, cultural awareness, and fostering mutually beneficial international arts contacts and activities at national, regional, local and institutional levels. Founded 1977.

Visual Communication Association, International (IVCA)

Bolsover House, 5-6 Clipstone Street, London W1P 8LD
tel 0171-580 0962 *fax* 0171-436 2606
e-mail 100434,1005@compuserve.com
Membership Secretary Bridget Conneely

For those who use or supply visual communication. Aims to promote the industry and provide a collective voice; provides a range of services, publications and events to help existing and potential users to make the most of what video, film, multimedia and live events can offer their business. Annual membership: from £150. Founded 1987.

Voice of the Listener & Viewer (VLV)

101 King's Drive, Gravesend, Kent DA12 5BQ
tel (01474) 352835
Chairman Jocelyn Hay, *Administrative Secretary* Linda Forbes

Independent association representing the citizen's voice in broadcasting and the interests of listeners and viewers on all broadcasting issues. Concerned to maintain the principle of public service plus independence, quality and diversity in British broadcasting. Has over 2000 individual members, 20 charities as corporate members and nearly 50 colleges in academic membership. Holds frequent public conferences. Publishes a quarterly newsletter and briefings on broadcasting developments. Founded 1983.

Wales, Arts Council of – see Arts Council of Wales

Edgar Wallace Society

Kohlbergsgracht 40, NL-6462 CD Kerkrade, The Netherlands
Organiser Kai Jörg Hinz

To promote an interest in the life and work of Edgar Wallace through the *Crimson Circle* magazine (quarterly). Annual subscription: Europe £15 (stu-

dents/senior citizens £10), rest of world £20 (students/senior citizens £10). Founded 1969.

The Walmsley Society

Secretary Fred Lane, April Cottage, 1 Brand Road, Hampden Park, Eastbourne, East Sussex BN22 9PX
Membership Secretary Mrs Elizabeth Buckley, 21 The Crescent, Hipperholm, Halifax, West Yorkshire HX3 8NQ

Aims to promote and encourage an appreciation of the literary and artistic heritage left to us by Leo and J. Ulric Walmsley. Founded 1985.

Water Colours, Royal Institute of Painters in

17 Carlton House Terrace, London SW1Y 5BD
tel 0171-930 6844 *fax* 0171-839 7830
President Ronald Maddox Hon. RWS

The Institute promotes the appreciation of watercolour painting in its traditional and contemporary forms, primarily by means of an annual exhibition at the Mall Galleries, London SW1 of members' and non-members' work and also by members' exhibitions at selected venues in Britain and abroad. Members elected from approved candidates' list. Founded 1831.

Watercolour Society, British

Director Leslie Simpson, Ralston House, 41 Lister Street, Riverside Gardens, Ilkley, West Yorkshire LS29 9ET
tel (01943) 609075

Promotes the best in traditional watercolour painting. Holds 2 open exhibitions p.a. Membership by selection. Founded 1830.

Watercolour Society, Royal

Bankside Gallery, 48 Hopton Street, London SE1 9JH
tel 0171-928 7521
President John Doyle MBE

Membership (RWS) open to British and overseas artists. An election of Associates is held annually, and applications for the necessary forms and particulars should be addressed to the Secretary. The Society gives lectures on watercolour paintings; organises residential/non-residential course; holds open exhibition in summer. Exhibitions: spring and autumn. Friends of the RWS open to all those interested in watercolour painting. Founded 1804.

Mary Webb Society

Secretary Miss M. Austin, Tansy Cottage,
Clunbury, Craven Arms SY7 0HF
tel (01588) 660565

For devotees of the literature and works
of Mary Webb and of the beautiful countryside of her novels. Publishes annual
journal in September, organises summer
schools in various locations related to
Webb's life and works. Archives, lectures; tours arranged for individuals and
groups. Founded 1972.

The H.G. Wells Society

Hon. General Secretary J.R. Hammond,
49 Beckingthorpe Drive, Bottesford,
Nottingham NG13 0DN

Promotes an active interest in and
encouragement of an appreciation of the
life, work and thought of H.G. Wells.
Publishes *The Wellsian* (annual) and
The Newsletter (bi-annual). Annual subscription £12, corporate £18. Founded
1960.

Welsh Books Council/Cyngor Llyfrau Cymru

Castell Brychan, Aberystwyth,
Ceredigion SY23 2JB
tel (01970) 624151 *fax* (01970) 625385
Director Gwerfyl Pierce Jones

Founded in 1961 to promote Welsh-language and English-language books of
Welsh interest. Editorial, design, marketing, distribution and children's books
promotion services provided for publishers.

Welsh Union of Writers

Secretary John Harrison, 4 Teilo Street,
Pontcanna, Cardiff CF1 9JN
tel (01222) 640041
web site via capitalnet

Independent union open to persons born
or working in Wales with at least one
publication in a quality outlet, fiction,
non-fiction or poetry. Lobbies for writing
in Wales; represents members in disputes;
annual conference; occasional events and
publications. Annual subscription: £10
plus £5 joining fee. Associate membership
now available for others with a committed
interest in writing: £5 plus £5 joining fee.
Founded 1982.

Welsh Writers, Union of – see Undeb Awduron Cymru

The West Country Writers' Association

President Christopher Fry FRSL, DLitt, *Chair* Bob
Cooper
Hon. Secretary Anne Double, Malvern View,
Garway Hill, Orcop, Hereford HR2 8EZ
tel/fax (01981) 580495

To foster love of literature in the West
Country and to give authors an opportunity of meeting to exchange news and
views. Holds Annual Weekend Congress
and Regional Meetings. Newsletter (2
p.a.). Membership open to published
authors. Annual subscription: £10.

West of England Academy, Royal

Queens Road, Clifton, Bristol BS8 1PX
tel (0117) 973 5129 *fax* (0117) 923 7874
President Peter Thursby PRWA, FRBS, *Academy
Secretary* Rachel Fear

Aims to further the interests of practising
painters and sculptors. Holds art exhibitions and is a meeting place for artists
and their work. Founded 1844.

The Oscar Wilde Society

154 Derwent Road, Leighton Buzzard,
Beds. LU7 7XT
tel (01525) 851481
Secretary Rosemary McGlashon

To promote knowledge, appreciation and
study of the life, personality and works
of the writer and wit Oscar Wilde.
Activities include exhibitions, readings,
meetings and lectures. Members receive
The Wildean journal (bi-annual), and a
Newsletter (6 p.a.). Annual membership:
£13 (UK), £15 (Europe), £20 (elsewhere);
student/unwaged £11; household £18.
Founded 1990.

Wildlife Artists, Society of

17 Carlton House Terrace,
London SW1Y 5BD
tel 0171-930 6844 *fax* 0171-839 7830
President Bruce Pearson

To promote and encourage the art of
wildlife painting and sculpture. Open
Annual Exhibition at the Mall Galleries,
The Mall, London SW1.

Charles Williams Society

26 Village Road, London N3 1TL
Secretary Gillian Lunn

To promote interest in the life and work
of Charles Walter Stansby Williams
(1886-1945) and to make his writings
more easily available. Founded 1975.

The Henry Williamson Society

Chairman and General Secretary Will Harris
Membership Secretary Mrs Margaret Murphy,
16 Doran Drive, Redhill, Surrey RH1 6AX
tel (01737) 763228

Aims to encourage a wider readership and greater understanding of the literary heritage left by Henry Williamson. Two meetings annually; also weekend activities. Publishes an annual journal. Annual subscription: £8.00; family, student and overseas rates available. Founded 1980.

Women Artists, Society of

Westminster Gallery, Westminster Central Hall,
Storey's Gate, London SW1H 9NU
web site http://www.nal.vam.ac.uk/
President Barbara Tate

Annual Exhibition of painting, sculpture, etc. Open to all women. Founded 1855.

Women in Publishing

c/o J. Whitaker, 12 Dyott Street,
London WC1A 1DF

Promotes the status of women within publishing; encourages networking and mutual support among women; provides a forum for the discussion of ideas, trends and subjects to women in the trade; offers practical training for career and personal development; supports and publicises women's achievements and successes. Annual subscription: £25. Founded 1977.

Women Writers and Journalists, Society of

Secretary Jean Hawkes, 110 Whitehall Road,
London E4 6DW
tel 0181-529 0886

For women writers: lectures, monthly lunchtime meetings; free literary advice for members. *The Woman Journalist* (3 p.a.). Annual subscription: town £25, country £21, overseas £15; joining fee £10. Founded 1894.

Women Writers Network

c/o Susan Kerr, 55 Burlington Lane,
London W4 3ET
tel 0181-994 0598
Membership Secretary Cathy Smith,
23 Prospect Road, London NW2 2JU
tel 0171-794 5861

London-based network with a branch in Manchester serving both salaried and independent women writers from all disciplines, and providing a forum for the exchange of information, support and networking opportunities. Holds monthly meetings, workshops and publishes a newsletter and members' Directory. Send A5 or A4 sae for information. Annual membership: £30. Meetings only: £5 at door. Founded 1985.

Worker Writers and Community Publishers, The Federation of

Box 540, Burslem, Stoke-on-Tent ST6 6DR
tel/fax (01782) 822327
e-mail writersfed@aol.com

A network of writers groups and community publishers which promotes working-class writing as an alternative to establishment literature. Annual membership: funded groups £40; unfunded £20. Founded 1976.

Writers' Circles

Contact Jill Dick, Oldacre, Horderns Park Road,
Chapel-en-le-Frith, High Peak SK23 9SY
tel (01298) 812305
e-mail Jillie@clx.compulink.co.uk

The *Directory of Writers' Circles*, containing addresses of over 600 writers' circles, guilds, workshops, literary clubs, societies and organisations, is published regularly. Copies of the 8th edition (£5 post free) are available from the compiler/editor, Jill Dick.

Writers' Groups, National Association of

The Arts Centre, Biddick Lane, Washington,
Tyne and Wear NE38 0AD
tel 0191-416 9751 *fax* 0191-415 7662
Secretary Brian Lister

Aims 'to advance the education of the general public throughout the UK, including the Channel Islands, by promoting the study and art of writing in all its aspects.' Annual membership: £14 per group. Founded 1995.

Writers Guild of America, East, Inc. (WGAE)

Executive Director Mona Mangan,
555 West 57 Street, Suite 1230, New York,
NY 10019, USA
tel 212-767-7800

Represents writers in screen and TV for collective bargaining. It oversees member services (pension and health) as well as educational and professional activities. Annual membership: 1.5% of covered earnings. Founded 1954.

Writers Guild of America (WGA), West Inc.

Executive Director Brian Walton,
7000 West 3rd Street, Los Angeles, CA 90048, USA
tel 213-951-4000 *fax* 213-782-4800
web site www.@wga.org

Union representing and servicing 9000 writers in film, broadcast, cable and multimedia industries for purposes of collective bargaining, contract administration and other services, and functions to protect and advance the economic, professional and creative interests of writers. Monthly publication, *Written by*, available by subscription. Membership: initiation $2500, quarterly $25, annually 1.5% of income. Founded 1933.

The Writers' Guild of Great Britain

430 Edgware Road, London W2 1EH
tel 0171-723 8074 *fax* 0171-706 2413
web site http://www.writers.org.uk/guild
General Secretary Alison V. Gray

Founded in 1959 as the Screenwriters' Guild, now a trade union affiliated to the TUC, representing writers' interests in film, radio, TV, theatre and publishing. Its scope extends into all areas of freelance writing and copyright protection and, where necessary, discusses at Government level policies on legislative matters affecting writers. The Guild's basic function is to negotiate minimum terms in those areas in which its members work. The Guild, by constitution non-political, employs a permanent secretariat and staff and is administered by an Executive Council of 26 members. There are also Regional Committees representing Scotland, Wales, the North and West of England. Full details of membership on request (see also page 485).

Writers in Oxford

41 Kingston Road, Oxford OX2 6RH
tel (01865) 513844 *fax* (01865) 510017
Membership Secretary Philip Pullman,
24 Templar Road, Oxford OX2 8LT

To promote valuable discussion and social meetings among all kinds of professional writers in and around Oxfordshire. Activities include: topical lunches and dinners, where subjects important to the writer are discussed; showcase evenings; parties. Quarterly newsletter, *The Oxford Writer*. Annual subscription: £15. Founded 1992.

Writers' Postal Workshops and Folios

Compiler Catherine M. Gill, Drakemyre Croft, Cairnorrie, Methlick, Ellon, Aberdeenshire AB41 7JN

Writers' postal workshops and folios provide criticism, guidance, encouragement and support to both published and unpublished writers and enable regular contact to be made by post with others of similar interests. *The Cottage Guide to Writers' Postal Workshops* contains full details of postal workshops, folios and similar organisations and is published and updated regularly by Croftspun Publications. Price £2 post free from the compiler.

Yachting Journalists' Association

3 Friars Lane, Maldon, Essex CM9 6AG
tel (01621) 855943 *fax* (01621) 852212
Secretary Peter Cook

Aims to further the interests of yachting, sail and power, and yachting journalism. Organises the annual Yachtsman of the Year Awards, currently sponsored by BT. Membership: £30 p.a. Founded 1969.

The Yorkshire Dialect Society

Hon. Secretary Michael Park, 51 Stepney Avenue, Scarborough YO12 5DW

Aims to encourage interest in dialect speech, the writing of dialect verse, prose and drama; the publication and circulation of dialect literature; the study of the origins and the history of dialect and kindred subjects. Organises meetings; publishes *Transactions* (annual) and *The Summer Bulletin* free to members; list of other publications on request. Annual subscription: £6. Founded 1897.

Young Book Trust – see Book Trust

Young Publishers, Society of

Contact The Secretary, c/o 12 Dyott Street, London WC1A 1DF

Provides a lively forum for discussion on subjects relevant to its members in publishing. Membership open to anyone employed in publishing, printing, bookselling or allied trades with associate membership available to those over 35. Meetings held at the Publishers

Association, usually on the last Wednesday of the month at 6.30pm The SYP also organises social and other events. Please enclose an sae when writing. Founded 1949.

Francis Brett Young Society
Secretary Mrs J. Pritchard, 52 Park Road, Hagley, Stourbridge, West Midlands DY9 0QF
tel (01562) 882973

To provide opportunities for members to meet, correspond, and to share the enjoyment of the author's works. Journal published 2 p.a. Annual subscription: £5 (individual), life membership £45 (other rates on application). Founded 1979.

The Society of Authors

The Society of Authors is an independent trade union, representing writers' interests in all aspects of the writing profession, including publishing, broadcasting, television and films, theatre and translation.

Founded over 100 years ago by Walter Besant, the Society now has more than 6000 members. It has a professional staff, responsible to a Management Committee of 12 authors, and a Council (an advisory body meeting twice a year) consisting of 60 eminent writers. There are specialist groups within the Society to serve the particular needs of broadcasters, literary translators, educational writers, medical writers and children's writers and illustrators. There are also regional groups representing Scotland, the North of England and the Isle of Man.

> 'When we begin working, we are so poor and so busy that we have neither the time nor the means to defend ourselves against the commercial organisations which exploit us. When we become famous, we become famous suddenly, passing at one bound from the state in which we are, as I have said, too poor to fight our own battles, to a state in which our time is so valuable that it is not worth our while wasting any of it on lawsuits and bad debts. We all, eminent and obscure alike, need the Authors' Society. We all owe it a share of our time, our means, our influence'
> – Bernard Shaw

What the Society does for members

Through its permanent staff (including a solicitor), the Society is able to give its members a comprehensive personal and professional service covering the business aspects of authorship, including:
• providing information about agents, publishers, and others concerned with the book trade, journalism, broadcasting and the performing arts;
• advising on negotiations, including the individual vetting of contracts, clause by clause, and assessing their terms both financial and otherwise;
• taking up complaints on behalf of

members on any issue concerned with the business of authorship;
• pursuing legal actions for breach of contract, copyright infringement, and the non-payment of royalties and fees, when the risk and cost preclude individual action by a member and issues of general concern to the profession are at stake;
• holding conferences, seminars, meetings and social occasions;
• producing a comprehensive range of publications, free of charge to members, including the Society's quarterly journal, *The Author*. *Quick Guides* cover many aspects of the profession such as: copy-

right, publishing contracts, libel, income tax, VAT, authors' agents, permissions, indexing, and the protection of titles. The Society also publishes occasional papers on subjects such as packaged books, revised editions, multimedia, and vanity publishing.

Membership benefits

Members have access to:
* the Retirement Benefit Scheme;
* a group Medical Insurance Scheme with BUPA;
* the Pension Fund (which offers discretionary pensions to a number of members);
* the Contingency Fund (which provides financial relief for authors or their dependents in sudden financial difficulties);
* automatic free membership of the Authors' Licensing and Collecting Society (ALCS);
* books at special rates;
* membership of the Royal Over-Seas League at a discount;
* use of the Society's photocopying machine at special rates.

The Society frequently secures improved conditions and better returns for members. It is common for members to report that, through the help and facilities offered, they have saved more, and some-times substantially more, than their annual subscriptions (which are an allowable expense against income tax).

What the Society does for authors

The Society lobbies Members of Parliament, Ministers and Government Departments on all issues of concern to writers. Recent issues have included the operation and funding of Public Lending Right, the threat of VAT on books, copyright legislation and European Community initiatives. Concessions have also been obtained under various Finance Acts.

The Society litigates in matters of importance to authors. For example, the Society backed Andrew Boyle when he won his appeal against the Inland Revenue's attempt to tax the Whitbread Award. It supported a number of members in proceedings against the BBC and Desmond Wilcox in connection with the publication of a book, *The Explorers*, and also in a High Court action over copyright infringement by *Coles Notes*.

The Society campaigns for better terms for writers. With the Writers' Guild, it has negotiated agreements with BBC Publications, Bloomsbury, Bodley Head, Jonathan Cape, Century, André Deutsch, Faber & Faber, Hamish Hamilton, HarperCollins, Hodder

---

Membership

The Society of Authors
84 Drayton Gardens, London SW10 9SB
tel 0171-373 6642

There are two categories of membership (admission to each being at the discretion of the Committee of Management):

Full Membership – those authors who have had a full-length work published, broadcast or performed commercially in the UK or have an established reputation in another medium.

Associate Membership – those authors who have had a full-length work accepted for publication, but not yet published; and those authors who have had occasional items broadcast or performed, or translations, articles, illustrations or short stories published.

Associate members pay the same annual subscription and are entitled to the same benefits as full members. The owner or administrator of a deceased author's copyrights can become a member on behalf of the author's estate.

The annual subscription (which is tax deductible under Schedule D) for full or associate membership of the Society is £70 (£65 by direct debit after the first year), and there are special joint membership terms for husband and wife. Authors under 35, who are not yet earning a significant income from their writing, may apply for membership at a lower subscription of £52. Authors over 65 may apply to pay at the reduced rate after their first year of membership.

Headline, Hutchinson, Michael Joseph, Methuen, Penguin Books, Sinclair-Stevenson, Transworld and Viking. Other publishers are now being approached, and the campaign is active. The translators' section of the Society has also drawn up a minimum terms agreement for translators which has been adopted by Faber & Faber, and has been used on an individual basis by a number of other publishers.

The Society is recognised by the BBC for the purpose of negotiating rates for writers' contributions to radio drama, as well as for the broadcasting of published material. It was instrumental in setting up the Authors' Licensing and Collecting Society (ALCS), which collects and distributes fees from reprography and other methods whereby copyright material is exploited without direct payment to the originators.

The Society keeps in close touch with the Arts Councils, the Association of Authors' Agents, the British Council, the Broadcasting Entertainment Cinematograph and Theatre Union, the Institute of Translation and Interpreting, the Secretary of State for National Heritage, the National Union of Journalists, the Publishers Association and the Writers' Guild of Great Britain.

The Society is a member of the European Writers Congress, the British Copyright Council, the National Book Committee and the International Confederation of Societies of Authors and Composers (CISAC).

Awards

The Society of Authors administers:
• two travel awards: the Somerset Maugham Awards and the Travelling Scholarships;
• four prizes for novels: the Betty Trask Awards, the Encore Award, the McKitterick Prize and the Sagittarius Prize;
• two poetry awards: the Eric Gregory Awards and the Cholmondeley Awards;
• the Tom-Gallon Award for short story writers;
• the Crompton Bequest for aiding financially the publication of selected original work;
• the Authors' Foundation and Kathleen Blundell Trust, which are endowed with wide powers to support work in progress;
• the Margaret Rhondda Award for women journalists;
• the Scott Moncrieff Prize for translations from French;
• the Schlegel-Tieck Prize for translations from German books published in Germany;
• the Teixeira-Gomes Prize for translations from Portuguese;
• the John Florio Prize for translations from Italian;
• the Francis Head Bequest for assisting authors who, through physical mishap, are temporarily unable to maintain themselves or their families.

The Writers' Guild of Great Britain

The Writers' Guild of Great Britain is the writers' trade union, affiliated to the TUC, and representing writers' interests in film, radio, television, theatre and publishing.

Formed in 1959 as the Screenwriters' Guild, the union gradually extended into all areas of freelance writing activity and copyright protection. In 1974 when book authors and stage dramatists became eligible for membership substantial numbers joined, and their interests are represented on the Executive Council. Apart from necessary dealings with Government and policies on legislative matters affecting writers, the Guild is, by constitution, non-political, has no involvement with any political party, and pays no political levy. The Guild employs a permanent secretariat and staff and is administered by an Executive Council of 26 members. There are also Regional Committees representing Scotland, Wales, the North and West of England.

The Guild comprises practising professional writers in all media, united in common concern for one another and regulating the conditions under which they work.

The Writers' Guild and agreements

The Guild's basic function is to negotiate minimum terms in those areas in which its members work. Those agreements form the basis of the individual contracts signed by members.

Television

The Guild has national agreements with the BBC and the commercial companies regulating minimum fees and going rates, copyright licence, credit terms and conditions for television plays, series and serials, dramatisations and adaptations. One of the most important achievements in recent years has been the establishment of pension rights for Guild members. The BBC pay an additional 7.5% of the going rate on the understanding that the Guild member pays 5% of his or her fee. ITV companies now pay an additional 8% and the writer 5%. The Guild Pension Fund amounts to well over £3 million at present.

In the late 1980s, comprehensive agreements were negotiated with the BBC and ITV to cover programme sales overseas and to cable and satellite stations. In addition, a special agreement was negotiated to cover the very successful serial *EastEnders*. In 1991, the first ever Light Entertainment Agreement was signed with the BBC. Most children's and educational drama has been similarly protected within the above industrial agreements. Rates of payment are updated from time to time.

Film

On 11 March 1985, an important agreement was signed with the two producer organisations: The British Film and Television Producers' Association and The Independent Programme Producers Association (now known as PACT, the Producers' Alliance for Cinema and Television). For the first time, there exists an industrial agreement which covers both independent television productions and independent film productions. Pension fund contributions have been negotiated for Guild members in the same way as for the BBC and ITV. The Agreement was

comprehensively renegotiated and concluded in February 1992. The areas of participation have been improved and the money paid upfront is considerably more than it was in the past. The Guild is also drawing up guidelines for the use of dramatic material in multimedia.

Radio

The Guild has fought for and obtained a standard agreement with the BBC, establishing a fee structure which is annually reviewed. The current agreement includes a Code of Practice which is important for establishing good working conditions for the writer working for the BBC. In December 1985 the BBC agreed to extend the pension scheme already established for television writers to include radio writers. It was also agreed that all radio writers would be entitled to at least one attendance payment as of right. Again, this brings the radio agreements more into line with the television agreements. In 1991 a comprehensive revision of the Agreement was undertaken and has been concluded.

Books

The Guild fought long, hard and successfully for the loans-based Public Lending Right to reimburse authors for books lent in libraries. This is now law and the Guild is constantly in touch with the Registrar of the scheme, which is administered from offices in Stockton-on-Tees.

The Guild, together with its sister union the Society of Authors, has drawn up a draft Minimum Terms Book Agreement which has been widely circulated amongst publishers. In 1984, the unions achieved a significant breakthrough by signing agreements with two major publishers; negotiations were also opened with other publishers. The publishing agreements will, it is hoped, improve the relationship between writers and publishers and help to clarify what writers might reasonably expect from the exploitation of copyright in their works.

Agreements have now been signed with

BBC Publications, Bloomsbury, Bodley Head, Jonathan Cape, Century, André Deutsch, Faber & Faber, Hamish Hamilton, HarperCollins, Hodder Headline, Hutchinson, Michael Joseph, Methuen, Penguin Books, Sinclair-Stevenson, Transworld and Viking. Negotiations are currently taking place with other leading publishers.

Theatre

In 1979, the Guild with its fellow union, the Theatre Writers' Union, negotiated the first ever industrial agreement for theatre writers. The Theatre National Committee Agreement covers the Royal Shakespeare Company, the Royal National Theatre Company and the English Stage Company. A new Agreement was concluded in April 1993.

On 2 June 1986, a new Agreement was signed with the Theatrical Management Association, covering some 95 provincial theatres. In 1991, negotiations opened for a comprehensive review of that Agreement and were concluded in 1993.

In 1991, after many years of negotiation, an Agreement was concluded between the Guild and Theatre Writers' Union, and the Independent Theatre Council, which represents some 200 of the smaller and fringe theatres as well as educational, touring companies. The Agreement breaks new ground. Only the West End is not covered by a union agreement.

Copies of all the above agreements are available to members and non-members at a small charge.

Other activities

The Guild is in constant touch with Government and national institutions wherever and whenever the interests of writers are in question or are being discussed. The Guild has been holding cross party Parliamentary lobbies since 1989 with its fellow arts unions, Equity, the Musicians Union, the NUJ and BECTU. The Guild and its fellow unions believe that it is important to keep in constant touch with all parties to ensure that the

various art forms they represent are properly cared for. The Guild held a lobby under the auspices of the Creators Copyright Coalition, an umbrella group representing creators in newspapers and publishing, focusing on the threat to copyright posed by digital technology. Most recently the Guild has submitted amendments to the Broadcasting Bill and proposals to the Arts Council of England concerning a New Writing Fund.

Proposals for changes in the law on copyright were published in a draft Bill in August 1986. The Guild along with other organisations made important submissions on behalf of the Guild and writers in general. The new Act came into effect in 1989. Moral rights have been granted to writers for the first time.

Perhaps one of the closest working relationships the Guild has established is with its fellow arts unions, Equity and the Musicians Union. The three unions have agreed to work much more closely together where they share a common interest. Representatives of the three governing bodies meet on a quarterly basis.

Regular Craft Meetings are held by all the Guild's specialist committees. This gives Guild members the opportunity of meeting those who control, work within, or affect the sphere of writing within which they work.

Internationally, the Guild plays a leading role in the International Affiliation of Writers' Guilds, which includes the American Guilds East and West, the Canadian Guilds (French and English) and the Australian and New Zealand Guilds. When it is possible to make common cause, then the Guilds act accordingly.

The Guild takes a leading role in the European Writers' Congress. It has been represented at every Congress since 1981. That body is becoming increasingly important and successful. An initiative from the Writers' Guild of Great Britain saw the setting up of a Copyright Committee to protect writers' interests within the EU in particular and through-

Membership

The Writers' Guild of Great Britain
430 Edgware Road, London W2 1EH
tel 0171-723 8074 *fax* 0171-706 2413
web site http://www.writers.org.uk/guild

Membership is by a points system. One major piece of work (a full-length book, an hour-long television or radio play, a feature film, etc) entitles the author to Full Membership; lesser work helps to accumulate enough points for Full Membership, while Associate Membership may be enjoyed in the meantime. Importantly, previously unpublished, broadcast or performed writers can apply for membership when they receive their first contracts. The Guild's advice before signature can often be vital. Affiliate Membership is enjoyed by agents and other professional advisers.

A new category of membership has recently been formed known as Candidate Membership. This is open to all those who are taking their first steps in writing but who have not as yet received a contract. Candidate Membership is £35.

The minimum subscription is £70 plus 1% of that part of an author's income earned from professional writing sources in the previous calendar year.

out Europe in general. With the harmonisation of Copyright Law, an opportunity has been seized to make representation directly to Brussels which could lead to an improvement for British writers.

The Guild in its day-to-day work takes up problems on behalf of individual members, gives advice on contracts, and helps with any problems which affect the lives of its members as professional writers.

The Guild publishes *The Writers' Newsletter* six times a year, which carries articles, letters and reports written by members.

Prizes and awards

This list provides details of many British prizes, competitions and awards for writers and artists, including grants, bursaries and fellowships, as well as details of major international prizes. On page 516 is a quick reference to its contents. Listings of Open exhibitions for artists start on page 519.

J.R. Ackerley Prize for Autobiography
Information PEN, 7 Dilke Street, London SW3 4JE
tel 0171-352 6303 *fax* 0171-351 0220

An annual prize given for an outstanding work of literary autobiography written in English and published during the previous year by an author of British nationality or an author who has been a long-term resident in the UK. No submissions please – books are nominated by the judges only. First awarded in 1982.

The Alexander Prize
Literary Director, Royal Historical Society, University College London, Gower Street, London WC1E 0DT
tel/fax 0171-387 7532

An annual award of £250. Candidates must either be under the age of 35 or be registered for a higher degree now or within the last 3 years. They may choose their own subject for a paper, but they must submit their choice for approval to the Literary Director. Closing date 1 November.

The Hans Christian Andersen Medals
Details International Board on Books for Young People, Nonnenweg 12, Postfach, CH-4003 Basel, Switzerland
tel (61) 272 29 17 *fax* (61) 272 27 57
e-mail ibby@eye.ch

The Medals are awarded every 2 years to a living author and an illustrator who by the outstanding value of their work are judged to have made a lasting contribution to literature for children and young people.

Aristeion Prizes
Details Mrs Enrica Varese, DGX, D1 Cultural Action, rue de la Loi 102, 4/25, 1040 Brussels, Belgium
tel (32) 2-299 94 19 *fax* (32) 2-299 92 83

Further information

In the UK, details of awards for novels, short stories and works of non-fiction, as they are offered, will be found in such journals as *The Author*.

Book Trust
Book House, 45 East Hill, London SW18 2QZ
tel 0181-870 9055

Publishes a list of prizes, *Guide to Literary Prizes 1997* (£3.99) and a free leaflet on grants and awards.

Candidates must be nationals of a member state of the European Union. Applications are not sought: nominations are made by an appointed authority from each member state and the winning titles are selected by a specially appointed jury of experts.

European Literary Prize
Founded in 1990, this annual award of 20,000 ecus is awarded for a single work, which may belong to any literary genre.

European Translation Prize
Founded in 1990, this annual award of 20,000 ecus is awarded to a translator for an outstanding translation of a significant work of contemporary European literature; the work may belong to any literary genre.

Rosemary Arthur Award
Details National Poetry Foundation, 27 Mill Road, Fareham, Hants PO16 0TH
tel (01329) 822218

An annual award for a book of poetry. The prize consists of the full cost of publishing the winner's book, £100 and an engraved clock. Founded in 1989.

The Arts Council/An Chomhairle Ealaíon, Ireland

Details The Arts Council (An Chomhairle Ealaíon), 70 Merrion Square, Dublin 2, Republic of Ireland
tel (01) 6611840 *fax* (01) 6761302

These literary awards are available only to Irish citizens, or to those who have been resident in Ireland for the previous 5 years.

Bursaries for Creative Writers
In 1996 awards totalling IR£80,000 were offered to creative writers of poetry, fiction and drama to enable them to concentrate on or complete writing projects. At least the same amount will be distributed in 1997. A limited number of literary non-fiction projects are also eligible.

Denis Devlin Memorial Award
This award, value IR£3000, is made triennially for the best book of poetry in the English language by an Irish citizen published in the preceding 3 years. The next award will be made in 1999.

Macaulay Fellowship
Fellowships, value IR£3500, are awarded once every 3 years to writers under 30 years of age (or in exceptional circumstances under 35 years) in order to help them to further their liberal education and careers. The cycle of awards is: Visual Arts (1997), Music (1998), Literature (1999).

The Marten Toonder Award
This award is given to an artist of recognised and established achievement on a rotating cycle as follows: Music (1997), Literature (1998), Visual Arts (1999). Candidates must be Irish-born (Northern Ireland is included). Value IR£4500.

An Duais don bhFilíocht i nGaeilge
This is Ireland's major award to Irish-language poetry; it is given triennially for the best book of Irish-language poetry published in the preceding 3 years. The next award will be made in 1999. Value IR£3000.

Travel Grants
Creative artists (including writers) may apply for assistance with travel grants to attend seminars, conferences, workshops, etc. Applications are assessed twice a year.

Arts Council of England

Details Arts Council of England, 14 Great Peter Street, London SW1P 3NQ
tel 0171-333 0100

Writers' Awards
The Arts Council gives annual bursaries to writers whose work is of outstanding quality. In 1997-98 there will be 15 such awards. They will be offered only to already published authors who are writing works of poetry, fiction, autobiography, biography, literature for young people and drama (intended for publication). At least one award will be reserved specifically for the Literature for Young People category. The value of each bursary is £7000. Closing date for applications: 30 September each year. Details are available from July onwards from the Literature Department.

Translation Fund
This fund supports the publication of translated work. Any text suggested for support should already have secured a publisher by whom nominations should be made. Grants may be given for specimen chapters of a work in progress. Grants are occasionally given to initiatives outside publishing which support an appreciation of translation. The budget for 1997-98 is just over £100,000 and there are 3 deadline dates each year. Further information from Jilly Paver, Literature Officer.

The Arts Council of Wales Awards to Writers

Literature Department, The Arts Council of Wales, Museum Place, Cardiff CF1 3NX
tel (01222) 394711 *fax* (01222) 221447

Book of the Year Award
A £3000 prize is awarded to winners, in Welsh and English, and £1000 to 4 other short-listed authors for works of exceptional merit by Welsh authors (by birth or residence) published during the previous calendar year in the categories of poetry, fiction and creative non-fiction.

Bursaries and competitions
Bursaries totalling about £75,000 are awarded annually to authors writing in both Welsh and English. In addition, the Council organises occasional competitions. Write for further details of the Arts Council of Wales' policies.

The Arts Foundation Fellowships

The Countess of Huntingdon's Chapel,
The Vineyards, Bath BA1 5NA
tel (01225) 315775 *fax* (01225) 317597
Director Prudence Skene

Fellowships worth £10,000 are awarded annually in various art form categories which change each year. The programme is not open to application: a network of nominators recommend individuals to be invited to apply. Established 1993.

Arvon Foundation International Poetry Competition

Details Arvon Foundation Poetry Competition,
Kilnhurst, Kilnhurst Road, Todmorden,
Lancs. OL14 6AX
tel (01706) 816582 *fax* (01706) 816359

A biennial competition for previously unpublished poems written in English. First prize £5000, plus at least £5000 in other cash prizes. Founded in 1980.

Authors' Club Awards

Details Ann Carter, Secretary, Authors' Club,
40 Dover Street, London W1X 3RB
tel 0171-499 8581 fax 0171-409 0913

Best First Novel Award

An award of £750 is presented at a dinner held in the Club, to the author of the most promising first novel published in the UK during each year. Entries (one from each publisher's imprint) are accepted during October and November and must be full-length novels – short stories are not eligible. Instituted by Lawrence Meynell in 1954.

Sir Banister Fletcher Award for Authors' Club

The late Sir Banister Fletcher, a former President of both the Authors' Club and the Royal Institute of British Architects instituted an annual prize 'for the book on architecture or the arts most deserving'. The award is made on the recommendation of the Professional Literature Committee of RIBA, to whom nominations for eligible titles (i.e. those written by British authors or those resident in the UK and published under a British imprint) should be submitted by the end of May of the year after publication. The prize of £750 is awarded by the Authors' Club during September. First awarded in 1954.

Marsh Award for Children's Literature in Translation

This biennial award of £750 is given to a British translator of a book for children (aged 4-16) from a foreign language into English and published in the UK by a British publisher. Electronic books, and encyclopedias and other reference books, are not eligible. Next award: October 1998. Founded in 1995.

Marsh Biography Award

This major national biography prize of £3500 plus a trophy is presented every 2 years. Entries must be serious biographies written by British authors and published in the UK. Next award: October 1997 (and then October 1999). Founded 1985-86.

The Authors' Foundation

Society of Authors, 84 Drayton Gardens,
London SW10 9SB

Grants are available to novelists, poets and writers of non-fiction who are published authors working on their next book. The aim is to provide funding (in addition to a proper advance) for research, travel or other necessary expenditure. Closing date: 30 April. Write for an information sheet. Founded in 1984 to mark the centenary of the Society of Authors.

BA/Bookseller Author of the Year

Details The Booksellers Association of Great Britain and Ireland, 272 Vauxhall Bridge Road, London SW1V 1BA
tel 0171-834 5477 *fax* 0171-834 8812

This annual award of £1000 is judged by members of the Booksellers Association of Great Britain and Ireland (4000 bookshops) in a postal ballot. Any living, British or Irish published writer is eligible and the award is given to the author judged to have had the most impact in the year. Founded in 1993.

Verity Bargate Award

Details Verity Bargate Award, The Soho Theatre Company, 21 Dean Street, London W1V 6NE

This bi-annual award is made to the writer of a new and previously unperformed full-length play. In addition to the cash prize of £1500, the winning play usually goes on to a full production by the Soho Theatre Company. Accordingly, the cho-

sen playwright is required to offer first option to produce the winning play to the Soho Theatre Company. It is also intended that emerging writers of interest – such as those whose plays are shortlisted – will be provided with workshop facilities to assist in their further development. Created as a memorial to the founder of the Soho Theatre Company. Send an sae for details.

H.E. Bates Short Story Competition

Details Events Team Office, Directorate of Environment Services, Cliftonville House, Bedford Road, Northampton NN4 7NR
tel (01604) 233500 ext 4243

This annual prize is awarded for a short story – maximum length 2000 words – to anyone resident in Great Britain. The first prize is for £200, other prizes to a total value of £150. Further details on receipt of sae from the Events Team.

BBC Wildlife Magazine Awards for Nature Writing

Details BBC Wildlife Magazine, Broadcasting House, Whiteladies Road, Bristol BS8 2LR
tel 0117-9738402 *fax* 0117-9467075
e-mail wildlifemag@gn.apc.org

BBC Wildlife Magazine awards prizes annually with the aim of reviving the art of nature writing, discovering and encouraging new essayists and focusing attention on those writers whose skills might otherwise be neglected. Entries are accepted from professional or amateur writers, and from young writers aged 17 and under. Send an sae for further information or see *BBC Wildlife Magazine*.

The BBC Wildlife Magazine Poet of the Year Contest

Details BBC Wildlife Magazine, Broadcasting House, Whiteladies Road, Bristol BS8 2LR
tel 0117-973 8402 *fax* 0117-946 7075
e-mail wildlifemag@gn.apc.org

An annual competition for poems (up to 50 lines) that express thoughts and feelings about the natural world. Prizes: winner £500, runners-up £75, winners of young poet categories £50. Closing date: varies from year to year. Founded 1991.

The Samuel Beckett Award

Details Editorial Department, Faber and Faber, 3 Queen Square, London WC1N 3AU

This award is open to residents of the UK and the Republic of Ireland for new dra-matic writing, professionally performed. The provisions of the award are currently under review. Founded in 1983.

The David Berry Prize

Council of the Royal Historical Society, University College London, Gower Street, London WC1E 6BT
tel/fax 0171-387 7532

Candidates may select any subject dealing with Scottish history, provided such subject has been previously submitted to and approved by the Council. Next closing date: 31 October 1998. Value of prize: £250.

The BFC Mother Goose Award

Books for Children, 4 Furzeground Way, Stockley Park, Middlesex UB11 1DP

Open to all artists having published a first major book for children during the previous year, only books first published in Britain will be considered, including co-productions where the illustration originated in Britain. The award, presented annually in April, is a bronze egg together with a cheque for £1000. Recommendations for the award are invited from publishers and should be sent to each panel member, whose names and addresses are available from the address above. Sponsored by Books for Children.

Big Book Cover Award

Details Jennifer Madden, Books+, Cultural Services HQ, Red Doles Lane, Huddersfield HD2 1YF
tel (01484) 226325 *fax* (01484) 226342
e-mail cultural-hq@geo2.poptel.org.uk
web site http://www.kirkleesmc.gov.uk

An annual award for the best jacket on a children's book published in the relevant year. Established 1995 by Yorkshire Libraries for Children.

The Bisto Book of the Year Award

Details The Administrator, Children's Books Ireland, Irish Writers' Centre, 19 Parnell Square, Dublin 1, Republic of Ireland
tel/fax (01) 8725854

This annual award is given for a children's book in English or Irish by an author or illustrator born or resident in Ireland, and first published between 1 January and 31 December of each judging year. Overall winner receives IR£1500, plus 3 category winners receive IR£500 each. Closing date: 31 January. Founded in 1990.

The James Tait Black Memorial Prizes

Submissions Department of English Literature, David Hume Tower, George Square, Edinburgh EH8 9JX
tel 0131-650 3619 *fax* 0131-650 6898

Two prizes of £3000 are awarded annually: one for the best biography or work of that nature, the other for the best novel, published during the calendar year. The adjudicator is the Professor of English Literature in the University of Edinburgh. Eligible novels and biographies are those written in English, originating with a British publisher, and usually first published in Britain in the year of the award. Both prizes may go to the same author, but neither to the same author a second time.

Publishers should submit a copy of any appropriate biography, or work of fiction, as early as possible with a note of the date of publication, marked 'James Tait Black Prize'. Closing date for submissions: 30 September. Founded in memory of a partner in the publishing house of A. & C. Black, these prizes were instituted in 1918.

The Kathleen Blundell Trust

Kathleen Blundell Trust, Society of Authors, 84 Drayton Gardens, London SW10 9SB

Awards are given to published writers under the age of 40 to assist them with their next book. Applications should be in the form of a letter giving reasons for the application, and must be accompanied by a copy of the author's latest book. The author's work must 'contribute to the greater understanding of existing social and economic organisation', but fiction is not excluded. Closing date: 30 April. Send sae for an information sheet.

The Boardman Tasker Prize

Details Mrs Dorothy Boardman, 14 Pine Lodge, Dairyground Road, Bramhall, Stockport, Cheshire SK7 2HS

This annual prize of £2000 is given for a work of fiction, non-fiction or poetry, the central theme of which is concerned with the mountain environment. Authors of any nationality are eligible but the work must be published or distributed in the UK. Entries from publishers only. Founded in 1983.

The Book Art Prize

Details Sophie Birula, Studio Administrator, Design Dept., Transworld Publishers Ltd, 61-63 Uxbridge Road, London W5 5SA
tel 0181-579 2652 *fax* 0181-231 6639

An annual prize (£1000) to promote excellence in book cover design and to build awareness of the art of illustration. Illustrators and photographers are both eligible. Founded 1997.

The Booker Prize

Book Trust, Book House, 45 East Hill, London SW18 2QZ
tel 0181-870 9055

This annual prize for fiction of £20,000 is awarded to the best novel published each year. It is open to novels written in English by citizens of the British Commonwealth and Republic of Ireland and published for the first time in the UK by a British publisher, although previous publication of a book outside the UK does not disqualify it. Entries only from UK publishers who may each submit not more than 2 novels with scheduled publication dates between 1 October of the previous year and 30 September of the current year, but the judges may also ask for other eligible novels to be submitted to them. In addition, publishers may submit one eligible title by authors who have been shortlisted or won the Booker Prize previously. Sponsored by Booker plc.

BP Natural World Book Prize

(in partnership with The Wildlife Trusts)
Details/entry form Book Trust, Book House, 45 East Hill, London SW18 2QZ
tel 0181-870 9055

Awards of £5000 to the winner and £1000 to the runner up for an adult book which most imaginatively promotes the conservation of the natural environment and all its animals and plants. Books must have been published in the UK between 1 October of the previous year and 31 October of the year of the award. An amalgamation of the BP Conservation Book Prize and the Natural World Book of the Year Award.

BP Portrait Award

Details National Portrait Gallery, St Martin's Place, London WC2H 0HE
tel 0171-306 0055 *fax* 0171-306 0056
web site http://www.npg.org.uk

An annual award to encourage young artists (EC citizens aged 18-41) to focus upon and develop the theme of portraiture within their work. 1st prize: £10,000 plus at the judges' discretion a commission worth £2000 to be agreed between the NPG and the artist; 2nd prize £4000; 3rd prize: £2000; Commendation: up to 5 entrants may be awarded £500 each. Closing date: April. A selection of entrants' work is exhibited at the National Portrait Gallery between June and September. Founded 1978.

Alfred Bradley Bursary Award

Details BBC Radio Drama Department, BBC North, New Broadcasting House, Oxford Road, Manchester M60 1SJ
tel 0161-244 4251

This biennial bursary of £6000 (spread over 2 years, plus a full commission for a radio play) is awarded to a writer resident or born in the North of England who has had a small amount of work published or produced. The focus for the 1996-97 award was verse drama. The scheme also allows for a group of finalists to receive small bursaries and participate in workshops. Founded in 1992.

The Bridport Prize

Details Competition Secretary, Arts Centre, South Street, Bridport, Dorset DT6 3NR
tel (01308) 427183 *fax* (01308) 424204

Annual prizes are awarded for poetry and short stories – 1st £2500, 2nd £1000, 3rd £500 in both categories. Entries should be in English, original work, typed or clearly written, and never published, read on radio/television/stage or entered for any other current competition. Closing date: 30 June each year. Winning stories are read by leading London literary agent, without obligation, and an anthology of winning entries is published each autumn. Founded as the Bridport Arts Centre Creative Writing Competition in 1980.

Katharine Briggs Folklore Award

Details The Convenor, The Folklore Society, University College London, Gower Street, London WC1E 6BT
tel 0171-387 5894

An award of £50 and an engraved goblet is given annually for a+k in English having its first, original and initial publica-

tion in the UK, which has made the most distinguished contribution to folklore studies. The term folklore studies is interpreted broadly to include all aspects of traditional and popular culture, narrative, belief, customs and folk arts.

British Academy Medals and Prizes

The British Academy, 20-21 Cornwall Terrace, London NW1 4QP
tel 0171-487 5966

A number of medals and prizes are awarded for outstanding work in various fields of the humanities on the recommendation of specialist committees: Burkitt Medal for Biblical Studies; Derek Allen Prize (made annually in turn in musicology, numismatics and Celtic studies); Sir Israel Gollancz Prize (in English studies); Grahame Clark Medal for Prehistory; Kenyon Medal for Classical Studies; Rose Mary Crawshay Prize (for English literature); Serena Medal for Italian Studies.

The British Academy Research Awards

Details/application form The British Academy, 20-21 Cornwall Terrace, London NW1 4QP
tel 0171-487 5966

These awards are made quarterly to scholars conducting advanced academic research in the humanities and social sciences, and normally resident in the UK. Applications are accepted for travel and maintenance expenses in connection with an approved programme of research, and costs of preparation of research for publication.

British Book Awards

Details Merric Davidson, 12 Priors Heath, Goudhurst, Cranbrook, Kent TN17 2RE
tel/fax (01580) 212041

Presented annually, major categories include: Author of the Year, Publisher of the Year, Bookseller of the Year, and Children's Book of the Year. Founded in 1989.

British Fantasy Awards

Details Robert Parkinson, Secretary, The British Fantasy Society, 2 Harwood Street, Stockport SK4 1JJ

Members of the British Fantasy Society vote annually for the best novel, short fiction, artist, small press and anthology of the preceding year. A further award,

the Committee Award, is decided separately. The awards take the form of a statuette. Closing date for nominations: end August each year. Founded in 1972.

Cardiff International Poetry Competition

Details/entry form Cardiff International Poetry Competition, PO Box 438, Cardiff CF1 6YA

Fourteen annual prizes totalling £5000 are awarded for unpublished poetry, written in English (1st prize £1000; 2nd £750; 3rd £500; 11 4th prizes of £250 each). Next closing date: 31 October 1997. Prizegiving: December 1997.

Children's Book Award

Details Marianne Adey, The Old Malt House, Aldbourne, Marlborough, Wilts. SN8 2DW
tel (01672) 540629 *fax* (01672) 541280

This award is given annually to authors of works of fiction for children published in the UK. Children participate in the judging of the award. 'Pick of the Year' booklist is published in conjunction with the award. Founded in 1980 by the Federation of Children's Book Groups.

Cholmondeley Awards

Administered by Cholmondeley Awards, Society of Authors, 84 Drayton Gardens, London SW10 9SB

These non-competitive awards are for the benefit and encouragement of poets of any age, sex or nationality. Submissions are not required. Total value of awards about £8000. Established by the then Dowager Marchioness of Cholmondeley in 1965.

Arthur C. Clarke Award

Details Paul Kincaid, 60 Bournemouth Road, Folkestone, Kent CT19 5AZ

An annual award of £1000 plus engraved bookend is given for the best science fiction novel with first UK publication during the previous calendar year. Titles are submitted by publishers. Founded in 1985.

The Cló Iar-Chonnachta Literary Award

Details Cló Iar-Chonnachta (Publishing Company), Indreabhán, Conamara, Co. na Gaillimhe, Republic of Ireland
tel (091) 593307

This award of £5000 is open to all writers in the Irish language. The subject of the award alternates from year to year; the 1997 prize is for Short Story Collection/Drama. Founded in 1985.

The David Cohen British Literature Prize

Details The Literature Department, Arts Council of England, 14 Great Peter Street, London SW1P 3NQ
tel 0171-333 0100

This prize of £30,000, currently the largest in the UK, will be awarded every 2 years to a living writer, novelist, short story writer, poet, essayist or dramatist in recognition of a lifetime's substantial body of achievement. Work must be written primarily in English and the writer must be a British citizen. In addition, the Arts Council will make available an extra £10,000 to enable the winner to encourage reading or writing among younger people. No application needed; the choice of the winner is made by a distinguished jury on the basis of its collective reading.

Commonwealth Writers Prize

Details/entry form Book Trust, Book House, 45 East Hill, London SW18 2QZ
tel 0181-870 9055 *fax* 0181-874 4790

This annual award is for the best work of fiction in English by a citizen of the Commonwealth published in the year prior to the award. A prize of £10,000 is awarded for best entry and a prize of £3000 for best first published book, selected from 8 regional winners who each receive prizes of £1000. Sponsored by the Commonwealth Foundation.

The Duff Cooper Prize

Details Artemis Cooper, 54 St Maur Road, London SW6 4DP
tel 0171-736 3729 *fax* 0171-731 7638

An annual prize for a literary work in the field of biography, history, politics or poetry published in English or French by a recognised publisher during the previous 12 months. The prize of £2000 comes from a Trust Fund established by the friends and admirers of Duff Cooper, 1st Viscount Norwich (1890-1954) after his death.

The Rose Mary Crawshay Prizes

One or more prizes are awarded each year to women of any nationality who, in the judgement of the Council of the British Academy, have written or published within the 3 calendar years immediately preceding the date of the award

an historical or critical work of sufficient value on any subject connected with English literature, preference being given to a work regarding Byron, Shelley or Keats. Applications are not sought in this competition. Founded in 1888.

CWA awards
Crime Writers' Association, 60 Drayton Road, Kings Heath, Brimingham B14 7LR

CWA Cartier Diamond Dagger
This award is for an outstanding contribution to the genre. Nominations are not required. Sponsored by Cartier in conjunction with the CWA. First awarded 1986.

CWA John Creasey Memorial Dagger
An award given annually for the best crime novel by an author who has not previously published a full-length work of fiction. Nominations by publishers only. Sponsored by Chivers Press. Founded in 1973 following the death of John Creasey, to commemorate his foundation of the CWA.

CWA Macallan Gold Dagger and Silver Dagger
An annual award for a crime novel published in the UK. Nominations by publishers only. Sponsored by The Macallan in conjunction with the CWA. Founded in 1955.

CWA Macallan Gold Dagger for Non-Fiction
An annual award for a non-fiction crime book to an author published in the UK. Chosen by 4 judges of different professions. Nominations by publishers only. Sponsored by The Macallan in conjunction with the CWA. Founded in 1977.

CWA Macallan Short Story Dagger
An award for the best published short story of the year, to be submitted by publishers. Panels of judges vary from year to year and the winner receives a cheque and a Dagger lapel pin. Sponsored by The Macallan. Instituted in 1993.

DT Charitable Trust Awards

David Thomas Self-Publishing Awards
Details/entry form Self-Publishing Awards, DT Charitable Trust, Writers News Ltd, PO Box 4, Nairn IV12 4HU
tel (01667) 454441

These awards are given annually to anyone resident in the UK who has self-published a book during the calendar year preceding the award. The awards are in 3 categories – novel, non-fiction, poetry – with a prize of £250 in each category. Next closing date: 15 January 1998. Established in 1993.

DT Charitable Trust Open Poetry Competition
Details/entry form Lorna Edwardson, Writing Magazine, PO Box 4, Nairn IV12 4HU
tel (01667) 454441
This annual award is open to anyone aged over 16 and writing in the English language. Poems can be up to 60 lines; there are no other restrictions on form or subject. The prize is £1200 and the winner holds the Silver Cup for one year. Established in 1994.

DT Charitable Trust Annual Ghost Story Competition
Details/entry form Lorna Edwardson, Writing Magazine (as above)
Open to anyone aged over 16, this competition is for a ghost story in 1600-1800 words. First prize is £1000 plus publication in *Writing Magazine*; 2 runners up of £100. The winner holds the Ghost Story Silver Cup for one year. Closing date: 15 January each year.

DT Charitable Trust Annual Love Story Competition
Details/entry form Lorna Edwardson, Writing Magazine (as above)
Open to anyone aged over 16, this competition is for a love story in 1600-1800 words. First prize is £1000 plus publication in *Writing Magazine*; 2 runners up of £100. The winner holds the Love Story Silver Cup for one year. Closing date: 15 January each year.

The Rhys Davies Trust
Details Mr Meic Stephens, The Secretary, The Rhys Davies Trust, 10 Heol Don, Whitchurch, Cardiff CF4 2AU
tel(01222) 623359 *fax* (01222) 529202
The Trust aims to foster Welsh writing in English and offers financial assistance to English-language literary projects in Wales, directly or in association with other bodies. It also supports the annual Rhys Davies Lecture at the University of Glamorgan.

The Dillons First Fiction Award

Details Dillons Publicity, Royal House, Prince's Gate, Homer Road, Solihull B91 3QQ

This annual award of £5000 (and substantial promotion through Dillons stores) is given to the best first-time novelist whose work, originally written in English, was published in the UK in the calendar year of the award. Shortlist of 6 titles is selected by panel of Dillons booksellers; the winning novel is chosen by panel of Dillons customers (selected through a competition in the Dillons magazine). Founded in 1995.

The Dundee Book Prize

Details Niall Scott, Beattie Communications, 4 Prospect House, Dundee Technology Park, Dundee DD2 1TY
tel (01382) 598408 *fax* (01382) 598442
e-mail beattiemedia-d@sol.co.uk
web sites http://www.dundee.ac.uk/pressreleases/dunpri.htm
http://dundeecity.gov.uk/dcchtml/cofd/bookprize.html

An annual prize (£6000 and the chance of publication by Polygon) awarded for an unpublished novel set in Dundee in the past or present. Founded 1996.

The T.S. Eliot Prize

Applications Poetry Book Society, Book House, 45 East Hill, London SW18 2QZ
tel 0181-870 8403

An annual prize of £5000 is awarded to the best collection of new poetry published in the UK or the Republic of Ireland during the year. Submissions are invited from publishers in the autumn. Founded in 1993.

Encore Award

Details The Society of Authors, 84 Drayton Gardens, London SW10 9SB
tel 0171-373 6642

This annual award of £7500 is for the best second novel of the year. The work submitted must be:
• a novel by one author who has had one (and only one) novel published previously, and
• in the English language, first published in the UK.
Closing date: 30 November.

The European Poetry Translation Prize

Administered by The Poetry Society, 22 Betterton Street, London WC2H 9BU

A prize of £1500 is given every 2 years for a published volume of poetry which has been translated into English from a European language. Next award 1997. Funded by the Arts Council of England. Founded in 1983.

Christopher Ewart-Biggs Memorial Prize

Details The Secretary, Memorial Prize, Flat 3, 149 Hamilton Terrace, London NW8 9QS
tel 0171-624 1863

This prize of £4000 is awarded once every 2 years to the writer, of any nationality, whose work is judged to contribute most to:
• peace and understanding in Ireland;
• to closer ties between the peoples of Britain and Ireland;
• or to co-operation between the partners of the European Union.
Eligible works must be published during the 2 years to 31 December 1998.

The Geoffrey Faber Memorial Prize

An annual prize of £1000 is awarded in alternate years for a volume of verse and for a volume of prose fiction, first published originally in the UK during the 2 years preceding the year in which the award is given which is, in the opinion of the judges, of the greatest literary merit. Eligible writers must be not more than 40 years old at the date of publication of the book and a citizen of the UK and Colonies, of any other Commonwealth state or of the Republic of Ireland. The 3 judges are reviewers of poetry or fiction who are nominated each year by the literary editors of newspapers and magazines which regularly publish such reviews. Faber and Faber invite nominations from reviewers and literary editors. No submissions for the prize are to be made. Established in 1963 by Faber and Faber Ltd, as a memorial to the founder and first Chairman of the firm.

The Eleanor Farjeon Award

An annual prize of (minimum) £750 may be given to a librarian, teacher, author, artist, publisher, reviewer, television producer or any other person working with or for children through books. Sponsored by Books for Children. Instituted in 1965 by the Children's Book Circle for distin-

guished services to children's books and named after the much-loved children's writer.

The Kathleen Fidler Award

Administered by Book Trust Scotland,
The Scottish Book Centre, 137 Dundee Street,
Edinburgh EH11 1BG

An annual award for an unpublished novel for children aged 8-12 years, to encourage authors new to writing for this age group. The work should be the author's first attempt to write for this age range. The winner will receive £1000 and the work will be published by Hodder Children's Books, the new sponsors of the award. Send sae for details.

E.M. Forster Award

The distinguished English author, E.M. Forster, bequeathed the American publication rights and royalties of his posthumous novel *Maurice* to Christopher Isherwood, who transferred them to the American Academy of Arts and Letters (633 West 155th Street, New York, NY 10032, USA), for the establishment of an E.M. Forster Award, currently $15,000, to be given annually to an English writer for a stay in the United States. Applications for this award are not accepted.

Forward Poetry Prizes

Details Forward Poetry Prize Administrator,
Colman Getty PR, Carrington House,
126-130 Regent Street, London W1R 5FE
tel 0171-439 1783 *fax* 0171-439 1784

Three prizes are awarded annually:
• best collection of poetry published between 1 October and 30 September (£10,000);
• best first collection of poetry published between 1 October and 30 September (£5000); and
• best individual poem, published but not as part of a collection between 1 May 1996 and 30 April 1997 (£1000).

All poems entered are also considered for inclusion in the *Forward Book of Poetry*, an annual anthology. Entries must be submitted by book publishers and editors of newspapers, periodicals and magazines in the UK and Eire. Individual entries from poets will not be accepted. Established in 1992.

Miles Franklin Literary Award

Details Arts Management Pty Ltd,
Station House, Rawson Place, 790 George Street,
Sydney, NSW 2000, Australia
tel (02) 9212 5066

This annual award of $28,000 is for a novel or play first published in the preceding year, which presents Australian life in any of its phases. More than one entry may be submitted by each author, and collaborations between 2 or more authors are eligible. Biographies, collections of short stories or children's books are not eligible. Closing date: approx. 31 January each year. Founded in 1957.

The Fulbright Commission Awards

Fulbright House, 62 Doughty Street,
London WC1N 2LS
tel 0171-404 6880 *fax* 0171-404 6834
web site www.fulbright.co.uk

Application forms are available on the web site or on receipt of sae (39p).

Fulbright Postgraduate Student Awards

Awards are made to outstanding graduate students who are able to demonstrate leadership qualities. There are about 20 annual awards to cover travel and maintenance costs. Closing date: usually end October/beginning November of the preceding academic year of study.

Fulbright Scholarship Grants

Awards are made to potential or established leaders of professional, academic and artistic excellence. Subjects which provide an opportunity for collaborative innovation of international significance or a focus on Anglo-American relations are of particular interest. Awards are for £1750 and applicants must have an invitation to lecture or research at an approved US institution. Closing date: early Spring.

The Lionel Gelber Prize

Details Prize Manager, The Lionel Gelber Prize,
c/o Meisner Publicity, 112 Braemore Gardens,
Toronto, Ontario M6G 2C8, Canada
tel 416-652-1947 *fax* 416-658-5205
e-mail oomfpub@pathcom.com

This international prize of $50,000 is awarded annually in Canada to the author of the year's most outstanding work of non-fiction in the field of international relations. Submissions must be published in English or in English trans-

lation between 1 September and 31 August of following year. Submissions deadline: 31 May, i.e. 3 months before the end of the period in question. Established in 1989.

The Alasdair Gilchrist-Fisher Memorial Award

Cadogan Contemporary, 108 Draycott Avenue, London SW3 3AE

tel 0171-581 5451 *fax* 0171-589 9120

e-mail artcad@dircon.co.uk

Biennial prize (approx. £3500) awarded to a young artist (aged under 30) for a landscape painting. Founded 1987.

The Glenfiddich Awards

Details The Glenfiddich Awards, 27 Fitzroy Square, London W1P 5HH

tel 0171-383 3024 *fax* 0171-383 4593

Awards are given annually to recognise excellence in writing, publishing and broadcasting relating to the subjects of food and drink. £800 is given to each of 12 categories, together with a case of Glenfiddich Single Malt Scotch Whisky and an engraved quaich. The overall winner receives The Glenfiddich Trophy and an additional £3000. Founded in 1970.

Juliet Gomperts Memorial Scholarship

Enquiries B.D. Gomperts, 31 Addison Avenue, London W11 4QS

e-mail rmka101@ucl.ac.uk

Established in honour of Juliet Gomperts who was tragically killed when she was an art student in Pakistan. The 5 annual scholarships (value £600) provide tuition, board and lodging for 2 weeks in the summer at the Verrocchio Arts Centre in Italy. Open to artists aged 18-40. Closing date: end of February. Send sae for details. Founded 1990.

E.C. Gregory Trust Fund

Details Society of Authors, 84 Drayton Gardens, London SW10 9SB

A number of substantial awards are made annually for the encouragement of young poets who can show that they are likely to benefit from an opportunity to give more time to writing. An eligible candidate must:

• be a British subject by birth but not a national of Eire or any of the British dominions or colonies and be ordinarily resident in the UK or Northern Ireland;

• be under the age of 30 on 31 March in the year of the Award (i.e. the year following submission);

• submit for consideration a published or unpublished work of belles-lettres, poetry or drama poems (not more than 30 poems). Entries: no later than 31 October.

The Guardian Children's Fiction Prize

The Guardian's annual prize of £1500 is for a work of children's fiction (usually for children over 8) published by a British or Commonwealth writer. The winning book is chosen by the Children's Book Editor together with a team of 3 or 4 other authors of children's books.

The Guardian Fiction Prize

The Guardian's annual prize of £3000 is for a work of fiction showing originality and promise published by a British or Commonwealth writer. The winning book will be chosen by the Literary Editor in conjunction with *The Guardian's* regular reviewers of new fiction.

The Hawthornden Prize

Details The Administrator, 42A Hays Mews, Berkeley Square, London W1X 7RU

This prize is awarded annually to the author of what, in the opinion of the Committee, is the best work of imaginative literature published during the preceding calendar year by a British author. Books do not have to be specially submitted.

Hawthornden Writers' Fellowships

Details The Administrator, Hawthornden Castle International Retreat for Writers, Hawthornden Castle, Lasswade, Midlothian EH18 1EG

tel 0131-440 2180

Applications are invited from novelists, poets, dramatists and other creative writers whose work has already been published. Four-week fellowships are offered to those working on a current project.

The Felicia Hemans Prize for Lyrical Poetry

Submissions The Registrar, The University of Liverpool, PO Box 147, Liverpool L69 3BX

tel 0151-794 2458 *fax* 0151-794 2454

This annual prize of books or money, open to past and present members and students of the University of Liverpool only, is awarded for a lyrical poem, the

subject of which may be chosen by the competitor. Only one poem, either published or unpublished, may be submitted. The prize shall not be awarded more than once to the same competitor. Poems, endorsed 'Hemans Prize', must be sent on or before 1 May.

Heywood Hill Literary Prize
Administration Heywood Hill Booksellers, 10 Curzon Street, London W1Y 7FJ

An award of £10,000 is given annually to a person chosen for their lifetime's contribution to the enjoyment of books. No applications. Established in 1995.

David Higham Prize for Fiction
Entry form Book Trust, Book House, 45 East Hill, London SW18 2QZ
tel 0181-870 9055

This prize of £1000 is awarded annually to a citizen of the British Commonwealth or Republic of Ireland for a first novel or book of short stories written in English and published during the current year. Publishers only may submit books. Founded in 1975.

William Hill Sports Book of the Year Award
Details Graham Sharpe, William Hill Organisation, Greenside House, 50 Station Road, London N22 4TP
tel 0181-918 3731

This award is given annually in November for a book with a sporting theme (record books and listings excluded). The title must be in the English language, and published for the first time in the UK during the relevant calendar year. Total value of prize is £6000, including £5000 in cash. An award for the best cover design was introduced in 1991, value £500. Founded in 1989.

The Calvin and Rose G. Hoffman Memorial Prize for Distinguished Publication on Christopher Marlowe
Applications The Headmaster, The King's School, Canterbury, Kent CT1 2ES
tel (01227) 595501 *fax* (01227) 595595

This annual prize of between £5000 and £6000 is awarded to the best unpublished work that examines the life and works of Christopher Marlowe and the relationship between the works of Marlowe and Shakespeare. Closing date: 1 September.

Royal Society of Literature Award under the Winifred Holtby Memorial Bequest
Submissions The Royal Society of Literature, 1 Hyde Park Gardens, London W2 2LT

This prize (value £800) is awarded for the best regional novel of the year written in the English language. The writer must be of British or Irish nationality, or a citizen of the Commonwealth. Translations, unless made by the author of the work, are not eligible for consideration. If in any year it is considered that no regional novel is of sufficient merit the prize may be awarded to an author, qualified as aforesaid, of a literary work of non-fiction or poetry, concerning a regional subject. Novels published during the current year should be submitted by 31 October.

Hunting Art Prizes
Details Parker Harris & Co., PO Box 1390, London SW8 1QZ
tel (01372) 462190 *fax* (01372) 460032
Contact Jane Sowerby

An annual national art competition open to all artists resident in the UK. Total prize monies: £20,500. Entry fee is £10 (£4 students) per work and artists may submit up to 3 works. Closing date: mid-November. 1997 winning entries will be exhibited at the Royal College of Art 5-15 Feb 1998 and at the Newport Museum and Art Gallery 21 March-2 May 1998. Established 1980.

The Richard Imison Memorial Award
Details/entry form The Secretary, The Broadcasting Committee, The Society of Authors, 84 Drayton Gardens, London SW10 9SB
tel 0171-373 6642

This annual prize of £1000 is awarded to any new writer of radio drama first transmitted within the UK during the period 1 January-31 December 1997 by a writer new to radio. Founded in 1993.

The Independent/Scholastic Story of the Year Competition
Prizes are awarded annually for the best short stories (1500-2500 words) for 6-9-year-old children. Prizes: £2000 winner, £500 each to runners up, £200 each to up to 7 finalists, whose entries are included in an anthology which is published each autumn. Full entry details are advertised

in *The Independent* each spring (February). Founded in 1993.

International IMPAC Dublin Literary Award

Details The International IMPAC Dublin Literary Award Office, Dublin City Public Libraries, Administrative Headquarters, Cumberland House, Fenian Street, Dublin 2, Republic of Ireland
tel (01) 6619000 *fax* (01) 6761628
e-mail dublin.city.libs@iol.ie
web site http://www.iol.ie/~dubcilib

An annual award of IR£100,000 is presented to the author of a work of fiction, written and published in the English language or written in a language other than English and published in English translation, which in the opinion of the judges is of high literary merit and constitutes a lasting contribution to world literature. Nominations accepted from library systems of major cities from all over the world, regardless of national origin of the author or the place of publication. Founded in 1995.

International Playwriting Festival

Details/entry form Warehouse Theatre, Dingwall Road, Croydon CR0 2NF
tel 0181-681 1257 *fax* 0181-688 6699

An annual competition for full-length plays which must be previously unperformed. Plays are accepted from all around the world and from both new and established writers. Deadline for entries: 6 July. Finalists are given a professionally directed and acted rehearsed reading in November (most winners have later had a full production). Established in 1986.

Irish Times Literary Prizes

Details Gerard Cavanagh (administrator)
tel (3531) 6792022 *fax* (3531) 6709383

These biennial prizes are awarded from nominations submitted by literary editors and critics. The 1997 Irish Literature Prizes were IR£5000 for each of 3 categories:
• fiction (novel, novella or collection of short stories);
• non-fictional prose (history, biography, autobiography, criticism, politics, sociological interest, travel, current affairs and belles-lettres);
• poetry (collection of works or long poem or sequence of poems or revised/

updated edition of previously published selection or collection of a poet's work). The work must be published in English or Irish. Launched in 1989.

International Fiction Prize

A biennial prize of IR£7500 is awarded for a work of fiction written in the English language and published in Ireland, the UK or the USA.

Jewish Quarterly Literary Prizes

Details The Administrator, Jewish Quarterly, PO Box 2078, London W1A 1JR
tel 0171-629 5004 *fax* 0171-629 5110

Prizes are awarded annually for a work of fiction (£4000) and non-fiction (£3000) which best stimulate an interest in and awareness of themes of Jewish concern among a wider reading public. Founded in 1977.

Kent & Sussex Poetry Society Open Poetry Competition

Submissions The Organiser, 8 Edward Street, Southborough, Kent TN4 0HP

This competition is open to all unpublished poems, no longer than 40 lines in length. Prizes: 1st £300, 2nd £100, 3rd £50, 4th 5 at £20. Closing date: 31 January. Entries should include an entry fee of £2 per poem, the author's name and address and a list of poems submitted. Founded in 1985.

The John Kobal Photographic Portrait Award

The John Kobal Foundation, PO Box 3838, London NW1 3JF
tel 0171-383 2979 *fax* 0171-383 0044

Portrait photography is defined here as 'photography concerned with portraying people with the emphasis on their identity as individuals' and the award is open to anyone over the age of 18. Total prize monies: £5500. Established 1992.

Kraszna-Krausz Awards

Details A.J. Mahoney, 14 Brands Hill Avenue, High Wycombe, Bucks. HP13 5QA
tel (01494) 444052

Awards totalling £40,000 are made each year, alternating annually between the best books on:
• still photography: art and culture, educational, photographic innovations (1996); and

• moving picture media: culture, business, techniques and technology (1997). The prize in each category will be awarded to the best book published in the preceding 2 years. Closing date: 30 June. Instituted in 1985. The Foundation is also open to applications for grants concerned with the literature of photography.

The Lady Short Story Competition
The Lady, 39-40 Bedford Street,
London WC2E 9ER

This competition is open to anyone possessing a coupon from the first October issue of *The Lady*. First prize is £1000. Subjects for short stories change each year. Further information in the relevant issue – please do not contact the magazine office directly in connection with the competition. Founded in 1993.

The Laing Art Competition
Details Mrs J. Donlevy, John Laing plc (Art Competition), Page Street, London NW7 2ER
tel 0181-959 3636

An annual national open art competition (seascapes and landscapes) open to all artists resident in the UK and held at regional venues. 1st prize: £5000; 5 highly commended prizes: £1000; regional 1st prize: £1000. Closing date: January. Winning entries will be exhibited in the spring regionally and at the Mall Galleries, London. Founded 1972.

Leverhulme Research Fellowships and Grants
The Leverhulme Trust, 15-19 New Fetter Lane, London EC4A 1NR
tel 0171-822 6964 *fax* 0171-822 5084
e-mail jcater@leverhulme.org.uk
web site http://www.leverhulme.org.uk

The Leverhulme Trustees offer annually approx. 75 Fellowships and Grants to individuals in aid of original research. These awards are not available as replacement for past support from other sources. Applications will be considered in all subject areas. The maximum total of a Fellowship or Grant is £15,965. Completed application forms must be received by 13 Nov 1997. Founded 1933.

The Library Association Children's Book Awards
e-mail info@la-hq.org.uk
web site http://www.fdgroup.co.uk/la.htm

Recommendations for the following 2 awards are invited from members of the Library Association, who are asked to submit a preliminary list of not more than 2 titles for each award, accompanied by a 50-word appraisal justifying the recommendation of each book. The awards are selected by the Youth Libraries Group of the Library Association.

Carnegie Medal
Awarded annually for an outstanding book for children (fiction or non-fiction) written in English and first published in the UK during the preceding year or co-published elsewhere within a 3-month time lapse.

Kate Greenaway Medal
Awarded annually for an outstanding illustrated book for children first published in the UK during the preceding year or co-published elsewhere within a 3-month time lapse. Books intended for older as well as younger children are included, and reproduction will be taken into account.

The Library Association Reference Awards
e-mail info@la-hq.org.uk
web site http://www.fdgroup.co.uk/la.htm

The Besterman Medal
Awarded annually for an outstanding bibliography or guide to the literature first published in the UK during the preceding year either in print or in electronic form. Recommendations for the award are invited from members of the Library Association, who are asked to submit a preliminary list of not more than 3 titles, and submissions from publishers are welcome.

The McColvin Medal
Awarded annually for an outstanding reference work either in print or in electronic form first published in the UK during the preceding year. Works eligible for consideration are encyclopedias, general and special; dictionaries, general and special; biographical dictionaries; annuals, yearbooks and directories; handbooks and compendia of data; atlases. Recommendations for the award

are invited from members of the Library Association, who are asked to submit a preliminary list of not more than 3 titles, and submissions from publishers are welcome.

The Walford Award

Awarded annually to an individual who has made a sustained and continued contribution to the science and art of British bibliography over a period of years. The bibliographer's work can encompass effort in the history, classification and description of printed, written, audiovisual and machine-readable materials. Recommendations may be made for the work of a living person or persons, or for an organisation. The award can be made to a British bibliographer or to a person or organisation working in the UK.

The Wheatley Medal

Awarded annually for an outstanding index published during the preceding 3 years. Printed indexes to any type of publication may be submitted for consideration, providing that the whole work, including the index, or the index alone has originated in the UK. Recommendations for the award are invited from members of the Library Association and the Society of Indexers, publishers and others. The final selection is made by a committee consisting of representatives of the Library Association Cataloguing and Indexing Group and the Society of Indexers.

The Lichfield Prize

Details Tourist Information Centre, Donegal House, Bore Street, Lichfield, Staffs. WS13 6NE
tel (01543) 252109 *fax* (01543) 417308

Lichfield District Council's biennial prize of £5000 and the chance of publication, is for the best novel based recognisably on the geographical area of Lichfield District, Staffordshire. Next closing date expected to be 30 April 1999. Instituted in 1988.

The Livingstone Award for Travel

Details The Livingstone Award for Travel, PO Box 3821, London NW2 3DQ

This award is open to any writer of a travel guide printed in the English language and published in the 12 months prior to closing date (31 August). The prize is £1000 plus an engraved goblet. Founded in 1990.

The London New Writing Competition

Entry form London Arts Board, Elme House, 133 Long Acre, London WC2E 9AF
tel 0171-240 1313 *fax* 0171-240 4580

Open to adults resident in Greater London, this biennial competition offers awards of £200 each (plus publication in an anthology) for the best creative pieces about London. Next closing date: end November 1998. Founded in 1992.

The Sir William Lyons Award

Details General Secretary, 30 The Cravens, Smallfield, Surrey RH6 9QS
tel (01342) 843294 *fax* (01342) 844093

This annual award (trophy, £1000 and 2 years' probationary membership of The Guild of Motoring Writers) was set up to encourage young people in automotive journalism, including broadcasting, and to foster interest in motoring and the motor industry through these media. Open to any person of British nationality resident in the UK under the age of 23, it consists of writing 2 essays and an interview with the Award Committee.

The Macallan/Scotland on Sunday Short Story Competition

Details The Administrator, The Macallan/ Scotland on Sunday Short Story Competition, 20 North Bridge, Edinburgh EH1 1YT

These annual prizes (1st £6000; 2nd £600; 4 runners up £100 each; publication of winning entries in *Scotland on Sunday*) are awarded for the best short story of less than 3000 words written by a person born in Scotland, now living in Scotland or by a Scot living abroad. Instituted in 1990.

The McKitterick Prize

Details The Society of Authors, 84 Drayton Gardens, London SW10 9SB

This annual award of £4000-£6000 is open to first published novels and unpublished typescripts by authors over the age of 40. Closing date: 16 December. Endowed by the late Tom McKitterick.

The Enid McLeod Literary Prize

Details Executive Secretary, Franco-British Society, Room 623, Linen Hall, 162-168 Regent Street, London W1R 5TB
tel/fax 0171-734 0815

This annual prize of £250 is given for a full-length work of literature which con-

tributes most to Franco-British understanding. It must be written in English by
a citizen of the UK, British
Commonwealth, the Republic of Ireland,
Pakistan, Bangladesh or South Africa,
and first published in the UK.

The Macmillan Prize for a Children's Picture Book

Applications Marketing Director, Macmillan
Children's Books, 25 Eccleston Place,
London SW1W 9NF

Three prizes are awarded annually for
children's book illustrations by art students in higher education establishments
in the UK. Prizes: £1000 (1st), £500 (2nd)
and £250 (3rd).

Macmillan Silver Pen Award for Fiction

Details PEN, 7 Dilke Street, London SW3 4JE
tel 0171-352 6303 *fax* 0171-351 0220

This award of £500 is given annually for
an outstanding collection of short stories
written in English and published during
the previous year by an author of British
nationality or an author who has been a
long-term resident in the UK. No submissions please – books are nominated by
members of the PEN Executive
Committee. Sponsored by Macmillan
since 1986. Founded in 1969.

The Mail on Sunday/John Llewellyn Rhys Prize

Entry form The Mail on Sunday/John Llewellyn
Rhys Prize, c/o Book Trust, Book House,
45 East Hill, London SW18 2QZ
tel 0181-870 9055

This annual prize of £5000 is offered to
the author of the most promising literary
work of any kind published for the first
time during the current year. The author
must be a citizen of this country or the
Commonwealth, and not have passed his
or her 35th birthday by the date of the
publication of the work submitted.
Publishers only may submit books.
Inaugurated in memory of the writer
John Llewellyn Rhys.

The Kurt Maschler Award

Details Book Trust, Book House, 45 East Hill,
London SW18 2QZ
tel 0181-870 9055

This annual prize of £1000 is awarded to
a British author/artist or an author/artist
who has been resident in Britain for

more than 10 years for a children's book
in which text and illustrations are of
excellence and enhance and balance
each other. Founded in 1982.

The Somerset Maugham Awards

Details The Society of Authors,
84 Drayton Gardens, London SW10 9SB

These annual awards, totalling about
£15,000, are to encourage young writers
to travel. Mr Maugham urged that originality and promise should be the touch-
stones: he did not wish the judges to
'play for safety' in their choice. A candidate must be a British subject by birth
and ordinarily resident in the UK or
Northern Ireland, must be under 35 years
of age and must submit a published literary work in the English language, of
which the candidate is the sole author.
Poetry, fiction, non-fiction, belles-lettres
or philosophy, but not dramatic works,
are eligible. Four, non-returnable copies
of one published work should be submitted, and must be accompanied by a statement of the author's date and place of
birth, and other published works.
Closing date: 31 December.

MCA Book Prize

Details Andrea Livingstone, Administrator,
MCA Book Prize, 122 Fawnbrake Avenue,
London SE24 0BZ
tel/fax 0171-738 6701

An annual main prize of £5000, and a
Young Writers Award (under 35 years
old) of up to £2000, are given to books
which contribute stimulating, original
and progressive ideas on management
issues. Authors must be British subjects
domiciled in the UK. Next closing date:
15 November 1997. Founded in 1993.

Meyer-Whitworth Award

Details Theatre Writing Section, Drama
Department, Arts Council of England,
14 Great Peter Street, London SW1P 3NQ
tel 0171-333 0100 ext 431
e-mail info.drama.ace@artsfb.org.uk

Set up to help further the careers of UK
contemporary playwrights who are not
yet established, this award of £8000 is
given annually for an English-language
play which shows writing of individual
quality and the promise of a developing
new talent. Candidates will have had no
more than 2 of their plays professionally

produced. Nominated plays must have been produced professionally in the UK for the first time between 1 August and 31 July; closing date: last Friday in August.

Millfield Arts Projects

Atkinson Gallery, Millfield, Butleigh Road, Street, Somerset BA16 0YD
tel (01458) 442291 *fax* (01458) 447276
Director of Art Len Green

'The mandate of the Millfield Arts Project programme is to search for, promote and support, primarily but not exclusively, young aspiring artists at local, regional, national and international levels.' In a professional art context MAP offers:
• Sculpture Commission. Artists work on campus for 8 weeks (£7500). Deadline for entries: mid January.
• Summer Show. An open exhibition. Application forms available: March.
• Six Gallery exhibitions selected by the Director of Art. Interested artists should send slides and CV to the Director of Art.
• Sculpture Summer Show. Campus sculpture exhibition in July/August/September.

Mind Book of the Year/Allen Lane Award

Details Anny Brack, Mind Publications, Granta House, 15-19 Broadway, London E15 4BQ
tel 0181-519 2122 *fax* 0181-522 1725

This £1000 award is given to the author of any book (fiction or non-fiction) published in the UK in the current year which outstandingly furthers public understanding of the prevention, causes, treatment or experience of mental health problems. Entries by 31 December. Administered by Mind, the National Association for Mental Health. Inaugurated in memory of Sir Allen Lane in 1981.

John Moores Liverpool Exhibition

Walker Art Gallery, William Brown Street, Liverpool L3 8EL
tel 0151-478 4199 *fax* 0151-478 4190
Contact Barbara Webb

Biennial painting exhibition open to any artist living or working in the UK. Cash prize of £20,000 plus acquisition (by gift) of prize-winning painting by the Walker Art Gallery. Hand in Aug 1997. Exhibition Oct 1997-Feb 1998. Founded 1957.

Shiva Naipaul Memorial Prize

Details The Spectator, 56 Doughty Street, London WC1N 2LL

This annual prize of £3000 is given to an English language writer of any nationality under the age of 35 for an essay of not more than 4000 words describing a visit to a foreign place or people. Founded in 1985.

The National Art Library Illustration Awards

Enquiries The National Art Library, Victoria and Albert Museum, South Kensington, London SW7 2RL
tel 0171-938 8313 or
Dr Leo De Freitas *tel/fax* (01295) 256110

These annual awards are given to practising book and magazine illustrators, for work first published in Great Britain in the 12 months preceding the judging of the awards. Book covers, illustrations of a purely technical nature and photographs together with works produced as limited editions are excluded. Cover illustrations to magazines are eligible. Sponsored by The Enid Linder Foundation.

National Poetry Competition

Competition Organiser, The Poetry Society, 22 Betterton Street, London WC2H 9DU
tel 0171-240 4810 *fax* 0171-240 4818
e-mail poetrysoc@dial.pipex.com
web site http://www.poetrysoc.com

One of Britain's major annual open poetry competitions. Prizes: 1st £5000, 2nd £1000, 3rd £500, 10 runners up of £50 plus a Montblanc pen. Maximum length 40 lines. Closing date: 31 October 1997. Send an sae for rules and entry form.

National Poetry Competition (Ireland)

Poetry Ireland, National Poetry Competition, Bermingham Tower, Upper Yard, Dublin Castle, Dublin 2, Republic of Ireland
tel (01) 6714632 *fax* (01) 6714634
e-mail poetry@iol.ie

An annual poetry competition with a prizes of Ir£1000 for the best poem and Ir£250 for the best poem by a poet who has never been published in any form. Poems can be on any subject in either English or Irish. All poems should be previously unpublished and no longer than 40 lines. Entry fees: £3 for the first poem, £2 for each subsequent poem, and £1 for all entries from under 18-year-

olds. Closing date: 28 Nov 1997. Founded 1992.

The NCR Book Award for Non-Fiction
Details The Administrator, NCR Book Award, 206 Marylebone Road, London NW1 6LY
tel 0171-725 8325 *fax* 0171-724 6519

An annual award to stimulate more interest in non-fiction writing and publishing in the UK. The award carries a prize of £25,000, currently one of the highest non-fiction awards available in the UK. Additionally, each shortlisted author receives a prize bringing the overall value to £37,500. Applications welcomed from publishers. Sponsored by NCR Limited. Founded in 1987.

The Nobel Prize in Literature
Awarding authority Swedish Academy, Box 2118, S-10313 Stockholm, Sweden
tel (08) 10-65-24 *fax* (08) 24-42-25
e-mail sekretariat@svenskaakademien.se
web site http://svenska.gu.se/academy.html

This is one of the awards stipulated in the will of the late Alfred Nobel, the Swedish scientist who invented dynamite. No direct application for a prize will be taken into consideration. For authors writing in English it was bestowed upon Rudyard Kipling in 1907, W.B. Yeats in 1923, George Bernard Shaw in 1925, Sinclair Lewis in 1930, John Galsworthy in 1932, Eugene O'Neill in 1936, Pearl Buck in 1938, T.S. Eliot in 1948, William Faulkner in 1949, Bertrand Russell in 1950, Sir Winston Churchill in 1953, Ernest Hemingway in 1954, John Steinbeck in 1962, Samuel Beckett in 1969, Patrick White in 1973, Saul Bellow in 1976, William Golding in 1983, Wole Soyinka in 1986, Joseph Brodsky in 1987, Nadine Gordimer in 1991, Derek Walcott in 1992, Toni Morrison in 1993 and Seamus Heaney in 1995.

Northern Arts Writers' Awards
Details Sarah Mann, Published & Broadcast Arts Department, Northern Arts, 9-10 Osborne Terrace, Jesmond, Newcastle upon Tyne NE2 1NZ
tel 0191-281 6334
e-mail smn@norab.demon.co.uk

Up to £3000 is available annually to support previously published novelists, short story writers, poets and literary critics living in the Northern Arts region of Teesside, Cumbria, Co Durham, Tyne & Wear and Northumberland.

Northern Short Story Competition
Application form Rosemary Jones, Short Story Competition, Arc Publications, Nanholme Mill, Shaw Wood Road, Todmorden, Lancs. OL14 6DY
tel(01706) 812338 *fax* (01706) 818948

This competition (total prize money £500) is open to residents of the area covered by Northern Arts, North West Arts and Yorkshire and Humberside Arts Boards (see page 471), as well as Derbyshire and Lincolnshire. Stories may be on any subject, of no more than 3000 words. Closing date: 30 June each year; entry forms available from beginning of March. Founded in 1988.

The Observer Hodge Award/Exhibition
The Observer Hodge Award, The Observer, 119 Farringdon Road, London EC1R 3ER
tel 0171-278 2332 *fax* 0171-713 4368
e-mail sara@guardian.co.uk, rachel@guardian.co.uk
Contact Sara Rhodes or Rachel Cave

Set up in memory of photographer David Hodge who died aged 30, the award is given to student and professional photographers under 30. First prize: £3000 plus a photographic assignment for *The Observer*. Best student prize: £1000. Other prizes: 2nd, 3rd and highly commended. The exhibition will be at The Photographers' Gallery in autumn/winter. Deadline for entries: early spring. Founded 1986.

P.J. O'Connor Awards
P.J. O'Connor Awards, RTE Radio Drama, Donnybrook, Dublin 4, Republic of Ireland
fax (01) 2083304
Producer in Charge Michael Campion

An annual competition for a 30-minute original radio play, open to unproduced writers born in or living in Ireland. 1st prize: £1000, 2nd prize: £750, £3rd prize: £500. Closing date: 8 Nov 1997.

One Voice
Details One Voice, c/o Theatr Cwmtawe, Parc Ynysderw, Pontardawe, W. Glamorgan SA8 4EG
tel (01792) 830111 *fax* (01792) 862020

This competition is open to all writers. Finalists' work will be performed and published. The Catrin Collier Random House Prize enables a writer in the Short Story section to spend a day with Catrin Collier and an editor from Random

House and to attend a professional performance of the winning entries. There are 2 categories: Story and Monologue. Workshops and surgeries are available to all entrants. Founded in 1992.

Orange Prize for Fiction
Orange Prize for Fiction, Book Trust, Book House, 45 East Hill, London SW18 2QZ, *tel* 0181-870 9055 *fax* 0181-874 4790

This new award of £30,000 is for a full length novel written in English by a woman of any nationality and first published in the UK between 1 April 1996 and 31 March 1997.

George Orwell Memorial Prize
Details The Literary Editor, The Political Quarterly, 8A Bellevue Terrace, Edinburgh EH7 4DT *e-mail* brc@tattoo.ed.ac.uk

Two prizes of £1000 each are awarded in March each year – one for the best political book, and one for best political journalism – of the previous year, giving equal merit to content and good style accessible to the general public. Next closing date: 20 January 1997 for work published in 1996. Founded in 1993.

Catherine Pakenham Memorial Award
Entry form Lucy Goodwin, Public Relations Dept, The Sunday Telegraph, 1 Canada Square, Canary Wharf, London E14 5DT *tel* 0171-538 6259 *fax* 0171-513 2512

Young women journalists, or aspiring journalists (over 18 and under 25 years of age), resident in Britain, are eligible for this award of £1000. It is given for a non-fiction article between 750 and 2000 words long. Entry forms are available after 1 September. Founded in 1970 in memory of Catherine Pakenham, who died in a car crash while working for the *Telegraph Magazine*.

Peterloo Poets Open Poetry Competition
Details Peterloo Poets, 2 Kelly Gardens, Calstock, Cornwall PL18 9SA

This annual competition offers for 1998 a first prize of £4000 and 5 other prizes totalling £2100. Closing date: 2 March 1998. Founded in 1986.

Poetry Life Open Poetry Competition
14 Pennington Oval, Lymington, Hants SO41 8BQ *tel* (01590) 679269

A competition held 3 times a year with a first prize of £500. Any style is acceptable with an 80-line limit on each poem. Poems entered must be previously unpublished (in book form) and must have not won a competition or prize on any other occasion. Winning entries will be published in *Poetry Life*. Entry fee: £3 per poem. Send sae for further details. Founded 1994.

Poetry Update 'Poem of the Month' Competition
Poem of the Month Competition, Poetry Update, 3 Fulham Broadway, London SW6 1AA *e-mail* publish@poetry.net *web site* http://www.poetry.net *Writing on the Web* http://www.writing.co.uk *Poetry Parlour* http://www.poetry.co.uk

An ongoing monthly competition with a prize of £100 plus publication in *Poetry Update* on the Internet. Entry fee: £3 per poem. Closing date: last day of each month. Write for details. Founded 1996.

The Portico Prize
Details Miss Emma Marigliano, Librarian, Portico Library, 57 Mosley Street, Manchester M2 3HY *tel* 0161-236 6785

This biennial prize of £2500 (next prize 1997) is awarded for a published work of general interest and literary merit set wholly or mainly in the North-West of England (Lancashire, Manchester, Liverpool, High Peak of Derbyshire, Cheshire and Cumbria). Founded in 1985.

Dennis Potter Play of the Year Award
Details Tessa Ross, Head of Independent Commissioning, c/o BBC Television Centre, London W12 7RJ

This annual £10,000 development commission for a television play is awarded to a writer who has not previously had a single play or film produced on television, excepting short films under 30 minutes. Submissions accepted from an individual producer, a BBC producer or a production company. Next closing date: end September. Founded in 1994.

The Mathew Prichard Award for Short Story Writing
Details The Competition Secretary, The Mathew Prichard Award, 95 Celyn Avenue, Lakeside, Cardiff CF2 6EL

Prizes (1st £1000, 2 runner-up prizes of £250) are awarded annually in this open competition for original short stories in

English of not more than 2500 words. Adjudication is organised in May each year by the South and Mid Wales Association of Writers. Next closing date: 1 March 1997.

The Questors National Student Playwriting Competition
The Questors Theatre, 12 Mattock Lane, London W5 5BQ
tel 0181-567 0011 *fax* 0181-567 8736

An annual (but not 1997) playwriting competition open to full-time writing students for a play which has not been performed before. £1000 is awarded plus a full production of the play for one week. Founded 1986.

Trevor Reese Memorial Prize
Details The Seminar & Conference Secretary, Institute of Commonwealth Studies, 28 Russell Square, London WC1B 5DS
tel 0171-580 5876 *fax* 0171-255 2160

This prize of £1000 is awarded biennially, usually for a scholarly work by a single author in the field of Imperial and Commonwealth history. The next award (for a book published in 1995 or 1996) will be given in 1998.

The Margaret Rhondda Award
Details The Society of Authors, 84 Drayton Gardens, London SW10 9SB

This award, is given every 3 years to a woman writer as a grant-in-aid towards the expenses of a research project in journalism, in recognition of the service which women journalists give to the public through journalism. Closing date for next award: 31 December 1998. First awarded in July 1968 on the tenth anniversary of Lady Rhondda's death.

The Rhône-Poulenc Prizes for Science Books
Details COPUS, c/o The Royal Society, 6 Carlton House Terrace, London SW1Y 5AG
tel 0171-839 5561 *fax* 0171-451 2693
e-mail ezmb013@mailbox.ulcc.ac.uk
web site http://www.royalsoc.ac.uk/rs/

These prizes, established in 1988 by COPUS and the Science Museum and sponsored by Rhône-Poulenc, are awarded annually for the best popular science books for the non-specialist reader. Eligible books must be written in English and published for the first time in the UK in the year preceding the prize. The Rhône-Poulenc prize (£10,000) is for a book with a general readership; the Junior Prize (£10,000), is for a book written specifically for young people (under 14): publishers may enter any number of books for each prize. Entries may cover any aspect of science and technology, including biography and history, but books published as educational textbooks or for professional or specialist audiences are not eligible. A prize-winning author will be ineligible for another Rhône-Poulenc Prize for 2 years.

Rhyme International Annual Poetry Competition
Details/entry form Orbis Literary Magazine, 199 The Long Shoot, Nuneaton, Warks. CV11 6JQ
tel (01203) 327440

The only annual international competition exclusively devoted to rhymed poetry. Total annual prizes average around £1000, divided into 2 classes, 'formal' and 'open'. Entry fee: £2.50 per poem, minimum £5. Closing date: 30 September each year. Adjudicated by a different leading poet each year. Founded as Rhyme Revival in collaboration with Coventry Chamber of Commerce in 1981.

Romantic Novelists' Association Award
Details Mrs Jean Chapman, 3 Arnesby Lane, Peatling Magna, Leicester LE8 5UN
tel/fax (0116) 247 8330

This annual award for the best romantic novel of the year is open to both members and non-members of the Romantic Novelists' Association, provided they are domiciled in the UK. Novels must be published between the previous 1 December and 30 November of the year of entry. Three copies of the novel are required. Entry forms and details are available after July.

New Writers' Award
Details Marina Oliver, Half Hidden, West Lane, Bledlow, Princes Risborough, Bucks. HP27 9PF
tel (01844) 345973 *fax* (01844) 274661

This award is for writers previously unpublished in the romantic novel field and who are probationary members of the Association. MSS are submitted each September under the New Writers' Scheme. All receive a critique. Any MSS which have passed through the Scheme and which are subsequently accepted for publication become eligible for the Award.

The Rooney Prize for Irish Literature

Details J.A. Sherwin, Strathin, Templecarrig, Delgany, Co. Wicklow, Republic of Ireland
tel (01) 287 4769 *fax* (01) 287 2595
e-mail jsherwin@iol.ie

This prize is to encourage young Irish writing talent. IR£5000 is awarded annually to a different individual, who must be Irish, published in either Irish or English and under 40 years of age. The prize is non-competitive and there is no application procedure or entry form. Founded in 1976.

The Royal Society of Literature Award under the W.H. Heinemann Bequest

Submissions Royal Society of Literature, 1 Hyde Park Gardens, London W2 2LT
tel 0171-723 5104

Set up to encourage the production of literary works of real worth, works in any branch of literature, originally written in the English language, may be submitted by their publishers for this annual award of £5000. Prose fiction is not excluded, but the Testator's intention was primarily to reward less remunerative classes of literature: poetry, criticism, biography, history, etc. The recipient of a Prize shall not be eligible again for 5 years. Closing date for entries: 31 October.

The Royal Society of Medicine Prizes

Details The Secretary, MWG, Society of Authors, 84 Drayton Gardens, London SW10 9SB

Closing date for submissions of medical textbooks, illustrated texts, atlases and electronic publications: 30 June 1998. The Medical Writers Group of the Society of Authors administers the prizes sponsored by The Royal Society of Medicine.

The RTZ David Watt Memorial Prize

Details/entry form The Administrator, The RTZ David Watt Memorial Prize, The RTZ Corporation plc, 6 St James's Square, London SW1Y 4LD

This £5000 prize is awarded for outstanding written contributions towards the greater understanding of international and political issues. Those eligible for the prize are writers actively engaged in writing for newspapers and journals in the English language. Entries should comprise a published article in English of not more than 5000 words. Closing date for entries and nominations: end March. Founded in 1988 and organised, funded and administered by The RTZ Corporation plc.

Runciman Award

Details Anglo-Hellenic League, Flat 4, 68 Elm Park Gardens, London SW10 9PB
tel 0171-352 2676 *fax* 0171-351 5657

Annual prizes of up to £9000 for books wholly or mainly about Greece or the Hellenic scene from antiquity to the present – history, archaeology, biography, the arts, fiction, poetry, etc. Funded by the Onassis Foundation and administered by the Anglo-Hellenic League. Established in 1985.

Saga Prize

Applications Saga Prize, Book Trust, Book House, 45 East Hill, London SW18 2QZ
tel 0181-870 9055

This annual award (£3000 plus publication by a different publisher each year) is eligible to black writers born in Great Britain or the Republic of Ireland who have a black African ancestor. Entrants submit an unpublished MS of a novel no longer than 80,000 words. Entry fee: £15.00. Founded in 1995.

The Ian St James Awards

Details/entry form The New Writers' Club, PO Box 60, Cranbrook, Kent TN17 2ZR
tel (01580) 212626

These annual awards are for writers of short stories: top prize £2000 and runner-up prizes of £200 each, plus publication in annual collection. The remaining 40 shortlisted writers are published throughout the year in the magazine, *The New Writer*. Eligible writers must be 18 or over and not have had a novel or novella previously published. Entries must be in English but can come from anywhere in the world. Closing date: 30 April. Founded in 1989.

Alastair Salvesen Art Scholarship

The Royal Scottish Academy, The Mound, Edinburgh EH2 2EL
tel 0131-225 6671 *fax* 0131-225 2349

The Scholarship consists of 2 parts:
- A 3-6 months travel scholarship of up to £8000 depending on the plan submitted; and
- An exhibition lasting about 3 weeks

(Nov/Dec) in the lower gallery of the Royal Scottish Academy.

Applicants must be painters aged 25-35 who have been trained at one of the 4 Scottish colleges of art; are currently living and working in Scotland; have worked for a minimum of 3 years outside a college or student environment; and have during 1997 had work accepted for an exhibition in the Annual Exhibition organised by certain Scottish institutes or, in a recognised gallery, have held a one-artist exhibition or participated in a group exhibition. Founded 1989.

Scoop of the Year Award

Details The Hon. Secretary, London Press Club, Freedom Forum, Stanhope House, Stanhope Place, London W2 2HH
tel 0171-262 5003 *fax* 0171-262 4631

Chosen by a panel of senior editors, this annual award of a bronze statuette is given for the reporting scoop of the year, appearing in either a newspaper or electronic media. Founded in 1990.

The Scottish Arts Council

Writers' Bursaries
Contact Jenny Brown, Literature Director, The Scottish Arts Council, 12 Manor Place, Edinburgh EH3 7DD
tel 0131-226 6051
e-mail jenny.brown.sac@arts.fb.org

A limited number of bursaries – of between £3000 and £8000 each – are offered to enable professional writers to devote more time to writing. Priority is given to writers of fiction and verse, but writers of literary non-fiction are also considered. Application normally open only to writers who have been living and working in Scotland for at least 2 years. Applications may be discussed with Jenny Brown.

Book Awards
Details Shonagh Irvine, Literature Officer, The Scottish Arts Council, 12 Manor Place, Edinburgh EH3 7DD
tel 0131-226 6051
e-mail shonagh.irvine.sac@arts.fb.org

Five awards of £1000 each are made in both spring and autumn. Preference is given to literary fiction and verse, but literary non-fiction is also considered. Authors should be Scottish or resident in Scotland, but books of Scottish interest by other authors are eligible for consideration. Books by Scottish writers for children are eligible for a new annual award. Publishers should apply for further information.

The Scottish Book of the Year and Scottish First Book

Details The Saltire Society, 9 Fountain Close, 22 High Street, Edinburgh EH1 1TF
tel 0131-556 1836 *fax* 0131-557 1675

These 2 annual awards (£5000 and £1500) are open to any author of Scottish descent or living in Scotland, or for a book by anyone which deals with the work or life of a Scot or with a Scottish problem, event or situation. Nominations are made by literary editors of Scottish newspapers and periodicals. Supported by The Scotsman Publications Ltd and the Post Office. Established in 1982 and 1988 respectively.

The Scottish International Open Poetry Competition

Details The Secretary, Ayrshire Writers' and Artists' Society, 42 Tollerton Drive, Irvine, Ayrshire KA12 0QE

An annual competition open to all poets over the age of 16 with no restriction on style or length. 1st prize UK section: £100 plus The MacDiarmid Trophy; 1st prize Scots section: The Clement Wilson Trophy; 1st prize international section: The International Trophy. Entry fee: none. Closing date 31 Dec 1997. Founded 1972.

Scottish Writer of the Year

Details Scottish Writer of the Year, Book Trust Scotland, Scottish Book Centre, 137 Dundee Street, Edinburgh EH11 1BG
tel 0131-229 3663 *fax* 0131-228 4293

An annual prize of £1000 is awarded to each of 5 shortlisted writers, plus a further £9000 to the winner. Submissions include novels, volumes of short stories, poetry, biography, autobiography, journalism, science fiction and children's books as well as theatre, cinema, radio and television scripts. Open to writers who were born or have been resident in Scotland, who have Scottish parents, or who take Scotland as their inspiration. Closing date: 31 July for work first made public during the previous 12 months.

The Seebohm Trophy – Age Concern Book of the Year
Application form Age Concern England, Astral House, 1268 London Road, London SW16 4ER
tel 0181-679 8000 ext 2353

An annual award is made to the author and publisher of a non-fiction title (published in the previous calendar year) which, in the opinion of the judges, is most successful in promoting the wellbeing and understanding of older people. The author receives £1000, the publisher the silver Seebohm Trophy. Nominations must be received before the middle of March each year. Founded in 1995 in memory of Frederic, Lord Seebohm, President of Age Concern, 1971-1989.

The Signal Poetry for Children Award
Details The Thimble Press, Lockwood, Station Road, South Woodchester, Stroud, Glos. GL5 5EQ

A prize of £100 is given annually for an outstanding book of poetry published for children in Britain and the Commonwealth during the previous year, whether single poem or anthology and regardless of country of original publication. Articles about the winning book are published in *Signal* each May. Not open to unpublished work.

The André Simon Memorial Fund Book Awards
Details Tessa Hayward, 5 Sion Hill Place, Bath BA1 5SJ
tel (01225) 336305 *fax* (01225) 421862

Two awards (£2000 each) are given annually, one each for the best new book on food and on drink, plus one Special Commendation of £1000 in either category. Closing date: November each year. Founded in 1978.

Singer & Friedlander/Sunday Times Watercolour Competition
Details PO Box 1390, London SW8 1QZ
tel (01372) 462190 *fax* (01372) 460032

An annual competition 'to promote the continuance of the British tradition of fine watercolour painting'. Total prize money: £25,000. Open to artists born or resident in the UK. Closing date: May 1998. Winning entries will be exhibited in London, Manchester, Leeds and Birmingham. Launched 1987.

Smarties Book Prize
Details Book Trust, Book House, 45 East Hill, London SW18 2QZ
tel 0181-870 9055

A prize (Gold Award) of £2500 is awarded to each of the 3 age category winners (0-5, 6-8 and 9-11 years). Runners-up (Silver Award) receive £1500 each, and third prize (Bronze Award) winners receive £500 each. Eligible books must be published in the UK in the 12 months ending 30 September of the year of presentation and be a work of fiction or poetry for children written in English by a citizen or resident of the UK. Closing date for entries: 31 July of the year of presentation. Sponsored by Nestlé Smarties. Established in 1985.

The W.H. Smith Annual Literary Award
Details W.H. Smith Group, Audrey House, Ely Place, London EC1N 6SN
tel 0171-404 4242

A prize of £10,000 is awarded annually to a Commonwealth author (including a citizen of the UK) whose book is judged to make the most outstanding contribution to literature. Books must be written in English and published in the UK within 12 months ending on 31 December preceding the date of the Award. Submissions are not accepted; the judges make their decision independently.

W.H. Smith Thumping Good Read Award
An annual award of £5000 is presented to the best new fiction author of the year. The award is judged by a panel of WHS customers. Founded in 1992.

W.H. Smith Young Writers' Competition – The Inky Foot Award
tel (01793) 451300 (Competition Hotline)

This competition is open to anyone aged 16 or under on 28 February of year of entry. Any original writing (poetry, prose, short fiction, drama) is accepted but must not exceed 3500 words. Winners' work is published by Macmillan in a paperback book. Founded in 1959.

The Jill Smythies Award
The Linnean Society of London, Burlington House, Piccadilly, London W1V 0LQ
tel 0171-434 4479 *fax* 0171-287 9364
e-mail john@linnean.demon.co.uk
web site www.linnean.org.uk

Established in honour of Jill Smythies whose career as a botanical artist was cut short by an accident to her right hand. The rubic states that 'the Award, to be made by Council usually annually consisting of a silver medal and a purse (currently £1000) ... is for published illustrations, such as drawings and paintings, in aid of plant identification, with the emphasis on botanical accuracy and the accurate portrayal of diagnostic characteristics. Illustrations of cultivars of garden origin are not eligible.' Closing date for nominations: 30 September. Founded 1988.

Southern Arts Literature Prize

Details The Literature Department, Southern Arts, 13 St Clement Street, Winchester, Hants SO23 9DQ
tel (01962) 855099 *fax* (01962) 861186

This prize is awarded annually on a rotating basis for a published novel, poetry collection, or work of literary non-fiction to writers living within the Southern Arts region. Prize: £1000 plus a craft commission to the value of £600. The 1998 award is for literary non-fiction. Closing date: 30 June 1998.

Stand Magazine Awards

Details Stand Magazine, 179 Wingrove Road, Newcastle upon Tyne NE4 9DA
tel/fax 0191-273 3280

Stand Magazine Short Story Competition

This biennial short story competition – with prizes to the value of £2500 – is open to any writer for an original, untranslated story in English, not longer than 8000 words, not previously published, broadcast or under consideration elsewhere. Next competition opens January 1999 and closes June 1999. Entry forms available from November 1998 on receipt of a UK sae or 2 IRCs. Founded in 1980.

Stand Poetry Competition

A new international biennial competition with prizes to the value of £2500. Entrants may submit as many poems as they wish but each poem must be accompanied by a donation of at least £3.50/$7.50 for the first, and £3.00/$7.00 for each subsequent poem. Competition opens 1 January 1998 and closes 30 June 1998. For further details and entry form on receipt of a UK sae or 2 IRCs.

The Steinbeck Award

Details William Heinemann, Michelin House, 81 Fulham Road, London SW3 6RB
tel 0171-581 9393 *fax* 0171-225 9095

This bi-annual award is given to a writer under the age of 40 for a new work of fiction in English, written in the spirit of Steinbeck, e.g. a work dedicated to issues of poverty, race or political injustice. The award is £10,000, half of which goes to a charity of the winner's choice. Closing date: 1 March. Founded in 1994.

The James Stern Silver Pen Award for Non-Fiction

Details PEN, 7 Dilke Street, London SW3 4JE
tel 0171-352 6303 *fax* 0171-351 0220

This award of £1000 is given annually for an outstanding work of non-fiction written in English and published during the previous year by an author of British nationality or an author who has been a long-term resident in the UK. No submissions please – books are nominated by members of the PEN Executive Committee. Sponsored by the Stern family since 1996. Founded in 1969.

The Suspended Sentence Award

Details The James Joyce Foundation, PO Box 104, Kings Cross, NSW 2011, Australia
tel (02) 9332 3649 *fax* (02) 9363 2038

An award for accomplishment in writing. James Joyce believed that it wasn't simply a matter of getting the right words but of getting those words in the right order. The Award will be given to that piece of writing which in the opinion of the judges most closely approximates to Joyce's standard of musical precision and significant content. It may be in prose or verse and can be in the form of fiction or non-fiction. Applicants must have had work previously published in book form or had 60 minutes of material produced (radio, TV, film or theatre), or must be recommended by a literary agent, publisher, producer or director. Entry fee: $20. Closing date: May 1998. Send sae for details.

Reginald Taylor and Lord Fletcher Essay Competition

Submissions Hon. Editor, Dr Martin Henig, British Archaeological Association, Institute of Archaeology, 36 Beaumont Street, Oxford OX1 2PG

A prize of a medal and £300 is awarded biennially for the best unpublished essay, not exceeding 7500 words, which shows original research on a subject of archaeological, art-historical or antiquarian interest within the period from the Roman era to ad 1830. The successful competitor may be invited to read the essay before the Association and the essay may be published in the Association's *Journal*. Competitors should notify the Hon. Editor in advance of the intended subject of their work. Next award: November 1998 (to be presented as one of the British Archaeological Awards), and the essay should be submitted not later than 1 June 1998, enclosing an sae. Founded in memory of E. Reginald Taylor FSA and Lord Fletcher FSA.

The Thomas Cook Travel Book Award
Details Travel Book Award, Thomas Cook Publishing, PO Box 227, Thorpe Wood, Peterborough PE3 6PU
tel (01733) 503566

This annual award is given to encourage the art of travel writing. Travel narrative books (150pp minimum) written in English and published between 1 January and 31 December of the preceding year are eligible. Established in 1980.

Anne Tibble Poetry Competition
Details Events Team Office, Directorate of Environment Services, Cliftonville House, Bedford Road, Northampton NN4 7NR
tel (01604) 233500 ext 4243

This annual prize is awarded for a poem, maximum length 20 lines, to anyone resident in Great Britain. The first prize is £200; other prizes to a total value of £200.

The Times Educational Supplement Book Awards
Details The Literary Editor, The Times Educational Supplement, Admiral House, 66-68 East Smithfield, London E1 9XY
tel 0171-782 3000 *fax* 0171-782 3200

There are 2 annual awards for the best books used in schools: Primary and Secondary categories. The books must be published in Britain or the Commonwealth.

Tir Na N-og Awards
Details Welsh Books Council, Castell Brychan, Aberystwyth, Ceredigion SY23 2JB
tel (01970) 624151 *fax* (01970) 625385

There are 3 annual awards to children's authors and illustrators:
• best Welsh fiction, including short stories and picture books;
• best Welsh non-fiction book of the year;
• best English book with an authentic Welsh background.
Total prize value is £3000. Founded in 1976.

The Tom-Gallon Trust
Submissions The Secretary, The Society of Authors, 84 Drayton Gardens, SW10 9SB

A biennial award is made to fiction writers of limited means who have had at least one short story accepted for publication. An award of £500 was made in 1995. Authors wishing to enter should send to the Secretary:
• a list of their already published fiction, giving the name of the publisher or periodical in each case and the approximate date of publication;
• one published or unpublished short story;
• a brief statement of their financial position;
• an undertaking that they intend to devote a substantial amount of time to the writing of fiction as soon as they are financially able to do so;
• an sae for the return of the work submitted.
Next closing date: 20 September 1998.

The Translators Association Awards
Details Kate Poole, The Translators Association, 84 Drayton Gardens, London SW10 9SB

The Translators Association of the Society of Authors administers a number of prizes for translations into English. They include prizes for translations of Dutch and Flemish, French, German, Italian, Japanese, Portuguese, Spanish and Swedish works.

The Betty Trask Awards
Details The Society of Authors, 84 Drayton Gardens, London SW10 9SB

These awards are for the benefit of young authors under the age of 35 and are given on the strength of a first novel (published or unpublished) of a romantic or traditional nature. It is expected that prizes totalling at least £25,000 will be present-

ed each year. The winners are required to use the money for a period or periods of foreign travel. Closing date: 31 January. Made possible through a generous bequest from Miss Betty Trask.

The Travelling Scholarships

These are non-competitive awards administered by the Society of Authors. Submissions are not required.

T.E. Utley Memorial Fund Award
Details Virginia Utley, 111 Sugden Road, London SW11 5ED
tel 0171-228 3900

Prizes of £2500 and 2 of £1500 are awarded annually for an essay on a given subject.

'Charles Veillon' European Essay Prize
Details The Secretary, Charles Veillon Foundation, CH 1017 Lausanne, Switzerland
tel (021) 701 4147

A prize of 20,000 Swiss francs is awarded annually to a European writer or essayist for essays offering a critical look at modern society's way of life and ideology. Founded in 1975.

Ver Poets Open Competition
Organiser May Badman, Ver Poets, 61-63 Chiswell Green Lane, St Albans, Herts. AL2 3AL
tel (01727) 867005

A competition open to anyone for poems of up to 30 lines of any genre or subject matter, which must be unpublished work in English. Prizes: £500 (1st), £300 (2nd), £100 (2 x 3rd). Entry fee: £2 per poem (each year a gift to charity is made). Closing date 30 April 1998.

Edgar Wallace Award
Details The Hon. Secretary, London Press Club, Freedom Forum, Stanhope House, Stanhope Place, London W2 2HH
tel 0171-262 5003 *fax* 0171-262 4631

Chosen by a panel of senior editors, this annual award of a silver inkstand is given for outstanding writing or reporting by a journalist. Founded in 1990.

Wandsworth London Writers Competition
Details Assistant Director of Leisure and Amenity Services (Community Services), Wandsworth Town Hall, High Street, London SW18 2PU
tel 0181-871 7037 *fax* 0181-871 7630

Open to writers of 16 years and over who live, work or study in the Greater London Area. Awards are made annually in 2 classes, Poetry and Short Story, the prizes totalling £1000 in each class. Entries must be previously unpublished work. Judging is under the chairmanship of Martyn Goff, Chairman of the Poetry Book Society.

Whitbread Literary Awards
Details The Booksellers Association, Minster House, 272 Vauxhall Bridge Road, London SW1V 1BA
tel 0171-834 5477 *fax* 0171-834 8812
e-mail 100437.2261@compuserve.com

Judged in 2 stages and offering a total of £31,000 prize money, the awards are open to 4 categories: Novel, First Novel, Biography/Autobiography, Poetry. The winner in each category receives a Whitbread Nomination Award of £2000. These 4 nominations are judged for the Whitbread Book of the Year, the overall winner receiving an additional £21,000. Writers must have lived in Great Britain and Ireland for 3 or more years. Submissions only from publishers. Closing date: mid July.

Whitbread Children's Book of the Year
Run in parallel to the Book of the Year Award, the overall winner receives £8000. Founded 1996.

The Whitfield Prize
Submissions Executive Secretary, Royal Historical Society, University College London, Gower Street, London WC1E 6BT
tel/fax 0171-387 7532

The Prize (value £1000) is announced in July each year for the best work on a subject within a field of British history. It must be its author's first solely written history book, an original and scholarly work of historical research and have been published in the UK in the preceding calendar year. Three non-returnable copies of an eligible book should be submitted before 31 December to the Executive Secretary.

John Whiting Award
Details Drama Dept, Arts Council of England, 14 Great Peter Street, London SW1P 3NQ
tel 0171-333 0100 ext 431
e-mail info.drama.ace@artsfb.org.uk

This prize of £6000 is given annually. Eligible to apply are any writers who have received during the previous 2 calendar years an award through the Arts Council new theatre writing schemes, or who have had a commission or premier production by a theatre company in receipt of an annual subsidy. Founded in 1965.

The Raymond Williams Community Publishing Prizes

Details The Secretary, Literature Department, The Arts Council of England, 14 Great Peter Street, London SW1P 3NQ
tel 0171-973 6442

These annual prizes are awarded to non-profit making publishers for work which offers outstanding imaginative and creative qualities and which exemplifies the values of ordinary people and their lives. First prize: £2000 to publisher, £1000 to writer/group, runner-up: £1500 to publisher, £500 to writer/group. Founded in 1990.

David T.K. Wong Fellowship

Details David T.K. Wong Fellowship, School of English & American Studies, University of East Anglia, Norwich NR4 7TJ
tel (01003) 592010 *fax* (01603) 507728

Founded by David Wong, retired senior civil servant, journalist and businessman, the annual Fellowship (worth £25,000) at the University of East Anglia will give writers of exceptional talent the chance to produce a work of fiction in English which deals seriously with some aspect of life in the Far East. Write for further details. Closing date: 31 Oct 1997. Founded 1997.

Write A Story for Children Competition

Entry forms The Academy of Children's Writers, PO Box 95, Huntingdon, Cambs. PE17 5RL
tel (01487) 832752

Three prizes are awarded annually (1st £1000, 2nd £200, 3rd £100) for a short story for children, maximum 1000 words, by an unpublished writer of children's fiction. Founded in 1984.

The Writers' Guild Awards

Details 430 Edgware Road, London W2 1EH
tel 0171-732 8074 *fax* 0171-706 2413

There are 5 categories of awards:
• radio – original drama, comedy/light entertainment, dramatisations, children's;
• theatre – West End, fringe, regional, children's;
• books – non-fiction, fiction, children's;
• film – best screenplay;
• television – original play/film, original drama series, original drama serial, dramatisation/adaptation, situation comedy, light entertainment, children's.

There are also awards for Non-English Language, New Writer of the Year, and Lifetime Achievement. The various shortlists are prepared by a different jury in each category and presented to the Guild Membership for its final vote.

Nominations are made from works which have been published, performed or broadcast during the period 1 August-31 July each year. No nominations are required from the public. Established 1961; relaunched 1991.

Xenos Annual Short Story Competition

29 Prebend Street, Bedford MK40 1QN
tel (01234) 349067
e-mail xenos@xenos.demon.co.uk
web site http://www.xenos.demon.co.uk

Short stories of 2000-10,000 words of all genres are considered, except graphic horror/blood and gore or anything with an explicit sexual content. Cash prizes and/or publication in *Xenos* magazine, a bi-monthly platform for both new and established writers. Write for details. Founded 1990.

Yorkshire Post Literary Awards

Submissions Margaret Brown, Yorkshire Post Literary Awards, Yorkshire Post Newspapers Ltd, PO Box 168, Wellington Street, Leeds LS1 1RF

Submissions are accepted only from publishers. For the first 2 awards, authors should be British or resident in the UK; for the third, authors need not be British, nor residents.

Yorkshire Post Book of the Year
A prize of £1200 annually for the Best Book, either fiction or non-fiction. Next closing date: 31 December.

Yorkshire Post Best First Work Award
A prize of £1000 is awarded for the Best First Work by a new author, either fiction or non-fiction. Next closing date: 31 December.

Yorkshire Post Art and Music Book Award
Prizes of £1000 each are given to authors whose books are judged to have contributed most to the understanding and appreciation of Art and of Music. Next closing date: 31 January.

Young Writers' Festival: Write Your Play
Details Young Writers' Festival, Royal Court Young People's Theatre, 309 Portobello Road, London W10 5TD
tel 0181-960 4641 *fax* 0181-960 1434

Anyone aged 23 or under can submit a play on any subject. A selection of plays is professionally presented by the Royal Court Theatre biennially (next festival takes place autumn 1998) with the writers fully involved in rehearsal and production. Workshops are run by professional theatre practitioners and designed to help everyone attending to write a play.

Prizes and awards by subject area

This list provides a quick reference to the main listings of prizes, competitions and awards which starts on page 488.

Biography

J.R. Ackerley Prize
Authors' Club Marsh Biography
  Award
James Tait Black Memorial Prize
The Duff Cooper Prize
The Royal Society of Literature
  Award under the W.H.
  Heinemann Bequest
The Runciman Award
Scottish Writer of the Year
The Whitbread Literary Awards

Children

Hans Christian Andersen Medal
Big Book Cover Award
The Bisto Book of the Year
  Award
Children's Book Award
The Eleanor Farjeon Award
The Kathleen Fidler Award
The Guardian Children's
  Fiction Prize
The Independent/Scholastic
  Story of the Year Competition
The Library Association
  Children's Book Awards
The Macmillan Prize for a
  Children's Picture Book
Kurt Maschler Award
The BFC/Mother Goose Award
The Signal Poetry for Children
  Award
Smarties Book Prize
The Times Educational
  Supplement Book Awards
Tir Na N-og Awards
Write a Story for Children
  Competition

Drama

The David Cohen British
  Literature Prize
Verity Bargate Award

Samuel Beckett Award
The Cló Iar-Chonnachta
  Literary Award
Miles Franklin Literary Award
The Richard Imison Memorial
  Award
Meyer-Whitworth Award
P.J. O'Connor Awards
Dennis Potter Play of the Year
  Award
Questors National Student
  Playwriting Competition
W.H. Smith Young Writers'
  Competition
John Whiting Award
Young Writers' Festival: Write
  Your Play

Essays

The David Cohen British
  Literature Prize
Shiva Naipaul Award
Reginald Taylor and Lord
  Fletcher Essay Competition
T.E. Utley Memorial Fund
  Award
Charles Veillon European Essay
  Prize

Fiction

Aristeion Prizes
Authors' Club Best First Novel
  Award
James Tait Black Memorial Prize
The Booker Prize
Arthur C. Clarke Award
The David Cohen British
  Literature Prize
Commonwealth Writers Prize
CWA Awards
Dillons First Fiction Award
The Dundee Book Prize
Encore Award
Christopher Ewart-Biggs
  Memorial Prize

The Geoffrey Faber Memorial
  Prize
Miles Franklin Literary Award
Mind Book of the Year/Allen
  Lane Award
The Guardian Fiction Prize
The Hawthornden Prize
David Higham Prize for Fiction
Royal Society of Literature
  under the Winifred Holtby
  Memorial Bequest
International IMPAC Dublin
  Literary Award
Irish Times Literary Prizes
Jewish Quarterly Literary Prizes
The Lichfield Prize
The McKitterick Prize (pub-
  lished/unpublished)
The Enid McLeod Literary Prize
Macmillan Silver Pen Award
  for Fiction
The Mail on Sunday-John
  Llewellyn Rhys Prize
The Somerset Maugham
  Awards
Mind Book of the Year/Allen
  Lane Award
Orange Prize for Fiction
Romantic Novelists'
  Association Awards
The Runciman Award
Saga Prize
Scottish Arts Council Book
  Awards
Scottish Writer of the Year
W.H. Smith Annual Literary
  Award
W.H. Smith Thumping Good
  Read Award
Southern Arts Literature Prize
The Steinbeck Award
The Suspended Sentence
  Award
The Betty Trask Awards (pub-
  lished/unpublished)
Whitbread Literary Awards
David T.K. Wong Fellowship
Yorkshire Post Literary Awards

Fine art – see Visual art

Grants, bursaries and fellowships

Arts Council of England
The Arts Council of Ireland
Arts Council of Wales
The Arts Foundation Literary
and Visual Arts Fellowships
Authors' Foundation
Kathleen Blundell Trust
Alfred Bradley Bursary
British Academy Research
Awards
The Rhys Davies Trust
E.M. Forster Award
The Fulbright Commission
Awards
E.C. Gregory Trust Fund
Hawthornden Writers'
Fellowships
Leverhulme Research
Fellowships and Grants
Northern Arts Writers' Awards
The Margaret Rhondda Award
Scottish Arts Council
The Travelling Scholarships
David T.K. Wong Fellowship

Illustration

Hans Christian Andersen Medal
Big Book Cover Award
Bisto Book of the Year Award
The Book Art Prize
British Fantasy Awards
The Eleanor Farjeon Award
The Macmillan Prize for a
Children's Picture Book
Kurt Maschler Award
The BFC/Mother Goose Award
The National Art Library
Illustration Awards
The Jill Smythies Award
Tir Na N-og Awards

Journalism

George Orwell Memorial Prize
Catherine Pakenham Memorial
Award
Scottish Writer of the Year
Margaret Rhondda Award
Scoop of the Year Award
Edgar Wallace Award

Non-fiction

Alexander Prize (History)
Aristeion Prizes
Authors' Club Sir Banister
Fletcher Award (Architecture)
BBC Wildlife Magazine Awards
for Nature Writing
David Berry Prize (History)
BP Natural World Book Prize
Katharine Briggs Folklore Award
British Academy Medals and
Prizes
The Duff Cooper Prize
The Rose Mary Crawshay Prizes
CWA Awards
Christopher Ewart-Biggs
Memorial Prize
Glenfiddich Awards (Food and
Drink)
The Calvin and Rose G.
Hoffman Memorial Prize
Irish Times Literary Prizes
Jewish Quarterly Literary Prizes
Kraszna-Krausz Awards
The Library Association
Reference Awards
The Livingstone Award for
Travel
The Mail on Sunday-John
Llewellyn Rhys Prize
The Somerset Maugham
Awards
MCA Book Prize (Management)
Enid McLeod Prize
Mind Book of the Year/Allen
Lane Award
The NCR Book Award for Non-
Fiction
The Portico Prize
Trevor Reese Memorial Prize
The Rhône-Poulenc Prizes for
Science Books
The Royal Society of Literature
Award under the W.H.
Heinemann Bequest
The Royal Society of Medicine
Prizes
The RTZ David Watt Memorial
Prize
Runciman Award
Scottish Arts Council Book
Awards
The André Simon Memorial
Fund Book Awards (Food and
Drink)
W.H. Smith Annual Literary
Award
Southern Arts Literature Prize
The James Stern Silver Pen
Award for Non-Fiction
The Suspended Sentence Award

The Thomas Cook Travel Book
Award (Travel writing)
The Times Educational
Supplement Book Awards
The Whitfield Prize (History)
Yorkshire Post Literary Awards

Poetry

Rosemary Arthur Award
Arvon Foundation
BBC Wildlife Magazine Poet of
the Year Contest
The David Cohen British
Literature Prize
Denis Devlin Memorial Award
Arts Council of Ireland
Arts Council of Wales
The Bridport Prize
Cholmondeley Award
Cardiff International Poetry
Competition
DT Charitable Trust Open
Poetry Competition
The T.S. Eliot Prize
Geoffrey Faber Memorial Prize
Forward Poetry Prizes
The Felicia Hemans Prize for
Lyrical Poetry
Irish Times Literary Prizes
Kent & Sussex Poetry Society
Open Poetry Competition
The Somerset Maugham
Awards
National Poetry Competition
National Poetry Competition
(Ireland)
Peterloo Poets Open Poetry
Competition
Poetry Life Open Poetry
Competition
Poetry Update Poem of the
Month Competition
Rhyme International Annual
Poetry Competition
The Royal Society of Literature
Award under the W.H.
Heinemann Bequest
The Runciman Award
Scottish Arts Council Book
Awards
The Scottish International
Open Poetry Competition
Scottish Writer of the Year
The Signal Poetry for Children
Award
Smarties Book Prize
W.H. Smith Young Writers'
Competition
Southern Arts Literature Prize
Stand Poetry Competition

Anne Tibble Poetry
Competition
Ver Poets Open Competition
Wandsworth London Writers
Competition
Whitbread Literary Awards

Short stories

H.E. Bates Short Story
Competition
The Bridport Prize
The Cló Iar-Chonnachta
Literary Award
The David Cohen British
Literature Prize
CWA/The Macallan Short Story
Dagger
David Higham Prize for Fiction
The Lady Short Story
Competition
Macallan/Scotland on Sunday
Short Story Competition
Macmillan Silver Pen Award
for Fiction
Scottish Writer of the Year
Northern Short Story
Competition
One Voice
The Matthew Prichard Award
for Short Story Writing
The Ian St James Awards
W.H. Smith Young Writers'
Competition
Stand Magazine Short Story
Competition
The Tom-Gallon Trust Award
Wandsworth London Writers
Competition
Write A Story for Children
Competition
Xenos Annual Short Story
Competition

Translation

European Translation Prize
Arts Council of England
Authors' Club Marsh Award
The European Poetry
Translation Prize
The Translators Association
Awards

Specialist

BA/Bookseller Author of the
Year Award
European Literary Prize
(Literature)
The Boardman Tasker Prize
(Mountain Literature)
British Academy Medals and
Prizes
British Book Awards
British Fantasy Awards
DT Charitable Trust Awards –
Self-Publishing Award
The Lionel Gelber Prize
(International Relations)
The Writers' Guild Awards
Heywood Hill Literary Prize
William Hill Sports Book of the
Year Award
The Library Association
Wheatley Medal (Indexing)
The London New Writing
Competition
The Enid McLeod Literary
Prize
The Somerset Maugham
Awards
The Nobel Prize in Literature
One Voice
The Portico Prize
The Rooney Prize for Irish
Literature

The Runciman Award (Greece)
Saga Prize (Black Writers)
Scottish Arts Council Book
Awards
Scottish Book of the Year and
Scottish First Book
The Seebohm Trophy – Age
Concern Book of the Year
The W.H. Smith Annual
Literary Award
W.H. Smith Young Writers'
Competition
Times Educational Supplement
Book Awards
The Raymond Williams
Community Publishing Prizes

Visual art

The Book Art Prize
BP Portrait Award
The Alasdair Gilchrist
Memorial Award
Juliet Gomperts Memorial
Scholarship
Hunting Art Prizes
The John Kobal Photographic
Portrait Award
Laing Art Prize
Millfield Arts Projects
John Moores Liverpool
Exhibition
The Observer Hodge
Award/Exhibition
Alastair Salvesen Art
Scholarship
Singer & Friedlander/Sunday
Times Watercolour
Competition

Open art exhibitions

This list should be used as a guide only. Many handing-in and exhibition dates had not been finalised as the Yearbook went to press. Send an sae to the relevant address for further information and entry forms. A handling fee is normally charged for each work entered. See Societies, associations and clubs section on page 437 for general information on the societies listed here.

Artists, Royal Birmingham Society of
69A New Street, Birmingham B2 4DU
tel 0121-643 3768 *fax* 0121-644 5298
Oil and Sculpture (February); Watercolour and Craftwork (May); RBSA Prize Competition (June); Pastel and Drawing (November).

Botanical Artists, Society of
1 Knapp Cottages, Wyke, Gillingham, Dorset SP8 4NQ
tel (01747) 825718; 0171-222 2723 (during exhibitions)
Held annually (Easter) at the Westminster Gallery, Westminster Central Hall, London SW1. Hand in on 23 February 1998 for 24 April-2 May exhibition.

BP Portrait Award – see Prizes and awards, page 488

British Artists, Royal Society of
17 Carlton House Terrace, London SW1Y 5BD
tel 0171-930 6844 *fax* 0171-839 7830
Held annually at the Mall Galleries, London SW1. Hand in August for exhibition in September. Prizes and awards.

The Discerning Eye
17 Carlton House Terrace, London SW1Y 5BD
tel 0171-930 6844 *fax* 0171-839 7830
Held annually at the Mall Galleries, London SW1. Hand in 5-6 September 1997 for 19-30 November exhibition. Work selected by a panel of 2 critics, 2 collectors, and 2 artists. Prizes, including the Discerning Eye New Discovery Art Prizes.

Graphic Fine Art, Society of
15 Willow Way, Hatfield, Herts. AL10 9QD
Held annually (September) at the Art Connoisseur Gallery. Hand in by 16

August 1998 for 14-26 September exhibition.

Hunting Art Prizes – see Prizes and awards, page 488

Illustrators, The Association of
First Floor, 32-38 Saffron Hill, London EC1N 8FN
tel 0171-831 7377
Held annually: The Best of British Illustration. Call for entries March/April. Prizes and awards.

Laing Art Prize – see Prizes and awards, page 488

Marine Artists, Royal Society of
17 Carlton House Terrace, London SW1Y 5BD
tel 0171-930 6844 *fax* 0171-839 7830
Held annually at the Mall Galleries, London SW1. Hand in September for exhibition in October. Prizes and awards.

Millfield Summer Show – see Prizes and awards, page 488

Miniature Painters, Sculptors and Gravers, Royal Society of
1 Knapp Cottages, Wyke, Gillingham, Dorset SP8 4NQ
tel (01747) 825718; 0171-222 2723 (during exhibitions)
Held annually (November) at the Westminster Gallery, Westminster Central Hall, London SW1. Hand in on 21 September 1998 for 13-28 November exhibition.

Miniaturists, British Society of
Ralston House, 41 Lister Street, Riverside Gardens, Ilkley, West Yorkshire LS29 9ET
tel (01943) 609075

Two per year: summer (6-14 June 1998) and Christmas (28 November-6 December 1998).

John Moores Liverpool Exhibition – see Prizes and awards, page 488

New English Art Club
17 Carlton House Terrace, London SW1Y 5BD
tel 0171-930 6844 fax 0171-839 7830
Held annually at the Mall Galleries, London SW1. Hand in October for exhibition in November. Prizes and awards.

Oil Painters, Royal Institute of
17 Carlton House Terrace, London SW1Y 5BD
tel 0171-930 6844 fax 0171-839 7830
Held annually at the Mall Galleries, London SW1. Hand in October for exhibition in December. Prizes and awards.

Oils, Pastels and Acrylics, British Society of Painters in
Ralston House, 41 Lister Street, Riverside Gardens, Ilkley, West Yorkshire LS29 9ET
tel (01943) 609075
Two per year: spring (14-22 March 1998) and autumn (19-27 September 1998).

Oriel Mostyn Open
12 Vaughan Street, Llandudno LL30 1AB
tel (01492) 879201/870875 fax (01492) 878869
Held annually (December-February). Purchase Prize: £6000. For entry forms, send sae in August.

Painters in Water Colours, Royal Institute of
17 Carlton House Terrace, London SW1Y 5BD
tel 0171-930 6844 fax 0171-839 7830
Held annually at the Mall Galleries, London SW1. Hand in end of February for exhibition in April.

The Pastel Society
17 Carlton House Terrace, London SW1Y 5BD
tel 0171-930 6844 fax 0171-839 7830
Held annually at the Mall Galleries, London SW1. Hand in January for exhibition in March.

Portrait Painters, Royal Society of
17 Carlton House Terrace, London SW1Y 5BD
tel 0171-930 6844 fax 0171-839 7830
Held annually at the Mall Galleries, London SW1. Hand in March for exhibition in May.

Ridley Art Society
37 James Street, Hounslow, Middlesex TW3 1SP
tel 0181-570 6419
Held annually.

Royal Academy of Arts
Piccadilly, London W1V 0DS
tel 0171-439 7438
Summer Exhibition held annually. Closing date for entry forms: 1 April. Hand in during April for June-August exhibition.

Royal Over-Seas League
Park Place, London SWA 1LR
tel 0171-408 0214 fax 0171-499 6738
Open to artists aged up to and including 35 years who are UK and Commonwealth citizens. Awards of more than £7000 in prizes and travel scholarships. Exhibition held annually September-October. Deadline for submissions: July.

Scottish Academy, Royal
The Mound, Edinburgh EH2 2EL
tel 0131-225 6671 fax 0131-225 2349
Exhibition held annually (April-July) for painting, sculpture and architecture.

Singer & Friedlander/Sunday Times Watercolour Competition – see Prizes and awards, page 488

Stockport Art Gallery
Wellington Road South, Stockport SK3 8AB
tel 0161-474 4453 fax 0161-480 4960
Held annually (summer); open to artists in the northwest. Four merit award prizes.

Watercolour Society, British
Ralston House, 41 Lister Street, Riverside Gardens, Ilkley, West Yorkshire LS29 9ET
tel (01943) 609075
Two per year: summer (6-14 June 1998) and Christmas (28 November-6 December 1998).

Watercolour Society, Royal
Bankside Gallery, 48 Hopton Street, London SE1 9JH
tel 0171-928 7521
Held annually in the summer. Hand in 23-24 June 1997 for 10 July-8 August exhibition. Prizes and awards.

West of England Academy, Royal
Queens Road, Clifton, Bristol BS8 1PX
tel 0117 973 5129 fax 0117 923 7874
Held annually. Hand in 2-3 October 1997 for 2 November-19 December exhibition.

Wildlife Artists, Society of
17 Carlton House Terrace, London SW1Y 5BD
tel 0171-930 6844 *fax* 0171-839 7830
Held annually at the Mall Galleries,
London SW1. Hand in June for exhibition in July.

Women Artists, Society of
Westminster Gallery, Westminster Central Hall,
London SW1H 9NU
Held annually for painting and sculpture. Hand in 20 January 1998 for 6-21 March exhibition.

Literature festivals

There are hundreds of arts festivals held in the UK each year – too many to mention in this Yearbook and many of which are not applicable specifically to writers. We give here a selection of literature festivals and general arts festivals which include literature events. Space constraints and the nature of an annual publication together determine that only brief details are given; contact festival organisers for a full programme of events.

Aldeburgh Poetry Festival
Aldeburgh Poetry Trust, Goldings, Goldings Lane,
Leiston, Suffolk IP16 4EB
tel (01728) 830631 *fax* (01728) 832029
Festival Co-ordinator Michael Laskey
Takes place 31 Oct-2 Nov 1997
The 9th annual international festival of contemporary poetry. A celebratory weekend including readings, workshops, a public masterclass, a lecture and a children's event. Twenty different poets as well as fringe events. Preceded by an extended residency for one of the invited poets. Festival prize for the year's best first collection.

Aspects Festival
North Down Borough Council, Town Hall,
The Castle, Bangor, Co. Down BT20 4BT
tel (01247) 270371 *fax* (01247) 271370
Festival Director Kenneth Irvine
Contact Paula Clamp (Arts Officer)
Takes place Autumn
An annual celebration of contemporary Irish writing with novelists, poets, playwrights and non-fiction writers. Includes readings, discussions, workshops and a children's day.

Ballymena Arts Festival
Ballymena Borough Council, Ardeevin,
80 Galgorm Road, Ballymena,
Co. Antrim BT42 1AB
tel (01266) 44111 *fax* (01226) 46296
Takes place 2-18 Oct 1997

A general arts festival which includes literature events.

Bath Literature Festival
Bath Festivals Trust, 2 Midland Bridge Road,
Bath BA2 3EQ
tel (01225) 462231 *fax* (01225) 445551
Programme Director Laurence Staig
Takes place 20-28 Feb 1998
An annual 9-day festival with leading guest writers. Includes readings, debates, discussions and workshops, and children's activities. Education and community programme includes author visits to schools and a children's writing competition. Each year has a chosen theme.

Belfast Festival at Queen's
Festival House, 25 College Gardens,
Belfast BT9 6BS
tel (01232) 667687 *fax* (01232) 663733
Marketing Manager Rosie Turner
Takes place November
The largest annual arts event in Ireland. Includes literature events. Programme available mid-September.

Birmingham Readers & Writers Festival
Festival Office, Central Library,
Chamberlain Square, Birmingham B3 3HQ
tel 0121-235 4244 *fax* 0121-233 9702
e-mail readers.writers@dial.pipex.com
Festival Director Jonathan Davidson
Takes place May

An annual 9-day festival which aims to promote the best in contemporary literature, both from within the city and internationally. Over 100 events are on offer: workshops, performances, talks, discussions, plus a special day of events for children. Leading guest writers and poets; poet in residence; BBC tie-ins. The festival runs the *Midlands Poetry Competition* and organises the *TSB Birmingham Children's Book Awards*.

Book Now!

Leisure Service Department,
London Borough of Richmond upon Thames,
Langholm Lodge, 146 Petersham Road,
Richmond, Surrey TW10 6UX
tel 0181-332 0534 *fax* 0181-940 7568
Principal Arts Officer Nigel Cutting
Takes place throughout November

An annual literature festival covering a broad range of subjects. Leading British guest writers and poets hold discussions, talks, debates and workshops and give readings. There are also exhibitions, storytelling sessions and a schools programme.

Brighton Festival

Brighton Festival Society Ltd, 21-22 Old Steine,
Brighton BN1 1EL
tel (01273) 713875 *fax* (01273) 622453
Takes place May

An annual general arts festival with a large literature programme. Leading guest writers cover a broad range of subjects in a diverse programme of events. Programme published end of February.

Broadstairs Dickens Festival

c/o Rooftops, 58 High Street, Broadstairs,
Kent CT10 1JT
tel (01843) 863453
Contact Honorary Festival Organiser
Takes place June

An annual festival held annually since 1937 with a variety of events inspired by Dickens. Includes walks, talks, dramatic readings, and a festival play of a Dickens work.

Cambridge Conference of Contemporary Poetry

c/o Ian Patterson, King's College,
Cambridge CB2 1ST
tel (01223) 327455
e-mail ikp1000@cam.ac.uk
Takes place April

An annual weekend of poetry readings, discussion and performance of international poetry in the modernist tradition.

Canterbury Festival

Festival Office, Christ Church Gate,
The Precincts, Canterbury, Kent CT1 2EE
tel (01227) 472820 *fax* (01227) 781830
Takes place 11-25 Oct 1997

An annual general arts festival with a literature programme and open poetry competition with £2000 in prizes. Programme published in July.

Chaucer Festival

Chaucer Heritage Trust, 22 St Peter's Street,
Canterbury, Kent CT1 2BQ
tel (01227) 470379 *fax* (01227) 761416 or
tel/fax 0171-229 0635
Manager and Events Organiser Philippe Wibrotte
Takes place Spring and Summer

An annual festival which includes commemoration services, theatre productions, exhibitions, readings, recitals, Chaucer site visits, medieval fairs, costumed cavalcades, educational programmes for schools. Takes place in London, Canterbury and the County of Kent in the Spring (Easter Chaucer Pilgrimage) and Summer (June-July).

Cheltenham Festival of Literature

Town Hall, Imperial Square, Cheltenham,
Glos. GL50 1QA
tel (01242) 521621 *fax* (01242) 256457
Festival Organiser Sarah Smyth
Takes place 10-19 Oct 1997

An annual festival with a chosen theme each year; 1997 focuses on Irish writing and post-colonial literature from all over the world. Includes themed days with talks around one specific subject and 3-hour 'Write Away' sessions with a team of writing tutors. *Book It!* is a festival for children within the main festival and for the second year will include a Multimedia Room. Programme available in August.

Chichester Festivities

Canon Gate House, South Street, Chichester,
West Sussex PO19 1PU
tel (01243) 785718 *fax* (01243) 528356
Takes place June/July

An annual general arts festival with a programme of literature events. Programme published in April.

City of London Festival

City Arts Trust, Bishopsgate Hall,
230 Bishopsgate, London EC2M 4QD
tel 0171-377 0540 *fax* 0171-377 1972
Takes place 23 June-9 July 1998

An annual general arts festival with a programme of literature events, including leading guest writers. Programme published in April.

Durham Literature Festival

c/o Durham City Arts Ltd, Byland Lodge,
Hawthorn Terrace, Durham DH1 4TD
tel (0191) 386 6111 ext. 338 *fax* (0191) 386 0625
Festival Co-ordinators Anna Barker, Paul Rubinstein
Takes place May/June

A showcase for major international writers. This annual festival offers a wide range of events covering the finest literature and poetry to the best in popular fiction and children's writing. Readings and performances, talks, discussions and workshops for adults and children, with contributions from leading guest writers. Also a special day for aspiring writers and poets.

Edinburgh Book Festival

Scottish Book Centre, 137 Dundee Street,
Fountainbridge, Edinburgh EH11 1BG
tel 0131-228 5444 *fax* 0131-228 4333
Director Jan Fairley, *Assistant Director* Alison Plackitt
Takes place 9-25 Aug 1997

Now regarded as Europe's largest book event for the public. In addition to the displays of books, over 250 international writers contribute to the programme of events. Programme details available in June. Runs concurrently with Edinburgh International Festival.

Edinburgh International Festival

21 Market Street, Edinburgh EH1 1BW
tel 0131-473 2001 *fax* 0131-473 2002
Takes place 16 Aug-5 Sept 1998

An annual international arts festival including world class theatre, dance, opera and music. Programme published late March.

Exeter Festival

Festival Office, Civic Centre, Exeter EX1 1JN
tel (01392) 265200 *fax* (01392) 265265
web site http://www.exeter.ac.uk/festival97
http://www.zynet.co.uk/festival
City Centre Marketing Officer Gerri Bennett
Takes place July

An annual general arts festival which includes a programme of literary evenings. Programme of events available in April.

Federation of Worker Writers and Community Publishers Festival of Writing

PO Box 540, Burslem,
Stoke-on-Trent ST6 6DR
tel/fax (01782) 822327
Takes place April

The Federation was formed in 1976 to promote working-class writing as an alternative to establishment literature. An annual weekend festival of readings, workshops, discussions and an opportunity to meet writers from different communities.

Female Eye National Festival of Women's Writing

Female Eye, Watersmead, Norwood Green Hill,
Halifax, West Yorkshire HX3 8QX
tel/fax (01274) 670181
Takes place June

Female Eye is a non-profit-making organisation set up to encourage and promote writing by women. Each year has a chosen theme and the festival comprises performance, writing workshops and discussion. Female Eye also runs collaborative events with other festivals and provides a networking base.

Festival at the Edge

c/o The Old Salt House, Bower Yard, Ironbridge,
Telford, Shropshire TF8 7JP
tel (01952) 883936
Contact Genevieve Tudor
Takes place second full weekend of July

'Tales at the Edge' story club hosts an annual weekend of storytelling, music, dance and song.

Guildford Book Festival

c/o Arts Office, University of Surrey,
Guildford GU2 5XH
tel (01483) 259167
Festival Organiser Joan König
Takes place 24 Oct-7 Nov 1997

An annual festival on a chosen theme, with a programme of over 40 events at 12 different venues. Includes readings, literary lunches and dinners, discussions, performance poetry, writing competitions, a writer in residence, the annual University of Surrey Poetry Lecture and children's events.

Harrogate International Festival

The Festival Office, Royal Baths, Harrogate,
North Yorkshire HG1 2RR
tel (01423) 562303 *fax* (01423) 521264
e-mail info@harrogate-festival.org.uk
web site http://www.harrogate-festival.org.uk
Takes place July/Aug

An annual international general arts festival which includes a programme of literary events. Programme available in May.

Hastings Poetry Festival

c/o Burdett Cottage, 4 Burdett Place,
George Street, Hastings, East Sussex TN34 3ED
tel (01424) 428855 *fax* (01424) 428855
Organiser and Editor of First Time Josephine
Austin
Takes place 2-3 Nov 1996

Started in 1968, this national festival is now held in the Sussex Hall, White Rock Theatre, Hastings. Includes the prize-giving of the *Hastings National Poetry Competition*. Poems are invited for consideration for the bi-annual *First Time* poetry magazine. Please include sae.

The Hay Festival

Festival Office, Hay-on-Wye HR3 5BX
tel (01497) 821217 *fax* (01497) 821066
Takes place May/June

This annual festival aims to celebrate the best in writing and performance from around the world, to commission new work, and to promote and encourage young writers of excellence and potential. Over 100 events in 10 days with leading guest writers. Programme published mid-March.

Huddersfield Poetry Festival

The Word Hoard Ltd, 46-47 Byram Arcade,
Westgate, Huddersfield HD1 1ND
tel (01484) 452070
Contact Dianne Darby
Takes place Spring and Autumn

This annual festival consists of two seasons. The Spring season consists of readings at various locations. The Autumn season (spread over 3 weekends in September and October) also includes readings but is more participatory, with workshops leading to performances.

Ilkley Literature Festival

Manor House, Ilkley, West Yorkshire LS29 9DT
tel (01943) 601210
Director David Porter
Takes place Events promoted throughout 1998

Into its 25th season, this annual festival has 3 seasons: Spring, Summer and Autumn. Includes readings, talks, lectures, workshops, story-telling, children's and family events; also accredited courses run in association with the University of Leeds in creative poetry writing, short story writing and understanding literature. Brings the best new and established writers from Britain and abroad.

International Playwriting Festival

Warehouse Theatre, Dingwall Road,
Croydon CR0 2NF
tel 0181-681 1257 *fax* 0181-688 6699
Contact Rose Marie Vernon

Takes place in 2 parts. The competition has a script submission deadline in July (see page 500). The November festival includes performed excerpts from the shortlisted plays, workshops and discussions, a performance from our partner's festival in Italy, the Premio Candoni Arta Terme, and a staged reading of the winning play.

King's Lynn Festival

27-29 King Street, King's Lynn, Norfolk PE30 1HA
tel (01553) 774725 *fax* (01553) 770591
Press and Marketing Officer Catherine Moore
Takes place 18 July-1 Aug 1998

An annual general arts festival with literature events featuring leading guest writers.

Lancaster Literature Festival

67 Church Street, Lancaster LA1 1ET
tel (01524) 62166
Contact Andrew Darby
Takes place end of October

Annual festival featuring readings, performances and workshops by contemporary writers for adults, young people and children. The LitFest also acts as a year-round literature development agency, organising readings and workshops, and offering advice and information to writers and readers in Lancashire.

Leicestershire Literature Festival

Leicestershire Libraries and Information Service,
County Hall, Glenfield, Leicester LE3 8SS
tel 0116-265 7386 *fax* 0116-265 7370
Takes place to be confirmed

A biennial festival with a set theme each year. Includes readings, discussions, exhibitions, workshops and competitions, with contributions from leading guest writers.

Lincolnshire Literature Festival

Education and Cultural Services Directorate,
Lincolnshire County Council, County Offices,
Lincoln LN1 1YL
tel (01522) 552831
County Arts Development Officer David Lambert
Takes place throughout the year

A series of festivals (March-June/July-October) focusing on specific genres, cultures and topical issues. Also a monthly series of literary events at Lincoln Central Library.

Norfolk and Norwich Festival

16 Princes Street, Norwich NR3 1AE
tel (01603) 614921 *fax* (01603) 632303
Festival Director Marcus Davey
Takes place 10-20 Oct 1996

A general arts festival with some literary events. Programme published in June.

North East Lincolnshire Literature Festival – Fishing for Words

Arts Development Unit, North East Lincolnshire
Council, Knoll Street, Cleethorpes,
Lincs. DN35 8LN
Festival Programmer Camilla Goddard
Takes place February/March

Reflecting the fishing heritage of the area, this annual festival aims to make literature accessible to all ages and abilities through a varied and unusual programme. Write for details.

Off the Shelf Festival of Reading and Writing

c/o Sheffield Libraries and Information Services,
Central Library, Surrey Street, Sheffield S1 1XZ
tel 0114-273 6645 *fax* 0114-273 5009
Contact Judith Adam
Takes place 18 Oct-1 Nov 1997

The festival comprises a wide range of events for adults and children, including writing workshops, talks, storytelling, drama sessions, illustration workshops and exhibitions. Programme available in September.

Poetry International

Literature Department, Royal Festival Hall,
London SE1 8XX
tel 0171-921 0906 *fax* 0171-928 2049
Contact Caroline Hughes
Takes place 10 days in Oct/Nov 1998

The biggest poetry festival in the British Isles, bringing together a wide range of poets from around the world. Includes readings, workshops, discussions and events for children. Poetry International is a biennial festival.

Poets and Small Press Festival

Contact for 1998 Festival Stuart A. Paterson,
c/o Dumfries and Galloway Arts Association,
Gracefield Arts Centre, 28 Edinburgh Road,
Dumfries GG1 1JQ
tel (01387) 260000

The festival celebrates the role that small presses have played in the current resurgence of poetry. Includes readings, performances, debates, live music and a magazine and book fair.

Royal Court Young Writers' Festival

The Royal Court Young People's Theatre,
309 Portobello Road, London W10 5TD
tel 0181-960 4641
Contact Aoife Mannix
Takes place varies

Each festival targets a different area of the UK. Anyone up to the age of 23 can attend workshops at various locations within these areas. Promising plays which arise from the workshops are then developed and performed at the Royal Court's Theatre Upstairs and at venues in the participating area (see page 515).

Salisbury Festival

75 New Street, Salisbury, Wilts. SP1 2PH
tel (01722) 323883 *fax* (01722) 410552
Director Helen Marriage
Takes place May/June

An annual general arts festival with a literature programme of events. Each year has a chosen theme. Programme published in March.

Shots on the Page

Broadwords, Broadway Media Centre,
14 Broad Street, Nottingham NG1 3AL
tel 0115-955 7171 *fax* 0115-952 6622
e-mail millward@broadwords.org.uk
web site http://www.broadwords.org.uk/broadwords

Taking place at the same time as the *Shots in the Dark* annual festival, this crime-writing convention is for writers and fans. Includes talks, workshops and discussions with leading guest writers.

The Torrington Literature Festival

The Plough Arts Centre, Fore Street, Torrington,
Devon EX38 8HQ
tel (01805) 622552 *fax* (01805) 624624
Contact Sharon Walters
Takes place 1-4 Oct 1997

The festival comprises workshops (including children's), readings, performances and exhibitions.

Warwick & Leamington Festival

Warwick Arts Society, Northgate,
Warwick CV34 4JL
tel (01926) 410747 *fax* (01926) 407606
Festival Director Richard Phillips, *Literary Consultant* Pauline Prior-Pitt
Takes place first half of July

A music festival which includes some literature and poetry events: readings, performances and workshops.

Ways With Words Literature Festival

Droridge Farm, Dartington, Totnes, Devon TQ9 6JQ
tel (01803) 867311 *fax* (01803) 863688
Contact Kay Dunbar
Takes place 8-15 July 1998

The festival includes readings, talks, interviews, discussions, seminars, workshops with leading guest writers. Literary weekends and writing courses also organised.

Wells Festival of Literature

Tower House, St Andrew Street, Wells,
Somerset BA5 2UN
tel (01749) 673385
Takes place late October

This annual festival features leading guest writers and poets; includes writing workshops and competitions.

Writearound: Cleveland's Annual Festival for Writers and Readers

c/o Cleveland Arts, Gurney House, Gurney Street, Middlesbrough, Cleveland TS1 1JL
tel (01642) 262429 *fax* (01642) 262424
Contact Mark Robinson
Takes place 10-19 Oct 1997, 9-18 Oct 1998

Writearound is an independent non-profit-making organisation dedicated to encouraging, promoting and developing literary activity on Teesside and surrounding areas, through an annual literary festival. A programme of events is offered throughout Middlesbrough, including workshops, performances, poetry, open readings and children's events.

Preparing for publication

Preparing and submitting a manuscript

A well-presented manuscript will make a good impression on the publisher's reader. Guidelines on how best to present your manuscript are given here.

Even though the majority of material for potential publication is originated on disk, the text is still referred to as a manuscript – after all, it is the printout which is read. A well-presented manuscript will make a good impression on the publisher's reader. Many publishers refuse even to consider handwritten manuscripts; and no publisher will accept them as final copy.

Typing

A neatly typed manuscript (or typescript – the words are interchangeable in present usage) is essential not only to make a good impression on a publisher, but also for the publisher's copy editor to work on. The typesetter must be able to read the manuscript with any amendments quickly and accurately, plus interpret the code of marks made by the copy editor or designer. Wide margins are therefore essential to accommodate all these additions. The left-hand margin should be a minimum of 3cm, and the right-hand, top and bottom margins should all be generous. Use the same margins throughout, so that the type on each page is of the same width and, except at the beginning and end of each chapter, there will be the same number of lines on each page. If you use a word processor, do not use its facility for 'justifying' the type on the right-hand side.

Lay out the text in double spacing, i.e. a full line of space between two lines of copy – not half a line of space. This will allow space for any last minute changes you wish to make and for the copy editor's amendments. Indent the first line of each paragraph a few spaces and do not leave a blank line between paragraphs unless you want to indicate a change of subject, scene, time or viewpoint.

Be as consistent as possible in your choice of variant spellings, use of subheadings, etc. For example, use either -ise or -ize suffixes consistently throughout.

Number the pages (or 'folios' as publishers prefer to call them to distinguish them from the pages of the final book) straight through from beginning to end – don't start each chapter at folio 1. If you need to include an extra folio after, say, folio 27, call it 27a and write at the foot of folio 27: 'Folio 27a follows'. Then write at the foot of 27a: 'Folio 28 follows'. Don't do this too often or you will confuse and irritate your readers.

Create a front page (unnumbered) for your manuscript. Type the title about halfway down the page, with your name (or pen name) immediately beneath. In the bottom left-hand corner, type your name and address, plus the word count (see below). It is worth including your name and address on the last page as well, in case the first folio becomes detached.

Most authors use a word processor for writing and/or for presenting the finished material (see *Word processing* on page 531). Use standard A4 paper, rather than

---

Manuscript checklist

- Allow generous margins
- Use double spacing
- Number each folio
- Include a front page
- Keep a duplicate of the manuscript

continuous listing paper, for your print-out and use one side only. This printout is referred to as 'hard copy', or more traditionally, the 'manuscript'. Work prepared on a typewriter should also be on A4 paper, using only one side of each sheet.

Corrections to your manuscript

Keep your corrections to the final printout to a minimum. Often the publisher's editor will suggest a few additional changes, and once these are included, the manuscript may have become very messy. If the publisher then feels it is not in a fit state for the typesetter to work from they may well ask you incorporate the changes and make a new printout.

Presentation

Publishers prefer to handle each folio separately, so do not use a binder which will make this impossible; ring binders are acceptable. It is best to place the separate sheets in a cardboard envelope folder, obviating the need for pins (which scratch), paperclips (which pick up other papers from an editor's desk), or staples (which make it awkward to read the typescript). The typescript can be protected by placing a piece of stiff card at front and back. Do not use a plastic folder as they tend to slip when placed in a pile, and both publishers and literary agents keep manuscripts piled on their desks.

Word count

The length of a book is referred to by publishers as the 'extent'. It is usual to give an approximation of the number of words

contained in a typescript. You do not have to count every word yourself. Use the word count facility on your word processor, or make a rough calculation, counting the number of words on a few pages to get an average and multiplying that figure by the number of pages in the typescript.

Submitting your manuscript

Choosing the right publisher

You will save time and postage if you check first that you are sending your manuscript to a publisher that will consider it. Publishers specialise – it is no use sending a work of romantic fiction to a firm that specialises in high-brow novels translated from obscure languages. It is still less use to send it to a firm which publishes no fiction at all. (For an index of *Publishers of fiction* see page 222.) By studying the entries in the *Yearbook*, examining publishers' lists of publications, or by looking for the names of suitable publishers in the relevant sections in libraries and bookshops, you will find the names of several publishers which might be interested in seeing your material. (Remember, though, that paperbacks are often editions of books published first in hardback editions.)

It is important how you approach a publisher. Many publishers will not accept unsolicited material – you must enquire first if they would be willing to read the whole manuscript. A few publishers are prepared to speak on the telephone, allowing you to describe, briefly, the work on offer. Most prefer a preliminary letter; and many publishers, particularly of fiction, will only see material submitted through a literary agent (listings of literary agents start on page 334). It has to be said that some publishing houses, the larger ones in particular, may well employ all three methods!

There is no point whatsoever in asking for an interview: the publisher will prefer to consider the manuscript on its own merits. In the event of a manuscript being rejected, the publisher will not be willing to discuss the reasons in person.

Treatment for plays

For plays, use capitals for character names and underline stage directions in red by hand. If a traditional typewriter is employed, use red for names of characters, stage directions, etc, and black for dialogue. See also *Presenting scripts for television and film* on page 293.

Preliminary letter

This will save you time, money and probably frustration. Most publishers prefer to see a brief preliminary letter together with a synopsis of the book and the first couple of chapters (enclose postage for their return). From this material the publisher can judge whether the book will fit the list, in which case you will be asked to send the complete manuscript. This is especially advisable in the case of non-fiction – most non-fiction books are commissioned as the result of an initial submission in the form of a synopsis and specimen chapters. Writers have been known to send out such letters in duplicated form, an approach unlikely to stimulate a publisher's interest. However, simultaneous submission to more than one publisher is permissible, provided that you inform each publisher that the book is being considered elsewhere at the same time. Always enclose return postage, even for a letter, when approaching a publisher. Remember, also, that whilst every reasonable care will be taken of material in the publishers' possession, responsibility cannot be accepted if material is lost or damaged. At all costs, keep a copy of your manuscript with all the most recent changes to the text included on it.

In the hands of the publisher

There is usually a considerable interval between submission and the publisher's decision. Most publishers acknowledge receipt of manuscripts; if you do not receive one it is advisable to check that your manuscript has arrived. Apart from that, it is not worth chasing the publisher for a quick decision: if pressed, the publisher will probably reject, purely because this is the safer decision.

You should hear from the publisher within about two months. During this time the manuscript will either have been read in-house or it will have been sent to one or more advisers whose opinions the publisher respects. Favourable readers' reports may mean that the publisher will immediately accept the manuscript, par-ticularly if it fits easily into the current publishing programme.

On the other hand, a reader's report may be glowing, but the publisher may still hesitate. Publishers want to be sure they will be able to sell a book profitably, so may obtain further opinions, and/or explore the financial viability, before making a final decision.

If you have not had a decision after two months, write either a tactful letter saying 'I don't want to rush you, but ...' or, alternatively, request an immediate decision and be prepared to start again with another publisher. If your book is topical you have a right to a speedy decision, but it is as well to establish this early on.

Illustrations

If illustrations form a large part of your proposed book and you expect to provide them yourself, then they should be included with the manuscript. If you are sending specimen pages you should include also some sample illustrations: this applies largely to children's picture books and to travel and technical books. Do not send the originals – send duplicate photographs, photocopies of line drawings and so on so that little harm is done if illustrations go astray.

In the case of a children's book, if you intend to illustrate it yourself, obviously one finished piece of artwork is essential, plus photocopies of roughs for the rest (the final artwork may have to be drawn to a particular size and the number of illustrations fixed according to the format chosen by the publisher). If you have written a children's story, or the text for a picture book, do not ask a friend to provide the illustrations; the publisher who likes your story may well not like your friend's artwork. Of course this does not apply when an artist and author work closely together to develop an idea, but in that case it is best to start by finding a publisher who likes the artist's work before submitting the story. See *Writing and illustrating children's books* on page 245 and *Children's book publishers and packagers* on page 249.

Travel manuscripts should be accompanied by a sketch map to show the area you are writing about, so the publisher has sufficient detail with which to follow your manuscript.

Many illustrated books these days have illustrations collected by the publishers. It is best to establish early on who is responsible for the illustration costs: a seemingly generous royalty offer might be less attractive if you have to gather the pictures, obtain permission for use, and foot the bills.

Quotations

It is normally the author's responsibility to obtain (and pay for) permission to quote written material which is still in copyright. Permission should always be sought from the publisher of the quoted work, not from the author. Fees for quotation vary enormously: for fashionable modern writers permission may be costly, but in other cases only a nominal fee is charged. There is no standard scale of fees. It is permissible to quote up to about 200 words for the purpose of criticism or review, but this does not apply to use in anthologies, nor does it apply to poetry. And it is a concession, not a right. Even though this is your area of responsibility, your publisher will be able to give you some advice.

Proofs for the author

When the publisher accepts your manuscript, if you have typed it on a word processor they may well ask you to supply the text on disk. The files containing your manuscript should be unformatted plain text – doing a fancy layout is a waste of time as it will be unformatted by the publisher or typesetter. Having the material on disk will save time and money in production costs, as well as cut down the margin for errors creeping in. Today, it is unusual for large publishing houses to take text which is not on disk.

As author you will see either one or two stages of proofs. Sometimes you will be shown the finalised copy of the manuscript immediately before it goes to the typesetter. If so, this is really your last chance to make changes which will not tend to sour relations with your publisher! Take the opportunity to comb through the manuscript, and if there are changes which you suspect you will want to make in proof, make them now. There was a time when authors could virtually rewrite their books in galley proof, and revise them again at page, but those days are long gone! (See *Correcting proofs* on page 539 for the conventional proof-correcting marks.)

Making corrections at proof stage is time-consuming and costly. You will probably have signed a contract undertaking to pay the cost of corrections (other than typesetter's errors) over say 10-15% of the cost of composition. This does not mean that you can change 10 or 15 lines in every 100.

Increasingly often only one stage of proofs is used in book production, and there is rarely any need for the author to see more than one stage. The proofs may be in several forms. You may only see a computer printout which has had all the amendments incorporated; this will bear no resemblance to the finished book but will contain everything that will appear in that book. Galley proofs are produced by the typesetter and are columns of continuous text. Page proofs have been made up into pages, including page numbers, headlines, illustrations, and so on. It is prohibitively expensive to make corrections at this stage, except to the printer's own errors.

The production of highly illustrated books, such as children's or 'coffee table' books, is dealt with differently. The fitting together of the pictures and text on each page is an important stage when the designer and the editor work together, modifying the text to make the final result come together happily.

Word processing

*There is little need to explain the basic ideas and advantages of moving words about on a screen before we print them. In this article, **Randall McMullan** considers how to write more effectively and more professionally while using a word processor.*

Methods of writing are very personal but they all involve a comfortable interaction between yourself and something mechanical, even if the equipment has to be a pad and pencil on your knee in front of the fire. But before you become set in the way you use the keyboard and screen of your word processor, do consider the information in the following sections. They contain techniques used by authors which may improve your efficiency, your income, your sanity – and even your writing.

Creating

If your creative habit depends upon letting the words flow, like Enid Blyton in her hidey-hole, then the word processor is an ideal companion. You can be a 'sprinter' or a 'fingertip' writer and rapidly get your narrative or ideas onto the screen. There is no need to stop; the layout and the order doesn't matter, you can work on those later.

Ordering your thoughts

More reflective methods of creation involve the use of reference materials, notes, outlines, ordering and assembly of portions of text. Any word processor allows you to develop personalised routines for these actions but you can also try some of the software packages which support these operations.

For example, many word processors have an 'outliner' which helps you to order your thoughts by using hierarchies of headings or 'layers' of text. If such ordered working is too much of a straightjacket then you may like the type of writing tool which searches your notes and offers links between sections containing similar words and ideas.

Writers' tools

A thesaurus can lead you through pleasant webs of cross-references. Other programs will analyse your writing and give a report on content and style. The grammatical comments are often debatable and a report on your sexism or pomposity may irritate you, but a correct analysis of the reading age of your text may surprise you.

A sample of writers' tools which have been on the market have names which give a clue to their purpose: Storyspace, Plot unlimited, Poetry Processor, WordPerfect Rhymer, Idea Fisher, IdeaList, Quotemaster, Lexica, StyleWriter, Readability Plus, Concise Oxford Dictionary, Oxford Concordance, Oxford Science Shelf.

Now that CD-Roms are standard in modern computers, the size, speed and utility of these reference works have increased dramatically. Available, for example, is a single CD-Rom which contains complete texts of out-of-copyright classics from Aristotle through Shakespeare to Wilde. The texts can be quickly searched for key words, displayed in a window on screen, and pasted into your own work as desired.

The Internet has various web sites devoted to the cares and concerns of authors. For example, if you enter a

'forum' and ask advice about general or particular software tools for writers, you will be guaranteed many direct and personal responses. There are also sites where you can download freeware packages or demonstration versions of commercial software packages for authors.

The well-known word processing programs include an indexing tool which may sound more useful than it may prove to be. You will still have to provide the thought, make the decisions, flag words or insert flagged phrases in the text. The indexer will then automatically sort and merge all your references with correct page numbers and update this index if you change the text.

Inputting text

You should abandon two habits from typewriter days: correcting errors as you enter, and typing 'over' existing text. You can't truly 'process' the words until all the words are there on the screen. Correcting, polishing and rearranging text are more efficient when done later as separate editing operations.

Don't stop for a typing mistake, even when you know you have just made one. Errors can be fixed automatically by the spell checker at an editing stage. On some word processors, typos can be automatically corrected as you write. The software can be set by you to change 'hte', for example, into 'the' – as you type.

Save, save, save your work as you write. It costs nothing and secures everything. Your creation on screen is transient until it is magnetically saved onto the hard disk or onto a floppy disk. A save command is usually a simple keystroke which should be given at the end of every page, every ten minutes, when the phone rings, and when the cat approaches the keyboard.

The physical aspects of putting text into the word processor should also be considered. You can learn or improve your typing skills from the various cheap and popular programs which use your screen and keyboard to train the eyes and fingers. If you intend to remain a two-finger typist, then at least keep each hand on its correct side of the keyboard.

Editing

Copy your work before making changes. Duplicate your work before and after making changes as you may be glad to go back to yesterday's version. Let the spell checker run through your entire text to correct the typos and the misspelt words. Remember that this tool can't correct for sense and that a correctly spelt word may still be the wrong word. Some of these wrong words can only be detected when your brain is in a different mode. The best editing is often done by reading and marking up a printout while away from your work area, preferably the next day.

As you make changes to text you need not 'overwrite' old text, as in typewriter days. Keep the word processor in normal 'insert' mode and let any text in front of your screen cursor be 'pushed along' in front of your new writing. The two versions can then be compared on the screen before deleting the unwanted text. A modern word processor also allows you to control revisions using coloured underlining and strike-through lines.

Become fluent in the commands of your word processor which allow you to mark 'blocks' of text and then copy or move them to new locations. A block of text can also be copied into a separate file docu-

---

RSI

The pain and disability of repetitive strain injury (RSI) has always been a risk for non-stop keyboardists, quill pen clerks and other repetitive workers such as chicken pluckers. Take heed of the following points to help minimise the risk of RSI to the hands and arms:
- ensure that your chair and your posture are comfortable and correct;
- locate the phone and the files away from the computer – moving and stretching is good for you;
- take regular breaks from working at the keyboard;
- do stretching exercises.

ment for use in future documents or for repeated insertion into your current document. Any stored text can be 'inserted' into the current text at the place where you have left the screen cursor. You can therefore open a new blank document and 'boilerplate' a new assembly of text out of existing saved text.

Formatting

The final layout and the style of print on the page should be thought of as a separate process carried out after the creation and the editing of text. A publishing house will prefer to receive your work as totally unformatted plain text, as do desktop publishing programs described in *Desktop publishing* (see page 535).

Ideally, your plain text should contain:
- no indents
- no padded word spaces
- no alignments
- no centring
- no line spaces
- no carriage returns except to start new paragraphs.

Save to 'text only' or 'plain text' – the save command of your word processor should have this type of option. Seek the agreement of the final publisher before using underlining, emboldening, large font and other effects.

Plain text looks cramped and uninspiring so you may, for creative reasons, wish to work with a copy of your text laid out in a form which resembles the final page. After inputting your text unformatted you can keep a copy of the plain text version before doing your fancy version. To control some writing projects you may need to set up your page to a certain width of line and length. Word processors can save these personal formats as blank templates.

Many word processing programs have desktop publishing features which allow you to do final page layout on the word processor screen if you wish. These activities, which require the skills and knowledge described in the desktop publishing article, are inspiring to some writers and of little interest to others.

Housekeeping

Authors can never be too rich, too thin, or have too many computer copies of their work. Each electronic document is stored as an electronic file or folder on the magnetic disk with a file or folder name chosen by yourself. Use a document or file 'copy' command to make a clone copy of your work but with a different filename.

If your work is being stored on the hard disk fitted inside your computer, then make a copy onto a portable floppy disk at daily intervals. Keep several floppy disk copies, some of them in a different room or building. If the computer fails, or is stolen, then you will be glad to go back to last week's version of your work.

Word processing files take up relatively little disk space compared to other computer files such as graphics. You can probably fit your entire year's writing onto one floppy disk but please don't do so as the disk may develop a fault and trap your masterpiece in a magnetic limbo. Floppy disks are so cheap that they are given away on magazine covers.

Training

Please *read* about your word processor; other writers have written to you! If you don't have a manual or a book then display the screen help items, print them out, and read them in bed. You don't need to spend money on a training course as you can't damage your word processor by experimenting. But you can remain ignorant of a feature which is just what you have been wanting to know about.

All modern word processors offer high level features such as automated routines (macros), printing envelopes and labels, and mail shots. If you want to use these features you should learn about them and try them.

Equipment

The simple broad aim is to use the same hardware as those people with whom you work or from whom you can obtain support. It is a fact that around 90% of the

market for business PCs belongs to the IBM PC/Intel families of machines made by a wide variety of manufacturers, not usually IBM.

The ability to gain information, swap disks, share equipment is often more important than other considerations. For most people that choice will be an IBM-compatible PC. For some it will be an Apple. The Apple Macintosh range has always used a 'graphical interface' which executes commands by moving a pointer on screen and 'clicking' the mouse. PC-compatible machines are now supplied with Microsoft Windows which provides a graphical interface similar to that of the Macintosh.

The PC and the Apple 'platforms' are slowly converging and the leading word processing packages work on both types of machine with minimal differences. The most common word processor package being bought for modern offices is Microsoft Word for Windows.

However, there are several dozen other word processing packages which have been in use over the years and they all do everything that most writers require. Conversion software allows you to convert text in one major format to another major format, although fancy layouts may become mangled. Most word processors should also be able to exchange information via the plain text or ASCII format.

The purchase of computer goods often relates to how you personally buy an item like a washing machine or television. You may purchase at a John Lewis department store and arrange for full delivery and installation, or you might bring the equipment home from a discount warehouse in an unopened box and set it up yourself.

It is common to buy computer equipment by mail order and credit card from reputable discount warehouses, so you should use the Internet or buy a magazine like *MicroMart* (Micromart UK Ltd) or *Personal Computer World* (VNU Business Publications) to get an idea of prices. Otherwise choose a dealer in a convenient location and use your magazine prices to negotiate a suitable package of price and help.

Randall McMullan is a writer and educational adviser who has been using word processors for over 20 years. He is the author of various works in the fields of fiction, busines computing, environmental science and construction.

Desktop publishing

*Ten years ago, preparing the words to be printed on the pages of a publication was the domain of the typesetter. Since then, the use of desktop publishing has become widespread and has opened up a whole range of opportunities for producing publications. However, no matter how sophisticated the program may be, it cannot plan and design a publication. **Richard Williams** introduces design considerations and describes how to prepare for publication using desktop publishing.*

Essential equipment

Because of the rapid pace of change, this article gives only general guidance on buying desktop publishing (DTP) equipment and software. For more detailed and up-to-date information, read the specialist computer magazines.

When buying a new computer, choose a machine which more than meets your current needs, and preferably one that can be upgraded since each release of a program is likely to require more power, machine memory and hard disk capacity than the last. Also take into account all the other things you may want to use a computer for: video editing, playing games, running CD-Roms, e-mailing, surfing the Internet, etc.

IBM-compatible PCs can probably run the greatest number of programs, but the Macintosh is favoured by the DTP and graphics professionals, so programs which they use tend to come out first on the Mac (and some specialised ones never make it to the IBM machines). In either case, opt for a larger-than-average sized monitor screen. Monitors are classified by the screen diagonal measurement and the smallest useful size is 15in. For sustained work 17in is probably the minimum and professionals tend to use 20in or 21in screens.

A mouse is essential for DTP work. These have always been provided with Macs, and nowadays IBM-compatible machines usually include one. If not, resist the temptation to buy a cheap model.

A printer is essential for proofing your work and can also be used to produce camera-ready copy (CRC). With the virtual disappearance of dot matrix printers, the choice now lies between injet and laser printers. Each has its advantages: inkjets are cheaper and quieter but laser printers give the best quality and a lower consumables cost per page. If you are using a printer to proof work for commercial printing, it is probably worth paying the extra cost for PostScript. This is almost universally used to produce the final bromide or film and gives a much better match between proof and final output. If you want to produce CRC, a 1200 dots per inch laser printer is the ideal, but PostScript is not essential.

Proofing full-colour printing still needs a costly printer for real accuracy, but the standard of colour now achieved by inexpensive injets makes these a practical proposition, either for preliminary layouts, or to produce prints from a digital camera.

Optional extras

A CD-Rom drive gives you access to illustrations in electronic form, ready to drop into the page. These can be either your

own photos transferred to Photo CDs, or commercial collections of stock photos and drawn 'clip art'. You can also use the huge range of fonts now available in this format. CD-Rom drives are now relatively inexpensive to buy, and are generally provided as part of a new computer. If not, one can be easily added. If you also want to use it for multimedia and games, make sure that it is at least an eight speed drive and buy a sound card as well (these often come bundled with drives).

A scanner, to convert existing paper illustrations or photographs into electronic form, is another useful extra. Now that flatbed scanners are more affordable, the choice between these and compact scanners depends more on convenience and type of media than on price. Compact scanners save space, and often come with sophisticated document management software, but flatbeds are better for scanning in colour and can cope not only with loose sheets but with transparencies, books and even objects.

Optical character reading (OCR) software can convert scans of existing typed or printed text directly into electronic format, avoiding the need to retype it.

A digital camera cuts out the scanning stage by producing images in electronic form, ready for immediate use. Affordable models are still restricted to relatively low definition (equivalent to a standard computer screen) but are useful if you need a lot of small-scale pictures quickly.

Software

Desktop publishing programs have tended to polarise between the inexpensive but competent, and the expensive and fully professional. For anyone doing a significant amount of DTP work the extra cost of the high end programs will be worthwhile, just for their power and ease of use (though not necessarily ease of learning). If you are not sure, start with one of the low end programs which will give you a clearer idea of your requirements if, or when, you come to buy a more powerful program.

Most high-end DTP programs now

enable you to publish on the Internet, as well as in more conventional form. This is particularly useful if you want to convert existing documents for Web use; for creating a Web site from scratch, the specialist authoring programs offer more flexibility and power.

Designing the publication

Planning is the most important first step in creating a document or publication. Before starting work you need to be clear what kind of document it is, and who it is aimed at. At the practical level you should decide, roughly at least, how many pages there will be, what size, and how they are to be printed and bound. Obviously, these decisions are often interlinked – your choice of page size will be limited if it is to be produced by laser printer, photocopier or quick printer, but much wider if it is to be commercially printed. Before you set up the page layout, spend as much time as you can looking critically at other publications. See what works, and what doesn't, and don't be afraid to copy a design that pleases you.

Try to avoid over-elaborate page designs. Use elements such as lines and boxes with a purpose, to clarify rather than ornament, and remember that white space has a vital role to play. Most programs allow you to set up a grid of guidelines, so use these to give pages a structure, particularly important in illustrated works.

When you start, work on just a few pages at first, the minimum needed to show all the possibilities in the document as a whole. For something simple, like a novel, you only need a double page spread of ordinary text, another spread for chapter start and finish, and possibly a single page for the table of contents. Non-fiction is usually more complex, and may require extra pages to show the treatment of headings and illustrations plus an index, if present. Work on these pages until you are happy with the result, then try a sample chapter as a check before laying out the rest of the book. In this way, problems can be solved at an early stage, and changes made, with a minimum impact on the work already done.

Using typefaces sensibly

Because DTP programs allow access to lots of typefaces, beginners tend to use too many. The basic rule is to use no more than two individual typefaces on a page, and get the necessary variety with different sizes and weights. One popular scheme is to combine a sans-serif face for headings with a serif face for text. This gives both variety and readability (serif faces are generally reckoned to be more legible for large amounts of text, except at very small sizes).

Beginners also err by carrying over the conventions of the typewriter, with plentiful use of capitals and underlining. In print this is unnecessary – use upper case (capital letters) sparingly, and don't use underlines at all. Instead use either bold or italics for emphasis: bold for an isolated word or phrase but italics for a longer passage, which would otherwise be over-emphatic.

Other common mistakes are using two spaces after a full stop, two hyphens for a dash, and the normal typewriter single and double quotation marks. For professional looking results, make sure there is only a single space, use proper dashes and opening and closing quotation marks, and avoid indents in the first paragraph after a heading.

The right spacing

The correct balance of spacing between letters, words and lines is crucial for legibility. Here the basic rule is that spacing between letters should be less than between words, and that between words less than between lines. Provided the relationship between these elements is correct, the actual amount of spacing is a matter of taste.

The ideal page should have an even texture, avoiding obvious variations in spacing from line to line. Letter spacing should normally be fixed, and word spacing should not be less than two thirds, or more than one and a half times the average setting. This may cause problems with shorter lines, but the solution here is

intelligent use of hyphenation (avoiding more than two successive hyphens) and the use of unjustified text for short lines. The ideal line length is generally reckoned to be about 60 to 70 characters – much less gives problems with spacing, whilst longer lines are more difficult to read.

Space should be used to differentiate headings from body text; there should be at least as much space below a heading as between paragraphs, and more above, so that it clearly relates to the following text. To ensure that text in adjoining columns lines up across the page, the total space occupied by a heading (the type itself, plus space above and below) must always be a multiple of the point size of the body text. Resist the temptation to use too many different levels of heading – three should be enough for almost any purpose.

Even with these rules to guide you, experimentation will be necessary to get a satisfactory combination of typefaces and spacing. Don't skimp this, but persevere until you are really happy with the result – if it doesn't look right, then it probably isn't. If you are not sure, put the sample page on one side for a day or more, so that you come back to it with a fresh eye.

Adding text and illustrations

Once you are happy with the layout and typography of your sample pages, you are ready to apply these to the whole text. You should be able to do this by creating 'styles' which format a paragraph in a single operation by 'tagging' it. The foolproof method is to prepare text in the word processor without any formatting at all, then use the appropriate style to format it in the DTP program. Text can also be tagged in a word processor, but this requires more expert knowledge.

Although simple graphics can be created in many DTP programs, it is better to use a separate program to create illustrations – a drawing program for diagrams and charts, a spreadsheet for graphs. Avoid the so-called paint programs if pos-

sible – these can give a jagged look to the finished result. If you must use one of these, make sure you create the illustration at least the size of the printed version and preferably larger.

Photographs can liven up a text page, but only if properly handled. Two common faults are to include too much detail for the size of the picture, and to print it too dark. Cropping can get rid of extraneous detail, and most DTP or graphics programs can do this.

Dot gain (the tendency of half-tone dots to be larger on paper than on the printing plate) causes photos to print darker than the original. This can be compensated for either in scanning or in the DTP program itself. Conventionally screened photos should take this into account, and pasting these into a bromide rather than scanning them may be the simplest solution.

Final stages

Make sure that you check the final proofs carefully – any mistakes not found at this stage will be expensive to correct later. Spell checkers need to be used intelligently – they are great for catching obvious errors but are no substitute for careful conventional proofreading.

One task that normally has to wait for this stage is the preparation of an index. Although DTP programs can help in this, the process still requires human intervention, and for anything more than a simple index a professional indexer will give a much better result.

Final output

Conventional printing is expensive for short runs, so consider using either a high quality copier in a quick printer, or one of the new machines which are a hybrid of copier and printer. For longer runs it is better to use a commercial printer. The first time you do so, get some sample pages (the ones you produced for deciding on layout and typography) run off by the printer or service bureau. Any sensible firm will be happy to do this, knowing that snags found at this stage will avoid much worse problems later.

Although some service bureaux will accept files in the format of the DTP program, PostScript files are easier for them to handle and the final output is more likely to match your proofs. If you are using a Windows-based program, make sure that the bureau can handle output in this format and has the appropriate fonts (Mac fonts may not be compatible.)

When you send a job to a service bureau or printer, list the files that you want to be output, and enclose proofs with the disks so that they can see how the finished job should look. For anything more than a short document, break it up into separate files of a few pages each, which makes it easier to recover from any problems. Doing this and getting sample pages printed beforehand should cope with most potential problems, but make sure they have a telephone number to contact you if necessary.

Richard Williams is the author of several books on desktop publishing and other computer applications and works as a consultant.

Correcting proofs

The following notes and table are extracted from BS 5261: Part 2: 1976 (1995) and are reproduced by permission of the British Standards Institution. Copies of the complete Standard are available from the British Standards Institution, 2 Park Street, London W1A 2BS.

The marks to be used for marking up copy for composition and for the correction of printers' proofs shall be as shown in table 1.

The marks in table 1 are classified in three groups as follows.
(a) Group A: general.
(b) Group B: deletion, insertion and substitution.
(c) Group C: positioning and spacing.

Each item in table 1 is given a simple alpha-numeric serial number denoting the classification group to which it belongs and its position within the group.

The marks have been drawn keeping the shapes as simple as possible and using sizes which relate to normal practice. The shapes of the marks should be followed exactly by all who make use of them.

For each marking-up or proof correction instruction a distinct mark is to be made:
(a) in the text: to indicate the exact place to which the instruction refers;
(b) in the margin: to signify or amplify the meaning of the instruction.

It should be noted that some instructions have a combined textual and marginal mark.

Where a number of instructions occur in one line, the marginal marks are to be divided between the left and right margins where possible, the order being from left to right in both margins.

Specification details, comments and instructions may be written on the copy or proof to complement the textual and marginal marks. Such written matter is to be clearly distinguishable from the copy and from any corrections made to the proof. Normally this is done by encircling the matter and/or by the appropriate use of colour (see below).

Proof corrections shall be made in coloured ink thus:
(a) printer's literal errors marked by the printer for correction: green;
(b) printer's literal errors marked by the customer and his agents for correction: red;
(c) alterations and instructions made by the customer and his agents: black or dark blue.

Table 1. Classified list of marks

NOTE. The letters M and P in the notes column indicate marks for marking-up copy and for correcting proofs respectively.

Group A General

Number	Instruction	Textual mark	Marginal mark	Notes
A1	Correction is concluded	None	/	P Make after each correction
A2	Leave unchanged	------ under characters to remain	(√)	M P
A3	Remove extraneous marks	Encircle marks to be removed	✗	P e.g. film or paper edges visible between lines on bromide or diazo proofs
A3.1	Push down risen spacing material	Encircle blemish	⊥	P
A4	Refer to appropriate authority anything of doubtful accuracy	Encircle word(s) affected	(?)	P

Group B Deletion, insertion and substitution

B1	Insert in text the matter indicated in the margin	⋏	New matter followed by ⋏	M P Indentical to B2
B2	Insert additional matter identified by a letter in a diamond	⋏	⋏ Followed by for example ⟨A⟩	M P The relevant section of the copy should be supplied with the corresponding letter marked on it in a diamond e.g. ⟨A⟩
B3	Delete	/ through character(s) or ├────┤ through words to be deleted	♂	M P
B4	Delete and close up	⌢ / through character ⌣ or ├────┤ through characters e.g. chara͡cter chara͡cter	⌒♂	M P

Table 1 *(continued)*

Number	Instruction	Textual mark	Marginal mark	Notes
B5	Substitute character or substitute part of one or more word(s)	/ through character or ├────┤ through word(s)	New character or new word(s)	M P
B6	Wrong fount. Replace by character(s) of correct fount	Encircle character(s) to be changed	⊗	P
B6.1	Change damaged character(s)	Encircle character(s) to be changed	✕	P This mark is identical to A3
B7	Set in or change to italic	───── under character(s) to be set or changed	⊔	M P Where space does not permit textual marks encircle the affected area instead
B8	Set in or change to capital letters	═════ under character(s) to be set or changed	≡	
B9	Set in or change to small capital letters	════ under character(s) to be set or changed	═	
B9.1	Set in or change to capital letters for initial letters and small capital letters for the rest of the words	≡ under initial letters and ══ under rest of the word(s)	≋	
B10	Set in or change to bold type	∿∿∿∿ under character(s) to be set or changed	∿	
B11	Set in or change to bold italic type	∿∿∿∿ under character(s) to be set or changed	⊔∿	
B12	Change capital letters to lower case letters	Encircle character(s) to be changed	╪	P For use when B5 is inappropriate

Table 1 *(continued)*

Number	Instruction	Textual mark	Marginal mark	Notes
B12.1	Change small capital letters to lower case letters	Encircle character(s) to be changed	≠	P For use when B5 is inappropriate
B13	Change italic to upright type	Encircle character(s) to be changed	山	P
B14	Invert type	Encircle character to be inverted	∩	P
B15	Substitute or insert character in 'superior' position	/ through character or ∧ where required	⌐ under character e.g. ²⟓	P
B16	Substitute or insert character in 'inferior' position	/ through character or ∧ where required	L over character e.g. /₂	P
B17	Substitute ligature e.g. ffi for separate letters	├────┤ through characters affected	⌒ e.g. ffi	P
B17.1	Substitute separate letters for ligature	├────┤	Write out separate letters	P
B18	Substitute or insert full stop or decimal point	/ through character or ∧ where required	⊙	M P
B18.1	Substitute or insert colon	/ through character or ∧ where required	⊙	M P
B18.2	Substitute or insert semi-colon	/ through character or ∧ where required	;	M P

Table 1 *(continued)*

Number	Instruction	Textual mark	Marginal mark	Notes
B18.3	Substitute or insert comma	/ through character or ⋏ where required	,	M P
B18.4	Substitute or insert apostrophe	/ through character or ⋏ where required	⸮	M P
B18.5	Substitute or insert single quotation marks	/ through character or ⋏ where required	⸮ and/or ⸮	M P
B18.6	Substitute or insert double quotation marks	/ through character or ⋏ where required	⸮ and/or ⸮	M P
B19	Substitute or insert ellipsis	/ through character or ⋏ where required	•••	M P
B20	Substitute or insert leader dots	/ through character or ⋏ where required	(•••)	M P Give the measure of the leader when necessary
B21	Substitute or insert hyphen	/ through character or ⋏ where required	⊢⊣	M P
B22	Substitute or insert rule	/ through character ⋏ where required	⊢⊣	M P Give the size of the rule in the marginal mark e.g. ⊢1 em⊣ ⊢4 mm⊣

Table 1 *(continued)*

Number	Instruction	Textual mark	Marginal mark	Notes
B23	Substitute or insert oblique	/ through character or ⋋ where required	Ⓘ	M P
Group C Positioning and spacing				
C1	Start new paragraph			M P
C2	Run on (no new paragraph)			M P
C3	Transpose characters or words	between characters or words, numbered when necessary		M P
C4	Transpose a number of characters or words	3 2 1	1 2 3	M P To be used when the sequence cannot be clearly indicated by the use of C3. The vertical strokes are made through the characters or words to be transposed and numbered in the correct sequence
C5	Transpose lines			M P
C6	Transpose a number of lines		—— 3 —— 2 —— 1	P To be used when the sequence cannot be clearly indicated by C5. Rules extend from the margin into the text with each line to be transposed numbered in the correct sequence
C7	Centre	⌐enclosing matter to be centred ⌐	[ ]	M P
C8	Indent			P Give the amount of the indent in the marginal mark

Table 1 *(continued)*

Number	Instruction	Textual mark	Marginal mark	Notes
C9	Cancel indent			P
C10	Set line justified to specified measure	and/or		P Give the exact dimensions when necessary
C11	Set column justified to specified measure			M P Give the exact dimensions when necessary
C12	Move matter specified distance to the right	enclosing matter to be moved to the right		P Give the exact dimensions when necessary
C13	Move matter specified distance to the left	enclosing matter to be moved to the left		P Give the exact dimensions when necessary
C14	Take over character(s), word(s) or line to next line, column or page			P The textual mark surrounds the matter to be taken over and extends into the margin
C15	Take back character(s), word(s), or line to previous line, column or page			P The textual mark surrounds the matter to be taken back and extends into the margin
C16	Raise matter	over matter to be raised under matter to be raised		P Give the exact dimensions when necessary. (Use C28 for insertion of space between lines or paragraphs in text)
C17	Lower matter	over matter to be lowered under matter to be lowered		P Give the exact dimensions when necessary. (Use C29 for reduction of space between lines or paragraphs in text)
C18	Move matter to position indicated	Enclose matter to be moved and indicate new position		P Give the exact dimensions when necessary

Marked galley proof of text

(B9.1)	⇥/
(B13)	⊥/
(C7)	[ ]/
(C9)	⅃/

At the sign of the red plate

The Life and Work of William Caxton, by H W Larken

[An Extract]

Few people, even in the field of printing, have any clear conception of what William Caxton did or, indeed, of what he was. Much of this lack of knowledge is due to the absence of information that can be counted as factual and the consequent tendency to vague generalisation.

Though it is well known that Caxton was born in the county of Kent, there is no information as to the precise place. In his prologue to the *History of Troy*, William Caxton wrote 'for in France I was never and was born and learned my English in Kent in the Weald where I doubt not is spoken as broad and rude English as in any place of England.' During the fifteenth century there were a great number of Flemish cloth weavers in Kent; most of them had come to England at the instigation of Edward III with the object of teaching their craft to the English. So successful was this venture that the English cloth trade flourished and the agents who sold the cloth (the mercers) became very wealthy people. There have been many speculations concerning the origin of the Caxton family and much research has been carried out. It is assumed often that Caxton's family must have been connected with the wool trade in order to have secured his apprenticeship to an influential merchant.

W. Blyth Crotch (*Prologues and Epilogues of William Caxton*) suggests that the origin of the name Caxton (of which there are several variations in spelling) may be traced to Cambridgeshire but notes that many writers have suggested that Caxton was connected with a family at Hadlow or alternatively a family in Canterbury.

Of the Canterbury connection a William Caxton became freeman of the City in 1431 and William Pratt, a mercer who was the printer's friend, was born there. H. R. Plomer suggests that Pratt and Caxton might possibly have been schoolboys together, perhaps at the school St. Alphege. In this parish there lived a John Caxton who used as his mark three cakes over a barrel (or tun) and who is mentioned in an inscription on a monument in the church of St. Alphege.

In 1941, Alan Keen (an authority on manuscripts) secured some documents concerning Caxton, these are now in the British Museum. Discovered in the library of Earl Winterton at Shillinglee Park by Richard Holworthy, the documents cover the period 1420 to 1467. One of Winterton's ancestors purchased the manor of West Wratting from a family named Caxton, the property being situated in the Weald of Kent.

There is also record of a property mentioning Philip Caxton and his wife Dennis who had two sons, Philip (born in 1413) and William.

Particularly interesting in these documents is one recording that Philip Caxton junior sold the manor of Little Wratting to John Christemasse of London in 1436, the deed having been witnessed by two aldermen, one of whom was Robert Large, the printer's employer. Further, in 1439 the other son, William Caxton, conveyed Wratting to John Christemasse, and an indenture of 1457 concerning this property mentions one William Caxton conveyed his rights in the manor Bluntes Hall at Little alias Causton. It is an interesting coincidence to note that the lord of the manor of Little Wratting was the father of Margaret, Duchess of Burgundy.

In 1420, a Thomas Caxton of Tenterden witnessed the will of a fellow townsman; he owned property in Kent and appears to have been a person of some importance.

¹ See 'William Caxton'.

Ⓐ attached to Christchurch Monastery in the parish of

(B12)	≠/
(B18.5)	⌄/
(B18.5)	⌄/
(B6)	Ⓚ/
(B17)	ﬔ/
(C8)	⊐/
(B14)	∩/
(A4)	⦵?/
(B7)	ɯ/
(A3.1)	⊥/
(B18.1)	⊙/
(B16)	⌄/
(C26)	⋎/
(B8)	≡/
(B6)	Ⓚ/
(C27)	
(B18)	⊙/
(C27)	
(B18.3)	'/
(C21)	◠/
(C19)	‖/

(C22)	Υ/
(B10)	⌇/
(B9)	≡/
(B1)	i⋀/
(A2)	⊘/
(B19)	…/
(C23)	Υ/
(C1)	⌐/
(B5)	t/
(B3)	⅁/
(C3)	⊔⊓/
(B7)	⊔⊔/
(C20)	≡/
(B2)	⋀Ⓐ/
(A3)	✗/
(B12.1)	≠/
(C2)	⌐/
(B4)	⅁/
(B22)	1e ⊢/
(C14)	⊢/
(B21)	⊢⊣/
(C6)	2 3 1
(C25)	⇑/
(C28)	(+1pt
(C29)	) −1pt

Revised galley proof of text incorporating corrections

At the Sign of the Red Pale

The Life and Work of William Caxton, *by H W Larken*

An Extract

FEW PEOPLE, even in the field of printing, have any clear conception of what William Caxton did or, indeed, of what he was. Much of this lack of knowledge is due to the absence of information that can be counted as factual and the consequent tendency to vague generalisation.

Though it is well known that Caxton was born in the county of Kent, there is no information as to the precise place. In his prologue to the *History of Troy*, William Caxton wrote '. . . for in France I was never and was born and learned my English in Kent in the Weald where I doubt not is spoken as broad and rude English as in any place of England.'

During the fifteenth century there were a great number of Flemish cloth weavers in Kent; most of them had come to England at the instigation of Edward III with the object of teaching their craft to the English. So successful was this venture that the English cloth trade flourished and the agents who sold the cloth (the mercers) became very wealthy people.

There have been many speculations concerning the origin of the Caxton family and much research has been carried out. It is often assumed that Caxton's family must have been connected with the wool trade in order to have secured his apprenticeship to an influential merchant.

W. Blyth Crotch (*Prologues and Epilogues of William Caxton*) suggests that the origin of the name Caxton (of which there are several variations in spelling) may be traced to Cambridgeshire but notes that many writers have suggested that Caxton was connected with a family at Hadlow or alternatively a family in Canterbury.

Of the Canterbury connection: a William Caxton became freeman of the City in 1431 and William Pratt, a mercer who was the printer's friend, was born there. H. R. Plomer[1] suggests that Pratt and Caxton might possibly have been schoolboys together, perhaps at the school attached to Christchurch Monastery in the parish of St. Alphege. In this parish there lived a John Caxton who used as his mark three cakes over a barrel (or tun) and who is mentioned in an inscription on a monument in the church of St. Alphege.

In 1941, Alan Keen (an authority on manuscripts) secured some documents concerning Caxton; these are now in the British Museum. Discovered in the library of Earl Winterton at Shillinglee Park by Richard Holworthy, the documents cover the period 1420 to 1467. One of Winterton's ancestors purchased the manor of West Wratting from a family named Caxton, the property being situated in the Weald of Kent. There is also record of a property mentioning Philip Caxton and his wife Dennis who had two sons, Philip (born in 1413) and William.

Particularly interesting in these documents is one recording that Philip Caxton junior sold the manor of Little Wratting to John Christemasse of London in 1436— the deed having been witnessed by two aldermen, one of whom was Robert Large, the printer's employer. Further, in 1439, the other son, William Caxton, conveyed his rights in the manor Bluntes Hall at Little Wratting to John Christemasse, and an indenture of 1457 concerning this property mentions one William Caxton alias Causton. It is an interesting coincidence to note that the lord of the manor of Little Wratting was the father of Margaret, Duchess of Burgundy.

In 1420, a Thomas Caxton of Tenterden witnessed the will of a fellow townsman; he owned property in Kent and appears to have been a person of some importance.

[1] See 'William Caxton'.

Table 1 *(continued)*

Number	Instruction	Textual mark	Marginal mark	Notes
C19	Correct vertical alignment	‖	‖	P
C20	Correct horizontal alignment	Single line above and below misaligned matter e.g. mi<u>s</u>aligned		P The marginal mark is placed level with the head and foot of the relevant line
C21	Close up. Delete space between characters or words	linking ⌣ characters	⌣	M P
C22	Insert space between characters	| between characters affected	Y	M P Give the size of the space to be inserted when necessary
C23	Insert space between words	Y between words affected	Y	M P Give the size of the space to be inserted when necessary
C24	Reduce space between characters	| between characters affected	⋀	M P Give the amount by which the space is to be reduced when necessary
C25	Reduce space between words	⋀ between words affected	⋀	M P Give amount by which the space is to be reduced when necessary
C26	Make space appear equal between characters or words	| between characters or words affected	ⱷ	M P
C27	Close up to normal interline spacing	(each side of column linking lines)		M P The textual marks extend into the margin

Table 1 *(continued)*

Number	Instruction	Textual mark	Marginal mark	Notes
C28	Insert space between lines or paragraphs			**M P** The marginal mark extends between the lines of text. Give the size of the space to be inserted when necessary
C29	Reduce space between lines or paragraphs			**M P** The marginal mark extends between the lines of text. Give the amount by which the space is to be reduced when necessary

Editorial, literary and production services

The following specialists offer a wide variety of services to writers (both new and established), to publishers, journalists and others. Services include advice on manuscripts, editing and book production, indexing, translation, research and writing. For an index of the services offered here, see page 565.

'A Feature Factory' Editorial Services

(incorporating Academic Projects)
4 St Andrews Court, 53 Yarmouth Road, Norwich NR7 0EW
tel (01603) 435229
Editor Dr Dennis Chaplin
Produces company magazines, brochures, company histories, press releases/features (including sameday turnaround), advertisement features, ghostwriting, DTP, research briefs for press/broadcasting, backgrounders, writing and research tuition. Extra researchers often needed for projects.

Abbey Writing Services

Portsmouth Cottage, St Mary Bourne, Andover, Hants SP11 6BP
tel/fax (01264) 738556
Director John McIlwain
Comprehensive writing, project management and editorial service. Writing of most non-fiction types: areas of expertise include guidebooks, dictionaries and education. Founded 1989.

Academic File (The Centre for Near East Afro-Asia Research) (NEAR)

Wallorton Gardens, London SW14 8DX
tel 0181-392 1122 *fax* 0181-392 1422
Director Sajid Rizvi
Research, advisory and consultancy services related to politics, economics and societies of the Near and Middle East, Asia and North Africa and related issues in Europe. Risk analysis, editorial assessment, editing and publishing design and production. Founded 1985.

Adkins Archaeology

Longstone Lodge, Aller, Langport, Somerset TA10 0QT
tel (01458) 250075 *fax* (01458) 250858
web site http://ourworld.compuserve.com/homepages/adkins_archaeology
Contact Lesley and Roy Adkins
Work with an archaeological, historical and heritage theme undertaken, including all types of research, critical assessment of MSS, contract writing for publishers, project management, copy-editing, indexing, some illustration, and picture research.

Advice and Criticism Service

5 St Agnes Gate, Wendover, Bucks. HP22 6DP
tel (01296) 623260 *fax* (01296) 623601
Contact Hilary Johnson
Authors' consultant: detailed and constructive assessment of typescripts/practical advice regarding publication. Recent organiser of Romantic Novelists' Association's New Writers' Scheme and publishers' reader. Specialities: crime/thrillers/popular women's fiction.

Alpha Word Power

3 Bluecoat Buildings, Claypath, Durham DH1 1RF
tel 0191-384 7219 *fax* 0191-384 3767
e-mail peter_hughes@compuserve.com
Publishing services: camera-ready copy, word processing, text from and/or to disk, desk editing, proofreading, liaison with printers/binders/graphic design; full secretarial services; business services. Specialise in versatility and speed of turnaround. Founded 1985.

Lucia Alvarez de Toledo MITI, MTG
138B Melrose Avenue, London NW2 4JX
tel 0181-450 5344 *fax* 0181-452 9005

Research, interpreting, translation, subtitles, voice overs, proofreading, editing, copy-writing, into/from English, Spanish, French, Italian. Founded 1979.

Anvil Editorial Associates
Lleifior, Malltraeth, Bodorgan, Anglesey LL62 5AF
tel/fax (01407) 840688
Director Dr H. Bernard-Smith

Comprehensive editorial service, including editing, copy-editing, and proofreading. Planning, preparation, writing and editing of books, house journals, company histories, reports, brochures, promotional literature, pamphlets, and scripts. In-house photography. Full MS service. Founded 1966.

Arioma Editorial Services
Gloucester House, High Street, Borth, Dyfed SY24 5HZ
tel/fax (01970) 871 296
Partners Moira Smith, Patrick Smith

Research, co-writing, ghost-writing, DTP, complete book production service. Specialities: military, naval, aviation history and autobiography.

Arkst Publishing
1 Lindsey House, Lloyd's Place, London SE3 0QF
tel/fax 0181-297 9997
Director James H. Willis FRCP (Edin)

General editing of MSS; also rewriting. Independent appraisal of MSS – fiction and non-fiction. Founded 1995.

Linda Auld Associates
Ashley House, Mill Road, Peasenhall, Saxmundham, Suffolk IP17 2LW
tel/fax (01728) 660550
Proprietor Linda Auld

Project management, managing editing, rewriting, copy-editing, proofreading, indexing, on-screen editing. All subjects. Member of Society of Freelance Editors and Proofreaders. Founded 1981.

Authors' Advisory Service
21 Campden Grove, London W8 4JG
tel 0171-937 5583

All typescripts professionally evaluated in depth and edited by long-established publishers' reader specialising in constructive advice to new writers and with wide experience of current literary requirements. Critic and reader for literary awards. Lecture service on the craft and technique of writing for publication. Founded 1972.

Authors' Aid
46 Cartier Close, Westbrook, Warrington, Cheshire WA5 5TD
tel (01925) 445196 and 838431
Partners Mrs C.A. Sawyer and Miss D.E. Ramage

Provides an honest critical appraisal of MSS and offers advice and guidance on such topics as style, presentation, characterisation, plot and marketability. A personalised service by an established writer with the aim of getting the work published. Other services: word processing, editing, reappraisal. Established 1991.

Authors Appraisal Service
12 Hadleigh Gardens, Boyatt Wood, Eastleigh, Hants SO5 4NP
tel (01703) 368863
Literary consultant J. Evans

Critical appraisal of all types of manuscript, specialising in romantic and historical fiction. Competitive rates. Preliminary letter please. Founded 1988.

Authors' Research Services
32 Oak Village, London NW5 4QN
tel 0171-284 4316
Contact Richard Wright

Offers comprehensive research service to writers, academics and business people worldwide, including fact checking, bibliographical references and document supply. Specialises in English history, social sciences, business. Founded 1966.

Ayrshire Business Services
48 Main Street, Loans, Ayrshire KA10 7EX
tel/fax (01292) 319006
Owner/Manager Janet Spufford

Full manuscript service – word processing or desktop publishing; assists new authors with placement of book and liaises with agent/publisher on behalf of author. Founded 1989.

Richard A. Beck
49 Curzon Avenue, Stanmore, Middlesex HA7 2AL
tel 0181-933 9787

Editing, proofreading, indexing, research, writing and rewriting. Reduced rates for new authors, senior citizens, the unemployed, etc. Founded 1991.

Beswick Writing Services

19 Haig Road, Stretford M32 0DS
tel 0161-865 1259
Contact Francis Beswick

Editing, research, information books. Special interests: religious, ecology, outdoor activities, philosophical and educational. Expertise in correspondence courses and Open Learning materials. Founded 1988.

Black Ace Book Production

PO Box 6557, Forfar DD8 2YS
tel (01307) 465096 *fax* (01307) 465494
Directors Hunter Steele, Boo Wood

Book production and text processing, including text capture (or scanning), editing, proofing to camera-ready/film, printing and binding, jacket artwork and design. Delivery of finished books; can sometimes help with distribution. Founded 1990.

Blair Services

Blair Cottage, Aultgrishan, Melvaig, Gairloch, Wester Ross IV21 2DG
tel/fax (01445) 771228
Director Ian Mertling-Blake MA, DPhil

Editing and revision: fiction and non-fiction (such as prospectus for schools and other educational purposes). Also specialist academic revision for books/articles on archaeology and associated subjects. Founded 1992.

Book Production Consultants

25-27 High Street, Chesterton, Cambridge CB4 1ND
tel (01223) 352790 *fax* (01223) 460710
e-mail apl@bpccam.demon.co.uk
Directors A.P. Littlechild, C.S. Walsh

Complete publishing service: writing, editing, designing, illustrating, translating, indexing, artwork; production management of printing and binding; specialised sales and distribution; advertising sales. For books, journals, manuals, reports, magazines, catalogues, electronic media. Founded 1973.

Book-in-Hand Ltd

20 Shepherds Hill, London N6 5AH
tel/fax 0181-341 7650
Contact Ann Kritzinger (managing), Kim Spanoghe (technical), Amanda Little (secretary)

Production of cost-effective short-run books for small and self-publishers, from typescript (or disk) to bound copies (hardbacks or paperbacks, sewn or unsewn).

Bookwatch Ltd

15-up, East Street, Lewin's Yard, Chesham, Bucks. HP5 1HQ
tel (01494) 792269 *fax* (01494) 784850
Directors Peter Harland, Jennifer Harland

Market research, bestseller lists, syndicated reviews, features. Publishers of *Books in the Media*, weekly for booksellers and librarians. Founded 1982.

David Bradley Science Writer

67 Vicarage Close, Waterbeach, Cambridge CB5 9QG
tel/fax (01223) 440834
e-mail bradley@enterprise.net, bradders1@aol.com
web site http://homepages.enterprise.net/bradley/bradhome.html
Partners David Bradley BSc (Hons) CChem, MRSC and Patricia Bradley BSc (Hons), GIPD, Dip RSA

General and specialist articles and scripts on scientific, technology and medical subjects. Editing and rewriting of articles, newsletters, scripts, brochures and technical MSS. Member of ABSW and recipient of several writing awards. Most word processing and picture formats handled; HTML aware. Established 1989.

Brittan Design Partnership

Clarence House, 35 Clarence Street, Market Harborough, Leics. LE16 7NE
tel (01858) 466950 *fax* (01858) 434632
Partners Derek W. Brittan MCSD, Jean E. Brittan, Nick J. Brittan

Complete editorial design and publishing service; in-house typesetting; high end computer graphics and pre-press; film production. Founded 1978.

Brooke Projects

21 Barnfield, Urmston, Manchester M41 9EW
tel 0161-746 8140 *fax* 0161-746 8132
e-mail urmston@brooke.u-net.com

Research, editing and contract writing. Specialises in business, management, tourism, history, biography and social science.

Mrs D. Buckmaster

51 Chatsworth Road, Torquay, Devon TQ1 3BJ
tel/fax (01803) 294663

General editing of MSS, specialising in traditional themes in religious, metaphysical and esoteric subjects; also success and inspirational books or articles. Founded 1966.

John Button

14 Manor House Way, Brightlingsea, Colchester,
Essex CO7 0QN
tel/fax (01206) 302769

Copy-editing and proofreading, specialising in legal, financial, taxation, business education and corporate identity publications; Legal Reference Library series. Founded 1991.

Calderbridge Associates

3 Lion Chambers, Huddersfield,
West Yorkshire HD1 1ES
tel/fax (01484) 512817
Directors R. Sharp, B. Bedar

MSS criticism and advice; editing; proofreading; word processing; multimedia/internet services. Founded 1995.

Cambridge Language Services Ltd

64 Baldock Street, Ware, Herts. SG12 9DT
tel/fax (01920) 486526
e-mail paul@oakleaf.demon.co.uk
Managing Director Paul Procter

Suppliers to publishers, societies and other organisations of customised database management systems, with advanced retrieval mechanisms, and electronic publishing systems for the preparation of dictionaries, reference books, encyclopedias, catalogues, journals, archives. PC (windows) based. Founded 1982.

Causeway Resources

8 The Causeway, Teddington,
Middlesex TW11 0HE
tel/fax 0181-977 8797
Director Keith Skinner

Genealogical, biographical and historical research, specialising in police history and true crime research. Founded 1989.

Central Office of Information

Hercules Road, London SE1 7DU
tel 0171-928 2345

The Government executive agency which procures and provides publicity and information services to government departments, other executive agencies and public sector bodies.

Vanessa Charles

38 Ham Common, Richmond, Surrey TW10 7JG
tel/fax 0181-940 9225
e-mail 101361,1176@compuserve.com

Design and book production services. Founded 1975.

Karyn Claridge Book Production

244 Bromham Road, Biddenham,
Bedford MK40 4AA
tel (01234) 347909

Complete book production management service offered from MS to bound copies; graphic services available; sourcing service for interactive book projects. Founded 1989.

Combrógos

Mr Meic Stephens, 10 Heol Don, Whitchurch,
Cardiff CF4 2AU
tel (01222) 623359 *fax* (01222) 529202

Specialises in books (including fiction and poetry) about Wales or by Welsh authors, providing a full editorial service and undertaking arts and media research. Founded 1990.

Copywriting One-to-One

Cowieslinn, Eddleston, Peeblesshire EH45 8QZ
tel/fax (01721) 730 350
Director Patrick Quinn

Correspondence course in copywriting with telephone helpline. Founded 1994.

Ingrid Cranfield

16 Myddelton Gardens, London N21 2PA
tel 0181-360 2433

Advisory and editorial services for authors and media, including critical assessment, rewriting, proofreading, copy-editing, writing of marketing copy, indexing, research, interviews, transcripts. Special interests: geography, travel, exploration, adventure (own archives), language, education, youth training, Japanese art. Translations from German and French. Founded 1972.

Clarissa Cridland

4 Rock Terrace, Coleford, Bath, Somerset BA3 5NF
tel (01373) 812705 *fax* (01373) 813517
e-mail cridland@telecall.co.uk

Full service on all aspects of author and publisher contracts, including but not limited to reading, typing and negotiating contracts. Established 1994.

David A. Cross

75 Croslands Park, Barrow-in-Furness,
Cumbria LA13 9LB
tel (01229) 822694

Research and information service; editing texts, specialising in art history, English literature, biography and genealogy; creative writing tutorials; lectures on artists and writers of the Lake District.

Margaret Crush Associates
Moonfleet, Burney Road, West Humble,
Dorking, Surrey RH5 6AU
tel (01306) 884347

Editing, copy-editing, writing, rewriting
and proofreading for publishers, especially illustrated books. Founded 1980.

D & N Publishing
Membury Business Park, Lambourn Woodlands,
Hungerford, Berks. RG17 7TJ
tel (01488) 71210 *fax* (01488) 71220
Partners David and Namrita Price-Goodfellow

Complete project management including
commissioning, editing, picture research,
illustration and design, page layout,
indexing, printing and repro. All stages
managed in-house and produced on
Apple Macs running Quark XPress,
FreeHand and Photoshop. Founded 1991.

Meg and Stephen Davies
31 Egerton Road, Ashton, Preston, Lancs. PR2 1AJ
tel (01772) 725120 *fax* (01772) 723853

Indexing at general and post-graduate
level in the arts and humanities. Can
offer indexes on PC disk. Also proofreading and copy-editing. Registered indexer
with Society of Indexers since 1971.

Editorial/Visual Research
21 Leamington Road Villas, London W11 1HS
tel 0171-727 4920
Contact Angela Murphy

Comprehensive research service including historical, literary, film and picture
research for writers, publishers, film and
TV companies. Services also include
copy-writing, editing, and travel and feature writing. Founded 1973.

Dr Martin Edwards
2 Highbury Hall, 22 Highbury Road,
Weston-super-Mare, North Somerset BS23 2DN
tel/fax (01934) 621261

Specialist editorial and research service
in the medico-scientific field: copy-editing, co-editorial/-authorship, proofreading, abstracting and conference productions. Special interest in the improvement of foreign texts. Founded 1985.

Lewis Esson Publishing
45 Brewster Gardens, London W10 6AQ
tel 0181-969 0951 *fax* 0181-968 1623
e-mail 101465.2252@compuserve.com

Project management of illustrated books
in areas of food, art and interior design;
editing and writing of food books.
Founded 1989.

etr (Edward Twentyman Resources)
4 Little Green, Cheveley, Newmarket CB8 9RG
tel (01638) 731332 *fax* (01638) 731152
e-mail freelance@etr.co.uk
web site www.etr.co.uk
Proprietor Edward Twentyman

Employment agency specialising solely
in freelance people in publishing.
Founded 1992.

First Edition Translations Ltd
6 Wellington Court, Wellington Street,
Cambridge CB1 1HZ
tel (01223) 356733 *fax* (01223) 321488
Directors Judy Boothroyd, Sarah Walsh

Translation, interpreting, voice recording,
editing, proofreading, indexing, DTP;
books, manuals, reports, journals and
promotional material. Founded 1981.

FJN Associates
Little Theobald, Sandy Cross, Heathfield,
East Sussex TN21 8BT
tel (01435) 866653 *fax* (01435) 868998
Partners Frederick J. Nixon, Brenda Mellen
Nixon

Comprehensive DTP and editorial service including magazine and newsletter
design and production; advice to
authors, editing and preparation of manuscripts for submission to publishers/
editors; proofreading. Founded 1990.

James Wilson Flegg
via Paolini 11, 10138 Turin, Italy
tel/fax (011) 4331192

Language consultant; writing, ghosting,
copy-editing, translation, abstracting;
projects and commissions undertaken.
Founded 1970.

Christine Foley Secretarial Services
Glyndedwydd, Login, Whitland,
Carmarthenshire SA34 0TN
tel/fax (01994) 448414
Partners Christine Foley, Michael Foley

Word processing service: preparation of
MSS from handwritten/typed notes and
audio-transcription. Complete secretarial
support. Founded 1991.

Brian J. Ford
Rothay House, 6 Mayfield Road, Eastrea,
Cambs. PE7 2AY
tel/fax (01733) 350888
e-mail bjford@kixcix.co.uk
web site http//www.sciences.demon.co.uk

Scientist and adviser on scientific matters; author, producer/director scientific films and programmes in addition to editor/contributor to many leading books and journals. Has hosted many leading BBC TV and radio programmes, and overseas documentaries.

Freelance Editorial Services
45 Bridge Street, Musselburgh,
Midlothian EH21 6AA
tel 0131-665 7825
Contact Bill Houston BSc, DipLib, MPhil

Editing, proofreading, indexing, abstracting, translations, bibliographies; particularly scientific and medical. Founded 1975.

Freelance Market News
Sevendale House, 7 Dale Street,
Manchester M1 1JB
tel 0161-237 1827 *fax* 0161-228 3533

Market Research Department for freelance writers issues a monthly Market News service the *Freelance Market News*; £29 p.a. A good rate of pay made for news of editorial requirements. UK agents for the Writers' Digest Books, including the American *Writer's Market*. Founded 1967.

Shelagh Furness
Hallgarth Farmhouse, The Hallgarth, Durham,
Co. Durham DH1 3BJ
tel 0191-384 3840

Research and information service, specialising in environmental, scientific and geographical topics, also North East England; word processing service. Founded 1992.

Roy Gaylor
4 Spring Shaw Road, Orpington, Kent BR5 2RH
tel 0181-300 0139

Copy-editing, proofreading, writing and rewriting. Special interests: sport, social history, history and travel. Established 1991.

Geo Group & Associates
4 Christian Fields, London SW16 3JZ
tel/fax 0181-764 6292

Visual aid production services: slide packs, packaging. Photo library. Commission photography (including aerial photography). Research and publishing consultancy. Copy-editing. Advisers to author-publishers.

C.N. Gilmore
52B St Michael's Road,
Bedford MK40 2LT
tel (01234) 346142

Sub-editing, copy-editing, slush-pile reading, reviewing. Will also collaborate. Undertakes work in all scholarly and academic fields as well as fiction and practical writing. Founded 1987.

Graham-Cameron Publishing
The Studio, 23 Holt Road, Sheringham,
Norfolk NR26 8NB
tel (01263) 821333 *fax* (01263) 821334
Partners Helen Graham-Cameron, Mike Graham-Cameron

Complete editorial, including writing, illustration and production services. Founded 1984.

Grahame & Grahame Editorial
18 Chichester Place, Brighton,
East Sussex BN2 1FF
tel (01273) 699533 *fax* (01273) 621262
Directors Tony and Anita Grahame

Copy-editing; quality typesetting; complete book production service. Founded 1989.

Guildford Reading Services
17 Burwood Gardens, Ash Vale, Aldershot,
Hants GU12 5HN
tel (01483) 504325/(01252) 317950
Director B.V. Varney

proofreading, press revision, copy preparation, sub-editing. Founded 1978.

Bernard Hawton
6 Merdon Court, Merdon Avenue,
Chandler's Ford, Hants SO53 1FP
tel (01703) 267400

Proofreading, copy-editing.

Heath Associates
Garden Flat, 15 South Hill Park Gardens,
London NW3 2TD
tel/fax 0171-435 4059
Proprietor Richard Williams

Consultancy on desktop publishing, word processing and graphics programs for IBM PC; design and illustration specialising in academic and technical works; writing and editing for computing and related topics. Founded 1988.

Antony Hemans
Maranatha, 1 Nettles Terrace, Guildford,
Surrey GU1 4PA
tel (01483) 574511

Biographical and historical research, specialising in industrial archaeology – railways, canals and shipping, air, military and naval operations – genealogy and family history. Founded 1981.

Robert Holland-Ford Associates
103 Lydyett Lane, Barnton, Northwich, Cheshire CW8 4JT
tel (01606) 76960
Director Robert Holland-Ford

Impresarios, concert/lecture agents.

Rosemary Horstmann
1 Kinmond Court, Kenilworth Street, Leamington Spa CV32 4QU
tel (01926) 883689

Broadcasting scripts evaluated; general consultancy on editorial and marketing matters; lectures, writing workshops. Send sae for brochure.

E.J. Hunter
6 Dorset Road, London N22 4SL
tel 0181-889 0370

Editing, copy-editing, proofreading; appraisal of MSS. Special interests: novels, short stories, drama, children's stories; primary education, alternative medicine, New Age.

Hurst Village Publishing
Henry and Elizabeth Farrar, High Chimneys, Davis Street, Hurst, Reading RG10 0TH
tel (01734) 345211 *fax* (01734) 342073

Offers design, photography, typesetting, printing and binding services, using the latest desktop publishing programs, photographic equipment and high resolution colour and laser printers. Founded 1989.

Society of Indexers
Mermaid House, 1 Mermaid Court, London SE1 1HR
tel 0171-403 4947

See pages 567 and 458 for further details.

Indexing Specialists
202 Church Road, Hove, East Sussex BN3 2DJ
tel (01273) 738299 *fax* (01273) 323309
e-mail indspec@pavilion.co.uk
Director Richard Raper BSc, DTA

Indexes for all types of books, journals and reference publications on professional, scientific and general subjects; copy-editing, proofreading services; consultancy on indexing and training projects. Founded 1965.

The Information Bureau
(formerly Daily Telegraph Information Bureau)
51 The Business Centre, 103 Lavender Hill, London SW11 5QL
tel 0171-924 4414 *fax* 0171-924 4456
Contact Jane Hall

Offers an on-demand research service on a variety of subjects including current affairs, business, marketing, history, the arts, media and politics. Resources include range of cuttings amassed by the bureau since 1948.

Ken Jackson
30 The Boundary, Langton Green, Tunbridge Wells, Kent TN3 0YB
tel (01892) 545198

Copy-editing, proofreading, indexing, particularly of technical, historical or religious MSS. Founded 1985.

JG Editorial
54 Mount Street, Lincoln LN1 3JG
tel (01522) 549180 *fax* (01522) 575883
Directors Janet Goss, Jenni Goss, John Goss

Independent critique service for fiction, general non-fiction (no poetry), academic/business/professional books; rewriting/ghosting; word processing/presentation/keying (MSS/audio); project management; editorial reports; copy and disk editing (PC/Mac); proofreading. Design/indexing/PR by arrangement. Founded 1988.

Library Research Agency
Burberry, Devon Road, Salcombe, Devon TQ8 8HJ
tel (01548 84) 2769
Directors D.J. Langford MA, B. Langford

Research and information service for writers, journalists, artists, businessmen from libraries, archives, museums, record offices and newspapers in UK, USA and Europe. Sources may be in English, French, German, Russian, Serbo-Croat, Bulgarian, and translations made if required. Founded 1974.

Miles Litvinoff
104 Doyle Gardens, London NW10 3SR
tel/fax 0181-965 3427

Writer and editor on environment, human rights and development. Writing, editing, commissioning, co-authorship, project management, editorial advice; especially environment, Third World, human rights, and development, including books for young people. Founded 1984.

Dr Kenneth Lysons
Lathom, Scotchbarn Lane, Whiston, Nr Prescot,
Merseyside L35 7JB
tel 0151-426 5513
Contact Dr Kenneth Lysons MA, MEd, DPA, DMS, FCIS,
FInstPS, FBIM

Company and institutional histories,
support material for organisational management and supervisory training, house
journals, research and reports service.
Full secretarial support. Founded 1986.

Duncan McAra
28 Beresford Gardens, Edinburgh EH5 3ES
tel/fax 0131-552 1558

Consultancy on all aspects of general trade
publishing; editing; proof correction. Main
subjects include art, architecture, archaeology, biography, film, military and travel.
See also Literary agents. Founded 1988.

McText
Denmill, Tough, By Alford,
Aberdeenshire AB33 8EP
tel/fax (019755) 62582
e-mail mctext@highland-pony.demon.co.uk
web site http://www.highland-pony.demon.co.uk
Partners K. and Duncan McArdle

Editing, copy-editing, proofreading, web
site authoring. Specialist interests:
archaeology, equestrian. Founded 1986.

Manuscript Appraisals
Quill Cottage, Penffordd, Narberth,
Pembs SA66 7HU
tel (01437) 563822
Proprietor Raymond J. Price
Consultants N.L. Price MBIM, Mary Hunt

Independent appraisal of authors' MSS
(fiction and non-fiction, but no poetry)
with full editorial guidance and advice.
In-house editing, copy-editing, rewriting
and proofreading if required. Interested in
the work of new writers. Founded 1984.

Marlinoak
22 Eve's Croft, Birmingham B32 3QL
tel/fax 0121-475 6139
Proprietor Hazel J. Billing JP, BA, DipEd

Preparation of scripts, plays, books, MSS
service, ghostwriting, proof reading,
research; also audio-transcription, word
processing and full secretarial facilities.
Founded 1984.

M.C. Martinez
60 Oakwood Avenue, London N14 6QL
tel 0181-886 5829
Partners Mary Martinez, Françoise Budd

Advice and evaluation of MSS; critical
assessment of MSS specialising in fiction
and children's books; full desktop publishing service; translation in French and
Spanish. Possible change of address;
please telephone first. Founded 1988.

James Moore Associates
51 Firs Chase, West Mersea, Essex CO5 8NN
tel/fax (01206) 382073
Partners James Moore BCom, Inge Moore

Advisory/consultancy services, editing of
MSS, proofreading, translation from/into
German, from French, Dutch, Spanish.
Special subjects: educational (especially
language courses), music, travel (espe-
cially France), sailing, ships and the sea.
Founded 1975.

Susan Moore Editorial Services
65 Albion Road, London N16 9PP
tel/fax 0171-923 2480

Troubleshooting service for publishers,
packagers and agents: co-authorship with
specialists, ghostwriting, rewiting, translation fine tuning, re-drafting. Founded
1994.

Morley Adams
20 Spectrum House, 32-34 Gordon House Road,
London NW5 1LP
tel 0171-284 1433 *fax* 0171-284 4494
Editor Mike Hutchinson

Specialists in the production of crosswords and other puzzles, quizzes, etc.
Founded 1917.

MS-S
Julia MacRae, 13 Pattison Road, London NW2 2HL
tel/fax 0171-435 7882 and
Christopher Sinclair-Stevenson, 3 South Terrace,
London SW7 2TB
tel/fax 0171-581 2550

Full editorial/advisory service. Fees
negotiable. Founded 1996.

Murder Files
Marienau, Brimley Road, Bovey Tracey,
Devon TQ13 9DH
tel (01626) 833487 *fax* (01626) 835797
Director Paul Williams

Crime writer and researcher specialising
in UK murders. Holds information on
thousands of well-known and less well-
known murders dating from 1400 to the
present day. Copies of press cuttings on
murder cases available from 1920 to date.
Research also undertaken for general

enquirers, writers, TV, radio, video, etc.
Founded 1994.

Elizabeth Murray

3 Gower Mews Mansions, Gower Mews,
London WC1E 6HR
tel/fax 0171-636 3761

Literary, biographical, historical, crime,
military, cinema, genealogy research for
authors, journalists, radio and TV from
UK, European and USA sources.
Founded 1975.

My Word!

138 Railway Terrace, Rugby, Warks. CV21 3HN
tel (01788) 571294 *fax* (01788) 550957
e-mail roddie@compuserve.com
Partners Roddie Grant, Janet Grant

Complete DTP service; word processing
service either to hard copy or disk; editing, copy-editing and proofreading. Work
done includes books, magazines, theses
and CVs. Founded 1994.

Paul Nash

Munday House, Aberdalgie, Perth PH2 0QB
tel/fax (01738) 621584

Indexer specialising in sciences, technology, environmental science. Winner of
Library Association Wheatley Medal (1992)
for outstanding index. Founded 1979.

Paul H. Niekirk

40 Rectory Avenue, High Wycombe,
Bucks. HP13 6HW
tel (01494) 527200

Text editing for works of reference and
professional and management publications, particularly texts on law; freelance
writing. Founded 1976.

Northern Writers Advisory Services

77 Marford Crescent, Sale, Cheshire M33 4DN
tel 0161-969 1573
Proprietor Jill Groves

Offers word processing, copy-editing,
proofreading and typesetting to small
publishers, societies and authors.
Founded 1986.

Northgate Training

Scarborough House, 29 James Street West,
Bath BA1 2BT
tel (01225) 339733 *fax* (01225) 429151
Directors M.R. Lynch, J.M. Bayley

Writing and design of management
games and training exercises. Specialists
in distance and open learning training
packages. Founded 1978.

Oakleaf Systems Ltd

64 Baldock Street, Ware,
Herts. SG12 9DT
tel/fax (01920) 486526
e-mail sue@oakleaf.demon.co.uk
Managing director Paul Procter BA

Suppliers to publishers, societies and
other organisations of customised database management systems, with
advanced retrieval mechanisms, and
electronic publishing systems for the
preparation of dictionaries, reference
books, encyclopedias, catalogues, journals, archives. PC (Windows) based.

Oriental Languages Bureau

Lakshmi Building, Sir P. Mehta Road, Fort,
Bombay 400001, India
tel 2661258/2665640 *fax* 2664598
Proprietor Rajan K. Shah

Undertakes translations and printing in
all Indian languages and a few foreign
languages.

Ormrod Research Services

Weeping Birch, Burwash,
East Sussex TN19 7HG
tel (01435) 882541
and at 4 Croftleigh Gardens, Solihull B91 1TG
tel 0121-711 7200

Comprehensive research service; literary,
historical, academic, biographical, commercial. Critical reading with report,
editing, indexing, proofreading, ghosting.
Founded 1982.

Oxprint Design

Aristotle House, Aristotle Lane,
Oxford OX2 6TR
tel (01865) 512331 *fax* (01865) 512408
Directors Per Saugman, John Webb (managing),
Peter Lawrence BA (Hons), Andrew King (company
secretary)

Design, typesetting, editorial, illustrating
scientific, educational and general books.
Specialists in project management.
Macintosh desktop and bureau facilities,
computer aided design and illustration.
Founded 1974.

Pageant Publishing

1 Weir Gardens, Bridge Street, Pershore,
Worcs. WR10 1AJ
tel (01386) 561125 *fax* (01386) 561119
Director Gillian Page

Consultancy on all aspects of academic
publishing: publication of academic journals. Founded 1978.

Pages Editorial & Publishing Services

Ballencrieff Cottage, Ballencrieff Toll, Bathgate, West Lothian EH48 4LD
tel/fax (01506) 632728
Director Susan Coon

Editorial and production service of magazines/newspapers for companies or for commercial distribution; promotional literature; publishing service for authors wishing to self-publish. Founded 1995.

Geoffrey D. Palmer

47 Burton Fields Road, Stamford Bridge, York YO4 1JJ
tel/fax (01759) 372874
e-mail gdp@cix.compulink.co.uk

Editorial and production services, including STM and general copy-editing, artwork editing, proofreading and indexing. Prepress project management. Founded 1987.

Roger Palmer Ltd

18 Maddox Street, London W1R 9PL
tel 0171-499 8875 *fax* 0171-499 9580
Director Roger Palmer, *Senior Consultant* Stephen Aucutt

Drafts, advises on and negotiates all media contracts for publishers, agents, packagers, authors and others; operates outsourced contracts department functions; undertakes contractual audits and devises contracts systems; provides advice on copyright and related issues; provides training and seminars. Special terms for members of the Society of Authors. Founded 1993.

Penman Literary Service

Mark Sorrell, 185 Daws Heath Road, Benfleet, Essex SS7 2TF
tel (01702) 557431

Advisory, editorial and typing service for authors. Rewriting, re-drafting, ghostwriting, proofreading; critical assessment of MSS.

Phoenix 2

Lantern House, Lodge Drove, Woodfalls, Salisbury, Wilts SP5 2NH
tel (01725) 512200 *fax* (01725) 511819
Partners Bryan Walker, Amanda Walker

Writing, editing, sub-editing, typesetting and design of magazines, newsletters, journals, brochures and promotional literature. Specialist areas are business, tourism, social affairs and education. Founded 1994.

Christopher Pick

41 Chestnut Road, London SE27 9EZ
tel 0181-761 2585 *fax* 0181-761 6388

Publications consultancy advice, project management, writing and editing for companies and private-sector, public-sector and voluntary-sector organisations: e.g. brochures and booklets, training manuals, strategy documents, research reports, company histories. Author and editor of non-fiction books for all popular markets. Special interests: modern social and political history, travel (especially UK), heritage and current affairs.

Picture Research Agency

Jasmine Cottage, Spring Grove Road, Richmond, Surrey TW10 6EH
tel 0181-940 5986
Contact Pat Hodgson

Illustrations found for books, films and TV. Written research also undertaken particularly on historical subjects, including photographic and film history. Small picture library.

Picture Research Service – see Rich Research

Reginald Piggott

Decoy Lodge, Decoy Road, Potter Heigham, Norfolk NR29 5LX
tel (01692) 670384

Cartographer to the University Presses and academic publishers in Britain and overseas. Maps and diagrams for academic and educational books. Founded 1962.

PJ Typecraft

21 Kingsbury Road, St John's, Worcester WR2 4JH
tel (01905) 426393
Partners P.M. Jones, J.L. Jones

Proofreading and copy-editing, all subjects but specialising in science and mathematics; complete word processing and typesetting service, including design and page layout. Founded 1990.

Keith Povey Editorial Services

Stoneleigh House, South Brentor, Tavistock, Devon PL19 0NW
tel (01822) 810190 *fax* (01822) 810191

Copy-editing, indexing, proofreading, publisher/author liaison. Partnership with:

T & A Typesetting Services

Suite 2, Tramway Offices, Mellor Street, Rochdale, Lancs. OL12 6AA
tel (01706) 861662 *fax* (01706) 861673

Specialist book-typesetting to CRC and negs, graphic design. Founded 1980.

Victoria Ramsay

Abbots Rest, Chilbolton, Stockbridge, Hants SO20 6BE
tel (01264) 860251 *fax* (01264) 860026

Freelance editing, copy-editing and proofreading; non-fiction research and writing of promotional literature and pamphlets. Any non-scientific subject undertaken. Special interests: education, cookery, travel, Africa and Caribbean and works in translation. Established 1981.

Reading and Righting (Robert Lambolle Services)

618B Finchley Road, London NW11 7RR
tel/fax 0181-455 4564

MSS/script analysis and evaluation service: fiction, non-fiction, stage plays and screenplays; editorial services; one-to-one tutorials, creative writing courses, lectures and research. Send sae for leaflet. Founded 1987.

S. Ribeiro Literary Services

42 West Heath Court, North End Road, London NW11 7RG
tel 0181-458 9082
Contact S. Ribeiro BA

Experienced editor, writer and writing tutor. MSS reading and criticism, including detailed analysis and suggestions. Writing, rewriting, ghost writing. Editing: MS copy or author's disk (all systems). New writers welcome. Guidance in submission to publishers and in self-publishing. Creative writing tuition. Experience: fiction, autobiography, travel, poetry, fine-tuning style and usage. Founded 1986.

Rich Research

One Bradby, 77 Carlton Hill, London NW8 9XE
tel/fax 0171-624 7755
Contact Diane Rich

Picture research service. Visuals found for all sectors of the media and publishing. Artwork and photography commissioned. Rights and permissions negotiated. Founded 1978.

Anton Rippon Press Services

20 Chain Lane, Mickleover, Derby DE3 5AJ
tel (01332) 512379/384235 *fax* (01332) 292755

Writer and researcher on historical, sociological and sporting topics. Features,

programmes, brochures produced; ghost writing. Radio and film documentary scripts. Complete book production service available.

Vernon Robinson Editorial Services

22 Granhams Close, Great Shelford, Cambridge CB2 5LG
tel (01223) 840391

Copy-editing and proofreading of all educational books, specialising in science, maths, engineering, economics, computer science, biology, etc. Also English correction of technical MSS translated into English for European publishers. Founded 1973.

Sandhurst Editorial Consultants

36 Albion Road, Sandhurst, Berks. GU47 9BP
tel (01252) 877645 *fax* (01252) 890508
e-mail mail@sand-con.demon.co.uk
web site http://www.sand-con.demon.co.uk
Partners Lionel Browne, Janet Browne

Specialists in technical, professional and reference work. Project management, editorial development, writing, ghosting, text processing, and general editorial consultancy. Founded 1991.

Sandton Literary Agency

PO Box 785799, Sandton 2146, South Africa
tel (011) 442-8624
Directors J. Victoria Canning, M. Sutherland

Evaluating, editing and/or indexing book MSS. Preparing reports, company histories, house journals, etc. Ghost writing and ghost painting. Critical but constructive advice to writers. Lecture agents. Please write or phone first. Founded 1982.

Sarratt Information Services

68 St Andrews Road, Henley-on-Thames, Oxon RG9 1JE
tel 0181-422 4384
Directors D.M. Brandl NIInfSci, G.H. Kay BSc, CEng, MIChemE, MBCS

Research bibliographies compiled, references checked, indexes compiled. Specialists in bioengineering, bio materials and disability information research. Founded 1986.

Science Unit

Rothay House, 6 Mayfield Road, Eastrea, Cambs. PE7 2AY
tel/fax (01733) 350888
e-mail bjford@kixcix.co.uk
web site http//www.sciences.demon.co.uk

Independent scientific consultancy specialising in microscopical matters and new directions in science. Advises on programmes and publications in general scientific field. Activities are worldwide, with publications in many overseas and foreign-language editions.

SciText
18 Barton Close, Landrake, Saltash, Cornwall PL12 5BA
tel/fax (01752) 851451

Dr Brian Gee. proofreading and editing in science, engineering and the history of science and technology; IBM compatible PC. Founded 1988.

Scriptmate
20 Shepherd's Hill, London N6 5AH
tel/fax 0181-341 7650
Contact Ann Kritzinger

An editing service in conjunction with **Book-in-Hand Ltd** for selected work in fiction and non-fiction. Founded 1985.

Mrs Ellen Seager
3 Hereford Court, Hereford Road, Harrogate, North Yorkshire HG1 2PX
tel (01423) 509770

Critical assessment of fiction and non-fiction work with helpful direction, tuition and advice; creative writing tutor; ghost writing; publishing and market information.

SeaStar Editorial Services
10 Trinity Road, Rothwell, Northants NN14 6HY
tel (01536) 710129
Proprietor Terry Scott

MSS revision and rewriting; compilation, layout, keying-in for floppy disk, disk conversion; photography; desktop publishing services; printer liaison.
Proprietor has held senior editorial posts, and has about 2 million words in print.

Serpentine Editorial
50 Quaker's Hall Lane, Sevenoaks, Kent TN13 3TU
tel/fax (01732) 457360
Partners Molly Perham, Julian Rowe

Publishing service for children's books: editing, writing and rewiting, planning and management of complete projects to CRC; DTP on PC or Apple Mac. All subjects, but science a speciality. Founded 1991.

SFEP (Society of Freelance Editors and Proofreaders) – see page 455

Joan Shannon – Freelance Services
41A Newal Road, Ballymoney, Co. Antrim, Northern Ireland BT53 6HB
tel (012656) 62953 *fax* (012656) 65019

Writing, editing, copy-editing, proofreading, desktop design and book production. Photography; postcard publisher. Founded 1991.

I.R. Sinclair
Saltire, Livermere Road, Gt Barton, Bury St Edmunds, Suffolk IP31 2RZ
tel (01284) 788312
e-mail iansinclair@mail.on-line.co.uk

Technical writing (electronics and computing). Typesetting to CRC, particularly mathematical setting. Founded 1984.

Small Print
The Old School House, 74 High Street, Swavesey, Cambridge CB4 5QU
tel (01954) 231713 *fax* (01954) 232777
e-mail info @smallprt.demon.co.uk
Proprietor Naomi Laredo

Editorial, project management, and audio production services, specialising in ELT and foreign language courses for secondary schools and home study; also phrase books, travel guides, general humanities. Translation from/to and editing in many European and Asian languages. Photography and picture research. Founded 1986.

Roger Smithells Ltd, Editorial Services
Garth Cottage, 26 High Street, Buriton, Petersfield, Hants GU31 5RX
tel (01730) 262369 *fax* (01730) 260722

Journalistic specialists in everything relating to travel and holidays; newspaper and magazine articles; TV and radio scripts; compilers of travel books.

Robert and Jane Songhurst
3 Yew Tree Cottages, Grange Lane, Sandling, Nr Maidstone, Kent ME14 3BY
tel (01622) 757635

Literary consultants, authors' works advised upon (fees by agreement), literary and historical research, feature writing, reviewing, editing, proofreading. Founded 1976.

Special Edition Pre-press Services

Partners Romilly Hambling, 17 Almorah Road,
London N1 3ER
tel/fax 0171-226 5339 and
Corinne Orde, 2 Caledonian Wharf,
London E14 3EW
tel/fax 0171-987 9600

Integrated Mac-based editing and page
make-up for publishers of general and
STM titles. Linguistics and music a speciality. Design and project management
undertaken. Established 1993.

Mrs Gene M. Spencer

63 Castle Street, Melbourne, Derbyshire DE73 1DY
tel (01332) 862133

Editing, copy-editing and proofreading;
feature writing; theatrical profiles; book
reviews; freelance writing. Founded 1970.

SPREd (Society of Picture Researchers and Editors) – now The Picture Research Association – see page 435

Stationers' Hall Registry Ltd

Stationers' Hall, Ave Maria Lane,
London EC4M 7DD
tel 0171-248 2934 *fax* 0171-489 1975

The Registry exists for those requiring
proof of existence of their material for
ownership of copyright purposes.
Written works or those on tape, record,
video or computer disk can be registered.
Established 16th century.

Strand Editorial Services

16 Mitchley View, South Croydon,
Surrey CR2 9HQ
tel/fax 0181-657 1247
Joint Principals Derek and Irene Bradley

Provides a comprehensive service to
publishers, editorial departments, and
public relations and advertising agencies.
Proofreading a speciality. Founded 1974.

Streetwise Town Plans Ltd

3 Rayleigh Road, Basingstoke, Hants RG21 7TJ
tel (01256) 328186
Contacts P.J. Corcoran, Rosemary Corcoran

Top quality computer-generated maps of
almost every town in Europe, plus major
towns and cities throughout the world.
All maps personalised to order.

Hans Tasiemka Archives

80 Temple Fortune Lane, London NW11 7TU
tel 0181-455 2485 *fax* 0181-455 0231
Proprietor Mrs Edda Tasiemka

Comprehensive newspaper cuttings
library from 1850s to the present day on
all subjects for writers, publishers, picture researchers, film and TV companies.
Founded 1950.

Lyn M. Taylor (UK)

(Eve-Line Proofs)
1 Eglinton Crescent, Edinburgh EH12 5DH
tel 0131-225 6152 *fax* 0131-467 6260
e-mail 106253.3476@compuserve.com

National comprehensive editorial service
for publishers and printers: copy-editing
and proofreading in all subjects.
Specialises in complex scientific and
medical. Hard copy or disk.

Teamwork

Unit 5, Spurlings Yard, Spurlings Road,
Fareham PO17 6AB
tel (01329) 827672, (0421) 417499
fax (01329) 829136
Proprietors Mrs D. Emmerson, N. Emmerson

Typesetting, paste-up, camera-ready artwork, design and preparation of books to
print stage, illustration, proofreading,
indexing, general editing and research
services. Founded 1973.

Tecmedia Ltd

Bruce House, 258 Bromham Road, Biddenham,
Beds. MK40 4AA
tel (01234) 325223 *fax* (01234) 353524
Managing Director J.D. Baxter

Specialists in the design, development
and production of training and information packages, newsletters and promotional material. Founded 1972.

Teral Research Services

111 The Avenue, Bournemouth, Dorset BH9 2UX
tel (01202) 519220
Contact Alan C. Wood
45 Forest View Road, Bournemouth,
Dorset BH9 3BH
tel/fax (01202) 516834
Contact Terry C. Treadwell

Research and consultancy on military
aviation, army, navy, defence, space,
weapons (new and antique), police, intelligence, medals, uniforms and armour.
Founded 1980.

3 & 5 Promotion

Crag House, Witherslack, Grange-over-Sands,
Cumbria LA11 6RW
tel (015395) 52286 *fax* (015395) 52013
e-mail musicbks @rdooley.demon.co.uk
Proprietor Rosemary Dooley

Collaborative publishers' exhibitions: music books. Advertising: music and dance. Founded 1985.

Felicity Trotman
Downside, Chicklade, Salisbury, Wilts. SP3 5SU
tel/fax (01747) 820503

Editing, copy-editing, proofreading, writing, rewriting, assessment of MSS. Specialises in children's books, fiction and non-fiction, all ages. Established 1982.

John Vickers
27 Shorrolds Road, London SW6 7TR
tel 0171-385 5774

Archives of British Theatre photographs by John Vickers, from 1938-1974.

Valerie Vogel Picture Research
141 Chestnut Street, Montclair, NJ 07042, USA
tel 201-746-8560 *fax* 201-746-8471
e-mail vvpics@adsight.com
web site http://adsight.com/vvpics

Freelance picture researcher/photo editor. Diverse experience in wide range of subjects for books, magazines, advertising, corporate and film. Uses traditional and online sources. Established 1980.

Gordon R. Wainwright
22 Hawes Court, Sunderland SR6 8NU
tel/fax 0191-548 9342

Criticism, advice and revision for publishers. Articles on education and training matters supplied to newspapers, journals and magazines. Training in report writing, rapid reading, effective meetings, etc. Lecture service. Consultancy service in all aspects of communication. Travel writing assignments undertaken.

Caroline White
78 Howard Road, London E17 4SQ
tel/fax 0181-521 5791

Research and writing of features for newspapers, magazines and radio, specialising in health and social issues. Corporate literature and reports. Press and public relations. Written and spoken Italian, Spanish and French. Project management of illustrated books. Founded 1985.

David L. Williams
7 Buckbury Heights, Newport,
Isle of Wight PO30 2LX
tel (01983) 528729 *fax* (01983) 822116

Picture and text research. Specialises in transport, particularly maritime and aviation; military and naval, particularly the World Wars. Also indexing and proofreading. Established 1982.

David Winpenny
17 Newlands Drive, York YO2 5PQ
tel/fax (01904) 784616
e-mail 101456.1270@compuserve.com

Writer and editor, including research and writing of features, news stories, brochures, speeches, advertising copy. Special interest in architectural history, the arts, music, landscape, heritage, business and the North. Founded 1991.

Rita Winter Editorial Services
'Kilrubie', Eddleston, Peeblesshire, EH45 8QP
tel/fax (01721) 730353
e-mail rita@ednet.co.uk

On-screen editing, copy-editing and proofreading (English and Dutch). Academic and general material, books, dictionaries, company literature. Special interests: art, art history, exhibition catalogues.

The Word Service
Bob Gallagher, 143 Sirdar Road, London N22 6QS
tel 0181-888 6962

Radio drama script analysis, evaluation and polishing; copy-editing and proofreading; research, specialising in Irish history, literary lives and the history of psychiatry. Founded 1994.

Wordwise
37 Elmthorpe Road, Wolvercote, Oxford OX2 8PA
tel (01865) 510098 *fax* (01865) 310556
e-mail wordwise@mendes.demon.co.uk
Director Valerie Mendes

Provides a range of publishing services, including creative writing (particularly for children); editing; educational, arts and humanities and English Language Teaching publishing; report analysis and full project management. Founded 1990.

WordWise Editorial Services
66 Russell Road, Lee-on-the-Solent,
Hants PO13 9HP
tel (01705) 359960 *fax* (01705) 552950
e-mail wordwise@cix.compulink.co.uk
Contact Martyn Yeo

Copy-editing, rewriting, proofreading, DTP, indexing, onscreen editing, project management, database publishing. Copy typing and typesetting services. Member of Corel Ventura Users and the SFEP. Established 1984.

Richard M. Wright

32 Oak Village, London NW5 4QN
tel 0171-284 4316

Indexing, copy-editing, specialising in politics, history, business, social sciences. Founded 1977.

Write Line Critical Service

130 Morton Way, London N14 7AL
tel 0181-886 1329

Criticism and assessment of poetry and serious fiction (including short stories). Suggestions for revision/development of work. Special interest: poetry. Sae essential. Founded 1988.

Write on ...

62 Kiln Lane, Oxford OX3 8EY
tel (01865) 761169
Contact Yvonne Newman

Writing seminars and holiday workshops. Freelance Open Learning writing. Founded 1989.

Writerlink

Bolsover House, 5 Clipstone Street,
London W1P 7EB
tel 0171-323 4323 *fax* 0171-323 0286
Director Charles Dawes, *Chief Reader* Paul Usiskin

Expert individual reports made and issued to authors by a team of readers widely experienced in publishing. Founded 1984.

The Writers Advice Centre for Children's Books

Palace Wharf, Rainville Road, London W6 9HN
tel/fax 0181-874 7347
Directors Louise Jordan, Nancy Smith, Jane Baker

Editorial and marketing advice to children's writers; training; reading and consultancy service for children's book publishers/agents. Founded 1994.

The Writers' Exchange

14 Yewdale, Clifton Green, Swinton,
Manchester M27 8GN
tel 0161-281 0544
Secretary Mike Wright

Copywriting, ghostwriting and editorial services, including appraisal service for amateur writers preparing to submit material to literary agents/publishers. Offers 'constructive, objective evaluation service, particularly for those who cannot get past the standard rejection slip barrier, or who have had work rejected by publishers and need an impartial view of why it did not sell'; fee £5 per 1000 words. Novels, short stories, film, TV, radio and stage plays. Send sae for details. Founded 1977.

Hans Zell, Publishing Consultant

11 Richmond Road, PO Box 56, Oxford OX1 2SJ
tel (01865) 511428 *fax* (01865) 311534

Consultancies, project evaluations, market assessments, feasibility studies, research and surveys, funding proposals, freelance editorial work, commissioning, journals management, exhibition services. Specialises in services to publishers and the book community in Third World countries and provides specific expertise in these areas. Founded 1987.

Editorial, literary and production services by specialisation

Addresses for editorial, literary and production services start on page 550.

Complete editorial, literary and book production services

'A Feature Factory' Editorial
   Services
Academic File
Linda Auld Associates
Book Production Consultants
Brittan Design Partnership
Central Office of Information
Karyn Claridge Book
   Production
D & N Publishing
Graham-Cameron Publishing
Grahame & Grahame
Northern Writers Advisory
   Services
Oxprint Design
Christopher Pick
Keith Povey Editorial Services
Anton Rippon Press Services
Small Print
Teamwork
Rita Winter Editorial Services
Wordwise

Advisory and consultancy services, critical assessments, reports

Academic File
Adkins Archaeology
Advice and Criticism Service
Arkst Publishing
Authors' Aid
Authors Appraisal Service
Authors' Advisory Service
Blair Services
Bookwatch Ltd
Calderbridge Associates
Ingrid Cranfield
Clarissa Cridland
Lewis Esson Publishing
FJN Associates

James Wilson Flegg
Geo Group & Associates
C.N. Gilmore
Heath Associates
Rosemary Horstmann
E.J. Hunter
Indexing Specialists
JG Editorial
Miles Litvinoff
Duncan McAra
Manuscript Appraisals
M.C. Martinez
James Moore Associates
Susan Moore Editorial Services
MS-S
Pageant Publishing
Penman Literary Service
Christopher Pick
Reading and Righting
S. Ribeiro Literary Services
Sandhurst Editorial Consultants
Sandton Literary Agency
Science Unit
Scriptmate
Mrs Ellen Seager
Robert and Jane Songhurst
Teral Research Services
Felicity Trotman
Gordon R. Wainwright
Caroline White
Joan Wilkins Associates
The Word Service
Wordwise
Write Line Critical Service
Writerlink
The Writers Advice Centre for
   Children's Books
The Writers' Exchange
Hans Zell, Publishing
   Consultant

Editing, copy-editing, proofreading

Abbey Writing Services
Alpha Word Power
Lucia Alvarez de Toledo
Anvil Editorial Associates
Arkst Publishing
Linda Auld Associates
Authors' Advisory Service
Authors' Aid
Richard A. Beck
Beswick Writing Services
Black Ace Book Production
Blair Services
David Bradley Science Writer
Brooke Publications Ltd
Mrs D. Buckmaster
John Button
Calderbridge Associates
Combrógos
Ingrid Cranfield
David A. Cross
Margaret Crush Associates
Meg and Stephen Davies
Editorial/Visual Research
Dr Martin Edwards
Lewis Esson Publishing
First Edition Translations Ltd
FJN Associates
James Wilson Flegg
Freelance Editorial Services
Roy Gaylor
C.N. Gilmore
Guildford Reading Services
Bernard Hawton
Heath Associates
E.J. Hunter
Indexing Specialists
Ken Jackson
JG Editorial
Miles Litvinoff
Duncan McAra
McText
Manuscript Appraisals
Marlinoak
James Moore Associates
My Word!

Paul H. Niekirk
Geoffrey D. Palmer
Penman Literary Service
Phoenix 2
Christopher Pick
PJ Typecraft
Victoria Ramsay
Reading and Righting
S. Ribeiro Literary Services
Vernon Robinson Editorial
  Services
Sandhurst Editorial Consultants
Sandton Literary Agency
SciText
SeaStar Editorial Services
Serpentine Editorial
Joan Shannon Freelance
  Services
Small Print
Roger Smithells Ltd, Editorial
  Services
Robert and Jane Songhurst
Mrs Gene M. Spencer
Strand Editorial Services
Lyn M. Taylor (UK)
Felicity Trotman
Gordon R. Wainwright
Caroline White
David L. Williams
David Winpenny
Rita Winter Editorial Services
The Word Service
Wordwise
WordWise Editorial Services
Richard M. Wright
The Writers' Exchange
Hans Zell, Publishing
  Consultant

Design, typing, word processing, DTP, book production

'A Feature Factory' Editorial
  Services
Alpha Word Power
Arioma Editorial Services
Authors' Aid
Ayrshire Business Services
Black Ace Book Production
Book-in-Hand Ltd
Calderbridge Associates
Cambridge Language Services
Vanessa Charles
First Edition Translations Ltd
FJN Associates
Christine Foley Secretarial
  Services
Shelagh Furness
Heath Associates

Hurst Village Publishing
JG Editorial
Marlinoak
M.C. Martinez
My Word!
Oriental Languages Bureau
Pageant Publishing
Pages Editorial & Publishing
  Services
Penman Literary Service
Phoenix 2
PJ Typecraft
Sandhurst Editorial Consultants
SeaStar Editorial Services
Serpentine Editorial
Joan Shannon Freelance
  Services
I.R. Sinclair
Special Edition Pre-press
  Services
Tecmedia Ltd
WordWise Editorial Services

Research and/or writing, rewriting, picture research

'A Feature Factory' Editorial
  Services
Abbey Writing Services
Adkins Archaeology
Lucia Alvarez de Toledo
Anvil Editorial Associates
Arioma Editorial Services
Arkst Publishing
Linda Auld Associates
Authors' Research Services
Beswick Writing Services
Blair Services
Bookwatch Ltd
David Bradley Science Writer
Brooke Publications Ltd
Causeway Resources
Combrógos
Ingrid Cranfield
David A. Cross
Margaret Crush Associates
Editorial/Visual Research
Dr Martin Edwards
Lewis Esson Publishing
First Edition Translations Ltd
James Wilson Flegg
Shelagh Furness
Roy Gaylor
Geo Group & Associates
Heath Associates
Antony Hemans
The Information Bureau
Library Research Agency
Miles Litvinoff

Kenneth Lysons
Manuscript Appraisals
Marlinoak
Susan Moore Editorial Services
Murder Files
Elizabeth Murray
Paul H. Niekirk
Ormrod Research Services
Penman Literary Service
Phoenix 2
Christopher Pick
Picture Research Agency
Victoria Ramsay
S. Ribeiro Literary Services
Rich Research
Anton Rippon Press Services
Sandhurst Editorial Consultants
Sandton Literary Agency
Sarratt Information Services
SeaStar Editorial Services
Serpentine Editorial
Joan Shannon Freelance
  Services
I.R. Sinclair
Small Print
Roger Smithells Ltd, Editorial
  Services
Robert and Jane Songhurst
Mrs Gene M. Spencer
Teral Research Services
Valerie Vogel Picture Research
Caroline White
David L. Williams
David Winpenny
The Word Service
The Writers' Exchange
Hans Zell, Publishing
  Consultant

Indexing

Adkins Archaeology
Linda Auld Associates
Richard A. Beck
Ingrid Cranfield
Meg and Stephen Davies
First Edition Translations Ltd
Freelance Editorial Services
Society of Indexers
Indexing Specialists
Ken Jackson
Paul Nash
Geoffrey D. Palmer
Sandton Literary Agency
Sarratt Information Services
David L. Williams
WordWise Editorial Services
Richard M. Wright
The Writers' Exchange

Translations

Lucia Alvarez de Toledo
Central Office of Information
Ingrid Cranfield
First Edition Translations Ltd
James Wilson Flegg
Freelance Editorial Services
Library Research Agency
M.C. Martinez
James Moore Associates
Oriental Languages Bureau
Small Print
Caroline White

Specialist services

Archives

Murder Files
Hans Tasiemka Archives
John Vickers

Cartography, artwork, cartoons, puzzles

Morley Adams
Reginald Piggott
Streetwise Town Plans Ltd

Cassettes, visual aids

Geo Group & Associates
Small Print

Contracts and copyright services

Clarissa Cridland
Roger Palmer Ltd
Stationers' Hall Registry Ltd

Database services

WordWise Editorial Services
Cambridge Language Services

Freelance employment agency

etr

Interpreting

First Edition Translations Ltd

Lecture agents

Holland-Ford Associates
Sandton Literary Agency

Media and publicity services

Central Office of Information
Freelance Press Services
3 & 5 Promotion

Tuition, lectures, conference services

Authors' Advisory Service
Copywriting One-to-One
David A. Cross
Rosemary Horstmann
Northgate Training
Reading and Righting
S. Ribeiro Literary Services
Mrs Ellen Seager
Gordon R. Wainwright
Joan Wilkins Associates
Write on...
The Writers Advice Centre for
  Children's Books

Voice overs, subtitles

Lucia Alvarez de Toledo
First Edition Translations Ltd

Indexing

A good index is a joy to the user of a non-fiction book; a bad index will downgrade an otherwise good book. The function of indexes, together with the skills needed to compile them, are examined here.

An index is a detailed key to the contents of a document, in contrast to a contents list, which gives only the titles of the parts into which the document is divided (chapters, for example). Precisely, an index is 'A systematic arrangement of entries designed to enable users to locate information in a document'. The document may be a book, a series of books, an issue of a periodical, a run of several volumes of a periodical, an audiotape, a map, a film, a picture, a computer disk, an object, or any other information-carrying artefact in print or non-print form.

The objective of an index is to guide enquirers to information on given subjects in a document by providing the terms of their choice (single words, phrases, abbreviations, acronyms, dates, names, and so on) in an appropriately organised list which refers them to specific locations using page, column, section, frame, figure, table, paragraph, line or other appropriate numbers.

An index differs from a catalogue, which is a record of the documents held in a particular collection, such as a library; though a catalogue may require

an index, for example to guide searchers from subject words to class numbers.

A document may have separate indexes for different classes of heading, so that personal names are distinguished from subjects, for example, or a single index in which all classes of heading are interfiled.

The Society of Indexers

The Society of Indexers is a non-profit organisation founded in 1957 and is the only autonomous professional body for indexers in the UK. It is affiliated with the American Society of Indexers, the Australian Society of Indexers, the Indexing and Abstracting Society of Canada, and the Association of South African Indexers and Bibliographers, and has close ties with the Library Association and the Society of Freelance Editors and Proofreaders.

The main objectives of the Society are to promote all types of indexing standards and techniques and the role of indexers in the organisation of knowledge; to provide, promote and recognise facilities for both the initial and the further training of indexers; to establish criteria for assessing indexing standards; and to conduct research and publish guidance, ideas and information about indexing. It seeks to establish good relationships between indexers, librarians, publishers and authors both to advance good indexing and to improve the role and well-being of indexers.

Services to indexers

The Society publishes a learned journal *The Indexer*, a newsletter and *Occasional Papers in Indexing*. Meetings are held regularly on a wide range of subjects while local and special interest groups provide the chance for members to meet to discuss common interests. A weekend conference is held every year. All levels of training are supported by regular workshops held at venues throughout the country.

Professional competence is recognised in two stages by the Society. Accredited Indexers who have completed the open-learning course qualification (see 'Training in indexing' below) have shown theoretical competence in indexing while Registered Indexers have proved their experience and competence in practical indexing through an assessment procedure and admission to the Register of Indexers. The services of Registered Indexers are actively promoted by the Society while all trained and experienced members have the opportunity of an annual entry in *Indexers Available*, a directory published by the Society and distributed without charge to over 1000 publishers to help them find an indexer.

The Society sets annually a minimum recommended indexing rate (£12.00 per hour in 1997) and provides advice on the business side of indexing to its members.

Services to publishers and authors

Anyone who commissions indexes needs to be certain of engaging a professional indexer working to the highest standards and able to meet deadlines.

Indexers Available only lists members of the Society and gives basic contact details (name, address, etc), subject specialisms and indexing experience. Those accepted for listing need to fall into the following categories:

• Registered Indexers who have had

What makes a good indexer?

An index compiler needs:
• the ability to analyse the text on behalf of a wide range of users who may want to locate information on a particular topic;
• the ability to scan the index to assess the scope of the book;
• the ability to find out how particular themes or ideas are developed;
• the ability to return to passages they remember reading;
• a good knowledge of the subject matter;
• the ability to devise suitable terms expressing the concepts in the text concisely and precisely;
• the ability to organise the entries in the index in the most appropriate and retrievable fashion;
• a passion for accuracy.

their competence in practical indexing recognised by the Society;

• Accredited Indexers who have passed the Society's tests of technical competence; and

• others who have successfully completed two other recognised training courses.

Advice on the selection of indexers is available from the Registrar, who may also be able to suggest names of professionals able to undertake related tasks such as thesaurus construction, terminology control or database indexing. The Registrar will also advise on relations with indexers.

The Society co-operates with The Library Association in the award of the Wheatley Medal for an outstanding index.

Training in indexing

The Society's course is based on the principle of open learning with Units, tutorial support and formal tests all available separately so that individuals can learn in their own way and at their own pace. The Units cover five core subjects and contain practical exercises and self-administered tests. Members of the Society receive a substantial discount on the cost although anyone can purchase the Units. Only members of the Society can apply for the formal tests or for tutorial support.

Further information

Society of Indexers, Mermaid House, 1 Mermaid Court, London SE1 1HR
tel 0171-403 4947
Secretary Mrs C. Shuttleworth
Write to The Secretary for further information. Enquiries from publishers and authors seeking to commission an indexer should be made to The Registrar.

Further reading

British Standards Institution, *British Standard recommendations for examining documents, determining their subjects and selecting indexing terms*,

BSI, 1984 (BS6529:1984)
Information and documentation – guidelines for the content, organization and presentation of indexes (ISO 999:1996)

Translation

The role of the translator in enabling written work to pass beyond national frontiers is receiving growing recognition. In view of the general increase of activity in this field, it is not surprising that many people with writing ability and a knowledge of languages should think of adopting freelance translating as a full- or part-time occupation. This article is for such would-be translators.

The first difficulty the beginner will encounter is the unwillingness of publishers to entrust a translation to anyone who has not already established a reputation for sound work. The least the publisher will demand before commissioning a translation is a fairly lengthy specimen of the applicant's work, even if unpublished. The publisher cannot be expected to pay for a specimen sent in by a translator seeking

work. If, on the other hand, a publisher specifically asks for a lengthy specimen of a commissioned book the firm will usually pay for this specimen at the current rate.

Perhaps the best way would-be translators can begin is to select some book of the type which they feel competent and anxious to translate, ascertain from the foreign author or publisher that the English-language rights are still free, translate a sub-

stantial section of the book and then submit the book and their specimen translation to an appropriate publisher. If they are extremely lucky, this may result in a commission to translate the book. More likely, however – since publishers are generally very well informed about foreign books likely to interest them and are rarely open to a chance introduction – the publisher will reject the book as such. But publishers who are favourably impressed may commission a translation of some other book of a similar nature which they already have in mind.

In this connection it is important to stress that translators should confine themselves to subjects of which they possess an expert knowledge. In the case of non-fiction, they may have to cope with technical expressions not to be found in the dictionary and disaster may ensue if they are not fully conversant with the subject. The translation of fiction, on the other hand, demands different skills (e.g. in the writing of dialogue) and translators should be confident that they possess these skills before taking steps to secure work of this nature.

Having obtained a commission to translate a book, the translator will be faced with negotiating terms. These vary considerably from publisher to publisher but are usually based on a rate per 1000 words. Translators should be able to arrange that the advance is on account of a royalty of 2.5% and a small share of the proceeds from secondary uses such as paperback reprint and American rights. However, some publishers avoid paying royalties to the translator even after reducing the royalties they pay to the original author. In the past it was common practice for translators to assign their copyright to the publisher outright, but this is no longer the rule. Most reputable publishers will now sign agreements specifying the rights they require in the translation and leaving the copyright in the translator's hands.

Advice regarding contracts for full-length works, copyright, Public Lending Right and other matters may be obtained from the Translators Association of the Society of Authors (see page 482). The Institute of Translation and Interpreting (see page 476) offers membership to all categories of qualified translators, in particular technical and commercial translators.

Annual or biennial prizes are awarded by the Translators Association for translations from German, Italian, French and other languages (see page 512).

Resources for writers

Books, research and reference

Almost every writing project will involve the use of books or research at some stage. Some references are quickly found; other projects require numerous books or information files on a specific topic, visits to specialist libraries and to other relevant places or people. **Margaret Payne** ALA *gives an introduction to printed sources.*

Although research can be an interest or pleasure in itself, it can also be time-consuming, cutting into writing or earning time. Even checking a single fact can take hours or days if you ask the wrong question or check the wrong source first. No article or book can hope to solve all problems – sometimes there are no answers, or the lack of information is itself the answer – but a few guidelines as to routines and sources may save much time and money.

This article is an introduction to printed sources. For a more detailed approach, Ann Hoffmann's *Research for Writers* (A&C Black, 5th edn 1996, £11.99) includes guides to original and unpublished material, and covers methods, sources, specific organisations and specialist libraries.

Suggestions for a core collection of reference books to own are given under 'A writer's reference bookshelf' on page 574. The final choice of title often depends on personal preference and interests, space, the frequency with which it needs to be consulted, its cost and the proximity of your nearest public reference library. Anyone living in or near a large city has an advantage over the country dweller, with a choice of major reference libraries; a variety of specialist sources such as headquarters of various societies, companies and organisations; academic and other specialist libraries and the government. Often a question can be answered much nearer home, but you may find the further back in time you go, or the more detailed your research, the further afield you need to travel.

Checking a fact

What do you really want to know?

Clarifying your question in advance can save much work for you or your researcher. If you want to check someone's date of birth and know the person is alive or very recently dead and in *Who's Who*, then ask for that book, or phrase your telephone request so that the librarian goes straight to that source. Do not start with general questions such as 'Where are the biographies?' In a branch library you may be shown sections of individual lives; on the telephone you are adding unnecessarily to your telephone bill, as well as wasting time. If the person is dead, did he or she die recently enough to have a newspaper obituary – it often mentions the date of birth – or long enough ago to be in a volume of *Who Was Who* or the *Dictionary of National Biography*? Never assume that information that you know is necessarily common knowledge; it needs to be specified.

Go straight to the index

Most reference books are arranged in alphabetical order but, if not, they should have an index. Some indexes may seem inadequate, but have you used the right key word? A good index should refer you from the one not used. For example, some will use carpentry and ignore woodwork as an entry. Others will ignore both and go straight to the object to be made or

repaired. If there is no index, turn first to the contents page, as in some books the index is at the front rather than the back.

Is it important to be up to date?

Most books have the date of publication on the back of the title page. Is the answer given in the book one which may be surpassed or superseded? Despite some instant publishing, when dealing with statistics most books have a built-in obsolescence. There is a cut-off date when the text goes to the printer and the updating must wait for the next edition. Some current events are too recent to be found in books at all, although well documented at the time in newspapers and magazines (see below).

If in doubt, re-check your answer

If the answer is of importance, try not to depend on one source. Mistakes can occur in print or in transcribing. Sometimes it is necessary to check another source for verification or to obtain another point of view. In all cases you should ...

Note your source

Even if you think you will remember, always note where you find your information, preferably next to the answer, or in a card file or book where it can be easily found. Note the title, author, publisher and date of publication as well as the page number. Nothing is more annoying than having to undertake the same search twice.

Researching a subject

Reference has already been made to Ann Hoffmann's book for detail, but Kipling's six honest serving men can still be the basis for any subject: What? Why? When? How? Where? Who? cover aspects of most enquiries. The starting point depends on the writer's personal knowledge of the subject. Where it is unfamiliar always start from the general and go on to the particular. An article in an encyclopedia can

fill in the background and often recommend bibliographies or other references. If an article in the *Encyclopaedia Britannica* is too detailed or too complex, try *The World Book* which can be found in the children's library. Because *The World Book* has to appeal to a wider readership, the text and illustrations are clearer. Avoid a detailed book on the subject until you need it; it may tell you more than you want to know.

Sources of information

Reference libraries. Use the largest one in your vicinity for encyclopedias, specialised reference books, annuals and for back numbers of newspapers and periodicals. Ask for *Walford's Guide to Reference Material*: three volumes list the standard reference works of subjects, most of which should be available for consultation.

Lending libraries. Find the place number of the books you want, and see what is available.

Special libraries. The *Aslib Directory of Information Sources in the United Kingdom* should be available in your reference library. It gives details of special libraries of industries, organisations and societies.

Catalogues, bibliographies and subject guides. Most library catalogues are now on-line, with author, title or key word access. There is a series of subject catalogues to the British Library up to 1975 and the *British National Bibliography* updates this (see 'Compiling a bibliography' on page 573).

Newspapers and bibliographies. There is a monthly index to *The Times*, cumulated annually, which often provides the date of an event. The index also includes the *The Times Supplements*. For periodical articles, begin with the *British Humanities Index*, and, if necessary, check also the specialist indexes and abstracting journals such as *Current Technology Index*. Your public library can often locate runs of periodicals and magazines, and the interloan service can obtain specific periodical articles if you have the details. *Profile*, an on-line index to quality newspapers, is the most up to date available, but retrospective only to 1985 and few libraries have the facility as yet. *Clover* is a printed index to the same broadsheet press.

Compiling a bibliography

Checking what books are already available may reveal both the range of titles already in print and the potential market for your work. If yours is to be the tenth book on the subject published in the last two years, saturation point may be near. On the other hand, if you know the books and believe you can do better, or have evolved a different approach, you can mention this in a covering letter to a potential publisher. A quick way to evaluate what is available is by checking the shelves of a public library or bookshop, but it should be remembered that in a library, many of the best books will be on loan. This practice also makes one aware of publishers' interests.

A more comprehensive and systematic list of recent books can be compiled by consulting the *British National Bibliography*, a cumulating list based on the copyright books in the British Library, with advance notice (up to three months) of new books through the Cataloguing in Publication scheme. The arrangement is by the Dewey Decimal Classification used in all public libraries. Other subject lists are less satisfactory to consult. The British Museum (now British Library) has a series of subject indexes up to 1975, and many British books are included in the American *Cumulative Book Index* (1928 on). *Whitaker's Books in Print* is predominantly an author-title list, but does index some books under the key word of a subtitle; as its name implies, out-of-print books are excluded.

Facilities now exist to obtain a bibliography on any subject by using one of the computer data banks based on the British Library, the Library of Congress or commercial firms. The difficulties are expense and finding local access points.

Obtaining books

Books in print

In 1996 101,504 different books were published in the United Kingdom alone, joining the many thousands of other titles still in print from previous years. The number of books available means that the chances of finding a copy of what you want on your bookseller's shelf, when you want it, may be slim. But if it is in print it can be ordered for you, although delivery times vary with each publisher. Most large bookshops and libraries now have the monthly microfiche or CD-Rom editions of *Whitaker's Books in Print* giving details of author, publisher, price, number of pages and ISBN. Supplying the ISBN number is often useful for speeding the order.

Out of print books

Out of print books present more difficulty. Generally the older the book, the more difficult it may be to obtain. Such books are no longer available from the publishers, who retain only a file copy, all other stocks having been sold. Therefore unless you are lucky enough to find an unsold copy on a bookseller's shelves, it must be sought in the second-hand market or through a library loan. There are many specialist second-hand and antiquarian booksellers, and a number of directories listing them and their interests. The most well known are *Sheppard's Book Dealers in the British Isles*, now published by R. Joseph. Copies of these should be in your local reference library. Many advertise in *Book and Magazine Collector*, a monthly magazine, which has an extensive 'wants' column.

Public libraries

Public libraries should be able to obtain books for you, whether or not they are in print, either from their own stock, from other libraries in the system or through the interloan scheme. This operates through the British Lending Library, but all requests must go through your library as you cannot apply direct. Your local library tickets may sometimes be used in other libraries, but different issuing systems have discouraged this in recent years. Most library systems now have a databased catalogue of all branch stock.

A writer's reference bookshelf

The increasing use of personal computers and the Internet is extending the sources of information from print to multimedia. Some reference books are available on CD-Rom and much knowledge can be accessed through web sites. But as yet few libraries in the UK have the funds, expertise or space to make such sources available, and in the meantime there is a growing division between individuals who prefer or only have access to print and those who are computer literate and can afford and have the time to explore what knowledge is available electronically, as well as what is not.

However good and accessible a public library may be, there are some books required for constant or instant consultation, which should be within easy reach of your work area. The choice of title may vary, but the following list is offered as suggestions for a core collection.

Dictionaries

With the use of word processor packages, a dictionary is no longer quite so essential for spelling checks, although still needed to clarify definitions and meanings. A book is often easier to consult, and portable. The complete Oxford English Dictionary is not, and although the definitive work, neither the full nor the compact edition with its magnifying glass, nor the two volume *Shorter Oxford Dictionary* is easy to handle for quick reference, so a one volume dictionary is more practical. The number of new words and meanings coming into vogue suggests a replacement every five years or so, or supplementing your choice by a good paperback edition. If you use an old copy, you will be surprised by the improved format and readability of the new editions.

The most popular one volume dictionaries are the *Concise Oxford Dictionary* (8th edn 1991, £15.99 – 80,000 definitions), *Chambers' English Dictionary* (6th edn 1993, £19.99 – 150,000 entries, appealing to crossword addicts), *The Collins English Dictionary* (Harper-Collins, 4th edn 1994, £25.00 – 110,000 entries). A recommended paperback dictionary is the *Oxford Paperback Dictionary and Thesaurus* (1997, £5.99 – 50,000 entries). If you write for the American market, it is advisable also to have an American dictionary to check variant spellings and meanings. The equivalent of the Oxford family of dictionaries is Webster's, the most popular one volume edition being Webster's *New World Dictionary* (Prentice-Hall, 4th edn 1994, £17.95).

Roget's Thesaurus

When the exact word or meaning eludes you, a thesaurus may help clear a mental block. There are many versions of Roget available, both in hardback and paperback, including a revision by E.M. Kirkpatrick (Longman, 1987, £15.99) and a paperback edition from Penguin (1984, £4.99). *The Bloomsbury Thesaurus* (Bloomsbury, 1993, £15.99) is a new compilation which includes 1000 knowledge categories and 1500 quotations.

Grammar and English usage

A wide choice is available but *New Fowler's Modern English Usage* remains a standard work (3rd edn 1996, revised R.W. Burchfield, Oxford UP, £16.99). Many prefer Sir Ernest Gowers' *Complete Plain Words* (4th edn 1994, rev. Sidney Greenbaum and Jane Whitcut, Penguin, £6.99). More recent works are *The Oxford Guide to English Usage* (Oxford UP, 2nd edn 1994, £4.99), and Michael Legat's *The Nuts and Bolts of Writing* (Hale, 1989, £9.95 and £5.99).

Encyclopedias and annuals

Multi-volume encyclopedias are both expensive and space consuming. They are best left for consultation at the nearest reference library, where the most up-to-date versions should be available, unless your need justifies ownership or you prefer the

CD-Rom version. Of the single volumes, *Pears Cyclopaedia* contains a surprising amount of general information and a new edition is issued annually (Pelham Books, 1997-8, £14.99). For those concerned with current affairs, the complete edition of *Whitaker's Almanack* has valuable statistics and information on government and countries, as well as many miscellaneous facts not found elsewhere. For annual replacement if constantly used.

Atlases, gazetteers and road maps

These also need replacing with updated editions from time to time. An old edition can be misleading with recent changes of place names and metrication. The *The Times Atlas of the World* is the definitive work, but it is expensive and bulky for quick reference. The *The Times Concise Atlas of the World* (Times Books, 7th edn 1995, £45.00) has the most comprehensive gazetteer-index. It is a little more manageable but still requires special shelving.

With the building of the M25 and other motorways, many existing road atlases of Britain may be out of date and need replacing. There are many paperback editions at 3 miles to 1 inch (1:190,080) for less than £5.00, but most detailed is *A-Z Great Britain Road Atlas* (Geographers A-Z, 1994, £6.95; 1:250,000) with 31,000 place names and 56 town maps. For London and environs *Greater London Street Atlas* (Nicholson, rev. edn 1997, £26.99 and £14.99) is a detailed 3.17 miles to 1 inch, 1:20,000 street map for the whole M25 area.

Literary companions and dictionaries

There are many to choose from, and frequency of consultation will determine whether all or some of the following are desirable. *Brewer's Dictionary of Phrase and Fable* (Cassell, 15th edn 1994, £25.00 and £16.99) and its companion volume *Brewer's Twentieth Century Dictionary of Phrase and Fable* (Cassell, 1991, £16.95 and £10.99 paperback) avoid many distractions by settling queries, as does The

Oxford Companion to English Literature (6th edn edited by Margaret Drabble, Oxford UP, 1995, £25.00). This new edition complements rather than replaces Sir Paul Harvey's earlier editions. Either can be used for checking an author's work, but the definitive and exhaustive lists are to be found in the *New Cambridge Bibliography of English Literature*. The four volumes and the index volume can be found in major reference libraries.

Books of quotations

Once divorced from their text and unattributed, quotations are not easy to trace. This should be a warning to any writer or researcher to note author, title and page number to any item copied. Tracing quotations often needs resort to more than one collection, but the most popular anthologies are *The Oxford Dictionary of Quotations* (4th edn, Oxford UP, 1992, £25.00) and the *Bloomsbury Dictionary of Quotations* (Bloomsbury, 2nd edn 1991, paperback, £12.99) and *The New Penguin Dictionary of Quotations* (Penguin, 1993, £6.99).

Biographical dictionaries

Pears Cyclopaedia contains a brief but useful section, but for a fuller working tool the standard works are *Chambers' Biographical Dictionary* (Chambers, 6th edn 1997, £40.00 – 15,000 entries) or the American-biased *Webster's New Biographical Dictionary* (Merriam-Webster Inc., 1990, £17.95 – 150,000 entries). Frequency of consultation will determine whether you need a personal copy of *Who's Who* or the *Concise Dictionary of National Biography*, which are available in most libraries.

Dates, anniversaries and names

A brief guide to current anniversaries is included in the *Journalists' calendar* (see page 576). *Dent's Everyman's Dictionary of Dates* (Weidenfeld, 8th edn, 1995, £20.00) and *The Independent Book of Anniversaries* (Headline, 1993, o.p.) are

useful. For historical facts *The Companion to British History* by Charles Arnold-Baker (Longcross Press, 1997, £48.00) is a comprehensive dictionary of events and people. Leslie Dunkling's *Guinness Book of Names* (Guinness, 7th edn 1995, £11.99) is an encyclopedic source on its subject from first names to places and pubs, with a comprehensive index.

Working directories for writers

A current copy of *Writers' & Artists' Yearbook* is essential, as recent moves and mergers have made so many publishers' details out of date. It is useful for very much more information besides that found in the first section. Browse through,

or use the index, in spare moments to familiarise yourself with its contents for future reference.

Frequency of consultation will determine whether you also need *Willings Press Guide* (annual, Hollis Directories Ltd) or *Benn's Media Directory* (2 vols. annual, Benn). Both are expensive but very comprehensive in their coverage of British and overseas newspapers, magazines and other media information. *Cassell's Directory of Publishing* complements all the above, but gives more information about publishing personnel not found elsewhere.

Margaret Payne ALA has worked in public and academic libraries in the UK and Canada and also as a librarian in a book trade library, in which subject she retains a special interest.

Journalists' calendar 1998

This Journalists' calendar has been compiled by the Information Bureau from a variety of sources and is designed as a guideline only. As some anniversary dates are disputed in different sources, all dates should be checked further before embarking on any major project involving any of these dates.

January

1 Union of Soviet Socialist Republics established, 1923

Colonel Patrick Porteous won the VC for his part in the raid on Dieppe in 1942

British Railways formed from four existing companies, 1948

Great Britain and Denmark joined the EEC, 1973

John Birt became director-general of the BBC, 1993

The oil tanker *Braer* ran aground in storms off Shetland and finally broke up on 12 January, causing a 20-mile slick, 1993

Czechoslovakia became two independent states, the Czech Republic and the Slovak Republic, 1993

The Single European Market came into being, 1993

2 David Bailey, photographer, born 1938

3 Michael Barratt, broadcaster and gardener, born 1928

Margaret Thatcher became the longest continuously serving Prime Minister this century with eight years 244 days, 1988

Bill Gibb, fashion designer, died 1988

4 Brian Josephson, Professor of Physics at Cambridge, won the Nobel Prize, 1973

5 HM King Juan Carlos of Spain born 1938

The first regular news programme in the UK, BBC TV's *Newsreel*, a 15-minute news round-up presented twice a week, was transmitted, 1948

Walter Mondale, US Vice President (Democrat) 1977-81, born 1928

Rowan Atkinson launched the charity appeal 'Comic Relief' 1988

6 John Croft, head of Home Office Research and Planning Unit (1981-3) and painter in his spare time, born 1923

Dizzy Gillespie, jazz trumpeter, died 1993

Rudolf Nureyev, ballet dancer, died 1993

7 Trevor Howard, actor, died 1988

US marines stormed weapons arsenal in Mogadishu, 1993

8 Alfred Wallace, naturalist and biologist, born 1823

Richard Tauber, tenor, died 1948

USSR launched unmanned spacecraft *Luna 21*, 1973

9 Simone de Beauvoir, French feminist writer and philosopher, born 1908

David Holbrook, author, born 1923

Dame Gracie Fields, singer, born 1898

11 Acquittal of Major Esterhazy in trial for alleged forgery of document in the Dreyfus case provoked Zola's *J'accuse* (13 January), an open letter to the President of France, for which he was later imprisoned (23 February), 1898

The Representation of the People Bill was passed by the House of Lords giving women the vote, 1918

Rt Rev John Baker, Bishop of Salisbury, born 1928

Alan Bowness, director of the Tate Gallery, born 1928

Thomas Hardy, novelist and poet, died 1928

British Airways issued an unconditional apology to Virgin Airlines and Richard Branson and agreed to pay damages and costs following the settlement of a libel action in which Virgin alleged that BA was conducting a 'dirty tricks' campaign against it, 1993

12 The first full-size supermarket in Britain opened by the London Co-operative Society at Manor Park, 1948

Launch of the 'Next Directory' 1988

13 Lord (Ted) Willis, novelist, playwright and TV scriptwriter, born 1918

US, British and French aircraft attacked and destroyed Iraqi missile sites and radar installations in response to Iraqi raids along its border with Kuwait, 1993

14 Most Rev Derrick Childs, Bishop of Monmouth and Archbishop of Wales, born 1918

Professor Sir Hans Kornberg, biochemist and Master of Christ's College, Cambridge, born 1928

Rev Charles Dodgson, better known as Lewis Carroll, died 1898

15 Mrs Golda Meir became the first Israeli Prime Minister to have an audience with the Pope, 1973

An earthquake in northern Japan registering 7.5 on the Richter scale killed two people and injured 360, 1993

Sammy Cahn, songwriter, died 1993

16 Sir Robin Dunn, Appeal Court judge, born 1918

Keith Shackleton, artist and naturalist, born 1923

Lady (Marina) Vaizey, art critic of *The Sunday Times*, born 1938

17 Vidal Sassoon, hair stylist, born 1928

Merger announced between Leyland Motors and British Motor Corporation, 1968

18 Jean (Eleanor Hibbert) Plaidy, who also wrote as Victoria Holt and Philippa Carr, novelist, died 1993

20 Richard Nixon inaugurated for a second term as President of the USA, 1973

Baron Philippe de Rothschild, French banker, vintner and entrepreneur, died 1988

Bill Clinton inaugurated as the 42nd President of the USA, 1993

Audrey Hepburn, film actress and UNICEF ambassador, died 1993

22 George Foreman, former heavyweight boxing champion, born 1948

L.B. Johnson, former President of the USA, died 1973

23 Jeanne Moreau, French actress, born 1928

Helgafell volcano on Heimaey island off Iceland erupted leaving 500 homeless, 1973

24 Desmond Morris, zoologist and writer, born 1928

25 Viscount Blakenham, chairman of Pearson plc, born 1938

Charles Wilson, one of the UK Great Train Robbers, recaptured at Rigaud, Quebec, 1968

26 Stephane Grapelli, jazz violinist, born 1908

Eartha Kitt, singer, born 1928

Vaclav Havel voted the first President of the new Czech state, 1993

27 Michael Craig, actor and playwright, born 1928

Charlie Fenwick, Baltimore banker who won the Grand National on *Ben Nevis* in 1980, born 1948

USA and Soviet Union signed agreement on development of cultural and other exchanges, 1958

Edward G. Robinson, actor, died 1973

William Randolph Hearst, American newspaper magnate and journalist, born 1908

28 Mikhail Baryshnikov, ballet dancer, born 1948

Arthur Hellyer, horticulturist and writer, died 1993

30 Orville Wright, pioneer aviator, died 1948

Mahatma Gandhi, Indian Nationalist Leader, killed in Delhi, 1948

Dr Emil Fuchs, East German spy, died 1988

31 Nauru ceased to be a UN trust territory and became independent, 1968

John Poulson, architect, imprisoned for bribery and corruption, died 1993

February

1 Leonard Gribble, thriller writer, born 1908

Muriel Spark, Scottish writer, born 1918

Lisa Marie Presley, daughter of Elvis, born 1968

2 Sir Norman Fowler, former Conservative MP, born 1938

West German government imposed series of foreign exchange controls following massive flight from the dollar and buying of Deutschmarks, 1973

Bernard Braden, Canadian-born actor and broadcaster, died 1993

3 Announcement of agreement for use by USA of air bases in the Azores, 1948

4 Hylda Baker, comedienne, born 1908
   Ida Lupino, British-born Hollywood actress, born 1918
   The Australian government abandoned colour bar in admission of new settlers, 1973

5 J.K. Huysmans, author, born 1848
   Arthur Ashe, US tennis player and Wimbledon champion in 1975, died 1993
   Lord Sidney Berstein, founder of Granada Television and the Granada Group, died 1993
   Joseph Mankiewicz, screenwriter and film director, producer, died 1993

6 Marghanita Laski, British broadcaster and writer, died 1988

7 Earl of Harewood, President of the British Board of Film Classification, born 1923

8 Osian Ellis, harpist, born 1928

9 Professor Steen Rasmussen, Danish architect, born 1898
   Sandy Lyle, British golfer, born 1958

10 Bertolt Brecht, German dramatist, born 1898

11 The Miracle of Lourdes: St Bernadette had her first vision of Our Lady, 1858
   Sir Vivian Fuchs, geologist, explorer, born 1908
   Sir Ronald Arculus, Italophile, born 1923

12 Henry Lindfield was the first car driver to be killed in a motoring accident, 1898
   Lord Moyola (James Chichester-Clark) former Prime Minister of Ulster, born 1923
   Franco Zeffirelli, film producer and designer, born 1923
   Leon Goossens, British oboist, died 1988
   Two-year-old James Bulger was abducted from a shopping centre in Liverpool; his body was later found on a railway embankment and two 10-year-old boys were charged with his murder, 1993
   The South African government and the ANC agreed plans for an elected black and white interim government, 1993

13 Oliver Reed, actor, born 1938
   Dame Christabel Pankhurst, suffragette daughter of Emmeline, died 1958
   US dollar devalued by 10%; Japanese yen floated, 1973
   Darius Guppy and Benedict Marsh were convicted of a £1.8 million jewellery insurance fraud and sentenced to five years' imprisonment, 1993

15 Jeremy Bentham, philosopher and writer, born 1748
   Herbert Asquith, former Prime Minister, died 1928
   First Polaris missile to be fired from a British submarine launched from Resolution off Cape Kennedy, 1968
   Michal Kovak voted the first President of the new Slovak state, 1993

16 Lord Carnarvon entered the tomb of Tutankhamen at Luxor, 1923

17 John Allegro, author and expert on the Dead Sea Scrolls, born 1923

18 Sinead Cusack, actress, born 1948
   Leslie Norman, film producer and director, died 1993

20 Ferruccio Lamborghini, founder of the Lamborghini car company, died 1993

21 Dr Oonagh McDonald, former Labour MP, born 1938
   America's leading TV evangelist Jimmy Swaggart confessed to his past sin of consorting with a prostitute, 1988

22 The first radio discussion programme was broadcast by the BBC. It was the first BBC programme to take notice of party politics and the first in which an MP, J.T. Walton Newbold, participated, 1923
   Bruce Forsyth, comedian and game-show host, born 1928

23 Kathleen Harrison, actress, born 1898
   Duke of Beaufort, born 1928

24 *The Flying Scotsman*, steam locomotive, went into service, 1923
   Dennis Waterman, actor, born 1948
   Bobby Moore, footballer, died 1993

25 Sir Christopher Wren, architect, died 1723

26 Fats Domino, rhythm and blues singer, born 1928
   Sir Donald Farquharson, judge, born 1928
   A bomb exploded in a car park beneath the World Trade Centre in New York, killing five and injuring over 1000, 1993

27 Dame Ellen Terry, actress, born 1848
   Sir (Charles) Hubert (Hastings) Parry, composer, born 1848
   Lillian Gish, American actress, died 1993

28 Alfred Burke, actor, born 1918
   The last British troops left India, 1948
   Three IRA bombs caused a huge explosion at a gasworks in Warrington, Cheshire, 1993
   Joyce Carey, OBE, actress, died 1993
   Ruby Keeler, dancer and actress, died 1993

29 Victor von Hagen, author and explorer, born 1908
   Joss Ackland, actor, born 1928
   Alan Loveday, violinist, born 1928

March

1 An internal UN report stated that the organisation was rife with overmanning, waste, corruption and bureaucratic patronage, 1993

2 Cardinal Basil Hume, born 1923

The British Commonwealth Trans-Antarctic expedition led by Sir Vivian Fuchs arrived at the New Zealand base on Ross Island having crossed the South Pole, 1958

3 Peter O'Sullevan, racing commentator, born 1918

Liberals and SDP formed Social & Liberal Democrats, 1988

Eddie 'The Eagle' Edwards returned to the UK from the Winter Olympics to a hero's welcome. Eddie, a plasterer from Cheltenham, came last in the ski jump, 1988

Richard Chipperfield, circus owner, died 1988

4 Patrick Moore, astronomer, born 1923

Alan Sillitoe, poet, playwright and novelist, born 1928

5 Rex Harrison, actor, born 1908

6 Pearl S. Buck, writer, died 1973

Three IRA members were shot dead by the SAS in Gibraltar after a bomb plan was uncovered, 1988

7 Bangladesh held its first general election, 1973

Divine (Harris Glenn Milstead), US film actor, died 1988

8 Two car bombs exploded outside the Old Bailey and Great Scotland Yard, 1973

Billy Eckstine, US singer and bandleader, died 1993

10 Death in Prague of Jan Masaryk, Czech diplomat and statesman 1948

Prince of Wales narrowly escaped death when his ski party at Klosters was caught by an avalanche. Major Hugh Lindsay was killed, 1988

11 The German army entered Austria, 1938

12 Revolution in Vienna began, 1848

Max Wall, comedian, born 1908

Edward Albee, American dramatist, born 1928

Mauritius became independent within the Commonwealth, 1968

13 Walter Annenberg, publisher, born 1908

Tessie O'Shea, comedienne, born 1918

14 Superman, comic strip hero, first appeared, 1938

15 Sir Henry Bessemer, inventor who modernised the process of making steel, died 1898

Earl Haig, painter, born 1918

16 Aubrey Beardsley, artist, died 1898

A loyalist gunman opened fire into a crowd of mourners at the IRA funerals of the IRA members shot dead in Gibraltar, killing three and injuring 50, 1988

18 Five-day revolution in Milan against Austrian rule and Joseph Radetzky was forced to abandon the city, 1848

Percy Thrower, gardener and broadcaster, died 1988

19 Patrick McGoohan, actor, born 1928

Two British soldiers were lynched in the vicinity of a Republican funeral in West Belfast, 1988

20 Sir Michael Redgrave, actor, born 1908

Two IRA bombs exploded in the centre of Warrington, killing three-year-old Jonathan Ball and injuring 56 people. Timothy Parry, aged 12, later died from his injuries, 1993

21 Patrick Steptoe, gynaecologist and test-tube baby pioneer, died 1988

22 Marcel Marceau, master of mime, born 1923

Andrew Lloyd Webber, composer, born 1948

23 Edward Middleditch, painter, born 1923

24 John Hersey, American war correspondent and novelist, died 1993

25 Dame Bridget D'Oyly Carte, born 1908

David Lean, film director, born 1908

26 Elizabeth Jane Howard, novelist and broadcaster, born 1923

Daily weather forecasts first broadcast by the BBC, 1923

Sarah Bernhardt, actress, died 1923

Kyung-Wha Chung, Korean violinist, born 1948

Mrs Susan Shaw became the first woman to set foot on the floor of the London Stock Exchange for 171 years, 1973

Sir Noel Coward, playwright, composer and singer, died 1973

27 John Burke, genealogist and founder of 'Burke's Peerage and Baronetage of the UK', died 1848

Victor Hochhauser, impressario, born 1923

Sir James Dewar, chemist and physicist, died 1923

Yuri Gagarin, Soviet astronaut and first man to fly in space, was killed in an aircraft crash, 1968

29 John Jacob Astor, founder of the Astor dynasty, died 1848

Pearl Bailey, actress and jazz singer, born 1918

A consortium of independent TV companies headed by Carlton Communications took over control of ITN, 1993

30 Ian Botham, cricketer, set out to emulate Hannibal's trek across the Alps , 1988

31 William Waldorf, Viscount Astor, born 1848

Sir David Steel, former MP and co-founder of Social and Liberal Democrats, born 1938

April

1 British electricity industry transferred to national ownership, 1948

Ali MacGraw, American actress, born 1938

The Royal Flying Corps and the Royal Navy Air Service officially became the Royal Air Force, 1918

VAT introduced in Great Britain, 1973

Lord Zuckerman, chief scientific adviser to the Government 1964-71, died 1993

4 Grinling Gibbons, English woodcarver, born 1648

The judgement in the Zola trial (11 January) was quashed on appeal, 1898

Martin Luther King, Civil Rights leader, died 1968

Broadcast of the final episode of the TV soap opera *Crossroads*, 1988

5 Bette Davis, actress, born 1908

Herbert von Karajan, conductor, born 1908

6 Professor James D. Watson, US biologist, born 1928

7 Percy Faith, composer and conductor, born 1918

8 Gaetano Donizetti, composer, died, 1848

Horatio Kitchener's victory at Atbara River, 1898

Pablo Picasso, artist, died 1973

Sir Clough Williams-Ellis, architect and town planner, died 1978

9 Paul Robeson, actor and singer, born 1898

Tom Lehrer, songwriter, born 1928

Jess Yates, former TV personality and producer, died 1993

10 The first photograph of a topical event in Britain was taken by W.E. Kilburn of the Chartist meeting held on Kennington Common, London; a crowd of 20,000 had gathered to petition Parliament for reform, 1848

11 Leo C. Rosten, US author and social scientist, born 1908

12 Hardy Kruger, actor, born 1928

Feodor Ivanovich Chaliapin, Russian operatic bass, died 1938

13 Joseph Bramah, inventor, born 1748

Alan Clark, Conservative MP, born 1928

14 John Stonehouse, politician and author, died 1988

15 Kenneth Williams, comedian found dead at his flat, 1988

Leslie Charteris, writer and creator of *The Saint*, died 1993

16 Spike Milligan, comedian and founder member of the *Goon Show*, born 1918

Gordon Wilson, former Scottish Nationalist MP, born 1938

Abu Jihad, military commander of the PLO was murdered in Tunisia, 1988

17 Two of the four officers accused of beating the black motorist Rodney King were found guilty of violating his civil rights; the other two officers were acquitted, 1993

18 Gustave Moreau, painter, died Paris, 1898

Roger de Grey, artist, born 1918

John Demjanjuk found guilty on Treblinka charges, 1988

19 Henry Newbolt, poet, died 1938

The siege of the Branch Davidian cult compound at Waco, USA ended after 51 days when the FBI stormed the compound, 1993

20 Hijack of Kuwait Airways 747 ended after 16 days. It began in Iran (5 April), moved to Cyprus and ended in Algiers, 1988

21 The 18th Earl of Derby, born 1918

22 Glen Campbell, country singer, born 1938

Eighteen-year-old Stephen Lawrence was murdered by white youths in a racially motivated attack in Eltham, London, 1993

23 James Kirkup, writer, born 1923

Shirley Temple Black, former child star, born 1928

Bill Cotton, former MD of BBC TV, born 1928

24 Ralph Brown, sculptor, born 1928

An IRA bomb exploded in the City of London killing a newspaper photographer and injuring 37 people. Later two minicabs were hijacked in separate incidents and ordered to take bombs to Downing Street and New Scotland Yard. The drivers alerted police before reaching their destinations, 1993

Oliver Tambo, President of the African National Congress 1978-91, died 1993

25 Ella Fitzgerald, jazz singer, born 1918

26 Ferdinand Delacroix, French painter, born 1798

Sir Oliver Millar, art historian and surveyor of the Queen's Pictures, born 1923

Duane Eddy, guitarist, born 1938

28 The first FA Cup final was played at Wembley, 1923

Fenner Brockway, politician and pacifist, died 1988

George Walker, former chairman of the Brent Walker leisure group declared bankrupt with debts of £180 million, 1993

29 Andrew Cruickshank, Scottish actor, died 1988

30 The Land Rover was introduced by the Rover Company at the Amsterdam Motor Show, 1948

The first national commercial pop radio station, Virgin 1215, went on air, 1993

May

1 The first women's college in Britain, Queen's College, Harley Street, opened 1848

Commodore George Dewey destroyed the Spanish fleet at Manila, 1898

The Marquis of Montaignac became the first motor racing fatality, 1898

Pierre Beregovoy, Prime Minister of France April 1992-March 1993, committed suicide, 1993

2 Henry Hall, former bandleader, born 1898

Dr Patrick Hillery, former President of Ireland, born 1923

3 Peter Oosterhuis, golfer, born 1948

4 Eric Sykes, comedian, born 1923

Muhammad Hosni Mubarak, President of Egypt, born 1928

The UN officially took command of the multinational peace-keeping force in Somalia, 1993

5 Dr Hugh Jolly, paediatrician, born 1918

6 Ian Mikardo, Labour MP, and former Party Chairman, died 1993

Ann Todd, film actress and documentary film-maker, died 1993

8 Duncan Grant, artist, died 1978

9 Pancho Gonzalez, tennis player, born 1928

Penelope Gilliatt, writer, died 1993

Dame Freya Stark, writer and traveller, died 1993, aged 100

11 Tom Cribb, pugilist, died 1848

Richard Feynman, physicist and Nobel Prize winner, born 1918

Kim Philby, British spy, died 1988

13 Chet Baker, US jazzman, died 1988

Tyneside shipbuilders Swan Hunter went into receivership after the Government awarded a £170 million order to Vickers, 1993

14 Bob Woolmer, cricketer, born 1948

End of the British Mandate in Palestine, 1948

William Randolph Hearst Jr, US newspaper magnate and journalist, died 1993

15 Communist rising in Paris, after news of suppression of Polish revolt; workmen overturned the Government and set up a provisional administration which immediately collapsed, 1848

16 Stuart Bell, Labour MP, born 1938

17 Rebecca Stephens became the first British woman to climb Mount Everest, 1993

Beverley Allitt, a nurse, was convicted of the murder of four babies in her care at Grantham and Kesteven Hospital in 1991, the attempted murder of three other babies and causing grievous bodily harm to six others; she was given 13 life sentences, 1993

18 Norman Hepple, painter, born 1908

Toyah Willcox, actress, born 1958

The siege of the Golden Temple at Amritsar ended with the surrender of 46 Sikh militants, 1988

Danish Maastricht Referendum: 56.8% in favour, 1993

19 William Gladstone, statesman, died 1898

Three former detectives were cleared of conspiring to pervert the cause of justice by fabricating evidence against one of the Guildford Four in 1975, 1993

20 James Stewart, actor, born 1908

Ronald Colman, actor, died 1958

21 Leo Sayer, pop singer, born 1948

22 Charles Aznavour, French singer, born 1923

Richard Benjamin, actor, 1938

23 Girolamo Savonarola, political reformer, was hanged and burnt, 1498

Denis Compton, cricketer, born 1918

Peter Preston, former editor of *The Guardian*, born 1938

24 Siobhan McKenna, actress, born 1923

William Trevor, writer, born 1928

Lord Jellicoe, Lord Privy Seal resigned over prostitution scandal, 1973

25 Geoffrey Robinson, Labour MP and HM Paymaster General, born 1938

26 Robert Morley, actor, born 1908

The Le Mans 24-hour race was inaugurated 26-27 May, 1923

27 Elizabeth Harwood, operatic soprano, born 1938

A car bomb exploded outside the Uffizi Gallery in Florence, damaging the building and many works of art, 1993

Lord Gormley, President of the National Union of Mineworkers 1971, died 1993

28 Albert Booth, former Labour MP, born 1928

29 Wisconsin became the 30th US state, 1848

Five Turks were killed by German neo-Nazi youths in an arson attack in Solingen; their deaths sparked riots throughout Germany, 1993

31 HRH Prince Ranier of Monaco, born 1923

John Prescott, Deputy Prime Minister, born 1938

Esmé Gordon, architect, died 1993

June

1 Charles de Gaulle became Prime Minister of France, 1958

Jason Donovan, singer, born 1968

Helen Keller, the deaf-blind scholar and author, died 1968

Trevor McDonald became the first black TV newscaster for ITN, 1973

The *Spycatcher* saga ended after a three-year legal battle. The Government failed in its attempt to prevent the publication of Peter Wright's book, 1988

2 Raj Kapoor, Indian film producer and director, died 1988

3　Samuel Plimsoll, social reformer who gave his name to the Plimsoll Line which governs the loading of ships, died 1898

Michael Jaffe, art historian, born 1923

4　Casanova, the world's most famous lover, died 1798

Dorothy Gish, star of silent screen, died 1968

5　Tony Richardson, film director, born 1928

Robert Kennedy, US senator, assassinated, 1968

Conway Twitty, American rock and country and western singer, died 1993

6　Dame Ninette de Valois, former ballerina, born 1898

Louis Lumière, younger of the two brothers who in 1895 perfected an apparatus embodying the features of the modern cinematograph, died 1948

7　James Ivory, film director, born 1928

Norman Strouse, composer, born 1928

Woody Allen failed to win custody of his three children after a bitter case against his partner, Mia Farrow, 1993

8　Russell Harty, writer and broadcaster, died 1988

10　Robert Maxwell, former publisher and chairman of Mirror Group Newspapers, born 1923

Maurice Sendak, American author, born 1928

Les Dawson, comedian, died 1993

In Vitez, Muslim gunmen forced British UN troops to surrender weapons, 1993

11　Sisters Michelle and Lisa Taylor, who were sentenced to life imprisonment in 1991 for the murder of Alison Shaughnessy, were released by the Court of Appeal after their convictions were found to be 'unsafe and unsatisfactory', 1993

Bernard Bresslaw, comic actor, died 1993

12　In Nigeria elections for a civilian President were held but on 23 June the military government declared the elections invalid, 1993

13　Peter Scudamore, jockey, born 1958

14　Edna Healey, biographer (married to Denis), born 1918

Che Guevara de la Serna, known as Che, born 1928

Julie Felix, folk singer, born 1938

15　Attempted assassination of Count Arco-Valley, Secretary of the German Embassy in London, 1898

James Hunt, world Formula 1 motor racing champion in 1976 and TV commentator, died 1993

16　James Bolam, actor, born 1938

The first aeroplane to be hijacked was the Cathay Pacific Airways Catalina flying boat *Miss Macao*; it was seized shortly after take-off from Macao during a flight to Hong Kong, 1948

17　Edward Burne-Jones, Pre-Raphaelite painter, died 1898

19　Sir William Golding, novelist and Nobel Laureate, died 1993

21　The German Fleet was scuttled at Scapa Flow, 1918

First broadcast by a US President, Warren G. Harding, 1923

Departure of Lord Mountbatten from India and the swearing-in of Mr Rajagopalachari as Governor-General, 1948

22　Dame Cicely Saunders, founder of St Christopher's Hospice, born 1918

Lloyds of London announced record losses of £2.91 billion for 1990, 1993

23　First Open University graduates received their degrees at a ceremony held at Alexandra Palace, London, 1973

The Tate Gallery at St Ives, Cornwall, opened by the Prince of Wales, 1993

24　Soviet prohibition of all railway traffic between Berlin and Helmstedt, 1948

26　Willy Messerschmitt, German designer of the first jet-propelled aircraft to be used in combat during the Second World War, born 1898

The Western powers began airlifts to Berlin, 1948

John Cranko, choreographer, died 1973

27　Tommy Cannon, comedian, born 1938

Alan Coren, journalist and broadcaster, born 1938

Shirley Ann Field, actress, born 1938

28　Cyril Smith, former Liberal MP, born 1928

Buckingham Palace announced that the Duke and Duchess of York had agreed the terms of their legal separation, 1993

29　Ian Bannen, actor, born 1928

30　Departure of the last British troops from Palestine, 1948

Nancy Mitford, writer, died 1973

July

1　Charles Darwin announced his theory of evolution to the Linnean Society, 1858

2　John Timpson, broadcaster, born 1928

Lord Owen, former MP, former Labour Foreign Secretary and former leader of the SDP, born 1938

3　Baroness Ryder of Warsaw, Sue Ryder, founder of homes for the disabled, born 1923

Evelyn Anthony, novelist, born 1928

Betty Grable, actress, died 1973

USS Vincennes shot down Iranian airbus 'by mistake': more than 200 dead, 1988

4　Vicomte Françoise de Chateaubriand, writer and diplomat, died 1848

Gertrude Lawrence, actress, born 1898

Lord Wyatt of Weeford, (Woodrow Wyatt) journalist and former Labour MP, born 1918

René Arnoux, Grand Prix racing driver, born 1948

5 Pierre Mauroy, former Prime Minister of France, born 1928

Major-General Sir Jeremy Moore, commander of the British Forces during the Falklands campaign, born 1928

The National Health Service began, 1948

6 Peter Glossop, opera singer, born 1928

Otto Klemperer, German conductor and composer, died 1973

An explosion on the North Sea oil rig *Piper Alpha* killed 170 workers, 1988

7 Charles Dyer, playwright, born 1928

Jimmy Edwards, comedian and actor, died 1988

8 Sir Henry Raeburn, artist, died 1823

9 Barbara Woodhouse, animal trainer and broadcaster, died 1988

10 H.J. Heinz II, Chairman of H.J. Heinz, born 1908

Russian blockade of Berlin by land and water made absolute, 1948

11 Sir Geoffrey Agnew, born 1908

Greville Janner, QC, born 1928

Mark Lester, actor, born 1958

12 Sir Alastair Burnet, broadcaster, born 1928

The first jet aircraft to fly across the Atlantic were six RAF de Havilland Vampires of No 54 Squadron, 1948

13 Sir Alec Rose, who sailed round the world in 1968, born 1908

Mark Tully, the BBC's former India correspondent, in a speech strongly criticised the BBC's Director General, John Birt, 1993

14 Ingmar Bergman, Swedish film-maker, born 1918

Lord Rees-Mogg, former editor of *The Times*, born 1928

15 Carmen Callil, publisher and founder of Virago, born 1938

16 The Prince of Wales unveiled RAF War Memorial at Whitehall Stairs on Thames Embankment, 1923

Anita Brookner, novelist, born 1938

Pinchas Zukerman, violinist, born 1948

Roger Woddis, satiric writer and versifier, died 1993

17 Elizabeth Quinn, actress, born 1948

Wayne Sleep, dancer and entertainer, born 1948

18 Dr W.G. Grace, cricketer, born 1848

Sir Brooks Richards, former diplomat, born 1918

Hugh Stephenson, former editor of the *New Statesman*, born 1938

Jack Hawkins, actor, died 1973

20 Diana Rigg, actress, born 1938

Mark Boxer, cartoonist and journalist, died 1988

Karyn Smith and Patricia Cahill, two British women who had been sentenced in Thailand for drug smuggling in 1990 were granted a royal pardon, 1993

21 The first press report by radio was the Kingstown Regatta report transmitted to the *Dublin Daily Express*, 1898

Cat Stevens, singer now known as Yusaf Islam, born 1948

22 Battle of Falkirk, 1298

Jimmy Hill, football commentator, born 1928

23 D.W. Griffith, pioneer film-maker of the silent screen, died 1948

24 The first life barons and baronesses were named, 1958

25 The steam engine was patented by Thomas Savery in London, 1698

Louise Brown, the first test-tube baby, born, 1978

26 Stanley Kubrick, film director, born 1928

Bernice Rubens, novelist, born 1928

27 Christopher Dean, ice dance champion, born 1958

28 Paddy Ashdown appointed the new SLD leader, 1988

29 Nicholas II, last Tzar of Russia, murdered at Ekaterinburg together with his wife and children, 1918

30 Count Otto von Bismarck, founder of the German Empire in 1870, died 1898

Henry Moore, sculptor, born 1898

Daley Thompson, athlete, born 1958

31 King Badouin of Belgium, died 1993

August

1 The Battle of the Nile: the English fleet, commanded by Nelson, destroyed the French fleet in Aboukir Bay, 1798

Completion of British withdrawal from Palestine, 1948

Dave Lee Travis announced his resignation as Radio 1 DJ on air in protest at recent changes, 1993

Joy Gardner, who collapsed after a violent struggle with police officers serving her with a deportation order on 28 July, died in hospital, 1993

2 James Craigen, former Labour and Co-op MP and freelance writer, born 1938

The UK ratified the Maastricht Treaty, 1993

3 Sir Osbert Lancaster, cartoonist, born 1908

Terry Wogan, TV presenter, born 1938

5 Ray Clemence, former footballer, born 1948

6 Sir David Madel, Conservative MP, born 1938

Buckingham Palace opened to the public for the first time, 1993

7 Greg Chappell, Australian cricketer, born 1948

Launch of newspaper *Scotland on Sunday*, 1988

8 The City and Waterloo Electric Railway opened for traffic, 1898

Iran-Iraq ceasefire; Soviet troops withdrew from Kabul, 1988

The Duchess of York gave birth to her first child, Beatrice, 1988

9 Frederick Marryat, sailor and novelist, died 1848

Rod Laver, Australian tennis player, born 1938

An injured Bosnian girl Irma Hadzimuratovic was flown from Sarajevo to London; she later underwent an operation at Great Ormond Street hospital. 'Operation Irma' was set up to airlift seriously injured people from Sarajevo, 1993

10 Eddie Fisher, American singer and Elizabeth Taylor's fourth husband, born 1928

12 George Stephenson, locomotive engineer, designer of the Rocket, died 1848

The islands of Hawaii transferred to the US, 1898

13 Jean Borotra, French tennis player, born 1898

Dr Frederick Sanger, Noble Prize-winning chemist, born 1918

14 Enzo Ferrari, racing car magnate, died 1988

15 Hans Feibusch, church mural painter, born 1898

16 Elvis Presley, pop star, died 1977

Stewart Granger, actor, died 1993

17 Pakistan's military ruler President Zia ul-Haq was killed in plane crash, 1988

19 Groucho Marx, film actor, died 1977

Sir Frederick Ashton, choreographer, died 1988

21 Chris Brasher, former athlete, born 1928

22 The first coloured MP to sit in a European legislature was M. Mathieu Louisi from Guadeloupe. He was elected to the French National Assembly as representative for Guadeloupe, 1848

Karlheinz Stockhausen, German composer and conductor, born 1928

Rob Buckman, TV doctor/presenter, born 1948

All-day opening of British and Welsh pubs, 1988

25 Leonard Bernstein, conductor, composer and pianist, born 1918

Frederick Forsyth, novelist, born 1938

26 Ralph Vaughan Williams, composer, died 1958

Anton van Leeuwenhoek, Dutch painter, died 1723

27 Sir Donald Bradman, former Test cricketer, born 1908

Lord Winstanley, former Liberal MP, born 1918

28 E.P. Thompson, historian and author, died 1993

29 Sir Richard Attenborough, actor, producer and director, born 1923

Marmaduke Hussey, former chairman of the Board of Governors of the BBC, born 1923

Elliott Gould, actor, born 1938

Lenny Henry, comedian, born 1958

31 Alan Jay Lerner, American writer and lyricist, born 1918

James Coburn, American actor, born 1928

Sir Garry Sobers became the first cricketer to score six sixes with six balls, 1968

September

1 John Ford, film director, died 1973

British Sky Broadcasting satellite TV launched, 1993

Ffyona Campbell became the first woman to walk the length of Africa, 1993

2 The Battle of Omduran won by an Anglo-Egyptian Army under Lord Kitchener in 1898

Michael Hastings, playwright, born 1938

J.R.R. Tolkien (John Ronald Reuel Tolkien), died 1973

Terry Venables resigned from the board of Tottenham Hotspur Football Club, 1993

8 Professor Sir Derek Barton, organic chemist who was joint winner of the Nobel Prize in 1969, born 1918

9 Israel and the Palestine Liberation Organisation officially exchanged letters under which the PLO recognised the right of Israel to exist, renounced violence, promised to end the intifada and remove offending articles from the PLO charter. Israel recognised the PLO as the representative of the Palestinian people, 1993

10 Assassination of the Empress of Austria by an Italian anarchist at Geneva, 1898

Hurricane Gilbert caused havoc in the Caribbean 1988

11 Death of Mahomed Ali Jinnah, Governor General of Pakistan, 1948

12 Raymond Burr, actor, died 1993

Roger Hargreaves, creator of the *Mister Men*, died 1988

13 Israel-PLO agreement signed at the White House, in Washington, 1993

16 Lee Kuan Yew, Prime Minister of Singapore, born 1923

The British National Party won its first local council seat in a by-election on the Isle of Dogs, 1993

17 Roddy McDowell, actor, born 1928

Paul Keating, Prime Minister of Australia, had an audience with the Queen at which he outlined his plans for Australia to become a republic by 2001, 1993

18 Derek Pringle, cricketer, born 1958

Salvador Allende, President of Chile, died 1973

19 Pete Murray, DJ/presenter, born 1928

Rosemary Casals, tennis player, born 1948

Jeremy Irons, actor, born 1948

20 Roy Kinnear, actor, died 1988

Leonard Parkin, former ITN newscaster, died 1993

21 Jimmy Young, radio presenter, born 1923

President Boris Yeltsin dissolved the Russian parliament and announced rule by decree, the parliament swore in Speaker Alexander Rutskoi as President, 1993

22 Captain Mark Phillips, former husband of Princess Royal, born 1948

23 Pablo Neruda, Chilean poet, died 1973

24 Howard Florey, British pathologist, born 1898

25 Sir John Moores, founder of Littlewoods Organisation and former chairman, died 1993

26 George Gershwin, composer, born 1898

Lucette Aldous, prima ballerina with the Australian Ballet, born 1938

Kenny Sansom, former footballer, born 1958

27 Queen Elizabeth, the Queen Mother, launched the Cunard liner *Queen Elizabeth*, 1938

Michèle Dotrice, actress, born 1948

Olivia Newton-John, singer and actress, born 1948

28 Ellen Malcolm, artist, born 1923

Marcello Mastroianni, actor, born 1923

The *Radio Times* first published, 1923

W.H. Auden, poet, died 1973

Demonstrators supporting the Russian parliament clashed with police in Moscow, 1993

29 Greer Garson, actress, born 1908

Palestine mandate began, 1948

The Munich Agreement between Germany and the European powers was signed in 1938 by Hitler, Chamberlain, Daladier and Mussolini

30 Donald Swann, entertainer, born 1923

Johnny Mathis, singer, born 1938

31 Mikhail Gorbachev became the new Soviet President, 1988

October

1 Admiral of the Fleet, Sir Varyl Begg, born 1908

George Peppard, American actor, born 1928

The famous Model T car was introduced by Henry Ford, 1908

Sir Sacheverell Sitwell, writer, died 1988

2 Trevor Brooking, former West Ham and England footballer, born 1948

Vice-Admiral Sir Anthony Tippet, Chief of Fleet Support, born 1928

Car designer and inventor of the mini, Sir Alexander Issigonis, died 1988

3 Ray Lindwall, cricketer and former Australian fast bowler, born 1921

Sir Shridath (Sonny) Ramphal, QC, born 1928

Sir Arthur Whitten-Brown, aviator, born 1948

4 The first transatlantic passenger jet service went into service, 1958

Russian troops stormed the White House: Alexander Rutshoi, Ruslan Khabulatov and other leaders surrendered: more than 170 were killed and 600 injured, 1993

5 Glynis Johns, South African-born actress, born 1923

President Boris Yeltsin declared a state of emergency in Moscow and banned all political parties and newspapers who had supported the rebellion, 1993

6 Admiral Sir Derek Reffell, Controller of the Navy, born 1928

In the Chilean election General Pinochet was defeated in his attempt to win another eight years of power, 1988

7 Sir Hubert Parry, composer, died 1918

Sir John Stocker, High Court judge, born 1918

Cyril Cusack, Irish actor-manager, died 1993

Mass graves containing the bodies of 576 Muslims massacred by Bosnian Croats were discovered near Mostar, 1993

8 Bill Maynard, TV actor, born 1928

Godfrey Talbot, first and longest-serving BBC court correspondent and President of the Queen's English Society, born 1908

Peter Wood, theatre and TV director, born 1928

Marriage of Viscount Linley and Hon. Serena Stanhope, 1993

9 Denzil Davies, Labour MP for Llanellli, born 1938

Donald Sinden, English actor, born 1923

10 Lord Kincraig, born 1918

Nicholas Parsons, radio and TV quizmaster, born 1928

11 Richard Clements, former editor of the *Tribune*, born 1928

Jerome Robbins, former choreographer and associate artistic director of the New York Ballet, born 1918

First TV outside broadcast from 10 Downing Street: Commonwealth Conference, 1948

13 The Turin Shroud revealed as a medieval fake by specialists who carried out carbon-dating tests at Oxford University, 1988

14 Lord Barnett, former Labour MP, born 1923

John Dean, President Nixon's legal counsel involved in the Watergate conspiracy, born 1938

15 Professor J.K. Galbraith, US economist, born 1908

Sir John Vinelott, High Court judge, born 1923

17 Sir Denis Dobson, former Permanent Secretary to the Lord Chancellor, born 1908

Rita Hayworth, Hollywood actress, born 1918

Ann Jones (née Haydon), tennis player, born 1938

The state of emergency lifted in Moscow, 1993

18 Melina Mercouri, former Greek Minister of Culture and film actress, born 1923

20 The Sydney Opera House was officially opened by Queen Elizabeth II, 1973

Sheila Scott, aviator, died 1988

A Health and Safety Executive report showed that children whose fathers worked at Sellafield and who lived in Seascale ran a risk 14 times the national average of developing leukaemia and non-Hodgkins lymphoma, 1993

22 Sir Hugh Wontner, former Savoy Hotel boss, born 1908

Derek Jacobi, actor, born 1923

Mike Hendrick, cricketer, born 1948

Pablo Casals, cellist, died 1973

23 President Nixon agreed to hand over Watergate tapes to Judge Sirica, 1973

24 Franz Lehar, Hungarian composer, died 1948

Phil Bennett, former Wales and British Lyons fly-half, born 1948

Sir Robin Day, TV interviewer, born 1923

The Thirty Years War ended in 1648 with the signing of the Treaty of Westphalia

Lord (Jo) Grimond, leader of the Liberal Party 1956-67, died 1993

25 Donald Wiseman, Professor of Assyriology at London University, born 1918

Vincent Price, film actor, died 1993

26 Sir Percy Cradock, former British ambassador to Peking, born 1923

27 Roy Lichenstein, US artist, born 1923

Charles Hawtrey, actor, died 1988

Sir Peter Quenell, writer and editor, died 1993

28 David Dimbleby, broadcaster, born 1938

William Rodgers, former Deputy President of the SDP and one of the original 'gang of four', born 1928

Dennis Taylor, snooker player, born 1948

29 Richard Dreyfuss, US actor, born 1948

Pietro Annigoni, painter, died 1988

At a summit in Brussels the 12 EC heads of government agreed that the European Monetary Institute should be based in Frankfurt and confirmed that economic and monetary union should be achieved by 1997 or 1999, 1993

30 The Bosphorus Bridge linking Europe and Asia opened by President Koruturk of Turkey, 1973

31 Raymond Novarro, film actor, died 1968

Frederico Fellini, Italian film-maker, died 1993

River Phoenix, film actor, died 1993

November

1 Victoria de los Angeles, Spanish lyric-soprano, born 1923

European Union established as Maastricht Treaty came into force, 1993

2 Sir John Daring, former chairman of the family merchant bank, born 1928

Paul Johnson, former author and editor of the *New Statesman*, born 1928

Peter Newsam, former chairman of the Commission for Racial Equality, born 1928

3 Lulu, pop singer and actress, born 1948

4 Lord Kitchener of Khartoum was presented with the Freedom of the City of London, 1898

Wilfred Owen, poet, killed in action, 1918

6 P.J. Proby, rock singer, born 1938

Richard Jeffries, author and naturalist, born 1848

7 Dr Billy Graham, US evangelist, born 1918

The *Sunday Mirror* published photographs of the Princess of Wales which were taken by a hidden camera while she was exercising in a London gym, 1993

Adelaide Hall, jazz singer, died 1993

8 Edward Goldsmith, ecologist, born 1928

The Beer Hall Putsch in Munich, marked the start of Hitler's rise to power, 1923

George Bush elected President of the USA, 1988

9 Spiro T. Agnew, former Vice-President of the USA, born 1918

The Prime Minister's speech at the Guildhall Banquet was broadcast by wireless for the first time, 1923

10 Kemal Ataturk, Turkish general, statesman, founder and first President of the Republic of Turkey, died 1938

Robert Carrier, US anglophile, born 1923

Sir Yue-Kong Pao, multi-millionaire Hong Kong shipping magnate, born 1918

Anne Shelton, singer and wartime forces sweetheart, born 1923

Launch of *The Post* by Eddy Shah, 1988

11 At the 11th hour on the 11th day of the 11th month in 1918, the Armistice that ended the First World War was signed

12 Hermione Baddeley, who first appeared on the London stage in 1918, born 1908

H.R. Haldeman (Harry), White House Chief of Staff under President Nixon and leading figure in the Watergate Scandal, died 1993

Jill Tweedie, journalist and author, died 1993

13 David Gower announced his retirement from cricket, 1993

14 Joe McCarthy, anti-Communist witch-hunting senator, born 1908

HRH Prince Charles, born 1948

Marriage of Princess Anne and Captain Mark Phillips, 1973

16 Burgess Meredith, US film actor, born 1908

17 General Sani Abacha replaced Ernest Shonekan as Head of State and Government in Nigeria in what was effectively a *coup d'etat*, 1993

The US House of Representatives approved the North American Free Trade Agreement, 1993

President de Klerk and Nelson Mandela ratified South Africa's first democratic constitution, 1993

18 Alan Shepherd, the first American in space (5 May 1961), born 1923

19 Auriol Sinclair, first official lady National Hunt trainer, born 1918

Christina Onassis, Greek ship owner, died 1988

20 Alistair Cooke, journalist and broadcaster and the BBC's commentator on US affairs since 1938, born 1908

21 René Magritte, surrealist painter, born 1898

Construction of the Forth Road Bridge began in 1958, the largest suspension bridge in Europe at the time

22 Anthony Burgess, novelist, essayist and composer, died 1993

23 Jerry Bock, composer, born 1928

The Mexican Senate ratified the North America Free Trade Agreement, 1993

24 Robert Thompson and Jon Venables, both 11 years old, were convicted of the murder of two-year-old James Bulger in February, 1993

25 Isaac Watts, hymn writer, died 1748

Upton Sinclair, American novelist and journalist, died 1968

Mauno Koivisto, former President of Finland, born 1923

27 Rodney Bewes, actor, born 1938

Walter Klein, Austrian concert pianist, born 1928

Chaim Weizmann became the first President of Israel, 1948

28 Claude Levi-Strauss, guru of anthropology, born 1908

Polaroid Land Camera, designed by Edwin Land, first marketed in Boston, 1948

29 David Rintoul, actor, born 1948

30 Efrem Zimbalist Jr, actor, born 1923

December

1 Keith Michell, actor, born 1928

David Ben-Gurion, first Prime Minister of Israel, died 1973

The electronics group Ferranti called in the receivers, 1993

Pablo Escobar, leader of the Medellin cocaine cartel, shot dead by Colombian police, 1993

2 Patricia Hewitt, Labour MP, born 1948

3 Trevor Bailey, former cricketer, born 1923

John Major and Albert Reynolds began talks in Northern Ireland, 1993

4 Frank Zappa, rock musician, died 1993

5 Miss Ethel Mary Charles was the first woman architect to qualify professionally in Britain. Elected an Associate Member of RIBA, 1898

Preston bypass, Britain's first section of motorway, officially opened, 1958

6 The first Labour woman MP, Susan Lawrence, elected for East Ham North, 1923

Keke Rosberg, former Finnish racing driver, born 1948

Don Ameche, film actor, died 1993

7 Gian Lorenzo Bernini, painter, sculptor and architect and designer of the colonnade of St Peter's Rome, born 1598

Noam Chomsky, inventor of transformational grammar, born 1928

Earthquake in Armenia measuring 6.9 on the Richter scale, 1988

The Transitional Executive Council was inaugurated in Cape Town, 1993

8 Paul Gauguin, artist, born 1848

Golda Meir, former Prime Minister of Israel, died 1978

President de Klerk was received in audience at Buckingham Palace; he was the first South African leader to meet the Queen since 1961, 1993

9 Joel Chandler Harris, creator of Brer Rabbit, born 1848

10 Louis Napoleon elected President of France, 1848

12 Connie Francis, singer, born 1938

Faulty installation of signalling was confirmed as the cause of the Clapham rail crash, 1988

13 Andy Peebles, DJ, born 1948

Edward Heath announced that industry would work a three-day week in the New Year to conserve energy, 1973

14 Women voted for the first time in a General Election in Britain, 1918

Myrna Loy, actress, died 1993

15 Michael Bogdanov, director, born 1938

Paul Getty III was freed after kidnappers received a ransom reported to be over £1 million, 1973

Downing Street Declaration was announced by John Major and Taoiseach Albert Reynolds on the future of Northern Ireland, 1993

18 Car bomb exploded in Horseferry Road, London, injuring 52 people, 1973

Sam Wanamaker, actor, director and founder of the Shakespeare Globe Trust, died 1993

19 Emily Brontë, novelist, died 1848

Gordon Jackson, actor, born 1923

Sir Anthony Buck, QC, born 1928

20 Uri Geller, bender of spoons, born 1948

John Steinbeck, writer, died 1968

21 PanAm jumbo jet crashed on Lockerbie killing 281 people. The cause is thought to have been a terrorist bomb, 1988

22 Noel Edmonds, TV personality, born 1948

23 The first Christmas edition of a magazine published, by the *Illustrated London News*, 1848

25 Karel Capek, playwright and novelist, died 1938

A 59-year-old British woman gave birth to twins after being implanted with a test-tube embryo in Italy, 1993

26 First Reith Lecture given: 'Authority and the Individual' by Bertrand Russell, 1948

27 Adam Mickiewicz, Polish poet, born 1798

29 First transatlantic radio broadcast: dance music from the Savoy Hotel was broadcast by WJZ in New York, 1923

Harvey Smith, former international show jumper, born 1938

30 Irving 'Swifty' Lazar, US literary and talent agent, died 1993

31 First broadcast of Big Ben's chimes to usher in the New Year, 1923

Sir Malcolm Campbell, racing motorist, died 1948

Former President Gamsakhurdia of Georgia committed suicide after the defeat of his rebellion in western Georgia, 1993

Government offices and public services

Enquiries, accompanied by a sae, should be sent to the Public Relations Officer. The names and addresses of many other public bodies can be found in Whitaker's Almanack.

Advertising Standards Authority
2 Torrington Place, London WC1E 7HW
tel 0171-580 5555 *fax* 0171-631 3051

AEA Technology
Harwell, Didcot, Oxon OX11 0RA
tel (01235) 821111 *fax* (01235) 432916

Agriculture, Fisheries and Food, Ministry of
3-8 Whitehall Place, London SW1A 2HH
Helpline (01645) 335577
tel 0171-270 3000 *fax* 0171-270 8125

Arts Council of England
14 Great Peter Street, London SW1P 3NQ
tel 0171-333 0100
Library/enquiry line 0171-973 6517
fax 0171-973 6590
e-mail information.ace@artsfb.org.uk
web site www.artscouncil.org.uk
For full details, see page 439.

Arts Council of Northern Ireland
185 Stranmillis Road, Belfast BT9 5DU
tel (01232) 381591 *fax* (01232) 661715

Arts Council, Scottish
12 Manor Place, Edinburgh EH3 7DD
tel 0131-226 6051 *fax* 0131-225 9833

Arts Council of Wales
9 Museum Place, Cardiff CF1 3NX
tel (01222) 394711 *fax* (01222) 221447

Australian High Commission
Australia House, Strand, London WC2B 4LA
tel 0171-379 4334 *fax* 0171-240 5333

Austrian Embassy
18 Belgrave Mews West, London SW1X 8HU
tel 0171-235 3731 *fax* 0171-344 0292

Bahamas High Commission
Bahamas House, 10 Chesterfield Street,
London W1X 8AH
tel 0171-408 4488 *fax* 0171-499 9937

Bangladesh High Commission
28 Queen's Gate, London SW7 5JA
tel 0171-584 0081-4 *fax* 0171-225 2130
e-mail bdesh-Lon@dial.pipex.com

The Bank of England
Threadneedle Street, London EC2R 8AH
tel 0171-601 4444

Barbados High Commission
1 Great Russell Street, London WC1B 3JY
tel 0171-631 4975 *fax* 0171-323 6872

Belgian Embassy
103 Eaton Square, London SW1W 9AB
tel 0171-470 3700 *fax* 0171-259 6213

Benefits Agency, Pensions and Overseas Benefits Directorate (POD) – see Social Security, Department of

Bodleian Library
Oxford OX1 3BG
tel (01865) 277000 *fax* (01865) 277182

Bosnia-Hercegovina, Embassy of
320 Regent Street, London W1R 5AB
tel 0171-255 3758 *fax* 0171-255 3760

Botswana High Commission
6 Stratford Place, London W1N 9AE
tel 0171-499 0031

British Broadcasting Corporation
Broadcasting House, London W1A 1AA
tel 0171-580 4468
web site http://www.bbc.co.uk

British Coal – see The Coal Authority

The British Council
10 Spring Gardens, London SW1A 2BN
tel 0171-930 8466 *fax* 0171-839 6347

British Film Commission
70 Baker Street, London W1M 1DJ
tel 0171-224 5000 *fax* 0171-224 1013

British Film Institute
21 Stephen Street, London W1P 2LN
tel 0171-255 1444 *fax* 0171-436 7950
web site www.bfi.org.uk

The British Library
96 Euston Road, London NW1 2DB
tel 0171-412 7111 *fax* 0171-412 7268

British Library
Document Supply Centre, Boston Spa, Wetherby,
West Yorkshire LS23 7BQ
tel (01937) 546060 *fax* (01937) 546333
e-mail dsc.customer.services@bl.uk

British Library Newspaper Library
Colindale Avenue, London NW9 5HE
tel 0171-412 7353 *fax* 0171-412 7379
e-mail newspaper@bl.uk
web site http://portico.bl.uk/newspaper

British Museum
Great Russell Street, London WC1B 3DG
tel 0171-636 1555 *fax* 0171-323 8118
e-mail pr-bm@mailbox.ulcc.ac.uk
web site http://www.britishmuseum.ac.uk

British Railways Board
Euston House, 24 Eversholt Street, PO Box 100,
London NW1 1DZ
tel 0171-928 5151 *fax* 0171-922 6545

British Standards Institution
Information Centre, 389 Chiswick High Road,
London W4 4AL
tel 0181-996 7111 *fax* 0181-996 7048

British Tourist Authority/English Tourist Board
Thames Tower, Black's Road, London W6 9EL
tel 0181-846 9000 *fax* 0181-563 0302
web site http://www.bta.org.uk

The Broadcasting Complaints Commission – see Broadcasting Standards Commission

Broadcasting Standards Commission
7 The Sanctuary, London SW1P 3JS
tel 0171-233 0544 *fax* 0171-222 3172

Bulgaria, Embassy of the Republic of
186-188 Queen's Gate, London SW7 5HL
tel 0171-584 9400/9433, 0171-581 3144 (5 lines)
fax 0171-584 4948

The Cabinet Office
70 Whitehall, London SW1A 2AS
tel 0171-270 1234

Cadw: Welsh Historic Monuments
Crown Building, Cathays Park, Cardiff CF1 3NQ
tel (01222) 500200 *fax* (01222) 826375

Canadian High Commission
Cultural Affairs Section, MacDonald House,
1 Grosvenor Square, London W1X 0AB
tel 0171-258 6366 *fax* 0171-258 6322

Central Office of Information
Hercules Road, London SE1 7DU
tel 0171-928 2345

In the UK conducts press, television, radio and poster advertising; produces booklets, leaflets, films, radio and television material, exhibitions and other visual material on behalf of other government organisations.

Central Statistical Office – now part of National Statistics, Office for

Centre for Information on Language Teaching and Research (CILT)
20 Bedfordbury, London WC2N 4LB
tel 0171-379 5101 *fax* 0171-379 5082
web site http://www.campus.bt.com/campusworld/pub/cilt

Supports the work of all professionals concerned with language teaching and learning throughout the UK, across every sector and stage of education. Offers a full conference programme, plus free on-site INSET for teachers, a complete range of publications and the CILT Teaching Resources Library with extensive IT and AV facilities. CILT also provides a comprehensive information service and knowledge of research and developmental activity

Charity Commission
St Alban's House, 57-60 Haymarket,
London SW1Y 4QX
tel 0171-210 4556 *fax* 0171-210 4545
2nd Floor, 20 King's Parade, Queen's Dock,
Liverpool L3 4DQ
tel 0151-703 1500 *fax* 0151-703 1555
Woodfield House, Tangier, Taunton,
Somerset TA1 4B1
tel (01823) 345000 *fax* (01823) 345003

The Coal Authority
200 Lichfield Lane, Mansfield, Notts. NG18 4RG
tel (01623) 427162 *fax* (01623) 22072

College of Arms (or Heralds' College)
Queen Victoria Street, London EC4V 4BT
tel 0171-248 2762 *fax* 0171-248 6448

The Commonwealth Institute
Kensington High Street, London W8 6NQ
tel 0171-603 4535 *fax* 0171-602 7374

e-mail info@commonwealth.org.uk
web site http://www.commonwealth.org.uk

For full details, see page 450.

Contributions Agency, International Services (InS) – see Social Security, Department of

Copyright Tribunal
Room 148, 25 Southampton Buildings,
London WC2A 1AY
tel 0171-438 4776 *fax* 0171-438 4780

Countryside Commission
John Dower House, Crescent Place, Cheltenham,
Glos. GL50 3RA
tel (01242) 521381 *fax* (01242) 584270

Court of the Lord Lyon
HM New Register House, Edinburgh EH1 3YT
tel 0131-556 7255 *fax* 0131-557 2148

Crafts Council
44A Pentonville Road, London N1 9BY
tel 0171-278 7700 *fax* 0171-837 6891
web site http://www.craftscouncil.org.uk

Exhibition gallery, picture library, reference library, reference service, shop, education workshop, café.

Croatia, Embassy of the Republic of
21 Conway Street, London W1P 5HL
tel 0171-387 1790 *fax* 0171-387 3289

Cyprus High Commission
93 Park Street, London W1Y 4ET
tel 0171-499 8272 *fax* 0171-491 0691

Czech Republic, Embassy of the
26 Kensington Palace Gardens, London W8 4QY
tel 0171-243 1115 *fax* 0171-727 9654

Royal Danish Embassy
55 Sloane Street, London SW1X 9SR
tel 0171-333 0200 *fax* 0171-333 0270

Data Protection Registrar, Office of the
Wycliffe House, Water Lane, Wilmslow,
Cheshire SK9 5AF
tel (01625) 545745(enquiries) (01625) 545700
(switchboard) *fax* (01625) 524510
e-mail data@wycliffe.demon.co.uk
web site http://www.open.gov.uk/dpr/dprhome.htm

Defence, Ministry of
Main Building, Whitehall, London SW1A 2HB
tel 0171-218 9000

The Design Council
Haymarket House, 1 Oxendon Street,
London SW1Y 4EE
tel 0171-208 2121 *fax* 0171-839 6033
web site www.design-council.org.uk

DTI: Department of Trade and Industry
1 Victoria Street, London SW1H 0ET
tel 0171-215 5000 (general enquiries)
fax 0171-222 2629
Business in Europe (0117) 944 4888
The Innovation Enquiry Line 0171-215 1217

Economic and Social Research Council
Polaris House, North Star Avenue, Swindon,
Wilts. SN2 1UJ
tel (01793) 413000 *fax* (01793) 413001
web site www.esrc.ac.uk

Education and Employment, Department for
Sanctuary Buildings, Great Smith Street,
London SW1P 3BT
tel 0171-925 5000 (switchboard) 0171-925 5555
(public enquiries)

Electricity & Gas Regulation Northern Ireland, Office of (OFREG)
Brookmount Buildings, 42 Fountain Street,
Belfast BT1 5EE
tel (01232) 311575 *fax* (01232) 311740

Electricity Regulation, Office of
Hagley House, Hagley Road, Edgbaston,
Birmingham B16 8QG
tel 0121-456 2100 *fax* 0121-456 4664

Engineering and Physical Sciences Research Council
Polaris House, North Star Avenue, Swindon,
Wilts. SN2 1ET
tel (01793) 444000 *fax* (01793) 444010
e-mail infoline@epsrc.ac.uk
web site http://www.epsrc.ac.uk

English Heritage
23 Savile Row, London W1X 1AB
tel 0171-973 3000 *fax* 0171-973 3001

English Regional Arts Boards
5 City Road, Winchester, Hants SO23 8SD
tel (01962) 851063 *fax* (01962) 842033
e-mail info.erab@artsfb.org.uk

Representative body for the 10 Regional Arts Boards in England; see page 470.

English Sports Council
16 Upper Woburn Place, London WC1H 0QP
tel 0171-273 1500 *fax* 0171-383 5740

The Environment Agency
Hampton House, 20 Albert Embankment,
London SE1 7TJ
tel 0171-587 3000 *fax* 0171-587 5258
Rio House, Waterside Drive, Aztec West,
Almondsbury, Bristol BS12 4UD
tel (01454) 624400 *fax* (01454) 624409

Carries out work formerly undertaken by

the National Rivers Authority, HM Inspectorate of Pollution, the waste regulation authorities and some technical units of the Dept of the Environment.

Environment, Department of the
Eland House, Bressenden Place, London SW1E 5DU
tel 0171-890 3000

Environment, Transport and the Regions Department of
76 Marsham Street, London SW1P 4DR
tel 0171-271 4800

Equal Opportunities Commission
Overseas House, Quay Street, Manchester M3 3HN
tel 0161-833 9244 *fax* 0161-835 1657

The European Commission
8 Storey's Gate, London SW1P 3AT
tel 0171-973 1992 *fax* 0171-973 1900

European Parliament
UK Office 2 Queen Anne's Gate, London SW1H 9AA
tel 0171-227 4300 *fax* 0171-227 4302
library fax 0171-227 4301
web site http://www.europarl.eu.int
http://www.cec.org.uk

Fair Trading, Office of
Field House, 15-25 Bream's Buildings, London EC4A 1PR
tel 0171-242 2858 *fax* 0171-269 8800
e-mail enquiries @oftuk.demon.co.uk

Finland, Embassy of
38 Chesham Place, London SW1W 8HW
tel 0171-838 6200 *fax* 0171-235 3860 (general)
0171-259 5602 (press and information)

Foreign and Commonwealth Office
King Charles Street, London SW1A 2AL
tel 0171-270 3000

Forestry Commission
231 Corstorphine Road, Edinburgh EH12 7AT
tel 0131-334 0303 *fax* 0131-334 4473

French Embassy
58 Knightsbridge, London SW1X 7JT
tel 0171-201 1000
Cultural Department 23 Cromwell Road, London SW7 2EL
tel 0171-838 2055

Gambia High Commission
57 Kensington Court, London W8 5DG
tel 0171-937 6316/7/8 *fax* 0171-937 9095

Gas Supply, Office of (OFGAS)
Stockley House, 130 Wilton Road, London SW1V 1LQ
tel 0171-828 0898 *fax* 0171-932 1600

General Register Office – now part of the National Statistics, Office for

German Embassy
23 Belgrave Square, London SW1X 8PZ
tel 0171-824 1300 *fax* 0171-824 1435
e-mail mail@german-embassy.org.uk
web site http://www.german-embassy.org.uk

Ghana, High Commission for
104 Highgate Hill, London N6 5HE
tel 0181-342 8686 *fax* 0181-342 8566

Government Offices for the Regions
23rd Floor, Portland House, Stag Place, London SW1E 5DF
tel 0171-890 3000 *fax* 0171-890 5019
Combination of the former regional offices of the Depts of the Environment, Trade and Industry, Education and Employment, and Transport. Established April 1994.

Greece, Embassy of
Press and Information Office, 1A Holland Park, London W11 3TP
tel 0171-727 3071 *fax* 0171-727 8960

Guyana High Commission
3 Palace Court, Bayswater Road, London W2 4LP
tel 0171-229 7684 *fax* 0171-727 9809

Hayward Gallery
Belvedere Road, London SE1 8XZ
tel 0171-928 3144 *fax* 0171-401 2664

Health, Department of
Richmond House, 79 Whitehall, London SW1A 2NS
tel 0171-210 3000

Health and Safety Executive
Rose Court, 2 Southwark Bridge, London SE1 9HS
tel (0541) 545500 *fax* 0114-289 2333
web site http://www.open.gov.uk/hte/hsehome.htm

Historic Scotland
Longmore House, Salisbury Place, Edinburgh EH9 1SH
tel 0131-668 8600 *fax* 0131-668 8888

HMSO Books – see The Stationery Office

Home Office
Queen Anne's Gate, London SW1H 9AT
tel 0171-273 4000
Director, Communication M.S.D. Granatt

Housing Corporation
149 Tottenham Court Road, London W1P 0BN
tel 0171-393 2000 *fax* 0171-393 2111

Hungary, Embassy of the Republic of
35 Eaton Place, London SW1X 8BY
tel 0171-235 4048/7191 *fax* 0171-823 1348

Independent Television Commission
33 Foley Street, London W1P 7LB
tel 0171-255 3000 *fax* 0171-306 7800

High Commission of India, Press & Information Wing
India House, Aldwych, London WC2B 4NA
tel 0171-836 8484 ext 147, 286, 327
fax 0171-836 2632
e-mail 106167.1470@compuserve.com

Inland Revenue, Board of
Somerset House, London WC2R 1LB
Library tel 0171-438 6648 *fax* 0171-438 7562

International Services (InS) – see Social Security, Department of

Ireland, Embassy of
17 Grosvenor Place, London SW1X 7HR
tel 0171-235 2171 *fax* 0171-245 6961

Israel, Embassy of
2 Palace Green, London W8 4QB
tel 0171-957 9500 *fax* 0171-957 9555
e-mail isr-info@dircon.co.uk
web site http://www.israel-embassy.org.uk/london/

Italian Embassy
14 Three Kings Yard, Davies Street,
London W1Y 2EH
tel 0171-312 2200 *fax* 0171-312 2230

Jamaican High Commission
1-2 Prince Consort Road, London SW7 2BZ
tel 0171-823 9911 *fax* 0171-589 5154

Japan, Embassy of
101-104 Piccadilly, London W1V 9FN
tel 0171-465 6500 *fax* 0171-491 9347 (information)
0171-491 9348 (other departments)
e-mail jicc@jicc.demon.co.uk
web site http://www.embjapan.org.uk

Kenya High Commission
45 Portland Place, London W1N 4AS
tel 0171-636 2371 *fax* 0171-323 6717

HM Land Registry
Lincoln's Inn Fields, London WC2A 3PH
tel 0171-917 8888 *fax* 0171-955 0110
web site http://www.open.gov.uk/landreg/
home.htm
Head of Information Eric Davies

Law Commission
Conquest House, 37-38 John Street,
Theobalds Road, London WC1N 2BQ
tel 0171-453 1220 *fax* 0171-453 1297
Covers England and Wales.

Law Commission, Scottish
140 Causewayside, Edinburgh EH9 1PR
tel 0131-668 2131 *fax* 0131-662 4900

The Legal Deposit Office
The British Library, Boston Spa, Wetherby,
West Yorkshire LS23 7BY
tel (01937) 546267/546268 *fax* (01937) 546176

Legal Services Ombudsman, Office of the
22 Oxford Court, Oxford Street,
Manchester M2 3WQ
tel 0161-236 9532 *fax* 0161-236 2651

Lesotho, High Commission of the Kingdom of
7 Chesham Place, London SW1 8HN
tel 0171-235 5686 *fax* 0171-235 5023

London Museum – see Museum of London

London Records Office, Corporation of
Guildhall, London EC2P 2EJ
tel 0171-332 1251 *fax* 0171-332 1119

London Transport
55 Broadway, London SW1H 0BD
tel 0171-222 5600 (administration) 0171-222 1234
(travel information) *fax* 0171-222 5719

Luxembourg, Embassy of
27 Wilton Crescent, London SW1X 8SD
tel 0171-235 6961 *fax* 0171-235 9734

Malawi High Commission
33 Grosvenor Street, London W1X 0DE
tel 0171-491 4172/7 *fax* 0171-491 9916

Malaysian High Commission
45 Belgrave Square, London SW1X 8QT
tel 0171-235 8033 *fax* 0171-235 5161

Malta High Commission
Malta House, 36-38 Piccadilly, London W1V 0PQ
tel 0171-292 4800 *fax* 0171-734 1831

Mauritius, High Commission for the Republic of
32-33 Elvaston Place, London SW7 5NW
tel 0171-581 0294/5 *fax* 0171-823 8437
Commercial Section
tel 0171-225 3331 *fax* 0171-225 1580
Tourist Information
tel 0171-584 3666 *fax* 0171-823 8437

Medical Research Council
20 Park Crescent, London W1N 4AL
tel 0171-636 5422 *fax* 0171-436 6179
e-mail firstname.surname@hq.mrc.ac.uk
web site http://www.nimr.mrc.ac.uk

Millennium Commission
Portland House, Stag Place, London SW1E 5EZ
tel 0171-880 2001 *fax* 0171-880 2000

Monopolies and Mergers Commission
New Court, 48 Carey Street, London WC2A 2JT
tel 0171-324 1467/8 *fax* 0171-324 1400

Museum of London
London Wall, London EC2Y 5HN
tel 0171-600 3699 *fax* 0171-600 1058

Comprises the collections of the London Museum and the Guildhall Museum.

Museum of Mankind
6 Burlington Gardens, London W1X 2EX
tel 0171-323 8043 (information)
fax 0171-323 8013

Ethnography Department of the British Museum. Closing 31 December 1997.

Museum of the Moving Image
South Bank, London SE1 8XT
tel 0171-928 3535 *fax* 0171-815 1419

National Audit Office
157-197 Buckingham Palace Road,
London SW1W 9SP
tel 0171-798 7000 *fax* 0171-828 3774
e-mail nao@gtnet.gov.uk
22 Melville Street, Edinburgh EH3 7NS
tel 0131-244 2736 *fax* 0131-244 2721
Audit House, 23-24 Park Place, Cardiff CF1 3BA
tel (01222) 378661 *fax* (01222) 388415

Provides independent information, advice and assurance to Parliament and the public about all aspects of the financial operations of government departments and many other bodies receiving public funds.

National Consumer Council
20 Grosvenor Gardens, London SW1W 0DH
tel 0171-730 3469 *fax* 0171-730 0191

National Gallery
Trafalgar Square, London WC2N 5DN
tel 0171-839 3321, 0171-747 2885 (general information) *Press Office fax* 0171-930 4764

National Heritage, Department of
2-4 Cockspur Street, London SW1Y 5DH
tel 0171-211 6000 *fax* 0171-211 6270

National Lottery, Office of the (OFLOT)
2 Monck Street, London SW1P 2BQ
tel 0171-227 2000 *fax* 0171-227 2005

National Maritime Museum
Greenwich, London SE10 9NF
tel 0181-858 4422 *fax* 0181-312 6632

Information also for the Queen's House and the Old Royal Observatory.

National Savings
Marketing Division, Charles House,
375 Kensington High Street, London W14 8SD
tel 0171-605 9300 *fax* 0171-605 9432/9481
web site http://www.open.gov.uk/ns

National Statistics, Office for
1 Drummond Gate, London SW1V 2QQ
tel 0171-533 5725 (economic statistics); 0171-533 5702 (social statistics) *fax* 0171-533 5719

Natural Environment Research Council
Polaris House, North Star Avenue, Swindon,
Wilts. SN2 1EU
tel (01793) 411500 *fax* (01793) 411501

The Natural History Museum
Cromwell Road, London SW7 5BD
tel 0171-938 9123 *fax* 0171-938 9290

Royal Netherlands Embassy
38 Hyde Park Gate, London SW7 5DP
tel 0171-590 3200
Press and Cultural Affairs fax 0171-581 0053

New Zealand High Commission
New Zealand House, Haymarket,
London SW1Y 4TQ
tel 0171-930 8422 *fax* 0171-839 4580

Nigeria High Commission
Nigeria House, 9 Northumberland Avenue,
London WC2N 5BX
tel 0171-839 1244 *fax* 0171-839 8746

Northern Ireland Office
Whitehall, London SW1A 2AZ
tel 0171-210 3000
Stormont Castle, Belfast BT4 3ST
tel (01232) 520700
web site http://www.nio.gov.uk/index.htm

Northern Ireland Tourist Board
59 North Street, Belfast, Northern Ireland BT1 1NB
tel (01232) 231221 *fax* (01232) 240960
e-mail general.enquiries.nilb@nics.gov.uk

Royal Norwegian Embassy
25 Belgrave Square, London SW1X 8QD
tel 0171-591 5500 *fax* 0171-245 6993
e-mail embassy@embassy.norway.org.uk

Oftel – see Telecommunications, Office of

OFWAT – see Water Services, Office of

Ordnance Survey
Romsey Road, Maybush,
Southampton SO16 4GU
tel (01703) 792000 *fax* (01703) 792452
Press Officer tel (01703) 792635

Particle Physics and Astronomy Research Council
Polaris House, North Star Avenue, Swindon,
Wilts. SN2 1SZ
tel (01793) 442000 *fax* (01793) 442002
e-mail pr_pus@pparc.ac.uk

Patent Office
General enquiries (designs, patents, trade marks)
Concept House, Cardiff Road, Newport,
South Wales NP9 1RH
tel (0645) 500505 *text phone* (0645) 222250
e-mail enquiries@patent.gov.uk
Copyright enquiries Copyright Directorate, The
Patent Office, Hazlitt House, 25 Southampton
Buildings, Chancery Lane, London WC2A 1AR
tel 0171-438 4777
e-mail copyright@patent.gov.uk

Pensions Ombudsman, The
11 Belgrave Road, London SW1V 1RB
tel 0171-834 9144 *fax* 0171-821 0065

Pensions and Overseas Benefits Directorate (POD) – see Social Security, Department of

PLR Office
Bayheath House, Prince Regent Street,
Stockton-on-Tees TS18 1DF
tel (01642) 604699 *fax* (01642) 615641
e-mail registrar@plr.octacon.co.uk
web site http://www.earl.org.uk/earl/members/plr/
Enquiries Registrar of Public Lending Right

Poland, Embassy of the Republic of
47 Portland Place, London W1N 4JH
tel 0171-580 4324 *fax* 0171-323 4018
e-mail pol-emb@dircon.co.uk
web site http://www.poland-embassy.org.uk/
Polish Cultural Institute
34 Portland Place, London W1N 4HQ
tel 0171-636 6032 *fax* 0171-637 2190

Police Complaints Authority
10 Great George Street, London SW1P 3AE
tel 0171-273 6450 *fax* 0171-273 6401
web site www.coi.gov.uk/coi/depts/deptlist.html

Population Census and Surveys, Office of – now Office for National Statistics

Portuguese Embassy
11 Belgrave Square, London SW1X 8PP
tel 0171-235 5331 *fax* 0171-245 1287 and
0171-235 0739

Post Office Headquarters
5th Floor, 148 Old Street, London EC1V 9HQ
tel 0171-490 2888

Privy Council Office
Whitehall, London SW1A 2AT
tel 0171-270 3000

Public Record Office
Ruskin Avenue, Kew, Richmond, Surrey TW9 4DU
tel 0181-876 3444 *fax* 0181-878 8905
Records of Government Departments and
central courts of law.

Public Service, Office of (OPS)
Horse Guards Road, London SW1P 3AL
70 Whitehall, London SW1A 2AS
tel 0171-270 1234

Public Trust Office
Stewart House, 24 Kingsway, London WC2B 6JX
tel 0171-269 7000 *fax* 0171-831 0060

Racial Equality, Commission for
Elliot House, 10-12 Allington Street,
London SW1E 5EH
tel 0171-828 7022 *fax* 0171-931 0429

The Radio Authority
Holbrook House, 14 Great Queen Street,
London WC2B 5DG
tel 0171-430 2724 *fax* 0171-405 7062

Regional Arts Boards – see English Regional Arts Boards

Romania, Embassy of
4 Palace Green, London W8 4QD
tel 0171-937 9666 *fax* 0171-937 8069
e-mail romania@roemb.demon.uk.co

Royal Commission on the Ancient and Historical Monuments of Scotland
(with National Monuments Record of Scotland)
John Sinclair House, 16 Bernard Terrace,
Edinburgh EH8 9NX
tel 0131-662 1456 *fax* 0131-662 1477/1499
e-mail rcahms.jsh@gtnet.gov.uk

Royal Commission on the Ancient and Historical Monuments of Wales
(with National Monuments Record of Wales)
Crown Building, Plas Crug, Aberystwyth,
Ceredigion SY23 1NJ
tel (01970) 621200 *fax* (01970) 627701

Royal Commission on Historical Manuscripts
Quality House, Quality Court, Chancery Lane,
London WC2A 1HP
tel 0171-242 1198 *fax* 0171-831 3550
e-mail nra@hmc.gov.uk
web site http://www.hmc.gov.uk

Royal Commission on the Historical Monuments of England
(with National Monuments Record)
National Monuments Record Centre,
Kemble Drive, Swindon, Wilts. SN2 2GZ
tel (01793) 414700 *fax* (01793) 414707
e-mail info@rchme.gov.uk
web site http://www.rchme.gov.uk

Royal Fine Art Commission
7 St James's Square, London SW1Y 4JU
tel 0171-839 6537 *fax* 0171-839 8475

Royal Fine Art Commission for Scotland
Bakehouse Close, 146 Canongate,
Edinburgh EH8 8DD
tel 0131-556 6699 *fax* 0131-556 6633

Royal Mint
Llantrisant, Pontyclun,
Mid-Glamorgan CF72 8YT
tel (01443) 222111

Royal National Theatre Board
South Bank, London SE1 9PX
tel 0171-928 2033 *fax* 0171-620 1197
e-mail rnteduc@gn.apc.org (education department)
Chairman Christopher Hogg

Russian Federation, Embassy of the
13 Kensington Palace Gardens,
London W8 4QX
tel 0171-229 3628 *fax* 0171-727 8625

Science and Technology, Office of
Department of Trade and Industry, Albany House,
Petty France, London SW1H 9ST
tel 0171-271 2000

Science Museum
Exhibition Road, London SW7 2DD
tel 0171-938 8000
Information Desk tel 0171-938 8080/8008
Press Office tel 0171-938 8188/8181
fax 0171-938 9790
web site http://www.nmsi.ac.uk

Scotland, National Galleries of
National Gallery of Scotland
The Mound, Edinburgh EH2 2EL
Scottish National Portrait Gallery
1 Queen Street, Edinburgh EH2 1JD
Scottish National Gallery of Modern Art
Belford Road, Edinburgh EH4 3DR
tel 0131-556 8921 *fax* 0131-556 9972 or
0131-343 3250 (press office)

Scotland, National Library of
George IV Bridge, Edinburgh EH1 1EW
tel 0131-226 4531 *fax* 0131-220 6662
e-mail enquiries@nls.uk
web site www.nls.uk

Scottish Natural Heritage
12 Hope Terrace, Edinburgh EH9 2AS
tel 0131-447 4784 *Press Office fax* 0131-446 2279

The Scottish Office
Dover House, Whitehall, London SW1A 2AU
tel 0171-270 3000

The Scottish Office Information Directorate
St Andrew's House, Edinburgh EH1 3DG
tel 0131-244 1111
Dover House, Whitehall, London SW1A 2AU
tel 0171-270 6744

Scottish Record Office
HM General Register House, Edinburgh EH1 3YY
tel 0131-535 1314 *fax* 0131-535 1360

Scottish Tourist Board
Thistle House, Beechwood Park North,
Inverness IV2 3ED
tel (01463) 716996 *fax* (01463) 717299

The Security Service (MI5)
PO Box 3255, London SW1P 1AE

Serpentine Gallery
Kensington Gardens, London W2 3XA
tel 0171-402 6075/0343 *fax* 0171-402 4103
Recorded information 0171-723 9072
International exhibitions of modern and contemporary art.

Seychelles High Commission
2nd Floor, Eros House, 111 Baker Street,
London W1M 1FE
tel 0171-224 1660 *fax* 0171-487 5756

Sierra Leone High Commission
33 Portland Place, London W1N 3AG
tel 0171-636 6483-5 *fax* 0171-323 3159

Singapore High Commission
9 Wilton Crescent, London SW1X 8SA
tel 0171-235 8315 *fax* 0171-245 6583

Slovak Republic, Embassy of the
25 Kensington Palace Gardens, London W8 4QY
tel 0171-243 0803 *fax* 0171-727 5824

Slovenia, Embassy of
Suite One, Cavendish Court,
11-15 Wigmore Street, London W1H 9LA
tel 0171-495 7775 *fax* 0171-495 7776

Social Security, Department of
POD at DSS, Benefits Agency, Tyneview Park,
Newcastle Upon Tyne NE98 1BA
tel 0191-218 7777 *fax* 0191-218 7293
web site a.grant@tvp001.dss.gov.uk
InS at DSS, Contributions Agency, Longbenton,
Newcastle Upon Tyne NE98 1BA
tel (0645) 154 811 *fax* (0645) 157 800
e-mail a.moy@new040.dss.gov.uk
web site www.open.gov.uk/dssca/cahome.htm
Contact Benefits Agency, Pensions and Overseas Benefits Directorate (POD) for queries about benefits being paid abroad, and Contributions Agency, International Services (InS) for queries about working abroad and paying National Insurance contributions.

South Africa, Republic of
South African High Commission, South Africa
House, Trafalgar Square, London WC2N 5DP
tel 0171-451 7299 *fax* 0171-451 7283/7284

Spanish Embassy
39 Chesham Place, London SW1X 8SB
tel 0171-235 5555 *fax* 0171-259 5392

Sri Lanka, High Commission of the Democratic Socialist Republic of
13 Hyde Park Gardens, London W2 2LU
tel 0171-262 1841 *fax* 0171-262 7970

Standards in Education, Office for (OFSTED)
Alexandra House, 33 Kingsway,
London WC2B 6SE
tel 0171-421 6800 *fax* 0171-421 6707

The Stationery Office
St Crispins, Duke Street, Norwich NR3 1PD
tel 0171-873 0011

Swaziland High Commission
20 Buckingham Gate, London SW1E 6LB
tel 0171-630 6611 *fax* 0171-630 6564

Sweden, Embassy of
11 Montagu Place, London W1H 2AL
tel 0171-724 2101 *fax* 0171-724 4174
Cultural Section fax 0171-917 6477

Swiss Embassy
16-18 Montagu Place, London W1H 2BQ
tel 0171-616 6000 *fax* 0171-724 7001

Tanzania High Commission
43 Hertford Street, London W1Y 8DB
tel 0171-499 8951 *fax* 0171-491 9321

Tate Gallery
Millbank, London SW1P 4RG
tel 0171-887 8000 *fax* 0171-887 8007
Albert Dock, Liverpool L3 4BB
tel 0151-709 3223
Porthmeor Beach, St Ives, Cornwall TR26 1TG
tel (01736) 796226

Telecommunications, Office of
50 Ludgate Hill, London EC4M 7JJ
tel 0171-634 8700 *fax* 0171-634 8943

Theatre Museum
National Museum of the Performing Arts,
1E Tavistock Street, London WC2E 7PA
tel 0171-836 7891 *fax* 0171-836 5148
See page 418 for reprographic services.

HM Treasury
Parliament Street, London SW1P 3AG
tel 0171-270 5000
Press Office tel 0171-270 5238 *fax* 0171-270 5244
Public Enquiry Unit tel 0171-270 4860

Trinidad and Tobago High Commission
42 Belgrave Square, London SW1X 8NT
tel 0171-245 9351 *fax* 0171-823 1065
e-mail trintogov@tthc.demon.co.uk

Trinity House, Corporation of
Tower Hill, London EC3N 4DH
tel 0171-480 6601 *fax* 0171-480 7662
The General Lighthouse Authority for England, Wales and the Channel Islands and a Deep Sea Pilotage Authority.

Turkish Embassy
43 Belgrave Square, London SW1X 8PA
tel 0171-393 0202 *fax* 0171-393 0066

Uganda High Commission
Uganda House, 58-59 Trafalgar Square,
London WC2N 5DX
tel 0171-839 5783 *fax* 0171-839 8925

United States Embassy
24 Grosvenor Square, London W1A 1AE
tel 0171-499 9000
web site http://www.usembassy.org.uk

Victoria and Albert Museum
South Kensington, London SW7 2RL
tel 0171-938 8500 *fax* 0171-938 8379

Visiting Arts Office of Great Britain and Northern Ireland
11 Portland Place, London W1N 4EJ
tel 0171-389 3015 *fax* 0171-389 3016
web site http://www.britcoun.org/visitingarts/
Director T. Sandell

Vocational Qualifications, National Council for
222 Euston Road, London NW1 2BZ
tel 0171-387 9898 *fax* 0171-387 0978

Wales, The National Library of
Aberystwyth, Dyfed SY23 3BU
tel (01970) 623816 *fax* (01970) 615709
e-mail glenwen.jones@llgc.org.uk

Wales Tourist Board
Brunel House, 2 Fitzalan Road, Cardiff CF2 1UY
tel (01222) 499909 *fax* (01222) 485031

Water Services, Office of (OFWAT)
Centre City Tower, 7 Hill Street,
Birmingham B5 4UA
tel 0121-625 1300 *fax* 0121-625 1400
web site http://www.open.gov.uk/ofwat

Wellington Museum
Apsley House, 149 Piccadilly, London W1V 9FA
tel 0171-499 5676 *fax* 0171-493 6576
web site http://www.vam.ac.uk/apsley/welcome.html
Open Tues-Sun, 11.00am-17.00pm.

Welsh Office
Gwydyr House, Whitehall, London SW1A 2ER
tel 0171-270 0565 *fax* 0171-270 0577
Cathays Park, Cardiff, CF1 3NQ
tel (01222) 825111 *fax* (01222) 823807

West India Committee (The Caribbean)
Nelson House, 8-9 Northumberland Street,
London WC2N 5RA
tel 0171-976 1493 *fax* 0171-976 1541

Women's National Commission
6th Floor, Adelphi, 1-11 John Adam Street,
London WC2 6HT
tel 0171-712 2462 *tel* 0121-626 2018 (media
enquiries) *fax* 0121-626 2041 (media enquiries)

An independent advisory committee to
the Government with the remit to ensure
that the informed opinions of women are
given their due weight in the delibera-
tions of the Government.

**Yugoslavia, Embassy of the Federal
Republic of**
5-7 Lexham Gardens, London W8 5JJ
tel 0171-370 6105 *fax* 0171-370 3838

Zambia High Commission
2 Palace Gate, London W8 5NG
tel 0171-589 6655 *fax* 0171-581 1353

**Zimbabwe, High Commission of the
Republic of**
Zimbabwe House, 429 Strand, London WC2R 0SA
tel 0171-836 7755 *fax* 0171-379 1167

Publishing practice

Publishing agreements

Publisher's agreements are not a standard form. Before signing one, the author must check it carefully, taking nothing for granted. **Michael Legat** *navigates the reader through this complex document.*

Any author, presented with so complex a document as a publisher's agreement, should read it carefully before signing, making sure that every clause is understood, and not taking anything for granted. Bear in mind that there is no such thing as a standard form. A given publisher's 'standard' contract may not only differ substantially from those of other publishers, but will often vary from author to author and from book to book. Don't be fooled into believing that it is a standard form because it appears to have been printed – each agreement can be individually produced on a word processor to give exactly that effect.

A fair and reasonable agreement

You should be able to rely on your agent, if you have one, to check the agreement for you, or – if you are a member – you can get it vetted by the Society of Authors or the Writers' Guild of Great Britain. But if you are on your own, you must either go to one of the solicitors who specialise in publishing business (probably expensive) or Do It Yourself. In the latter case it will help to compare the contract you have been offered, clause by clause, with a typical Minimum Terms Agreement such as those printed in my own books, *An Author's Guide to Publishing* and *Understanding Publishers' Contracts*.

Minimum Terms Agreement

The Minimum Terms Agreement (MTA), developed jointly by the Society of Authors and the Writers' Guild, is signed by a publisher on the one hand and the Society and the Guild on the other. It is not an agreement between a publisher and an individual author. It commits the publisher to offering his or her authors terms which are at least as good as those in the MTA. The intention is that only members of the Society and Guild should be eligible for this special treatment, but in practice publishers who sign the agreement tend to offer its terms to all their authors. There is no standard MTA, and most signatory publishers have insisted on certain variations in the agreement; nevertheless, the more important basic principles have always been accepted. It must be pointed out that the MTA does not usually apply to:

- books in which illustrations take up 40% or more of the space;
- specialist works on the visual arts in which illustrations fill 25% or more of the space;
- books involving three or more participants in royalties; or
- technical books, manuals and reference books.

Since its origins in 1980, comparatively few publishers have signed a Minimum Terms Agreement, although the signatories include several major publishing houses. Some publishers have refused, claiming to treat their authors quite well enough already, while others say that each author and each book is so different that standard terms cannot be laid down. Nonetheless, the MTA has been a resounding success. Almost all non-signatory publishers have adopted some or all of its provisions, and even in the case of

the excluded books mentioned above, the terms have tended to improve. All authors can now argue, from a position of some strength, that their own agreements should meet the MTA's standards.

The provisions of the MTA

The MTA is a royalty agreement (usually the most satisfactory form for an author), and it lays down the minimum acceptable royalties on sales, and the levels at which the rate should rise. These royalties are expressed as percentages of the book's retail price but can easily be adjusted to apply to royalties based on price received, a system to which a number of publishers are changing, increasing the percentages so that the author's earnings are not adversely affected. The MTA also covers the size of the advance (calculated in accordance with the expected initial print quantity and retail price), and recommended splits between publisher and author of moneys from the sale of subsidiary rights (including US and translation rights).

However, the MTA is not by any means concerned solely with money, but with fairness to the author in all clauses of a publishing agreement, special attention being paid to provisions designed to make the author/publisher relationship more of a partnership than it has often been in the past. While recognising the publisher's right to take final decisions on such matters as print quantity, publication date, retail price, jacket or cover design, wording of the blurb, promotion and publicity, and remaindering, the MTA insists that the author has a right to consultation (which should not be an empty formality but should mean that serious consideration is given to his or her views), in all such cases. Also the author's approval must be sought for the sale of any subsidiary rights.

Some essential clauses

Any publisher's agreement you sign should contain, in addition to acceptable financial terms, clauses covering:

- **Rights licensed.** A clear definition of which rights you are licensing to the publisher. The publisher will normally require volume rights but the agreement must specify whether such rights will apply in all languages (or perhaps only in English) and throughout the world (or only in an agreed list of territories). The duration of the publisher's licence should be spelt out; commonly this is for the period of copyright (currently the author's lifetime plus 70 years), although some publishers now accept a shorter term. A list of those subsidiary rights of which control is granted to the publisher must be included (make sure that the splits of moneys earned from these rights are in accordance with, or approximate reasonably to, those in the MTA, especially in the currently growing area of merchandising). Because the development of non-traditional forms of publishing, such as the Internet, continues to be so rapid, it may be advisable for the author not to grant the publisher control of electronic and multimedia rights, or of any additional rights as yet unknown resulting from advances in technology, but to reserve them, allowing the split of income from such sources to be negotiated as and when their sale occurs.
- **Publication date.** Commitment by the publisher to publication of the book by a specific date (usually within a year or 18 months from the delivery of the typescript). Avoid signing an agreement which is vague on this point, saying, for instance, only that the book will be published 'within a reasonable period'.
- **Copyright.** Confirmation that in all copies of the book the publisher will print a copyright notice in the author's name and a statement that the author has asserted his or her 'Right of Paternity' (the right to be identified as the author in future exploitation of the material in any form), and that a similar commitment will be required from any subsidiary licensee.
- **Fees and permissions.** Clarification, if the book is to include a professionally prepared index or material the copyright of which does not belong to the author,

of whether the author or the publisher will be responsible for the fees (or if costs are to be shared, in what proportions) and the clearance of permissions.

• **Acceptable accounting procedures.** Most publishers divide the year into two six-month periods, accounting to the author, and paying any sums due, three months after the end of each period. Look askance at any less frequent accounting or longer delay after the royalty period. The publisher should also agree to pay the author the due share of any subsidiary moneys promptly on receipt, provided that the advance on the book has been earned.

• **Termination.** A clear definition of the various conditions under which the agreement shall be terminated, with reversion of rights to the author.

Clauses to question

You can question anything in a publisher's agreement before you sign it. Provided that you do so politely and are not just being difficult, the publisher should be prepared to answer every query, to explain, and where possible to meet your objections. Most publishing contracts are not designed to exploit the author unfairly, but you should watch out for:

• **Rights assigned elsewhere.** It is unwise to accept a clause which allows the publisher to assign the rights in your book to another firm or person without your approval.

• **Non-publication.** The contract for a commissioned book often includes wording which alludes to the publisher's acceptance of the work, implying that there is no obligation to publish it if he or she deems it unacceptable. It may be understandable that the publisher wants an escape route in case the author turns in an inferior work, but he or she should be obliged to justify the rejection, and to give the author an opportunity to revise the work to bring it up to standard. If, having accepted the book, the publisher then wishes to cancel the contract prior to publication, the author can usually expect to receive financial compensation,

which should be non-returnable even if the book is subsequently placed with another publisher. However, this point is not normally covered in a publishing agreement.

• **Sole publisher.** Some agreements prohibit the author from writing similar material for any other publisher. This may clearly affect the author's earning ability.

• **Editing consultation.** Don't agree to the publisher's right to edit your work without any requirement for him or her to obtain your approval of any changes made.

• **Royalty rate.** While it is normal practice for an agreement to allow the publisher to pay a lower royalty on books which are sold at high trade discounts, the disappearance of the Net Book Agreement increases the likelihood of such sales, and you should therefore make sure the royalty rate on high discount sales is not unfairly low.

• **Future books.** The Society of Authors and the Writers' Guild are both generally opposed to clauses giving the publisher the right to publish the author's next work, feeling that this privilege should be earned by the publisher's handling of the earlier book. If you accept an option clause, at least make sure that it leaves all terms for a future book to be agreed.

Joint and multiple authorship

In the case of joint authorship (a work so written that the individual contributions of the authors cannot be readily separated), the first written agreement should be between the authors themselves, setting out the proportions in which any moneys earned by the book will be split, specifying how the authors' responsibilities are to be shared, and especially laying down the procedure to be adopted should the authors ever find themselves in dispute. The terms of any publishing agreement which they sign (each author having an identical copy) should reflect their joint understanding. The total earnings should not be less than would be paid were the book by a single author, and the authors

should have normal rights of consultation.

In the case of multiple authorship (when the work of each contributor can be clearly separated), each author is likely to have an individual contract, and may not be aware of what terms are offered to the others involved. Because of the possibility of disagreement between the authors, the publisher will probably offer little in the way of consultation. All the individual author can do is to ensure that the agreement appears to be fair in relation to the amount of work contributed, and that the author's responsibilities indicated by the contract refer only to his or her work.

Outright sale

As a general rule no author should agree to surrender his or her copyright to the publisher, although this may be unavoidable in the case of a book with many contributors, such as an encyclopedia. Even then, give up your copyright with great reluctance and only after an adequate explanation from the publisher of why you should (and probably a substantial financial inducement). The agreement itself will probably be no more than a brief and unequivocal letter.

The Net Book Agreement

In the autumn of 1995 a small number of publishers decided no longer to enforce the provisions of the Net Book Agreement (NBA), which required booksellers to adhere to the published price of books fixed by the publisher and shown on the jacket or cover. Other publishers followed this lead, and the NBA was swiftly abandoned so that, with a very few exceptions, booksellers in the UK are now free to offer discounts on the published price of the books they sell. It was predicted that sales of books generally would rise (which does not appear to have happened except in supermarkets) and that many independent booksellers would be forced out of business (which has not occurred as frequently as expected). The main results of the disappearance of the NBA would seem to be an all-round rise in recommended retail prices – although books are of course still cheap – and an increase in sales by publishers at high discounts, mostly affecting bestsellers.

Subsidies and vanity publishing

Few commercial publishers will be interested in publishing your book on a subsidy basis (i.e. with a contribution from you towards costs), unless perhaps it is of a serious, highly specialised nature, such as an academic monograph, when a publisher who is well established within that particular field will certainly behave with probity and offer a fair contract. Vanity publishers, on the other hand, will accept your book with enthusiasm, ask for 'a small contribution to production costs' (which turns out to be a very substantial sum, not a penny of which you are likely to see again), and will fail to achieve any sales for your book apart from the copies which you yourself buy. If you want to put your own money into the publication of your book, try self-publishing (see page 255) – you will be far better off than going to a vanity house. How do you tell which are the vanity publishers? That's easy – they're the ones who put advertisements in the papers saying things like, 'Authors Wanted!'. Regular publishers don't need to do that.

Michael Legat became a full-time writer after a long and successful publishing career. He is the author of a number of highly regarded books on publishing and writing.

Further reading

Clark, Charles (ed.), *Publishing Agreements: A Book of Precedents*, Butterworths, 5th edn, 1997

Flint, Michael F., *A User's Guide to Copyright*, Butterworths, 4th edn, 1997

Legat, Michael, *An Authors' Guide to Publishing*, Robert Hale, 3rd edn, 1991

Legat, Michael, *Understanding Publishers' Contracts*, Robert Hale, 1992

Unwin, Sir Stanley, *The Truth About Publishing*, Unwin Hyman, 8th edn, 1976, o.p. (An edition is available from the US publishers Lyons & Burford)

International Standard Book Numbering (ISBN)

The Standard Book Numbering (SBN) system was introduced in this country in 1967. Three years later, it became the International Standard Book Numbering (ISBN) system. The Standard Book Numbering Agency receives a large number of telephone calls, many of which follow a common pattern. The most common questions asked about ISBNs are answered here.

Who administers ISBNs?
The overall administration of the international system is done from Berlin by the International ISBN-Agentur. In the UK the system is administered by the Standard Book Numbering Agency Ltd in London, which was set up before the scheme became international – hence that word does not appear in its title.

Are they legal? Do we have to have them?
There is no legal requirement for a book to carry an ISBN. But it is useful to educational authorities, certain library suppliers, public libraries and distributors which use computers, and is now essential to booksellers using the teleordering system. The introduction of Public Lending Right has also made ISBNs of importance to authors.

I am about to publish a book. Must I deposit a copy with the ISBN Agency to obtain copyright?
No. Copyright is obtained by the simple act of publication. However, by law, a copy of every new book must be deposited at the Legal Deposit Office of the British Library, Boston Spa, Wetherby, West Yorkshire LS23 7BY. The Legal Deposit Office issues a receipt, and this has, in the past, proved useful when a dispute has arisen over the date of publication.

Titles deposited are catalogued by the British National Bibliography, which records ISBNs where available. Perhaps a confusion about copyright and ISBNs arises from this, but the ISBN, of itself, has nothing to do with copyright.

What are the fees for ISBNs?
No charge is made for the allocation of a publisher prefix. Publishers may ask the Agency to supply a computer printout of all the ISBNs available to the publisher, with check digits calculated. A small charge is made for this printout.

Are you a government department?
No. Our parent company pays taxes; we get no subsidy from anyone. In most other countries the costs are borne by the state, through the national library system which frequently administers the scheme overseas.

Do I need an ISBN for a church magazine?
No. But you may need an ISSN (International Standard Serial Number), obtainable from the UK National Serials Data Centre. Incidentally, a yearbook can have both an ISBN and an ISSN.

Should we have our own identifier? We do not consider ourselves within the English speaking group.
This comes from publishers with devolution in mind. Usually Welsh, less often Irish. The group system within the ISBN scheme is not quite so categoric as to be dictated by language considerations only.

A group is defined as a 'language, geographic or other convenient area'. There is no strict logic applied, just pragmatism as to what is most convenient for trading purposes.

I want my book to reach as wide a market as possible. Should I have an ISBN?
The ISBN will not automatically sell a book. If the book, like that famous mousetrap, is a better one, the world will beat a path to its door. However, the ISBN will oil the wheels of distribution and it is therefore advisable to have one.

Will you supply an ISBN for a carton of assorted painting books?
No. In the words of the ISBN manual (available from the SBN agency at £4.50, cash with order), 'an ISBN identifies one title, or edition of a title, from one specific publisher, and is unique to that title or edition'. It is now additionally used to identify computer software and maps. It is

Useful addresses

International ISBN-Agentur
Staatsbibliothek Preussicher Kulturbesitz, Potsdamer Str 33, 10785 Berlin, Germany

Standard Book Numbering Agency Ltd
12 Dyott Street, London WC1A 1DF
tel 0171-420 6008 *fax* 0171-836 434

UK National Serials Data Centre
The British Library, Boston Spa, Wetherby, West Yorkshire LS23 7BY

not designed for a carton of assorted painting books.

How does a publisher get an ISBN?
If they have not had ISBNs before, publishers should contact the SBN Agency. Written answers are required to some basic questions.

Reproduced by kind permission of the Standard Book Numbering Agency Ltd.

The Authors' Licensing and Collecting Society Ltd

The Authors' Licensing and Collecting Society Ltd (ALCS) is the British collecting society for writers in all genres. Its principal purpose is to ensure that hard-to-collect revenues due to authors are collected speedily and distributed to members.

The Society currently represents some 35,000 members and associates who are writers, writers' heirs and members of the Society of Authors, the Writers' Guild of Great Britain, the NUJ and the CIOJ (Chartered Institute of Journalists) and BAJ (British Association of Journalists). Foreign writers are also represented under reciprocal arrangements with overseas collecting societies.
The Society is a non-profit making organisation governed by a Council of Management, all of whom are active writers. Four are ALCS members, elected by the ordinary members, and four each are nominated by the Society of Authors and the Writers' Guild of Great Britain.

Powers

On joining, members license the ALCS to administer on their behalf those rights which an author is unable to exercise as an individual or which are best handled on a collective basis. Chief among these are:

- photocopying
- cable transmission
- lending (not British PLR)
- BBC Prime and BBC World Service
- off-air recording
- electronic rights
- private recording
- rental
- public reception of broadcasts.

The Society can administer these rights in Great Britain, Northern Ireland and the Irish Republic.

Sources of income/distributions

During the financial year 1996-97 the ALCS collected just over £9 million for distribution. The Society's main sources of income are:

- **Photocopying.** The ALCS, in co-operation with the Publishers' Licensing Society (PLS), established the Copyright Licensing Agency (CLA) to administer licenses for photocopying. The ALCS distributes the writers' share of copying fees. (See *The Copyright Licensing Agency Ltd* on page 606.)
- **Foreign Public Lending Right.** The ALCS makes annual distributions from VG WORT, the collecting society in Germany. Further money is held in Germany on behalf of British writers who have not yet joined the ALCS. Those eligible to receive German PLR through the ALCS are living British authors resident anywhere; heirs of British authors through successor membership; foreign writers resident in Britain.
- **Cable retransmissions.** The ALCS collects fees for the simultaneous cable retransmission of the UK's terrestrial channels. The Society also distributes fees for BBC World Service programming and BBC Prime, and collects fees from several European countries and Canada for British writers whose work is cabled in neighbouring countries.
- **Educational off-air recording.** The ALCS is part of the Educational Recording Agency Ltd (ERA), which was set up to license educational establishments to record off-air under the provisions of the 1988 Copyright Act. The

ALCS distributes the writers' share of recording fees for radio and television. The ALCS also distributes Australian off-air recording fees to British writers.

Allocation of funds

The ALCS has a sophisticated membership, distribution and accounting system and a unique database of literary, film and broadcasting information. However, it is essential that writers register with the Society so that funds can be correctly allocated and payments made speedily.

Policy and aims

In addition to its core activities, the ALCS maintains a watching brief on all matters affecting copyright, both in the UK and abroad, making representations to UK government authorities and the European Union.

The Society aims to foster a sense of writers' rights and to speak on behalf of groups of writers who do not yet benefit from union or agency efforts, particularly in tackling legal issues and those at the technological frontier. It is currently running a Higher Education and Academic Libraries Project which aims to provide a voice for the concerns of academic authors in copyright and intellectual property matters. A similar project will be mounted on behalf of journalists during the second half of 1997.

Membership

The Authors' Licensing and Collecting Society Ltd
Marlborough Court, 14-18 Holborn,
London EC1N 2LE
tel 0171-395 0600 *fax* 0171-395 0660
e-mail alcs@alcs.co.uk
web site http://www.alcs.co.uk
The current subscription is £5.00 (inc. VAT), £5.00 for European Economic Area residents, and £7.00 for overseas residents. Members of the Society of Authors, the Writers' Guild, the NUJ and the CIJ have free membership.

The Society is a member of CISAC (International Confederation of Authors and Composers Societies), IFRRO (International Federation of Reprographic Rights Organisations) and many other international rights organisations. It is also represented on the British Copyright Council and the PLR Advisory Committee. The ALCS is a lead partner in the EU-funded Imprimatur Project which aims to provide both the methodology and software tools for a safe electronic copyright trading environment.

The ALCS is increasingly active in the field of electronic rights and is a prime resource and leading authority on matters of copyright, intellectual property and writers' collective rights.

The Copyright Licensing Agency Ltd

In response to the need to regulate copying, the seeds were sown 25 years ago for today's laws on regulating copying from books, journals and periodicals. As a result, The Copyright Licensing Agency (CLA) was formed to oversee 'heavy user' groups.

In 1973, interest groups in the UK started to prepare submissions to the government-appointed committee under the Hon. Mr Justice Whitford about ways of regulating copying from books, journals and periodicals. These interest groups, representing owners of copyright, were seeking both a mechanism of control and just recompense for authors and publishers while at the same time continuing to satisfy the reasonable demands of a modern information-driven society.

The role of the CLA

When it was eventually published in 1977, the Whitford Report on Copyright and Designs Law suggested, as the best likely solution to the problem, a collective administration system for copying rights organised by the rightsholders themselves.

This recommendation spawned first the Wolfenden Committee that brought together representatives of authors' societies and publishers' associations, and then the de Freitas Committee that hammered out and fashioned, with these two sometimes antagonistic groups, a mutually acceptable constitution for such a licensing body. The outcome was the formation of the Copyright Licensing Agency (CLA) in April 1902 and its incorporation in January 1983 as a non-profit making company limited by guarantee. The Agency, which is primarily concerned with licensing 'heavy user' groups, issued its first licence in May 1984.

CLA is 'owned' by the Authors' Licensing and Collecting Society (ALCS) and the Publishers Licensing Society (PLS) in that they are its members. ALCS's members are members of the Society of Authors and the Writers' Guild of Great Britain and several thousand individual members; and PLS's members are the Publishers Association, the Periodical Publishers Association and the Association of Learned and Professional Society Publishers. All are represented on CLA's board of 12 directors, six being ALCS nominations and six PLS nominations.

Licence to copy

CLA sees its principal licensing areas in the UK as being education, government and industry. Each of these broad categories has three or four sub-groups. In company with nearly all other Reprographic Rights Organisations (RROs) around the world, CLA started licensing in the general education sector.

Functions of the CLA

The six main functions of the CLA are:
- to obtain mandates from publishers and authors in association with ALCS and PLS;
- to license users for copying extracts from books, journals and periodicals;
- to collect fees from licensed users for such copying;
- to implement a system of record-keeping sufficient to provide statistically acceptable information on which to calculate a fair apportionment of the distributable income;
- to pay ALCS and PLS their correct shares of the distributable income and provide sufficient data to enable these societies to pay individual authors and publishers; and
- to institute such legal proceedings as may be necessary for the enforcement of the rights entrusted to the Agency.

The first major development was in April 1986, when three-year voluntary licensing agreements with the country's local education authorities (LEAs) came into effect; in April 1989 these licences were extended for a further three years; copying in all 30,000 or so state colleges and schools is now covered by such licences. The Agency also licenses the independent education sector through its licensing scheme for independent schools.

CLA next turned its attention to higher and further education. In 1989 arrangements were finalised whereby universities, polytechnics, independent colleges and language schools, etc all became licensed for three years from 1 January 1990.

The LEA licences were negotiated with a joint committee of representatives appointed by the Association of County Councils, the Association of Metropolitan Authorities and the Convention of Scottish Local Authorities. A similar committee but expanded to include representatives of the Association of District Councils and the Association of London Authorities is now trying to license the non-LEA parts of local government.

The Agency intends dealing with central government on a ministry by ministry basis, starting with the Department of Trade & Industry as the sponsors of the Copyright, Designs and Patents Act 1988; the Department for Education; and the National Health Service, the largest employer in Europe.

Public bodies, i.e. those organisations for which government ministers have some accountability (e.g. The British Council), may have to be dealt with in some non-collective manner.

Trade, industry, commerce and the professions present CLA with its greatest challenge because of their size and diversity. A first step has already been taken, however, with the setting up of a joint task force with the Confederation of British Industry (CBI). This CBI/CLA working party, chaired by an industrialist, is examining the best way or ways forward, concentrating initially on manufacturing industry, with particular emphasis on R&D-driven sectors such as pharmaceuticals, chemicals, engineering, electronics, aerospace and oil fuel.

A banking role

Basically, CLA is a banking operation with legal overtones: it collects fees from licensed users in respect of acts of photocopying from books and serials and other copying such as microfiche printing and, after deducting its administration costs and any reserves or provisions the Board may decide, distributes the balance to ALCS and PLS for them to pay to authors and publishers.

CLA currently offers two basic services, i.e., licences to copy authorised by many individual owners of copyright, both of which offer the collective repertoire of copyright works mandated to CLA by those owners:

- **A collective user service** such as that made with the associations representing local education authorities for state colleges and schools.
- **A transactional user service** for those institutions where a suitable representative organisation, such as an LEA, is unable or unwilling to provide the level of administrative support that a collective

user scheme requires, e.g. implementation and supervision of a sampling system, single cheque payment, etc.

Both types of licence are valid for a specific period, usually two or three years.

Under a collective user arrangement the level of copying for a group of institutions is mutually agreed and a global fee set; this fee total is then apportioned by the organising body amongst its constituents and paid by them to CLA on presentation of the agency's invoice. With the transactional user scheme, fees are paid on a straight cost per copy-page basis; returns to CLA are made at regular, agreed intervals, and a self-billing system is used.

Who benefits?

The main advantage from the user community's standpoint is that CLA indemnifies all licensees against any inadvertent infringement of copyright.

Right from the outset, the authors' representatives insisted:
• that writers should benefit individually and directly from the copying of their works and that the money should not go to authors' societies for 'social benefit' purposes, as is the case in some parts of the world;
• that the individual authors' shares should be paid to them directly, and not through the accounting systems of their publishers.

Keeping records of copying

In order to fulfil these requirements, CLA had to devise a title-based distribution system and a form of record-keeping suitable for a geographically spread, stratified and statistically sound sample of the licensees. Some form of itemised record-keeping, therefore, is necessary on the part of both categories of licence holders. With collective user licensing, a rotating sample of about 5% of institutions in each broad category is required to maintain records of their copying, which are returned to CLA at agreed intervals, where they are checked and analysed. Transactional user licensees are required to keep records of all their copying.

Controlled record-keeping is crucial to CLA because the statistical information extracted from these records of copying is used as the basis for making payments to copyright owners whose works have been copied.

Once a licence has been issued, it has been relatively simple, so far, to collect fees. It is quite another matter, however, to edit, process and analyse the returns of copying, and to calculate the correct amounts due to copyright owners. On return to the Agency, the record-keeping forms, which are regarded and treated as strictly confidential documents, some of which are deemed to be personal data under the Data Protection Act 1984, are:
• checked by the licensing officer responsible to ensure that the conditions of the licence are being adhered to;
• scrutinised by the data preparation department to validate the information being submitted, e.g. missing ISBN/ISSNs etc are searched for;
• keyed for computer analysis;
• subjected to a final edit for data quality.

The results are analysed and summaries produced showing pages copied, by ISBN/ISSN and by title, by author and by publisher. Apportionments are then calculated, statements produced and cheques drawn. The existence of the ISBN and the ISSN systems is a great benefit to CLA in carrying out its tasks.

Distribution of fees

The first distribution to members was £1.4 million (US$2.3 million), paid in two parts: the first tranche of just over £500,000 in October 1987, and the balance in March/April 1988. According to a CLA Board decision, payments to rights owners have since been made every six months. At the time of writing, CLA has distributed over £50 million to members.

It must be emphasised that a CLA licence is not a carte blanche to copy without restrictions. The conditions are clearly set down and are required to be displayed alongside every copying

machine within the control of the licensee. The wording of the notices may vary slightly depending on the category of the licensee but the core message is always the same. CLA also produces various user guides for issue to employees, and there is a warning sticker that goes on top of machines to act as a reminder to copier users.

Agreements with other countries

For CLA there is comfort in knowing that it is not alone in pioneering the collective administration of copying rights. Counterpart organisations to CLA now exist in 19 other countries – Australia, Austria, Canada, Denmark, Finland, France, Germany, Iceland, Ireland, Italy, Japan, the Netherlands, New Zealand, Norway, South Africa, Spain, Sweden, Switzerland and the United States – nearly all of them in membership of IFRRO, the International Federation of Reproduction Rights Organisations. RROs are also presently being formed in Belgium and Israel.

Finally, the broader the repertoire an RRO can offer its licensees the better, and it is a priority of CLA to secure reciprocal agreements with counterpart organisations overseas, particularly those in English-speaking countries where UK books, journals and periodicals are being widely and extensively copied, and, equally, where much publishing in the English language takes place.

Administration

Critics of collecting societies say that they spend pounds to distribute pennies. From the start, this is a potential criticism of which the CLA directors were acutely conscious. As far back as November 1982 the board designate set down in its minutes that on no account were CLA's administration costs to exceed 20% of the fee income. The Agency has done much better than that: CLA's overhead is working out at about 10% of the fee income, and the Agency continually strives to reduce that level where possible. However, because it is in the business of handling large numbers of documents and processing a great deal of information, investment in technology has been inevitable.

CLA's aim is to distribute as much as it can, as fast as it can, and as efficiently as it can. It believes that over £50 million, distributed between October 1987 and March 1997, speaks louder than any words, and demonstrates better than anything else the Agency's resolve to achieve its objectives.

Further information

The Copyright Licensing Agency Ltd
90 Tottenham Court Road, London W1P 0LP
tel 0171-436 5931 *fax* 0171-436 3986
e-mail cla@cla.co.uk
web site http://www.cla.co.uk
Contact The Secretary

Public Lending Right

Under the PLR system, payment is made from public funds to authors (writers, translators, illustrators and some editors/compilers) whose books are lent out from public libraries. Payment is made once a year, in February, and the amount authors receive is proportionate to the number of times (established from a sample) that their books were borrowed during the previous year (July to June).

The legislation

PLR was created, and its principles established, by the Public Lending Right Act 1979 (HMSO, 30p). The Act required the rules for the administration of PLR to be laid down by a scheme. That was done in the Public Lending Right Scheme 1982 (HMSO, £2.95), which includes details of transfer (assignment), transmission after death, renunciation, trusteeship, bankruptcy, etc. Amending orders made in 1983, 1984, 1988, 1989 and 1990 were consolidated in December 1990 (S.I. 2360, £3.90). Some further amendments affecting author eligibility came into effect in December 1991 (S.I. 2618, £1.00).

How the system works

From the applications he receives, the Registrar of PLR compiles a register of authors and books which is held on computer. A representative sample of book issues is recorded, consisting of all loans from selected public libraries. This is then multiplied in proportion to total library lending to produce, for each book, an estimate of its total annual loans throughout the country. Each year the computer compares the register with the estimated loans to discover how many loans are credited to each registered book for the calculation of PLR payments. The computer does this using code numbers – in most cases the ISBN printed in the book.

Parliament allocates a sum each year (£4,903,000 for 1997-98) for PLR. This Fund pays the administrative costs of PLR and reimburses local authorities for recording loans in the sample libraries. The remaining money is then divided by the total registered loan figure in order to work out how much can be paid for each estimated loan of a registered book.

Limits on payments

Bottom limit. If all the registered interests in an author's books score so few loans that they would earn less than £1 in a year, no payment is due.

Top limit. If the books of one registered author score so high that the author's PLR earnings for the year would exceed £6000, then only £6000 is paid. No author can earn more than £6000 in PLR in any one year.

Money that is not paid out because of these limits belongs to the Fund and increases the amounts paid that year to other authors.

The sample

The basic sample represents only public libraries (no academic, school, private or commercial libraries are included) and only loans made over the counter (not consultations of books on library premises). It follows that only those books which are loaned from public libraries can earn PLR and make an application worthwhile. However, the feasibility of extending PLR to reference books is currently under review.

Most borrowed authors in UK public libraries

Based on PLR sample loans July 1995-June 1996. Includes all writers, both registered and unregistered, but not illustrators where the book has a separate writer. Writing names are used; pseudonyms have not been combined. (C) indicates a children's book author.

Authors with estimated loans over one million (4.8% of national loans)

Janet & Allan Ahlberg (C)	Dick Francis	Ruth Rendell
Enid Blyton (C)	René Goscinny (C)	Danielle Steel
Agatha Christie	Jack Higgins	R.L. Stine (C)
Catherine Cookson	Dick King-Smith (C)	Kate William (C)
Josephine Cox	Ann M. Martin (C)	
Roald Dahl (C)	Ellis Peters	

Authors with estimated loans over 500,000 (6.8% of national loans)

Ted Allbeury	Colin Forbes	Charlotte Lamb
Virginia Andrews	Christine Marion Fraser	Ed McBain
Evelyn Anthony	Iris Gower	Betty Neels
Jeffrey Archer	Cynthia Harrod-Eagles	Pamela Oldfield (C)
Rev W. Awdry (C)	Colin & Jacqui Hawkins (C)	Rosamunde Pilcher
Tessa Barclay	Hergé (C)	Terry Pratchett
Maeve Binchy	Georgette Heyer	Claire Rayner
Emma Blair	Eric Hill (C)	Miss Read
Harry Bowling	Victoria Holt	Sidney Sheldon
Barbara Taylor Bradford	Audrey Howard	Wilbur Smith
Tony Bradman (C)	Shirley Hughes (C)	Mary Jane Staples
Mary Higgins Clark	Mick Inkpen (C)	Jessica Stirling
Babette Cole (C)	P.D. James	Jamie Suzanne (C)
Bernard Cornwell	Penny Jordan	E.V. Thompson
John Cunliffe (C)	Marie Joseph	Joanna Trollope
Len Deighton	Lena Kennedy	Martin Waddell (C)
Colin Dexter	Stephen King	Mary Wesley
Elizabeth Ferrars	Dean R. Koontz	Margaret Yorke

The sample consists of the entire loans records for a year from libraries in 30 public library authorities spread through England, Scotland, Wales and Northern Ireland. Sample loans will be around 10% of the national total from 1 July 1997. Several computerised sampling points in an authority contribute loans data ('multi-site' sampling). This change has been introduced gradually, and began in July 1991. The aim has been to increase the sample without any significant increase in costs. In order to counteract sampling error, libraries in the sample change every two to three years. Loans are totalled every 12 months for the period 1 July to 30 June.

An author's entitlement to PLR depends, under the 1979 Act, on the loans accrued by his or her books in the sample. This figure is multiplied to produce regional and national estimated loans.

ISBNs

PLR depends on the use of code numbers to identify books lent and to correlate loans with entries on the register so that payment can be made. Principally the system uses the International Standard Book Number (ISBN). From July 1991 an ISBN has been required for all new registrations. Different editions (e.g., 1st, 2nd, hardcover, paperback, large print) of the same book have different ISBNs.

Authorship

In the PLR system the author of a book is the writer, illustrator, translator, compiler,

---

Summary of the 14th year's results

Registration: authors When registration closed for the 14th year (30 June 1996) the number of shares in books registered was 257,600 for 25,937 authors. This included 690 German authors.

Eligible loans Of the 534.6 million estimated loans from UK libraries, 234 million belong to books on the PLR register. The loans credited to registered books – 43.8% of all library borrowings – qualify for payment. The remaining 56.2% of loans relate to books that are ineligible for various reasons, to books written by dead or foreign authors, and to books that have simply not been applied for.

Money and payments PLR's administrative costs are deducted from the fund allocated to the Registrar annually by Parliament. Operating the Scheme this year cost £654,000, representing some 13.1% of the PLR fund. The Rate per Loan for 1996-97 increased to 2.07 pence and was calculated to distribute all the £4,346,000 available. The total of PLR distribution and costs is therefore the full £5,000,000 which the Government provided in 1996-97.

The numbers of authors in various payment categories are as follows:

98	payments at	6,000 maximum
34	payments at	5,000-5,999
250	payments between	2,500-4,999
616	payments between	1,000-2,499
805	payments between	500-999
3,712	payments between	100-499
15,540	payments between	1-99
21,055	TOTAL	

There were also 4882 registered authors whose books earned them nil payment. As a result of the £6000 maximum payment rule some £500,570 became available for redistribution to other authors.

---

editor or reviser. Authors must be named on the book's title page, or be able to prove authorship by some other means (e.g. receipt of royalties). The ownership of copyright (apart from crown copyright) has no bearing on PLR eligibility.

Co-authorship/illustrators

In the PLR system the authors of a book are those writers, translators, editors, compilers and illustrators as defined above. Authors must apply for registration before their books can earn PLR. There is no restriction on the number of authors who can register shares in any one book as long as they satisfy the eligibility criteria.

Writers and/or illustrators

At least one must be eligible and they must jointly agree what share of PLR each will take. This agreement is necessary even if one or two are ineligible or do not wish to register for PLR. Share sizes should be based on contribution. The eligible authors will receive the share(s) specified in the application. PLR can be any whole percentage. Detailed advice is available from the PLR office.

Translators

Translators may apply, without reference to other authors, for a 30% fixed share (to be divided equally between joint translators).

Editors and compilers

An editor or compiler may apply, either with others or without reference to them, to register a 20% share. Unless in receipt of royalties an editor must have written at least 10% of the book's contents or more than 10 pages of text in addition to normal editorial work. The share of joint editors/compilers is 20% in total to be divided equally. An application from an editor or compiler to register a greater percentage share must be accompanied by supporting documentary evidence of actual contribution.

Dead or missing co-authors

Where it is impossible to agree shares with a co-author because that person is dead or untraceable, then the surviving co-author or co-authors may submit an application without the dead or missing co-author but must name the co-author and provide supporting evidence as to why that co-author has not agreed shares.

The living co-author(s) will then be able to register a share in the book which will be 20% for the illustrator (or illustrators) and the residual percentage for the writer (or writers). If this percentage is to be divided between more than one writer or illustrator, then this will be in equal shares unless some other apportionment is requested and agreed by the Registrar.

The PLR Office keeps a file of missing authors (mostly illustrators) to help locate co-authors. Help is also available from publishers, the writers' organisations, and the Association of Illustrators.

Life and death

Authors can only be registered for PLR during their lifetime. However, for authors so registered, books can later be registered if first published within one year before their death or 10 years afterwards. New versions of titles registered by the author can be registered posthumously.

Residential qualifications

Eligibility for PLR is restricted to authors who are resident in the United Kingdom or Germany. A resident in these countries (for PLR purposes) has his or her only or principal home there. The United Kingdom does not include the Channel Islands or the Isle of Man.

Eligible books

In the PLR system each separate edition of a book is registered and treated as a separate book. A book is eligible for PLR registration provided that:
- it has an eligible author (or co-author);
- it is printed and bound (paperbacks counting as bound);
- copies of it have been put on sale (i.e. it is not a free handout and it has already been published);
- it is not a newspaper, magazine, journal or periodical;
- the authorship is personal (i.e. not a company or association) and the book is not crown copyright;
- it is not wholly or mainly a musical score;
- it has an ISBN.

Notification and payment

Every registered author receives from the Registrar an annual statement of estimated loans for each book and the PLR due.

Sampling arrangements

Libraries

To help minimise the unfairnesses that arise inevitably from a sampling system, the Scheme specifies the eight regions within which authorities and sampling points have to be designated and includes libraries of varying size. Part of the sample drops out by rotation each year to allow fresh libraries to be included. The following library authorities have been designated for the year beginning 1 July 1997 (all are multi-site authorities):
- Wales: Bridgend, Gwynedd, Newport;
- Scotland: Aberdeen, Glasgow, Highland;
- Northern Ireland: Southern Education & Library Board, Western Education & Library Board;
- London: Barking and Dagenham, Kensington and Chelsea, Richmond, Wandsworth;
- Metropolitan Districts: Birmingham, Kirklees, Liverpool, Manchester, Sunderland;
- Counties S&E: Cambridgeshire, Hertfordshire, Northamptonshire, Suffolk, West Sussex;
- Counties S&W: Cornwall, Somerset, Staffordshire, Wiltshire;
- Counties N: Cheshire, Cumbria, Hull, North Yorkshire.

Participating local authorities are reimbursed on an actual cost basis for additional expenditure incurred in providing loans data to the PLR Office. The extra PLR work mostly consists of modifications to computer programs to accumulate data already held in the local authority computer and to produce a monthly magnetic tape to be sent to the PLR Office at Stockton-on-Tees.

Reciprocal arrangements

In 1981-1982 reciprocal arrangements with West Germany were sought by British writers to help ensure that they did not lose the German PLR they had enjoyed since 1974. The German Scheme, although loan based, is very different in most other respects. Reciprocity was brought into effect in January 1985. Authors can apply for German PLR through the Authors' Licensing and Collecting Society. (Further information on PLR schemes internationally and recent developments within the EC towards wider recognition of PLR may be found in *Proceedings of the First International Conference on Authors' Lending Rights*, James Parker (ed), 1996, £8 plus UK postage, from the PLR Office.)

Further information

Public Lending Right
PLR Office, Bayheath House, Prince Regent Street, Stockton-on-Tees TS18 1DF
tel (01642) 604699 *fax* (01642) 615641
web site http://www.earl.org.uk/earl/members/plr/
Contact The Registrar

Application forms, information, publications and a copy of its *Annual Review* are all obtainable from the PLR Office. Further information on eligibility for PLR, loans statistics and forthcoming developments may be found on PLR's web site.

PLR Advisory Committee
Advises the Secretary of State for National Heritage and the Registrar on matters concerning PLR.

Copyright and libel

British copyright law

*Copyright is a creature of statute. There have been a series of Copyright Acts over the years, gradually extending the scope of this area of the law so as to offer protection to the widening range of media used by writers and artists of all types. In an article of this length, it is not possible to deal fully with all the changes in the law effected by the most recent Act, nor indeed with all the complexities of this technical area of the law. Rather, **Amanda L. Michaels**, barrister, sets out the basic principles of copyright protection, and identifies topics which may be of particular interest to readers of this Yearbook.*

On 1 August 1989, the Copyright Act 1956, previously the major Act in this field, was replaced by the Copyright, Designs and Patents Act 1988 ('the Act'). The Act restated the law of copyright, especially in so far as it related to the essentials of what may be protected as a copyright work and the nature of that protection. Section 172 of the Act, in particular, provided that mere changes of expression from the old law do not denote a substantive change in the law, whilst prior decisions may be referred to as an aid to the construction of the Act.

However, there was a good deal in the Act which was innovatory (see, for instance, the comments below on the new design right, and the repercussions upon infringement actions of section 51), as well as a number of provisions where one might well ask whether all that was intended was a change of expression from the old law, or whether a change of words implies a change of substance. Reference to Parliamentary debates as reported in Hansard may help to resolve such difficulties: see *Pepper* v. *Hart* [1993] AC 593.

Continuing effects of old law

There were complicated transitional provisions (in Schedule 1 to the Act) relating to pre-existing works and infringements, and reference will need to be made to these and to the old law for some years to come, as well as to numerous Orders in Council made under the Act. Users of this *Yearbook* particularly need to note that forms of publishing and licensing agreements suitable for use under the old law will probably need revision in the light of the Act. In particular, old texts on the subject may not apply to new copyright works.

Harmonising the law

Further recent changes to the law

On 1 January 1996, further important changes were made to UK copyright law, upon the implementation of EC Directive 93/98 ('the Term Directive') by the Duration of Copyright and Rights in Performances Regulations 1995 (S.I. 1995 No. 3297). The Term Directive harmonised copyright laws throughout the European Union as to the period of copyright protection offered to various types of copyright work, with a view to avoiding distortions within the internal market. Rather than take away vested rights in any one state, the term was harmonised 'upwards' to meet the longest protection already offered in Germany. The end result is that the term of copyright in the UK and in some other countries has been extended from the 'life of the author plus 50 years' provided by the

Berne Convention to life plus 70 years. Certain works may, as a result, benefit from a 'revived' term of copyright protection in the UK and this may well make the task of deciding whether a work is still protected by copyright fraught with difficulty (see below). The Regulations also deal with what is to happen to a variety of existing rights (e.g. publishing contracts) in the works offered an extended term of protection.

Copyright protection of works

Copyright protection has always protected the form in which the artist/author has set out his or her inspiration, not the underlying idea. So, plots, artistic ideas, systems and themes cannot be protected by copyright. Whilst an idea remains no more than that, it can be protected only by the law relating to confidential information (contrast the cases of *Green* v. *Broadcasting Corp. of New Zealand* [1989] RPC 700: no copyright in 'format' of *Opportunity Knocks*, and *Fraser* v. *Thames TV Ltd* [1984] QB 44: plot of a projected television series protected by law of confidence). The law of copyright prevents the copying of the material form in which the idea has been presented, or of a substantial part of it, measured in terms of quality, not quantity.

The Act therefore starts out, in section 1, by setting out a number of different categories of works which can be the subject of copyright protection. These are:
• original literary, dramatic, musical or artistic works,
• sound recordings, films, broadcasts or cable programmes, and
• typographical arrangements of published editions.

These works are further defined in sections 3 to 8 (see box for examples). The definitions are not identical to those in the 1956 Act.

The definitions of literary and musical works do not, however, contradict the basic rule that copyright protects the form (or the 'expression of the idea') and not the idea; works are not protected before being reduced into tangible form. Section

---

Definitions under the Act

Literary work is defined as: 'any work, other than a dramatic or musical work, which is written, spoken or sung, and accordingly includes: (a) a table or compilation, and (b) a computer program.'

A musical work means: 'a work consisting of music, exclusive of any words or action intended to be sung, spoken or performed with the music.'

An artistic work means: '(a) a graphic work, photograph, sculpture or collage, irrespective of artistic quality, (b) a work of architecture being a building or model for a building, or (c) a work of artistic craftsmanship.'

3(2) specifically provides that no copyright shall subsist in a literary, musical or artistic work until it has been recorded in writing or otherwise.

On the other hand, all that is required to achieve copyright protection is to record the original work in any appropriate medium. Once that has been done, copyright will subsist in the work (assuming that the qualifying features set out below are present) without any formality of registration or otherwise. As long as the work is recorded in some tangible form there is, for instance, no need for it to be published in any way for the protection to attach to it. (Please note, however, that although this lack of formality applies here and in most European countries, the law of the United States does differ – see *US Copyright* on page 625). The common idea that one must register a work at Stationers Hall, or send it to oneself or to, say, a bank, in a sealed envelope so as to obtain copyright protection is incorrect. All that this precaution may do is provide some proof in an infringement action (whether as plaintiff or defendant) of the date of creation and form of one's work.

Originality

Section 1 provides that in order to gain copyright protection, literary, dramatic,

artistic and musical works must be original. Similarly, there are provisions which exclude from copyright protection sound recordings or films which are mere copies of pre-existing sound recordings and films, broadcasts which infringe rights in another broadcast or cable programmes which consist of immediate retransmissions of broadcasts.

The test of originality may not be quite that expected by the layperson. Just as the law protects the form, rather than the idea, originality relates to the 'expression of the thought', rather than to the thought itself. A work need not be original in the sense of showing innovative or cultural merit, it needs only to have been the product of skill and labour on the part of the author. This can be seen from various sections in the Act, for instance in the definition of certain artistic works, and in the fact that it offers copyright protection to works such as compilations (like football pools coupons or directories) and tables (including mathematical tables).

There may be considerable difficulty, at times, in deciding whether a work is of sufficient originality, or has original features, where there have been a series of similar designs or amendments of existing works. See *L.A. Gear Inc* v. *Hi-Tec Sports Plc* [1992] FSR 121. A new edition of an existing work, or an adaptation of one, may therefore obtain a new copyright; this will not affect the earlier copyright protection. See *Cala Homes (South) Limited* v. *Alfred McAlpine Homes East Limited* [1995] FSR 818. What is clear, though, is that merely making a 'slavish copy' of a drawing will not create an original work: see *Interlego AG* v. *Tyco Industries* [1989] AC 217.

On the other hand, 'works' comprising the titles of books or periodicals, or advertising slogans, which may have required a good deal of original thought, generally are not accorded copyright protection, because they are too short to be deemed literary works.

See, too, the limited protection given to drawings of a functional or engineering type in the sections on infringement and design right below.

Qualification

The Act is limited in its effects to the UK (and to colonies to which it may be extended by Order in Council). It is aimed primarily at protecting the works of British citizens, or works which were first published here. However, in line with the requirements of various international conventions to which the UK is a party, copyright protection in the UK is also accorded to the works of nationals of many foreign states which are also party to these conventions, as well as to works first published in those states, on a reciprocal basis.

The position is somewhat different where copyright in works of nationals of other member states of the European Union are concerned, as there is a principle of equal treatment which applies to copyright protection, so that protection must be offered to such works here: see *Phil Collins* v. *Imtrat Handelsgesellschaft mbH* (Case C92/92) [1993] 2 CMLR 773.

The importance of these rules mainly arises when one is trying to find out whether a pre-existing foreign work is protected by copyright here, for instance, if one wishes to make a film based upon a foreign novel. Within the confines of this article, all that can be said is that there have been numerous different Orders in Council regulating the position for most of the major countries of the world, including the other member states of the EU and the USA, and further Orders continue to be made, but that in every case it will be wise to check the position.

Ownership

The general rule is that a work will initially be owned by its author, the author being the creator of the work, or in the case of a film or sound recording, the person who makes the arrangements necessary for it to be made. The Term Directive (in common with certain other EC Directives) provided that the 'principal director' of a film shall be deemed to be its author or one of its authors.

One essential exception to the general

rule is that the copyright in a work made by an employee in the course of his or her employment will belong to their employer, subject to any agreement to the contrary. However, this rule applies only to true employees, not to freelance designers, journalists, etc, and not even to nominally self-employed company directors. This obviously may lead to problems if the question of copyright ownership is not agreed (see box: Assignments).

Where a work is produced by several people who collaborate in such a way that each one's contribution is not distinct from that of the other(s), then they will be the joint authors of the work. Where two people collaborate to write a song, one producing the lyrics and the other the music, there will be two separate copyright works, the copyright of which will be owned by each of the authors separately. But where two people write a play, each rewriting what the other produces, there will be a joint work.

The importance of knowing whether the work is joint or not arises:
• in working out the duration of the copyright, and
• from the fact that joint works can only be exploited with the agreement of all the joint authors, so that all of them have to join in any licence, although each of them can sue for infringement without joining the other author(s) in the proceedings.

Duration of copyright

As a result of the amendments brought into effect on 1 January 1996, copyright in literary, dramatic, musical or artistic works expires at the end of the period of 70 years from the end of the calendar year in which the author dies (new section 12(1)). Where there are joint authors (see 'Ownership', above), then the 70 years runs from the year of the death of the last of them to die. If the author is unknown, there will be 70 years protection from the date the work was first made available to the public by being performed, etc.

The extended 70-year term also applies to films, and runs from the end of the calendar year in which the death occurs of the last to die of the principal director, the author of the screenplay, the author of the dialogue or the composer of any music especially created for the film (new section 13B). This could obviously be a nightmare to establish, and there are certain presumptions in section 66A which may help someone wishing to use material from an old film.

However, sound recordings are still protected by copyright for only 50 years from the year of making or release (new section 13A); similarly, broadcasts and cable programmes still get only 50 years protection. Computer-generated works keep a 50-year term of protection.

The new longer term obviously applies without difficulty to works created after 1 January 1996. Nor is the extension of term especially hard to apply to works which were in copyright here on 31 December 1995, as the term will simply be extended for a further 20 years, and the owner of that extended copyright will be the person who owned it on 31 December 1995, unless that person had only a limited term of ownership, in which case the extra 20 years will be added on to the reversionary term (see paragraph 18 of the Regulations).

Where copyright had expired here, but the author died between 50 and 70 years ago, the position is more complicated. The Term Directive provided that if a work was protected by copyright anywhere in the European Union on 1 July 1995, then copyright protection should revive for it in any other state in which it had expired, until the end of the same 70-year period (this was given effect by paragraph 16(d) of the 1995 Regulations). This is not, unfortunately, simply a question of looking at the date of the author's death, since protection may not have been offered to a particular work even by Germany, the state offering the 70-year period of protection prior to the Directive, for other reasons, e.g. lack of originality according to German law. It might therefore be necessary to look at the position in the other states offering a longer term of protection, namely France and Spain.

Ownership of the revived term of copyright will belong to the person who was the owner of the copyright when the initial term expired, save that if that person died (or a company, etc, ceased to exist) before 1 January 1996, then the revived term will vest in the author or his or her personal representatives, and in the case of a film, in the principal director or his personal representatives (paragraph 19 of the Regulations).

The increased term offered to works of other EU nationals as a result of the Term Directive is not offered automatically to the nationals of other states, but will only apply where an equally long term is offered in their state of origin (new subsections 12(6), 13A(4) and 13B(7)).

Where acts are carried out in relation to such revived copyright works, pursuant to things done whilst they were in the public domain prior to such revival, certain protection from infringement is available (see paragraph 23 of the Regulations). A licence as of right may also be available, on giving notice to the copyright owner and paying a royalty (see paragraph 24).

Finally, where one is dealing with a work made before the Act came into force, one needs to look at the law in force when it was made, as well as at the transitional provisions of the 1956 Act (for pre-1957 works) and/or of the Act (for pre-1989 works).

Dealing with copyright works

As will be seen below, ownership of the copyright in a work confers upon the owner the exclusive right to deal with the work in a number of ways, and essentially stops all unauthorised exploitation of the work. Ownership of the copyright is capable of being separated from ownership of the material form in which the work is embodied, whether the transfer of the latter includes the former will depend upon the terms of any agreement or the circumstances. Buying a copy of a book does not transfer the ownership of the copyright in the underlying work, but purchasing the original manuscript or a unique piece of sculpture might do so,

Assignments

The whole right in the work is sold, with the owner retaining no interest in it (except, possibly, for payment by way of royalties).

An assignment must be in writing, signed by or on behalf of the assignor, but no other formality is required. One can make an assignment of future copyright (under section 91). Where the author of a projected work agrees in writing that he will assign the rights in a future work to another, the copyright vests in the assignee immediately upon the creation of the work, without further formalities. This facility may be used where works are commissioned from the author, as the specific provisions as to ownership of commissioned works which existed in the 1956 Act are not reproduced as such in the new Act, save in respect of works protected by the new design right (see page 622).

These rules do not, apparently, affect the common law as to beneficial interests in copyright. Essentially, where someone has been commissioned to create a work for another, in circumstances in which copyright will not vest automatically in the latter, and the court finds that it was the parties' mutual intention that the copyright should belong to the 'commissioner', it will hold that the 'commissioner' is the equitable or beneficial owner of the copyright, and the author will be obliged to assign the copyright to him or her. 'Commission' in this context means only to order a particular piece of work to be done: see *Apple Corps. Ltd* v. *Cooper* [1993] FSR 286 (on the 1956 Act). If no sufficient agreement is found of this sort, then the arrangement is likely to be found to have conferred a licence, whether exclusive or not, upon the 'commissioner'.

depending upon the circumstances and/or any express agreement between the parties.

Copyright works can be exploited by their owners in two ways:

• Assignment: the whole right in the work may be sold, with the owner retaining no interest in it (except, possibly, for payment by way of royalties); or

• Licensing: the owner may grant a licence to another to exploit the right, whilst retaining overall ownership. Agreements dealing with copyright

Licensing

A licence is granted to another to exploit the right whilst retaining overall ownership.

Licences do not need to take any form in particular, and may indeed be granted orally. However, an exclusive licence (i.e. one which excludes even the copyright owner himself from exploiting the work in the manner authorised by the licence) must be in writing, if the licensee is to enjoy rights in respect of infringements concurrent with those of the copyright owner.

should make it clear whether an assignment or a licence is being granted, and should clearly define the scope of any assignment or licence. The question of moral rights (see below) will also have to be considered by parties negotiating an assignment or licence.

Both assignments and licences can, and frequently do, split up the various rights contained within the copyright. So, for instance, a licence might be granted to one person to publish a novel in hardback and to another to publish in softback, a third person might be granted the film, television and video rights, and yet a fourth the right to translate the novel into other languages.

Assignments and licences may also confer rights according to territory, dividing the USA from the EU or different EU countries one from the other. Two comments must be made about this. Firstly, it must be appreciated that any such agreement would be dealing with a bundle of different national copyrights, as each country's law extends only to its own borders; each country's law on copyright protection, on licensing and on infringement may differ and will continue to do so even after the implementation of the Term Directive. Secondly, when seeking to divide rights between different territories of the EU there is a danger that one will infringe the competition rules of the EU (in the main Articles 30-36 and 85-86 of the Treaty of Rome). Professional advice should be taken to ensure that one is not in breach of these rules, which would render the parties liable to be fined, as well as

making the agreement void in whole or in part.

Licences can also, of course, be of varying lengths. There is no need for a licence to be granted for the whole term of copyright; indeed this would be unusual, if not foolish. Well-drafted licences will provide for termination on breach, including the failure of the licensee to exploit the work properly, and on the bankruptcy or winding up of the licensee.

Copyright may be assigned by will, and where a bequest is given of an original document, etc embodying an unpublished copyright work, the bequest will carry the copyright.

Any licence affecting a copyright work which subsisted on 31 December 1995 and was then for the full term of the copyright, shall continue to have effect during any extended term, subject to any agreement to the contrary (paragraph 21 of the Regulations).

Infringement

Copyright is infringed by doing any of a number of specified acts in relation to the copyright work, without the authority of the owner. In all forms of infringement, it suffices if a substantial part of the original is used, and the question is one to be judged according to quality not quantity (e.g., see *Ravenscroft* v. *Herbert* [1980] RPC 193). The form of infringement common to all forms of copyright works is that of copying. This means reproducing the work in any material form. It is important to note that primary infringement, such as copying, can be done innocently of any intention to infringe.

Infringement may occur where an existing work provides the inspiration for a later one, if copying results, e.g. by including edited extracts from a history book in a novel (*Ravenscroft* v. *Herbert*, see above) or using a photograph as the inspiration for a painting (*Baumann* v. *Fussell* [1978] RPC 485). Infringement will not necessarily be prevented merely by the application of significant new skill and labour by the infringer, nor by a change of medium.

In the case of a two-dimensional artistic work, reproduction can mean making a copy in three dimensions, and vice versa, although there is an important limitation on this general rule in section 51 of the Act, which provides that in the case of a 'design document or model' (defined as a record of a design of any aspect of the shape or configuration, internal or external, of the whole or part of an article, other than surface decoration) for something which is not itself an artistic work, it is no infringement to make an article to that design. This would appear to mean that whilst it would be an infringement to make an article from a design drawing for, say, a sculpture, it will not be an infringement of copyright to make a handbag from a copy of the design drawing for it, or from a handbag which one has purchased. In order to protect such designs one will have to rely upon design right or upon a registered design (for both see below). However, under the transitional provisions, the right to rely upon copyright protection for any such designs made before the commencement of the new Act will continue until 1 August 1999 (see Schedule 1, paragraph 19) and see *Entec (Pollution Control) Ltd* v. *Abacus Mouldings* [1992] FSR 332.

Copying a film, broadcast or cable programme can include making a copy of the whole or a substantial part of any image from it (see section 17(4)). This means that copying one frame of the film will be an infringement, as it was under the previous law (see *Spelling Goldberg Productions* v. *BPC* [1981] RPC 283).

Copying is generally proved by showing substantial similarities between the original and the alleged copy, plus an opportunity to copy. Surprisingly often, minor errors in the original are reproduced by an infringer.

Copying need not be direct, so that, for instance, where the copyright is in a fabric design, copying the material, without ever having seen the original drawing, will still be an infringement, as will 'reverse engineering' of industrial designs e.g. to make unlicensed spare parts (subject to any defence of implied licence: see

---

'Secondary' infringements

Secondary infringements consist not of making the infringing copies, but of dealing with them in some way. So, it is an infringement to import an infringing copy into the UK, and to possess in the course of business, or to sell, hire, offer for sale or hire, or distribute in the course of trade an infringing copy. However, none of these acts will be an infringement unless the alleged infringer knew or had reason to believe that the articles were infringing copies. What is sufficient knowledge will depend upon the facts of each case (see *LA Gear Inc.* v. *Hi-Tec Sports Plc* [1992] FSR 121 and *ZYX Records* v. *King* [1997] 2 All ER 132). Merely putting someone on notice of a dispute as to ownership of copyright may not, however, suffice to give him or her reason to believe in infringement for this purpose: *Hutchison Personal Communications* v. *Hook Advertising* [1995] FSR 365.

Other secondary infringements consist of permitting a place to be used for a public performance in which copyright is infringed and supplying apparatus to be used for infringing public performance, again, in each case, with safeguards for innocent acts.

British Leyland Motor Corp v. *Armstrong Patents Co Ltd* [1984] FSR 591).

Issuing copies of a work to the public when it has not previously been put into circulation in the UK is also an infringement of all types of work.

Other acts which may amount to an infringement depend upon the nature of the work. It will be an infringement of the copyright in a literary, dramatic or musical work to perform it in public, whether by live performance or by playing recordings. Similarly, it is an infringement of the copyright in a sound recording, film, broadcast or cable programme to play or show it in public.

One rather different form of infringement is to make an adaptation of a literary, dramatic or musical work. An adaptation includes, in the case of a literary work, a translation, in the case of a non-dramatic work, making a dramatic work of it, and in the case of a dramatic work, making a non-dramatic work of it. An adaptation of a musical work is a tran-

scription or arrangement of it. There are also a number of 'secondary' infringements – see box on page 621.

Exceptions to infringement

The Act provides a large number of exceptions to the rules on infringement, many of which are innovatory. They are far too numerous to be dealt with here in full, but they include:

• fair dealing with literary, dramatic, musical or artistic works for the purpose of research or private study;
• fair dealing for the purpose of criticism or review or reporting current events;
• incidental inclusion of a work in an artistic work, sound recording, film, broadcast or cable programme;
• various educational exceptions (see sections 32-36);
• various exceptions for libraries (see sections 37-44); various exceptions for public administration (see sections 45-50);
• dealing with a work where the author cannot be identified and the work seems likely to be out of copyright;
• public recitation, if accompanied by a sufficient acknowledgement;
• recording broadcasts or cable programmes at home for viewing at a more convenient time.

Remedies for infringements

The copyright owner has all the remedies offered to other owners of property. Usually the owner will want two things: firstly, to prevent the repetition or continuation of the infringement, and, secondly, compensation.

In almost all cases an injunction will be sought at trial, stopping the continuation of the infringement. A very useful remedy offered by the courts is the 'interlocutory injunction'. This is a form of interim relief, applied for at short notice, with a view to stopping damaging infringement at an early stage, without having to await the outcome of a full trial. Interlocutory injunctions are not always granted in copyright cases, but it is always worth considering the matter as soon as an infringement comes to notice, for delay in bringing an interlocutory application may be fatal to its success. Where an infringement is threatened, the courts will in appropriate cases make a *quia timet* injunction to prevent the infringement ever taking place.

Financial compensation may be sought in one of two forms. Firstly, damages may be granted for infringement. These will usually be calculated upon evidence of the loss caused to the plaintiff, sometimes based upon loss of business, at others upon the basis of what would have been a proper licence fee had the defendant sought a licence for the acts complained of. Additional damages may be awarded in rare cases for flagrant infringements.

Under the old law, a plaintiff could also claim conversion damages, which were often assessed at a much higher level than infringement damages. However, these cannot be claimed under the Act.

Damages will not be awarded for infringement where the infringer did not know, and had no reason to believe, that copyright subsisted in the work. This exception is of limited use to a defendant, though, in the usual situation where he had no actual knowledge of the copyright, but the work was of such a nature that he should have known that copyright would subsist in it.

The alternative to a claim for damages is a claim for an account of profits, that is, the profits made by the infringer by virtue of his illicit exploitation of the copyright.

A copyright owner may also apply for delivery up of infringing copies of his or her work (sections 99 and 113-15).

Finally, there are various criminal offences relating to the making, importation, possession, sale, hire, distribution, etc of infringing copies (see sections 107-110).

Design right

Many industrial designs will now effectively be excluded from copyright protection, by reason of the provisions of sec-

tion 51 of the Act, described above. Alternatively, they may have the term of their copyright protection limited to 25 years from first industrial exploitation, by section 52 of the Act. However, they may instead be protected by the new 'design right' created by sections 213-64 of the Act. Like copyright, design right does not depend upon registration, but upon the creation of a suitable design by a qualified person.

The protection of the new right is given to original designs consisting of the shape or configuration (internal or external) of the whole or part of an article and not being merely 'surface decoration'. A design is not to be considered original if it was commonplace in the design field in question at the time of its creation. In *Ocular Sciences Limited* v. *Aspect Vision Care Limited* (unrep. 11/11/96), 'commonplace' was defined as meaning a design of a type which would excite no 'peculiar attention' amongst those in the trade, or one which amounts to a run-of-the-mill combination of well-known features. Designs will also not be protected if they consist of a method or principle of construction, or are dictated by the shape, etc of an article to which the new article is to be connected or of which it is to form part, the so-called 'must-fit' and 'must-match' exclusions. In *Ocular Sciences*, these exclusions had a devastating effect upon numerous design rights claimed for contact lens designs.

Design right will be granted to designs made by qualifying persons (in this part of the Act meaning UK and EU citizens or residents or others to whom the right may be extended) or commissioned by a qualifying person, or first marketed in the UK, another EU state or any other country to which the provision may be extended by Order in Council.

Design right lasts only 15 years from the end of the year in which it was first recorded or an article made to the design, or (if shorter) 10 years from the end of the year in which articles made according to the design were first sold or hired out.

The designer will be the owner of the right, unless he or she made it in pursuance of a commission, in which case the commissioner will be the first owner of the right. The same rule applies as in copyright, that an employee's designs made in the course of his or her employment will belong to the employer.

The right given to the owner of a design right is the exclusive right to reproduce the design for commercial purposes. The rules as to assignments and licensing and as to infringement, both primary and secondary, are substantially similar to those described above in relation to copyright, as are the remedies available.

Design right will coexist with the scheme of *registered* designs of the Registered Designs Act 1949 (as amended by the Act), which provides a monopoly right renewable for up to 25 years in respect of designs which have been accepted on to a register. Registered designs must contain features which appeal to and are judged by the eye, unlike designs protected by the design right.

Moral rights

The Act also provided for the protection of certain so-called 'moral rights', commonly known as the rights of 'paternity' and 'integrity'.

The right of 'paternity' is for the author of a copyright literary, dramatic, musical or artistic work, and the director of a copyright film, to be identified as the author/director in a number of different situations, largely whenever the work is published, performed or otherwise commercially exploited (section 77).

However, the right does not arise unless it has been 'asserted' by the author or director, by appropriate words in an assignment, or otherwise by an instrument in writing (section 78), or in the case of an artistic work by ensuring that the artist's name appears on the frame, etc. Writers should therefore aim to ensure that all copies of their works carry a clear assertion of their rights under this provision (see end). There are exceptions to the right, in particular where the first ownership of the copyright vested in the

author's or director's employer.

The right of 'integrity' is not to have one's work subjected to 'derogatory treatment'. This is defined as meaning an addition to, deletion from, alteration or adaptation of a work (save for a translation of a literary or dramatic work or an arrangement of a musical work involving no more than a change of key or register) which amounts to distortion or mutilation of the work or is otherwise prejudicial to the honour or reputation of the author/director.

Again, infringement of the right takes place when the maltreated work is published commercially or performed or exhibited in public. There are various exceptions set out in section 81 of the Act, in particular where the publication is in a newspaper, etc, and the work was made for inclusion therein or made available with the author's consent.

Where the copyright in the work vested first in the author's or director's employer, he or she has no right to 'integrity' unless he was identified at the time of the relevant act or was previously identified on published copies of the work.

These rights subsist for as long as the copyright in the work subsists.

A third moral right conferred by the Act is not to have a literary, dramatic, musical or artistic work falsely attributed to one as author, or to have a film falsely attributed to one as director, again where the work in question is published, publicly performed, etc. This right subsists until 20 years after a person's death.

None of these rights can be assigned during the person's lifetime, but all of them either pass on the person's death as directed by his or her will or fall into his residuary estate.

A fourth but rather different moral right is conferred by section 85. It gives a person who has commissioned the taking of photographs for private purposes a right to prevent copies of the work being issued to the public, etc.

The remedies for breach of these moral rights may again include damages and an injunction, although section 103(2) specifically foresees the granting of an injunction qualified by a right to the defendant to do the acts complained of, if subject to a suitable disclaimer.

Moral rights will be exercisable in relation to works in which the copyright has revived subject to any waiver or assertion of the right made before 1 January 1996 (see details as to who may exercise rights in paragraph 22 of the Regulations).

NOTICE

I, AMANDA LOUISE MICHAELS, hereby assert and give notice of my right under section 77 of the Copyright, Designs and Patents Act 1988 to be identified as the author of the foregoing article.

AMANDA MICHAELS

Amanda L. Michaels is a barrister in private practice in London, and specialises in copyright, designs, trade marks, and similar intellectual property and 'media' work. She is author of *A Practical Guide to Trade Mark Law* (Sweet & Maxwell, 2nd edn 1996).

Further reading

Skone James, Mummery, Rayner James and Garnet, *Copinger and Skone James on Copyright*, Sweet & Maxwell, 13th edn, 1991, and supplement 1994; 14th edn expected March 1998

Laddie Prescott and Vitoria, *The Modern Law of Copyright*, Butterworths, 2nd edn, 1995

Flint, *A User's Guide to Copyright*, Butterworths, 4th edn, 1997

Bainbridge, *Intellectual Property*, Pitman, 3rd edn, 1996

Cornish, *Intellectual Property*, Sweet & Maxwell, 3rd edn, 1996

Copyright acts

Copyright, Designs and Patents Act 1998

The Duration of Copyright and Rights in Performances Regulations 1995 (SI 1995 No 3297)

see also Numerous Orders in Council

US copyright law

*When authors and other artists take their work overseas, the complex subject of copyright can become even more daunting. **Gavin McFarlane**, barrister, introduces US copyright law and points out the differences, and similarities, of British copyright law.*

International copyright

International copyright conventions

There is no general principle of international copyright which provides a uniform code for the protection of right owners throughout the world. There are, however, two major international copyright conventions which lay down certain minimum standards for member states, in particular requiring member states to accord to right owners of other member states the same protection which is granted to their own nationals. One is the higher standard Berne Convention of 1886, the most recent revision of which was signed in Paris in 1971. The other is the Universal Copyright Convention signed in 1952 with lower minimum standards, and sponsored by Unesco. This also was most recently revised in Paris in 1971, jointly with the Berne Convention. To this latter Convention the United States has belonged since 1955. On 16 November 1988, the Government of the United States deposited its instrument of accession to the Paris Revision of the Berne Convention. The Convention entered into force as regards the United States on 1 March 1989. Together with certain new statutory provisions made in consequence of accession to Berne, this advances substantially the process of overhaul and modernisation of US copyright law which was begun in the 1970s.

Effect on British copyright owners

The copyright statute of the United States having been brought into line with the requirements of the Universal Copyright Convention, compliance with the formalities required by American law is all that is needed to acquire protection for the work of a British author first published outside the United States. Even these formality requirements have been largely removed now that the United States has joined the Berne Convention, although caution is still required. The Berne Convention Implementation Act of 1988 makes statutory amendments to the way foreign works are now treated in US law. These are now inserted in the US codified law as Title 17 – The Copyright Act. 'Foreign works' are works having a country of origin other than the United States. The formalities which were for so long a considerable handicap for foreign copyright owners in the American system have now become optional, though not removed altogether. Indeed the new system provides incentives to encourage such foreign right owners to continue to comply with formalities on a voluntary basis, in particular notice, renewal and registration.

US copyright law – summary

Introduction of new law

After many years of debate, the new Copyright Statute of the United States was passed on 19 October 1976. The greater

part of its relevant provisions came into force on 1 January 1978. It has extended the range of copyright protection, and further eased the requirements whereby British authors can obtain copyright protection in America. New Public Law 100-568 of 31 October 1988 has made further amendments to the Copyright Statute which were necessary to enable ratification of the Berne Convention to take place. The Universal Copyright Convention is now for all practical purposes moribund. The problems which derived from the old system of common law copyright no longer now exist.

The rights of a copyright owner

(1) To reproduce the copyrighted work in copies or phonorecords.
(2) To prepare derivative works based upon the copyrighted work.
(3) To distribute copies or phonorecords of the copyrighted work to the public by sale or other transfer of ownership, or by rental, lease or lending.
(4) In the case of literary, musical, dramatic and choreographic works, pantomimes, and motion pictures and other audiovisual works, but not sound recordings, to perform the copyrighted work publicly. However, in 1995 Congress granted a limited performance right to sound recordings in digital format in an interactive medium.
(5) In the case of literary, musical, dramatic, and choreographic works, pantomimes, and pictorial, graphic, or sculptural works, including the individual images of a motion picture or other audiovisual work, to display the copyrighted work publicly.
(6) By the Record Rental Amendment Act 1984, s.109 of the Copyright Statute is amended. Now, unless authorised by the owners of copyright in the sound recording and the musical works thereon, the owner of a phonorecord may not, for direct or indirect commercial advantage, rent, lease or lend the phonorecord. A compulsory licence under s.115(c) includes the right of a maker of a phonorecord of non-dramatic musical

work to distribute or authorise the distribution of the phonorecord by rental, lease, or lending, and an additional royalty is payable in respect of that. This modifies the 'first sale doctrine', which otherwise permits someone buying a copyright work to hire or sell a lawfully purchased copy to third parties without compensating the copyright owners, and without his or her consent.
(7) A further exception to the 'first sale doctrine' and s.109 of the Copyright Act is made by the Computer Software Rental Amendments Act. A similar restriction has been placed on the unauthorised rental, lease or lending of software, subject to certain limited exceptions. Both the phonocard and software exceptions to the first sale doctrine terminate on 1 October 1997.
(8) The Semiconductor Chip Protection Act 1984 adds to the Copyright Statute a new chapter on the protection of semiconductor chip products.
(9) The Visual Artists Rights Act 1990 has added moral rights to the various economic rights listed above. These moral rights are the right of integrity, and the right of attribution or paternity. A new category of 'work of visual art' is created, broadly paintings, drawings, prints and sculptures, with an upper limit of 200 copies. Works generally exploited in mass market copies such as books, newspapers, motion pictures and electronic information services are specifically excluded from these new moral rights provisions. Where they apply, they do so only in respect of works created on or after 1 June 1991, and to certain works previously created where title has not already been transferred by the author.

Manufacturing requirements

With effect from 1 July 1982, these ceased to have effect. Prior to 1 July 1982, the importation into or public distribution in the United States of a work consisting preponderantly of non-dramatic literary material that was in the English language and protected under American law was

---

Works protected in American law

Works of authorship include the following categories:
- Literary works. Note: Computer programs are classified as literary works for the purposes of United States copyright. In *Whelan Associates Inc.* v. *Jaslow Dental Laboratory Inc.* (1987) F.S.R.1, it was held that the copyright of a computer program could be infringed even in the absence of copying of the literal code if the structure was part of the expression of the idea behind a program rather than the idea itself.
- Musical works, including any accompanying words.
- Dramatic works, including any accompanying music.
- Pantomimes and choreographic works.
- Pictorial, graphic and sculptural works.
- Motion pictures and other audiovisual works – note: copyright in certain motion pictures has been extended by the North American Free Trade Agreement Information Act 1993.
- Sound recordings, but copyright in sound recordings is not to include a right of public performance.
- Architectural works: the design of a building as embodied in any tangible medium of expression, including a building, architectural plans or drawings. The Architectural Works Copyright Protections Act applies this protection to works created on or after 1 December 1990.

---

prohibited unless the portions consisting of such material had been manufactured in the United States or Canada. This provision did not apply where, on the date when importation was sought or public distribution in the United States was made, the author of any substantial part of such material was not a national of the United States or, if a national, had been domiciled outside the United States for a continuous period of at least one year immediately preceding that date.

Thus since 1 July 1982, there is no manufacturing requirement in respect of works of British authors. Certain interested groups in the United States still lobby for the restoration of the manufacturing clause in American law. Countries such as

Britain will no doubt oppose this vigorously through diplomatic channels. With American ratification of the Berne Convention, the formalities previously required in relation to copyright notice, deposit and registration have been greatly modified.

Formalities

Notice of copyright. Whenever a work protected by the American Copyright Statute is published in the United States or elsewhere by authority of the copyright owner, a notice of copyright should be placed on all publicly distributed copies. This should consist of:
- either the symbol © or the word 'Copyright' or the abbreviation 'Copr.' plus
- the year of first publication of the work, plus
- the name of the copyright owner.

Since the Berne Amendments, both US and works of foreign origin which were first published in the US after 1 March 1989 without having notice of copyright placed on them will no longer be unprotected. In general, authors are advised to place copyright notices on their works, as this is a considerable deterrent to plagiarism. Damages may well be lower in a case where no notice of copyright was placed on the work.

Deposit. The owner of copyright or the exclusive right of publication in a work published with notice of copyright in the United States must within three months of such publication deposit in the Copyright Office for the use or disposition of the Library of Congress two complete copies of the best edition of the work (or two records, if the work is a sound recording).

Registration. Registration for copyright in the United States is optional. However, any owner of copyright in a work first published outside the United States may register a work by making application to the Copyright Office with the appropriate fee, and by depositing one complete copy of the work. This requirement of deposit may be satisfied by using copies deposited

for the Library of Congress. Whilst registration is still a requirement for works of US origin and from non-Berne countries, it is no longer necessary for foreign works from Berne countries. But as a matter of practice there are procedural advantages in any litigation where there has been registration. On the whole, it is advisable. The United States has interpreted the Berne Convention as allowing formalities which are not in themselves conditions for obtaining copyright protection, but which lead to improved protection. Moreover, the law allows statutory damages and attorneys' fees only if the work was registered prior to the infringement.

Restoration of copyright

Works by non-US authors which lost copyright protection in the United States because of failure to comply with any of these formalities may have protection restored in certain circumstances. Works claiming restoration must still be in copyright in their country of origin. If a work succeeds in having copyright restored, it will last for the remainder of the period to which it would originally have been entitled in the United States.

Duration of copyright

An important change in the new American law is that in general, copyright in a work created on or after 1 January 1978 endures for a term of the life of the author, and a period of 50 years after the author's death. This brought the United States into line with most other advanced countries, and with the further amendments made by Public Law 100-568 of 31 October 1988 has enabled that government to ratify the higher standard Berne Convention. Copyright in a work created before 1 January 1978, but not published or copyrighted before then, subsists from 1 January 1978, and lasts for the life of the author and a postmortem period of 50 years.

Any copyright, the first term of which under the previous law was still subsisting on 1 January 1978, shall endure for 28 years from the date when it was originally secured, and the copyright proprietor or his or her representative may apply for a further term of 47 years within one year prior to the expiry of the original term. Until 1992, application for renewal and extension was required. Failure to do so produced disastrous results with some material of great merit passing into the public domain in error. However, by Public Law 102-307 enacted on 26 June 1992, there is no longer necessity to make a renewal registration in order to obtain the longer period of protection. Now renewal copyright vests automatically in the person entitled to renewal at the end of the 28th year of the original term of copyright.

The duration of any copyright, the renewal term of which was subsisting at any time between 31 December 1976 and 31 December 1977, or for which renewal registration was made between those dates, is extended to endure for a term of 75 years from the date copyright was originally secured.

These alterations are of great importance for owners of existing American copyrights.

All terms of copyright provided for by the sections referred to above run to the end of the calendar year in which they would otherwise expire.

Public performance

Under the previous American law the provisions relating to performance in public were less generous to right owners than those existing in United Kingdom copyright law. In particular, performance of a musical work was formerly only an infringement if it was 'for profit'. Moreover, the considerable American coin-operated record-playing machine industry (juke boxes) had obtained an exemption from being regarded as instruments of profit, and accordingly their owners did not have to pay royalties for the use of copyright musical works.

Now by the new law one of the exclusive rights of the copyright owner is, in the case of literary, musical, dramatic and choreographic works, pantomimes, and

US copyright law 629

motion pictures and other audiovisual works, to perform the work publicly, without any requirement of such performance being 'for profit'. By Section 114 however, the exclusive rights of the owner of copyright in a sound recording are specifically stated not to include any right of public performance.

The position of coin-operated record players (juke boxes) is governed by the new Section 116A, inserted by Public Law 100-568 of 31 October 1988. It covers the position of negotiated licences. Limitations are placed on the exclusive right if licences are not negotiated.

These extensions of the scope of the right of public performance should augment the royalty income of authors, composers and publishers of musical works widely performed in the United States. All such right owners should ensure that their American interests are properly taken care of.

Mechanical right

Where sound recordings of a non-dramatic musical work have been distributed to the public in the United States with the authority of the copyright owner, any other person may, by following the provisions of the law, obtain a compulsory licence to make and distribute sound recordings of the work. This right is known in the United Kingdom as 'the mechanical right'. Notice must be served on the copyright owner, who is entitled to a royalty in respect of each of his or her works recorded of either two and three fourths cents or one half of one cent per minute of playing time or fraction thereof, whichever amount is the larger. Failure to serve or file the required notice forecloses the possibility of a compulsory licence and, in the absence of a negotiated licence, renders the making and distribution of such records actionable as acts of infringement.

Transfer of copyright

Under the previous American law copyright was regarded as indivisible, which meant that on the transfer of copyright, where it was intended that only film rights or some other such limited right be transferred, the entire copyright nevertheless had to be passed. This led to a cumbersome procedure whereby the author would assign the whole copyright to his or her publisher, who would return to the author by means of an exclusive licence those rights which it was not meant to transfer.

Now it is provided by Section 201(d) of the Copyright Statute that (1) the ownership of a copyright may be transferred in whole or in part by any means of conveyance or by operation of law, and may be bequeathed by will or pass as personal property by the applicable laws of intestate succession and (2) any of the exclusive rights comprised in a copyright (including any subdivision of any of the rights set out in 'The rights of a copyright owner' above) may be transferred as provided in (1) above and owned separately. The owner of any particular exclusive right is entitled, to the extent of that right, to all the protection and remedies accorded to the copyright owner by that Statute. This removes the difficulties which existed under the previous law, and brings the position much closer to that existing in the copyright law of the United Kingdom. All transfers and assignments of copyright must be recorded in the US Copyright Office.

Copyright Arbitration Royalty Panels

In 1993, the Copyright Royalty Tribunal which had been established by the Copyright Act was eliminated by Congress. In its place a new administrative mechanism was established in the Copyright Office with the purpose of making adjustments of reasonable copyright royalty rates in respect of the exercise of certain rights, mainly affecting the musical interests. The newly formed Copyright Arbitration Panels are constituted on an ad hoc basis and perform in the United States a function similar to the new Copyright Tribunal in the United Kingdom.

The new American law spells out the economic objectives which its Copyright Tribunal is to apply in calculating the relevant rates. These are:

- to maximise the availability of creative works to the public;
- to afford the copyright owner a fair return for his or her creative work and the copyright user a fair income under existing economic conditions;
- to reflect the relative roles of the copyright owner and the copyright user in the product made available to the public with respect to relative creative contribution, technological contribution, capital investment, cost, risk, and contribution to the opening of new markets for creative expression and media for their communication.
- to minimise any disruptive impact on the structure of the industries involved and on generally prevailing industry practices.

Every final determination of the Tribunal shall be published in the Federal Register. It shall state in detail the criteria that the Tribunal determined to be applicable to the particular proceeding, the various facts that it found relevant to its determination in that proceeding, and the specific reasons for its determination. Any final decision of the Tribunal in a proceeding may be appealed to the United States Court of Appeals by an aggrieved party, within 30 days after its publication in the Federal Register.

Fair use

One of the most controversial factors which held up the introduction of the new American copyright law for at least a decade was the extent to which a balance should be struck between the desire of copyright owners to benefit from their works by extending copyright protection as far as possible, and the pressure from users of copyright to obtain access to copyright material as cheaply as possible – if not completely freely.

The new law provides by Section 107 that the fair use of a copyright work, including such use by reproduction in copies or on records, for purposes such as criticism, comment, news reporting, teaching (including multiple copies for classroom use), scholarship or research is not an infringement of copyright. In determining whether the use made of a work in any particular case is a fair use, the factors to be considered include:

- the purpose and character of the use, including whether such use is of a commercial nature or is for non-profit educational purposes;
- the nature of the copyrighted work;
- the amount and substantiality of the portion used in relation to the copyrighted work as a whole; and
- the effect of the use upon the potential market for or value of the copyrighted work.

It is not an infringement of copyright for a library or archive, or any of its employees acting within the scope of their employment, to reproduce or distribute no more than one copy of a work, if:

- the reproduction or distribution is made without any purpose of direct or indirect commercial advantage;
- the collections of the library or archive are either open to the public or available not only to researchers affiliated with the library or archive or with the institution of which it is a part, but also to other persons doing research in a specialised field; and
- the reproduction or distribution of the work includes a notice of copyright.

It is not generally an infringement of copyright if a performance or display of a work is given by instructors or pupils in the course of face-to-face teaching activities of a non-profit educational institution, in a classroom or similar place devoted to instruction.

Nor is it an infringement of copyright to give a performance of a non-dramatic literary or musical work or a dramatico-musical work of a religious nature in the course of services at a place of worship or other religious assembly.

It is also not an infringement of copyright to give a performance of a non-dramatic literary or musical work other than in a transmission to the public, without any purpose

of direct or indirect commercial advantage and without payment of any fee for the performance to any of the performing artists, promoters or organisers if either:
• there is no direct or indirect admission charge; or
• the proceeds, after deducting the reasonable costs of producing the performance, are used exclusively for educational, religious or charitable purposes and not for private financial gain.

In this case the copyright owner has the right to serve notice of objection to the performance in a prescribed form.

Note the important decision of the Supreme Court in *Sony Corporation of America* v. *Universal City Studios* (No. 81-1687, 52 USLW 4090). This decided that the sale of video recorders to the public for the purpose of recording a copyrighted programme from a broadcast signal for private use for time-switching purposes alone (not for archiving or 'librarying') does not amount to contributory infringement of the rights in films which are copied as a result of television broadcasts of them. Among other reasons for their decision advanced by the majority of the judges was their opinion that even unauthorised time-switching is legitimate fair use.

Remedies for copyright owners

Infringement of copyright

Copyright is infringed by anyone who violates any of the exclusive rights referred to in 'The rights of a copyright owner' above, or who imports copies or records into the United States in violation of the law. The owner of copyright is entitled to institute an action for infringement so long as that infringement is committed while he or she is the owner of the right infringed. Previously, no action for infringement of copyright could be instituted until registration of the copyright claim had been made, but this requirement has been modified now that the United States has ratified the Berne Convention. Under the new provision, US authors must register, or attempt to register, but non-US Berne authors are exempt from this requirement.

Injunctions

Any court having civil jurisdiction under the copyright law may grant interim and final injunctions on such terms as it may deem reasonable to prevent or restrain infringement of copyright. Such injunction may be served anywhere in the United States on the person named. An injunction is operative throughout the whole of the United States, and can be enforced by proceedings in contempt or otherwise by any American court which has jurisdiction over the infringer.

Impounding and disposition

At any time while a copyright action under American law is pending, the court may order the impounding on such terms as it considers reasonable of all copies or records claimed to have been made or used in violation of the copyright owner's exclusive rights; it may also order the impounding of all VCRs, tape recorders, plates, moulds, matrices, masters, tapes, film negatives or other articles by means of which infringing copies or records may be reproduced. A court may order as part of a final judgement or decree the destruction or other disposition of all copies or records found to have been made or used in violation of the copyright owner's exclusive rights. It also has the power to order the destruction of all articles by means of which infringing copies or records were reproduced.

Damages and profits

An infringer of copyright is generally liable either for the copyright owner's actual damage and any additional profits made by the infringer, or for statutory damages.
• The copyright owner is entitled to recover the actual damages suffered by him or her as a result of the infringement, and in addition any profits of the infringer which are attributed to the infringement and are not taken into account in computing the actual damages. In establishing the infringer's profits, the copyright owner is only required

Criminal proceedings in respect of copyright

- Anyone who infringes a copyright wilfully and for purposes of commercial advantage and private financial gain shall be fined not more than $10,000 or imprisoned for not more than one year, or both. However, if the infringement relates to copyright in a sound recording or a film, the infringer is liable to a fine of not more than $25,000 or imprisonment for not more than one year or both on a first offence, which can be increased to a fine of up to $50,000 or imprisonment for not more than two years or both for a subsequent offence.
- Following a conviction for criminal infringement a court may in addition to these penalties order the forfeiture and destruction of all infringing copies and records, together with implements and equipment used in their manufacture.
- It is also an offence knowingly and with fraudulent intent to place on any article a notice of copyright or words of the same purport, or to import or distribute such copies. A fine is provided for this offence of not more than $2500. The fraudulent removal of a copyright notice also attracts the same maximum fine, as does the false representation of a material particular on an application for copyright representation.

to present proof of the infringer's gross revenue, and it is for the infringer to prove his or her deductible expenses and the elements of profit attributable to factors other than the copyright work.

- Except where the copyright owner has persuaded the court that the infringement was committed wilfully, the copyright owner may elect, at any time before final judgement is given, to recover, instead of actual damages and profits, an award of statutory damages for all infringements involved in the action in respect of any one work, which may be between $500 and $20,000 according to what the court considers justified.
- However, where the copyright owner satisfies the court that the infringement was committed wilfully, the court has the discretion to increase the award of statutory damages to not more than

$100,000. Where the infringer succeeds in proving that he or she was not aware and had no reason to believe that his or her acts constituted an infringement of copyright, the court has the discretion to reduce the award of statutory damages to not less than $100.

Costs: time limits

In any civil proceedings under American copyright law, the court has the discretion to allow the recovery of full costs by or against any party except the Government of the United States. It may also award a reasonable sum in respect of an attorney's fee.

No civil or criminal proceedings in respect of copyright law shall be permitted unless begun within three years after the claim or cause of action arose.

Counterfeiting

By the Piracy and Counterfeiting Amendment Act 1982, pirates and counterfeiters of sound recordings and of motion pictures now face maximum penalties of up to five years imprisonment or fines of up to $250,000.

Colouring films

The United States Copyright Office has decided that adding colour to a black and white film may qualify for copyright protection whenever it amounts to more than a trivial change.

Satellite home viewers

The position of satellite home viewers is now controlled by the Satellite Home Viewer Act of 1988. (Title II of Public Law 100-667 of 16 November 1988.)

The Copyright Remedy Clarification Act has created s.511 of the Copyright Act, in order to rectify a situation which had developed in case law. By this, the component States of the Union, their agencies and employees are placed in the same position as private individuals and entities in relation to their liability for copyright infringement.

General observations

The copyright law of the United States has been very greatly improved as a result of the new statute passed by Congress on 19 October 1976. (Title 17, United States Code.) Apart from lifting the general standards of protection for copyright owners to a much higher level than that which previously existed, it has on the whole shifted the balance of copyright protection in favour of the copyright owner and away from the copyright user in many of the areas where controversy existed. But most important for British and other non-American authors and publishers, it has gone a long way towards bringing American copyright law up to the same standards of international protection for non-national copyright proprietors which have long been offered by the United Kingdom and the other major countries, both in Europe and elsewhere in the English-speaking world. The ratification by the United States of the Berne Convention with effect from 1 March 1989 was an action which at that time put American copyright law on par with the protection offered by other major countries.

Gavin McFarlane LLM, PhD is a barrister at Titmuss Sainer Dechert. He specialises in international trade law, and is particularly interested in the involvement of the World Trade Organisation in intellectual property matters.

Libel

Any writer should be aware of the law of libel. **Antony Whitaker** *gives an outline of the main principles, concentrating on points which are most frequently misunderstood. But this article is no more than that, and specific legal advice should be taken when practical problems arise.*

The law discussed is the law of England and Wales. Scotland has its own, albeit somewhat similar, rules. A summary of the main differences between the two systems appears in the box on page 639.

At the time of going to press, Parliament had passed the Defamation Act 1996, but only limited parts of it had been brought into force. The purpose of the Act is mainly to streamline and simplify libel litigation.

Libel: liability to pay damages

English law draws a distinction between defamation published in permanent form and that which is not. The former is libel, the latter slander. 'Permanent form' includes writing, printing, drawings and photographs and radio and television broadcasts. It follows that it is the law of libel rather than slander which most concerns writers and artists professionally, and the slightly differing rules applicable to slander will not be mentioned in this article.

Publication of a libel can result in a civil action for damages, an injunction to prevent repetition and/or in certain cases a criminal prosecution against those responsible, who include the author (or artist or photographer), the publishers and the editor, if any, in which the libel appeared. 'Innocent disseminators', such as printers, distributors, broadcasters, Internet service providers and retailers, who can show they took reasonable care and had no reason to believe what they were handling contained a libel, are now protected under the 1996 Act. Prosecutions are rare. Certain special rules apply to them and these will be

explained below after a discussion of the question of civil liability, which in practice arises much more frequently.

Libel claims do not qualify for legal aid, although the closely analagous remedy of malicious falsehood does. Most libel cases are usually heard by a judge and jury, and it is the jury which decides the amount of any award, which is tax-free. It is not necessary for the plaintiff to prove that he or she has actually suffered any loss, because the law presumes damage. While the main purpose of a libel claim is to compensate the plaintiff for the injury to his or her reputation, a jury may give additional sums either as 'aggravated' damages, if it appears a defendant has behaved malevolently or spitefully, or as 'exemplary', or 'punitive', damages where a defendant hopes the economic advantages of publication will outweigh any sum awarded. Damages can also be 'nominal' if the libel complained of is trivial. It is generally very difficult to forecast the amounts juries are likely to award, though recent awards against newspapers have disclosed a tendency towards considerable generosity. The Court of Appeal now has power to reduce excessive awards of damages.

In an action for damages for libel, it is for the plaintiff to establish that the matter he or she complains of:

• has been published by the defendant,
• refers to the plaintiff,
• is defamatory.

If this is done, the plaintiff establishes a *prima facie* case. However, the defendant will escape liability if he or she can show he has a good defence. There are five defences to a libel action. They are:

• Justification
• Fair Comment
• Privilege
• Offer of Amends: s. 4 of the Defamation Act, 1952, to be replaced by ss. 2-4 of the Defamation Act, 1996
• Apology, etc, under the Libel Acts, 1843 and 1845.

A libel claim can also become barred under the Limitation Acts, as explained below. These matters must now be examined in detail.

The plaintiff's case

The meaning of 'published'

'Published' in the legal sense means communicated to a person other than the plaintiff. Thus the legal sense is wider than the lay sense but includes it. It follows that the content of a book is published in the legal sense when the manuscript is first sent to the publishing firm just as much as it is when the book is later placed on sale to the public. Subject to the 'innocent dissemination' defence referred to above, both types of publication are sufficient for the purpose of establishing liability for libel, but the law differentiates between them, since the scope of publication can properly be taken into account by the jury in considering the actual amount of damages to award.

Establishing identity

The plaintiff must also establish that the matter complained of refers to him or her. It is of course by no means necessary to mention a person's name before it is clear that he or she is referred to. Nicknames by which he or she is known or corruptions of his name are just two ways in which his or her identity can be indicated. There are more subtle methods. The sole question is whether the plaintiff is indicated to those who read the matter complained of. In some cases he or she will not be unless it is read in the light of facts known to the reader from other sources, but this is sufficient for the plaintiff's purpose. The test is purely objective and does not depend at all on whether the writer intended to refer to the plaintiff.

It is because it is impossible to establish reference to any individual that generalisations, broadly speaking, are not successfully actionable. To say boldly 'All lawyers are crooks' does not give any single lawyer a cause of action, because the statement does not point a finger at any individual. However, if anyone is named in conjunction with a generalisation, then it may lose its general character and become particular from the context. Again, if one says 'One of the X Committee has been convicted of

murder' and the X Committee consists of, say, four persons, it cannot be said that the statement is not actionable because no individual is indicated and it could be referring to any of the committee. This is precisely why it is actionable at the suit of each of them as suspicion has been cast on all.

Determining what is defamatory

It is for the plaintiff to show that the matter complained of is defamatory. What is defamatory is decided by the jury except in the extreme cases where the judge rules that the words cannot bear a defamatory meaning. Various tests have been laid down for determining this. It is sufficient that any one test is satisfied. The basic tests are:

- Does the matter complained of tend to lower the plaintiff in the estimation of society?
- Does it tend to bring him or her into hatred, ridicule, contempt, dislike or disesteem with society?
- Does it tend to make him shunned or avoided or cut off from society? The mere fact that what is published is inaccurate is not enough to involve liability; it is the adverse impact on the plaintiff's reputation that matters. For example, merely to overstate a person's income is not defamatory; but it will be if the context implies he has not fully declared it to the tax authorities.

'Society' means right-thinking members of society generally. It is by reference to such people that the above tests must be applied. A libel action against a newspaper which had stated that the police had taken a statement from the plaintiff failed, notwithstanding that the plaintiff gave evidence that his apparent assistance to the police (which he denied) had brought him into grave disrepute with the underworld. It was not by their wrongheaded standards that the matter fell to be judged.

Further, it is not necessary to imply that the plaintiff is at fault in some way in order to defame him. To say of a woman that she has been raped or of someone that he is insane imputes to them no degree of blame, but nonetheless both statements are defamatory.

Sometimes a defamatory meaning is conveyed by words which on the face of them have no such meaning. 'But Brutus is an honourable man' is an example. If a jury finds that words are meant ironically they will consider this ironical sense when determining whether the words are defamatory. In deciding, therefore, whether or not the words are defamatory, the jury seeks to discover what, without straining the words or putting a perverse construction on them, they will be understood to mean. In some cases this may differ substantially from their literal meaning.

Matter may also be defamatory by innuendo. Strictly so called, an innuendo is a meaning that words acquire by virtue of facts known to the reader but not stated in the passage complained of. Words, quite innocent on the face of them, may acquire a defamatory meaning when read in the light of these facts. For example, where a newspaper published a photograph of a man and a woman, with the caption that they had just announced their engagement, it was held to be defamatory of the man's wife since those who knew that she had cohabited with him were led to the belief that she had done so only as his mistress. The newspaper was unaware that the man was already married, but some of its readers were not.

Defences to a libel action

Justification

English law does not protect the reputation that a person either does not or should not possess. Stating the truth therefore does not incur liability, and the plea of justification – namely, that what is complained of is true in substance and in fact – is a complete answer to an action for damages. However, this defence is by no means to be undertaken lightly. For instance, to prove one instance of using bad language will be insufficient to justify the allegation that a person is 'foul-mouthed'. It would be necessary to prove several instances, and the defendant is obliged in most cases to particularise in

his pleadings giving details, dates and places. However, the requirement that the truth of every allegation must be proved is not absolute, and is qualified by the 'multiple charge – no worse off' defence. This applies where two or more distinct charges are levelled against a plaintiff, and some of what is said turns out to be inaccurate. If his or her reputation in the light of what is shown to be true is made no worse by the unprovable defamatory allegations – for example, mistaken accusations that a convicted pickpocket and car thief is also a shoplifter – the publisher will be safe. This is the extent of the law's recognition that some individuals are so disreputable as to be beyond redemption by awards of damages regardless of what is said about them. Subject to this, however, it is for the defendant to prove that what he or she has published is true, not for the plaintiff to disprove it, though if he can do so, so much the better for him.

One point requires special mention. It is insufficient for the defendant to prove that he or she has accurately repeated what a third person has written or said or that such statements have gone uncontradicted when made on occasions in the past. If X writes 'Y told me that Z is a liar', it is no defence to an action against X merely to prove that Y did say that. X has given currency to a defamatory statement concerning Z and has so made it his own. His only defence is to prove that Z is a liar by establishing a number of instances of Z's untruthfulness. Nor is it a defence to prove that the defendant genuinely believed what he or she published to be true. This might well be a complete answer in an action, other than a libel action, based on a false but non-defamatory statement. For such statements do not incur liability in the absence of fraud or malice which, in this context, means a dishonest or otherwise improper motive. Bona fide belief, however, may be relevant to the assessment of damages, even in a libel action.

Special care should be taken in relation to references to a person's convictions, however accurately described. Since the Rehabilitation of Offenders Act, 1974, a person's convictions may become 'spent' and thereafter it may involve liability to refer to them. Reference to the Act and orders thereunder must be made in order to determine the position in any particular case.

Fair comment

It is a defence to prove that what is complained of is fair comment made in good faith and without malice on a matter of public interest.

'Fair' in this context means 'honest'. 'Fair comment' means therefore the expression of the writer's genuinely held opinion. It does not necessarily mean opinion with which the jury agree. Comment may therefore be quite extreme and still be 'fair' in the legal sense. However, if it is utterly perverse the jury may be led to think that no one could have genuinely held such views. In such a case the defence would fail, for the comment could not be honest. 'Malice' here includes the popular sense of personal spite, but covers any dishonest or improper motive.

The defence only applies when what is complained of is comment as distinct from a statement of fact. The line between comment and fact is notoriously difficult to draw in some cases. Comment means a statement of opinion. The facts on which comment is made must be stated together with the comment or be sufficiently indicated with it. This is merely another way of saying that it must be clear that the defamatory statement is one of opinion and not of fact, for which the only defence would be the onerous one of justification. The exact extent to which the facts commented on must be stated or referred to is a difficult question, but some help may be derived in answering it by considering the purpose of the rule, which is to enable the reader to exercise his own judgement and to agree or disagree with the comment. It is quite plain that it is not necessary to state every single detail of the facts. In one case it was sufficient merely to mention the name of one of the Press lords in an article about a newspaper though not one

owned by him. He was so well known that to mention his name indicated the substratum of fact commented upon, namely his control of his group of newspapers. No universal rule can be laid down, except that, in general, the fuller the facts set out or referred to with the comment, the better. All these facts must be proved to be true subject, however, to the flexibility of the 'proportionate truth' rule. This means that the defence remains available even if, for example, only three out of five factual claims can be proved true, provided that these three are by themselves sufficient to sustain, and are proportionate to, the fairness of the comment. The impact of the two unproven claims would probably fall to be assessed in accordance with the 'multiple charge – no worse off' rule in justification, set out above.

The defence only applies where the matters commented on are of public interest, i.e. of legitimate concern to the public or a substantial section of it. Thus the conduct of national and local government, international affairs, the administration of justice, etc, are all matters of public interest, whereas other people's private affairs may very well not be, although they undoubtedly interest the public, or provoke curiosity.

In addition, matters of which criticism has been expressly or impliedly invited, such as publicly performed plays and published books, are a legitimate subject of comment. Criticism need not be confined merely to their artistic merit but equally may deal with the attitudes to life and the opinions therein expressed.

It is sometimes said that a man's moral character is never a proper subject of comment for the purpose of this defence. This is certainly true where it is a private individual who is concerned, and some authorities say it is the same in the case of a public figure even though his or her character may be relevant to his or her public life. Again, it may in some cases be exceeding the bounds of fair comment to impute a dishonourable motive to a person, as is frequently done by way of inference from facts. In general, the imputation is a dangerous and potentially expensive practice.

Privilege

In the public interest, certain occasions are privileged so that to make defamatory statements upon them does not incur liability. The following are privileged in any event:

- fair, accurate, and contemporaneous reports of public judicial proceedings in England published in a newspaper;
- Parliamentary papers published by the direction of either House, or full republications thereof.

The following are privileged provided publication is made only for the reason that the privilege is given and not for some wrongful or indirect motive:

- fair and accurate but non-contemporaneous reports of public judicial proceedings in England, whether in a newspaper or not;
- extracts of Parliamentary papers;
- fair and accurate reports of Parliamentary proceedings;
- a fair and accurate report in a newspaper of the proceedings at any public meeting held in the United Kingdom. The meeting must be bona fide and lawfully held for a lawful purpose and for the furtherance or discussion of any matter of public concern. Admission to the meeting may be general or restricted. In the case of public meetings, the defence is not available, if it is proved that the defendant has been requested by the plaintiff to publish in the newspaper in which the original publication was made a reasonable letter or statement by way of explanation or contradiction, and has refused or neglected to do so, or has done so in a manner not adequate or not reasonable having regard to all the circumstances.

This list of privileged occasions is by no means exhaustive, and when s. 15 of the 1996 Act comes into effect the existing categories will be amended and extended. The privilege defence will be extended to the media generally, rather than, as at present, being confined simply to newspapers.

Offers of Amends under the 1952 and 1996 Acts

Section 4 of the 1952 Act was still in force at the time of going to press, but it is due

to be replaced by sections 2, 3 and 4 of the 1996 Act. The 1952 Act affords a degree of protection to the publisher of an 'innocent' defamation. 'Innocent' is narrowly defined: it means simply that the publisher, despite having exercised reasonable care, did not know that what he said might be read as a reference to the plaintiff – e.g. through an improbable coincience of name – or that circumstances existed which made an otherwise innocuous statement defamatory – e.g. by mistakenly depicting a married lady as her husband's 'fiancée', thus implying that she lived with him as his mistress rather than as his wife. This defence has proved somewhat rigid and unworkable over the years, mainly because of its technicality and the fact that it has to be put forward, together with a correction and an apology, as soon as the potentially defamatory impact of what has appeared has been drawn to the publisher's attention.

When they are operative, sections 2, 3 and 4 of the new Act will offer a rather more flexible method of nipping in the bud potential libel actions by those who have been unintentionally defamed. The range of libel meanings for which the new defence will cater is much wider than that covered by the current s. 4; and though it envisages the payment of damages (which the current provision does not) as well as costs, together with the offer of a correction and apology, the damages figure will be fixed by a judge if the parties cannot agree. He or she will do this bearing in mind the generosity of the correction and apology, and the extent of its publication. While recourse to this defence will exclude reliance on the defences of justification, privilege and fair comment, it is likely to offer a far greater incentive to settle compaints than the present provision, and should save substantially on costs.

Apology under 1843 and 1845 Acts

This defence is rarely utilised, since if any condition of it is not fulfilled, the plaintiff must succeed and the only question is the actual amount of damages. It only applies to actions in respect of libels in newspapers and periodicals. The defendant pleads that the libel was inserted without actual malice and without gross negligence and that before the action commenced or as soon afterwards as possible he inserted a full apology in the same newspaper, etc, or had offered to publish it in a newspaper, etc, of the plaintiff's choice, where the original newspaper is published at intervals greater than a week. Further a sum must be paid into court with this defence to compensate the plaintiff.

'Fast-track disposal' procedure

In its recognition of the generally cumbersome nature of libel litigation, the 1996 Act envisages a simplified mechanism for dealing with less serious complaints. When sections 8, 9 and 10 come into force, a judge alone will be able to dismiss unrealistic claims virtually at the outset; and he will also be able to dispose 'summarily' of relatively minor, but well-founded, claims, on the basis of an award of up to £10,000, a declaration that the publication was libellous, an order for an apology and an order forbidding repetition.

Apologies in general

Quite apart from the provisions concerning statutory apologies mentioned above, a swift and well publicised apology will always go some way towards assuaging injured feelings and help reduce an award of damages.

Limitation and death

As from September 1996, the new Act has reduced from three years to one the period within which a libel action must generally be started if it is not to become 'statute-barred' through lapse of time. But successive and subsequent publications, such as the issue of later editions of the same book, or the sale of surplus copies of an old newspaper, can give rise to fresh claims.

Civil claims for libel cannot be brought on behalf of the dead. If an individual living plaintiff or defendant in a libel case

> ### The main differences between English and Scottish law
>
> Much of the terminology of the Scots law of defamation differs from that of English law, and in certain minor respects the law itself is different. North of the border, libel and slander are virtually indistinguishable, both as to the nature of the wrongs and their consequences; and Scots law does not recognise the offence of criminal libel. Where individual English litigants enjoy absolute privilege for what they say in court, their Scottish counterparts have only qualified privilege. 'Exemplary', or 'punitive', damages are not awarded by the Scottish courts. Until recently, libel cases in Scotland were for the most part heard by judges sitting alone, but there is now a marked trend towards trial by jury, which has been accompanied by a significant increase in the levels of damages awarded.

dies before the jury gives their verdict, the action 'abates', i.e. comes to an end, so far as their involvement is concerned, and no rights arising out of it survive either for or against their personal representatives.

Insurance

For an author, the importance of at least an awareness of this branch of law lies first, in the fact that most book contracts contain a clause enabling the publisher to look to him should any libel claims result; and second, in the increasingly large awards of damages. It is therefore advisable to check what libel insurance a publisher carries, and whether it also covers the author who, if he or she is to have the benefit of it, should always alert the publisher to any potential risk. One company which offers libel insurance for authors is the Sun Alliance of 1 Leadenhall Street, London EC3V 1PP. Premiums start at £1000, and can be substantially higher if the book is tendentious or likely to be controversial. The company generally insists on the author obtaining, and paying for, a legal opinion first. Indemnity limits vary between £50,000 and £1 million, and the author is required to bear at least the first £5000, and 10% of the remainder, of any loss. It is worth remem-

bering that 'losses' include legal costs as well as damages, which they can often exceed. Libel insurance can also be obtained through a Lloyds broker.

Criminal liability in libel

Whereas the object of a civil action is to obtain compensation for the wrong done or to prevent repetition, the object of criminal proceedings is to punish the wrongdoer by fine or imprisonment or both. There are four main types of writing which may provoke a prosecution:

- defamatory libel;
- obscene publications;
- sedition and incitement to racial hatred;
- blasphemous libel.

Defamatory libel

The publication of defamatory matter is in certain circumstances a crime as well as a civil wrong. But whereas the principal object of civil proceedings will normally be to obtain compensation, the principal object of a criminal prosecution will be to secure punishment of the accused, for example by way of a fine. Prosecutions are not frequent, but there have been signs of late of a revival of interest. There are important differences between the rules applicable to criminal libel and its civil counterpart. For example, a criminal libel may be 'published' even though only communicated to the person defamed and may be found to have occurred even where the person defamed is dead, or where only a group of persons but no particular individual has been maligned. During election campaigns, it is an 'illegal practice' to publish false statements about the personal character or conduct of a candidate irrespective of whether they are also defamatory.

Obscene publications

It is an offence to publish obscene matter. By the Obscene Publications Act, 1959, matter is obscene if its effect is such as to tend to deprave and corrupt persons who are likely, having regard to all relevant cir-

cumstances, to read, see or hear it. 'To deprave and corrupt' is to be distinguished from 'to shock and disgust'. It is a defence to a prosecution to prove that publication of the matter in question is justified as being for the public good, on the ground that it is in the interests of science, literature, art or learning, or of other objects of general concern. Expert evidence may be given as to its literary, artistic, scientific or other merits. Playwrights, directors and producers should note that the Theatres Act, 1968, though designed to afford similar protection to stage productions, does not necessarily prevent prosecutions for indecency under other statutes.

Sedition and incitement to racial hatred

Writings which tend to destroy the peace of the realm may be prosecuted as being seditious or as amounting to incitement to racial hatred. Seditious writings include those which advocate reform by unconstitutional or violent means or incite contempt or hatred for the monarch or Parliament. These institutions may be criticised stringently, but not in a manner which is likely to lead to insurrection or civil commotion or indeed any physical force. Prosecutions are a rarity, but it should be remembered

that writers of matter contemptuous of the House of Commons, though not prosecuted for seditious libel are, from time to time, punished by that House for breach of its privileges, although, if a full apology is made, it is often an end of the matter. The Public Order Act 1986 makes it an offence, irrespective of the author's or publisher's intention, to publish, or put on plays containing, threatening, abusive or insulting matter if hatred is likely to be stirred up against any racial group in Great Britain.

Blasphemous libel

Blasphemous libel consists in the vilification of the Christian religion or its ceremonies. Other religions are not protected. The offence lies essentially in the impact of what is said concerning, for instance, God, Christ, the Bible, the Book of Common Prayer, etc; it is irrelevant that the publisher does not intend to shock or arouse resentment. While temperate and sober writings on religious topics however anti-Christian in sentiment will not involve liability, if the discussion is 'so scurrilous and offensive as to pass the limit of decent controversy and to outrage any Christian feeling', it will.

Antony Whitaker is Legal Manager at Times Newspapers Ltd.

Finance for writers and artists

Income tax

*Despite attempts by successive Governments to simplify our taxation system, the subject has become increasingly complicated. **Peter Vaines**, a chartered accountant and barrister, gives a broad outline of taxation from the point of view of writers and other creative professionals. At the time of writing the proposals in the July 1997 Budget have just been announced and these are reflected in this article.*

How income is taxed

Generally

Authors are usually treated for tax purposes as carrying on a profession and are taxed in a similar fashion to other professional persons, i.e. as self-employed persons assessable under Schedule D. This article is directed to self-employed persons only, because if a writer is employed he or she will be subject to the rules of Schedule E where different considerations apply – substantially to his or her disadvantage.

Attempts are often made by employed persons to shake off the status of 'employee' and to attain 'freelance' status so as to qualify for the advantages of Schedule D, such attempts meeting with varying degrees of success. The problems involved in making this transition are considerable and space does not permit a detailed explanation to be made here – individual advice is necessary if difficulties are to be avoided.

Particular attention has been paid by the Inland Revenue to journalists and to those engaged in the entertainment industry with a view to reclassifying them as employees so that PAYE is deducted from their earnings. This blanket treatment has been extended to other areas and, although it is obviously open to challenge by individual taxpayers, it is always difficult to persuade the Inland Revenue to change its views.

There is no reason why employed people cannot carry on a freelance business in their spare time. Indeed, aspiring authors, painters, musicians, etc, often derive so little income from their craft that the financial security of an employment, perhaps in a different sphere of activity, is necessary. The existence of the employment is irrelevant to the taxation of the freelance earnings although it is most important not to confuse the income or expenditure of the employment with the income or expenditure of the self-employed activity. The Inland Revenue is aware of the advantages which can be derived by an individual having 'freelance' income from an organisation of which he or she is also an employee, and where such circumstances are contrived, it can be extremely difficult to convince an Inspector of Taxes that a genuine freelance activity is being carried on.

For those starting in business or commencing work on a freelance basis the Inland Revenue produces a very useful booklet, *Starting in Business (IR28)*, which is available from any tax office.

Income

For income to be taxable it need not be substantial, nor even the author's only source of income; earnings from casual writing are also taxable but this can be an advantage, because occasional writers do not often make a profit from their writing. The expenses incurred in connection with writing may well exceed any income receivable and the resultant loss may then

be used to reclaim tax paid on other income. There may be deducted from the income certain allowable expenses and capital allowances which are set out in more detail below. The possibility of a loss being used as a basis for a tax repayment is fully appreciated by the Inland Revenue, which sometimes attempts to treat casual writing as a hobby so that any losses incurred cannot be used to reclaim tax; of course by the same token any income receivable would not be chargeable to tax. This treatment may sound attractive but it should be resisted vigorously because the Inland Revenue does not hesitate to change its mind when profits begin to arise. However, in the case of exceptional or non-recurring writing, such as the autobiography of a sports personality or the memoirs of a politician, it could be better to be treated as pursuing a hobby and not as a professional author. Sales of copyright cannot be charged to income tax unless the recipient is a professional author. However, the proceeds of sale of copyright may be charged to capital gains tax, even by an individual who is not a professional author.

Royalties

Where the recipient is a professional author, a series of cases has laid down a clear principle that sales of copyright are taxable as income and not as capital receipts. Similarly, lump sums on account of, or in advance of royalties are also taxable as income in the year of receipt, subject to a claim for spreading relief (see below).

Copyright royalties are generally paid without deduction of income tax. However, if royalties are paid to a person who normally lives abroad, tax will be deducted by the payer or his agent at the time the payment is made unless arrangements are made with the Inland Revenue for payments to be made gross.

Arts Council grants

Persons in receipt of grants from the Arts Council or similar bodies will be con-

---

Arts Council category A awards

- Direct or indirect musical, design or choreographic commissions and direct or indirect commission of sculpture and paintings for public sites.
- The Royalty Supplement Guarantee Scheme.
- The contract writers' scheme.
- Jazz bursaries.
- Translators' grants.
- Photographic awards and bursaries.
- Film and video awards and bursaries.
- Performance Art Awards.
- Art Publishing Grants.
- Grants to assist with a specific project or projects (such as the writing of a book) or to meet specific professional expenses such as a contribution towards copying expenses made to a composer or to an artist's studio expenses.

---

cerned whether or not such grants are liable to income tax. The Inland Revenue has issued a Statement of Practice after detailed discussions with the Arts Council regarding the tax treatment of such awards. Grants and other receipts of a similar nature have now been divided into two categories (see boxes) – those which are to be treated by the Inland Revenue as chargeable to tax and those which are not. Category A awards are considered to be taxable; awards made under category B are not chargeable to tax.

This Statement of Practice has no legal force and is used merely to ease the administration of the tax system. It is open to anyone in receipt of a grant or award to disregard the agreed statement and challenge the Inland Revenue view on the merits of their particular case. However, it must be recognised that the Inland Revenue does not issue such statements lightly and any challenge to their view would almost certainly involve a lengthy and expensive action through the Courts.

The tax position of persons in receipt of literary prizes will generally follow a decision by the Special Commissioners in connection with the Whitbread Literary

---

Arts Council category B awards

- Bursaries to trainee directors.
- In-service bursaries for theatre directors.
- Bursaries for associate directors.
- Bursaries to people attending full-time courses in arts administration (the practical training course).
- In-service bursaries to theatre designers and bursaries to trainees on the theatre designers' scheme.
- In-service bursaries for administrators.
- Bursaries for actors and actresses.
- Bursaries for technicians and stage managers.
- Bursaries made to students attending the City University Arts Administration courses.
- Awards, known as the Buying Time Awards, made not to assist with a specific project or professional expenses but to maintain the recipient to enable him or her to take time off to develop his personal talents. These at present include the awards and bursaries known as the Theatre Writing Bursaries, awards and bursaries to composers, awards and bursaries to painters, sculptures and print makers, literature awards and bursaries.

Award. In that case it was held that the prize was not part of the author's professional income and accordingly not chargeable to tax. The precise details are not available because decisions of the Special Commissioners were not, at that time, reported unless an appeal was made to the High Court; the Inland Revenue chose not to appeal against this decision. Details of the many literary awards which are given each year start on page 488, and this decision is of considerable significance to the winners of each of these prizes. It would be unwise to assume that all such awards will be free of tax as the precise facts which were present in the case of the Whitbread award may not be repeated in another case; however it is clear that an author winning a prize has some very powerful arguments in his or her favour, should the Inland Revenue seek to charge tax on the award.

Allowable expenses

To qualify as an allowable business expense, expenditure has to be laid out wholly and exclusively for business purposes. Strictly there must be no 'duality of purpose', which means that expenditure cannot be apportioned to reflect the private and business usage, e.g. food, clothing, telephone, travelling expenses, etc. However, the Inland Revenue does not usually interpret this principle strictly and is prepared to allow all reasonable expenses (including apportioned sums) where the amounts can be commercially justified.

It should be noted carefully that the expenditure does not have to be 'necessary', it merely has to be incurred 'wholly and exclusively' for business purposes. Naturally, however, expenditure of an outrageous and wholly unnecessary character might well give rise to a presumption that it was not really for business purposes. As with all things, some expenses are unquestionably allowable and some expenses are equally unquestionably not allowable – it is the grey area in between which gives rise to all the difficulties and the outcome invariably depends on negotiation with the Inland Revenue.

Great care should be taken when claiming a deduction for items where there is a 'duality of purpose' and negotiations should be conducted with more than usual care and courtesy – if provoked the Inspector of Taxes may well choose to allow nothing. An appeal is always possible although unlikely to succeed as a string of cases in the Courts has clearly demonstrated. An example is the case of *Caillebotte* v. *Quinn* where the taxpayer (who normally had lunch at home) sought to claim the excess cost of meals incurred because he was working a long way from his home. The taxpayer's arguments failed because he did not eat only in order to work, one of the reasons for his eating was in order to sustain his life; a duality of purpose therefore existed and no tax relief was due.

Other cases have shown that expenditure on clothing can also be disallowed if it is the kind of clothing which is in everyday use, because clothing is worn not only

Allowable expenses

(a) Cost of all materials used up in the course of preparation of the work.

(b) Cost of typewriting and secretarial assistance, etc; if this or other help is obtained from one's spouse then it is entirely proper for a deduction to be claimed for the amounts paid for the work. The amounts claimed must actually be paid to the spouse and should be at the market rate although some uplift can be made for unsocial hours, etc. Payments to a wife (or husband) are of course taxable in her (or his) hands and should therefore be most carefully considered. The wife's earnings may also be liable for National Insurance contributions and it is important to take care because otherwise you may find that these contributions may outweigh the tax savings.

(c) All expenditure on normal business items such as postage, stationery, telephone, e-mail, fax and answering machines, agent's fees, accountancy charges, photography, subscriptions, periodicals, magazines, etc, may be claimed. The cost of daily papers should not be overlooked if these form part of research material. Visits to theatres, cinemas, etc, for research purposes may also be permissible (but not the cost relating to guests). Unfortunately, expenditure on all types of business entertaining is specifically denied tax relief.

(d) If work is conducted at home, a deduction for 'use of home' is usually allowed providing the amount claimed is reasonable. If the claim is based on an appropriate proportion of the total costs of rent, light and heat, cleaning and maintenance, insurance, etc (but not the Council Tax), care should be taken to ensure that no single room is used 'exclusively' for business purposes, because this may result in the Capital Gains Tax exemption on the house as the only or main residence being partially forfeited. However, it would be a strange household where one room was in fact used exclusively for business purposes and for no other purpose whatsoever (e.g.

storing personal bank statements and other private papers); the usual formula is to claim a deduction on the basis that most or all of the rooms in the house are used at one time or another for business purposes, thereby avoiding any suggestion that any part was used exclusively for business purposes.

(e) The appropriate business proportion of motor running expenses may also be claimed although what is the appropriate proportion will naturally depend on the particular circumstances of each case; it should be mentioned that the well-known scale benefits, whereby one is taxed according to the size and cost of the car, do not apply to self-employed persons.

(f) It has been long established that the cost of travelling from home to work (whether employed or self-employed) is not an allowable expense. However, if home is one's place of work then no expenditure under this heading is likely to be incurred and difficulties are unlikely to arise.

(g) Travelling and hotel expenses incurred for business purposes will normally be allowed but if any part could be construed as disguised holiday or pleasure expenditure, considerable thought would need to be given to the commercial reasons for the journey in order to justify the claim. The principle of 'duality of purpose' will always be a difficult hurdle in this connection – although not insurmountable.

(h) If a separate business bank account is maintained, any overdraft interest thereon will be an allowable expense. This is the only circumstance in which overdraft interest is allowed for tax purposes and care should be taken to avoid overdrafts in all other circumstances.

(i) Where capital allowances (see page 645) are claimed for a personal computer, fax, television, video, CD or tape player, etc, used for business purposes the costs of maintenance and repair of the equipment may also be claimed.

---

to assist the pursuit of one's profession but also to accord with public decency. This duality of purpose may be sufficient to deny relief – even where the particular type of clothing is of a kind not otherwise worn by the taxpayer. In the case of *Mallalieu* v. *Drummond* a lady barrister failed to obtain a tax deduction for items of sombre clothing purchased specifically

for wearing in Court. The House of Lords decided that a duality of purpose existed because clothing represented part of her needs as a human being.

Despite the above, Inspectors of Taxes are not usually inflexible and the expenses listed in the box opposite are among those generally allowed. Clearly many other allowable items may be claimed in

addition to those listed. Wherever there is any reasonable business motive for some expenditure it should be claimed as a deduction although it is necessary to preserve all records relating to the expense. It is sensible to avoid an excess of imagination as this would naturally cause the Inspector of Taxes to doubt the genuineness of other expenses claimed.

The question is often raised whether the whole amount of an expense may be deducted or whether the VAT content must be excluded. Where VAT is reclaimed from the Customs and Excise (on the quarterly returns made by a registered person), the VAT element of the expense cannot be treated as an allowable deduction. Where the VAT is not reclaimed, the whole expense (inclusive of VAT) is allowable for income tax purposes.

Capital allowances

Allowances

Where expenditure of a capital nature is incurred, it cannot be deducted from income as an expense – a separate and sometimes more valuable capital allowance being available instead. Capital allowances are given for many different types of expenditure, but authors and similar professional people are likely to claim only for 'plant and machinery'; this is a very wide expression which may include motor cars, personal computers, fax and photocopying machines, modems, televisions, CD, video and cassette players used for business purposes, books – and even a horse! Plant and machinery generally qualify for a 25% allowance in the year of purchase and 25% of the reducing balance in subsequent years. However, a special 50% first year allowance was introduced in the July 1997 Budget on expenditure on plant and machinery incurred by small businesses before 1 July 1998. The 25% writing down allowance on the reducing balance will continue to be given in subsequent years. Where the useful life of an asset is expected to be short, it is possible to claim special treatment as a 'short life asset' enabling the allowances to be accelerated.

The reason these allowances can be more valuable than allowable expenses is that they may be wholly or partly disclaimed in any year that full benefit cannot be obtained – ordinary business expenses cannot be similarly disclaimed. Where, for example, the income of an author does not exceed her personal allowances, she would not be liable to tax and a claim for capital allowances would be wasted. If the capital allowances were to be disclaimed their benefit would be carried forward for use in subsequent years. Careful planning with claims for capital allowances is therefore essential if maximum benefit is to be obtained.

As an alternative to capital allowances, claims can be made on the 'renewals' basis whereby all renewals are treated as allowable deductions in the year; no allowance is obtained for the initial purchase, but the cost of replacement (excluding any improvement element) is allowed in full. This basis is no longer widely used, as it is considerably less advantageous than claiming capital allowances as described above.

Leasing is a popular method of acquiring fixed assets, and where cash is not available to enable an outright purchase to be made, assets may be leased over a period of time. Whilst leasing may have financial benefits in certain circumstances, in normal cases there is likely to be no tax advantage in leasing an asset where the alternative of outright purchase is available. Indeed, leasing can be a positive disadvantage in the case of motor cars with a new retail price of more than £12,000. If such a car is leased, only a proportion of the leasing charges will be tax deductible.

Books

The question of whether the cost of books is eligible for tax relief has long been a source of difficulty. The annual cost of replacing books used for the purposes of one's professional activities (e.g. the annual cost of a new *Writers' & Artists' Yearbook*) has always been an allowable expense; the difficulty arose because the initial cost of reference books, etc (e.g.

when commencing one's profession) was treated as capital expenditure but no allowances were due as the books were not considered to be 'plant'. However, the matter was clarified by the case of *Munby* v. *Furlong* in which the Court of Appeal decided that the initial cost of law books purchased by a barrister was expenditure on 'plant' and eligible for capital allowances. This is clearly a most important decision, particularly relevant to any person who uses expensive books in the course of exercising his or her profession.

Pension contributions

Personal pensions

Where a self-employed person pays annual premiums under an approved personal pension policy, tax relief may now be obtained each year for the following amounts:

Age at 6/4/97	Maximum %
35 and under	17.5% (max) £14,700
36 – 45	20% (max) £16,800
46 – 50	25% (max) £21,000
51 – 55	30% (max) £25,200
56 – 60	35% (max) £29,400
61 and over	40% (max) £33,600

These figures do not apply to existing retirement annuity policies; these remain subject to the old limits which are unchanged.

These arrangements can be extremely advantageous in providing for a pension as premiums are usually paid when the income is high (and the tax relief is also high) and the pension (taxed as earned income when received) usually arises when the income is low and little tax is payable. The reduction in the rates of income tax to a maximum of 40% makes this decision a little more difficult because the tax advantages could go into reverse. When the pension is paid it could, if rates rise again, be taxed at a higher rate than the rate of tax relief at the moment. One would be deferring income in order to pay more tax on it later. However, this involves a large element of guesswork, and many people will be content simply with the long-term pension benefits.

Class 4 NI contributions

Allied to pensions is the payment of Class 4 National Insurance contributions, although no pension or other benefit is obtained by the contributions; the Class 4 contributions are designed solely to extract additional amounts from self-employed persons and are payable in addition to the normal Class 2 (self-employed) contributions. The rates are changed each year and for 1997/98 self-employed persons will be obliged to contribute 6% of their profits between the range £7010-£24,181 per annum, a maximum liability of £1030 for 1997/98. This amount is collected in conjunction with the Schedule D income tax liability.

Spreading relief

Relief for copyright payments

Special provisions enable authors and similar persons who have been engaged on a literary, dramatic, musical or artistic work for a period of more than 12 months, to spread certain amounts received over two or three years depending on the time spent in preparing the work. If the author was engaged on the work for a period exceeding 12 months, the receipt may be spread backwards over two years; if the author was engaged on the work for more than 24 months, the receipt may be spread backwards over three years. (Analogous provisions apply to sums received for the sale of a painting, sculpture or other work of art.) The relief applies to:

- lump sums received on the assignment of copyright, in whole or in part;
- sums received on the grant of any interest in the copyright by licence;
- non-returnable advances on account of royalties;
- any receipts of or on account of royalties or any periodical sums received within two years of first publication.

A claim for spreading relief has to be made within eight years from 5 April following the date of first publication.

Relief: copyright sold after 10 years

Where copyright is assigned (or a licence in it is granted) more than 10 years after the first publication of the work, then the amounts received can qualify for a different spreading relief. The assignment (or licence) must be for a period of more than two years and the receipt will be spread forward over the number of years for which the assignment (or licence) is granted – but with a maximum of six years. The relief is terminated by death, but there are provisions enabling the deceased author's personal representatives to re-spread the amounts if it is to the beneficiaries' advantage.

The above rules are arbitrary and cumbersome, only providing a limited measure of relief in special circumstances. The provisions can sometimes be helpful to repair matters when consideration of the tax position has been neglected, but invariably a better solution is found if the likely tax implications are considered fully in advance.

Collection of tax

Self assessment

The year ended 5 April 1997, i.e. the tax year 1996/7, brought with it two profound changes to the method of taxing individuals, particularly those carrying out a self-employed activity such as writing. The old system of sending in a tax return showing all your income and the Inland Revenue raising an assessment to collect the tax has gone. So has the idea that you pay tax on your profits for the preceding year. Now, when you send in your tax return you have to work out your own tax liability and send a cheque; this is called 'self assessment'. If you get it wrong, or if you are late with your tax return or the payment of tax, interest and penalties will be charged.

Under the new system, the Inland Revenue will rarely issue assessments; they are no longer necessary because the idea is that you assess yourself. A new colour-coded tax return has been designed to help individuals meet their new tax obligations. This will be a daunting task but the term 'self assessment' is not intended to imply that individuals have to do it themselves; they can (and often will) engage professional help. The term is only intended to convey that it is the taxpayer, and not the Inland Revenue, who is responsible for getting the tax liability right and for it to be paid on time.

The deadline for sending in the tax return is 31 January following the end of the tax year; so for the tax year 1996/97, the tax return has to be submitted to the Inland Revenue by 31 January 1998. If for some reason you are unwilling or unable to calculate the tax payable, you can ask the Inland Revenue to do it for you, in which case it is necessary to send in your tax return by 30 September.

Income tax on self-employed earnings remains payable in two instalments but the payment dates have been moved to 31 January and 31 July each year. Because the accurate figures may not necessarily be known, these payments in January and July will therefore be only payments on account based on the previous year's liability. The final balancing figure will be paid the following 31 January together with the first instalment of the liability for the following year.

When the Inland Revenue receives the self-assessment tax return, it will be checked to see if there is anything obviously wrong; if there is, a letter will be sent to you immediately. Otherwise, the Inland Revenue has 12 months in which to make further enquiries; if it doesn't, it will have no further opportunity to do so and your tax liabilities are final – unless there is something seriously wrong such as the omission of income or capital gains. In that event, the Inland Revenue will raise an assessment later to collect any extra tax together with appropriate penalties. It is essential for the operation of the new system that all records relevant to your tax returns are retained for at least 12 months in case they are needed by the Inland Revenue. For the self employed, the record-keeping requirement is much more onerous because the records need to

be kept for nearly six years. One important change in the rules is that if you claim a tax deduction for an expenditure, it will be necessary to have a receipt or other document proving that the expenditure has been made. Because the existence of the underlying records is so important to the operation of self assessment, the Inland Revenue treats them very seriously and there is a penalty of £3000 for any failure to keep adequate records.

Transitional relief for the self employed

For people who were engaged in professional writing or other self-employed activities before 6 April 1994, there is a special relief in connection with the change to the current year basis of assessment. After all, it would be very unfair to replace the preceding year basis with a current year basis without some special rules because otherwise, two years' profits would be taxed in the same year. Accordingly, for the tax year 1996/97, the profits to be taxed will be only 50% of the profits for the two years ending in that tax year. So, for example, if accounts are made up to 31 December each year, the profits for the year ended 31 December 1995 and 31 December 1996 are added together and half the total charged to tax in 1996/97. This transitional relief obviously provides opportunities for tax saving but great care must be taken in trying to make the most of these opportunities because there are special provisions designed to prevent abuse.

Interest

Interest is chargeable on overdue tax at a variable rate, which at the time of writing is 8.5% per annum. It does not rank for any tax relief, which can make the Inland Revenue an expensive source of credit.

However, the Inland Revenue can also be obliged to pay interest (known as repayment supplement) tax-free where repayments are delayed. The rules relating to repayment supplement are less beneficial and even more complicated than the rules for interest payable but they do exist and can be very welcome if a large repayment has been delayed for a long time. Unfortunately, the rate of repayment supplement is only 4%, much lower than the rate of interest on unpaid tax.

Value added tax

The activities of writers, painters, composers, etc, are all 'taxable supplies' within the scope of VAT and chargeable at the standard rate. (Zero rating which applies to publishers, booksellers, etc on the supply of books does not extend to the work performed by writers.) Accordingly, authors are obliged to register for VAT if their income for the past 12 months exceeds £48,000 or if their income for the coming month will exceed that figure. (This registration threshold goes up to £49,000 on 1 December 1997.)

Delay in registering can be a most serious matter because if registration is not effected at the proper time, the Customs and Excise can (and invariably do) claim VAT from all the income received since the date on which registration should have been made. As no VAT would have been included in the amounts received during this period the amount claimed by the Customs and Excise must inevitably come straight from the pocket of the author.

The author may be entitled to seek reimbursement of the VAT from those whom he or she ought to have charged VAT but this is obviously a matter of some difficulty and may indeed damage his commercial relationships. Apart from these disadvantages there is also a penalty for late registration. The rules are extremely harsh and are imposed automatically even in cases of innocent error. It is therefore extremely important to monitor the income very carefully because if in any period of 12 months the income exceeds the £48,000 limit, the Customs and Excise must be notified within 30 days of the end of the period. Failure to do so will give rise to an automatic penalty. It should be emphasised that this is a penalty for failing to submit a form and has nothing to do with any real or potential loss of tax.

Furthermore, whether the failure was innocent or deliberate will not matter. Only the existence of a 'reasonable excuse' will be a defence to the penalty. However, a reasonable excuse does not include ignorance, error, a lack of funds or reliance on any third party.

However, it is possible to regard VAT registration as a privilege and not a penalty, because only VAT registered persons can reclaim VAT paid on their expenses such as stationery, telephone, professional fees, etc, even typewriters and other plant and machinery (excluding cars). However, many find that the administrative inconvenience – the cost of maintaining the necessary records and completing the necessary forms – more than outweighs the benefits to be gained from registration and prefer to stay outside the scope of VAT for as long as possible.

Overseas matters

The general observation may be made that self-employed persons resident and domiciled in the United Kingdom are not well treated with regard to their overseas work, being taxable on their worldwide income. It is important to emphasise that if fees are earned abroad, no tax saving can be achieved merely by keeping the money outside the country. Although exchange control regulations no longer exist to require repatriation of foreign earnings, such income remains taxable in the UK and must be disclosed to the Inland Revenue; the same applies to interest or other income arising on any investment of these earnings overseas. Accordingly, whenever foreign earnings are likely to become substantial, prompt and effective action is required to limit the impact of UK and foreign taxation. In the case of non-resident authors it is important that arrangements concerning writing for publication in the UK, e.g. in newspapers, are undertaken with great care. A case concerning the wife of one of the great train robbers who provided detailed information for a series of articles in a Sunday newspaper is most instructive. Although she was acknowledged to be resident in

Canada for all the relevant years, the income from the articles was treated as arising in this country and fully chargeable to UK tax.

The United Kingdom has double taxation agreements with many other countries and these agreements are designed to ensure that income arising in a foreign country is taxed either in that country or in the UK. Where a withholding tax is deducted from payments received from another country (or where tax is paid in full in the absence of a double taxation agreement), the amount of foreign tax paid can usually be set off against the related UK tax liability. Many successful authors can be found living in Eire because of the complete exemption from tax which attaches to works of cultural or artistic merit by persons who are resident there. However, such a step should only be contemplated having careful regard to all the other domestic and commercial considerations and specialist advice is essential if the exemption is to be obtained and kept; a careless breach of the conditions could cause the exemption to be withdrawn with catastrophic consequences.

Companies

When an author becomes successful the prospect of paying tax at the higher rate may drive him or her to take hasty action such as the formation of companies, etc, which may not always be to his advantage. Indeed some authors seeing the exodus into tax exile of their more successful colleagues even form companies in low tax areas in the naive expectation of saving large amounts of tax. The Inland Revenue is fully aware of the opportunities and have extensive powers to charge tax and combat avoidance. Accordingly, such action is just as likely to increase tax liabilities and generate other costs and should never be contemplated without expert advice; some very expensive mistakes are often made in this area which are not always able to be remedied.

To conduct one's business through the medium of a company can be a most

effective method of mitigating tax liabilities, and providing it is done at the right time and under the right circumstances very substantial advantages can be derived. However, if done without due care and attention the intended advantages will simply evaporate. At the very least it is essential to ensure that the company's business is genuine and conducted properly with regard to the realities of the situation. If the author continues his or her activities unchanged, simply paying all the receipts from his work into a company's bank account, he cannot expect to persuade the Inland Revenue that it is the company and not himself who is entitled to, and should be assessed to tax on, that income.

It must be strongly emphasised that many pitfalls exist which can easily eliminate all the tax benefits expected to arise by the formation of the company. For example, company directors are employees of the company and will be liable to pay much higher National Insurance contributions; the company must also pay the employer's proportion of the contribution and a total liability of over 20% of gross salary may arise. This compares most unfavourably with the position of a self-employed person. Moreover, on the commencement of the company's business the individual's profession will cease and the Inland Revenue has the power to revise tax liabilities for previous years; this is always a crucial factor in determining the best moment when the changeover to a company should take place.

The tax return

No mention has been made above of personal reliefs and allowances (e.g., the single and married couples allowances, etc); this is because these allowances and the rates of tax are subject to constant change and are always set out in detail in the explanatory notes which accompany the Tax Return. The annual Tax Return is an important document and should not be ignored because it is crucial to one's tax position. Indeed, it should be completed promptly with extreme care because the Inland Revenue treats failures to disclose income very harshly, invariably exacting interest and penalties – sometimes of substantial amounts. If filling in the Return is a source of difficulty or anxiety, comfort may be found in the Consumer Association's publication *Money Which? – Tax Saving Guide*; this is published in March of each year and includes much which is likely to be of interest and assistance.

Peter Vaines FCA, ATII, barrister, is a Partner at Brebner, Allen & Trapp Chartered Accountants, and writes and speaks widely on tax and related matters. He is Managing Editor of *Personal Tax Planning Review*, on the Editorial Board of *Taxation*, and tax columnist for *New Law Journal*.

Social security contributions

*In general, every individual who works in Great Britain either as an employee or as a self-employed person is liable to pay social security contributions. The law governing this subject is complicated and **Peter Arrowsmith** FCA gives here a summary of the position. Despite speculation that there might be some changes, no announcements affecting the above were made in the July 1997 Budget. This article should only be regarded as a general guide only.*

All contributions are payable in respect of years ending on 5 April. The classes of contributions are:

Class 1 These are payable by employees (primary contributions) and their employers (secondary contributions) and are based on earnings.

Class 1A Use of company car, and fuel, for private purposes.

Class 2 These are weekly flat rate contributions, payable by the self-employed.

Class 3 These are weekly flat rate contributions, payable on a voluntary basis in order to provide, or make up entitlement to, certain social security benefits.

Class 4 These are payable by the self-employed in respect of their trading or professional income and are based on earnings.

Employed or self-employed?

The question as to whether a person is employed under a contract *of* service and is thereby an employee liable to Class 1 contributions, or performs services (either solely or in partnership) under a contract *for* service and is thereby self-employed liable to Class 2 and Class 4 contributions, often has to be decided in practice. One of the best guides can be found in the case of *Market Investigations Ltd* v. *Minister of Social Security* (1969 2 WLR 1) when Cooke J. remarked:

'... the fundamental test to be applied is this: "Is the person who has engaged himself to perform these services performing them as a person in business on his own account?" If the answer to that question is "yes", then the contract is a contract for services. If the answer is "no", then the contract is a contract of service. No exhaustive list has been compiled and perhaps no exhaustive list can be compiled of the considerations which are relevant in determining that question, nor can strict rules be laid down as to the relative weight which the various considerations should carry in particular cases. The most that can be said is that control will no doubt always have to be considered, although it can no longer be regarded as the sole determining factor; and that factors which may be of importance are such matters as:

• whether the man performing the services provides his own equipment,
• whether he hires his own helpers,
• what degree of financial risk he takes,
• what degree of responsibility for investment and management he has, and
• whether and how far he has an opportunity of profiting from sound management in the performance of his task.'

The above case was also considered as recently as November 1993 by the Court of Appeal in the case of *Hall* v. *Lorimer*. In this case a vision mixer with around 20 clients and undertaking around 120-150 separate engagements per annum was held to be self-employed. This follows the, perhaps surprising, contention of the Inland Revenue that the taxpayer was an employee.

Further guidance

There have been three cases dealing with musicians, in relatively recent times, which provide further guidance on the question as to whether an individual is employed or self-employed.

• *Midland Sinfonia Concert Society Ltd* v. *Secretary of State for Social Services* (1981 ICR 454). A musician, employed to play in an orchestra by separate invitation at irregular intervals and remunerated solely in respect of each occasion upon which he does play, is employed under a contract for services. He is therefore self-employed, not an employed earner, for the purposes of the Social Security Contributions and Benefits Act 1992, and the orchestra which engages him is not liable to pay National Insurance contributions in respect of his earnings.

• *Addison* v. *London Philharmonic Orchestra Ltd* (1981 ICR 261). This was an appeal to determine whether certain individuals were employees for the purposes of section 11(1) of the Employment Protection (Consolidation) Act 1978.

The Employment Appeal Tribunal upheld the decision of an industrial tribunal that an associate player and three additional or extra players of the London Philharmonic Orchestra were not employees under a contract of service, but were essentially freelance musicians carrying on their own business. The facts found by the industrial tribunal showed that, when playing for the orchestra, each appellant remained essentially a freelance musician, pursuing his or her own profession as an instrumentalist, with an individual reputation, and carrying on his or her own business, and they contributed their own skills and interpretative powers to the orchestra's performances as independent contractors.

• *Winfield* v. *London Philharmonic Orchestra Ltd* (1979 ICR 726). This case dealt with the question as to whether an individual was an employee within the meaning of section 30 of the Trade Union and Labour Relations Act 1974. The following remarks by the appeal tribunal

are of interest in relation to the status of musicians:

'... making music is an art, and the co-operation required for a performance of Berlioz's *Requiem* is dissimilar to that required between the manufacturer of concrete and the truck driver who takes the concrete where it is needed ... It took the view, as we think it was entitled on the material before it to do, that the company was simply machinery through which the members of the orchestra managed and controlled the orchestra's operation ... In deciding whether you are in the presence of a contract of service or not, you look at the whole of the picture. This picture looks to us, as it looked to the industrial tribunal, like a co-operative of distinguished musicians running themselves with self and mutual discipline, and in no sense like a boss and his musician employees.'

Other recent cases have concerned a professional dancer and holiday camp entertainers (all of whom were regarded as employees). In two recent cases income from part-time lecturing was held to be from an employment.

Accordingly, if a person is regarded as an employee under the above rules, he or she will be liable to pay contributions even if his employment is casual, part time or temporary. Furthermore, if a person is an employee and also carries on a trade or profession either solely or in partnership, there will be a liability to more than one class of contributions (subject to certain maxima – see below).

Exceptions

There are certain exceptions to the above rules, those most relevant to artists and writers being:

• The employment of a wife by her husband, or vice versa, is disregarded for social security purposes unless it is for the purposes of a trade or profession (e.g. the employment of his wife by an author would not be disregarded and would result in a liability for contributions if her salary reached the minimum levels).

• The employment of certain relatives in

a private dwelling house in which both employee and employer reside is disregarded for social security purposes provided the employment is not for the purposes of a trade or business carried on at those premises by the employer. This would cover the employment of a relative (as defined) as a housekeeper in a private residence.

• In general, lecturers, teachers and instructors engaged by an educational establishment to teach on at least four days in three consecutive months are regarded as employees, although this rule does not apply to fees received by persons giving public lectures.

Freelance film workers

As regards the status of workers in the film and allied industries, the Inland Revenue made the following announcement on 30 March 1983:

'The Inland Revenue has recently carried out a review of the employment status of workers engaged on "freelance" terms within the industry. Following this review there has been an extensive series of discussions with representative bodies in the industry, including Independent Programme Producers Association, British Film and Television Producers Association, Advertising Film and Video Tape Producers Association, National Association of Theatrical and Kine Employees, and Association of Cinematograph, Television and Allied Technicians.

'As a result of that review and the subsequent discussions, the Inland Revenue considers that a number of workers engaged on "freelance" terms within the industry are engaged as employees under contracts of service, either written or oral, and should be assessed under Schedule E. Many workers in the industry already pay employee's National Insurance contributions.

'The Inland Revenue, however, accepts that a number of "freelance" workers in certain types of work within the industry are likely to be engaged under contracts for services, as people in self-employment, and should therefore be assessed under Schedule D. Any individual who does not agree with the Revenue's determination of his position has the normal right of appeal to the independent Income Tax Commissioners.'

There is a list of grades in the film industry in respect of which PAYE need not be deducted and who are regarded as self-employed for tax purposes.

Further information can be obtained from the March 1992 edition of the Inland Revenue guidance notes on the application of PAYE to casual and freelance staff in the film industry. In view of the Inland Revenue announcement that the same status will apply for PAYE and DSS purposes, no liability for employee's and employer's contributions should arise in the case of any of the grades mentioned above. However, in the film and TV industry this general rule has not always been followed in practice. In December 1992, after a long review, the DSS agreed that individuals working behind the camera and who have jobs on the Inland Revenue Schedule D list are self-employed for social security purposes. The Contributions Agency will accept claims for repayment of Class 1 contributions where persons were correctly to have been treated as self-employed. It was announced on 23 June 1995 that a provision had been included in the Pensions Bill to enable a self-employed person who had erroneously been charged Class 1 contributions to forego a refund of the employee's contributions and retain the right to earnings-related state pension entitlement and, if applicable, personal pension rebates. The provision does not prevent the 'employer' reclaiming the employer's portion of contributions. The individual's benefit position will be preserved provided that it is only the employer's contributions that are refunded. Individuals or employers wishing to seek refunds should write to The Contributions Agency Refunds Group (see page 658).

There are special rules for, *inter alia*, personnel appearing before the camera, short engagements, payments to limited companies and payments to overseas personalities.

Artistes, performers/non-performers

From 6 April 1990 to 5 April 1996 artistes and performers (excluding established performers with 'reserved Schedule D status' and guest artistes engaged by opera companies) working under standard Equity contracts were treated as employees for income tax purposes so far as earnings from such employments were concerned. This brought the income tax treatment into line with that of social security, as it has been the view of the DSS for many years that the vast majority of performers are employees for social security contribution purposes because of the general conditions under which they usually work.

However, from 6 April 1994 it is understood that the Inland Revenue accepts that the earnings of many artistes should be assessed under Schedule D Case I. This does not, of itself, affect the social security position but the DSS has always acknowledged that there is some scope for self-employment for performers (especially 'act as known' engagements), and specific claims to self-employment are looked into in detail. Accordingly 'act as known' engagements will normally be treated as self-employment for both social security and income tax purposes.

The DSS does, however, permit subsistence allowances to be paid without liability to contributions, and special rules apply to travelling expenses.

The industry also uses standard agreements for the engagement of non-performers. The Inland Revenue has looked at some of these and concluded that some are normally contracts for services (self-employed) and others contracts of service (employed).

Class 1 contributions

As mentioned above, these are related to earnings, the amount payable depending upon whether the employer has applied for his employees to be 'contracted-out' of the State earnings-related pension scheme; such application can be made where the employer's own pension scheme provides a requisite level of benefits for his or her employees and their dependants.

Contributions are only payable once earnings exceed the lower earnings limit but are then due on *all* such earnings up to the upper earnings limit by employees ('primary contributions') but without an upper limit for employers ('secondary contributions'). Contributions are normally collected via the PAYE tax deduction machinery, and there are penalties for late submission of returns and for errors therein. From 19 April 1993, interest will be charged automatically on unpaid PAYE and social security contributions.

Employees liable to pay

Contributions are payable by any employee who is aged 16 years and over (even though he or she may still be at school) and who is paid an amount equal to, or exceeding, the lower earnings limit (see below). Nationality is irrelevant for contribution purposes and, subject to special rules covering employees not normally resident in Great Britain, Northern Ireland or the Isle of Man, or resident in EC countries or those with which there are reciprocal agreements, contributions must be paid whether the employee concerned is a British subject or not provided he is gainfully employed in Great Britain.

Employees exempt from liability to pay

Persons over pensionable age (65 for men; 60 – currently – for women) are exempt from liability to pay primary contributions, even if they have not retired. However, the fact that an employee may be exempt from liability does not relieve an employer from liability to pay secondary contributions in respect of that employee.

Rate of employees' contributions

From 6 April 1997, the rate of employees' contributions, where the earnings are not less than the lower earnings limit, is 2%

of earnings to the lower earnings limit and 10% of earnings between the lower and upper earnings limits (8.4% for contracted-out employments).

Certain married women who made appropriate elections before 12 May 1977 may be entitled to pay a reduced rate of 3.85%. However, they will have no entitlement to benefits in respect of these contributions.

Employers' contributions

All employers are liable to pay contributions on the gross earnings of employees. As mentioned above, an employer's liability is not reduced as a result of employees being exempted from, or being liable to pay only the (3.85%) reduced rate of, contributions.

For earnings paid on or after 6 April 1997 employers are liable at rates of 3%, 5%, 7% or 10% on earnings paid (without any upper earnings limit) depending upon the particular band into which the earnings fall (see below). The rate of contributions attributable to the band into which the earnings fall is applied to all those earnings and not merely to the earnings falling into that band. The above four rates of secondary contributions are reduced to zero%, 2%, 4% and 7% in respect of earnings above the lower earnings limit and up to and including the upper earnings limit for contracted-out employments from 6 April 1997.

The above employers' rates become 1.5%, 3.5%, 5.5% and 8.5% where the scheme is a contracted-out *money purchase* scheme rather than being contracted out by virtue of a *salary-related* scheme.

The employer is responsible for the payment of both employees' and employer's contributions, but is entitled to deduct the employees' contributions from the earnings on which they are calculated. Effectively, therefore, the employee suffers a deduction in respect of his or her social security contributions in arriving at his weekly or monthly wage or salary. Special rules apply to company directors and persons employed through agencies.

Items included in, or excluded from, earnings

Contributions are calculated on the basis of a person's gross earnings from his or her employment. This will normally be the figure shown on the tax deduction working sheet, except where the employee pays superannuation contributions and, from 6 April 1987, charitable gifts – these must be added back for the purposes of calculating Class 1 liability. Profit-related pay exempt from income tax is not exempt from social security contributions.

Earnings include salary, wages, overtime pay, commissions, bonuses, holiday

---

Rates of Class 1 contributions and earnings limits from 6 April 1997

Earnings per week	Rates payable on all earnings			
	Not Contracted-out		Contracted-out	
	Employee	Employer	Employee	Employer
£		%		%
Below 62.00	—	—	—	—
62.00 – 109.99	2% to lower	3	2% to lower	*3/nil or 1.5
110.00 – 154.99	earnings limit,	5	earnings limit,	*5/2 or 3.5
155.00 – 209.99	10% between	7	8.4% between	*7/4 or 5.5
210.00 – 465.00	lower and	10	lower and	*10/7 or 8.5
Over £465.00	upper earnings	10	upper earnings	†10/7 or 8.5
	limits		limits	

* The first figure is the rate to the lower earnings limit and the second is to all the excess.
† 10% to lower earnings limit and above upper earnings limit; 7% or 8.5%between these limits.

pay, payments made while the employee is sick or absent from work, payments to cover travel between home and office, and payments under the statutory sick pay and statutory maternity pay schemes.

However, certain payments, some of which may be regarded as taxable income for income tax purposes, are ignored for social security purposes. These include:
- certain gratuities paid other than by the employer,
- redundancy payments and most payments in lieu of notice,
- certain payments in kind,
- reimbursement of specific expenses incurred in the carrying out of the employment,
- benefits given on an individual basis for personal reasons (e.g. wedding and birthday presents),
- compensation for loss of office, and
- meal vouchers which can only be redeemed for food or drink.

IR/CA booklet CWG 2 (April 1997 edition) gives a list of items to include in or exclude from earnings for Class 1 contribution purposes.

Maximum contributions

There is a limit to the total liability for social security contributions payable by a person who is employed in more than one employment, or is also self-employed or a partner.

Where only not contracted-out Class 1 contributions, or not contracted-out Class 1 and Class 2 contributions, are payable, the maximum contribution is limited to 53 primary Class 1 contributions at the maximum weekly non-contracted-out standard rate. For 1997/98 the maximum will thus be £2201.62.

However, where contracted-out Class 1 contributions are payable, the maximum primary Class 1 contributions payable for 1997/98 where all employments are contracted out are £1859.88.

Where Class 4 contributions are payable in addition to Class 1 and/or Class 2 contributions, the Class 4 contributions are restricted so that they shall not exceed the excess of £1356.15 (i.e. 53 Class 2 contributions plus maximum Class 4 contributions) over the aggregate of the Class 1 and Class 2 contributions.

Miscellaneous rules

There are detailed rules covering a person with two or more employments; where a person receives a bonus or commission in addition to a regular wage or salary; and where a person is in receipt of holiday pay. From 6 April 1991 employers' social security contributions arise under Class 1A in respect of the private use of a company car, and of fuel provided for private use therein. The rate is currently 10%.

Class 2 contributions

Class 2 contributions are payable at the weekly rate of £6.15 as from 6 April 1997. Exemptions from Class 2 liability are:
- A man over 65 or a woman over 60.
- A person who has not attained the age of 16.
- A married woman or, in certain cases, a widow who elected prior to 12 May 1977 not to pay Class 2 contributions.
- Persons with small earnings (see below).
- Persons not ordinarily self-employed (see below).

Small earnings

Application for a certificate of exception from Class 2 contributions may be made by any person who can show that his or her net self-employed earnings per his profit and loss account (as opposed to taxable profits):
- for the year of application are expected to be less than a specified limit (£3480 in the 1997/98 tax year); or
- for the year preceding the application were less than the limit specified for that year (£3430 for 1996/97) and there has been no material change of circumstances.

Certificates of exception must be renewed in accordance with the instructions stated thereon. At the Secretary of State's discretion the certificate may commence up to 13 weeks before the date on

which the application is made. Despite a certificate of exception being in force, a person who is self-employed is still entitled to pay Class 2 contributions if he or she wishes, in order to maintain entitlement to social security benefits.

Persons not ordinarily self-employed

Part-time self-employed activities (including as a writer or artist) are disregarded for contribution purposes if the person concerned is not ordinarily employed in such activities and has a full-time job as an employee. There is no definition of 'ordinarily employed' for this purpose but the DSS often regards a person who has a regular job and whose earnings from spare-time occupation are not expected to be more than £800 per annum as falling within this category. Persons qualifying for this relief do not require certificates of exception. It should be noted that many activities covered by this relief would probably also be eligible for relief under the small earnings rule (see above).

Method of payment

From April 1993, Class 2 contributions may be paid by monthly direct debit in arrears or by cheque, bank giro, etc following receipt of a quarterly (in arrears) bill from DSS.

Overpaid contributions

If, following the payment of Class 2 contributions, it is found that the earnings are below the exception limit (e.g. the relevant accounts are prepared late), the Class 2 contributions that have been overpaid can be reclaimed for tax years 1988/89 onwards, provided a claim is made between 6 April and 31 December immediately following the end of the tax year.

Class 3 contributions

Class 3 contributions are payable voluntarily, at the weekly rate of £6.05 per week from 6 April 1997, by persons aged 16 or over with a view to enabling them to qualify for a limited range of benefits if their contribution record is not otherwise sufficient. In general, Class 3 contributions can be paid by employees, the self-employed and the non employed.

Broadly speaking, no more than 52 Class 3 contributions are payable for any one tax year, and contributions are not payable after the end of the tax year in which the individual concerned reaches the age of 64 (59 for women).

Class 3 contributions may be paid in the same manner as Class 2 (see above) or by annual cheque in arrears.

Class 4 contributions

In addition to Class 2 contributions, self-employed persons are liable to pay Class 4 contributions. These are calculated at the rate of 6% on the amount of profits or gains chargeable to income tax under Schedule D Case I or II which exceed £7010 per annum but which do not exceed £24,180 per annum for 1997/98. Thus the maximum Class 4 contribution is 6% of £17,170 – i.e. £1030.20 for 1997/98.

For the tax year 1997/98, Class 4 contributions are based on the income tax assessment for 1997/98 (e.g., under the income tax rules for self assessment, the profits for the year ended 31 December 1997), and so on for subsequent years.

The income tax profits on which Class 4 contributions are calculated is after deducting capital allowances and losses, but before deducting personal tax allowances or retirement annuity or personal pension plan premiums.

Class 4 contributions produce no additional benefits, but were introduced to ensure that self-employed persons as a whole pay a fair share of the cost of pensions and other social security benefits without the self-employed who make only small profits having to pay excessively high flat rate contributions.

From 6 April 1996 no income tax relief is available for Class 4 contributions. Previously, half the liability attracted income tax relief.

Payment of contributions

In general, contributions are now self assessed and paid to the Inland Revenue together with the income tax under Schedule D Case I or II, and accordingly the contributions are due and payable at the same time as the income tax liability on the relevant profits. Under self-assessment, interim payments of Class 4 contributions are payable at the same time as interim payments of tax.

Class 4 exemptions

The following persons are exempt from Class 4 contributions:
• Men over 65 and women over 60 at the commencement of the year of assessment (i.e. on 6 April).
• An individual not resident in the United Kingdom for income tax purposes in the year of assessment.
• Persons whose earnings are not 'immediately derived' from carrying on a trade, profession or vocation (e.g., sleeping partners and, possibly, limited partners).
• A child under 16 on 6 April of the year of assessment.
• Persons not ordinarily self-employed (see above as for Class 2 contributions).

Married persons and partnerships

Under independent taxation of husband and wife from 1990/91 onwards, each spouse is responsible for his or her Class 4 liability.

In partnerships, each partner's liability is calculated separately. If a partner also carries on another trade or profession, the profits of all such businesses are aggregated for the purposes of calculating his or her Class 4 liability.

When an assessment has become final and conclusive for the purposes of income tax, it is also final and conclusive for the purposes of calculating Class 4 liability.

Further information

Further information can be obtained from the many booklets published by the Department of Social Security, available from local offices – refer to telephone directory under 'Contributions Agency' in the first instance.

Contributions Agency, International Services
Newcastle upon Tyne NE98 1YX
tel (06451) 54811 (local call rates apply)
Address for enquiries for individuals resident abroad.

The Contributions Agency Refunds Group
Employers Unit 4, Room 101E,
Benton Park Road, Longbenton,
Newcastle upon Tyne NE98 1YX
tel (06451) 54260 (local call rates apply)
Address for individuals or employers wishing to seek refunds.

Peter Arrowsmith FCA is National Insurance Consultant at Grant Thornton, Chartered Accountants, Northampton office. He is a member of the National Insurance Committee of the Institute of Chartered Accountants in England and Wales and Consulting Editor to *Tolley's National Insurance Contributions 1997/98*.

Social security benefits

*There are many leaflets produced by the Department of Social Security. However, due to the nature of the subject social security benefits can be quite difficult to understand. In this article, **K.D. Bartlett** FCA has summarised some of the more usual benefits that are available under the Social Security Acts.*

This article deliberately does not cover every aspect of the legislation but the references given should enable the relevant information to be easily traced. These references are to the leaflets issued by the Department of Social Security. No announcements affecting this article were made in the July 1997 Budget.

It is usual for only one periodical benefit to be payable at any one time. If the contribution conditions are satisfied for more than one benefit it is the larger benefit that is payable. Benefit rates shown below were those payable from week commencing 6 April 1997.

Employed persons (Category A or D contributors) are covered for all benefits. Certain married women and widows (Category B and E contributors) who elected to pay at the reduced rate receive only attendance allowance, guardian's allowance and industrial injuries benefits. Other benefits may be available dependent on their husbands' contributions.

Self-employed persons (Class 2 and Class 4 contributors) are covered for all benefits except earnings-related supplements, unemployment benefit, widow's and invalidity pensions, widowed mother's allowance and industrial injury benefits.

The major changes, which took place from the week beginning 6 April 1997, were:

- Contributory benefits, including retirement pension, rise by 2.1% in line with the Retail Price Index for September 1996.
- Income-related benefits rise by 2.6% in line with the Sept 1996 'ROSSI' index.
- Lone parent rates remain unchanged.

- Increases will be made to deductions, and the income thresholds, in income support, jobseekers' allowance, housing benefit and council tax benefit in respect of non-dependent adults living in the claimant's home.

Family benefits

Child benefits

Leaflet CH 1

Child benefit is payable for all children who are either under 16 or under 19 and receiving full-time education at a recognised educational establishment. The rate is £11.05 for the first or eldest child and £9.00 a week for each subsequent child. It is payable to the person who is responsible for the child but excludes foster parents or people exempt from UK tax. Furthermore, one-parent families receive £17.10 per week for the eldest child.

Maternity benefits

Help with maternity expenses is given to selected people from the social fund. To be eligible the claimant must be receiving income support or family credit. £100 is paid for each new or adopted baby, reduced by the amount of any savings over £500 held by the claimant or his or her family. A payment can be obtained from the social fund for an adopted baby provided the child is not more than 12 months old when the application is made. The claimant has three months to make the claim from when adoption has taken place.

Maternity pay

Leaflet NI 17A

Statutory maternity pay (SMP) was introduced for female employees who leave employment because of pregnancy. SMP is applicable to those who have worked for 26 weeks by the 15th week before the expected date of confinement. This 15th week is known as the qualifying week (QW). The other qualifying conditions are that the woman must:

• be pregnant at the 11th week before the expected week of confinement, or already have been confined;

• have stopped working for her employer wholly or partly because of pregnancy or confinement;

• have average earnings of not less than the lower earnings limit for the payment of National Insurance contributions which is in force during her QW;

• provide her employer with evidence of her expected week of confinement;

• provide her employer with notice of her maternity absence.

Rates of SMP

There is a higher and a lower rate. The higher rate of SMP is 90% of an employee's weekly earnings and is paid for the first six weeks for which there is entitlement to SMP. To be eligible for the higher rate, a woman must meet all the qualifying conditions and have been employed by the employer for a continuous period of at least two years (at between 8 and 16 hours a week). Her service must continue into the QW.

The lower rate of SMP is a set rate reviewed each year. The rate for the tax year beginning 6 April 1997 is £55.70 per week. It is paid for 18 weeks to those not entitled to the higher amount and for up to 12 weeks to those who receive the higher rate for the first six weeks.

SMP is taxable and also subject to National Insurance contributions. The gross amount of SMP and the employer's portion of National Insurance payable on the SMP can be recovered from the State by deducting the amounts from the amount normally due for PAYE and National Insurance deductions payable to the Collector of Taxes.

Guardian's allowance

Leaflet NI 14

This is paid at the rate of £9.90 a week. For each subsequent child the rate of benefit is £11.20 a week to people who have taken orphans into their own family. Usually both of the child's parents must be dead and at least one of them must have satisfied a residence condition.

The allowance can only be paid to the person who is entitled to child benefit for the child (or to that person's spouse). It is not necessary to be the legal guardian. The claim should be made within three months of the date of entitlement.

Disability living allowance

Disability living allowance (DLA) was introduced on 6 April 1992 and replaces attendance allowance for disabled people before they reach the age of 65. It has also replaced mobility allowance.

Those who are disabled after reaching 65 may be able to claim attendance allowance. The attendance allowance board decide whether, and for how long, a person is eligible for this allowance. Attendance allowance is not taxable.

The care component is divided into three rates whereas the mobility allowance has two rates. The rate of benefit from 6 April 1997 is:

	Per week £
Care component	
Higher rate (day and night, or terminally ill)	49.50
Middle rate (day or night)	33.10
Lower rate (if need some help during day, or over 16 and need help preparing a meal)	13.15
Mobility component	
Higher rate (unable or virtually unable to walk)	34.60
Lower rate (can walk but needs help when outside)	13.15

Attendance allowance
Attendance allowance has been replaced by DLA from 6 April 1992 for those aged under 65. For those aged 65 or over, attendance allowance will continue to be paid. The rate of benefit from 6 April 1996 is:
Higher rate (day and night)   49.50
Lower rate (day or night)   33.10

Benefits for the ill or unemployed

Statutory sick pay

Leaflets NI 27, NI 16, NI 244
In the majority of cases the employer now has the responsibility of paying sick pay to its employees. The payment is dependent on satisfying various conditions in respect of periods of incapacity, periods of entitlement, qualifying days and rules on notification of absence. The rules are quite complicated and reference should be made to the relevant booklets for further clarification but the key points are:
• Payment is made by the employer.
• There is a possibility of two rates of payment dependent on the employee's gross average earnings.
• The employee must not be capable of work and must do no work on the day concerned.
• SSP is not usually payable for the first three working days.
• The maximum entitlement is 28 weeks in any period of incapacity.
• Notification must be made by the employer but this procedure must be within statutory guidelines.
• Payment can be withheld if notification of sickness is not given in due time.
From 6 April 1996 most employers will no longer be able to reclaim any SSP back. Small employers may, in certain circumstances, receive compensation called the New Relief Scheme which will help all employers faced with exceptionally high levels of sickness absence.

Sickness benefit

DSS Leaflet NI 16
The majority of illnesses are now covered by statutory sick pay and sickness benefit now only applies to those employees who are excluded from statutory sickness pay and the self-employed. Sickness benefit is paid for up to 28 weeks for those who are off work. If a claimant is still ill after 28 weeks he or she is transferred to the long term benefit, invalidity benefit.

To be eligible for sickness benefit the claimant must have paid, in any one tax year ending before the calendar year in which the claim is made, Class I contributions on an amount of earnings at least 25 times the weekly lower earnings limit for that tax year (or the equivalent of Class 2 contributions for self-employed people).

There is another condition which must be satisfied in that the claimant must have paid, or been credited with, in the tax year ending before the benefit year in which he or she makes the claim, Class 1 contributions on an amount of earnings at least 50 times the weekly lower earnings limit for both the last two tax years (or the equivalent number of Class 2 contributions for self-employed people).

Incapacity benefit

Leaflet DS 700
Incapacity benefit replaced sickness benefit and invalidity benefit. The contribution conditions haven't changed but a new medical test has been brought in which includes a comprehensive questionnaire. The rates from 6 April 1997 are:

	£
Long-term Incapacity Benefit	62.45
Short-term Incapacity Benefit	
Higher rate	55.70
Lower rate	47.10
Increase of Long-term Incapacity	
Benefit for age:	
Higher rate	13.15
Lower rate	6.60

Severe disablement allowance

Leaflet NI 252
This is a benefit for people under pensionable age who cannot work because of physical or mental ill health and do not

have sufficient National Insurance contributions to qualify for sickness or invalidity benefit. The basic allowance is £37.75 a week. There are increases of £22.40 a week for adult dependants and £11.20 for each child.

Invalid care allowance

Leaflet NI 212

This is a taxable benefit paid to people of working age who cannot take a job because they have to stay at home to look after a severely disabled person. The basic allowance is £37.35 per week. An extra £22.35 is paid for each adult dependant and £11.20 for each child.

Jobseekers' allowance

Jobseekers' allowance (JSA) is a new social security benefit that came in force on 7 October 1996. It has taken the place of unemployment benefit and income support for unemployed people. JSA differs from unemployment benefit in that there are no additional amounts payable for dependants. The rates are:

Rates of JSA	Post-April 1997
Single under 18	£29.60
18-24	£38.90
25 or over	£49.15

Claimants will be able to claim JSA if they have paid National Insurance contributions equal to 25 times the lower earnings level in one of the last two complete tax years before the claim; and either paid or have been credited in respect of each of the last two complete tax years before the year of the claim 50 times the lower earnings limit for that tax year.

JSA is not normally paid for the first three waiting days. Exceptions are made for those under 18 who are considered to be in severe hardship or if a person has received income support, incapacity benefit or invalid care allowance in the 12 weeks prior to the claim for JSA. Contributory-related JSA is only payable for a maximum of 182 days.

People ineligible for contributory-related JSA may be able to claim income-related JSA. If a claimant satisfies the entitlement conditions he or she is entitled to income-related JSA indefinitely.

Eligibility conditions

In order to be eligible for JSA a potential claimant must not have capital exceeding £8000. If he or she has capital of £3000 or more, £1 is deducted for every £250 above the £3000. The claimant is not allowed to work more than 24 hours a week and his or her partner is only allowed to work 16 hours a week.

Claimants must usually be available to take up employment immediately unless they can show that they are doing part-time work and need to give notice. Once that notice has ended the claimant must take up work immediately afterwards.

Claims should be made at the nearest office of the Department for Education and Employment – in most cases this will be a job centre. Benefit is normally paid fortnightly in arrears via giro cheque either at a post office or via a bank account. JSA is a taxable benefit.

Seeking work

A claimant must agree to a 'jobseekers' agreement' based on the job search plan which will be discussed at the 'new jobseeker' interview. The jobseeker will attend thereafter for a job search review. If the conditions for JSA are still being met, benefit will be paid. If it seems that the jobseeker has made himself unemployed and refuses a job without good cause, payment of JSA can be stopped for up to 26 weeks. People unemployed for at least 13 weeks will not be subject to sanctions if they start a job and then leave it within a period of five to eight weeks after starting a full-time job.

Pensions and widow's benefits

Leaflets NP 23, NP 35, NP 31

The state pension is divided into two parts – the basic pension, presently £62.45 per week for a single person or

£99.80 per week for a married couple, and the State Earnings Related Pension Scheme (SERPS), which will after it matures on the present basis pay a pension of 25% of revalued earnings between the lower and upper earnings limits.

The cost of SERPS has been a major political consideration for some time. In order to reduce the long-term cost of the scheme, benefits will be reduced for those retiring or widowed after the year 2000. The benefits will be reduced as follows:
• The pension will be based on lifetime average earnings rather than the best 20 years as at present.
• The pension will be calculated on the basis of 20% of earnings between the lower and upper earnings limit rather than 25%. This will be phased in over 10 years from the tax year 2000/2001.
• Presently all of a member's state earnings-related benefit is inherited by a surviving spouse. For deaths occurring after April 2000 this will be reduced to 50%.

Women paying standard rate contributions into the scheme are eligible for the same amount of pension as men but five years earlier, from age 60. If a woman stays at home to bring up her children or to look after a person receiving attendance allowance she can have her basic pension rights protected without paying contributions.

The widow's pension and widowed mother's allowance also consists of a basic pension and an additional earnings-related pension. The full amount of the additional pension applies only if the husband has contributed to the new scheme for at least 20 years.

Widow's benefits

From 11 April 1988 there are three main widow's benefits:
• Widow's payment, which has replaced the widow's allowance.
• Widowed mother's allowance.
• Widow's pension.

Widow's payment
This is a new allowance, currently a lump sum payment of £1000 payable to widows who were bereaved on or after 11 April 1988. It is payable immediately on the death of the husband. Entitlement to this benefit is based on the late husband's contribution record but no payment will be made if the widow is living with another man as husband and wife at the date of death. The late husband must have actually paid contributions on earnings of at least 25 times the weekly or lower earnings limit for a given tax year in any tax year ending before his death (or ending before he reached pensionable age if he was over 65 when he died). The equivalent number of Class 2 or voluntary Class 3 contributions will be sufficient.

When claiming, the widow should complete the form on the back of the death certificate and send it to the local social security office. On receipt of this information the DSS will send the claimant a more detailed form (BD8) which, once completed, has to go back to the social security office. It is important to claim the benefit within 12 months of the husband's death.

Widowed mother's allowance
Leaflet NP 45
If a widow is left with children to look after, she is entitled to a widowed mother's allowance provided that her late husband had paid sufficient national insurance contributions. These contributions are:
• 25 Class 1, 2 or 3 contributions before age 65 and before 6 April 1975; or
• contributions in any one tax year after 6 April 1975 on earnings of at least 25 times the weekly lower earnings limit for that year.

It is important that the widow is looking after either her own child or her husband's child and that the child is under 16 or, if between the age of 16 and 19, is continuing in full-time education.

The allowance stops immediately if the widow remarries and will be suspended if she lives with a man as his wife. From April 1996 the amounts payable are:

	£
Basic allowance	62.45
Increase for each child	11.20

Where a husband's contributions only satisfied the first test above, the basic allowance may be payable at a reduced rate. This reduction does not alter the rate of an increase for a child.

Widow's pension
Leaflet NP 45

A widow who is over the age of 45 when her husband dies may be eligible for a widow's pension unless she is eligible for the widowed mother's allowance. In this situation the widow's pension becomes payable when the widowed mother's allowance ends, provided she is still under the age of 65. However, where a woman had been receiving the widowed mother's allowance, she becomes entitled to a widow's pension if she is between the ages of 45 and 65 when the allowance ends, no matter what her age may have been when her husband died. Before 11 April 1988 a widow aged 40 or over could qualify for a widow's pension.

Qualification conditions

• The contributions conditions must be satisfied and these conditions are the same as those for the widowed mother's allowance above.
• The widow must not be receiving the widowed mother's allowance.
• When her husband died she was aged between 45 and 65 or she was entitled to widowed mother's allowance and is aged between 45 and 65 when her widowed mother's allowance finished.

Cessation of widow's pension

• Entitlement finishes if the widowed mother's allowance stops because she has remarried.
• Widow's pension must not be claimed when the payment of the widowed mother's allowance has been suspended because the widow is in pension or is living with a man as his wife.

From 11 April 1988 both the basic and additional pension are paid at a reduced rate if the widow was aged under 55:
• when her husband died, if she did not subsequently become entitled to wid-

owed mother's allowance; or
• when her widowed mother's allowance ceased to be paid. The relevant rates from 6 April 1997 are as follows (the ages given in parentheses apply to women for whom widow's pension was payable before 11 April 1988):

Age related	£
Age 54 (49)	58.08
53 (48)	53.71
52 (47)	49.34
51 (46)	44.96
50 (45)	40.59
49 (44)	36.22
48 (43)	31.85
47 (42)	27.48
46 (41)	23.11
45 (40)	18.74

Funeral expenses

The death grant was abolished from 6 April 1987. It has been replaced by a payment from the social fund where the claimant is in receipt of income support, family credit or housing benefit. The full cost of a reasonable funeral is paid, reduced by any savings of over £500 held by the claimant or his or her family (£1000 for couples over 60).

Family credit

Family credit replaced family income supplement (FIS) with effect from 11 April 1988. Family credit is a tax-free benefit payable to families in Great Britain where:
• the claimant or partner is engaged in remunerative work for 16 hours or more per week; and
• there is at least one child under 16 in the family (or under 19 if in full-time education up to and including A level or OND standard) for whom the claimant and/or partner is responsible.

Entitlement to family credit is determined by comparing the family's normal income with a prescribed amount, known as the 'applicable amount'. The current applicable amount is £75.20. Eligible families fall into two income groups:

• those whose total income does not exceed the applicable amount. Such families will be entitled to the appropriate maximum amount of family credit payable; and
• those whose total income does exceed the applicable amount but by an amount which still allows some entitlement. To determine eligibility, a prescribed percentage (currently 70%) of the excess income (over and above the applicable amount) is deducted from the appropriate maximum family credit. If there is an amount left (i.e. the figure is a plus sum of at least 50p) the family will be able to receive family credit equal to this amount, rounded to the nearest penny.

Maximum family credit benefit rates (from 6 April 1997)	
Adult	£47.65
Child	
aged less than 11 years	£12.05
aged 11 to 15 years	£19.95
Young person	
aged 16 to 17 years	£24.80
aged 18 years	£34.70

An award is normally made for a period of 26 weeks. Changes of circumstances during this period will not usually affect the award.

Capital and income

Families where the claimant and partner together hold capital in excess of £8000 will not be entitled to family credit. The resources of a family taken into account as income for family credit are the aggregate of their normal net earnings and

Further information

This article does not set out to cover every aspect of the Social Security Acts legislation. Further information can be obtained from the local office of the Department of Social Security or from Accountants Digest No. 370 published by the Institute of Chartered Accountants in England and Wales. Readers resident abroad who have queries should write to the Department's Overseas Branch, Newcastle upon Tyne NE98 1YX.

other income plus any tariff income. Certain payments are disregarded in the calculation of income. For those with capital of between £3000 and £8000, the rate of benefit will be affected. For every £250 (or part of £250) held in excess of £3000, a 'tariff' income of £1.00 will be added to the family's other income.

Grants from local authorities

Council tax benefit

People will be able to claim benefit are those who:
• are on a low income, or
• are in receipt of income support
• share the house with certain other persons who are receiving income support.
The maximum benefit entitlement for a liable person claiming will be 100% of the liability.

K.D. Bartlett FCA qualified as a Chartered Accountant in 1969 and became a partner in a predecessor firm of Clark Whitehill in 1972.

Index

Order Form

Books in the 'Writing' series

—	Writing for Children 2nd edn	£7.99
—	Writing Crime Fiction 2nd edn	£7.99
—	Writing Erotic Fiction	£8.99
—	Writing Fantasy Fiction	£8.99
—	Writing about Food	£8.99
—	Writing Historical Fiction 2nd edn	£8.99
—	Writing Horror Fiction	£8.99
—	Writing for Magazines 2nd edn	£9.99
—	Writing a Play 2nd edn	£8.99
—	Writing Popular Fiction 2nd edn Oct '97	£9.99
—	Writing for Radio 3rd edn	£8.99
—	Writing for the Teenage Market	£8.99
—	Writing for Television 2nd edn	£9.99
—	Writing a Thriller 2nd edn	£9.99
—	Writing about Travel 2nd edn	£7.99

Other books for writers

—	Interviewing Techniques for Writers and Researchers	£7.99
	Research for Writers 5th edn	£11.99
—	Sports Writing July '97	£8.99
—	The Writer's Rights	£8.99

All these books can be ordered through your local bookshop or direct from the publisher.
Tick the titles you want and fill in the form below.
Prices and availability subject to change without notice

Please return to A & C Black (Publishers) Ltd,
Dept YB98, PO Box 19, Huntingdon, Cambs PE19 3SF *tel* **(01480) 212666** *fax* **(01480) 405014**

Send a cheque or postal order for the value of the book(s), adding (for postage and packing) 15%
UK and Eire; 20% overseas.
Airmail rates available on application.
OR please debit this amount from my Access/Visa Card (delete as appropriate)

Card number _____

Amount _____ Expiry date _____

Signed _____

Name (please print) _____

Address _____

_____

_____

Postcode _____

D0281447

Writers' & Artists' Yearbook 1998